NO-HITTERS

EDITED BY BILL NOWLIN
ASSOCIATE EDITORS LEN LEVIN AND CARL RIECHERS

Society for American Baseball Research, Inc.
Phoenix, AZ

NO-HITTERS
Edited by Bill Nowlin
Associate editors Len Levin and Carl Riechers

Copyright © 2017 Society for American Baseball Research, Inc.
All rights reserved. Reproduction in whole or in part without permission is prohibited.

ISBN 978-1-943816-51-4
(Ebook ISBN 978-1-943816-50-7)

Cover and book design: Gilly Rosenthol

Photo credits:
Cover photographs: Courtesy of the National Baseball Hall of Fame.
The scorecard of Lee Richmond's perfect game is courtesy of John R. Husman.

Photography: All photographs are courtesy of the National Baseball Hall of Fame, except the following:

Wilson Alvarez: Courtesy of Triple Play Sports Productions Archive (page 354)
and Team Venezuela/World Baseball Classic (page 357).
Al Atkinson: Courtesy of SABR.
Steve Barber: Courtesy of the Baltimore Orioles
Vida Blue: Courtesy of Dwayne Labakas.
Dallas Braden: Courtesy of Michael Zaganis/Oakland Athletics.
Steve Busby: Courtesy of Kansas City Royals Baseball Club.
Rollie Fingers: Courtesy of Dwayne Labakas.
Devern Hansack: Courtesy of the Boston Red Sox.
Andy Hawkins: Courtesy of the Texas Rangers.
Sam Kimber: Courtesy of SABR.
Ed Lafitte: Courtesy of Jim Leeke.
Paul Lindblad: Courtesy of Dwayne Labakas.
Derek Lowe: Courtesy of the Boston Red Sox.
Stu Miller: Courtesy of the Baltimore Orioles.
David Palmer: Courtesy of Russ Hansen.
Mike Witt: Courtesy of Angels Baseball
Matt Young: Courtesy of the Boston Red Sox.
The images of Joe Borden, Earl Hamilton, Bill Hawke, and Ed Head are all in the public domain.

Society for American Baseball Research
Cronkite School at ASU
555 N. Central Ave. #416
Phoenix, AZ 85004
Phone: (602) 496-1460
Web: www.sabr.org
Facebook: Society for American Baseball Research
Twitter: @SABR

CONTENTS

1. Introduction 1
2. JOE BORDEN 2
   Charlie Weatherby
3. *July 28, 1875* 8
   Casey Tibbitts
4. GEORGE BRADLEY 10
   Brian Engelhardt
5. *July 15, 1876* 18
   Parker Bena
6. LEE RICHMOND 20
   John R. Husman
7. *June 12, 1880* 25
   John R. Husman
8. LARRY CORCORAN 27
   Bob LeMoine
9. *August 19, 1882* 35
   Bob LeMoine
10. TONY MULLANE 38
    Ray Birch
11. *September 11, 1882* 43
    Ray Birch
12. GUY HECKER 45
    Bob Bailey
13. *September 19, 1882* 49
    Bob Bailey
14. SAM KIMBER 52
    David Nemec
15. *October 4, 1884* 55
    David Nemec
16. AL ATKINSON 58
    Chris Rainey
17. *May 1, 1886* 62
    Chris Rainey
18. AMOS RUSIE 64
    Charles F. Faber
19. *July 31, 1891* 70
    Gregory H. Wolf
20. THEODORE BREITENSTEIN 73
    Steve Rice
21. *October 4, 1891* 79
    Steve Rice
22. BILL HAWKE 81
    Jimmy Keenan
23. *August 16, 1893* 86
    Jimmy Keenan
24. NIXEY CALLAHAN 88
    James E. Elfers
25. *September 20, 1902* 92
    James E. Elfers
26. EARL HAMILTON 95
    Paul Hofmann
27. *August 30, 1912* 100
    Paul Hofmann
28. ED LAFITTE 102
    Jim Leeke
29. *September 19, 1914* 108
    Jim Leeke
30. FRED TONEY 110
    Mike Lynch
31. *May 2, 1917* 116
    Mike Lynch
32. CHARLIE ROBERTSON 119
    Jacob Pomrenke
33. *April 30, 1922* 124
    Jacob Pomrenke

34. BOBBY BURKE 127
    Gregory H. Wolf

35. *August 8, 1931* 132
    Gregory H. Wolf

36. BILL DIETRICH 135
    Gregory H. Wolf

37. *June 1, 1937* 142
    Gregory H. Wolf

38. BOB FELLER 145
    C. Paul Rogers III

39. *April 16, 1940* 161
    C. Paul Rogers III

40. ED HEAD 164
    Lyle Spatz

41. *April 23, 1946* 171
    Lyle Spatz

42. WILLIAM McCAHAN 173
    David E. Skelton

43. *September 3, 1947* 178
    David E. Skelton

44. BOBO HOLLOMAN 180
    Len Pasculli

45. *May 6, 1953* 185
    Joe Schuster

46. DON LARSEN 188
    Charles F. Faber

47. *October 8, 1956* 195
    Charles F. Faber

48. SANDY KOUFAX 198
    Marc Z Aaron

49. *June 30, 1962* 212
    Marc Z Aaron

50. *May 11, 1963* 214
    Marc Z Aaron

51. *June 4, 1964* 216
    Marc Z Aaron

52. *September 9, 1965* 218
    Mike Huber

53. KEN JOHNSON 220
    Steve Schmitt

54. *April 23, 1964* 225
    Steve Schmitt

55. BILL STONEMAN 227
    Norm King

56. *April 17, 1969* 233
    Adam J. Ulrey

57. *October 2, 1972* 235
    Norm King

58. STEVE BUSBY 238
    John DiFonzo

59. *April 27, 1973* 246
    John DiFonzo

60. *June 19, 1974* 249
    John DiFonzo

61. BOB FORSCH 251
    Ben Girard

62. *April 16, 1978* 262
    Ben Girard

63. *September 26, 1983* 265
    Ben Girard

64. KEN FORSCH 268
    Chip Greene

65. *April 7, 1979* 275
    Chip Greene

66. LEN BARKER 278
    Joe Wancho

67. *May 15, 1981* 282
    Joe Wancho

68. DAVID PALMER 285
    Norm King

69. *April 21, 1984 (second game)* 291
    Norm King

70. MIKE WITT 293
    Paul Hensler

71. *September 30, 1984* 308
    Paul Hensler

72. MIKE SCOTT 311
    Rory Costello

73. *September 25, 1986* 317
    Frederick C. Bush

74. TOM BROWNING 320
    Joe Cox

75. *September 16, 1988* 324
    Joe Cox

76. ANDY HAWKINS 327
    Stew Thornley

77. *July 1, 1990* 331
    Stew Thornley

78. DAVE STIEB 334
    Joe Cox

79. *September 2, 1990* 338
    Adrian Fung

80. DENNIS MARTINEZ 341
    Rory Costello

81. *July 28, 1991* 350
    Rory Costello

82. WILSON ALVAREZ 353
    Leonte Landino

83. *August 11, 1991* 360
    Leonte Landino

84. MATT YOUNG 363
    Alan Raylesburg

85. *April 12, 1992* 369
    Alan Raylesburg

86. KENNY ROGERS 372
    Ton Schott

87. *July 28, 1994* 379
    Tom Schott

92. HIDEO NOMO 382
    Bill Staples

93. *September 17, 1996* 392
    Bill Staples

94. *April 4, 2001* 395
    Bill Staples

88. DAVID WELLS 399
    Norm King

89. *May 17, 1998* 406
    Norm King

90. DAVID CONE 409
    Tara Krieger

91. *July 18, 1999* 424
    Tara Krieger

95. DEREK LOWE 428
    Bill Nowlin

96. *April 27, 2002* 433
    Bill Nowlin

97. RANDY JOHNSON 436
    Joe Wancho

98. *May 18, 2004* 442
    Joe Wancho

99. DALLAS BRADEN 444
    Dirk Lammers

100. *May 9, 2010* 448
    Dirk Lammers

101. ROY HALLADAY 450
    Alan Cohen

102. *May 29, 2010* 459
    Alan Cohen

103. *October 6, 2010* 462
    Alan Cohen

COMBINED NO-HITTERS

104. STEVE BARBER 465
    Warren Corbett

105. STU MILLER 471
    Warren Corbett

106. *April 30, 1967* 477
    Jimmy Keenan

FOUR PITCHERS COMBINE

107. VIDA BLUE 479
    Rich Puerzer
108. GLENN ABBOTT 486
    Clifford Corn
109. PAUL LINDBLAD 491
    Paul Hofmann
110. ROLLIE FINGERS 497
    Dale Voiss
111. *September 28, 1975* 502
    Mike Huber

SIX PITCHERS COMBINE

112. *June 11, 2003* 505
    Mike Huber

OTHER ARTICLES

113. Ahead of Their Time:
    Negro League No-Hitters 508
    Dirk Lammers
114. Pitchers Who Threw Complete-Game
    No-Hitters in Both the Minor and
    Major Leagues 512
    Chuck McGill
115. No-Nos Knocked Off the Books ... 517
    Dirk Lammers
116. When Is A No-Hitter Not A
    No-Hitter *(October 1, 2006)* 523
    Bill Nowlin
117. Devern Hansack 526
    Bill Nowlin
118. The Curse of King Korn 532
    John T. Saccoman
119. The "Most-Hitters" 534
    Bill Nowlin

120. Contributors 538

INTRODUCTION

PITCHING A NO-HITTER IS A dream for every major-league pitcher — once they have already realized their first dream, which is to make it to the big leagues in the first place.

Over the course of nearly 150 years of major-league baseball, and thousands upon thousands of games played, fewer than 300 pitchers have thrown an official no-hitter. The figure through the 2016 season is maybe 294 or 295 or so, depending on your definitions. And if you include a handful of no-hitters that were deemed not to be no-hitters, the figure climbs to a little over 300.

The number of games played, using Retrosheet standards for what constitutes a major-league game and counting forfeits (both played and unplayed) is 213,307 games through the end of the 2016 season.[1]

If we go by 295 no-hitters, that's more or less one no-hitter every 723 games, or 0.0013829. It's a rare thing.

Fewer than half the pitchers in the National Baseball Hall of Fame have thrown a no-hitter. Many of the biggest names in pitching have never done it. We won't mention names here, but chances are that our average reader can easily name a few.

Some pitchers have pitched more than one. It's just the way things are in baseball.

About a year or so after work for this book got underway, there appeared a book we would like to highly recommend: *Baseball's No-Hit Wonders*, by Dirk Lammers. It's a really fat book, and it takes on the story of the no-hitter, looking at it from various perspectives and with a lot of good humor. We are pleased that Dirk and his publisher at Unbridled Books have granted us permission to include his chapter on Negro League no-hitters here. There are a lot of angles from which he looks at no-hitters and, again, we highly recommend the book.

This book focuses on pitchers who threw no-hitters and the no-hitters they threw. Naturally, we couldn't present biographies of everyone who ever threw a no-hitter nor could we present Games Project accounts of all of them. That wasn't our goal. What we wanted to do is to put together a book that encouraged SABR biographers to add another 30 or 40 bios to SABR's BioProject and a similar number of games to the Games Project. Assembling the books we do is a labor of love meant to stimulate research and build up SABR's body of work.

We wanted the book to touch on a variety of matters, and we wanted to have it span the decades so that there was some representation of the earlier eras of baseball right up to more recent years. Why isn't Cy Young in the book? His bio was already written, and we were trying to stimulate new research so we selected some other people instead. We tried to hit certain themes — first no-hitter in each league; first no-hitter thrown at 60 feet 6 inches; first in which the losing team scored a run; first pitcher to debut with a no-hitter; first extra-inning no-hitter; etc. You'll find those all in here and maybe a surprise or two as well.

—Bill Nowlin

NOTES

[1] Email from Tom Ruane, March 15, 2017.

JOE BORDEN

By Charlie Weatherby

JOE BORDEN, AN AMATEUR who broke into professional baseball at the age of 21, had a short but notable two-year major-league pitching career, playing in 39 games and posting a record of 13-16 with an earned-run average of 2.56. Although his record appears unassuming, he is best known for pitching professional baseball's first no-hitter, in 1875, and winning the National League's first game, in 1876. He was also involved in a few other "firsts."

In an era when pitchers threw underhand from 45 feet and batters could request a pitch location, Borden's pitching style was described by pioneer baseball writer Henry Chadwick as "having speed, but with little strategy. … In addition to his swiftly moving fastball, he also delivered a curveball that moved down and away from right-handed batters. Both pitches he delivered from a low arm angle."[1] He was called "phenomenal" when he broke in, but was released in the middle of his second season, causing *Sporting Life* to note that Borden's career "went up like a rocket and came down like a stick."[2]

Joseph Emley Borden was born on May 9, 1854, in Jacobstown, Burlington County, New Jersey. He was the fourth of John H. and Sarah Ann (Emley) Borden's six children. His parents were New Jersey natives; his father was a prominent and well-to-do merchant who manufactured boots and shoes. Borden was a descendant of Henry Borden (1370-1469) of Headcorn, Kent, England. Researchers believe that the family (originally named DeBourdon) came from Normandy with William the Conqueror in 1066.

By 1870 the Borden family had relocated to Philadelphia, where 16-year-old Joe began to play baseball. In 1875 he was a member of the J.B. Doerr club, a crack amateur squad that played the best teams in Philadelphia and environs. On July 12, Doerr faced the professional Philadelphia Athletics of the National Association. With Borden in the box pitching under the name "Josephs," Doerr won 6-4. Borden's outing earned him widespread notice in the press.

Meanwhile, the White Stockings (also called the Pearls), another Philadelphia National Association club, needed a pitcher; Cherokee Fisher, who had started all 41 games up to July 22, was dismissed from the team for what author David Nemec called "drunkenness and general misbehavior."[3] George Zettlein, formerly of the Chicago White Stockings, was signed as a replacement but wasn't immediately available. Desperate for help, manager Mike McGeary invited Borden to pitch for a few days as a noncontract player.

Before his professional debut against the Athletics on July 24, Borden persuaded McGeary to enter his name on the lineup card as Josephs; baseball historian Rich Westcott wrote that "Borden's family… did not approve of his playing baseball. … Borden … used pseudonyms, pitching under the name of Nedrob (Borden spelled backward) or Joe Josephs."[4] In a game the *Philadelphia Inquirer* called "long and tedious, although closely contested in the first six innings," Borden surrendered eight runs in the seventh and eighth innings as the Pearls lost 11-4; "Joseph's pitching was swift but rather wild," the *Inquirer* said.[5] Teammate Tim Murnane, who later played with Borden in Boston and became a respected sportswriter for the *Boston Globe*, said Joe "was hammered all over the lot."[6]

Borden's second outing, an 8-1 loss, came two days later against Chicago; again, the *Inquirer* said, he was "rather wild."[7]

With two losses under his belt, no one could have expected what came next. On July 28 Borden threw major-league baseball's first no-hitter, a 4-0 shutout of the Chicago White Stockings before 500 spectators at Philadelphia's Jefferson Park. In the *Chicago*

Tribune's opinion, "The threatening appearance of the weather deterred many from witnessing one of the best games ever played. From the effective pitching of Josephs the Chicagos were unable to make a base hit throughout the entire game—a thing unparalleled in the annals of baseball."[8] The 1 hour and 40 minute contest was the National Association's only no-hitter during its five years of play.

Two early August contests with Boston, by far the best National Association team, made a big impact on Borden's short major-league career. On August 3 rainy weather in Boston forced cancellation of the day's game between the Pearls and Red Caps, but a large contingent of fanatics were treated to a muddy exhibition between the two clubs, with each team exchanging pitchers and catchers. Boston won the six-inning contest, 4-2, with the *Boston Globe* noting that Borden "bothered his own men so that they went out in one, two, three order" in the first and second innings.[9]

Though the weather was threatening on August 4, the 4-3 Boston victory in 11 innings was, in the *Globe's* opinion, "one of the most, if not *the* most exciting game ever played in this city."[10] According to the *Boston Journal*, "Josephs, for an amateur player, is certainly a marvel. Not only is he one of the finest pitchers which the Bostons have ever faced, but he is a splendid fielder and good batsman. His delivery is swift and accurate, and he has the strength to hold out, as his pitching of yesterday demonstrated, for in the eleventh inning he was, if anything, swifter than in the other innings. ... [He is] a pitcher, not a thrower."[11]

After a 2-0 loss to Chicago on August 5, Borden notched his second win of the year on August 9 with a 16-0 rout of the St. Louis Brown Stockings, surrendering just four hits. From August 18 through the end of the season on October 25, George Zettlein pitched 21 of the Pearls' remaining 23 games. Borden briefly returned to the box on September 2 against Boston, a contest that ended in an 8-8, 10-inning tie. He finished the season with a 2-4 record, pitching 66 innings and posting an ERA of 1.50, third in the league. His opponents' batting average of .181 and on-

base percentage of .203 were the lowest for a pitcher that season. (It was the last year of the National Association, a league that started with 13 teams and finished with seven.)

Borden came to be known as "the phenomenon" or "Josephus the Phenomenal." He again pitched for the Doerr club on September 3, but received lucrative offers from several professional teams, including the Philadelphia Pearls. Knowing that he could fall back on work in the boot and shoe business, with his father or otherwise, Borden sought a long-term contract. Nevertheless, on September 5, the Boston Red Caps' president Nathaniel Apollonio, and manager Harry Wright, signed Borden to a three-year contract worth $2,000 a year. According to baseball historian Peter Morris, this was one of the first multiyear contracts in major-league history.

The *Boston Daily Advertiser* was effusive in its praise of Borden, calling him "probably the best pitcher in the country next to [future Hall of Fame member Al] Spalding," who would soon sign with Chicago.¹²

With the National Association giving way to the new National League, the Boston club held its first 1876 practice at a YMCA on March 16. Borden was reported to be in splendid condition due to playing skittles during the winter. According to the *Globe*, all of the players were weighed and measured; Borden was listed at 5-feet-7¼-inches tall, (shorter than the 5-feet-9 listed in today's records) and 139¾ pounds.

The first game in National League history took place on April 22 at the Philadelphia Athletics' Jefferson Street Grounds. Borden and the Red Caps edged the Athletics, 6-5, before 3,000 spectators, making him the league's first winning pitcher. The Athletics stroked ten hits, but squandered a superior offensive attack by making 11 errors. In a rematch two days later, Philadelphia routed Boston, 20-3; according to the *Inquirer*, "Josephs … was hit with ease."¹³

On April 25 Borden was the winning pitcher in a 7-6 victory over the New York Mutuals; manager Harry Wright replaced him with Jack Manning in the fifth inning, after he had surrendered five runs, making Borden the first starting pitcher in the National League to be relieved.

Boston's first home game, on April 29, was a 3-2 loss to Hartford. The winning run scored on Borden's wild pitch with two outs in the 10th, a ball that sailed 10 feet over the catcher's head and into the grandstand, where, according to the *Globe's* Tim Murnane, "[it]made a hit with a swell society woman of Chicago … hitting her in the face. The game was delayed while Mr. Borden went into the stand and made a dignified apology, and later called at the woman's residence, where in due time he was royally entertained and pronounced a well-bred gallant."¹⁴

Borden's next game was also memorable. In the third inning of a 15-3 Hartford victory, he hit a leadoff single but became confused about who had the ball and was tagged out by first-baseman Everett Mills, thus becoming the first National Leaguer to be a victim of the hidden-ball trick. For the second game in a row, Borden was replaced at pitcher by Manning and spent the rest of the game in right field.

On May 23, 1876, Borden pitched what might have been the first no-hitter in National League history, blanking the Cincinnati Red Stockings, 8-0. Box scores indicate two hits for the Reds, but 75 years later, according to SABR researcher David Nemec, baseball historian Lee Allen found that the two hits charged to Borden were really walks called hits by official scorer Opie Caylor, who usually counted walks as hits. This conclusion continues to be controversial; scorekeeping was not uniform in that era. Other historians doubt Allen's interpretation and maintain that George Bradley threw the league's first no-hitter, in July 1876.

Borden's stock took a dive during June. Chicago, with Al Spalding pitching, won three straight against Boston and Borden between May 30 and June 3, putting to rest the assertion that Borden was anywhere near Spalding's equal. Joe's wild throws and his nervous demeanor were harshly criticized by fans and the press, which suspected that he had a sore arm. Others speculated that he had changed his delivery or "lost his cunning." In the *Chicago Tribune's* opinion, "These games should … convince the Bostonians that Borden is nothing more than a third-class player in the pitcher's position. If they don't believe it now, they will within two weeks."¹⁵ According to author Neil Macdonald, "It was plainly evident that [Borden's] future was becoming the substance of clouds. He was throwing so wildly that batsmen and umpires gyrated in turbulent terror dodging his errant throws. … He was throwing tantrums over his own inability to throw strikes."¹⁶

On June 29 Borden recorded his final major-league "first." Pop Snyder of the Louisville Grays hit a 10th-inning home run off him to give Louisville an 8-6 win over Boston. It was the first extra-inning game-winning home run in the National League.

Borden's final pitching appearance was on July 15, 1876, a 15-0 loss to Chicago and Al Spalding; Borden was relieved by Manning in the fifth after giving up four runs. The *Chicago Tribune* concluded that the two pitchers' performance represented "some of the worst pitching of the year. … Neither Manning nor Josephs were any sort of use against the Whites, who had their batting armor on and made things very lively in the field."[17] This was the final straw for Harry Wright, who had Manning make the next 11 starts. Foghorn Bradley replaced him for the final 17 games.

Borden made his final major-league appearance on July 19 in Philadelphia, where he played right field in a 10-7 win over the Athletics. It was his 16th game in the outfield, where he had seven errors and a miserable .462 fielding percentage. For the year, Borden was 11-12 in the box with a 2.89 ERA (10th in the league) in 218 1/3 innings. He had 22 errors as a pitcher (second in the league), 34 strikeouts (sixth), and 21 wild pitches (third).

Borden was mediocre as a hitter, posting a .188 average; extra-base hits were rare (three doubles) and RBIs (8) were hard to come by. One of his better days at the plate was against Al Spalding on June 3, when he was 2-for-4 with a run scored.

Although Borden was released by the Red Caps on August 17, there was the matter of the two-plus years remaining on his contract. According to Peter Morris, club management came up with a plan to deal with the situation. First, they tried to get Borden to abandon his contract, which failed. Next, they gave him twice-a-day groundskeeping duties while also requiring him to attend daily practices. Borden, who had obtained legal advice on the contract's validity, did all that was asked of him, including serving as an umpire for an exhibition game between Boston and Fall River on October 14. He continued to be employed by the Red Caps until February 1877, when club president and noted tightwad Arthur Soden negotiated a buyout.

With his exit, the press brutally reviewed Borden's tenure in Boston. The *Boston Herald* called his engagement "ill-advised, although he showed some talent as a pitcher. ... [He was] one of the most outrageous frauds who ever saw his name in a score sheet ... hired at a large salary to do certain work which he could not do, and the least spark of manhood or decency in him would have dictated his withdrawal when he could not carry out his contract. No one but a plug would have hung on and drawn money for which he returned no service. ... he was a glaring failure."[18]

In 1900 the *Globe's* Murnane called Borden "perhaps the greatest failure that ever came to the Boston club." He wrote that Borden's initial trial with the 1875 Philadelphia club was "as much for a joke as anything," suggesting that he "was cute enough to lay up for the rest of the season and pick the best offer for the next year."[19]

Done with professional baseball, Borden returned to Pennsylvania. In 1878 he was living in West Chester, near Philadelphia, and had his own business manufacturing and retailing boots and shoes. He briefly returned to baseball during the summer of 1883 when he joined West Chester's Brandywine Base Ball Club, a semipro team that played the region's best competition. On August 28 Borden pitched, played first base, and was 1-for-11 as Brandywine won games from two clubs, Christiana and the Alerts of Rock Run. His only other connection to baseball occurred in July 1888 when he was on a sales trip to Washington and ran into Boston Beaneaters' manager John Morrill, a former Red Cap teammate, on the train. Morrill introduced him to future Hall of Fame pitcher John Clarkson and catcher King Kelly.

In early June 1889, *Sporting Life* reported that Borden was a victim of the disastrous Great Johnstown (Pennsylvania) Flood, an error that was corrected in its June 19 issue, which said that he was "safe at his home in Philadelphia."[20]

On February 7, 1891, Borden married Henrietta S. Evans in West Chester. The *Inquirer* described the festivities as "a brilliant society wedding."[21] Evans was the daughter of newspaper publisher and politician Henry S. Evans and his wife, Jane, whose father was a doctor, historian, noted botanist, and former Congressman William Darlington. Her grandfather was Revolutionary War General John Lacey, who later served in the New Jersey legislature. The Bordens set up residence with her mother in West Chester. They had two children, Richard, who did not survive his first year, and Lavinia.

By the time of his marriage, Borden was out of the footwear business and was an officer of a Philadelphia bank, Guarantee Trust and Safe Deposit Company, a position he held for more than two decades. He was also the Philadelphia representative of the U.S. Shipping Board, a federal government agency. By 1900 the Bordens had moved to Fernwood, a neighborhood in Yeadon, a west Philadelphia suburb.

Although he wasn't involved in baseball, Borden took pride in being in good physical condition and trained regularly at the Philadelphia Boxing Academy, where he was an amateur boxer "as good as the best," in the opinion of the West Chester *Daily Local News*.[22] An avid hunter, Borden was a member of the Girard Kennel Club and owned some of the finest hunting dogs in the country, both beagles and bird hounds. One of his bird dogs, Ruby D III, won every show she was exhibited in and, according to the *Daily Local News*, "proved so finely drawn in all points that she became known world-wide and the standard of the class was raised by the dog authorities because of her showing."[23]

Borden died on October 14, 1929, at the home of his daughter, Lavinia Cook Borden Adams, in Lansdowne, Pennsylvania. He was 75; the cause of death was listed as paralysis. He was survived by his daughter and a sister, Florence Borden of Philadelphia. His death came on the same day the Philadelphia Athletics won the World Series with a 3-2 victory over the Chicago Cubs. He is buried in the Darlington family plot at West Chester's Oaklands Cemetery. According to Rich Westcott, "His grave site was unkempt and unnoticed for many years until located by SABR member Tom Taylor [in 1990]. The unadorned tombstone makes no mention [of his] baseball career."[24]

SOURCES

In addition to the items in the notes, the author also consulted Borden's player file at the National Baseball Hall of Fame and numerous other newspaper articles, as well as the following publications:

Creamer, Robert W. "Twas Time For A Change." *Sports Illustrated*, April 4, 1986.

Morris, Peter. *A Game of Inches: The Story Behind the Innovations That Shaped Baseball* (Chicago: Ivan R. Dee, 2010).

Prager, Joshua. *The Echoing Green: The Untold Story of Bobby Thomson, Ralph Branca and The Shot Heard Round The World*. (Random House Digital, Inc., 2008).

Vincent, David, and Jayson Stark. *Home Run: The Definitive History of Baseball's Ultimate Weapon* (Dulles, Virginia: Potomac Books, 2008).

ACKNOWLEDGEMENT

Thanks to Karen Zindel for her research at the Chester County Historical Society, West Chester, Pennsylvania.

NOTES

1. Neil W. Macdonald, *The League That Lasted: 1876 and the Founding of the National League* (Jefferson, North Carolina: McFarland, 2004), 74.
2. "Philadelphia News," *Sporting Life*, June 27, 1888: 2.
3. David Nemec. *The Great Encyclopedia of Nineteenth Century Major League Baseball* (Tuscaloosa: University of Alabama Press, 2006), 7.
4. Rich Westcott. "Joe Borden: The First No-Hit Pitcher and National League Winner," *The National Pastime*, Vol. 23 (2003): 69-70.
5. "Philadelphia And Suburbs: Out Door Sports," *Philadelphia Inquirer*, July 26, 1875: 2.
6. T. H. Murnane, "Old-Time Baseball," *Boston Globe*, February 19, 1900: 6.
7. "Base Ball," *Philadelphia Inquirer*, July 27, 1875: 2.
8. "Chicagos-Philadelphias," *Chicago Tribune*, July 29, 1875: 5.
9. Undated *Boston Globe* newspaper clipping.
10. "Yesterday's Sports," *Boston Globe*, August 5, 1875: 5.
11. "Boston and Vicinity," *Boston Journal*, August 5, 1875: 4.
12. "Our New Pitcher," *Boston Daily Advertiser*, September 6, 1875: 57.
13. "Base Ball," *Philadelphia Inquirer*, April 25, 1876: 2.
14. T. H. Murnane.
15. "Base Ball, *Chicago Tribune*, June 4, 1876: 3.
16. Neil W. Macdonald. *The League That Lasted: 1876 and the Founding of the National League of Professional Baseball Clubs* (Jefferson, North Carolina: McFarland, 2004), 119, 123.
17. "Base Ball, *Chicago Tribune*, July 16, 1876: 3.
18. Undated *Boston Herald* newspaper clipping.
19. T. H. Murnane.
20. "One Saved, The Other Lost," *Sporting Life*, June 19, 1889: 1.
21. "Brilliant Society Wedding," *Philadelphia Inquirer*, February 8, 1891: 5.

22 *Daily Local News* (West Chester, Pennsylvania), October 16, 1929.

23 Ibid.

24 Westcott, 70.

THE FIRST PROFESSIONAL NO-HITTER
JULY 28, 1875: PHILADELPHIA 4, CHICAGO 0, AT JEFFERSON STREET GROUNDS, PHILADELPHIA

By Casey Tibbitts

PROFESSIONAL BASEBALL in the 19th century produced many notable firsts and many colorful characters, but rarely were the two combined as they were on July 28, 1875. On that warm midsummer day 21-year-old Joseph Emley Borden, in just his third start for the Athletics of Philadelphia of the National Association, etched his name firmly in the history books by pitching professional baseball's first no-hitter.

In July 1875 the National Association of Professional Base Ball Players, baseball's first professional league, was midway through its fifth and final season. Borden came to the Philadelphia club only because Cherokee Fisher, the team's hard-drinking pitcher, had clashed with team captain Mike McGeary and was released. To fill the hole the club lured away Chicago's George Zettlein, one of the better hurlers in the league. But Zettlein was slow to arrive in Philadelphia, so McGeary was forced to turn to the local amateur teams for an interim solution.[1] He found Borden, whose style John Morrill would later describe as "so entirely different from every one else that nobody could hit him."[2]

Borden agreed to pitch for Philadelphia but only if he was listed in game accounts and box scores as Joseph E. Josephs, evidently to keep his well-heeled family in New Jersey from discovering that he was playing baseball for pay. (He was also known to have played as Joseph Nedrob, Borden spelled backwards).[3]

McGeary agreed, and Borden, now Josephs, joined the club on July 24 for its game against the crosstown rival Athletics at the Jefferson Street Grounds. It was an inauspicious debut, as Borden and the White Stockings lost 11-4 before a crowd estimated at 1,000. Two days later the Chicago White Stockings arrived for the first of two scheduled games, and Borden again was defeated, this time by a score of 5-1.

The clubs squared off again for the series finale two days later, on Wednesday, July 28, and this time Borden's fortunes took a dramatic turn. He defeated the visitors 4-0 and in the process pitched the first no-hit game in the short history of professional baseball. His performance instantly made him a star.[4]

Borden, still known as Joe Josephs, started four more games for Philadelphia. His first two outings after the no-hitter were losses, but he earned his second win of the season with an outstanding 16-0 shutout of St. Louis on August 9, defeating an 18-year-old Pud Galvin. At this point Zettlein arrived and took over the pitching chores. Borden started one last game, on September 2, tying Boston and Albert Spalding 8-8. He left the team with a record of two wins and four losses in seven starts. But Borden still had two significant games to play.

In 1876 the National Association folded and the National League was formed to take its place. Harry Wright moved his champion Boston team into the new league, but in the process lost Spalding to Chicago. To fill the void created by the defection of his star pitcher, he signed Borden to an unheard-of three-year contract at the princely sum of $2,000 per season. Local sportswriters immediately hailed him as Spalding's successor and dubbed him "Josephus the Phenomenal."[5]

On April 22, 1876, Borden, now playing under his real name, beat Philadelphia 6-5 in the first game in National League history, making him the league's first winning pitcher.[6]

The following month Borden narrowly missed out on yet another first when Boston defeated the Cincinnati Red Stockings 8-0, with Borden allowing only two hits. The official scorer that day was O.P. Caylor, whose practice it was to count bases on balls as hits. In 1950 historian Lee Allen researched the game and argued that the hits had actually been walks, and that Borden should have been credited with the National League's first no-hitter. It remains uncertain how Caylor actually scored the game.[7]

Borden started 18 of Boston's first 19 games in 1876 before showing signs of arm soreness and fatigue. He yielded the box for five starts, then returned for five more. On July 15 he pitched an embarrassing 15-0 loss to Chicago and Spalding. Frustrated with his performance, Wright dropped Borden, still only 22, from the team. His final totals for the year were 11 wins and 12 losses in 24 starts.

Since Borden was still under contract, the club put him to work taking tickets, cutting the grass, and mending the fences, hoping he would quit and void the agreement. But he went about his new job cheerfully, and the club bought him out at the end of the season.[8] He later found work stitching baseballs, and was erroneously reported to have died in the Johnstown Flood of 1889.[9] In fact he passed away in 1929 at the age of 75, his name firmly written in baseball lore as the man who pitched professional baseball's first no-hitter.

This essay was originally published in Inventing Baseball: The 100 Greatest Games of the 19th Century *(SABR, 2013), edited by Bill Felber.*

NOTES

1. David Nemec and David Zeman, *The Baseball Rookies Encyclopedia* (Dulles, Virginia: Brassey's, 2004), 7.
2. A.G. Spalding, *Spalding's Official Base Ball Guide for 1896* (New York: American Sports Publication, 1896).
3. William A. Cook, *The Louisville Grays Scandal of 1877: The Taint of Gambling at the Dawn of the National League* (Jefferson, North Carolina: McFarland, 2005), 42.
4. Nemec and Zeman, 7.
5. Harold Kaese, *The Boston Braves, 1871-1953* (Boston: University Press of New England, 2004), 19.
6. Rich Westcott, *Philadelphia's Old Ballparks* (Philadelphia: Temple University Press, 1996), 5.
7. Cook, 50.
8. George V. Tuohey, *A History of the Boston Base Ball Club* (Boston: M. F. Quinn & Co., 1897), 202.
9. Cook, 166.

Phil.	R	H	PO	A	Chicago	R	H	PO	A
Murnane, 1b	0	1	13	0	Higham, c	0	0	5	2
McGeary, 2b	1	1	5	4	Devlin, 1b	0	0	13	0
Addy, rf	1	2	0	0	Hines, cf	0	0	2	0
Meyerle, 3b	1	2	0	0	Glenn, lf	0	0	3	0
Snyder, c	0	0	4	1	Peters, ss	0	0	0	7
Fulmer, ss	0	0	0	4	Miller, 2b	0	0	1	2
McMullin, cf	0	0	3	0	Golden, p	0	0	2	1
Josephs, p	0	0	1	2	Warren, 3b	0	0	1	0
Treacey, lf	1	1	1	0	Bielski, rf	0	0	0	0
	4	7	27	11		0	0	27	12
Chicago	0 0 0				0 0 0	0 0 0 – 0			
Philadelphia	1 2 0				0 0 0	1 0 0 – 4			

Runs earned – None. First base on errors – Chicago 4, Philadelphia 1. Umpire – N.E. Young. Time – 1:35.

GEORGE WASHINGTON BRADLEY

By Brian C. Engelhardt

GEORGE WASHINGTON Bradley[1] of the St. Louis Brown Stockings shut out (or, in the baseball parlance of the time, "Chicagoed") the Hartford Dark Blues by a score of 2-0 on July 15, 1876. Aside from their being Chicagoed, the Blues also failed to get any hits in the process (although Bradley did walk two) establishing this game as the first no-hitter in the history of the recently formed National League. Bradley's nickname, "Grin," came from the constant smile he showed to batters as he pitched. It apparently made a striking impression. Years after he retired, an article in *The Sporting News* mentioned that "no one before ever had such a tantalizing smirk."[2]

While being the architect of the National League's inaugural no-hitter is Bradley's most noted accomplishment, during that same 1876 season besides shutting out the Dark Blues, he did the same to 15 other teams—a total of 16 shutouts in the season: a record that was matched only by Grover Cleveland Alexander in 1916 (it must be those presidential names). Referring to Bradley as the "Chicago King," baseball historian David Nemec suggested that the term may have arisen because Bradley's first shutout victim that season was the Chicago White Stockings, who succumbed 1-0 on May 5.[3] The unlikelihood that this record will ever be surpassed is underscored by the fact that since Juan Marichal threw 10 shutouts in 1965, only three pitchers have reached double figures: Bob Gibson with 13 in 1968, Jim Palmer with 10 in 1975, and John Tudor with 10 in 1985.

Bradley's professional career extended over 15 years, including 11 seasons with nine different teams in four different major leagues—in many ways mirroring Organized Baseball's state of flux at the time. Appearing in 347 games as a pitcher, Bradley compiled 171 victories. He played in 269 other games as a position player—mostly at third base, where his fielding skills were quite accomplished. In addition to his major-league travels, Bradley played for eight minor-league teams.

Born in Reading, Pennsylvania, on July 13, 1852, to George and Margaret Bradley,[4] George was the first native of the city to play in the major leagues. Although references to Bradley in Reading newspapers during his career occasionally mentioned his having been "born and raised in Reading," there is otherwise little information available about his life before he started playing in Philadelphia in 1872, the same year in which he married Philadelphia native Charlotte Heavener.

Early in the 1874 season, while playing for Philadelphia's Modoc club (described as a "third-rate amateur club"[5]) against an independent team from Easton, Pennsylvania, Bradley showed skills that caught the eye of Easton's manager, Jack Smith, who signed him as an infielder who would also pitch batting practice. When Smith observed that Bradley's new teammates couldn't handle his pitches during batting practice, he tried him out as a starting pitcher. That experiment went so well that that Smith, who had been the starting pitcher, benched himself in favor of Bradley. Bradley and catcher Tom Miller developed a fine relationship, which would lead to their both playing for the St. Louis Brown Stockings the next season. The chemistry between the two was noted by the *Easton Daily Express* after a 14-0 Easton victory over the Collins Club of Philadelphia in August. "Bradley and Miller worked together like a charm, many people remarking that it was their best game this year," the paper said, also describing Bradley's pitches in the game as "lightning bolts."[6]

Later that month Bradley returned to his hometown of Reading when Easton came to play the semipro Reading Actives. Before a crowd of about 4,000, Easton won the game, 11-6, in what the *Reading Eagle* described as "one of the most closely contested (games) that either club has ever played." With the score tied, 4-4, Easton broke the game open with five runs in the eighth inning. (*The Reading Times* account attributed the rally to Easton "doing some heavy batting,"[7] while the *Eagle* found Easton's runs to be the product of "bad luck, overthrows and a general demoralization"[8] on the part of the home team.) Although no statistics on the 1874 Actives or its players can be found, must have been a good one; the game account in the *Eagle* was headlined "Actives' First Defeat."[9] The account related that Bradley's "balls came in very swiftly and during the first part of the game were not hit."[10]

The *Eagle* said the Easton club was "regarded by knowing professional players to be the very best club in the country not on the professional lists,"[11] and said Easton clearly came to town as "enemy" in the eyes of the Reading locals. The *Easton Daily Express* complained that followers of the Actives "were in danger of life and limb from the blackguards and roughs of Reading, (unable) to praise the Eastons without being insulted and threatened."[12]

In a return match a few weeks later, Easton again won, 34-18, with the *Express* declaring that Reading did not appear "to get the hang of Bradley until the ninth inning."[13]

In early August Easton lost at home in front of a crowd of 2,000 to the National Association Brooklyn Atlantics by 30-11 in a game in which Bradley gave up 19 hits but was victimized by 16 Easton errors that resulted in only 4 of the Atlantics' 30 runs counting as earned runs.[14] At the end of the season Easton achieved consecutive exhibition victories over three National Association teams: the Atlantics in a rematch, then the Philadelphia Whites and finally the Philadelphia Athletics. As a result, Bradley was invited to pitch for the Athletics in an October exhibition against the Boston Red Stockings. In the game he impressed enough that St. Louis signed him after the season.

The 1875 Brown Stockings were managed by 39-year-old shortstop Dickey Pearce, and its roster included a number of players besides Bradley with Easton connections, starting with his batterymate

Tom Miller, who had played four games with the Athletics near the end of the 1874 season. Also signed from the 1874 Easton team were third baseman Bill Hague, a light hitter known for his strong throwing arm and light-hitting outfielder Charlie Waitt. Browns second baseman Joe Battin played for Easton in 1873 before signing with the Philadelphia Athletics, where he spent the 1874 season.

Bradley's major-league debut was as the Opening Day pitcher on May 4, 1875, pitching the team to a 15-9 victory over the St. Louis Red Stockings. Two days later, on May 6, Bradley became an instant St. Louis fan favorite, shutting out the hated Chicago White Stockings, 10-0, in front of 8,000 fans at Grand Avenue Park in St. Louis, with another 2,000 peeking through knotholes or perched in trees outside the park.[15]

On June 2 Bradley suffered his first loss of the season, 10-3 to a Boston Red Stockings team that went an amazing 71-8 that season. Boston's lineup featured future Hall of Famers Harry and George Wright, Al Spalding, Orator Jim O'Rourke, and

Deacon White, who would hit a league-leading .367. Also in the Boston lineup were White's closest competitors in the batting race, Ross Barnes (.364) and Cal McVey (.355). The Red Stockings' victory boosted their record so far to 25-0.

Three days later Bradley avenged the loss by handing the Red Stockings their first defeat as he pitched St. Louis to a 5-4 win. The *Boston Globe* said that Bradley and "the 'Brown Sox' were carried off the field on the shoulders of their friends."[16]

On June 7, with St. Louis in a frenzy over "Brown Stocking fever," a crowd described by the *Globe* as "the largest ever seen on a ball field in this city, about 8,000"[17] saw the Red Stockings pound Bradley for 24 hits (he was said to be suffering from an attack of vertigo), with Spalding holding the home team to six hits as the visitors won, 15-2.

Just as was the case during their season in Easton, Bradley worked well with Miller, the duo being credited for much of the Browns' success. A contemporary commentator wrote that the two constituted "the main strength of the club," adding, "They are not supported by a first class field but, if their work of to-day is a criterion, they do not need one. The field(ers) were called upon to do but the easiest kind of play… and scarcely a ball was struck that would bother an ordinary player."[18] The leading hitter on the team was outfielder Lip Pike, while outfielder Jack Chapman exhibited such skill in the field that he earned the nickname of "Death To Flying Things."

A number of factors contributed to Bradley's success on the mound. At 5-feet-10 and 175 pounds, he was a big man for the times (in 1876 he was the fourth-tallest pitcher in the National League) and he used his size to power his delivery. Equally imposing from a psychological

standpoint was the "smile" Bradley showed batters. In his analysis of Bradley's pitching technique, baseball historian Neil MacDonald declared the rather innocuous moniker of "Grin" to be a nickname that "belied a serious, savagely determined … man who wanted to play and win as much as any man alive."[19]

MacDonald wrote that Bradley combined the abilities of a "straight pitcher like Al Spalding, considered to be the best in the game, with the ingenuity of a breaking ball specialist like Candy Cummings, the consummate chucker of curves."[20] An additional factor contributing to Bradley's success during the 1876 season involved a new tactic learned from Browns teammate Mike McGeary: crushing game balls in a vise.

On October 26, 1875, Bradley returned to Reading with the Browns for an exhibition game against the semipro Reading Actives. Bradley and catcher Tom Miller were featured in ads in the *Times* and the *Eagle* referring to him as "The famous Bradley" and proclaiming, "The old foes are coming. Bradley and Miller—St. Louis professionals versus Actives."[21] Upon Bradley's arrival in Reading the day before the game, the *Eagle* described him as "the best looking ballplayer in the profession."[22]

The next day the Browns defeated the Actives 18-11 in a sloppy game in which the Actives committed 20 errors and the Browns 12. Bradley entered the game in relief of the Browns backup pitcher, Pud Galvin, who surrendered eight runs in five innings, allowing the Actives to pull ahead at one point, 8-7. Bradley quieted the Actives' bats and the Browns erupted for 11 runs in the final four innings. (The *Eagle* headlined its game story "One of the Worst Games Yet,"[23] but failed to provide the score. Without the *Reading Times's* game account, posterity would never have known the score.)

The 18-year-old Galvin had been signed at the start of the season to back up Bradley after he had pitched impressively for the Niagara amateur team of St. Louis in a preseason game against the Browns.[24] Galvin pitched in three games in a row in late May, winning two, when Bradley was sidelined with health problems. Bradley returned the lineup on May 29, after which Galvin made only four more pitching starts. On his way to becoming baseball's first 300-game winner, over the next 17 years Galvin won another 361 games en route to his induction into the Baseball Hall of Fame.

The National Association of 1875 suffered from a great disparity between the haves and have-nots. The Browns finished in fourth place with a record of

39-29, a distant 26½ games behind the Red Stockings. As the winning pitcher in all but six of the Browns' victories, Bradley finished his rookie season with a record of 33-26, starting 60 games and finishing 57, with 5 shutouts. In 535⅔ innings pitched, Bradley struck out 60 and gave up a remarkably low 17 walks.

During the tumultuous offseason that followed, the National League was created, the National Association dissolved, a number of former National Association teams (the Browns among them) joining the new league, and a multitude of players moving to new teams. Although Bradley remained with the Browns, his surrounding cast underwent changes, the most dramatic being catcher Tommy Miller contracting a disabling illness over the winter from which he died on May 29, 1876.[25] Miller's replacement, Honest John Clapp, was signed away from the Philadelphia Athletics in the offseason and is viewed as one of the most talented catchers in baseball at the time. Despite the success Bradley enjoyed over the two seasons Miller was his batterymate, at least one commentator credited Clapp for helping Bradley go from very good in 1875 to superlative in 1876.[26]

Other changes to the Browns lineup included Bill Hague and "Death To Flying Things" Chapman both signing with Louisville, and 40-year-old Dicky Pearce being replaced as shortstop by Denny Mack. Pearce and as manager by Mase Graffen. (With superior fielding skills, Pearce returned as the starting shortstop later in the season even though he was 14 years older than Mack.)

Also moving on was Pud Galvin, leaving his role as Bradley's understudy to become the primary pitcher with the St. Louis Red Stockings, an unaffiliated team made up mostly of members of the team's 1875 National Association entry. Galvin was not replaced as Bradley's backup, or change pitcher; during the 1876 season Bradley threw every inning for the Browns except for four innings of relief pitched by Joe Blong.

On April 25, 1876, just before the start of the season, the *Louisville Courier-Journal* declared that Bradley was the hardest man in the profession to bat against.[27] This did not appear to be the case at the season's outset, as the Browns and Bradley lost the first two games of the season to a bad Cincinnati Reds club that won only seven more games that season. As the season progressed, Bradley did his best to confirm the *Courier-Journal's* analysis. During a series in late May against the New York Mutuals, he threw only 24 balls in 27 innings.[28] A 17-0 shutout of the Athletics on June 1 was his sixth of the year. He pitched two more shutouts in June, four in July, three in August, and one in September on his way to setting the record of 16 in a season.

In early July Bradley signed a contract with the Philadelphia Athletics for the following year. When word of this came out, the St. Louis press criticized him for "treachery," and the *Chicago Tribune* speculated that he would not try to win games in a coming series against the Hartford Blues. Bradley's response to this was to shut out Hartford three times in five days, culminating with the 2-0 victory on July 15 in which the Dark Blues failed to get a hit. The *Tribune* ran a retraction.[29]

Appreciation of no-hitters was in its nascent state at the time, and most accounts of the game focused on Hartford's poor hitting, with little attention given to the fact that Bradley had not allowed a hit, with some accounts not even mentioning that it was a no-hitter.[30]

On May 23 Boston's Joe Borden had shut out the Cincinnati Reds, giving up only two walks, which were recorded as hits consistent with scoring rules at that time. Bradley's gem has been considered the first no-hitter in the National League. (The previous season Borden, pitching for the Philadelphia Pearls in the National Association, threw the first major-league no-hitter, 4-0 against the Chicago White Stockings. As for his 1876 shutout of Cincinnati, sportswriters and league officials disagreed over categorizing as walks as hits, but, as Neil W. McDonald wrote, "Enough doubt has been cast on Borden's efforts against Cincinnati to erase his honor of tossing the first National League no-hitter. Only God and the ghosts of '76 know if Borden was sinned against."[31]

Along with Bradley's range of pitches, pinpoint control, having the best catcher in the league, and having a withering grin, an unseemly side to his success in 1876 involved gamesmanship (or cheating, depending upon one's view). According to Bradley's former manager Frank Bancroft, the pitcher learned from teammate Mike McGeary how to steam open the sealed box containing the new ball to be used for the game, put the ball in a vise to crush it, and then reseal the box, creating a new mushy ball.[32] Aside from the process enhancing Bradley's curve, the ball usually lost its shape over the course of the game, allowing a crafty pitcher like Bradley to alter its plateward course with more trickery.[33]

With the Browns in third place for much of the season behind Chicago and Hartford, on August 17 Bradley shut out the visiting White Stockings, 3-0, culminating a stretch in which the team went 14-3 and moved past Hartford into second place, six games behind Chicago. The Browns took another game from Chicago and moved within five games of first, the closest they would get that season. (They finished in second place also with a record of 45-19, six games behind the White Stockings. Bradley pitched 573 innings, all but four innings of the St. Louis season, and every decision was his. In addition to his record-setting 16 shutouts, he had a league-low 1.23 earned-run average. He also led the league with 34 wild pitches.

Although Bradley had signed with Philadelphia for the 1877 season, the A's were expelled from the National League for failing to complete their full schedule, and Bradley was able to nullify the contract. Instead he signed with Chicago, but tried to avoid burning bridges in St. Louis, sending the following letter to the *St. Louis Globe-Democrat* (published October 18, 1876), expressing his sentiments to St. Louis fans:

To the Editor of the Globe-Democrat:

Dear Sir: In leaving St. Louis I think it due to myself to make a few remarks in explanation of contracting in Chicago when I did so. I had a private misunderstanding with some of the officers of the St. Louis Club, this being the prime cause of my signing in Chicago.

I desire to say that my relations in St. Louis have been of the most pleasant character and to the hosts of warm friends I have acquired I desire to leave the most sincere expression of gratitude for the kind appreciation of my poor services. I shall always remember St. Louis with the liveliest feelings of respect and can never readily forget the generous treatment I have received in this city, where my professional reputation has to a great extent been made

Yours, etc. G. W. Bradley[34]

The plan with the White Stockings was that Bradley would succeed Al Spalding as the pitcher, with Spalding moving to first base. The plan didn't work out well. Bradley finished the season with a disappointing 18-23 record, with Chicago making no attempt to keep him for the next season. Reasons advanced for the falloff in Bradley's performance were that his former teammate McGeary, who had taught him the crushed-ball ploy, warned other teams of the trick,[35] and that the White Stockings made the mistake of not signing John Clapp to catch Bradley.[36]

After his season with the White Stockings, Bradley set out on an odyssey that would see him switch teams 16 times over the next 12 seasons, playing in 16 cities in various major and minor leagues. Bradley began the 1878 season with New Bedford of the fledgling International Association (which was meant to rival the National League but never did), signed by its manager, Frank Bancroft. When things didn't work out with the league to Bancroft's satisfaction, after just three games he pulled the club from the league and instead played an independent schedule for the season.[37] The team played 130 games against teams on the East Coast, with Bradley logging in more than 760 innings.[38]

The next season (1879) Bradley pitched for the last-place Troy Trojans of the National League, posting 13 wins to go with a league-leading 40 losses. In 1880 he moved to the Providence Grays of the National League, where he alternated playing third base and pitching with John Montgomery Ward. After signing with the Detroit Wolverines of the National League for 1880, he was released because of health issues after playing one game at shortstop. He then signed with the Cleveland Blues, but negotiated a release that resulted in his being sold for $500[39] to the Philadelphia Athletics of the American Association (Bradley's third major league) in June of 1883.[40]

With the A's Bradley won 16 games as the team's primary backup pitcher to Bobby Mathews; when not pitching he played third base. In September, when Mathews was out with arm problems, Bradley and Jumping Jack Jones put together a string of pitching performances that enabled the A's to win seven in a row on their way to the pennant. Despite his heroics, Bradley was released after the season, telling one interviewer, "They sent me adrift, just as you would a broken down horse. But that was strictly business, you know."[41]

The next year Bradley signed with the Cincinnati Outlaw Reds of the ill-fated Union Association, which existed only in 1884 (Bradley's fourth and final major league). His record was 25-15 as the team's primary pitcher. After the dissolution of the UA, for his playing in that league and jumping his contract with the Philadelphia, Bradley found himself blacklisted from other major-league teams for the 1885 season. Adding financial insult to career injury, Bradley never received what the Cincinnati team agreed to pay him, leading him to sue the defunct team. He eventually settled for $1,500 in cash, considerably less than what he was owed, since the team had gone bankrupt.

In 1886 Bradley signed with the Philadelphia Athletics again, as a shortstop, but was released after 13 games with an average of .083. Despite letting him go, Athletics manager Bill Sharsig called him "the hardest working and most conscientious player for his club that we ever had."[42] Despite these fine intangibles, Sharsig said, Bradley's hitting was too weak to keep him on the team.

Over the remainder of 1886 and the next four seasons Bradley played for seven minor-league teams, beginning with Nashville of the Southern League. At the outset of the next season he not only played for Nashville, but managed the team as well, where he played third base, and also envisioned making a pitching comeback.[43] Replaced as manager at the end of May,[44] he moved on to play with the New Orleans Pelicans of the same league, then appeared briefly with the Baltimore Orioles of the American Association before finishing the season with Danville in a league in Illinois.[45] In 1888 he played third base and first base for the New Orleans Pelicans of the Southern League. When the league disbanded in July, New Orleans joined the independent Texas League. Bradley moved north for the 1889 season, playing third base (and pitching one inning) for the Sioux City Corn Huskers of the Western Association. In 1890 he went full circle and finished his career in Easton of the Eastern Interstate League, playing 21 games at third base and batting .299.

With his baseball career over, Bradley first worked as a night watchman and then joined the Philadelphia police force. His son George W. Jr. apparently showed some baseball talent, and in 1907 Bradley talked of his son's growing abilities, referring to him as a, "keeper" (who) …will make good either at third-base or behind the bat.[46] No records could be found relating to a baseball career for George Jr.

In 1915 Bradley made an appearance at a revival in Philadelphia conducted by the former major leaguer Billy Sunday, whose career overlapped Bradley's. Seeing Bradley, on duty and in uniform, Sunday encouraged him to come forward, calling out to him, "Brad, God bless you, old scout."[47] An account of the event described how Bradley "gulped hard as he transferred his mace to his left hand and reached up to grip the reaching hand of his former rival. Then … said simply, 'Bill, I feel better now. Thanks.'"[48]

Bradley retired from the police in 1930.[49] He died of liver cancer on October 2, 1931, and was buried in Norwood Cemetery in Philadelphia. He was survived by his wife, Charlotte; his daughter, Lottie Crouse; and three sons, George W. Jr., John, and Morris. His obituary in the *Philadelphia Inquirer* called him "a close friend of many prominent men connected with big-league baseball today."[50] His hometown *Reading Eagle* ran a brief item noting that he pitched the first no-hitter in the National League, with no mention of his local connection.[51]

SOURCES

In addition to the sources cited in Notes, the author accessed Bradley's player file from the National Baseball Hall of Fame.

Some of the material in this article was also used were used in "Days of Grin and Heck: Berks County's First Two Major Leaguers," which appeared in *The Historical Review of Berks County*, Summer, 2014, Volume 79, Number 5.

Thanks to David Nemec for information and guidance in correspondence with the author, April 21, 2014.

NOTES

1 Not to be confused with George H. "Foghorn" Bradley, a former umpire who won nine games for the 1876 Boston Red Stockings, who, like the subject of this article, is buried in Philadelphia.

2 *The Sporting News*, April 23, 1892, quoted in David Nemec, *Major League Baseball Profiles 1871–1900, Vol. 1*, (Lincoln: University of Nebraska Press, 2009), 18.

3 David Nemec, *The Great Encyclopedia of 19th Century Baseball* (New York: Donald I. Fine Books, 1997), 86.

4 "The Boys Stock Up Again," *Reading Eagle*, September 2, 1876: 1.

5 John David Cash, *Before They Were Cardinals* (Columbia, Missouri: University of Missouri Press, 2002), 26-35.

6 "Baseball—Eastons Again Victorious—Reading Disgraced," *Easton Daily Express*, August 1, 1874.

7 "An Exciting Game Yesterday Between the Eastons, of Easton, Pa., and the Actives of Reading," *Reading Times*, August 4, 1874: 1

8 "Actives First Defeat," *Reading Eagle*, August 4, 1874: 1.

9 Ibid.

10 Ibid.

11 "An Exciting Game."

12 "Baseball," *Easton Daily Express*, August 4, 1874.

13 "Baseball—Easton—Reading," *Easton Daily Express*, August 14, 1874.

14 "Baseball," *Easton Daily Express*, August 19, 1874.

15 Cash, 35.

16 "Summer Sports: The Bostons Defeated by St. Louis Club," *Boston Globe*, June 7, 1875: 5.

17 "Bat and Ball: The Bostons Slaughter the Brown Stockings," *St. Louis Daily Globe-Democrat*, June 8, 1875: 8.

18 Quoted in David Nemec, *Major League Baseball Profiles 1871–1900, Vol. 2* (Lincoln: University of Nebraska Press, 2009), 295.

19 Neil W. McDonald, *The League That Lasted: 1876 and the Founding of the National League of Professional Baseball Clubs* (Jefferson, North Carolina: McFarland and Co., 2004), 143.

20 McDonald, 149.

21 "St. Louis Team in This City," *Reading Eagle*, October 26, 1875: 1.

22 Ibid.

23 "One of Worst Games Yet," *Reading Eagle*, October 27, 1875: 1.

24 Jeffrey Kittel, "This Game of Games, Bradley vs. Galvin, October 3, 2009. thisgameofgames.blogspot.com/search/label/Pud%20Galvin.

25 Nemec, Vol. 2, 296.

26 Section on Clapp written by Peter Morris in Nemec, Vol. 1, 222.

27 McDonald, 105.

28 Ibid.

29 Jeffrey Kittel, "This Game of Games, Bradley's Gratitude," April 27, 2010. thisgameofgames.blogspot.com/search/label/George%20Bradley.

30 McDonald, 152.

31 Ibid.

32 Nemec, Vol. 1, 18.

33 Nemec, Vol. 1, 15.

NO-HITTERS

34 Jeffrey Kittel, "This Game of Games, the 1876 Brown Stockings: The Clubs Might Have Played Until the Resurrection, January 20, 2010. thisgameofgames.blogspot.com/search/label/George%20Bradley.

35 Nemec, Vol. 1, 18.

36 Nemec, Vol. 1, 222.

37 Nemec, Vol. 2, 117.

38 Chapter by Jim Rygelski in Frederick Ivor-Campbell, Robert L. Tiemann, and Mark Rucker, eds, *Baseball's First Stars* (Cleveland: Society for American Baseball Research, 1996), 9.

39 John Shiffert, *Baseball in Philadelphia* (Jefferson, North Carolina: McFarland, 2006), 108.

40 "Bradley Obtains His Release," *Cleveland Leader,* May 19, 1883.

41 Ivor-Campbell, Tiemann, and Rucker, 9.

42 Rygelski.

43 "The Smiling Nashville Manager Talks About His Club," March 9, 1887, Article in unidentified newspaper in Bradley's file at the National Baseball Hall of Fame.

44 "Baseball Notes," *Philadelphia Times,* May 23, 1887: 1.

45 "Baseball Club Disbanded," *Decatur Herald*, September 13, 1887: 3.

46 "Brad the Second," *Sporting Life,* May 25 1907: 6.

47 "Sunday Converts Another Player," *Pittsburgh Press*, February 4, 1915: 24.

48 Ibid.

49 "Old Time Hurler Is Retired as Officer," *Lewiston Evening Journal,* October 2, 1930: 7.

50 "First No Hit Pitcher Struck Out by Death," *Philadelphia Inquirer,* October 3, 1931.

51 "First No Hit No Run Pitcher Passes Away," *Reading Eagle,* October 4, 1931: 13.

WEARIN' OF THE 'GRIN': GEORGE BRADLEY'S NO-HITTER

JULY 15, 1876: ST. LOUIS BROWN STOCKINGS 2, HARTFORD DARK BLUES 0, AT GRAND AVENUE PARK, ST. LOUIS

By Parker Bena

SINCE 1876 MARKED THE US Centennial, it was only fitting that a man given the name of George Washington should play a starring role in that summer's events.

This George Washington—his surname was Bradley—wasn't a politician but a baseball pitcher. On July 15, 1876, less than two weeks after the Centennial observance took place in Philadelphia and less than three weeks after George Armstrong Custer met his doom at Little Bighorn, Bradley became the first pitcher in National League history to throw a no-hit game.

Granted, it was a young National League history at that point. Only the previous February, Chicago businessman William A. Hulbert had gathered together a group to form what would become the National League of Professional Base Ball Clubs.

Bradley pitched for the St. Louis Brown Stockings, and he accomplished his pitching feat against the Hartford Dark Blues at Grand Avenue Park in St. Louis. In two previous meetings that week— one of them coming on his 24th birthday—Bradley had already shut out the Hartfords, both times besting the man who was his pitching opponent again on the 15th, Tommy Bond. Described as a perpetually happy fellow, Bradley was rarely called George or George Washington by those who knew him, but more commonly "Grin." By whatever name, Bradley entered the game in the midst of an amazing streak that would extend to 37 consecutive shutout innings.

His teammates gave Bradley the only run he would need in the top of the first inning. With one out, catcher John Clapp drove a clean single to center, reached third on a wild throw by Bond, and scored on Mike McGeary's fly ball.

Bradley's duties were made more challenging by his teammates' lack of fielding support. The Brown Stockings committed eight errors that day, the first coming in the opening inning when shortstop Dickey Pearce threw badly to first on a groundball by Jack Burdock. A passed ball sent Burdock to second, but he died at third base.

The Browns added another run in the second. Right fielder Joe Blong's one-out single got things going, and he took second on left fielder Tom York's slow fielding. Bradley hit a grounder that should have been played by first baseman Everett Mills, but Mills let the ball slip between his legs, allowing Blong to trot home.

Over the next 7½ innings, Bradley and Bond matched each other goose egg for goose egg, Bradley overcoming sloppy fielding to hold his two-run edge. St. Louis threatened twice. In the third John Clapp doubled to left with one out. He died at second as Mike McGeary popped up to Jack Burdock at second and Lip Pike sent a liner to York in left for the third out. In the sixth Pike beat out a grounder to Burdock at second. He stole second, but got no farther as Joe Battin went down on strikes for the third out.

Going into the eighth inning, the Browns still led 2–0 and Bradley's consecutive scoreless innings streak had reached 25. Despite the no-hitter being intact, a lapse of control presented Hartford with a golden opportunity to score in its half of the eighth. The frame started out with Tom York reaching first on a base on balls. He was sacrificed to second, and made it to third on a wild pitch. There he remained as catcher Bill Harbridge grounded to McGeary at short, who threw it to Dutch Dehlman at first. Inning over. Threat over. Golden opportunity wasted for the Hartfords.

The St. Louises went quietly in their half of the ninth, leaving Hartford one final opportunity. Jack Remsen grounded to Dickey Pearce at short for the first out, but Battin muffed Burdock's groundball for the Brown Stockings' eighth error of the game. Dick Higham was the next man up for the Hartfords and he hit a shot to Battin at third, who caught it and doubled Burdock off first to end the game. Grin Bradley now had his no-hitter and his place in baseball history.

For a while, it looked as though Bradley was going to secure yet another place in baseball history in his next start, three days later against Cincinnati, also at Grand Avenue Park. He was perfect through seven innings and took another no-hitter into the ninth. Center fielder Charley "Baby" Jones broke up that opportunity with a double. Jones scored on a hit by catcher Amos Booth, and although the Brown Stockings won 5–1, Bradley's scoreless innings streak ended at 37. That mark stood until Christy Mathewson tossed 39 straight scoreless innings for the New York Giants in 1901.

Pitching virtually every game, as was the custom of the time, Bradley won 45 games that season for the Brown Stockings, who finished second in the new league, six games behind the champions from Chicago. His 1.23 earned-run average was the lowest in the league, although the profusion of fielding errors made behind him (and behind all pitchers in those days) gave that statistic less importance than it has today.

Bradley never approached the same performance levels after 1876. Signing with Chicago in 1877, he started 44 games, but won just 18 and saw his ERA climb to 3.31, the highest among pitchers with at least 20 starts. He remained in the big leagues for six more seasons, but usually as a sort of a spare part, winning 75 games but losing 83. After one season with Philadelphia in the American Association, he closed his big-league career pitching for Cincinnati in the 1884 Union Association and worked in the minors until 1890. He became a Philadelphia police officer after his baseball career ended and was retired on a pension when he died in Philadelphia on October 2, 1931.

But if his career as a whole was undistinguished, Bradley certainly distinguished himself by heading a list that is now well into the 200s — the roster of major-league pitchers who have thrown a no-hitter. It was exactly the sort of accomplishment the game might have expected from somebody named George Washington in the summer of '76.

This essay was originally published in Inventing Baseball: The 100 Greatest Games of the 19th Century *(SABR, 2013), edited by Bill Felber.*

LEE RICHMOND

By John R. Husman

J. LEE RICHMOND, MAJOR-league baseball's first full-time* left-handed pitcher, is best known for pitching the first perfect game. He also accomplished a number of other noteworthy firsts during his six-year major-league career. Because he played concurrently as an amateur and as a professional, the first rules were promulgated that banned a professional from participating in amateur sports. His heart-side delivery caused changes in baseball strategy that are integral to every game played today.

Lee Richmond was the last of nine children and the last of six sons of Cyrus R. Richmond, a Baptist minister, and Eliza (Tinan) Richmond. He was born on May 5, 1857, in Sheffield, Ohio. He attended public and normal schools in Geneva, Ohio. Richmond enrolled in the (college) Preparatory Department of Oberlin College of Ohio as a 16-year-old in 1873. His three-year Oberlin experience focused mutually on education and baseball—a combination that he employed for a decade. He followed Willis, an older brother by seven years, as a member of Oberlin's baseball club and pitched for the college nine.

Richmond enrolled at Brown University in 1876, performing in the fall season as an outfielder for the varsity nine and playing occasionally for the Rhode Islands of Providence. Richmond was elected class president, played on the school's first football team and spent the next two seasons as an outfielder and pitcher for Brown. He labored in Brown's gymnasium the winter of 1878-1879, developing several curve deliveries. His curves broke up and down, rather than in and out and were known as a jump ball and a drop ball. Combined with his rare left-handed delivery, the pitches produced devastating results. Richmond, slight in stature at 5-feet-10 and 142 pounds, did not overpower hitters and consequently allied his unusual pitches with cunning, deception and strategy. He studied hitters and kept a book on them.

Richmond burst upon the baseball scene in 1879. He held the Chicago White Stockings hitless in his professional debut, led his Brown University nine to the college championship, pitched a professional no-hit game, and made his major-league debut. He ended the season as he began it, playing as an amateur and captaining Brown's team. His composite record for the 1879 season included 47 wins and a .350 plus batting average. After much entreating by manager Frank Bancroft, Richmond agreed to pitch an exhibition game for Worcester of the National Baseball Association against Cap Anson's White Stockings on June 2. He was paid $10 for the appearance and so became a professional baseball player on that day. In the game, Richmond walked the first Chicago batter and then did not allow another base runner as Worcester prevailed, 11-0, in seven innings. After the contest Anson and Bancroft both sought to make a contract with Richmond. Bancroft closed the deal for $100 per month. One week later, Richmond rejoined his college mates for the college championship game against Yale and again prevailed. He struck out the final Yale batter with runners on second and third in the ninth inning to preserve a 3-2 win in what Ronald A. Smith described as "one of the great college games of the nineteenth century" in his *Sports & Freedom: The Rise of Big-Time College Athletics.*[1] Back in the professional ranks, Richmond threw a two-hitter against the Washington Nationals, the leader of the National Baseball Association, on June 11. On July 28 he no-hit Springfield and contributed four hits himself as Worcester romped, 14-0. Still participating in Worcester's and Brown's fall schedules, Richmond was retained by Harry Wright of Boston (NL) to pitch his team's final home game. After a shaky first inning against Providence, he pitched a solid 12-6 win, allowing but a single base hit over the final eight innings. He recorded a league-record five consecutive strikeouts in his National League debut.

Since Richmond had played concurrently as an amateur and professional, his eligibility was the focus of the December 1879 meeting of the American College Base Ball Association (Amherst, Brown, Dartmouth, Harvard, Princeton, and Yale). After lengthy discussion, the body agreed to allow Richmond (and his Brown catcher, Winslow) to play but banned future professionals from participating. Still smarting from its losses to Brown and Richmond in the previous season, Yale walked out of the meeting in protest and later withdrew its membership. This rule continues as the basic tenet of amateurism for virtually all sports worldwide.

Richmond's remarkable 1879 season so revitalized the Worcester franchise that the small New England city was admitted to the National League for 1880. According to the *Toledo Daily Times*, Richmond signed with Worcester for "the unheard-of salary of $2,400"[2] in 1880. He pitched for Worcester for the franchise's entire three-year history, accounting for 78.8 percent of the club's wins. He pitched and played the outfield for the Providence Grays (NL) in 1883 and briefly for the Cincinnati Red Stockings (AA) in 1886. Besides being the first truly successful left-handed pitcher in major-league baseball, Richmond established a number of initial milestones. He gave up the first grand slam, won 20 games for a last-place team, and contributed a home run to the first three-home-run inning and four-home-run game for a team. He was the first left-hander to win 30 games for a season. He pioneered the use of a variety of pitches that included a rising fastball, a drop ball, and a change of pace. The milestone event of Richmond's career came on June 12, 1880, when his perfect game, another first, beat Cleveland 1-0 at Worcester. Richmond's left-handedness caused teams to stack their right-handed batters at the top of the lineup and left-handed batters to cross over when facing him, as baseball very quickly adapted to the left-handed pitcher. Worcester's manager, Frank Bancroft, also instituted new pitching strategies when he alternated Richmond and right-hander Fred Corey according to which box a batter used. The game adapted quickly.

A perfect game is the rarest of single-game pitching feats. Taken in context with the events preceding the game, Richmond's gem was even more unlikely. Two days before this Saturday contest, Richmond had shut out the Clevelands, 5-0. He was in the midst of a streak of 42 consecutive innings during which he would not allow an earned run, and the perfect game would be his third shutout in nine days. He returned to Providence for graduation festivities and parties, passing up Worcester's Friday exhibition game with the Yale nine. Graduation events included a class baseball game played at 4:50 A.M. on Saturday. Richmond had been up all night following the class supper at Music Hall. He took part in the ballgame and went to bed at 6:30 A.M. He rose in time to catch the 11:30 A.M. train for Worcester to pitch in the afternoon contest against Cleveland. The train on which he rode was delayed, and he was forced to go to the field without his dinner. So his preparations for the game included forgoing food and sleep and playing another game earlier in the day.

Richmond and Cleveland's Jim McCormick locked up in a duel. Richmond himself got the first hit of the game in the fourth but was erased on a double play. Worcester got but two more hits on the day, both by shortstop Art Irwin. The only run of the contest scored in the fifth on a double error by Cleveland second baseman Fred "Sure Shot" Dunlap. Like so many classic games, this one featured a game-saving play. In the fifth inning Cleveland's Bill Phillips hit a ball through the right side for an apparent base hit. Lon Knight, captain, right fielder, and the second oldest man of the team at 26, charged, scooped up and fired to first. Umpire Foghorn Bradley called the runner out, and the perfect game was preserved. It was Richmond's third professional no-hitter before he graduated from college.

Richmond always kept his achievement in perspective. He once remarked in a newspaper interview that "(catcher Charlie) Bennett and the boys behind me gave me perfect support."[3] On another occasion he said, "I couldn't have pitched it if the fielders had not been so expert in handling the ball."[4] Richmond knew that an errorless game played by barehanded fielders was a rare achievement in itself. The game was called "the most wonderful on record"[5] by one writer and "unprecedented"[6] by another as the phrase "perfect game" had yet to be coined. However, several contemporary newspaper accounts referred to perfection in describing the play. The *Worcester Daily Spy* commented, "Richmond was most effectively supported, every position on the home nine being played to perfection."[7] The *Chicago Tribune* said, "The Clevelands were utterly helpless before Richmond's puzzling curves, retiring in every inning in one, two, three order, without a base hit. The Worcesters played a perfect fielding game."[8]

The ballplayer-student graduated from Brown University with a bachelor of arts degree on June 16, 1880, four days after his perfect game. He continued his education over the next three winters at the College of Physicians and Surgeons (now part of Columbia University) and the University of the City of New York (now New York University), and at medical facilities in Providence and New York City. His M.D. was conferred by University of the City of New York in March of 1883. He was awarded a master of arts degree in June of 1883 by Brown University. When he stepped on to the field for Providence (NL) in 1883, he became the first physician to play major-league baseball. For 10 years it was baseball in the summer and school in the winter for J. Lee Richmond. Presumably his baseball earnings provided him means to pursue his bachelor's and advanced degrees. After the 1883 season the tandem vocations ended when he hung up his spikes, shelved the books, and went about the business of his life's work.

The Worcester franchise ceased to exist after the 1882 season, and Richmond signed with the National League's Providence Grays for the following

J. LEE RICHMOND.

[With Portrait.]

This once famous left-handed pitcher, J. Lee Richmond, was born in Sheffield, Ashtabula Co., O., May 5, 1859.

season. His pitching successes had diminished over the course of his career, and he was now primarily an outfielder but was in the box occasionally for the Grays. His opposite-side delivery and the repertoire of pitches that had so surprised hitters when he first appeared on the scene had been combated by new strategies and familiarity. As was the custom of the day, Richmond was a virtual one-man pitching staff for the Worcesters, and he experienced arm problems as overwork took its toll on his slender frame. A rule change also affected Richmond's delivery. The pitching distance was changed from 45 to 50 feet beginning in 1881. These factors combined to reduce his effectiveness but he continued in the game in another role and until he was ready to leave baseball.

After the 1883 season Richmond continued his medical study with Dr. C.T. Gardner in Providence and then returned to his native northeast Ohio, where he established a practice. He used his vacation in 1886 to make a short and unsuccessful comeback with Cincinnati (AA). He continued his medical practice in Conneaut, Ohio, until he changed careers and became the principal of the Geneva, Ohio, schools in 1889. He moved west to Toledo in 1890 to become a teacher at Toledo High School. He continued his career in education in Toledo for nearly 40 years. In Toledo high schools he was a teacher of Greek, history, physics, chemistry, and mathematics, a baseball coach, an orchestra conductor, and a principal. The son of Addie Joss, the pitcher of baseball's fourth perfect game, was in Richmond's geometry class at Scott High School. According to the *Toledo Blade*, Richmond told young Norman Joss upon their first meeting, "Your father pitched a perfect game. Well, so did I. It doesn't mean anything around here and it isn't going to help you with your geometry."[9] In 1921, at age 65, he was forced to "retire." He then became professor of hygiene and dean of men at the University of the City of Toledo (now the University of Toledo). He remained at the university the rest of his years.

Richmond was a lifelong baseball fan and appeared in uniform in his late 60s at Toledo's Swayne Field. His perfect game gave him a kind of celebrity status in Toledo, and his baseball prowess was mentioned many times over his years in the city. He was the first Brown University athlete named to that school's Athletic Hall of Fame. He enjoyed golf throughout his life and was a scratch player.

J. Lee Richmond married Mary Naomi Chapin, a former high-school student of his, on December 27, 1892, and had three daughters, Ruth, Dorothy, and Jane. He died at age 72 on October 1, 1929, and is buried in Forest Cemetery in Toledo, Ohio.

*Bobby Mitchell pitched in 45 games mostly for Cincinnati from 1877-1882, but was never his team's primary pitcher.

SOURCES

In addition to the sources cited in the Notes, the author also consulted:

Brownlee, Kimberley. "The Most Wonderful Game: J. Lee Richmond's Perfect Game," *Timeline*, Vol 21, No. 3 (Columbus: Ohio Historical Society, 2004).

Goslow, Brian Charles. "Fairground Days: When Worcester Was a National League City," *Historical Journal of Massachusetts, Vol. 19, No. 2* (Westfield, Connecticut: The Historical Journal of Massachusetts, 1991).

Husman, John Richmond, "Baseball's First Perfect Game," *Toledo Magazine*, in the *Toledo Blade*, May 16, 1987.

_____. "J. Lee Richmond," in Mark Rucker and Robert L. Tiemann, eds., *Nineteenth Century Stars* (Kansas City, Missouri: Society for American Baseball Research, 1989).

_____. "J. Lee Richmond's Remarkable 1879 Season," *The National Pastime Vol. 4, No. 2* (Cooperstown, New York: Society for American Baseball Research, 1985).

Mayer, Ronald A., *Perfect*! (Jefferson, North Carolina: McFarland & Company, Inc., 1991).

Richmond, J. Lee. "Beating Harvard and Yale in Seventy-nine," in Robert Perkins Brown, Henry Robinson Palmer, Harry Lyman Koopman, and Clarence Saunders Brigham, eds., *Memories of Brown* (Providence: Brown Alumni Magazine Company, 1909).

Smith, Ronald A. "Lee Richmond, Brown University, and the Amateur-Professional Controversy in College Baseball," *NEQ 64* March 1991.

The Brunonian

General Catalogue of Oberlin College 1833-1908.

J. Lee Richmond file, National Baseball Library, Cooperstown, New York.

New York Tribune.

Toledo News Bee.

Worcester Evening Gazette.

NOTES

1. Ronald A. Smith, *Sports & Freedom: The Rise of Big-Time College Athletics* (New York: Oxford University Press, 1988), 60.
2. *Toledo Daily Times*, October 1, 1929: 1.
3. Alfred H. Spink, *The National Game* (St. Louis: National Game Publishing Company, 1910), 155.
4. John B. Foster, "Baseball's Biggest Firsts," *Providence Journal*, 1930. Date is for copyright. The newspaper clipping is from a Richmond scrapbook and not further identified.
5. *Cleveland Leader*, June 13, 1880.
6. *New York Clipper*, June 19, 1880: 98.
7. *Worcester Daily Spy*, June 14, 1880: 4.
8. *Chicago Tribune*, June 113, 1880: 8.
9. Seymour Rothman, "Baseball's Biggest "Firsts," *Toledo Blade*, April 20, 1976: P-1.

BASEBALL PERFECTION
CLEVELAND AT WORCESTER
JUNE 12, 1880

By John R. Husman

"THE MOST WONDERFUL game on record."[1] That's how contemporary newspaper reports described the no-run, no-hit, no-man-reach-first-base 1-0 triumph by Worcester's Lee Richmond over Cleveland. Although the term itself wouldn't be created for more than a quarter-century, it was the first "perfect game" ever pitched.[2] Actually, the "perfect" label was applied to one aspect of the game: the Worcester fielding. "Richmond was most effectively supported, every position on the home nine being played to perfection," reported the next day's *Worcester Daily Spy*.[3]

The National League game was played on Saturday, June 12, 1880, at the Worcester (Massachusetts) Agricultural Fairgrounds, also known as Driving Park, and was the second game of a three-game series. The Ohio team came to town in third place, just a half game behind the upstart Worcesters. Both teams were far behind runaway leader Chicago. In the first game of the series, on Thursday the 10th, Richmond and Worcester had shut out Cleveland, 5-0, the clubs swapping positions in the standings.

A 23-year-old left-hander in his first full season, Lee Richmond was a busy man both on and off the field that week. In fact, his activities prior to his perfect game made the outcome all the more unlikely. Besides being the Worcesters' front-line pitcher, he was wrapping up his college studies and was scheduled to graduate from Brown University in Providence, Rhode Island, 40 miles down the road from Worcester, on June 16. Richmond skipped Worcester's Friday exhibition game with Yale University, returning instead to Providence for Brown's graduation festivities. His classmate, Walter Angell, recorded Richmond's activities while in Providence in a scrapbook:

"I met them (Thursday night) at the depot … and rode out to the Messer St. ball grounds in a carriage. …We returned at midnight. Next day was Class Day. Richmond went to the Class Supper at Music Hall. He was up all night. He took part in the usual ball game about 4:50 Saturday morning; went to bed about 6:30; took the train for Worcester at 11:30. …."[4]

On Saturday, Richmond and Cleveland's Jim McCormick were matched in what became a classic duel. McCormick was outstanding, giving up three hits and one unearned run while striking out seven and walking one. Richmond, batting second in the order, got the first hit, in the fourth but was erased on a double play. Shortstop Art Irwin led off the fifth with a single. Catcher Charlie Bennett followed with a walk. Then Art Whitney hit a comebacker to McCormick, who threw to second only to see second baseman Fred Dunlap drop the ball. Alertly, Irwin rounded third and kept right on running. Dunlap recovered but threw home wildly for his second error on the play, allowing Irwin to score. McCormick allowed only one more baserunner. Dunlap was an unlikely source for decisive defensive miscues; he was considered a fine fielder. "I used to think Dunlap was the greatest defensive second baseman in the world," Richmond later said of him.[5]

As good as McCormick was, Richmond was even better. Of the 27 batters Richmond faced, only two hit fair balls beyond the infield and one of these resulted in a gem-saving play. Leading off the fifth inning, Cleveland first baseman Bill Phillips slapped a Richmond left-handed delivery into right field for an apparent base hit. Lon Knight, the Worcester right fielder and team captain, fielded the sharply hit ball and fired to first in time to retire Phillips.

The game was delayed by rain for about five minutes with one out in the bottom of the eighth inning. Richmond then finished the game with the aid of sawdust that he used to dry the ball before every pitch.[6] Richmond struck out five in the 1-hour 26-minute game.

The 700 people in attendance also witnessed what might have been the first instance of platooning. Richmond, the game's first regular left-hander, had been in the league for only about six weeks and Cleveland had not yet seen him but already the Clevelands knew that right-handed batters might have an edge against the left-handed heaver.[7] Because of this, the Cleveland team changed its batting order against Richmond. Immediately before and after the Worcester series, Cleveland's left-handed hitters, Orator Shaffer, Pete Hotaling, and Ned Hanlon, were second, third, and fourth in the lineup. For the June 10 game against Worcester, Shaffer was dropped to fourth, Hanlon to seventh, and Hotaling to ninth. For the games of June 12 and 14, Shaffer dropped to the number five slot, Hanlon moved to the ninth position and Hotaling was removed from the lineup. In addition, switch-hitting in order to face the pitcher from the opposite side was employed as a strategy in this game. The *Cleveland Leader* reported in its June 10 edition, "Hotaling in today's game will bat right-handed. …"[8] Game accounts do not reveal whether Hotaling did turn around against Richmond. Nonetheless, the seed was planted for using the strategies of switch-hitting and platooning that are integral in today's game.

Cleveland won the series' final game, 7-1, on Monday, McCormick defeating Richmond. By season's end, the 23-year-old rookie had won 32 games and lost an equal number as his team finished in fifth place. But the notoriety of pitching professional baseball's perfect game went with Richmond throughout his life. He remarked of it, "I can remember almost nothing except that my jump ball and my half stride ball were working splendidly and that Bennett and the boys behind me gave me perfect support."[9]

NOTES

1. *Sunday Herald* (unidentified clip in J. Lee Richmond file, National Baseball Library, Cooperstown, New York); *Cleveland Leader*, June 13, 1880.
2. Paul Dickson, Paul. *The Dickson Baseball Dictionary* (New York: W.W. Norton Company, Inc., 2009), 630.
3. *Worcester Daily Spy*, June 14, 1880.
4. Letter from Walter Angell to the Editor of the *Boston Post*, August 18, 1925, page 2.
5. Ronald A. Mayer. *Perfect!* (Jefferson, North Carolina: McFarland & Company, Inc., 1991), 17.
6. *Worcester Daily Spy*, June 14, 1880.
7. "Richmond's Debut In Professional Baseball," in *Brown Alumni Monthly*, 1910-1911; from the *New York Tribune*.
8. *Cleveland Leader*, June 10, 1880.
9. Alfred H. Spink. *The National Game* (St. Louis: National Game Publishing Co., 1910), 155.

LARRY CORCORAN

By Bob LeMoine

"**F**LINT AND CORCORAN HAD funny signals for changes of curves," recalled Tommy Burns, a teammate of catcher Frank "Silver" Flint and pitcher Larry Corcoran of the Chicago White Stockings of the 1880s. "(Corcoran) invariably carried a mammoth chew of tobacco in his mouth, and when he chewed he shifted it about with a movement that resembled the actions of an elephant begging peanuts of a crowd of children. Flint noticed this peculiarity and one day suggested to Larry that he make his curve signals by shifting the chew. It worked to a charm, and many an old-timer was fooled."[1]

Larry Corcoran was a dominant pitcher in the early 1880s despite a less-than-intimidating 5-foot-3, 127-pound frame that gave him the nickname "Little Corcoran." One of baseball's early curveball masters, Corcoran was a part of three pennant-winning Chicago teams. He was a true workhorse, averaging 456 innings pitched and 34 wins per season for five years, until his arm, understandably, burned out. Unable to adjust to life outside of baseball, he turned to alcohol and died at the age of 32.

Lawrence J. "Larry" Corcoran was born on August 10, 1859 in Brooklyn, New York, to William and Ann (Boylan) Corcoran, Irish immigrants. According to the 1860 US Census, William worked as a butcher. Lawrence was listed as a 19-year-old "ballplayer." He had six siblings: older brothers William and Michael, younger sisters Frances, Margaret, and Mary, and a younger brother, Thomas.

In 1897 Bennett Wilson recalled the 1870s when he pitched on a Brooklyn Lurlines amateur team that included Corcoran and fellow future major-league pitchers Terry Larkin and Mickey Welch. They would gather "in a big back yard almost every day and used a clothes line horse, which was used by an old widow on which to dry her washing, with which to gain control of the various curves. The horizontal bar across the horse was supposed to represent the height of a batter's waist and the ball was curved around the main sticks. This afforded an effective means of practice."[2]

Corcoran pitched in the spring of 1877 for two Brooklyn teams, Chelsea and the Mutuals. On May 19 the *New York Clipper*, in an article on a Chelsea game, mentioned "that fine young player and pitcher Corcoran."[3] The *Brooklyn Eagle* earlier reported that the Mutuals had "an excellent pitcher in Corcoran—a player well worthy a position in a strong professional nine."[4] The Mutuals played on the Capitoline Grounds. In June Corcoran moved on to play for the Livingston Club of Genesco, New York. While there was no pitching line for the game, the June 30, 1877, *Clipper* noted that "Corcoran, their new pitcher, made his first appearance with them in this game, and played well."[5]

Corcoran joined the Springfield (Massachusetts) club in 1878. "He is a swift, effective pitcher, one of the best curves in the business, a sure infielder and excels in watching the bases. His only fault is too great an anxiety not to give his opponents a hit, which causes him to pitch wildly and to put too much work upon himself and the catcher" wrote the *Springfield Republican*.[6] In August Corcoran moved to the Buffalo Bisons, at the time an independent "minor-league" team.[7] He returned to Springfield in 1879 because no catcher in Buffalo could be fund who could handle his pitching.[8] Corcoran may have thrown a no-hitter on May 14, 1879; the *Springfield Republican* reported, "Not a base hit was made from Corcoran's pitching," although it is not known if he pitched the entire game.[9] The Springfield Club disbanded on September 6, 1879, and Corcoran was briefly with the Holyoke (Massachusetts) club, before being released on the 23rd.[10] He joined the Worcester (Massachusetts) club for just a few days and was asked to join the major-league Chicago

White Stockings on a trip to California in October.[11] Chicago pitcher Terry Larkin had a sore arm, giving Corcoran a chance in the major leagues.[12]

"He was a very little fellow," Chicago manager Cap Anson recalled of Corcoran in his memoirs, published in 1900, "with an unusual amount of speed, and the endurance of an Indian pony. As a batter he was only fair, but as a fielder in his position he was remarkable, being as quick as a cat and as plucky as they made them."[13] Despite his height, Corcoran was a tough scrapper. "I remember a set-to that he had one night in the old clubhouse with Hugh Nichols, in which he all but knocked Hughy out, greatly to that gentleman's surprise, as he had fancied up to that time that he was Corcoran's master in the art of self-defense," Anson recalled.[14]

As the White Stockings gathered for the start of the 1880 season, the *Chicago Tribune* mentioned that their new pitcher, Corcoran, "has developed into a left-handed pitcher, and it is expected that his double method of delivery will prove extremely puzzling to batsmen."[15]

Corcoran won his first major-league start, on Opening Day, May 1, in Cincinnati, a game called "one of the most exciting ever seen here."[16] Chicago rallied in the ninth inning for a 4-3 win. Corcoran pitched the first five games of the season, and Fred Goldsmith pitched the next four games. Beginning on May 18, manager Cap Anson alternated the two pitchers in 15 of the next 16 starts, the very first formation of a pitching rotation in professional baseball. The two pitchers started 84 of 86 games, Corcoran throwing 536⅓ innings and Goldsmith 210⅓. Anson liked the contrast between Corcoran, a hard-throwing pitcher, and Fred Goldsmith, a "slow-baller."[17]

The *Tribune* called the White Stockings-Providence Grays game on June 4 "the most extraordinary game of ball ever played." Corcoran and John Montgomery Ward of Providence pitched all 16 innings before the game was ended by darkness with the teams tied, 1-1.[18] On August 5 Corcoran threw a two-hitter against Boston, outdueling Tommy Bond.[19] On August 10 he pitched a one-hitter against Providence. The *Tribune* said, "(T)he heavy

hitters of the visiting team were completely baffled by Corcoran's slow and swift curves."[20] The win put Chicago in first place by 12½ games over the Grays.

On August 19, in the days before the phrase "no-hitter" was used, Corcoran defeated the Boston Red Stockings who, as the *Tribune* put it, "obtained neither a tally nor a base-hit," adding, "Corcoran was never in such form before, and Flint caught him superbly." A rain delay in the third inning made the ball "mushy and shapeless for the greater part of the play," but Chicago, the *Tribune* added, had 13 hits.[21] Corcoran finished the season 43-14 with a 1.95 ERA. His 268 strikeouts, 4.5 strikeouts per nine innings, and 99 walks (the fewest) led the league. Goldsmith was 21-3 with a 1.75 ERA, and Chicago easily won the pennant.

Corcoran and Goldsmith again formed a two-man starting rotation in 1881. Corcoran shut out Cleveland on May 3, allowing only three hits, and pitched a three-hitter against Providence on June 24.[22] On August 4 he pitched a two-hitter against Buffalo in what the *Tribune* called "perhaps the best game of all his life," adding, "His headwork and his consummate control of the ball he never abated for an instant."[23] Corcoran pitched a four-hit, 5-1 victory over Buffalo on August 17. Corcoran and Goldsmith were said to be trying a "snake ball" as their curves were dominating the league.[24] On August 23 Goldsmith sprained an ankle in the third inning, so Corcoran came "in from the turnstile" and pitched the rest of the game with Chicago defeating Detroit in the 12th inning.[25] The White Stockings easily won the pennant again, and Corcoran was 31-14 with a 2.31 ERA in 396⅔ innings pitched. His 31 victories tied Boston's Jim "Grasshopper" Whitney for the league lead, but Whitney lost 33 games.

Chicago struggled in the early part of the 1882 season, falling to 12-14 and fifth place on June 15. Corcoran hit a grand slam on June 20 against Worcester, "a tremendous drive to the seats in centre field," according to the *Tribune*, and driving in seven of the 13 runs Chicago scored.[26] Then the White Stockings got hot, going 21-6, and at the end of July were 33-20. Chicago scored six or more runs in 23 of Corcoran's 40 starts.[27] Corcoran won 10 consecutive starts from June 29 to July 29, including wins of 23-4, 35-4, and 17-1.

Chicago went on an Eastern road trip from July 27 to August 24 and didn't return home until August 29. By the time the White Stockings returned home, Corcoran was a married man. The exact date is unknown, but two user-created family trees on Ancestry.com list August 20 or August 25, 1882, with no official documentation given. After a 15-4 pounding of the White Stockings by Worcester on August 23, the *Cincinnati Enquirer* wrote, "Corcoran was off being married … and Goldsmith is Chicago's only pitcher."[28] The *Boston Herald* on August 29 wrote that Corcoran was "enjoying his honeymoon, having been recently married."[29] His bride was Gertrude Grork of Newark, New Jersey.[30]

At the end of August, Chicago trailed first-place Providence by 2½ games, and then went on a 16-2 streak. Corcoran again won 10 straight starts, including his second no-hitter, against Worcester on August 20. The day was "raw and disagreeable" with 1,500 spectators, wrote the *Tribune*, and "play began at 3:30 sharp in order to enable the Worcesters to take an early train for the East." The 90-minute, 5-0 win showed that Corcoran "has been pitching a great game of late—perhaps the best of his life."[31] Corcoran finished the season 27-12 with a league-best 1.95 ERA in 355⅔ innings pitched, and Chicago won its third straight pennant, by three games over Providence.

On May 22, 1883, a freezing cold day, Corcoran defeated Boston 4-3 to put the White Stockings a half-game ahead of Providence in first place. The game featured the debut of Chicago left fielder Billy Sunday, who struck out in all four at-bats.[32] Chicago swooned in June, tumbling out of first place on June 11 and falling seven games behind on the 23rd. Corcoran threw shutouts on June 9, July 18 (a one-hitter versus Boston), and August 29.[33]

Chicago won 11 in a row from August 22 to September 8, including 10 straight home victories, and moved into first place 1½ games over Boston.[34] Then the White Stockings traveled to Boston for a four-game series. They dropped the first game. The next day Corcoran pitched hitless ball through four innings in a duel with Jim Whitney. Two runs in the ninth inning gave the Beaneaters the 3-2 win and sole possession of first place, a lead they did not relinquish as they won the pennant.[35] Corcoran finished 34-20 with a 2.49 ERA in 473⅔ innings pitched. This was the first year in which he did not league the league in wins, ERA, or strikeouts.

American Sports (reprinted in the *Chicago Tribune*) reported on a debate between Corcoran and Anson over "place-hitting." "Anson took the ground that he could hit a ball in any direction he chose. Corcoran held the contrary, and offered to bet a dollar on every ball hit that Anson couldn't do it." Anson attempted to prove it in that afternoon's game, but went hitless in six at-bats, with only half of his batted balls going in the intended direction.[36]

For 1884 the White Stockings offered Corcoran a contract for $2,100, a raise of $300 from 1883. He wanted $4,000. This was "an outrageous demand," wrote Chicago's *Inter Ocean* on December 9.

Corcoran demanded his release, but was refused, so he threatened to sit out the 1884 season. Go ahead and sit out, the club said. Corcoran reconsidered and accepted the $2,100. "The National League is to be congratulated on the wisdom displayed in the adoption of this reserve rule," the *Inter Ocean* commented, "for without it the position of pitcher or catcher would soon command a higher salary than the President of the United States receives."[37]

But Corcoran wrote to team president Albert Spalding that he was withdrawing his request and had signed with the Chicago team in the new Union Association. The National League expelled Corcoran.[38] The *New York Clipper* published a letter from Corcoran explaining his actions. He wrote, "I asked the large salary not because I thought I would get it, but in hopes of inducing the management to give me my release. After a short consideration Mr. Spalding informed me he would pay me no such exorbitant salary, and, as we could not come to satisfactory terms, I started for my home without signing." Corcoran entertained an offer from the Chicago Unions president, Albert H. Henderson. Then he saw a story in a Boston paper claiming he was in a conspiracy with fellow White Stockings Flint and George Gore to grab higher salaries from management, which Corcoran denied. The story said Chicago would do just fine without Corcoran, prompting him to sign with Henderson. "For four years I have fulfilled my contracts to the letter and have worked hard and faithfully for the Chicago Club, but as my contracts never spoke of a reserve-rule or made any mention of one, I do not feel I am breaking my word in any way to that club. … Leaving the public to judge my action, I am, respectfully, Lawrence J. Corcoran."[39] Henderson's contract to Corcoran was said to be $3,000.

But Spalding threatened to blacklist Corcoran if he failed to sign by January 6, 1884, so on January 4 Corcoran re-signed with the White Stockings for $2,100.[40] Apparently Corcoran wasn't too perturbed at the new contract because six days later he was pitching in a baseball game played on ice skates in Brooklyn. The team captains were Henry Chadwick and George Taylor, and players were both amateur and professional. It was played at the Washington Skating Park in South Brooklyn and "the diamond was laid out on the Fourth-avenue and Third-street corner, there being a clear space for the regular skaters in front of the grand-stand." Corcoran's team won 41-12.[41]

The White Stockings had a forgettable 1884 season. They were 5-14 on May 26. Injuries contributed to the slow start. "A nine composed about one-third of 'has-been' material will not win the championship this year," whined the *Tribune*.[42] Chicago never spent a day in first place, finishing 62-50 in fourth-place, 21½ games behind. Corcoran won only two of his first 12 starts before pitching a one-hitter on May 23.

On June 16, with Goldsmith in Canada, Corcoran, suffering a sore pitching hand, alternated his left and right hands in a desperate attempt to pitch a game in Buffalo. The *Buffalo Commercial Advertiser* said Corcoran had a "felon" on his right index finger and had "no business in the box. Why in the name of common sense Anson permitted Goldsmith to go to Canada and persisted in playing Corcoran, when the little man was suffering excruciating pain, is a question no one can answer. It was an act at once brutal and stupid. Larry used his right and left hands alternately, but it was no go."[43] He was removed after four innings.

Corcoran came back to throw a no-hitter against Providence on June 27. "The fact that Chicago has at least one pitcher was demonstrated very plainly in yesterday's game," wrote the *Tribune*, "in which the Providence team, composed of the heaviest batters in the league, failed to earn a single base in nine innings."[44] It was Corcoran's third no-hitter and a 6-0 victory. Corcoran was the first pitcher to throw three no-hitters.[45] Corcoran also pitched shutouts on July 1 and 7.

"The Chicagos, thinking they could win with any pitcher, presented a brother of Larry Corcoran's and the home team made him think he had better sign with amateurs," wrote the *Inter Ocean* on July 16 after the White Stockings lost to Detroit, 14-0, the day before.[46] Corcoran's older brother, Mike, made his debut against Detroit and pitched a complete game giving up 16 hits, seven walks, five wild pitches, and 14 earned runs. It was Mike Corcoran's only major-league appearance.

Larry Corcoran finished the 1884 season 35-23 with a 2.40 ERA, his fifth straight year of 27-plus wins, and the fourth year out of five in which he won over 30 games. He pitched 516⅔ innings, his most since 1880, as Goldsmith pitched only 188 innings and was released on August 7. Both pitchers, not surprisingly, suffered from tired arms. Goldsmith had pitched 1,516⅔ innings in five years for Chicago, Corcoran 2,279. Goldsmith was 107-63, Corcoran 170-83, but the days of the first pitching rotation were over. Newcomer John Clarkson, who was 10-3 with a 2.14 ERA in 14 games, "already ranks as one of the foremost of league pitchers, and Corcoran will have to look to his laurels next season," wrote the *Tribune*.[47]

Corcoran pitched his last shutout on May 14, 1885, at Philadelphia, one of the last highlights of his career. Anson began using Clarkson as the predominant starting pitcher, abandoning any sort of rotation. Corcoran's last Chicago start was an 11-10 win at Boston on May 26, in which he surrendered 15 hits and in the sixth inning "handed the ball to [Fred] Pfeffer and refused to be hammered any longer."[48] Corcoran was nursing a sore arm and was "impatient to get into his uniform, and says he is quite confident of being able to take the field within a few days' time," reported the *Tribune* on June 22.[49] But he was only 5-2 with a 3.64 ERA in 59⅓ innings, and was released on July 11, "ordered to keep his arm in a sling for two months," wrote the *Inter Ocean*, adding, "He will leave for his home in Newark, N.J., this evening, and will be seen no more upon the ball field for a time."[50] Corcoran complained that Chicago had not paid him for the 41 days he had been out injured. Spalding replied, "I paid him $750 for the seven games in which he played. … I bought him his railroad ticket from Chicago to New York … and I loaned him $100 on my personal account, and he was profuse with his thanks."[51]

Corcoran quickly signed with the New York Giants. "It is insinuated that Corcoran's arm is as good as it ever was, and that the 'sore arm' business was simply an excuse to get his release," the *Inter Ocean* complained.[52] "This is a wise move," the *New York Times* commented. "In condition Corcoran is a first-class pitcher."[53] New York was in second place, trailing first-place Chicago by 2½ games. Corcoran started three games at the end of the season, pitching well, going 2-1 with a 2.88 ERA. He got his last major-league win on October 8 at St. Louis. He left the game in the eighth inning with to a sprained ankle.[54]

Corcoran never again pitched for New York, and played in only one game as an outfielder for the Giants in 1886. He was "loaned" to the Washington Nationals for $2,200 "to use him while the New-Yorks could get along without his services."

"I feel in good condition. … I think I will get a good chance to show that I can curve a ball with as much skill as I did when I was a member of the Chicago Club," Corcoran told the *Times*.[55] Corcoran played shortstop for nine games and the outfield for 11 games, batting .185. He pitched in two games for the Nationals in 1886, losing 10-4 in Kansas City on July 6. "Corcoran pitched for Washington," the *Washington Daily Critic* wrote, "and demonstrated that his best days are over. … We don't want any more of New York's cast-off players."[56] In early August, Corcoran was released, and spent the winter focusing on becoming a full-time left-handed pitcher in 1887.[57]

On March 22, 1887, Corcoran signed with Nashville of the Southern League.[58] He pitched in three games and fell into controversy. Memphis players Bob Black and John Sneed were paid by gamblers to coax Corcoran to a bar and get him drunk. Corcoran failed to appear for his start on June 30, and betting was high on Memphis. Nashville manager George Bradley was on to the scheme and pitched the game, beating Memphis. Corcoran was fined $50 and suspended.[59] On May 9, however, he was on his way back to the major leagues, signed by the Indianapolis Hoosiers, who paid $1,000 to Nashville for his release, and gave Corcoran a $2,000 salary. "He says that he is in first-class form, physically," the *Indianapolis News* reported, "and thinks he is as capable of pitching effectively as he ever was—at least he is going to try it."⁶⁰

Indianapolis was playing a three-game series in Chicago, so Corcoran went straight there to pitch on May 11. It was a rude homecoming. "'Little Larry' who used to twirl for us down on the Lake-Front—faced the champions, and when he stepped into the box it was plain to be seen that he had a great many admirers among the spectators," wrote the *Tribune*. "He lost most of them, before the game was over."⁶¹ Corcoran surrendered 11 runs on 12 hits and 10 walks in the Hoosiers' 11-6 defeat. "Corcoran labored under the fatigue of a long ride from Nashville," wrote the *Indianapolis News*.⁶²

Corcoran made his last major-league start on May 17 at New York. "A study of the score is suggestive of profanity," commented the *Indianapolis News* on the Giants' 26-6 win. Ironically, he was "presented a floral harp by his eastern admirers."⁶³ "It was a sad day for Larry Corcoran," wrote the *New York Herald*, "The little favorite was a rattling good pitcher—once."⁶⁴ Corcoran played in center field on May 20, his last major-league game, and was released by the end of the month.⁶⁵

In 1888 Corcoran signed with the London (Ontario) Tecumsehs of the International Association. He played in 28 games, pitching in only six and playing 22 in left field. He was again fined and suspended for intoxication, then was in a fight with teammate Shorty Howe, biting Howe's finger so badly that the fingernail came off.⁶⁶ Both players were released, and Corcoran's baseball career was over. *Sporting Life* noted at the end of 1888, "Larry Corcoran has come to that dernier resort of decayed ball players—bar-tending. He hands out drinks in a Newark saloon."⁶⁷

Corcoran umpired in the Atlantic League in 1890 and the Illinois-Iowa-Indiana League in 1891, but stepped down due to poor health.⁶⁸ The fledgling Brotherhood of Professional Base Ball Players, an early and unsuccessful attempt to organize a baseball players union, was able to send $300 to Corcoran "in his last days," *Sporting Life* reported.⁶⁹

Corcoran died on October 14, 1891, at the age of 32 at his home at 24 Cherry Street in Newark after suffering for several months from Bright's disease, a kidney ailment that today is called nephritis. His funeral was held at St. John's Catholic Church in Newark. He was survived by Gertrude and four children, Margarete, Walter, Mary, and Sarah Corcoran.

Corcoran died broke and was buried in an unmarked grave in Holy Sepulchre Cemetery in Newark. In 2009 Captain John Melody and a group of baseball-loving police officers and firefighters in Essex County, New Jersey, stumbled upon Corcoran's story on the website thedeadballera.com and raised money for a headstone. It was dedicated in September 2009. "We felt he deserved a gravestone based on his accomplishments in the big leagues," Melody said. "Plus, his last name was Corcoran, and most of us are Irish, so we felt a connection."⁷⁰

SOURCES

In addition to the sources cited in the text, the author consulted John O'Malley's article, "Lawrence J. Corcoran," in Robert L. Tiemann and Joseph Overfield, eds., *Nineteenth Century Stars* (Phoenix: Society for American Baseball Research, 2012), 63-64. Special thanks also to the Baseball Hall of Fame in Cooperstown, New York, for access to Larry Corcoran's file, and Jacob Pomrenke for research assistance in writing this article.

NOTES

1 "Between the Lines," *Boston Herald*, November 15, 1891: 22.

2 "Special to the Eagle," *Brooklyn Eagle*, April 2, 1897: 4; Peter Morris, *Game of Inches: The Story Behind the Innovations That Shaped Baseball* (Chicago: Ivan R. Dee Publishers, 2010), 93.

3 "Enterprise vs. Chelsea," *New York Clipper*, May 19, 1877: 59.

4 "Base Ball," *Brooklyn Eagle*, May 4, 1877: 2.

5 "Livingston vs. Rochester," *New York Clipper*, June 30, 1877: 107.

6 "The Springfields for 1879. Something About the Previous Work of the Men Constituting the Nine," *Springfield* (Massachusetts) *Republican*, April 11, 1879: 8.

7 SABR researcher Joseph M. Overfield called the 1878 Bisons "The First Great Minor League Club." See research.sabr.org/journals/first-great-minor-league-club. Retrieved July 28, 2015.

8 "The Springfields for 1879."

9 "Sporting Matters. Base Ball," *Springfield Republican*, May 14, 1879: 5.

NO-HITTERS

10 "Sporting Matters. Base Ball. Exit Springfield Ball Club," *Springfield Republican*, September 8, 1879: 5; "Sporting Matters," *Springfield* Republican, September 24, 1879: 5.

11 "Sporting Matters. Rowell Wins the Walking Match, with Merritt Second and Hazael Third," *Springfield Republican*, September 29, 1879: 5.

12 David L. Fleitz, *Cap Anson: The Grand Old Man of Baseball* (Jefferson, North Carolina: McFarland, 2005), 88.

13 Adrian C. Anson, *A Ball Player's Career. Being the Personal Experiences and Reminiscences of Adrian C. Anson* (Chicago: Era Pub, 1900), 109-110.

14 Anson, 110.

15 "Sporting. Base Ball," *Chicago Tribune*, April 2, 1880: 3.

16 "Base-Ball. Opening of the League Championship Season Yesterday," *Chicago Tribune*, May 2, 1880: 7.

17 David Quentin Voigt, *American Baseball: From Gentleman's Sport to the Commissioner System* (Norman, Oklahoma: University of Oklahoma Press, 1966), 102.

18 "Sporting Events. The Most Extraordinary League Championship Game on Record," *Chicago Tribune*, June 5, 1880: 11.

19 "Athletic Amusements. Model Exhibitions on the Base Ball Diamond Yesterday," *Boston Globe*, August 5, 1880: 4.

20 "Sporting Events. The League Championship Struggle Resumed on the Chicago Grounds," *Chicago Tribune*, August 11, 1880: 3.

21 "Sporting Events. A Game of Ball In Which Boston Scored Neither a Run Nor a Base-Hit," *Chicago Tribune*, August 20, 1880: 8.

22 "Sporting Events. Slashing Defeat of the Clevelands by the Chicago Champions," *Chicago Tribune*, May 4, 1881: 5; "Sporting Events. Providence Smothered by the Chicago Champions—Score, 8 to 0," *Chicago Tribune*, June 25, 1881: 6.

23 "Sporting Events. A Model Game of Base-Ball in Which the Chicagos Were Victorious," *Chicago Tribune*, August 5, 1881: 3.

24 "Wild Play and 'Snake' Balls," *Inter Ocean* (Chicago), August 12, 1881; Morris, 97.

25 "Sporting Events. Chicago Successful in a Twelve-Inning Game Against Detroit," *Chicago Tribune*, August 24, 1881: 3.

26 "Base-Ball Games. Return of the Chicago Team for a Series on Their Own Grounds," *Chicago Tribune*, June 21, 1882: 8.

27 John O'Malley, "Lawrence J. Corcoran," in Mark Rucker and Robert L. Tiemann, eds., *Nineteenth Century Stars* (Kansas City: Society for American Baseball Research, 1989), 31.

28 "Corcoran Was Off Being Married," *Cincinnati Enquirer*, August 24, 1882: 5.

29 "Base Ball Matters," *Boston Herald*, August 29, 1882: 5.

30 An obituary listing "Gertrude A. Corcoran nee Grork, widow of Lawrence J. Corcoran" as having died on March 9, 1898, appeared in the *Springfield Republican*, March 12, 1898.

31 "Base-Ball Games. Brilliant Close of the Championship Season by the Chicagos at Home," *Chicago Tribune*, September 21, 1882: 8.

32 "Sporting. Chicago vs. Boston," *Chicago Tribune*, May 23, 1883: 6.

33 "Base-Ball. Chicago 9; Boston 0," *Chicago Tribune*, July 19, 1883: 8; "Base-Ball. The Cleveland Club Neatly Whitewashed By the Home Team," *Chicago Tribune*, August 30, 1883: 2.

34 "Sporting. The Chicago Team Now Clearly in the Lead for the Championship," *Chicago Tribune*, September 9, 1883: 3.

35 "Base-Ball. The Champions Defeated in a Close and Exciting Game at Boston," *Chicago Tribune*, September 11, 1883: 6.

36 "Placing the Ball," *Chicago Tribune*, September 9, 1883: 3; Morris, *Game of Inches*, 45.

37 "Base Ball. Corcoran Knocked Out," *Inter Ocean* (Chicago), December 9, 1883: 19.

38 "To Be Expelled From the League," *New York Times*, December 15, 1883: 4.

39 "Corcoran and the Chicago Club," *New York Clipper*, December 15, 1883: 647.

40 *New York Clipper*, January 12, 1884: 727; "At His Old Post," *Wheeling* (West Virginia) *Register*, January 8, 1884: 1.

41 "Baseball. A Game on Skates," *New York Clipper*, January 19, 1884: 745.

42 "Sporting News. The Chicago League Team Again Defeated—Providence the Victor," *Chicago Tribune*, May 11, 1884: 11.

43 *Buffalo Commercial Advertiser*, June 17, 1884; cited in Al Kermisch, "Corcoran Pitched With Both Hands in Regular Game," in *Baseball Research Journal* 10 (SABR, 1982), 66.

44 "Base-Ball. Chicago, 6; Providence, 0," *Chicago Tribune*, June 28, 1884: 6.

45 The feat was tied twice (Cy Young in 1908 and Bob Feller in 1951) and broken in 1965 by Sandy Koufax.

46 "Base Ball. League Club Contests," *Inter Ocean* (Chicago), July 16, 1884: 8.

47 "Base-Ball. The Chicago Program for 1885," *Chicago Tribune*, October 12, 1884: 15.

48 "All in Sport. The Chicagos Win an Uphill Game From the Willow-Wielders of the Hub," *Chicago Tribune*, May 27, 1885: 3.

49 "Sporting Affairs. Anson's Team in the Lead in the League Championship Race—Corcoran's Condition," *Chicago Tribune*, June 22, 1885: 3.

50 "Diamond Dust," *Inter Ocean* (Chicago), July 12, 1885: 3.

NO-HITTERS

51 Henry Clay Palmer [Remlap], "From Chicago. Our Interest in the Game—Al Spalding and the Chicago Club—Larry Corcoran's Release," *Sporting Life*, July 29, 1885: 4.

52 "Corcoran Signs With New York. His Sore Arm Suddenly Healed," *Inter Ocean* (Chicago), July 19, 1885: 2.

53 "Baseball News," *New York Times*, July 20, 1885: 5.

54 "Baseball. The New-York Team Win a Second Victory in St. Louis," *New York Times*, October 9, 1885: 5.

55 "Transfer of a Player," *New York Times*, June 29, 1886: 2.

56 "Out-Door Sports. Base Ball," *Washington Daily Critic*, July 7, 1886: 1.

57 "Base Ball Briefs," *Kansas City Times*, August 7, 1886: 6; "Baseball. Remarkable Pitching Performances in 1886," *New York Clipper*, January 29, 1887: 729.

58 "Larry Corcoran Signs With Nashville," *New Orleans Times-Picayune*, March 23, 1887: 2.

59 "Around the Bases," *Chicago Tribune*, May 6, 1877: 3; *New York Sun*, May 8, 1887: 14; "Tennessee Troubles," *New Orleans Times-Picayune*, May 3, 1887: 2.

60 "A Change Pitcher. Larry Corcoran Engaged," *Indianapolis News*, May 10, 1887: 1.

61 "Base-Ball. A Long Game Between Chicago and Indianapolis," *Chicago Tribune*, May 12, 1887: 3.

62 "Corcoran's Trial. Kindly Received by Chicago," *Indianapolis News*, May 12, 1887: 1.

63 "Oh, What a Game! The Lamented Corcoran Knocked out of the Box—General Ball Talk," *Indianapolis News*, May 18, 1887: 1.

64 "Ball Gossip," *Indianapolis News*, May 20, 1887: 1.

65 "Base Ball Gossip," *Indianapolis News*, May 23, 1887: 1.

66 "Baseball Small-Talk," *The Critic*, June 7, 1888: 3; "Chips From the Diamond," *New York Sun*, August 6, 1888: 3.

67 "Notes and Comments," *Sporting Life*, December 19, 1888: 2.

68 "Notes and Gossip," *Sporting Life*, June 21, 1890: 4; "News, Gossip, and Comment," *Sporting Life*, June 27, 1891.

69 "Still on Earth," *Sporting Life*, December 12, 1891: 12.

70 Tom Meagher, "Essex County police, firefighters raise money to mark grave of forgotten baseball player," nj.com/news/local/index.ssf/2009/09/cops_raise_money_to_mark_grave.html, retrieved August 1, 2015.

LARRY CORCORAN'S FIRST NO-HITTER

AUGUST 19, 1880: CHICAGO WHITE STOCKINGS 6, BOSTON RED CAPS 0

By Bob LeMoine

"THE REDS WERE WOEFULLY weak with the willow, not being able to hit beyond the diamond and not scoring a base hit in thirty times at bat."[1] That was the brief description by the *Boston Globe* of Larry Corcoran's no-hitter on August 19, 1880, the first of three in his career. These were the days before the phrase "no-hitter" was even used. The *Cincinnati Enquirer* wrote "There were no special features of interest," although "the Bostons received a most thorough trouncing from the Chicagos today, the visitors failing to secure a single hit off Corcoran."[2] While a modern no-hitter would be analyzed by studio hosts and top defensive plays of the game regularly repeated, in 1880 most newspapers didn't have a summary of the game, let alone a mention of a great pitching feat.

The *Chicago Tribune* gave a little more detail, writing that the 2,000 fans present "saw something that never before occurred on the Chicago grounds,— that is, a game in which the defeated team obtained neither a tally nor a base-hit."[3] The *Cincinnati Commercial Tribune* spent two of its six sentences of coverage in a lackluster comment that "Rain also caused a cessation of play. All this prolonged the game to nearly three hours."[4]

While a pitcher throwing a no-hitter today is a top story on sports stations, the *Tribune* simply concluded, "the game of yesterday merits little in the way of description."[5] The *Chicago Inter-Ocean* said, "The Boston nine were treated to a fine, though unwelcome, basketful of goose-eggs."[6] They surely didn't make much ado about nothing … nothing in the hit column, that is. In his short career, Corcoran still became the first pitcher to throw three no-hit gems, a feat matched only by Cy Young and Bob Feller, and surpassed by Sandy Koufax and Nolan Ryan.

Corcoran had actually thrown a one-hitter nine days earlier against Providence, "but it remained for the Bostons to suffer the extreme effect of his great skills as a pitcher," the *Tribune* wrote.[7] His rookie season of 1880 saw him throwing (unfathomable by today's standards) 536⅓ innings, on his way to a 43-14 record and a 1.95 ERA with 268 strikeouts. He completed 57 of 60 starts. Keeping up this torrid pace for five years, Corcoran was essentially finished because of a dead arm at the age of 25.

The White Stockings at 47-11 and 12½ games ahead of second-place Providence had all but won the National League pennant already. They had taken sole possession of first place on May 13 and hadn't looked back since. They had a 21-game winning streak from June 2 to July 8, and finished the season an amazing 50 games over .500 (67-17). It was a Chicago year, as were the next two seasons, as the White Stockings won three pennants in a row.

The Red Caps had struggled the entire season, and were entering the game 26-32 and in the sixth-place position they would finish the year in. Boston pitching allowed the most earned runs and had the second highest ERA in the league, 3.08 (Buffalo had 3.09). That looks excellent to the modern fan, but in 1880 three clubs had ERAs below 2.00. The Red Caps's starting pitcher this day, Tommy Bond, had also been a workhorse the past three years, throwing over 500 innings and winning over 40 games each year.

Chicago scored a run in the first inning "through a base-hit and [Abner] Dalrymple's good running,"[8] along with a muffed throw by John Morrill at first base. In the third inning Joe Quest singled and stole second, and Dalrymple walked. Hits by George Gore and Ned Williamson brought in two runs, only one being earned. "A fine running catch by [Charley] Jones was much applauded."[9] Chicago took a 3-0 lead. The rain delay in the third inning made the ball "mushy and shapeless for the greater part of the play," the *Tribune* commented, "but that did not prevent the White Stockings from making eleven hits and thirteen totals off Bond and [Curry] Foley."[10] It is not known when right fielder Foley and Bond swapped places. Chicago, wrote the *Inter Ocean*, "batted Bond freely and would have similarly treated Foley, but for the soggy condition of the ball in the last two innings."[11]

In the fourth inning Boston shortstop John Richmond, who had sprained a knee in Cincinnati the week before, reinjured himself and had to leave the game. Jim O'Rourke moved to center field and his brother John took over at shortstop.

Chicago scored three more runs in the sixth inning. Tom Burns singled, stole second, and scored on Corcoran's hit. Corcoran wound up at third on Morrill's muff of a throw from Tommy Bond. Corcoran scored on Quest's single. Dalrymple reached on Jim O'Rourke's error. Gore "sent the mushy ball over to [the] right-field fence for two bases,"[12] and Quest scored. Gore went 4-for-4 in the game with two doubles.

The Red Caps were retired in order in seven of their nine innings. They had their first real chance in the ninth, courtesy of two errors.

With one out in the ninth, John O'Rourke grounded to Quest, who bobbled the ball and threw wildly to first. O'Rourke made second. Jim O'Rourke followed with a grounder of his own to Quest "and he muffed this one too," wrote the *Tribune*, placing the brothers at first and third. Sometime during the inning, Chicago catcher Silver Flint had "his right thumb put out of joint in the ninth inning, and in trying to pull it back to place the flesh was badly lacerated. It will probably disable Flint altogether for a fortnight at least."[13] Jim O'Rourke raced to second on an attempted hit-and-run, but Jack Burdock "batted Quest a fly, and Joe had the satisfaction of closing the inning and atoning for his bungling by a clever double play."[14] Jim O'Rourke was doubled up, the game was over, and Corcoran had his no-hitter on the wet Chicago grounds.

Others injured besides Flint were Boston's second baseman Burdock, catcher Sam Trott, and Corcoran himself. Burdock "was hit in the ribs by one of Corcoran's twisters. Trott had his finger banged by a foul tip … and Corcoran injured his ankle in running the bases—quite enough accidents for one day," wrote the *Inter Ocean*.[15]

The *Inter Ocean* noted that Chicago's King Kelly "had neither run, base-hit, fielding play, nor error," but Cap Anson "retired twenty-one of the twenty-seven Boston men without an error, equaling the best first-base record ever made. Add to these unusual features the fact that four men were seriously injured during its progress, and it might truly be said that it was a remarkable game."[16]

The time of game was 2 hours and 30 minutes. "The umpiring was unexceptional," the *Inter Ocean* commented.[17]

NOTES

1. "What Is the Score? The Bostons Chicagoed and the Providences Winners," *Boston Globe*, August 20, 1880.
2. "Thoroughly Trounced," *Cincinnati Enquirer*, August 20, 1880: 8.
3. "A Game of Ball in Which Boston Scored Neither a Run Nor a Base-Hit," *Chicago Tribune*, August 20, 1880: 8.
4. "Harry Wright Again Disgusted," *Cincinnati Commercial Tribune*, August 20, 1880: 6.
5. "A Game of Ball."
6. "Boston's Goose Eggs, Which the Hub Nine Received Yesterday at the Hands of the Chicago Club," *Inter-Ocean* (Chicago), August 20, 1880.
7. "A Game of Ball."
8. "Boston's Goose Eggs."
9. "A Game of Ball."
10. Ibid.
11. "Boston's Goose Eggs."
12. "A Game of Ball."
13. Ibid.

14 Ibid.
15 "Boston's Goose Eggs."
16 Ibid.
17 Ibid.

TONY MULLANE

By Raymond Birch

AMONG THE BASEBALL accomplishments in Tony Mullane's career, two events in 1882 stand out in particular: becoming the first ambidextrous pitcher in major-league history on July 18, while with the Louisville Eclipse of the American Association, and tossing a no-hit game on September 11.

Anthony John Mullane, also known by the nicknames the Count and the Apollo of the Box, was born on January 30, 1859, in County Cork, Ireland. He pitched for four teams in the National League (Detroit, Cincinnati, Baltimore, and Cleveland) and four in the American Association (Louisville, St. Louis, Toledo, and Cincinnati) between 1881 and 1894. Well known as a ladies' man, Mullane also was a proficient boxer, as well as a competitive roller skater and ice skater.

Mullane was the oldest son of Dennis Mullane, a laborer born in 1827, and Elizabeth (Behan) Mullane (born 1828), a homemaker. Anthony had two brothers, John (born in 1874 in Pennsylvania), and Sam (born in 1865 in New Jersey), and a sister, Nora (born in 1860 in Ireland). In 1862, when Anthony was 3, the family emigrated to the United States.

In his book *A Fine-Looking Lot of Ball-Tossers*, Richard McBane wrote that, while living with his family in Erie, Pennsylvania, Mullane "would run away from home and play ball. He wouldn't learn a trade. He imagined he was cut out for a ball player and he undoubtedly was. He filled the box in several amateur games in Erie, and then became discontented because no pay was attached."[1]

Mullane is said to have begun his professional baseball career in Ohio, where he played for a number of local teams, including Cambridge and Akron during the 1880 season. But McBane wrote that Mullane signed a professional contract in 1876 with the Geneva, Ohio, team for $1 a day plus room and board; between 1876 and 1880, he apparently drifted from club to club in eastern Ohio and western Pennsylvania before joining the Akron team.[2] Early in the 1881 season, Mullane played for Akron again, against other amateur teams in Ohio as well as National League teams that would play Akron when they were playing near Cleveland, which had a National League franchise. There also is a record of Mullane playing with the local White Sewing Machine team in 1881 as a center fielder.[3]

As of May 1881 Mullane was playing again with Akron, a member of the League Alliance, which placed the Akron team under the rules of the National League and allowed the team to play League teams. Among the League teams that they played during the 1881 season were Cleveland, Boston, and Worcester, with Mullane playing well as a pitcher, first baseman, and outfielder. In July of 1881 it was rumored that Mullane would leave the Akron team to play for the Louisville Eclipse of the American Association.[4] Instead Mullane went to the Detroit Wolverines of the National League in August and played in five games as a change pitcher, with a 1-4 record and a .263 batting average.[5]

In 1882 Mullane went to the Eclipse. He played in 77 games, 55 of them as a pitcher, and also played first base, second base, and the outfield; he batted .257 and compiled a 30-24 record on the mound, with a 1.88 ERA. He pitched in particularly memorable games. On July 18 in Baltimore, after giving up seven runs in three innings to the lowly Orioles, the right-hander began pitching with his left hand, becoming the first ambidextrous pitcher in major-league baseball. And on September 11 Mullane pitched a no-hit game against the Cincinnati Reds, the first no-hitter in the American Association.

Mullane's talents attracted the interest of other teams and in August 1882, the *Cleveland Dealer* reported that he had signed with the St. Louis Browns of the American Association for the 1883

season. Mullane continued his winning ways with his new team, posting a 35-15 record with a 2.19 ERA. After the season the Browns reserved his contract for the 1884 season. However, a new league, the Union Association, was forming, with a franchise in St. Louis, and the new team, the Maroons, reportedly signed him as a pitcher, giving him $500 in advance money. The president of the Browns, Chris Von der Ahe, said he would not punish Mullane for breaking the reserve rule as he himself opposed the rule. Meanwhile, before the 1884 season began, the Toledo club of the American Association offered Mullane a contract reported at between $4,000 and $5,000 to jump back from the Union Association and he did so, with Von der Ahe's blessing.

Mullane became much sought after. The *Boston Herald* described him as "a most effective pitcher; his delivery is low and his command of the ball wonderful. He pitches with left or right arm equally well."[6]

One of Mullane's catchers in Toledo was Moses Fleetwood Walker, who is credited by some as the first African American to play major-league baseball. While pitching for Toledo in a game in St. Louis on May 4, Mullane felt the wrath of the crowd. He was called a contract breaker and cheat, and was hissed when he hit and raucously cheered when he struck out. To the crowd's disappointment, Mullane showed little or no reaction.[7] The next day the Browns applied to the circuit court in St. Louis for a restraining order preventing Mullane from playing for any team other than the Browns. The issued the restraining order, but it was immediately overturned by a federal judge who said the courts' time should not be occupied by baseball matters and that it was beneath the dignity of the courts to notice.[8] Mullane rejoined Toledo on May 14 and in 95 games hit .276 and won 36 games while losing 26, with an ERA of 2.52 and a career-high 325 strikeouts.

In August 1884, it was reported that several clubs, including Cincinnati of the American Association, anticipating that the Toledo club would fold, were interested in acquiring Mullane's services. On November 5 Mullane signed with Cincinnati for an estimated $5,000, with a $2,000 advance; however, his signing by the Reds violated an agreement Mullane had made with the St. Louis Browns. Mullane was subsequently suspended for a year and fined $1,000 for jumping his contract with Toledo. An attempt to reinstate Mullane fell flat when a satisfactory agreement between representatives of the teams could not reached. Mullane pitched some games for local games in Ohio in 1885 and was reinstated at the end of the American Association season on October 2. He pitched for Cincinnati against St. Louis in a series of exhibition games, but not in St. Louis because of an injunction granted to the Browns. Mullane, who had trained hard despite not pitching in the major leagues, was in great shape and pitched well against St. Louis.

Signing Mullane for the 1886 season proved difficult for Cincinnati and he threatened to quit baseball for business if his salary demands were not met. But on March 4 he signed with the Reds and later opened a pool room in Cincinnati, which the *Cincinnati Commercial Tribune* called a "first-class, orderly place."[9] Despite showing up for the season in great physical shape, Mullane was hit hard at the beginning of the season and expressed disgust at his performance, threatening to retire from pitching for good.[10] By mid-May, though, he began to pitch like the Mullane of old.

Controversy erupted when the *Cincinnati Times-Star* reported an accusation that Mullane and four other Cincinnati players had thrown a game on June 4 at Brooklyn.[11] The accuser, Patrick J. McMahon, alleged that Mullane told him to bet as much money as he could on Brooklyn to win after the fourth, fifth, and sixth innings, despite the fact that Cincinnati was ahead 7-0 at the end of the seventh inning. With Mullane pitching, Brooklyn scored eight runs in the eighth and four in the ninth to win the game, with 10 of the 12 runs being earned. The Brooklyn club was connected to some New York gambling houses with which Mullane was alleged to have made a bargain. Mullane sued the *Cincinnati Times-Star* in Ohio superior court, asking for $20,000 for alleged slanderous and malicious libel.[12] Meanwhile, an American Association panel cleared Mullane of any charges.[13] Mullane finished the season with 33 wins and 27 losses with a 3.70 ERA.

After being reserved again by Cincinnati, and signed for the 1887 season, Mullane was suspended without pay in May and fined $100 for insubordination after refusing to play until his salary was increased. The Red Stockings placed Mullane on their reserve list. If he had merely been released, he could have been claimed by another club. The situation became more complicated when Mullane threatened the president of the Cincinnati club, Aaron Stern, with violence because of the $100 fine.[14] Mullane then went to Rutland, Vermont, in early June to play for a local unaffiliated club there for $200 a month.[15] But by mid-June, cooler heads had prevailed and Mullane was reinstated by the Red Stockings. Despite the disrupted season, he won 31 games and lost 17.

The 1888 season was relatively uneventful for Mullane, although on August 2 he was arrested at the Brooklyn ballpark on a charge of contempt for failure to appear regarding a charge of not paying for some whiskey, but he eventually paid his bill and the case was closed.[16] Statistically, he posted a 26-16 record, increased his strikeout total to 186 from 97 the previous year and reduced his ERA to 2.84 from 3.24; he also umpired in three games. But by 1889 Mullane appeared to be on the decline as a pitcher. His record dropped to 11-9 in only 33 appearances as a pitcher; he also played 34 games as a third baseman, outfielder, and first baseman and batted .296, a career high.

In 1890 Cincinnati moved to the National League. Mullane played outfield, third base, shortstop, and first base while pitching in 25 games. He came back strong on the mound in the second half of the season, posting a 12-10 record with a 2.24 ERA. That strong finish gave the club the confidence that he might be returning to his dominant form of previous years.

In an article written in *The Sporting News* of July 12, 1890, Mullane spoke of how he was able to prevent "dead arm." He said:

"… I have had a bad arm on two occasions. Once in Akron my arm went back on me entirely. I did not set around and give it a rest. Neither did I bathe it in arnica or high wines. I simply put on two heavy sweaters, and although it hurt me even to raise my arm, I went to work and pitched ball after ball … and it hurt me so badly that I had to grit my teeth. … Had I sat around nursing my sore arm I am confident that I would not now be solid as a pitcher."

However, after an 1891 season when he won 23 games but lost 26 and saw his ERA rise by a full run to 3.23, the pressure was on Mullane to produce better statistics in 1892 or risk not pitching regularly again, especially since he was an active participant in dissension that had riddled the Cincinnati team. Perhaps contributing to that dismal season was the fact that Mullane's son had died in July and that Mullane had played injured. After the season Mullane was very close to signing with the Chicago Colts of the National League before his wife intervened and said no to the proposed deal.[17]

Mullane came back to Cincinnati, won 21 games and lost 13 in 1892, and lowered his ERA to 2.59. In May of 1893, Mullane's wife of seven years, Barbara, filed for divorce, alleging that he beat her when she criticized his play after a game. In turn Mullane filed for alimony from his wife, with whom he had one child, saying that she smoked cigarettes, drank beer, and lost much of his money in "wild schemes."[18] Cincinnati was enjoined from paying him any money pending resolution of the suit. After a 6-6 start to the 1893 season with Cincinnati, Mullane was traded to the Baltimore Orioles for Piggy Ward and $1,500 on June 16. He finished the season at 18-22, with an ERA of over 4.00. In January of 1894 his wife accused him of threatening to kill her after a dispute and she wanted him arrested for contempt of court, for failure to pay her alimony after a judge had thrown out his attempt to refrain from paying it.[19] The *Chicago Tribune* wrote that Mullane had developed a "sulky temper" in Baltimore, and had been sued for $2,000 by a hotel proprietor for hitting him with a baseball bat, a claim Mullane disputed.[20] Perhaps the low point of Mullane's career on the field came when he was tagged for 16 runs in the first inning of a game against Boston on June 18 en route to a 24-7 shellacking by the Beaneaters. On July 24, 1894, Mullane's wife was granted a divorce on grounds of extreme cruelty against her and their young daughter. The Orioles traded Mullane to the Cleveland Spiders on July 15, and the Spiders released him on August 4, in part because of an ingrown nail on his left index finger that brought about blood poisoning

After the 1894 season Mullane played 11 games with Oakland in the California Winter League, then in March of 1895 he signed with the St. Paul Apostles of the Western League, disappointed that he was not signed by a National League team. He played in 95 games for St. Paul, batting .320, and compiling a 16-10 pitching record in 218 innings. He played for St. Paul until May 27, 1898, when he became captain and manager of the Detroit Tigers of the Western League. He was released by the Tigers on June 12. He signed with Toronto of the Eastern League for 1899 but retired after only playing seven games.

In December 1896, *Sporting Life* had reported that Mullane filed an application to the National League to become an umpire.[21] A few weeks after the Tigers released him in 1898, the Western League hired him as an umpire. *Sporting Life* initially reported in August that Mullane was "umpiring good ball,"[22] but an article three weeks later indicated that writers in Western League cities felt that "his umpiring is extremely poor" and he "does not seem to have his lines cast in easy parts."[23] Numerous controversies involving Mullane's calls led to his resignation after the season. After his short stint as a player in Toronto ended in 1899, he became an umpire in the Atlantic League,[24] where his umpiring skills showed great improvement. In 1901 he sold a saloon he owned in Chicago and announced that he would resume his quest for an umpiring position in the National League, where the salary was higher. He was hired as an umpire by the Western Association in 1901 season, and took an umpiring job in the Pacific Northwest League in 1902. He left that job because of poor performance, and joined the league's Spokane Smoke Eaters as a player, appearing in 20 games.

Mullane took a job with the Chicago Police Department as a complaint sergeant in January 1903, but continued to umpire, first in the American Association in 1903, then in the Southern Association in 1904. In 1911 Mullane suffered a near-fatal abscess of the brain. After recovering, he continued working for the Police Department. He died on April 26, 1944. He was survived by his daughter, Ina; his brother, John; and a granddaughter, Dorothy.

NOTES

1. Richard L. McBane, *A Fine-Looking Lot of Ball-Tossers: The Remarkable Akrons of 1881* (Jefferson, North Carolina: McFarland & Company, Inc., 2005), 34-35. McBane cited an 1886 article in *The Sporting News*.
2. McBane, 34-35.
3. "Akron's Annihilators," *Cleveland Plain Dealer*, April 27, 1881.
4. "Just Like Him," *Cleveland Plain Dealer*, August 29, 1881.
5. *Cleveland Plain Dealer*, August 30, 1881. A change pitcher is defined by the *Dickson Baseball Dictionary* as a relief or substitute pitcher.
6. *Boston Herald*, April 8, 1884.

7 "A One-Sided Game Between St. Louis and Toledo—A Prize Fight of Seventeen Rounds –Sullivan," *Kansas City Times*, May 5, 1884.

8 "Mullane's Victory," *Cincinnati Commercial Tribune,* May 13, 1884.

9 "Baseball—Tony Mullane Signs to Play With the Cincinnatis," *Cincinnati Commercial Tribune*, March 7, 1886.

10 *Kansas City Times*, May 11, 1886.

11 "Charges of 'Throwing,'" *Boston Herald*, June 19, 1886.

12 *Kansas City* (Missouri) *Times*, June 17, 1886.

13 "Mullane Vindicated," *Cincinnati Commercial Tribune*, July 1, 1886.

14 "Struck Out," *Sporting Life*, May 25, 1887.

15 *Sporting Life*, June 8, 1887.

16 "Tony Mullane's Arrest," *Sporting Life*, August 8, 1888.

17 "Cincinnati Chips—Mullane's Wife Settles His Case," *Sporting Life*, November 21, 1891.

18 "More Troubles for Mullane," *Chicago Tribune*, May 26, 1893.

19 "Mullane's Troubles," *Sporting Life*, January 20, 1894.

20 "Tony Mullane Sued for Damages," *Chicago Tribune*, May 8, 1894.

21 "Mullane's Ambition," *Sporting Life*, December 5, 1896.

22 *Sporting Life*, August 20, 1898.

23 *Sporting Life*, August 27, 1898.

24 *Sporting Life*, July 8, 1899.

SEPTEMBER 11, 1882

LOUISVILLE ECLIPSE 2, CINCINNATI RED STOCKINGS 0, AT BANK STREET GROUNDS, CINCINNATI

By Raymond Birch

IF YOU HAD MENTIONED THE name Tony Mullane to his teammates and opponents during his baseball-playing days, many differing opinions of his actions might come to mind. For example, Mullane, who came to the United States with his family from Ireland in 1864, was handsome and is said to be one of the reasons that ladies' day games became popular in the 1880s. He was also willing to bend the rules of baseball, pitching above the shoulder at a time when this was considered an illegal pitch; he was also considered to be tightfisted with his money, often wearing clothes until they became raggedy. But one thing that was universally acknowledged about him was that Tony Mullane was one of the dominant pitchers in professional baseball of his time, posting 284 career wins.

After a five-game pitching debut with the Detroit Wolverines of the National League in 1881, during which his won-loss record was 1-4, Mullane appeared to be a long shot to succeed in professional baseball. But despite his less-than-impressive first season, the Louisville Eclipse of the American Association sought his services as a change pitcher and first baseman, and signed him for the 1882 season, the Association's inaugural season. The circuit adopted the same dimensions for the pitcher's box (6 feet by 4 feet) and the distance from the front of the pitcher's box to the center of home plate (50 feet) as the rival National League.[1] Mullane, having pitched in the National League in 1881, had already adjusted to the distance to home, and compiled a 30-24 won-lost record with a 1.88 ERA in 1882.

Mullane was involved in two particularly noteworthy games during the 1882 season. First, on July 18 he used both hands to throw to batters, (throwing left-handed to left-handed batters and right-handed to right-handed batters), becoming professional baseball's first ambidextrous pitcher, in a 9-8 loss to the Baltimore Orioles.[2] On September 11 he pitched a no-hit game against the Cincinnati Red Stockings, the Association's first.

In the no-hit game, Mullane's pitching opponent was Will White of the Red Stockings, an accomplished hurler in his own right, who would win 229 games over a 10-season career with a lifetime 2.28 ERA; in 1882, he would go 40-12 with a 1.54 ERA. The game was played at Bank Street Grounds in Cincinnati before 1,922 fans with the temperature in the high 60s on a day when Cincinnati was beginning to close in on the first American Association pennant.[3] Cincinnati, the home team, opted under the rules of the day to bat first.

Cincinnati's leadoff batter, Joe Sommer, drew a base on balls. But he was doubled up on an outfield fly, his mistake compounded when the next batter, Hick Carpenter, reached base on a two-base error and went to third on a passed ball; no damage was done, as Carpenter was left stranded at third. After the visiting Eclipse went out in order in the first, the Red Stockings failed to capitalize on a muffed fly by John Reccius in center field in the second inning; in the bottom of the inning, the Eclipse wasted a single by Mullane when he was thrown out by catcher Pop Snyder trying to advance on a passed ball.

The third and fourth innings were uneventful for both teams, and the Red Stockings were retired in order in the fifth and sixth. The Eclipse, however, in the sixth inning, provided some excitement when Samuel Maskrey, known by his middle name, Leech, reached on an error by Red Stockings third baseman Carpenter. Reccius hit to right field, and he and

Maskrey both advanced a base on Harry Wheeler's throw to home. With no outs and runners at second and third, a big inning appeared imminent, but pitcher White of the Red Stockings bore down and retired Pete Browning, Guy Hecker, and Dan Sullivan to end the threat.

After a scoreless seventh frame, the Eclipse scored two runs in the eighth. Leadoff batter Bill Schenck reached on an error by shortstop Chick Fulmer. Maskrey flied out but Reccius swatted a three-base hit to right center, scoring Schenck, and scored himself when right fielder Wheeler threw wild attempting to get Reccius at home. The next batter, Pete Browning, made history of his own when he became the first American Association player to reach base safely but getcalled out for being an illegal baserunner.[4] Browning, who had a pulled leg muscle, had requested that someone run for him when he was hitting, his teammate Hecker. With Hecker standing behind him ready to run to first when the ball was hit, Browning stroked a hit to right field. But in his excitement at getting a hit, Browning began to run to first. Hecker, confused at seeing Browning begin to run, stopped and ran off the field, while Browning continued to first, and eventually was declared out for being an illegal baserunner. Browning batted .378 and won the Association's batting title by a whopping 36 points in 1882. The lost hit affected his career batting average by one point (.341), preventing him from tying Dan Brouthers (.342) for the highest career batting average among players active primarily before 1893, when the pitching distance was lengthened.[5]

Sommer struck out to lead off the Cincinnati ninth, but got to first when catcher Sullivan missed the third strike. Wheeler flied out and Carpenter forced Sommer at second. With two out, Reccius muffed a fly ball by Snyder, and Carpenter went to third and Snyder to first. However, Dan Stearns forced Snyder at second, ending the game. Both White and Mullane pitched well, and umpire Mike Walsh was praised for his fairness in calling balls and strikes. the game was completed in 1 hour and 40 minutes. No matter what people thought of the antics of Mullane over the years, it cannot be denied that pitching a no-hit game in your first full year of professional baseball is a great way to start your career.

NOTES

1. Eric Miklich, "The Pitcher's Area," 19cbaseball.com/rules.html
2. Jerry Grillo, "Mullane Goes Both Ways," Bill Felber, ed., *Inventing Baseball: The 100 Greatest Games of the 19th Century* (Phoenix: Society for American Baseball Research, 2013).
3. "Mullane's Mash," *Cincinnati Tribune,* September 12, 1882.
4. David Nemec, *The Great Encyclopedia of 19th Century Major League Baseball* (New York: Penguin Books, 1997), 175.
5. Ibid.

GUY HECKER

By Bob Bailey

GUY HECKER HAS BEEN regarded as the best combination of hitter and pitcher during the nineteenth century.[1] In a major-league career that lasted from 1882 to 1890 he won 175 games and compiled a .282 batting average. But when one looks at his year-by-year record, two seasons stand out. Fittingly, one was as a hitter and one was as a pitcher.

Guy Jackson Hecker was born April 3, 1856, to Thomas and Lucinda Hecker near Youngsville, Pennsylvania, in Warren County. Guy was the eldest of two brothers (Charles was a year younger), and his father worked as a laborer in Warren County. Guy was born three years prior to Edwin Drake drilling the first successful oil well in nearby Titusville, Pennsylvania, in 1859. This event set off an oil boom in the area during the 1860s, and Thomas Hecker relocated his family up the Allegheny River to the prosperous town of Oil City in Venango County where he became the Superintendent of Streets for the borough of Venango.

Guy Hecker, who threw and batted right-handed, was a regular on the ball fields of Oil City and in 1877 landed a spot on his first professional team in Springfield, Ohio. He returned to Oil City after one season to marry and entered the business world while still playing in the amateur and semipro ranks in and around Oil City. In 1879 a young pitcher joined the team who would play a key role in getting Hecker to the majors. The pitcher was Tony Mullane, who won 284 games in his own major league career. Mullane became friendly with Hecker in his only season with Oil City, and when Tony joined the 1882 Louisville Eclipse in the newly formed American Association, he convinced the Louisville management to sign Hecker as a first-baseman and backup pitcher just before the start of the 1882 season.

In Hecker's first big-league season he hit .276 in 78 games and split 12 decisions as a pitcher. The six-foot, 190-pounder split his major-league time as a pitcher (336 games) and first baseman (322 games) and spent 75 games in the outfield. The highpoint of his 1882 season came on September 19 when he threw the second no-hitter in American Association history, against the Alleghenys of Pittsburgh. He missed having the first no-hitter by a week when his teammate Mullane no-hit the Cincinnati club.

Mullane moved on to St. Louis in 1883 and Hecker became Louisville's top pitcher. He posted a 28-23 record while pitching 469 innings. As a hitter he continued to hit in the .270s. In 1884 he exploded as a pitcher and began to develop as a major-league hitter. He raised his batting average to .297 and slugged at a .430 clip. But in the pitcher's box Hecker was the dominant pitcher in the American Association. He set the American Association single-season records for wins (52), innings pitched (670 2/3 in 1884), and complete games (72). He completed the pitcher's triple crown by leading the Association in ERA (1.80), and strikeouts (385). Only two other pitchers in major league history have won as many as 50 games in a season. A year after Hecker's 50-win season, John Clarkson won 53. But Hecker's real misfortune was that the all-time single-season wins record was set the same season Hecker won 52, as Charley Radbourn won 59 for Providence in the National League. Hecker's 52-20 record in 1884 included a game against Washington in June in which he struck out the first seven batters he faced, and a one-hitter against St. Louis in August.

But records were not something players or fans thought much about in the 1800s, and Hecker opened the 1885 campaign ready to continue his mastery of the American Association. However, after a game on April 21 he complained of a sore arm. He tried to pitch though the arm trouble and had flashes of his old brilliance. There were various conjectures as to the cause of his troubles, including the enforcement of the rule requiring a pitcher to keep his delivery below his shoulder level. But no medical cause was ever announced, and Hecker compiled a 30-23 record in 480 innings pitched. His decline concerned the Louisville management enough that they purchased the contract of a young lefty from Chattanooga, Tom (Toad) Ramsey, late in the season. Hecker's decline as a pitcher was matched in the batter's box as his average dropped to .273 and his slugging average dropped nearly 100 points to .337.

Over the winter Hecker did two things. He allowed his arm to rest, and he opened the Hecker Supply Company in Louisville. During the 1885 season he had indicated his dissatisfaction with his salary, and it had been rumored that he was seeking his release from Louisville. It is probable that, instead of a higher salary, someone in the Louisville management agreed to help finance Hecker's sporting goods company to keep him in Louisville. By January he was on the road hawking sporting goods across the South. The combination of resting his arm and starting a new business allowed him to miss much of the team's preseason training routine. He never liked playing in cold weather and blamed the 1885 preseason for some of his arm troubles.

The 1886 season started well for Hecker as he was named team captain and won his Opening Day start with a three-hitter against Cincinnati. But within a week of that win he was diagnosed with an inflamed nerve in his right arm. Some on the Louisville team thought his pitching days were over. Through May he pitched about once a week and had compiled a 3-4 record. Most of the pitching load fell to Ramsey, who was 38-27 in 588 2/3 innings for the season. As Ramsey's status with the team grew, he became more at odds with Hecker. Ramsey said that Hecker was jealous of Ramsey's success and it would be good for the team if Hecker were released.[2]

An anti-Hecker clique grew, and Guy was soon replaced as team captain. But the dissension on the club continued. Hecker's reputation as a gentleman and Ramsey's as a hard drinker got prominent play in the local press. In the midst of this turmoil, Hecker found himself off to the best hitting season of his

career. Hitting .417 in June, he raised his season's average to .341.

But Hecker's immediate problem was his arm. He tried corn plasters and massages. He tried rest and a lighter pitching load. In July he finally found a treatment that helped. Twice daily he would soak his arm in "electric-baths" at the *Courier-Journal* press room. He was so convinced of the benefits of this early "electronic-stimulation" treatment that he carried a galvanic battery on road trips. Hecker was back and he began pitching as well as he hit. Starting in July he won 11 straight games en route to a 26-23 pitching record.

During this period of rejuvenation, Hecker had the greatest hitting day any pitcher has ever experienced in the majors. In the second game of an August 15 doubleheader with Baltimore Hecker won the game as the starting pitcher while hitting three home runs and three singles with seven runs scored. His 15 total bases was a major-league record at the time, as was his three-homer game as a pitcher (matched by Jim Tobin in 1942). His seven runs scored remain the major-league single-game record by any player.

As his contribution in the pitcher's box resumed, his batting was the best of his career. In July he hit .379. He upped that to .500 in August and found himself on top of the batting leaders list with a .378 average starting September. With the temperatures turning cooler Hecker's average began to drop, and he closed the season with a .342 average. It took several weeks for the American Association office to announce the final averages and crown the season's batting champ. When they did in November, standing atop the league was New York's Dave Orr with a .346 average followed by Hecker and Caruthers at .342 and Browning and Tip O'Neill of St. Louis at .339. But many decades later, as statisticians researched and corrected baseball records for the publication of the *Baseball Encyclopedia*, the revised averages put Hecker's .342 at the top of the list followed by Browning (.340), Orr (.338), Caruthers (.334), and O'Neill (.328). So Guy Hecker did not win the American Association batting title in 1886 but, as it turns out, he did post the highest batting average. Subsequent research has found that Hecker's league-leading average in 1886 was actually .341. In 1886 Guy Hecker appeared in 49 games with 378 plate appearances. Modern readers may question Hecker's eligibility for a batting championship but during the 19th century no league had any rules for minimum games, plate appearances, or at-bats for eligibility for the batting title.

In correspondence with David Nemec, author of the *Great Nineteenth Century Baseball Encyclopedia* and *The Rules of Baseball*, he states that "the best that can be said is that in every season the winner was at least a reasonable choice (if not always a correct one)." So someone in the league office assessed the final numbers and chose the champion based on whatever criteria seemed appropriate at the time. Nemec notes that in 1883 the American Association announced Tom Mansell as the batting champion "until media derision forced it to go with [Ed] Swartwood." In the 1887 *Reach's Official American Association Base Ball Guide* Hecker makes the list as Reach used a 20-game standard to be included in the publication. The 1887 *Spalding Guide* does not include Hecker as they used a 100-game standard.

After 1886 Hecker showed a rapid decline as both a hitter and a pitcher. Although his batting average in 1887 could be seen as a lusty .366, during that one season walks counted as hits. Without the 31 walks he hit .319 on a comparable basis with 1886.[3] His pitching record fell to 18-12. There are two reasons given for his pitching decline. Having averaged over 500 innings pitched for four seasons could have ended his effectiveness. But 1887 also saw a shrinking of the pitcher's box. Hecker's pitching style included making a "hop, skip, and jump winding his arm beautifully about his head" to deliver a pitch.[4] Having to change his pitching style to accommodate the smaller pitching area could also have contributed to his decline.

By 1889 the Louisville team that had been a first-division team in the early years of the American Association was now a perennial tail-ender. Undercapitalized and beset by seemingly annual ownership changes, the team sunk to a 27-111 record in 1889. Things took a particularly bad turn after the parsimonious Mordecai Davidson took over control of the club. Davidson squeezed what money he could out of the franchise, even naming himself manager for a brief period. When he instituted a series of fines for errors and poor play, the players began to revolt. After one payday where several players owed the club money due to fines and only one player received a full paycheck, they issued an ultimatum: either the fines were returned or they would refuse to play. Davidson refused and on June 14, 1889, Guy Hecker was one of six Louisville players to participate in the first major-league strike when they refused to take the field in Baltimore. The players returned the next day when the American Association agreed to mediate the dispute.

Most of the dispute was resolved with new ownership in August, but Guy Hecker's Louisville run was about over. Pete Browning played his last game that season for Louisville in early September, and on September 17 Guy Hecker was released with a month to go in the season. The new management had decided to develop a younger team, and there was no place for the hero of 1884 and 1886.

Hecker left the American Association with his name high on several career pitching category lists. His Association record included 173 wins (third), 15 shutouts (eighth), 1078 strikeouts (fourth), 322 pitching appearances (second), and 137 losses (first).

In 1890 he replaced Ned Hanlon as the manager of the National League's Pittsburgh club. But this was the year of the Players League revolt and Hecker presided over a ragtag bunch that lost 113 games. Over the next two seasons he was player-manager for Fort Wayne in the Northwestern League and Jacksonville in the Illinois-Indiana League. He returned to Oil City in 1893 to enter the oil business but kept active in baseball by managing the local team for several seasons. The locals called the independent team "Hecker's Hitters."

Guy Hecker died at the age of 82 on December 3, 1938, in Wooster, Ohio. He had settled in Wooster to operate a grocery store after leaving Oil City. At the time of his death the strong right arm that produced 52 major-league wins in 1884 was almost useless as a result of injuries suffered in an automobile accident in 1931. He was buried in Wooster Cemetery.

SOURCES

In addition to the sources cited in the notes, the author also relied on:

Nemec, David. *The Beer and Whiskey League* (New York: Lyons & Burford, 1994).

Thorn, John, Pete Palmer & Michael Gershman, eds., *Total Baseball, 7th ed.* (Kingston, New York: Total Sports Publishing, 2001).

Louisville Commercial

Louisville Times

Oil City (Pennsylvania) *Derrick*

The Daily Record (Wooster, Ohio)

NOTES

1 L. Robert Davids, ed. *Great Hitting Pitchers* Cooperstown: Society for American Baseball Research, 1979).

2 *Courier-Journal* (Louisville, Kentucky), May 25, 1886.

3 Depending on the standard used, one could find a batting average as high as .403: 149 hits and ealks / 407 PA = .366 BA; 149 hits and walks / 370 AB = .403 BA; 118 hits / 370 at-bats = .319 BA.

4 *Courier-Journal*, June 21, 1886.

GUY HECKER NO-HITS PITTSBURGH

SEPTEMBER 19, 1882: LOUISVILLE 3, PITTSBURGH 1, AT EXHIBITION PARK, PITTSBURGH

By Bob Bailey

WHEN GUY HECKER tossed a no-hitter against the Alleghenys of Pittsburgh on September 19, 1882, it was a first in several ways:

- It was the first time the losing team scored a run in a no-hitter.
- It was the first time a team recorded a second no-hitter for the franchise.
- It was the first time a team recorded two no-hitters in a single season.

Eight days earlier, Hecker's Louisville teammate Tony Mullane had pitched Louisville's first no-hitter, against Cincinnati. Mullane's game was the first American Association no-hitter and matched the previous five no-hitters tossed by National League pitchers. It was also the first no-hitter thrown from the new 50-foot pitching distance. Mullane and Hecker had a long-running association. After playing one season for a professional team in Springfield, Ohio, Hecker returned home to Oil City, Pennsylvania, to get married and join the local labor force. He continued to play with local semipro teams and in 1879 Tony Mullane joined his Oil City team. When Mullane signed with Louisville for the 1882 season he recommended Hecker to the management for the position of change pitcher. Hecker was signed and primarily played first base, pitching in 13 games in 1882.

Hecker's sixth start of the season was at Pittsburgh's Exposition Park on September 19, 1882. Neither team was more than a middle-of-the-pack squad at this point of the season. The Alleghenys entered the game in fourth place with a 37-36 record. Louisville was slightly better at 37-32 in second place. But it was mostly academic as Cincinnati had clinched the pennant the day before. The Allegheny team was a solid hitting team with Ed Swartwood being the most productive batter. Swartwood led the American Association that season in total bases (161); runs scored (87), and doubles (18). He was third in batting average (.331), second in slugging average (.498), tied for second in hits (109), and third in home runs (4). The Association's premier batter that season was on the other side. Pete Browning won the batting (.378) and slugging (.510) titles and finished second in home runs (5) while tieing Swartwood for second in hits (109). Hecker's mound opponent was Denny Driscoll. Driscoll was signed by the Alleghenys in June and developed into the second starter behind Harry Salisbury. Driscoll posted a 13-9 record with a league-leading 1.21 ERA.

Both pitchers were effective and the game was scoreless through the fifth. Driscoll retired Leech Maskrey to open the sixth inning and then walked John Reccius. At this point in the reporting on the game one runs into a chronic problem with recording events in 19th-century baseball. Each reporter of a game kept his own scorecard. The assignment of hits, errors, and other scoring decisions can and does vary from one paper to another. With Reccius on second and one out, Browning came to the plate and either singled home Reccius after Reccius stole second with Browning advancing to second on an error by Mike Mansell, or Reccius scored on Browning's double. The consensus of the Pittsburgh writers (the Louisville paper's stories were dispatches by Pittsburgh writers) was that Browning doubled Reccius home with the first run of the game. Hecker followed Browning with an RBI single and Louisville was up 2-0 entering the bottom of the sixth.

The scoring confusion continued in the bottom of the sixth. With two outs Swartwood lifted a fly ball to left-center. Reccius misplayed the fly and then threw wildly to second, with the ball skipping past all the fielders and allowing Swartwood to score. Or after Reccius muffed the fly, center fielder Maskrey threw wildly to the infield or Maskrey's throw was misplayed by second baseman Denny Mack, allowing Swartwood to score. The reporting consensus was that Reccius committed a pair of errors on the play.

The scoring differences of opinion popped up again in the top of the seventh. Mack singled to open the inning and was forced at second by Mullane. Then either Mullane stole second and scored from second on a routine groundout to shortstop or … when Mack was forced at second, George Strief tried to complete the double play and threw wildly to first, putting Mullane on third, from where he scored on Schenck's groundout to short. As it seems improbable that Mullane scored from second on a routine groundball, it is more likely that Strief's error put him on third. From this point, each team was retired in order through the end of the game.

The final scoring discrepancy questions the number of hits Hecker surrendered. According to the *Pittsburgh Telegraph*, *Pittsburgh Commercial-Gazette*, *Pittsburgh Times* and the *Louisville Commercial*, it was a no-hitter. But Louisville's *Courier-Journal* records one hit for Pittsburgh. As with all the other variances, only the *Courier-Journal* deviates from the consensus of all the other papers. The *Courier-Journal* credits Pittsburgh shortstop John Peters with a single. There are two possibilities where this might have happened. In the fifth and seventh innings, Peters reached base on what were reported as Browning errors at shortstop. But the *Courier-Journal* box score records a pair of errors charged to Browning and the *Commercial-Gazette* and *Pittsburgh Times* game stories give no other situation where Browning might have picked up an error. Since the *Courier-Journal* is the sole source for all the scoring questions, it is likely that the correspondent who sent the paper the Pittsburgh game story was either unfamiliar with scoring a game or had a different set of standards to judge scoring decisions. In any case, treating the *Courier-Journal* as an outlier among the five papers consulted, Hecker gets his no-hitter.

Although Hecker's feat was acknowledged as worthy of note in the game stories, it was still just a single game with no future reference to it later in the week or later in the season. The Reach and Spalding Guides that cover the 1882 season make no reference to any no-hitter recorded in 1882. The *Pittsburgh Times* noted that no hits were made off Hecker in a sub-headline, but no other papers made any reference to it until late in their game story. In the last sentence of the story, the Times wrote, "The home nine failed to get a base hit off Hecker during the entire game. …"

The *Louisville Commercial* said, "Not one base hit was scored by them [Pittsburgh]. …"

The term no-hitter appears in no story about the game.

Skip McAfee, editor of the *Dickson Baseball Dictionary*, notes that the earliest reference he knows for the use of the term "no-hitter" is in a story appearing in the *Lincoln* (Nebraska) *Evening News* on August 31, 1911. No-hitters in the 19th century were viewed neither by fans nor sportswriters as the sort of significant events they became in later years. By and large, they were just another ballgame.

The various difficulties in dealing with the reporting and scoring of this game underscore the challenges faced by 19th-century researchers to assemble accurate statistics for the period. Even with multiple contemporary newspaper sources, we cannot determine with much confidence the details of many games played. We only have the comfort that scoring decisions do not change the outcome of the games.

Four years later, Hecker also achieved note when he homered three times in one game, and set single-game records for runs scored (7), total bases (15), and home runs (3), in the August 15, 1886, game for Louisville.[1]

SOURCES

Courier-Journal (Louisville), *Louisville Commercial*, *New York Clipper*, *Pittsburgh Commercial-Gazette*, *Pittsburgh Times*, and *Pittsburgh Telegraph*, all dated September 20, 1882.

Bevis, Charlie. "Denny Driscoll," SABR Baseball Biography Project, sabr.org/bioproj/person/c7e1352a.

Bailey, Bob. "Guy Hecker," SABR Baseball Biography Project, sabr.org/bioproj/person/4b471b76

Thanks to Bruce Allardice, Craig Britcher, Gary Collard, Bob LeMoine, Tom Mueller, Ron Selter, Andrew Terrick, and Bob Tholkes for their assistance to gather Pittsburgh newspaper stories on the game. Thanks to Skip McAfee for his help on the use of the term "no-hitter."

NOTES

1. Bob Bailey, "August 15, 1886: Guy Hecker: hitting pitcher," at sabr.org/gamesproj/game/august-15-1886-guy-hecker-hitting-pitcher.

SAM KIMBER

By David Nemec

SAMUEL JACKSON KIMBER'S childhood might have been the stuff of a Dickens novel and his short but distinctive major-league pitching career the scaffolding for a film script. He was born in Philadelphia to Richard R. and Sarah (Jaret) Kimber on October 29, 1852.[1] His father worked as a paper stainer but died suddenly the day before Sam's first birthday, on October 28, 1853, of a hemorrhage. Left to struggle as a single parent, Sarah Kimber appears to have died in 1859 of unknown causes, orphaning young Sam. He was soon thereafter placed in Girard College in Philadelphia, "a school for poor, orphaned or fatherless white boys who would live on campus."[2] Kimber is registered as an "inmate" at the school in the 1860 US Census.[3]

Girard in the 1860s was a dreary station for a young boy, but it had one saving grace. Baseball was a popular sport among the inmates. Led by Lon Knight, an outfielder and pitcher who first began making a living at the diamond sport in the mid-1870s, Girard had produced an abundance of professional ballplayers by the end of the 19th century, and Kimber proved to be one of them although none might have predicted his success at the game during his years at the orphanage school. The circumstances that enabled him to leave Girard are unknown, as are his movements in the 1870s after he can be presumed to have struck out on his own at age 18 or so. But by the time he was 28, when the 1880 census was taken, he was working purportedly as a blacksmith and living with his wife, Sarah (Kelley) Kimber, like him a native of Philadelphia. They had a young son, William, born in June 1879. Kimber seems to have abandoned blacksmithing soon after the 1880 census and begun working as a laborer in Philadelphia. He nonetheless still found time to play baseball, albeit only at the sandlot or amateur level. Samuel Jr., the couple's second child, was born in 1881 and a daughter, Sadie, joined the family in 1888.

Kimber continued to hurl on his days off for a string of local amateur and semipro clubs in Philadelphia until he was past 30. If he had ever entertained professional aspirations, his time to explore them seemingly had come and gone. Moreover, thus far nothing has emerged to suggest that he cut much of a swath in Philadelphia amateur or semipro circles. He may in fact have been a virtual nonentity. Yet he suddenly appears to have tried to shave two years off his birth date —some sources have listed his birth year as 1854—in an effort to appeal to one of the burgeoning number of professional teams in the Philadelphia area. The ruse succeeded in gaining him a pitching post with the powerful Merritt club of Camden, New Jersey, at age 28 (really 30) in 1883. What's more, he swiftly made the most of his chance, displaying talents in the box that heretofore had never received public mention. He went to the Brooklyn Greys of the Interstate Association in July when the Merritts disbanded while leading the IA by a comfortable margin. Kimber had been 14-3 with Camden and was subsequently 14-7 with Brooklyn, enabling him to finish the season a composite 28-10 with the two clubs, with a combined (retrospective) 1.27 earned-run average.

The 5-foot-10½, 165-pound right-hander accompanied Brooklyn when it joined the major-league American Association in 1884. The Brooklyns, known at the time as the Greys, are the distant predecessors of the present-day Los Angeles Dodgers franchise. Kimber started the franchise's first game as a major-league entity on May 1, 1884, working under manager George Taylor at Brooklyn's Washington Park. He lost egregiously to Washington rookie John Hamill in a 12-0 blowout. For Hamill, it was his best day; he finished his one and only big-league season with a 2-17 record. Kimber quickly turned himself around

second-division club when he lost his final start of the season to Cincinnati, 5-2, on October 13.

On October 4, 1884, Kimber achieved a famous first that has never been equaled. It was on his home ground in Brooklyn when he was caught by fellow rookie Jack Corcoran and held eighth-place Toledo hitless for 10 innings before the game was called by darkness with the score still 0-0 as his teammates managed just four hits off Toledo's kingpin, Tony Mullane.[4] Kimber's achievement was not only the first extra-inning no-hitter in professional baseball history but through 2015 he remained the only hurler to fashion a major-league complete-game no-hitter of nine or more innings without being credited with a decision.

Brooklyn reserved Kimber for 1885 but then cast him adrift along with most of its regular 1884 cast when it bought out the disbanding Cleveland National League team in order to acquire the majority of its players deemed more desirable. In most times, his 18 wins and the monumental no-hitter as a rookie would almost certainly have earned him a shot with another major-league team, but the aftermath of the 1884 season was one of a kind. With the major leagues reduced from 28 franchises to just 16 after the rebel Union Association threw in the towel after just one season and the American Association cut its ranks from 12 teams to eight for 1885, major-league pitching jobs were reduced by 40 percent. Kimber thus began 1885 with the Virginia club of the Eastern League but was dropped in August with a 28-8 ledger. It was scarcely a month after he fashioned an 8-0 no-hit win against Alexandria, Virginia, on July 22 in which he was caught by his old Brooklyn batterymate Corcoran and registered just one strikeout. Kimber added icing to the cake by hammering a gigantic three-run homer over the distant center-field fence in Alexandria, the first man ever to accomplish that feat.[5]

After leaving the Virginias, Kimber joined the Newark club in the same loop and was 3-3 with the New Jersey entry when the 1885 Eastern League season ended. His final major-league game, in answer to an emergency summons from the pitching-deplet-

and emerged as the Brooklyn staff ace, winning 18 games for a team that finished ninth in a 12-franchise league with a 40-64 record. He missed his 19th win and a chance to finish with a .500 record for a poor ed Providence Grays (who were already on the brink of folding even though the 1885 National League season had not yet closed), is best forgotten, as he lost 13-1 at Detroit to Wolverines lefty Lady Baldwin on September 29.

In light of what transpired over the remainder of Kimber's professional baseball career, one can reasonably surmise that his precipitous decline late in the 1885 campaign was the result of an injury, quite possibility to his arm, as he was never again a commanding pitcher. He began the 1886 season with Atlanta of the Southern League but was ineffective and finished the year with Williamsport of the Pennsylvania State Association. Kimber then pitched two more seasons in the lower minors before turning his offseason job driving a streetcar in Philadelphia into a full-time profession for a time. In his first season, spent mostly with Wheeling, West Virginia, of the Ohio State League, he experienced a climate of discontent in midsummer when members of the Nail Cities were publicly accused by local fans of playing to lose. The controversy was highlighted for several days in the *Wheeling Register* and quickly put to rest when Parson Nicholson, who had replaced the unpopular John Crogan as player-manager, published a letter in the July 29, 1887, edition of the *Register* avowing his club's honesty. The letter drew ardent support from his entire team, including Kimber.[6]

Kimber returned to Wheeling for the 1888 season. The Nail Cities were now in the Tri-State League under player-manager Al Buckenberger and had pennant aspirations (they ultimately finished second). After winning six of his first 10 starts Kimber was summarily released when Buckenberger suspected him of coveting the club's managerial post. Owing to a bizarre rule the Tri-State League legislated in the spring of 1888 (to the dismay of other minor-league circuits) that prohibited any other league from signing a player released by a Tri-State entry until the 1888 season closed, Kimber sat idle for several weeks at his home in Philadelphia.[7] He hooked on later in the summer with Portland, Maine, of the New England League but dropped his professional aspirations entirely after losing four straight starts. Earlier, while still active in the game, Kimber had spent his winters working as a watchman (what we might now call a security guard) in various Philadelphia mills. He seems to have found steady work as a watchman with the railroad sometime in the first decade of the new century and worked as such for the remainder of his life.

Kimber died of bronchial pneumonia brought on by influenza, in Philadelphia on November 6, 1925, at age 73.

NOTES

1 Her surname is also found rendered as Jarett, and might today more typically be spelled Jarrett.

2 girardcollege.com/page.cfm?p=359.

3 He is listed as a laborer in the Philadelphia City Directory in 1882 and as late as 1890.

4 *Sporting Life,* October 11, 1884: 4.

5 *Sporting Life,* July 29, 1885: 2.

6 "The Bobbies Win," *Wheeling Register,* July 29, 1887: 4.

7 *Sporting Life,* August 29, 1888: 1; under pressure the Tri-State League lifted the ban on signing any of its released players before the 1888 season ended.

SAM KIMBER'S ONE-OF-A-KIND NO-HITTER

OCTOBER 4, 1884: BROOKLYN GREYS 0, TOLEDO BLUE STOCKINGS 0, AT ECLIPSE PARK

By David Nemec

THERE ONCE WAS A MAJOR-league game that served up all of these delectable ingredients:

- The first no-hitter by a pitcher representing one of major-league baseball's longest standing and most storied franchises.
- The first major-league no-hitter that went extra innings.
- The first major-league no-hitter in which the pitcher who was the victim of it had previously thrown a no-hitter himself.
- The only major-league no-hitter to date in which the pitcher who was the victim of it did not suffer a loss even though his team was shut out.
- The only pitcher to date to hurl a complete-game major-league no-hitter of nine or more innings and not be credited with a decision.
- The only scoreless no-hit major-league game to date that lasted nine or more innings.
- The first major-league no-hitter that occurred in the month of October.
- The first no-hitter in major-league history by a rookie pitcher who had passed his 30th birthday.
- The only major-league no-hitter to date that highlighted a pitcher and an umpire who were once major-league teammates and later were business partners.

Any one of these distinctions would have been sufficient in the present day to draw momentous attention, some of course substantially more than others. That there are no less than *nine* on the list of unique and meritorious feats in this superlative game is in itself perhaps the most remarkable distinction of all.

Yet, with all that, there is another first that may prove a shock to most readers. To our knowledge this is both the first account of that game in the 131 years since its occurrence and the first ever to tabulate its many extraordinary features.

The 31-year-old rookie author of this one-of-a-kind game was a 5-foot-10½, 165-pound right-hander named Samuel Jackson Kimber, who had joined the minor-league Brooklyn Greys of the International Association midway through the 1883 season and accompanied the City of Churches club when it boldly cast its lot with the major-league American Association the following year. By the conclusion of spring practice sessions in 1884, Kimber in manager George Taylor's estimation was the Greys' best pitcher, thereupon earning the honor of starting the present Los Angeles Dodgers franchise's first official game as a major-league entity, on May 1, 1884, at Brooklyn and losing in a most embarrassing manner to Washington rookie John Hamill in a 12-0 blowout. Hamill would win only one more game in the process of sculpting a horrendous 2-17 ledger in his lone big-league season, but Kimber quickly put the egregious Opening Day pasting behind him and logged a team-best 18 wins for an otherwise lackluster second-division team.

Far and away Kimber's most significant pitching performance in 1884 was not a win, however, but a tie. It came on October 4, 1884, at Brooklyn, when he was caught by fellow rookie Jack Corcoran and held the Toledo Blue Stockings hitless for 10 innings before the game was called by darkness with the score still

0-0 as his Brooklyn mates managed just four hits off Toledo's kingpin, Tony Mullane. Two of the hits came off the bat of the offensive star of the game, Greys first baseman Charlie Householder, including the contest's lone extra-base hit, a double. Kimber fanned six and gave up three walks, one of which was issued to his box opponent, Mullane, who was the only Toledo baserunner to reach second base, after a Kimber wild pitch. In its account of the game in its October 15, 1884, issue, *Sporting Life* marveled that in a battle between two second-division teams not only had the pitching been exceptional but "not a single fielding error was charged to either nine, all the errors committed—and they were few—being batting errors, bases on called balls and wild pitches."[1] The paper added: "Darkness stopped play just as the eleventh inning was about to be commenced. The contest abounded in good plays. There were good catches, clever stops and beautiful throws to the bases, all of which tended to make the game a most interesting one."

According to the *New York Times* of October 5, 1884, a crowd of 1,200 attended the Saturday-afternoon game. The *Times* recounted: "During the past nine years the feat of retiring a club for nine innings without a safe hit has been accomplished 35 times, but there is no record of a man's pitching 10 innings in one game without having a safe hit charged against him."[2] Among the 35 previously recorded no-hitters[3] was one by Mullane on September 11, 1882, that was a famous first in its own right. Mullane, with Louisville at the time, registered the first no-hitter in American Association history when he blanked the eventual inaugural AA pennant winner, the Cincinnati Reds, 2-0 at Cincinnati.

The October 5 issue of the *Brooklyn Daily Eagle* echoed in its headline: "An Unprecedented Base Ball Contest at Washington Park."[4]

The umpire in the Kimber no-hitter was Louisville native John Dyler, a one-game outfielder with the fledgling Louisville American Association entry in 1882.[5] The Louisville team also numbered Mullane, then in the first full season of a checkered career that nonetheless would almost certainly have brought him a plaque in the Baseball Hall of Fame long before now had he not been suspended for one full season and lost half of another when he jumped his team in a contract dispute, thereby sacrificing a probable 30 to 40 victories that would have put him well over the magic figure of 300, a number that has assured Hall of Fame entry thus far for every pitcher who has reached it. Dyler would join with Mullane in 1886 to open a combination saloon and poolroom on Vine Street in Cincinnati that was dubbed The Base-Ball Headquarters. The "bar fixtures" were "of cherry wood and the beveled-edged, plate-glass mirror behind the bar" was "cut in the shape of a baseball diamond."[6]

- Historians will quickly observe after examining the box score of the Kimber game that missing from the Toledo lineup that day was the Blue Stockings' largest contribution to baseball lore, their African-American catcher Moses Walker. Walker's last appearance with Toledo (and final major-league appearance) had come exactly a month earlier in a home game against Pittsburgh when he caught Mullane in a 4-2 win over Jack Neagle of the Allegheny club.

Through 2015, Kimber remained the only hurler to fashion a major-league complete-game no-hitter of nine or more innings without being credited with a decision, a distinction one could say with almost utter assurance will be his forever.

NOTES

1 *Sporting Life*, October 15, 1884: 6.

2 *New York Times*, October 5, 1884: 2.

3 The *Times's* proclamation that Kimber had hurled the 35th no-hitter to that point is provided without any substantiation. Nor did the *Times* offer its criteria for what constituted a no-hitter in its estimation—i.e., nothing about the level of competition, the number of innings pitched, etc. Starting with Joe Borden's no-hitter in 1875, the first recorded at any level of competition, Kimber's no-hitter was the 19th full-length no-hitter in major-league history, including two perfect games. There were also three no-hitters previous to Kimber's in 1884 that were curtailed to less than nine innings either by rain or darkness; these were the first abbreviated no-hitters in the major leagues. The *Encyclopedia of Minor League Baseball*, 3rd Edition, lists only two no-hitters in the minors prior to October 4, 1884, bringing the number of full-length professional no-hit games to 21 at the time of Kimber's achievement.

4 *Brooklyn Daily Eagle*, October 5, 1884: 1.

5 *Sporting Life*, the *Brooklyn Eagle*, and the *New York Times*, the author's three primary research sources, all credit Dyler with umpiring the Kimber no-hit game in Brooklyn on October 4, 1884, along with Brooklyn's last previous game, on October 1 versus Louisville. However, *Sporting Life* also credits Dyler with a physical impossibility: umpiring an American Association game in Richmond that day, as does Retrosheet.org, which credits the Kimber game to John Valentine even though Valentine umpired no other Brooklyn home games in September or October 1884. For the moment we trust most the *Brooklyn Eagle* and the *New York Times* since both papers provided daily coverage of the Brooklyn team throughout the 1884 season.

6 *Sporting Life*, February 24, 1886: 4.

AL ATKINSON (AKA ATKISSON)

By Chris Rainey

THE PHILADELPHIA Athletics of the American Association assembled in Philadelphia in early April of 1884. They welcomed four rookies, including pitcher Al Atkinson. The *Philadelphia Inquirer* wrote that the right-hander was "from an Illinois village and has his reputation to make as little is known of him."[1] He was quick to make an impression two days later by beating Yale 10-5 with 10 strikeouts. Exhibition games were played over the next three weeks and Atkinson showed enough talent to join the pitching rotation with Bobby Mathews and Billy Taylor. He got his first start on May 1 against the Pittsburgh Alleghenys. In front of 7,000 fans at the Jefferson Street Grounds, he limited the Alleghenys to seven hits and won, 9-2. A fair hitter, he added a single and scored a run.

Pittsburgh got revenge two days later, besting Atkinson 9-8. He split a pair of decisions with Baltimore before beating Washington despite his own three errors. That started a four-game win streak highlighted by a no-hitter on May 24 against the Alleghenys. Pittsburgh did manufacture an unearned run in the first inning, but that was the extent of the damage in the 10-1 defeat. Atkinson issued only one walk, struck out two, and had two hits. It should be noted that pitchers in 1884 were not allowed to have their hand above their shoulder. Atkinson had a curve and a fastball in his repertoire. At the end of May, he had a 6-2 won-lost mark. Atkinson probably went from a one-day-a-week amateur pitcher to part of a rotation in the majors, taking the box every third game. Fatigue soon set in and in July he went home to rest from an illness.

Atkinson returned to the Athletics, but on July 24 he jumped to the Union Association. The Chicago Unions had been overworking One-Arm Daily and turned to Atkinson for help. Atkinson shut out Kansas City, 4-0, in his first outing, putting up a 4-4 record before the franchise was moved to Pittsburgh. There he went 2-6 before that team went belly-up and he was added to the Baltimore roster. With Baltimore, he added three more wins. He tossed 393⅔ innings in the two leagues. In the American Association, he was 11-11 and in the Union he went 9-15. He did finish in the top 10 in WHIP (walks and hits per inning pitched) in the Union at 1.051. His biggest deficiency was fielding; he made 31 errors for a .785 fielding percentage.

Atkinson was born in Clinton, Illinois, on March 9, 1861. His mother was the former Mary E. Wright; the identity of his father is unknown. The Wrights had moved west from New York, through Pennsylvania, where Mary was born, before settling in Illinois. In 1870 Mary and Al lived with her mother and brothers in Mount Pulaski, in central Illinois. She worked as a milliner. Atkinson got four years of elementary-school education before going to work as a farm laborer.

Central Illinois was a hotbed for baseball. Peoria and Springfield fielded minor-league teams in the 1880s when few leagues existed. Newspaper coverage of baseball was also in its infancy, so when and how Atkinson was discovered is a mystery. He is listed as 5-feet-11 and 165 pounds.

Atkinson was blacklisted for his jump to the Union Association. He was eligible to return contingent upon re-signing with the Athletics. He seemed content to return to Illinois instead and play semipro ball. There was one report that Milwaukee of the Western League might try to get him reinstated.[2] No deal ever materialized and Atkinson joined the Gem City club in Quincy, Illinois, before moving to St. Joseph, Missouri.[3] He may also have played for a team called the Chicago Blues. In October, he agreed to terms with Philadelphia and was reinstated for the 1886 season.

After tending bar all winter, Atkinson joined the Athletics in late March of 1886. The highlight of their training season was a seven-game series against the Phillies of the National League. Early in the regular season the Athletics used four pitchers: Bobby Mathews, Ted Kennedy, Sam Weaver, and "Atkisson." Weaver was jettisoned quickly after allowing 30 hits in 11 innings. Kennedy posted a 5-15 mark before his release. Atkinson, who appeared in print as Atkisson for most of the season, won his first two starts and took the box on May 1 against the New York Metropolitans. A first-inning error led to a run for the Mets, but Atkinson walked and scored in the third to knot the score. He took a 3-1 lead into the ninth when a two-base error, a grounder, and a fly scored a second run for the Mets. Atkinson slammed the door and recorded his second no-hitter in the process. The next day Mathews allowed 22 hits and 19 runs against Brooklyn. Atkinson took over as the ace of the staff.

Atkinson was the first American Association pitcher to toss two no-hitters. Adonis Terry of Brooklyn duplicated the feat in 1888. Larry Corcoran of the Chicago White Stockings in the National League had three no-hitters from 1880-84 which might explain the lack of excitement about Atkinson's feat. He went on to compile a 25-17 record in 396⅔ innings, nearly 200 fewer than league leader Toad Ramsey of Louisville. He led the league in hit batters (22) and home runs surrendered (11). Once again overwork wore Atkinson down and he ended the season when "the Cincinnatians pounded the life out of Atkisson today."[4] He returned to St. Joseph and the saloon business uncertain about his future. In late November, the Athletics finally decided to reserve him for 1887.

The Athletics and Phillies opened the exhibition season in April. The Athletics tested Atkinson and were pleased with the results, especially a four-hit shutout on April 12. They opened the season with a two-man rotation of Ed Seward and Atkinson.

Atkinson lost to Baltimore, but then beat the Mets and Ed Cushman twice. Curiously, he saw no action for the next 18 days as Cannonball Titcomb and rookie Gus Weyhing joined Seward in the rotation. When he took the box on May 14 the *Inquirer* called him Atkinson, but soon reverted to calling him Atkisson for the remainder of the season. He won on the 14th, besting Louisville in 10 innings. Seward and Weyhing were given the bulk of the work. Atkinson was used on doubleheader days and when there were three games in three days. This meant that he would often sit a week or more between starts. On August 10 and 13 he lost consecutive games, surrendering 13 runs in each. The Athletics released him. Weyhing and Seward pitched over 900 innings; Atkinson made 15 starts and tossed 124⅔ innings with a 6-8 record.

Atkinson's major-league career was over. He had a 51-51 record and a 3.96 earned-run average.

Atkinson returned to Missouri, but soon joined the Lincoln (Nebraska) Tree Planters in the Western League. Former Athletics Orator Shaffer (his box-score name, Baseball-reference uses only one "f") and Bill Hart were members of the team. Atkinson had a 2-2 mark with Lincoln. In 1888, he went north to join the Toronto Canucks in the International Association. For the first time in his career, he was in a league that was not dominated by powerful hitting. The Canucks and Syracuse staged a great pennant race until Atkinson fell ill in September and Syracuse pulled away to win by 3½ games. Atkinson compiled eye-popping statistics. He hurled 444 innings, second in the league, and his 34-13 record was the fourth highest wins' total. He finished second in ERA and WHIP and led the league with 307 strikeouts, nearly double his competition. He also hit .219, a career high for him in a full season. Atkinson was well compensated for his work. He was signed for the maximum salary allowed but manager Charlie Cushman "engaged his wife and other relatives as clerks, stenographers, etc. so as to make up the salary he wanted."[5] None of the relatives was ever put to work. There is one other reference to Atkinson being married during the 1880s. Because the 1890 census was destroyed by a fire, the name of his spouse is uncertain.

As in past seasons, the 1889 Canucks went to Cincinnati in April for exhibition games with the Reds. Atkinson was so wild in his first outing that he was yanked early. The poor pitching haunted him into the regular season. In 30 innings he issued 20 walks, hit four batters, and unleashed eight wild pitches. It is uncertain whether this is related to his illness or was a case of "Steve Blass disease," but his career was essentially over. He played a game with Toronto in 1890 and then five games with Rochester in the Eastern league in 1892. There were rumors that Atkinson might have been considered as manager for the Canucks in 1890, but nothing materialized.

Leaving his baseball career behind, Atkinson moved to McDonald County, Missouri. He worked in the lead and zinc mines. He also did carpentry work on the side. Eventually he purchased farmland near McNatt and raised grain. In 1903, he wed Nancy Jane (Wasson) Paschall, a divorcee with two children, Forest and Agnes. The marriage lasted until Nancy's death in 1951. They helped to raise both of Agnes's children, Wincel and Glenn Pogue, and Al kept farming into his 80s.

Atkinson gained local notoriety in the late 1920's and 1930's with his artwork. Most notably was a piece he called "Star of America." He had heard on the radio that there was a contest with a $500 prize for the best radio console. He created a magnificent piece made from over 15,000 pieces of wood from 72 different, native Ozark woods. The effort took nearly two years to complete. As fate would have it, he did not enter the contest because of the entry fee. The console was displayed locally and gained attention. It went on display at the Missouri Museum in Jefferson City for about a dozen years.[6]

In addition to his carpentry, Atkinson became a self-taught painter and created landscapes and portraits. His reputation grew and he was even interviewed by *The Sporting News* in 1951. He died in his McNatt, Missouri, home on June 17, 1952. He and Nancy are buried in Macedonia Cemetery near Stella, Missouri.[7]

SOURCES

In addition to the sources cited in the notes, the author also consulted *The Baseball Encyclopedia*, Atkinson's player questionnaire at the National Baseball Hall of Fame, and the *Baltimore Sun*, *Daily Illinois State Journal* (Springfield, Illinois), *New York Herald*, *Pittsburgh Post-Gazette*, *Philadelphia Times*, and *The Sporting News*.

NOTES

1. *Philadelphia Inquirer*, April 5, 1884: 2.
2. *Kansas City Times*, May 5, 1885: 2.
3. *Sporting Life*, June 3, 1885: 7.
4. *Sporting Life*, October 11, 1886: 2
5. *Omaha World-Herald*, May 15, 1892: 13.
6. "True History of an Ozark Radio Console," *Neosho Daily News* (Neosho, Missouri), December 28, 1929: 4.
7. *Joplin* (Missouri) *Globe*, June 18, 1952: 6.

MAY 1, 1886
PHILADELPHIA ATHLETICS 3, NEW YORK METROPOLITANS 2, AT THE JEFFERSON STREET GROUNDS

By Chris Rainey

FROM 1875 TO 1899 THERE were 50 complete-game no-hitters thrown in the "major" leagues.[1] The hitless team scored in seven of those games. The first of these was in 1882 when Guy Hecker of Louisville beat Pittsburgh 3-1 in American Association action. The next two cases, also in the American Association, saw the hitless team actually score first and both times against the same pitcher, Al Atkinson (aka Atkisson). On May 24, 1884, he beat Pittsburgh 10-1, allowing an unearned run in the first. On May 1, 1886, Atkinson (who appeared in box scores of the game as Atkisson) tossed his second career no-hitter.[2]

When Al Atkinson toiled, the rules of the game were very different than in the game we know today. The 1886 season was the last in which a batter could ask for a high or low pitch. A low pitch was between the knees and belt, high was from the belt to the shoulders. In Atkinson's first no-hitter, in 1884, he was restricted to having his pitching hand below his shoulder. That restriction was lifted by 1886. "By 1886 finger gloves were in fairly widespread use" and the chest protector was two years old.[3] Pitchers were helped by a six-ball/three-strike rule for walks and strikeouts, but even so Atkinson issued 101 walks for the season.

The New York Metropolitans took the field on May 1 at Philadelphia's Jefferson Street Grounds, in last place with a 2-8 record. Powerful Dave Orr was their star; he would hit 31 triples, bat .338 and finish second in the league in OPS. The Mets sent Ed Cushman to the box. In 1884 while pitching in the Union Association, Cushman had tossed a no-hitter. He started 1885 with Philadelphia but was released after 10 games and joined the Mets. Cushman would record a 17-21 mark with a team-leading 3.12 ERA in 1886. The Athletics entered the game in second place with a 7-4 record. Bobby Mathews was coming off three consecutive 30-win seasons and was the featured pitcher early in the season. Atkinson came into the game with a 2-0 mark after wins over Brooklyn and Baltimore. The Athletics boasted the veteran slugging duo of Harry Stovey and Henry Larkin, both of whom would be in the top 10 in OPS. The rest of the lineup on May 1 was far from the norm. Utilityman Jack O'Brien caught and catcher Jocko Milligan made a rare start at third. Two veterans, Orator Shafer and George Bradley, played center field and shortstop respectively. Both were dropped soon after. Bradley had been a star pitcher in 1876 at the birth of the National League and is credited with pitching the first no-hitter in the league. Umpiring the game was Billy Carlin, a Philadelphia native working one of his 35 games in 1886.

The Mets scored in the first inning; with one out, outfielder Chief Roseman walked, went to second on a passed ball, and scored when Athletics right fielder John Coleman muffed a fly ball hit by Orr. Atkinson tied the game in the third inning when he drew a walk, went to third on a hit by Stovey, and scored on a wild throw by second baseman Elmer Foster. Foster's throw was so wild that the speedy Stovey also came around to score. In the sixth Stovey and Coleman ripped doubles to account for the Athletics' third run. Meanwhile Atkinson had calmed down and allowed two more walks. He struck out seven (well above his 3.5 per-game average). In the ninth the Mets staged a rally of sorts when Orr reached on a two-base error by Bradley, advanced on a grounder and scored on a long fly. Atkinson disposed of the last batter to win the game, 3-2, and chalk up his second no-hitter in front of 2,700 fans. The *Philadelphia Inquirer* said "a contest of this kind is always dull for the onlookers" but that two "phenomenal plays" by Bradley caused great excitement.[4]

The *Cleveland Plain Dealer* wrote, "The game was a most interesting one, and while there were no particularly brilliant plays the clean and sharp work of both teams in the field drew forth frequent bursts of applause."[5]

By season's end the Athletics had slipped to sixth place. They finished 10 games ahead of the seventh-place Mets. Atkinson lost 3-1 to Brooklyn in his next outing. He became the staff ace and posted a 25-17 record. He pitched sparingly in 1887 and then disappeared from the major-league scene.

SOURCES

In addition to the sources cited in the notes, the author also consulted the *Louisville*

Courier-Journal, Pittsburg Post-Gazette, The Times (Philadelphia), and *Sporting Life*.

NOTES

1 The first no-hitter is credited to Joe Borden in the National Association in 1875. There were also six no-hitters prior to 1900 that did not go nine innings.

2 *New York Times,* May 2, 1886: 2.

3 travel-watch.com/oldtimebaseballequipment.

4 *Philadelphia Inquirer,* May 3, 1886: 2.

5 *Cleveland Plain Dealer,* May 2, 1886: 3.

AMOS RUSIE

By Charles F. Faber

THE VELOCITY OF HIS FAST-balls earned him the nickname "The Hoosier Thunderbolt." Amos Rusie played long before the invention of the radar gun, so we don't know how fast his pitches were. John McGraw said of Rusie's fastballs, "You can't hit 'em if you can't see 'em."[1] Sportswriters of the day claimed that batters were so terrified of being hit by Rusie's pitches that they insisted the distance from the pitcher's box to the plate be increased.[2] As a pitcher for the New York Giants he was the biggest star on the biggest stage and he enjoyed life to the hilt.

Amos Wilson Rusie was born on May 30, 1871, in Mooresville, Morgan County, Indiana, a village about 20 miles southwest of Indianapolis. He was the second of the four children of Mary Elizabeth "Lizzie" Donovan and William Asbury Rusie. Amos's father must have been quite a man. Born in Mooresville in 1847, he joined the 33rd Indiana Volunteer Infantry on December 18, 1863, at the age of 16. During the war he lost his left leg above the knee. Available military records do not identify the battle in which he was wounded, but it was probably in Georgia or the Carolinas.[3] After his discharge William Rusie returned to Indiana and, despite the loss of his leg, worked for many years as a brick mason in Mooresville and Indianapolis. He died in a home for disabled veterans in 1925.

The Rusie family moved from Mooresville to Indianapolis during Amos's childhood. At the age of 16 Amos dropped out of school to work in a variety of jobs, including one in a factory and one as a varnisher in an Indianapolis furniture store. After working hours and on Sundays the teenager played for a number of amateur or semipro teams in the Indianapolis area. At first he played only in the outfield. One day when he was with the Grand River club in the City League, the regular pitcher was knocked out of the box, and Rusie relieved him. He found the position where he belonged, and he never played in the outfield again.[4] While pitching for an outfit called the Sturm Avenue Never Sweats in 1888, he shut out two touring National League clubs, the Boston Beaneaters and the Washington Nationals. After these stellar performances, John T. Brush, owner of the National League's Indianapolis Hoosiers signed Rusie to a professional contract.[5] At the start of the 1889 season, Frank Bancroft, manager of the Hoosiers, sent Rusie to Burlington, Iowa, for seasoning. He pitched four games for the Burlington Babies in the Central Inter-State League before being called up to Indianapolis. That was the extent of his minor-league career.

Amos Rusie made his major-league debut for the Hoosiers on May 9, 1889, at the age of 17. The 6-foot-1, 200-pound right-hander entered the game in relief of Jim Whitney in a 13-2 loss at Cleveland. He made his first start on June 15 at home as Indianapolis defeated Pittsburgh, 16-11. In his rookie season, he had a 12-10 record for the seventh-place Hoosiers. The Indianapolis club folded after the 1889 season. The National League distributed the Hoosiers players among other clubs in the league. Rusie was fortunate to be assigned to the New York Giants.

During his first month with the Giants, Rusie hooked up with Boston's Kid Nichols at the Polo Grounds in one of the great pitching duels of all time. On May 12 the two young hurlers each held their opponents scoreless for 12 innings. Going into the 13th, each pitcher had allowed only three hits. The Giants had elected to bat first. With one out in the top of the 13th, Mike Tiernan hit a tremendous line drive that cleared the fence in the deepest part of the Polo Grounds. Rusie quickly set the Beaneaters down in the bottom of the frame to claim a 1-0 victory. The game has been honored as one of the 100 greatest games of the 19th century.[6] Rusie became an instant

celebrity in New York. Later he and Nichols were two of the three pitchers of the 1890s named to the National Baseball Hall of Fame. (Cy Young was the other.)

Rusie's star continued to shine brightly in New York. He won 29 games in 1890 and led the league in strikeouts. He started 62 games, pitched 56 complete games, and allowed the fewest hits per inning pitched of any hurler in the league. He also led the league in losses, walks, and wild pitches. He allowed 289 bases on balls, a major-league record that has never been broken and probably will never be approached. (The 208 walks given up by Bob Feller in 1938 is the closest to that number in the last 125 years.)

But it was Rusie's strikeouts that caught the fancy of the public. His 341 strikeouts in 1890 were the most in the decade of the 1890s. Only Bob Feller, Sandy Koufax, Randy Johnson, and Nolan Ryan have rung up more K's in a season since then. Rusie said it was not easy. "It took a lot of pitchin' to strike a man out in those days. The foul strike rule hadn't come in. A guy had to miss three of 'em clean before he was out."[7]

The Hoosier Thunderbolt became a sensation in the Big Apple. Restaurants named drinks after him, and vaudevilleans included skits about him in their acts. It was reported that Lillian Russell, the most famous Broadway star of the day, clamored to meet him. The young man lived it up. He enjoyed drinking and carousing in the big city, but the night life apparently did not interfere with his pitching. Sportswriter Sam Crane wrote, "Rusie went through his active pitching days as though on a continuous joy ride. He broke training whenever he felt like it and never looked upon life as a serious matter."[8]

Rusie's fastball was the stuff of legends. It was reputed to be the fastest pitch ever thrown up to that time. Outfielder Jimmy Ryan said, "Words fail to describe the speed with which Rusie sent the ball. … The giant simply drove the ball at you with the force of a cannon. It was like a white streak tearing past you."[9]

Connie Mack, whose major-league career spanned more than 60 years, saw all of the great fastball pitchers from Rusie to Feller. He batted against some and managed against the others. "Rusie was the fastest without a doubt," Mack said. "Maybe that is because I had to hit against him. And they looked like peas as they sailed by me. All I saw of them was what I heard when they went into the catcher's mitt."[10]

Dick Buckley, who had been Rusie's catcher in both Indianapolis and New York, tried inserting into his glove a sheet of lead, covered with a handkerchief and a sponge, to cushion the impact of the fastball.[11]

On November 8, 1890, Rusie married Susie May Smith in Muncie, Indiana. They had a daughter, Jeannette, born in 1897. At age 19 and enjoying the high life in New York City, Rusie at first was perhaps not an ideal husband. On January 9, 1899, May filed for divorce. The couple reconciled temporarily, but little more than a year later May filed for divorce again. On May 9, 1900, the court awarded May her divorce. Amos was devastated. He promised to stay sober and behave himself and agreed to leave the Giants and settle down in Indiana permanently. May had detested living in New York and hated what she perceived the city was doing to her husband's lifestyle.¹² Less than three months later the couple married for the second time. Amos kept his word. This union lasted until May's death on October 7, 1942.

In 1891 Rusie won 33 games, the first of four consecutive seasons in which the fireballer posted more than 30 victories. On July 31, 1891, Rusie pitched a no-hitter, shutting down Brooklyn, 6-0. It was the first no-hitter ever pitched by a New York hurler. Year after year he was atop the leader board.

The Hoosier Thunderbolt led the National League in strikeouts five times, in shutouts four times, and in bases on balls five times.

Rusie's blazing fastball combined with his wildness intimidated batters. Some were so terrified at the prospect of being hit in the head by one of his thunderbolts that the league agreed in 1893 to move the pitcher's box farther from the plate. The change from 55 feet to 60 feet 6 inches instituted in1893 was the last alteration in the configuration of the baseball diamond.

The change in the location of the pitcher's box did not diminish Rusie's effectiveness. Although his strikeout numbers decreased, he still led the league in that category in 1893 and each the next two seasons. In 1894 Rusie had a career-high 36 victories and won the pitcher's Triple Crown by leading the National League in wins, strikeouts, and earned-run average.

At the end of the 1894 season William Temple, president of the Pittsburgh Pirates, proposed that a postseason series be played between the top two finishers in the National League. He donated an $800 cup, the Temple Cup, to be awarded to the winner of the best-of seven-series. The Baltimore Orioles had won the pennant, with the Giants second. Sparked by the pitching of Rusie and Jouett Meekin, the Giants swept the Temple Cup series in four straight games. The Hoosier Thunderbolt won Games One and Three by identical scores of 4-1, giving up only two runs, one of which was unearned, for an ERA of 0.50. Meekin pitched a shutout in Game Two, winning 9-0, and wrapped up the series by winning Game Four, 16-3. Both pitchers threw complete games in their starts; no other Giants pitchers appeared in the series.¹³ A New York reporter wrote, "The alleged mighty hitters of the league's pennant winners are but putty in the hands of Rusie and Meekin."¹⁴

In the games of the Temple Cup series played at the Polo Grounds, which had no center-field fence, large crowds ringed the outfield. A rope was strung between posts to separate the fans from the playing field. Some patrons sat in carriages and viewed the game by looking over the heads of the standees.¹⁵ Other horse-drawn vehicles were left unattended on Eighth Avenue below the field. In the eighth inning of Game Three, one of the horses bolted, climbed up the embankment, smashed the buggy, and charged into people standing around the rope. The horse ran through the crowd, jumped over the ropes, and charged onto the playing field. It headed straight across the field toward Giants left fielder Eddie Burke. A reporter wrote, "Burke had shown the Polo Grounds patrons some pretty fast running in his time, but he never equaled the sprint he made to get under the left field bleachers."¹⁶ The runaway horse was caught; Rusie resumed pitching and finished his 4-1 victory.

In 1895 Giants owner Andrew Freedman deducted $200 from Rusie's pay. One hundred dollars was cut for allegedly being out after curfew one night and another hundred for "not trying hard enough" while pitching.¹⁷ An irate Rusie protested the fines. Two hundred dollars was a very large chunk out of his $3,000 salary. He told Freedman he would not sign a contract for 1896 unless the fines were restored. The owner refused. Rusie sat out the entire 1896 season. Represented by a famous baseball personality and attorney, John Montgomery Ward, Rusie sued Freedman for $5,000 and release from his Giants contract. Owners of other National League clubs, worried that the courts might invalidate the reserve clause, gave Rusie $5,000 to drop the suit. Rusie agreed. "That $5,000 I got for not playing was almost $2,000 more than I would have been paid for playing all season," he said.¹⁸ He remained a Giant, and Freedman paid him $3,000 for 1897.

Batters' fear of being hit by the Hoosier Thunderbolt's pitches was justified. Baltimore's

Hughie Jennings, one of baseball's top shortstops, was hit in the head by a Rusie fastball in 1897. He was unconscious for four days.[19] Although he survived, his baseball-playing days were in jeopardy.

In 1898 Rusie suffered an injury that ended his effectiveness as a pitcher. He was pitching against the Chicago Cubs one day in August. Chicago's speedy outfielder Bill Lange was on first base. Lange had led the National League in stolen bases the previous year. Although his productivity was down in 1898, due to physical and attitude problems, he was still a threat on the basepaths.[20] Rusie resolved to pick the speedster off base. Instead of taking the usual step when throwing to a base, Rusie made a quick throw to first base without moving his feet. Something snapped in his shoulder. He got his out, but never regained his fastball. "My arm felt dead," Rusie said. "I finished the game throwing floating curves. The following day saw the start of a parade of doctors. Each examined my arm. Each had a different diagnosis The x-ray was unknown then, so their job wasn't an easy one."[21]

Rusie took five weeks off. "When I returned to the firing line, my arm felt okay," he said. "The zip in my fast one was still there; my curve crackled and snapped. For the rest of the season, everything was fine. But the following spring, when I tried to pitch, my arm felt dead. I took my turn on the hill, but every effort was followed by nights of torture, during which I walked the floor. So I had to hang up my glove."[22]

More than 40 years after his injury, Rusie put his hand on his shoulder and told an interviewer, "Even today I'm often bothered by twinges of pain here."[23]

After 1898 Rusie never won another game in the major leagues. He blamed his snap pickoff move for his downfall. He was quoted as saying, "I coulda lasted as long as Cy Young what with my strength and all. That's what happens when you try to act smart."[24]

The Hoosier Thunderbolt pitched nary a game in Organized Baseball in 1899 or 1900. He rested his arm for two years and used the time trying to repair his relationship with his estranged wife. On December 15, 1900, the New York Giants traded Rusie to the Cincinnati Reds for Christy Mathewson, in perhaps the most lopsided transaction in the entire history of baseball. One future Hall of Fame pitcher for another may not sound out of line, but it certainly was. Matty was a youngster on his way up; Rusie was all but finished as a pitcher. Mathewson went on to win 372 games for the Giants, the most any pitcher has ever won for any National League club. Rusie won no games for Cincinnati or anybody else.

At the time of the census in June 1900, Rusie was living with his widowed father in Indianapolis. The census taker listed him as a ballplayer, although he was playing no baseball that summer. May was living near Muncie with her brother Edward Smith. In less than two months Amos and May would be together again, this time 'til death did them part.

In 1901 Rusie started two games for the Reds and relieved in one. His record was 0-1, with an ERA of 8.59. He made his final major-league appearance on June 9, 1901, at the age of 30. The game was played at Cincinnati's League Park against Rusie's former team, the New York Giants. An overflow crowd of 17,000 fans surrounded the field and pushed toward the diamond. Balls that outfielders normally could have caught fell among the onlookers and went for two-base hits. In the bottom of the ninth inning the crowd overran the field and caused so much confusion that umpire Bob Emslie forfeited the game to the Giants.[25] The Giants were leading 25-13 at the time, and that was recorded as the official score. (Forfeited games are usually scored 9-0, but if the home team is at fault and visiting team is leading the actual score is recorded.)

After he retired from baseball, Rusie returned to his native Indiana. He worked at a pulp and paper mill in Muncie until the mill closed. He then moved to Vincennes, Indiana, where he worked as a laborer. He also did some pearling, that is, hunting for pearls in mollusks retrieved from the Wabash River or other bodies of water in the area. According to his obituary in *The Sporting News*, Rusie worked as a ticket taker at a Seattle ballpark in 1907 and 1908, and as a bottle layer in a bottle factory in Olean, Illinois, in 1910, and umpired in the Northwestern League for two weeks in 1911. The obituary contains several inaccuracies. His actual whereabouts in 1910 cannot be ascertained. Neither he nor May can be located in 1910 census records released by Ancestry.com. Nor can he be found in available city directories for that year.

It is known that in 1911 Amos and May moved to Seattle, where he worked for 10 years as a gas fitter for a lighting company and as a steamfitter in a shipyard.

In 1921 John McGraw, now the manager of the New York Giants, brought Rusie back to New York, where he worked as a night watchman and later as superintendent of grounds at the Polo Grounds. Did he like the job? Accounts vary. In a SABR book published in 1996, Richard Puff wrote that he enjoyed the position.[26] Rusie's obituary in the *New York Times* stated that he didn't care much for the job.[27] Living in New York was difficult for May. She was partly paralyzed from an undisclosed cause and confined to a wheelchair. The couple moved back to Washington State in 1929.

Perhaps with help from McGraw, Rusie purchased a chicken ranch in Auburn, Washington, but it failed during the Great Depression. In July 1934 he was injured in an automobile accident that left him unconscious for four days. He suffered a brain concussion and several broken ribs. Unable to work, he fell behind on his house payments. In February 1935 a notice appeared in the Seattle newspapers announcing the mortgage foreclosure of the 5-acre farm of Amos Rusie and wife in Auburn by the Home Owners Loan Corporation.

A moratorium loan on the little farm for $1,932.32 had been closed on November 29, 1933, and provided for interest payments of $8.05 in June 1934, and $17.87 monthly thereafter. Rusie was unable to make payments on the principal, interest, or taxes. The Rusies' income consisted of a $35 pension paid monthly to Amos by the Association of Professional Ball Players of America and a $28-a-month old-age payment for May.[28] The *Seattle Post-Intelligencer* instituted a fundraising campaign. Although unable to prevent the foreclosure, the paper, assisted by *The Sporting News*, raised enough money to provide the Rusies with an income for the rest of their lives and a little house in which to live.[29]

Because of their declining health, the Rusies stayed in the house only a few years. Before 1940 they moved in with their daughter Jeannette and her husband, Clarence E. Spaulding, an upholsterer in a Seattle department store.

May died on October 7, 1942. Amos suffered from chronic myocarditis, and two months after May's death, he died at Ballard General Hospital on December 6, 1942, at the age of 71. May and Amos were buried side-by-side in Acacia Memorial Park in the city of Lake Forest Park, just north of the Seattle city limits on the shores of Lake Washington.

In 1977 Rusie was elected by the Veterans Committee to the National Baseball Hall of Fame. The inscription on his plaque at Cooperstown reads:

AMOS WILSON RUSIE
"THE HOOSIER THUNDERBOLT"
INDIANAPOLIS N.L, NEW YORK N.L.,
CINCINNATI N.L. 1889-1895
1897-1898 AND 1901
GENERALLY CONSIDERED FIREBALL KING OF NINETEENTH-CENTURY MOUNDSMEN. NOTCHED BETTER THAN 240 VICTORIES IN TEN-YEAR CAREER. ACHIEVED 30-VICTORY MARK FOUR YEARS IN A ROW AND WON 20 OR MORE GAMES EIGHT SUCCESSIVE YEARS. LED LEAGUE IN STRIKEOUTS FIVE YEARS AND LED OR TIED FOR MOST SHUTOUTS FIVE TIMES.

SOURCES

In addition to those cited in the Notes, the most useful sources included Ancestry.com and Baseball-reference.com.

NOTES

1 Richard Puff, "Amos Wilson Rusie," in Frederick Ivor-Campbell, Robert L. Tiemann, and Mark Rucker, eds., *Baseball's First Stars* (Cleveland: Society for American Baseball Research, 1996), 143.

2 Ibid.

3 William Rusie was a private in Company C. See 33rdindiana.org/roster/c/warusi.html.

4 *The Sporting News,* December 28, 1939: 5.

5 Puff.

6. Peter Mancuso, "The Kid, the Bolt, and Silent Mike," in Bill Felber, ed., *Inventing Baseball*, (Phoenix: Society for American Baseball Research, 2013), 225-27.
7. Charles F. Faber, *Major League Careers Cut Short* (Jefferson, North Carolina: McFarland, 2011), 50.
8. the baseballpage.com/players/rusieam/01/bio.
9. baseball-reference.com/players//r/ryanji01.shtml.
10. *The Sporting News*, December 25, 1946: 5.
11. Puff, 143.
12. Findagrave.com.
13. Tom Schott and Nick Peters, *The Giants Encyclopedia*, 2nd ed. (Champaign, Illinois: Sports Publishing, 2003), 276.
14. *New York World*, October 7, 1894.
15. Philip J. Lowry, *Green Cathedrals* (New York: Walker, 2006), 150.
16. *New York World*, October 7, 1894.
17. Puff.
18. Ibid.
19. John Thorn, *Baseball in the Garden of Eden* (New York: Simon & Schuster, 2011), 250.
20. Bill Lamb, "Bill Lange," sabr.org/bio/proj.
21. *The Sporting News*, December 28, 1939: 5.
22. Ibid.
23. Ibid.
24. *New York Times*, December 7, 1942.
25. *New York Times*, June 10, 1901.
26. Puff, 144.
27. *New York Times*, December 7, 1942.
28. *The Sporting News*, April 15, 1937.
29. *The Sporting News*, June 3, 1937.

NEW YORK'S 20-YEAR-OLD AMOS RUSIE BLANKS BROOKLYN FOR FIRST NO-HITTER IN GIANTS HISTORY

JULY 31, 1891: NEW YORK GIANTS 6, BROOKLYN BRIDEGROOMS 0, AT THE POLO GROUNDS

By Gregory H. Wolf

"IT WAS THE CLEVEREST PIECE of pitching ever seen in the Polo Grounds," opined the *New York Times* about the Giants' 20-year-old Amos Rusie's no-hitter against the Brooklyn Bridegrooms in July 1891.[1] "At times [Brooklyn] shrank away from his balls which curved over the plate," wrote the *Brooklyn Daily Eagle* of the right-hander's command performance and the first no-hitter in the history of the Giants club. "[T]he speed of the delivery was swift and wild at times and marked by curves which puzzled the batsman."[2] As of the end of the 2015 season, Rusie was the youngest big-leaguer to author a no-hitter (20 years, 2 months).

Friday, July 31, was a "perfect day" for baseball, according to the *New York Tribune*, which estimated that 2,580 spectators filed into the Polo Grounds, which had just opened in April 1890, to see a clash between Gotham City rivals the Giants and Bridegrooms.[3] Brooklyn, the reigning NL pennant-winner, had struggled this far in '91 under first-year player-manager John Montgomery Ward, and were in sixth place (36-42) in the eight-team league. Coincidentally, Ward, a former hurler who had transitioned to shortstop and second base, had himself been the youngest pitcher (20 years, 3 months) to spin a big-league no-hitter when the future Hall of Famer held the Buffalo Bisons hitless as a member of the NL Providence Grays on June 17, 1880. After a disappointing sixth-place finish the previous season, veteran skipper Jim Mutrie's New York club was in second place (47-32), just 3½ games behind the Chicago Colts.

The Giants' hopes to capture their third pennant in the last four seasons seemed dashed on July 24 when Rusie hurt the index finger of his right hand attempting to field a grounder in the second inning of an eventual victory over Philadelphia.[4] The *New York Times* reported that the club feared "he would not be able to play for some time to come."[5] The loss of Rusie, often considered the hardest thrower in the game, would indeed have been a disaster. "[Rusie's] pitching alone has saved the club," suggested the *Times*. "[I]f he has to retire for any length of time the team will do a little tobogganing."[6] The Indiana-born hurler, known as the Hoosier Thunderbolt, had debuted as a 17-year-old in 1889, and made headlines the following season by posting a 29-34 record, completing 56 of 62 starts while striking out 341 and walking 289, both league bests. The competitive Rusie was not the type to rest, and, according to the *Times*, "he urged Capt. Ewing to allow him to play" against the Bridegrooms.[7] Long John Ewing, the team's captain and secondary starter, was happy to oblige. About five weeks earlier, on June 22, Ewing was on the mound when Brooklyn's Tom Lovett held the Giants hitless at Eastern Park in Brooklyn.[8]

Since its inception in 1876, the National League had showcased pitchers who racked up strikeouts, like Old Hoss Radbourn, John Clarkson, Jim Whitney, and Tim Keefe, but hitters had never seen anything like the speed and wildness of Rusie's pitches. In fact, Rusie's pitching was considered among the reasons why major-league baseball decided to replace the pitcher's 5½-by-4-foot box with a 12-by-4-inch pitching rubber in 1893, thereby increasing the distance of the plate from about 55 feet to 60 feet 6 inches.[9] Pitchers threw from a flat surface in Rusie's era. The pitcher's mound was introduced around 1903; Monte Ward is often given credit for the idea.

Under the rules of time, the home team had the option of batting or taking the field to start the game. The Giants defied common convention by sending Brooklyn to the plate first (a fact noted by the local newspapers).[10] Rusie set the tone of the game by striking out leadoff batter Ward. "Brooklyn's batsmen were at Rusie's mercy during the rest of the game," opined the *Tribune*.

New York wasted no time pressuring slumping Brooklyn hurler Adonis Terry, who had entered the season with a 120-123 record in seven seasons. Leadoff hitter George Gore drew a walk, but was forced at second on Silent Mike Tiernan's grounder. After Charley Bassett walked, 40-year-old Orator Jim O'Rourke bunted to load the bases. Roger Connor's "puny effort," according to the *Tribune*, led to a double play, but still Tiernan scored the game's first run.[11] The *Times* described it as a sacrifice bunt by Connor; with Bassett subsequently getting "caught off third."[12]

The Giants maintained a precarious 1-0 lead until the bottom of the sixth, when they "began to find Terry's curves."[13] O'Rourke led off with another bunt and then scored when Connor smashed one of "his favorite extra hits," a triple in the left-center field gap.[14] The career leader in triples with 157 entering the '91 season, Connor had led the NL in three-baggers twice and finished second four times in the previous nine campaigns. Dick Buckley connected for a two-out double to plate Connor for a 3-0 Giants lead.

Described by the *Brooklyn Daily Eagle* as "fearfully intimidating," the stout, 6-foot-1, 200-pound Rusie continued to mow down Brooklyn's hitters.[15] In the bottom of the seventh, Rusie's teammates doubled his lead, effectively sealing the Bridegrooms' fate and leaving them at the altar. Gore, who began the season as the NL career leader in walks (576), took a free pass, moved to third on consecutive sacrifice bunts by Tiernan and Bassett, and then scored on O'Rourke's hit described variously as a liner to left field by the *Times* and *Tribune*, or a sacrifice bunt by the *Brooklyn Daily Eagle*. O'Rourke stole second, "aided by a passed ball" by catcher Con Daily.[16] After Connor drew a walk, the Giants attempted a double steal. Daily's bad throw sailed into left field, enabling O'Rourke to score. Seemingly indifferent to the errant orb rolling in his direction, left fielder Darby O'Brien was, according to the *Times*, "slow in retrieving the ball"; this allowed Connor to scamper home for the Giants' sixth and final run.[17]

Rusie, lauded as a "gallant young pitcher" by the *Tribune*, held Brooklyn hitless in the ninth to fashion the maiden no-hitter in Giants history in one hour and 45 minutes. The *Times* gushed about the most popular player on the team, if not metropolitan New York, in its account of the game. "[Rusie] sent balls to the plate with rare speed, and he curved the sphere in a manner to behold," winning with "apparent ease."[18] Though Rusie fanned only four and issued seven bases on balls, he overpowered Brooklyn's hitters, who pounded his curveball into the dirt throughout the game. The Bridegrooms hit only one ball out of the infield; O'Brien popped up to shallow center where Gore easily snared the ball. [Neither the *Times*, *Tribune*, nor *Eagle* reported in which inning that putout occurred]. There was "no question of a base hit being made," pronounced the *Times*.[19]

Local newspapers gave credit to the Giants' exceptional fielding for the no-hitter as much as they did Rusie's hurling. The *Tribune* described the game as a "scientific contest" with New York's "unusually brilliant" fielding.[20] In an era when teams averaged more than three fielding errors per game (excluding passed balls by catchers), New York committed just one, by second baseman Danny Richardson. [New York finished the '91 season with 384 errors and a .933 fielding percentage; both marks were second best to the Boston Beaneaters' 358 and .938.] The *Brooklyn Daily Eagle* gushed that "never before have [the Giants] given such a fine exhibition of fielding"; the *Times* claimed that the Giants "fielded the ball with unaccustomed skill."[21] New York retired 16 of 27 batters on what the *Times* considered "grounders of a very weak character."[22] Though baseball gloves and mitts had become commonplace about a decade earlier, padding had been used only since the late mid- to late 1880s; fielding was still a dangerous and awe-inspiring art at a time when the game was defined by bunting and infield hits. The *Tribune*, for example, singled out New York's second baseman Charley Bassett whose "throwing across the infield [was] especially fine."[23]

Rusie's no-hitter cemented his reputation as one of baseball's best hurlers and a genuine celebrity. The future Hall of Famer finished the season with 33 victories, tied with the Beaneaters' John Clarkson for second most behind Chicago's Bill Hutchinson's 44. It was also the first of four consecutive seasons in which Rusie notched at least 30 wins, including a league-best and career-high 36 in 1894. Over a dominating six-year stretch from 1890 to 1895, the Hoosier Thunderbolt paced the circuit in strikeouts and walks five times each and shutouts four times for Giants teams that finished in the top half of the standing only twice.

NOTES

1. "Rusie's Wonderful Feat," *New York Times*, August 1, 1891: 13.
2. "Giants Win," *Brooklyn Daily Eagle*, August 1, 1891: 2.
3. "Rusie Himself Again," *New York Tribune*, August 1, 1891: 3.
4. "Pitcher Rusie Disabled," *New York Times*, July 25, 1891: 3.
5. "Rusie's Wonderful Feat."
6. "Pitcher Rusie Disabled."
7. "Rusie's Wonderful Feat."
8. "The Giants Worst Defeat," *New York Tribune*, June 23, 1891: 3.
9. For more on the history of the pitcher's mound, see Eric Miklich, The Pitcher's Area, *19th Century Baseball*. 19cbaseball.com/field-8.html. See Tim Wendel's essay on Amos Rusie at the *National Pastime* for more on Rusie's role in the changes of 1893, thenationalpastimemuseum.com/article/amos-rusie.
10. Rusie Himself Again."
11. Ibid.
12. "Rusie's Wonderful Feat."
13. Ibid.
14. "Giants Win."
15. Ibid.
16. "Rusie's Wonderful Feat."
17. Ibid.
18. Ibid.
19. Ibid.
20. Rusie Himself Again."
21. "Giants Win"; "Rusie's Wonderful Feat."
22. "Rusie's Wonderful Feat."
23. Rusie Himself Again."

THEODORE BREITENSTEIN

By Stephen V. Rice

LIKE STEVE CARLTON, WHO won 27 of his team's 59 victories in 1972, Theodore Breitenstein was a left-handed ace on a weak team. Breitenstein was credited with 43 percent of the St. Louis Browns' victories from 1893 to 1896. In 21 seasons of professional baseball from 1891 to 1911, the durable southpaw won more than 325 games.[1]

"Theodore Breitenstein was at one time the greatest left-handed pitcher in America."

– Alfred H. Spink, founder of *The Sporting News*[2]

"Breitenstein is one of the few left-handers who can locate the plate when he wants to, and in addition to this he has terrific speed, sharp curves, and there is not a pitcher in the league that fields his position better."

– Wee Willie Keeler, 1897[3]

Breitenstein was a freckled-faced redhead. His nickname was "Breit" (rhymes with write). He was also called Red, Theo, and "The," the first syllable of Theo.[4] Unlike Carlton, Breitenstein was small, 5-feet-9, and weighed between 137 and 150 pounds early in his career, increasing to 167 pounds later on.[5]

Born on June 1, 1869, in St. Louis, Theodore J. Breitenstein was the youngest of the three children of German immigrants Louis Breitenstein (1822-1888, a cabinet maker) and Elizabeth (Moore) Breitenstein (1825-1883).[6] Louis and Elizabeth died when Theodore was a teenager. Theodore went to work making cookstoves for the Wrought Iron Range Company of St. Louis and played on the Home Comforts, a baseball team named for the company's brand of ranges and furnaces. With Theodore pitching, the team won the 1889 St. Louis Baseball League championship game.[7]

In 1890 Breitenstein was one of the Brown Reserves, a group of promising amateurs permitted by St. Louis Browns owner Chris Von der Ahe to practice at the Browns' ballpark.[8] This led to Breitenstein joining the Browns in 1891. He made his major-league debut on April 28, pitching two scoreless innings in relief against the Louisville Colonels.[9] He went to the Grand Rapids (Michigan) Shamrocks in May and returned to the Browns in August.[10] On October 4, the last day of the season, Breitenstein made his first major-league start and threw a no-hitter against the Colonels. Except for one base on balls, it was a perfect game. The 22-year-old hurler did not realize he had a no-hitter going until the game was over; his teammates had kept mum so that he would not get rattled.[11]

After hearing "tales of pitcher Breitenstein's drinking," Von der Ahe had doubts about his future.[12] Breitenstein pitched erratically for the Browns in 1892. On April 15 he hurled a three-hitter against the Pittsburgh Pirates, but a week later the Pirates hammered him for 12 runs in the first inning.[13] On April 24 Breitenstein allowed 12 hits and nine walks in a 10-2 loss to the Cincinnati Reds, yet on May 6, he had a no-hitter through eight innings against the Brooklyn Grooms en route to a two-hitter, albeit with seven walks.[14] On May 14 he walked 10 batters in a 5-3 loss to the Chicago Colts, but a week later he outpitched Cy Young in a 4-1 victory over the Cleveland Spiders.[15]

The roller-coaster continued throughout the season. In early June Breitenstein was knocked out in blowout losses to the Philadelphia Phillies and Baltimore Orioles.[16] Then he tossed a two-hitter against Louisville on June 20, and four days later went the distance against Cy Young in a 16-inning, 3-3 tie.[17] *Sporting Life* cautioned Breitenstein in July:

"Breitenstein and jag juice [hard liquor] have been trotting a rapid heat lately. ... He is the only player on the team who has been fined this season, and if he insists on dallying with the stuff that purloins the brain an indefinite suspension will be the result. But he is a good-natured, hard-working lad, and he ought to think it over a couple of times before following ... the ruddy road to ruin."[18]

Von der Ahe suspended Breitenstein for part of August and September.[19] The Browns finished in 11th place in the 12-team National League. Breitenstein compiled an unimpressive 9-19 record and 4.69 ERA in 282⅓ innings, yet his nine wins were second most on the Browns' pitching staff.

In 1893 the pitching distance was increased from 50 feet to 60 feet 6 inches. This sparked a 29 percent increase from 1892 in National League scoring per game. The new distance suited Breitenstein. He pitched 382⅔ innings in 1893, led the league with a 3.18 ERA, and posted a 19-24 record for the 10th-place Browns. Highlights included a two-hit shutout of Cap Anson's Chicago Colts on May 7, and a two-hitter against John Ward's New York Giants on the Fourth of July.[20] Breitenstein's favorite catchers were Dick Buckley and Heinie Peitz; he credited Buckley for his success as a pitcher.[21] The German duo of Breitenstein and Peitz became known as the Pretzel Battery.[22]

After a doubleheader in St. Louis on August 1, 1893, the Browns traveled to Louisville for a three-game series. Along the way, they stopped to play an exhibition game at Vincennes, Indiana. Breitenstein "filled up on Indiana whisky" and refused to board the train to Louisville; three teammates "attempted by main force to put Breitenstein on the train, but failed."[23] After sobering up, he returned to the team and apologized to Von der Ahe.[24]

In 1894 Breitenstein was overworked, underpaid, and bullied by Von der Ahe. He pitched 447⅓ innings, the most innings in one season by a National League pitcher from 1894 to 2014. His 27-23 record was remarkable on a team with a 56-76 record. His ERA jumped to 4.79 but was better than the league average of 5.33. *Sporting Life* said, "Breitenstein is one of the lowest-salaried and most effective pitchers in the League."[25] Breitenstein's contract paid him a meager $1,350 for the season and included a "temperance" clause that permitted Von der Ahe to fine him $100 for each time he was caught drinking; this fine was levied once during the season.[26] According to reporter O.P. Caylor, Von der Ahe liked to swear at Breitenstein in German and "know that he is understood."[27]

Breitenstein's relentless workload and rocky relationship with Von der Ahe were demonstrated during a doubleheader against Brooklyn on September 9, 1894. He pitched a complete game in the first game, and the Browns won, 7-5. He had thrown complete games on September 1, 3, 6, and 9, and pitched in relief on September 4 and 8.[28] Nonetheless, after two St. Louis hurlers were battered in the second game of the doubleheader, Von der Ahe wanted to put Breitenstein into that game, too, and was angered that he had changed out of his uniform. Von der Ahe ordered him to put his uniform on and go in to pitch. Breitenstein refused, so Von der Ahe fined him $100 and suspended him.[29] Breitenstein explained:

"The cranks [baseball fans] have but a slight appreciation of the fearful strain a pitcher's arm is subjected to. A man who takes his regular turn in the box ought to be asked to do extra work only in case of an emergency. I have had but little trouble with my arm and seldom complain when called on to go into the points. I make it a rule to trust the straight ball and change of pace until a man gets on base, when I resort to the [more strenuous] drop and curved ball to outwit an opponent. ... I don't loaf in the box, but I adopt this system of saving my arm."[30]

Breitenstein returned to action on September 15 in St. Louis and was defeated 7-2 by the Giants.[31] That evening the 25-year-old pitcher married 18-year-old Ida L. Uhlmansick. Like Breitenstein, Ida was

THEODORE BREITENSTEIN, Pitcher.
CINCINNATI 1900.

a native of St. Louis and a child of German immigrants.[32] She was "a pretty German girl, with eyes that are blue and hair that is blond."[33] Breitenstein promised to be a model husband, and Ida said she would lock him in at night if necessary.[34] The couple resided in St. Louis. In the offseason Breitenstein worked at a stove foundry as a machinist.[35] He was said to be "a first-class workman" with "not a lazy bone in his body."[36]

Breitenstein rejected Von der Ahe's initial offer of $1,800 and signed for $2,000 for the 1895 season.[37] The Browns were even weaker in 1895 than in 1894. Statistics published by the *Pittsburgh Daily Post* on August 5, 1895, indicate that Breitenstein's won-lost record was 16-18 when the rest of the St. Louis pitching staff had a combined record of 12-41.[38] Von der Ahe turned down offers of $10,000 for Breitenstein from both the Phillies and Pirates, an enormous sum for that era.[39] Breitenstein was the most popular player in St. Louis, and "St. Louis patrons were up in arms against" any sale of the hometown favorite.[40] *Sporting Life* said, "The League should insist on making Von der Ahe keep his great pitcher, Breitenstein, as the sale of this young man will be the deathblow to base ball in St. Louis."[41]

Breitenstein finished the 1895 season with a 19-30 record in 438⅔ innings, and the Browns landed in 11th place with a 39-92 record. He was credited with 49 percent of the team's wins (19 of 39); no pitcher won a greater percentage of his team's victories from 1893 to 2014.[42] Reportedly, Breitenstein "dissipated" (abused alcohol) on one road trip.[43] Despite losing 30 games, he was wanted by every team in the league. *Sporting Life* said: "What a good-natured, hardworking little wonder he is. The balls come in over the plate like a zig-zag streak of lightning, and there is not a moment's rest for him in the whole nine innings. ... He has the nerve and the heart and the equilibrium of temper and the modesty, and yet with it all the confidence, too."[44]

In 1896 St. Louis again finished in 11th place, with Breitenstein earning 18 of the team's 40 victories. The Cincinnati Reds acquired him after the season for a reported $10,000. Thrilled to leave Von der Ahe, Breitenstein demonstrated what he could do on a good team. In 1897 he compiled a 23-12 record for the fourth-place Reds, including 10 consecutive victories from June 11 to July 18. The *Cincinnati Enquirer* said, "Some of those who in the early spring used to refer to Breit as a ten-cent counterfeit, are now quite ready to take off their hats to him as the only genuine, blown-in-the-glass, Ten-Thousand-Dollar-Beauty in the business."[45] Breitenstein enjoyed his three-hit shutout of St. Louis on June 30, with Von der Ahe looking on.[46] Without Breitenstein, St. Louis won only 29 games; the 1897 Browns, with a .221 winning percentage, rank as the second worst major-league team between 1891 and 2014.

The Pretzel Battery was reunited when Breitenstein joined the Reds. He and Peitz were a clever pair. They would "argue" with each other during pivotal moments of a game. Breitenstein described the ploy:

> "The batter, of course, is interested in the supposed quarrel, and when he sees that Peitz apparently is not ready to catch, he

takes his eye off the ball. Then Heinie gives me the sign, and I shoot it over. The batter either hits late at the ball and pops it up, or misses it entirely. I tell you, we have pulled out of many a tight hole with that trick."[47]

With Peitz behind the plate, Breitenstein out-dueled Cy Young on Opening Day in 1898.[48] A week later, against Pittsburgh, Breitenstein hurled his second career no-hitter.[49] After shutting out Cleveland on September 4, he had an 18-8 record and the Reds were in first place with a 1½-game lead over the Boston Beaneaters. The Beaneaters won 30 of their remaining 35 games to capture the pennant, while the Reds fell to third place, 11½ games back. Breitenstein finished the season with a 20-14 record. He was bothered by a sore arm late in the season, and an X-ray revealed a bone spur near his left elbow.[50]

Breitenstein's arm troubled him in the spring of 1899,[51] but he pitched well for the Reds in 1899 and 1900. In February 1901, the *St. Louis Republic* lobbied for his return to St. Louis.[52] The Reds complied by releasing Breitenstein, and he signed with the St. Louis Cardinals. After he pitched poorly in three starts, though, the Cardinals released him. Breitenstein "gave no indication of any of his former prowess, and the necessity of reducing [the Cardinals] to the League limit of 16 men by May 15 forced his release."[53] This ended his major-league career, a few weeks before his 32nd birthday. Breitenstein had thrown 301 complete games in the major leagues, establishing a record for southpaws that has been exceeded by only Eddie Plank and Warren Spahn in major-league history through 2015.

Beginning in June 1901, Breitenstein pitched for the St. Paul (Minnesota) Saints of the Western League, but the team released him in August "in the interests of good discipline."[54] He finished the season with the semipro Alton (Illinois) Blues.[55] In December Breitenstein was thrown from a horse-drawn carriage and broke his right (nonpitching) arm.[56] That winter was a low point in his life, both physically and mentally, and he said he would never again play baseball.[57]

Breitenstein's friend and former teammate Charlie Frank, who managed the Memphis Egyptians of the Southern Association, persuaded him to return to baseball as a member of the Egyptians.[58] Breitenstein posted a 21-11 record for Memphis in 1902. One of his six shutouts was a three-hitter against the New Orleans Pelicans on June 24; the "New Orleans left-handed batters found Breitenstein an unsolvable proposition" and opted to bat right-handed against him.[59]

Breitenstein still had the stuff to pitch in the major leagues, but he turned down a chance to join Connie Mack's Philadelphia Athletics in the spring of 1903.[60] With six shutouts and a 17-11 record, Breitenstein helped the Egyptians win the 1903 Southern Association pennant. On September 19 his triple knocked in two runs in his 3-0 shutout of the Atlanta Crackers; the Memphis "crowd went frantic and a subscription of $75 was taken up for the pitcher."[61] Despite the appreciation shown in Memphis, Breitenstein was loyal to manager Frank and followed him the next season to New Orleans.

Breitenstein pitched spectacularly for the New Orleans Pelicans from 1904 to 1906, with a 57-20 record and a 1.50 ERA. The Pelicans won the 1905 Southern Association pennant. The Philadelphia Athletics and St. Louis Browns tried to lure Breitenstein back to the major leagues, but he declined.[62] Earning a $2,700 salary in New Orleans, he was better paid than many major-league hurlers.[63]

Following an offyear in 1907, Breitenstein was exceptional in 1908, with a 17-6 record and a minuscule 1.05 ERA. Over the final two months of the season, he threw seven shutouts. A dramatic showdown occurred on September 19, the last day of the season. The Pelicans needed to defeat the Nashville Volunteers to win the pennant; otherwise, Nashville would take the flag. Nashville won the game, 1-0, in "a brilliantly contested pitchers' battle between [Carl Vedder] Sitton and Breitenstein."[64] Sportswriter Grantland Rice called it "the greatest game ever played in Dixie."[65]

Breitenstein was known as "The Grand Old Man" of the Southern Association. The *Cleveland Plain*

Dealer said: "He is a little, weazened up old man with furrows on his face. ... His looks are typical of a player who has baked beneath the boiling suns on a ball field season after season."[66] At age 40, "the wise old owl" pitched a no-hitter against the Montgomery (Alabama) Senators on August 15, 1909; the Senators "were utterly unable to connect" with his offerings.[67] It was the third no-hitter of his professional career, and it came 18 years after his first. On August 27 Breitenstein threw an 11-inning, two-hit shutout against the Birmingham Barons.[68] He followed that with a 12-inning, three-hit shutout of Montgomery on September 5.[69]

New Orleans won the 1910 Southern Association pennant by a comfortable eight-game margin over second-place Birmingham. Breitenstein compiled a 19-9 record and a 1.53 ERA, with eight shutouts; however, the brightest star on the Pelicans was Shoeless Joe Jackson, a sensational 22-year-old center fielder who led the league with a .354 batting average. The next season was Breitenstein's last as a player, and at age 42, he helped the Pelicans win another pennant. He stayed in the Southern Association as an umpire from 1912 to 1918.

After leaving baseball, Breitenstein was employed at a Ford assembly plant, and later at Forest Park, in St. Louis. He enjoyed watching major-league games at Sportsman's Park,[70] but felt the pitchers were pampered. "Now, if a boy is hit in the first couple of innings, they put the blankets on him and he's through for four days," he said in 1929. "We worked three or four times a week, and lots of times played the outfield when we weren't pitching."[71]

Breitenstein offered advice to young pitchers:

- "More batsmen are fooled by change of pace than by all the speed, curves or shoots in the world. A good change of pace is the most valuable faculty a pitcher can possess."[72]
- "Study your batters. If you know he likes a high ball give him a low one and vice versa. Not all the time, of course, for if they know what is coming they are liable to lay for it. Mix them up at unexpected moments."[73]
- "Never pitch for strike-outs. Their day is over. Always remember that you have eight men to help you."[74]

Ida Breitenstein died on April 25, 1935. Heartbroken over the loss of his wife, Theodore died eight days later of heart failure, at the age of 65.[75] They are buried at St. Peter's Cemetery in St. Louis.[76]

"Over the hills to the Old Men's Home
Rattles the dismal car.
Famous fielders and willow wielders
Have made the journey far.
Countless the inmates all down and out,
Never again to star.
But silky fine is T. Breitenstein,
The Grand Old Man ain't that!"[77]

– *Pointers from Pelicanville*, 1910

NOTES

1. In 2015 Baseball-reference.com indicated that Breitenstein had earned 160 major-league wins and 165 minor-league wins, for a total of 325 wins in professional baseball; however, his 1891 minor-league record is not included in this tally.
2. Alfred H. Spink, *The National Game, 2nd Edition* (St. Louis: National Game Pub. Co., 1911), 124.
3. *Harrisburg* (Pennsylvania) *Daily Independent*, July 9, 1897.
4. Although record books give his name as Ted Breitenstein, the research for this biography found no evidence that he was called Ted by his contemporaries.
5. *The Sporting News*, April 5, 1934.
6. Ancestry.com. Theodore's middle initial is given as "J" in the 1910 US Census and in 1895 and 1917 St. Louis city directories.
7. Spink, *The National Game*, 53.
8. *The Sporting News*, April 5, 1934; *St. Louis Post-Dispatch*, March 16, 1890.
9. *Chicago Tribune*, April 29, 1891.
10. *Fort Wayne* (Indiana) *Sentinel*, August 6, 1891.
11. *The Sporting News*, February 21, 1929. Breitenstein (1891), Bumpus Jones (1892), and Bobo Holloman (1953) were the only pitchers to throw a no-hitter in their first major-league start, through 2014.
12. *Sporting Life*, March 12, 1892.
13. *Pittsburgh Dispatch*, April 16 and 23, 1892.
14. *Sporting Life*, April 30, 1892; *Brooklyn Daily Eagle*, May 7, 1892.

15. *Brooklyn Daily Eagle*, May 15, 1892; *Los Angeles Herald*, May 22, 1892.
16. *Chicago Inter Ocean*, June 7, 1892; *Pittsburgh Daily Post*, June 11, 1892.
17. *St. Paul Globe*, June 21, 1892; *San Francisco Call*, June 25, 1892.
18. *Sporting Life*, July 2, 1892.
19. *St. Paul Globe*, September 19, 1892.
20. *Chicago Tribune*, May 8, 1893; *Cleveland Plain Dealer*, July 5, 1893.
21. *Sporting Life*, January 25, 1896.
22. *New York World*, July 12, 1893.
23. *Sporting Life*, August 12, 1893.
24. *Chicago Tribune*, August 5, 1893.
25. *Sporting Life*, May 12, 1894.
26. *Sporting Life*, March 17, 1894; *Pittsburgh Post-Gazette*, July 17, 1894.
27. *Kansas City* (Kansas) *Gazette*, May 13, 1894.
28. *Washington Times*, September 2 and 5, 1894; *Philadelphia Times*, September 4, 1894; *Pittsburgh Post-Gazette*, September 7, 1894; *Chicago Inter Ocean*, September 9, 1894.
29. *Sporting Life*, September 13, 1894; *Scranton* (Pennsylvania) *Tribune*, September 14, 1894.
30. *Springfield* (Missouri) *Leader*, September 17, 1894.
31. *Richmond* (Virginia) *Dispatch*, September 16, 1894.
32. Ancestry.com.
33. *Sporting Life*, September 22, 1894.
34. Ibid.
35. *Sporting Life*, December 9, 1893, and November 24, 1894.
36. *Sporting Life*, October 31, 1896.
37. *Philadelphia Times*, January 26, 1895; *Sporting Life*, March 9, 1895.
38. *Pittsburgh Daily Post*, August 5, 1895.
39. *New York Tribune*, June 9, 1895; *Pittsburgh Daily Post*, July 9, 1895.
40. *Brooklyn Daily Eagle*, July 25, 1895; *Sporting Life*, August 3, 1895.
41. *Sporting Life*, July 20, 1895.
42. SABR, *The SABR Baseball List & Record Book: Baseball's Most Fascinating Records and Unusual Statistics* (New York: Scribner, 2007), 266.
43. *Sporting Life*, July 13, 1895.
44. *Sporting Life*, June 22, 1895.
45. *Cincinnati Enquirer*, July 19, 1897.
46. *The Sporting News*, July 3, 1897.
47. *Sporting Life*, August 13, 1898.
48. *Cincinnati Enquirer*, April 16, 1898.
49. *Chicago Tribune*, April 23, 1898.
50. *Sporting Life*, August 27 and September 10, 1898; *Kansas City Journal*, December 18, 1898. X-rays were discovered in 1895 by Wilhelm Roentgen. The X-ray of Breitenstein's arm in 1898 is an early example of the use of X-rays in sports medicine.
51. *Louisville Courier-Journal*, May 8, 1899.
52. *St. Louis Republic*, February 3, 1901.
53. *St. Louis Post-Dispatch*, May 12, 1901.
54. *Minneapolis Journal*, June 3 and August 16, 1901.
55. *St. Louis Republic*, August 31, 1901.
56. *Sedalia* (Missouri) *Democrat*, December 9, 1901.
57. *Sporting Life*, January 25, 1902.
58. *Atlanta Constitution*, March 31, 1902.
59. *New Orleans Times-Picayune*, June 25, 1902.
60. *Mansfield* (Ohio) *News*, May 16, 1903.
61. *Atlanta Constitution*, September 20, 1903.
62. *Washington Times*, September 2, 1905; *Atlanta Constitution*, September 9, 1905.
63. *Washington Post*, December 12, 1905.
64. *Sporting Life*, October 3, 1908.
65. John A. Simpson, *The Greatest Game Ever Played in Dixie: The Nashville Vols, Their 1908 Season, and the Championship Game* (Jefferson, North Carolina: McFarland, 2007), 25.
66. *Cleveland Plain Dealer*, March 28, 1909.
67. *New Orleans Times-Picayune*, August 16, 1909.
68. *Sporting Life*, September 4, 1909.
69. *Sporting Life*, September 18, 1909.
70. *The Sporting News*, April 5, 1934.
71. *The Sporting News*, February 21, 1929.
72. *St. Louis Post-Dispatch*, May 10, 1896.
73. Ibid.
74. Ibid.
75. *Cleveland Plain Dealer*, May 4, 1935.
76. stpeterschurch.org/cemetery/cemetery_SearchResults.php?S=2&L=124.00&LO=1.
77. *New Orleans Times-Picayune*, July 30, 1910.

BREITENSTEIN NO-HITS THE LOUISVILLE COLONELS IN HIS FIRST MAJOR-LEAGUE START

OCTOBER 4, 1891: ST. LOUIS BROWNS 8, LOUISVILLE COLONELS 0, AT SPORTSMAN'S PARK, ST. LOUIS

By Stephen V. Rice

IT WAS SUNDAY, OCTOBER 4, the last day of the 1891 season, when Charlie Comiskey, the St. Louis Browns' first baseman and manager, let Theodore Breitenstein pitch the first game of a doubleheader against the Louisville Colonels in St. Louis. Breitenstein was a 22-year-old rookie, a little redhead from St. Louis. He stood 5-feet-9 and weighed barely 140 pounds.[1] The Browns had already clinched second place in the American Association, and it was not possible to catch the first-place Boston Reds, so why not give the youngster a try? He had pitched well for the Browns in five relief appearances during the season and had earned this opportunity.

For the Louisville Colonels, it had been a tough year. After winning the 1890 American Association pennant, the team had fallen to eighth place in 1891. Manager Jack Chapman selected Jouett Meekin, a promising 24-year-old right-hander, to face the Browns in the first game of the doubleheader. The previous Sunday, in the second game of a doubleheader, Meekin fired a six-inning, two-hit shutout of the Browns in Louisville.[2] Chapman hoped Meekin would repeat this effort in St. Louis.

It was a cold and blustery day in the Mound City, yet close to 5,000 fans came to Sportsman's Park for the doubleheader.[3] Before the first game, Comiskey advised Breitenstein to let the Colonels hit the ball and to trust "Heaven and the outfield."[4] Browns right fielder Tommy McCarthy said: "Bear down on the first man, kid. Get him away each inning and you won't have to worry."[5]

Breitenstein did bear down; he focused on each batter with great concentration. He was a left-hander with a whirling motion, and the Louisville hitters were baffled by his delivery. Breitenstein retired the Colonels inning after inning: Monk Cline, Farmer Weaver, and Captain Harry Taylor at the top of the order; the impressive rookie Hughie Jennings and veterans Chicken Wolf and Bill Kuehne in the heart of the order; and Tim Shinnick, Tom Cahill, and pitcher Meekin at the bottom of the order. To the surprise of everyone, Breitenstein delivered a nine-inning no-hitter! Except for a base on balls given to Taylor, it was a perfect game. Breitenstein faced 28 batters, one over the minimum, in his first major-league start. He struck out Taylor, Shinnick, and Meekin, and fanned Wolf twice. Only three balls were hit to the outfielders. The Browns backed him with flawless defense and scored eight runs off Meekin.[6]

Breitenstein did not realize he had a no-hitter going. He said:

"[Browns third baseman] Jack Boyle … and McCarthy gave me a big hand every inning. But they never mentioned the no-hit angle, and nobody on the bench said anything. Afraid I'd get excited. I was too busy worrying about the next batter to care what had happened before, so I never knew what was going on. It wasn't until after the game that Boyle … started pounding me on the back. 'Attaboy, kid, that's showin' 'em how,' he says. I says, 'Well, I was pretty lucky, I guess.' 'Lucky, hell,' he says, 'you shut 'em out without a hit.' And while I was trying to figure it out they carried me into the clubhouse on their shoulders."[7]

The next day a headline in the *Louisville Courier-Journal* read, "An Amateur Pitcher Shuts the Colonels Out Without a Single Hit."[8] That "amateur" Breitenstein would have a successful professional career, winning more than 300 games over the next 20 seasons.

NOTES

1. *The Sporting News*, April 5, 1934.
2. *Louisville Courier-Journal*, September 28, 1891.
3. *St. Louis Post-Dispatch*, October 5, 1891.
4. *The Sporting News*, February 21, 1929.
5. Ibid.
6. *Louisville Courier-Journal* and *St. Louis Post-Dispatch*, October 5, 1891. In a 1934 mention, *The Sporting News* said it had been just 27 batters, that one had walked but was then erased trying to steal. Contemporary reports and box scores reflect 28 batters.
7. *The Sporting News*, February 21, 1929.
8. *Louisville Courier-Journal*, October 5, 1891.

BILL HAWKE

By Jimmy Keenan

FROM HIS EARLY DAYS AS an amateur, pitcher Bill Hawke mowed down opposing batters with a lightning-quick fastball and tantalizing off-speed pitches. When the distance between the batter and pitcher was expanded to 60 feet 6 inches in 1893, Hawke changed his strategy and began to induce outs with grounders and pop flies. In addition to his overpowering heater, Hawke's pitching arsenal consisted of what baseball writers of the day described as "drops and shoots." Hawke himself used the term "sinker" when describing his deceptive drop ball to a reporter from the *Baltimore Sun*.[1]

A severely broken wrist put an end to Hawke's big-league career after only three seasons. Modern medical treatment would have had him back in the lineup in a few months, but this would not be the case for the man who threw the first major-league no-hitter at the present-day pitching distance.

William Victor "Bill" Hawke was born in Elsmere, Delaware, on April 28, 1870. His parents were John and Jane Hawke, and the 1870 census shows him as the youngest of seven children. Bill attended public school in Wilmington, Delaware, until the age of 14. At that time, he got a job at a local wheelwright's shop. Later he was employed at a morocco factory. (Morocco was the term for the process of turning goatskin into shoe leather.)

Hawke, who was occasionally referred to in some newspaper accounts as Dick Hawke,[2] first made his mark on the diamond as a third baseman and catcher for the Defiance team from Wilmington. By 1889 he had moved on to a nine in nearby Middleton. The following season he joined the Elkton, Maryland, club and became a pitcher, striking out 20 of his former Middleton teammates in a nine-inning game. During this time, Hawke also pitched for a team from Chestertown, Maryland.

On July 2, 1891, the *Baltimore Sun* noted that Baltimore Orioles vice president Billy Waltz received a letter from a sender the newspaper described as "a well known resident of Elkton," recommending Hawke for the Baltimore pitching staff. The letter said that on the previous Saturday, Hawke, pitching for Elkton, threw a no-hitter against a very talented team from Chester, Pennsylvania, striking out 23. A dispatch to the *Sun* the day before noted that on that day Hawke shut out the Columbias from Wilmington 19-0, fanning 20 batters in the process.

The Orioles, who were playing in the American Association at this time, were not keen on signing amateur pitchers and rushing them into the fast-paced competition of major-league baseball. Hawke didn't sign with Baltimore, although an article in the July 6 *Sun* noted that he had been offered a trial by Orioles manager Billie Barnie but hadn't undecided whether to accept. Hawke eventually chose not to sign with Baltimore.

On August 8 Hawke led Elkton to a 2-0 victory over the Rising Sun club for the championship of Cecil County, allowing just three hits while striking out 24 batters. On August 12 he struck out 26 in a 13-inning contest while pitching for an aggregation from Pocomoke City, Virginia. Three days later he was back pitching for the Elkton nine in a 5-3 loss to a local Baltimore team called the Pastimes at Union Park. Of Hawke's pitching that day, the *Baltimore Sun* of August 17 wrote, "Hawke has good speed, curves and control and made a favorable impression."

The following week, the speedballer posted 19 strikeouts in a game against the Schuylkill Navy Yard team and soon after whiffed 16 in an 18-3 victory over New Castle.

With performances like this, it did not take long for minor-league teams to come calling. In late May of 1892, Hawke inked his first professional contract, with the Reading Actives of the Pennsylvania State

League for an annual salary of $1,500. Hawke's brother Harry, who was a catcher, joined the team on June 27.

The *Chestertown Transcript* of June 16, 1892 wrote of Hawke, "He differs from most professional ball players, in that he is quiet and gentlemanly, two qualifications too seldom found in professional players."

When the Actives folded in July, Hawke joined the Pocomoke City team. One of the games Hawke pitched for Pocomoke was an 18-inning victory over Norfolk in which he struck out 29.

A short time later, Hawke traveled to Baltimore to inquire about a pitching job with the major-league Orioles. When he arrived at Union Park, the Baltimore front office made it clear that the team was not interested in his services. Rejected, Hawke walked to the visiting team's clubhouse to ask the St. Louis Browns for a tryout. By chance the Browns' scheduled starting pitcher, Kid Gleason, had come down with a sore arm and the team needed an immediate replacement. St. Louis owner Chris von der Ahe agreed to give Hawke a trial.

Shaking off any nervousness he may have had over his first major-league start, the 5-foot-8, 169-pound Hawke strode out to the pitcher's box and went to work. He had his good stuff that afternoon. He gave up four hits and struck out four while leading the Browns to a 2-1 victory over the team that had turned him down. This stellar performance earned Hawke a contract with St. Louis for the rest of the season. Of Hawke's pitching, the *Sun* wrote, "He has good curves, fine speed and above all, excellent control of the sphere."[3]

After spending about a month with the Browns, Hawke left the club in Baltimore, went back home to Wilmington, and sat out the season after a disagreement over a fine that had been levied on him by Von der Ahe.[4] He had compiled a 5-5 record with a 3.70 earned-run average for a St. Louis club that finished 56-94, 11th in the 12-team National League. Hawke rejoined the Elkton squad for the remainder of the 1892 campaign.

Over the following winter, the Browns hired former major leaguer William Henry "Watty"

Watkins as their new manager. Part of his preseason duties was to settle any past differences between Von der Ahe and some of his players. Watkins traveled around the country signing new players while visiting a number of disgruntled Browns including Jack Glasscock, King Crooks, Kid Gleason, and Hawke. After a lengthy meeting with Watkins in Wilmington, Hawke agreed to return to the Browns.

To spur more offense, the National League moved the pitcher's rubber from 55 feet to 60 feet 6 inches from home plate at the start of the 1893 season.[5] This led to higher batting averages and more scoring, making the games more exciting for the fans.

That spring, Hawke didn't report to the Browns because of a disagreement over his salary. After a brief holdout, he came to terms with the club and agreed to join the team. Upon his arrival, he immediately made his presence known, striking out 12 in an April 8 exhibition game against a local amateur club.

As it turned out, Von der Ahe was still harboring ill feelings toward Hawke, presumably for walking out on the team the previous season, and possibly his latest holdout. Whatever the reason, after trying to sell Hawke's contract to Baltimore for $500, Von der Ahe released him after just one unsuccessful start.

Hawke was given his 10 days' notice by the Browns on May 14. Von der Ahe was going with Kid Gleason (21-22), Pink Hawley (5-17), Ted Breitenstein (19-24), and John Dolan (0-1) as his starting pitchers so he felt that Hawke was expendable. When Baltimore manager Ned Hanlon heard that the right-hander might be available, he told a reporter for the *Baltimore Sun*, "I did not know of Hawke's release, but if he can come we will take him as a member of the Oriole team."[6] True to his word, Hanlon signed Hawke to a contract.

In his first start with Baltimore, on June 9, Hawke bested Cap Anson's Chicago Colts, 11-9. For the next two months his work for Orioles was credible but not spectacular. It also soon became apparent that the headstrong pitcher was not enamored with the pitch calling of Orioles catcher Wilbert Robinson. On July 3 the *Sun* observed, "If Hawke would follow Robinson's instructions as to what kind of balls to pitch he would be 50 percent more effective than he is."[7]

There is no way to know if Hawke started taking Robinson's advice, but the burly backstop was behind the plate on Wednesday, August 16, 1893, when Hawke became the first pitcher to toss a no-hitter from the new pitching distance. The Orioles defeated the Washington Senators, 5-0, that day as Hawke's drop ball worked with pinpoint accuracy. His overwhelming command of the elusive pitch led to a number of Senators tapping the ball weakly to a waiting infielder or popping up an easy fly to an outfielder. Hawke also took care of a few of the Washington batters himself, striking out six Senators and making one putout from the pitcher's box. Hawke, who was a bit superstitious, attributed his good luck that day to a new felt hat he had recently purchased. He finished the 1893 season with a record of 11 wins and 16 losses for a Baltimore team that finished eighth in the National League. (His record with St. Louis was 0-1.)

Pitching from a greater distance and facing professionals instead of amateurs, Hawke was no longer racking up high strikeout totals. Instead, he pitched to contact and let his fielders do the rest. Even so, his 2.74 strikeouts per nine innings was the fifth highest in the National League.

In late February of 1894, Hawke declined to join the Oriole team when it left Baltimore for spring training in Macon, Georgia. *Sporting Life* wrote that Hawke vowed not to leave his home in Elkton until manager Ned Hanlon restructured his contract.[8] He held out until the beginning of May, eventually garnering a substantial raise from Hanlon. In his first game back with the club, on May 17, Hawke defeated the Washington Senators 10-2, giving up only three hits.

As the season progressed, Hawke battled a sore arm for most of the year but continued to pitch well, going 16-9 while completing 17 of his 25 starts. The Orioles captured their first National League pennant, and Hawke averaged three strikeouts per game.

Discussing Hawke's pitching, *Sporting Life* noted in October, "He is what is called a 'phenom' and pitches a very swift, puzzling ball, difficult to fathom."[9]

In an article in the same edition of *Sporting Life*, St. Louis Browns pitcher Ted Breitenstein commented on the toughness of his former teammate: "Hawke of Baltimore has lots of sand. When he was with the Browns, a knot the size of an egg would form near the elbow of his pitching arm after every game. I told him he must quit using his drop ball so often or he would lose his arm. How he stands the pain and suffering which he goes through after every game is a source of wonder to me. You seldom find him in two games in the same week."[10]

Hawke started Game Four of the Temple Cup Championship for Baltimore against the New York Giants in the fall of 1894.[11] The wear and tear on his arm from the regular season possibly contributed to his giving up nine hits and four runs in just four innings. Kid Gleason took over in the fifth inning, and the hot-hitting Giants scored 11 more runs on their way to a four-game sweep of the Orioles.

Hawke notified the Orioles in the spring of 1895 that he would not report to the team until he received a raise in his salary. Because this had become a yearly ritual, Baltimore's management was not unduly alarmed. But this time was different; Hawke had suffered a severely broken wrist when he fell off a horse about a week before he was scheduled to report to the team. Keeping the injury under wraps, he hoped to buy himself some recuperating time by prolonging his contract negotiations. By early June the Orioles were ready to meet Hawke's demands, but his wrist still had not healed sufficiently so he had no choice other than to make the Orioles aware of his injury.

While attending a game at Union Park in Baltimore on June 19, Hawke spoke to reporters about the status of his wrist injury. He said that he could barely close his hand, but he had been pitching a bit and hoped to come around in a few weeks. Unfortunately for Hawke, the broken bone never did mend correctly. The January 18, 1896, edition of *Sporting Life* reported that his wrist was going to be rebroken and set again in order for it to heal properly.

To supplement his income, Hawke went to work at a Wilmington saloon. In late March of 1996 he got a contract offer from Al Lawson, manager of the Pottsville team in the Pennsylvania State Association. But Hawke's slow recovery prevented him from joining the club. A short time later, Hawke returned to the game as a substitute umpire in the Atlantic League.

By 1898 Hawke was working at a local feed shop and still not pitching. He was an avid outdoorsman who liked hunting and fishing. He also enjoyed attending and betting on the bantam rooster fights that were held around the Wilmington area. A brief line in *Sporting Life* noted that Hawke would "walk five miles on stilts through a swamp" to watch two roosters go at it.[12]

In 1899 Hawke returned to the diamond, with the Brockton Shoemakers of the New England League. His good work in the box for the Shoemakers was noted in July: "Hawke has improved steadily since joining the team, until now he is pitching the best ball of all the pitchers. He is the speediest man in

the league. Besides having a wonderful drop ball, he is steady and seldom gives a base on balls."[13]

Hawke seemed to regain his old form, going 11-6 before the club disbanded in early August. A lifetime .230 hitter in the minors, Hawke batted .277 for Brockton with 18 hits and one home run.

After the Shoemakers folded, Hawke signed with the Albany Senators of the New York State League on August 13. The Senators won the league pennant and Hawke went 3-2 in 84 innings of work. When the New York State League season ended, he finished out the year pitching for an independent team from McClure, Pennsylvania.

Hawke started out the 1900 season with Albany. On June 30 *Sporting Life* reported that he and teammate Lem Bailey had been suspended from the team.[14] He never gained reinstatement, and his professional baseball career ended.[15]

At that time Hawke's health began to deteriorate rapidly, and on December 11, 1902, he died at his home from carcinoma at the age of 32.[16] His death certificate lists his last occupation as saloon keeper. His funeral was held on December 15 at his residence at Cedar and Brown Streets in Wilmington. Numerous friends and family along with the Wilmington Chapter of the Fraternal Order of Eagles, attended the service. Hawke's obituary in the *Wilmington News* showed him as being married, but his wife's name was not mentioned, nor were any children listed in the obituary or on the death certificate.[17] He is buried at the Brandywine and Wilmington Cemetery. During his days on the diamond, Hawke was evidently willing to share his knowledge of the game with aspiring ballplayers in the Wilmington area. Ninety-three years after his death, in 1995, he was elected to the Delaware High School Baseball Coaches Hall of Fame.

SOURCES

Newspapers consulted include the *Wilmington News*, the *Wilmington Sunday News*, *Sporting Life*, the *Baltimore American*, the *Baltimore Sun*, and the *Chestertown Transcript*.

Special thanks to Frank Russo for providing me with Bill Hawke's death certificate, Marty Payne and Reed Howard for providing information on Hawke's career, and Ben Prestianni, Wilmington Public Library Reference Department.

NOTES

1. *Baltimore Sun*, August 3, 1894: 6.
2. A line in the April 5, 1894, edition of the *Chestertown Transcript* noted that Richard (R.V.) Hawke had not yet signed with Baltimore. There are numerous other instances in newspaper accounts of Hawke's first name being given as Dick, but his given name on all documents I located was William Victor Hawke.
3. *Baltimore Sun*, July 29, 1892.
4. St. Louis owner Chris Von der Ahe was well known throughout baseball circles for issuing frivolous fines to his players for a variety of minor infractions.
5. In 1892 the composite batting average for the National League was .245. The next season, after the pitching distance had been expanded from 55 feet to 60 feet 6 inches, the batting average jumped to .280. On the pitching side, the cumulative earned-run average went from 3.28 in 1892 to 4.66 in 1893.
6. *Baltimore Sun*, May 15, 1893.
7. *Baltimore Sun*, July 3, 1893.
8. *Sporting Life*, March 31, 1894.
9. *Sporting Life*, October 6, 1894.
10. Ibid.
11. The Temple Cup tournament was a best-of-seven postseason series between the first- and second-place teams in the National League from 1894 through 1897.
12. *Sporting Life*, March 16, 1895.
13. *Sporting Life*, July 29, 1899.
14. We were unable to locate the reason for Hawke's suspension from the Albany team in 1900.
15. We found no other mention of Hawke playing professionally, but it is possible he continued to play amateur ball in the Wilmington area.
16. Carcinoma is a subtype of cancer that arises from the epithelial cells, which form the linings of the internal organs, cavities, glands, and skin.
17. The 1900 US Census lists William V. Hawke as single and living at his father's residence. Hawke was married after the census was taken; we were unable to find out his wife's first name.

BILL HAWKE'S NO-HITTER
AUGUST 16, 1893: BALTIMORE ORIOLES 5, WASHINGTON SENATORS 0, AT BOUNDARY FIELD, WASHINGTON

By Jimmy Keenan

IN THE EARLY DAYS OF BASEball, a multitude of changes occurred over time in relation to how far the pitcher stood from the batter when he released the ball. Originally, the pitcher was positioned behind a line that was 45 feet from the center of home plate. As time went on, rules changed, and the line was modified to a box that was moved back to 50 feet from home plate with the pitcher working from the back line five-and-a-half feet further back.

In 1893, the National League replaced the pitcher's box with a rubber slab 12 inches by four inches that was set in the ground 60 feet, 6 inches from the back of home plate. Batting averages had been on the decline for years and the extra distance was meant to handicap the pitcher, thus making the game more exciting. The added distance had its desired effect; more than 30 batters hit .300 or better in 1893, after nine reached the mark the previous year.

On Wednesday, August 16, 1893, Bill Hawke of the Baltimore Orioles became the first pitcher to toss a no-hitter from the new distance, defeating the Washington Senators, 5–0. Based on his lackluster major-league pitching record up to that point, the 23-year-old right-hander was an unlikely candidate to achieve this milestone. The Delaware native started out his amateur career as a catcher and third baseman. In 1890, Hawke began pitching on a fulltime basis for a team from Elkton, Maryland. He signed his first professional contract with Reading of the Pennsylvania State League in the spring of 1892 and in late July signed with the St. Louis Browns. Hawke finished out the season with the Browns, going 5–5 with a 3.70 earned-run average. St. Louis released him the next season after he was hit hard in his first start. Hawke signed with Baltimore in June and his work with the club had been creditable but not spectacular during the weeks leading up to his no-hit game.

It was a clear, humid summer day in Washington with temperatures ranging in the high 80s when the Baltimore Orioles took the field against the Washington Senators. Neither team had been setting the league on fire. Baltimore was struggling, 12 games below .500, and the Washington club, which was floundering in last place, had 33 wins and 59 losses. The game was played at Boundary Park, which was on the future site of Griffith Stadium. The umpire was Bob Emslie, who had been an outstanding pitcher, winning 32 games for Baltimore in 1884, and now in his fourth year as an umpire.

The starting pitchers were Hawke for Baltimore and Ben Stephens, who was making his debut with the Senators. Stephens had been a rising star in the Midwestern leagues before signing a major-league contract with Baltimore in July 1892. He had won 18 and lost seven for the Western League champion Columbus team before joining the Orioles. Washington's left-fielder, Charles Abbey, also made his major-league debut in this game.

Washington batted first and lead-off hitter William "Dummy" Hoy drew a base on balls off Hawke. Hoy attempted to steal second base, but Orioles catcher Wilbert Robinson threw him out. Washington's only other baserunner was catcher Duke Farrell, who walked in the fourth inning but was left stranded at second.

Hawke was backed by a number of fine defensive plays. Orioles third baseman Billy Shindle and shortstop John McGraw made a number of outstanding stops and throws that cut down batters. Hawke himself hustled over and covered first base on a sharply hit ball to first-baseman Harry Taylor. Baltimore outfielders Joe Kelley and George Treadway also made clutch grabs that helped preserve Hawke's no-hit bid.

The Orioles scored two runs in the second inning. George Treadway singled and advanced to second on a passed ball by Farrell. Jim Long sacrificed Treadway to third and he scored on a single by second baseman Heinie Reitz. The next hitter, Wilbert Robinson, drilled a groundball that caromed off Washington shortstop Joe Sullivan and ended up in center field. Reitz advanced to third. Hawke hit a sacrifice fly to center that sent Reitz home.

Stephens settled down after that and the Orioles didn't score again until the eighth inning. Shindle reached on an error by Washington second baseman Cub Stricker and Taylor walked. Both runners scored when Jim Long smashed a double to left field, and Reitz followed with a double to right that plated Long.

Stephens deserved a kinder fate, working all nine innings, allowing seven hits and just two earned runs. The 25-year-old struck out two (the first two batters he faced), walked two, and uncorked a wild pitch. Stephens also went winless in his next five starts, and was released after appearing in three games for the Senators in 1894. He returned to the minors and pitched for the Milwaukee Brewers of the Western League for two seasons before dying of tuberculosis at the age of 28 on August 5, 1896.

Hawke's sinkerball kept the Senators off-balance for the entire game. He struck out six and walked two. Hawke finished the 1893 campaign with an 11–17 record (including one loss with St. Louis). He hit his stride the next season, going 16–9 for the National League champion Orioles. *Sporting Life* said of him on October 6, 1894, "He is what is called a 'phenom' and pitches a very swift, puzzling ball, difficult to fathom." Unfortunately for Hawke, he suffered a broken wrist before the start of the 1895 season and never won another major-league game. He made a short-lived comeback in the minors in 1899 but was never the same pitcher. Like his pitching opponent on August 16, 1893, Hawke died young, a victim of cancer at the age of 32 on December 11, 1902.

This essay was originally published in Bill Felber, ed., Inventing Baseball: The 100 Greatest Games of the 19th Century *(Phoenix: Society for American Baseball Research, 2013).*

SOURCES

Baseball-reference.com

Thorn, John, Phil Birnbaum, Bill Deane, *et al.*, eds. *Total Baseball: The Ultimate Baseball Encyclopedia.* 8th ed. (Toronto: Sport Media Publishing, Inc., 2004).

Baltimore Morning Herald, August 17, 1893.

Baltimore Sun, August 17, 1893.

The Sporting Life, October 6, 1894: 4.

Washington Evening Star, August 17, 1893: 3.

NIXEY CALLAHAN

By James E. Elfers

THOUGH KNOWN TODAY AS "Nixey" Callahan, the slim, 5-feet-10, 180-pound, right-handed jack of all trades rarely used that moniker during his big league days. Nixey was a childhood nickname that Jimmy largely left behind when his baseball skills took him from his native Fitchburg, Massachusetts to the pinnacle of the sport —although the local papers continued to use "Nixey" throughout his life. The child of Irish immigrants, born on March 18, 1874, James Joseph Callahan, Jr lost his father at age 15. A year before that, he was already helping to support his mother Margaret and his two sisters. At 14, he entered the local clothing mills. Though a certificate in his scrapbook indicates that Jimmy qualified for high school, it is unclear if he ever attended a secondary institution.[1] For 75 cents a day, he toiled as a "bobbin boy." It was dusty, dangerous work that might have ruined the lad had he not proved more valuable to his employer on the baseball diamond.

Something of a prodigy on the sandlot, Jimmy began playing for his company team while in his mid-teens. Even at that age he was outclassing the locals. Over the next two years, his reputation and abilities increased. At age 16, about the same time as he had apprenticed to a local plumber, Jimmy's professional career essentially began. He was promised a dollar if he won a game against another local team. Jimmy won the game, pocketed the dollar, and was soon hurling regularly for the semiprofessional team in Pepperell, Massachusetts. Because the plumber frowned on moonlighting, Jimmy played under the inventive alias of William Smith.

"Smith's" chicanery went undiscovered for three years. Jimmy was found out, however, and dismissed from his apprenticeship. That really was no hardship, because by this point he was earning between $30 and $40 a game pitching for Pepperell, his high point being the recording of 22 strikeouts in a single game.

At the age of 19, he was spotted by Arthur Irwin, manager of the Philadelphia Phillies. Irwin signed Callahan and brought him south. Jumping directly to the Phillies lineup in 1894, he appeared in nine games, compiling a 1-2 record with a terrible 9.89 ERA. "They didn't pay me enough salary to wreck them or make me," Callahan later joked to John J. Ward of *Baseball Magazine*. "That way they could afford to take a chance with such a green youth as myself. I pitched a few games but I wasn't a Walter Johnson with speed or a Christy Mathewson with skill so at the end of the season they decided that Philly would muddle along as best it could without my services. In short, they wished me well, propelled me gently through the door and carefully closed the door in my face. I was alone in the wide world."[2]

What would have been a moment of profound doubt and loss of self-esteem to most rookies became a bolt of inspiration for Jimmy Callahan. Realizing there were plenty of jobs to be had in the minor leagues, he wrote a letter to the Springfield (Massachusetts) Ponies of the Eastern League informing them that he "was a player of rare promise."[3] The ploy worked and he was given a starting position on the team.

Jimmy certainly lived up to his own billing, winning 32 out of the 41 games he started, helping Springfield to the pennant. When not pitching, Callahan played the outfield and second base. Kansas City of the Western League drafted Jimmy off of Springfield's roster in 1896. He lasted one season with the Blues before being bought by the Chicago Colts of the National League prior to the 1897 season. Callahan impressed the Colts not only with his pitching, but also with his running ability, despite the fact that he rarely stole bases.

Perhaps the best thing for Jimmy in joining the Chicago Colts was his teammate and life-long friend Clark Griffith. Callahan adapted his pitching motion

and style to resemble that of the "The Old Fox." It was just what the young player needed. Jimmy's confidence and abilities swelled under the instruction of the veteran. Like Griffith, he also relied heavily on his defense, never posting more than 77 strikeouts in an individual season. Callahan pitched well, but the Colts were not going anyplace in the standings.

The collapse of the American Association had created a bloated 12-team National League as the only game in town. The Colts could make little headway in such a congested league, finishing each season respectably but well out of first place. As the new century dawned, baseball was about to undergo a revolution and Jimmy determined to be a part of it. Of the nascent American League of 1900, Jimmy said, "I thought I had a special call to go to the American League. I was not under contract but, of course, I was held by the reserve rule. This rule is a good thing for baseball all right, just as the law that it's wrong to take human life is a good and necessary thing, but in war time that very rule may be reversed, and so it is in baseball war. I figured that if anybody had been specially appointed to look after my interests his name was Callahan. I figured that if Callahan didn't look after my interests there was something wrong with his noodle. So I told him to get busy."

"I decided with myself that Mr. Comiskey looked like a white man of large ambition and good prospects. I was getting X dollars with the Cubs. Comiskey offered me X plus Y dollars. I compared the two salaries and found that one would buy more collars and shirts than the other. While never noted as a mathematician in my school studies my mind was able to grasp that salient fact. So I decided to change my Sox, putting on the more or less white ones that Comiskey furnished, and was duly

branded as a rebel, traitor and undesirable citizen by the National League after the accepted manner of baseball tradition."[4]

Led by Griffin and Callahan the White Sox won the first American League pennant, though in 1900, the league was still considered outlaw and minor. It was no longer minor the following year but it was still treated as an outlaw by the National League. Unfortunately for Callahan, his actual appearance in the newly organized American League in 1901 was delayed for a few weeks due to a broken bone in his forearm. Post-recovery, he compiled a sparkling 15-8 record with a 2.42 ERA. He was just as impressive at the plate, where the right-handed batter hit a career-best .331 for the season, with 11 extra-base hits in 132 plate appearances. The combination of Griffith and Callahan on the pitching mound helped Chicago win a second consecutive American League pennant, taking the flag by four games over the Boston Americans.

The following season, Callahan slumped to a 16-14 mark with a subpar 3.60 ERA. But he also pitched the best game of his career, a no-hitter against the Detroit Tigers on September 20. In what marked his final hurrah as a major-league pitcher, Callahan set down the Tigers in just one hour and 20 minutes, becoming the first American Leaguer to toss a no-hitter. Named manager of the White Sox the following season, Callahan pitched in just three games in 1903, posting a mediocre 4.50 ERA. Callahan transitioned to third base, where he registered a poor .895 fielding percentage but batted a solid .292. Under

Callahan's leadership the Sox finished a disappointing seventh.

Callahan remained Chicago's manager for the first 42 games of the 1904 season before he was replaced by Fielder Jones. Nonetheless, he went on to play in 132 games for the White Sox that year, batting .261 and splitting his time between left field and second base. In 1905 he appeared in 96 games, mostly in left field, and finished the year with a .272 average and 26 steals

Callahan's career path in baseball then took a very unusual trajectory, as he related in his inimitable style. "It was in 1906 I decided that Comiskey was drawing down his ten or twelve dollars every week (or it may have been fourteen) and was laying by a few shekels in the bank for a rainy day. In other words, he was getting fat around the waist line and every year brought a bulge in his bank account. I felt that I had given him five good years and that it was about time I began to work for James Callahan. Callahan might not be as good a man to work for as Comiskey but I was more interested in his welfare and the thought occurred to me that it wouldn't be a bad plan if he had a bank account himself."[5]

Thus began his career as semipro magnate, the sandlot king of Chicago He bought the Logan Squares semipro team and their stadium at the corner of Diversey and Milwaukee in the Logan Square section of Chicago. The club very quickly established itself as one of the finest if not the premier semipro baseball team in the country. Often called "Callahan's Logan Squares," [6] Callahan's club beat both participants in after the conclusion of the 1906 World Series, the White Sox and Cubs, although the team's "semipro" lineup was augmented by several major leaguers, some of whom played under assumed names.

Callahan's business venture did not endear him to organized baseball. The Logan Squares were declared "outlaws" by Ban Johnson and major-league teams faced fines or censure if they played the Logan Squares. Walter Johnson was once fined $100 for pitching in an exhibition game against them. Such machinations did little to curb the enthusiasm Chicago had for the local boys. On August 27, 1910, Callahan's club won the first night game ever played at Comiskey Park, defeating the Rogers Park semipro club, 3-0, under portable lights, with Callahan himself driving in two of the three runs. Callahan amassed quite a nice bit of money in his role as stadium owner and team president.

After a few years, however, attendance started to lag and Callahan began looking for an opportunity to get back into organized baseball. He ran into Comiskey during the winter of 1910. "Commy" offered him the job of president of the White Sox but Callahan, then nearing 37 years of age, convinced him that he was not through as a player. To return to the majors, he had to get his name cleared from the ineligible list. This was accomplished by paying a fine of $700. His return to baseball in 1911 was one of the era's most remarkable comeback stories. In a season Callahan considered his best in the major leagues, he played left field and hit .281 in 120 games, while also posting career highs in hits (131), home runs (3), RBIs (60), and stolen bases (45). Not bad for a man who had been out of the majors for five years.

During the offseason he added stage performer to his repertoire, taking a turn in front of the flood lights in Chicago as a monologist. His specialty was telling funny Irish stories, complete with the brogue. It wasn't great theater, but it satisfied his audience. Ring Lardner noted, "Jimmy Callahan tells Irish Stories admirably and deserves the laughs he gets."[7]

So impressed was Comiskey with Callahan's on-field performance in 1911 that he re-appointed him manager of the club in 1912. The team finished in fourth place that year with a 78-76 record, and Jimmy, in his last full season as a player, batted .272 in 111 games. The following year, manager Callahan confined himself to the bench for all but six games, and the White Sox again won 78 games, though the club dropped to fifth place.

From October 1913 to March 1914 Callahan's White Sox and the New York Giants took their baseball teams on a world exhibition tour. Along with Comiskey and McGraw, Callahan was a major force behind the tour, putting up an undisclosed amount of money to help pay the teams' traveling expenses. The teams barnstormed across the United States then set out for Japan, China, Hong Kong, the Philippines, Australia, Sri Lanka, Egypt, Italy, France, and Great Britain, with a personal side trip to Ireland. As far as Callahan was concerned the best parts of the tour were the teams' visit with the Pope and the game in London, played before 20,000 fans, including King George V.

The tour was wearying, however, and the White Sox got off to a flat start in 1914 and finished the year a disappointing tied for sixth. Just before Christmas 1914, Callahan was bumped up to the White Sox front office to make room for Eddie Collins, whom Comiskey had just acquired, to serve as player-manager. (Collins didn't want the job, however; it later ended up going to Pants Rowland.) The Pirates selected Callahan as manager in 1916. He led the team to a sixth-place finish. Callahan was dismissed midway through the 1917 season with the Buccos mired in last place.

Following his baseball career, Callahan became one of Chicago's most successful contractors, building the entire waterworks for the Great Lakes Naval Station. On October 4, 1934, Callahan died of natural causes while visiting friends in Boston. Survived by his wife, the former Josephine Hardin, two sons, and a daughter, Callahan was buried in St. Bernard's Cemetery in his hometown of Fitchburg.

SOURCES

In addition to the sources cited in the Notes, the author consulted Baseball-Reference,com, Callahan's obituaries in the *Chicago Tribune* and *New York Times*, and the following:

"Who's Who on the Diamond," *Baseball Magazine*, May, 1909.

Lee, Bill. *The Baseball Necrology* (Jefferson, North Carolina: McFarland, 2003).

McGlynn, Frank. "*Striking Scenes from the Tour Around the World*," *Baseball Magazine*, August 1914 to December 1915.

Assorted clippings from Callahan's personal scrap book provided by Don Bunce of Arlington Heights, Illinois. He is Callahan's foster grandson and the closest thing to a living relative Jimmy Callahan has. All three of Callahan's natural children have passed on and all were childless. Don was very giving of his time during a visit to Chicago as well.

NOTES

1 Jimmy Callahan's personal scrapbook

2 John J. Ward, "Callahan, The Cast Off Manager," *Baseball Magazine*, August 1916.

3 Ibid.

4 Ibid

5 Ibid

6 Undated clipping in Jimmy Callahan's scrap book. "Callahan's Logan Squares" recounting the history of the team

7 Ring Lardner, "The Biggest Bugs In Baseball," *Baseball Magazine*, January 1912: 36.

WHITE SOX WIN AND TIE
SEPTEMBER 20, 1902: CHICAGO WHITE SOX 3, DETROIT TIGERS 0, AT SOUTH SIDE PARK, CHICAGO

By James E. Elfers

WHEN SEVENTH-PLACE teams visit fourth-place teams in the third week of September, they usually hope to play the role of spoiler. As such, the Detroit Tigers hoped to vanquish the Chicago White Sox in at least one game of a scheduled doubleheader. The American League pennant had already been claimed by Connie Mack's Philadelphia Athletics. The White Sox were determined to remain in fourth and maintain their hold on the first division.

Abysmal weather, which had marred the entire 1902 American League schedule, made its presence known this day as well. Gray clouds hung overhead, threatening showers that would deliver rain on Sunday, and the temperature never exceeded 55 degrees. A steady wind also blew out of the south. It was the kind of raw, dour day that put everyone's minds on thoughts of next spring. Despite the threatening skies, a healthy crowd of 3,300 passed through the gates of South Side Park. Chicago had taken a shine to Comiskey's team in a big way and wanted to bid them a fond adieu. Just four home games remained in the season.

The game promised to be interesting. The Tigers starter, 21-year-old Aloysius Jerome "Wish" Egan, of Evart, Michigan, was in only his second big-league game. He had impressed in a 5-3 loss to the Athletics on September 3. The 6-foot-3, 185-pound right-handed hurler would be facing off against 5-foot-10, 180-pound right-handed pitcher James Joseph "Nixey" Callahan.

Jimmy Callahan had thus far compiled a 15-12 record for the season, fairly undistinguished for him; in most years he racked up twice as many wins as losses. Callahan was a control pitcher who modeled his delivery on that of teammate and friend Clark Griffith. Like many of the pitchers of that era, including stars such as Christy Mathewson, he was content to have the men behind him do the job of recording outs. Strikeouts just weren't his bag.

Portly, walrus-mustached home-plate umpire Jack Sheridan, who spent the offseason as a mortician, settled himself and his massive chest protector behind catcher Ed McFarland, currently in his 10th season. He was virtually the same height and weight as his batterymate.

As with a fair number of other American League players, a legal cloud clung to McFarland. Rejecting the reserve clause of the National League, he had jumped from the Phillies to the White Sox at the beginning of 1902. The Phillies sued to try to retain his services. McFarland was in such a legal quagmire that when the White Sox journeyed to Philadelphia on June 3, both he and Wiley Piatt, who had jumped from the Phils to the White Sox in 1901, were left behind in Chicago, lest the Phillies' lawsuit-happy owner, Colonel John Rogers, find some legal chicanery to keep the players in the City of Brotherly Love and force them back into the Phillies fold.[1]

No one on either end of the battery put in much effort. Callahan set the first three Tiger batters, Dick Harley, combative Kid Elberfeld, and the slight Jimmy Barrett, down in order. Jimmy made his way off the mound hoping for some early support.

That is just what happened. Singing Sammy Strang immediately took it to the tall rookie by firing a hot single past third. Fielder Jones followed, fouling out. Danny Green punched a single through, sending Strang to third. George Davis tripled to deep left field, plating two runs. Sam Mertes became the inning's second foul out. Tom Daly's grounder should have ended the inning, but shortstop Kid Elberfeld made a wild toss past first, sending Davis home. Those three runs would be all that Callahan would need.

Callahan's perfect first five had their share of drama. Lew McAllister left off the second with a nasty grounder on which Davis at shortstop made a spectacular grab. In the fourth, Elberfeld smashed a wicked liner that knocked down third baseman Strang. Saving the day again was Davis, who retrieved the ball in time to nail Kid at first.

The sixth frame was Callahan's most troublesome. John O'Connell whiffed, Callahan's first K. Jim McGuire grounded to Davis, but the shortstop's spectacular play to this point was marred when his toss to first went wide of the bag. Behind the plate, McFarland allowed a costly passed ball, giving McGuire second. Wish Egan tried to aid his own cause; his groundout sent McGuire to third. That would be the high-water mark for Detroit. Dick Harley popped out to crotchety Frank Isbell at first, dousing the flames.

The seventh began with Callahan's first walk—to Kid Elberfeld. Jimmy Barrett grounded to shortstop Davis for a force out and Lew McAlister flied out to Fielder Jones in center. Joe Yeager received Callahan's second and final walk. Pete LePine ended the inning with a grounder to first that was handled by Isbell, who lobbed the ball to Callahan.

To his considerable credit, Wish Egan had little trouble with the White Sox after that first inning. His biggest spot of trouble occurred in the fifth. Pitcher Callahan was safe at first on Elberfeld's second error. Sammy Strang went to first on Egan's first walk. Usually reliable Fielder Jones and Danny Green produced consecutive outs, but George Davis delivered a single that loaded the bases. The inning ended when Dick Harley made a running catch of Sam Mertes' very long drive to left center.

The only other time the White Sox came close to scoring again was the eighth. George Davis got Egan's second walk; two outs later, he tried to score on a nifty double by Frank Isbell but was out at the plate when Quebec-born Peter LePine, in right field, made an equally nifty throw to McGuire.

The eighth found Jimmy Callahan in firm control. Tigers first baseman John O'Connell hit one to right, where it was flagged by Danny Green. Jim McGuire sent a dribbler to third for the second out, and Wish Egan lived up to the reputation of pitchers as hitters by becoming Callahan's second and final strikeout victim.

Callahan's ninth frame mirrored his first. Harley led off with a pop out to third, Elberfeld lofted a fly to Mertes in left, and when Barrett hit a grounder to third, Strang tossed the ball to Callahan, who tagged first, recording the final out of the first no-hitter in the American League. Technically, one had been tossed on Opening Day two years before, by Doc Amole. However, the American League at that time was not considered more than a glorified minor league.

The game consumed a brisk one hour and 20 minutes.

One question that cannot be answered at this remove is whether the fans at South Side Park really appreciated how momentous the event they had just witnessed was. No-hitters were not unknown, but they did not seem to inspire the same intensity of focus as one does today. In a media-driven age when cable, radio, satellite, and the Internet flash word of no-hitters in progress to every interested eye and ear on the planet, the understated reaction to Callahan's no-hitter seems positively surreal. The *St. Paul Globe*'s coverage on September 21, 1902, was a succinct piece of understatement: "Callahan was in rare form in the first game today and accomplished the unusual feat of shutting out his opponents without the semblance of a hit."[2] With just one more sentence describing how the White Sox scored all of their runs in the first inning, the newspaper's coverage of the first American League no-hitter closed.

Even the local papers were sedate. The *Chicago Tribune* offered no banner headlines, not much heralding at all, Under the main headline, "White Sox Win And Tie," was a subhead that said simply, "Callahan Pitches No Hit Game In First

Contest."3 With that, Chicago's largest newspaper moved on to what it considered the far more important event of the day—the parade of 200 local baseball clubs before the game and "the presentation of a handsome fishing outfit" to Charles Comiskey.

Lost in the milestone's glare, this was the second no-hitter of catcher McFarland's career. The conclusion of the twin bill was decidedly underwhelming, a 3-3 tie called on account of darkness. Saving the best for last, Callahan effectively concluded his career as a pitcher. He won his last season outing, for a 16-14 record. In 1903 he appeared in just three games, his ERA swelling ominously. Jimmy, who at one point had played every position except catcher, and was a fairly good hitter, transitioned to becoming a position player, spending most of his subsequent time at third base and second base.

NOTES

1 Bill Nowlin, "Ed McFarland," SABR BioProject, sabr.org/bioproj/person/0826b933.

2 "One Shutout and One Tie," *St. Paul Globe*, September 21, 1903: 8.

3 *Chicago Sunday Tribune*, September 21, 1902: 9.

EARL HAMILTON

By Paul Hofmann

EARL HAMILTON, SAD SAM Jones, and Ken Holtzman. What do these three pitchers have in common? Hamilton, Jones, and Holtzman are the only three major-league pitchers to pitch a no-hitter without striking out a single batter. Hamilton was the first to achieve the feat when he no-hit Ty Cobb and the Detroit Tigers on August 30, 1912.

Earl Hamilton was an undersized, free-spirited southpaw who pitched for the St. Louis Browns (1911-17), Detroit Tigers (1916), Pittsburgh Pirates (1918-1923), and Philadelphia Phillies (1924) in a major-league career that spanned 14 years. Hamilton's career can be divided into two distinct periods: the pre-World War I years spent with the St. Louis Browns and a career revival with the Pittsburgh Pirates.

Earl Andrew Hamilton was born in Gibson City, Illinois, on July 19, 1891. He was the fourth child born to Albert and Ida (Merritt) Hamilton. US census records identify Albert as a postmaster and Ida as a homemaker and mother of eight children.[1] The family moved to Oswego, Kansas, when Earl was young and he lived there for much of his major-league career.[2]

Hamilton began his journey in Organized Baseball as a 17-year-old in 1909 with the Springfield Midgets of the Class-C Western Association. He showed great promise as he made 24 appearances and finished with a 13-9 record. His 13 victories ranked second on the Midgets behind Marc Hall's 19.

The tandem teamed up again on the Western Association's Joplin Miners in 1910. The Miners were widely considered one of the strongest minor-league teams of the era. They posted a record of 90-34 (.726) and won the Western Association pennant by a whopping 22½ games.[3] The team's seven-man pitching staff was bolstered by five hurlers, including Hall, who would eventually make it to the majors. Hamilton appeared in a team-high 36 games on his way to earning 19 victories against 8 defeats. By this time the 5-foot-8, 160-pound Hamilton had attracted the attention of the St. Louis Browns brass.

Coming off a dismal 1910 season in which the team used 20 different pitchers and finished with a 47-107 record, the Browns needed pitchers who could eat innings and get major-league hitters out. They turned to the 19-year-old Hamilton to help remedy their pitching woes. Hamilton made his major-league debut on April 14, 1911, when he came on in relief of Lefty George in a 7-5 loss to Cleveland. Ten days later Hamilton made his first start and absorbed his first loss, a 7-6 defeat at the hands of the Detroit Tigers at Detroit's Bennett Park. On April 29 Hamilton earned his first major-league victory with a 1-0 shutout of the White Sox in Chicago. Overall, his rookie campaign was a struggle and he finished with a 5-12 record and a 3.97 ERA. The Browns were no better and finished 45-107, two wins shy of the team's total victories in 1910.

Hamilton established himself as a mainstay in the Browns' pitching rotation in 1912. Trimming his ERA to 3.24, Hamilton led the Browns in innings pitched (249⅔) and strikeouts (a career-high 139) on his way to posting an 11-14 record. On August 30 he wrote his name in the annals of baseball history in indelible ink when he no-hit the Detroit Tigers at Navin Field to become the first St. Louis Browns pitcher to author a no-hitter. The feat carried added significance; it was the first no-strikeout no-hitter in major-league history.

Hamilton recorded his only winning record with the Browns in 1913. He pitched in 31 games, 24 as a starter, and posted a 13-12 record. Despite making his final appearance of the season on August 8, Hamilton managed to toss 19 complete games, three shutouts, and two one-hitters on his way to recording a 2.57 ERA. At the ripe young age of 22, his stock was clearly on the rise and it was widely reported that the Philadelphia Athletics' Connie Mack had interest in signing Hamilton for the coming season.[4]

Before the 1914 season the upstart Federal League began raiding major-league rosters in an effort to challenge the senior and junior circuits' monopoly on major-league status. Hamilton was one of the players targeted by the Federal League's Kansas City Packers. On April 9 he accompanied former teammate and now Packers player-manager George Stovall to Kansas City after signing a three-year, $21,000 contract with the club, which included a $5,000 cash bonus. This infuriated the Browns and elicited a strong response from team president Robert Hedges. Hedges declared, "You can say for me that President Johnson, the American League, the National Commission, and organized baseball in general will never permit Earl Hamilton to play with the Kansas City Federals."[5] AL President Ban Johnson himself responded by stating, "The American League will stop Hamilton if it takes every dollar in the treasury. He signed a most liberal three-year contract with the St. Louis Browns, and nothing will be left undone to check him for his willful violation of his contract."[6]

Hamilton's association with Federal League, like that of many of his major-league colleagues, was short-lived, as he began to get cold feet. On the eve of the season opener, Hamilton took the train to Oswego under the pretense of visiting family. Instead, he met there with the Browns' owner and agreed to return to St. Louis. A disappointed Stovall reacted by telling the *Kansas City Times*, "I can go out and get these ball players, but I can't chain 'em down."[7] Hamilton had become a "double jumper."[8]

Hamilton's initial desertion of the Browns and subsequent flip-flop back to the club was followed by bitter accusations between the feuding parties and ultimately the filing of a lawsuit by the Packers against him. The suit charged Hamilton with violating his contract and sought $25,000 in damages from the hurler to compensate for the "great loss" the club suffered by his return to the Browns. The petition explained the loss by stating, "He is a wonderful pitcher and a great draw."[9]

The 1914 season was one of Hamilton's finest in the majors. He pitched in 44 games for the Browns, starting 35 and completing a career-high 20 while recording five shutouts. He finished the season with a 16-18 mark and a 2.50 ERA for a Browns club that finished in fifth place with a record of 71-82. The season personified Hamilton's years with the Browns. While he was generally considered one of the better left-handed pitchers in the American League during these years, playing for a team that typically ranked near the bottom in batting average, runs scored, and fielding did not result in the number of wins one might expect.

Hamilton made headlines after the 1914 season when a car he was driving, with five female passengers, was involved in a predawn single-car accident on the Eads Bridge in St. Louis. Hamilton was badly injured, suffering a fractured arm, broken ribs, a broken collarbone, and facial lacerations. The left-hander was hospitalized for nearly two weeks and it was originally feared that his pitching career might be over. All five passengers were also seriously injured, and one died from her injuries.[10]

Recovered from his injuries, Hamilton reported to spring training in March 1915 and declared his left arm fit for duty. He made three starts to start the season before being suspended indefinitely and fined $500 on May 7 for "alleged misbehavior off the field" that led to a heated exchange with Browns manager Branch Rickey.[11] After a three-week period in which he continued to "assiduously" work out with the Browns each morning, he was reinstated.[12] Rickey's eagerness to welcome any winning equation to his pitching staff helped secure Hamilton another chance. Hamilton finished the 1915 season with a record of 9-17 and an ERA of 2.87.

Hamilton started the 1916 season with the Browns and made a single relief appearance for the club before the Tigers "purchased" his contract off waivers on May 29. In reality Tigers manager Hughie Jennings agreed to take Hamilton on a trial basis for a period to determine if he was worth the stipulated price of $7,500.[13] Hamilton made five starts for the Tigers, finishing with a mark of 1-2 with a respectable 2.65 ERA. Though he posted an ERA more than a third of a run better than the Tigers' 1916 team ERA, Jennings decided the waiver price was too high and instead St. Louis claimed him back off waivers from the Tigers.[14] Hamilton finished the 1916 campaign with St. Louis, going 5-7 with a 3.05 ERA.

The 1917 season was Hamilton's last with the Browns. The left-hander failed to win a game, finishing 0-9, despite posting a relatively average ERA of 3.14. Before the start of the 1918 season, Hamilton was sold to the Pittsburgh Pirates. The 26-year-old's career with the Browns was over. His seven-year totals with the Browns were modest in light of the promise his career had held at the start. He finished with a mark of 59-89 and a 3.00 ERA.

Hamilton thrived in his new environment and for the first month of the season enjoyed the best stretch of his career. He made six starts for the Pirates, all complete-game victories. In 54 innings he yielded just five earned runs. He finished 6-0 with a 0.83 ERA. But in May, with the World War I "work-or-fight" order in effect, he enlisted in the Navy.

In previewing the 1919 season, *Spalding's Official Base Ball Guide* speculated that Pittsburgh might have won the pennant in 1918 had Hamilton been available for the entire season. While it is inconceivable that he could have single-handedly closed the 17-game gap between the first-place Chicago Cubs and fourth-place Pirates, the return from the war of Hamilton and other Pirates regulars increased expectations among the Pittsburgh faithful.

But both Hamilton and the Pirates took a step back in 1919. Hamilton's setback started in spring training when the southpaw reportedly suffered from a bad cold and a loss of appetite that resulted in a 15-pound weight loss from the time training camp opened.¹⁵ He didn't make his first start of the season until April 27 and pitched in only 28 games, finishing the year with an 8-11 record and a 3.31 ERA.

Hamilton had a resurgent 1920 season. His 230⅓ innings pitched were the most he had thrown since 1914. He pitched 16⅓ of these innings in a single game when he squared off with the New York Giants' Rube Benton in a marathon pitchers' duel on July 16. Both pitchers held their opposition scoreless for 16 innings. But in the 17th inning Hamilton got only one out before surrendering seven earned runs and being relieved by Wilbur Cooper.¹⁶ Benton retired the Pirates in the 17th to secure the win. Hamilton recorded only a single strikeout in his 16⅓ innings of work. He finished the season with a 10-13 mark.

The 1921 season brought a renewed optimism to the Pirates. Along with Wilbur Cooper, Whitely Glazner, Babe Adams, and Johnny Morrison, Hamilton formed the nucleus of the rotation that would lead the Pirates to a second-place finish, four games behind the pennant-winning New York Giants. This was the closest Hamilton would ever get to the World Series. He started 30 games for the Pirates that season and finished with a record of 13-15 and a 3.36 ERA.

Love was in the air during the spring of 1922. On May 11 newspapers reported that Hamilton was engaged to marry Edna Noonan of Alexandria, Minnesota. The announcement traced the start of the romance to the Pirates' spring training in Hot Springs, Arkansas.¹⁷ On the mound, meanwhile, Hamilton enjoyed only the third (and final) winning season of his career. Despite an ERA that had grown to 3.99, largely due to the new livelier ball, the now 31-year-old posted 11 victories against 7 defeats.

Hamilton made 28 appearances and 15 starts for the Pirates in 1923. The 141 innings he pitched were his lowest total since his abbreviated 1918 season. He finished his final full season in the majors at 7-9 with a 3.77 ERA. In his six-year stint with the Pirates he was 55-55 with a 3.35 ERA.

In December of 1923 the Philadelphia Phillies claimed Hamilton off waivers from the Pirates. The Phillies were coming off a disastrous last-place finish that saw the team win only 50 games and finish 45½ games behind the first-place Giants. Unbeknownst to the Phillies, Hamilton's days as a major-league pitcher where behind him. He struggled in three appearances in early May before being released.

His major-league career over, Hamilton finished the 1924 season and spent the entire 1925 season with the Minneapolis Millers of the American Association. In 1926 and 1927 he pitched for the Los Angeles Angels of the Pacific Coast League, notching 24 and 7 victories respectively. At the age of 41, Hamilton returned to the Joplin Miners, now in the Class-A Western League, for his last season as a player in Organized Baseball. Pitching against players averaging more than 15 years younger, he finished with a record of 6-7.

In 20 professional seasons, Hamilton finished with a combined record of 195-213. At the major-league level, the diminutive left-hander logged 2,342⅔ innings and posted a career record of 115-147 with a 3.16 ERA. As of 2016 his 115 victories ranked fourth behind Jesse Tannehill (197), Dolf Luque (194), and Bobby Shantz (119) for pitchers who were 5-feet-8 and shorter.

Hamilton remained active in baseball as a minor-league manager, scout, and club owner. Later in life he moved to Anaheim, California, and opened a lumberyard.¹⁸ He died of emphysema at Memorial Hospital in Anaheim on November 17, 1968, and is buried in Anaheim's Melrose Abbey Cemetery. He was survived by his second wife, Clyde Mae Hamilton, who died in 1985.

NOTES

1 US Census, 1900.

2 Kansas Historical Society, kshs.org.

3 Bill Weiss and Marshall Wright, "Top 100 Teams." Retrieved from milb.com/milb/history/top100.jsp?idx=66.

4 "Topics of the Sport World," *Ekalaka* (Montana) *Eagle*, September 26, 1913.

5 "Federal Raid on St. Louis Browns," *New York Times*, April 10, 1914.

6 "Earl Hamilton, Pitcher, Taken by Federals," *Harrisburg* (Pennsylvania) *Telegraph*, April 13, 1914.

NO-HITTERS

7 Peter Grathoff, "Long-Forgotten KC Packers Will Take Center Stage at Wrigley Field for Centennial," *Kansas City Star*, April 22, 2014.

8 Steve Steinberg, "Robert Hedges," sabr.org/bioproj/person/b91246d7.

9 "Pitcher Hamilton Sued for $25,000," *New York Times*, April 17, 1914.

10 "Pitcher Hamilton Hurt," *New York Times*, October 11, 1914.

11 "Earl Hamilton Suspended," *Pittsburg Press*, May 7, 1915.

12 "Earl Hamilton Is Reinstated," *Pittsburg Press*, May 30, 1915.

13 "Earl Hamilton May Be Returned to St. Louis, "*Pittsburg Press*, June 23, 1916.

14 Earl Hamilton, baseball-reference.com.

15 "Earl Hamilton Is on Invalid List: Star Southpaw Can't Eat and Has Lost Fifteen Pounds Since Reporting at Camp," *Pittsburgh Press*, April 4, 1919.

16 Frank Jackson, "No Runs, No Hits, No Strikeouts," hardballtimes.com/no-runs-no-hits-no-strikeouts/.

17 "Local Baseball Star Is Engaged to Marry," *Pittsburgh Press*, May 11, 1922.

18 Paul Batesel, *Major League Baseball Players of 1916: A Biographical Dictionary* (Jefferson, North Carolina: McFarland & Co., 2007), 67.

THE FIRST NO-STRIKEOUT NO-HIT GAME

AUGUST 30, 1912
ST. LOUIS BROWNS 5, DETROIT TIGERS 1, AT NAVIN FIELD, DETROIT

By Paul Hofmann

THE DETROIT TIGERS played in Bennett Field in 1911. Immediately after the last game of the 1911 season, the small wooden structure was demolished and replaced with a $300,000 steel and concrete ballpark named Navin Field after the club's owner, Frank Navin. Navin Field officially opened its doors to Tigers fans on April 20, 2012.[1]

Given the fact that Navin Field had been open for less than four months, it could easily be assumed that visiting pitcher Earl Hamilton's gem on August 30 was the first no-hitter thrown at Navin Field. However, this honor went to the Tigers' George Mullin. Mullin, who recorded 209 victories for the Tigers in 12 years with the club, celebrated his 32nd birthday by pitching a no-hitter during the second game of a doubleheader against the St. Louis Browns on July 4, 1912. The Browns returned to Detroit on August 30 and Hamilton tossed the second no-hitter in Navin Field history. Though the two games were separated by 57 days of travel and baseball, they were consecutive games in the season series between the Tigers and Browns.

Although Navin Field was constructed with a capacity of 23,000 to accommodate the growing numbers of fans, only 2,150 spectators were on hand on the 30th. Unseasonably cool temperatures and a matchup between two second-division clubs may have kept some fans away. The temperature in Detroit that Friday afternoon topped out at 70 degrees[2] and the fifth-place Tigers and last-place Browns entered the game 29 and 45 games off the pace respectively.

Earl Hamilton entered the game with an 8-11 mark for the Browns, managed by George Stovall. He was opposed by the Tigers' Jean Dubuc, who brought a record of 16-8 into the tilt. A native of Vermont, Dubuc was enjoying run support from his teammates to the tune of 5.65 runs per nine innings and on his way to a career-best 17-10 mark. The right-hander pitched for the Cincinnati Reds, Detroit Tigers, Boston Red Sox, and New York Giants during a nine-year major-league career and finished with record of 84-76 with a 3.04 ERA.

The Browns jumped on the Tigers' Dubuc quickly. With one out in the top of the first, left fielder Pete Compton reached on a hit and came around to score on right fielder Gus Williams's double to stake Hamilton to a 1-0 lead. The Browns added a pair of runs in the third and another in the fourth to take a 4-0 lead.

Hamilton walked two batters in the game. Hughie Jennings' Tigers managed to scratch out a fourth-inning run without the benefit of a hit when Ty Cobb walked and raced around to third, ahead of the relay throw, when Browns rookie second baseman Del Pratt booted Sam Crawford's groundball. Third baseman Jimmy Austin alertly threw the ball to second in an attempt to catch the trailing Crawford while the ever-aggressive Cobb took off for home. Cobb slid safely around Walter Alexander's tag.[3] The *Grand Rapids Press* headlined its brief story, "Cobb's Daring Dash Prevents a Shutout."[4]

Hamilton continued to baffle the Tigers with his fine control, puzzling delivery, and excellent curveball.

He also was the benefactor of strong defensive play behind him. Center fielder Burt Shotton made two fine catches and shortstop Heine Smoyer and Austin "on more than one occasion made splendid stops and throws" on difficult drives.[5]

After Hamilton retired Donie Bush and Cobb to start the bottom of the ninth, only Crawford stood between him and baseball immortality. The Tigers' future Hall of Famer came to the plate and laced a liner to left field. Fortunately for Hamilton, Browns left fielder Pete Compton was able to catch up to it and haul it in to preserve the first no-hitter in St. Louis Browns history.[6]

Hamilton, who came from Oswego, Kansas (only about "a score of miles from the home of the great Walter Johnson"), was 21 years old.[7] In 1 hour and 35 minutes he was the first to prove that on any given day, if all things are in alignment and the breaks go your way, it is possible to pitch a no-hitter without striking out a single batter. While numerous pitchers have thrown no-hitters with modest strikeout totals, only two duplicated Hamilton's feat of pitching a no-hitter without fanning a single batter.[8]

Hamilton's career statistics suggest he was a good candidate to potentially throw a no-strikeout no-hitter. Eight years later, in 1920 as a member of the Pittsburgh Pirates, he struck out only one man while throwing 16 shutout innings in a game against the New York Giants.[9] For his entire career, Hamilton averaged only 3.03 strikeouts per nine innings. However, a closer examination of his 1912 statistics suggests he may not have been the most likely candidate. Hamilton finished the season sixth in the American League with 139 strikeouts, an average of 5.01 K's per nine innings.

SOURCES

In addition to the sources cited in the Notes, the author also relied on Baseball-Reference.com and Retrosheet.org.

NOTES

1. Jim Wohlenhaus, "Frank Navin's Field of Dreams," *Tigers by the Tale: Great Games at Michigan and Trumbull* (Phoenix: Society for American Baseball Research, 2016).

2. Official Weather: Detroit, Michigan, Retrieved from weathersource.com/account/official-weather?location=Detroit%2C+Michigan&start-date=08%2F30%2F1912&end-date=09%2F02%2F1912&subscription-demo=1&sid=02rfqmqhdnkqjjtq2dcf42rsv1&search=1&station-id=15390&latitude=42.3634&longitude=-83.0835.

3. "Hamilton Is Puzzle to Tiger Crew in Game: St. Louis Browns Have No Trouble in Coping, Pitching a No-Hit Contest," *Kalamazoo* (Michigan) *Gazette,* August 31, 1912.

4. "Cobb's Daring Dash Prevents a Shutout," *Grand Rapids* (Michigan) *Press*, August 31, 1912: 8.

5. "Hamilton Holds Detroit Hitless: St. Louis Hurler Pitches Remarkable Ball, Browns Winning Game, 5-1," *Chicago Tribune*, August 31, 1912.

6. "Hamilton of Browns Twirls No-Hit Game: St. Louis Boxman Fails to Stop Cobb from Scoring—Detroit Beat 5-1—Red Sox Down Athletics, 7-4," *Pawtucket* (Rhode Island) *Times*, August 31, 2012.

7. "Hamilton Young for No Hit Fame," *Jackson* (Michigan) *Patriot*, August 31, 1912: 7.

8. The two are by Sad Sam Jones of the New York Yankees against the Athletics at Shibe Park, Philadelphia, on September 4, 1923, and Ken Holtzman of the Chicago Cubs on August 19, 1969, against the Atlanta Braves at Wrigley Field, Chicago.

9. In the 17th inning, he collapsed, giving up seven earned runs and losing the game.

ED LAFITTE

By Jim Leeke

A PRACTICING DENTIST IN the offseason, pitcher Ed Lafitte was a lanky, square-jawed journeyman in the American and Federal Leagues during the Deadball Era. No one knew just what to expect when righty Doc Lafitte took the mound. His hurling was often wild and occasionally brilliant, sometimes both in the same game. His historic contributions to his sport and his profession, however, came after his big-league career had ended, while he was an officer in the US Army serving overseas in World War I.

Edward Francis Lafitte was born in New Orleans on April 7, 1886, son of James A. Lafitte and Jane Templar Huger Lafitte. The family soon relocated to Atlanta, where Ed's father became the superintendent of a private social club. The city always considered Ed an adopted son. His older brother, Jim, was a city firefighter-turned-catcher who for many years played and managed in the Southern minor leagues. The brothers occasionally formed the starting battery for local semipro teams.

The younger Lafitte began his hurling career by accident in 1904, when he tried out for baseball at Atlanta's Marist College. (Marist at the time offered both secondary and college educations.) The team had no pitchers. "What are you, son?" asked the coach, former big-leaguer Joe Bean. Hearing that Ed was a catcher, like his big brother, Bean replied, "No, you must be wrong. You look like a pitcher. In fact, you've *got* to be a pitcher."[1]

The rangy right-hander learned quickly. Lafitte starred at Marist for two years, becoming the best pitcher in the Georgia Prep League in 1905. The following year he entered Georgia Tech, where he played for the legendary John Heisman, who also coached the school's football and basketball teams. Heisman was startled the first time he saw Lafitte throwing fastballs. "Heavens, man, the football season is over and this is gentle baseball," Heisman said. "Slow 'em down a little."[2]

At 6-feet-2 and 185 pounds, Big Ed Lafitte was a star and mainstay of Heisman's pitching staff in 1906 and was elected captain in 1907. During a memorable 1-0, 11-inning win over Mercer, he walked only two men and struck out 20. He struck out 18 in a game in Knoxville against Tennessee. In addition to his hurling, he played every infield position, hit nearly .300, and was a forward on the basketball team. (He also pitched four no-hitters in the Atlanta City League in 1907.) The *Atlanta Constitution* called Lafitte the "greatest college pitcher the South had ever seen."[3]

After his father died, Lafitte left Georgia Tech to turn pro, signing in 1908 with Jersey City in the Eastern League. Again playing for Joe Bean, he went 12-19 in 33 games on a weak Skeeters team and accounted for nearly one-fourth of its victories. On July 5 Lafitte tossed 19 scoreless innings against Newark. The sensational game ended in a 0-0 tie, called due to darkness after 3 hours and 40 minutes. He struck out 14 batters, gave up only three hits, two walks, and two hit batsmen, and stretched a personal streak of consecutive scoreless innings to 27. Lafitte was particularly effective with runners on base. "I have hit against Mathewson and some of the old Baltimore Oriole pitchers," Bean recalled years later, "but Ed had as much stuff that day as any pitcher I ever saw."[4]

The scoreless game caught the attention of a Detroit Tigers scout. The Tigers acquired Lafitte from Jersey City for $5,000, a very large sum at the time. This was a big stride forward, but Lafitte didn't invest all of his hopes in baseball. He enrolled that fall in the Southern Dental College in Atlanta, "not because he wants to quit the baseball game," the *Constitution* explained, "but rather to have something for his arm to do when it becomes feeble from the strenuous twirling."[5]

Lafitte began the 1909 season with Detroit, making his debut in relief on April 16 at home against Chicago. His stay in the major leagues was brief, however. He appeared in just three games, including a blowout loss to Cy Young on a raw spring day better suited to football. "I guess I didn't have anything that they couldn't see," the pitcher said afterward.[6] The Tigers shipped him off to Providence for more seasoning.

Luck didn't accompany Lafitte to the Eastern League. Although a star for the Providence Grays, he lost one shutout after being ejected in the ninth inning for questioning the umpire. He tossed a no-hitter against his old Jersey City club on July 12, but lost 2-0, "robbed of a well-deserved victory through the misplays" of his infielders, according to *Sporting Life*.[7] Lafitte ended the season at 13-11. An opposing manager noted that Lafitte had abandoned his spitball to become "twice as good as he was last spring."[8]

The Rochester Bronchos bought Lafitte's contract that fall. Although sold to the New York Highlanders in July 1910, the pitcher remained with Rochester the whole season, finishing a very respectable 23-14. The Tigers reacquired him in September, and he never saw New York. Lafitte made the Detroit club a second time the following spring. This time he stuck.

Detroit got off to a fast 21-2 start in 1911, prompting the rookie to quip that he guessed the Tigers needed the World Series money. Having fellow Georgian Ty Cobb playing behind him certainly didn't hurt. Cobb was having an MVP season in which he would bat .420. Cobb and Lafitte were both members of what a Detroit paper called the Baseball Brothers' Society—each had a brother playing in the minors. (Ed and Jim Lafitte, in fact, had both played with Cobb's brother Paul on a team outside Atlanta.) Ed quickly proved almost untouchable for Detroit, losing only a single game during the first half. Sportswriters began calling him "Chateau Lafitte."

The pitcher achieved another goal in May when he returned briefly to Atlanta to graduate from dental college. This inevitably led to his other, more lasting nickname, Doc. (While he wasn't a direct descendant of pirate Jean Lafitte, it was a shame the big right-hander never pitched for Pittsburgh.) By July he had amassed a 10-1 record to lead the American League in wins. Lafitte's season had started to sour, however, with a serious bout of tonsillitis in late June. He didn't recover his form and finished the year a disappointing 11-8. Lafitte did have one bright moment late in August in an otherwise regrettable loss to Washington. He hit his first big-league home run (he would hit only one more) off Walter Johnson.

The 1912 season also went badly for Lafitte. He announced that he would again leave the team for a few days in May to take an exam for his dentist's certificate in Georgia. Manager Hugh Jennings was never happy about his right-hander taking time away from the team. "If you go home, you can continue on to Providence," Jennings told him.[9] Lafitte went, and finished the season in the minors.

"Ed Lafitte belongs to that class of players who are about two points shy of the major league standard," opined the *Milwaukee Journal*.[10] But he was hardly the only Tiger hurler to fall by the wayside in that era. As the *Detroit Free Press* pointedly noted of the pitching staff in 1917, the club "has purchased and inspected over half a hundred men in the last six seasons."[11]

The Atlanta Crackers in the Southern Association wanted to acquire Lafitte, but the $3,000 asking price was too high. He wound up back in Providence after a brief holdout. He pitched with the Grays for the remainder of 1912 and finished 15-17. He was there during all of 1913 as well, going 15-15. Like many unhappy ballplayers in the major and minor leagues, Lafitte jumped to the new Federal League the following year, signing with the Brooklyn Tip-Tops for 1914.

Lafitte found modest success in Brooklyn, pitching with what the *New York Tribune* called his "space devouring stride."[12] On September 19, facing the visiting Kansas City Packers at Washington Park, he threw his second no-hitter, the league's first. Again, his outing was exceptional but imperfect. The *Tribune* noted that "his own wildness and errors in the field let the Packers score a brace of runs" in the 6-2 win.[13] "Lafitte pitched a peculiar game," wrote the *New York Times*. "He was wild and gave six bases on balls, but the Kansas City batters could not seem to connect with him when he did get them over the plate."[14] Lafitte's season in the Federal League typified his entire career. He and the Tip-Tops were evenly matched, finishing 16-16 and 77-77, respectively. (Some record books suggest that Lafitte's record was actually 18-15.) Lafitte pitched more than 290 innings, second-most on the team, and led the league in walks with 127.

The 1915 season would be the Federal League's last. It went poorly for Brooklyn, with dissension between players and management apparent as early as the Mississippi training camp. On July 5 the Tip-Tops had lost 17 of their previous 19 games. "I have a lot of incompetent players, and I am going to get rid of them in a hurry," player-manager Lee Magee declared.[15] With a 6-9 record, Lafitte was on Magee's list. Newspapers speculated that manager Joe Tinker of the Chicago Whales might try to engineer a trade for Lafitte and Brooklyn outfielder Benny Kauff. In the end, the right-hander went to the last-place Buffalo Blues on the strong recommendation of a former Tip-Top teammate.

Lafitte returned to Brooklyn on July 9 to face his old team at Washington Park. He beat the Tip-Tops 9-1 in the second game of a doubleheader sweep. "About the happiest person leaving New York for Buffalo last night was Dr. Edward F. Lafitte, formerly a Brookfed twirler," the *Brooklyn Eagle* said the next day. "Lafitte pitched fine ball and inning after inning he just kidded his former team mates along and took many a merry verbal shot at Magee."[16]

But the pitcher wore a Blues uniform for just seven weeks. Lafitte's record was 2-2 when he and three other players were released on August 28, after a rain-shortened game in Buffalo. Lafitte had "no place to go but home," the *Eagle* reported. His big-league record was 35-36, with an ERA of 3.34. "I was about ready to call it quits as far as baseball was concerned," he later admitted.[17]

But the former Georgia Tech star wasn't finished. Always a popular figure in Atlanta, he received a good, unexpected offer from the hometown Crackers of the Southern Association. Lafitte accepted and was the first man to report to camp in 1916. He got himself into great shape and won the home opener, 2-1. For a while, his season looked promising. "I won the first 11 of 12 games [I] pitched for the Crackers," he recalled. "I pitched three or four times a week until my arm could stand it no longer."[18]

He developed a sore arm, and Atlanta went into a slide. A headline writer noted in mid-July that as a pitcher Ed Lafitte was a fine young dentist. Manager Charley Frank benched him to rest him, unwilling to lose a popular player on a struggling team. Lafitte saw the end coming. "I told him the expense of paying me and not getting any results was too much on a club that was not drawing at the gate and I suggested he release me," Lafitte said of Frank. "He did, but not until after I threatened to quit."[19]

Lafitte's record was 11-12 when he left the Crackers, bringing his minor-league totals to 89-88. That made his combined record for nine major- and minor-league seasons exactly even at 124-124, plus six big-league saves (counted retrospectively). But the pitching dentist still wasn't finished. He went north to Pennsylvania to hurl for Ridgway in the semipro Interstate League. There he occasionally still summoned big-league stuff. In an exhibition game against Connie Mack's Philadelphia Athletics in September, *Sporting Life* reported, Lafitte "pitched excellent ball … striking out nine in the five innings he pitched."[20]

In the spring of 1917 Lafitte was practicing and teaching dentistry in Philadelphia. Although the Tigers had bought his Ridgway contract, he decided not to report back to Detroit. Instead, he worked on teeth during the week, then twirled for Chester in the Delaware County (Pennsylvania) League on Saturdays and for the Doherty Silk Sox in the Paterson (New Jersey) Industrial League on Sundays. These were two strong semipro leagues with a number of former major leaguers on their rosters. Lafitte also pitched for an itinerant all-star team fielded by former big leaguer Red Murray.

When America entered the World War in April 1917, Lafitte's thoughts turned from baseball. His late father had hoped Ed might attend West Point. The pitcher did have some military experience, having drilled as a cadet at Marist and served in 1912 in a militia company called the Marist Rifles. On July 19, 1917, Dr. Edward Lafitte became one of the first current or former major leaguers to volunteer for the Army. He received a commission in the Dental Reserve Corps and reported for duty at Camp Jackson, South Carolina. Shortly before Christmas, First Lieutenant Ed Lafitte got orders to the Army's School of Plastic and Oral Surgery in St. Louis. He was promoted to captain in February and shipped out in April 1918 for England and France. The *Brooklyn Eagle* reported that he specialized in "the remaking of faces maimed in the war, one of the highest and most important developments of recent military surgery."[21]

Across the Atlantic, eight American and Canadian military teams made up the Anglo-American Baseball League, founded by American businessmen to play on cricket grounds in and around London. Playing on weekends and holidays before decent crowds, its proceeds going to war charities, the league constituted what the *Atlanta Constitution* later called "the crest of a baseball mania which has followed American soldiers and sailors wherever they are based in Europe."[22] Many former professional and collegiate ballplayers took the field. Naturally, Captain Lafitte was soon drafted to pitch for the AEF Base Section (Army headquarters) team.

A growing British enthusiasm for baseball mounted almost to a frenzy with the announcement of a game between the American Army and Navy headquarters teams at Stamford Bridge, London, on the Fourth of July, 1918. A baseball diamond was squeezed onto the Chelsea Football Grounds, normally home to a soccer team. King George V, who took a genuine interest in baseball, accepted an invitation to attend and let it be known that he was practicing to throw out the first ball. Newspapers trumpeted the game in England and America, *The Times* of London predicting that it would "undoubtedly become historic."[23] Coverage spread beyond the sporting pages in publications around the world.[24]

An immense crowd of soldiers, sailors, and curious British civilians descended on the soccer grounds on the Fourth. Attendance far outstripped capacity, with estimates running as high as 55,000. In the royal box, protected by netting from foul balls, sat King George, Queen Mary, the Queen Mother, Winston Churchill, many other politicians, industrialists, and diplomats, the American Army and Navy commanders, and what *Ladies' Home Journal* described as "a huge group of generals, a scattering of princesses and other royalties."[25] Newsreels caught Captain Lafitte surrounded by Army officers and VIPs, wearing his Army baseball flannels and a Detroit Tigers cap.

The Navy pitcher was Yeoman Herb Pennock, a lanky young southpaw late of the Boston Red Sox. The game he and Lafitte pitched was remarkable even to the uninitiated. The *Ladies' Home Journal* correspondent (whose article, published a year later, indicated the widespread interest in the game) recalled a young British officer who was "amazed at the swiftness of Lafitte's practice pitching. He could believe, he said, that the ball might be hit by mere accident, but never by intention."[26]

Lafitte gave up just five hits to the Navy. Pennock struck out 14 Army batters. Neither team scored until the fourth inning, when the Navy scratched out a run. In the sixth, another Navy yeoman, former Red Sox utility infielder Mike McNally, doubled in Ensign Charles Fuller, a young naval aviator and former Harvard catcher, for Navy's second and final run. "The pitching and fielding were brilliant," *The Times* said, and in the late innings "it looked as if the Army would be beaten pointless."[27] But in the bottom of the ninth, the Army first baseman doubled off Pennock, then stole third. Lafitte followed him to the plate, perhaps remembering the day he had batted against Walter Johnson. He doubled, scoring the runner and pulling the Army to within one run of the Navy. Pennock left Lafitte stranded, however, and recorded the final outs in a 2–1 victory. After the game, both pitchers were summoned to the royal box to shake hands with King George. The amiable monarch chatted with Lafitte about the "receiver being padded up like an armchair when the cricketer bowled."[28]

The effects of the game were profound. The *New York Tribune* agreed that it was "bound to become historic."[29] In London, *The Times* marveled at the "REMARKABLE SCENES AT CHELSEA," and added, "Nothing really dimmed the brilliance of yesterday afternoon."[30] Three eventful months later, with an American army in the field and the Allied victory in sight, a newspaper in faraway Tasmania concluded that the "Anglo Saxon fellowship was sealed on the Fourth of July, 1918. … [T]he most characteristic gathering was in the afternoon at Stamford Bridge, where the United States Navy defeated the United States Army at baseball." The contest, the writer concluded, had been "some match!"[31]

Although they lost the game, Lafitte and his teammates captured the Anglo-American league title that year. Each received a wristwatch inscribed *Army Baseball Team Champions, 1918. Presented by Major the Hon. Waldorf Astor, M.P.* (Member of Parliament).

Lafitte's real mission overseas wasn't to pitch, however. The dentist reconstructed the teeth and jaws of wounded doughboys, first at Queen's Hospital outside London, then at American Base Hospital No. 202 in

France. He liked the work and received numerous citations. The *Brooklyn Eagle* noted Captain Lafitte's return to the United States on the transport ship *Patria* on March 17, 1919. Two weeks later it reported his promotion to major and added that, with one exception, he was "the only baseball player who has risen to the rank of major by actual work instead of by appointment on his reputation." The paper said in another piece: "Many a soldier today with apparently normal features owes the restoration of his face to Maj. Lafitte's skill."[32]

"I'm not going to play ball any time soon," the major said while in Atlanta on furlough. "The Army don't seem to be able to do without me, and I'm headed from here to St. Louis for the base hospital there. Don't know when I'll get out." The *Constitution* tactfully forgot its own earlier wisecrack about the pitcher being a fine dentist. "The army has certainly agreed with Ed," its writer reported. "He looks in the greatest kind of form. When he does break back into baseball, Ed is going to do some hurling the like of which he himself has never seen."[33]

After his Army discharge, Lafitte returned to Philadelphia but not to professional baseball. He resumed his dental practice and in 1920 pitched for Lansdale in the Montgomery County (Pennsylvania) Baseball League. That spring he also became the baseball coach at nearby Swarthmore College, "one of the most experienced coaches now handling college squads," according to the *Brooklyn Eagle*.[34] During the early 1920s, he coached for both Swarthmore and the Montgomery School for Boys.

Dr. Ed Lafitte practiced dentistry in Philadelphia for more than 42 years, retiring in 1961. He was inducted into the Georgia Tech Athletics Hall of Fame in 1958. He died at his home outside Philadelphia on April 12, 1971, shortly after his 85th birthday, survived by his second wife, Natalie Blizard Lafitte, two grandchildren, and two great-grandchildren.

SOURCES

In addition to the sources mentioned in the notes, the author also consulted:

Buffalo Express, *Detroit News*, *New London Day*, *Philadelphia Bulletin*, *Philadelphia Inquirer*, *Philadelphia Public Ledger*, and *The Sporting News*.

NOTES

1. *Atlanta Constitution*, March 9, 1934.
2. *Atlanta Constitution*, May 13, 1906.
3. *Atlanta Constitution*, March 21, 1908.
4. *Atlanta Constitution*, March 9, 1934.
5. *Atlanta Constitution*, November 4, 1908.
6. *Atlanta Georgian and News*, April 23, 1909.
7. *Sporting Life*, July 24, 1909.
8. *Atlanta Georgian and News*, October 1, 1909.
9. *Atlanta Constitution*, March 29, 1936.
10. *Milwaukee Journal*, April 26, 1912.
11. *Detroit Free Press*, February 13, 1917.
12. *New York Tribune*, May 1, 1914.
13. *New York Tribune*, September 20, 1914.
14. *New York Times*, September 20, 1914.
15. *Brooklyn Eagle*, July 2, 1915.
16. *Brooklyn Eagle*, July 10, 1915.
17. *Atlanta Constitution*, March 29, 1936.
18. Ibid.
19. Ibid.
20. *Sporting Life*, September 23, 1916.
21. *Brooklyn Eagle*, April 10, 1918.
22. *Atlanta Constitution*, October 13, 1918.
23. *The Times* (London), July 4, 1918.
24. For much more on this visit to England, see Jim Leeke, *Nine Innings for the King: The Day Wartime London Stopped for Baseball, July 4, 1918* (Jefferson, North Carolina: McFarland, 2015).
25. George Earle Raiguel, "The Fourth of July That Rang Round the World: The Greatest Baseball Game Ever Played," *Ladies' Home Journal*, July 1919.
26. Ibid.
27. *The Times* (London), July 5, 1918.
28. *Atlanta Constitution*, March 29, 1919.
29. *New York Tribune*, July 5, 1918.
30. *The Times* (London), July 5, 1918.
31. *Hobart* (Tasmania) *Mercury*, October 5, 1918.
32. *Brooklyn Eagle*, April 1, 1919.
33. *Atlanta Constitution*, March 29, 1919.
34. *Brooklyn Eagle*, March 9, 1920.

DOC LAFITTE TOSSES THE FEDERAL LEAGUE'S FIRST NO-HITTER

SEPTEMBER 19, 1914: BROOKLYN TIP-TIPS 6, KANSAS CITY PACKERS 2, AT WASHINGTON PARK, BROOKLYN

By Jim Leeke

THE BROOKLYN TIP-TOPS had just lost five games at Washington Park to the visiting Indianapolis Hoosiers, who now stood atop the Federal League standings. Today the Brooklyn nine faced a doubleheader with player-manager George Stovall's Kansas City Packers. Ed Lafitte, a big right-hander, took the mound for the first game against Kansas City left-hander Nick Cullop.

A rangy (6-feet-2) graduate of Georgia Tech, Lafitte was an Atlanta dentist during the offseason, winning him the nickname Doc. He and his club were nearing the end of a mediocre season in which they would finish at 18-15 and 77-77, respectively. Lafitte had shown occasional flashes of brilliance during an uneven professional career, and would shine again today.

A "goodly crowd of fans" watched the Brooklyn nine burst from the dugout to put the embarrassing sweep behind them.[1] Their hurler, whom the hometown *Brooklyn Standard Union* referred to jokingly as the "Dixie dentist" and "Monsieur Edouard Lafitte, the French reservist," dominated the game from the start.[2] Lafitte set down the first 13 Packers he faced, despite a second-inning walk to first baseman Stovall, who was quickly doubled off following "a great one-handed catch of a line fly" by shortstop Al Halt.[3] The Tip-Tops, meanwhile, "took kindly to Cullop," scoring a run in the first when second baseman Jim Delahanty tripled and center fielder Felix Chouinard singled him in.[4]

The game went along uneventfully until the fifth inning. With one out, Lafitte walked Kansas City third baseman George Perring, who had lined into the double play back in the second. Perring now stole second, but was stranded there following two easy outs. Brooklyn then scored twice in its half of the frame. Packers shortstop Johnny Rawlings fielded Halt's grounder but threw wildly. One out later, Lafitte helped his own cause by singling in Halt. A sacrifice moved Doc up and Delahanty's double sent him home.

The sixth inning was scoreless, and by now Lafitte surely knew he was working on a no-hitter. "The crowd was keyed up to a high state of excitement … hoping to see Lafitte complete the game without a hit, after his brilliant start," the *New York Times* reported.[5] Lafitte had tossed a previous professional no-hitter, on July 12, 1909, for the Providence Grays of the Eastern League at Jersey City. Despite surrendering no hits to the Skeeters, he'd lost the game, 2-0, "robbed of a well-deserved victory through the misplays" of the Grays' infield.[6]

Now facing Kansas City in Brooklyn, "Lafitte was alternately wild and effective in the seventh"—a neat summary of Doc's entire career.[7] He alternated two foul outs with free passes to second baseman Duke Kenworthy and Perring, then plunked Kansas City catcher Ted Easterly to load the bases. Rawlings grounded to Tip-Tops third baseman Tex Westerzil, "who let the ball go through him, allowing Kenworthy to score."[8] Lafitte got the third out on a fly ball to right by Cad Coles, a pinch-hitter for Cullop. Brooklyn's shutout was gone, but the no-hitter was intact.

Right-hander Dwight Stone took the mound for Kansas City in the bottom of the inning. Neither side scored again until the bottom of the eighth, when

Brooklyn "enthusiastically mauled" Stone.[9] The Tip-Tops scored three runs on hits by Delahanty, first baseman Solly Hofman, and Westerzil, compounded by two Kansas City errors.

Lafitte struggled again in the top of the ninth. He started with another walk to Stovall, who advanced to second on Perring's out. Delahanty then fumbled a grounder by Packers center fielder Art Krueger, moving Stovall to third. The Kanfeds skipper crossed the plate on a force out of Krueger at second. Lafitte ended the scoring there and came away with a 6-2 no-hitter, the contest taking just one hour and 47 minutes. The Tip-Tops also won the nightcap, 12-6.

In his second professional no-hitter, Lafitte had faced 35 batters, walked seven, and hit one with a pitch. The *New York Times* found it "a peculiar game," but added that Lafitte "was in superb form, and the Packers did not make anything that even resembled a safe clout."[10] Lafitte's achievement was "somewhat tarnished by the fact that the visitors scored two runs against him, but there was no question about the absence of a base-hit of any description," agreed the *Brooklyn Eagle*.[11]

Lafitte's was the league's only no-hitter of 1914. Federals Frank Allen, Claude Hendrix, Alex Main, and Dave Davenport each tossed a no-hitter in 1915, the second and final season in the league's brief history. These four no-hitters were all of the traditional sort, with the opponents held scoreless, but Lafitte's tarnished masterpiece at Washington Park is the one most remembered today.

An unidentified someone had suggested sending Lafitte back out for the second game of the doubleheader, to attempt "the unheard-of feat of pitching two no-hit games in one day," an *Eagle* sportswriter wrote. Manager Bill Bradley wouldn't hear of it. "Thus was the Georgian euchered [sic] out of an opportunity to have his name handed down in baseball history as a wonder-maker."[12]

Lafitte would become an international wonder-maker four years later, during World War I, while serving as a US Army captain at a hospital for wounded soldiers in England. He faced Red Sox left-hander Herb Pennock, pitching for a US Navy team, in a special Fourth of July "baseball match" at Stamford Bridge, Chelsea. Pennock won a 2-1 thriller, after which he and Doc Lafitte chatted with King George V, who had enjoyed the game from the grandstand with Queen Mary and other members of the royal family.

NOTES

1   *New York Tribune*, September 20, 1914.
2   *Brooklyn Standard Union*, September 20, 1914.
3   *Brooklyn Eagle*, September 20, 1914.
4   *Kansas City Star*, September 20, 1914.
5   *New York Times*, September 20, 1914.
6   *Sporting Life*, July 24, 1909.
7   *Brooklyn Eagle*, September 20, 1914.
8   *Kansas City Star*, September 20, 1914.
9   Ibid.
10 *New York Times*, September 20, 1914.
11 *Brooklyn Eagle*, September 20, 1914.
12 Ibid.

FRED TONEY

By Mike Lynch

FRED TONEY WAS A BIG, strong, temperamental right-handed pitcher who authored two of the best performances in baseball history. Pitching for the Winchester Hustlers of the Class-D Blue Grass League, the 6-foot-2, 195-pounder tossed a 17-inning no-hitter in 1909. But it was his 10-inning no-hitter against the Chicago Cubs on May 2, 1917, that put him on the map and made him a household name. Toney was more than just a two-trick pony, however, and was one of the better pitchers in the National League during his prime. In fact, from 1915 to 1921 only Grover Cleveland Alexander had a better ERA in the National League than Toney's 2.39, and only Walter Johnson and Eddie Cicotte were better in the American League.

Fred Alexandra Toney was born on December 11, 1888, in Nashville, Tennessee, to John A. and Alice (Richardson) Toney. Fred's father worked as a railwayman, first for the Louisville & Nashville Railroad, and later for the Nashville, Chattanooga and St. Louis Railway, while his mother stayed home to raise their family.[1] When Fred was a boy there wasn't enough level ground for a baseball diamond in his neighborhood and he spent his childhood playing a game called "drop 'em dead" (pronounced "drap 'em daid" in Nashville), in which he and his friends threw fist-sized rocks at tin cans or bottles mounted on sticks.[2]

Legend has it that Toney would challenge his friends, with the winner getting rifle ammunition from his opponents, and was so good that "he kept his whole family supplied with cartridges."[3] When Toney was a teenager, a furrier from Winchester, Kentucky, spotted him playing "drap 'em daid" and the Tennessean was invited to Winchester, where he learned to pitch.[4]

Toney's professional career began in 1908 when he signed with Winchester at only 19. He was very good in 1909, going 22-15, throwing the aforementioned no-hitter, in which he fanned 19 batters, and leading the team to a first-place finish, then followed that up with a 23-10 season in 1910. The Chicago Cubs purchased Toney in August 1910 for $1,000,[5] reportedly the largest sum ever paid for a Class-D player.[6]

In 1911 Toney impressed fans and writers alike in spring training, particularly after a three-inning performance against the University of Notre Dame on April 7. Sam Weller of the *Chicago Tribune* compared him to Rube Waddell, the left-handed flamethrower who won six consecutive strikeout crowns for the Philadelphia Athletics from 1902 to 1907.[7] Toney showed "so much smoke that he almost clouded a clear sky," wrote Weller.[8]

Toney made his major-league debut on April 15, 1911, and appeared in 18 games for the Cubs, finishing second on the team with a 2.42 ERA. On June 17 the *Chicago Defender* reported that the Cubs thought they'd found the next Amos Rusie (the New York Giants star dubbed "The Hoosier Thunderbolt" because of his exceptional fastball that resulted in five strikeout crowns from 1890 to 1895.[9]) "He possesses a huge, powerful frame and has speed to burn when working," wrote the *Defender*.[10]

The paper also reported that catchers Jimmy Archer and Johnny Kling were "preparing Toney for the hill," before Kling was traded to the Boston Rustlers (later the Braves).[11] The two backstops were considered the best of the era, Kling for his intelligence and Archer for his strong arm that he used to gun down baserunners from his knees. Needless to say, Toney was in good hands.

In January 1912 the powerful righty won the long-distance throwing contest at a field day held at Chicago's Comiskey Park, which featured a 100-yard dash, run around the bases, fungo hitting distance, and accurate throwing contest, among others. Toney's throw went more than 392 feet and beat runners-up

Joe Tinker, his Cubs teammate, and Boston Red Sox right fielder Harry Hooper.

Despite his success Toney threatened to quit and go into business, notifying Cubs owner Charles Murphy that he wanted to "devote his time to developing a system for reducing the switching cost of freight traffic."[12] He married Alice Walker on May 16, and changed his mind about his baseball career, although he spent most of the season with Louisville of the Double-A American Association, with whom he went 10-11 with a 2.70 ERA before rejoining the Cubs late in the season. He went only 1-2 with a 5.25 ERA in nine appearances with Chicago and reports in early 1913 claimed that Cubs manager Johnny Evers was going to convert Toney into a spitball pitcher.[13]

Toney began the 1913 season with the Cubs but went 2-2 with a 6.00 ERA in seven appearances before he was sent back to Louisville in early July. He went 13-8 with a 2.30 ERA for Louisville, then won 21 games for the Colonels in 1914. After the season the NL's Brooklyn Robins drafted Toney in the Rule 5 draft, but it was reported that he'd signed a contract with the Pittsburgh Rebels of the Federal League, claiming he "would rather play with the Feds for cigarette money than the salary the Brooklyn club is offering him."[14]

Toney denied the reports and early in 1915 he was selected off waivers by the Cincinnati Reds. He made his Cincinnati debut on June 1 and his first five appearances came as a reliever before he earned his first start on June 17 against the Philadelphia Phillies. He was 17-6 with a 1.58 ERA, second-best behind Pete Alexander's 1.22. Brooklyn's star outfielder Zack Wheat attributed Toney's success to a new approach. Where he relied mostly on his fastball with the Cubs, he was a different pitcher with the Reds.

"He had five or six styles, all sorts of deceptive motions, and as good a change of pace as there is in the National League," Wheat told *The Sporting News* in December. "Side-arm, overhand and under-hand were all the same to him. Instead of that constant fast ball, he had a half dozen speeds. … Don't let any one kid you into thinking Toney is fluking through."[15]

Before the 1916 season Toney demanded $6,000, almost double what he earned in 1915, or his unconditional release, but Reds president Garry Herrmann countered with $4,000 and told his hurler he'd pitch for that amount or not at all.[16] The sides split the difference and Toney signed his contract in late February.[17] The Reds ace enjoyed another excellent season, tossing a then-career-high 300 innings and posting a 2.28 ERA, but he went only 14-17 thanks to a paucity of run support.[18] He insisted he'd win 25 games a year if the Reds would give him four runs per game.

Toney proved prophetic when he won 24 games in 1917 while averaging 3.81 runs of support, but it was his performance on May 2 that put his name in the record books. On a cold, windy day in Chicago, Toney held the Cubs hitless for nine innings. But Cubs southpaw Jim "Hippo" Vaughn matched him and also went nine innings without allowing a hit. The Reds finally broke through in the 10th when shortstop Larry Kopf shot a clean single to right field, then came around to score on an error by center fielder Cy Williams and an infield hit by legendary athlete Jim Thorpe.

Toney threw one more hitless inning to win the game, 1-0, and became only the second pitcher of the Modern Era to win a 10-inning no-hitter.[19] He was almost as impressive on July 1 when he started both games of a doubleheader against the Pittsburgh Pirates, completed both of them and allowed only six hits and one earned run in 4-1 and 5-1 victories that ran his record to 13-8. That kicked off a run of excellence in which Toney pitched to a 1.81 ERA in his last

24 appearances, and when he shut out the St. Louis Cardinals on August 12 to win his league-leading 20th game, he was rewarded with a $1,000 bonus.

Toney looked to be the front-runner to pace the NL in wins, holding a two-win lead over Alexander, but "Old Pete" won 12 of his last 15 decisions to win 30 for the third consecutive year and easily outpaced the Reds ace. That 1917 campaign would prove to be Toney's best season on the field. Things took a drastic turn in December when he was arrested for allegedly dodging the World War I draft. When he registered under the Draft Act he falsely swore that his wife, child, mother, stepfather, and sister were dependent on his $5,000 salary. According to reports, Toney and his wife had lived apart for three years and he had provided little support to her while she worked as an operator for the Cumberland Telephone and Telegraph Company.[20]

Toney was held on a $2,500 bond but released when a Nashville restaurateur put up the money. The penalty for "conspiring to make fraudulent representation of dependencies" was a year in prison followed by military service. In March 1918 Toney swore before a judge that his mother, stepfather, brother, niece, and deceased sister had been dependent on him for their livelihood and would suffer if he was imprisoned or forced into military service.[21]

The *Washington Post* reported that Toney would be lost to the Reds for the 1918 season,[22] and that appeared to be true when witnesses for the prosecution insisted that Toney wasn't supporting his family as much as he'd claimed.[23] But his estranged wife, Alice, testified that Toney had been sending her and their child $70 a month during the 1917 campaign and a mistrial was declared on April 10.[24] The pitcher's troubles were far from over, however; during his trial he was indicted for violating the Mann Act, also known as the White Slave Traffic Act, for transporting a woman across state lines for the purpose of having sex.[25] The sex was consensual, but still against the law.

Before Toney returned to the Reds, the club put him on waivers, fearing that public opinion would be harsh. Any team in either league could have claimed the pitcher for the waiver price of $1,500, but all passed, not wanting the backlash that might come with his signing.[26] Those fears turned out to be unfounded. Toney wasn't with the Reds to start the season, but he made his first start on May 5 and beat the Pirates 3-1. Perhaps more important is that the Cincinnati crowd greeted him with a rousing ovation and cheered him throughout the game.

"The greeting he got was a tribute to him," wrote Jack Ryder in the *Cincinnati Enquirer*, "and showed that the fans had finally learned to understand his case and to realize that he was simply the victim of circumstances and not an intentional slacker." Ryder also wrote, "(T)here had been talk of booing him off the field, but none of the patriots who threatened such a thing made a public appearance."[27]

Toney won his first five decisions but lost 10 of his next 11 to fall to 6-10 and was sold to the New York Giants on July 22. He threatened to go home to Nashville if he didn't get a cut of the purchase price, but made his first start for the Giants on August 1. He was overweight when he joined the Giants—some reports listed him at 250 pounds and newspapers began to refer to him as "Man Mountain"[28]—and lost his first two decisions with New York, but rebounded and finished strong, going 6-0 with a save in his last 11 appearances and dropping his ERA from 3.03 to 2.43.

Giants skipper John McGraw predicted that once Toney lost weight he'd be the best pitcher in the National League.[29] But legal troubles hounded him again and he went on trial for the Mann Act violation in early January 1919. He was also retried for dodging the draft in 1917. Toney's ex-sister-in-law testified that his sister worked in Gallatin, Tennessee, and didn't require assistance from Toney as he'd stated when he applied for draft exemption.[30]

Toney was acquitted of evading the draft on January 4, but sentenced to a four-month jail term for violating the Mann Act. By this time he had remarried, making Goldie May Strange his wife. After spending three months in jail, the hurler decided to retire from baseball, but had a change of heart and made his first appearance of the season on May 31.

He went 13-6 with a 1.84 ERA that was second best on the Giants behind Art Nehf's 1.50 and fourth best in the NL among qualifiers.

Toney and Nehf paced the Giants in wins in 1920 with 21 apiece and Toney pitched to a 2.65 ERA, good for second on the team, a tick behind Jesse Barnes's 2.64. He was mostly mediocre through mid-July, going 9-8 with a 3.22 ERA, and challenged catcher Frank Snyder to a fight when the backstop berated his batterymate for his careless pitching against the Cubs on July 8, an 8-5 loss. But Toney went 12-3 with a 2.04 ERA down the stretch to save his season.

Then, in the wake of the Black Sox Scandal that rocked Organized Baseball when it was discovered that eight members of the Chicago White Sox conspired to throw the 1919 World Series to the Reds, Toney testified before a grand jury that former teammate Heinie Zimmerman offered him a bribe to throw a game against the Cubs. Giants outfielder Benny Kauff also implicated Zimmerman, and second baseman Larry Doyle testified that first baseman Hal Chase offered him a bribe to throw an exhibition game against a team of "colored" players from Philadelphia.[31]

Zimmerman and Chase were both blackballed from major-league baseball after the 1919 season and Kauff, ironically enough, was linked to the Black Sox Scandal and eventually banned from the majors for auto theft. Even though McGraw lost three of his better players, he wasn't done cleaning house and it was reported that Toney had "outlived his usefulness" in Gotham.[32]

Despite the reports, Toney stayed with the Giants and enjoyed another solid season in 1921, going 18-11 with a 3.61 ERA, and finishing among the top 10 in several categories. In July he was implicated in the Black Sox Scandal when Sleepy Bill Burns testified that the hurler had been present during meetings between the players and gamblers at the Ansonia Hotel in New York.[33] But NL President John Heydler issued a statement that called Burns's testimony misleading and saying Toney had nothing to do with the conspiracy.[34]

The McGraws won their sixth pennant since 1905 and faced the Yankees in the World Series, but Toney wasn't up to the task. He started Game Three but lasted only two innings in which he surrendered four runs before Jesse Barnes relieved him and stopped the bleeding in a 13-5 victory that pulled the Giants to a two-games-to-one deficit.

Toney started again in Game Six with the Yankees up three games to two and allowed three runs in two-thirds of an inning before being pulled in favor of Barnes again, who saved him for the second time with 8⅓ brilliant innings in an 8-5 win that tied the Series at three wins apiece. The Giants won the Series in eight games in a best-of-nine format, but Toney was dismal, pitching to a 23.63 ERA and establishing a record for futility that still stands.[35]

The 1922 campaign started off inauspiciously when Toney developed a sore arm during spring training and was sent home to get in shape. He didn't make his debut until May 16 and struggled through his worst season, going 5-6 with a 4.17 ERA in 13 games. According to Ralph McGill of the *Atlanta Constitution*, Toney could be volatile and was the only player John McGraw ever managed whom he truly feared.

And for good reason. Toney once punched Reds teammate Greasy Neale in the face after criticizing the outfielder for his shoddy play in the field and at bat.[36] But "Little Napoleon" wasn't one to mince words and he had some choice ones for Toney, who'd struggled in his last three starts, going 1-2 with an 8.41 ERA.[37] Toney threw a water bottle at his manager and let him know with "cold, knife-like words" how he felt about McGraw.[38]

A day later, on July 30, Toney was traded to the Boston Braves along with pitchers Larry Benton and Harry Hulihan and $100,000 for pitcher Hugh McQuillan. A few days later it was reported that Toney would rather quit than play for a last-place club. "I have $50,000 and don't have to play baseball with the Braves," he told friends.[39]

The *Boston Globe* thought Toney was bluffing in an effort to get cash considerations from the Braves, but he stood firm and was placed on waivers. The

St. Louis Cardinals claimed Toney on August 17 and hoped he'd help bolster a club that was only 3½ games out of first place. But he refused to report, citing an illness in the family, and not even a two-day visit to Nashville by Cardinals president Branch Rickey, during which "he had used every effort, both financial and persuasive, to induce Toney to report immediately," could convince the pitcher to change his mind.[40]

St. Louis finished in a tie for third place, eight games behind the Giants, but Rickey held no grudges and insisted Toney was in good standing with the team and expected him to report for work in 1923. The hurler told reporters that after spending the winter "in the open, he would be in grand shape for a comeback,"[41] but the hurler surprised the Cards when he announced in February that he was through with baseball.[42]

Sportswriter John B. Sheridan tore into Toney in *The Sporting News* soon after. "Toney never much appealed to me as a player," he opined. "He seemed to be a big, fat food-destroying animal, eating as much as would keep three better men." He also called him a "jail bird" and a "large, fat draft dodger," and concluded, "As I see it, Toney is pretty well shot as a pitcher. Not at any time would I want him for a baseball team."[43]

Toney changed his mind and joined the Cards, for whom he was consistently inconsistent, trading wins and losses with equal measure and staying within two decisions of .500 throughout the season en route to an 11-12 mark and a 3.84 ERA. His season wasn't without controversy and he threatened to quit again in June after fans jeered him for reprimanding young shortstop Specs Toporcer for not heeding his advice about where to position himself.

Toney knew how he wanted to pitch to Chicago Cubs batter Cliff Heathcote and tried to get Toporcer to play closer to third base. Toporcer refused and when Heathcote shot a hit through the area where Toney wanted Toporcer stationed, the pitcher laid into the much smaller shortstop, who took off his glasses and offered to settle the argument with his fists. Toney scoffed at the idea, boasting that "he could meet a dozen Toporcers in a room, lick them all at once and come out without a scratch."[44] But when the fans turned on Toney and cheered Toporcer, the mercurial pitcher left the game and claimed he was through with the Cardinals.

In typical fashion, Toney reversed field and decided to stay with the team, but the 1923 season proved to be his last in the majors. Rickey gave Toney his unconditional release on April 6, 1924. He sat out the '24 season, then appeared in nine games with the Nashville Volunteers of the Southern Association in 1925, with whom he went 4-3 with a 4.09 ERA before he quit in a huff after his teammates kicked away three straight games in which he pitched brilliantly. After the third loss, "Fred Toney said not a word," wrote Ralph McGill. "He walked out of the box and into the clubhouse. He took a bat and knocked the lock off the locker, put on his clothes and went home. He never pitched again."[45]

Toney made headlines in December 1925 when he was arrested for violating Tennessee game laws after being found with two red fox pelts in his possession.[46] In 1926 his wife, Goldie, gave birth to a son named Rogie.[47] In his post-playing life, Toney worked as a spinner in a textile mill, coached for Nashville, ran a roadhouse 14 miles west of his hometown,[48] operated a soft-drink and sandwich stand, worked as a security guard, and finally as a court officer for the Davidson County Sheriff's Office.[49]

He died of a heart attack in Nashville on March 11, 1953. He was 64.

NOTES

1. There were multiple John A. Toneys listed in the city directories who lived in Nashville. One was listed as a carpenter and another, listed under John Toney, was an engineer. Fred Toney had siblings, at least two sisters and a brother, but census records haven't been found that list their names, nor were they mentioned in newspapers by name.
2. *Charlotte News*, July 31, 1922.
3. Ibid.
4. Ibid.
5. Deadball Era Committee of the Society for American Baseball Research, *Deadball Stars of the National League* (Washington, D.C.: Brassey's, Inc., 2004), 262.

6. *Sporting Life*, August 27, 1910.
7. *Chicago Tribune*, April 8, 1911.
8. Ibid.
9. *Chicago Defender*, June 17, 1911. Rob Neyer ranked Rusie's fastball number two among starting pitchers behind only Walter Johnson in *The Neyer/James Guide to Pitchers: An Historical Compendium of Pitching, Pitchers, and Pitches* (New York: Simon & Schuster, Inc., 2004), 24.
10. Ibid.
11. Ibid.
12. *Sporting Life*, March 9, 1912.
13. *Sporting Life*, April 12, 1913.
14. *Sporting Life*, January 9, 1915.
15. *The Sporting News*, December 16, 1915.
16. *Chicago Tribune*, January 23, 1916.
17. *Hartford Courant*, February 23, 1916.
18. Toney insisted in August that if he could get four runs of support per game he'd win 25 games (*The Sporting News*, August 17, 1916). Lee Sinins' Complete Baseball Encyclopedia credits Toney with 17 wins had he received average run support (3.45 runs per game).
19. On July 4, 1908, New York Giants hurler George Wiltse tossed 10 no-hit innings against the Philadelphia Phillies, setting a new modern-day record. Dodgers pitcher Harry McIntyre threw 10 no-hit innings against the Pittsburgh Pirates on August 1, 1906, but allowed a hit in the 11th and lost in 13 innings.
20. *Chicago Tribune*, December 24, 1917.
21. *Atlanta Constitution*, March 12, 1918.
22. *Washington Post*, March 22, 1918.
23. *Washington Post*, April 9, 1918.
24. *Atlanta Constitution,* April 11, 1918.
25. Ibid. The Mann Act was enacted in 1910 to stop the interstate trafficking of women for the purposes of prostitution, "debauchery, or any other immoral purpose," but those who engaged in consensual sex could also be prosecuted under the law. Toney eventually married a woman from Kentucky named Goldie May Strange and it might have been his relationship with her that resulted in his indictment.
26. *The Sporting News*, January 13, 1927.
27. *Cincinnati Enquirer*, May 6, 1918.
28. *New York Times*, August 2, 1918
29. *St. Louis Post-Dispatch*, November 11, 1918.
30. *Washington Post*, January 3, 1919.
31. *New York Times*, October 6, 1920.
32. *Atlanta Constitution*, November 3, 1920.
33. *New York Times*, July 22, 1921.
34. *Chicago Tribune*, July 24, 1921.
35. Among pitchers with at least two World Series starts in a single Series, Toney holds the record for the worst ERA. The best-of-nine format was used in 1903, 1919, 1920, and 1921 before it went back to a best-of-seven format.
36. *Pittsburgh Post-Gazette*, September 11, 1943.
37. *Atlanta Constitution*, June 22, 1935.
38. Ibid.
39. *New York Times*, August 3, 1922.
40. *St. Louis Post-Dispatch*, August 22, 1922.
41. *The Sporting News*, February 15, 1923.
42. *Christian Science Monitor*, February 9, 1923.
43. *The Sporting News*, February 22, 1923.
44. *The Sporting News*, June 28, 1923.
45. *Atlanta Constitution*, June 22, 1935.
46. *Washington Post*, December 20, 1925.
47. The 1930 census is difficult to read and it's unclear if the last letter in Rogie's name is an e. But the pop-up preview window lists him as "Rogie" and the first four letters are clear on the census sheet.
48. *Chicago Tribune*, September 29, 1938.
49. *Deadball Stars of the National League,* 263.

FRED TONEY DEFEATS HIPPO VAUGHN IN EPIC DUEL

MAY 2, 1917: CINCINNATI REDS 1, CHICAGO CUBS 0, AT WEEGHMAN PARK, CHICAGO

By Mike Lynch

On May 2, 1917 the Cincinnati Reds and Chicago Cubs squared off at Chicago's Weeghman Park for the first game of a four-game series. At 10-7 the Cubs sat in second place, only a half-game back of the eventual National League champion New York Giants. The Reds were in sixth place with a mark of 9-10, but were only 2½ games off the pace in the still young season.

On the mound for the Reds was Fred Toney, a big, powerful right-hander known for his strength and arsenal of pitches.[1] The Tennessee native began his pro career with Winchester of the Blue Grass League in 1908 and quickly established himself as a top hurler, winning 45 games in 1909-1910, including a 17-inning no-hitter against Lexington on May 10, 1909, in which he fanned 19 batters.

Toney made his major-league debut with the Cubs on April 15, 1911, but it wasn't until he was claimed off waivers by the Reds in 1915 that he finally blossomed, going 17-6 with a 1.58 ERA that was second best in the NL. Only Grover Cleveland Alexander had a better ERA than Toney's 1.98 in 1915-1916, and he was one of the circuit's best pitchers again in 1917, going 4-1 with a 2.30 ERA prior to the May 2 tilt.

His mound opponent was Jim "Hippo" Vaughn, a 6-foot-4 left-handed behemoth known for his hard fastball and competitiveness.[2] Vaughn's pro career began a year before Toney's, in 1907 with Corsicana of the North Texas League, and he made his major-league debut with the New York Yankees on June 19, 1908.

But, like Toney, it took a change of scenery before Vaughn became a consistent winner; from 1913, his first season with the Cubs, until 1920, his last winning season, Vaughn won 148 games and posted a 2.14 ERA, second in the NL to Alexander over that period. On May 2 Vaughn was 3-1 with a 2.25 ERA and had just beaten the Reds on April 25, striking out a season-high 11 batters in a 4-2 complete-game victory.

Conditions were less than favorable for a ballgame. It was cold and blustery as a stiff breeze blew off Lake Michigan, and the field was "soggy and slow" from recent rains.[3] Jack Ryder of the *Cincinnati Enquirer* reported that only 2,500 brave souls were there to witness baseball history, over 2,000 less than average for Weeghman Park that year.[4]

Third baseman Heinie Groh led off the game for the Reds and fanned, then shortstop Larry Kopf grounded out. Greasy Neale, Cincinnati's regular left fielder who was in center to fill in for an injured Edd Roush, belted a long drive to center field, but Cy Williams corralled it for the third out of the inning. It would be the only Cincinnati ball to leave the infield for the next nine innings. Toney retired Rolly Zeider, Harry Wolter, and Larry Doyle in order to send the game to the second.

Toney said later that he didn't like the conditions and didn't have his usual stuff, but he continued to baffle Cubs batters with his assortment of pitches.[5] Vaughn set down Hal Chase, Jim Thorpe, and second baseman Dave Shean in order in the second. Toney ran into a spot of trouble in his half, but worked out of a jam. Fred Merkle led off with a hot liner that was speared by Groh, Williams walked with one out and advanced to second on a grounder to third, but Art Wilson, the Cubs backstop, popped out to Kopf to end the threat. It would be the only time a Cub reached second.

Both pitchers easily retired the side in the third, then Vaughn had to escape a jam of his own when he walked Groh to lead off the fourth. Kopf bounded into a double play to clear the bases, but Zeider muffed Neale's grounder to give the Reds a runner on first with two outs. Neale attempted to steal second, but was gunned down by Wilson to end the frame.

Toney had no issues in the bottom of the fourth, and Vaughn narrowly escaped with his no-hitter intact when Thorpe clubbed a long liner down the left-field line that landed just foul. But the big southpaw set the Reds down again without allowing a hit. Williams drew another free pass in the bottom of the fifth, Les Mann lined out to left fielder Manuel Cueto, then Wilson hit a pop fly to Shean, who purposely dropped the ball in hopes of turning a double play. He retired Williams at second but Wilson was safe at first. Cubs third sacker Charlie Deal smacked a long fly to center, but Neale made a nifty running catch to retire the side.

Through six innings neither team had sniffed a hit or gotten past second base. The fans sensed what was happening and began rooting for both pitchers.[6]

Vaughn took the hill for the seventh and ran the count on Groh to 1-and-2 before Groh snapped and gave home-plate umpire Al Orth his unsolicited opinion about Orth's strike zone. Groh was ejected and replaced by Gus Getz, who walked in Groh's stead. But Kopf grounded into his second double play of the game, and Vaughn easily retired Neale. Toney dispatched the Cubs again in the bottom of the seventh, and Vaughn did the same to the Reds in the top of the eighth.

It was during the bottom of the eighth that Vaughn realized he was throwing a no-hitter.[7] The Cubs lefty was so focused on keeping the game "well in hand" that he hadn't realized he was only one inning away from tossing his first no-hitter. Toney was of the same mindset, just trying to keep the Cubs off the scoreboard until his boys finally broke through against Vaughn.[8]

Vaughn dispatched the Reds in the ninth, then Toney set down the Cubs in order and the game went into extra frames with both sides still without a hit. Getz led off the top of the 10th and skied a foul pop to Wilson for the first out. That brought up Larry Kopf, who had grounded out three times, including twice into rally-killing double plays. By his own admission Vaughn "grew careless" and took one chance too many.[9]

Kopf shot a drive between Doyle and Merkle, the latter making a diving effort to no avail. It was a clean hit and the double no-hitter was over. Though the hometown throng was disappointed, the fans gave Kopf a nice ovation for ending Vaughn's masterpiece. Neale poked a fly ball to Williams for out number two and it looked as if Vaughn would escape with his shutout intact, but Williams misplayed Chase's line drive and suddenly there were Reds at first and third with two outs.[10] Chase stole second while Wilson wisely held the ball rather than risk Kopf scoring on a throw.

With two on and two out, Jim Thorpe topped a short grounder in front of the plate that rolled up the third-base line. Vaughn went after it, figuring Deal wouldn't be able to race in from third in time to record the out. He also knew he wouldn't get Thorpe, a former Olympic gold medalist, at first base, so he tried to scoop the ball to Art Wilson in an effort to nab Kopf at the plate.

Kopf slid safely past Wilson, who then dropped the ball. Chase attempted to score as well, but Wilson recovered in time to tag him out and end the inning.[11] The Reds went up 1-0 and Toney needed only three outs to complete his no-hitter. He began the bottom of the 10th by fanning Larry Doyle. Up stepped Fred Merkle, the Cubs' cleanup hitter, and he delivered a blow to left that looked as though it would not only end Toney's no-hit bid, but also tie the score. "It looked like a home run into the left bleachers," wrote the *Commercial Tribune*, "but little Mr. Cueto of Cuba dashed back until he hit the wall and then speared the ball over his head."[12]

With two outs and a near miss it was up to Cy Williams to keep the Cubs alive. Williams wasn't the hitter he'd been in 1916 when he led the National League in home runs, but he was still dangerous. In fact, he showed how dangerous he was when he fouled off two two-strike pitches, including a long line drive down the right-field line that landed a foot foul. Toney threw another ball to run the count full and some speculated he was going to walk Williams again to face the less threatening Leslie Mann, but he came back with a side-arm curve and Williams swung and missed to complete Toney's historic no-hitter.

Never before or since have two pitchers thrown nine no-hit innings in the same contest.

NOTES

1. ourgame.mlblogs.com/2012/02/04/. "He threw a variety of stuff," wrote John Thorn, Major League Baseball's official historian, "spitballs, fastballs, curves, and an overhand sinker that faded away from left-handed batters just as [Christy Mathewson's] 'fadeaway,' or screwball, once had."

2. Bill James and Rob Neyer, *The Neyer/James Guide to Pitchers: An Historical Compendium of Pitching, Pitchers, and Pitches* (New York: Fireside, 2004), 411-412. "Big Jim Vaughn used to pitch the particular kind of ball a batter liked best just to show him that he couldn't hit it," Pete Alexander told *Baseball Magazine* in 1925, as reported by Neyer/James.

3. "The weather was bitterly cold," wrote Jack Ryder of the *Cincinnati Enquirer*, "and it was a wonder that even so many fans turned out to shiver in the arctic breezes off the lake," May 3, 1917.

4. Baseball-Reference.com and Retrosheet.org list that day's attendance at 3,500; the Cubs averaged 4,678 fans per game at Weeghman Park in 1917.

5. "It was rather a cold day and I was not feeling in my best form when the game started," Toney said. "I didn't have so much stuff as I sometimes do for the first six innings." Vaughn concurred. "The boys said [Toney] didn't seem to have as much on the ball as usual," *Baseball Magazine*, July 1917.

6. "Toney and Vaughn were both in magnificent form," wrote Ryder, "working with the precision of a machine. As round after round went by without either side getting the suspicion of a safety the crowd became wildly excited, urging on both the great pitchers to continue their wonderful work," Jack Ryder, *Cincinnati Enquirer*, May 3, 1917.

7. "I was sitting on the bench and happened to make a remark that we weren't hitting Toney very much," Vaughn told *Baseball Magazine*. "One of the fellows assented to this and then added that [the Reds] weren't hitting me very much either. Then I recalled that they hadn't made a safe hit off my delivery," *Baseball Magazine*, July 1917.

8. "I didn't fully realize it was a no-hit game until the ninth inning," Toney explained later. "Then I took time to get my breath and my bearings and made up my mind to put all I had on whatever other balls I pitched." Ibid.

9. "I had been putting a fastball over the plate for my first strike right along and put over one too many," Vaughn explained. Ibid.

10. Rich Coberly, *The No-Hit Hall of Fame: No-Hitters of the 20th Century* (Newport Beach, California: Triple Play Publications, 1985), 48. "Cy scarcely had to move," reported the *Cincinnati Commercial Tribune*, per Coberly's book, "but if he had advanced two steps he could have taken it in front of his belt buckle. Instead, he had to catch it at his ankles, and he muffed the ball."

11. *Cincinnati Enquirer*, May 3, 1917. The *Commercial Tribune* reported that Vaughn's toss hit Wilson in the shoulder and that Kopf crashed into the catcher before he scored. Kopf himself told John Thorn that (in Thorn's words) he "stopped dead in his tracks" when he saw Vaughn shovel the ball to Wilson and it was only after he realized that Wilson was frozen with confusion that he continued home to score. "Kopf, seeing Wilson standing there like a zombie as the ball rolled a few steps away, dashed home with the run," wrote Thorn. See Coberly, 48, and ourgame. mlblogs.com/2012/02/04/.

12. Coberly.

CHARLIE ROBERTSON

By Jacob Pomrenke

IF THERE WAS ONE THING THE Detroit Tigers could do under player-manager Ty Cobb, it was hit. They set an American League record with a .316 team batting average in 1921, and six of their eight starters in 1922 finished over .300. Even four of their backups hit over .300 that year. They were strong up and down the lineup.

So when the 25,000 fans at Navin Field in Detroit rose for the seventh-inning stretch on Sunday, April 30, 1922, and word spread throughout the overflow crowd that the Tigers still had not recorded a single hit, they turned their attention to the opposing pitcher: 26-year-old Chicago White Sox rookie Charlie Robertson.

Robertson was the last pitcher anyone — least of all the Detroit faithful — expected to be shutting out the mighty Tigers offense. He was a journeyman with an unremarkable résumé who had recorded his first major-league victory just four days earlier. But here was Robertson following up future Hall of Famer Red Faber's shutout the day before with one of his own.

So in the seventh inning, the Navin Field fans let him have it, in one final effort to unsettle the rookie right-hander.[1] Nursing a 2-0 lead, Robertson was unfazed. In the seventh he set down Lu Blue, George Cutshaw, and Ty Cobb — the latter on a called strike three. Cobb was furious and loudly accused Robertson of doctoring the ball. Umpire Dick Nallin didn't take the bait. In the eighth Bobby Veach took Robertson to a full count but anxiously chased a pitch out of the strike zone and flied out. Harry Heilmann and Bob Jones also went down in order. By the ninth, the crowd's mood had changed. History was being made, and now they were rooting for Robertson to finish the job.

Cobb sent Dan Clark to pinch-hit for rookie Topper Rigney. Clark struck out for the first out. Clyde Manion lifted an easy pop fly to second base for the second out. Only pinch-hitter Johnny Bassler, the regular starting catcher, stood in Robertson's way now. Robertson called timeout and walked behind the mound to prepare himself. Shortstop Eddie Mulligan was startled to hear Robertson talking to him: "Do you realize that little fat man up there is the only thing between me and a perfect game?"[2] Mulligan was too stunned to reply. He pushed Robertson back toward the mound.

Robertson wound up and delivered a fastball to Bassler, who looped it into short left field. Johnny Mostil squeezed the ball in his glove for the 27th out. Charlie Robertson's perfect game — perhaps the most unlikely perfect game in major-league history — was officially in the books.

After Robertson's second major-league victory, there was nowhere to go but down.

Charles Culbertson Robertson, who pitched in one game for the 1919 White Sox, was born on January 31, 1896, in Dexter, Texas, on the Red River in the northeastern part of the state. He was the eighth of nine children born to Mathias and Nancy Robertson, farmers from Tennessee who moved to Texas around 1890 and eventually settled in Montague County.[3] Not much is known of Charlie's early life, but he was well educated for his time. He graduated from Nocona High School in 1915 and began studying for the ministry at Austin College in Sherman, Texas. According to his file at the National Baseball Hall of Fame Library, he played baseball, football, and basketball at Austin College and graduated around 1918.[4]

While in college, Robertson was signed by the Sherman team of the low-level Western Association in 1917 and developed a reputation as a "shine ball expert."[5] He reportedly pitched shutouts in both games of a doubleheader against Ardmore, and won 23 out of 27 starts.[6] This drew the attention of the Chicago White Sox and Robertson was invited to spring training with the major-league club in 1918 at Mineral Wells, Texas. Manager Pants Rowland and coach Kid Gleason "thought he was not quite ready" and sent him to the Minneapolis Millers of the American Association.[7] He went 2-7 with a 1.94 ERA in nine games for the Millers before enlisting in the U.S. Army Air Service as baseball players and other non-essential employees were ordered to "work or fight" during World War I. He saw no combat and returned to Minnesota after the war ended.

In early 1919 Robertson was called up to the White Sox for the first time. With a critical series against the defending World Series champion Boston Red Sox approaching in mid-May, Gleason — who had replaced Rowland as White Sox manager — gave his rookie pitchers a chance to show off their abilities against the lowly St. Louis Browns at Comiskey Park. Robertson made his major-league debut on May 13 against the Browns. He lasted just two innings, allowing five hits and two runs, and was replaced by fellow rookie Dickey Kerr, who pitched seven shutout innings in a 2-1 loss.[8] Kerr stayed with the White Sox and became a relief ace of sorts for Gleason as Chicago went on to win the American League pennant. The two innings were all Robertson pitched in the majors until 1922. Robertson was sent back to the Minneapolis Millers and struggled to an 11-13 record and a 3.10 ERA in the minor leagues.

Robertson watched from afar as the White Sox lost the tainted 1919 World Series to the Cincinnati Reds — and later as eight of his former teammates were implicated in throwing the Series for a promised $100,000 bribe from gamblers in what became known as the Black Sox Scandal. The eight Black Sox implicated in the fix were banned from Organized Baseball for life following the 1920 season.

As the scandal unfolded in Chicago, Robertson spent two more years with the Minneapolis Millers. He was a solid but unspectacular prospect, logging more than 300 innings apiece in 1920 and 1921 and compiling 35 wins to 31 losses. In the offseason he went home to Nocona, Texas, and worked as a salesman at a rubber company.[9]

In 1922, with the depleted White Sox searching for dependable pitchers, the 26-year-old Robertson finally earned a spot in Kid Gleason's starting rotation. His early-season performances gave no indication that he was about to make history. He pitched two innings of mop-up relief in a 14-0 loss to the Browns on April 15 and was pulled after six innings in a 10-5 win at St. Louis on April 21. Five days later Robertson hurled his first complete game, pitching in and out of trouble in a 7-3 win at Cleveland. It was his first major-league victory. No one could have predicted the historic nature of his second.

Robertson's perfect game on April 30 against the Tigers was the third in American League history, after those of Cy Young in 1904 and Addie Joss in 1908. With a lineup powered by Hall of Famers Ty Cobb and Harry Heilmann and the great Bobby Veach, Detroit was an unlikely no-hit victim. Robertson's feat included an added degree of difficulty because of the overflow crowd at Navin Field. With spectators on the field, ground rules dictated that any ball hit into the crowd would be ruled a double. Only one ball came close. In the second inning Bobby Veach lined a sharp drive toward the roped-off boundary in left field. But as Johnny Mostil backed up, the crowd parted, allowing him to make the catch with ease. In the same inning Harry Hooper made a splendid running catch of a hard-hit ball by Bob Jones.[10] The Tigers hit only five balls out of the infield and struck out six times.

Led by manager Cobb, a master of gamesmanship, the Tigers seemed to spend more time worrying about the legality of Robertson's pitches than in actually trying to hit them. Cobb stopped the game on several occasions to complain to umpire Nallin, accusing Robertson of using oil or grease to make the ball jump noticeably, a charge the White Sox mocked afterward. The next day Nallin dutifully took two game balls to American League President Ban Johnson's office in Chicago. Johnson quickly denied the Tigers' protest, stating, "I consider Robertson one of the cleanest pitchers in organized baseball today."[11]

April 30 wasn't the only shining moment in Robertson's rookie season. On June 13 he took a no-hitter into the eighth inning against the Red Sox, settling for a two-hit shutout. His third shutout of the year was a rain-shortened, five-inning affair against the Indians on September 1. He would record just three more shutouts in his major-league career. For the most part, Robertson rarely found the magic touch he possessed that Sunday afternoon in Chicago. His 1922 season could best be described as erratic; he allowed at least 10 hits in 11 of his 34 starts and finished with a 14-15 record and a 3.64 ERA in 272 innings. The Tigers, in particular, took pleasure in beating up on the right-hander, who struggled to a 5.58 ERA in 17 appearances against Detroit after the perfect game, his worst against any American League club.[12]

Some reporters and teammates said the early success went to Robertson's head, because in 1923 he staged a lengthy holdout during spring training and threatened to jump to a semipro team in Chicago, as teammate Dickey Kerr had done.[13] *The Sporting News* reported that the White Sox' offer to Robertson was just $100 more than what he had been making ($3,750) in 1922; he figured his performance entitled him to a raise of about ten times higher than that.[14] He got what he was asking for and signed a contract worth $5,000, but didn't get over the slight quickly.

In late June of 1923, White Sox manager Kid Gleason suspended a petulant Robertson after a poor start against the Tigers in Detroit. Gleason claimed his pitcher was "not trying" — an accusation now taken extremely seriously by the White Sox since the World Series scandal — by pitching side-arm and walking three batters in the first inning. Robertson was sent home to Chicago and did not make another appearance for two weeks.[15]

Despite pitching well after his return, Robertson was put on the trading block in the offseason. The Sox and Yankees nearly agreed to a blockbuster deal sending future Hall of Famer Eddie Collins and Bibb Falk to New York for Bob Meusel, Aaron Ward, and Waite Hoyt (another future Hall of Famer), but the Yankees demanded an extra pitcher from the White Sox and were not willing to accept Robertson. Gleason "insisted that if one (pitcher) had to go Robertson would have to be the man."[16] The talks ended without a deal and Collins — and Robertson — stayed in Chicago for the time being.

An elbow injury limited Robertson to 97⅓ innings in his third full season with the White Sox, 1924. He walked nearly twice as many batters as he struck out and finished 4-10 with a 4.99 ERA.[17] He had surgery to remove bone chips that fall, and felt well enough to join some of his White Sox teammates on an around-the-world tour organized by White Sox owner Charles Comiskey and Giants manager John McGraw. It was a reprise of their successful tour held during the offseason of 1913-14. Stars like Red Faber, Willie Kamm, Stuffy McInnis, Sam Rice, Johnny Evers, Heinie Groh, Frank Frisch, Ross Youngs, and Casey Stengel participated. Games were scheduled in England, Ireland, France, Japan, Hong Kong, the Philippines, and Australia, but poor weather and even worse crowds — fewer than 20 people showed up for an exhibition in Dublin — abruptly ended the tour overseas after seven games. The group sailed back to New York in late November.[18]

Healthy again, Robertson showed a brief resurgence early in 1925, recording two shutouts. But he went 1-6 in his final nine appearances for the White Sox and was claimed off waivers by the St. Louis Browns in the offseason.

Robertson's first appearance for the Browns in 1926 was against his old teammates at Comiskey Park; he lasted just two innings against the White Sox. In June, with Robertson sporting an atrocious 8.36 ERA, the Browns sent him down to the minor leagues for the first time in five years. He pitched well for the Milwaukee Brewers of the American Association, and the Boston Braves took a flyer on him in the Rule 5 draft that fall. But Robertson had nothing left. He went 7-17 for the Braves in 1927 and 2-5 in 1928 before the Braves sold his contract. He lost 34 games in two forgettable seasons with the Brewers in 1929 and '30, then hung up his spikes for good.

Robertson's eight-year major-league career ended with a 49-80 record, the worst winning percentage (.380) by any pitcher who has thrown a perfect game. His crowning achievement was one of the White Sox' lone bright spots in the decade after the World Series scandal, but he didn't have the ability or temperament to succeed consistently in the majors.

He retired to his native Texas with his wife, the former Fay Redus, whose ancestors were early settlers in Palo Pinto County, where Robertson had first been invited to spring training with the White Sox at Mineral Wells. Robertson became a prosperous pecan broker in Fort Worth and ignored the baseball world until 1956, when Don Larsen of the New York Yankees threw the major leagues' first perfect game — in the World Series, no less — since Robertson had done it 34 years before. Reporters across the country sought out Robertson for interviews and he reluctantly appeared on the CBS television show *What's My Line?*[19]

Robertson told *The Sporting News* he was glad to be out of the limelight:

"[If I] had known then what I know now, I wouldn't have been in baseball," he said. "It isn't sour grapes. Baseball didn't give me a particularly bad break, but I went through it and found out that it's ridiculous for any young man with qualifications to make good in another profession to waste time in professional athletics. … When they get through with an athlete, he has to start over and at an age when it's the wrong time to be starting. … Just forget my name. It was long ago."[20]

But Charlie Robertson is still remembered, then and now. His name resurfaces on the rare occasion when a major-league pitcher throws a perfect game. When he died at age 88 on August 23, 1984, at a Fort Worth nursing home, his niece Nancy Ward said he "still gets fan mail from all over the world. He got three letters last week."[21] Baseballs, photos, and other mementos often show up at his gravesite in Palo Pinto Cemetery.

Robertson's one shining moment was just that: a moment. For one afternoon, as unlikely as it was, he could say he was perfect.

SOURCES

Special thanks to the National Baseball Hall of Fame Library in Cooperstown, New York, for making Robertson's player file available. Other sources, in addition to those cited in the endnotes, include Baseball-Reference.com, Retrosheet.org, Ancestry.com, the *Chicago Tribune*, and *The Sporting News*.

NOTES

1 Edward Prell, "Thirty Years Ago Today: Sox Pitcher Was Perfect," *Chicago Tribune*, April 30, 1952, B2.

2 Norman Kronstadt, "The Perfect Game," Undated article in Charlie Robertson player file, National Baseball Hall of Fame Library, Cooperstown, New York.

3 1900 United States Census, accessed at Ancestry.com; McDaniel, Robert Wayne. "Dexter, TX," Handbook of Texas Online, Published by the Texas State Historical Association.

4 An uncredited May 2, 1922, article in Robertson's Hall of Fame player file said he graduated in January 1918. A January 30, 1981, letter from Mike Barry, director of alumni relations at Austin College, to SABR founding member Joe Simenic, available in Robertson's Hall of Fame player file, stated that "Mr. Robertson graduated in 1920."

5 *Paris* (Texas) *News*, August 30, 1917. Charlie Robertson player file, National Baseball Hall of Fame Library, Cooperstown, New York.

NO-HITTERS

6 Uncredited article from July 26, 1917, Charlie Robertson player file, National Baseball Hall of Fame Library, Cooperstown, New York.

7 "Robertson No Juvenile Wonder," uncredited article from May 2, 1922, Charlie Robertson player file, National Baseball Hall of Fame Library, Cooperstown, New York. This article and another by Edward Prell of the *Chicago Tribune* said the White Sox paid $250 to the Sherman (Texas) team in 1918 for Robertson's contract, with an additional $1,750 to be paid if they kept him. When the White Sox sent him to Minneapolis for seasoning, they got no response from Sherman and the additional money was never paid. In 1922, after Robertson's perfect game, the Sherman club suddenly "came to life and demanded the payment." On advice from Commissioner Kenesaw Mountain Landis, the White Sox settled with Sherman rather than fight the case.

8 Irving Sanborn, "Old Man Horseshoes Helps Browns Lick White Sox, 2-1," *Chicago Tribune*, May 14, 1919, 19.

9 Baseball-Reference.com; 1920 United States Census, Ancestry.com.

10 "Sox Close First Series Here With Monday Game," uncredited article from May 1, 1922, Charlie Robertson player file, National Baseball Hall of Fame Library, Cooperstown, New York.

11 "Absolves Pitcher of All Suspicion." *Spartanburg* (South Carolina) *Herald*, May 3, 1922.

12 Charlie Robertson pitching splits, Retrosheet.org, accessed online on February 20, 2012.

13 "'No-Hit Bobby' Holdout As Sox Arrive In Camp," *Chicago Tribune*, March 1, 1923. Dickey Kerr, the 1919 World Series hero, spent two seasons out of major-league baseball pitching for a Chicago semipro team, was suspended for the entire 1924 season, and made an aborted comeback in 1925.

14 "'Reward' For Perfect Game," *The Sporting News*, February 8, 1923; salary data from SABR member Michael Haupert's study of the National Baseball Hall of Fame Library contract cards.

15 "Disciplined," *Chicago Tribune*, June 25, 1923.

16 "Big Deal Depends on One Player," *New York Times*, December 19, 1922; "Yankees and White Sox End All Negotiations for Big Trade Involving Collins," *Providence News*, February 20, 1923.

17 Irving Vaughan, "Crooked Arm Lays Up Robertson, Sox Ace," *Chicago Tribune*, May 1, 1924.

18 Ancestry.com; "Players Named For Tour," *The Sporting News*, October 9, 1924, 1; John Mullin, "Comiskey Rewarded Pals With Sox-Giants World Tours," *Chicago Tribune*, March 30, 1998.

19 "Robertson on 'What's My Line?'" *The Sporting News*, October 24, 1956, 28. "Introduced only as C.C. Robertson of Fort Worth, Texas, his identity was guessed immediately by panelist Bennett Cerf but the panel nearly ran out of time before guessing his present occupation as a pecan broker."

20 "Robertson Would Turn Down Game If He Had New Chance," *The Sporting News*, October 17, 1956, 7.

21 "Enduring Popularity," uncredited article dated August 26, 1984, Charlie Robertson player file, National Baseball Hall of Fame Library, Cooperstown, New York.

APRIL 30, 1922
CHARLIE ROBERTSON THROWS A PERFECT GAME IN FOURTH CAREER START
CHICAGO WHITE SOX 2, DETROIT TIGERS 0, AT NAVIN FIELD, DETROIT

By Jacob Pomrenke

AFTER THROWING THE third perfect game in American League history, Charlie Robertson said he didn't realize the magnitude of his feat until "that funny little fat guy," pinch-hitter Johnny Bassler, came to bat for the pitcher with two outs in the ninth inning.[1] Robertson admitted that he was barely paying attention to the Detroit Tigers lineup — and what a lineup it was, led by future Hall of Famers Ty Cobb and Harry Heilmann, with a team batting average over .300.

Bassler lifted a lazy fly ball to left field for the game's final out and set off one of baseball's most unlikely celebrations. In his fourth career start, on three days' rest, the Chicago White Sox' rookie right-hander Robertson earned his second major-league win in historic fashion.

His performance was so unbelievable that nobody — not his opponents, nor even some of his own teammates — believed he could have done it without a little subterfuge. Even before the game ended, Robertson was accused of applying crude oil, grease, or rubber cement to the baseball during his masterpiece.[2] While he was officially absolved of any wrongdoing, he never again reached the heights he did on April 30, 1922, in front of 25,000 fans at Detroit's Navin Field.

Entering the game, Robertson had shown no signs that he was capable of perfection. He had recorded his first career victory (and first complete game) on April 26 in a lackluster 7-3 win over the Cleveland Indians, scattering 12 hits and walking four. With manager Kid Gleason's pitching rotation still decimated by the Black Sox Scandal, that was good enough to earn the 26-year-old Robertson another start against the Tigers four days later.

Under player-manager Ty Cobb, the Tigers were one of the best-hitting clubs in major-league history. In 1921 Detroit set an American League record with a team batting average of .316. Although they were off to a tough start in 1922, losing 10 of their first 14 games as they prepared to face Robertson, the Tigers would go on to hit .306 that season — one of just two .300-hitting teams to ever be the victim of a no-hitter.[3] Cobb himself finished above .400 for the third and final time in his illustrious career, while Heilmann, Bassler, Bobby Veach, Topper Rigney, and Lu Blue all hit above .300. "That Detroit club," Robertson later said, "looked as pleasant as a cage full of lions."[4]

But after Robertson set down the first 12 hitters in order, the Tigers got angry. In the fifth inning Heilmann called timeout during his at-bat and asked umpire Dick Nallin to inspect the ball. Nallin found nothing wrong, but the Tigers continued to protest. At one point, the *Chicago Tribune* reported, Cobb went out to first base and looked at Earl Sheely's glove to see if he was concealing any foreign substances. Robertson's uniform was also inspected during the game.[5]

Robertson relied mostly on a high fastball and uncharacteristically good control to induce the Detroit hitters to pop the ball up. Only five balls left the infield, which was fortunate because the outfield boundary was closer than usual that afternoon. The overflow crowd of 25,000 spilled into the outfield grass, and spectators were standing just a hundred feet or so from where the fielders were positioned. In the second inning the White Sox' Johnny Mostil chased down a long drive by Bobby Veach and "the crowd in that sector spread to make the left fielder's feat easier to perform."[6] Any ball hit into the crowd would have been a ground-rule double. Two batters later, Chicago right fielder Harry Hooper made a difficult running catch of a hard-hit ball by Bob Jones to end the inning. The Tigers did not come close to a base hit again.

In the seventh, "when they rose for the traditional stretch," the hometown Tiger fans tried one last time to rattle Robertson, who was protecting a 2-0 lead thanks to Earl Sheely's two-run single in the second inning.[7] After Robertson "set down their favorites, their sentiment quickly changed."[8] By the ninth, Detroit fans were openly cheering for Robertson to make history.

Cobb sent up the left-handed Danny Clark to hit for his shortstop Rigney to open the ninth inning. Robertson fanned him, one of his six strikeouts that day. Clyde Manion lunged at the first pitch and popped up to White Sox second baseman Eddie Collins for the second out. Another pinch-hitter, Johnny Bassler, went up to hit for Tigers pitcher Herman Pillette, who had pitched a fine game, allowing just seven hits and the two early runs. On Robertson's 92nd pitch,[9] Bassler's pop fly settled in Mostil's glove just as he passed the left-field foul line — and the Chicago pitcher had achieved perfection. A swarm of Detroit fans rushed to congratulate the lanky right-hander and carried him off the field, "an ovation that an athlete seldom is granted on a foreign field," the *Chicago Tribune* reported.[10]

Robertson's perfect game was the first in the major leagues since Hall of Famer Addie Joss pitched one in 1908. No pitcher would turn the trick again until Don Larsen in the World Series 34 years later.

Afterward, the Tigers still weren't convinced about the legitimacy of Robertson's achievement. Cobb held onto a few game balls that he claimed were discolored or smeared with a foreign substance, sending them to American League President Ban Johnson for further observation. A Detroit writer added fuel to the fire by stating, "It is a pity that such a magnificent game ... should be tainted."[11] But Johnson immediately dismissed the Tigers' complaints. "I consider Robertson one of the cleanest pitchers in organized baseball today," he said.[12]

More than four decades later, Robertson's teammate Eddie Mulligan — the White Sox shortstop was one of two players, along with center fielder Amos Strunk, who didn't handle a single chance during the perfect game — accused his pitcher of hiding a pinch of rubber cement in the corner of his glove. "There was no tampering with the *ball*," Mulligan insisted. "Robertson merely applied the cement to his first two fingers ... this gave him an extra amount of backspin on the fastball."[13]

Whether Robertson tampered with the ball remains a matter of conjecture, but one of the reasons the controversy won't die is that he remains one of the unlikeliest pitchers to have thrown a perfect game. His 49-80 career record (a .380 winning percentage) over eight major-league seasons is the worst of any pitcher with a perfect game to his name.[14] He retired to Fort Worth, Texas, and worked quietly as a pecan broker until Don Larsen brought him reluctantly back into the limelight in 1956. Tracked down by a reporter after the World Series, Robertson refused to pose for a photograph and said, "Just forget my name. It was long ago."[15]

NOTES

1. John Kieran, "Modest 'No-Hit' Robertson Gives Teammates Most Credit," *New York Tribune*, May 14, 1922.
2. Bert Walker, "Tigers Protest Star Chisox Hurler," *Detroit Times*, May 1, 1922; Scott Baillie, "Sly Charley Robertson Cemented Perfect Game Against Tigers," *Fresno Bee*, June 28, 1964.
3. The 1929 Pirates are the other. They hit .303 as a team and were no-hit by Carl Hubbell of the New York Giants on May 8.
4. Associated Press, "Texan Recalls His '22 Perfect Game,'" *Abilene Reporter-News*, June 23, 1964.
5. Irving Vaughan, "Kid Robertson Flings Perfect Game for Sox," *Chicago Tribune*, May 1, 1922.

6 "Sox Close First Series Here With Monday Game," uncredited article from May 1, 1922, in Charlie Robertson player file, National Baseball Hall of Fame Library.

7 The box score at Retrosheet.org, as of August 2015, claims that Mostil and Hooper each scored one run and each drove in one run, even though both White Sox runs came in the second inning. Unless they both hit home runs, this cannot be true. While RBIs were not listed in any box scores the next day, play-by-play accounts in various newspapers from May 1, including the *Chicago Tribune* and *Rockford* (Illinois) *Republic*, confirm that Mostil and Hooper scored on a ball hit by Earl Sheely that deflected off third baseman Bob Jones's glove.

8 Edward Prell, "Thirty Years Ago Today: Sox Pitcher Was Perfect," *Chicago Tribune*, April 30, 1952.

9 "Robertson Hero of Perfect Game," *Christian Science Monitor*, May 1, 1922.

10 Vaughan, "Kid Robertson Flings Perfect Game for Sox."

11 Walker, "Tigers Protest Chisox Hurler."

12 "Absolves Pitcher of All Suspicion," *Spartanburg* (South Carolina) *Herald*, May 3, 1922.

13 Baillie, "Sly Charley Robertson Cemented Perfect Game Against Tigers."

14 As of 2015, six perfect-game pitchers had finished their careers with losing records: Robertson, Lee Richmond, Don Larsen, Len Barker, Dallas Braden, and Phil Humber. Humber was also a journeyman right-hander for the White Sox who threw an unlikely perfect game against the Seattle Mariners on April 21, 2012, and then won four more games the rest of his career. Humber's 16 major-league wins are the fewest of any pitcher with a perfect game.

15 "Robertson Would Turn Down Game if He Had New Chance," *The Sporting News*, October 17, 1956: 7.

BOBBY BURKE

By Gregory H. Wolf

THE WASHINGTON Senators played in Griffith Stadium for 50 years (1911-1960). But only once, on August 8, 1931, did a Senators pitcher toss a no-hitter in the nation's capital. The author of that gem was southpaw Bobby Burke, who fashioned a 38-46 record in parts of 10 seasons as a spot starter and reliever (1927-1935, 1937).

Robert James Burke was born on January 23, 1907, in Joliet, then a gritty industrial city of 30,000 about 40 miles southwest of Chicago. His Illinois-born parents of Irish heritage were Bernard E. and Mary A. Burke, proprietors of a retail grocery store. According to various census reports, the Burkes welcomed six children into the world; Bobby was the third son and last child. Bobby's first introduction to baseball appears to be on local town teams.[1] "His ambition is to be a professional baseball player," read a description of Burke in his senior class yearbook upon graduation from Joliet Township High School in 1926. "He's not only a good pitcher, but an artist as well."[2]

Burke drew the attention of the Chicago White Sox, who signed the teenager soon after he completed school. Burke was sent to the Class-A Little Rock Travelers (Southern Association), where he was teammates with another 19-year-old future big leaguer, catcher Bill Dickey. Competing against players who averaged more than 10 years his senior, Burke held his own, posting the only winning record (11-8) for the last-place club (65-98), and logged 203 innings with a 5.54 ERA. Manager Joe Cantillon, who had skippered the Washington Senators for three seasons (1907-1909), probably thought he had a diamond in the rough. Based on scout Joe Engel's recommendation, Washington selected Burke on October 1 in the Rule 5 draft.

Washington's pitching staff was in transition when spring training convened in Tampa in 1927, with their biggest squad ever assembled—41 players, including 22 pitchers.[3] The Senators had captured pennants in 1924 and 1925 propelled by a staff that had led the league in team ERA both seasons. But skipper Bucky Harris's squad fell to fourth place in 1926, as age and injuries caught up to the staff and it finished a disappointing fifth in team ERA. The team's longtime stalwart, 39-year-old Walter Johnson, was back for his 21st and final season in 1927, but was suffering from arm pain. Dependable southpaw Dutch Ruether had been traded the previous August to the New York Yankees, and workhorse Stan Coveleski, a 37-year-old right-hander, was on his last legs and would be released in June.

Some grizzled veterans like Tris Speaker, Sam Rice, and "Big Train" Johnson might have thought Burke was a batboy. The 20-year-old, baby-faced hurler stood an even 6 feet tall, but weighed just 138 pounds. He eventually packed on another 10-12 pounds over the next few seasons, but descriptions such as "skinny," "string bean," and "bean pole" would accompany him throughout his career. "I like the style of Bob Burke," wrote umpire-turned-sportswriter Billy Evans. "He reminds you in action of Herb Pennock."[4] Despite the premature comparison to the Yankees' formidable southpaw who had racked up 79 victories in the previous four seasons, Burke seemed to be in the right position at an opportune time. The Senators desperately needed a left-hander to join the only other veteran southpaw in camp, reliever Garland Braxton, acquired in the Ruether trade. Burke debuted on April 16, recording the final four outs, but also yielding two hits, a walk, and a run in an 8-7 loss to Philadelphia in the nation's capital. Burke spent most of the season in the major's busiest bullpen, joining Braxton and Firpo Marberry, who paced the league in appearances with 58 and 56 respectively. Burke emerged victorious in the first of his six starts among his 36 appearances, holding Philadelphia to eight hits and two runs in eight innings on July 2.

"There's no chance of a shortage of left-handed pitching talent," wrote the AP's Brian Bell about a group of at least eight southpaws at Washington's spring training in 1928. Though Burke had an even 100 innings (and 3.96 ERA) under his belt, there was no guarantee that he would make the squad. Washington had re-acquired left-handed starter Tom Zachary the previous July from the St. Louis Browns and Braxton was primed to play a bigger role. Confined to mop-up duty on a crowded staff, Burke was loaned to the Birmingham Barons of the Southern Association in mid-May. "Ordinarily a pitcher wouldn't be of very much use to a ball club if he was to pitch just four games and then pack his portmanteau," opined sportswriter Harold C. Burr of the transaction. "The Barons are glad to get Burke on these terms."[5] Burke made a statement in his return to the big leagues a month later by tossing the first of his four career shutouts in what Les Conklin of the International News Service called a "brilliant 1-0 duel" with Red Ruffing of the Boston Red Sox at Fenway Park on June 22.[6] Burke's success, however, proved to be short-lived. After lasting just two thirds of an inning two starts later, he resumed his customary role as a mop-up artist with an occasional start, often in a doubleheader. The modest hurler finished with a 2-4 record and 3.90 ERA in 85⅓ innings while Washington dropped to 75-79, its first losing season since 1923.

Walter Johnson, only a season removed from tossing the last of 5,914⅓ innings for the Senators, took over as skipper in 1929. Like his predecessor and typical for the era, Johnson employed his hurlers as starters and relievers, often going with the hot hand or playing match-ups. Eight pitchers started at least 10 games; first-year player Bump Hadley led the staff with 27. Seven pitchers logged at least 125 innings. Burke, a spot starter in the first three months of the season, enjoyed the busiest stretch in his big-league career, making 11 consecutive starts from July 17 to August 31. After Burke tossed complete games and yielded only five earned runs to win the first three of those, he was hailed by Washington sportswriter Paul E. Eaton as "having arrived."[7] Harold C. Burr noted

that Burke, who now weighed about 150 pounds, seemed stronger. "He has learned to cut the corners and mix up his offerings," wrote Burr. "[H]e has one of the easiest pitching motions in baseball."[8] But in an offensive era (the AL set a new league record for runs scored, averaging 10 per game), Burke was also hit hard during that stretch (5.40 ERA). While Washington's franchise-record five-year stretch of first-division finishes ended with the club winding up in fifth place. Burke started a career-high 17 of 37 appearances, won six of 14 decisions, and owned a 4.79 ERA in 141 innings.

The Senators surprised the baseball world by challenging Connie Mack's reigning World Series champion Philadelphia Athletics for much of the 1930 season, finishing in second place (94-60), eight games off the pace. Washington's success was largely due to its pitching staff and especially a quintet of hurlers (Hadley, Marberry, General Crowder, Lloyd Brown, and Sad Sam Jones) who led the AL in team ERA in cavernous Griffith Stadium. While each member of that quintet notched at least 15 victories, Burke seemed lost on the far end of the bench. He made just four starts and appeared in 24 games, logged 74⅓ innings and carved out a robust 3.63 ERA, well below the league average of 4.65. Sportswriter Thomas Holmes of the *Brooklyn Daily Eagle* thought Burke could become a "full-fledged" star if he had the opportunity to pitch regularly;[9] however, the consensus was that the frail-looking hurler "lacked the stamina to go the full route" in an era when pitchers were expected to complete games and regularly relieve.[10]

Acknowledged as serious challengers to end Philadelphia's two-year stranglehold on the AL pennant, Washington was once again led by what Les Conklin described as a "well-rounded mound staff capable of winning close to 100 games."[11] A septet of hurlers (Brown, Crowder, Marberry, Jones, Hadley, first-year southpaw Carl Fisher, and Burke) started 154 of the club's 156 games, and logged 1,359⅓ of 1,394⅓ innings. In a precursor to what would happen later that season, Burke held the Detroit Tigers hitless into the seventh inning on June 3 in an eventual three-hit, 2-1 victory. Described as a "valuable asset" by D.C. sportswriter Denman Thompson, Burke won a career-high five straight decisions, in June.[12] Saturday afternoon, August 8, seemed like an unlikely date for Burke to etch his name into the history books. According to Ronald Valentine of the AP, the hurler had severely burned his back the day before when he fell on an exhaust pipe while on a fishing boat.[13] Overcoming the "depressing summer heat" and back pain, Burke became just the 20th major-league southpaw to toss a no-hitter, blanking the Boston Red Sox, yielding five walks in a 5-0 victory.[14] Not only was Burke's masterpiece the Senators' first no-hitter since the Big Train's gem at Fenway Park in 1920, it was the first and only no-hitter ever thrown in the 50-year history of Griffith Stadium (1911- 1960). Burke was bounced after retiring just four batters in his next outing, but returned two days later, on August 15, to toss 10 innings of seven-hit ball, yielding two runs in a 12-inning victory over the St. Louis Browns in Sportsman's Park. After yielding 14 earned runs in only 12 innings in his last three starts, Burke pitched just once after September 7. He concluded the season with an 8-3 record, 13 starts among 30 appearances, and a 4.27 ERA in 128⅔ innings for the third-place Nationals, as the Senators were affectionately known.

A holdout in 1932, Burke reported late to spring training.[15] Sportswriter Harold C. Burr reported that team owner Clark Griffith as well as skipper Johnson had grown tired of Burke's inconsistencies. Nonetheless the 25-year-old started off well, tossing a complete-game five-hitter with no walks to defeat the Red Sox, 4-3, in his season debut, on April 20. With two outs in the ninth inning, Burke (a career .194 hitter with 54 hits) slashed the game-winning single to drive in Ossie Bluege. In his next start, Burke issued a career-high 12 free passes to the New York Yankees, yet somehow managed to surrender just one earned run in a 6⅔-inning no-decision. He was erratic and often roughed up in his occasional starts. Burke's big-league career seemed to be at a crossroad after a disastrous relief appearance on August 5 (seven runs in 4⅔ innings). "[Burke] is about washed up after six years in Washington regalia," wrote Denman Thompson.[16] Burke was optioned to Chattanooga in the Southern Association; however, he complained of a sore arm, did not pitch for the Lookouts, and was ultimately placed on the voluntarily retired list.[17]

Burke was reinstated in the offseason, but his future with the club remained murky under first-year player-manager Joe Cronin. Coming off a dismal season (5.14 ERA in 91 innings), Burke was playing for his career. Thompson reported excitedly that Burke was "one of the most pleasant surprises" at Washington's spring training in Biloxi, Mississippi.[18] Once described as a "lobby sitter, his interests in the game negligible," Burke seemed, according to Harold C. Burr, "refreshed,"[19] while Thompson noted a different "attitude."[20] Unfortunately, Burke's arm and shoulder pain returned by the end of camp. He was sent to Selma, Alabama, for medical treatment, and also trained with Chattanooga before returning to Washington for the start of the season. In limited action, Burke went 4-3 with a 3.23 ERA in 64 innings for the surprising pennant-winning Senators, who won a franchise-record 99 games. Burke did not pitch in Washington's World Series loss to the New York Giants in five games.

After winning 90 or more games for four consecutive seasons for the first and only time in club history (as of 2015), the Senators dropped to 66-86 and seventh place in 1934. The franchise would manage only four more winning seasons (and one .500 season) in the next 25 seasons in Washington before relocating to Minneapolis-St. Paul for the 1961 campaign. Burke, suffering from what *The Sporting News* reported as his "annual sore shoulder," assumed his role as reliever and spot starter in 1934.[21] In the second game of a doubleheader against Cleveland on August 17, Burke tossed a three-hitter to record his fourth and final shutout. That victory initiated the best stretch in Burke's career. He completed five of seven starts and posted a 1.43 ERA in 63 innings, earning the designation of the "new Senators ace" by Theon Wright of the United Press.[22] In what proved to be Burke's most productive, but also final full season in the majors, the 27-year-old hurler split 16 decisions, made 15 starts in 37 appearances, and set career bests in innings (168) and ERA (3.21, fourth lowest in the AL).

Described as a "perennial question mark" by UP, Burke began the 1935 campaign in the starting rotation, but was clobbered.[23] He went 1-6 in eight starts and yielded 34 earned runs in 47 innings (6.51 ERA). "[He's] lost his effectiveness," opined Denman Thompson.[24] The Associated Press reported in early July that Washington released Burke (1-8, 7.46 ERA in 66⅓ innings) to Chattanooga.[25] But Burke refused to report, and was ultimately transferred to Albany in the Double-A International League.

Burke posted a 12-16 record for cellar-dwelling Albany in the eight-team IL in 1936 and earned another shot at the big leagues despite his 4.65 ERA in 180 innings when the Albany club (which had acquired his rights from Washington) sold him on a conditional basis to the Philadelphia Phillies in the offseason.[26] The Phillies had enjoyed just one winning season since trading pitcher Pete Alexander following a contract dispute with owner William Baker after the 1917 season, and were seemingly in perpetual need of pitchers. The 30-year-old Burke, "nursing a sore arm," wasn't the answer.[27] After two relief appearances in which he failed to retire any of the four batters he faced, Burke was sent to Jersey City of the IL, where he made his last four appearances in Organized Baseball. Released by Jersey City, Burke signed with the St. Paul Saints of the Double-A American Association, but was released in spring training in 1938, bringing his professional baseball career to an end.

"Ordinarily when a pitcher failed to win more games than I did," said Burke in retirement, "he found himself back in the minors. But I was allowed to hang around, start a game occasionally, and wait for a relief assignment." In parts of 10 big-league seasons, Burke won 38, lost 46, started 88 of 254 appearances, and carved out a 4.29 ERA in 918⅔ innings. His no-hitter against the Red Sox was the last thrown by a Washington pitcher in the nation's capital until Jordan Zimmerman of the Washington Nationals no-hit the Miami Marlins on September 28, 2014. [The 1961 expansion Washington Senators, who replaced the relocated Senators to the Twin Cities in Minnesota, played one season in Griffith Stadium before moving into D.C. Stadium (later renamed Robert F. Kennedy Stadium). The second reincarnation of the Senators did not have a no-hitter until 1973 when Jim Bibby turned the trick two years after the club had moved to Texas].

According to John Jevitz of the Old Timers' Baseball Association of Joliet, Burke was a "very quiet man and would fade into a crowd."[28] Shy and even withdrawn, Burke did not talk much about himself or his career in baseball. He attended the McGowan-Ormsby Umpire school in Florida in 1940, and umpired for one season in the Southeastern League. He served in the Navy during World War II, after which he returned to his childhood home in Joliet, and became active in coaching baseball in a local park district league. He later owned and operated Bob Burke's Plainfield Fishing Resort.

Burke eventually retired with his wife, Virginia (nee Greif), to Port St. Lucie, Florida. On February

8, 1971, Burke died at his home in Florida at the age of 64. According to his Florida death certificate, the causes were natural. He is buried St. Patrick's cemetery in Joliet.

SOURCES

In addition to the sources noted in this biography, the author also accessed Burke's player file and player questionnaire from the National Baseball Hall of Fame, the *Encyclopedia of Minor League Baseball*, Retrosheet.org, Baseball-Reference.com, Bill Lee's *The Baseball Necrology*, the SABR Minor Leagues Database, accessed online at Baseball-Reference.com, *The Sporting News* archive via Paper of Record, and Ancestry.com.

NOTES

1 Don Hazen, "Bob Burke: a Senator of old," *Joliet Herald-News*, February 14, 1971.

2 *The J. 1926*. The Yearbook of Juliet Township High School. mocavo.com/The-J-Joliet-Township-High-and-Junior-College-1926-Volume-1926/902178/25#2.

3 Billy Evans, "Pitching Will Make or Break the Senators," *Alton* (Illinois) *Telegraph*, March 29, 1927: 8.

4 Ibid.

5 Harold C. Burke, "Shirley Slated For a Comeback by Freak Trade," *Brooklyn Daily Eagle*, June 7, 1928: 30.

6 Les Conklin (International News Service). "Youthful Browns May Be Successors to New York," *Huntington* (Indiana) *Herald*, June 23, 1928: 6.

7 *The Sporting News*, August 1, 1929: 1.

8 Harold C. Burr, "Mack Blames Cover On Ball For Slugging," *Brooklyn Daily Eagle*, August 10, 1929: 6.

9 Thomas Holmes, "Johnson and Griffith Believe 1931 Senators A 'Team of Destiny,'" *Brooklyn Daily Eagle*, November 26, 1930: 20.

10 *The Sporting News*, August 13, 1931: 1.

11 Les Conklin (International News Service). "Washington To Be Contenders For A.L. Flag," *Santa Ana* (California) *Register*, January 27, 1931: 8.

12 *The Sporting News*, June 4, 1931:3.

13 Ronald Valentine (Associated Press), "No-Hit, No-Run Gem Pitched By Youngster," *Anniston* (Alabama) *Star*, August 9, 1931: 12.

14 Ibid.

15 Associated Press, "Nats Troubled With Holdouts," *Post-Crescent* (Appleton, Wisconsin), February 23, 1932: 13.

16 *The Sporting News*, August 18, 1932: 3.

17 Associated Press, "Charles Jamieson is Voluntarily Retired," *Lincoln* (Nebraska) *Evening Journal*, August 19, 1932: 19.

18 *The Sporting News*, March 9, 1933: 2.

19 Harold C. Burr, "Detroit Boss Still Stands Behind Harris," *Brooklyn Daily Eagle*, March 1, 1933: 19.

20 *The Sporting News*, March 9, 1933: 2.

21 *The Sporting News*, March 29, 1934: 6.

22 Theon Wright (United Press), "Joe Moore Ends Dean Indian Sign on Giants Batters To Win, 5-3," *Dunkirk* (New York) *Evening Observer*, August 24, 1934: 10.

23 United Press, "Capital Fans Not Optimistic Over '35 Team," *Ogden* (Utah) *Standard-Examiner*, February 3, 1935: 11.

24 *The Sporting News*, June 13, 1935: 1.

25 Associated Press, "Nats Release Bob Burke," *Montana Butte Standard*, July 12, 1935: 11.

26 *The Sporting News*, November 26, 1936: 5.

27 *The Sporting News*, April 8, 1937: 6.

28 Hazen.

AN UNMATCHABLE FEAT

BOBBY BURKE FIRST AND ONLY WASHINGTON SENATOR TO TOSS NO-HITTER IN GRIFFITH STADIUM

AUGUST 8, 1931: WASHINGTON SENATORS 5, BOSTON RED SOX 0, AT GRIFFITH STADIUM

By Gregory H. Wolf

GRIFFITH STADIUM WAS THE home of the Washington Senators from 1911 until the club relocated to Minneapolis-St. Paul after the 1960 season, and then for the inaugural campaign of the expansion Senators in 1961; but only one Senators hurler ever fired in a no-hitter in that mammoth steel and concrete structure. The author of that gem was spot starter and reliever Bobby Burke, described by the Associated Press as an "in-an-outer,"[1] who fashioned a record of 38-46 and made just 88 starts in his 10-year big-league career (1927-1935, 1937), all but the last of those with Washington.

As Washington prepared to take the field on August 8, 1931, against the lowly Boston Red Sox, their third-year manager and the greatest former player in franchise history, Walter Johnson, probably recognized that his second-place club (64-39) had just a slim chance to catch the two-time reigning World Series champion Philadelphia Athletics, whom they trailed by 11 games. Sixth-place Boston (41-63), skippered by rookie pilot Shano Collins, was battling the Chicago White Sox and Detroit Tigers for the worst record in the league, and trailed the eventual pennant-winning A's by 34½ games.

Toeing the rubber for Boston was 34-year-old Wilcy Moore, who had made national headlines in 1926 by winning 30 games for the Greenville (South Carolina) Spinners in the Class-B South Atlantic League. The following season, he won 19 games and led the AL in ERA for the world-champion New York Yankees. Acquired by Boston prior to the '31 campaign from the St. Paul Saints in the Rule 5 draft, the right-handed sinker-ball pitcher known as "Cy" sported a career record of 38-23, including 9-8 thus far in '31.

Described by sportswriter Ronald Valentine as a "tall and bashful youngster, his name not outstanding in the minds of baseball fans,"[2] the 24-year-old left-handed Burke had been the eighth pitcher on Washington's eight-man staff since the rail-thin, 6-foot, 150-pounder debuted with the club in 1927. The fifth-year hurler seemed to reach his stride earlier in the '31 season, winning five straight decisions in June to improve his record to 7-1, but had been hit hard since. A most unlikely candidate to join his manager as the only Senators to pitch no-hitters (the Big Train turned the trick on July 1, 1920, against Boston at Fenway Park), Burke was making his first start since a disastrous outing against the St. Louis Browns on July 2 in which he yielded four runs and walked five in just 2⅓ innings, and had been victimized for 16 runs (all earned) in his last 26 innings. If that weren't cause for concern, the United Press reported that Burke was "working under a handicap" after he supposedly fell on an exhaust pipe the previous day while boating, and suffered a serious burn on his back.[3]

Only 5,000 spectators braved "depressing summer heat" to take in a Saturday afternoon of baseball and witness history.[4] After Burke retired leadoff hitter Jack Rothrock, Hal Rhyne smashed what the *Boston Globe* considered the Red Sox' only hard-hit ball of the game, a sharp liner that center fielder Sam West snared in "handy fashion" for the second out.[5] Burke "frequently had himself in trouble," reported the Associated Press, and struggled at times with control for the remainder of the game;[6] however, the Joliet, Illinois, native mesmerized the Red Sox hitters with what the *Boston Herald* called a "barrel of stuff."[7]

Wilcy Moore's hope to replicate his success from his previous outing, a career-best three-hit shutout against the Yankees on August 2 at Fenway Park, was dashed in the first inning. Sam Rice, a 41-year-old with 2,715 hits in his 17-year career, executed a one-out bunt. Former AL batting champ Heinie Manush, who had entered the season with a .340 batting average in eight seasons, lined to short for what seemed to be a routine double-play ball.[8] According to the *Boston Herald*, shortstop Hal Rhyne broke too soon to cover second base, and the ball went through the gap, enabling Rice to scamper to third.[9] He subsequently scored Washington's first run on Joe Cronin's force out.

A "broad grin from Dame Fortune," opined the *Herald*, led to Washington's second run, in the third inning.[10] Buddy Myer walloped a high fly ball under which, according to the *Globe*, left-fielder Rothrock "camped almost directly."[11] Blinded by the sun, Rothrock lost sight of the ball, which hit the ground and bounced. By the time he retrieved it, Myer was on his way to third. No error was charged to Rothrock. Rice followed with a whistling single (his 10th hit in his last 19 at-bats) past the pitcher to drive in Myer.

Both teams threatened in the fourth inning. With a "tendency toward unsteadiness," Burke issued free passes to rookie Urbane Pickering and Bill Sweeney, but escaped unscathed.[12] It was the only time Boston had two runners on base. After Washington's Joe Kuhel belted a two-out double, Moore intentionally walked Roy Spencer to play the percentages against his hurling counterpart. Burke obliged by making the third out.

Save for two scratch safeties in the first and a fluke hit in the third, Moore pitched well enough to keep Boston in the game. He escaped a scare in the seventh, stranding Kuhel at third after he had reached on a one-out single. But the stout, 6-foot, 200-pound Moore seemed to be wilting in the heat and humidity in the nation's capital. The Nationals, as Washington was affectionately called by both sportswriters and fans, broke the game open in the eighth when Rice, Manush, Cronin, and West connected for four consecutive singles resulting in two runs; Cronin and West were each credited with an RBI. Kuhel knocked in Cronin on a force play to give Washington a 5-0 lead.

Burke took the mound in the ninth with the Washington faithful on their feet cheering him on. He was in unusual territory. The softspoken hurler had completed only 11 of his 41 starts in his career thus far, and had only one shutout to his credit—a seven-hitter against Boston on June 22, 1928. Wiping the sweat from his brow, Burke quickly retired Rothrock on a routine liner to center fielder Sam West, and then dispatched Rhyne on a weak roller to shortstop Joe Cronin.

Club owner Clark Griffith supposedly had a soft spot in his heart for Burke, yet was concerned that the southpaw's frail frame and stamina would keep him from becoming a bona-fide big-league starter. But on this day, Burke was just one out away from baseball immortality. Nonetheless, both the players and fans had to endure a few minutes of suspense before the game concluded. Undoubtedly feeling a rush of adrenaline and perhaps some jitters, Burke issued his fifth walk of the game—and third to Pickering—to prolong the game. Boston's most dangerous hitter, Earl Webb, who set a major-league record with 67 doubles that season, took two strikes and a ball as Pickering strolled unmolested to second and third. (No stolen bases were credited.) Needing one more strike, Burke heaved a fastball; Webb kept the bat on his left shoulder as he watched the ball rocket over the plate. Home-plate umpire George Moriarty yelled strike three to end the game in just one hour and 39 minutes.

Mobbed by his teammates on the mound, Burke finished with a career-high eight punchouts while becoming, in the words of the *Boston Herald*, "one of the heroes of the national pastime."[13] Burke's gem earned him another shot as a starter, but success proved to be elusive. In his subsequent five starts, he surrendered 30 hits, 19 walks, and 19 earned runs in just 23⅓ innings. Winless after his no-hitter, Burke finished the season with an 8-3 record and 4.27 ERA in 128⅔ innings.

Major-league baseball was played for another 30 years in Griffith Stadium, but only Bobby Burke can lay claim to be the sole Senators hurler to toss a no-hitter in the history of that park. The next no-hitter by a Washington pitcher in the nation's capital came 83 years later, when 28-year-old All-Star right-hander Jordan Zimmerman of the Washington Nationals turned the trick on September 28, 2014, against the Miami Marlins in the club's last game of the season.

NOTES

1 Associated Press, "Bobby Burke, an In and Outer With Washington for 4 Years, Pitches No-Hit, No-Run Game," *Jacksonville* (Illinois) *Daily Journal*, August 9, 1931: 10.

2 Ronald Valentine (Associated Press), "No-Hit, No-Run Gem Pitched by Youngster," *Anniston* (Alabama) *Star*, August 9, 1931: 12.

3 Ibid.

4 Ibid.

5 "No Hit for Red Sox Against Burke," *Boston Globe*, August 9, 1931: A1.

6 Associated Press, "Bobby Burke, an In and Outer With Washington for 4 Years, Pitches No-Hit, No-Run Game," *Jacksonville* (Illinois) *Daily Journal*.

7 "Senators Bunch Hits to Emerge Victorious, 5-0," *Boston Herald*, August 9, 1931: 1.

8 As a member of the Detroit Tigers, the 24-year-old Manush led the majors with a .378 batting average in 1926.

9 "Senators Bunch Hits to Emerge Victorious, 5-0," *Boston Herald*.

10 Ibid.

11 No Hit for Red Sox Against Burke."

12 Ibid.

13 "Senators Bunch Hits to Emerge Victorious, 5-0." Burke also had eight strikeouts against the St. Louis Browns in an eight-inning relief outing on May 12, 1934, at Griffith Stadium.

BILL DIETRICH

By Gregory H. Wolf

HARD-THROWING RIGHT-hander Bill Dietrich battled wildness, struggled with his temper, and endured chronic elbow pain that resulted in two operations to fashion a 108-128 record and log in excess of 2,000 innings in parts of 16 injury-plagued big-league seasons (1933-1948) while playing for primarily second-division clubs. Twice waived out the American League in 1936, Dietrich signed with the Chicago White Sox, with whom his career was revived by skipper Jimmy Dykes and coach Muddy Ruel. The following season Dietrich seemed like an unlikely candidate to throw a no-hitter; however, two days after surrendering 10 runs and 14 baserunners in a disastrous 3⅓-inning start, Dietrich ignored his bloated 10.13 ERA to hold the St. Louis Browns hitless at Comiskey Park on June 1.

A lifelong resident of Philadelphia, William John Dietrich was born on March 29, 1910, in the City of Brotherly Love. His Pennsylvania-born parents of German ancestry were Charles, an accountant, and Berth (Hopes) Dietrich. The family also had an older son, Charles, and a younger daughter, Mable. By all accounts Bill was a small and unathletic child who began wearing glasses by the age of 8. Despite weighing only about 115 pounds when he enrolled in Frankford High School in the Near Northeast Side of the city in 1925, Bill tried out for the freshman baseball team. "I was not much good [as an infielder]," recalled Dietrich, "but it was noticed that I could throw the ball hard. I was advised to take up pitching … and my progress was quick."[1] Aided by a growth spurt that packed about 60 pounds onto his eventual 6-foot frame, young Bill became one of the best athletes in school history. He lettered in football, basketball, and baseball for three years each, and developed into one of the area's best hurlers. As a senior in 1929 he led his high-school nine to the Philadelphia Public League championship, fanning 20 batters in a 13-inning complete game and scoring the winning run in the title game.[2] By that time, scouts from big-league teams routinely watched him pitch. After graduating, Dietrich worked out at Shibe Park at the invitation of Athletics manager Connie Mack, who signed him to a contract for the 1930 season. Dietrich supposedly rejected more lucrative offers from both the New York Giants and the New York Yankees to sign with the reigning champions.[3]

After competing in various semipro leagues in the summer and fall of 1929 and during an abbreviated college experience at Villanova, Dietrich joined the A's in spring training in Fort Myers, Florida, in 1930. Practicing with the likes of 20-game winners Lefty Grove and George Earnshaw, the teenage Dietrich held his own. Mack, who thought the youngster could benefit by being around big leaguers, took an unorthodox approach by retaining Dietrich as a batting-practice pitcher at home game during the season, instead of optioning him to the minors. Dietrich continued hurling in Philadelphia's semipro league the entire season.

Dietrich's career in Organized Baseball officially got under way in 1931 when he was optioned to the Harrisburg Senators of the Class-B New York-Pennsylvania League after participating in spring training with the big-league club. En route to an 18-11 season and a sturdy 2.89 ERA (but also 130 walks in 209 innings) for the league champions, Dietrich tossed a no-hitter on June 6 against Wilkes-Barre in just his eighth professional start.[4]

Described by the *Harrisburg Telegraph* as possessing an "extremely fast ball" but also being "very erratic," Dietrich began the 1932 season with the Portland Beavers in the Double-A Pacific Coast League.[5] In mid-July, sporting a 5-7 record, Dietrich was sent back to the New York-Penn League (by one account he asked to pitch closer to home),[6] where he twirled for Wilkes-Barre, winning nine of 13 decisions.

In spring training with the A's for the first time in two seasons, the 23-year-old Dietrich impressed Connie Mack with his speed, and broke north with the club to start the 1933 season. He debuted in the second game of the campaign, on April 13, relieving Earnshaw with one out in the sixth inning at Washington. He yielded three hits and two walks to the five batters he faced, and was charged with three earned runs in a forgettable outing. It didn't get much better for the native son, who was optioned to Montreal in the Double-A International League in late May. Despite struggling north of the border (5.19 ERA and 104 walks in 156 innings), Dietrich returned as a September call-up to the A's, who finished in third place with 79 wins, their lowest total since 1924.

Mack, whose primary income was his baseball club, continued dismantling the team in light of the financial hardships brought on by the Great Depression. After selling Al Simmons to the Chicago White Sox after the 1932 season, the "Tall Tactician" dealt two more future Hall of Famers after the '33 season: Lefty Grove to the Boston Red Sox and Mickey Cochrane to the Detroit Tigers. Mack counted on Dietrich to shore up a young, inexperienced staff that included two first-year players who had respectable seasons: Johnny Marcum (14-11, 4.50 ERA) and Joe Cascarella (12-15, 4.68) and three-year veteran, Sugar Cain (9-17, 4.41). Dietrich got off to a horrible start (10 runs in 10⅔ innings of relief), then lacerated his right thumb on a bottle in mid-May. According to sportswriter Frank Reil, Dietrich was on the verge of being optioned when he pitched a complete-game four-hitter to pick up his maiden big-league victory, 4-2 over the St. Louis Browns.[7] Frustratingly inconsistent, Dietrich was either very good (he tossed four shutouts, including a sparking two-hitter against Washington in his next to last start of the year) or horrible. He surrendered at least five earned runs in 11 of his 23 starts, including 11 in a complete-game loss to the Yankees. He finished with an 11-12 record and a 4.68 ERA in 207⅔ innings, and issued a career-high 114 free passes for the fifth-place

A's. Twice that season he walked a career-high nine batters; one of those games was on July 28 against the Yankees, whom he defeated in a distance-going outing, 4-3, despite yielding 17 baserunners.

Dietrich was among the few players who wore spectacles, and rarely did a sportswriter refer to him without mentioning his cheaters. Like Will White of Cincinnati in the American Association in the 1880s and later Lee Meadows of the National League (1915-1929), widely considered the first pitchers to don glasses on the mound, Dietrich's glasses were not shatterproof. Luckily he was never hit in the face by a batted ball. "I had my cap knocked off lots of times," recalled Dietrich. "Line drives would come so close to my ear that they would actually draw blood."[8] Throughout his career, Dietrich was known as "Bullfrog," given his moon-shaped face punctuated by his round eyeglasses.

Dietrich slipped to 7-13 in 1935 as the A's finished in last place for the first time since 1921. "[He] had a very bad year, both as a starting pitcher and relief pitcher," opined Philadelphia sportswriter James C. Isaminger.[9] Of Dietrich's 18 starts in a career-best 43 appearances, five came within a 20-day span in August. A six-hit shutout against Cleveland at League Park IV on August 22 was sandwiched between four losses during which he yielded 30 runs in 32 innings. In the final of those defeats, Dietrich surrendered career highs in runs (13), earned runs (11), and hits (17), and also walked eight in a loss to Detroit. Dietrich's 5.39 ERA (in 185⅓ innings) was the third-highest in the AL.

Dietrich's big-league career was in peril in 1936. An exasperated Mack finally cut ties with the walk-prone "problem child" of his staff, placing Dietrich on waivers about a week after the right-hander tossed 11 innings of relief against Chicago on June 19, yielding only two unearned runs in the 13th inning to lose the game.[10] Despite Dietrich's unsightly 6.53 ERA in 71⅔ innings, the Washington Senators claimed him. Dietrich made only five ineffective relief appearances (nine earned runs in 8⅓ innings) before he was given his outright option to Albany of the International League. Unexpectedly, the Chicago White Sox blocked the move by claiming him off waivers. Thrust into the starting rotation, Dietrich tossed a complete game in his first start in a 19-6 drubbing of the A's, then blanked the Boston Red Sox on two hits in his next start.

Notwithstanding Dietrich's dismal 5.75 ERA in 162⅔ innings for three teams in 1936, Chicago skipper Jimmy Dykes and his trusted coach Muddy Ruel saw a reclamation project. Ruel, a former catcher, thought that Dietrich's wildness resulted from clenching the ball too tightly, and suggested a lighter grip. That advice helped Dietrich harness his control enough to be a productive hurler for the next decade despite two elbow operations and a host of other injuries.

While Ruel worked on Dietrich's mechanics, Dykes addressed his attitude. Dietrich had a reputation as a hothead. "[He] had one of the worst tempers in baseball," said Dykes. "It was the thing that beat him day after day. ... I told him I thought he had the makings of a great pitcher except for his temper. 'You break your temper or I'll break you,' I said to him."[11]

Dietrich responded to Dykes's tough love and reined in his temper.

Dietrich got off to a dismal start in 1937, suffering from flu-like symptoms and sinus problems. On May 29 Cleveland assaulted him for nine hits and 10 runs in just 3⅓ innings, raising his ERA to 10.13 in 16 innings. Undeterred by the humiliating loss, Dykes sent the Bullfrog back to the mound on two days' rest to face the St. Louis Browns at Comiskey Park on June 1. Defying expectations, Dietrich tossed the game of his life, a headline-grabbing no-hitter, and issued just two free passes. The victory was part of what Chicago sportswriter Irving Vaughan called a "sensational spurt" of 10 consecutive wins that catapulted the White Sox into a tie with the Yankees for first place on June 8 and ignited pennant fever.[12] The team eventually settled for third place and 86 victories, their best marks since 1920 when the Black Sox scandal broke. Dietrich, bothered by a sore elbow most of the season, went 8-10 and carved out a 4.90 ERA in 143⅓ innings.

In the offseason Dietrich underwent surgery on his right elbow to remove bone chips and growths. The presiding surgeon, Dr. Phillip H. Kreuscher of Philadelphia, expected the hurler to be able to pitch in 1938. However, Dietrich's recovery was slow and his elbow swelled every time he threw. By mid-June Dietrich had made only eight mostly ineffective appearances (5.44 ERA with 31 walks in 48 innings) and was placed on the voluntarily retired list a month later.[13]

In the next two seasons Dietrich saw action primarily as a spot starter and occasional reliever as the White Sox recorded consecutive fourth-place finishes. He went 7-8 (5.22 ERA in 127⅔ innings) in 1939, then enjoyed his first winning season (10-6) with a more respectable 4.03 ERA in 149⅔ innings in 1940. In the last five weeks of that season, a finally healthy Dietrich flashed the kind of heater that once made Connie Mack compare him to Walter Johnson and Lefty Grove. In his best stretch of ball since 1934, the Bullfrog completed four of seven starts, relieved once and posted a stellar 2.44 ERA in 66⅓ innings.

In an oft-repeated refrain in White Sox history, the 1941 club was characterized by the league's lowest-scoring offense and stingiest staff (3.52 team ERA). The result was a .500 record, yet a third-place finish. The mound corps included All-Stars Thornton Lee (22-11, with a league-leading 2.37 ERA and 30 complete games) and Eddie Smith, as well as 40-year-old Sunday hurler Ted Lyons. Dietrich, described by Stan Baumgartner in *The Sporting News* as one of the "backbones" of the squad, took the mound on Opening Day in front of more than 46,000 partisan fans at Cleveland's Municipal Stadium to face off against Bob Feller, coming off a 27-win season.[14] In the second inning, Feller hit Dietrich with a fastball on his right elbow. "Closest call I ever had," recounted Dietrich years later. "I just got my hands up to protect my face."[15] Courtesy pinch-runner Don Kolloway took first while trainers tended to Dietrich. Surprisingly, Dietrich came back to the mound the next inning and outdueled Bullet Bob, spinning a seven-hitter to win, 4-3. Never one to back down, Dietrich also plunked Feller, in the fifth with a changeup. Apparently feeling no ill effects from Feller's errant throw, Dietrich held Detroit hitless for 8⅓ innings in an eventual 6-3 victory in his next start. But bad luck always seemed to find Dietrich, who the *Chicago Tribune* suggested was a "child of repeated misfortune."[16] One start after yielding only a fourth-inning single in a shutout against the Browns on May 29 for his fourth victory of the season (all by complete game), Dietrich injured his thumb in a bunt attempt against Washington and was sidelined almost four weeks.[17] In his second start after returning, he injured the same thumb while bunting and also suffered a leg injury in a collision at first base, and was scratched for three more weeks.[18] Dietrich's once promising season ended with a 5-8 record with a bloated 5.35 ERA in 109⅓ innings.

After the White Sox' sixth-place finish in 1942, sportswriter Irving Vaughan of the *Chicago Tribune* opined ominously that "only a super-optimist would endeavor to paint a picture showing the Sox ready for what is coming in 1943."[19] Dietrich, who had won six of 17 decisions with the fourth-highest ERA in the league (4.89) in 160 innings the previous season, was named Opening Day starter. He lost his first three starts despite yielding just seven earned runs in 24 innings, then was hit on the right arm by a liner off the bat of Washington's Rip Radcliff on May 9.[20] Dietrich suffered no broken bones, but his arm was put in splints. Over the next seven weeks he made only four abbreviated starts before hurling a four-hit shutout on July 1 against Early Wynn and the Senators, completed in one hour and 39 minutes. Bullfrog finished the season in a flurry, winning all five of his decisions by complete game in September with a stellar 1.29 ERA in 56 innings. Included among his six starts were consecutive 10-inning outings (in the former of which he scored the winning, walk-off run after being hit by a pitch), as well as a seven-hit shut-out against New York in Yankee Stadium.[21] In his hitherto best season in the big leagues, Dietrich set new personal bests in wins (12; he also lost 10), starts (26), and ERA (2.80 in 186⅔ innings) for the surprisingly competitive fourth-place White Sox (82-72).

In 1944 the White Sox conducted spring training for the second consecutive season in the southern Indiana spa town of French Lick, about 280 miles from Chicago. Baseball Commissioner Kenesaw Mountain Landis had instituted travel restrictions and ordered all teams to conduct camp north of the Mason-Dixon Line and east of the Mississippi River in order to conserve resources for the war effort. (The St. Louis teams were excepted.) The White Sox and their NL brethren, the Cubs, shared a site at the French Lick Spring hotel, and battled cold, wet weather.[22]

While the White Sox lost defending AL batting champion shortstop Luke Appling and workhorse southpaw Eddie Smith to military service, the pitching staff remained relatively intact for the '44 season. Dietrich, who had been given a 1-B classification (fit for limited service because of previous injury and his family),[23] was joined by the top winner from '43, Orval Grove, Johnny Humphries, and a highly touted 26-year-old rookie, southpaw Eddie Lopat. That group impressed Chicago beat writer Irving

Vaughan, who boldly predicted that the club would win the AL pennant.[24]

After dropping his first two starts of the '44 season, Dietrich finally won in exciting fashion. Described by *Tribune* writer Ed Burns as "the big man on offense and defense," Dietrich held Cleveland to five hits, singled in the 10th, and subsequently tallied the walk-off run with two outs on a "brilliant sprint" from second base in a 3-2 victory.[25] Not known for his hitting or running, Dietrich batted just .150 (94-for-627) in his career. For what seemed like the first time since his rookie season, Dietrich hurled an entire season without suffering a serious injury. To be sure, he still occasionally let his temperament get the best of him; he often argued with skipper Jimmy Dykes and bawled out teammates who muffed plays. Ed Burns described Dietrich as "high-strung" and "allergic to nagging";[26] however, the 34-year-old Bullfrog enjoyed a career year in 1944. Over a nine-week stretch from May 27 to August 3, he was one of the best twirlers in the league, completing eight of 17 starts, winning 12 of 17 decisions, and carving out a stellar 2.17 ERA in 124⅓ innings. On July 9 he was honored in his hometown after the first game of a doubleheader against the A's at Shibe Park. Dietrich picked up the win (one run in six innings) and also war bonds and a travel bag, while friends and families made public tributes. Despite Vaughan's optimistic prediction, the White Sox finished in seventh place as the offense sputtered, finishing last in batting average, home runs, and slugging percentage, and seventh in runs scored. In what proved to be Dietrich's last full season in the majors, he set personal bests in practically every pitching category, including wins (16) starts (36), innings (246), and complete games (15) while posting a 3.62 ERA. He was also a hard-luck loser; in 16 of his league-leading 17 defeats (tied with Early Wynn), Chicago scored just 22 runs, including nine games of one run or less.

Dietrich was the object of fierce trading rumors in the offseason. Most reports had him going to the Cleveland Indians as part of a four- or six-player deal, but neither skipper Dykes nor player-manager Lou Boudreau could agree on what they considered an equitable transaction.[27] Nonetheless, when Chicago opened spring training in Terre Haute, Indiana, about 180 miles south of the Windy City, Dietrich was nowhere to be found. [As Don Zminda has pointed out, the Cubs' and White Sox' two-year experiment conducting joint spring training in French Lick ended because of players and coaching staffs arguing about space, facilities, and even the golf course.[28]] Demanding a raise, Dietrich finally arrived in camp at the end of March after accepting a contract worth $9,500, a substantial $2,500 salary increase. But after his first start, Dietrich complained of soreness in his elbow. Irving Vaughan reported that an examination by team physician John Claridge determined that the 35-year-old hurler had bone chips in his elbow that required surgery.[29] Despite optimistic predictions that the hurler would miss only three weeks, Dietrich made his next start two months later. In that dramatic return on June 18, Dietrich spun a four-hit shutout against Dizzy Trout and the Detroit Tigers, earning the 1-0 victory when Mike Tresh hit a one-out walk-off single. He tossed two more 1-0 shutouts in a three-start span in July, blanking Philadelphia on nine hits and hurling 11 frames against New York in Yankee Stadium, allowing seven hits and walking just one. The latter was the ninth and final time Dietrich pitched at least 10 innings in a game. Suffering from arm pain throughout the season, Dietrich was limited to 16 starts, finishing with a 7-10 record and 4.19 ERA in 122⅓ innings for the sixth-place White Sox.

Named Opening Day starter in 1946, Dietrich squared off against Bob Feller in a rematch from five years earlier, on April 16 at Comiskey Park. Dietrich "pitched with brilliance," opined Ed Burns, striking out a career-high nine and allowing only six hits in a distance-going outing.[30] However, Feller, who had tossed the first and (as of 2015) only no-hitter on Opening Day, was better, hurling a three-hitter and whiffing 10 in a 1-0 victory. Given some extra time between assignments, Dietrich was off to a good start before suffering a season-ending injury against Washington on June 25. A liner back to the mound by Cecil Travis hit Dietrich in the thumb, breaking it. According to the *Tribune*, Dietrich returned home to Philadelphia after initial x-rays and examinations; however, his relationship with Ted Lyons, who had replaced Dykes as skipper after 30 games, soon turned toxic. When Dietrich failed to report to Chicago for treatment, Lyons suspended him on August 15. "I acted in good faith when I left Chicago after the team physician told me I would have to wait for several weeks for additional x-rays," said Dietrich, who also added defiantly, "I'll just stay home even if I don't get paid."[31] About a month later, Chicago gave Dietrich his unconditional release. He had posted a 3-3 record and robust 2.61 ERA in 62 innings.

Despite Dietrich's age and an injury-prone career, the venerable Connie Mack signed the hurler. But it didn't take long for the injury bug to reappear as a member of the A's in '47. According to *The Sporting News*, Dietrich tore a back muscle in spring training.[32] After two relief outings, Dietrich made his first start on May 6 against the White Sox at Comiskey Park. Relying on guile and probably a desire for revenge, Dietrich tossed his 17th and final shutout, blanking his former team on five hits. Plagued by arm pain all season, Dietrich made only eight more starts, finishing with a 5-2 record, a 3.12 ERA and 40 walks 60⅔ innings. In his last victory of the season, as well as a big-league starting pitcher, Dietrich tossed a five-hitter to beat Chicago at Shibe Park.

The dean of AL hurlers in 1948, Dietrich tossed only 15⅓ innings before he was released on June 14, bringing an 18-year career in Organized Baseball to a conclusion (except for an abbreviated comeback attempt with Triple-A Oakland in 1950). He compiled a 108-128 record, started 253 of 366 appearances, and posted a 4.48 ERA in 2003⅔ innings as a big leaguer.

Dietrich settled into his post-playing career with his wife, Doris, his former high-school sweetheart, and their two children, Bill Jr. and Lynne. Save for his brief spell with Oakland, Dietrich had very little contact with major-league baseball after his playing days. He worked as a salesman for the Frankford-Unity grocery-store chain, retiring in 1957. "I'm through with baseball," Dietrich said in 1952.[33] According to Philadelphia sportswriter Harold Rosenthal, Dietrich was bitter because he had played on poor clubs.[34] He discouraged his son from playing baseball, too. "I always said that if I caught him playing baseball, I'd break his arm … his pitching arm."[35] Despite his father's disapproval, Bill Jr. became a stalwart pitcher at Frankford High School and signed with the New York Yankees in 1952. In seven years spent primarily in the low minors, Junior went 40-41. As a member of the Monroe (Louisiana) Sports in the Class-C Cotton States League, Bill joined his father on April 28, 1955, by tossing a no-hitter against the Greenville (Mississippi) Bucks.[36]

Dietrich died at the age of 68 on June 20, 1978, at his home in Philadelphia.

SOURCES

In addition to the sources noted in this biography, the author also accessed Dietrich's player file and player questionnaire from the National Baseball Hall of Fame, the *Encyclopedia of Minor League Baseball*, Retrosheet.org, Baseball-Reference.com, Bill Lee's *The Baseball Necrology*, the SABR Minor Leagues Database, accessed online at Baseball-Reference.com, *The Sporting News* archive via Paper of Record, and Ancestry.com.

NOTES

1. Unattributed and undated article in Bill Dietrich's Hall of Fame file.
2. "Philadelphia High School Baseball Recaps of Public School Title Games," TedSilary.com; tedsilary.com/BASEPLtitlerecaps.htm.
3. "Dietrich to Pitch Against Black Sox," *Mount Carmel* (Pennsylvania) *Item*, August 15, 1929: 4.
4. "Bill Dietrich Hangs Up No-Hit, No-Run Record Saturday," *Harrisburg* (Pennsylvania) *Telegraph*, June 8, 1931: 12.
5. *Harrisburg* (Pennsylvania) *Telegraph*, July 8, 1932: 12.
6. Ibid.
7. Frank Reil, "Tigers, Hustling Team Under Cochrane, Look Good To Mack," *Brooklyn Daily Eagle*, July 6, 1934: 18.
8. *The Sporting News*, November 19, 1952: 5.
9. *The Sporting News*, August 29, 1935: 2.
10. *The Sporting News*, July 9, 1936: 1.
11. *The Sporting News*, June 5, 1941: 1.
12. *The Sporting News*, June 10, 1937: 2.
13. Associated Press, "Bill Dietrich Is On Retired List," *Shamokin* (Pennsylvania) *News-Dispatch*, July 14, 1938: 10.

14 *The Sporting News*, June 5, 1941: 1.

15 *The Sporting News*, November 19, 1952: 5.

16 "Bill Dietrich To Pitch Today in Boston Final," *Chicago Tribune*, July 24, 1941: 17.

17 "Chicago Fans Give Watch To Connie Mack," *Chicago Tribune*, June 5, 1941: 31.

18 "Bill Dietrich To Pitch Today in Boston Final," *Chicago Tribune*, July 24, 1941: 17.

19 Irving Vaughan, "White Sox Lead with Dietrich; Play St. Louis," *Chicago Tribune*, April 21, 1943: 31.

20 Judson Bailey, "Lively Ball Brings Lively Disputes to Big Leagues Sunday," *Dixon* (Illinois) *Evening Telegraph*, May 10, 1943: 6.

21 Irving Vaughan, "Sox Win, 3-2, Over Browns in 10 Innings," *Chicago Tribune*, September 18, 1943: A1.

22 "Sports Flashback: White Sox and Cubs spring training in French Lick," *Chicago Tribune*, February 20, 2015. Chicagotribune.com/sports/baseball/ct-flashback-cubs-sox-spring-training-spt-0222-20150220-story.html.

23 "Bill Dietrich Accepted For Limited Service," *Alton* (Illinois) *Telegraph*, March 3, 1944: 16.

24 Irving Vaughan, "Sox Rated as Team to Beat for the A.L. Crown," *Chicago Tribune*, April 16, 1944: A1.

25 Ed Burns, "Cubs Face Reds; Sox Win in 10th," *Chicago Tribune*, May 2, 1944: 25.

26 Ed Burns, "Bill Dietrich Yields 7 Hits in 9-5 Triumph," *Chicago Tribune*, September 9, 1944: 19.

27 Ed Burns, "Sox and Indians Pilots Weigh 6 Player Deal," *Chicago Tribune*, December 7, 1944: 31.

28 Don Zminda, "The White Sox in Wartime," in *Who's On First. Replacement Players in World War II*, eds. Mark Z. Aaron and Bill Nowlin (Phoenix, Arizona: Society for American Baseball Research, 2015), 221.

29 Irving Vaughan, "Dietrich Lost to White Sox for Three Weeks," *Chicago Tribune*, April 26, 1945: 25.

30 Ed Burns, "Cubs Win, 4-3; Indians, Feller Whip Sox, 1-0," *Chicago Tribune*, April 16, 1946: 25.

31 "Suspension Irks Dietrich," *Chicago Tribune*, August 17, 1946: 17.

32 *The Sporting News*, April 16, 1947: 18.

33 *The Sporting News*, November 19, 1952: 5.

34 Ibid.

35 Ibid.

36 Associated Press, "No-hit Game Pitched by Bill Dietrich, Jr.," *Terre Haute* (Indiana) *Tribune*, April 29, 1955: 2.

"BULLFROG" DIETRICH RESUSCITATES CAREER WITH A NO-HITTER
JUNE 1, 1937: CHICAGO WHITE SOX 8, ST. LOUIS BROWNS 0, AT COMISKEY PARK

By Gregory H. Wolf

THE CHICAGO WHITE SOX' bespectacled 27-year-old right-hander Bill Dietrich's five-year big-league career was at a crossroads when he took the mound against the St. Louis Browns on June 1, 1937, in the Windy City. In his last start, just two days earlier, Dietrich was "battered almost beyond recognition," opined *Chicago Tribune* sportswriter Irving Vaughn, surrendering 10 runs in just 3⅓ innings to the Cleveland Indians.[1] With an ERA of 10.12, Dietrich probably recognized that his days on skipper Jimmy Dykes' staff were numbered.

The last year had been a trying one for Dietrich. The previous June Philadelphia Athletics owner Connie Mack, who had signed the local phenom out of high school in 1929, finally gave up on the erratic hard-thrower and sold him to the Washington Senators in a waiver transaction. When Washington attempted to send Dietrich outright to Albany in the International League after five relief appearances and just three weeks, Chicago blocked the move. Dykes and his trusted coach, former big-league catcher Muddy Ruel, were known to take chances on pitching reclamation projects, and acquired Dietrich despite his 22-33 career record and ERA well in excess of 5.00. Dietrich, whom coaches and teammates called "Bullfrog" because of his round face and slightly protruding eyes magnified by his glasses, split his eight decisions for the White Sox in '36, but had thus far struggled in '37 while battling the flu and sinus problems.

Undoubtedly suppressing the memories of his last start, Dietrich enjoyed a 1-2-3 inning against manager Rogers Hornsby's Browns on a warm Tuesday in Comiskey Park. Chicago had kicked off a 14-game homestand the day before by sweeping last-place St. Louis (10-24) in a doubleheader to increase its winning streak to three games and move a game over .500 (18-17). The White Sox wasted no time pummeling 33-year-old left-hander Chief Hogsett, owner of a 53-66 record in his nine-year career, including 1-4 with a 5.79 ERA thus far in '37. Leadoff hitter Rip Radcliff drew a walk and scampered to third on "Iron Mike" Kreevich's double to left; both scored on Dixie Walker's double to right. After retiring Zeke Bonura and Luke Appling, Hogsett walked Jackie Hayes and Tony Piet to load the bases. His third consecutive walk, to Luke Sewell, resulted in the third run of the game. Hogsett dispatched Dietrich to end the frame.

Following another three-up-three-down inning by Dietrich, Hogsett returned to the mound, still smarting from his rude welcome in the first inning. Hogsett "started to work himself into another spasm of wildness," wrote Irving Vaughn, and walked Radcliff again. A seemingly perpetually perturbed Hornsby yanked Hogsett in favor of swingman Russ Van Atta, who had led the AL in pitching appearances in each of the previous two campaigns. The 31-year-old left-hander with a 28-32 record in five seasons induced Kreevich to hit a grounder that forced Radcliff at second, before he "was bitten by the control bug." Van Atta walked Walker, then received a boost from shortstop Bill Knickerbocker, who fielded Bonura's lazy grounder to initiate an inning-ending 6-4-3 double play.

After Dietrich retired his 12th straight batter, Chicago's leadoff hitter reached base for the fourth consecutive time when Sewell drew a walk in the fifth. [Appling had singled to start the third but was erased in a failed stolen-base attempt]. Sewell took off on contact as Dietrich attempted a sacrifice bunt. Third baseman Harlond Clift fielded the ball and "foolishly attempted a force play at second," opined Vaughn. Both runners were safe and subsequently advanced on Radcliff's sacrifice bunt. Kreevich, who had gone 26-for-73 in his previous 17 games to raise his batting average from .176 to .322, singled to drive in Sewell and Dietrich, and advanced to second when left fielder Joe Vosmik fumbled the ball. Bonura drew a two-out walk, but Appling failed to pad Chicago's 5-0 lead, flying out to right.

Dietrich's perfect game ended in the sixth inning when he walked the leadoff batter, Rollie Hemsley, on four pitches. The slow-footed catcher was retired one batter later when Tom Carey hit a bouncer to shortstop Luke Appling, who started a 6-4-3 twin killing. Dietrich committed a cardinal sin by walking his mound counterpart, Van Atta, then ended the inning by inducing Harry Davis to ground out to first baseman Zeke Bonura.

Sam West led off the top of the seventh with what Vaughn called the "most treacherous" hit of the game, a screeching liner to first base. But fourth-year veteran Bonura, who had led AL first sackers in fielding percentage in two of his first three seasons, made a leaping catch to keep the no-hitter intact. It was his second spectacular defensive play of the game. In the fifth inning he snared Knickerbocker's slashing liner. Hot-hitting Beau Bell, who eventually led the AL in hits (218) and doubles (51) while batting .340 in 1937, smashed a two-out liner to third baseman Tony Piet, who juggled the ball just long enough to permit Bell to reach first safely. Piet was charged with an error. Unshaken by Bell's presence on the basepaths, Dietrich fanned Clift to close out the seventh.

The White Sox battered Van Atta for three more runs in the eighth. Sewell led off with a double. Kreevich connected for his third hit, a two-out single to left field, to drive in Sewell. The fleet-footed, 5-foot-7, 165-pound Kreevich stole second and moved to third on Hemsley's errant throw. Dixie Walker took advantage of the situation by singling Kreevich home. After Bonura singled, Appling slapped Chicago's fourth consecutive two-out single, driving in Walker and increasing Chicago's lead to 8-0.

Known throughout his career as a hothead whose temper often got the better of him, Dietrich took the mound in the ninth just three outs from becoming the first big-league pitcher since his Chicago teammate Vern Kennedy held Cleveland hitless on August 31, 1935, at Comiskey Park. An unusually calm Dietrich revealed to Irving Vaughn after the game that he was not nervous in the last two-plus innings because he had a feeling that the error charged to Piet in the seventh would be overturned and Bell credited with a hit. Nonetheless, Dietrich knew the pressure of a no-hitter. In just his fourth professional start, in 1931, the Bullfrog spun a no-hitter against Wilkes-Barre in the Class-B New York-Pennsylvania League as a member of the Harrisburg Senators.

Dietrich began the ninth by retiring Sunny Jim Bottomley, in the final campaign of a 16-year Hall of Fame career, on a routine fly to center fielder Kreevich. Given his recent struggles, Dietrich was in unusual terrain. He had not hurled a nine-inning complete game since defeating the Browns at Sportsman's Park on August 6 of the previous year. The knock against Dietrich was his lack of command and his frustrating inconsistency. But when the stout, 6-foot, 185-pound hurler could harness his fastball, he enjoyed moments of brilliance, and had tossed six shutouts, including two two-hitters, in just 54 career starts entering the '37 campaign. Dietrich retired Harry Davis on an "easy bounder" to second baseman Jackie Hayes for the second out. As the White Sox faithful stood cheering, Dietrich threw a fastball by Sam West, who swung and missed to end the game in one hour and 48 minutes.

Mobbed by teammates, Dietrich finished with five punchouts. "His fastball was on the inside corner for both right- and left-hand hitters," said batterymate Luke Sewell, who caught his third no-hitter. "As a result, they were hitting the ball with the handle of their bats and easy fly balls followed."[2] Undoubtedly aided by Dykes and Ruel, Dietrich pitched consistently enough to maintain his spot in the rotation, and concluded the campaign with an 8-10 record and 4.90 ERA in 143⅓ innings. Plagued by myriad injuries throughout his 16-year career (1933-1948), Dietrich enjoyed his greatest success in the war years with the White Sox, retiring with a 108-128 record.

Dietrich's gem was the White Sox' fourth of 10 consecutive victories that catapulted the club from sixth place on May 29 into a tie with the New York Yankees for first place on June 8. It was the first time Chicago had been at the top of the AL standings that late in the season since August 31, 1920, just four weeks before former White Sox players Eddie Cicotte and Shoeless Joe Jackson confessed their participation in a scheme to fix the 1919 World Series to a grand jury. Manager Jimmy Dykes' '37 club ultimately finished in third place with an 86-68 record, their best marks since their fateful and history-altering 1920 season.

NOTES

1 All quotations are from Irving Vaughn, "Dietrich Hurls No-Hit Game; Sox Win, 8-0," *Chicago Tribune*, June 2, 1937: 23.

2 Joe Wancho, "Luke Sewell," SABR BioProject; sabr.org/bioproj/person/3fcde47d. In addition to Dietrich's no-hitter, Sewell also caught Vern Kennedy's in 1935 and Wes Ferrell's as a member of the Cleveland Indians on April 29, 1931.

BOB FELLER

By C. Paul Rogers III

BOB FELLER WAS A 35-year-old veteran of 15 major-league seasons in 1954 when the Cleveland Indians won 111 games and swept to the American League pennant by eight games over the New York Yankees. His fastball had lost a good deal of its luster and manager Al Lopez had reportedly wanted to release him during spring training. Lopez, however, was overruled by general manager Hank Greenberg, who was worried about fan reaction, particularly since Feller had pitched pretty well in 1953, winning 10 while losing seven.[1]

Still, Lopez was reluctant to rely on Feller and sat him on the bench until the third week of the season, when he started Feller in the first game of a doubleheader against the Washington Senators. Feller was gone by the fifth inning but escaped with a no-decision. His next opportunity was not until two weeks later, and this time he made it only until the third inning, again ending with a no-decision as the Indians won. Fortunately, Lopez gave him another chance a week later. This time Feller showed he had something left in the tank, pitching a complete-game 14-3 win over the Baltimore Orioles for the 250th win of his storied career.

After a complete-game loss to the White Sox, Feller got on to a roll, winning six consecutive starts to stand at 7-1 on July 21. Lopez was starting him every six days to great effect. In those six wins he allowed a grand total of only seven runs. His fastball revived to the extent that, if not back to 1940s standards, it was above average. He had developed a sinker to go with his curveball and slider, and sometimes even broke out a knuckleball.[2] For the season, Feller finished with 13 victories against just three losses. He threw nine complete games in 19 starts and allowed only 127 hits in his 140 innings of work.

Feller was naturally quite anxious to win his first World Series game, accurately thinking the 1954 World Series would be his last chance.[3] Lopez originally penciled Feller to start Game Three against the New York Giants, the first game to be played in Cleveland. When the Indians lost the first two games in the Polo Grounds, however, Lopez opted to start Mike Garcia, who had won 19 games and had the lowest earned-run average in the American League, in Game Three. Feller was hopeful of starting Game Four, but when Cleveland lost Game Three to go down three games to zero, Lopez selected 23-game-winner Bob Lemon to go on short rest. Unhappily for the Tribe, that didn't work either as the Giants won to sweep the Series.

Feller continued to be perplexed as to why Lopez did not use him at all in the Series, noting that Lopez used seven pitchers, including all the principal starters and relievers but him. In his second memoir, he pointed out that those seven gave up 21 runs in four games.[4] His real last chance for a World Series victory, he lamented, had been in 1948, the last time the Indians had been in the Series.[5] It was indeed, for the Indians would finish second in both 1955 and 1956, the last two years of Feller's career.

Robert William Andrew Feller was born on November 3, 1918, in Van Meter, Iowa, the first of two children to the former Lena Forrett, a schoolteacher and registered nurse, and William Feller, a farmer. The boy was perhaps the first to be raised by his father to be a major-league star.[6] Before little Bobby could walk, his father would roll a ball to him and use a pillow to catch the return tosses.[7] From the age of 4 on, playing catch with his father was a daily routine. By the time he was 9, Bobby could throw a baseball more than 270 feet.[8] Although he was an excellent hitter and fielder, his father saw his promise as a pitcher and set up arc lights in the barn so that the two could play catch there during cold winter evenings.[9]

During the summer of 1930, when Bobby was 11, the Van Meter High School team played several games against the elementary school team. Since Feller could throw harder than anyone else, he pitched and more than held his own against the older boys.[10] By the fall of 1931, Bill Feller and son took the extraordinary step of building a ballpark on the farm to give local players a place to play and to better showcase young Bobby's talent. Soon the field, which they called Oak View Park, was hosting games, charging 25 cents admission, and sometimes drawing 1,000 fans.[11]

Initially, Bobby played mostly shortstop for the Oak View team, batting .321 in the summer of 1933. In 1934, when he was 15, however, he began having exceptional success on the mound, striking out 35 batters in his first 18 innings as a starter for Oak View. He was soon pitching for the American Legion team in nearby Adel as well, with similar results. His batterymate there was often Nile Kinnick, who later won the Heisman Trophy at the University of Iowa before being killed in World War II.[12]

The following summer, 1935, after reportedly throwing five no-hitters for Van Meter High,[13] the 16-year-old Feller graduated to the semipro Farmers Union team in Des Moines, where the competition was tougher and scouts more plentiful. His meteoric rise continued. According to statistics kept by his father, Bob struck out 361 hitters in 157 innings that summer, allowing only 42 hits and compiling an earned-run average of under 1.00.[14]

In early September Farmers Union traveled to Dayton, Ohio, for the national amateur baseball tournament. Before at least eight scouts, Feller pitched the opening game against Battle Creek, Michigan. He lost, 1-0, but allowed just two hits while striking out 18 batters. Suddenly Feller was besieged with offers that included sizeable bonuses. He couldn't accept, however, for the fact was that he had secretly signed a contract with Cy Slapnicka of the Cleveland Indians earlier in July.[15] A Des Moines semipro umpire had tipped the Indians about Feller and Slapnicka was dispatched to check out the young phenom.[16] He was impressed and on July 21 Feller (and his dad since

Bobby was 16) signed for a bonus of one dollar and an autographed Indians baseball.[17]

Feller was to report the following spring to the Fargo-Moorhead Twins of the low-rung Class-D Northern League. While in Van Meter that winter for his junior year of high school, however, he somehow developed a sore arm. The Indians transferred Feller's contract to the New Orleans Pelicans of the Southern League, where he was placed on the "voluntarily retired" list while he finished his spring semester of school. After the school year, Slapnicka, whom the Indians had promoted to the equivalent of general manager, had Feller take the train to Cleveland, ostensibly to work in concessions but in reality so that the Indians could monitor the health of his arm.[18]

After a couple of weeks, Slapnicka arranged for Feller to start two games for the Rosenblums, a fast Cleveland semipro team sponsored by a clothing store. In the second game he struck out 16 while allowing only four hits. Then on July 6, Feller made his professional debut, entering an Indians-St. Louis Cardinals exhibition game in the fourth inning.[19] His first pitch was a fastball strike to Bruce Ogrodowski, a rookie catcher. Ogrodowski bunted the second pitch and was thrown out by third baseman Sammy Hale. The second hitter was Leo Durocher, the Cardinals' shortstop, who attempted to intimidate Feller, yelling, "Keep the ball in the park, busher." Feller did, striking Durocher out swinging on three fastballs. The third hitter, reserve infielder Arthur Garibaldi, did the same.[20]

In his three innings of work, Feller gave up an unearned run and struck out eight batters, including Rip Collins, Pepper Martin, and Durocher twice. On his second trip to the plate, Durocher told the umpire, "I feel like a clay pigeon in a shooting gallery."[21] Afterward, a photographer asked Cardinal ace Dizzy Dean it he would pose for a picture with the kid pitcher. Diz responded, "If it's all right with him, it's all right with me. After what he did today, he's the guy to say."[22]

Feller was still technically on the Rosenblums roster and started one more game for them, losing 3-2 while striking out 15. Finally, on July 14, the Indians officially put him on the big-league roster, sending him to Philadelphia to join the club there. The 17-year-old's first official major-league appearance came a few days later, on July 19 in the eighth inning of a game against the Washington Senators in Griffith Stadium that the Indians were losing 9-2. Feller plunked the first batter, Red Kress, in the ribs with a wild curveball. Then, throwing only fastballs, Feller retired the side around two walks on a strikeout and two popups to end his one inning of work.[23] His second appearance was six days later, on July 24 in Cleveland. With the Tribe ahead of the Philadelphia Athletics 15-2, manager Steve O'Neill brought the 17-year-old into the game in the eighth inning. In two innings, he gave up three hits and one run while striking out two. He got mop-up duty again two days later in the ninth inning of a 13-0 loss, allowing three hits, a walk, and two runs.[24]

O'Neill continued to use Feller sporadically in relief before giving him his first start, against the seventh-place St. Louis Browns on August 23 in Cleveland. The fireballer began by striking out Lyn Lary on three pitches, giving up a single to Harlond Clift, and then striking out the number three and four hitters, Moose Solters and Beau Bell. Pitching in 90-degree heat, Feller continued to be overpowering and struck out a total of 15 hitters in a complete-game 4-1 victory, one shy of Rube Waddell's American League record. He gave up six hits.[25]

O'Neill knew he had something special on his hands and resolved to start Feller about once a week for the balance of the season. Bob had control problems during his next two starts, losing both and failing to get out of the first inning against the Yankees on September 3. He then defeated the Browns again on September 7, striking out 10 in a complete-game seven-hitter. On the 13th he defeated the Athletics 5-2 on two hits, but walked nine and allowed seven stolen bases. He was virtually unhittable that afternoon, striking out 17 batters to set the American League record and tying Dizzy Dean's major-league record.[26]

Young Feller won two of his last three starts as the 1936 season wound down, with the Indians settling in fifth place with an 80-74 record. For his rookie year, the teenager threw 62 innings in 14 appearances, including eight starts. He posted a 5-3 record, allowing 52 hits, with 76 strikeouts and 47 walks. His 3.34 earned-run average was the best on the club. After the season Feller signed on for a brief barnstorming tour, pitching against Satchel Paige in Des Moines and traveling into the Dakotas and Canada.[27]

Although one would assume that Feller would not have a worry in the world after his impressive beginning, he in fact did. Pursuant to a complaint from E. Lee Keyser, the owner of the Des Moines Demons, the closest minor-league team to Van Meter, Commissioner Kenesaw Mountain Landis was investigating alleged irregularities in his signing by Cleveland, with the threat of declaring him a free agent.[28] After summoning Bob and his father to his Chicago office shortly after the end of the season, Landis waited until December to decide that Feller could remain Cleveland property.[29]

In the meantime, Feller spent the winter finishing high school, taking physics, English literature, American history, and government, before leaving for spring training in New Orleans.³⁰ The Indians and New York Giants annually barnstormed north out of spring training, playing games in places like Vicksburg and Jackson, Mississippi; Thomaston, Georgia; Decatur, Alabama; Little Rock and Fort Smith, Arkansas; Tyler, Texas; and Shawnee, Oklahoma.

Feller first pitched against the Giants in Vicksburg and in three hitless innings struck out six Giants, four in succession. Everyone was impressed except Giants shortstop Dick Bartell, who said, "He's not so fast. We've got several pitchers in the National League who can throw just as hard. I know he isn't as fast as [Van Lingo] Mungo." As the caravan moved on, Feller proceeded to strike out Bartell 16 out of 19 times. One sportswriter noted that Bartell went all the way to Fort Smith before he got a loud foul off Feller.³¹

Overall, Feller had a terrific spring and was dubbed the "schoolboy wonder" in several national publications. *Time* magazine put him on its April 19 cover, only the second time a baseball player had been so honored.

It all came to a screeching halt on April 24. Feller, in pitching to the first batter in his first start of the year, felt a sharp pain in his elbow when throwing a curveball. He managed to get by only with fastballs for six innings before finally telling manager Steve O'Neill that he had hurt his arm. The Indians sent him to several specialists, most of whom recommended rest. He made national news when he flew home in May to attend his high-school graduation, but on his return to Cleveland was still not ready to take the mound. Finally, in June, Cy Slapnicka sent Feller to A.L. Austin, a chiropractor just a few blocks from League Park, the Indians' home ballpark. He diagnosed a dislocated ulna bone as the problem, gave Feller's arm a sudden twist, and pronounced him ready to pitch after one more day's rest.³²

Two days later Feller threw in the bullpen and was pain-free. He returned to action on June 22 with two inning of work and then on July 4 threw four innings against the St. Louis Browns. He was wild but as fast as ever, giving up three runs but only one hit. A week later he pitched an eight-inning complete game against the Tigers, losing 3-2. By late July he was back in the rotation, starting every fifth day. He was 0-4 in his first four starts, but still overpowering most of the time. In August, he threw a 12-strikeout, 10-walk game against the Yankees in Yankee Stadium. Later in the month he struck out 16 Red Sox while walking only four and allowing just four hits.

For the 1937 season, Feller finished 9-7 despite his 0-4 start. In just under 149 innings, he allowed only 116 hits. His 3.39 earned-run average was second on the team to that of Johnny Allen, who won 15 while losing only a single game that season. Feller's 150 strikeouts were fourth in the league even though he had missed three months of the season.

Incredible as it seems today, especially considering his sore arm, Feller again embarked on a barnstorming trip after the season, pitching against Paige and other top Negro League players. This tour was more extensive and wound through the hinterlands before arriving in Los Angeles.³³

So high had been the expectations for Feller that the Associated Press had unfairly named him "flop of the year" for 1937.³⁴ The Indians still had faith in him and backed it with a salary of $17,500 for 1938, right in line with Joe DiMaggio and the highest-paid players on the Indians. New manager Oscar Vitt did not use Feller much in spring training, instead attempting to improve his delivery by shortening his leg kick in bullpen work.³⁵ He started the second game of the season, on April 20 in League Park against the Browns, and pitched the first of 12 one-hitters of his career.³⁶ The only hit was a sixth-inning bunt single that Billy Sullivan barely beat out.³⁷

In late June Feller defeated the legendary Lefty Grove of the Red Sox to run his won-loss record to 9-2 and, on the same day, was named to his first American League All-Star team. Still only 19 years old, he was the youngest player named to the Midsummer Classic. Although he did not appear in the game, won by the National League, 4-1, he was warming up in the bullpen to come in for the bottom of the ninth had the American League been able to tie the score.³⁸

Cleveland Indians Bob Feller and catcher Frankie Hayes who caught Feller's no-hitter and won the game with a homer in the ninth inning, 1946.

Feller was not as effective after the All-Star break as the Indians faded to third place. The Yankees ran away with the 1938 pennant and as the season wound down, all attention was focused on Hank Greenberg's run at Babe Ruth's single-season home-run record of 60. The season concluded on October 2 with Feller starting the first game of a Sunday doubleheader against the Tigers and Greenberg needing two home runs to tie Ruth. Rapid Robert lived up to his name that day, striking out 18 Tigers to set a new major-league strikeout record and steal the thunder from Greenberg, who went without a home run.[39] It was almost anti-climactic that Feller lost the game, 4-1.

For the year, his first full big-league season, Feller won 17 and lost 11. His 240 strikeouts led the league as did his hard-to-believe 208 walks, which no doubt contributed to his 4.08 earned-run average.[40] All this and Feller was still a teenager. As if 278 innings weren't enough wear and tear on a 19-year-old arm, Feller took a brief barnstorming trip after the season.[41]

Feller was given his first Opening Day start in 1939 and defeated Detroit, 5-1, fanning 10.[42] Although the Indians were playing about .500 baseball, Feller had won five of his first six starts leading into his May 14 start against the White Sox in Cleveland. That day happened to be Mother's Day and Feller's mother was attendance, along with his father and sister. In the third inning, Chicago third baseman Marv Owens sliced a foul ball into the stands, striking Mrs. Feller flush in the face above her left eye and shattering her glasses. Cleveland officials rushed her to the hospital while a visibly shaken Feller managed to complete a 9-4 victory.[43]

Undaunted, Feller continued to dominate the league, and by late June had put together an 11-3 record. On June 27 he started the first night game in Cleveland history, pitching against the Detroit Tigers. He proceeded to strike out 13 batters and allowed only one hit, a fifth-inning humpback drive off the bat of the recently traded Earl Averill that fell in front of center fielder Ben Chapman.[44] By the All-Star break Feller was 14-3 and a shoo-in for the Midsummer Classic. This time he pitched in the game, entering in the fifth inning at Yankee Stadium with a 3-1 lead and holding the National League scoreless in 3⅔ innings of one-hit relief.[45]

While the Indians finished the season in third place, Feller established himself as the top pitcher in the American League. He led the league with 24 wins, almost 297 innings pitched, 246 strikeouts, 24 complete games, and fewest hits allowed per nine innings.[46] Still only 20 years old, he was the youngest starting pitcher in the league and the youngest ever to win 20 games.[47] Never one to turn down an extra payday, Feller headed back to California after the season to barnstorm up and down the California coast.[48]

In 1940 Feller was again the Opening Day hurler, this time with historic results. On April 16 in 40-degree weather in Comiskey Park in Chicago with his mother, father, and sister present, the 21-year-old Feller tossed a no-hitter to win, 1-0. As of 2012 it remained the only Opening Day no-hitter in major-league history.[49] Feller continued to dominate as the Indians played themselves into the middle of the pennant race. On June 20 he defeated the Senators, 12-1, to push the club into first place. But while the team was playing well, at the same time Feller and others were revolting against their caustic manager, Oscar Vitt. The press got wind of the revolt and dubbed the team "the Crybabies."[50]

The team nonetheless held first place at the All-Star break. Feller, with a 13-5 record, was named to the All-Star team. He pitched two innings in the game, allowing one run in a 4-0 loss to the National League. In his next regular-season start, on July 12, he nearly had another no-hitter, allowing only an eighth-inning single to Dick Seibert of the Philadelphia A's.

The pennant race was a tight one and the Indians went into the final series of the season against the Tigers trailing them by two games.[51] Feller thus pitched the biggest game of his career to that point on September 27 in the first game of the series. The Tigers, essentially conceding the game and saving their best pitchers for the second and third games of the series, started unknown rookie Floyd Giebel. Although Feller gave up only three hits and two runs on a homer by Rudy York, Giebel pitched the game of his life and shut out the Indians to clinch the pennant for the Tigers.[52]

For the year, the 21-year-old Feller won 27 games to lead the league, while losing 11. In one of the most dominating performances in history, he also led the league in six other categories, including strikeouts (261), earned-run average (2.61), innings pitched (320⅓), games (43), games started (37), complete games (31), and fewest hits per nine innings (6.9).[53] He finished second in the league MVP voting and was named the 1940 *Sporting News* Player of the Year. Even with his prodigious regular-season workload, Feller could not resist a brief barnstorming tour into Montana and North Dakota before returning home to Van Meter for the winter.[54]

The Indians' 1941 spring training was in Fort Myers, Florida, and there Feller began dating Virginia Winther, the daughter of a wealthy Chicago family attending college at nearby Rollins. The Indians had finally fired Oscar Vitt in the offseason, replacing him with Roger Peckinpaugh. The club played well out of the gate and held first place into early June when it began to slump. But Feller had a spectacular first half and by the All-Star break was 16-4. That earned him his first All-Star Game start and he did not disappoint, striking out four and allowing only a single to Lonnie Frey in three innings.[55]

While the Indians stumbled to a tie for fourth place, Feller again led the American League with 25 wins, against 13 losses. He repeated as the league leader in most major categories including innings pitched (343), strikeouts (260), shutouts (6), games pitched (44), and games started (40).[56] Still only 22 years old, Feller now had 107 big-league victories.

He would remain stuck on that number for 3½ years, thanks to World War II. On December 7, 1941, Feller was driving from Van Meter to Chicago to meet with Cleveland officials about his 1942 contract. When he heard on the radio about the attack on Pearl Harbor, he immediately decided to enlist in the Navy and was sworn in at a Navy recruiting office in Chicago on December 9.[57]

After a couple of weeks back home in Van Meter, Feller reported for basic training at the Norfolk Training Station in Virginia. When he completed basic training, he was given the rank of chief petty officer and became a physical-drill instructor. Beginning in March 1942, Feller played for the Training Station baseball team, playing minor-league clubs and other service teams.[58] Feller estimated that the team won 92 of about 100 games played that spring and summer.[59]

Feller, however, was not content with his light military duty and volunteered for gunnery school after he was turned down for pilot training because he failed a high-frequency-hearing test. He was assigned to the battleship Alabama, stationed in Norfolk,[60] where he learned in early January 1943 that his father had died. He was granted a 10-day emergency leave to attend the services. Also, as his father had wished, Feller went ahead with wedding plans and married Virginia Winther in Waukegan, Illinois, before returning to his ship in Norfolk.[61]

That spring and summer the Alabama was dispatched to the British Home Fleet to escort convoys along the North Atlantic corridor.[62] In early August the Alabama was called home to Norfolk and dispatched to the Pacific, traveling through the Panama Canal before arriving at Efate in the New Hebrides Islands on September 14. For the first time since the previous September, Feller was able to play some baseball, pitching for the Alabama's baseball team and playing first base for the softball team.[63]

Beginning in November, however, the Alabama went into combat and over the next six months saw action off the Gilbert Islands, the Marshall Islands, Truk, Tinian, Saipan, and Guam. While at sea, Feller occasionally played catch on deck, but in the main was completely away from baseball. In late April and May, the Alabama went for refitting on the island of Majuro, where Feller was again able to pitch for the ship's baseball team. He threw 47 consecutive scoreless innings at one juncture and continued to work on the slider he'd first developed in Norfolk.[64]

In early June, the Alabama was out to sea again, participating in the invasion of Saipan. Feller participated in the Battle of the Philippine Sea, one of the most lopsided American victories in the war. In charge of a gunnery crew, he was in the heat of combat and later called the battle "the most exciting 13 hours of my life," adding, "After that, the dangers of Yankee Stadium seemed trivial."[65] The Alabama continued to see action in and around the Philippines until it finally returning to Seattle for repairs and crew rotation in January 1945. Feller's combat duties would be over.

After reuniting with his bride,[66] Feller received a leave in early February and visited his mother in Van Meter. He was then assigned to the Great Lakes Naval Training Station and in April succeeded Mickey Cochrane as manager of the base's crack baseball team.[67] During the summer of 1945 Feller pitched about 100 innings for Great Lakes, with the highlight coming on July 21, when he threw a 10-strikeout no-hitter before a crowd of 10,000 sailors.[68]

Finally, on August 21, one week after VJ Day, Feller received his honorable discharge from the Navy. He had served for 44 months and accumulated eight battle stars.[69] He was still only 26 years old.

Feller immediately signed a contract with the Indians for the balance of the 1945 season and was treated to a hero's welcome before his first start, on August 24, just three days after his discharge.[70] Before a crowd of more than 45,000 fans, Feller notched a complete-game 4-2 victory over the Detroit Tigers and their ace southpaw Hal Newhouser. Using his new slider with his fastball and curveball, Feller struck out 12 and allowed only four hits. It was his first big-league game in almost four years, but he had announced in no uncertain terms that he was back.[71]

Feller made eight more starts for Cleveland in 1945, compiling a 5-3 record with a fine 2.50 earned-run average. He struck out 59 in 72 innings, allowing only 50 hits. His best game came on September 19 when, again facing the Tigers, he allowed only a bloop third-inning single by Jimmy Outlaw to finish with the sixth one-hitter of his career.[72]

Feller was eager to make up some of his lost income from the war[73] and organized a monthlong barnstorming trip[74] which featured a number of matchups against Satchel Paige and other Negro League stars.[75] Then on December 10, Virginia gave birth to the Fellers' first child, a baby boy they named Stephan and called Stevie.[76] In late January Feller organized and held a "free school" in Tampa, Florida, for baseball players returning from the war. More than 180 former players attended the three-week course and 66 eventually signed professional contracts.[77]

During spring training Jorge Pasquel, a Mexican millionaire who was trying to create another major league south of the border, reportedly offered Feller a three-year contract at $100,000 a year to pitch in his new league. Feller was not anxious to leave the US after two years in the Pacific and turned it down, telling the press, "No chili con carne baseball for me."[78] He opened the 1946 season with a 1-0 shutout of the White Sox. Then, in his fourth start of the year, he threw his second career no-hitter, this time against the New York Yankees in Yankee Stadium in another tense 1-0 win.[79] Those starts propelled Feller to one of the greatest seasons of pitching in major-league history. By the All-Star break Feller had 15 wins, half the way to the coveted 30.[80] He pitched one-hitters on July 31 and August 8 to bring his career total to eight and break Addie Joss's major-league record of seven.[81] On August 14 he surpassed his personal season strikeout record of 261 and set his sights on Rube Waddell's major-league record of 349.[82]

With eight games left in the season, Feller stood at 320 strikeouts. Of the next seven games, he started two on short rest and relieved in another to tie the record at 343 heading in the final game of the season against the Tigers. His opponent was Hal Newhouser, who sported a 26-8 record. A tired Feller didn't strike out anyone until the fifth inning, but then managed to fan five to break the record and finish at 348 strikeouts.[83] For the season, he finished with 26 wins against 15 losses. The sixth-place Indians won only 68 games, meaning that Feller was the winning pitcher in more than 38 percent of his team's wins.[84] He threw an incredible 371⅓ innings in 48 games and 42 starts, 36 of which were complete games. He also led the league with 10 shutouts and his 2.18 earned-run average was the third lowest in the league.[85]

While putting together this prodigious record, the tireless Feller was organizing an extensive postseason barnstorming trip in which "Bob Feller's All-Stars" would play 34 games in 27 days. Feller rented two DC-3 airliners for the tour, which started in Pittsburgh and ended in Long Beach, California. Most of the opposition was provided by the "Satchel Paige All-Stars" with Paige and Feller toeing the mound for a few innings in virtually every game. In all the tour covered around 13,000 travel miles and drew an estimated 250,000 fans.[86]

In January Feller signed a contract with new Indians owner Bill Veeck for 1947, which at $70,000 plus attendance bonuses, was reputed to surpass Babe Ruth's $80,000 salary as the largest in sports history.[87] Although Feller battled injuries in 1947 and elected not to pitch in the All-Star Game because of back pain, he put together another stellar campaign for the improving fourth-place Indians. He pitched two more one-hitters to bring his career total to 10, and finished the season with 20 wins against 11 losses. He led the league in games started (37), shutouts (5), strikeouts (196), and innings (299), and was second in earned-run average (2.68).[88] After the season Feller, despite his heavy workload, went barnstorming again, competing mostly against Satchel Paige and other Negro League stars.[89]

With the Indians in a pennant race in 1948, Feller, at least for him, struggled during the first half of the season and was only 9-10 by the All-Star break.[90] He battled arm fatigue after the break and was inconsistent, sometimes showing his old form and sometimes getting rocked. On October 3, the last day of the season, manager Lou Boudreau sent Feller to the mound against Hal Newhouser and the Tigers with a one-game lead. If the Indians won, they would win the pennant. Feller did not survive the third inning, however, and the Indians lost, 7-1, forcing a one-game playoff with the Red Sox in Boston.[91]

The Indians won the playoff game, 8-3, behind the pitching of southpaw Gene Bearden, pitching on just one day's rest.[92] The following day, October 6, Boudreau tapped Feller to start the first game of the World Series against the National League champion Boston Braves. He was on his game and didn't allow a hit until the fifth inning before retiring nine more Braves in a row. He headed into the bottom of the eighth inning locked in a scoreless tie against Braves ace Johnny Sain, who had scattered four hits. In the eighth Feller walked leadoff batter Bill Salkeld, who was replaced by pinch-runner Phil Masi, who was sacrificed to second. With two out, Feller turned and picked Masi off second by at least a foot; the only problem was that umpire Bill Stewart called Masi safe. Unfortunately for Feller and the Indians, Tommy Holmes then singled to left, scoring Masi and sending Feller to a 1-0 defeat.[93]

Later, with the Indians leading the World Series three games to one, Feller toed the rubber for Game Five back in Cleveland with a chance to close out the Series. He was anything but sharp and struggled to a 5-5 tie into the seventh, when the roof really caved in on him and four relievers. The game ended in an 11-5 defeat. The Indians clinched the Series the next day in Boston but Feller had the ignominy of being the losing pitcher in the only two games the Indians lost in the Series.[94]

Feller was no better than the third-best pitcher on the crack Indians staff in 1948, finishing with a 19-15 record and a 3.56 earned-run average.[95] He did start 38 games, to lead the league, and although his strikeout total dropped to 164, that, too, was first in the league. After the season, Feller did not barnstorm, other than throwing seven shutout innings in an exhibition game to celebrate "Feller Day" in his hometown.[96]

Named Opening Day starter in 1949, Feller strained a shoulder muscle warming up and lasted only two innings. By the All-Star break, he was only 6-6 and was not named to the AL team for the first time since 1937 (excepting the war years). He finished the season 15-14 with a 3.75 earned-run average as the Indians, beset with injuries, fell to third place. In 211 innings, Feller's strikeouts fell to 108.[97] He improved to 16-11 in 1950, with his ERA dropping to 3.43. At 31, Feller was no longer overpowering, but was still a quality starting pitcher and was again named to the All-Star team.[98]

Feller started the 1951 season with a vengeance, and on June 30 stood 10-2 with a league-leading ERA of under 3.00. Yankees manager Casey Stengel nonetheless left him off the All-Star team. The day after the team was announced, Feller answered the slight by pitching the third no-hitter of his career, defeating the Tigers 2-1.[99] Although Feller was not as sharp in the second half of the season, he still finished 22-8, leading the league in wins for the second-place Indians.[100]

Unhappily, Feller's 1952 season was a dud. He finished at 9-13 for the first losing record of his career. He also walked more than he struck out and gave up more hits than innings pitched, both also for the first time. His ERA was an unsightly 4.74 and his disappointing year had a lot to do with the Indians' second consecutive second-place finish behind the Yankees. Although he had long had his sights set on 300 career victories, Feller was now resigned to falling short of that mark.[101]

At 34, Feller was able to bounce back in 1953, becoming a serviceable once-a-week starter. He won 10 games, lost seven, and dropped his earned-run average over a run to 3.59 as the Indians again finished in second place behind the Yankees. He continued his success as a weekly starter in the Indians' runaway 1954 pennant year,[102] but in 1955 was restricted to spot starting and long relief. Finishing 4-4, he had a very serviceable 3.47 earned-run average in 83 innings of work. He still showed flashes of his old self, throwing the 12th one-hitter of his career, against the Red Sox on April 16.

Feller was back for more in 1956 and emerged from spring training as the Indians' fifth starter. But after one ineffective start in April and another in May, he was relegated to the bullpen, where he was used mostly in mop-up duty. The Indians threw a day for him on September 9, honoring him with a new car and various other gifts. President Dwight Eisenhower sent a telegram lauding Feller for his military service and work with charities, which "makes a fine example of American manhood."[103]

The final start of Feller's career was on September 30, the last day of the season. He pitched a complete game against the Detroit Tigers, losing 8-4 and failing to strike out a single batter. For the season, he appeared in only 19 games and threw only 58 innings, finishing 0-4 with a 4.97 earned-run average. Amid much speculation, Feller met on December 28 with Indians general manager Hank Greenberg. When he emerged he announced his retirement to the assembled press.[104] He was 38 years old.

Although no one knew it at the time, Feller's wife, Virginia, had become addicted to barbiturates and amphetamines shortly after the war ended. For the last 10 years of his playing career, Virginia was a constant worry and distraction for Feller. The couple had three sons and Feller had to hire a live-in maid to take care of them. Virginia had several stays in the Mayo Clinic, but couldn't stem her addiction, which caused insomnia and other behavioral problems as well as stretching the family's finances. Finally, in 1971 the couple divorced.[105]

Feller did not slow down upon his retirement as an active player. He got into the insurance business in Cleveland and also joined Motorola as "consultant on youth activities," crisscrossing the country supporting Little League programs by giving speeches and conducting baseball seminars and camps.[106] In August 1957 he appeared on the *Mike Wallace*

Interview program on ABC Television and created controversy by roundly criticizing baseball's reserve clause.[107] He became the first president of the Major League Players Association and helped develop its first pension plan.

In 1958 Feller briefly joined the Mutual Radio Network to help broadcast the *Game of the Day*.[108] He was elected to Baseball's Hall of Fame in 1962, his first year of eligibility, receiving 150 of 160 votes cast.[109] After his divorce, Feller was married again in 1974 to Anne Thorpe, a woman he had met in church. He sometimes participated in old-timer's games and was a frequent guest at sports memorabilia shows around the country. In 1994 the Cleveland Indians erected a 10-foot bronze statue of him at their new Jacobs Field home and in 1995 the Bob Feller Museum, designed by Feller's architect son, Steve, opened in Van Meter. Feller was still throwing a baseball every day well into his 80s and claimed to have thrown a baseball more often than any man in history.[110] The last time he pitched was at an exhibition game in Cooperstown in June 2009, at the age of 90.

Feller was diagnosed with leukemia in August 2010 and died on December 15 of that year. He was 92 years old.

For his 18-year major-league career, Feller won 266 games against 162 losses.[111] At 6 feet tall and 185 pounds, he was on the short side for a right-handed pitcher by contemporary standards. Both Ted Williams and Joe DiMaggio labeled him the greatest pitcher either had ever seen.[112] Although he lost almost four full seasons to service in World War II during the prime of his career, he still led the American League in victories six times and in strikeouts seven times. With his three no-hitters, 12 one-hitters, 279 complete games, and 44 shutouts, he was the dominant pitcher of his generation and one of the greatest of all time.

SOURCES

In addition to the sources cited in the Notes, the author also consulted:

Addie, Bob. "Indians Almost Axed Feller!," *Baseball Digest*, July 1954.

Berkow, Ira. *The Corporal Was a Pitcher: The Courage of Lou Brissie* (Chicago: Triumph Books, 2009).

Bloodgood, Clifford. "All-Star Double Feature," *Baseball Magazine*, September 1942.

Bloodgood, Clifford. "Has Another Walter Johnson Come Along?," *Baseball Magazine*, March 1937.

Boudreau, Lou with Russell Schneider, *Lou Boudreau—Covering All the Bases* (Champaign, Illinois: Sagamore Publishing, 1993).

Boudreau, Lou with Ed Fitzgerald, *Player-Manager* (Boston: Little, Brown & Co., 1949).

Bryson, Bill. "Iowa's Favorite Son," in Sidney Offit, ed., *Best of Baseball* (New York: G.P. Putnam's Sons, 1956).

Burr, Harold C. "Indians Cross the Border," *Baseball Magazine*, December 1939.

Calhoun, Ralph. "Can Feller Come Back?," *Baseball Digest*, August 1945.

Cannon, Jimmy. "Feller's Legend Bows to Materialism," *Baseball Digest*, 1947.

Connor, Anthony J. *Baseball for the Love of It—Hall of Famers Tell It Like It Was* (New York: Macmillan Publishing Co., 1982).

Cobbledick, Gordon. "Is It True About Bob Feller?," *Sport Magazine*, June 1948.

Crissey, Harrington E. Jr., *Athletes Away* (Philadelphia: Self-Published, 1984).

Dempsey, Jack. "Why Bob Feller Is a Champion," *Liberty Magazine*, August 9, 1941.

Dickson, Bill. *Bill Veeck—Baseball's Greatest Maverick* (New York: Walker Publishing Co., 2012).

DiMaggio, Joe. *Lucky to Be a Yankee* (New York: Rudolph Field, 1946).

Fehler, Gene. *When Baseball Was Still King—Major League Players Remember the 1950s* (Jefferson, North Carolina: McFarland & Co., Inc., 2012).

Feller, Bob as told to Edward Linn, "The Trouble With the Hall of Fame," *Saturday Evening Post*, January 27, 1962.

Feller, Bob as told to Ken W. Purdy, "I'll Never Quit Baseball," *Look Magazine*, March 20, 1956.

Feller, Bob as told to Ed McAuley, "My Greatest Game—Feller," *Baseball Digest*, January 1951.

Feller, Bob as told to Ed Fitzgerald, "Who Says I'm Finished?," *Sport Magazine*, April 1949.

Feller, Bob. "The Pitcher and the Preacher," *Guideposts*, 1949.

Feller, Bob et. al., "The Players Report Their Doings," *Baseball Magazine*, January 1938.

Feller, Virginia, as told to Hal Lebovitz, "He's My Feller!" *Baseball Digest*, May 1952.

Flaherty, Vincent X. "Feller Goes to Sea," *Baseball Digest*, March 1943.

Gibbons, Frank. "Determined Mr. Feller," *Baseball Digest*, September 1951.

Goldstein, Richard. *Spartan Seasons—How Baseball Survived the Second World War* (New York: Macmillan Publishing Co., 1980).

Halberstam, David. *The Teammates - Portrait of a Friendship* (New York: Hyperion, 2003).

Halberstam, David. *The Summer of '49* (New York: William Morrow & Co., 1989).

Hayes, Gayle. "Fanning With Feller," *Baseball Magazine*, December 1938.

Holtzman, Jerome. "An American Hero," *Baseball Digest*, December 2000.

Johnson, William H. "The Crybabies of 1940," in Brad Sullivan, ed., *Batting Four Thousand—Baseball in the Western Reserve* (Cleveland: Society for American Baseball Research, 2008).

Katz, Lawrence S. *Baseball in 1939: The Watershed Season of the National Pastime* (Jefferson, North Carolina: McFarland & Co., 1994).

Kelley, Brent. *The Early All-Stars—Conversations with Standout Baseball Players of the 1930s and 1940s* (Jefferson, North Carolina: McFarland & Co., Inc., 1997).

Kirksey, George. "When a Feller Needs a Fella," *Baseball Magazine*, June 1938.

Lebovitz, Hal. "Mr. Robert, Master Herbie," in Brad Sullivan, ed., *Batting Four Thousand—Baseball in the Western Reserve* (Cleveland: Society for American Baseball Research, 2008).

Lebovitz, Hal. "Bob Feller's Disappointment," *Sport Magazine*, October 1959.

Mansch, Larry. "Hitting Bob Feller," *The National Pastime*, Vol. 17 (Cleveland: Society for American Baseball Research, 1997).

MacFarlane, Paul, ed., *Daguerreotypes—The Complete Major and Minor League Records of Baseball's Immortals* (St. Louis: The Sporting News Publishing Co., 1981).

McAuley, Ed. "Feller's a Whiz Promoting Two," *Baseball Digest*, September, 1946.

McKelvey, Richard G. *Mexican Raiders in the Major Leagues—The Pasquel Brothers vs. Organized Baseball, 1946* (Jefferson, North Carolina: McFarland & Co., 2006).

Markoe, Arnold, ed., *The Scribner Encyclopedia of American Lives—Sports Figures*, Vol. 1, A-K (New York: Charles Scribner's Sons, 2002).

Moore, Joseph Thomas, *Larry Doby—the Struggle of the American League's First Black Player* (Mineola, New York: Dover Publications, 2011).

Nason, Jerry. "Feller Slides—Halfway," *Baseball Digest*, July 1948.

Oakley, J. Ronald. *Baseball's Last Golden Age: The National Pastime in a Time of Glory and Change* (Jefferson, North Carolina: McFarland & Co., 1994).

Peary, Danny, ed., *We Played the Game—65 Players Remember Baseball's Greatest Era, 1947-1964* (New York: Hyperion, 1994).

Pietrusza, David. *Judge and Jury: The Life and Times of Judge Kenesaw Mountain Landis* (South Bend, Indiana: Diamond Communications, 1998).

Pluto, Terry. *Our Tribe—A Baseball Memoir* (New York: Simon and Schuster, 1999).

Porter, David L., ed. *Biographical Dictionary of American Sports—Baseball, Revised and Expanded Edition A-F* (Westport, Connecticut: Greenwood Press, 2000).

Povich, Shirley. "A Chat with Mr. Feller," *Baseball Digest*, August 1946.

Powers, Jimmy. *Baseball Personalities* (New York: Rudolph Field, 1949).

Schneider, Russell. *The Cleveland Indians Encyclopedia* (New York: Sports Publishing, 2001).

Stockton, J. Roy. "Bob Feller—Storybook Ball Player," *Saturday Evening Post*, February 20, 1937.

Szalontai, James D. *Teenager on First, Geezer at Bat, 4-F on Deck—Major League Baseball in 1945* (Jefferson, North Carolina: McFarland & Co., Inc., 2009).

Thorn, John and John Holway, *The Pitcher* (New York: Prentice-Hall Press, 1987).

Van Blair, Rick. *Dugout to Foxhole—Interviews with Baseball Players Whose Careers Were Affected by World War II* (Jefferson, North Carolina: McFarland & Co., Inc., 1994).

Westcott, Rich. *Diamond Greats—Profiles and Interviews with 65 of Baseball's History Makers* (Westport, Connecticut: Meckler Books, 1988).

Wilson, Nick. *Voices from the Pastime* (Jefferson, North Carolina: McFarland & Co., Inc., 2000).

NOTES

1 John Sickels, *Bob Feller—Ace of the Greatest Generation* (Dulles, Virginia: Brassey's, Inc., 2004), 236.

2 John Sickels, op. cit., 239.

3 Bob Feller with Bill Gilbert, *Now Pitching—Bob Feller* (New York: Birch Lane Press, 1990), 198.

4 *Now Pitching—Bob Feller,* 201. When asked years later why he had not pitched Feller in the 1954 Series, Lopez responded, "He wasn't that good of a pitcher anymore." Wes Singletary, *Al Lopez—The Life of Baseball's El Senor* (Jefferson, North Carolina: McFarland & Co., Inc., 1999), 171.

5 *Now Pitching—Bob Feller,* 198.

6 Frank Deford, "Robert Can Still Bring It," *Sports Illustrated*, August 8, 2005: 63. Another early example of a father raising a son to be a star athlete is Colonel Robert Jones, who cultivated his son Bobby from an early age to be a champion

NO-HITTERS

golfer. Grantland Rice, "Reg-lar Fellers," *Sport Magazine*, September 1946: 18.

7   Donald Honig, *Baseball When the Grass Was Real* (New York: Coward, McCann & Geoghegan, Inc., 1975), 261.

8   John Sickels, 11.

9   Feller's dad was quoted as saying, "I don't want him to be a farmer." Bob Feller, *Strikeout Story* (New York: A.S. Barnes & Co., 1947), 4; Arthur Daley, *Times at Bat: A Half-Century of Baseball* (New York: Random House, 1950), 202. The arc lights were used about 15 years before power lines came to the farm. When Feller was 14 or 15 he threw his father a fastball in the barn when he was expecting a curve. The result was three broken ribs for his father. Donald Honig, 263; Fay Vincent, *The Only Game in Town—Baseball Stars of the 1930s and 1940s Talk About the Game They Love* (New York: Simon and Schuster, 2006), 37.

10   *Strikeout Story*, 9.

11   *Strikeout Story*, 11-13; John Sickels, 15-17; Bob Feller, with Burton Rocks, *Bob Feller's Little Blue Book of Baseball* (Chicago: Triumph Books, 2009), 7. In 1946 after Feller's second major-league no-hitter, sportswriters asked him who was the greatest figure in his baseball career. "My father," was Feller's response. Arthur Daley, 202-03.

12   *Now Pitching—Bob Feller*, 36; John Sickels, 18-20; Bob Feller, "Bob Feller and American Legion Baseball," *American Legion Magazine*, June 1963, 14-15, 45-46.

13   David Pietrusza, Matthew Silverman, and Michael Gershman, eds., *Baseball—The Biographical Encyclopedia* (New York: Total/Sports Illustrated, 2000), 346.

14   John Sickels, 22.

15   John Sickels, 24-26.

16   Art Rust, Jr. with Mike Marley, *Legends—Conversations With Baseball Greats* (New York: McGraw-Hill Publishing Co., 1989), 38-40.

17   Both are today in the Bob Feller Museum in Van Meter.

18   John Sickels, 30-31.

19   The game was played during the All-Star break. The Cardinals' 38-year-old manager, Frankie Frisch, reportedly took himself out of the game after watching Feller warm up, saying, "They're not gonna get the old Flash out there against that kid." Tom Meany and Tommy Holmes, *Baseball's Best—The All-Time Major League Baseball Team* (New York: Franklin Watts, Inc., 1964), 38; Tom Meany, *Baseball's Greatest Pitchers* (New York: A.S. Barnes & Co., 1951), 53. For other versions of the Frisch story, see Bob Broeg, *Super Stars of Baseball* (St. Louis: The Sporting News, 1971), 74; Dick "Rowdy Richard" Bartell, with Norman L. Macht, *Rowdy Richard—A Firsthand Account of the National Baseball Wars of the 1930s and the Men Who Fought Them* (Berkeley, California: North Atlantic Books, 1987), 190-91.

20   *Strikeout Story*, 24.

21   *Strikeout Story*, 25. In his first at-bat, Durocher supposedly took two strikes, dropped his bat, and turned toward the dugout. The umpire said, "You've still got a strike left." "You can have it," Durocher said, "I don't want it." Bob Feller as told to Ken W. Purdy, "Baseball a Game? What a Laugh!" *Look Magazine*, February 11, 1956: 38.

22   *Strikeout Story*, 27; Arthur Daley, 201.

23   John Sickels, 38.

24   It was an appearance Feller wanted to forget. He did not mention it in either of his autobiographies. John Sickels, 39.

25   *Strikeout Story*, 40-42.

26   Adding to his record-setting performance was the fact that his father was in the stands that day. *Strikeout Story*, 54-58.

27   Timothy Gay, *Satch, Dizzy, & Rapid Robert* (New York: Simon and Schuster, 2010), 163-67. Hall of Fame pitcher Robin Roberts remembered that Feller came to Springfield, Illinois, that year to throw out the first pitch for the Illinois State Amateur Baseball Championship. Roberts, who was 9 years old, managed to get a Feller autograph but lost it before he got home. Robin Roberts with C. Paul Rogers, III, *My Life in Baseball* (Chicago: Triumph Books, 2003), 5.

28   *Now Pitching—Bob Feller*, 41. Although Feller would have been the subject of a huge bidding war if declared a free agent, he was comfortable with the Cleveland organization and very much wanted to stay there. John Sickels, op. cit., 51-52; Franklin Lewis, *The Cleveland Indians* (New York: G.P. Putman's Sons, 1949), 195-97; J.G. Taylor Spink, *Judge Landis and 25 Years of Baseball*, 193-95.

29   During the face-to-face meeting Bill Feller had threatened a lawsuit if Judge Landis declared his son a free agent. David Pietrusza, *Judge and Jury: The Life and Times of Judge Kenesaw Mountain Landis* (St. Louis: The Sporting News Publishing Co., 1974), 354; William Marshall, *Baseball's Pivotal Era—1945-1951*, (Lexington: University Press of Kentucky, 1999), 5-6. Landis required Cleveland to pay the Des Moines franchise $7,500 in damages. John Sickels, op. cit., 57; Ed Fitzgerald, "Feller Incorporated," *Sport Magazine*, June 1947: 62.

30   Feller's high-school principal arranged for a tutor and allowed him to graduate with his class if he "could pass the usual tests." *Strikeout Story*, 61.

31   Bob Broeg, "No Fireball's Any Swifter Than Feller's," *The Sporting News*, July 3, 1971: 18; Ed Fitzgerald, 63.

32   John Sickels, 67-71.

33   Timothy Gay, 170-78. The Indians did send trainer Lefty Weisman along to watch over their prized property.

34   John Sickels, 75.

35   Feller initially had trouble holding runners on base with his high leg kick. He was also tipping when he was going to throw to first base with a runner on. Ben Chapman reportedly told Feller he could steal second base on him anytime he wanted and, after

36 They are listed in Paul MacFarlane, ed., *Daguerreotypes—The Complete Major and Minor League Records of Baseball's Immortals* (St. Louis: The Sporting News Publishing Co., 1981), 92.

37 By his own estimation, Feller threw 136 pitches in his one-hitter, striking out and walking six. He also got two base hits and drove in two runs. *Now Pitching—Bob Feller*, 68-69.

38 *Now Pitching—Bob Feller*, 78.

39 Greenberg did touch Feller for a double while twice striking out. *Now Pitching—Bob Feller*, 83-85; *Strikeout Story*, 143-47; Hank Greenberg and Ira Berkow, ed., *The Story of My Life* (New York: Times Books, 1989), 106-22.

40 Feller's wildness in his early years was legendary. In one oft-told incident, Lefty Gomez was batting against Feller late in the second game of a doubleheader at Yankee Stadium. The afternoon shadows were long and when Gomez stepped into the batter's box, he promptly pulled a cigarette lighter out of his pocket, flicked up a light, and held it in front of his face. The umpire was not pleased and said, "C'mon Lefty, are you trying to make a joke out of the game? You can see Feller just fine." The quick-witted Lefty responded, "Hell, I can see him. I just want to make sure that wild man out there can see me." Bill Werber and C. Paul Rogers, III, *Memories of a Ballplayer—Bill Werber and Baseball in the 1930s* (Cleveland: Society for American Baseball Research, 2001), 99; Elden Auker, *Sleeper Cars and Flannel Uniforms* (Chicago: Triumph Books, 2001), 197; Arthur Daley, 128.

41 Arthur Daley, 148.

42 The Detroit game was the first game of the season. The actual Opening Day in St. Louis, which Feller was to start, was rained out. John Sickels, 84.

43 Mrs. Feller required some stitches but was not seriously injured. Talmage Boston, *1939—Baseball's Pivotal Year* (Fort Worth: The Summit Group, 1994), 140; John Sickels, 84; Ira Smith, *Baseball's Famous Pitchers* (New York: A.S. Barnes & Co., 1954), 284-85.

44 The trade of Averill, who had been openly critical of manager Oscar Vitt, to the Tigers was very unpopular in Cleveland. *Strikeout Story*, 157-59; John Sickels, 85.

45 *Strikeout Story*, 159-161; David Vincent, Lyle Spatz, and David W. Smith, *The Mid-Summer Classic—A Complete History of Baseball's All-Star Game* (Lincoln: University of Nebraska Press, 2001), 39-43. When Feller struck out Stan Hack in the ninth inning to end the game, 63,000 Yankee Stadium fans gave him a rousing standing ovation. Ed Fitzgerald, 63.

46 Lefty Gomez told the story of batting against Feller and taking the first two pitches for strikes on fastballs he could barely see. When the umpire called strike three on the third pitch, Lefty turned and said, "C'mon. That one sounded a bit low." Ed Fitzgerald, 64.

47 Feller also tied for the most shutouts with four and was third with a 2.85 earned-run average. He would finish third in the voting for the Most Valuable Player. John Sickels, 87.

48 Commissioner Landis had set forth an edict limiting postseason barnstorming tours to ten days, thus limiting Feller's West Coast excursion. Timothy Gay, 178-80; Thomas Barthel, *Baseball Barnstorming and Exhibition Games, 1901-1962* (Jefferson, North Carolina: McFarland & Co., Inc., 2007), 132, 142.

49 John Klima, *Pitched Battle—35 of Baseball's Greatest Duels from the Mound* (Jefferson, North Carolina:, McFarland & Co., Inc., 2002), 63-67; Rich Westcott and Allen Lewis, *No-Hitters—the 225 Games, 1893-1999* (Jefferson North Carolina: McFarland & Co., Inc., 2000), 142-44.

50 The Cleveland fans largely took the side of management and several times threw diapers and baby bottles onto the field during games. John Sickels, 92-98; John Phillips, *The Crybaby Indians of 1940* (Cabin John, Maryland: Capital Publishing Co., 1990); William H. Johnson, "The Crybabies of 1940," in Brad Sullivan, ed., *Batting Four Thousand—Baseball in the Western Reserve* (Cleveland: Society for American Baseball Research, 2008), 37.

51 Feller had pitched on short rest several times during September and at one point threw 27 innings in eight days. John Sickels, 99-100.

52 Giebel never won another major-league game. John Sickels, 100-01; Frederick G. Lieb, *The Detroit Tigers* (New York: G.P. Putnam's Sons, 1946), 244; Gene Schoor, *Bob Feller—Hall of Fame Strikeout Star* (Garden City, New York: Doubleday & Co., 1962), 132; Brent Kelley, *The Pastime in Turbulence—Interviews with Baseball Players of the 1940s* (Jefferson, North Carolina: McFarland & Co., Inc., 2001), 41-50.

53 He also tied for the lead in shutouts with four and reduced his walks to 118 to avoid the league lead in that category for the first time since he became a full-time starter.

54 Feller teamed with Earle Mack and Johnny Mize and played games in Little Falls, Billings, Missoula, and Great Falls, Montana, and in Fargo, North Dakota. Thomas Barthel, 144.

55 Feller promptly picked Frey off first. David Vincent, Lyle Spatz, and David W. Smith, 50-55.

56 Feller also led in hits allowed (284) and walks (194).

57 John Sickels, 115-16; Gary Bloomfield, *Duty, Honor, Victory—America's Athletes in World War II* (Guilford, Connecticut: Lyons Press, 2003), 288-89. Feller was already wrestling with whether to enlist or not even before Pearl Harbor. Mike Vaccaro, *1941—The Greatest Year in Sports* (New York: Doubleday, 2007), 270; *Strikeout Story*, 218.

58 Other professional baseball players on the team included Ace Parker, Sam Chapman, Fred Hutchinson, Jack Conway, Vinnie Smith, and Max Wilson. *Strikeout Story*, 221.

NO-HITTERS

59 In one game against Wilson, North Carolina, a Class-C team in the Bi-State League, Feller struck out 21 batters. *Strikeout Story*, 221.

60 Feller requested assignment to the battleship Iowa but apparently there was not room there for everyone from the Hawkeye State. *Strikeout Story*, 222.

61 Former Indians outfielder Soup Campbell was best man and teammates Lou Boudreau and Rollie Hemsley also attended the wedding. The newlyweds managed a three-day honeymoon in New York City before Feller returned to active duty. John Sickels, 120-22.

62 There Feller recalled playing softball in Iceland at 2 in the morning with the sun still up. He also helped a woman stack her peat moss and milk her cows in exchange for a quart of fresh milk. William B. Mead, *Even the Browns—the Zany, True Story of Baseball in the Early Forties* (Chicago: Contemporary Books, 1978), 193.

63 Feller took the lead in constructing a more proper baseball field than the primitive one they found. Led by his pitching, the Alabama's squad won the 3rd Fleet championship. John Sickels, 123.

64 John Sickels, 125.

65 *Strikeout Story*, 213.

66 Feller had by now been married almost two years and had spent just five nights with his wife, Virginia. She immediately flew out from Norfolk to reunite with her husband. *Strikeout Story*, 228; Todd Anton and Bill Nowlin, eds., *When Baseball Went to War* (Chicago: Triumph Books, 2008), 105-09; Todd Anton, *No Greater Love—Life Stories of the Men Who Saved Baseball* (Burlington, Massachusetts: Rounder Books, 2007), 116-33.

67 Although the roster changed continually, the club was stocked with big leaguers like Ken Keltner, Dick Wakefield, Clyde Shoun, Walker Cooper, Denny Galehouse, and Johnny Gorsica. *No Greater Love*, 230; John Sickels, 128.

68 John Sickels, 129.

69 *Strikeout Story*, 230-31; According to Feller, although he had enough points, an admiral at Great Lakes was dragging his heels about his discharge. So Feller called the secretary of the Navy and was discharged the next morning, along with 19 others who had enough points. William B. Mead, *Even the Browns*, 225-26.

70 In pregame ceremonies, Cleveland great Tris Speaker presented Feller with a new Jeep for use back in Iowa. Feller in turn contributed $1,000 to the Press Memorial Fountain Fund. John Sickels, 133. Cy Young was also present for the occasion. *Strikeout Story*, 232.

71 Feller had pitched an exhibition game in Cleveland for an all-star service team against the American League All-Stars on June 7, losing 5-0. *Strikeout Story*, 231-32.

72 *Strikeout Story*, 234-35; John Sickels, 134.

73 Feller believed he had lost about $250,000 due to the war. "The trick," he told his wife, "was to make it up." Gene Schoor, *Bob Feller—Hall of Fame Strikeout Star*, 141.

74 Commissioner Happy Chandler waived the ten-day postseason barnstorming limit to allow ballplayers returning from the service a chance to earn extra money *Strikeout Story*, 236.

75 Paige and Feller pitched before a crowd of 20,000 in St. Louis and 23,000 in Wrigley Field, Los Angeles, where 10,000 fans were reportedly turned away. Timothy M. Gay, 205; Thomas Barthel, 146.

76 *Strikeout Story*, 237.

77 Feller recruited former major leaguers such as Dizzy Dean, Bill Dickey, and Lou Fonseca as well as current stars like Joe DiMaggio, Lou Boudreau, Spud Chandler, Eddie Miller, Charlie Keller, Hugh Mulcahy, Rollie Hemsley, and Tommy Bridges to act as coaches. Ed Fitzgerald,, 65; John Sickels, 137-39; William Marshall, 84.

78 *Strikeout Story*, 238; William Marshall, 49.

79 The game went into the ninth inning a scoreless tie until Frankie Hayes homered off Floyd Bevens for the only run of the game. Feller threw 133 pitches in the game, which ended with Snuffy Stirnweiss on third base for the Yankees in the bottom of the ninth. *Strikeout Story*, 241-44; John Sickels, op. cit., 140-41; *Now Pitching—Bob Feller*, 130-32; Rich Westcott and Allen Lewis, 154-55; Don Schiffer, *My Greatest Baseball Game* (New York: A.S. Barnes & Co., 1950), 75-79; Bob Feller as told to Ed McAuley, "My Greatest Game—Feller," *Baseball Digest*, January 1951, 85-87.

80 Feller started the All-Star Game for the American League, which was held at Fenway Park. He pitched three shutout innings, allowing two hits and striking out three, and was the winning pitcher in a 12-0 American League victory. David Vincent et. al., 76-82.

81 *Strikeout Story*, 245.

82 *Strikeout Story*, 250; John Sickels, 142; Frederick Turner, *When the Boys Came Back—Baseball and 1946* (New York: Henry Holt & Co., 1996), 186-89; *Now Pitching—Bob Feller*, 133-35.

83 *Strikeout Story*, 253-55. Research later revealed that Waddell had struck out 349 rather than 343 batters, snatching the record back. John Sickels, op. cit., 145. Frederick Turner, op. cit., 204. It has since been broken by Sandy Koufax and Nolan Ryan.

84 The next winningest Indians pitcher was Allie Reynolds with 11 victories.

85 Surprisingly, Feller probably would not have won the American League Cy Young Award had it existed. Hal Newhouser finished 26-9 for the second-place Tigers and led the league with a 1.94 earned-run average.

86 Feller's club included Stan Musial, Phil Rizzuto, Ken Keltner, Jeff Heath, Charlie Keller, Johnny Sain, Bobo Newsom, and Spud Chandler among others. Paige's team had Monte Irvin, Max Manning, Buck O'Neil, Sam Jethroe, Hilton Smith,

Willard Brown, and Quincy Trouppe. John Sickels, 149-57; Timothy M. Gay, 219-45; Thomas Barthel, 146-52; *Now Pitching—Bob Feller*, 136-44; Larry Tye, *Satchel—The Life and Times of an American Legend* (New York: Random House, 2009), 170-75.

87 Feller's total 1947 income including barnstorming and endorsements may have exceeded $150,000, although high postwar tax rates cut into that amount by as much as two-thirds. John Sickels, 163; Burton Hawkins, "Bob Feller's $150,000 Pitch," *Saturday Evening Post*, April 19, 1947: 25, 148, 170. For Bill Veeck's account of his salary negotiations with Feller see Bill Veeck, with Ed Linn, *Veeck—As in Wreck* (New York: G.P. Putnam's Sons, 1962), 133.

88 In 1947 Billy Goodman, who would win the 1950 American League batting title, was a rookie. He was sent up to hit against Feller and told to make Feller throw him a strike. Goodman later said, "I did better than that. I made him throw me three strikes. I went back and sat down and said to myself, 'Man, you're in the wrong league.' I had never seen anything like that." Robert W. Creamer, *Baseball in '41* (New York: Viking Press, 1991), 167.

89 The 1947 version of the "Bob Feller All-Stars" included Andy Pafko, Ralph Kiner, Ferris Fain, Ken Keltner, Eddie Lopat, Ewell Blackwell, Jeff Heath, Jim Hegan, and Bill McCahan. It included several games in Mexico but overall was not a financial success. John Sickels, 177-81; Timothy M. Gay, 246-60; Thomas Barthel, 152-55.

90 Feller was nonetheless selected for the All-Star team. He elected not to participate, drawing a firestorm of controversy. John Sickels, 193-94; *Now Pitching—Bob Feller*, 152-53. American League All-Star manager Bucky Harris was particularly vocal, saying that if he had his way, Feller would never be asked to another All-Star Game. Frank Graham, *Baseball Extra* (New York: A.S. Barnes & Co., 1954), 143-44. For Feller's side of the story, see Bob Feller, "When the Crowd Boos!," *American Weekly*, July 6, 1952: 1.

91 David Kaiser, *Epic Season—the 1948 American League Pennant Race* (Amherst, Massachusetts: University of Massachusetts Press, 1998), 229-30; Russell Schneider, *The Boys of Summer of '48* (Champaign, Illinois: Sports Publishing, 1998), 62.

92 Gary R. Parker, *Win or Go Home—Sudden Death Baseball* (Jefferson, North Carolina: McFarland & Co., Inc., 2002), 39-75.

93 *Now Pitching—Bob Feller*, 163-67; Eddie Robinson with C. Paul Rogers, III, *Lucky Me—My 65 Years in Baseball* (Dallas: SMU Press, 2011), 65; Joseph Reichler, *Baseball's Great Moments* (New York: Bonanza Books, 3rd ed. 1983), 32-34; Russell Schneider, 63.

94 *Now Pitching—Bob Feller*, 170-71; Eddie Robinson with C. Paul Rogers, III, 67.

95 Bob Lemon finished 1948 with a 20-14 record and a 2.82 earned-run average while Gene Bearden went 20-7 with a 2.43 ERA to lead the league.

96 John Sickels, 205.

97 Feller did participate in a brief, unsuccessful barnstorming tour of the West Coast after the 1949 season. John Sickels, 212; Timothy M. Gay, 273-74. The average attendance was about 3,000 but a game in Tijuana, Mexico, attracted a reported 125 fans. Thomas Barthel, 158.

98 In 247 innings, he recorded 119 strikeouts but walked 103.

99 The Tigers' run was aided by Feller's throwing error in the fourth inning. That tied the score, 1-1, where it remained until Luke Easter singled in a go-ahead run in the eighth. Afterward Stengel was quoted as saying, "How did I know the guy would pitch a no-hitter? I'm better off dead." John Sickels, 218-20; Rich Westcott and Allen Lewis, 167-69.

100 In honor of his great season, the Cleveland sportswriters named Feller "Man of the Year." John Sickels, 222.

101 John Sickels, 231.

102 He often pitched on Sundays, to maximize his still considerable drawing power. *Now Pitching—Bob Feller*, 210.

103 John Sickels, 247.

104 John Sickels, 248.

105 *Now Pitching—Bob Feller*, 206-08, 215-17.

106 For example, Feller spoke at the author's Little League banquet in Casper, Wyoming, in the summer of 1959 and gave an autographed postcard-sized photo to every Little Leaguer in attendance.

107 Wallace took Feller to task since he had been one of baseball's highest-paid players for many years, but Feller stuck to his guns, noting that the reserve clause very negatively affected the average ballplayer, who averaged only four-plus years in the big leagues. John Sickels, 252-54.

108 In later years, he had a sports radio show in Cleveland and also did some cable-television broadcasting for the Indians. *Now Pitching—Bob Feller*, 211.

109 John Sickels, 255-56. Feller was elected with Jackie Robinson. They were the first first-ballot inductees since the inaugural Hall of Fame elections in 1939. Feller was the first pitcher elected on the first ballot since Walter Johnson. For Feller's view of the Hall of Fame in 1962, the year before he was elected, see Bob Feller, as told to Edward Linn, "The Trouble with the Hall of Fame," *Saturday Evening Post*, January 27, 1962: 49-52.

110 David Pietrusza, Matthew Silverman, and Michael Gershman, eds., 348.

111 Feller was a lifetime .151 hitter with eight career home runs. One was a pop fly that just fell into the right-field pavilion in Sportsman's Park in St. Louis against Elden Auker. Auker later reported that every time he saw Feller, "that home run gets a little longer." Elden Auker with Tom Keegan, 120.

112 Robert W. Creamer, 167.

NO-HITTERS

BOB FELLER'S OPENING DAY NO-HITTER

APRIL 16, 1940: CLEVELAND INDIANS 1, CHICAGO WHITE SOX 0, AT COMISKEY PARK

By C. Paul Rogers III

IN ALL OF BASEBALL HISTORY through 2015, only one no-hitter was pitched on Opening Day. Perhaps not surprisingly, it was thrown by the 21-year-old prodigy Bob Feller on April 16, 1940, against the Chicago White Sox on a blustery 40-degree day in Comiskey Park. The masterpiece was the first of three no-hitters Feller threw in his illustrious career, along with a remarkable 12 one-hitters.

Feller was coming off his second dominant season, having gone 24-9 in 1939 for the third-place Cleveland Indians. They had, however, finished 20½ games in arrears of the powerful New York Yankees, who had blown away the rest of the league with 106 wins. The White Sox had finished fourth, two games back of the Indians, and both squads had high hopes for 1940.

The unseasonably cold day, even for Chicago, held the Opening Day crowd down to just over 14,000. Three of them, however, were Feller's father, Bill; his mother, Lena; and his sister, Marguerite, who had all traveled from Van Meter, Iowa, to take in the first game of the season.

Feller didn't feel particularly sharp warming up and wondered how the strong wind blowing in from center field would affect his curveball.[1]

He began by retiring leadoff hitter Bob Kennedy on a fly to right and then sandwiched a walk between two strikeouts to retire the side. The second inning proved more problematic. With one out, Taft Wright, who was something of a Feller nemesis, hit a fly ball to Roy Weatherly in center field that Weatherly dropped. The official scorer, Ed Burns of the *Chicago Tribune*, took a moment or two before ruling an error.[2] Feller struck out the next batter, but then issued consecutive walks to Mike Tresh and opposing pitcher Edgar Smith to load the bases with two outs. He then bore down to strike out Kennedy and escape the jam.

The weather was making it difficult for Feller to grip his curveball, and after the second inning he threw almost all fastballs. Joe Kuhel led off the third with a walk and stole second. Feller managed the first two outs on a flyball to right and a popup to first, bringing the dangerous Luke Appling to the plate. Appling connected solidly, driving a hard, low line drive to right field. But Ben Chapman, covering ground quickly, made a nice running catch to end the inning.

Meanwhile, the Indians had managed only an infield single and a couple of walks against Edgar Smith, a southpaw who had engaged in several duels against Feller in previous seasons. In the top of the fourth, however, Indians first baseman Hal Trosky smashed a mighty blast to right field that the wind knocked down enough for Taft Wright to catch against the fence. Jeff Heath followed with a single through the left side of the infield, and with two outs catcher Rollie Hemsley lined a long drive over Wright's head in right. Hemsley rumbled into third with a triple, scoring Heath for what would be the only run of the game.[3]

Feller had by now found his rhythm and after his walk to Kuhel he retired 20 White Sox in a row. Other than Appling's liner, the only other hard-hit ball was a similar line drive by Wright in the fourth, also run down by Chapman in right field. In the eighth second baseman Ray Mack made a nice play on a slow roller to nip the speedy pinch-hitter Larry Rosenthal by a step.[4]

Feller already had three one-hitters in his three-plus years in the big leagues and the crowd was by now hoping this would be the day he broke through, even against the home team. By the eighth inning the fans were standing, rooting for Feller to complete his gem, and in the ninth they were in an uproar. He managed to give them plenty of drama, beginning by running the count to Mike Kreevich to 2-and-2 before retiring him on a popup to second baseman Mack. Moose Solters was next and Feller retired him on the third pitch on a routine groundout to shortstop Lou Boudreau. Now only "Old Aches and Pains" Luke Appling stood between Feller and immortality. Appling was known for his bat control and his penchant for fouling off pitches. With two strikes, he fouled off four Feller fastballs before working a 10-pitch walk to become the first White Sox baserunner since the third inning.[5]

The free pass brought Taft Wright to the plate. Feller threw ball one and then, on the second pitch, Wright hit a screaming groundball to the left of second baseman Mack. He managed to lunge and knock it down with his glove hand, get up and retrieve it on the grass with his bare hand, and throw a perfect peg to Trosky at first to nail the speedy Wright by a half-step. Just like that, the game was over and Feller had his first no-hitter. His teammates rushed to congratulate him, shaking his hand and slapping him on the back, while leading him through the fans, who were racing onto the field.[6]

Surprisingly, Feller's first no-hitter wasn't one of his most dominating performances. He struck out eight, modest by his standards, and allowed five walks. After the game, his catcher, Hemsley, said, "I've seen Bob better, but he was plenty good enough."[7]

For his part, Feller thought his stuff was "just about normal." He related that he tired in the fourth, but got his second wind the next inning.[8]

The next day the Indians returned to Cleveland by train and an estimated 7,000 greeted them at Union Terminal. The throng included Mayor Harold Burton, a uniformed band, and Cleveland immortal Tris Speaker. The next day an article ran in a local paper about 8-year-old Paul Hauschultz, a huge Indians fan who had been in the hospital with spinal meningitis, a mastoid infection, and streptococcus for about a month. The article mentioned how much he'd improved while listening on the radio to Feller's no-hitter. As a result, Feller surprised the youngster with a visit in the hospital, armed with a ball signed by the entire team and another signed by himself.[9] According to Feller's 1990 memoir, the youngster was able to go home that afternoon.[10]

The Indians soon found themselves in a tight pennant race with the Detroit Tigers and New York Yankees. Their season, and Feller's, however, was tainted by a June player revolt against their caustic manager, Oscar Vitt. A number of Indians, Feller among them, went to Alva Bradley, the owner of the club, to try to get Vitt fired. Bradley refused but when the press got wind of the attempted revolt, they dubbed the team "the Crybabies."[11] Even with all the drama, the Indians led the league much of the first half of the season and finished in second place, just a game behind the Tigers.

Feller would go on to have a gargantuan season, winning 27 games and leading the league in wins, innings pitched, strikeouts, earned-run average, games started, and complete games while tying for the lead in shutouts. He finished second in the MVP voting to Hank Greenberg, but was voted the American League Player of the Year by *the Sporting News*.

NOTES

1 Bob Feller, *Strikeout Story—Bob Feller* (New York: A.S. Barnes & Co., 1947), 175.

2 Feller, *Strikeout Story*, 176.

3 Gordon Cobbledick, "Feller Hurls No-Hitter to Win, 1 to 0, *Cleveland Plain Dealer*, April 17, 1940: 21.

4 Charles Bartlett, "Indians Put on a Big Celebration After No-Hitter," *Chicago Tribune*, April 17, 1940: 27.

5 Cobbledick, 1. In his second autobiography, published in 1990, Feller claimed that after Appling fouled off four or five straight 2-and-2 pitches, he threw two fastballs outside on purpose to in effect intentionally walk him and get him out of the way. Bob Feller with Bill Gilbert, *Now Pitching—Bob Feller* (New York: Birch Lane Press, 1990), 96; Bob Feller with Burton Rocks, *Bob*

Feller's Little Black Book of Baseball Wisdom (New York: McGraw-Hill, 2001), 29.

6 Cobbledick, 21.

7 John Sickels, *Bob Feller — Ace of the Greatest Generation* (Dulles, Virginia: Brassey's, Inc., 2004), 91.

8 Bartlett, 25.

9 John Phillips, *The Crybaby Indians of 1940* (Cabin John, Maryland: Capital, 1990), 5; Sickels, 91.

10 Feller with Gilbert, 97.

11 Franklin Lewis, *The Cleveland Indians* (New York: G.P. Putman's Sons, 1949, reprinted by Kent State University Press, 2006), 206-13; Phillips, 26-32.

ED HEAD

By Lyle Spatz

ON A SUMMER AFTERNOON in 1935, 17-year-old Ed Head was on a bus to Mer Rouge, Louisiana. Head, a left-handed pitcher for the semipro Pioneer (Louisiana) team, was on his way to play a game against the Mer Rouge team. He and his girlfriend were seated on the left side of the bus (facing forward), Head in the aisle seat and the girl in the window seat. As teenage boys typically do, Head had his left arm draped over her shoulders.

Unfortunately, they were seated almost directly in the path of another bus that rammed theirs. Head was knocked unconscious. When he awoke, he saw that his girlfriend was dead and his left arm, wrenched loose from its socket, was "a mass of shattered bone and mangled flesh."[1] He was taken to the Willys Clinic in Mer Rouge, where the local doctor told him he would have to amputate the arm.

Head was still conscious, and though weak and in shock, he argued against amputation. He pleaded to have his uncle, Dr. L.E. Larche, who had the only fluoroscope in the area, come look at the injury. "It was the only fluoroscope in Northern Louisiana," Head said several years later.[2] A philanthropist had donated it to the clinic in the late 1920s. Dr. Larche determined that he could save the arm, which he did following many hours of surgery.

For several days Head's life was in danger and the thought of his ever pitching again was dismissed. His lifetime goal had always been to be a major-league pitcher, but with his left arm nearly useless, that would be impossible. Head realized there was only one way he could reach his goal, by throwing right-handed. The dedication and effort needed to make this happen would have discouraged most people, but Head worked and practiced until he succeeded.

"It was tough at first, but not as bad as it might have been for some kids," he remembered. "I had fooled around a lot throwing right-handed even though I was a natural left-hander. It took me about three years though, before I could throw with any real speed."[3] Head eventually regained full use of his left arm and continued to write left-handed.

Edward Marvin Head was born on January 25, 1918, in Selma, Louisiana. His parents, Marvin Redwine Head (1890-1959), a timber cutter, and Ida Maude Rawls Head (1898-1990) were married on May 3, 1917. Two more sons followed Ed, Jack, and Roy Lee, who died at age 16 in 1944. The couple also had a stillborn daughter named Margaret Ann, who was born and died on July 30, 1940.

Head, who described his nationality as Scotch-Irish-French and Indian, attended Crosley High School through the eighth grade and graduated from Ouachita Parish High School. Both schools were in Monroe, Louisiana. He began his professional career in 1939 with the Abbeville (Louisiana) A's of the Class-D Evangeline League. He went 19-8 for the A's, a Philadelphia Athletics farm team.

After the season the Brooklyn Dodgers bought his contract, but there are two versions of how that purchase came about. Head's obituary in the *New York Times* said Brooklyn signed him on the advice of its top scout, Ted McGrew.[4] But Larry MacPhail, then the Dodgers' president, told a different story.

According to MacPhail, "A guy named Goldberg, who owned the Abbeville club, came to me with two telegrams. One was from Branch Rickey [GM of the St. Louis Cardinals], the other was from Earl Mann, the Atlanta [Crackers] owner. Both dealt with Head. Rickey offered Goldberg $3,000 for Head and Mann offered $4,000. Goldberg asked me what he should do. Now, I had never heard of Head," he said. "None of our scouts had turned in any report on him, in fact."[5]

However MacPhail knew Rickey and Mann were two of the smartest operators in baseball. So although he knew nothing about Head, he decided that if the

164

young pitcher was worth $3,000 to Rickey and $4,000 to Mann, he would offer $5,000. Goldberg accepted the offer, but only after MacPhail agreed to also purchase Head's batterymate for $1,500.

The percentage of players who make it from Class D to the major leagues is very low, but there were three pitchers in the Evangeline League in 1939 who not only reached the major leagues, but became stars: Virgil Trucks and Hal Newhouser for the Detroit Tigers and Howard Pollet for the St. Louis Cardinals.

The Dodgers sent the 6-foot-1, 175-pound Head to the Elmira (New York) Pioneers of the Class-A Eastern League for the 1940 season. Through late July, he had justified the jump of three levels in the minor-league chain with a 12-7 record, 116 strikeouts, and a 2.56 earned-run average. He also had taken a wife that month, having married Johnnie Mae Womack on July 2.

After years of mediocrity, the Dodgers were attempting to win their first pennant since 1920. Much to the dismay of the fans in Elmira, they called up Head and the Pioneers' sensational young outfielder Pete Reiser, who was batting .378 at the time of the recall. In the season's final two months, Reiser gave Brooklyn fans a glimpse of what was to come. He batted .293 in 58 games, mostly as a replacement for Cookie Lavagetto at third base.

Head had pitched in an exhibition game for Elmira against the Dodgers a few weeks earlier. He had impressed Dodgers coach Charlie Dressen, who was managing the team for that game, by allowing only one hit and striking out five in three innings.

"He has more stuff than any pitcher I've seen this year," said Brooklyn's veteran outfielder Dixie Walker. "His curve dropped like something rolling off a table and his fastball sailed. So far as I was concerned, the ball might just as well have disappeared."[6]

Catcher Gus Mancuso also was impressed with Head's pitching. "He not only has a fastball," said Mancuso, "but if he has good control over that hook I know he is going to be tough to hit."[7]

Dressen said that in addition to Head's outstanding fastball, he pitched with authority and never showed a trace of nervousness in facing the big

leaguers.[8] The Dodgers players all raved about the composure the youngster had shown.

Head made his major-league debut with a scoreless inning against St. Louis in the first game of a July 27 doubleheader at Ebbets Field. Three days later he made his first start, at home against Pittsburgh. Heavy rain and lightning almost made for a postponement, but the weather cleared just before game time—unfortunately for Head. The Pirates scored four first-inning runs on their way to an 8-2 victory. Dodgers manager Leo Durocher pulled Head after two innings, during which he allowed three hits and walked four.

After a day off, the Dodgers and Pirates played a doubleheader on August 1. After Brooklyn won the first game, Durocher started Head again in the nightcap in what might have been a ploy to get Pirates manager Frankie Frisch to start a left-handed-hitting lineup. After Head began the game by walking Lloyd Waner on four pitches, Durocher replaced him with left-hander Lee Grissom.

Dixie Walker continued to encourage Head after he joined the Dodgers. The youngster was trying to develop a slider similar to the one Brooklyn ace Whit Wyatt threw. He asked the Dodgers batters for their reaction, and Walker had given him the most positive advice. "Pretty good, but stay with it and you'll make it better," he told Head. "And that's all you need—a pitch with some quality of deception to go with your other stuff. You've got everything else."[9]

Head's first big-league win also came against the Pirates, a complete-game 8-2 victory on September 13. In two months with the Dodgers, Head got into 13 games, finishing with a 1-2 record. The club invited him to Havana for spring training in 1941, and his excellent work there appeared to have earned him a place on the club.

"I'm keeping that kid," Durocher said after Head pitched an outstanding game against Shreveport of the Texas League. "He has great stuff," Leo said. "They can't hit his fastball. Every hit they made off him in Havana and in yesterday's game was off his curve. It isn't a bad curve, but he hasn't got good enough control of it, and besides he throws it to the wrong spots."[10]

Brooklyn's oldest pitcher, Fred Fitzsimmons, had been working with Head to improve that curve. But if his curveball was a problem, there was much to praise about his fastball. New Dodgers catcher Mickey Owen, who caught Head in the game against Shreveport, said, "His fastball was as live as a basket of snakes."[11]

Yet the suspicion remained that Durocher might change his mind and let Head spend the year with Brooklyn's top farm team in Montreal, where Clyde Sukeforth, an excellent teacher of pitchers, was the manager. The writers who traveled with the team were almost evenly split as to whether the Dodgers should keep him or let him gain the benefit of one more year of seasoning. While Durocher agreed Head was ready for the big leagues, he wanted him to get more seasoning and sent him to Montreal.

The 23-year-old Head won his first seven games for the 1941 Royals, on his way to an 18-8 season. The Royals finished second to the Newark Bears and met the Buffalo Bisons in the first round of the 1941 Governor's Cup series.[12] Head shut out Buffalo, 7-0, in Game Two to even the seven-game semifinal series at 1-1. With the Royals trailing three games to two, he came back to win the sixth game, 4-3, with ninth-inning relief help from Van Mungo. The Royals won Game Seven, and then defeated Newark, four games to three, in the championship series.

The Dodgers had edged out the St. Louis Cardinals in the National League pennant race, but Montreal was not able to duplicate that against the Cardinals' top farm team in the Junior World Series. The Burt Shotton-managed Columbus (Ohio) Red Birds of the American Association won the title in six games. Head made two appearances, both in relief, without a decision.

At spring training in 1942, the Dodgers were again working on Head's curveball while also attempting to improve his control. (He had walked 92 batters in 209 innings at Montreal.) He made the club, and his control improved once the season started. As he had the previous year, Head started strong. In his first five starts of the season, through May 16, he was 5-0, with an ERA of 2.74 and 28 strikeouts with only 17 walks.

"During spring training, I felt pretty miserable," he said after winning his fifth game. "I had a touch of grippe. And then there was the added worry of my wife's condition. When Eddie Jr. was born … everything took a turn for the better. The curveball I was developing for a change of pace began to nip the corners consistently and my fastball hopped as well as ever."[13]

Like many ballplayers, Head had an unusual superstition. He would not begin to warm up before a game until coach John Corriden handed him the ball. And if he was going, for his fourth victory, Corriden would have to slap the ball four times with his right palm, and say: "There it is for you."[14] This means that Corriden was doing six ball snaps for quite a while. Head lost his next four decisions and did not win his sixth game until June 29.

Head had his strongest outing of the season on May 29 against the Giants. He retired the New Yorkers in order through six innings. Billy Werber ended any hopes of a perfect game when he walked to lead off the seventh and eventually came around to score an unearned run. Head was now trailing Tom Sunkel of the Giants, 1-0, but he still had a no-hitter working. That ended when Harry Danning singled to lead off the eighth. The Dodgers tied the score in the bottom of the ninth, but Hugh Casey, who replaced Head in the ninth, gave up two runs in the 10th to take the loss.

Overall, Head finished with a 10-6 record in 36 games: 15 starts and 21 relief appearances. It was a frustrating season for the Dodgers, who led the league by 10 games in early August and finished with 104 victories, but wound up second to St. Louis.

The 1942 baseball season had been a mostly normal one, but by 1943 the war's impact was being felt in players lost to the military and in travel restrictions. The Dodgers trained at Bear Mountain, New York, not far from the US Military Academy at West Point. After catching Head one afternoon, Mickey Owen said: "Ed's much faster than this time a year ago. A year ago they were comparing him with [Dodgers pitcher] Chet Kehn. I always thought Head was faster than Kehn — and I thought his curve was better, too, although some people said the opposite. Head should get off to a great start this spring. He's a much better pitcher."[15]

Brooklyn opened the 1943 season at Ebbets Field against the Giants. It was the Dodgers' first game under new president Branch Rickey, who had replaced Larry MacPhail, now in the military. Head's excellent spring had earned him the honor of pitching the opener, which he won, 5-2. He allowed just six hits, four of which were by the Giants' manager, future Hall of Famer Mel Ott.

The highlight of Head's 1943 season came in May when he pitched back-to-back shutouts against Chicago and Cincinnati. In his next start, he shut out Pittsburgh through six innings, and had compiled a streak of 26⅔ consecutive scoreless innings before Vince DiMaggio ended it with a home run.

Head's third consecutive win was also his third consecutive complete game. He tailed off after that, failing to pitch a complete game after May 29. He regained his old form in late August with consecutive complete-game wins against the Pirates (6-1) and the Phillies (8-0).

Both this season and last, he had pitched well in the beginning and at the end of the season, but had faltered in midseason. Head was a Southerner, so it could not be the heat that was affecting him, according to some convoluted reasoning by sportswriter Tim Cohane. "Head simply has not yet learned to use his equipment," said Cohane, making sense. "Essentially, he is a fastball pitcher. His fastball is live. It does things, hopping or dipping or swerving as it approaches the plate. But a live fastball is not enough to get by in the majors unless a fellow is a Walter Johnson."[16]

Head's problem was that he had never developed a major-league curveball, and his experiment with a slider this season had not succeeded, Cohane concluded. After the win over Pittsburgh, Durocher informed Rickey that Head had made use of a change of pace to complement his fastball. He used it again in the shutout of the Phillies. Head had been instructed to use a change of pace all season but had stubbornly resisted.

Durocher was using him more in relief this season. Head's 47 appearances, second most on the club, included only 18 starts. Yet both his 9-10 record and ratio of strikeouts (83) to walks (66) were disappointments.

Because he expected to be drafted before the 1944 season began, Head never reported to Bear Mountain for spring training. He finally joined the team four days before the season opener, and he did not make his first appearance until May 29. His first start was on June 2, when he held the Chicago Cubs to one run in six innings, but was not involved in the decision. On June 8 he pitched a complete game victory over the Philadelphia Phillies, 8-1, in the second game of a doubleheader. As in past seasons, he started off well and then faded. He pitched five straight complete games, winning four, before he slumped like the rest of the Dodgers. From June 28 through July 16, the Dodgers lost a franchise record 16 consecutive games. Three of those losses were charged to Head in games he started.

On July 13, during the All-Star break, Head received orders from his draft board in Monroe, Louisiana, to report for Army induction immediately. He took his basic training at Camp Hood, Texas, and then served with the Tank Destroyers Recruit Training Corps at Camp Hood North. His main role, however, was as the physical training instructor and athletic director.

There were 20,000 soldiers at Camp Hood North, most of whom had little athletic or physical training opportunities. Head, with the commanding general's approval, organized leagues for softball, basketball, and volleyball. He also managed and pitched for the post's baseball team and took care of all the athletic equipment.

"I took care of all athletics and inspected physical training," Head wrote. "I managed the post baseball team that finished third in the Texas semipro tournament. We finished the season with 22 victories and 11 defeats."[17] For his efforts in this area, he received a letter of commendation from his commanding officer. In the first week of November 1945, at Fort Hood, Head, who had risen to the rank of Tech/5, received his official discharge from the Army.

The return of servicemen helped swell the record number of players at spring training camps in 1946, including that of the Dodgers in Daytona Beach, Florida. Head had been gone for two years and his arm was still a little sore from absorbing the recoil from a 57-millimeter antitank gun while at Fort Hood.

But he opened the season with Brooklyn and made his postwar debut on April 23, starting against the Boston Braves at Ebbets Field. The game, played on a Tuesday afternoon, drew a near-capacity crowd of 26,787. Fans had endured three full years of subpar baseball during the war and this was an early sign they would turn out in record numbers this season. For Head, it would be the game of his career, as he no-hit the Braves, 5-0, in the first no-hitter in Brooklyn since Cincinnati's Johnny Vander Meer's second consecutive no-hitter in 1938.

Using an assortment of fastballs, curveballs, sliders, and changeups, Head struck out only two, but he kept the opposing batters off stride all day. The Braves had four baserunners, three walks, and a fifth-inning error by shortstop Pee Wee Reese, while Brooklyn's defense turned two double plays.

This was a knowledgeable crowd, aware of what was happening. There were two close calls, one in the seventh inning and one in the eighth. Tommy Holmes led off the Boston seventh with a long drive to right-center field, but rookie center fielder Carl Furillo ran it down and made the catch in front of the exit gate. In the eighth Whitey Wietelmann slashed a line drive between Reese and third baseman Reiser that Reiser was able to grab with his glove hand.

The crowd was quiet when Chuck Workman, batting for Boston pitcher Mort Cooper, led off the ninth with a walk. But they rose in joy when, as Connie Ryan was striking out, catcher Ferrell Anderson threw to first baseman Ed Stevens to double up Workman. Johnny Hopp made the final out on a groundball to second baseman Billy Herman as the crowd erupted in cheers.

The day before the no-hitter, Ed's wife, Johnnie Mae, had given gave birth to a baby boy they named Rickey. "Boy, what a day, what a day," Head said in the Dodgers dressing room after the game. "First I celebrate the birth of my son and then I pitch a no-hitter. And would you believe it," he added, "I knew I was going to do it all the time. I felt great right from the start. I threw only one bad pitch all game—that one to Holmes—I meant to keep it on the outside. You can bet I was saying to myself, 'Come on Furillo.'"[18]

Head said he did not think he had anything extra, but just threw harder and harder as the game progressed. "All I used was my fastball, curve, slider, and change of pace. The slider is the only thing I didn't have before the war."[19]

But there was one other thing Head now had that he did not have before the war: a sore arm. A few weeks after the no-hitter he reinjured his arm, ending his major-league career. Head pitched in 13 games for Brooklyn in 1946, winning three and losing two. His last big-league appearance was a one-inning mop-up job in the second game of a doubleheader at St. Louis on August 25.[20]

He spent all of spring training with the Dodgers in 1947, but was unable to stick with the club. On Opening Day he was sent to the Fort Worth Cats of the Double-A Texas League. He split the season between Fort Worth, where he lost all three of his decisions, and the St. Paul Saints of the Triple-A American Association, where he won three and lost three.

Head spent his final three active seasons in baseball as the general manager and field manager of the Monroe (Louisiana) Sports.[21] Monroe was a member of the Cotton States League in 1954 and 1955, winning the pennant in '55. In 1956 the Sports moved to the Evangeline League, where Head had started his career in 1939.[22]

After baseball, Head lived in Bastrop, Louisiana, and worked as a preventive maintenance coordinator for the International Paper Company. He was still in their employ when he died in Bastrop on January 31, 1980, six days past his 62nd birthday. Head was survived by his mother, his wife, three sons, and three grandchildren.

NOTES

1. Tom Meany, "Fluoroscope Helped to Avoid Amputation; Youth, Now a Dodger, Then Learned to Throw With Other Hand," *PM*, April 30, 1942.
2. Ibid.
3. Ibid.
4. "Ed Head, an Ex-Dodger; Pitched No-Hit Game," *New York Times*, February 1, 1980.
5. Tom Meany.
6. *Brooklyn Eagle*, July 12, 1940.
7. Undated 1940 article from the *New York Sun* in Head's Hall of Fame file.
8. Head often claimed he threw much harder as a left-hander than he did as a right-hander.
9. *Brooklyn Eagle*, July 12, 1940.
10. Jerry Mitchell, "Rookie Ed Head Hurls His Way To Regular Pitching Staff," *New York Post*, April 2, 1941.
11. Tommy Holmes, "Ed Head May Crash Flock Mound Staff," *Brooklyn Eagle*, April 2, 1940.
12. The Governor's Cup format was to have the first- and fourth-place finishers and the second- and third-place finishers meet in a best-of-seven series. The two winners would then play a best-of-seven series to decide which International League team would meet the American Association representative in the Junior World Series.
13. Johnnie Mae Head gave birth to a boy, their first child, on March 22, 1942, in Louisiana. They named him Edward Marvin Head Jr. Unsourced clipping from Head's Hall of Fame file.
14. Unsourced clipping from Head's Hall of Fame file.
15. Harold Parrott, "Both Sides," *Brooklyn Eagle*, March 22, 1943.
16. Tim Cohane, "Head May Have Caught On," *New York World Telegram*, September, 2, 1943.
17. From a 1960 questionnaire Head filled out for the commissioner's office.
18. Joseph M. Sheehan, "Head Of Dodgers Wins No-Hitter, 5-0," *New York Times*, April 24, 1946.

19 Ibid.

20 The Dodgers were trailing 10-4 when Head came in to pitch the seventh inning. He allowed one run in Brooklyn's 14-8 loss.

21 Head began the 1954 season as the manager of the Tri-City Braves of the Class-A Western International League.

22 *The Sporting News* of February 23, 1980, wrote that Head scouted for the Houston Astros for three years in the early 1960s.

ED HEAD'S NO-HIT GAME
APRIL 23, 1946: BROOKLYN DODGERS 5, BOSTON BRAVES 0, AT EBBETS FIELD

By Lyle Spatz

FOR THE FIRST TIME SINCE 1941, the 1946 baseball season opened with the United States at peace. Fans, who had endured subpar baseball for the previous three years would turn out in record numbers this season. In Brooklyn, the Dodgers would shatter their previous attendance record, drawing just under 1.8 million. An early indication of what was to come was the near-capacity crowd of 26,787 that showed up at Ebbets Field on April 23 for a Tuesday afternoon game against the Boston Braves. Weekday afternoon games, particularly in the spring, were typically not well attended. But the Dodgers had gotten off to a 5-1 start and pennant fever was already being felt in Brooklyn.

On the mound for the Dodgers was Ed Head, a 28-year-old right-hander, who was making his first major-league appearance since 1944. After two years in the Army's Tank Destroyer Corps at Fort Hood, Texas, he had made the team out of spring training, though his arm was still sore from absorbing the recoil from a 57-millimeter antitank gun.

That Head had ever made it to the major leagues was a miracle in itself. In 1935, when he was 17, Head was a left-handed pitcher for a semipro team in Louisiana. One afternoon he was on a bus for scheduled game against another team. He and his girlfriend, who accompanied him, were seated on the left side of the bus; Head in the aisle seat and the girl in the window seat. As teenage boys typically do, Head had his left arm draped over her shoulders.

Unfortunately, they were seated almost directly in the path of another bus that rammed theirs. Head was knocked unconscious. When he awoke, he saw his girlfriend was dead and his left arm, wrenched loose from its socket, was "a mass of shattered bone and mangled flesh."[1] The local doctor told him he would have to amputate the arm.

Head argued against amputation and pleaded to have his uncle, who had the only fluoroscope in the area, to come look at the injury. His uncle, a doctor, determined that he could save the arm, which he did following many hours of surgery.

For several days Head's life had been in danger and the thought of his ever pitching again had been dismissed. His lifetime goal had always been to be a major-league pitcher, but with his left arm nearly useless, that would be impossible. At that point, Head realized there was only one way he could reach his goal, by throwing right-handed. The dedication and effort needed to make this happen would have discouraged most people, but Head worked and practiced until he succeeded.

The day before Head's return to baseball, his wife, Johnnie Mae, had given birth to their second son, whom they named Rickey. So before he took the mound, he was handing out cigars in the clubhouse. When he did take the mound, he pitched the game of his career, a 5-0 no-hitter. Head had flirted with a no-hitter once before. On May 29, 1942, he retired the first 18 New York Giants before walking Bill Werber, ending the possibility of a perfect game. The no-hitter ended when Harry Danning led off the eighth inning with a single.

Head was not overpowering this afternoon, striking out only two, but he used an assortment of fastballs, curveballs, sliders, and changeups to keep the opposing batters off stride. The Braves had only four baserunners, three walks, and a fifth-inning error by shortstop Pee Wee Reese, while Brooklyn's defense turned two double plays. Reese's error was clearly a bobble, with no controversy on the scoring.

The Dodgers used four straight hits to take a two-run lead in the third inning. They added two more in the fifth on a two-run double by Ed Stevens. Ferrell Anderson's solo home run in the sixth accounted for Brooklyn's fifth run.

Meanwhile, Head kept getting easy outs. He had only two close calls, one in the seventh inning and one in the eighth. Tommy Holmes led off the seventh with a long drive to right center field that rookie center fielder Carl Furillo ran down and caught in front of the exit gate. In the eighth Whitey Wietelmann slashed a line drive between Reese and third baseman Pete Reiser that Reiser was able to grab with his glove hand.

This was a knowledgeable crowd, aware of what was happening. They were silent when Chuck Workman, batting for Boston pitcher Mort Cooper, led off the ninth with a walk. But they rose in joy when, as Connie Ryan was striking out, catcher Ferrell Anderson threw to first baseman Stevens to double up Workman. Johnny Hopp made the final out on a groundball to second baseman Billy Herman as the crowd erupted in cheers.

In true baseball tradition, none of the other Dodgers mentioned to Head that he was throwing a no-hitter. Herman said he hadn't realized it until the later innings when the crown began loudly cheering every putout. Reese and Stevens claimed they first learned about it when they reached the dressing room.

"Boy, what a day, what a day," Head said in the Dodgers clubhouse after the game. "First I celebrate the birth of my son and then I pitch a no-hitter. And would you believe it," he added, "I knew I was going to do it all the time. I felt great right from the start. I threw only one bad pitch all game—that one to Holmes—I meant to keep it on the outside. You can bet I was saying to myself, 'Come on Furillo.'"[2]

Head said he did not think he had anything extra, but just threw harder and harder as the game progressed. "All I used was my fastball, curve, slider, and change of pace. The slider is the only thing I didn't have before the war."[3]

Head's no hitter was the first by a Dodger since Tex Carleton's at Cincinnati on April 30, 1940. It was the first in Brooklyn since June 15, 1938, when Johnny Vander Meer of the Reds pitched his second consecutive no-hitter in the first night game at Ebbets Field.

A few weeks after the no-hitter, Head reinjured his arm, ending his major-league career.

NOTES

1 Tom Meany, "Fluoroscope Helped to Avoid Amputation; Youth, Now a Dodger, Then Learned to Throw With Other Hand," *PM*, April 30, 1942.

2 Joseph M. Sheehan, "Head Of Dodgers Wins No-Hitter, 5-0," *New York Times*, April 24, 1946.

3 Ibid.

BILL MCCAHAN

By David E. Skelton

IN JUNE 1947, THREE MONTHS before his husky right-handed hurler delivered the fifth no-hitter in franchise history, Philadelphia Athletics manager Connie Mack forecast the expected stardom of 26-year-old Bill McCahan. "[Y]ou will see another great pitcher in this boy," Mack said. "Let me make a prediction. He will be another [Spud] Chandler."[1]

Being compared to the American League's 1943 Most Valuable Player was heady stuff for a blue-eyed, ruddy-cheeked rookie who had entered the 1947 season with just one major-league win under his belt. But McCahan had been in the manager's sights for years. In 1938 his uncle Izzy Hoffman,[2] who three decades earlier had brief stints in the outfield with the Washington Senators and Boston Doves, arranged a tryout for McCahan in Philadelphia's Shibe Park in front of Mack's watchful gaze. Shortly thereafter, the future Hall of Fame skipper sent his former ace hurler Jack Coombs, who was managing the Duke University baseball team, to McCahan's suburban Philadelphia home with an offer to pay the youngster's four-year tuition to the prestigious college.

The "can't-miss" label ascribed to the righty over the next nine years was built in part upon the illustrious career McCahan established in college and while pitching for US Army Air Corps teams during World War II. Tabbed by *Washington Post* sportswriter Shirley Povich as "an amazing member of Connie [Mack]'s fantastic [1948] pitching staff,"[3] the youngster appeared poised to take his place among the long roster of great Athletics hurlers. But predictions of greatness quickly disappeared when arm and shoulder problems surfaced after McCahan's rookie season, ailments that held him to just 107⅓ innings pitched over the remainder of his four-year major-league career.

William Glenn McCahan Jr. was born in Philadelphia on June 7, 1921, the only child of William Glenn McCahan Sr. and Madeline Sarah (Snell) McCahan. Around the turn of the nineteenth century his third great-grandfather, John McCahan, left the town of Ballycastle, on the northeastern tip of what is now Northern Ireland, with his wife and eight children and emigrated to the United States. The family initially settled in Bradford County in northern Pennsylvania before moving to regions west of Harrisburg, the state capital. Bill's grandfather John A. McCahan was a captain in the 205th Pennsylvania Infantry in the Civil War before moving to Philadelphia after the conflict. He married Lucy Glenn, a Pennsylvania native 12 years his junior. (The Glenn name would be carried by their son and grandson.) Their third child, William—Bill's father—spent two years in France as a sergeant in the US Army during World War I before being discharged on April 22, 1919. A year later he married Madeline Snell. William launched a long career as a civil servant and, after a move to suburban Bucks County in 1927, became the county highway superintendent.[4] When he died in February 1935, Hoffman, Bill's uncle, stepped in as his surrogate father.

McCahan attended Langhorne Middletown High School (now Neshaminy High) in Langhorne, Pennsylvania, where his nickname, "Wheezer," may have come from his exhaustive schedule. He participated in the student council (he was the 1938 class vice president), the glee club, and an extensive list of athletic pursuits including soccer, track, volleyball, basketball, baseball, and especially football—all while holding down part-time jobs as a golf caddy or working on a farm.[5] A three-time All-County halfback, McCahan received a dozen athletic scholarship offers to play football in college. These offers were spurned in favor of the youngster's singular desire to follow his uncle's path into professional baseball.

McCahan pursued this passion at a dizzying pace by playing shortstop or third base for his high school, an American Legion squad, and two semipro clubs. In his senior year of high school, McCahan, who disdained pitchers, reluctantly took to the mound after his uncle convinced him he would not reach the professional ranks as a hitter. The youngster went 12-2, missing out on a 13th win though he pitched a 12-inning no-hitter against Bristol High School. (The game ended in a scoreless tie.)

McCahan graduated from high school in 1938 and proceeded to Durham, North Carolina, where he split his extracurricular time playing basketball and baseball for the Duke Blue Devils. (His benefactor, Connie Mack, forbade football for fear of a permanent injury). Among the fastest players on the hardwood court, McCahan helped the basketball team to the Southern Conference championship in 1940 and 1942. In the latter season, he scored 163 of his 219 career points to earn selection as the starting guard on the United Press all-conference first team.[6] But McCahan's primary interest was on the diamond, where he formed an effective mound duo with New York Giants hurler Frank Seward. Using nothing but heat, McCahan had a career record of 24 wins against seven losses. During his four years at Duke he also spent at least one summer pitching for the Bennington (Vermont) Generals in the collegiate Northern League.

After graduating from college in 1942, McCahan was assigned to the Wilmington (Delaware) Blue Rocks in the Interstate League (Class B), the Athletics' second highest minor-league affiliate. Working closely with Blue Rocks manager Duke Brett, a former Chicago Cubs right-hander, McCahan tried unsuccessfully to master a curveball and changeup (something he never fully achieved throughout his career). He surrendered 35 walks in 77 innings—walks were another career-long challenge—to finish the season with an unremarkable record of 5-3, 3.51 in 22 appearances. Opportunities to expand upon his debut campaign were interrupted on February 24, 1943, when the righty entered the US Army Air Corps during World War II.

McCahan was sent to the 21st College Training Detachment at Colby College in Waterville, Maine, where he received flight instruction. His first assignment was as a B-29 bomber test pilot at Spence Air Base in Moultrie, Georgia. On August 4, 1944, he received a commission as a second lieutenant before being transferred to Maxwell Air Base in Montgomery, Alabama. Throughout his service McCahan earned a record of 61-2 pitching for base teams. During the winter of 1943-44 he also put in a brief stint playing professional basketball with the champion Wilmington Bombers in the American Basketball League. On November 9, 1945, with the war over, he was discharged. McCahan waited out the winter by returning to the Bombers, commuting from his home in Prospect Park, a Philadelphia suburb. He would continue his basketball pursuits over four of the next five seasons.

On the morning of February 17, 1946, McCahan traveled from his home to the North Philadelphia station, where he was among the first players departing on the 11:30 train bound for the Athletics' West Palm Beach, Florida, spring-training camp. During the camp's opening weeks, he and fellow pitching prospect Joe Coleman captured great attention as the club looked to improve upon one of the AL's worst mound staffs. But far less success ensued for both youngsters. On March 31, in the club's last Grapefruit League exhibition, McCahan was one of three Athletics hurlers clobbered by the International League's Baltimore Orioles in an 11-10 loss. Shortly thereafter, he and Coleman were assigned to the Triple-A Toronto Maple Leafs. McCahan was among the team's leaders in all pitching categories and among the league leaders with a 2.76 ERA — a yield that got him only 11 wins for the league's worst offense. On June 21, this was made up in part by the club's strong defense, which turned an International League-record six double plays to aid McCahan in a 10-inning complete-game win over the Syracuse Chiefs. When the season ended, McCahan was among the Athletics' late season call-ups.

On September 15, 1946, McCahan made his major-league debut in Cleveland Stadium, starting the second game of a doubleheader against the Indians. He scattered seven hits and three walks in a 2-0 shutout win over Bob Feller. Two weeks later, following two successful relief appearances, McCahan made his second start, this time against the New York Yankees in Shibe Park. A second-inning leadoff single by Joe DiMaggio ignited a two-run rally. McCahan yielded just three more hits in a heartbreaking 2-1 complete-game loss on the last day of the season. During the offseason, he moved to New York to play basketball with the Syracuse Nationals in their inaugural season in the National Basketball League. McCahan was not a tall man, listed at 5-feet-11 and 200 pounds. Around this same time Mack, who was considering his options for the 1947 season said, "McCahan made a good impression on me at the close of last season. I think he is ready."[7]

The mound youth movement that Mack began in 1946 yielded dividends in 1947 as six pitchers, ranging in age from 20 to 26 years old, collected 60 percent of the Athletics' starting assignments to help bring an end to the team's 13 straight losing seasons. The six, who entered the season with a combined .288 winning percentage, included the 26-year-old McCahan who, due to eight rain-canceled assignments, was unable to string two consecutive starts until July. "All I have to do is pick up my glove and it starts to drizzle," a frustrated McCahan said.[8] A strong July 10 performance against the Indians ended in defeat when Cleveland righty Don Black no-hit the Athletics. Six days later, in a four-hit gem against the St. Louis Browns, an error by center-field teammate Sam Chapman was the only thing that stood between McCahan and his second major-league shutout. Another whitewash was lost on July 28 when a streak of wildness ruined eight innings of two-hit shutout pitching. He rebounded from this disappointment with six straight wins in August.

"It was all my fault," Athletics first baseman Ferris Fain said in a postgame interview on September 3. "I threw the ball while I was still pivoting, and it was five full feet from the bag."[9] The 26-year-old rookie was lamenting his second-inning error on a groundball off the bat of Stan Spence that allowed the Senators center fielder to gain first base. The miscue proved to be the difference between McCahan and the sixth perfect game in major-league history. When the day started, the chances of such a historic event being played out before a tiny crowd of 2,816 seemed most unlikely.

Thirty years had passed since the Senators were handcuffed by a no-hitter when Boston Red Sox righty Ernie Shore famously relieved Babe Ruth after just one batter on June 23, 1917. The odds were even greater considering that until 1947 only six no-hitters had been twirled by a rookie. (The mark is made even more astounding because McCahan is the first of only two pitchers in major-league history to be on both the winning and losing ends of a no-hitter; the other being St. Louis Cardinals great Bob Gibson.) McCahan's gem was aided by right fielder Elmer Valo who, in his first game back from an August 9 beaning, accounted for two-thirds of the offense with a seventh inning two-run double after robbing Senators first baseman Mickey Vernon of a sure extra-base hit with a spectacular catch against Shibe Field's right-field scoreboard. Not until Catfish Hunter's perfect game in 1968 would the Athletics — by then relocated in Oakland—have a pitcher deliver another no-hitter.

Within two weeks of the 3-0 no-hit win, Mack, who was often strapped for cash, was compelled to publicly deny rumors of a $500,000 offer from the Yankees for McCahan, Fain, and Chapman. The Athletics manager was adamant about not parting with any of the trio, especially the rookie hurler, who finished the season among the team's leaders in wins (10), ERA (3.32), complete games (10) and innings pitched (165⅓). In October McCahan was selected to *The Sporting News* All Rookies team alongside future Hall of Famers Yogi Berra and Jackie Robinson while also garnering some consideration for the AL Most Valuable Player Award.

When the season ended, McCahan was prepared to sign an attractive offer from the Boston Celtics to play in the Basketball Association of America (predecessor to the present-day NBA) before Mack interceded. Wanting his promising hurler to rest over the winter, he proffered a $1,000 bonus to persuade McCahan to forgo the offer. The bonus did not cover expenses incurred by the youngster for a new car and a new home. After barnstorming through the United States and Mexico with the Bob Feller All-Stars, McCahan took a job with an oil company loading and unloading drums weighing over 100 pounds. Moreover, McCahan's successful campaign earned him a regular spot on the rubber-chicken circuit where he gained considerable weight. "I played at many more dinner plates than home plates," he later confessed. When McCahan reported to Florida in the spring of 1947, tight arm, shoulder, and chest muscles from lifting the heavy oil drums, combined with the added weight, had him struggling "like a man pushing a shot instead of [throwing] a baseball."[10]

On April 23, 1948, in his first appearance of the new season, McCahan was fortunate to avoid the decision in a 5-3 loss to the Senators after yielding eight hits and four walks through eight laborious innings. Six days later he was unable to survive the second inning in an 11-5 Red Sox win. Complaining of a sore arm and shoulder stiffness, McCahan took the mound just once over the next 10 weeks. In August he appeared to have found himself with three wins in five starts before imploding with a 12.00 ERA in his last three starts of the season. He finished the year with a disappointing record of 4-7, 5.71 in 86⅔ innings. When the season ended, Mack, eager to ensure that McCahan would not be hoisting oil drums again, readily approved the youngster's request to play basketball during the offseason.

But a season with the Philadelphia SPHAs (South Philadelphia Hebrew Association) in the American Basketball League, preceded by a two-week barnstorming tour of Eastern Pennsylvania with fellow Keystone State natives Del Ennis, Carl Furillo, and Curt Simmons, did little to alleviate McCahan's sore arm. When the 1949 season opened, he was brought along very slowly. On May 8, with only one inning of work under his belt, McCahan provided a glimpse of his former potential with seven strong innings against the Chicago White Sox in a 3-2 win. It proved to be his last victory in the major leagues. On June 5, after a 12-day rest, McCahan offered an encouraging performance through two innings against the Indians before his arm gave way in the third. Two weeks later he worked one inning of relief at home against the St. Louis Browns before he was sent to the Buffalo Bisons in the International League. On September 28 the Athletics sent McCahan and $25,000 to the Brooklyn Dodgers for utility infielder Kermit Wahl.

In February 1950 McCahan reported to the Dodgers spring training where, for the first time in three years, he could throw pain-free. "If his arm is sound, he can help us win the 1950 pennant," Brooklyn GM Branch Rickey said.[11] But his restored arm did little in the way of results and McCahan spent the 1950 season bouncing among three of the Dodgers minor-league affiliates. After the season, he traveled south to play winter ball in Venezuela, where he got more than he bargained for following the November 13 assassination of the country's provisional president. In the ensuing chaos, police stormed Caracas's Hotel Savoy, where McCahan and other US players were staying. The players "took a severe punching and shoving" before order was finally restored. Within days, most of the US players, presumably including McCahan, left the country.[12]

There was far less drama in 1951 when McCahan was pitching for the Fort Worth Cats in the Double-A Texas League. He placed among the circuit leaders with a record of 19-9, 2.76 in 228 innings, missing an opportunity for a 20th win when he was called to Philadelphia after his mother contracted a serious illness. (She died two months later.) In 1952 McCahan, seeing little chance of ever returning to the major leagues, accepted a demotion to Class A as player-manager of the Pueblo (Colorado) Dodgers in the Western League. When right-handed pitching prospect Joe Stanka approached his rookie skipper to help him develop a curve, McCahan with only slight exaggeration said, "Joe, I've never thrown a curveball in my life. I don't know how to help you."[13] He led the club to a respectable 81-73 record before retiring from baseball.

McCahan returned to Fort Worth, where he launched a 26-year career with the General Dynamics Corporation, eventually heading an F-16 fighter project. Around 1953, he married Addie Marie Shipp, a Texas native one year his senior.[14] The union remained intact until he died 33 years later. On July 3, 1986, McCahan died of cancer one month after his 65th birthday. He was buried at Greenwood Memorial Park in Fort Worth. Three years later, his prep-school exploits on the gridiron were acknowledged with his induction into the Neshaminy High School Hall of Fame.

In the postgame glow of his brilliant September 3, 1947, no-hitter McCahan said, "[s]ome day someone may batter my brains in, and it's possible I'll lose a few."[15] The words proved sadly prophetic when the righty lost nine of his last 14 major-league decisions. McCahan never attained the stardom that was once predicted for him. He concluded his four-year career with a record of 16-14, 3.84 in 290⅔ innings.

SOURCES

In addition to the sources cited in the Notes, the author consulted Ancestry.com and Baseball-Reference.com. The author wishes to thank SABR member Bill Mortell for his valuable assistance.

NOTES

1. "Mack Finding New Marvels at 84—A's Play to 'Standing Room Only,'" *The Sporting News*, July 9, 1947: 9.
2. Some sources have incorrectly identified McCahan's uncle as former Philadelphia Athletics centerfielder Danny Hoffman.
3. "Curvers Cutting Fancy Figures in Connie Mack's Hill Setup," *The Sporting News*, April 14, 1948: 9.
4. The September 10, 1947, edition of *The Sporting News* suggests that as a young man Bill's father appeared in silent films as a cowboy actor, a claim the author was unable to substantiate.
5. Charles W. Lauble Jr., "Langhorne Trivia," Historic Langhorne Association. Accessed November 13, 2016 (bit.ly/2etx1Vu).
6. John Roth and Ned Hinshaw, *The Encyclopedia of Duke Basketball* (Durham, North Carolina: Duke University Press, 2006), 255.
7. "Thin-Man Russ of A's Weighs Plan to Retire," *The Sporting News*, November 27, 1946: 8.
8. "Rain Balks McCahan of Eight Starts," *The Sporting News*, July 23, 1947: 11.
9. "Bill Didn't Think About No-Hitter Until Ninth," *The Sporting News*, September 10, 1947: 13.
10. "McCahan Takes Case to Court (Basketball)," *The Sporting News*, November 10, 1948: 7.
11. "McCahan in Dodger Bid," *The Sporting News*, March 29, 1950: 18.
12. Bob Lemke, "American Ballplayers Caught in 1950 Venezuela Police Riot," January 14, 2014. Accessed November 17, 2016 (bit.ly/2fjXjWJ).
13. C. Paul Rogers, III, "Joe Stanka." The Baseball Biography Project, Society of American Baseball Research. Bob Lemke's Blog, accessed November 15, 2016. (http://bit.ly/2geCobl).
14. One source indicates that when McCahan was in college he was engaged to Amityville, New York, native Charlotte Crump. The author was unable to find evidence that they married.
15. "McCahan, Prof. Coombs' Diligent Dukester, Makes Varsity Grade on No-Hitter Over Nats," *The Sporting News*, September 10, 1947: 13.

ATHLETICS ROOKIE MCCAHAN ONE MISCUE AWAY FROM A PERFECT GAME

SEPTEMBER 3, 1947: PHILADELPHIA ATHLETICS 3, WASHINGTON SENATORS 0, AT SHIBE PARK

By David Skelton

"IT WAS ALL MY FAULT," Philadelphia Athletics first baseman Ferris Fain said in a postgame interview. "I threw the ball while I was still pivoting, and it was five full feet from the bag."[1] The 26-year-old rookie was lamenting his second-inning error on a groundball off the bat of Stan Spence that allowed the Washington Senators center fielder to gain first base. The miscue proved to be the difference between Athletics rookie Bill McCahan and the sixth perfect game in major-league history. Even the opposition took a conciliatory tone afterward. "I'm sorry I had to be the one to spoil [it]," Spence said. "I was just trying to make a base-hit."[2]

When this day started, the chances of such a historic event being played out in Philadelphia's Shibe Park before the tiny crowd of 2,816 seemed most unlikely. Thirty years had passed since the Senators were handcuffed by a no-hitter when Boston Red Sox righty Ernie Shore famously relieved Babe Ruth after just one batter on June 23, 1917. The odds were even greater considering that up until this year only six no-hitters had been twirled by a rookie. The mark is made even more astounding because right-hander McCahan, who two months earlier was on the losing end of Cleveland Indians righty Don Black's gem, remains as of 2016 the only pitcher ever to be on both the winning and losing ends of a no-hitter.

Neither team was in contention for the American League pennant. Entering the day, Philadelphia was at exactly .500 (65-65) and in fifth place, 18 games behind the Yankees. The Senators were seventh, 27½ games back, with a record of 55-74.

It was a close game nonetheless. The game's outcome remained in doubt throughout the entire 1- hour and 26-minute affair as Senators hard-luck hurler Ray Scarborough kept the Athletics popgun offense in check for most of the game. In the second inning, Philadelphia capitalized on two of Scarborough's four walks to take a 1-0 lead before the righty settled down to hold the Athletics scoreless over the next four frames. But a one-out single by McCahan in the seventh ignited a two-run rally with the key blow being a bases-loaded double to right by outfielder Elmer Valo. In the top half of the inning Valo, who was appearing in his first game since an August 9 beaning by Senators right-hander Sid Hudson, had provided the fielding heroics with a spectacular catch against the right-field scoreboard that robbed Senators first baseman Mickey Vernon of a sure extra-base hit. Other fielding gems were recorded by second baseman Pete Suder and center fielder Sam Chapman. But the true hero this day was McCahan, who claimed afterward that he had not given a thought to a no-hitter before the ninth inning. "Then I bore down," the husky hurler said. "[U]ntil that time I was just trying to win a ballgame."[3]

Senators manager Ossie Bluege brought in three consecutive pinch-hitters to face McCahan in the ninth. None of the three got the ball out of the infield. The first flied out to shortstop, the second grounded to second, and McCahan struck out Cecil Travis to win the game. He'd faced 28 batters in all, one over the minimum, Spence reaching on the error in the second inning.

McCahan's journey from a former high-school phenom to a promising major-league hurler began in

1938 when his uncle Izzy Hoffman, a former major-league outfielder, arranged a tryout for his nephew in front of Athletics skipper Connie Mack. Immediately enamored, Mack arranged for McCahan's four-year tuition at Duke University, where the youngster could develop under Blue Devils manager and former Athletics ace Jack Coombs. A successful collegiate career, followed by an equally successful stint pitching for US Army Air Corps clubs during World War II, quickly made McCahan a "can't miss" prospect. The label appeared even more fitting on September 15, 1946, when, in his major-league debut, he outdueled Bob Feller in a 2-0 shutout win.

In 1947 McCahan's path to stardom was slowed by the extraordinarily large number of rainouts he was forced to endure through the first half of the season. In July, when the weather finally began to cooperate, McCahan established himself as one of the Athletics' prized young hurlers as he won seven of nine decisions prior to his historic September performance.

But fate would not shine as brightly throughout the remainder of McCahan's career. An offseason job lifting 100-pound oil drums increased his muscle tone to the point where it adversely affected his delivery. By the following spring he was struggling "like a man pushing a shot instead of [throwing] a baseball."[4] McCahan compiled a record of 5-8, 5.11 over the next two seasons before being demoted to the minor leagues. He never returned.

In the postgame glow of his brilliant September 3, 1947, performance McCahan said, "[s]ome day someone may batter my brains in, and it's possible I'll lose a few."[5] The words proved sadly prophetic following his rookie season as McCahan never attained the stardom that was once predicted for him.

SOURCES

In addition to the Sources cited in the Notes, the author relied on Baseball-Reference.com.

NOTES

1 "Bill Didn't Think About No-Hitter Until Ninth," *The Sporting News*, September 10, 1947: 13.

2 Ibid.

3 Ibid.

4 "McCahan Takes Case to Court (Basketball)," *The Sporting News*, November 10, 1948: 7.

5 "McCahan, Prof. Coombs' Diligent Dukester, Makes Varsity Grade on No-Hitter Over Nats," *The Sporting News*, September 10, 1947: 13.

BOBO HOLLOMON

By Len Pasculli

WHO IS THE ONLY MAJOR league pitcher in the modern era to throw a no-hitter in his first start? The answer is the St. Louis Browns' big right-hander Alva Lee "Bobo" Holloman. "Improbable" was the adjective most often used to describe Holloman's gem of May 6, 1953 — and its odd distinction would come to stand out more. As is always recounted, that was the only complete game Bobo pitched in his short career — he was out of the majors before the end of the 1953 season with only three victories to his name.[1]

It is one of those records that may never be broken, although 14 years later Billy Rohr of the Boston Red Sox came very close. In his first major-league appearance, a start against the New York Yankees on April 14, 1967, the 21-year-old Rohr came within a single strike of pitching a no-hitter when Elston Howard singled in the bottom of the ninth. But like Bobo Holloman, Rohr won only two other games in his career.

As of 2009, 21 no-hitters have been tossed by rookies since 1900 (of course, no others came in their first start).[2] Holloman was only the eighth rookie to do so, and from then on, the newspapers have told the tale of "Bobo's No-No."

Some will qualify Holloman's feat, noting that two other men before him pitched no-hitters in their first big-league start. However, they came before 1893, the year in which the pitching mound was moved back to its current location 60 feet 6 inches from home plate. On October 4, 1891, 22-year-old Ted Breitenstein of the St. Louis Browns in the old American Association allowed no hits in an 8-0 win over the Louisville Colonels. Just over one year later, on October 15, 1892, 22-year-old Charley "Bumpus" Jones pitched a no-hitter in his major-league debut as the Cincinnati Reds defeated the Pittsburgh Pirates, 7-1. To date, in the modern era, the runners-up are Wilson Alvarez (August 11, 1991) and Clay Buchholz (September 1, 2007). Both men were making their second start.[3]

Alva Lee Holloman Jr., was born in Thomaston, Georgia, to Alva Lee Sr. and Hattie Holloman on March 7, 1923.[4] Alva Lee was the fourth of six children — Edward, Baynard, Connie, Alva, Richard, and Carol — and he soon came to be called "Junior."

As a boy, Junior helped his father, a truck farmer. In fact, amid the Great Depression, he was forced to quit high school after just one year. Father and son hauled sweet potatoes and watermelons to Florida and brought oranges back to Georgia.

In 1940, the Hollomans moved about 100 miles northeast to Athens, Georgia. There Junior met Nan Stevens, daughter of Jessie and Maxine Stevens. Nan recalls the Sunday night "that good-looking, coal-black haired, brown-eyed 'new' boy in town" gave her a ride home from the Mars Hill Baptist Church.[5] They were married on January 24, 1942. Holloman served in the United States Navy, and early in their marriage he was stationed at Port Hueneme near Oxnard, California. He then shipped overseas for 11 months until his discharge in December 1945.

Holloman played sandlot baseball as a youth; while at Port Hueneme, he pitched for the base's team. Back at home in 1946, he tried out for the Macon Peaches, a Class-A baseball team affiliated with the Chicago Cubs in the "Sally" (*i.e.*, South Atlantic) League. The team liked what they saw in the 6-feet-2, 200-pound hard-throwing right-hander, and assigned him to the Moultrie Packers, a Class-D team in the Georgia-Florida League. There he enjoyed an all-star season, striking out 184 batters in 216 innings and compiling a 20-5 record with a 2.33 ERA for his favorite manager, Jim Poole. At one point, he pitched a doubleheader to make up a turn, so he could come home for the birth of his son, Gary Lee, on July 4, 1946. Six weeks later, young Gary, nicknamed "Little Papoose" since his papa was "Big Indian Chief" to the Moultrie fans, witnessed his first baseball game. The Big Chief pitched and won and hit a home run.

That winter, Holloman pitched in Cuba with the Oriente team in La Liga de la Federación (an "alternate" league that existed for one season in the wake of the Mexican League's player raids). It was not an especially successful season, as he lost a league-leading six games in a brief 40-game schedule.[6] Back in the United States in the summer of 1947, Holloman won 18 games and lost 17 for Macon. He began the 1948 season with Macon but was promoted to the Nashville Vols, the Cubs' Double-A affiliate in the Southern Association. He played there on and off through 1951. His combined record in 1948 was 15-5; in 1949, spent entirely with Nashville, he was 17-10.

It was in "Music City" that Alva Lee became "Bobo." At the time, 6-feet-2, 220-pound righthander Bobo Newsom was an American League All-Star pitcher. Larry Gilbert, the Vols' owner, gave Holloman the same nickname saying, "You're big, you have a strong arm, you like to pitch and you like to talk. You remind me of Bobo Newsom."[7] Holloman was a boastful, overenthusiastic, harmonica-playing, hot-headed man. Bobo was also superstitious: each time he entered a game, he would stop near the foul line on his way to the mound, bend down and draw the initials "GN" in the dirt — letters that stood for his son Gary and wife Nan. He considered using "NG"— but that, he said, did not connote a positive outcome.

In 1950 Bobo pitched over 200 innings for the fourth time in the first five years of his professional career. He picked up 13 wins against 13 losses while pitching for both Nashville and Shreveport, Louisiana, a Texas League team. In 1951, after a poor start at Nashville, Holloman and the Cubs parted ways. They sold his contract to Albany of the Eastern League, which in turn sold him on to Augusta, an unaffiliated club in the South Atlantic League. With an 11-9 record, he pitched well enough to be noticed by fellow Athens, Georgia, resident Spud Chandler. The former New York Yankee pitcher, then

a scout, influenced Augusta to sell Bobo's contract to the Syracuse Chiefs (also unaffiliated) of the International League in 1952. At age 29, he was at last just a step away from the majors.

During the '52 season Holloman had an appendectomy and lost about one month of playing time. Yet he put together a rather impressive 16-7 record and 2.51 ERA in 183 innings pitched, with 12 complete games including a one-hitter. He allowed 123 hits, the fewest of any pitcher in the International League that year — and only *six* of them were extra-base hits.[8]

Bobo Holloman loved to throw. In the days before pitch counts and relief specialists, he averaged more than 210 innings per year over the first seven seasons of his pro career (1946-1952), not counting winter ball or spring training.

The best of those winter seasons came in 1952, right after his success with Syracuse. At the suggestion of his International League opponent, future Brooklyn Dodger Junior Gilliam, Bobo played for the Santurce Cangrejeros club in Puerto Rico. Holloman was both the Crabbers' ace and workhorse, leading the league with 15 wins.[9] In the Puerto Rican league finals against San Juan, he pitched a 13-inning 7-5 victory on two days' rest, enabling Santurce to reach the Caribbean World Series in Cuba. Despite his heavy workload, he got two of the team's six wins in the round robin, both over the Caracas Leones.[10] The Crabbers were undefeated.

Coupling his regular-season and postseason output for Santurce with his Syracuse victories, he probably had more wins that year than any other professional pitcher. On the strength of that outstanding performance, Big Bobo was finally headed to the big leagues. In October 1952 he had been traded by Syracuse to the St. Louis Browns for pitcher Duke Markell and $35,000 ($10,000 up front and $25,000 if Holloman remained on the Brownies roster past June 15). The Browns had resided in or near the basement of the American League since 1946, and Bobo was hoping to make a difference.

Bobo Holloman made his major-league debut on April 18, 1953, in relief. He thought he was best as a starter, but manager Marty Marion used Holloman only out of the bullpen. And even at that, Bobo was not very effective in April. In four brief outings, he pitched 5 1/3 innings, allowing five runs on 10 hits and three walks. His ERA was nearly 9.00.

Nevertheless, Holloman nagged his manager on several occasions begging for a chance to start. A few times in early May when Marion thought he might start Bobo, the game got rained out. But finally "Slats" yielded to Holloman's constant pleas and started him against the Philadelphia Athletics in a night game on May 6 at old Sportsman's Park in St. Louis. Team owner Bill Veeck explained why he agreed with Marion to start Holloman. He said the Athletics were the "softest competition we could find" and if the Browns didn't give Bobo his chance, "he'll be on our ears all the way to the train station."[11]

May 6, 1953, was a rainy night. Only 2,473 fans were in attendance — including Gary and Nan — when Holloman took the mound for the home team. Veeck gives one of the best accounts of what happened next in his autobiography *Veeck — As In Wreck*:

[E]verything he threw up was belted. And everywhere the ball went, there was a Brownie there to catch it. It was such a hot and humid and heavy night that long fly balls which seemed to be heading out of the park would die and be caught against the fence. Just when Bobo looked as if he was tiring, a shower would sweep across the field, delaying the game long enough for him to get a rest. Allie Clark hit one into the left-field stands that curved foul at the last second. A bunt just rolled foul on the last spin. Our fielding was superb. The game went into the final innings and nobody had got a base hit off Big Bobo. On the final out of the eighth inning, Billy Hunter made an impossible diving stop on a ground ball behind second base and an even more impossible throw. With two out in the ninth, a ground ball was rifled down the first base line — right at our first baseman, Vic Wertz. Big Bobo had pitched the quaintest no-hitter in the history of the game.[12]

The Browns won, 6-0. Holloman struck out three, but six batters reached base — one on an error (Holloman's own) and five on walks. Three of those walks were in the ninth inning. And to top off this amazing night, Bobo's improbable pitching performance was matched only by his improbable batting performance. He collected three RBIs that night with two singles — his only hits and RBIs in his major-league career.

Bobo Holloman never pitched another complete game. He came close on June 21 when he defeated the Red Sox on two hits, 2-0 — his third and last major-league victory — but he needed relief help from Satchel Paige in the ninth inning. Plagued with a sore arm, Bobo pitched in his final major-league game on July 19, 1953. His pitching line for that season — and for his career — is 22 appearances, 10 starts, 65 1/3 innings, 3 wins, 7 losses, 25 strikeouts, 50 walks, 5.23 ERA…with one complete-game shutout.

On July 23, 1953, the Toronto Maple Leafs, a Triple-A team in the International League, purchased Holloman's contract from Bill Veeck. Holloman appeared in 13 games, starting eight of them, but he clearly was not regaining his form. He allowed 53 hits and 31 earned runs and walked 43 batters in 55 innings. Bobo returned to Puerto Rico for the Winter League, but left early with an 0-2 record and a sore arm.[13] The following summer he bounced around playing for five different teams in five different minor leagues. But by the end of 1954 Holloman was out of baseball entirely at age 31.

He returned to Georgia and made a living driving trucks for a while, as he had done during his playing days. He then worked as a foreman at Roper Hydraulics, a tool and die company in Commerce, Georgia. The local hero stayed involved in athletics in a small way by coaching Little League baseball and officiating high school football, but he kept his competitive juices flowing in a big way by taking up golf. He soon became a par golfer, and along the way, he imparted the love of the game to his son, Gary. At about age 14, the Little Papoose caddied for the Big Chief until Gary himself became quite good in his own right. Following his collegiate golfing career at the University of Georgia, Gary got his Professional Golf Association card in 1974. Over the years, father and son entered and won several tournaments in Georgia.

But Bobo was a disappointed and resentful man when his powerful right arm betrayed him and forced him out of baseball. Always combative on the field, now his battle was with alcoholism. Yet, just as he fought through the ninth inning in his miracle game on that rainy night in St. Louis, he fought off his sickness in 1972. On the 30th anniversary of his marriage to Nan, Bobo swore off drinking forever.[14]

He turned his energy to starting his own advertising company which he called BoNanGa, named, of course, after Bobo, Nan, and Gary. In 1974, he also worked as a part-time scout for the Baltimore Orioles in the Georgia area. He was invited back to participate in several Old-Timers games in major league parks. On May 1, 1987, Alva Lee "Bobo" Holloman Jr. died of a sudden heart attack at his home in Athens, Georgia. He was 64.

In February 2006, Bobo was inducted into the Thomaston-Upson Sports Hall of Fame. His adoring widow, Nan, accepted the plaque.

AUTHOR'S NOTE

I cannot write this biography without acknowledging the truly spiritual joy I experienced by meeting Bobo's widow Nan Holloman. Nan spoke with me by phone from her home in Athens, Georgia, on May 23, 2005. To help my research, she sent me one of her last remaining autographed copies of *This One and That One: The True Life Story of BoBo "No-hit" Holloman*, the book she wrote in 1975 (printed by Southeastern Color Lithographers, Athens, Georgia). Thank you, Nan.

However, with apologies to Nan, in this biography I spell Alva Lee's nickname as "Bobo." Although in her book and in her letters to me, Nan spelled her husband's nickname as "BoBo," in all other published accounts that I found, his nickname was spelled as "Bobo."

SOURCES

In addition to the sources in the notes, the author relied on Holloman's player file from the National Baseball Hall of Fame Library, as well as to several baseball-related websites and, accessed online, from the *New York Times*, *Chicago Daily Tribune*, and *Baseball Digest*. Other resources not already cited in the endnotes include:

Various Authors. *The Ol' Ball Game: A Collection of Baseball Characters and Moments Worth Remembering* (New York: Barnes and Noble, 1990).

Graham, Frank. *Great No-Hit Games of the Major Leagues* (New York: Random House, 1968).

NOTES

1. The second-fewest wins by a major-league pitcher who threw a no-hitter: 7, by George Davis.

2. This article was written at the beginning of the 2009 season. This list of 21 rookies includes pitchers who pitched their no-hitters in a year after their debut year — in the case of Sam "Toothpick" Jones, *four* years after his MLB debut! — in accordance with MLB rules.

3. Charlie Robertson threw his on April 30, 1922, which was his third start; and two others threw their no-hitters in their fourth major-league start — Bo Belinsky on May 5, 1962, and Burt Hooton on April 16, 1972 (the first start of his first full major league season).

4. Published accounts of Holloman's date of birth vary from 1923 through 1926. For the March 7, 1923, date of birth used in this biography, the author relies on: (1) *This One and That One* (1975, Self-published: Third Print 2006) by Nan Holloman, at page 3; (2) the presentation at Holloman's induction into the Thomaston-Upson Sports Hall of Fame (*see* http://www.tusportshalloffame.com/ALVA%20LEE%20HOLLOMAN.htm); and (3) the online player profiles published at www.baseball-almanac.com, www.baseball-reference.com, and www.retrosheet.org.

5. Nan Holloman. *This One and That One* (1975, Third Print 2006), 5.

6. Jorge S. Figueredo. *Béisbol Cubano: a un Paso de Las Grandes Ligas, 1878-1961* (Jefferson, North Carolina: McFarland & Company, 1995), 251-252.

NO-HITTERS

7 Lowell Reidenbaugh. "Holloman, Facing Axe, Hurls No-Hitter," *The Sporting News*, May 13, 1953. See also Nan Holloman, 23. However, some accounts say it was Holloman who named himself "Bobo."

8 Holloman, 40.

9 Jose A. Crescioni Benítez. *El Béisbol Profesional Boricua* (San Juan, Puerto Rico: Aurora Comunicación Integral, Inc., 1997), 86.

10 Thomas Van Hyning. *The Santurce Crabbers* (Jefferson, North Carolina: McFarland & Company, 1999), 41-42.

11 Bill Veeck, with Ed Linn. *Veeck — As In Wreck* (Chicago: University of Chicago Press ed., 2001), 297.

12 *Ibid.*, loc. cit. Veeck's memory was a bit faulty, as it was elsewhere in his memoir. It was Vic Wertz who recorded the last out, but he was the right fielder for the Browns that night, not the first baseman.

13 Thomas Van Hyning. *Puerto Rico's Winter League* (Jefferson, North Carolina: McFarland & Company, 1995), 55.

14 Holloman, 85.

BOBO HOLLOMAN THROWS A NO-HITTER IN HIS FIRST MAJOR-LEAGUE START

MAY 6, 1953: ST. LOUIS BROWNS 6, PHILADELPHIA ATHLETICS 0, AT BUSCH STADIUM, ST. LOUIS

By Joe Schuster

BEFORE THE 1953 SEASON, pitcher Alva "Bobo" Holloman predicted great things for himself. Acquired by the St. Louis Browns from the Triple-A Syracuse Chiefs the previous October, he immediately started a campaign to assure himself a spot as a starter, telling team owner Bill Veeck that he would be his number-one pitcher and asking, "Am I going to be a regular starter?"[1]

Holloman continued pursuing a shot at starting throughout the early spring. "The guy's a real character," Veeck said. "Every night since the season's opened, he's come pounding on [manager] Marty Marion's door. 'When you gonna start me?' he'd ask."[2]

Holloman gave little evidence early on that he deserved to start. In his first four relief outings, covering 5⅓ innings, he allowed five earned runs on 10 hits.[3] He justified his poor performance by claiming he was naturally a starter and insisting that if Marion did not accede to his wishes, he wanted a trade. Finally, largely to put an end to his wheedling, Marion gave in, a move many thought was a prelude to the Browns shedding the pitcher when the May 14 cutdown deadline required teams to reduce their rosters to 25: Holloman would prove no better a starter than reliever and the team would release him.[4]

Marion initially scheduled Holloman to start an April 28 home game against the New York Yankees, but with rain falling as Holloman finished his warm-up and Yankees leadoff hitter Phil Rizzuto stepping into the batter's box, home-plate umpire Bill Summers called the game, deferring Holloman's start.[5]

As it turned out, the delay likely kept him in the majors beyond the cutdown day, since in his eventual start, against the Philadelphia Athletics on May 6, Holloman threw an improbable no-hit, no-run game, the only one in the majors that season.

Opening the day, the Browns were 9-9, on their way to finishing last with their third 100-loss season in five years. The Athletics came in 10-8, bound for a seventh-place finish in the eight-team league. Opposing Holloman was southpaw Morrie Martin, in the fourth season of a 10-season major-league career, making his second start after missing a year of baseball when a line drive broke the index finger of his pitching hand the previous May.[6] In Martin's first appearance, on May 1, he pitched a complete-game 4-1 victory over Detroit.

As with Holloman's earlier attempt to start, it was raining and chilly at game time. The weather kept the crowd down to 2,473, such a poor showing that in the fifth inning, Veeck told his public-relations director, Bob Fishel, to announce that, due to the "bad night," the team would honor the rain checks for the game, even though by then it was official.[7]

As the game started, Holloman went through his usual ritual, scratching the initials of his wife and son into the foul line, "N" for Nancy and "G" for Garry.[8] The superstition seemed to pay immediate dividends. Relying primarily on his sinker and curve, with an occasional slider because his fastball lacked zip, he was perfect through the first two innings, although he needed a spectacular play by Browns left fielder Jim Dyck for the last out in the second, when A's slugger Gus Zernial hit a deep line drive. Dyck made what one writer described as a "circus performance" catch, leaping against the wall to make a one-handed grab.[9]

In the bottom of that inning, Browns catcher Les Moss hit a one-out double down the right-field line. After first baseman Roy Sievers struck out, Moss went to third when second baseman Bobby Young reached on an error, bringing up Holloman for his first major-league plate appearance. He singled, scoring Moss and giving the Browns a 1-0 lead. They added single runs in the third, fifth, and sixth innings before closing out the scoring with two in the seventh on Holloman's second and last major-league hit, also a single.

While game accounts describe most of the plays behind Holloman as routine, there were moments that challenged the eventual gem, including a few plays one writer characterized as "perils of Pauline fielding."[10] In the fifth, with one down, A's right fielder Allie Clark hit a fly to deep left that cleared the wall, but foul by a few feet. After Clark grounded to short, Zernial again threatened to end the no-hitter, sending a high bouncer back up the middle, which Holloman leaped to snag but it got caught in his glove. When he shook it out, it hit the ground and Zernial was safe, but the official scorer ruled it an error.[11]

Leading off in the sixth, A's catcher Joe Astroth trickled a groundball down the third-base line. Knowing he would be unable to throw Astroth out, Browns third baseman Bob Elliott hovered over it, hoping it would go foul, which it did; Astroth walked on the next pitch.[12] Astroth threatened the no-hitter again in the eighth, when he hit a hard grounder far to the left of shortstop Billy Hunter, who made what one reporter hyperbolically called "a 1000-yard dash," dropped to a knee to stop the ball and threw to first, nabbing Astroth.[13]

As Holloman went to the mound for the ninth, he was nervous and, for luck, touched his wife's and son's initials again in the foul line.[14] This time, it seemed to fail him, as he hit a streak of wildness, walking the first two, pinch-hitter Elmo Valo and shortstop Eddie Joost. When center fielder Dave Philly hit into a 4-6-3 double play, sending pinch-runner Joe DeMaestri to third, Holloman was one out away from his no-hitter, but extended things by walking third baseman Loren Babe, bringing up first baseman Eddie Robinson, who watched a strike go by and then fouled the next pitch before smashing a Holloman curve down the first-base line, only inches foul.[15]

Holloman and Moss figured that Robinson would be looking for a fastball and decided to come back with the curve instead. It was wise: Robinson flied out to right fielder Vic Wertz.[16] Holloman was in the record books as the first pitcher in the century to throw a no-hitter in his first start; the 6-0 victory was the first win of his major-league career.

After the game, Marion seemed to revise his opinion of Holloman, saying, "Some people would call him a screwball. ... But I'm mighty happy that he pestered me into giving him his chance to start. ... He proved to me that he's just about as good as he thinks he is."[17]

As it turned out, he wasn't. In Holloman's next start, on May 12, against the Athletics in Philadelphia, he lasted 1⅓ innings, walking the first three batters and giving up two runs and three hits before departing with a blister on his pitching hand.[18] Over his next four starts, he managed a total of 14⅓ innings, allowing 14 runs on 18 hits and 15 walks. From early June until late July, Holloman bounced between starting and relieving, finding one more moment of small glory, when he went eight innings against the Boston Red Sox on June 21, surrendering just two hits and no runs, earning what was his last major-league victory, 2-0, when Satchel Paige came on to save it.

On July 23, with his record at 3-7 with a 5.23 ERA, Holloman was sold to Toronto of the International League. Characteristically, he at first refused to report, saying he would devote himself to a Nashville trucking company he co-owned, However, he relented and reported to Toronto.[19] A bit more than a year later, after playing for five minor-league teams in the 1954 season, Holloman was out of baseball. By then the

Browns were gone, too — moved to Baltimore, where they became the Orioles.

NOTES

1. "Veeck Limits Holloman Pitching in Puerto Rico," *The Sporting News*, January 14, 1953: 23.
2. Lowell Reidenbaugh, "Holloman, Facing Axe, Hurls No-Hitter," *The Sporting News*, May 13, 1953: 13.
3. Unless otherwise noted, all stats and game accounts come from Retrosheet or Baseball Reference.
4. Reidenbaugh.
5. Louis Effrat, "Rain Washes Out 'Bout' at St. Louis," *New York Times*, April 29, 1953: 45.
6. Stan Opdyke, "Morrie Martin," sabr.org/bioproj/person/08084fff, accessed December 23, 2015.
7. Reidenbaugh.
8. "Bobo Does Some Boasting But It's About His Hitting," *St. Louis Post-Dispatch*, May 7, 1953: 4B.
9. Dent McSkimming, "Holloman Hurls No Hitter in His First Start," *St. Louis Post-Dispatch*, May 7, 1953: 4B.
10. Jack Rice, "Holloman Throws No-Hitter," *St. Louis Globe-Democrat*, May 7, 1953: 2B.
11. Reidenbaugh.
12. Ibid.
13. Rice.
14. "Bobo Does Some Boasting."
15. Ibid.
16. McSkimming.
17. Ibid.
18. "Browns Trounce Athletics, 7-3," *New York Times*, May 13, 1953: 35.
19. "Great Bobo Gives In, Goes to Toronto — and is Routed." *The Sporting News*, August 5, 1953: 32.

DON LARSEN

By Charles F. Faber

HE IS A BUNDLE OF CONtradictions, this imperfect man who pitched a perfect game. Don Larsen disdained training rules and had a mediocre major-league career; yet he pitched the greatest game in World Series history. He married out of a sense of duty; yet he refused to support his wife and baby daughter. He kept his marriage secret as long as he could, preferring to be viewed as a carefree bachelor. He loved the night life; yet he was living out his retirement years (as of 2015) in a quiet village in northern Idaho, far from the crowded bars of his youth. This man who turned down college scholarships because he didn't like to study, the same man who had to be compelled by a court order to support his family, auctioned off one of his most prized possessions to raise money to support his grandchildren's college education. Don Larsen is truly a bundle of contradictions.

Don James Larsen was born on August 7, 1929, in Michigan City, on the shores of Lake Michigan in extreme northwestern Indiana. He was the second child and only son of Charlotte and James Larsen. During his childhood his mother worked as a waitress in a restaurant, His father, son of Norwegian immigrants, was a watchmaker in a retail jewelry store. Years later Don Larsen remembered, "My first introduction to baseball was watching my father play sandlot ball."[1] When he was 4 years old Don started playing baseball with his father. James encouraged Don in his childhood ambition to become a professional baseball player. However, the youngster showed more talent in basketball than baseball. As a freshman, Don made the Michigan City High School basketball team.

In 1944 Don moved with his family to San Diego, where his mother worked as a housekeeper in a retirement home and his father became a jewelry salesman. At Point Loma High School Don became a star in basketball and baseball. He made the All-Metro Conference basketball team and received several scholarship offers to play college basketball, which he declined. He said, "I was never much with studies, and I didn't really have an interest in going to college and studying my life away."[2] Art Schwartz, a scout for the St. Louis Browns, saw Larsen pitching for an American Legion team and offered him a contract. He signed for an $850 bonus.

The Browns sent the 17-year-old right-handed pitcher to Aberdeen in the Class-C Northern League. Larsen pitched two seasons for the Pheasants, winning four games in 1947 and 17 in 1948. He started the 1949 season with the Globe-Miami Browns in the Class-C Arizona-Texas League and was promoted in midseason to Springfield in the Class-B Three-I League. Another promotion came in 1950, as he moved from the Wichita Falls Spudders in the Class-B Big State League to the Wichita Indians in the Class-A Western League. He was described by Bob Turley, one of his teammates in both the minors and majors, as a "fun-loving guy who liked to go out and have a beer or two and talk to people in bars."[3]

In 1951 Larsen was drafted into the US Army. He spent two years during the Korean War in noncombat roles. After basic training at Fort Ord, he was sent to Hawaii. When an officer learned that Larsen was a professional baseball player, he assigned him to a Special Services unit at Fort Shafter. He pitched and played first base for an Army team during 1951 and 1952. Corporal Larsen was discharged in 1953 and went to spring training in 1953 on the roster of the San Antonio Browns. After several good pitching performances, he was promoted to the big-league Browns. "I'll never forget how excited I was when I found out I made the club," he said. "It was like Christmas in springtime."[4]

The 23-year-old stood 6-feet-4 and weighed 215 pounds. His teammates gave him the nickname

New York Yankee Don Larsen presenting Yogi Berra a bronzed replica of the catcher's glove he used in Larsen's perfect game in the 1956 World Series.

Gooney Bird. Writer Lew Paper said it was because of his protruding ears, pear-shaped body, and long, dangling arms.[5] Another writer, Peter Golenbock, said the nickname was bestowed because of Larsen's antics.[6]

Larsen made his major-league debut on Saturday, April 18, 1953, in the first game of a doubleheader against the Detroit Tigers at Briggs Stadium. The first batter he faced, Harvey Kuenn, touched him for a single, but he settled down and pitched shutout ball for five innings. He was knocked out of the box in the sixth, as the Tigers scored three runs to take a 3-2 lead. However, the Browns rallied to win the game, 8-7, with Larsen receiving no decision. He collected his first major-league win at Connie Mack Stadium on May 12, pitching 7⅔ innings and giving up one earned run in the Browns' 7-3 win over the Philadelphia Athletics.

The Browns moved to Baltimore in 1954. That season Larsen led the league in losses with 21, while winning only three games, but fortunately for him two of the wins were over the New York Yankees, and Yankees manager Casey Stengel remembered those two wins. Larsen did not honor the midnight curfew set by the Browns. His motto was, "Let the good times roll. You give the best you can on the field. Who cares what you do afterwards, as long as you show up and do well."[7] Jimmy Dykes, his manager in Baltimore, said, "The only thing Don fears is sleep."[8]

During the season Larsen met the future Vivian Larsen, a 27-year-old telephone operator in Baltimore. At the end of the season he intended to break off the affair, but Vivian called him in California and told him she was pregnant. Abortion was out of the question. Larsen suggested she put the baby up for adoption. She refused. Vivian was determined to keep the baby. Larsen then did what he thought was the honorable thing. They were married on April 23, 1955. Don insisted that the marriage be kept secret; he was marrying her only for the sake of the child. Three months later he left her with no intention of returning because he was not ready to settle down and preferred "a life of free and easy existence."[9]

Larsen was traded to the New York Yankees on November 17, 1954, in a huge transaction involving 17 players. He reported to spring training in 1955 with a sore shoulder and was soon sent down to the Yankees' farm club in Denver. He won 9 of 10 decisions for the Bears and after four months in the Triple-A American Association, he was recalled to New York. Between New York and Denver he had won 18 games that year, against only three losses. One of his teammates said, "He probably had a lot more ability than 95 percent of all the pitchers in baseball, He was a good hitter. He could run the bases. He could field the ball. But he was a lazy type."[10]

The Yankees won the American League pennant in 1955 and faced the Brooklyn Dodgers in the World Series. The Dodgers were playing in Brooklyn's eighth World Series. They had seven losses to show for their first seven attempts. The Ebbets Field faithful were hoping for a different outcome in 1955. The Dodgers were a powerful club, featuring four future Hall of Famers—Roy Campanella, Pee Wee Reese, Jackie Robinson, and Duke Snider—plus perennial all-star Gil Hodges and former Rookies of the Year Jim Gilliam and Don Newcombe. The Yankees won the first two games, but Brooklyn took Game Three. Larsen started Game Four for the Yankees and did not fare well. Although staked to a 3-1 lead, he gave up a leadoff home run to Campanella in the fourth inning. Larsen then walked Carl Furillo, and Hodges hit a two-run homer to put the Dodgers ahead. In the fifth inning Gilliam led off with a walk and stole second while Reese was batting, At this point Stengel replaced Larsen with Johnny Kucks, who gave up a single to Reese and a three-run homer to Snider, one run of which was charged to Larsen. When Yankees were unable to catch up, Larsen was tagged as the losing pitcher, with a line for the game of five earned runs on five hits and two walks.

Brooklyn won Game Five to go ahead in the Series, three games to two. New York evened it up by taking Game Six. The Series came down to Game Seven. Johnny Podres pitched a masterpiece, shutting out the Yankees, 2-0, thereby earning Brooklyn its first-ever world championship.

Larsen was thrilled to have pitched in the Series: "I had stretched beyond my childhood dreams by playing for the Yankees in the World Series. Even though we lost the championship to the Dodgers, I was thankful to have been even been there in the first place."[11]

Larsen's appetite for strong drink and exuberant night life did not diminish. Mickey Mantle said of him, "Don had a startling capacity for liquor. Larsen was easily the greatest drinker I've known and I've known some pretty good ones in my time."[12] During spring training 1956 Larsen wrecked his brand-new Oldsmobile by driving it into a St. Petersburg telephone pole at 4 or 5 o'clock one morning. He admitted that he had been drinking at several bars earlier in the night and said he had fallen asleep at the wheel.

His teammates thought Larsen was a bachelor, a devil-may-care playboy.[13] They were shocked to learn of his secret marriage. Although Don and Vivian did not live together, she had moved to New York, attempting to collect some child-support money. On July 16, 1956, Justice Henry Greenberg of the Bronx Superior Court awarded Vivian $60 a week from Don in support of herself and their daughter, Caroline Jean.[14] Don didn't deliver. Living the high life that he enjoyed can be very expensive in New York City. He was having trouble making ends meet.[15] He certainly didn't have any spare cash to spend on a wife or child. He even asked the Yankees' traveling secretary, Bill

McCorry, for an advance on his World Series share: "I've got to get home to California when this is over, and I don't have a nickel."[16] McCorry promised to deliver the cash if the Yankees won.

In October Vivian filed a complaint over Larsen's failure to pay child support. (He had made four payments, then stopped paying.) He owed $420, for seven weeks in arrears at $60 per week.) Vivian's lawyer, Harry Lipsig, said, "While this baseball hero is enjoying the luxuries of life and the plaudits of the public, he is subjecting his 14-month-old baby girl and his wife to the pleasures of a starvation existence."[17] Bronx Superior Court Justice Sam H. Hofstadter filed a filed an order requiring the Yankees, Larsen, and Baseball Commissioner Ford Frick to show cause why his World Series share should not be seized by the Bronx Supreme Court.[18]

The court order was in Larsen's locker when he took the mound in Yankee Stadium and pitched the most incredible game in World Series history. The Yankees had won the pennant for the second straight year in a streak that was to yield four consecutive flags. They faced the defending World Series champion Brooklyn Dodgers.

The Dodgers won Game One at Ebbets Field behind the pitching of Sal Maglie. Larsen pitched briefly in Game Two. He faced only 10 batters, six of whom reached base safely, one on a base hit, one on an error, and four by means of walks. Larsen was charged with four unearned runs. The Dodgers won a slugfest. The Series then moved to Yankee Stadium. The home team won Games Three and Four to even the Series at two games apiece. Given Larsen's poor performances in the 1955 fall classic and Game Two of the present match, there was little reason to expect him to start another game in the Series.

On the night before Game Five, Larsen went out for a few beers with Arthur Richman, a sportswriter for the *New York Daily Mirror*. Before midnight they headed back toward Larsen's hotel apartment. During the cab ride Larsen told Richman, "I'm gonna beat those guys tomorrow. And I'm just liable to pitch a no-hitter."[19] It was typical Larsen bluster. Actually, he had no idea he was going to pitch. Stengel had not yet announced the starting pitcher for the next day's game. Following the Yankees custom at the time, whenever the starter had not been determined the night before, in the morning coach Frankie Crosetti would place the warm-up ball for the day's game in one of the starting pitcher's shoes.[20]

Earlier that evening Herman Carey, father of Yankees third baseman Andy Carey, entered a novelty shop on Times Square that printed fake newspaper headlines. He purchased two. One read "Larsen Pitches No-hitter." The other stated "Gooney Birds Pick Larsen to Win Fifth Game." He returned to the hotel and taped the one about the no-hitter to the door of Larsen's room. Then he had second thoughts. He didn't want to risk jinxing the pitcher. So he shredded the paper and disposed of it. He kept the other one, without showing it to Larsen at the time.

It turned out that the fake headlines were prescient. To the surprise of most of the Yankees, manager Stengel chose Larsen to start Game Five. The pitcher arrived at the ballpark early in the morning of October 8, saw the ball, and learned he would be the starting pitcher.[21] He took a whirlpool bath and a cold shower, and had a rubdown.[22] He lay down for a short nap in the clubhouse.[23] Larsen was opposed by the tough Sal "The Barber" Maglie. Both men were at the top of their games. Using his new no-windup delivery, Larsen was unhittable. Maglie was almost as good, retiring the first 11 batters in a row until Mantle hit a solo blast in the fourth inning. By the end of the sixth inning it began to dawn on viewers that they might be watching history in the making. In keeping with baseball superstition, nobody on the Yankee bench mentioned a possible no-hitter, but surely it was on everybody's mind.

Larsen said he knew he was pitching a no-hitter, since every pitcher knows when he is throwing one. He said, "I tried to engage in conversation with some of our players on the bench during the game, but they all avoided me like the plague.[24]

Larsen mowed the Dodgers down, through the seventh, eighth, and into the ninth inning. He retired the first two batters in the ninth. Up came Dale Mitchell to pinch-hit for Maglie. Larsen's first pitch was a ball, high and outside. Next came a slow curve over the plate for a called strike. Mitchell swung at another curve and missed for strike two. He fouled off a fastball. Then he took a quarter-swing at a fastball that seemed to some to be eye-high.[25] Umpire Babe Pinelli called him out. Don Larsen had pitched the first no-hitter in World Series history. Not only was it a no-hitter, but it was a perfect game—no hits, no runs, with no one reaching base.

"Damn," said sports reporter Dick Young. "The imperfect man just pitched a perfect game."[26]

Shirley Povich of the *Washington Post* wrote, "The million-to-one shot came in. Hell froze over. A month of Sundays hit the calendar. Don Larsen today pitched a no-hit, no-run, no-man-reach-first game in a World Series."[27]

The *San Francisco Chronicle* wrote about "madcap Don Larsen, a carefree soul who breaks automobiles, likes bright lights, reads comic books…and is just about the last person in baseball who might be expected to pitch a perfect game."[28]

Larsen sent $420 to Harry Lipsig to give to his wife and daughter. "This man is still no hero," the lawyer said. "In these proceedings, he has brazenly suggested when his daughter was born she was immediately to be given out for adoption."[29]

The Dodgers won Game Six, but the Yankees took Game Seven and again reigned as baseball's world champions.

One month after Larsen's perfect game, he and Vivian divorced.

In 1957 Larsen got off to a poor start, but improved toward the end of the season, winding up with a commendable 10-4 record. The Yankees won the pennant again. In the World Series against the Milwaukee Braves, Larsen won one and lost one. In Game Three he relieved Bob Turley in the second inning and pitched well throughout the game, getting credit for the win as the Yankees prevailed, 12-3. In Game Seven Larsen was the starting pitcher, but was knocked out of the box in the third inning. With one out and a man on base, shortstop Tony Kubek made an errant throw to second base on a grounder hit by Johnny Logan. Eddie Mathews then doubled, and Larsen was out of the game. Lew Burdette pitched a shutout for his third win of the Series. The Braves were world champions for the first time since the Miracle Braves of 1914.

On December 7, 1957, Larsen married Corrine Bruess, a 26-year-old flight attendant from Minnesota, whom he had met on a flight out of Kansas City. This marriage endured. Apparently Corinne brought some much-needed stability to his life. The union produced one son, Scott, born October 5, 1962.

Both New York and Milwaukee repeated as pennant winners in 1958. Larsen started two games in the 1958 World Series. In Game Three he pitched shutout ball until relieved by Ryne Duren in the eighth inning and received credit for the win in the Yankees' 4-0 victory. In Game Seven Larsen was removed in the third inning with one out and two Braves on base and the Yankees leading, 2-1. Bob Turley erased the Braves threat and was credited with the win as the Yankees won the game, 6-2, for their 18th triumph in the fall classic.

The Yankees slipped to third place in the 1959 standings and Larsen had a losing record at 6-7. On December 11, 1959, he was traded, along with Hank Bauer, Norm Siebern, and Marv Throneberry, to the Kansas City Athletics for Joe DeMaestri, Roger Maris, Kent Hadley, and Gerry Staley.

Larsen had very little success in Kansas City, losing 10 out of 11 decisions. The A's sent him down to Dallas-Fort Worth in the Triple-A American Association, where he won two of three decisions, earning another shot at the majors. He appeared in only eight games for the A's before being traded with Andy Carey, Ray Herbert, and Al Pilarcik to the Chicago White Sox for Wes Covington, Stan Johnson, Bob Shaw, and Gerry Staley. He had a combined 8-2 record for the two clubs.

Soon he was on the move again. On November 30, 1961, Larsen was traded with Billy Pierce to the San Francisco Giants for Bob Farley, Eddie Fisher, Dom Zanni, and Verle Tiefenthaler. In the City by the Bay, Larsen became a full-time reliever, winning five games and saving 10. The Giants finished the regular season tied for first place with the Los Angeles Dodgers. In the deciding game of the three-game playoff for the pennant, Larsen relieved Juan Marichal in the eighth inning and received credit for the win, as the Giants won their first championship after their move to the West Coast. In Game Four of the 1962 World Series against the New York Yankees, Larsen picked up a win, even though he pitched only one-third of an inning. He entered the game in the bottom of the sixth inning, with two outs, runners on first and second, and the game tied, 2-2. Larsen walked Yogi Berra to load the bases and then induced Tony Kubek to ground out, ending the inning. In the top of the seventh, Larsen was lifted for a pinch-hitter, as the Giants took a lead they did not relinquish.

In 1963 Larsen had a 7-7 record with four saves for the Giants. The much-traveled pitcher was sold to the Houston Colt .45's on May 20, 1964, and was traded less than a year later to the Baltimore Orioles for Bob Saverine and cash. He won only one game for the Orioles before being released on April 11, 1966. He spent much of the next three seasons in the minors, toiling for clubs in Phoenix, Dallas-Fort Worth, Tacoma, and San Antonio.

Before the 1967 season began, the Chicago Cubs signed Larsen as a free agent. He pitched only four innings for the Cubs. His final major-league appearance came on July 7, 1967, at Houston's Astrodome in an 11-5 Cubs loss. He entered the game in the sixth inning and pitched two innings, giving up one run and one base on balls. On the last pitch the 37-year-old Larsen threw in the major leagues, Jim Wynn flied out to Billy Williams in left field to end the seventh inning. Larsen was removed for a pinch-hitter in the eighth inning, and his major-league career was over.

After retiring from baseball, Larsen worked for about 25 years as a salesman for the Blake, Moffett & Towne Paper Company in the San Jose area. When he retired from this occupation, he, Corinne, and Scott moved to the shores of Hayden Lake, not far from Coeur d'Alene in Idaho's scenic Panhandle, about 100 miles from the Canadian border. "I like Idaho because it's peaceful and quiet," Larsen said.[30]

Don's son, Scott, as of 2015 was a maintenance technician for an aerospace company in Idaho. Scott and his wife, Nancy, gave Don two grandsons, Justin and Cody. Don, his sons, and grandsons enjoy trout fishing and frogging together, hunting by spotlights in the cool of a northern Idaho morning.[31]

In 2012 Larsen announced that he was retrieving the uniform he had worn when pitching the perfect game. He had loaned it to the San Diego Hall of Champions, but he intended to auction off his most prized possession to raise money for his grandchildren's college educations. He listed it with Steiner Sports Marketing for an online auction that ran from October 8 to December 2 at steinersports.com. "I really don't know what it's worth," Larsen said. "But what I do know is that in terms of historic importance, my uniform is a part of one of the greatest moments in the history of sports. I have thought about that perfect game, more than once a day, every day of my life since the day I threw it."[32]

The auction attracted 22 bids. The uniform sold for $756,000. The winning bidder was Pete Seigel, CEO of Gotta Have It, a New York City gallery that collects and displays pop-culture memorabilia. Seigel said that Larsen's uniform would be a welcome addition to a collection of Yankees memorabilia that his company was building.[33]

Three-quarters of a million dollars is surely enough to pay Justin and Cody's college expenses. There may be enough extra cash to enable the Larsen family to take their hoped-for trip to Alaska.

NOTES

1 Don Larsen and Mark Shaw, *The Perfect Yankee: The Incredible Story of the Greatest Miracle in Baseball History* (Champaign, Illinois: Sagamore Publishing, 1996), 37.

2 Lew Paper, *Perfect: Don Larsen's Miraculous World Series Game and The Men Who Made It Happen* (New York: New American Library, 2009), 12.

3 Paper, 13.

4 Larsen and Snow, 77.

5 Larsen and Snow, 1.

6. Peter Golenbock, *Dynasty: The New York Yankees 1949-1964* (Mineola, New York: Dover Publishing, 201), 292.
7. Paper, 13.
8. Paper, 14.
9. Paper, 17.
10. Paper, 14.
11. Paper, 15.
12. Paper, 16.
13. Paper, 17
14. Ron Rembert. "Baseball Immortals: Character and Performance On and Off the Field," in Peter Carino, ed., *Baseball/Literature/Culture Essays* (Jefferson, North Carolina: McFarland, 2004), 139.
15. Roger Kahn. *The Era, 1948-1957, When the Yankees, the Giants, and the Dodgers Ruled the World* (New York: Ticknor and Fields, 1993), 331.
16. Paper, 17.
17. Ibid.
18. Rembert.
19. Paper, 5.
20. Don Larsen, "The Game I'll Never Forget." *Baseball Digest*, October 2003: 54.
21. Ibid.
22. Kahn, 332.
23. Paper, 6.
24. Larsen, *op. cit.*, 55-56.
25. Kahn, 332.
26. Ibid.
27. Ibid.
28. Larsen and Shaw, 209.
29. Ibid.
30. Larsen, 56.
31. *Newark Star-Ledger*, October 9, 2012.
32. *New York Times*, May 26, 2012.
33. New York *Daily News*, December 6, 2012.

OCTOBER 8, 1956: DON LARSEN'S PERFECT GAME

NEW YORK YANKEES 2, BROOKLYN DODGERS 0, AT YANKEE STADIUM

By Charles F. Faber

IT WAS A PERFECT DAY FOR A perfect game. Under a clear blue sky 64,519 fans trooped into historic Yankee Stadium to witness a World Series contest between the two dominant teams of the era. The world champion Dodgers were facing the club that had won more World Series titles than any other two clubs combined. The Dodgers had won the first two games of the 1956 Series, but the Yankees had taken the next two.

Facing each other on the mound that day were two pitchers with vastly different career records. Brooklyn started Sal Maglie, who had 108 major-league victories and only 49 losses, for a sparkling .688 winning percentage. New York countered with Don Larsen, who had a record of 30-40, .429. In the 1955 World Series Larsen had started Game Four against the Dodgers and became the losing pitcher when he was removed from the mound in the fifth inning with the Yankees trailing 4-3. In 1956 Larsen had started Game Two for the Yankees and was knocked out of the box in the second inning. It is only natural that some of his teammates were "flabbergasted" that manager Casey Stengel elected to go with Larsen in Game Five.[1] One factor in Larsen's favor was his strong finish in the 1956 regular season, abetted by a no-windup delivery that he developed near the end of the campaign.

The night before Game Five, Larsen had told sportswriter Arthur Richman, "I'm gonna beat those guys tomorrow. And I'm just liable to pitch a no-hitter."[2] It was typical Larsen braggadocio. Actually he didn't expect to pitch again in the Series. The next morning he learned he was to be the starting pitcher in Game Five when he arrived at the clubhouse and found the warm-up ball in one of his shoes, placed there by coach Frankie Crosetti in conformity with a Yankee ritual. He took a whirlpool bath and a cold shower, and had a rubdown.[3] Then he lay down in the clubhouse for a short nap.[4]

Many years later Larsen remembered: "I felt confident as I prepared to face the Dodgers because we were in Yankee Stadium and we had won eight of our last nine games there."[5] (Larsen's memory wasn't quite accurate. The Yankees had actually won six of their last nine home games.)

Larsen started the game by striking out the first two batters, Junior Gilliam and Pee Wee Reese. Then he retired Hank Bauer on a soft fly to right field. In the second inning Jackie Robinson led off for the Dodgers with a hot smash toward third base that bounced off Andy Carey's glove and ricocheted straight to shortstop Gil McDougald, who threw to first base. At age 37 Robinson had lost some of the speed for which he had been noted. The throw beat him to the bag by a step. Larsen got through the rest of the second and the third inning unscathed.

Maglie matched Larsen pitch for pitch. Neither pitcher allowed a hit through the first three innings. In the bottom of the fourth Mickey Mantle made the first hit of the game, a home run that gave the Yankees a 1-0 lead. The Dodgers threatened to tie it up in the top of the fifth. Gil Hodges drove a pitch to the deepest part of left-center field. It appeared that the ball might leave the field for a home run or at least hit the wall for extra bases. However, Mantle raced back and made a spectacular catch for the out. "It was," Mantle said, "the best catch I ever made."[6]

Larsen wasn't out of the woods yet. Sandy Amoros drove the ball into the right-field stands. Umpire Ed Runge signaled that it was foul. Bauer said, "When I saw the ball heading for the right-field seats I was ready to concede the homer. But when it hooked foul … I was the happiest guy in the park."[7] Amoros then grounded out to end the threat.

Larsen said, "I knew I was pitching a no-hitter, since every pitcher knows when he is throwing one. I tried to engage in conversation with some of our players on the bench during the game, but they all avoided me like the plague."[8] (Baseball superstition requires that nobody mention a no-hitter while a possible one is in progress.)

Throwing mostly fastballs, with some sliders and a few curves, Larsen held the Yankees hitless, inning after inning. Furthermore, he walked nobody. He said, "I never had such good control in all my life as I had in that game. That was the secret to my success. … I was throwing the ball right on the black of the plate."[9]

Nearly everyone in the stadium knew what was going on. Most, even some Dodgers players, were rooting for Larsen to achieve perfection. Brooklyn pitcher Clem Labine admitted that in the late innings he began to subconsciously root for Larsen. "As the game went on," he said, "I thought to myself that this could be the one I'd tell my grandchildren about. I truly believe it's the first time I ever rooted for the opposition. And certainly for a Yankee. In fact, I wanted to be out there in Larsen's shoes."[10]

Most Dodger players, however, were rooting hard against Larsen. If anything, they bore down harder trying to prevent the no-hitter. Baseball teams hate to have a no-hitter pitched against them. As Larsen said, "It's bad enough to lose, but no team wants to think that a pitcher is that much better than they are on a given day."[11]

Sportswriter Arthur Daley wrote, "Tension kept mounting until it was as brittle as an electric light bulb. The slightest jounce and the dang thing might explode."[12]

Mantle said that by the ninth inning the crowd was on its feet and his knees were shaking. "I played in more than 2,400 games in the major leagues. But I was never as nervous as I was in the ninth inning of that game."[13]

Carl Furillo led off the top of the ninth for Brooklyn by flying out to deep right field. Bauer chased the ball down in an outstanding defensive play. The next batter, Roy Campanella, grounded out second to first. Two outs, one to go. Larsen said the fans were delirious and "I was a nervous wreck."[14]

Pitcher Sal Maglie was due up next, but there was no way he was going to bat at this crucial juncture of the game. For pinch-hitting duties Brooklyn manager Chuck Dressen selected the veteran Dale Mitchell. Larsen said, "He really scared me up there. Looking back on it, though, I know how much pressure he was under. He must have been paralyzed. That made two of us."[15]

When Mitchell stepped to the plate, Larsen looked at Yogi Berra. He had confidence in his catcher and had seldom shaken him off during the game. He said, "I also took a deep breath, trying to somehow calm the nerves that threatened to blow my stomach apart."[16]

As Mitchell readied for the pitch, broadcaster Vin Scully told the television audience, "I think it would be safe to say no man in the history of baseball has ever come up to home plate in a more dramatic moment."[17] The first pitch was high and outside, ball one. Next came a slow curve over the plate for a called strike. Mitchell swung at another curve and missed for strike two. He fouled off the next pitch, a fastball. The count remained 1-and-2. Another fastball from Larsen, and Mitchell started to swing, but held up. Mitchell thought the ball was high, but umpire Babe Pinelli called him out.

Catcher Yogi Berra rushed out to the mound and leaped into his pitcher's arms. Don Larsen had pitched the first no-hitter in World Series history. Not only was it a no-hitter, but it was a perfect game—no hits, no runs, no walks, nobody reaching base.

"Damn," said sports reporter Dick Young, "The imperfect man just pitched a perfect game."[18]

Shirley Povich of the *Washington Post* wrote: "The million-to-one shot came in. Hell froze over. A month of Sundays hit the calendar. Don Larsen today pitched a no-hit, no-run, no-man-reach-first game in a World Series."[19]

In the locker room after the game, Larsen paid tribute to his manager: "When it was over, I was so happy I felt like crying. I wanted to win this one for Casey. After what I did in Brooklyn, he could have forgotten about me and who would blame him? But he gave me another chance and I'm grateful."[20]

Vin Scully expressed the opinion of millions when he said, "Ladies and gentlemen, it's the greatest game ever pitched in baseball history."[21]

NOTES

1. Lew Paper, *Perfect: Don Larsen's Miraculous World Series Game and The Men Who Made It Happen* (New York: New American Library, 2009), 5.
2. Ibid.
3. Roger Kahn, *The Era, 1947-1957, When the Yankees, the Giants, and the Dodgers Ruled the World* (New York: Ticknor & Fields, 1993), 32.
4. Paper, 6.
5. Don Larsen, "The Game I'll Never Forget," *Baseball Digest*, October 2003: 54.
6. Paper, 163.
7. Miscbaseball.wordpress.com, June 4, 2010. Accessed August 14, 2014.
8. Don Larsen and Mark Shaw, *The Perfect Yankee: The Incredible Story of the Greatest Miracle in Baseball History* (Champaign, Illinois: Sagamore Publishing, 1996), 55-56.
9. Larsen and Shaw, 54-55.
10. Larsen and Shaw, 151.
11. Larsen and Shaw, 183.
12. Larsen and Shaw, 180.
13. Ibid.
14. Larsen and Shaw, 183.
15. Larsen and Shaw, 187.
16. Ibid.
17. Larsen and Shaw, 187-88.
18. Kahn, 332.
19. Ibid.
20. Baseball-almanac.com/quotes. Accessed August 9, 2015.
21. Larsen and Shaw, 190.

SANDY KOUFAX

By Marc Z Aaron

"MYSTIQUE" IS A WORD often linked with Sandy Koufax. He was dubbed "The Left Arm of God" for his pitching feats—especially over the five years from 1962 to 1966. A litany of statistics attests to his brilliance during this period, but perhaps the most salient points are these: Koufax became the first man to win three Cy Young Awards, and was the only pitcher to do so when the prize was given to just one major leaguer. He also won the Triple Crown of pitching in each of those seasons (1963, 1965, and 1966). He pitched four no-hitters, one of them a perfect game.

The great Ernie Banks described what it was like to face Koufax. "It was frightening. He had that tremendous fastball that would rise, and a great curveball that started at the eyes and broke to the ankles. In the end you knew you were going to be embarrassed. You were either going to strike out or foul out."[1] Banks said, "He was the greatest pitcher I ever saw. Most of the time we knew what was coming. He held his hands closer to his head when he threw a curveball, but it didn't matter."[2]

Koufax's build—huge back, long arms, and exceptionally long fingers—enabled him to put extra spin on his pitches. According to Dodgers catcher Norm Sherry, Koufax could "do things with a baseball nobody has been able to do before or since."[3] Pictures show that the baseball was as low as the top of his left ankle when he reached back to throw. He then propelled the ball with a fluid over-the-top delivery that utilized the weight and force of his body.[4]

Koufax believed his natural gifts required him to work hard at his job of winning games. His personal integrity was deep. It took six seasons for him to master his wildness, however, and his career was halted after the 1966 season by an arthritic left elbow. His decision to retire at the age of 30 after such a dominant run left many, both inside and outside of baseball, wondering why he would leave at the top of his game. Yet this too contributed to his aura. When he was elected to the Baseball Hall of Fame in 1972, he was just 36 years old—the youngest man ever inducted. Decades after his retirement, debate still stirs over Koufax's dazzling peak vs. his career totals.

Two other factors fueled Koufax's legend. As one of the greatest Jewish baseball players ever, he became a hero in that community, especially after refusing to pitch the opening game of the World Series in 1965 because it fell on the High Holy Day of Yom Kippur.[5] The other was his deep sense of privacy. Koufax was, and still is, a greatly admired figure—yet he chose to make few public appearances. Remaining out of the spotlight gave Koufax sightings extra cachet. "Awestruck" is another word frequently attached to this man. Opponents and fans felt that way watching him on the mound, and he retained a unique personal presence.

Sandy Koufax was born as Sanford Braun on December 30, 1935. His parents were Evelyn (née Lichtenstein) and Jack Braun, Sephardic Jews of Hungarian descent.[6] The family lived in the Bensonhurst section of Brooklyn. Koufax had an older stepsister, Edith, who died in November 1997.

When Sandy was 3, Evelyn (an accountant) divorced Jack Braun.[7] She and the children lived with her parents in Brooklyn. Sandy's grandfather, Max Lichtenstein, was a plumber. The boy's street activities were stoop ball, punch ball, and stickball.[8]

Sandy was 9 when Evelyn married Irving Koufax, the lawyer whom Sandy affectionately came to call his dad.[9] The Koufaxes moved to Rockville Centre, New York. They lived on the first floor of a two-story home owned by his uncle, Sam Lichtenstein, an architect.[10]

The young Koufax had just completed ninth grade, when—after a Long Island Railroad train derailment—the Koufax family moved back to

Bensonhurst. It was then, at the age of 14, that Koufax took up another sport in which he had a lot of talent: basketball. He was a strong rebounder who demonstrated his jumping ability in front of the New York Knicks when the Police Athletic League of Bath Beach arranged for a benefit game to be played at the gym in Lafayette High School, which Sandy began to attend in 10th grade.[11]

During summer vacations from school, Koufax worked as a waiter and counselor at Camp Chi-Wan-Da, near Kingston, New York. He had been going to this camp since the age of 3. His mother was its bookkeeper.[12]

Milton Laurie, a delivery driver for the *New York Journal American*, is believed to be the first man to uncover Koufax's pitching ability. Laurie, a longtime sandlot manager who had years before been signed by the Boston Braves, spotted Koufax pitching for the Tomahawks in the Ice Cream League, a counterpart of the Little League and Babe Ruth League.[13] Even though Koufax walked nine men in two innings, Laurie had his son Walter, who was a classmate, invite Koufax to join his sandlot team. Koufax at first refused, but after much begging by Laurie, he changed his mind. Laurie's team, the Parkviews, were part of the Coney Island Sports League.[14] Koufax was busy working in summer camp. As such, he did not play much, but when he did, he would strike out 16 to 18 batters.

It thrilled Sandy to see Irving Koufax arrive one day at a game. That night, at the dinner table, Irving related how impressed he was and said Evelyn should hand Sandy some money to buy a new pair of spikes. This was a complete surprise to the young Koufax, who had repeatedly heard his father say that "spending on baseball is a waste of money" and "a baseball player you will never be." His parents wanted him to follow in the footsteps of his uncles, who were architects.

Yet it was his interest and skill in basketball that won Koufax a university scholarship. His parents were excited when he accepted the offer from the University of Cincinnati, where the basketball program had a strong reputation. The Bearcat scouts had

Koufax celebrating his four no-hitters.

seen Koufax playing both at high school and at the Jewish Community House.[15]

At the urging of friends, Koufax did go out for baseball in his senior year at Lafayette. He played first base. The team captain was Fred Wilpon, a lefty with a "crackling" curveball, who decades later became the owner of the New York Mets.[16] Their coach was Charlie Sheerin, a utility infielder for the 1936 Phillies.[17]

Koufax stood 6-feet-2 when fully grown. (During his major-league career, he weighed as much as 210 pounds.) When he went to Cincinnati, he was a starting forward on the freshman team. He was known to be a "savage" rebounder and able to dunk.[18] He was the team's third-leading scorer with a 9.7-point average. The team won 12 of 14 games, and according to the coach, Ed Jucker, Koufax could have made it in professional basketball. Jucker led the Bearcats varsity squad to NCAA championships in 1961 and 1962; he later coached the NBA's Cincinnati Royals.[19]

Jucker was also the Bearcats' baseball coach. The team lacked pitchers, so Koufax volunteered to help out. He threw hard but was so wild that catchers wanted no part of him. In his debut game, at Keesler Air Force Base in Biloxi, Mississippi, Koufax struggled. He returned to the Cincinnati campus to pitch a four-hitter against Wayne, striking out 16. He next took on Louisville, striking out 18, a school record. He finished his first college season with a record of 3-1, 51 strikeouts and 30 walks in 31 innings.[20] He caught the eye of major-league scouts.

Koufax interested each of the three New York City big-league clubs — the Yankees, Giants, and Dodgers — not only because he could throw hard but also because of his religion. Since the days of John McGraw, the New York teams had desired Jewish drawing cards. His faith may have had something to do with it — the bigger factor was his performance — yet it was said in the 1960s that when Koufax pitched, regardless of where, there would be 10,000 more fans in attendance.[21]

The Yankees sent a Jewish scout, which offended the Koufax family. They offered only $4,000 and a Class-D assignment.[22] Koufax had a tryout with the Giants at the Polo Grounds. He showed up without his glove and had to borrow one from Johnny Antonelli.[23] The team lost interest; tense and frightened, Sandy was wild.[24]

Jimmy Murphy, who covered school sports for the *Brooklyn Eagle*, tipped off Dodgers scout Al Campanis to Koufax. This led to a workout at Ebbets Field before the general manager, Buzzie Bavasi, and the manager, Walt Alston.[25] Campanis offered a $14,000 bonus and a $6,000 salary. Branch Rickey, who by then was general manager of the Pittsburgh Pirates, authorized one of his scouts to top the Dodgers by $5,000. The Milwaukee Braves offered $30,000.[26] But they were too late. Sandy had talked with Irving Koufax frequently, and they decided to sign with Brooklyn. Irving sealed the deal with a handshake. It was on December 14, 1954, that Koufax signed as a bonus baby.

Sandy then dropped out of Cincinnati and transferred to Columbia University to take some courses at the school of architecture.[27] The demands of playing baseball and the requirement that Koufax fulfill his military service obligation of six months between playing seasons eventually caused him to drop out of Columbia.[28]

Koufax's bonus was rather modest compared to what many bonus babies got in that era. Yet the rules then in effect denied clubs the right to send any player to the minors who was given more than $6,000 to sign.[29] Thus, Koufax never spent a day in the minors.[30]

According to teammate Carl Erskine, even as a rookie Koufax showed a quiet sense of humor. Erskine related how in the spring of 1955, the Dodgers were on a city bus heading back to their hotel after an exhibition game in Miami. The Dodgers had lost and it was a hot night. The bus stopped to let a very slow freight train pass. The passengers grew impatient; coach Billy Herman, sitting across the aisle from Koufax, let out, "Darn, you can give this town back to the Jews." The entire bus went silent. Koufax, not even 20 then, very softly said, "Now Billy, you know we already have it." This defused the situation with no carryover.[31]

It was more than two months into the 1955 season before Koufax made his major-league debut. Early in the season, he injured his ankle and wound up on the disabled list. Tommy Lasorda was the odd man out on June 8, when he was demoted to the Montreal Royals to make room for Koufax. Lasorda liked to say, "It took the greatest left-handed pitcher in baseball history to get me off that Brooklyn club — and I still think they made a mistake."[32]

Once off the DL, another reason for Koufax's idleness emerged: Alston favored experience over youth. This was true of many big-league managers then, but Alston's tendency was more pronounced because the Dodgers were a World Series contender.

Also, in those days, big-league pitching staffs were smaller and structured differently. There were four regular starters, and they were expected to pitch deep into the game if not complete it. There were two long-relief men in case a starter got into early trouble. Although the "closer" role was evolving and the concept of saves was just emerging, there was also one short man, used sometimes to wrap up the game or often to put out late-inning fires. The eighth and ninth pitchers were the low men on the totem pole. In the normal course of events, they did not get into games. They awaited a blowout by either side or some catastrophe (injury) to occur.[33]

Finally, on June 24, 1955, against the Braves at Milwaukee's County Stadium, Koufax got into a game for Brooklyn. He entered at the start of the fifth inning with the Dodgers trailing, 7-1, and pitched two scoreless innings, striking out two.

After one more relief outing, Koufax got his first start, on July 6, 1955. It was the first game of a doubleheader in Pittsburgh. He lasted just 4⅔ innings. He walked eight batters and gave up three hits but allowed only one run. He was not the pitcher of record. After that, he pitched just three times in a span of 50 days.

Koufax's first win came on August 27, 1955. He started and went the distance, shutting out the Cincinnati Reds on two hits and five walks. He fanned 14, including Gus Bell four times. In his next start, on September 3, Koufax threw another shutout, over Pittsburgh. He allowed just five hits. Those were his only two wins as a rookie.

Koufax was on the World Series roster in 1955 but did not pitch. He took night classes at Columbia while the Series was in progress, then attended in the day after Johnny Podres finished off the Yankees.[34] Brooklyn won the pennant again in 1956; once more Koufax was on the postseason roster, but Alston did not call upon him.

During his first two years as a Dodger, Koufax gained little experience—just 28 appearances (15 starts) and barely 100 innings pitched. He was frustrated and quick to blame his wildness and unsteadiness on the lack of regular work.[35] It was a vicious cycle. He couldn't pitch until his control improved—but the less he pitched, the worse his control became. While in Brooklyn for three years, Koufax considered himself not a pitcher but an arm. He could not help but feel that some potentially prime years were wasted.[36]

Koufax got a boost in May 1956, however, with the arrival of Sal Maglie. Koufax and Don Drysdale (then a 19-year-old rookie) sat in the bullpen with the savvy veteran and listened to analysis of what was happening on the field.[37]

During the 1956-57 offseason, rather than touring Japan with most of the Dodgers, Koufax got a chance to practice his "lessons" in winter ball. The Dodgers arranged for him to pitch in Puerto Rico with the Caguas Criollos. The manager was Ben Geraghty, from the Braves organization, a renowned developer of young talent. Although Koufax posted a won-lost record of just 3-6, he showed more glimpses of brilliance—a one-hit shutout and a two-hit shutout. The great Roberto Clemente got the only hits off Koufax in the latter game, Sandy's last in Puerto Rico. Caguas had to release him because a league ruling precluded teams from having more than three imported players with big-league experience.[38]

Koufax got more work with Brooklyn in 1957. He pitched in 34 games, starting 13 of them, and logged over 100 innings. That season ended on a distinctive note: Koufax became the last man to throw a pitch in a Brooklyn Dodgers uniform. In relief of Roger Craig at Philadelphia, he struck out Willie Jones on three pitches.

During the 1958 season, with the Dodgers now ensconced in Los Angeles, Koufax told Carl Erskine that he was going to quit baseball and pursue an opportunity to buy into a radio station. But at the end of the season, Koufax felt appreciative of the way the Dodgers had treated him. He had been used more than ever before—40 games, 26 starts, nearly 160 innings pitched. He said he would give it one more year (1959) before making a final decision.

Erskine believed that because basketball had been Koufax's favorite sport, he did not possess the inner fire for baseball that other rookies and players in general had. Koufax would not approach the other pitchers for advice or ask any questions. He was being self-taught. There was no one trying to show him how to pace himself or how to hold a runner. In addition to the bonus rule, which prevented Koufax from getting seasoning, Erskine talked about competition. In the 1950s, players generally had one-year contracts, and thus were not inclined to take a rookie under their wing and show him the ropes. Each man was fighting for his own job. It was not uncommon for players to be released in midyear and be replaced by one of the many minor-league aspirants.

Erskine said Koufax may have felt some guilt about leapfrogging over the other pitchers that each of the 15 farm teams in the Dodgers organization had. Koufax had taken a spot on the roster that another deserved more. His sensitivity played a role in his image of himself.[39]

Koufax started poorly in 1959. By May 2 he had started four games — not getting past the fourth inning in any — and relieved once. In just 11 innings, he had allowed 19 hits and 17 walks, and his ERA was a dismal 12.27. Koufax felt that the Dodgers were very close to getting rid of him. Pitching coach Joe Becker said, "He has no coordination and he has lost all his confidence. His arm is sound, but mechanically he is all fouled up. ..."

Even though Walt Alston said not to give up on Koufax, Sandy believed those were the words of the front office, not the field manager. At this point Koufax was hoping that some other team would claim him on waivers so he could continue in the big leagues.[40] In mid-June, though, it started to come together. Koufax improved his control and pitched three consecutive complete-game victories. He had a similar run in late August. On August 31, against the Giants at the Los Angeles Coliseum, Koufax struck out 18 batters. It was his final win of the season. In the bottom of the ninth with the score tied, Koufax was allowed to hit and singled to left field off Giants starter Jack Sanford. After Junior Gilliam singled, Wally Moon launched a three-run walk-off home run. The win streak ended September 6 when, after matching zeroes with Chicago's Art Ceccarelli for nine innings, Koufax gave up a three-run homer to Ernie Banks in the 10th and lost.

Koufax was continuing to mature as a pitcher. In 1959 the Dodgers won another pennant, and so he appeared in a World Series at last. After pitching two innings in Game One, a blowout victory for the White Sox, Koufax started Game Five. On October 6, in front of 92,706 spectators at the Coliseum, he pitched seven innings of five-hit ball, striking out six. He walked only one batter and allowed the game's only run when Sherm Lollar grounded into a double play. The White Sox may have won, but Erskine believed that Koufax realized that he could be truly successful in the major leagues.[41] What also transformed him from an inconsistent pitcher to a Hall of Famer was coming to grips with fear of failure on such a big stage.[42]

The Dodgers realized more fully what they had in 1960, when Yankees GM George Weiss tried to get Koufax in a trade for catcher Elston Howard. Bavasi turned the deal down.[43] The original offer for Howard was Duke Snider and Johnny Podres.[44] Koufax himself may not have agreed. When the 1960 season ended, he was again uncertain about his future. He was disgusted with his performance over 175 innings. Despite 197 strikeouts, both his control (100 walks allowed) and ERA (3.91) had improved just marginally.[45]

It's often observed that the two halves of Koufax's 12-year career stand in stark contrast. From 1955 through 1960, he won 36 and lost 40, with 405 walks in 691⅔ innings. His ERA was 4.10. But Koufax burst into prominence in 1961, winning 18 games and leading the National League with 269 strikeouts.

During spring training in 1961, Norm Sherry, sitting with Koufax on a bus filled with reserves heading out of Vero Beach to an exhibition game, had suggested to Koufax that he ease up a bit — the harder he threw, the wilder he became. Koufax would then tense his massive muscles, and thus his fastball would lose life and his control would erode further. Joe Becker stated, "He needs a loose wrist to get snap in the ball at the position of release, not more muscular tension than he was already creating."[46] Sherry said, "Why not have some fun out there, Sandy? Don't try to throw so hard and use more curveballs and changeups."[47]

Heeding this suggestion was truly the turning point in Koufax's career. He economized effort, retained velocity, and gained better control of both his pitches and himself. In other words, he went from thrower to pitcher. The mental dimension of his game was prominent.

- At times Koufax put on an act to fool batters into looking for a different pitch. He did not like to shake off signs in a regular manner; he believed it was a tip-off. So he would purposely shake off a series of signs only to come back to where he wanted to be.
- Koufax would not think of the other team's lineup before warming up. He believed that thinking about the hitters that late forced him to concentrate upon them completely.[48]
- He focused on retiring the average hitters, rather than getting out the best opposing batter. His philosophy was that allowing the star(s) to reach base three or four times in a game did not matter if no one else preceded or followed with a hit.
- To be at his best, on the two days before a start Koufax abstained from any activity that might interfere with his performance.[49]

Of interest, however, Koufax believed that luck had a lot to do with success on the mound—particularly line shots hit right at an infielder. Some other noteworthy points include these:

- When Koufax wasn't pitching, he liked to hold a ball with his fastball and curveball grips to strengthen his muscles and tendons.[50]
- He could never throw a slider—it hurt his arm.
- For leverage and push, Koufax pitched from atop the rubber rather than in front of it.
- He believed it necessary to establish the outer half of the plate with a fastball and not get beaten in a close game by throwing a strike on the inner half.[51]
- Koufax never blamed any single play or player for costing him a game, because that same player got him out of trouble in another game.[52]

Koufax's last win in 1961 came in the last big-league game played at the LA Coliseum. He earned a complete-game victory after 13 innings and 205 pitches. He struck out 15 and walked only three, not allowing a hit over the final five innings.

During his last five seasons, 1962-1966, Koufax ascended to a new level—one of the best peak periods from any pitcher ever (though he did benefit from a notably pitcher-friendly home park in Dodger Stadium). Over that span, he won 111 games and lost only 34, with a 1.95 ERA. He led the National League in ERA in each of those five seasons. *The Sporting News* named him NL Pitcher of the Year from 1963 through 1966. In each of his Cy Young Award/Triple Crown seasons (1963, 1965, and 1966) he won at least 25 games and struck out over 300 batters. In 1963 he was also the NL's Most Valuable Player, and he was the runner-up in the MVP voting of 1965 and 1966.

Koufax enjoyed his fame, but only from afar. Though always elegantly dressed, poised, and articulate, he was a basically shy and repressed person. He did not welcome all the commotion that came with his success. He tried very hard to stay out of the news. He would on occasion avoid answering the phone. On urgent matters, a call was often replaced by a wire to Koufax's home.[53] He would often dine in gourmet restaurants at his own expense rather than eat the club's traditional fare, "Dodger steaks."[54] However, he almost never left his hotel room in his final two seasons, preferring to order room service to avoid the attention.[55]

Koufax's 1962 season was off to a good start. On April 24 at Wrigley Field he struck out 18 Cubs as the Dodgers won 10-2. His progress was then interrupted by a career-threatening injury—not to his elbow or shoulder, but to his index finger. It happened in his next start, on April 28 against Pittsburgh at Dodger Stadium. By nature a right-handed batter, Koufax decided to protect his throwing arm by swinging lefty instead. In this unfamiliar stance, a pitch from Pirates starter Earl Francis jammed his hand—oddly enough, Koufax got an infield single on the play. He remained in the game, earning a complete-game 2-1 victory. However, the trauma led to the circulatory condition called Raynaud's phenomenon.[56] It got so bad that if he pressed the finger, it would turn white for hours. His thumb was also affected to a degree.

Despite this numbness, Koufax pitched a no-hitter against the Mets on June 30, 1962. On July 12 he won his 14th game of the season, also against the Mets. (He feasted on the expansion club in its weak early years, going 17-2 with a 1.44 ERA.) He did not win another game that year. On July 17 Koufax left a game against the Reds after the first inning. He was out of the lineup until September 21. The doctors tried various drugs and intravenous injections designed to dissolve the blood clot in his finger. It alleviated the condition, but at one point the threat of amputation existed.[57]

In the heat of a pennant race with the Giants, Koufax returned, but the layoff had cost him endurance. The Dodgers faded down the stretch, and a three-game playoff for the flag ensued. Koufax took the ball for Game One but was knocked out of the box in the second inning.

Going into the 1963 season, there were some lingering doubts about Koufax's condition. He missed three starts in late April and early May with a sore shoulder. His first game back was a victory over the Cardinals, followed by his second career no-hitter, on May 11 against the San Francisco Giants. Koufax was perfect until he walked Ed Bailey with one out in the eighth. Surprisingly, he struck out only four. After the game Koufax said, "Because of my finger and shoulder injuries and caliber of the Giants, this would have to be my biggest thrill."[58]

The opposing pitcher at Dodger Stadium that night was one of the other premier pitchers in the NL, Juan Marichal. Koufax and the Dominican ace started against each other four times, and this was Koufax's second triumph before losing the next two.

Koufax finished the 1963 season 25-5. He fired 11 shutouts—since then only five other pitchers have had seasons with double-digit shutout totals, and none since 1985.[59]

The Dodgers went on to sweep the World Series against the Yankees. Koufax was named Series MVP, going all the way to win both Game One (5-2) and Game Four (2-1). In Game One, he struck out 15, breaking his old friend Carl Erskine's record, set exactly a decade before. Koufax was aware of it; when he saw Erskine he actually apologized.[60] Koufax set another Series record that day by striking out the first five batters he faced.

By the end of the 1963 season, Koufax had developed traumatic arthritis in his left elbow. Pictures often showed him with his left arm in an ice bath after games. Some experts speculated that the elbow problem came from throwing a few pitches side-arm in his early years. Koufax believed that it happened over a period of 10 to 12 years and may have started in high school when he fell on the basketball court.[61]

The general public had been unaware of the heat treatments that followed.[62] Koufax went to the trainer about an hour before his starts to have Capsolin—basically, chili pepper salve—rubbed on his arm. Capsolin irritates the skin to increase circulation; it burns until the arm goes numb. Excessive application would cause the skin to start peeling.[63] Originally, when his arm blew up, Koufax was given phenylbutazone alka, an anti-inflammatory pill.[64] The nonsteroidal drug was intended for animals and is no longer approved for human use. Today's equivalent is Ibuprofen.

During 1964 Koufax's arthritis became exacerbated. On April 22 he lasted only one inning. He took 12 days off and returned to pitch a complete-game 10-inning win. A month later in Philadelphia, he pitched his third career no-hitter (and only shutout ever against the Phillies).

In Milwaukee on August 8, Koufax dove back to second base on a pickoff attempt and landed on his elbow. The chronic throbbing after he pitched became more acute; eventually everywhere from his shoulder to wrist swelled up. The team's orthopedic surgeon, Dr. Robert Kerlan, took X-rays that revealed the extent of the arthritis. The treatment was aspirating the fluid build-up with a needle, cortisone injections, and oral medications to relieve the inflammation.[65]

Koufax's final start that season came on August 16. Yet despite taking the mound just 29 times in 1964, he won 19 games.

Koufax came up with the idea that if he skipped his customary sideline throwing between starts it would help lessen the pain.[66] The idea seemed to work, as shown by his 1965 record, including a career-high 335⅔ innings pitched. His 382 strikeouts shattered the modern-era record of 349 that Rube Waddell had set in 1904.

Another memorable matchup against Juan Marichal took place on August 22, 1965—the game in which Marichal took a bat to Johnny Roseboro's head. Marichal, ejected in the third inning, got no decision. Koufax retired Bob Schroder (who finished Marichal's turn at bat) and Tito Fuentes, but he was still shaken. He walked two and then gave up a three-run homer to Willie Mays that gave the Giants a 4-3 victory.[67]

Koufax, knowing the deadly force of his own deliveries, refrained from beanball wars and never sought to hurt a batter. According to his co-author, Ed Linn, he would not intentionally throw at a hitter and did not try to make batters look bad.[68] Over his career, he hit just 18 batters.

By contrast, the National League's other premier pitcher of the day, Bob Gibson, hit 102 batters over his career 3,884 innings. Gibson (and Don Drysdale) believed that brushback pitches had a valuable purpose. Yet in his five matchups against Gibson from 1961 through 1966, Koufax was 4-1 with a 0.92 ERA and three shutouts. (His 10 shutouts against the Cardinals were the most he threw against any team.)

With his perfect game at Dodger Stadium on September 9, 1965, Koufax became the first major-league pitcher to throw a fourth no-hitter, surpassing Bob Feller. The Cubs' pitcher, Bob Hendley, allowed just one hit—the teams' combined totals of just one hit and two baserunners are records that have not since been approached.

But the left-arm pain remained at times unbearable for Koufax, despite the Capsolin, ice baths, and pain relievers. He found that his left arm was shortening. He had to lean over to reach his face when shaving.

Nonetheless, down the stretch, in yet another heated pennant race with the Giants, Koufax had four complete-game wins in his last five starts. He then pitched two shutouts against Minnesota in the World Series. Though he lost Game Two, he threw a four-hitter in Game Five, striking out 10. In Game Seven, on just two days' rest, he fired a three-hitter. For the second time, he won Series MVP honors.

Koufax's personal decision not to pitch on Yom Kippur, which fell on October 6 in 1965, has been well chronicled. According to media reports, supposedly Koufax was going to consult a rabbi to determine whether he could play. But on October 2 he said simply, "I didn't want to say anything about it before because we were not in a position to clinch the pennant. But at no time did I ever consider it. I will definitely not pitch."[69]

Sports Illustrated named Koufax its Sportsman of the Year for 1965, and writer Jack Olsen asked what drove him. Koufax responded, "I think it's just competition. I want to win, and I want to do things well. And I want to be capable of doing my best. If I were to go out and get beat and then realize after the game that I got beat because of something I did the day before … to me, that's the worst way to lose. … I'd be ashamed of myself."[70]

Before the 1966 season, Koufax became embroiled in contract negotiations. He and the Dodgers' other pitching mainstay, Don Drysdale, had grown weary of being played against each other in the process. The two decided to pool their strength and make their salary demands together. The sides were far apart at first; eventually, Buzzie Bavasi made a final offer of $240,000 as a package. This was at the time the largest sum ever paid two pitchers on one club for one season—Koufax's portion, $130,000, was then the highest salary in baseball history.[71] However, Koufax and Drysdale had to give up the no-cut clauses in their contracts.[72] Club owner Walter O'Malley was ready to let them both walk if they did not accept that final offer. He mentioned that the Mets were interested in them both.[73]

In 1966 Koufax matched his career highs of the preceding season with 41 starts and 27 complete games. During that season, though, it became necessary for him to receive cortisone injections directly into the elbow joint. The injections became more frequent as the inflammation and fluid in the elbow became more and more difficult to contain. Dr.

Kerlan had warned that the traumatic arthritis was incurable. By the end of the 1966 season, Koufax's left arm was bent at a 22.5-degree angle and the bone spurs in the elbow had grown to almost a quarter-inch. Every pitch would bring pain. Combing his hair had become a painful effort. He had his suit jackets retailored so that the malformation of his left arm would be hidden.[74]

Yet Koufax never missed a turn—his competitive fire continued to drive him. In midseason Bob Hunter of the *Los Angeles Times* reported that Koufax had said, "I go out to pitch a no-hitter every game. Of course that can't be, but after I allow one hit, I shoot for a shutout."[75] That dovetailed with his comment the previous year: "And when I give up a run, I want to pitch a one-run game."[76]

In echoes of the 1951 stretch drive, the Giants got hot late in the 1966 race—the threat of a playoff for the Dodgers loomed. But Koufax turned the rivals away in the season's last game. Pitching on two days' rest in the nightcap of a doubleheader at Philadelphia, he hurled a complete-game 6-3 victory over Jim Bunning to clinch the pennant.[77]

In the 1966 World Series against Baltimore, Koufax started Game Two, going on three days' rest after his October 2 pennant-clincher. He pitched six innings and allowed four runs; meanwhile, 20-year-old Jim Palmer threw a shutout. The Orioles swept the Series in four games, and so that was the last mound appearance ever by Sandy Koufax.

Before the season was over, the autobiography *Koufax*, written in conjunction with Ed Linn, was published. Among many detailed insights was the following: "I do not think the ballplayer is of an extraordinary importance in our national life. We do not heal the sick or bring peace and comfort to a troubled world. All we do is to provide a few hours of diversion to the people who want to come to the park, and a sort of conflict to those who identify their fortunes with ours through the season. ... [B]y its nature, it is a brief, self-liquidating life. It is a temporary life, really, a period between the time of our youth and the beginning of our lifetime career."[78] While Koufax's decision to retire has often been portrayed as "abrupt," this passage supports the idea that he had been contemplating retirement for some time.

It's noteworthy that in 1964, Koufax commented that to be considered a great pitcher, you need to show that you can win games for 10 to 15 years. To be a great ballplayer, your accomplishments need to span not just a couple of years but a whole career.[79]

With this in mind, Carl Erskine's take on Koufax's early retirement becomes even more intriguing. In Erskine's view, once Koufax established his pitching records, he had reached a point where he had nothing more to prove and wanted to leave at the top of the heap. Erskine believed that Koufax never felt totally comfortable as a major-league pitcher. He had never heard or seen any medical report that said Koufax could not go out and pitch.[80]

In his 12 seasons, Sandy Koufax amassed the following notable statistics:

- Winning percentage of .655
- ERA of 2.76
- 40 shutouts, including 10 1-0 victories
- Along with his four no-hitters, two one-hitters, eight two- hitters, and 17 three-hitters
- 9.28 strikeouts per nine innings
- Eight regular-season games with 15 or more strikeouts
- Opponents' batting average of .205
- 6.79 hits allowed per nine innings during his career

Koufax never won a Gold Glove, but in 1965 he did not commit an error.[81]

As noted, Ernie Banks had a hard time facing Koufax. In 143 plate appearances, Banks had only 23 hits (they did include seven home runs) and struck out 31 times. One player who had great success against Koufax was Bill Virdon—.404 in 60 plate appearances despite swinging left-handed, well above his career .267 average.

Even for a pitcher, Koufax was a weak hitter, batting just .097 in his career. He did have two home runs. Both came at County Stadium in Milwaukee against the Braves and both were off left-handers. His first, on June 13, 1962, was a solo shot to left center in the fifth inning off Warren Spahn. It proved to be the winning run. The second came a year later off Denny Lemaster. Other batting highlights include a home game against Houston on July 20, 1965. In the ninth with the score tied, Walt Alston allowed Koufax to bat with two out and two on. Koufax delivered a walk-off single to left. Also, in a game against the Mets on June 5, 1966, Koufax had two hits in one inning.

In December 1966, Koufax joined NBC as a broadcaster. His contract (which also called for him to do other work for the network) was for an estimated $1 million over 10 years.[82] Koufax was reassigned to the second broadcasting team in 1969 to gain more experience; Tony Kubek was promoted to join Curt Gowdy, and Pee Wee Reese's contract was not renewed.[83]

After the 1968 season, the Dodgers made a formal offer to Koufax to return. He politely turned it down, telling Bob Hunter that he did not want to wind up a cripple and not be able to play a normal game of golf.[84]

According to Carl Erskine, Koufax wanted to have a successful marriage with children. Sandy was regularly seen in the presence of beautiful young women, yet he wondered why he could not meet someone like Erskine's wife. He confessed that his dates had usually been introduced to him at cocktail parties. Erskine told Koufax that was the problem. "You should go to your synagogue or other such similar places to meet a different kind of woman."[85]

Koufax never became a father, but he got married three times. His first wife was Anne Widmark, daughter of actor Richard Widmark. Their wedding was on New Year's Day, 1969.[86] They lived in East Holden, near Ellsworth, Maine. They bought what was known as the Winkumpaugh Farm on October 4, 1971, then proceeded to buy the 300 adjacent acres. Koufax joined the Bucksport Golf Club and got his handicap down to six. He was able to advance to the championship flights in the 1973 Maine State Amateur Championship. He continued his interest in electronics and dabbled in carpentry and gourmet cooking.[87] Sandy's sister Edith related that when they were growing up, her brother was a pretty good cook and handy around the family home, which he wired for sound. When Edith married, he even came over to the newlyweds' home and spent three hours fixing a sewing machine.[88]

It was at his Maine home that Koufax received the news that he had been voted into the Hall of Fame.[89] At the time his 344 votes were the most ever. In his Hall of Fame acceptance speech on August 7, 1972, Koufax referred to his old pitching coach, Joe Becker: "Becker pushed me, shoved me, embarrassed me and made me work and thank God for him. Being a pitcher I feel that it is sometimes very solitary, very lonely. … You feel like, well, everybody on the other team is against you, and they are. The only one that seems to be close, the only friend you have is the catcher, and I'd like to thank every catcher who ever caught in any ballgame I was ever in, two in particular, Roy Campanella, who caught the very first one, and John Roseboro, who caught most of the others."

Koufax's contract with NBC was terminated by mutual consent before the start of the 1973 season.[90] From Koufax's side, the decision to leave the broadcast booth stemmed in part from difficulty in talking baseball to people who had not played the game professionally. Other challenges for him were describing pitchers whose repertoires differed from his, and being honest and critical of the men he played with and against. As a result, he was uncomfortable on the air.[91]

In 1974 the Koufaxes sold the Maine property and moved back to California. Koufax played golf, invested in real estate and enjoyed listening to music at home. He rarely attended a baseball game, instead watching on television. He admitted that he missed playing, stating, "It's hard not to miss the one thing in your life you've done very well."[92]

After his retirement, Koufax spent much of his time on a ranch outside Paso Robles. He eventually ran into financial difficulties. Thus, he returned to baseball in 1979 as a special pitching coach for the Dodgers.[93] Over the following 11 years he worked with prospects during spring training, paying follow-up visits in Double A and Triple A. Keeping a low profile, he had no name on the back of his jacket when on the practice field. During the offseason he retreated to his ranch and eventually to southern Idaho to keep away from the press and baseball.[94]

Anne Widmark and Koufax divorced in 1982. In 1985 Koufax married his second wife, Kimberly Francis, a fitness enthusiast with a passion for the arts. For a time, they lived in Oregon, where she had a gallery. Their marriage ended in the winter of 1998-1999.[95] Koufax married a third time, to Jane Purucker Clarke, a sorority sister of Laura Bush, former President George W. Bush's wife.[96]

The 1989 season was the last of Koufax's 11 years with the Dodgers as minor-league pitching instructor, although he continued to visit unofficially in spring training. For many years, well into the 21st century, he would also visit the Mets in spring training to catch up with old friend Fred Wilpon and offer sage advice to young pitchers. Sometimes he would disappear, though, before players had a chance to shake his huge hand.

Many books have been written about Sandy Koufax over the years, a testament to enduring public interest in the man. Not a day goes by without his name appearing on the World Wide Web.[97] The year 2002 brought *Sandy Koufax: A Lefty's Legacy*, by Jane Leavy. Koufax authorized the book but declined to be interviewed; thus, Leavy interviewed more than 400 people to gain perspective on the player and person, from the standpoints of both baseball and Judaism. It became a bestseller and was praised for the quality of its writing.

Alas, after the book came out, Koufax's relationship with the Dodgers became severely strained. The *New York Post*, then owned—as were the Dodgers—by News Corp., planted a blind item insinuating that Koufax was gay. The paper quickly withdrew the item and apologized, but Koufax severed his ties with the club for a couple of years. In 2004, however, Frank McCourt bought the Dodgers, and Koufax resumed his unofficial spring-training visits to work with pitchers.[98]

In 2007, 41 years after he retired from baseball, Koufax was the final player chosen in the draft to stock the six teams for the first (and only) season of the Israel Baseball League. Koufax, then 71, was picked by the Modi'in Miracle in the draft conducted by the head of the league's operations, Dan Duquette. Miracle manager Art Shamsky (another noted Jewish big leaguer) stated, "His selection is a tribute to the esteem with which he is held by everyone associated with this league. It's been 41 years between starts for him. If he's rested and ready to take the mound again, we want him on our team."[99]

Koufax remained a frequent newsmaker. In 2010 President Barack Obama likened himself in jest to Koufax at a White House gathering that honored Jewish Americans. Obama said, "We are both lefties. He can't pitch on Yom Kippur. I can't pitch." Obama started his introduction by saying "This is a pretty fancy ... pretty distinguished group and Sandy Koufax."[100] The mention of Koufax's name brought the biggest cheer at this event, which included members of the House and Senate, two justices of the Supreme Court, Olympic athletes, entrepreneurs, and rabbinical scholars.

Koufax's reputation for privacy endured for decades. Even his own mother saw him as a mystery. When she heard that Sandy was writing his autobiography, she asked if she could get one of the first copies so she could learn about her son. "You never told me anything," she said.[101] One 1999 report noted, "Koufax's tight band of friends ... call him The Ghost because of the way he suddenly appears and disappears."[102] Yet this report and others over the years emphasized his loyalty. Fellow Brooklyn native Joe Torre said that once you were in Koufax's inner circle, you were in for good.[103] For example, even though Fred Wilpon got Sandy to become one of the investors in Bernard Madoff's notorious Ponzi scheme, Koufax publicly supported Wilpon. He would have testified on behalf of the Mets' ownership, had a settlement not averted a civil trial.

Koufax himself added balance to the portrait. "I'm trying to figure out who says I'm private," he said with a grin. "I'm at the Final Four. I go to golf tournaments. I go to the movies. I go to dinner. I live my life. Somebody wrote that 50 years ago, and they're still writing that. ... I don't care what anybody says. I'm past caring."[104]

In the spring of 2012, Guggenheim Baseball bought the Dodgers, and co-owner Earvin "Magic" Johnson reached out to Koufax. Previously, Sandy had thrown out the first pitch at Dodger Stadium on Opening Day 2008, but in 2013, he forged closer ties with the club again. He continued to impart his wisdom to pitchers and became a special adviser to Chairman Mark Walter. Koufax expressed his delight and said that some of his most cherished memories came at Dodger Stadium. But Ned Colletti, who was then the team's general manager, summed it up perfectly.

"He's as iconic a player as we'll ever have."[105]

NOTES

1 Ira Berkow, "Koufax Is No Garbo," *New York Times,* July 3, 1985.

2 Tom Verducci, "The Left Arm of God," *Sports Illustrated,* July 12, 1999.

3 Maury Allen, "Koufax Labors in Obscurity of Dodger System," *New York Post,* September 15, 1983.

4 Verducci.

5 Ed Guver, "Two Southpaws—the Best of Their Eras," *Philadelphia Inquirer.* April 9, 2000.

6 Milton Gross, "Call Him Lucky," *New York Post,* October 10, 1965.

7 According to an Associated Press clipping in Koufax's Hall of Fame player file, "Braun Real name of Sandy Koufax," Jack Braun was a 6-footer with features that resembled his son's. Braun was part-owner of a business that distributed records. With his second wife, he had a daughter named Marie, born in 1946.

8 Sandy Koufax with Ed Linn, *Koufax* (New York: Viking Press, 1966), 16-28.

9 Bob Broeg, "Sandy Started Slowly ... But Oh What a Finish," *The Sporting News,* August 14, 1971.

10 Koufax with Linn.

11 Koufax with Linn, 16-28.

12 Koufax with Linn, 38.

13 Phil Pepe, "Koo: At First He Succeeded," *New York Daily News,* August 6, 1971.

14 infinitecardset.blogspot.com/2010/10/52-sandy-koufax-and-coney-island.html.

15 Broeg.

16 Pepe.

17 Ibid.

18 Broeg; Richard Sandomir, "Koufax's Change-Up: He Talks With ESPN," *New York Times,* April 2, 1999.

19 Associated Press, "Sandy Was Sometimes Special," *New York Post,* April 2, 1974.

20 Koufax and Linn, 43-44.

21 Broeg.

22 Koufax and Linn, 49-50.

23 Koufax and Linn, 47.

24 "Sandy Finally Signed With Persistent Dodgers," *The Sporting News,* August 14, 1971.

25 Broeg.

26 "Sandy finally Signed."

27 Broeg.

28 Ibid.

29 Ibid.

30 Ibid.

31 Carl Erskine, telephone interview with Marc Z. Aaron, October 26, 2012 (hereafter Erskine telephone interview).

32 Joe Resnick, Associated Press, "Lasorda Remembers Being Replaced by Koufax," June 7, 2005.

33 Koufax and Linn, 110-111.

34 *The Sporting News,* January 4, 1956: 33. *The Sporting News,* October 26, 1955: 11.

35 Melvin Durslag, "Sandy Koufax the Strikeout King," *The Saturday Evening Post,* July 14, 1962.

36 Koufax and Linn, 113-114.

37 Koufax and Linn, 114-118.

38 Thomas E. Van Hyning, *The Santurce Crabbers* (Jefferson, North Carolina: McFarland & Co., 1999), 77.

39 Erskine telephone interview.

40 Koufax and Linn, 134.

41 Erskine telephone interview.

42 Joel Sherman, "Mets Soak in Some Koufax Greatness," *New York Post,* March 17, 1998.

43 Durslag, "Sandy Koufax."

44 Bill Libby, "The Sophistication of Sandy Koufax," *Sport,* September 1963.

45 Koufax and Linn, 142.

46 Broeg.

47 Ibid.

48 Koufax and Linn, 187.

49 *Sports Illustrated*, "Koufax on Koufax," December 20, 1965.

50 Verducci.

51 Sherman.

52 Koufax and Linn, 8-9.

53 Melvin Durslag, "Challenging Sandy Was Fascination and Hopeless," *The Sporting News*, February 12, 1972.

54 Richard Lamparski, *Whatever Became of…* (seventh series) (New York: Crown Publishers, April 1978).

55 Verducci.

56 *Sports Illustrated*, "Koufax on Koufax."

57 Broeg.

58 Ibid.

59 The others: Dean Chance, Juan Marichal, Bob Gibson, Jim Palmer, and John Tudor.

60 Erskine telephone interview.

61 *Sports Illustrated*, "Koufax on Koufax."

62 Ibid.

63 Sandy Koufax with Ed Linn, "My Special World Series Memories," *Sport*, October 1966.

64 Koufax and Linn, 237.

65 Broeg.

66 Koufax and Linn, 228.

67 Peter C. Bjarkman, "Dandy Sandy and the Summer of '65'," *Elysian Fields Quarterly*, Winter 1998.

68 Ed Linn, "Koufax Remembered," *Sports Illustrated*, January 20, 1972.

69 Associated Press, "Koufax to Miss Opener, Will Observe Holy Day," October 2, 1965.

70 "Koufax on Koufax"; Sportsman of the Year," *Sports Illustrated*, December 20, 1965.

71 Hunter.

72 *New York Post*, April 11, 1966.

73 Koufax and Linn, 288.

74 Linn, "Koufax Remembered."

75 Bob Hunter, "No-Hit Game Koufax Goal Every Start," *Los Angeles Times*, June 18, 1966.

76 Phil Pepe, "Burden on Sandy," *New York World Telegram*, March 18, 1965.

77 Jeff Meyers, United Press International, "Koufax Comes Through and Dodgers Clinch Pennant," September 30, 1966.

78 "Koufax 'Right On,' " *Binghamton* (New York) *Press*, January 2, 1972.

79 Leonard Koppett, "The Greatest Pitcher of Them All," *New York Times Magazine*, October 4, 1964.

80 Erskine telephone interview.

81 Bob Gibson was the winner even though he made three errors and had fewer assists than Koufax.

82 Associated Press, "Koufax to Broadcast Baseball," December 30, 1966.

83 Milton Richman, Associated Press, "Pee Wee Reese Gets Word From Network," March 7, 1969.

84 Bob Hunter, "Sandy Says Nix to Comeback Pitch by Dodgers," *Los Angeles Times*, November 9, 1968.

85 Erskine telephone interview

86 Associated Press, "Sandy Koufax, Ann [sic] Widmark Are Married," January 2, 1969.

87 Verducci.

88 Broeg.

89 Included among the clippings in Koufax's Hall of Fame library file was a copy of an uncashed check, dated January 26, 1972, made out to Vic Lapiner with a handwritten note that stated, "Dear Vic, Here's your blood money. Honestly I can say it is a bet I'm happy to lose. I don't think it would be fun to be judged yearly. Hope all are well, and have a good year. As always, Sandy." In a telephone interview on May 16, 2012, Lapiner said that shortly before the Hall of Fame voting he bet Koufax that he would get into the Hall on the first ballot in January 1972. Lapiner was a pitcher in the Cleveland and Kansas City farm systems and a star athlete at USC. He met Koufax when he continued his baseball career by throwing batting practice for various teams including the Dodgers. They built up a strong friendship, possibly in part because Lapiner is also Jewish.

90 Maury Allen, "Koufax Return Stirs memories," *New York Post*, February 6, 1979.

91 Jack Craig, SporTView column, *Boston Globe*, March 17, 1973; Ralph Bernstein, "Sandy Koufax Says Transition from Playing Field to Telecasting Was Not an Easy Move," *Utica Daily Press*, February 8, 1968.

92 Maury Allen.

93 Gordon Verrell, "Recluse Koufax Steps Back Into the Game," *The Sporting News*, February 17, 1979.

94 Edvins Beitiks, "Koufax Says He's Happy to Be Compared With Gooden," *San Francisco Examiner*, undated clipping from 1986 or 1987 in Koufax's Hall of Fame player file.

95 Verducci.

96 Third marriage confirmed with Sandy Koufax by telephone on November 17, 2015. old.nationalreview.com/interrogatory/kessler200604032246.asp; Ronald Kessler, *Laura Bush: An Intimate Portrait of the First Lady* (New York: Broadway Books, 2007).

97 This is the author's observation after a lengthy subscription to Google Alerts.

NO-HITTERS

98 Dylan Hernandez, "Dodgers and Sandy Koufax Team Up Again After Years Apart," *Los Angeles Times*, January 22, 2013.

99 cbsnews.com/2100-500290_162-2735685.html.

100 Mark Knoller, "Obama Honors Jewish Americans at White House Reception," cbsnews.com, May 27, 2010.

101 Koufax and Linn, 39.

102 Jeff Jacobs, "At 63, Koufax Still Elusive," *Hartford Courant*, October 26, 1999.

103 Jeff Arnold, "Joe Torre Reflects on Sandy Koufax in Advance of Dodger Legend's Pump Foundation Honor," ThePostGame.com, August 8, 2012 (thepostgame.com/blog/men-action/201208/sandy-koufax-joe-torre-tony-larussa-pump-brothers-foundation-cancer).

104 Greg Beacham, Associated Press, "Sandy Koufax a Commanding Presence in Dodgers' Spring Training," February 24, 2013.

105 Hernandez.

SANDY KOUFAX'S FIRST NO-HITTER
JUNE 30, 1962: LOS ANGELES DODGERS 5, NEW YORK METS 0, AT DODGER STADIUM, LOS ANGELES

By Marc Z Aaron

THE LOS ANGELES DODGERS (50-29), in second place a half-game behind the San Francisco Giants, were eager to host the last-place New York Mets at Dodger Stadium. The Mets, in their inaugural season, had won just 20 games and lost 52.

The last time the Dodgers' starting pitcher, Sandy Koufax, faced the Mets was Memorial Day at the Polo Grounds. Koufax went the distance as the Dodgers won, 13-6. The Mets had come up with 13 hits that day, one of them a home run by Gil Hodges. Hodges would not be facing Koufax on this day; he was out with an injured foot.

Koufax (10-4, 2.48 ERA) did not waste any time in getting down to business. Nine pitches were all he needed to set down the first three Mets hitters — Richie Ashburn, Rod Kanehl, and Felix Mantilla — on strikes. Mantilla took his looking. You could have heard each of them muttering some expletives as they left the batter's box.[1] As Koufax walked to the dugout, he received a standing ovation from the fans behind the Dodgers dugout.[2] Mets third-base coach Solly Hemus was good-naturedly needling Koufax, yelling, "It isn't really that easy, is it?" Koufax could be heard responding, "No, it surely isn't."[3]

Relief pitcher Ron Perranoski, sitting in the Dodgers bullpen, could see that Koufax had wicked stuff going. He later said, "From my angle back there … his curveball used to break from the first deck, it looked like. And all of a sudden it's breaking from the second deck."[4]

In the bottom half of the first inning, the Dodgers exhibited their appreciation and support of what Koufax had just done. Bob Miller (0-5, 4.46 ERA) was on the mound for the Mets. With two out, Willie Davis tripled to left-center and then scored on a single that gave Tommy Davis his 81st run batted in and 108th hit of the season, both of them tops in the majors. On the first pitch to Ron Fairly, Davis stole second. Fairly then drew a four-pitch walk, bringing big Frank Howard to the plate. Howard had homered in the previous night's loss to the Mets. With a one-ball count, Howard delivered a groundball single up the middle that scored Davis. John Roseboro smacked a long line drive to right field that went off the fence. Fairly and Howard scored as Roseboro moved easily into second with a double. The Dodgers led 4-0 and after the next batter, Larry Burright, singled, that was it for the starter Miller. Montreal native Ray Daviault, a rookie with a 7.97 ERA, relieved and retired Koufax on a foul pop, ending the inning.

In the top of the second, Frank Thomas swung on the first pitch and smashed a ball into the hole between third and short that looked as though it might get through, but Maury Wills got to the ball moving to his right, made a backhand stop, and threw Thomas out.[5] First baseman Ron Fairly made a sweeping catch of the tough hop on the long, hurried throw by Wills.[6] The next two batters, Cliff Cook and Jim Hickman, took called third strikes.

In the third, Koufax went to a full count on Elio Chacon but got him swinging. Chris Cannizzaro, the Mets catcher, also worked a full count before flying out to center. (He was the third batter in a row who had gone to 3-and-2; by the end of the game Koufax had gone to full counts on nine batters.) Pitcher Daviault went down swinging on three pitches. Koufax had now fanned seven and was perfect through three innings.

Leading off the fourth, Richie Ashburn became the first Mets baserunner as he walked.

In the fifth inning two Mets reached the outfield. Cook flied out to left and Hickman flied out to center.

In the sixth, on another full count, Cannizzaro went down swinging; Daviault swung and missed on the final pitch of his at-bat. That gave Koufax 11 strikeouts and marked the 39th time in his career and eighth time in the 1962 season that he had reached double figures. Looking for his 12th strikeout and third of the inning, Koufax had two strikes on Ashburn. But Ashburn struck a curving liner that Tommy Davis appeared to have momentarily lost in the lights. Davis snared the ball on the run to keep the no-hitter alive. Koufax had abandoned his changeup at the start of the fifth inning, and was relying on his fastball and curve.

Each time Koufax passed Hemus as he walked off the mound, Hemus would heckle Koufax by reminding him that he still had a no-hitter going.[7]

With one out in the bottom of the seventh, Daviault threw a slow curve that Frank Howard lined into the left-field bleachers, 374 feet away. It was his second home run in two games and his eighth of the season. The Dodgers now led 5-0.

When Koufax stepped to the plate to lead off the eighth, the crowd uttered quiet hoorays and hurrahs.

The Dodgers made two defensive replacements in the top of the ninth. Ron Fairly moved from first base to right field, replacing Howard, and Tim Harkness replaced Fairly at first. Daviault, who was still pitching for the Mets, was scheduled to lead off, and Gene Woodling—who rarely hit against a lefty—pinch-hit for him. After the game the 16-year major-league veteran said manager Casey Stengel had told him to "grab a bat, this will be a new experience for you."[8] Woodling walked. Joe Christopher ran for him. The spectators then held their breath as Ashburn again hit a liner toward left that Tommy Davis had no chance to snare. But it landed foul by about six feet. With a runner at first, Koufax got three groundballs in a row. Ashburn grounded to shortstop, forcing Christopher at second. Kanehl's grounder to third forced Ashburn at second, and on a 2-and-1 count Mantilla grounded to short, forcing Kanehl at second.

Game over! It was the first no-hitter of the season in the National League and the first for Koufax.

After the final out a message flashed on the scoreboard, reading, "Koufax, report to Buzzie Bavasi and have your contract torn up."[9] Sandy was engulfed by his teammates and Solly Hemus, under his breath, congratulated him.[10]

When it was all over the Mets had hit only five balls out of the infield—Cannizzaro, Cook, Ashburn, and Hickman (twice). Koufax had struck out 13 Mets.

Looking back at the great fielding plays of the game and the five walks issued, Koufax attributed luck playing a big part in pitching a no-hitter. Koufax was quoted as saying "In essence, every pitcher takes the mound trying to pitch a no-hitter. The main idea is to keep the batter from getting a base-hit, isn't it? But you have to be lucky to keep 27 batters from dunking one in or hitting one on the nose."[11]

NOTES

1. Dick Young, "A Wing for Sandy's Motel?" *New York Daily News*, appearing in *San Francisco Chronicle*, July 6, 1962.
2. Frank Finch, "13 Mets Strike Out in Classic," *Los Angeles Times*, July 1, 1962.
3. Bob Hunter, "Dazzling Dodger Southpaw Fans 13 Mets, Walks Five," *The Sporting News*, July 14, 1962.
4. Jane Leavy, *Sandy Koufax, A Lefty's Legacy* (New York: HarperCollins, 2002), 119.
5. Joe McDonnell, "Dodger Stadium's Most Memorable Moments … Koufax's Three No-Hitters," *1987 Dodger Scorebook*.
6. Young.
7. Sandy Koufax with Ed Linn, *Koufax* (New York: Viking Press, 1966), 188.
8. Ibid.
9. Leavy, 119.
10. Ibid.
11. Finch.

SANDY KOUFAX'S SECOND NO-HITTER
MAY 11, 1963: LOS ANGELES DODGERS 8, SAN FRANCISCO GIANTS 0, AT DODGER STADIUM, LOS ANGELES

By Marc Z Aaron

IT WAS A GREAT PITCHING match-up as the fifth-place Los Angeles Dodgers (15-15) hosted the National League-leading San Francisco Giants (19-11) on May 11. It was a great pitching match-up: Juan Marichal (4-2) and Sandy Koufax (3-1).

Koufax had missed two weeks at the end of April into May with stiffness in his shoulder. A couple of weeks later, he said, "Guess I'm getting old. I'm just falling apart, piece by piece."[1]

In Koufax's first no-hitter, the season before, the Dodgers supported him with four runs in the first inning. Koufax had not had great control, going to full counts on nine New York Mets batters and walking five while striking out 13.

This game was a much different story. Going to the bottom of the sixth inning, the score was 1-0 in favor of the Dodgers. The lone run was produced by a Wally Moon fly-ball home run down the right-field line. Koufax had not yet walked a batter. He only had one three-ball count—in the first inning to Willie Mays, who then flied out to center. Koufax was perfect through six. The only close play came in the fifth when Orlando Cepeda hit a slow roller that shortstop Dick Tracewski barehanded to throw out Cepeda at first.

In the bottom of the sixth, Junior Gilliam lined a single to right to open the inning. Ron Fairly tried to advance Gilliam with a bunt but popped it to first base for the first out. Tommy Davis singled to right and then Wally Moon lined a run-scoring single to right and advanced to second on the throw from the outfield. With runners on second and third and one out, Frank Howard was intentionally walked. John Roseboro, with a career average under .200 against Marichal, lined a single to center, scoring Davis and Moon. After an infield hit by Tracewski loaded the bases, Marichal was replaced by John Pregenzer, who struck out Koufax and got Willie Davis on a groundball.

At the start of the seventh, Nate Oliver went in to play second base. Second baseman Gilliam moved to third and Tommy Davis switched from third base to left field, replacing Wally Moon, who came out of the game.

This turned out to be a key move. Koufax ran into lady luck in the seventh inning when Harvey Kuenn smashed a liner to right, but squarely into the mitt of Frank Howard. Felipe Alou, the league's leading hitter, then sent a high, hard shot to left. Tommy Davis took it about two feet short of the stands. Next, Willie Mays cracked a blistering liner that Jim Gilliam stabbed behind the third base bag."[2] When Davis caught Alou's ball, the bullpen kept yelling, "You got room, you got room."[3]

Don Larsen, the last man to pitch a perfect game, was watching from the San Francisco bullpen.[4]

None of the players on the bench said anything about the possible no-hitter but Koufax was aware all the time and knew he was close to a perfect game.[5]

Leading off the eighth, Orlando Cepeda hit a hot shot off Koufax's glove to second baseman Nate Oliver, who threw out Cepeda by a step.[6] The next man up was catcher Ed Bailey. Bailey had not much success previously against Koufax. Bailey took three balls, then two hard, straight fastballs for strikes before fouling one off. The pressure was agonizing.[7] "Finally, he threw one I couldn't reach," Bailey said later, "and he walked me."[8] Koufax, aware of the no-hitter all the way, kicked the mound and thumped his glove as the perfect game got away.[9] Then Bailey was taken off the basepaths as Jim Davenport grounded into a double play.

It was ladies night at Dodger Stadium. The crowd of 55,350 (49,807 paid) was the largest of the season thus far in the major leagues.[10] From the sixth inning on, fans were aware of the no-hitter and a possible perfect game. They applauded every time Koufax retired a batter.[11]

In the bottom of the eighth with one out, Roseboro and Tracewski singled. As Koufax approached the plate he received a standing ovation from the crowd.[12] He drew a walk and scored the sixth run of the game on a double by Ron Fairly.

In the ninth Joe Amalfitano popped out to first baseman Fairly. Jose Pagan flied out to Willie Davis in deep center. Willie McCovey pinch-hit for Pregenzer and walked on four pitches. Koufax got one strike on Kuenn, who hit a bouncer right back to him. Koufax carefully lobbed the ball over to Fairly after running almost to first for the putout.

Koufax was mobbed by his teammates as the crowd roared and sent a shower of seat cushions onto the field.[13] Koufax could be seen anxiously looking for his parents, who had recently relocated to the West Coast, but they were not to be seen as Koufax had forgotten to leave them tickets.[14]

Koufax believed that in his first no-hitter he had exceptional stuff, but did not think he had overpowering stuff this night. It was good but not great. Strikeouts tell the story. In his first no-hitter he had 13, but against the Giants only four, and none after the sixth inning.[15] He threw 111 pitches, relying more on breaking balls.[16]

When it was all over, Koufax had become the only active pitcher other than Warren Spahn with two no-hitters. He also joined Carl Erskine as the second pitcher in Dodgers history to pitch two no-hitters. It was the third no-hitter pitched at Dodger Stadium.[17]

Notably, Koufax had not yet allowed a run at Dodger Stadium in 1963 after having pitched 24⅔ innings.

The victory was the second and final time Koufax beat Marichal.

NOTES

1. Bob Hunter, "Koufax' No-Hit Voodoo Kayoes Injury Hex," *Los Angeles Herald-Examiner*, May 25, 1963.
2. Frank Finch, "Dodger Lefty Retires First 22 Batters in 8-0 L.A. Win," *Los Angeles Times*, May 12, 1963.
3. United Press International, "Koufax Triumphs on No-Hitter, 8-0," *New York Times*, May 12, 1963.
4. Melvin Durslag, "Perfecto Larsen Viewed Sandy's Classic Curving," *Los Angeles Herald-Examiner*, May 25, 1963. Larsen was a relief pitcher for the Giants in 1963.
5. "Koufax Rates 2nd No-Hitter First," *New York Times*, May 13, 1963.
6. Joe McDonnell, "Dodger Stadium's Most Memorable Moments … Koufax's Three No-Hitters," *1987 Dodger Scorebook*; Durslag.
7. Durslag.
8. Jane Leavy, *Sandy Koufax, A Lefty's Legacy* (New York: HarperCollins, 2002), 123.
9. Hunter.
10. Finch.
11. "Koufax Rates 2nd No-Hitter First."
12. Finch.
13. Ibid.
14. Leavy, 122.
15. Sandy Koufax with Ed Linn, *Koufax* (New York: Viking Press, 1966), 181-183.
16. "Koufax Rates 2nd No-Hitter First."
17. Bo Belinsky pitched a no-hitter for the Los Angeles Angels in Dodger Stadium on May 5, 1962.

SANDY KOUFAX'S THIRD NO-HITTER
JUNE 4, 1964: LOS ANGELES DODGERS 3, PHILADELPHIA PHILLIES 0, AT CONNIE MACK STADIUM, PHILADELPHIA

By Marc Z Aaron

THE LOS ANGELES DODGERS (21-25, and in eighth place) came to Philadelphia to play the league-leading Philadelphia Phillies (27-15). It was a great pitching matchup: Sandy Koufax (5-4) and Chris Short (3-2, 0.64 ERA).

Both pitchers set the side down in order in the first inning. In the second inning Tommy Davis singled but was erased on an inning-ending double-play ball. Koufax looked dominant from the beginning of the game, needing only six pitches to set the Phillies down in order in the second and picking up his third strikeout. Johnny Callison, Dick Allen, and Gus Triandos had all gone down swinging.

In the top of the third, Koufax lined a single to center with two out, but Willie Davis fouled out to third baseman Dick Allen. In the bottom half, Tony Taylor went down looking, Ruben Amaro hit a popup to first baseman Ken McMullen, and Chris Short went down swinging.

In the bottom of the fourth with two out, Koufax fell behind in the count 3-and-0 to Dick Allen. Two strikes and one foul ball later, Koufax walked Allen on a fastball that was three inches below the strike zone. Koufax later commented that he shook off the curve to throw the fastball.[1] Allen was erased from the basepaths when he attempted to steal on a 2-and-2 count with Danny Cater at bat. After the game Koufax said, "(Doug) Camilli had called for a curve, but I shook him off … then right in the middle of my windup I realized I had made a mistake, that Allen would be looking for the fast one. But just like you don't stop a golf shot on the backswing, I kept right on going. There was no doubt about the call. It was a ball."[2]

In the fifth inning Cater went down swinging, Triandos flied to center, and Sievers fouled out to first. In the sixth Taylor hit a grounder back to Koufax, and both Amaro and Short went down swinging at the air.

After six innings there had been only three hits, one error allowing a base, and just the one walk to Allen. A real pitching duel. The Dodgers had not scored a run in 19 straight innings.

In the top of the seventh, Gilliam grounded a ball up the middle and went to third on a line-drive single to right by Tommy Davis. On the next pitch from Chris Short, Frank Howard crushed his 14th home run of the season, the ball taking one hop on the arched roof of the left-field pavilion. Ken McMullen then singled to left but was out trying to stretch it into a double. Doug Camilli hit a fly ball to right for the second out. Dick Tracewski doubled to left, chasing Short from the mound. Ed Roebuck came in and got Koufax, his former teammate on the Dodgers, to ground out to short.

The Dodgers made some lineup changes in the bottom of the seventh. Wes Parker was now the right fielder and Ron Fairly came in to play first base. They replaced Frank Howard and Ken McMullen. Koufax faced Cookie Rojas and with two strikes Rojas flied out to left. Johnny Callison grounded back to Koufax and Allen hit a high chopper to Gilliam at third. Gilliam came running hard to grab it on the short hop and throw Allen out by three steps.

In the eighth Ray Culp replaced Roebuck. The Dodgers went down in order. In the bottom half of the inning Cater was out on a hard liner to right on the first pitch, and Triandos and Sievers went down swinging.

In the ninth, Tony Taylor struck out. Amaro, swinging at the first pitch, fouled out to first baseman Fairly, who caught the ball about 20 feet behind first. With two outs, Bobby Wine, batting .205 and 1-for-17 against Koufax, batted for Culp. With the count 1-and-2, Wine went down swinging. But not before he had fouled off the second pitch into the dirt. The ball bounced up and hit home-plate umpire Ed Vargo in the throat. Vargo didn't want to hold up the game and allow Koufax to cool off, even though he was having trouble breathing.[3]

Final score: Dodgers 3, Phillies 0. A crowd of 29,704, the biggest of the season so far, witnessed Koufax's third no-hitter. (The crowd for the game against the San Francisco Giants the next night exceeded the Dodgers' crowd by 2,000.) The game took 1 hour 55 minutes to play as Koufax faced the minimum 27 batters. He threw just 97 pitches and the only three-ball count was the one to Allen that resulted in Koufax's lone walk. Koufax struck out 12 Phillies in what was to be the only time he was to shut out the Phillies during his career. It was the 54th time he had struck out 10 or more batters. He joined Bob Feller as the only pitchers to throw three no-hitters in the twentieth century.[4]

Before the no-hitter the Dodgers had been defeated by the Phillies in eight of their nine previous contests.

Koufax remarked after the game, "This was the first time this season that I have been able to put everything together."[5] He was throwing differently than he had earlier in the season. He wasn't stepping as far to the left and not throwing as much across his body. He seemed to have better leverage on his follow-through. He had his old rhythm back. The fastball was overpowering and the curve cut the corners.[6]

Prior to this start, Koufax came across an issue of *Sport* magazine that featured a photo of him during his 1963 no-hitter against the Giants. From the photo angle, Koufax was able to detect a flaw in his stride.[7] He could see that he had to open up a little.[8]

On the bus from the stadium, Koufax remarked to pitcher Joe Moeller, "You know, I got away with a pitch. I hung a curve to Wine."[9] He faced the minimum number of batters and all he could think about was the one pitch that got away. Typical Koufax.

Don Drysdale, who lost 1-0 in 11 innings the night before, was not traveling with the team. When he heard the announcer reporting that Koufax had pitched his third no-hitter, Drysdale asked impatiently, "But did he win?"[10]

SOURCES

In addition to the sources cited in the Notes, the author also consulted Baseball-Reference.com and an article by Bob Hunter in the June 20, 1964, issue of *The Sporting News*.

NOTES

1. John Brogan, "Sandy Shook Off Curve, Fast Ball Walked Allen," *Philadelphia Bulletin*, June 5, 1964.
2. Associated Press, "Koufax Pitches His 3rd No-Hitter," June 4, 1964.
3. Allen Lewis, "Ump Vargo Refused to Leave Contest in spite of Painful Injury From Foul," *The Sporting News*, June 20, 1964. (Vargo would again be behind the plate when Koufax pitched his perfect game against the Cubs in 1965.)
4. Larry Corcoran and Cy Young accomplished the feat in the nineteenth century.
5. Associated Press, "Sandy Found a Flaw, Corrected It, and…," *Los Angeles Times*, June 5, 1964: B1.
6. "Koufax Pitches His 3rd No-Hitter."
7. Jane Leavy, *Sandy Koufax, a Lefty's Legacy* (New York: HarperCollins, 2002), 152.
8. Sandy Koufax with Ed Linn, *Koufax* (New York: Viking Press, 1966), 220.
9. Leavy, 154
10. Ibid.

"A MILLION BUTTERFLIES" AND ONE PERFECT GAME FOR SANDY KOUFAX
SEPTEMBER 9, 1965: LOS ANGELES DODGERS 1, CHICAGO CUBS 0, AT DODGER STADIUM

By Mike Huber

ON SEPTEMBER 9, 1965, Sandy Koufax became the first major-league pitcher to throw four no-hitters, and his record-setting accomplishment was a 1-0 perfect game.[1] In front of a relatively small crowd of 29,139 fans at Dodger Stadium, Koufax, who came into the contest against the Chicago Cubs with a 21-7 record, locked in a pitchers' duel with a fellow lefty, Bob Hendley, with a record of 2-2. As of the end of the 2015 season, this was the only perfect game thrown by a Dodgers pitcher.[2]

Hendley, just recalled from the minors, also pitched a brilliant game, giving up only one hit, and the only run scored off him was unearned. Koufax went him one better.

Cubs center fielder Don Young, in his major-league debut, led off the game with a popout to second baseman Jim Lefebvre. Koufax then struck out Glenn Beckert and Billy Williams looking. Hendley was equally sharp, getting the first three Los Angeles batters in order. Koufax was in top form, striking out at least one Chicago batter in every inning. Future Hall of Famer Ernie Banks struck out three times, all swinging. According to announcer Vin Scully, the first Banks strikeout came in the second inning on a forkball. Every Cubs batter except shortstop Don Kessinger struck out at least once. On the other side, Hendley had only three strikeouts, Koufax and Lefebvre (twice).

Hendley was in no danger though the first four innings. The only run came in the fifth. The Dodgers' Lou Johnson led off with a walk and advanced to second on a sacrifice by Ron Fairly. Vin Scully told his listeners that Hendley might have had a play at second base when he fielded the bunt, but he dropped the ball and got the sure out at first. With Lefebvre batting, Johnson stole third base and then continued home as Cubs catcher Chris Krug couldn't handle Hendley's pitch.

The Cubs had a chance in the sixth inning, when Chris Krug hit a groundball to shortstop Maury Wills. Wills's throw to first was in the dirt, but Wes Parker dug the ball out for the first out of the inning, preserving the string of consecutive outs. Kessinger then hit a grounder to third and was just erased, as third baseman Jim Gilliam was playing in for a possible bunt. Koufax then struck out Hendley to end the inning.

Both pitchers had no-hitters intact until the seventh inning, when the Dodgers had several exciting at-bats. Lead-off batter Gilliam hit a grounder to third baseman Ron Santo, who fielded the high bouncer and threw out Gilliam at first. Willie Davis followed with a slow grounder to first. Banks fielded the ball and then tagged out Davis, who tried sliding into the bag to avoid the tag. Johnson then hit a ball past first base that barely made it to the outfield grass before rolling into foul territory. By the time Banks retreated to field it, Johnson had motored to second base for a two-out double. However, he was stranded there as Fairly grounded out to short, and the Dodgers did not score, but Hendley's bid for a no-hitter was gone.

In the top of the eighth inning Koufax, facing the middle third of the Cubs' order, struck out Santo looking and Banks and Byron Browne swinging. The Dodgers tried to add a run in their half of the

eighth, but Jeff Torborg's long fly to left was caught by Browne in front of the bullpen gate.

Before the ninth inning, Vin Scully told his producers, "Let's make a recording."[3] Fans can still hear Scully call the final three outs. The Cubs had sent up two pinch-hitters. After Chris Krug struck out, Joey Amalfitano came on to bat for Kessinger and struck out swinging. The broadcast climaxed when Scully exclaimed, "Swung on and missed, a perfect game!" as Harvey Kuenn, who batted for Hendley, struck out to end the game.[4] The game lasted one hour and 43 minutes. The final six Chicago batters (and seven of the final nine) went down on strikes.

With his perfect game, Koufax surpassed Bob Feller's record of three no-hitters. Koufax's record stood for 16 years, until Houston Astros fireballer Nolan Ryan pitched his fifth no-hitter on September 26, 1981, against the Los Angeles Dodgers.

Hendley faced only 26 batters in his eight-inning gem. On any other day, his performance would have grabbed the top headlines. Five days after Koufax's perfect game, on September 14, 1965, he and Hendley faced each other again, this time at Chicago's Wrigley Field. The Cubs prevailed, as Hendley beat Koufax 2-1.

The Cubs had only three groundball outs. Koufax's 14 strikeouts were the highest strikeout total in a perfect game (equaled by Matt Cain on June 13, 2012). Koufax finished the season with 382 strikeouts, which bested Rube Waddell's 20th-century record of 349 set in 1904. But Nolan Ryan topped his record eight years later, striking out 383 in 1973.

Koufax finished the 1965 campaign with a record of 26-8. His earned run average was 2.04, and he pitched 27 complete games out of 41 starts.

SOURCES

In addition to the items cited in the notes, the author also consulted:

"The Cubs haven't been no-hit since Sandy Koufax pitched," http://ftw.usatoday.com/2013/08/the-cubs-havent-been-no-hit-since-sandy-...

"Sandy Koufax pitches perfect game," http://history.com/this-day-in-history/sandy-koufax-pitches-perfect-game.

"Sept. 9, 1965 — Sandy Koufax perfect game," http://latimes.com/local/.

http://baseballsiscokidstyle.blogspot.com/2014/09/sandy-koufax-becomes-first-pitcher-to.html

NOTES

1 Koufax's other no-hit games were pitched on June 30, 1962, May 11, 1963, and June 4, 1964.

2 A complete listing of all Dodgers no-hitters may be found at: "Los Angeles Dodgers no-hitters," http://nonohitters.com/los-angeles-dodgers-no-hitters/.

3 "Recorded History: Vin Scully Calls a Koufax Milestone," at http://npr.org/templates/story.php?storyId=9752592.

4 Harvey Kuenn, who struck out to end the perfect game, also made the last out in Koufax's 1963 no-hit game against the San Francisco Giants. In that game, Kuenn grounded out to the pitcher, Koufax.

KEN JOHNSON

By Steven D. Schmitt

EARLY IN 1966, WHEN IT WAS still unclear whether the Braves would take root in Atlanta or return to Milwaukee because of a pending court ruling, Ken Johnson was not worried. "If we have to go back to Milwaukee, it will be all right with me," Johnson said. "I liked it there. I like anyplace in the big leagues where I'm pitching."[1]

Born on June 16, 1933, Kenneth Travis Johnson grew up in West Palm Beach, Florida, the son of Ernest and Margie Johnson. His father was a bank teller. Johnson's brother, Ernest Jr., also called "Buddy," worked for the Pratt & Whitney aircraft plant before retirement. A sister, Shirley, died of breast cancer at age 45. Johnson was actually born left-handed but his father, out of habit, put Ken's baseball glove on his left hand and taught him to throw right-handed. Johnson eats and writes as a lefty but pitched professional baseball right-handed for 19 seasons. He played baseball at Palm Beach High School, where the coaches said, "If you're a serious baseball player, don't play any other sport." Like many high-school players, Johnson played American Legion baseball in the summer.[2] At age 18, he was a professional. At 32 he was a 16-game winner in the major leagues.

Johnson took a long road to the major leagues. In 1952 he reported to spring training in his hometown of West Palm Beach, Florida (where he had been a scoreboard boy), as an 18-year-old pitching prospect for the Philadelphia Athletics. He won 14 games for the Class A Savannah (Georgia) Indians of the South Atlantic League. Before joining the Army, Johnson pitched an 18-0 shutout against Charleston.[3] Back from the service in 1956, Johnson won 12 games for the Columbia (South Carolina) Gems, also of the South Atlantic League. Johnson started 30 games for the Little Rock Travelers of the Double-A Southern Association in 1957 and had 30 starts and 12 relief outings for the Buffalo Bisons of the Triple-A International League in 1958 before making his major-league debut for the Kansas City Athletics on September 13. Johnson gave up a second-inning grand slam to Washington Senators catcher Clint Courtney in a relief role. He made one more relief appearance against the Chicago White Sox and returned to the minors in 1959.

Johnson won 16 games for the Portland Beavers of the Triple-A Pacific Coast League with five shutouts and a 2.82 ERA. Called up late in the season, he lost his first major-league decision to Detroit's Jim Bunning at Briggs Stadium on September 22. Johnson lasted four innings and gave up a three-run home run to Harvey Kuenn. Four days later Johnson earned his first win in a start at Cleveland. Used mostly as a reliever in 1960, Johnson won his fifth game when the A's were 40 games under .500 and hurting at the gate, too.

By 1961, the Athletics had given up on Johnson, who had learned to throw a knuckleball pitching winter ball in Puerto Rico. When Dick Schofield homered off Johnson on a knuckler in spring training, manager Joe Gordon told him to stop throwing it. By May 6, Johnson was 0-4 with a 10.61 ERA and the Athletics sold him to the Toronto Maple Leafs of the International League, where he posted a 5-5 mark. In what Johnson later called the "biggest break of my career," he was traded to the Cincinnati Reds on July 21 for pitcher Orlando Pena and cash. Johnson joined the Reds immediately and helped them win the National League pennant with a 6-2 record and 3.25 ERA in 83 innings, three complete games in 11 starts, and one save.[4] Johnson won his first two starts, beat Mike McCormick, Bob Gibson, and Don Drysdale in August, and shut out the Phillies on September 4. The Reds won 14 of 22 games at the end of the regular season to win the pennant by four games over the Los Angeles Dodgers. In the World Series, which the Reds lost to the Yankees in five games, Johnson retired both batters he faced in former Kansas City teammate Bud Daley's Series-clinching victory for New York. (Roger Maris and Hector Lopez had played with Johnson, too.) Johnson looked forward to a full season with the National League champions in 1962.

Instead, the Houston Colt .45s selected him 29th in the National League expansion draft. The move reunited Johnson with Harry Craft, the Colt .45s' inaugural manager and Johnson's first skipper in Kansas City. Johnson took his new situation in stride, saying he would have had a tough time making the Reds' staff with prospects Ken Hunt and Jim Maloney joining an experienced group of starters. Johnson started throwing his knuckleball again, saying it made his other pitches more effective. Once, St. Louis third baseman Ken Boyer asked Johnson why he didn't throw his knuckler anymore. "The next time I faced him, I struck him out with the knuckler," Johnson said. Pitching for San Juan in the Puerto Rican League, Johnson fanned Giants slugger Orlando Cepeda twice on knuckleballs, pitched two 1-0 games and had a 4-2 record.

At the Colt .45s' spring-training camp at Apache Junction, Arizona, Johnson won two starts against the Los Angeles Angels, as Houston won the Cactus League. Craft named Johnson his second starter. In his first four starts, Johnson allowed nine earned runs in 29 innings but lost each game. His record was 0-5 when he won his first game on May 18 with a 10th-inning single after allowing a Willie McCovey tape-measure homer in the bottom of the ninth that tied the score, 2-2. Five days later Johnson became the first pitcher to beat Bob Purkey, who would go 23-5 for Cincinnati in 1962, with a 2-0 shutout. On June 3 Pittsburgh's Bob Skinner drove a Johnson delivery onto the right-field roof of Forbes Field, becoming only the fifth player to reach such heights, but Johnson had a respectable 4-7 record and 3.00 ERA through June 17.

Johnson objected to sportswriters calling him a hard-luck pitcher: "If people call me that long enough, that's what I'll become." But he had his share of hard luck during the season.[5] On September

12 Johnson stopped Maury Wills' 19-game hitting streak but lost his 15th game (against six wins), 1-0, at Colt Stadium on Frank Howard's fifth-inning home run. Until then, Johnson had not allowed a baserunner. There were some positive highlights as well that season. On August 14 against St. Louis, Johnson struck out 12 Cardinals batters, tying Turk Farrell for the club's single-game strikeout record. On September 18 Johnson's three sacrifice bunts along with an RBI helped beat Casey Stengel's "Amazin' Mets" for his seventh victory. Johnson (7-16) had a respectable 3.84 ERA and led the National League in strikeout/walk ratio with 178 strikeouts and 46 walks in 197 innings for an eighth-place team. The Colt .45s became the second franchise in major-league history with a pitching staff that recorded 1,000 strikeouts, and the club awarded each pitcher, including Johnson, a 14-karat-gold tie clasp with the engraving "1,000 Ks" at a pregame ceremony in August 1963.[6]

Johnson won 11 and lost 17 with a 2.65 ERA in 1963 for a ninth-place club that never reached the .500 mark. On April 17 he started against the San Francisco Giants and pitched 12 innings for a 2-1 victory as the .45s scored the deciding run in the top of the 13th.

On April 27 Johnson lost 1-0 to the Cincinnati Reds when Frank Robinson was awarded first base when rookie catcher John Bateman was called for interference after bumping into Robinson at the plate, and then scored on Johnny Edwards's single.[7] On July 15 at the Polo Grounds, the Mets' Carlton Willey hit a grand slam off Johnson, becoming the first Mets pitcher ever to hit a bases-loaded homer.[8] After a 3-2 complete-game loss to Bob Gibson and the Cardinals on August 14, and a 1-0 loss to Cincinnati's Joe Nuxhall on August 20, Johnson had a 6-17 record but won his last five decisions to end the season. On Opening Day 1964 in Cincinnati, Johnson became the first pitcher to put Houston in first place. He beat the Reds' Jim Maloney, 6-3, but it was a solemn occasion. Houston players wore black armbands in memory of Johnson's best friend and road roommate, pitcher Jim Umbricht, who had died of cancer five days earlier at the age of 33. Johnson dedicated the game to Umbricht. "I thought about him before the game," Johnson said. "All the fellows did." In his next start, Johnson beat another ace, Milwaukee's Tony Cloninger, one of four different Braves starters Johnson defeated that season.

Johnson's third start of 1964 was normally good enough to beat anyone. On April 23 he no-hit the Reds but lost, 1-0, when second baseman Nellie Fox's ninth-inning error scored Pete Rose, who had tried to bunt to break up the no-hitter and reached on Johnson's own throwing error. Johnson even suffered a bruised shin when Chico Ruiz hit a line drive to the mound in the ninth inning that turned into an out. "It's amazing," he said the next day, "how many people come up to me and start their sentences off the same way: 'Congratulations, Ken. That was sure a lousy break.' See what I mean? They give me congratulations and condolences at the same time. They don't know whether to feel glad or sad for me."[9] The 10th no-hit loss in major-league history got Johnson a guest appearance on the popular CBS *I've Got a Secret* game show four nights later. (Baseball buff Henry Morgan guessed Johnson's secret, that he had pitched a no-hitter and lost.)[10]

Johnson's lack of hitting support even drew the interest of a Mexican voodoo practitioner who had called the Colt .45s' Spanish-language radio announcer, Rene Cardenas, claiming that he could cast a good-luck spell on Johnson if he could obtain one of Johnson's old baseball gloves.[11]

During the second game of a twi-night doubleheader on May 23, Johnson fired a five-hit, 4-0 shutout against the Mets in a game that did not start until 11 P.M. due to several rain delays.

"We could have had him but I thought he was a seven-inning pitcher and now I see I'm right," said Casey Stengel. "After seven innings, he gives up a hit."[12] Johnson had lost his next two starts after the April 23 no-hitter and later lost two 1-0 games and another, 2-1. On July 18 he finally won a close one with some medical help. During a start at San Francisco's Candlestick Park, Johnson complained, "Every time the wind blows out on the mound, it feels like somebody is holding an ice cube against my back." Trainer Jim Ewell applied a thick coating of oil to Johnson's back between the fifth and sixth innings and Johnson won, 2-1.[13] In 11 of his 16 losses in 1964, Houston was either shut out or managed just a single tally.

The Braves must have remembered what Johnson had done against them when they traded outfielder Lee Maye for him and first baseman-outfielder Jim Beauchamp on May 23, 1965. The Colt .45s had become the Astros and were playing in the Harris County Domed Stadium, better known as the Houston Astrodome. Johnson had a 3-2 record for the Astros when he left for Milwaukee and had his first winning season for a lame-duck team that would move to Atlanta in 1966. Milwaukee had winning records at home and on the road, led the loop in home runs, and contended until early September, but the impending move kept fans away. The Braves drew just over 555,000 fans, last in the league. Johnson won 13 and lost 8 as the Braves' third starting pitcher and finished 16-10 overall. He beat the powerful Cincinnati Reds three times and the Pittsburgh Pirates twice, but lost twice to the Phillies' Ray Culp and twice to the eighth-place Cubs. Johnson's wife,

Lynn, recalled a family atmosphere in Milwaukee where wives got together for coffee and went to the games. The move to Atlanta was heavy on the minds of Milwaukee residents. "The Braves were leaving and the people there were upset about it," Lynn Johnson said. "They didn't do a lot of booing."[14]

Relocating to Atlanta meant the Johnsons would live closer to family. Mrs. Johnson's parents lived in Augusta, Georgia. "The wives would get apartments in the same complex," she added. "When the players went on the road, the wives would plan things to do together."[15]

On April 8, 1966, Johnson pitched the opening game of a three-game preseason exhibition series in Atlanta Stadium against the Yankees. In the second regular-season game, Johnson lasted just three innings and lost, 6-0, to the Pirates on Willie Stargell's two-run homer and RBI single. Three days later, Johnson was among 11 Braves fined for fraternizing with opposing players before a game with the Mets. On May 18 Johnson stopped Vernon Law's personal 10-game winning streak that stretched over two seasons. Johnson was the last to beat Law, on July 15, 1965.[16]

For the next month, Johnson struggled with tendinitis in his right shoulder but returned to beat the Pirates on June 10. Two weeks later, he ended the Braves' five-game losing streak, beating the Dodgers, 5-4, in the day half of a day-night twin bill at Dodger Stadium that drew 79,289 paid customers. Johnson went the distance, hit a home run, and had a 6-5 record. Manager Bobby Bragan said, "When Johnson goes out there, you know you're going to be in the game." Johnson replied, "Plenty of guys have more ability than I do. But I've worked hard to get where I am. I've put in plenty of long hours."[17]

In 1967 the Braves embraced the knuckleball, moving Phil Niekro into a starting role with Johnson and reacquiring catcher Bob Uecker to catch the dazzling deliveries. Niekro led the NL in earned-run average and Johnson won 13 games. The "Year of the Pitcher" in 1968 was not a good one for Johnson, who dropped to 5-8 on a .500 team on which he was reunited with former Houston manager Lum Harris. On May 10 Johnson was the winning pitcher and tossed a complete game in a 2-1 Braves victory in Atlanta over Los Angeles Dodgers' ace Don Drysdale, who proceeded to pitch a then-record 58⅔ scoreless innings and six shutouts over his next seven starts. The Braves won the NL West Division and faced the Eastern Division champion New York Mets in the 1969 NLCS, but Johnson was not there. The Braves sold him to the Yankees on June 10, but he was with them only two months before the Cubs bought him on August 11 as extra bullpen help for their NL East Division championship drive. Johnson had a 1-2 record in nine games including eight relief appearances. He was on the mound on September 7 when Don Kessinger's error and Richie Hebner's single produced two unearned runs in the 11th inning as the Cubs lost in extra innings to the Pirates at Wrigley Field before going on the road and free-falling out of first place. "It was fun until they started losing," Lynn Johnson remembered. Released by the Cubs in April 1970, Johnson pitched briefly for the Montreal Expos, his second expansion team, and pitched his last game on April 18, 1970.[18]

After his baseball career ended, Johnson returned to West Palm Beach and supervised the Work Ship program at Palm Beach Atlantic College. He found work sites for students to get real-world experience for a certain number of hours that the college required for graduation. Some of the assignments involved assisting those with disabilities, Lynn Johnson said. After that, Johnson coached baseball at Louisiana College in Pineville, where his son, Kenneth Travis Johnson Jr., got a baseball scholarship and later became a family practice physician. Another son, Russell "Rusty" Johnson, became a certified public accountant, while daughter Janet taught kindergarten in Alexandria, just across the Red River from Pineville, where the Johnsons lived in 2014. A grandson, Jason Johnson, a pediatric cardiologist in Memphis, lost an 11-month-old son to a severe heart condition. All three graduated from Louisiana Baptist College, where Ken had been assistant baseball coach for 10 years before retiring. "We babysat grandchildren so that the wives could work," Lynn Johnson said.[19]

On November 21, 2015, Johnson passed away at the age of 82 at his home in Pineville, Louisiana. His son, Kenneth, Jr., said that his father had been bedridden with Alzheimer's and Parkinson's diseases and that he died after contracting a kidney infection.[20] Most of Johnson's baseball experiences in recent years remained lost or clouded in his mind and he was unable to share them for purposes of this article because of Alzheimer's disease, which Lynn said he inherited from his father. In a brief conversation in the summer of 2014, Johnson did express appreciation to the author that an article would be published on his career, also intimating that Rose may have beaten out the play that was called an error.

Sadly, the *New York Times* online obituary is titled, "Ken Johnson, Only Loser of 9-Inning No-Hitter, Dies at 82."[21] His accomplishments thus deserve more attention, especially considering a professional baseball career that began at age 18, included 13 big-league seasons, and finally ended in 1970. How many ballplayers can say they started out with Connie Mack, pitched for two expansion teams and two jilted franchises, appeared in a World Series, threw a no-hitter, were part of a controversial franchise shift and a memorable collapse—and still coached his son in baseball and was able to enjoy six grandchildren and four great-grandchildren? The grand-kids got a big charge out of reading about Grandpa on the Internet, sitting on his lap as they did it. That is another memory Johnson shared and was able to take with him.

NOTES

1. Bob Wolf, "Milwaukee Just 'Two-Bit Town,' Bragan Spouts After Decision," *The Sporting News*, April 30, 1966: 6.
2. Lynn Johnson, telephone interview, December 12, 2013 (Lynn Johnson interview).
3. "Sally League Class A," *The Sporting News*, May 13, 1953: 32.
4. Clark Nealon, "Vet Server Johnson Shoots for No. 1 Job on Colts' Hill Corps," *The Sporting News*, February 21, 1962: 29.
5. Mickey Herskowitz, "'They'll Talk About It for 30 Years,' Says Loser Johnson," *The Sporting News*, May 9, 1964: 5.
6. "Colt 45s," *The Sporting News*, August 17, 1963: 18.
7. Major Flashes, "Interference Call Costly," *The Sporting News*, May 11, 1963: 27.
8. "Willey Slams Historic Blow," *The Sporting News*, July 27, 1963: 21.
9. *The Sporting News*, May 9, 1964.
10. Lynn Johnson interview; imdb.com/title/tt1212755/, accessed December 12, 2013; Mickey Herskowitz, "Woody Warns Hill Fraternity—'The Hitters Are Out to Get Us,'" *The Sporting News*, May 16, 1964: 13.
11. Mickey Herskowitz, "Colts Fire Salutes to Johnson's Start," *The Sporting News*, April 25, 1964: 25.
12. Dick Young, "Young Ideas," *The Sporting News*, May 30, 1964: 18. Not surprisingly, Casey's quote is somewhat misleading; Johnson actually gave up two hits in the second inning of that contest.
13. "Oiled Back Helps Johnson," *The Sporting News*, August 1, 1964: 25.
14. Lynn Johnson interview.
15. Lynn Johnson interview.
16. "Johnson Deals Law His Only Two Losses Since July '65," *The Sporting News*, June 4, 1966: 15; "National League," *The Sporting News*, July 9, 1966: 22.
17. Wayne Minshew, "Johnson Rare Jewel—Steady Teepee Hurler," *The Sporting News*, July 16, 1966: 8.
18. Lynn Johnson interview.
19. Lynn Johnson interview.
20. Bruce Weber, "Ken Johnson, Only Loser of 9-Inning No-Hitter, Dies at 82," *New York Times*. Obituary. November 23, 2015. http://www.nytimes.com/2015/11/24/sports/baseball/ken-johnson-82-only-loser-of-9-inning-no-hitter-dies.html?_r=1. Accessed November 25, 2015.
21. Ibid.

KEN JOHNSON NO-HITTER

APRIL 23, 1964: CINCINNATI REDS 1, HOUSTON COLT .45S 0, AT COLT STADIUM, HOUSTON, TEXAS.

By Steven D. Schmitt

MAKING BASEBALL HIS-tory is usually a shining moment or a dream come true.

For the Houston Colt .45s' knuckleball specialist, it was a nightmare.

On Thursday night, April 23, 1964, Ken Johnson pitched a brilliant nine-inning no-hitter against his former team, the pennant-contending Cincinnati Reds—and lost, 1-0. No major-league pitcher had ever met such a frustrating fate, though nine mound artists before him had lost no-hit games in extra innings. "It's a heady feeling to know that you have a niche in history," Johnson said. "So I made history tonight," grinning as he said it. "Heck of a way to get into the books, isn't it?"[1]

Ten days earlier, Johnson had beaten the Reds on Opening Day in Cincinnati for his sixth straight victory, dating back to 1963 when he was 10th lowest in National League earned-run average (2.65). He had dedicated the game to his fellow pitcher, road roommate, and best friend Jim Umbricht, who died of cancer just five days before.[2] Seeking his third win of the season, Johnson pitched a spectacular game before 5,426 fans at makeshift Colt Stadium. He recorded 12 groundball outs, nine strikeouts, and three infield popouts. Only three times did Reds batters reach the outfield. Johnson walked only two batters, both on full counts.[3]

By the seventh inning, Johnson was aware he had a no-hitter. He asked teammate Don Nottebart, who had pitched the first no-hitter in Colts history against the Philadelphia Phillies 11 months earlier, "How's a guy supposed to feel, Notty? What do you do?" Nottebart replied, "Stay loose and keep going."[4] The next inning, Johnson could have won his own game with a two-run homer when he sent left fielder Bob Skinner back to the base of the fence, a 365-foot drive that was caught for the third out.[5]

The game began with Johnson's strikeout of 1963 National League Rookie of the Year Pete Rose, who became the central figure in this history-making event. Winning pitcher Joe Nuxhall—who almost ruined the no-hitter when he nearly beat out a bunt—led off the ninth with a groundout to third baseman Bob Aspromonte.[6] Rose came up next and dropped a bunt on the third-base side of the mound, 15 to 20 feet in front of home plate. Johnson pounced on it, half straightened up and threw wildly to first baseman Pete Runnels and Rose made it to second. In the bottom of the inning, Houston coach Jimmy Adair asked first-base umpire Stan Landes if Rose could have beaten the throw. Landis answered curtly, "I don't have to tell you. If the (official scorer) wants to know, I'll tell him." Adair responded, "Why you chicken blanketyblank," and Landes gave him the heave-ho.[7]

With Rose on second, Chico Ruiz smashed a line drive off Johnson's shin that left a mark the shape and color of a large plum. Aspromonte fielded the carom and fired to Runnels at first to nip the speedy Ruiz as Rose took third. Needing one out to preserve the no-hitter and shutout, Johnson delivered to Vada Pinson, who hit a routine grounder to second baseman Nellie Fox. The normally surehanded Fox (in his first year with the Colts and 18th in the majors) fumbled the ball, allowing Rose to score as Pinson reached first.

Fox was near tears for making the error that caused Johnson to make history by losing. He approached Johnson in the Houston dressing room immediately afterward. "Ken, I'm sorry I had to mess it up," Fox said. "Don't feel bad about it, Nellie," Johnson replied as he put his arm around Fox's shoulder. "I put the guy on myself. I came up throwing. A good throw would have nailed him."[8]

Johnson confessed that he could not have continued into extra innings anyway because of the injury suffered on Ruiz's smash. "Even if we had tied it," he said, "I couldn't have gone on."[9] Frank Robinson flied out to Jimmy Wynn in left field to end the inning. The Colts had one last gasp in the bottom of the ninth when Runnels reached on Deron Johnson's error at first base with two outs. Landes called Runnels out but home-plate umpire Augie Donatelli overruled Landes, saying Johnson did not have control of the ball when he stepped on the first-base bag. The Reds played the game under protest.[10] Bob Lillis came in to run for Runnels but pinch-hitter Johnny Weekly was called out on strikes to end the game.

Johnson got both congratulations and condolences from teammates and fans but did not want sympathy and was not bitter. "What else can I do? I pitched the best game of my life," he said. "I can't feel bad because I lost it. I feel worse for the guys on the club. I guess that sounds funny but it's true."[11]

Johnson's modesty and class were one of many things unique about this game. Johnson had no-hit the team that gave him a chance to pitch in the 1961 World Series. Both pitchers went the distance in a snappy 1 hour and 56 minutes, Nuxhall pitching a five-hit shutout. Fox, who made the fateful error that decided the game, was the only player on either side to get two hits. Four days later, Johnson appeared on the CBS-TV game show *I've Got a Secret*. Panelist Henry Morgan, an avid baseball fan and a regular on the show, guessed that Johnson—referred to as "Mr. X"—had pitched a no-hitter and lost.[12]

Kenneth Travis Johnson spent 18 seasons in professional baseball and pitched for seven major-league clubs with a 91-106 lifetime record. Born in West Palm Beach, Florida, on June 16, 1933, Johnson died on November 21, 2015, at his home in Pineville, Louisiana, from complications of Alzheimer's disease. He was 82 years old.

SOURCES

In addition to the sources cited in the Notes, the author consulted Baseball-Almanac.com, Baseball-Reference.com, and some additional newspapers. Thanks to Lynn Johnson for an interview on December 12, 2013.

NOTES

1 Mickey Herskowitz, "A No-Hitter Nobody Could Ever Forget," *The Sporting News*. May 9, 1964: 5.

2 *The Sporting News*, April 25, 1964: 22.

3 Ibid; "Colt Spins No-Hitter, Loses," *Dallas Morning News*. April 24, 1964: Sec. 2, p. 1.

4 Murray Chass, "Ken Johnson Makes History in Losing Nine-Inning No-Hitter," *Portsmouth* (Ohio) *Times*, April 24, 1964: 18.

5 "Colts' Johnson Loses No-Hit Game, 1-0," *Chicago Tribune*, April 24, 1964: C1.

6 "Colt Spins No-Hitter, Loses."

7 Herskowitz.

8 "My Fault, Says Colts' Big Loser," *Chicago Tribune*, April 24, 1964: C1.

9 Herskowitz.

10 "Colt Spins No-Hitter, Loses."

11 Murray Chass.

12 carsonscrafts.com/igas/igas_1964.htm#4-27. I've Got a Secret Episode Guide. Week 620. April 27, 1964. Accessed April 5, 2016.

BILL STONEMAN

By Norm King

BILL STONEMAN STARTED out as a Vandal and ended up as an Angel. No, Stoney, as he was known, was not a wayward soul who found redemption. Rather, he has had a long, successful career in baseball and business, during which he took some Lip, put a franchise that was barely out of diapers on the map, made some Canadian history, and built a World Series champion for good measure. His varied résumé includes an eight-year career as a major-league pitcher with a fall-off-the-table curveball, a stint in the banking industry, and success in management with the Montreal Expos and the Anaheim Angels.

William Hambly Stoneman III was born on April 7, 1944, in Oak Park, Illinois, a suburb of Chicago, to William Hambly Stoneman Jr. and his wife, Kathryn. His father did mechanical engineering, although he did not have a degree in the field. Bill also had three brothers, Rick, Jim, and John. Stoneman's family had deep roots both in the Windy City and baseball. "My mother's mother and a good friend of hers all attended the Babe Ruth "called shot" game [in the 1932 World Series at Wrigley Field]," he said. "She was a Cubs fanatic."[1]

The family moved to West Covina, California, east of Los Angeles, in 1954. Stoneman began playing in local Little League and Pony League programs, and, contrary to conventional wisdom, started throwing curveballs while still a boy. "They say that kids shouldn't be allowed to throw curves until they're in their late teens," he said, "but I've been throwing them since I was 10."[2] Stoneman took his curveball to West Covina High School, then to nearby Mount San Antonio Junior College, where the local media selected him to the Eastern Conference First All-Star team team.

After one year at Mount San Antonio, Stoneman enrolled at the University of Idaho in 1963, and joined the rotation of the school's baseball team. The club was called the Vandals, but the only things Stoneman broke were the school's record for victories by a pitcher, and the confidence of more than one opposing hitter. In 1965 he led the league in strikeouts and ERA and was chosen to the Big Sky Conference's First All-Star Team. He followed that up in 1966 by leading the Vandals to a 34-9 record and the conference championship, posting a 7-2 record with a 0.45 ERA.

Stoneman put up amazing numbers during his three seasons in Idaho, going 17-10 with a 1.44 ERA and 245 strikeouts in 192⅔ innings pitched. His last start as a Vandal was not memorable, as he lost 3-2 to the University of Arizona Wildcats in the first game of a two-game district playoff. The 'Cats won the next game as well and went on to the College World Series.

Despite that loss, Stoneman's numbers got him some attention, and after graduating with a bachelor's degree in business, Stoneman entered the June 1966 amateur draft. He was noticed by Chicago Cubs scout Gene Handley, who had been sent to scout another player, and Handley recommended that the Cubs draft him. They chose Stoneman in the 31st round, but would have selected him sooner had it not been for human error.

"Somehow [Stoneman's] card was misplaced [on draft day] and we had concluded our draft calls when the card was finally found," explained Cubs vice president John Holland. "It was then we made the call, very much surprised that he was still available."[3]

Stoneman may have set a record for change-of-address-card usage in 1966 by playing at three levels in three states during his first year as a professional. His first assignment was with Chicago's Rookie-level Pioneer League affiliate in Caldwell, Idaho, known as the Treasure Valley Cubs. From there he joined the Class-A Lodi Crushers of the California League, then moved up to the Dallas-Fort Worth Spurs of

the Double-A Texas League. Overall he appeared in 22 games, but started only twice, compiling a 1-2 record with a respectable 2.70 ERA in just 40 innings.

"I think relief is Stoneman's best asset," said Treasure Valley manager George Freese. "He has a sharp breaking curve and is quick enough."[4]

If the technology were available in those days, Stoneman would have kept the moving companies on speed dial again in 1967. After missing spring training while attending graduate school at the University of Oklahoma (where he received a master's in education), he started the season in Dallas-Fort Worth. He pitched 12 innings in five relief appearances before getting called up to the Tacoma Cubs of the Triple-A Pacific Coast League. As fate would have it, the parent Cubs, in desperate need of pitching, played an exhibition game against Tacoma on July 12. Despite being in only his second year of professional baseball, Stoneman turned heads when he came on in the sixth with the score tied 5-5, and held the big leaguers scoreless for three frames. Chicago won the game 7-5 in 10 innings, but more importantly for Stoneman, he earned a trip to "The Show" a few days later and made his major-league debut on July 16, 1967.

Cubs manager Leo "The Lip" Durocher didn't mind giving Stoneman a baptism by fire, starting him in the second game of a doubleheader against the power-laden San Francisco Giants.[5] Stoneman had an impressive outing, giving up only two earned runs in 5⅓ innings as the Cubs won 3-2. Stoneman did not get the win. He pitched well in his second start, five days later, also against the Giants, giving up only one earned run in 4⅓ innings. Again, he didn't get the win. Despite two very respectable starts, Durocher used Stoneman as a reliever the rest of the season. He went 2-4 with four saves and had a 3.29 ERA. He also acquired the nickname "Toy Tiger" from his teammates for both his tenacity on the mound and his relatively slight (5-foot-10) stature.

Uncle Sam had a big impact on Stoneman's 1968 season. This was still the era of the military draft, and Stoneman spent most of spring training again, except for a few weekends, fulfilling his commitment to the Arizona National Guard. With his chance to prepare for the season off-kilter, Stoneman had a tough time getting on track, and with two weeks of active National Guard duty looming in June, the Cubs sent him back to Tacoma on May 23 after he had pitched in only seven games, with a record of one blown save and a 6.75 ERA. That blown save occurred on April 30 against Pittsburgh when he hung a curveball to Manny Mota with two out and two on in the bottom of the ninth and the Cubs leading 3-2. Mota smacked the pitch for a two-run double, giving the Pirates a 4-3 win. Stoneman got plenty of lip from Leo the next day.

"They didn't give you that signing bonus of $100,000 for your curveball," said Durocher. "They gave it to you because of your fastball. I want you to throw your fastball late in the game until they hit it off the [scoreboard] clock in center field."

The problem with Durocher's tirade was that he thought he was talking to the Cubs' number-one draft pick, Dean Burk. Nonetheless, Stoneman was restricted from using his curveball the rest of the year.

He returned to the Cubs on June 27, and worked only sporadically for the remainder of the season. For the year, Stoneman pitched only 29⅓ innings (all in relief), and had an 0-1 record, two blown saves (the second one came against the Cardinals), and a 5.52 ERA. Not surprisingly, he was left off of the Cubs' protected list for the 1968 expansion draft. On October 14, 1968, the brand-new Montreal Expos selected him with the 19th pick.

"Really, I wasn't surprised the Cubs didn't protect me in the draft, and I had a feeling I would go to the Expos," Stoneman said. "Especially after Gene Mauch was named Montreal manager. I'd been told Mauch liked my style of pitching."

It would be hard to find a player who had a rougher start than Stoneman to a season only to reach unheard-of peaks within the first two weeks of a new franchise's existence. He started the second game of the opening series against the Mets and lasted only a third of an inning, giving up four earned runs and leaving the game with an ERA of 108.00. He was better in his second start, a tough 7-6 loss to his former team, the Cubs. He pitched 8⅓ innings and was charged with all seven Cubs runs, but only one was earned.

Then came his third start.

The New York Mets joined the National League in 1962 and didn't have a pitcher throw a no-hitter until 2012. The Expos' expansion cousins, the San Diego Padres, were still awaiting their first no-no as of 2016. That makes what Stoneman did on April 17, 1969, all the more remarkable, as he pitched a no-hitter against the Philadelphia Phillies in just the ninth game of the Expos' existence.

Stoneman walked five and struck out eight in what proved to be his first win as an Expo and only the fourth in the team's history. It was also the first complete game of Stoneman's career. Jerry Johnson took the loss for the Phillies in front of only 6,496 fans at old Connie Mack Stadium in Philadelphia.

The Expos' reaction to the no-hitter seems almost quaint by today's standards. Management ripped up Stoneman's contract and gave him a new one with a $2,000 raise. Then, between games of an April 20 doubleheader against the Cubs, the public-address announcer asked fans to stay in their seats and then called Stoneman out of the dugout. Team president John McHale pointed to a new Renault car in center field, a gift from the Renault Company. However, the big surprise came when one of the car's doors opened and out stepped Stoneman's mother and a brother just back from Vietnam.

The no-hitter was one of the few pitching bright spots for the first-year Expos. Stoneman went 11-19 with a 4.39 ERA, leading the team in both wins and losses. He led the league in walks with 123, and hit batsmen with 12. He did pitch five shutouts, which remains the franchise record (later tied by Steve Rogers twice and by Dennis Martinez and Carlos Perez).

Despite having such a poor record, and enduring the team's 52-110 season, Stoneman said he had fond memories of his early days with the Expos. "The early years of the Expos were a great time," said Stoneman. "Even though we only won 52 games in 1969, people cheered from the first out to the last, and we drew 1.4 million, which was pretty good attendance then." (The Expos' attendance in their debut year was actually 1.2 million.)

"Being on an expansion team didn't matter. We were happy to be in the majors and in Montreal. We loved playing there. It was like going to Europe and getting paid for it. We got a taste of a culture we didn't even know was there."[6]

On the flight that brought the Expos to Montreal after they opened the season on the road, Stoneman met Diane Falardeau, an Air Canada stewardess, as they were called in those days. He offered her two tickets to an Expos game and she went, even though she didn't know anything about baseball. It seemed that fastballs worked better than fast talk, and they were married in December 1969. They have two children, daughter Jill and son Jeff.

Maybe it was newlywed's euphoria, but for whatever reason, Stoneman had a poor season in 1970, going 7-15 with a 4.59 ERA. Control was again a problem, as he issued 109 walks (tied for third in the NL with Steve Carlton of the Phillies) and he led the league in hit batsmen with 14.[7] Typical of Stoneman's season was his four-hitter against San Francisco on May 5 in a 4-1 loss at Jarry Park. More specifically, he hit four batters in that game, Ken Henderson (twice), Dick Dietz, and future teammate Ron Hunt. Responding to charges that Stoneman was hitting the batters deliberately, the Expos' Gene Mauch defended his pitcher, sort of. "If Stoneman could throw the ball exactly where he wanted to, he wouldn't have walked 160 batters last year," Mauch said.[8] (As noted, Stoneman walked 123 batters in 1969.)

Prior to the 1971 season, Mauch seemed to have developed a different opinion of Stoneman's potential, telling UPI sports editor John Griffin that he was ready to "blossom out" any time.[9] Mauch's comment was prescient; Stoneman was hot right out of the gate, building up a 9-4 record by mid-June. He finished with a 17-16 record, a 3.15 ERA, and 294⅔ innings pitched, the only season of his career in which he won more games than he lost. He also led the league again in walks allowed with 146 (still a franchise record as of 2015). Two slumps prevented Stoneman from reaching the 20-win mark. He lost five of six decisions from June 20 to July 10, including three one-run games, and five of seven from August 10 to September 5. Still, all in all, it was a career year. Stoneman felt that pitching a lot of innings was necessary for success.

"I feel that if I pitch 300 innings, the other things will take care of themselves," he said. "To pitch 300 innings, there have to be so many complete games and you'd have to think so many wins."[10]

Stoneman followed up his 1971 season by earning two honors in 1972, both for the only time in his career. His only career Opening Day start on April 15 was a showdown against Bob Gibson and the St. Louis Cardinals. Gibson was gone after six, but Stoney was masterful, going all the way for a 3-2 win in which he struck out eight and walked only one. Al Santorini took the loss.

Stoneman also received his only All-Star selection in 1972, becoming the first Expo not named Rusty Staub to make the team.[11] He went to the mound for the seventh inning with the NL leading 2-1 and set down Dick Allen, Carl Yastrzemski (via strikeout), and Bobby Grich in order. He wasn't so lucky in the eighth, allowing a single to Carlton Fisk and a two-run homer to Cookie Rojas to give the American League squad a 3-2 lead. His NL teammates bailed him out by tying it up in the ninth and winning in the 10th.

Aside from the Opening Day start and the All-Star appearance, the 1972 season was frustrating for Stoneman because he didn't win consistently. He won four of five decisions between May 23 and July 7, then lost eight of his next 11 decisions. He had an 11-14 record going into his last start of the season, on October 2 in the first game of a twi-night doubleheader against the Mets at Jarry Park. Despite giving up seven walks that night, Stoneman pitched the second no-hitter of his career, a historic 7-0 win that was the first such gem ever pitched in the majors outside the U.S. It was also the last complete game of Stoneman's career, making him the only pitcher in major-league history to pitch no-hitters in his first and last complete games.[12]

Stoneman's 1973 season started off poorly and only got worse from there. He held out for five days, then bursitis in his shoulder prevented him from pitching in spring training until March 19, when he went 1⅔ innings against the Baltimore Orioles. The Expos put him on the 21-day disabled list on March 30, and he didn't make his first appearance of the year until May 5, when he went 4⅓ innings and got a no-decision in an 8-6 Expos win over Cincinnati. Things didn't get much better, as he lost four of his first five starts.

Stoneman got his last win as an Expo in the first game of a doubleheader against the Braves in Atlanta on July 13, and even with the victory, his day was a complete disaster. He left the first game after five innings trailing 7-1 (all runs were earned), but the Expos scored seven in the top of the sixth to taker an 8-7 lead. Having thrown enough innings to qualify for the win, and being the pitcher of record when the Expos rallied, Stoneman got the W despite a poor performance. Since Mauch had probably never heard of pitch counts, he decided to use Stoneman again in the eighth inning of the second game, with the Expos trailing 9-6. Stoneman gave up six earned runs, and while he wasn't tagged with the loss, he ruined any chance the Expos had of making a comeback. Stoneman's ERA on July 12 was 6.29; after that day's shellacking, it was 7.52. Stoneman finished the year with a 4-8 record and a 6.80 ERA.

Stoneman signed his 1974 contract before spring training started. When asked why he didn't use an agent to negotiate on his behalf, Stoneman said, "You don't need a lawyer to tell the club you had a lousy year."[13]

That "lousiness" continued into spring training, and on April 4 the Expos sold the 30-year-old former All-Star to the California Angels for an undisclosed amount of cash. After going 1-1 in his first two decisions, Stoneman lost seven straight. By July 1, he was 1-8 with a 6.14 ERA. The Angels cut him on July 12 and his playing career was over.

"I just don't have the stuff any more. It wasn't like 1970 when I had a bad season. I didn't know how to pitch then, but I knew I had a good curveball.

"This time I knew how to pitch, but my curve wasn't sharp any more. It wasn't a matter of a sore arm. I had just picked up too many bad habits to shake."[14]

Unlike most former Expos players, Stoneman continued to live in Canada after his baseball career ended. He got into a management training program with Royal Trust, a Canadian financial institution; he spent the first few years of his new career in Montreal before being transferred to Toronto. One day in 1983, while returning home from a family vacation, he stopped at Montreal's Olympic Stadium to say hello to some friends and former teammates. Expos president John McHale asked Stoneman to drop by his office. "When I saw John McHale, he said, 'Have you ever thought about coming back into baseball?' I kind of looked at him and said, 'No! I hadn't.' I was telling the truth—I hadn't."[15] He joined the Expos on November 28, 1983, to work in the areas of player relations and contract negotiations.

Stoneman remained with the Expos until 1999, climbing the corporate ladder until he eventually became the team's vice president of baseball operations. He left the Expos that year to join the Angels as their general manager.

"It was time to do something different," explained Stoneman about the move. "There was an ownership change in Montreal that was going to happen. It was a natural time to leave."[16]

The Angels had finished last in the American League West with a 70-92 record. One of Stoneman's first acts was to hire Mike Scioscia as manager. Together, they took the team to its first-ever World Series championship when the Angels defeated the San Francisco Giants in 2002. Stoneman stepped down as GM in 2007, but remained with the team as a consultant. He briefly took over the reins again in 2015 when incumbent Jerry DiPoto stepped down, but left after the season. As of 2016, Stoneman and his wife lived in the Anaheim area.

Special thanks to Tim Mead of the Los Angeles Angels for his assistance.

SOURCES

In addition to the sources cited in the Notes, the author also used the following:

Brandon (Manitoba) *Sun.*

Chicago Tribune.

Daily InterLake (Kalispell, Montana).

Lewiston (Idaho) *Morning Tribune.*

Los Angeles Daily News.

Mtsac.edu.

San Bernardino County Sun.

WestCovina.org.

NOTES

1. George Castle, *Where Have All Our Cubs Gone?* (Lanham, Maryland: Taylor Trade Publishing, 2005), 90.
2. Ted Blackman, "It's as Easy—or Easier Than Building a TV set," *Montreal Gazette*, May 27, 1971.
3. James Enright, "Toy Tiger 34th Cub Draft Pick in '66," *The Sporting News*, May 3, 1969.
4. "Cubs Near Door of Leader Ogden," *Idaho Free Press* (Nampa, Idaho), August 31, 1966.

NO-HITTERS

5   The Giants were second in the National League in home runs in 1967 with 140. The Atlanta Braves led with 158.

6   Al Doyle, "Bill Stoneman: The Game I'll Never Forget: Right-Hander Who Tossed Two No-Hitters During His Career Recalls Victory Over Padres in Which He Fanned 14 Batters," *Baseball Digest*, June 2005.

7   The Expos' starting rotation was a free-pass factory in 1970. Carl Morton led the National League with 125 walks and Steve Renko was fifth with 104. The staff as a whole gave up 716 bases on balls, far and away the highest number in the NL.

8   Ted Blackman, "Red Hair, Strong Arm—Morton Ticket to Montreal," *The Sporting News*, May 23, 1970: 26.

9   John G. Griffin, "Expos Fans Have High Hopes; Mauch Shooting for 81 Wins," *News-Herald* (Franklin, Pennsylvania): 13.

10 Ian MacDonald, "Stoney Shuns Goals, Piles Up Victories," *The Sporting News*, August 7, 1971: 21.

11 Staub represented the Expos at the All-Star Game during the franchise's first three seasons, 1969-71. The Expos traded him to the New York Mets prior to the 1972 season.

12 baseball-reference.com/bullpen/Bill_Stoneman.

13 "Walton's Skin Color Surprises Black Coach," *La Crosse (Wisconsin) Tribune*, March 9, 1974: 22.

14 Tim Burke, "Stoneman Calls It a Career With 'Too Many Bad Habits," *Montreal Gazette*, August 14, 1974: 19.

15 Bill Stoneman, Bill Kirwin, "Interview With Bill Stoneman, General Manager, Anaheim Angels," *Nine: A Journal of Baseball History and Culture*, Volume 10, Number 2, Spring 2002: 172.

16 Murray Chass, "Baseball: Inside Baseball; Stoneman Maneuvers Out of the Angels' Spotlight," *New York Times*," November 3, 2002.

STONEY SETS RECORD FOR FASTEST NO-HITTER BY A FRANCHISE

APRIL 17, 1969: MONTREAL EXPOS 7, PHILADELPHIA PHILLIES 0, AT CONNIE MACK STADIUM

By Adam J. Ulrey

IT SEEMS THAT THE EXPOS wanted to give their fans a lifetime of memories as quickly as possible.

As if the inaugural game at Shea Stadium or the first home win at Jarry Park weren't memorable enough, the Expos quickly adopted a flair for the dramatic in just the franchise's ninth game, on April 17, 1969. That night, Bill Stoneman pitched a no-hitter against the Philadelphia Phillies, allowing *Nos Amours*–a French expression meaning Our Loves–to achieve the feat more quickly than any other team.[1]

Montreal came into the game at Connie Mack Stadium with a 3-5 record and was playing its seventh game on the road after two at Jarry Park. What made this game more improbable was Stoneman's career to date. Drafted in 1966 in the 31st round by the Chicago Cubs, he was called up to the big leagues in 1967 and went 2-5 over the next two years, mostly as a reliever. He earned the nickname Toy Tiger as much for his size (5-feet-10), as for his determination. Chicago manager Leo Durocher gave Stoneman only two starts, while using him in relief 44 times. The Expos selected Stoneman with the 10th pick in the 1968 expansion draft, viewing him as a starter even though he had only two starts in his major-league career. Going into this contest, he had an 0-2 record and a 5.00 ERA.

Stoneman's inexperience showed in his first appearance of the season, when he gave up four earned runs in 1/3 of an inning against the Mets and left the game with a 108.00 ERA. His second outing was slightly better: He pitched 8⅔ innings and gave up all seven runs (but only one earned) in a 7-6 loss to the Cubs. His teammates made three errors behind him.

In this game, though, the defense was excellent from the beginning. Center fielder Don Bosch recovered from a late jump to grab a sinking fly ball by Don Money in the second. In the next inning, Rusty Staub preserved the no-hitter when he snared a liner off the bat of Tony Taylor.

As historic a night as it was for Stoneman, some of his teammates also had noteworthy evenings. In addition to his fielding heroics, Staub put on a batting clinic with four hits, including three doubles and a fourth-inning home run, his third of the season. Staub had 10 total bases in the game and drove in three runs. Le Grand Orange was blossoming.

Also joining the hit parade was rookie Coco Laboy, who rapped out four singles and drove in a run to help the Expos to their fourth win of the year.

Phillies pitchers had forgettable nights. Starter Jerry Johnson went eight innings and gave up four runs (three earned) on 11 hits. The Expos opened the scoring with an unearned run in the third. Laboy singled and went to second when Gary Sutherland reached on an error. After Stoneman struck out, Laboy scored when Tony Taylor made the Phillies' second error of the inning, this time on a Bosch grounder.

Staub homered leading off the fourth inning and with the Expos in front 2-0 in the sixth, run-scoring singles by Ty Cline and Laboy upped the lead to 4-0. In the ninth the Expos put the game away for good with three more runs off Bill Wilson. Staub doubled with the bases loaded, plating Stoneman and Bosch and moving Maury Wills to third. Turk Farrell replaced Wilson and allowed Wills to score on a wild pitch to make the score 7-0.

Stoneman's determination showed in the ninth inning as he finished the game in style, striking out Ron Stone and Johnny Briggs, and then inducing the dangerous Deron Johnson to ground out to Wills. Overall, Stoneman faced 31 batters, struck out eight and walked five. Stoneman later admitted that he wasn't overpowering that night.

"People think that a pitcher who throws a no-hitter totally dominates the game, but that isn't always true," he said. "I had trouble with my control and gave up five walks, which is something that happened a lot in my career."[2]

As sweet as the win was for the players, this game also provided some revenge for Expos manager Gene Mauch, who was fired by the Phillies after 53 games the previous season. Not only did his new team lay a beating on his old one, but he was serenaded by the fans chanting "we want Mauch" from the seventh inning until the end of the game.[3]

The Expos' reaction to the event seems almost quaint by today's standards. Management ripped up Stoneman's contract and gave him a new one with a $2,000 raise. Then, between games of an April 20 doubleheader against the Cubs, public address announcer Claude Mouton asked fans to stay in their seats and then called Stoneman out of the dugout. Team president John McHale pointed to a new Renault car in center field, a gift from the Renault Company. However, the big surprise came when one of the car's doors opened and out stepped Stoneman's mother along with a brother just back from Vietnam.

Nonetheless, Stoneman's first no-hitter was no fluke. He repeated the feat on October 2, 1972, at Montreal's Jarry Park against the Mets, winning by the same 7–0 score. Stoneman struck out nine, but had control problems, walking seven. Ironically, this was the last complete game of his career. He is the only pitcher in major league history to pitch no-hitters in his first and last career complete games.

SOURCES

In addition to the sources listed in the notes, the author consulted:

Ballparks.com

Blackman, Ted. "Stoney Staggered by Montreal Huzzahs Over No-Hitter," *The Sporting News*, May 3, 1969.

Baseball-reference.com.

Conniemackstadium.com.

King, Norman. "Expos get first franchise no-hitter right out of the gate," *Baseball Research Journal*, Spring 2002.

Philadelphia Athletics Historical Society.

NOTES

1. In the expansion era, the California Angels held the previous record, when Bo Belinsky pitched a 2-0 no-hitter against Baltimore on May 5, 1962, in the franchise's 181st game.
2. Al Doyle, "Bill Stoneman: The Game I'll Never Forget: Right-Hander Who Tossed Two No-Hitters During His Career Recalls Victory Over Padres in Which He Fanned 14 Batters," *Baseball Digest*, June 2005.
3. Jacques Doucet and Marc Robitaille, *Il était une fois les Expos, Volume I* (Montreal: Éditions Hurtubise Inc., 82.

STONEY'S SECOND NO-NO
OCTOBER 2, 1972: MONTREAL EXPOS 7, NEW YORK METS 0, AT JARRY PARK

By Norm King

ON SEPTEMBER 28, 1972, the entire country of Canada ceased to function. Businesses closed. Kids were let out of school. The occasion was Game Eight of the epic hockey series between a team of Canadian National Hockey League players and the Soviet national team. The series, which Team Canada was expected to win in a skate, had come down to the final game with the series tied at three wins each and one tie. Canucks from coast to coast to coast watched intently as the final minutes ticked away with the score tied 5-5. Finally, Paul Henderson scored with 34 seconds left to play to seal the series victory for Canada and send an entire nation into a state of delirium. Take the Miracle on Ice, multiply by 10, and you will understand the elation Canadians felt after Henderson scored that goal.

Perhaps it was because of the afterglow of that event, or the cool October weather, that only 7,184 hardy souls attended a twi-night doubleheader between the Montreal Expos and the New York Mets at Jarry Park on October 2, 1972. They saw something in the first game that no one had ever seen before–the first major-league no-hitter ever pitched on other than American soil.

"There was only one way, it seems, that we could knock Team Canada from the front page," said Expos president John McHale. "That was for Stoneman to throw a no-hitter—and he did."[1]

The Mets and Expos were winding down disappointing seasons. The Mets had a 79-72 record, good for third place in the National League East Division, 15 games behind the eventual division champion Pittsburgh Pirates. Since coming from nowhere to win the World Series in 1969, they had won 83 games in 1970 and 1971, and would do so again in 1972.

The Expos were 69-82 in their fourth season of existence. Since winning 73 games in 1970 when manager Gene Mauch "predicted "70 in 70" for what was then a second-year franchise, the Expos hadn't improved at all. They went 71-90 in 1971 and were on their way to a 70-86 season in 1972 (the season was shortened by a players' strike at the beginning of the year).[2]

The two starting pitchers had both been slumping. Mets starter Jim McAndrew was in the midst of a losing streak. After defeating the Phillies on September 12 to go 11-5, he had lost his next two starts, including a 4-0 whitewash in St. Louis. Similarly, Stoneman would never sing "Try to Remember That Kind of September" after the month he went through. In seven appearances, he went 1-5 with a 3.86 ERA. Somebody was due to have a good game.

It was clear from the get-go that that somebody was not to be McAndrew. After Stoneman struck out the side in the first (he also walked John Milner), the Expos struck quickly in the bottom of the inning. Leadoff hitter Ron Hunt doubled, moved to third on a Tim McCarver fly ball, and scored on a wild pitch. He would have come home anyway because after Ken Singleton struck out, Ron Fairly gave Montreal a 2-0 lead with a home run.

The Expos put it away in the bottom of the third. McAndrew plunked Hunt to lead off the inning.[3] Hunt moved to third on McCarver's single to center, and scored on Ken Singleton's single; Singleton advanced to second on the throw to the plate. One out later, Jim Fairey was walked intentionally to load the bases for Boots Day. Boots belted the ball to right for a bases-clearing triple to give the Expos a 6-0 lead after three.

The Expos' final run, off Mets reliever Brent Strom in the fourth, was a singular achievement. Singleton singled home Hunt, who had singled and moved to second on McCarver's single. That made the score 7-0.

A big lead after four innings certainly doesn't guarantee a no-hitter. It doesn't even assure victory, at least not in baseball. The Mets came close to scoring in the fifth when Bill Sudakis walked with one out, moved to second when Stoneman flubbed a Don Hahn grounder and to third when Ted Martinez hit into a fielder's choice. With two on and two out, Stoneman fanned pinch-hitter Dave Marshall to end the Mets' only real scoring threat.

Stoneman's performance from the sixth inning on was marked by an oddity in that he didn't have a single three-up-three-down inning. He walked two batters in the sixth and one in each in the seventh, eighth, and ninth. He also left one runner on base in each frame (Lute Barnes, who received the first base on balls in the sixth, was erased on a double play).

The Mets' relief corps did a fine job. Strom, who came on with one out in the third, allowed one run. Bob Rauch pitched three scoreless innings and Ray Sadecki gave up one walk in working the eighth.

This was the second no-hitter of Stoneman's career, making him the 16th pitcher in the 20th century to pitch two gems. His first no-hitter was also historic as it came in the ninth game of the Expos' existence on April 17, 1969, and was the first ever thrown in an expansion team's debut season. When he left the major leagues he was the only pitcher to toss no-hitters in his first and last career complete games.

The two games were also similar statistically. In the 1969 game, Stoneman struck out eight and walked five. He struck out nine and walked seven in the 1972 one. Seven walks sounds high, but according to Expos manager Gene Mauch, they were the result of smart pitching rather than of poor control.

"Most of his walks tonight were because he made certain he didn't give the batters anything decent to hit after he fell behind," Mauch explained. "He simply said to hell with this and just gave them nothing to hit."[4]

As with any no-hitter, a pitcher has to rely on his defense to make outstanding plays. Tim Foli made two quality plays to keep the goose egg in the hit column. The first came in the fourth when he went far to his right to snag a blooper off Milner's bat that went behind third baseman Coco Laboy. The second came on the game's last out when Hahn—a former Expo—smacked a grounder that bounced crazily after hitting the edge of the grass. Foli was able to snare it and throw to Fairly at first for the out.

"Both [no-hitters] ended with tough groundballs to shortstop," Stoneman said. "Foli stayed with it. He made the play look easy and it wasn't that easy."[5]

Expos management deserves kudos for arranging to show Stoneman the team's appreciation the very next night between games of another Expos-Mets doubleheader. They gave him a $2,000 bonus check and two Air Canada plane tickets to anywhere the airline flew. His wife, Diane, a former Air Canada stewardess, received a gold watch and his batterymate, McCarver, received a $500 gift certificate.

For his part, Stoneman was happy to have pitched his second no-hitter in the *milieu familier* of Jarry Park for the hometown crowd.[6] "I heard the people yelling. It felt great," he said after the game. "Having pitched one on the road, I know that I'm happier to have pitched it here."[7]

Years later, Stoneman evaluated the two no-hitters not just in terms of what they meant to the fans or the team, but what type of pitcher threw them. "There were a lot of similarities to both games," he said, "but the pitcher who threw the first no-hitter and the pitcher who threw the second were two different pitchers in terms of experience."[8]

SOURCES

In addition to the sources listed in the notes, the author consulted:

Baseball-reference.com.

SI.com.

NO-HITTERS

NOTES

1. Ian MacDonald, "Stoneman repeats his no-hit gem," *The Gazette* (Montreal), October 3, 1972.
2. This was the first players' strike in major-league baseball history.
3. Hunt led the National League in HBP seven straight years, from 1968 to 1974. He set the 20th-century single-season major-league record of 50 in 1971. Hughie Jennings set the all-time record when he was hit 51 times in 1896.
4. MacDonald.
5. Video, *Les Expos, Nos Amours*, Volume I, produced by TV Labatt, 1989.
6. *Milieu familier* is the French translation of *friendly confines*.
7. MacDonald.
8. *Les Expos, Nos Amours*.

STEVE BUSBY

By John DiFonzo

ON JUNE 18, 1974, PAUL Splittorff threw a two-hit shutout against the Brewers in Milwaukee. After the game Splittorff and his roommate, Steve Busby, were talking about no-hitters. Splittorff did not consider himself to be a no-hit-type pitcher. But he had a list of pitchers who he considered could throw a no-hitter every time out—which included Nolan Ryan and Busby. Busby, who had pitched a no-hitter the previous season, said, "I got all over him for saying this because I really don't consider myself to be a no-hit pitcher. I think I've been more fortunate than a lot of other pitchers because obviously it takes a lot of luck to pitch one."[1] The next day Busby threw his second no-hitter. Busby would be forever associated with the no-hitter and rotator cuff surgery, but there is much more to his story.

Steven Lee "Buzz" Busby was born on September 29, 1949, in Burbank, California, to Marvin and Betty Busby, who were of English and German descent. Marvin played football at USC and professionally for the Los Angeles Dons of the All-American Football Conference.[2] This had an influence on his son, Steve, who grew up preferring football to baseball. When Marvin's football days were over, he worked as a petroleum and chemical engineer. Betty taught American history at the University of California at Berkeley before leaving to raise their children. Busby said he was raised to believe that the team was more important than the individual and that individual accomplishments didn't mean much if they didn't contribute toward the team winning.[3]

Busby grew up in Fullerton, California, and was a three-sport star at Union High, excelling in basketball, baseball, and football. (Hall of Famers Arky Vaughan and Walter Johnson also attended the school.) While in high school, Busby threw two no-hitters. He cited his baseball coach there as one of his early influences. "Jim Bass is the best teacher of fundamentals … catching, throwing, pitching mechanics," Busby said. "I learned pitching mechanics from him, learning to win from him."[4]

Playing football during his senior year, Busby suffered a knee injury that required an operation. In 1967 the San Francisco Giants selected Busby in the fourth round of the June draft. When Busby's knee gave out during a workout, the Giants discovered that there were still lingering effects from the injury and cut their bonus offer in half. Busby decided to accept a scholarship to the University of Southern California and to play for the legendary coach Rod Dedeaux.

In 1968 Busby went 8-3 and batted .422 and was named the team's most valuable player for the USC freshman team.[5] In 1969, his sophomore year, Busby required surgery to relocate the ulnar nerve in his right arm. His arm strength was gone and he realized that he had to start developing other pitches. Before the surgery he threw 80 percent fastballs; after, he developed a slider and made the transition from thrower to pitcher. Busby's arm strength eventually returned and he became a more complete pitcher.

In 1971 Busby compiled an 11-2 record for the Trojans with a 1.92 ERA in 21 games and made the All-American team. Busby was the team's leading pitcher, and though he lost an early-round game to Southern Illinois University in the College World Series, he redeemed himself in the deciding game. Busby struck out Southern Illinois' Bob Blakely with the bases loaded to seal the 7-2 victory for the Trojans.

Busby's major at USC was business administration He also studied computer technology because he enjoyed the mathematical analysis. While at USC, Busby took a creative writing class taught by the creator of *The Twilight Zone,* Rod Serling,[6] and was inspired to write science-fiction novels. Busby thrived on challenges, and he wanted to see if he could "make all the pieces fit together."[7] His novels were described as not the "stars and galaxy kind, but the Rod Serling type … the psychological experience … and some occult."[8]

Busby was selected by the Kansas City Royals in the second round of the secondary phase (June) of the amateur draft in 1971. Despite being one semester short of graduating and having a year of college eligibility left, Busby signed with the Royals for a $37,500 bonus. He was described in *The Sporting News* as "not merely being early maturity, rather a happy blend of intelligence, perspective and competitive intensity, tempered with self control. He seemed already to know how to pitch. If he didn't pitch well, he knew why not and he knew how to accept victory or defeat."[9] Busby credited Dedeaux, saying, "I attribute a lot of my attitude to Coach Dedeaux. He always emphasized that you should do the best you can and not blame anyone else for failure. Don't downgrade anyone else."[10] He added, "I didn't appreciate the things Rod Dedeaux taught us until I got into pro ball. He taught me how to win including the psychological part of the game, how to recognize the small things: whether the outfielder was left-handed or right-handed, watching people in the infield, and looking at every possible way to beat you, whether it was good fielding, a good pickoff move, by intimidation or being lucky."[11]

Pitching for the Royals' San Jose farm team (California League), Busby compiled a 4-1 record with an 0.68 ERA, giving up only three earned runs in 40 innings and striking out 50. In the Florida Instructional League he continued to impress, with a 5-2 record, 1.50 ERA, and a league-leading 67 strikeouts in 60 innings.

It was felt that Busby had a shot to make the major-league roster out of spring training in 1972; he was the talk of the newcomers and had the poise of a veteran. He started the season at Triple-A Omaha. On May 4 Busby struck out eight consecutive Tulsa batters and broke up the opposing pitcher's no-hitter in the fifth inning en route to a 7-1 victory. In another game against Tulsa he struck out 16 in a pitching duel he won over Jim Bibby. Busby twice came close to

pitching no-hitters during the season. The first time his bid was broken up with one out in the ninth, the second in the seventh. His manager, Jack McKeon prophetically counseled Busby "not to worry, that I'd pitch a couple of no-hitters and it'll be in the big leagues."[12] Busby led the league in strikeouts (221), innings pitched (217), and complete games with 17. He compiled a 12-14 record with a 3.19 ERA, for a team that the Royals felt victimized its pitchers with its poor defense. Busby said he benefited from McKeon's counsel, particularly on pitch selection..[13]

Busby got a surprise call-up after Omaha's season after Dick Drago's jaw was broken by a line drive on September 1. He made his major-league debut on September 8, 1972, started against the Minnesota Twins at Kansas City's Municipal Stadium. Cesar Tovar and Rod Carew greeted Busby with singles and the Twins took an early 1-0 lead. Busby settled down and pitched a complete-game 3-2 victory, striking out seven and allowing only five hits.

In Busby's third start, against the California Angels in Anaheim, just a 15-minute drive from his childhood home in Fullerton (and the first time his parents saw him pitch in the majors), he lost a grand slam after smacking pitcher Lloyd Allen's offering over the left-field fence. First-base umpire John Rice had called time before the pitch to eject Jerry May for suggesting that Rice speak to his tailor about "adding an extra panel in his suit." Royals manager Bob Lemon and Dick Drago also were ejected. When play resumed, Busby singled to center for his first major-league hit and collected two RBIs. Busby got two other hits, and the three were his only major-league base hits, because the American League adopted the designated hitter the next season. (A good all-around athlete, Busby was against the DH.) Busby started five games for the Royals in '72 and was 3-1 with a 1.58 ERA.

In 1976 Busby found out what happened on that night when he was convalescing in the hospital. Busby's roommate and best friend on the team, Paul Splittorff, came to see him. Busby recalls years later with a chuckle, "My arm is strapped to my chest and I'm still kind of woozy from all the medication they were giving me… He said hey I got to fess up to you and he told me the story about what he had said and he hid behind somebody as he was yelling it. He was the one who suggested to Rice about the tailor. He said you know I feel terrible about it. I was completely out of it. 'I said yah, whatever.' It was a month later, I finally came to and realized what he had told me. I had to corner him about it. He said, 'I figured you're not going to come back and pitch anymore anyways so I might as well get it out of the way and I'm not going to have to worry about rooming together.' That was kind of my impetus to get back to pitch the major league level and room with him again so I can give him a hard time."[14]

At the start of the 1973 season expectations were high for Busby. He was slated to be in the starting rotation and there was speculation from McKeon, the Royals new manager, that Busby had the makeup to win 20 games. "There isn't a hitter that can intimidate Busby," McKeon said.[15] Busby and Doug Bird combined to no-hit the Detroit Tigers in an exhibition game, Busby pitching the first six innings. He followed with seven hitless innings against the Cardinals. Busby was the Opening Day starter, but struggled, losing to California. In his first four starts he was 1-2 with an 8.04 ERA. He lasted only one inning and gave up five runs in a 16-2 defeat by the Chicago White Sox. Busby had some stiffness in his shoulder and was held back a few days before his next start. He recalled McKeon telling him that if he didn't show improvement in his next start, he would be sent down to work it out in Omaha.[16]

Did he ever show improvement! On April 27, a cold evening that Busby described as perfect for pitching, he threw the Royals' first no-hitter, beating the Detroit Tigers, 3-0. Busby became the 14th rookie to throw a no-hitter. He was wild, walking six. He had trouble locating his breaking pitches and threw mostly fastballs. At the time Busby downplayed the individual achievement, noting that first baseman John Mayberry bailed him out with a line-drive double play in the ninth. "It was blind luck. It had nothing to do with skill," Busby said of his feat.[17] More recently he said, "It was less than 40 degrees, I was wilder than a Marsh hare, the Tigers were a veteran ballclub that didn't feel like swinging the bats."[18] (The umpire whose time-out call cost Busby his grand slam, John Rice, was the home-plate umpire for the no-hitter.)

Busby pitched well in his next game but then slumped and his record was 4-9 on July 2. But from then until the end of the season he was 12-6, helping the Royals to finish in second place in the American League West. Against Milwaukee on July 10 Busby struck out 13, tying the Royals team record at the time. He finished the season with a 16-15 record and a 4.23 ERA. It was the most wins by an American League rookie since 1968 and Busby was named *The Sporting News* American League Rookie Pitcher of the Year.

Despite high expectations for 1974, the Royals struggled early in the season and were two games under .500 and 4½ games behind Oakland on June 11. Owner Ewing Kaufman fired general manager Cedric

Tallis, whose trades were credited with making the Royals the most successful expansion team in baseball history at the time. The timing was disruptive and the team was also grumbling about manager Jack McKeon and his handling of the pitching staff.

Busby got off to a better start in 1974, 8-6 with a 3.66 ERA going into his June 19 start in Milwaukee. Busby threw a gem. He walked only George Scott to lead off the second inning and retired the final 24 batters to record his second no-hitter, defeating the Brewers 2-0. Busby became the first and as of 2016 the only pitcher to throw no-hitters in his first two major-league seasons. Modestly, he said, "There were some outstanding plays behind me. I had good stuff but it could have been a four- or five-hitter."[19] Busby recalled that both no-hitters were low-scoring games and he had to focus on keeping the opposition off the boards rather than thinking about the no-hitter.[20]

Busby started his next game by retiring the first nine batters he faced. He broke the American League record by retiring 33 consecutive batters. (The record was tied in 1977 and broken in 1998.[21]) In both of Busby's starts after his no-hitters he pitched 5⅓ no-hit innings.

Busby started the season 13-9 with a 3.31 ERA to earn his first All-Star Game selection, but did not pitch. The Royals were a streaky team and won 16 of 22 games in late August to pull to within four games of the division-leading A's. But on a long homestand they lost 10 of their next 11 games to fall out of contention.

On September 17, Busby became the Royals second 20-game winner, but it was bittersweet as he hadn't won a game in three weeks as the Royals slid from contention. "It has no value because we didn't accomplish what I consider valuable, a championship," he said.[22]

Controversy struck the club again when McKeon fired hitting coach Charlie Lau before the last home game of the season. The move was sharply criticized by the players. Busby, the team's player representative, was very critical of the move. "We'll never win a pennant with this type of thinking," he said. "… If this organization is not interested in winning, then I don't want to be part of it. … You can't win a championship without horses … and they have taken away one of the very best horses they've had available."[23] It was rumored that McKeon was jealous of Lau and that the players went to Lau for help rather than McKeon.

Busby finished the season at 22-14 with a 3.39 ERA and a club record 292⅓ innings pitched. Busby was in the top 10 in almost every pitching category including WAR (seventh) and strikeouts per nine innings (fourth). The innings pitched may seem high by today's standards but Busby was only ninth in the league in innings pitched.

Controversy followed the Royals into the 1975 campaign. Busby resigned as player representative in May. Rumors were swirling that he threatened to leave the team in New York on May 18, because he had been at odds with McKeon and he wanted Buck Martinez and not Fran Healy, who caught both his no-hitters, to catch him. Busby dispelled any rumors of quitting after his meeting with McKeon and general manager Joe Burke.[24]

Busby was having his best season and started out 10-5 with a 2.57 ERA. He began to experience pain in the front of his shoulder, tendinitis, but a new pain in the rear of his shoulder began to appear. He compensated by altering his pitching motion, a step that caused mechanical issues. In a *Sports Illustrated* article in August 1978, Busby detailed what happened next: "On the 25th of June I threw 12 innings in Anaheim and won 6-2, but I struggled for the last seven. It was really a chore to throw. The next time I pitched was July 1 against Texas. Normally I recuperate fast between starts, but this day I just couldn't throw well. I was having strength problems: I couldn't grip the ball well and I had a lessened ability to snap my wrist. I couldn't even make a tight fist. … I pitched on through the middle of September with very little success."[25]

Busby was named to his second All-Star Game and pitched two innings in relief. After two months of speculation, Jack McKeon was fired as manager of the Royals on July 24 and was replaced by Whitey Herzog. GM Burke cited McKeon's poor relationship with his players and the media as the main reason.

The club was a disappointing 50-46, 11 games behind the A's. Herzog brought back hitting coach Charlie Lau.

The Royals finished seven games behind Oakland. Busby was held out the last week of the season because of shoulder soreness. He recalled, "By that time, I had no sensation of strength when I threw the ball."[26] He finished with an 18-12 record and a 3.08 ERA 260⅓ innings.

After the season Busby saw Dr. Frank Jobe, who prescribed different therapies. Busby thought his problems had been caused by bad mechanics and began an offseason training program. Busby was counted on to be a key contributor to the Royals' hopes to win the American League West crown in 1976. Dr. Jobe recommended that Busby pitch until he could no longer be effective. He started the season on the disabled list, joined the team in early April and pitched his first game on April 18. The Royals lost, 6-0; Busby gave up two runs in six innings but walked seven. After the game he was optimistic: "There is no doubt in my mind I'm healthy. My arm is fine."[27] Herzog added, "Busby threw freely and had no pain. He threw better than he did all last September."[28] Busby pitched an impressive game against the Yankees on May 1 and "removed any doubts about the condition of his arm."[29] But the relief over Busby's arm was short-lived. He left his May 12 start in the fifth inning as a precaution. At the time the seriousness of his arm condition was not known. Busby said, "It's not really serious. It's a muscle problem, an injury most pitchers suffer during spring training."[30] At the time it was reported that Busby was recovering from an elbow problem that he suffered late in the 1974 season.

Busby was held out of his next start and then was put on a pitch count. He pitched 15 innings in his next three starts restricted to 100 pitches and gave up only one run. (Though Busby has been said to be the first pitcher held to a pitch count, this was common practice at the time for a pitcher recovering from an injury.) Through June 2 Busby pitched in only seven games, but the Royals were off to a great start and were leading the American League West.

By June 15 Busby's season was described "an on again off again comeback" in *The Sporting News*.[31] Herzog summed up the situation: "We can't go on like this not knowing what his status is. If he needs complete rest, than let's go that route."[32] On June 22 Busby gave up nine runs to the White Sox; he said, "The arm feels good, but the results aren't."[33] On July 6 Busby gave up four runs in seven innings to the Yankees. One of the Yankees said, "He had nothing, no fastball, no curveball."[34] Both Busby and Herzog knew this, too, and decided to find out what was wrong.

Busby recalled, "[Dr. Robert] Kerlan [Dr. Jobe's partner] ordered me to have a shoulder arthrogram. Dye is injected into the joint, and if it leaks out into the surrounding tissue, there is a problem—and it showed that I had a tear in the rotator cuff. Rest wouldn't help an injury that serious. If I were to pitch again, I would have to have surgery."[35] Busby was done for the season; he finished with only 13 starts, a 3-3 record with a 4.40 ERA in 71⅔ innings. The tear in his rotator cuff was caused by the upper bone in the arm rubbing up against the top bone in the shoulder. Surgery lasting 3½ hours was required to cut the shoulder open, sew up the hole, cut three-quarters of an inch off the shoulder bone and shave off the back of the upper arm bone to reduce the friction.[36] This was the first time this procedure was performed on an active pitcher. Dr. Jobe performed the groundbreaking surgery on July 19, 1976. Jobe had previously done the surgery on tennis players and it was expected that Busby would regain full use of his arm, but his future effectiveness as a pitcher was unknown. A torn rotator cuff had ended many pitchers' careers including that of Don Drysdale. Dr. Jobe recommended that Busby seek other employment, but Busby wasn't ready to give up.

Meanwhile, the Royals went on to win their first American League West Division title and Busby found solace in the team's accomplishment. Busby said, "It was such a great feeling."[37] The Royals lost the ALCS to the Yankees on Chris Chambliss's walk-off home run. Busby worked on a rehab program overseen by Dr. Jobe. Given the nature and severity of the injury the Royals were not counting on him. They took a gamble and left Busby exposed to the 1977 expansion draft. Busby was not selected at least for two rounds (24 players selected) by the Toronto Blue Jays and Seattle Mariners.

There was no timetable for Busby's return; there was no one to whom one could compare his situation. He was confident he would return and could be effective with reduced velocity if he could control his breaking pitches. Busby appeared in one minor-league game and fared poorly. He reinjured his left knee while altering his pitching delivery and strengthening his shoulder. Dr. Jobe operated on the knee.

Baseball had taken a toll on Busby's personal life. He had placed baseball as his first priority, which led to a separation from his wife. During the summer of 1977 he got back together with his wife and two daughters and placed family as his first priority.

Although the Royals were not counting on Busby for the 1978 season, he showed up in camp after more rehabilitation to his arm and knee and made the staff out of spring training. He started out well with a shutout, then was hit hard in his next three starts and was sent to the minors. Busby was called up in September and appeared in three games.

During spring training 1979 the 29-year-old Busby was competing for the fifth starter/long reliever role for Kansas City. He made the squad and posted a 6-6 record and 3.63 ERA, appearing in 22 games and starting 12.

During the offseason, Busby had arthroscopic surgery on his oft-injured right knee. In 1980 he competed again for the fifth starter/long reliever role. He made the staff and appeared in relief until he was sent to the minors in April. While in the minors, Busby was impressive with Omaha, posting a 2.48 ERA and throwing a one-hitter. He was recalled by the Royals and started six games. Busby posted a 1-3 record with a 6.17 ERA. The Royals wanted to use left-handed reliever Ken Brett in the playoffs and released the 30-year-old Busby on August 29, just two days before he would have been playoff eligible. Busby expressed his frustration. "It was disappointing watching the playoffs, not being able to pitch every year through 1980. I wanted to pitch so bad, I could taste it."[38] It is one of the great what-ifs: If Busby had been healthy from 1976 to 1980, would the fortunes of the Royals had been different? They lost the ALCS to the Yankees three times and lost the 1980 World Series to the Phillies.

In 1981 Busby was reviewing his business options, including broadcasting, a car dealership, and a beverage distributorship, when Herzog invited him to spring training with the St. Louis Cardinals as a nonroster player. Busby did not make the team and he retired. In 1984, at age 34, Busby was considering a comeback. "It's been nagging at me for three years," he said.[39] But he decided against pitching winter ball and his pitching days were over. In 1986 Busby and Amos Otis were inducted as the inaugural members of the Royals Hall of Fame.

While Busby was rehabilitating, former Royals play-by-play announcer Buddy Blattner recommended that he get into broadcasting. In 1981 Busby worked as a weekend sports anchor with the local Kansas City NBC affiliate. In 1982 he had two job offers, from the Boston Red Sox and Texas Rangers. He chose the Rangers because they were closer to home, and in Boston he would be filling the big shoes of the legendary Ken "Hawk" Harrelson.[40] Busby became one of the rare ex-athletes to become a play-by-play announcer. He described how this came to be: "When I first started out, I was very fortunate to have one of the all-time greats in broadcasting, Merle Harmon, that I was paired with down here in Texas, and Merle made it a point to get me to learn how to do play-by-play and help him out during ballgames. He didn't have to do it for nine innings of play-by-play. So the first spring training that we worked together, he and I went out to games that we weren't broadcasting and took a tape recorder and Merle made me do five, six, seven innings of play-by-play. Then we would go back to the hotel after the game and listen to it. He would critique me and give me pointers and really got me going. If it hadn't been for someone like that taking the time and making the effort to help me get settled in to being a broadcaster, I never would have done it. Merle was one of the nicest people in the world. You don't find many people in this business or for that matter in most competitive businesses who are willing to take the time to train somebody else and help them advance themselves."[41]

In 1996 Busby worked as the play-by-play announcer for the Royals alongside his close friend, Paul Splittorff. Busby struggled with his retirement from baseball for many years even though he had made a career as a broadcaster. "I always said that it doesn't bother me and that it was part of the game, and that was a bunch of garbage," he said. "It bothered me. It hurt. That injury and the subsequent injuries stripped me of my identity."[42] Busby had what he would describe as a "rebirth" in late 1997. "I finally got OK with me being me. Just saying, 'OK this is who you are, this where you are, and what do we do from here on out?'"[43] Busby spent more time with his children. He took a year off from broadcasting and began working with high-school pitchers, teaching them the finer points of pitching.

As of 2016, Busby was the play-by-play announcer for the Rangers. He said being a former player gave him the advantage of having a very comfortable conversation with his partner, Tom Grieve.[44] Their broadcasts have been described as "watching baseball, telling stories, eating cookies and pastries, and most of all, having fun."[45]

NOTES

1. Gib Twyman, "No-Hit Hurler? 'Not Me! Says Busby," *The Sporting News*, July 6, 1974: 13.
2. Wil A. Linkugel and Edward J. Pappas, *They Tasted Glory: Among the Missing at the Baseball Hall of Fame* (Jefferson, North Carolina: McFarland, 1998), 128.
3. Author's interview with Steve Busby on April 20, 2016 (hereafter Busby interview).
4. Randy Covitz, "Busby's heart lasted longer than his arm," *Kansas City Star* June 5, 1986: 3B.
5. Busby player file at the National Baseball Hall of Fame library.
6. Busby interview.
7. Rosemarie Ross, "Busby: Can He Win 20 in His First Full Season?" *The Sporting News*, April 21, 1973: 20.
8. William Barry Furlong, "0-Hit Kid Steve No Stereotype," unidentified newspaper clipping from Busby player file.
9. Twyman.
10. Ibid.
11. Covitz.
12. Sid Bordman, "'Steve Buzz's Bomb Act Captures Tigers Again," *The Sporting News*, May 12, 1973: 12.
13. Ross.
14. April 2014 interview with Steve Busby, clubhouseconversation.com/2014/05/steve-busby/.
15. Ross.
16. Busby interview.
17. Covitz.
18. Busby interview.
19. Covitz.
20. Busby interview.
21. Seattle Mariners relief pitcher John Montague tied the mark in 1977, and David Wells of the New York Yankees broke the record and set a new mark of 38 innings on May 24, 1998. Busby's USC teammate, Jim Barr, held the National league record of 41 set in 1972 and this wasn't broken until 2009 by Mark Buehrle. Yusmeirio Petit of the San Francisco Giants set a new record of 46 in 2014.
22. Joe McGuff, "20-Win Champagne Has Flat Taste for Busby," *The Sporting News*, October 5, 1974: 22.
23. McGuff, "Player Yelps Following the Bouncing of Lau," *The Sporting News*, October 19, 1975: 30.
24. Bordman, "Healy Gets Healthy and So Does Royals Catching," *The Sporting News*, June 14, 1975: 14.
25. Ron Fimrite, "Stress, Strain and Pain," *Sports Illustrated*, August 14, 1978.
26. Bill Reiter, "Finding Steve Busby," *Kansas City Star*, April 1, 2007.
27. McGuff, "Busby, Little Spruce Up Royals' Hill Staff," *The Sporting News*, May 8, 1976: 18.
28. Ibid.
29. McGuff, "Swift Wolhford's Magic Glove Wows Royals," *The Sporting News*, May 22, 1976: 19.
30. "Busby Hurt Again," *The Sporting News*, May 29, 1976: 30.
31. "Busby Still a Puzzle," *The Sporting News*, July 3, 1976: 24.
32. Ibid.
33. "Royals," *The Sporting News*, July 10, 1976: 30.
34. McGuff, "Pitching Shy Royals Storm Heights with Bats," *The Sporting News*, July 24, 1976: 13.
35. Fimrite.

NO-HITTERS

36 "Busby Rebuilding Family Life, Career," *Chicago Tribune*, April 21, 1978.

37 Covitz.

38 Ibid.

39 Jim Reeves, "Rangers Roundup," *The Sporting News*, July 20, 1984: 49.

40 Busby interview.

41 April 2014 interview with Steve Busby, clubhouseconversation.com/2014/05/steve-busby/.

42 Bill Reiter, "Finding Steve Busby," *Kansas City Star*, April 1, 2007.

43 Ibid.

44 Busby interview.

45 Jim Reagan, "Steve Busby: Locked Into the Job He Loves," *Durant* (Oklahoma) *Democrat*, March 19, 2016.

ROOKIE BUSBY THROWS A NO-HITTER
APRIL 27, 1973: KANSAS CITY ROYALS 3, DETROIT TIGERS 0, AT TIGER STADIUM

By John DiFonzo

THE DETROIT TIGERS AND the Kansas City Royals were two contending teams heading in opposite directions when they met on the cold, raw evening of April 27, 1973. The Detroit Tigers were an aging ballclub that had won the 1968 World Series and made the playoffs in 1972. Starting pitcher Joe Coleman and third baseman Aurelio Rodriquez were the only regular contributors under the age of 30.

By contrast, the Kansas City Royals were an expansion team that quickly rose to contender status through a series of skillful trades by their general manager, Cedric Tallis. In the 1968 expansion draft, the Royals selected key assets including Dick Drago, Al Fitzmorris, Fran Healy, and Joe Foy.[1]

Tallis also chose well in the regular draft. He selected Paul Splittorf in the 25th round in 1968 and Doug Bird in 1969. Frank White was signed as an amateur free agent in 1970. The Royals' best draft to date was in 1971, when they selected a pair of California natives, Steve Busby and George Brett.

Busby showed very well in September 1972, working 40 innings for the Royals with a 1.58 ERA. In spring training in 1973, he pitched six innings of a combined no-hitter with Doug Bird against Detroit. Busby pitched seven no-hit innings against the St. Louis Cardinals in his next start. Busby was named the Opening Day starter, but struggled, starting the season 1-2 with an 8.04 ERA. In a start on April 20 he lasted only one inning and gave up five runs. Busby had some stiffness in his shoulder and was held back a few days before his next start, against Detroit. It was revealed afterward that Busby could have been demoted to Omaha if he did not show improvement in that start. Busby was opposed by 37-year-old right-hander Jim Perry.[2]

Busby, a three-sport star in high school who was also a good hitter, became the first major-league pitcher to throw a no-hitter without an at-bat because this was the year the American League adopted the designated hitter. Busby's batterymate for the game was catcher Fran Healy.

The Royals pitcher induced three groundouts in the first inning, and three outfield flies in the second. He got a strikeout, a foul out, and a groundout in the third.

Busby changed his grip about the fourth inning. He explained, "I couldn't control my fastball, it was sinking too much. So I changed and it started running in on left-handers. I had better success against them. I was still throwing the ball all over the place. Maybe I was wild enough to keep the hitters loose."[3] This was the first American League no-hitter since rookie Vida Blue's against the Minnesota Twins on September 21, 1970. Jim Perry was the victim that night as well.

Ed Kirkpatrick hit a solo home run in the fifth inning and Amos Otis did likewise in the eighth. The Royals added another run in the ninth. Busby walked six batters, two of whom were eliminated via double plays. Only two runners made it past first base. In the fourth, Rich Reese walked and took second on a passed ball by Healy. Busby walked Bill Freehan to lead off the seventh. Freehan advanced to second on a groundout to first and went to third on a wild pitch. With one out, Busby struck out Norm Cash and got Dick McAuliffe to fly out to left field. "We were swinging at a lot of bad balls," Cash said after the game. "We were trying to hack it over the roof."[4]

The closest the Tigers came to a hit was in the ninth. Busby walked Duke Sims to lead off the inning. Rich Reese hit a line drive. "My cap flew over my head when I threw the ball," Busby said. "I hurried to pull my cap up because I thought it was coming at me. When I looked over at first I saw John stepping on the bag for the double play."[5] Mayberry was playing a few feet behind first base, in perfect position to make the play. Reese said, "If Sims wasn't on base Mayberry would not have playing next to the bag. The ball would have been a hit."[6] Mayberry countered, "I don't know if it would have been a hit without a runner on. I would have been playing deeper and it would have made the play tougher. But I still might have knocked the ball down after it bounced and tagged first. I think we were ready to catch anything,"[7]

Fran Healy, who was catching Busby for the first time, said, "He deserves all the credit. We were thinking the same way most of the time. He shook me off maybe three or four times."[8]

With his six walks, Busby was far from dominant.[9] However, he made the right pitches when he needed to. The 23-year-old rookie threw an estimated 75 to 90 percent fastballs with the remainder being sliders and an occasional changeup or curveball. It was the first no-hitter in Royals history and also the first no-hitter for a Kansas City major-league team. (The Athletics played there for 13 years before moving to Oakland.)

"This is the greatest thrill of my life," said Busby.[10] "I felt stronger because of the cold weather. I always pitch better when it's cool."[11]

Busby compared his spring-training no-hitter with this one and said, "Down there I tried to hit spots. Today I threw as hard as I could for as long as I could."[12] This was the first no-hitter pitched in Tiger Stadium since Virgil Trucks defeated the Washington Senators 1-0 on May 15, 1952. Jim Busby, Steve's cousin, was the starting center fielder for the Senators that day.

Busby's no-hitter was one of two thrown against the Tigers in 1973. Nolan Ryan pitched one in Tiger Stadium on July 15, and once again Jim Perry was the victim. This was the first time an American League team was no-hit twice in one season since it happened to the 1923 Philadelphia Athletics.[13] The Tigers finished in third place in the American League East in 1973 and in the bottom half of the division the following seven seasons. They returned to the postseason in 1984, capping off the one of the most dominant seasons with a World Series victory. The Royals won the American League West crown four out of five years from 1976 through 1980.

Busby became the 14th of 22 rookies to throw a no-hitter. Jim Bibby became the 15th later in 1973, the only time that two rookies threw no-hitters in the same season.[14] Busby pitched another no-hitter in 1974, becoming the first pitcher to throw no-hitters in his first two full seasons in the major leagues. Pitching at Omaha in 1972, Busby lost a no-hitter in the ninth inning against Evansville. His prophetic manager at Omaha (and Kansas City), Jack McKeon, told Busby, 'You'll pitch a couple of no-hitters and it will be in the big leagues.'"[15]

NOTES

1 Tallis then made a series of moves to build up the new team. On April 1, 1969, Tallis acquired Lou Piniella from the Seattle Pilots for John Gelnar and Steve Whitaker. Tallis traded Joe Foy to the New York Mets in December for Amos Otis and Bob Johnson. The following June he acquired Cookie Rojas from the St. Louis Cardinals for Fred Rico. On December 2, 1970, Tallis acquired Freddie Patek, Bruce Dal Canton, and Jerry May from the Pittsburgh Pirates for Jim Campanis, Jackie Hernandez, and Bob Johnson. Tallis got Houston's John Mayberry and Dave Grangaard for Lance Clemons and Jim York on December 2, 1971. On November 30, 1972, he acquired Hal McRae and Wayne Simpson from the Cincinnati Reds for Roger Nelson and Richie Scheinblum.

2 Joe McGuff, "Fear of Omaha Demotion Drove Busby to Success," *The Sporting News*, May 19, 1973: 9.

3 Sid Bordman, "Steve's Buzz Bomb Act Captures Tigers Again," *The Sporting News*, May 12, 1973: 3.

4 Ibid.

5 Bordman.

6 Associated Press, "Rookie Busby's No-Hitter Inevitable," unidentified newspaper clipping in Busby's player file at the National Baseball Hall of Fame, dated April 28, 1973: 10

7 Bordman.

8 Ibid.

9 This accomplishment is not common. Clyde Wright was the previous pitcher to throw a no-hitter while walking more batters (3) than he struck out (1) for the California Angels when he defeated the Oakland A's on July 3, 1970.

NO-HITTERS

10 "Rookie Busby's No-Hitter Inevitable."

11 Bordman.

12 "Rookie Busby's No-Hitter Inevitable."

13 On September 4 New York Yankees hurler Sad Sam Jones pitched a no-hitter against the Athletics, winning 2-0. Three days later, on September 7, Howard Ehmke of the Boston Red Sox held the Athletics hitless and won 4-0.

14 On July 30, 1973, Texas Rangers right-hander Jim Bibby no-hit the Oakland A's in the Oakland-Alameda Coliseum, 6-0.

15 Bordman.

BUSBY MAKES HISTORY

JUNE 19, 1974: KANSAS CITY ROYALS 2, MILWAUKEE BREWERS 0, AT MILWAUKEE COUNTY STADIUM

By John DiFonzo

THE KANSAS CITY ROYALS were in Milwaukee for a two-game series against the American League East's last-place team, the Milwaukee Brewers. The Royals got stellar pitching performances from their two best pitchers, who happened to be roommates. On June 18 Paul Splittorf pitched a gem; facing only 30 batters, he allowed just two hits and walked one to win, 7-0. The next night, not to be outdone by his roommate, Steve Busby pitched the second no-hitter of his career. Busby walked only one batter and faced just 28 Brewers. As of 2016 Busby was the only pitcher to throw no-hitters in each of his first two full major-league seasons.

In a pitchers' duel with the Brewers' Clyde Wright, Busby had complete command of his fastball, mixing in his slider and newly developed curveball. After the game, he said, "I was much more aware of what was going on this time. I wasn't nervous as much as I was fighting myself to keep my concentration. When I lose my concentration, I pipe the ball, throw it down the middle and give up maybe four or five hits in a row or else walk everybody. For about the last three innings I really had to fight myself to keep my head in the game. But this was the biggest thrill of all, bigger than last time because this was my type of game."[1] Busby considered himself a control pitcher. In Busby's first no-hitter, the season before against the Detroit Tigers, he was wild and walked six batters.

Against Milwaukee, George Brett drove home John Mayberry with a single to center field in the second inning for the only run Busby would need. The Royals added an unearned run in the fourth inning when Jim Wohlford scored on a throwing error by the Brewers' 18-year-old rookie shortstop and future Hall of Famer, Robin Yount. Busby's walk came in the second inning. He got ahead of George Scott 0-and-2, then threw four straight balls. As Busby sailed a head-high pitch for ball four, he kicked the dirt in front of the pitching rubber and turned in anger toward center field. "No way I was thinking of the perfect game then. It was losing a man that I had 0-and-2 that made me mad," he said.[2]

Excellent fielding by Busby's teammates helped preserve the no-hitter. Al Cowens chased line drives to the warning track in the second and fourth innings by Darrell Porter and George Scott respectively. In the third inning, George Brett backhanded a groundball behind third base and made a perfect throw to get Bob Coluccio. Freddie Patek took two steps to his right to catch Robin Yount's line drive in the seventh. Scott missed a double when his checked-swing line drive landed inches foul outside first base in the seventh inning.

In a 2007 interview, Busby pointed out two specific plays. In the bottom of the sixth inning, Don Money hit a groundball down the third-base line. Brett backhanded the ball and threw across the diamond to get Money by half a step to end the inning. Busby called it one of the best defensive plays he had ever seen from behind third base.[3] In the bottom of the eighth, Brewers DH Bob Hansen hit a sharp two-hopper that appeared destined for right field. The Royals' 35-year-old second baseman, Cookie Rojas, took three quick steps and dove head-first to his left to grab the ball, then sprang to his feet to throw out Hansen. "It was the play of the game," Busby said. "I don't think I've ever seen him go so far that way or dive for a ball quite like that, even for Cookie."[4]

The Brewers went quietly in the ninth. Don Money popped out to Rojas for the final out. Busby received a standing ovation from the crowd of 9,019, who saw the first major-league no-hitter pitched at County Stadium since April 28, 1961, when Warren Spahn of the Milwaukee Braves outdueled Sam Jones of the San Francisco Giants, 1-0. Fran Healy, who also caught Busby's first no-hitter, observed, "He also had a pretty good curve, and when he has that, well then the rest is history for the hitters."[5]

In his 58th major-league start, Busby became the third youngest pitcher to throw two no-hitters. Johnny Vander Meer was the youngest when he threw the second of his consecutive no-hitters on June 15, 1938, at age 23 years, 7 months, and 13 days. Don Wilson of the Houston Astros was 24 years, 2 months, and 19 days old when he pitched his second on May 1, 1969. Busby was 24 years, 8 months, and 21 days old. He became the 25th pitcher to throw multiple no-hitters.[6] Busby's second no-hitter came 418 days after his first no-hitter, which he pitched on April 27, 1973.

Despite the fact that he threw two no-hitters in the major leagues, two one-hitters in Triple-A ball, and two no-hitters in high school, Busby told a sportswriter he did not consider himself to be a no-hit pitcher, but said, "I think I've been more fortunate than a lot of other pitchers because obviously it takes a lot of luck to pitch one."[7]

Busby started his next game by retiring the first nine batters he faced, setting an American League record of 33 consecutive batters retired. That mark was tied later that year but was not broken for 24 years.[8]

Bill James created a formula to predict the number of no-hitters a pitcher would throw based on their hits per nine innings and games started.[9] Based on this formula, Busby was the least likely pitcher to throw multiple no-hitters of the pitchers who actually threw two or more. Busby had the best hits per nine innings of the four deemed least likely by James's formula, but he had the fewest starts.

As of 2016 no other pitcher has thrown two no-hitters in his first two seasons. The closest anyone has come was when Wilson Alvarez lost his second possible no-hitter with no outs in the seventh inning. Jim Bibby had the second best no-hit bid, going 4⅓ no-hit innings in his next start after pitching a no-hitter.

NOTES

1. Associated Press, "Steve Busby Hurls His 2d No-Hitter," *Chicago Tribune*, June 20, 1974: Section 3, 1.

2. Gib Twyman, "No-Hit Hurler? 'Not Me! Says Busby," *The Sporting News*, July 6, 1974: 13.

3. Dave Brandon, Royal Curve, "Then and Now: Q&A With Steve Busby," April 9, 2007, scout.com/mlb/royals/story/633993-then-and-now-rc-q-a-with-steve-busby.

4. Twyman.

5. Ibid.

6. As of 2016 there were 30, including Roy Halladay, who pitched one in the postseason.

7. Twyman.

8. Busby's 33 consecutive batters retired broke the record of 32 held by Vic Raschi of the New York Yankees (1950) and Lindy McDaniel of the Yankees (1968). Seattle Mariners relief pitcher John Montague tied the mark in 1977. David Wells of the Yankees set a new record of 38 consecutive batters retired on May 24, 1998. Busby's University of Southern California teammate Jim Barr set a National League record of 41 in 1972, but this was broken by Mark Buehrle of the Chicago White Sox, who retired 45 consecutive batters in 2009, and again by Yusmeiro Petit of the San Francisco Giants (46 in 2014).

9. Bill James, "Expected No-Hitters," November 8, 2004, robneyer.com/baseball-books/neyer-james-guide-to-pitchers/expected-no-hitters/?doing_wp_cron=1460599985.6001229286193847656250.

BOB FORSCH

By Ben Girard

ON OCTOBER 28, 2011, THE St. Louis Cardinals prepared to play Game Seven of the World Series against the Texas Rangers at Busch Stadium. The organization asked Whitey Herzog, the manager of the last Cardinals team to play a World Series Game Seven at home, to throw the ceremonial first pitch. He had fallen ill, however, and was recovering in the hospital. Bob Forsch filled in for his former manager.

Forsch pitched major-league baseball for the St. Louis Cardinals from 1974 to September 1988, and for the Houston Astros from September 1988 until his last major-league game, in 1989. Over his career he started 422 games. He won 168 games and lost 136, pitched 19 complete-game shutouts, and posted 3 saves. He compiled a career ERA of 3.76, and a career WHIP of 1.291.

Forsch did not have overpowering velocity. He won 20 games in only one of his 16 seasons in the majors. He was never selected for the All-Star Game. A newspaper article in 1982 described him using such words as "gutty ... humble ... underrated ... self-conscious ... analytical ... unassuming ... .understated."[1] Friends and teammates won't hesitate to describe him as reliable, witty, and loyal. Cardinals fans, not to mention his family, would be quick to add *loved*.

That night in 2011, as Bob Forsch walked to the mound and received a round of applause, Cardinals fans saw something they had previously seen only off the mound: Forsch's characteristic broad, warm smile. "When you're on the mound," Forsch wrote, "nobody has a sense of humor. You have to understand: the game's serious."[2] This time, his smile was unrestrained as he threw the ceremonial pitch, accepted another ovation, and waved goodbye.

Robert Herbert Forsch was born on January 13, 1950, in Sacramento, California, to Herbert and Freda (Roth) Forsch.[3] Herb Forsch had played semipro baseball; he "played shortstop and third base, and ... pitched, too."[4] Herb, a South Dakotan, and Freda Roth from Alberta, Canada moved to Sacramento after their marriage.[5] There, Herb opened Forsch Electric Motors, an agricultural repair shop.[6]

In the family's yard, Herb taught his two sons, Bob and Ken, baseball's fundamentals. In the midst of homework and family dinners, they routinely installed games of "pepper," during which the Forsch brothers formed a sibling rivalry that was both competitive and (mostly) healthy. Despite growing up in a home so filled with baseball, Bob Forsch attended only one major-league game as a kid: a Giants game against, appropriately, the Cardinals.[7]

Bob, the younger of the Forsch brothers by 3½ years, was both a talented pitcher and a talented hitter. He made the all-city team[8] and led Hiram Johnson High School to a city championship in 1968.[9] That year the Houston Astros selected Ken in the 18th round of the amateur draft. 195 selections later, in the 26th round, Bob was selected by the Cardinals.[10]

Cardinals scout Bill Sayles, himself a former major-league pitcher, believed that Forsch had genuine batting talent, and that his greatest potential was as an infielder.[11] Forsch turned down a full scholarship from Oregon State University and joined the Cardinals' minor-league system as an infielder-outfielder-pitcher.[12]

On Forsch's first day in the Cardinals farm system, "He was drowsing in the dugout when an old man with glasses asked him for the count and outs. ... [Forsch] looked around a pillar in the dugout and relayed the game info. ... Don't ever let me catch you in here without knowing the count and outs, snapped the old guy. It was George Kissell," the most famous instructor and respected mentor of the Cardinals farm system.[13] (In 2015 Kissell and Forsch were both inducted to the Cardinals Hall of Fame.)

Forsch bounced around the minor leagues for three years and never impressed as a hitter. Ken Forsch, on the other hand, received a September call-up in 1970 and made the Astros roster out of spring training in 1971. That spring, Bob was "playing infield and not doing well."[14]

One day, during spring training, Cardinals farm director Bob Kennedy asked Forsch to follow him. Forsch recalled, "We were at our complex in St. Petersburg, and … he took me out to the garage where they kept the tractors that mowed the field[.]" Kennedy pulled open the garage door and went inside. He emerged a few moments later, holding a broom.

"[O]ne of those really big ones with the thick bristles and a handle that's like five feet long. … He stood the broom on end, with the bristles on the floor, and he held the handle with one hand. Then he started lifting it gradually until he was holding it straight out away from him. … It looks like it should be real easy to do. It's just a broom, right? … I tried it, and I couldn't lift it an inch. … Bob just looked at me and said, 'That's your problem. You're not strong enough.'"[15]

Forsch started over. Maybe Bill Sayles had been wrong. If Forsch couldn't hit, maybe he could pitch. With the help of the organization's instructors, especially Bob Kennedy and Bob Milliken, Forsch transformed himself into a professional pitcher. He gradually separated himself from the minor-league pack, throwing two no-hitters along the way. Tom Barnidge later wrote in the *St. Louis Post-Dispatch*, "Non-hitting third basemen who turn into winning pitchers are about as common as quarterbacks who decide to play defensive end."[16] Forsch, though, did just that.

It was also in 1971, while Forsch was playing at Cedar Rapids, that he struck up a conversation with Mollie Jane Knaau at a local restaurant.[17] They married in June of 1972.[18]

Forsch received his own major-league call-up and started his first game for the Cardinals on July 7, 1974, at Riverfront Stadium in Cincinnati. Facing Cincinnati's Big Red Machine, Forsch pitched 6⅔ innings, giving up four hits and walking five; he took a 2-1 loss.

Forsch's next start, and his first game at the Cardinals' Busch Memorial Stadium (now known commonly as *Busch II*), came five days later, in the second game of a doubleheader against the Atlanta Braves. He struck out five, walked none, and gave up no runs on four hits—a complete-game shutout. The Cardinals won, 10-0.

Over his next five starts, Forsch posted a no-decision, two losses, and two wins, both of which were complete games. He took a mid-August assignment to the bullpen before returning to the starting rotation on August 31. He was a starter for the rest of the season, posting a 4-1 record, which included another complete-game shutout.

The last start of Forsch's first season was a high-stakes game for a rookie. With the Cardinals making a September push to claim the National League East from the Pittsburgh Pirates, he started the first game of the team's final regular-season series against the Montreal Expos. The Cardinals and Pirates were tied for the division lead. Forsch later recalled a brief conversation in the men's room before the game with Cardinals pitching legend and notoriously fierce competitor Bob Gibson:

"I went in to take a pee before I went out to warm up. Gibson came in and stood at the urinal next to me and asked if I was nervous. … Here was a man who hadn't talked to me all year, and this is the question I got. … For some reason, I was honest and said yes. Gibby said, 'Good! I always pitch better when I'm nervous. There's a difference between being nervous and being scared.' … And then he left. … I couldn't believe that he would ever have been nervous. But I thought if Gibson said it, that was good enough for me."[19]

Forsch gave up only three hits and one run in a complete game, pitching the Cardinals to a 5-1 win. Gibson, however, lost his start the next day. Once the Pirates then completed a 10-inning comeback win over the Cubs, the Cardinals were eliminated.

In his sophomore season, 1975, Forsch secured his place as a Cardinals starter. He was impressive, posting a record of 15-10, at .600 the team's best won-lost percentage among starters, and tied for the team's most wins. He posted an ERA of 2.86, also the best among Cardinals starting pitchers.

In spring training of 1976 Forsch injured his throwing arm.[20] He received medical attention, but hid much of the pain and powered through it. "[I]f you don't pitch, you don't get paid. At least not the next year, when your one-year contract is up."[21] Forsch was 8-10, and his ERA and WHIP both jumped significantly.

Forsch rebounded in 1977. During a season in which the Cardinals' owner, August (Gussie) Busch Jr., installed disciplinarian Vern Rapp as manager and the team came close to mutiny,[22] Forsch became a 20-game winner with a 3.48 ERA. (He lost seven games.) The Cardinals finished third in the NL East.

April 16, 1978, was not an ideal day for baseball in St. Louis. A cold front had blown in, bringing thunderstorms and persistent fog.[23] As a sparse crowd sauntered into Busch II that afternoon, the temperature was under 45 degrees.

The Cardinals had been losing crowd appeal throughout the 1970s—their home opener, six days earlier, drew only 19,241. "The Cardinals' tradition took a hike in the '70s. … I kept hearing about the baseball tradition in St. Louis; at the time, I didn't understand it. We were playing bad baseball, and people weren't going to pay for it. … I always had fun, though."[24] Only 11,495 showed up to watch Forsch start his third game of the season, against the defending National League East champion Philadelphia Phillies.

In his second start of the season, he had struck out nine Pirates, walked three, and allowed four hits in a complete game. The Cardinals won, 5-1. Forsch's parents had made the trip from California to see that game, which Forsch described as one of the best he ever pitched; "I really felt proud," he recalled.[25]

Against the Phillies, Forsch was at the top of his game, though when he arrived at the ballpark he didn't feel like it. "My arm just felt weak, like I'd spent it all the game before."[26]

Nevertheless, in the fifth inning, Forsch was protecting a 1-0 Cardinals lead. With one out, he walked Richie Hebner—the Phillies' first baserunner. Hebner put himself in scoring position by stealing second. Although Forsch had struck out no one to that point, he ended the threat by striking out the next two batters.

As the game progressed, none of Forsch's teammates wanted to talk to him—they were honoring an age-old baseball tradition. When he retreated into the Cardinals' clubhouse, however, a radio was on and tuned to local station KMOX. "'They were saying … that no no-hitter had been pitched by a Cardinal in St. Louis in 54 years.'"[27]

By the top of the eighth inning, the Cardinals led 4-0 and the Phillies had managed only one more baserunner—another base on balls. Leading off the eighth, Garry Maddux hit a hard groundball to Cardinals third baseman Ken Reitz. Reitz "reached for the ball but it went under his glove."[28] "Everybody in the stadium was watching the scoreboard to see whether it was called a hit or an error."[29] Without delay, a number *1* appeared, not under the Phillies'

H column, but under the Cardinals' *E* column. The crowd erupted.

"Neal Russo of the *St. Louis Post-Dispatch*, —who was the official scorer—called it an error[,]" Forsch recalled; "I later asked Neal about it. ... He told me, 'That far along in the game, the first hit has to be a clean hit.'"[30] Maddux was eliminated in a 6-4-3 double play. Ted Sizemore then hit a line drive directly to shortstop Garry Templeton, ending the Phillies half of the eighth. Forsch was just three outs away.

Pinch-hitting and leading off the top of the ninth was the Phillies' Jay Johnstone. Ted Simmons, the Cardinals' catcher and Forsch's good friend, said a pivotal pitch that inning was "'the first pitch to Johnstone. ... [I]f he took that pitch for a strike, we had him.'"[31] They did, on a groundout to Templeton. Next up was Bake McBride. "He hadn't hit at all during the series. We kept feeding him slow stuff,'" Simmons said.[32] McBride grounded out to second base.

Larry Bowa batted for the Phillies with two outs.. He beat the ball into the turf for the fourth time that day, this time to Ken Reitz, who threw for the out at first. Forsch had his no-hitter. After the game he received a congratulatory telegram from the last Cardinal to throw a no-hitter, Bob Gibson. "I thought that was really neat[,]" Forsch said; "Nobody sends telegrams anymore[.]"[33]

A little less than a year later, at the Astrodome in Houston, Ken Forsch celebrated a no-hitter of his own. "I thought of all the great brother acts in baseball[,]" he said; "[T]he Niekros, the Perrys, and Dizzy and Daffy Dean."[34] He and his brother had now done something none of those others ever did: Bob and Ken Forsch became the first brothers each to throw a major-league no-hitter.

Between celebratory hugs and champagne-soaked interviews, Ken Forsch received a telegram. It read: "Congratulations on your no-hitter. I know how it feels. Enjoy every minute of it. Your Little Brother."[35]

Things changed quickly for the Cardinals starting in August of 1980, when Whitey Herzog took over as manager and general manager. Though not the most offensively powerful team, Herzog's Cardinals were a defensive juggernaut. With a solid infield anchored by the acrobatic future Hall of Famer Ozzie Smith at shortstop, a groundball pitcher like Bob Forsch was perfectly in his element. In fact, of the starting pitchers in St. Louis before Herzog's arrival, only Forsch was left 18 months later.[36]

A player strike split the 1981 season. Despite finishing 1981 with the best record in the National League East, the Cardinals were denied a spot in the playoffs by a convoluted playoff format. The shortened season also denied Forsch the ability to play out what statistics suggest could have been one of his best years.

Forsch, Herzog, and the Cardinals waited until 1982 to experience the postseason—the franchise's first such appearance since 1968. Forsch's first postseason start came in Game One of the National League playoff against the Atlanta Braves. He pitched one of the games of his life: a complete game in which he allowed no runs, walked no one, and gave up just three hits. The Cardinals won, 7-0. Bob Gibson, then the Braves' pitching coach, said, "This is the best I've ever seen him pitch. ... But with guys like Forschy, this is the time of year they pitch like that."[37] The Cardinals swept the Braves in three games to advance to the World Series. Forsch, though, would never pitch so well again in the postseason.

The 1982 World Series was a competition between polar opposites: The St. Louis Cardinals' speed and defense, and the Milwaukee Brewers' power. The Cardinals started Forsch in Game One.

By the fifth inning, Forsch had allowed three runs on six hits. He did not have his best stuff, but he was getting by. In the top of the fifth, Forsch gave up a home run to his former teammate Ted Simmons, who had been traded to the Brewers in 1980. Forsch recovered and kept himself in the game until the top of the sixth, when Robin Yount ended his game by hitting a two-out, two-run double. The Brewers scored four more times on three more pitchers, besting the Cardinals, 10-0.

The Cardinals, however, won two of the next three games. Forsch had a chance to give them the Series lead in Game Five.

Forsch was better than in Game One, but struggled nonetheless, allowing runs in four of the seven innings he pitched. He made a wild throw attempting to pick off Robin Yount at second base in the bottom of the first, allowing Yount to take third. He scored on a Ted Simmons groundout.

Yount menaced Forsch again in the bottom of the seventh with a solo home run. The Cardinals' closer, Bruce Sutter, replaced him in the eighth. The Cardinals lost, 6-4.

With only two games left at most, Forsch had thrown his last pitch of the year. He did have at least one more important role to play in the Cardinals' 1982 World Series run, though: host.

"Game 5 was on a Sunday afternoon and there was an off day Monday. We were on the flight home and all of a sudden Bruce [Sutter] said, 'Party at the Forsches' house!' … I guess Bruce figured everybody needed to relax. He picked our house because it was the best venue. We had a basement with a full bar."[38]

After a sparsely attended optional practice on Monday, the Cardinals tied the Series by routing the Brewers in Game Six, 13-1. Bruce Sutter struck out Gorman Thomas to close out the decisive Game Seven, and Forsch was halfway to a dogpile at the pitcher's mound before Cardinals' announcer Jack Buck could shout, "That's a winner!" It was the happiest moment of Forsch's career.[39]

1983, however, was a hangover year for the Cardinals. Forsch, who sued a former agent that year for fraud, experienced control problems.[40] On September 26, as the *St. Louis Post-Dispatch* ran an article disclosing that Herzog wanted Forsch to work on a knuckleball in the Florida Instructional League, Forsch took the mound against the Montreal Expos."[41]

Forsch had yet to allow a baserunner when he faced Expos catcher Gary Carter in the second inning. Forsch later recalled, "You know how some guys just bug you? Gary Carter bugged me … bad!"[42]

Forsch's previous start had also been against the Expos, five days earlier, in Montreal.

"You always had to pitch Gary inside so he couldn't get his arms out and pound the ball … I threw a pitch that … just ran in on him for ball four. … He went down to first base. And on the way he said something like, 'throw the ball over the plate.' … I wasn't feeling great. So I said, 'The next one you get will hit you.' … I ended up getting knocked out of that game before he came up again."[43]

True to his word, Forsch hit Carter with a fastball. "He went to first base and didn't say a word."[44] The home-plate umpire warned both benches. Carter went from first base to third when Chris Speier sent a groundball through Ken Oberkfell's legs — an error. Forsch averted the crisis by striking out shortstop Angel Salazar for the third out.

The Cardinals scored all of their runs in the fifth inning, when Ozzie Smith, Lonnie Smith, and Willie McGee each batted in a run.

Forsch later said, "You don't even think about a no-hitter until after the sixth inning, when you only have to go through the lineup one more time."[45] That time had come after he retired the Expos in the top of the sixth on a strikeout, a groundout, and a pop fly. Mollie Forsch didn't remember being nervous during Bob's 1978 no-hitter until the seventh inning; this time, she admitted, "I started getting nervous in the fifth."[46]

Dan Schatzeder replaced Expos starter Steve Rogers on the mound in the bottom of the sixth. He was ejected for hitting the first Cardinals batter he faced, Andy van Slyke. After an argument with the home-plate umpire, Expos manager Bill Virdon was also given an early exit. Expos coach Vern Rapp took over the team's managerial duties. (Rapp had still been the Cardinals manager when Forsch threw his no-hitter against the Phillies.)

The Expos were still hitless with two outs in the top of the ninth inning. "[E]very time I threw a pitch, there was a crowd reaction."[47] With two outs, Oberkfell, now at third base, found himself in the path of another sharply hit groundball, this one off Manny Trillo's bat. After the game, Oberkfell said,

"I'm glad I didn't make an error on the last one."[48] When Oberkfell threw out Trillo at first base, Forsch became the 25th major-league pitcher to throw multiple no-hitters.[49]

Five days later, in his final start of the season, Forsch again pitched well, and improved his record to 10-12. By that evening, he had "definitely ... decided not to experiment with the knuckleball in the Florida Instructional League[.]"[50]

The epilogue came the following year, on April 21. Forsch recalled, "[T]he first time we played the Expos, George Hendrick came into the clubhouse before the game and said, 'Hey, Gary Carter wants to talk to you outside on the runway.' ... So I went out there, and to his credit, Gary said, 'I play hard. Every day.' ... And he did. ... I told Gary, 'I pitch hard. Every day.' ... And I did. ... I respected him for coming up and saying that. And we never had a problem after that."[51]

"In 1984 the [Cardinals] stopped hitting altogether," wrote Peter Golenbock,[52] and Forsch was treated for nerve problems in his back. Forsch rebounded in 1985, and the Cardinals won 101 games to beat the New York Mets in a tight race for the NL East.

After losing Bruce Sutter to free agency, Whitey Herzog had elected to use a "bullpen by committee." Herzog made Forsch part of the committee and went to a four-man starting rotation. Forsch was a near-perfect fit as a spot starter and long reliever. By September he found his way back into the rotation.

Forsch started Game Five of the National League Championship Series, against the Los Angeles Dodgers. He allowed two runs on three hits and two walks in 3⅓ innings. He was relieved by Ken Dayley in the top of the fourth. The game, tied 2-2, gained a permanent place in Cardinals history in the bottom of the ninth, when shortstop Ozzie Smith hit a walk-off home run off the Dodgers' Tom Niedenfuer.

The Cardinals, who trailed the Dodgers 5-4 in the top of the ninth inning of Game Six at Dodger Stadium, went to the World Series on a three-run Jack Clark home run—also hit off Niedenfuer.

The 1985 World Series, against the Kansas City Royals, started promisingly enough for the Cardinals. They won the first two games in Kansas City on strong starts by Danny Cox and John Tudor. Although Royals ace Bret Saberhagen overpowered the Cardinals in Game Three, John Tudor shut out the Royals in Game Four to give the Cardinals a lead of three games to one.

Forsch started Game Five. Whitey Herzog told television broadcaster Tim McCarver, who had caught the first game of Forsch's major-league career, that he would be satisfied if Forsch got through three or four innings.[53] After allowing six of the first 11 Kansas City batters to reach base, Forsch exited after 1⅔. It was not Forsch's day, nor the Cardinals'. In fact, it proved to be the first of three games that Cardinals fans would rather forget. In the eighth inning of Game Six, the Cardinals took a 1-0 lead, then retired the Royals in short order. Whitey Herzog's "bullpen by committee," a categorical success, had not given up a ninth-inning lead during the whole of the 1985 regular season.[54]

In the bottom of the ninth, Todd Worrell got Royals pinch-hitter Jorge Orta to chop a high pitch into the ground, then covered first base and received Jack Clark's throw for the out. First-base umpire Don Denkinger awarded the base to Orta anyway. In 2010, MLB Network called it the most controversial call in the history of modern major-league baseball.[55] Later, with one out and the bases loaded, former Cardinal Dane Iorg hit a single to right field, scoring two and evening the Series.

Game Six was frustrating for the Cardinals. Game Seven, however, was utterly depressing. Cardinals starter John Tudor exited the game in the third inning, after walking in a run—his third earned. Two more inherited runners scored in the next at-bat.

When Tudor's replacement, Bill Campbell, was replaced by Jeff Lahti in the fifth inning, the score was 5-0. When Ricky Horton replaced Lahti, it was 9-0. Joaquin Andujar, normally a starter, was next. Notorious for his temper, Andujar erupted at Denkinger. Herzog, too, left the dugout to express his frustration. Manager and pitcher both were ejected, and Forsch took Andujar's place on the mound.

Bob Costas recalls, "When Bob Forsch took the ball, a sense of professionalism, pride and dignity was restored[.]"[56] Forsch induced a fly ball to (finally) end the fifth inning. He calmed the situation further by retiring the Royals in order in the sixth before being replaced by a pinch-hitter in the seventh. "[The World Series] went up in flames. It was tough to take, especially since we should have won Game Six—with or without the bad call by Don Denkinger at first base."[57]

Although the 1986 Cardinals were a shell of their 1985 selves, Forsch had a career year. Anchoring the rotation, he started more games (33) and pitched more innings (230) than any other Cardinals pitcher. His WHIP, 1.213, was lower than it had been since the strike-shortened season of 1981.

By 1987, though, Forsch showed signs of wear. He and two other pitchers each won 11 games in '87—no Cardinals starter that year won more.[58] The team won 95 games anyway, took the top spot in the National League East, and advanced to the NLCS against the San Francisco Giants. When Whitey Herzog constructed his postseason roster, Forsch's role was that of a reliever.

Recalling his times in the bullpen, " 'I think it's kind of fun,' [Forsch] said. 'It's kind of different. That's the way I approach it. To me, it's not downgrading. You know when you come to the ball park that you have a chance to get in the game.' "[59]

Forsch pitched in Games Two, Three, and Five of the 1987 NLCS. While Game Five was arguably the roughest outing of his postseason career, Forsch's teammates remember his Game Three performance most. San Francisco's Jeffrey Leonard was giving fits to the Cardinals pitchers, and flaunting it. He hit a home run in each of the Series' first three games, and mockingly followed each one by circling the bases slowly with his characteristic "one flap down" trot.

Forsch, who entered Game Three in relief of starter Joe Magrane, faced Leonard in the bottom of the fifth. Magrane recalled, "On the first pitch … [Forsch] knocked him on his ass. … and I thought that changed the entire series right there."[60] More than one of the 1987 Cardinals agree.[61] The Cardinals started a comeback the next inning. Being a team player, at least during Forsch's time, sometimes involved throwing at another player. Bob Forsch was, first and foremost, a team player.

The Cardinals continued their rally and won Game Three, 6-5. The Giants won Games Four and Five before the Cardinals advanced to the World Series by shutting them out in Games Six and Seven.

The 1987 World Series was the first to be played partially indoors. The Cardinals' opponent, the Minnesota Twins, played their home games in the Hubert H. Humphrey Metrodome. When Forsch entered Game One in the bottom of the fourth, the bases were loaded with no outs. Catcher Tim Laudner hit Forsch's second pitch for a single, scoring one. Just as starter Joe Magrane removed his earplugs on the Cardinals bench, the crowd erupted as Forsch allowed the first grand slam during a World Series since 1970. He retired nine of the next 14 batters, giving up two more runs on a Steve Lombardozzi home run, before he was replaced by Rick Horton. The Cardinals lost, 10-1.

They lost the second game in Minnesota, as well, before recovering to win Game Three in St. Louis. Greg Mathews, the Cardinals' starter in Game Four, had experienced trouble with an upper leg muscle in preceding weeks, but told Forsch before the game that it wasn't a problem.[62] It was. Forsch relieved him in the middle of an at-bat in the fourth inning. After completing a walk, which was charged to Mathews, Forsch struck out the next hitter and ended the Twins' fourth-inning threat.[63]

In the bottom of the fourth the Cardinals offense exploded. Because Forsch had entered the game in the previous half-inning, he received credit for the win. After pitching major-league baseball for 13 years, and after appearing in three World Series, Forsch's record finally included a World Series *W*.

The Cardinals also won Game Five in St. Louis, giving them a lead of three games to two. They led 5-2 going into the bottom of the fifth inning of Game Six, when the proverbial wheels fell off. By the bottom of the sixth inning, Ricky Horton, who had relieved a frustrated John Tudor in the fifth, was having issues of his own. Forsch entered with a runner on first and no outs. A walk and a passed ball put Minnesota runners on second and third. Forsch, however, bracketed an intentional walk of Don Baylor with a pair of infield popups from Gary Gaetti and Tom Brunansky.

Forsch may just have been able to get out of the jam. Herzog, though, opted to have lefty Ken Dayley pitch to Kent Hrbek, a left-handed hitter. Dayley followed Forsch's Game One example and gave up the second grand slam of the 1987 World Series. The Cardinals lost Game Six, 11-5.

Things looked promising for the Cardinals in Game Seven, as well, until the Twins tied it in the fifth inning and went ahead in the sixth. They added an insurance run in the eighth before their closer, Jeff Reardon, retired the Cardinals in order in the top of the ninth to lock up the World Series.

On August 28, 1988, Forsch pitched six innings in Cincinnati, giving up six hits, walking five, and allowing three earned runs. When he was relieved in the top of the seventh by Ken Dayley, the Cardinals led the Reds, 5-3. The score had not changed by game's end, and Forsch recorded his 163rd major-league win. He and the Cardinals then flew to Atlanta to start a three-game series with the Braves.

At about 3:00 p.m. the following day, Forsch got a phone call.

"I was already at the ballpark and in uniform. … I'd rather get to the ballpark. There was always a card game or something going … you know, the fraternity, the roadshow. … And I get called to the phone in the clubhouse. And [Cardinals GM Dal Maxvill] said, 'We've made a trade and you're going to Houston.' … Except I told him, 'Hey, you can't trade me without my consent.' … Dal told me, 'Well, if you stay here you're not going to pitch again.'"[64]

Having amassed more than 10 years of major-league service and having spent the last five years with the same club gave Forsch the right, at least technically, to veto any trade arranged by the Cardinals.

"I was a little shocked, to say the least. I told [Whitey Herzog] that I was … thinking of vetoing the trade. … Whitey said, 'It's my team. And nobody's telling me who I'll pitch and who I won't pitch.' … Then I asked Whitey what my [contract] situation would be for the next year, the '89 season. He said, 'The same situation that it's been for the last three years.' … Which meant I'd have to make the team in spring training."[65]

Forsch did not have long to make up his mind. In order to be eligible for the playoffs, he would have to make it onto the Astros roster before August 31.

"[The Astros] said I'd have a guaranteed contract for the next season, 1989. … So I decided to okay the trade. … I wasn't ready to quit. I wanted to see what another organization was like. … My brother had played in Houston and had liked it down there. And the Astros had a really good team that was going for a championship."[66]

On September 5, 1988, Forsch pitched the first game of his major-league career for a team other than the Cardinals. He won the game, giving up five hits, walking one, and allowing no runs through eight innings before Dave Smith closed out the ninth. The Astros, however, did not make the playoffs. After Forsch won his Astros debut, they won only eight of their last 25 games. They finished fifth in the National League West, just two games over .500.

August Busch Jr. died on September 29, 1989. He was succeeded as team president by his son, August Busch III, who made no secret of his dislike for ownership of the Cardinals. The club's ownership situation would be in a state of flux until 1996.

The Cardinals started the 1990 season poorly. "Whitey [Herzog] wanted certain players [each in the last year of his contract] signed, or in the alternative, traded. With the death of Gussie Busch … Whitey was unable to get the front office to act. Frustrated, he quit."[67] Herzog's departure, coupled with the death of Gussie Busch, signaled the end of an era for the Cardinals.

As promised, the Houston Astros extended Forsch's contract through 1989. He spent most of the year as a starter, but his performance declined. The Astros did not offer him another contract extension.

Forsch later explained that the decision to retire was a relatively easy one: "[W]hen I was young and

I'd lose … I always thought I'd win the next game, and I always knew when that game would be. … When I reached the end of my career … I didn't know when I could redeem myself."[68]

After retiring, Forsch turned down opportunities to coach with at least two clubs, the Cardinals and the Phillies.[69] Once his playing days were over, Forsch loved the time he was able to spend with his family. Whenever he was home during his career, he had always made sure to drive his daughters, Amy and Kristin, to school; "that's the only time I see them," he had lamented in 1986.[70] He could now give them the time he'd always wanted.

Forsch also spent time fishing and golfing, sometimes for charity, but always preferably with one or more of the many friends he made during his career. Additionally, he enjoyed sitting comfortably at home on his couch.[71] "He is so desiring to be at home and with his family that he's a real tough one to get to do things[,]" his wife once said.[72] Doing nothing, Forsch never hesitated to admit, was among his favorite pastimes. "And I'm *reaaaaaal* good at it."[73] He perennially delayed returning to baseball as a coach, although it never strayed too far from his mind.[74]

Forsch took up one activity in the fall of 2002 that he had never previously imagined; Bob Wheatley wrote, "He had no plans to do a book. Ever. … 'Oh no,' he said, 'I can't write a book.' … 'You don't have to,' I said. 'You just tell stories.' … It took some convincing but he agreed to give it a try. … He talked … I wrote and munched through his stash of cashews and peanut M&Ms, as Forschie complained that his meager book royalties wouldn't cover his snack bill."[75] The book they wrote is called *Tales From the St. Louis Cardinals Dugout: A Collection of the Greatest Cardinals Stories Ever Told*. No source has been more useful in the writing of this biography.

Success returned to the Cardinals after their sale in 1995 and '96. Ten years later, they began construction of a new ballpark to succeed Busch II. Shortly after their last game of 2005, with their new home halfway finished across the street, demolition crews brought down the old stadium.

Forsch's first no-hitter, in 1978, was the first no-hitter ever pitched at Busch II. The stadium's demolition ensured that Forsch's second no-hitter, in 1983, had been the last—no one else ever pulled it off, even once.

Forsch became fond of spending time as an instructor in the Cardinals fantasy camp each spring in Jupiter, Florida…[76] Florida's climate, apparently, suited him. His daughters having both left home and graduated from college, Forsch's marriage of three decades ended while he was writing his book.[77] He got a fresh start when he married his second wife, Janice, and moved with her to their new home north of Tampa.[78]

In 2007, former Cardinals general manager Walt Jocketty offered Forsch a coaching job with the Cincinnati Reds. This time, Forsch said yes.[79] He spent the next five years as a pitching coach in the Reds' minor-league organization.

Forsch was inducted to the Cardinals Hall of Fame on August 15, 2015. At the ceremony, Amy Forsch displayed a very familiar broad, warm smile as she spoke on behalf of her father. "[A]fter my dad retired," she said, "the thing he missed the most was being part of the team. He loved being part of the team."[80]

A little less than four years earlier, at home in Florida, Bob Forsch had collapsed. He died on November 3, 2011, at the age of 61.[81] It had been less than a week since he relieved his former manager and threw the ceremonial first pitch before Game Seven of the World Series.

He had watched that game in a suite at the new Busch Stadium, with former teammates Danny Cox and Joe Magrane.[82] The Cardinals won, 6-2. "He was happy[,]" Danny Cox said; "He was loving what he was doing."[83] He was probably a little nostalgic, as well, seeing the Cardinals reenact the happiest moment of his career. Surely, as Bob Forsch watched the last game he ever saw, his smile had never been broader or warmer.

SOURCES

In addition to the sources cited in the Notes, the author also consulted baseball-reference.com and the following:

NO-HITTERS

1982 World Series. Dir. Harry Coyle. Perf. Joe Garagiola, Dick Enberg, and Tony Kubek. NBC Sports; Major League Baseball. 1982.

Baseball. Dir. Ken Burns. PBS. 1994, 2009.

"Fans Speak Out." *Baseball Digest*, November/December 2015.

Feldmann, Doug. *Gibson's Last Stand: The Rise, Fall, and Near Misses of the St. Louis Cardinals, 1969-1975* (Columbia: University of Missouri Press, 2011).

Hummel, Rick. "Forsch Locks Self out for Summer." *St. Louis Post-Dispatch*, March 5, 1990: 5C.

McDermott, Mark, et al. "History." 2010. *BaseballSacramento.com*. August 2 2014. baseballsacramento.com/History-All-City_1961-1970.html.

National Baseball Hall of Fame and Museum. "Bill Sayles." *Diamond Mines*. August 2, 2014. scouts.baseballhall.org/scout?s-sabr-id=58bff33a.

Simmons, Ted. Remarks at the 2015 Cardinals Hall of Fame Induction Ceremony. St. Louis, August 15.

"Fanfare," *Washington Post*, January 23, 1988: B2.

Sutter, Bruce. Remarks at the 2015 Cardinals Hall of Fame Induction Ceremony. St. Louis, August 15.

NOTES

1 Tom Barnidge, "Forsch's Pitching Outclassed Reviews," *St. Louis Post-Dispatch*, October 8, 1982: 1B.

2 Bob Forsch and Tom Wheatley, *Tales From the St. Louis Cardinals Dugout: A Collection of the Greatest Cardinals Stories Ever Told* (New York: Sports Publishing, 2006), 168.

3 Forsch and Wheatley, 55, 90.

4 Tom Wheatley, "Forsches Wisely Heeded Pa's Pitch," *St. Louis Post-Dispatch*, July 7, 1987: C1.

5 Bob Broeg, "Forsch's Maturity Key Factor in Cards' Title Quest," *St. Louis Post-Dispatch*, March 27, 1975: 2C.

6 Nelson Greene, "Ken Forsch" (forthcoming), SABR BioProject.

7 Forsch and Wheatley, 26.

8 Forsch and Wheatley, 52.

9 Joe Davidson, "A Look Back at All D-1 Baseball Champions Since 1968," *Sacramento Bee*, May 27, 2009. blogs.sacbee.com/preps/archives/2009/05/a-look-back-at-all-d.html.

10 Forsch wrote, in *Tales From the Cardinals Dugout*, that he was selected in the 38th round of the draft (Forsch and Wheatley, 52); *Baseball Almanac* and *Baseball-Reference.com*, however, both list him as being drafted 594th overall, in the 26th round.

11 Forsch and Wheatley, 27.

12 Ibid.

13 Tom Wheatley, "Forschie" (2013), in Forsch and Wheatley, xii.

14 Forsch and Wheatley, 5.

15 Forsch and Wheatley, 5-6.

16 Tom Barnidge, "Forsch's Pitching Outclassed Reviews," *St. Louis Post-Dispatch*, October 8, 1982: 1B, 4B.

17 Broeg, "Forsch's Maturity."

18 Carolyn Olson, "Bob Forsch Makes a Pitch to Stay in St. Louis," *St. Louis Post-Dispatch*, December 17, 1986: 3W.

19 Forsch and Wheatley, 15.

20 Forsch and Wheatley, 144.

21 Ibid.

22 Peter Golenbock, *The Spirit of St. Louis: A History of the St. Louis Cardinals and Browns* (New York: Spike/Avon Books, 2000), 526.

23 Weather Underground. "Weather History for St. Louis, MO," wunderground.com.

24 Mike Eisenbath, "Malaise ... Cardinals' Winning Tradition Took a Hike in 1970s," *St. Louis Post Dispatch*, August 23, 1992: 3F.

25 Forsch and Wheatley, 132.

26 Ibid.

27 Neal Russo, „Forsch Avoids Jinxes, Gets No-Hitter, *St. Louis Post-Dispatch*, April 17, 1978: 1C, 4C.

28 Allen Lewis, "Tainted No-Hitters." *Baseball Digest*, February 2002: 60.

29 Forsch and Wheatley, 132.

30 Ibid.

31 Russo, "Forsch Avoids Jinxes, Gets No-Hitter," 4C.

32 Ibid.

33 Tom Wheatley, "Complete Game: Forsch Enjoys Retirement With No Regrets," *St. Louis Post Dispatch*, August 23, 1990: 1D, 3D.

34 "Ken Forsch Makes Little Brother Proud," *St. Louis Post-Dispatch*, April 9, 1979: 2B.

35 Ibid.

36 Golenbock, 538.

37 Barnidge, "Forsch's Pitching Outclassed Reviews," 4B.

38 Forsch and Wheatley, 171-172.

39 "Where Are They Now? Bob Forsch," *St. Louis Post-Dispatch*, August 15, 2003: D8.

40 "Forsch Files Fraud Charge against His Former Agent," *St. Louis Post Dispatch*, May 6, 1983: 6B.

41 Ibid.

42 Forsch and Wheatley, 76.

43 Ibid.

44 Ibid.

45 Forsch and Wheatley, 132.

NO-HITTERS

46 Hummel, "Forsch Adds Some Taste to an Unpalatable Season," 6C.

47 Rick Hummel, "Forsch Hurls His 2nd No-Hitter," *St. Louis Post Dispatch*, September 27, 1983: 1C, 6C.

48 Hummel, "Forsch Hurls His 2nd No-Hitter," 6C.

49 Hummel, "Forsch Hurls His 2nd No-Hitter," 1C.

50 Rick Hummel, "Forsch Hurls Another Gem, 3-2," *St. Louis Post-Dispatch*, October 2, 1983: 1F, 6F.

51 Forsch and Wheatley, 76.

52 Golenbock, 552.

53 *1985 World Series*. Dir. Harry Coyle. Perf. Al Michaels, Jim Palmer, and Tim McCarver. ABC Sports; Major League Baseball.

54 Golenbock, 562.

55 *MLB Network Countdown*, "The Most Controversial Calls in MLB History," MLB Network. 2010.

56 Bernie Miklasz, "Bernie Bytes: Remembering Bob Forsch." *St. Louis Post-Dispatch*, November 4, 2011. stltoday.com/sports/baseball/professional/bernie-bytes-remembering-bob-forsch/article_94654ad2-06f5-11e1-a395-0019bb30f31a.html.

57 Forsch and Wheatley, 40.

58 Golenbock, 569.

59 Malcolm Moran, "Forsch Was Ready for Call," *New York Times*, October 22, 1987.

60 Golenbock, 572.

61 Rick Hummel, "Forsch was 'Icon in Cards' History,'" *St. Louis Post-Dispatch*, November 5, 2011. stltoday.com/sports/baseball/professional/cardinal-beat/cardinals-pitcher-forsch-dies-at-age/article_bdfb18cc-06f5-11e1-a7f4-001a4bcf6878.html#ixzz1cku6QvBa.

62 Moran, "Forsch Was Ready for Call."

63 *1987 World Series*, Game Four.

64 Forsch and Wheatley, 83.

65 Forsch and Wheatley, 83-84.

66 Forsch and Wheatley, 84.

67 Ibid.

68 Golenbock, 580.

69 Tom Wheatley, "Complete Game: Forsch Enjoys Retirement With No Regrets," *St. Louis Post-Dispatch*, August 23, 1990: 1D, 3D.

70 Olson, "Forsch Makes a Pitch to Stay in St. Louis."

71 Wheatley, "Complete Game: Forsch Enjoys Retirement with No Regrets."

72 Olson, "Forsch Makes a Pitch to Stay in St. Louis."

73 Tom Wheatley, "The Cardinal Way" (2013), in Forsch and Wheatley, xiv.

74 Ibid.

75 Wheatley, "Forschie," xi-xii.

76 "Where Are They Now? Bob Forsch," D8.

77 Wheatley, "The Cardinal Way," xiv.

78 Ibid.

79 Ibid.

80 Amy Forsch, remarks at the St. Louis Cardinals Hall of Fame Induction Ceremony. St. Louis, August 15, 2015.

81 Rick Hummel, "Former Cardinals Pitcher Bob Forsch Dies at 61," *St. Louis Post-Dispatch* November 5, 2011. STLToday.com. stltoday.com/sports/baseball/professional/cardinal-beat/former-cardinals-pitcher-bob-forsch-dies-at/article_d448e11e-0753-11e1-b253-0019bb30f31a.html.

82 Hummel, "Forsch was 'Icon in Cards' History."

83 Ibid.

BOB FORSCH THROWS THE CARDINALS' FIRST NO-HITTER AT HOME SINCE 1924

APRIL 16, 1978: ST. LOUIS CARDINALS 5, PHILADELPHIA PHILLIES 0, AT BUSCH MEMORIAL STADIUM, ST. LOUIS

By Ben Girard

APRIL 16, 1978, WAS NOT an ideal day for baseball in St. Louis. As a sparse crowd sauntered into Busch Memorial Stadium (*Busch II*) that afternoon, the temperature was under 45 degrees.[1] The Cardinals had been losing crowd appeal throughout the 1970s. Their home opener, six days earlier, had drawn only 19,241. Only 11,495 showed up to watch Bob Forsch start his third game of the season, against the defending National League East champion Philadelphia Phillies.

Unlike the Cardinals' ticket sales, Forsch was in a good place. He had rebounded from a shoulder injury in to win 20 games in 1977. He started on Opening Day 1978, and gave up just one run on five hits through 7⅓ innings as the Cardinals won, 5-1. His second start was even better: With his parents on hand, he struck out nine Pirates, walked only three, and allowed just four hits in a complete game. Again the Cardinals won, 5-1. Forsch described it as one of the best games he ever pitched.[2] "I really felt proud," he recalled.[3]

Although Forsch was at the top of his game on April 16, he didn't feel like it. "My arm just felt weak, like I'd spent it all the game before."[4] A start against the Phillies in 1978 was not the best time to have a tired arm. They had an impressive lineup, and had their eyes on a third consecutive division title.

After Forsch retired Bake McBride and Larry Bowa, Schmidt gave him an early scare by pounding a high fly ball deep to center field. Outfielder Tony Scott hauled it in at the warning track, ending the top of the first inning. The Cardinals threatened in the bottom of the first when Phillies starter Randy Lerch walked the Cardinals leadoff hitter, speedster Lou Brock. Three pop flies, however, kept the Cardinals off the scoreboard.

Two pop flies then worked in Forsch's favor before the Phillies' Garry Maddux pounded a pitch into the infield turf. Cardinals catcher Ted Simmons handled it and threw to first baseman Keith Hernandez, bringing the Cardinals back to the plate for the bottom of the second. They too were retired in order. Forsch then set down the bottom of the Phillies order in the top of the third, via a pop fly and two infield groundballs, before he struck out to lead off the bottom of the third. Brock and shortstop Gary Templeton each lined out.

With the top of the Phillies order due in the fourth to get its second look at Forsch, now was as likely a time as any for Forsch's tired arm to falter. McBride flied to center, however, and Bowa hit a hard grounder to Hernandez, who tossed to Forsch, covering first base. Mike Schmidt again scared the Cardinals by taking a pitch deep to center; it was caught, again, by Tony Scott.

The Cardinals broke the deadlock in the bottom of the fourth when catcher Ted Simmons doubled, advanced to third on a grounder by Hernandez, and scored on a single by Ken Reitz. Forsch took the mound for the top of the fifth with a one-run lead.

After the Phillies' leadoff hitter ground out to first, Forsch walked Richie Hebner. The first Phillies baserunner of the game, Hebner put himself in scoring position and removed himself from double-play candidacy by stealing second. With a runner on second, a groundball could advance the runner to third or tie the game, especially on the thin Astroturf of Busch II. Forsch reached back for more power, and found it. He struck out Garry Maddux and Bob Boone to strand Hebner on second.

The next three Cardinals hitters went down in order. The bottom of the Phillies lineup returned the favor in the top of the sixth. "You don't even think about a no-hitter until after the sixth inning," Forsch wrote, "when you only have to go through the lineup one more time."[5]

With two outs in the bottom of the sixth, Hernandez appeared to ground out. Lerch bobbled the ball, however, extending the inning and allowing Garry Templeton (who had doubled) to take third base. Lerch then hit Reitz to load the bases before Roger Freed, pinch-hitting for Tony Scott, doubled to right field, clearing the bases and giving the Cardinals a 4-0 lead.

In the top of the seventh, Forsch faced the heart of the Phillies order. After Larry Bowa ground out—again—Mike Schmidt hit a pitch deep to center field—again. This time it was Jerry Mumphrey, Scott's replacement in center field, who hauled it in. If Cardinals manager Vern Rapp eyed the bullpen phone when Forsch issued his second walk of the day, he would have stopped when the next batter popped up harmlessly to short. Lerch rediscovered his footing in the bottom of the seventh and retired Forsch, Brock, and Templeton in order.

Leading off the top of the eighth, Garry Maddux hit a hard groundball to Reitz at third base. Reitz "reached for the ball but it went under his glove."[6] Forsch wrote, "I knew I had a no-hitter. So did everybody who was there. Everybody in the stadium was watching the scoreboard to see whether it was called a hit or an error. ... Neal Russo of the *St. Louis Post-Dispatch*—who was the official scorer—called it an error. ... I later asked Neal about it. ... He told me, 'That far along in the game, the first hit has to be a clean hit.'"[7]

The next Phillies batter, Bob Boone, hit a groundball to the shortstop. Templeton threw quickly to second baseman Mike Tyson, who forced out Maddox and threw to Hernandez, completing a 6-4-3 double play. Ted Sizemore then hit a line drive directly to Templeton. Forsch was just three outs away.

Whenever Forsch made it into the Cardinals clubhouse between innings, he could hear a radio tuned to local station KMOX; "he heard plenty about [his performance;] ...'They were saying on the radio that no no-hitter had been pitched by a Cardinal in St. Louis in 54 years.'"[8]

In the bottom of the eighth, right fielder Jerry Morales led off with a single. Keith Hernandez appeared to hit a double-play ball to the Phillies' shortstop, but Bowa committed an error that allowed the runners to advance to third and second. Lerch was replaced by reliever Gene Garber, who intentionally loaded the bases before retiring the next two batters. Close as he was to getting out of the jam, Garber then walked Dane Iorg, pinch-hitting for Tyson. The Cardinals led 5-0. With the bases loaded, Forsch flied out to center field.

The crowd "'pumped me up,' Forsch said. 'It was a tremendous feeling. With all that cheering when I went out in the ninth, I felt like I could lick the world.'"[9] Hitting for the pitcher, the Phillies' Jay Johnstone led off. Cardinals catcher Ted Simmons said a pivotal pitch that inning was "'the first pitch to Johnstone. ... [I]f he took that pitch for a strike, we had him.'"[10] They did, on a groundout.

The Phillies' number-one and number-two hitters, McBride and Bowa, were next. "'McBride?'" Simmons said, "He hadn't hit at all during the series. We kept feeding him slow stuff.'"[11] McBride grounded out to Mike Phillips, who came in for Dane Iorg and took Tyson's spot at second base. Bowa then hit a groundball to Reitz, who threw to first for the out. "Forsch said he didn't remember the last inning. 'But I did know there were three outs and it was over.'"[12] He had shut out the Phillies, 5-0, on two walks, three strikeouts, one error, and no hits: a no-hitter.

As Forsch and the Cardinals celebrated, the Phillies protested. They claimed Garry Maddox's grounder in the eighth inning beat Ken Reitz for a hit, despite the score keeper's ruling. Lucky or not, Forsch had thrown a complete game on just 96 pitches.[13] That day he had been a very good pitcher at his very best.

A little less than a year later, Bob Forsch's brother, Ken, celebrated his own no-hitter in Houston. "I thought of all the great brother acts in baseball[,]'" he said; "'The Niekros, the Perrys, and Dizzy and Daffy Dean.'"[14] On April 7, 1979, the Forsch brothers did something none of those others ever did: They became the only brothers to throw no-hitters in major-league baseball.

Between celebratory hugs and champagne-soaked interviews, Ken received a telegram. It read: *"Congratulations on your no-hitter. I know how it feels. Enjoy every minute of it. Your Little Brother."*[15]

SOURCES

In addition to the sources in the Notes, the author also consulted baseball-reference.com and Amy Forsch's remarks at the Cardinals Hall of Fame Induction Ceremony, St. Louis, August 15, 2015.

NOTES

1. Weather Underground, "Weather History for St. Louis, MO," wunderground.com/history/airport/KSTL/1978/4/16/DailyHistory.html?req_city=&req_state=&req_statename=&reqdb.zip=&reqdb.magic=&reqdb.wmo=&MR=1.
2. Bob Forsch and Tom Wheatley, *Tales From the St. Louis Cardinals Dugout: A Collection of the Greatest Cardinals Stories Ever Told* (New York: Sports Publishing, 2006), 131.
3. Forsch and Wheatley, 132.
4. Ibid.
5. Ibid.
6. Allen Lewis, "Tainted No-Hitters," *Baseball Digest*, February 2002: 60.
7. Forsch and Wheatley, 132.
8. Neal Russo, "Forsch Avoids Jinxes, Gets No-Hitter," *St. Louis Post-Dispatch*, April 17, 1978: 4C.
9. Ibid.
10. Ibid.
11. Ibid.
12. Neal Russo, "Freed Breaks Ice: 'I Know I Can Hit,'" *St. Louis Post-Dispatch*, 1978: 4C.
13. Ibid.
14. News Services, "Ken Forsch Makes Little Brother Proud," *St. Louis Post-Dispatch*, April 9, 1979: 2B.
15. Ibid.

BOB FORSCH SETTLES THE SCORE, DODGES THE KNUCKLEBALL, AND THROWS HIS SECOND NO-HITTER

SEPTEMBER 26, 1983: ST. LOUIS CARDINALS 3, MONTREAL EXPOS 0, AT BUSCH MEMORIAL STADIUM, ST. LOUIS

By Ben Girard

ON SEPTEMBER 26, 1983, AN article in the *St. Louis Post-Dispatch* read, "Cardinals Manager Whitey Herzog would like to have veteran Bob Forsch go to the Florida Instructional League this offseason to work on a knuckleball. But Herzog said he hadn't received an answer from the 33-year-old Forsch, who has struggled to an 8-12 record this season. ... He is to start tonight against the Montreal Expos."[1]

The Expos battled with the Philadelphia Phillies in 1983 for the NL East. Since a 13-inning walk-off win against the Cardinals on September 16, however, the Phillies had been on a winning streak that Montreal couldn't match. On September 26 the Expos were readying to play the Cardinals in St. Louis when the Phillies won their 11th straight. That was it—regardless of the outcome of their own game that night, the Expos had been eliminated from playoff contention.

The temperature rested comfortably in the mid-70s as Bob Forsch took the mound to start the game. Terry Francona led off for the Expos; it was only the third time the Expos pinch-hitter had started in the number one spot that season. After he grounded out to second, Manny Trillo popped up to right field. Andre Dawson sent a shot to center field that looked like trouble, but Willie McGee made an exceptional catch to put the Expos away in order. The Cardinals' Ken Oberkfell tripled to center in the bottom of the inning but, the Cardinals were unable to bring him home.

After retiring the first two batters in the second inning, Forsch looked ready to put away the Expos in order once again. The next Expos batter, however, was catcher Gary Carter, and Forsch did not intend for him to make an out.

Forsch recalled, "You know how some guys just bug you? Gary Carter bugged me ... bad!"[2] Forsch's previous start had also been against the Expos, five days earlier, in Montreal.

„You always had to pitch Gary inside so he couldn't get his arms out and pound the ball. ... I threw a pitch that was sort of tight. It just ran in on him for ball four. He went down to first base. And on the way he said something like, "throw the ball over the plate." ... I wasn't feeling great. So I said, 'The next one you get will hit you.' ... I ended up getting knocked out of that game before he came up again."[3]

The second inning in St. Louis was the next time they saw each other. True to his word, Forsch hit Carter with a fastball. "He went to first base and didn't say a word"[4] as home-plate umpire Harry Wendelstedt warned both benches. The next batter, third baseman Chris Speier, reached base when he sent a groundball through the legs of Oberkfell, playing second base in place of the injured Tom Herr. Carter went from first base to third on the error. With Carter now 90 feet from home plate, Forsch averted the crisis by striking out shortstop Angel Salazar.

The Cardinals and Expos then traded 1-2-3 half-innings. In the bottom of the third, after Ozzie

Smith and Forsch each grounded out, Lonnie Smith reached base with an infield single. He was caught stealing to end the inning. In the top of the fourth, Forsch retired Andre Dawson and Al Oliver on fly balls to left field, and got Tim Raines to ground out.

In the bottom the fourth, with one out, Willie McGee singled, stole second, then advanced to third on a fly ball to right by Darrell Porter. Andy Van Slyke, playing in Ken Oberkfell's regular spot at third base, struck out to end the inning. Gary Carter led off the Expos half of the fifth with a fly ball in foul territory to first baseman Jim Adduci, a Cardinals September call-up. Speier and Salazar both then grounded out.

Cardinals right fielder David Green led off the bottom of the fifth with a walk, and avoided a double play by making it safely to second base when Adduci grounded out to first base. Ozzie Smith singled to center field, scoring Green, and advanced to second base on the throw home. Bob Forsch played an offensive part of his own by flying out to right field, allowing Smith to advance to third base. Smith scored when left fielder Lonnie Smith doubled to left. Willie McGee brought Lonnie Smith home with a single to right before Darrell Porter ended the inning by striking out.

Steve Rogers' day was over. With his spot up first in the top of the sixth, Warren Cromartie pinch-hit, and struck out. Forsch had now been through the Expos' lineup twice without allowing a hit. He promptly sat down Francona and Trillo on a ground-out and a pop fly.

Forsch said after the game, "After I finished the sixth inning, I figured I had a fairly decent chance."[5] His wife, Mollie, admitted, "I started getting nervous in the fifth."[6]

Steve Rogers' replacement on the pitcher's mound was Dan Schatzeder. He hit the first Cardinals batter he faced, Andy Van Slyke, and was promptly ejected from the game. After an argument with home-plate umpire Wendelstedt, Expos manager Bill Virdon also earned himself an early exit. Ray Burris replaced Schatzeder and Expos coach Vern Rapp took over managerial duties. (Rapp had been the Cardinals manager when Forsch threw his no-hitter on April 16, 1978.)

Ray Burris replaced Schatzeder and retired Adduci and Ozzie Smith on fly balls, then struck out Forsch to end the inning. Leading off the seventh, Andre Dawson grounded to Ozzie Smith. After Al Oliver did the same, Tim Raines connected with a pitch, sending it to right field, where it was caught by David Green. The Cardinals then went down in order for the first time since the second inning.

With Gary Carter due to lead off the eighth, Whitey Herzog substituted Bill Lyons, a defensive improvement at second base, for Lonnie Smith. Ken Oberkfell moved from second to his preferred third base, and Andy Van Slyke moved from third base to left field. With an improved defense behind him, Forsch promptly struck out Gary Carter and Chris Speier—the only back-to-back strikeouts Forsch achieved all game—then fielded the next out himself. The crowd, belying its size of 12,457, erupted as Forsch tossed to Adduci for out number three. For the second time in his life, Forsch was three outs away from a no-hitter.

Forsch's teammates gave him little chance to rest before the top of the ninth; in the bottom of the eighth they went down 1-2-3. Forsch later described the crowd: "Every time I threw a pitch, there was a crowd reaction. … That kind of thing makes you do more than you're capable of doing."[7] Francona kept the Cardinals' defense awake by flying out to right field. With two outs, Manny Trillo stepped to the plate.

Oberkfell, now at third, found himself in the path of another sharply hit groundball, this one off Trillo's bat. When Adduci received Oberkfell's throw at first base, Forsch became the 25th major-league pitcher to throw multiple no-hitters. In the clubhouse Oberkfell said, "I'm glad I didn't make an error on the last one."[8]

The no-hitter put Forsch at 9-12 for the season. On October 1, in his last start of the season, he pitched well enough to earn his 10th win. By that evening, he had "definitely … decided not to experiment with the knuckleball in the Florida Instructional League[.]"[9]

The epilogue came the following season. Forsch recalled, "[T]he first time we played the Expos, George Hendrick came into the clubhouse before the game and said, 'Hey, Gary Carter wants to talk to you outside on the runway.' ... So I went out there, and to his credit, Gary said, "I play hard. Every day." ... And he did. ... I told Gary, 'I pitch hard. Every day.' ... And I did. ... I respected him for coming up and saying that. And we never had a problem after that."[10]

SOURCES

In addition to the sources cited in the Notes, the author consulted Baseball-Reference.com.

NOTES

1 Rick Hummel, "Herzog Would Like Forsch to Work on Knuckleball," *St. Louis Post-Dispatch*, September 26, 1983: 8C.

2 Bob Forsch and Tom Wheatley, *Tales From the St. Louis Cardinals Dugout: A Collection of the Greatest Cardinals Stories Ever Told* (New York: Sports Publishing, 2006): 76.

3 Ibid.

4 Ibid.

5 Hummel, "Forsch Hurls His 2nd No-Hitter," *St. Louis Post-Dispatch*, September 27, 1983: 6C.

6 Hummel, "Forsch Adds Some Taste to an Unpalatable Season," *St. Louis Post-Dispatch*, September 27, 1983: 6C.

7 Hummel, "Forsch Hurls His 2nd No-Hitter."

8 Ibid.

9 Hummel, "Forsch Hurls Another Gem, 3-2," *St. Louis Post-Dispatch*, October 2, 1983: 1F, 6F.

10 Forsch and Wheatley, 76.

KEN FORSCH

By Chip Greene

ON SEPTEMBER 30, 2011, after his team's 91st victory of the season, Anaheim Angels general manager Tony Reagins resigned his position. Three days later, owner Arte Moreno announced that the team had declined to renew the contracts of assistant to the general manager Gary Sutherland and assistant general manager Ken Forsch. For the 65-year-old Forsch, his severance brought to an end not only a 30-year relationship with the Angels; it also marked the end of a 43-year affiliation with major-league baseball. His career had been quite a journey.

Fittingly, that journey had ended in a city, Anaheim, that was just a long day's drive down Interstate 5 from where Forsch had learned the game more than 60 years earlier. Forsch had been introduced to the game almost from the day he was born. On September 8, 1946, Herbert Forsch, the owner of Forsch Electric Motors, in north Sacramento, California, and his wife, Freda, welcomed their first child, whom they christened Kenneth Roth Forsch. In addition to the senior Forsch's business (he repaired electric motors that farmers used in their irrigation systems), the Forsches also owned a chicken farm in Sacramento, where the family lived on several acres of fertile land. In 2016 Ken remembered, "I had a baseball uniform and bat and mitt in my crib when I was brought home from the hospital."[1] Those implements were far more than simply an infant's toys, however. Indeed, baseball was central to Herb Forsch's life.

In his off-hours, Herb was a pitcher and third baseman on several semipro teams in the Sacramento area.[2] By all accounts he was quite a skilled player, too: In 1978 he was inducted into the La Salle Club Baseball Hall of Fame.[3] Ken Forsch provided an amusing anecdote about his father's career: "Dad would pitch on Sunday, and in order to keep in shape, my mother had to catch him, behind the garage of the house they lived in then." Asked once by Ken to confirm this story, Herb replied, "She sure did. I'd smoke 'em in there pretty good, too, and she'd catch 'em. I didn't have to worry about her. She could handle the glove."[4] Years later, as her son(s) developed their own baseball careers, they too asked their mother to catch them. "When [we] were small," Ken recalled, "she tried to catch us. But I think she'd lost her touch by then."[5]

In January 1950 the Forsches welcomed their second child, another son, whom they named Robert Herbert Forsch. Like his older brother, Bob too was destined to become a major-league pitcher.

Despite Herb's athletic career, the boys were never forced into baseball; their love for the game developed naturally. Still, if Herb never encouraged the boys to go out and practice, their parents provided their sons with everything they needed to succeed. On the acreage behind the house, Herb built a baseball diamond. During summers, all the kids in the neighborhood would play ball there from sunup to sundown. When Herb arrived home from work each evening, he and the boys would also play pepper for half an hour in the front yard. It became a ritual before they all went in to dinner.

Fully grown, Ken Forsch eventually reached a height of 6 feet 4 inches tall and maintained a weight of around 210 pounds. It took a while to reach that size, however. Throughout Little League and Babe Ruth League, from ages roughly 9 through 12, Forsch, who never played any position other than pitcher (although he did recall, "I played a little bit at shortstop") was "really small." Therefore, the 60 feet 6 inches from the pitcher's mound to home plate was "a challenge." By the time Forsch reached Sacramento's Hiram Johnson High School, he was still diminutive, which hampered his ability to make the varsity baseball team; "I kept getting cut," he recalled. By his junior year, Forsch had reached 5 feet 6 inches, and over the next year grew another six inches. Finally, in his senior year, Forsch made the varsity. With his newfound height he also played basketball, and in that senior season was named both Most Valuable Player in baseball and the school's Most Valuable Athlete. With his rapidly developing natural ability to throw hard, Forsch, who graduated in 1964, was now ready to take his game to the next level.

Asked in 2016 whether he had been scouted in high school, Forsch recalled, "I was not very strong then. ... I was still growing; had sore arm problems. ... I think the Pittsburgh Pirates were going to draft me [out of high school], but my father told [Pirates scout] Ronnie King, 'I don't think you should sign him because he's been battling a sore arm.' So (the Pirates) backed off."

Forsch had hurt his arm playing for the local American Legion team in the summer after graduation. The Legion team featured at shortstop future major leaguer Larry Bowa, whose father coached the team. Forsch had already enrolled at Sacramento City College, but when he hurt his arm, he said, "It hurt so bad, I couldn't throw for over a year. I couldn't even go out for the SCC baseball team." Instead, Forsch joined the basketball team, where he played guard. By midseason, after receiving therapy for his injury, he found that he could throw the basketball downcourt on fast breaks with no pain, so he went out for the varsity baseball team, made it, and later threw a no-hitter. (Larry Bowa was a teammate.) By then scouts were again interested in the tall right-hander.[6]

In 1966 Forsch was drafted by the California Angels in the ninth round of the amateur draft. While he talked to the Angels about signing, even traveled to Stockton, California, to watch their California League affiliate there play, he ultimately turned down the Angels' offer, deciding instead to remain in school. Soon, though, he received another offer, one he couldn't decline.

Gene Tanselli, the head baseball coach at Oregon State University, had kept an eye on Forsch during the pitcher's City College season; it's likely he was there when Forsch threw his no-hitter. So when Tanselli offered Forsch a scholarship, Forsch accepted, and

KEN FORSCH   PITCHER   HOUSTON ASTROS

headed to Corvallis, Oregon, for the 1967 baseball season.

The next two seasons ultimately propelled Forsch to the major leagues. (In 1991 he was inducted into the OSU Athletics Hall of Fame.[7]) At the time of his induction, Forsch held the school record for strikeouts in a season (121), amassed during a stellar 1968 campaign in which he also threw a stretch of 48 scoreless innings and was named a second-team All-PAC 8 selection. Bob Lillis, a Houston Astros advance scout, saw Forsch in a game against Arizona State University in which, Forsch later recalled, "I think I struck out just about everybody who came up for five innings." Impressed, Lillis told the Astros, and they sent scout Ray Coley to Oregon State to confirm the pitcher's talents. Coley signed Forsch to a contract. Subsequently, the Astros drafted Forsch in the 18th round of the 1968 amateur draft, and the 21-year-old's professional career began.

(According to Baseball-Reference.com, Forsch was also drafted in the 1967 by the Chicago Cubs but did not sign. When asked to confirm, Forsch was surprised. "Oh, OK, I had no idea I was even drafted by the Cubs," he said. "I don't think I was ever drafted by the Cubs. I know a number of teams were talking to me. The Dodgers called and I told them what I wanted for a bonus, and they quickly backed off. I think they signed Sandy Vance instead of me.")

Over the next 2½ years, Forsch worked his way through the Astros' minor-league system, making stops at every level: Single-A Greensboro (North Carolina), Williamsport (Pennsylvania), and Peninsula (Hampton, Virginia) in 1968 and '69 (when he also worked in the Florida Instructional League); and Double-A Columbus (Georgia) and Triple-A Oklahoma City in 1970. While his numbers proved impressive at each stop, Forsch also endured several notable physical ailments. In 1969, while pitching for Peninsula, Forsch was a member of the Oregon National Guard (he received basic training at Fort Lewis, Washington). Once a month he was required to fly to Corvallis for Guard meetings. One night in May 1969, after all-night maneuvers, Forsch and a Peninsula teammate, Jack Humphrey, were driving to Portland to catch a flight back to Hampton. En route, Humphrey, who was driving, fell asleep at the wheel, ran off the road and wrecked their car. The Astros sent Forsch, who had cut his knee, home for a week to recuperate, after which he returned to Peninsula. Later that season Forsch also suffered from a significant back problem, for which the team brought him to Houston for exploratory surgery. Following a diagnosis of a bulging muscle, Forsch stayed in Houston for a month to rehab, watched the Astros play, then completed the season at Peninsula. In all, he pitched just 17 games that season, but added another 10 in the Instructional League.

By 1970, after brilliant performances at Columbus and Oklahoma City, Forsch was ready for the big leagues. At Columbus he had tied for the Southern League lead in wins, with 13; a league-leading five of those were shutouts. After four more wins and a 1.58 ERA at Oklahoma City in September, the Astros called the right-hander to the National League. On September 7, 1970, the day before his 24th birthday, Forsch debuted in San Diego, as a starter. Taking a 10-0 lead and a one-hitter into the bottom of the ninth, he tired and allowed five hits and five runs, including a grand slam by the Padres' Ramon Webster. Forsch completed the game and won, 10-5, earning what would be his lone victory among four starts before the season ended. Forsch would be a mainstay of the Astros pitching staff for the next 11 years.

As Forsch's Astros pitching career progressed, he was destined, except for a few necessary occasions, rarely to settle into a permanent role. From starter to reliever then back to starter, over the course of his career Forsch's size, strength, durability, and, most importantly, consistency, assured the team that rarely with him on the mound would they be out of a ballgame. In spring training 1971, as Forsch battled for the first time to make the team, Astros manager Harry Walker offered his insights into the reason for the right-hander's effectiveness. Walker's sentiments held true throughout Forsch's tenure with the team.

"More important than his size," offered Walker when asked to explain how Forsch had overcome a number of shaky exhibition performances, "is his desire.... [W]hat attracted our attention was the way he always battled back the next time out [following a poor outing]. He didn't get discouraged and quit. He kept punching. He showed us a lot of courage under pressure. And he improved steadily."

In a word, said Walker, it was "poise — that describes him best, I suppose. Nothing ruffles him."

That quality was echoed that spring by Astros pitching coach Jim Owens, who said, "The first time I saw him, he was further along than most pitchers four or five years older. He must have been born with poise."

For his part, Forsch responded at the time, "What really happens, I think, is that I just get mad at myself and want to prove something. I can't wait for another chance after I've flubbed up."[8] Such a mentality would never dissipate.

Over his first two full seasons, 1971 and '72, Forsch was primarily a starter: 47 of his 63 appearances came in that role. For the most part he was basically a two-pitch pitcher, the fastball and the slider. "I try to get ahead of the hitter right away," Forsch said in 1972. "When you get behind, (the batter) knows you've got to come in to him and is looking for heat somewhere in the strike zone. If you get ahead, you can work on him a little, try for the corners or try to make him chase a slider."[9] That approach garnered Forsch 14 wins during the two seasons.

One game still stood out for Forsch in 2017. It was played on September 24, 1971, in San Diego. He pitched 13 innings and then Harry Walker "removed me for a pinch hitter in the 14th. I was livid. I always felt that as long as you were getting them out, you stayed on the mound till the end of the game. The 13 innings will always be special to me." (The Astros eventually won, in 21 innings.)[10]

In 1973, however, not for the last time, Forsch's role changed. Two factors prompted that move. The previous season, when Forsch had been the fifth starter in a rotation with Don Wilson, Larry Dierker, Dave Roberts, and Jerry Reuss, Leo Durocher had replaced Harry Walker as manager for the final 31 games of the season. Meanwhile, at Triple-A Oklahoma City, in 1972, 6-foot-8 right-hander J.R. Richard, whom the Astros had selected second overall in the 1969 draft, struck out 169 batters in 128 innings, a loud pronouncement that the Astros had to find a place in their starting rotation for their phenom. On top of that, Durocher, who had used a procession of pitchers in short relief, had no stopper in the bullpen; he wanted someone who could come in on short notice, throw hard, and get strikes. So Forsch became the Astros' closer.

On July 29, 1973, Forsch's season record as a starter stood at 8-9, with a 3.83 ERA. That night he made his first appearance in his new role, gaining a win in relief against Atlanta. On August 10 and 11, he earned his first two saves, first in relief of Richard, then Dierker. About his new role, Forsch later admitted, "I've always wanted to be a starter. Doesn't every pitcher? I still think I can be." However, he explained, in regard to his approach as a reliever, "I just went in and threw as hard as I could. ... There's not much new out there. Trouble is still trouble, no matter how you look at it. I've pitched out of enough jams in my life as a starter so I know what it's like when I'm out there in relief. I just go to my power pitches—my fastball and my slider. I give them my best."[11]

With few exceptions, that's what Forsch did for the next five years. Over that span he became one of the best closers in the game. In 1974 Forsch set a team record (later broken) with 70 appearances, all in relief; he won 8 games, saved 10, and tossed 103⅓ innings. In the days before closers evolved into primarily one-inning stoppers who entered only in the ninth inning with their team ahead, Forsch often threw multiple innings: included in his outings that year were single appearances of both five and four innings each, and multiple stints of three innings, a trend he continued throughout his time in the bullpen. In 1976, when Forsch registered a career-high 19 saves over 92 innings, he represented the Astros in the All-Star Game in Philadelphia, the first of what would be two such appearances in his career.

As Forsch solidified and refined his relief role during this period, so too did he adapt his pitching arsenal and mindset. Much of the credit for his development went to Roger Craig, the Astros pitching coach in 1974 and '75. "In the past," Forsch explained in 1974, "I gripped the ball across the seams and my fastball would rise." Instead, "Roger suggested I try gripping it with the seams. Now the ball is sinking instead of rising and they're hitting it on the ground instead of in the air and I'm getting 'em out."[12]

Additionally, Forsch suggested later that fall, "Roger has made me think more aggressively, and he's brought a change in my attitude. He's built my confidence up. I go at the hitters more and pitch quicker to [them]. This keeps the defense on their toes and I think it's a reason I've had so many good plays behind me."[13] That aggressive attitude eventually led to 50 saves in Forsch's Astros career.

While Forsch anchored the Houston bullpen for five years, he was occasionally called upon to start as well: Of the 250 games in which he appeared from 1974 to 1978, he started 20, typically during times when he briefly assumed a fifth-starter role. For those assignments, Forsch took to the mound a greater array of pitches, developed during his time warming up as a reliever, when he would experiment in the bullpen with changing speeds. "As a reliever," offered Craig in 1975, "he was using his fastball all the time. Now he's developed his overhand curve and changeup."[14] Forsch also developed a forkball as an off-speed pitch, and this expanded repertoire enhanced his effectiveness as a starter.

In September 1975, with the Astros in danger of suffering a 100-loss campaign, Bill Virdon had replaced Preston Gomez as the manager. Over the next two seasons under Virdon, the Astros won 80 and 81 games and posted consecutive third-place finishes. In 1978, though, the team regressed (they would win just 74 games), and in late August, Virdon inserted Forsch into the starting rotation. In six starts Forsch finished 4-2, with four complete games and two shutouts. So for 1979, Virdon announced that Forsch would once again be a starter. It took Forsch just one game in the new season to announce his return in the most impressive way imaginable.

The Astros opened the 1979 season in Atlanta. On Opening Day (actually night), April 6, J.R. Richard defeated the Braves' Phil Niekro in a 2-1 pitchers' duel. The next night was Forsch's turn. During the exhibition season he had scrapped his fastball and slider in order to work on his off-speed pitches. The result had been a miserable 0-3 record. Then, during Richard's win, Forsch had spent the entire day sick after an insect bite on his arm became infected. In spite of those factors, Forsch was magnificent, as he threw a no-hitter, on the earliest date ever in the major leagues, beating the Braves, 6-0.[15] What made the event even more meaningful was that Forsch's brother, Bob, who had begun his major-league career in 1974 with the Cardinals, had already thrown two no-hitters. The Forsches were thus the only brothers in history to each toss a no-hitter.

It said much about Ken's feelings toward his brother when he said after his no-hitter, "Bob's no-hitter last year was one of the greatest moments of my life. He's the greatest guy I know."[16]

If Forsch's no-hitter ultimately proved to be the individual capstone to his career, in 1980 he achieved a similarly gratifying team highlight. That season, under new Astros ownership, Nolan Ryan joined the club. Together with Ryan, Richard, and Joe Niekro, Forsch joined a stellar rotation which that year brought to Houston the Astros' first postseason appearance. After finishing the regular season with 12 wins and a 3.20 ERA, Forsch was rewarded by starting Game One of the National League Championship Series, against the Phillies. On October 7, at Philadelphia's Veterans Stadium, despite allowing just three runs and eight hits and tossing a complete game, Forsch lost, 3-1, to Steve Carlton.[17] Five days later, he entered in relief in the eighth inning of the decisive Game Five, played at the Astrodome, and allowed two hits and a run as the Astros took a heartbreaking 8-7 loss to the Phillies. Those appearances proved to be the only postseason action of Forsch's career. They were also his final appearances in an Astros uniform.

For many years Tal Smith had been a key figure in the Astros front office. In 1968, the year Forsch was drafted, Smith had been the vice president of player personnel. In 1973 Smith had moved to the Yankees, where he remained until August 1975, when he returned to Houston as the Astros' general manager and began to assemble a playoff team. It came as a shock to Astros fans, then, when several days after the team's loss in the 1980 NLCS, new owner John McMullen surprisingly fired Smith, long a Forsch advocate, and named Al Rosen the general manager.

Rosen's hiring signaled the end of the line for Forsch in Houston. To strengthen the pitching staff, Rosen signed free-agent pitcher Don Sutton and traded for Bob Knepper. Despite Forsch's 78 wins and 50 saves during 11 seasons with the Astros, in 1981 he was to be the odd-man-out of the rotation. Once again he would be sent to the bullpen. "If that's the way they reward loyalty," countered Forsch, "then I don't want to pitch for this club."[18] Instead, Forsch requested that the team trade him to a contender.

As a 10-and-5-year player (10 years of major-league service time and the last five years with the same team), Forsch had the right to reject any trade. Initially, during the Winter Meetings, Rosen tried to trade Forsch to the San Francisco Giants in exchange for outfielder Larry Herndon. When the Giants refused to renegotiate Forsch's contract, he rejected the trade. Subsequently, on April 1, the Astros sent Forsch to the Anaheim Angels in exchange for shortstop Dickie Thon. This time, when Forsch requested that some contractual clauses be reworded, the Angels, just hours prior to the deadline for acceptance, acceded to his request. So at 34 years old, Forsch returned home to California.

It took an injury to end Forsch's career. For three seasons he gave the Angels all he had. Indeed, almost immediately he became the team's ace, and his 86 starts and 35 wins over that span were crucial to the team's fortunes. Never was he better than in 1981. That season, a strike year, Forsch won six of his first seven decisions and stood 9-3 with four shutouts and a 2.27 ERA when the strike began. Named to his second All-Star team, this time as a starter, Forsch finished the season 11-7. The following season Forsch contributed 13 more wins, but agonizingly was removed from the rotation during the Angels' playoff series against the Milwaukee Brewers. In his last full season, 1983, he started 31 times and won another 11 games. But he was bound to win just one more.

On April 2, 1984, at home against Boston, Forsch won the 114th and, as it turned out, final game of his career, an impressive 2-1, complete-game six-hitter. Five days later, again at home, versus the Toronto Blue Jays, he again took the mound. Trailing 2-1 in the top of the eighth inning, Forsch allowed a home run to Lloyd Moseby. The next batter was Willie Upshaw. As Upshaw hit a squibber in front of the mound, Forsch fielded the ball and raced Upshaw toward first base. Diving to the bag, Forsch landed on his right elbow and immediately felt pain. He had dislocated his shoulder. After the game, x-rays proved negative; the joint appeared to have popped back into the socket and the prognosis was that Forsch would be out for a month. Instead, he missed the remainder of that season and all of the next. His career was effectively over.

Throughout the winter of 1985, Forsch worked out hard at Anaheim Stadium. In 1986 the Angels invited him to camp as a nonroster invitee, and in March they Forsch as a free agent. It was soon clear, however, that he had nothing left. On May 23, in relief of, ironically, Don Sutton, Forsch allowed five hits and four runs in 4⅔ innings against the Yankees, and two days later he was released. In July he signed with the Seattle Mariners, spent a month at their Calgary affiliate, but realized he was through. Forsch was 39 years old.

Back in Anaheim, Forsch settled into life with his wife, Jonnye Sue. They had met in 1971 when Forsch's good friend and roommate, Roger Metzger, ended up one evening with two dates, one of whom was Forsch's future wife. Ken and Jonnye Sue dated for six weeks, three of which were on the road, and were then married. As of January 2017, Stephanie, their only child, and her children, Jessie and Will, lived with Ken and Jonnye Sue in Anaheim.

After leaving baseball, Forsch went into commercial real estate, first with Grubb & Ellis, then with Lang Financial. After several years he got his broker's license and went out on his own. Throughout that time, 1986 to 1993, he stayed in touch with the game as a member of the Angels' Speakers Bureau; he gave speeches at Rotary Clubs and the like. "It was good for me," he recalled, "because I would meet people for my real estate business."

In 1994 Forsch learned that the Angels were looking for a new director of player development. At the time, Whitey Herzog was the general manager. Forsch didn't know Whitey, but his brother Bob had played for Herzog for years as a member of the Cardinals and "loved the guy." So Ken interviewed with Herzog, went back the next day, and two days later was on a plane to Arizona as the Angels director of player development, a post he held for four years. In 1998 he was promoted to assistant general manager, won a World Series ring in 2002, and held that position until his dismissal in 2011.

As of January 2017, the retired Forsch spent many of his days golfing and fly fishing. In 2017 he was nominated for induction into the Sacramento Sports Hall of Fame. Voting will take place in October 2017.

SOURCES

In addition to the sources cited in the Notes, the author also consulted Baseball-Reference.com, Retrosheet.org, and the Sacramento Sports Hall of Fame at sacsportshof.com/.

Thanks to Ken Forsch for email exchanges in November and December 2016 and January 2017. Thanks as well to T.C. Martin, founder, Sacramento Sports Hall of Fame, for email exchanges on December 6 and 15, 2016.

NOTES

1 Author interview with Ken Forsch, November 18, 2016. Unless otherwise noted, all Forsch quotes are from this interview.

2 In his 2016 interview, Forsch recalled that his father once played for the Roma Wines company team. "All the wineries had teams," he said.

3 baseballsacramento.com/LaSalle_Club_Baseball_HOF.html.

4 *Houston Post*, July 1, 1973 (article in Ken Forsch's player file at the National Baseball Hall of Fame Library, Cooperstown, New York).

5 Ibid.

6 In 2003 Forsch was inducted into the Sacramento City College Athletics Hall of Fame.

7 osubeavers.com/sports/2011/3/9/208343623.aspx.

8 Ed Rumill, "Houston's Forsch," *Christian Science Monitor*, July 6, 1971: 12.

9 John Wilson, "When Forsch Hurls Nine, Most He Earns Is a Draw," *The Sporting News*, June 24, 1972: 16.

10 Ken Forsch email to author, January 16, 2017.

11 Joe Heiling, "Forsch Takes Up New Pad in Astros Bullpen," *The Sporting News*, September 1, 1973: 13.

12 "N.L. Flashes," *The Sporting News*, May 11, 1974: 23.

13 Joe Heiling, "Fireman Ken Forsch an Astro Lifesaver," *The Sporting News*, October 12, 1974: 10.

14 Harry Shattuck, "Floundering Astros Find One Gem: Hitter Howard," *The Sporting News*, August 16, 1975: 18.

15 In 1940 Cleveland's Bob Feller threw an Opening Day no-hitter, but that had occurred on April 16.

16 Unidentified, undated article in Ken Forsch's Hall of Fame file.

17 Forsch allowed a two-run home run to Greg Luzinski and an RBI single to Greg Gross.

18 Dick Young, unnamed article in Forsch's Hall of Fame file, dated March 19, 1981.

KEN FORSCH HURLS EARLIEST NO-HITTER IN HISTORY

APRIL 7, 1979: HOUSTON ASTROS 6, ATLANTA VBRAVES 0, AT THE ASTRODOME

By Chip Greene

To relate each of the historical events that converged in the Houston Astrodome the night of April 7, 1979, to the unique accomplishment that followed, a historian has to traverse the previous 65 years of baseball history.

First, one has to stop in St. Louis. There, on April 14, 1917, Chicago White Sox pitcher Eddie Cicotte threw a no-hitter against the St. Louis Browns. It was the earliest date for a no-hitter in the regular season. It would remain so for the next 62 years.

The next stop through baseball history comes in Brooklyn. It was September 21, 1934. On their way to an eventual world championship, the St. Louis Cardinals visited the Dodgers for a doubleheader. This was no ordinary season for the Cardinals pitching staff. In addition to their young superstar, Dizzy Dean, who, as the game-one starter, was in search of his 27th win of the season, St. Louis also boasted Dizzy's 22-year-old brother, Paul, a 17-game winner in this, his rookie season. Paul would start game two.

On this day, the Dodgers batters never stood a chance in either game. In the opener, Dizzy poured fastball after fastball over the plate and throttled Brooklyn, 13-0. After no-hitting Brooklyn for seven innings, Dean allowed three singles in the final two innings to finish with a complete-game three-hitter. As if that weren't enough, however, in the nightcap, Paul completed what Dizzy couldn't — he threw a no-hitter, which prompted from Dizzy the quip: "If I had known you were going to pitch a no-hitter, I'd have pitched one too."[1] No-hitters from a pair of brothers would have to wait a while.

Finally, we return to St. Louis, where, on April 16, 1978, Cardinals right-hander Bob Forsch, in his third start of the season, defeated the Philadelphia Phillies, 5-0, in what would be the first of two career no-hitters. With that, the stage was set for a very special night in Houston almost exactly one year later.

There was little to suggest that Bob Forsch's older brother, Ken, was in for a particularly effective performance that day. After winning his first major-league game as a September call-up to the Astros in 1970, Ken had spent the next three seasons as a starter, amassing an unimpressive 23-28 record, before being mostly relegated to the bullpen for the next five years. He enjoyed some good years as a late-inning specialist, including a 1976 campaign in which he tallied 19 saves and made the NL All-Star team. In 1978 Forsch made just six starts but completed four, won 10 games and produced a 2.70 ERA, and as the 1979 season dawned, Forsch once again found himself as a member of the Astros' starting rotation.

He had endured a rocky spring, however. During the exhibition season, Forsch made just two starts, worked only 10 innings, and surrendered an abysmal 27 hits. In his final spring outing, on April 3 against the Montreal Expos, he allowed 13 hits in seven innings. Sometime during that game, too, Forsch suffered an insect bite on his left elbow, and as the Astros opened their season in the Astrodome on Friday night, April 6, against the Atlanta Braves, the bite had swollen so severely that Forsch, who was scheduled to start the season's second game the following day, was questionable.

On Friday night, Houston scored two runs in the bottom of the first inning and held on to defeat the

Braves, 2-1. The next day 24,325 fans were on hand as Forsch, with a career record of 55-62, overcame the bug bite and started the season's second contest. It would be the greatest game of his career.

Reflecting on his poor spring during an interview after the game, Forsch said, "After the spring I had, I figured I got it all out of my system. I said to myself, 'I've given up all the hits I'm going to give up.'"[2] And for this one night, he had.

On the mound for Atlanta was left-hander Larry McWilliams. Given his superb rookie season (9-3, 2.81) in 1978, the Braves undoubtedly felt McWilliams gave them a solid chance to even their record at 1-1. Yet after Forsch easily retired the first three batters to start the game, Houston plated two runs in the bottom of the inning, and that would be all the offense the Astros needed.

In the end, Forsch was never tested. Against the leadoff batter, Jeff Burroughs, in the top of the second inning, Forsch issued a walk on a 3-and-1 count, yet quickly retired the next three men on a foul popup, a groundout that forced Burroughs, and a strikeout. In the fourth inning, the Braves came closest to getting a hit when Glenn Hubbard stroked a sharp grounder to third baseman Enos Cabell, but Cabell fielded the ball cleanly on one hop and rifled a throw to first to beat Hubbard by two strides. With two outs in the eighth inning, Forsch issued his second walk, to Barry Bonnell, but a weak grounder to second by pinch-hitter Bob Beall snuffed out any chance Atlanta had of generating a rally. As the Braves came to the plate in the top of the ninth, trailing 6-0, Forsch stood just three outs away not only from the first no-hitter of his 10-year career, but also from joining his brother as the only siblings ever to throw one.

In the seventh inning, sensing the magnitude of what was evolving, the Astrodome crowd had begun cheering every out. Likewise, when Forsch came to bat with two outs in the bottom of the eighth, he received a 20-second standing ovation. Now, as Forsch stared in for the sign against the leadoff hitter, left-handed pinch-hitter Rowland Office, the whole stadium was abuzz with excitement. As Forsch delivered, Office watched the first pitch go by for strike one. Then he tapped a slow grounder to second and was easily thrown out at first. That brought to the plate right-handed-hitting Jerry Royster. As the crowd held its collective breath, Royster worked the count to 2-and-1. And then, swinging away, Royster drilled a searing liner down the third-base line, but it veered foul by 10 feet. It was the hardest-hit ball of the night and proved to be the Braves' last gasp. On the next pitch, Royster grounded out to shortstop Craig Reynolds, and finally, Hubbard, too, grounded out to Reynolds. As the ball smacked into the glove of first baseman Cabell (he had changed positions in the top of the eighth), the Astros charged from their dugout and mobbed Forsch halfway between the mound and the first-base line, while the crowd stood and roared its approval. Ken Forsch had thrown the sixth no-hitter in Houston franchise history[3] and the earliest gem in the history of the major leagues.

"I realized I had the no-hitter way back in the third inning," Forsch told the press, "and in the seventh, I smelled it."[4]

"I figured that my rhythm was going so well there was no way they were going to get a hit. Now I'm gonna try to pitch another one this year."[5] He never did. Just 356 days earlier, Bob Forsch had thrown his no-hitter. Bob was at his home in St. Louis when he learned of Ken's gem. "That's just great, isn't it?" Bob said when interviewed on the phone. "I think it's fantastic. The only bad part is that it's [Ken's] first game of the season so it's all downhill from here. I'm so happy that he pitched one—I know exactly how he feels. Now that we're the first brother act, it's unbelievable … just fantastic.[6]

"Right now," Bob said, "he's getting so many phone calls. You don't realize exactly what you've done until you get home. I'm gonna try to get ahold of him in a few hours and if I can't, I'll send him a telegram in the morning."[7]

In recognition of Ken's accomplishment, four days later the Texas House of Representatives designated April 11 Ken Forsch Day in the state. That evening the Astros presented Forsch a new car in honor of his no-hitter.

NO-HITTERS

NOTES

1. UPI, *Galveston* (Texas) *Daily News*, April 8, 1979.
2. UPI, *Daily Herald Suburban Chicago*, April 8, 1979.
3. The others: Don Nottebart, May 17, 1963 (Colt .45s); Ken Johnson, April 23, 1964 (Colt .45s - despite a no-hitter Johnson lost the game, 1-0); Don Wilson, June 18, 1967; Don Wilson, May 1, 1969; Larry Dierker, July 9, 1976.
4. UPI, *Daily Herald Suburban Chicago*, April 8, 1979.
5. Ibid.
6. As of October 31, 2015, the Forsches remain the only brothers to each throw a no-hitter
7. UPI, *Galveston Daily News*, April 8, 1979.

LEN BARKER

By Joseph Wancho

BASEBALL NIRVANA landed in Cleveland, Ohio, on May 15, 1981. And it landed smack-dab on the pitching mound. For the Cleveland Indians, a major-league franchise that was a consistent nonfactor for most of the 1960s into the 1990s, to be king of the mountain for even one day was heavenly.

Len Barker gave that feeling to the Tribe and their fans. On a cold and misty evening at Cleveland Stadium, Barker pitched the major leagues' 10th perfect game. The visiting Toronto Blue Jays sent 27 men to the plate, and they went down in order like a row of dominos. The key to Barker's perfecto was a dominating curveball, one that he threw 70 percent of the time. He was so much in command that he never had a three-ball count on a batter. Barker got stronger as the game went on, and struck out 11 of the last 17 batters he faced. All 11 went down swinging.

"That was one of the most unreal days of my life," said Barker. "I knew that I had good stuff, maybe even awesome stuff, when I began the game. But as the game went on, I had total command. I could throw anything, anywhere I wanted. My curveball was something else."[1]

Although only 7,290 were in attendance that night, many more would claim to have been there. It was an uplifting moment for a city in need of a baseball identity. It was something for Indians fans to hang their collective hat on, to rally around. Of course there were others who decided to still kick dirt on Barker's evening. A writer in Dallas asked "How can it be perfect if it happened in Cleveland?"[2]

"Imagine, a perfect game," said the Indians' Toby Harrah. "A perfect game and we're all part of it; all of us and the entire city of Cleveland! It's so great for everybody, especially this team."[3] Indeed it was pure perfection for one night in Cleveland Indians history.

Leonard Harold Barker II was born to Leonard and Emogene (Lockcart) Barker on July 7, 1955, in Fort Knox, Kentucky. Barker was a pitcher at a young age, starring in American Legion ball. Throwing no-hitters was not the problem, but his control was; he would walk up to a dozen players an outing.

The Barkers relocated to Pennsylvania, where Len enrolled at Neshaminy High School in Langhorne, about 26 miles north of Philadelphia. Barker was a three-sport star at Neshaminy (football, basketball, baseball), but it was his pitching that was his meal ticket. Specifically, he threw an overpowering fastball. Already 6-feet-4, "Large Lenny" was quite a presence on the mound. His control might have been lacking, but the speed he threw with could not be denied.

After his graduation from high school, the Texas Rangers drafted Barker in the third round of the 1973 amateur draft. The Rangers selected pitchers early, first picking high-school phenom David Clyde with the first pick, and then left-hander Rich Shubert in the second round.

Barker had early success. He went 7-1 in the Gulf Coast Rookie League, registering 54 strikeouts in 59 innings pitched. He was promoted to Gastonia of the Class-A Western Carolinas League in 1974. Barker emerged as the Rangers' top prospect, posting an 11-7 record, and led the league with five shutouts. He whiffed 140 batters in 124 innings pitched.

The big right-hander had a reputation for being a bit wild, on and off the diamond. In 1976 the Rangers brought him to spring training. Barker was not there long before he found trouble. After a few beers at the bar of the Surf Rider Hotel in Pompano Beach, Florida, Barker and bullpen coach Pat Corrales got into an altercation with some hotel guests. A fist fight broke out and Corrales was arrested. A Dallas sportswriter hid Barker in his room to avoid apprehension. The next day Barker was sent to the team's minor-league facility in Plant City.

Barker was promoted in 1976 to Triple-A Sacramento (Pacific Coast League). His record for the Solons in 1976 (11-10, 5.55 ERA) was not his best effort, and his walks (96) outnumbered his strikeouts (92). However, Barker started two games at the end of the season for Texas. He got a no-decision in his major-league debut, against California on September 14, 1976. Barker got his first major-league victory in the last game of the season, going the distance to defeat Rich Gossage and the Chicago White Sox, 3-0. He struck out six and scattered three hits. "I've got to show 'em I want a job here," said Barker. "My goal for next spring is to go down there to Florida and make that five-man rotation."4

During the offseason Barker played winter ball in Venezuela. His manager was the Rangers' bullpen coach, Pat Corrales. After the winter league season, Corrales said, "When he's throwing the ball over the plate, there ain't nobody hittin' him. And when he's right, nobody wants to hit against him. He'll scare hell out of a batter. That first pitch might be coming right at your ear then the next three are right out there on the corner of the plate.

"But is he ready now? No, I don't think so. Maybe later in the season, who knows? But consistency is the thing. The first six games in Venezuela this winter he was something else. He had great control. Then he came apart at the end of the season. He'd throw three good innings, then maybe walk five."5

Corrales' assessment was indeed correct. Barker was sent to Triple-A Tucson for the first half of the season. He was recalled by Texas and made three starts, but mostly pitched out of the bullpen. He made the most out the opportunity given him, going 4-1 with a 2.66 ERA. Barker struck out 51 in 47⅓ innings. After the season, on December 23, Barker and Bonnie Elwell were married.

The Rangers dealt closer Adrian Devine to Atlanta as part of a four-team deal. "At first, I couldn't believe it because (Devine had) had such a good year," Barker said. "I was trying to figure out why they would trade him. Then it finally sunk in; with Adrian gone this team was handing the job to me. When I finally did realize this was the case, it's about the nicest feeling I've ever had in baseball. I never thought I'd be able

to accept going to the bullpen. Of course, if they tell you to go, you've got to do it."6

But the plans went awry in 1978 spring training when Barker did not see much activity. He totaled about six innings of work the entire spring. "We were in a situation where we knew what he could do because he did it for us last year," said manager Billy Hunter. "We had a lot of new faces, and I needed to see what they could do so they got more work."7

In his third pitching appearance of the season, against Boston at Fenway Park on April 16, Barker raised eyebrows when he let go of a pitch that landed on the backstop screen just below the press box. "One year in the Instructional League a pitched slipped and I threw it *over* the press box," said Barker.8

With mixed results early in the season, Barker was sent to Tucson to could get some work in on a regular basis. "(Hunter) told me I'll be back in about three weeks," said Barker. "I'll go down, get some starts, get some work, then come back up. I need to get my arm loose, and this will help. I've thought about it, and I'd rather go down to Tucson rather than stay here and only pitch once every eight days."[9]

Barker went 4-0 in his abbreviated stay at Tucson, with a minuscule ERA of 1.04. But he was unable to duplicate his success when he was recalled to Texas. Reggie Cleveland took over the closer role. Although Barker earned four saves of his own, his overall record took a few steps backward (1-5, 4.82 ERA).

For a while, Texas coveted Jim Kern, Cleveland's stellar relief pitcher. From the beginning of the 1978 season the Rangers had intermittent negotiations with Cleveland about a deal. On October 3 the deal was done; Texas shipped Barker and outfielder Bobby Bonds to the Indians for Kern and infielder Larvell Blanks.

Bonds was the main subject of the trade, with his power and speed and his refusal to play in Cleveland. Barker was almost a footnote. Cleveland manager Jeff Torborg did acknowledge that Barker threw with more mustard on the ball than Kern did. Barker is capable of "throwing a strawberry through the side of a submarine," said Torborg.[10]

Barker started the 1979 season working out of the bullpen. He made his first start on June 14 against Oakland. He pitched well, giving up one earned run, but had a no-decision in the 2-1 Indians win. Steadily, he improved and he strung six wins together from July 31 through September 4. Included in that streak were two wins over Texas. Barker finished the year at 6-6.

Barker earned a spot in the Indians rotation for the 1980 season. He was given the role that he sought and he responded with his best year of his career. After the All-Star break, Barker reeled off an 11-1 record, lowering his ERA from 5.00 to 3.68. Included were two games in which he recorded double-digit strikeouts; at Chicago on August 18 (12) and at Minnesota on September 1 (11). "Lenny has the ability to be a big winner," said Indians pitching coach Dave Duncan. "Everyone knows that. Just how much he develops down the road will depend on how much he works on all of his pitches and how much he learns about the hitters throughout the league."[11]

Barker won his 19th game of the season on September 27 against Baltimore, but he was unable to get number 20 as he dropped his final two games of the season. He finished with a 19-12 record, and a 4.17 ERA. His 187 strikeouts led the league. "He's certainly one of the best pitchers in the American League," said Tribe skipper Dave Garcia, who had replaced Torborg the previous season.[12]

A month after Barker's perfecto on May 15, the players' strike halted the season, wiping out games for two months (June 12-August 10). Barker's record was 5-3 when play was halted. After the strike was settled, the season resumed with the All-Star Game in Cleveland on August 9. Barker was selected to the AL team and pitched two scoreless innings. "This was great," he said. "The fans were outstanding. It is a pleasure to play with these guys because you know they are a great bunch of ballplayers."[13] Three losses in September made Barker's season record 8-7, but he led the league again in strikeouts (127).

Cleveland put together a pretty good pitching staff for 1982 with Barker, Bert Blyleven, John Denny, and Rick Sutcliffe. But injuries to Blyleven and Denny curtailed their 1982 season. Sutcliffe led the league with a 2.96 ERA, and Barker was second in the league with 187 strikeouts. He pitched 244⅔ innings and had a 15-11 record. But it fell apart for the big right-hander in 1983. A bone spur in his right elbow caused his fastball to lose its zip, dropping from the low 90s to the mid-80s. Barker was in the last year of his contract and odds were long that he would remain with the Indians.

The Atlanta Braves were in a fight for the top spot in the National League West. The Braves front office believed that adding another arm to their rotation might give them the edge and targeted Barker. On August 28, 1983, Atlanta acquired Barker (8-13 at the time) for three players to be named later (Rick Behenna, Brook Jacoby, and Brett Butler) and gave him a five-year, $5 million contract. "I couldn't be happier," said Barker. I'm going to a first-place team. I got a five-year contract. Wouldn't you be happy to leave a last-place club?"[14] The Braves medical staff believed that the bone spur was not serious. Barker went 1-3 for the Braves in six starts. The Dodgers won the division by three games.

Barker spent the 1984 and 1985 seasons in Atlanta, suffering from pain in his elbow. The bone spurs were more serious than the Atlanta doctors thought and he underwent surgery in 1984. The rehabilitation caused him to work less in spring training the following year. He was shelved with the same elbow problems in the middle of the 1985 season. His record in Atlanta was 10-20 over parts of three seasons, including 2-9 in 1985.

The Braves released Barker at the end of spring training in 1986. He signed with Montreal, but pitched all season for Triple-A Indianapolis. Released after the season, Barker signed with Milwaukee, but was once again relegated to the minors, this time with Triple-A Denver. He did make 11 starts for the Brewers in 1987, posting a 2-1 record. He was plagued with arm problems that placed him on the disabled list. Barker filed for free agency at the end of the season, but there were no takers. He retired from baseball with a career record of 74-76 and a 4.34 ERA.

Barker founded Perfect Pitch Construction, a home-remodeling business. He remained a fan favorite in Cleveland and was a popular player at the yearly Indians fantasy camp. (That was where he met his second wife, Eve.)

In 2010 Barker joined the coaching staff at Notre Dame College in South Euclid, Ohio, and in 2012 he became the head coach. Former teammates Joe Charboneau and Ron Pruitt joined his coaching staff. "When I get around these guys I feel like a kid," said Barker.[15] As of 2016 he and Eve resided in Chardon, Ohio, 30 miles east of Cleveland.

On August 18, 1980, Len Barker was pitching no-hit ball against Chicago through five innings at Comiskey Park. In the bottom of the sixth inning, Leo Sutherland led off with a bunt that rolled past Barker to second baseman Alan Bannister. But the throw was late and the White Sox had their first hit. Barker finished with a three-hitter, as the Indians were victorious, 4-2 in the first game of a doubleheader. After the game, Barker was more upset that he did not get a shutout than he was about Sutherland's bunt. "I'll get a no-hitter sooner or later," said Barker. "At least I hope to be around a long time and one night I'll have one of those special nights."[16]

Perhaps Lenny Barker could add clairvoyance to his arsenal of talents.

NOTES

1 Terry Pluto, *The Curse of Rocky Colavito* (New York: Simon and Schuster, 1994), 237.

2 Pluto, 238.

3 Russell Schneider, "Wife and Brother Are Among Joyous Fans," *Cleveland Plain Dealer*, May 16, 1981: 6-C.

4 Randy Galloway, "Rangers End Year in Style, 3-0," *Dallas Morning News*, October 4, 1976: B-2.

5 Randy Galloway, "Rangers' Barker: He Keeps on Hummin'," *Dallas Morning News*, March 3, 1977: B-3.

6 Randy Galloway, "Pressure Falls on Barker," *Dallas Morning News*, February 25, 1978: 22.

7 Randy Galloway, "Reliever Barker Plans to Return," *Dallas Morning News*, May 28, 1978: 64.

8 Randy Galloway, "Bosox Run Down Texas, 8-6," *Dallas Morning News*, April 17, 1978: 21.

9 Randy Galloway, "Reliever Barker Plans to Return," *Dallas Morning News*, May 28, 1978: 64.

10 Bob Dolgan, "Slugger Refuses to Say if He'll Report to Tribe," *Cleveland Plain Dealer*, October 4, 1978: 7-E.

11 Burt Graeff, "Large Lenny's Head and Arm Give KayCee a Royal Blush," *Cleveland Press*, August 23, 1980: C-7.

12 Bob Sudyk, "Large Lenny Barker Gets the Message," *Cleveland Press*, September 2, 1980: C-3.

13 Terry Pluto, "Record Crowd Sees NL Win Again," *Cleveland Plain Dealer*, August 10, 1981: 5-C.

14 Terry Pluto, "Barker Is Traded to Braves," *Cleveland Plain Dealer*, September 29, 1983: 4-B.

15 Bill Lubinger, "Former Cleveland Indians Pitcher Len Barker Finds Perfect Fit at Notre Dame College," cleveland.com, May 6, 2010.

16 Terry Pluto, "Barker's Three-Hitter Jolts Chisox," *Cleveland Plain Dealer*, August 19, 1980: 1-C.

LEN BARKER PERFECT GAME
MAY 15, 1981: CLEVELAND INDIANS 3, TORONTO BLUE JAYS 0, AT CLEVELAND STADIUM

By Joe Wancho

WHO COULD HAVE FOREseen that the Friday evening matchup between the Toronto Blue Jays and the Cleveland Indians would be such a historic game? Certainly not the 7,290 who sat through a misty, wet game that began with a first-pitch temperature of 47 degrees, which fell to the 30s by the time the final out was recorded. Welcome to spring time in Cleveland. Years later many more Tribe fans would swear they were there. Certainly not the *Cleveland Plain Dealer*. Beat writer Terry Pluto had a conflict that evening and the paper assigned a green reporter just two years out of Ohio University named Tony Grossi to write up the ballgame. Grossi, who eventually went on to cover the Cleveland Browns and the NFL for the *Plain Dealer* and later ESPN, saw his byline crisscross the country.

Least of all could Indians starting pitcher Len Barker. He was anxious about his older brother, Chuck, who was flying in from Fort Lauderdale. "Lenny didn't want to come to the park," said his wife, Bonnie. "He was much more concerned about his brother coming in. He also didn't want to sit through rain delay after rain delay."[1] Barker was late getting to the park after picking up his brother from the airport.

Pitching coach Dave Duncan may have been the one person who had an inkling of how special a night it might be. "Lennie's curveball is better than I've ever seen. It's breaking quick and hard. He's going to have an outstanding game," Duncan told manager Dave Garcia after watching him warm up in the bullpen.[2]

The game was a contrast of teams. Cleveland sat atop the American League's East Division. The Blue Jays were scuffling at the bottom of the division, and riding a 21-inning scoreless streak. On May 6 Cleveland right-hander Bert Blyleven had pitched eight hitless innings against these same Blue Jays at Toronto's Exhibition Stadium. Dave Garcia replaced left fielder Joe Charboneau with rookie Larry Littleton in the bottom of the ninth inning. The move backfired as Lloyd Moseby lifted Blyleven's first offering to left field and Littleton misplayed it. Moseby was credited with a double. He scored on a single by George Bell to make the final score 4-1. Blyleven struck out nine in the win.

Toronto's speedy shortstop, Alfredo Griffin, led off the game and tapped a groundball over the pitcher's mound. Shortstop Tom Veryzer charged, gloved, and threw to nip him at first base. The next two outs were groundouts.

Luis Leal started for Toronto. Rick Manning led off the Cleveland first with a single. Mike Hargrove reached first on a fielding error by first baseman John Mayberry. Manning went to third on the play and scored on Andre Thornton's sacrifice fly. Ron Hassey singled home Hargrove for the second tally; both runs were unearned.

In the Blue Jays' second, Damaso Garcia sent a line drive to left-center that Manning ran down and snared for the final out. Six up, six down and on it went. In the fourth inning, Barker struck out Moseby and Bell, his first two strikeouts of the game.

Meanwhile, Barker's father-in-law, Bill Elwell, was having trouble picking up the broadcast of the game at his home in Norristown, Pennsylvania. The miserable weather forced Elwell to leave his home and find a spot where he could clearly listen to the ballgame. Elwell ended up at a golf course, hunched over the front seat of the car, listening to the remainder of the game.

The Blue Jays continued to march to the plate. Barker's fastball was humming and he seemingly could place it anywhere he wanted to. But it was his curve that was breaking and giving the Jays fits. Duncan's prediction proved prophetic; Barker never went to a three-ball count on any batter. He reached a two-ball count on only eight Toronto batters.

But Barker had help from his friends. In the fifth inning third baseman Toby Harrah drifted over in foul ground in pursuit of a pop fly off the bat of Willie Upshaw. The wind pushed it to the seats, but Harrah was not to be deterred. He leapt into the crowd to make the catch, lost his cap, but hung on to the ball. Harrah said, "You've got to dive in a situation like that. You never know if making a catch in the early innings will or won't mean something later."[3] In the sixth inning, second baseman Duane Kuiper ranged to his right on a one-hop groundball to throw out Rick Bosetti. In the seventh inning, Kuiper went to his left, took three steps, and then threw to first base to nip the speedy Griffin. "Because of the situation, it makes those plays seem better than they actually were. Griffin's groundball was the tougher of the two because he's running hard right out of the box," said Kuiper.[4]

Jorge Orta smacked his second home run of the year, to right field, to push the Indians' advantage to 3-0 heading to the ninth inning. As Barker took the mound, his nerves were understandably getting the best of him. "My legs were quivering," he admitted Barker, nicknamed Large Lenny for his 6-foot-5, 225-pound frame. "I might have seemed like I was relaxed, but I wasn't. It was a mental thing. I was concentrating like crazy to keep myself together."[5]

Bosetti stepped in to the batter's box to lead off the ninth for Toronto. He popped up to Harrah. Al Woods pinch-hit for Danny Ainge. He struck out on three pitches. "He looked awesome to me," said Woods of Barker.[6] It was the last of 11 strikeouts for Barker; all of them were of the swinging variety. Ernie Whitt pinch-hit for Buck Martinez. "I was thinking about going up and pointing to center field to show Barker where I was going to hit the ball," said Whitt. "I thought it might upset Barker's concentration."[7]

Whitt did hit the ball to center field, just not too deep. Manning settled under the harmless fly ball, catching it for the 27th consecutive out. "If I had to run to the pitcher's mound, I would have gotten it," said Manning.[8]

The celebration ensued. Len Barker had just thrown the 10th perfect game in major-league history. Catfish Hunter had been the last to record a perfect game, on May 8, 1968, against Minnesota. This was the second perfect game in the Cleveland team's history. The first was thrown by Addie Joss on October 2, 1908, against Chicago. It was the first Indians no-hitter since Dennis Eckersley blanked California on May 30, 1977. As of the start of the 2016 season, Barker's gem was the last no-hitter thrown by a Cleveland pitcher.

"I knew that I had good stuff, maybe awesome stuff," said Barker. "But I really didn't start thinking about it until the last inning. My big pitch was my curveball. I had total command. I could throw anything, anywhere I wanted. And (catcher) Ron Hassey called a great game. Everybody was great."[9] Hassey said, "Every time he goes out there with a good curveball, he's got the chance for something like this. He was placing it right where I aimed it. I mean the ball was breaking so much Toronto kept asking to see the ball."[10]

The Blue Jays were accepting and complimentary in defeat. "If you have to lose I'm glad to lose to a guy who pitched a perfect game to beat me," said Toronto starter Luis Leal. "It is the first time in my life (24 years) that I've seen a perfect game. I never had it in my mind he would do it until he did it. I'm very happy for him."[11] Pitcher Dave Stieb said, "I'm jealous. I wish I could have done it. Lenny Barker made it look easy."[12] (Stieb got a degree of revenge against Cleveland, pitching a no-hitter against the Indians on September 2, 1990, at Cleveland Stadium. It was the last no-hitter in the stadium's history.)

Barker's mother, Emogene McCurry, was listening to the game from her home in Trevose, Pennsylvania. "The game kept fading in and out," she said. "It came back in the eighth inning, but then we lost it in the ninth."[13] Unlike Bill Elwell, Emogene did not leave her home in search of better reception. When Barker's grandmother, Tokie Lockhart of Ona, West Virginia, heard the news, she remarked, "Tell Len I'm Proud. I hope he does better next time."[14] "I thought we had him in the ninth," Toronto pitcher Mark Bomback said. "He was so nervous. Then when they flashed the trivia question (on the center-field scoreboard), I was sure he was jinxed."[15] The trivia question, which had been selected that morning? Which two teams had never been involved in a no-hitter? The answer? Toronto Blue Jays and Seattle Mariners.

NOTES

1 Russell Schneider, "Wife and Brother Are Among Joyous Fans," *Cleveland Plain Dealer*, May 16, 1981: 1-C.
2 Ibid.
3 Burt Graeff, "Ah, that was perfect!" *Cleveland Press*, May 16, 1981: A56.
4 Graeff: A54.
5 Bob Sudyk, "Perfecto," *The Sporting News*, May 30, 1981: 11.
6 Dennis Lustig, "Barker Family," *Cleveland Plain Dealer*, May 16, 1981: 6-C.
7 Lustig, "Blue Jays," *Cleveland Plain Dealer*, May 16, 1981: 6-C.
8 Tony Grossi, "Barker Hurls Perfect Game," *Cleveland Plain Dealer*, May 16, 1981: 1.
9 Terry Pluto, "Barker's Night," *Cleveland Plain Dealer*, May 16, 1981: 6-C.
10 Grossi, 6-C.
11 Lustig, 6-C.
12 Ibid.
13 Associated Press, "Son Makes History, but Mrs. Barker Loses Game in 9th," *Cleveland Plain Dealer*, May 17, 1981: 8-B.
14 Sudyk.
15 Bruce Newman, *Sports Illustrated*, May 25, 1981.

DAVID PALMER

By Norm King

DAVID PALMER WAS AN example of local boy makes good. Sort of. Palmer, who played for the Montreal Expos, Atlanta Braves, Philadelphia Phillies, and Detroit Tigers, used to make the 3½-hour drive to Montreal from his hometown of Glens Falls, New York — which is halfway between Montreal and New York — to watch the Expos play at Jarry Park. On September 9, 1978, he became a player that other people from Glens Falls drove up to see.

"I don't know that I ever pitched a game in Montreal where family, coaches, and classmates and friends weren't there," said Palmer. "That made it so much more special to be able to share with the people I grew up with and the people who helped to influence my life and career."[1]

David William Palmer Jr. was born on August 19, 1957, the second of six children born to David Palmer Sr. and Gwen (Lewis) Palmer. His father was a corrections officer and his mother was a nurse. Although his father never played baseball because of a childhood illness, he coached Palmer all through his formative years.

"He coached my first Little League game and he coached my last amateur American Legion game," said Palmer. "Other than high school, he was the only coach I ever had."[2]

Palmer played all positions in his younger years before finally pitching full-time. He pitched for the Glens Falls High School Indians, where future major leaguer Dave LaPoint was a teammate and, it seems, a rival.

Coach Pete Davidson "had me and Palmer together," said LaPoint. "The competition we had between ourselves was better than what we had with other teams."[3]

That competition stood both pitches in good stead, as they both had successful major-league careers. For Palmer, that began when he caught the eye of Expos Canadian scout Bill McKenzie. McKenzie persuaded the Expos' scouting brain trust, which included minor-league director Jim Fanning, to draft Palmer, and they selected him in the 21st round of the 1976 amateur draft. He began his professional career with the Lethbridge Expos in the Rookie-level Pioneer League. The 18-year-old fared poorly, going 0-5 with a 7.20 ERA, tied for highest on the team; by his own assessment, he was the worst pitcher in the league. After the season, Palmer decided that he was going to have to stick to it, literally, if he was going to succeed.

"That winter, I went home and someone told me I needed to hold the fingers together to get the ball to move a little bit," Palmer recalled. "So I taped my fingers together and held a baseball all winter."[4]

It's hard to say whether that particular tactic was successful. It is true, though, that Palmer's career shifted because of a video game. More precisely, he broke off his fingernail while shifting down on a racing video game at a mall during spring training of 1977. He pitched the next day anyway because he wasn't sure if he was going to make the team. The injury forced Palmer to alter his grip on the ball to avoid putting pressure in the injured digit. Suddenly he had a very effective cut fastball and he started getting batters out.

The Expos promoted Palmer to the West Palm Beach Expos of the Class-A Florida State League for 1977. He joined a pitching staff that included Bill Gullickson and Scott Sanderson. (When the three of them eventually reached the Expos, they combined with veteran Steve Rogers — Rogers was Palmer's idol growing up — to form the nucleus of the great Expos pitching staffs of the late 1970s and early 1980s.) Palmer went 6-8, but his significantly improved 2.87 ERA showed how effective his new pitch was.

"Back then, (the Expos) didn't mind moving players up if they thought they were ready," said Palmer. Manager Dick Williams "always liked to have a young pitcher on his staff."[5]

Palmer began the 1978 season in West Palm Beach, and went 4-2 with a 1.94 ERA, then moved up to the Doublke-A Memphis Chicks, where he compiled a record of 8-10 with a respectable 3.05 ERA. Felipe Alou, who had managed him in West Palm Beach, was also Palmer's skipper in Memphis, and continued giving Palmer the benefit of his tutelage.

"To have someone like Felipe Alou as your manager in A ball and Double-A, you know, how special is that?" said Palmer. "He comes out to take me out of the game; I wanted him to sign the baseball and put it in my trophy case."[6]

It would be inaccurate to attribute Palmer's reverence for Alou simply to a young player's awe of a major leaguer. Gullickson and Sanderson were much higher draft picks than Palmer, yet Alou recognized Palmer's ability.[7]

"He believed in me and gave me the ball," said Palmer. "He was in my corner. … He gave me a chance to pitch."[8]

Alou's guidance and confidence in Palmer prompted the Expos to include him among the September call-ups that year. He got into his first game on September 9, 1978, pitching a scoreless ninth inning in a 6-3 loss to the Chicago Cubs at Olympic Stadium. Gene Clines was his first strikeout victim. Palmer ended up pitching in five games that September, all in relief, going 0-1 with a 2.79 ERA in 9⅔ innings pitched.

The 1979 season was a special one for the Expos as they took part in their first pennant race, going 95-65 and finishing two games behind the eventual world champion Pittsburgh Pirates. Palmer made the team out of spring training, but not before he learned a valuable lesson about how hard veteran major leaguers work to get ready for the season.

"The first day of spring training … the veteran pitchers—they don't need to run as hard as they're running, but they are," recalled Palmer. "When you see the franchise pitcher [Rogers] leading the guys in sprints at the end of practice and the way he went about his business, that really impressed me. There's no getting here and slacking off—if anything you've got to work harder to stay here."[9]

Palmer went north with the team, but didn't pitch much the first half of the season. He got his first major-league win on April 10 at Shea Stadium, pitching three scoreless innings as the Expos won, 3-2. He made 20 relief appearances before making his first career start against San Diego on July 13. The Expos won the game 10-7, but Palmer got a no-decision. He pitched several more times in relief before joining the rotation for the remainder of the season on July 30. He won that game, 5-1, over St. Louis to bring his record to 3-2.

Williams went to a seven-man rotation, including Palmer, to deal with the load. Palmer won again, and again, and again, eventually winning eight times in a row (including one in relief), to finish the season at 10-2, with a 2.64 ERA.[10] Palmer was positively blazing; he won three times during a team 10-game winning streak from August 28 to September 6, with a 0.82 ERA. That streak was invaluable in keeping the Expos in the race during September, when the team was forced to play a brutal schedule of eight doubleheaders due to rainouts early in the year.

After the season Palmer had the first in a series of medical procedures he would have to endure during his career. In this case, he had surgery to remove excess cartilage from his right knee. He had to spend several weeks on crutches, but he was ready for spring training for the 1980 season. However, it seems spring training wasn't ready for him. More precisely, the Players Association and Major League Baseball were in the midst of contentious labor negotiations, and the Association stopped the players from playing any exhibition games after April 1. Although players from other teams stayed in Florida or Arizona to continue training, chaos reigned supreme at the Expos' facility. Players were told that they wouldn't have access to the team facilities and to go home. Palmer returned to Glens Falls, only to find out that his teammates were working out and playing intrasquad games; he missed some valuable training time, and so wasn't ready to start when the season began.

Palmer spent the first month of 1980 working out of the bullpen in order to get in playing condition. He returned to the starting rotation on May 1, and proved that the winning streak of 1979 was no fluke by winning his first three decisions. The third one ended up being a nailbiter, as Palmer left after eight innings with an 11-1 lead, only to see reliever Fred Norman give up seven runs (six earned) before Stan Bahnsen and Woodie Fryman, who got the save, put out the fire.

By mid-July, however, Palmer began feeling soreness just below his right elbow. He pitched once in August and was pounded for five runs, four earned, in just one inning. He won two and lost two in September; one of the losses was a heartbreaking 2-1 decision in Philadelphia when he gave up a walk-off home run to Bake McBride. He finished with a flourish, pitching an 8-0 shutout against the Cardinals.

That soreness under the elbow ended up requiring surgery on a ligament that ultimately cost Palmer the entire 1981 season and, perhaps, a World Series berth for the Expos.[11] Without one of their best pitchers, they made it to the National League Championship Series before losing to the Los Angeles Dodgers on a ninth-inning home run by Rick Monday in the fifth and deciding game.

Missing those playoffs served as motivation when a nervous Palmer arrived at spring training in 1982. His initial Grapefruit League outing was encouraging, as he gave up one hit in two scoreless innings. More importantly, he felt no pain.

"I was nervous at first, and I had to adjust to a flatter mound than the one I'd been training on," he said. "But in my second inning I pitched with more confidence."[12]

Nonetheless, the Expos decided to go slowly on Palmer's comeback, and had him start the season with their Memphis affiliate during the cooler months of April and May. He went 3-2 with the Chicks with a 3.51 ERA in nine outings before returning to Montreal, where he made his first start on May 25 at Houston, going six innings and giving up only one run in a 6-1 Expos victory. It wasn't a classic—Palmer walked six batters and hit another—but it was pretty good for someone who hadn't faced a major-league hitter in more than 18 months and whose wife, Beverly, was late in giving birth to their first child (son John).

Palmer continued to pitch well into August. After 12 starts he had a 6-4 record with a 3.30 ERA. Then, in an August 13 start at Philadelphia, he had to leave the mound in the third inning due to arm soreness. The team physician, Dr. Larry Coughlin, told the media that Palmer had calcium deposits in his elbow and ordered rest. The Expos put him on the 21-day disabled list, but Palmer ended up missing the rest of the 1982 season and all of 1983 after Tommy John surgery.

Palmer returned for the beginning of the 1984 campaign, and began his first outing of the year on April 7 against the Braves with a bang, literally, as he blasted a two-run home run off his mound opponent, Pete Falcone, in the third inning. It was the first of five dingers Palmer hit in the majors. The Expos went on to win 7-2, with Palmer going six innings. But as Al Jolson used to say, you ain't seen nothin' yet.

Palmer's next start was in St. Louis in the second game of a doubleheader on a dark and stormy night in the Gateway City. He went only five innings, but he was perfect. No Cardinal got a hit or reached base. The game was called after five due to rain, but Palmer got the win, 4-0. (In 1991, MLB changed the rule regarding no-hitters, deeming that a game had to go at least nine innings to be considered a no-hitter. The rule was applied retroactively, which means that Palmer is no longer officially credited with a perfect game.) Of the 15 batters he faced, 11 grounded out, one lined out, one flied out, and two struck out.

"It was a long, long, long night," recalled Palmer. "There were two or three rain delays during the first game. The game went on until after midnight."[13]

Those two starts began a fine season for Palmer, who went 7-3 with a 3.84 ERA. He probably would have gone into double figures had he not missed the entire month of August because of shoulder stiffness.

Palmer seemed to be channeling the Alan Alda movie *Same Time Next Year*, because he went on the disabled list for a tender shoulder again in 1985. He attributed the problems to inconsistency with his delivery; he also had pitched more innings by that time, 118⅔, than he had since 1980, when he threw 129⅔ innings. The inconsistency in Palmer's motion may also have contributed to an inconsistent season. He went 7-10, with a 3.71 ERA, but he was streaky. He lost his first two decisions, won his next two, and had a three-game losing streak in July, during which his ERA climbed almost a full run, from 2.79 to 3.79. He also had control issues, having given up 67 walks.

"It was hard for me to stay in a groove," Palmer said. "I was trying too hard to show [the Expos] I was healthy and kept digging myself into a deeper hole."[14]

Palmer became a free agent after that season and decided it was time for a change, so he signed a one-year contract with the Braves, partly to get a change of scenery, and partly because his family lived in Memphis, one hour away from Atlanta.

"I wanted to leave Montreal," he said. "I want to find out what it's like to play for another team. Atlanta was really my first choice."[15]

Maybe it was the chance to eat grits instead of poutine, but the new environment worked out well for Palmer. Even though the Braves were an awful team—they finished last in the National League West with a 72-89 record—Palmer had career highs in starts (35), wins (11, to go with 10 losses and a 3.65 ERA) and innings pitched (209⅔). He also led the team with a 3.6 Win Above Replacement (WAR). Palmer's effectiveness depended on how much rest he got between starts. He was 1-6 with a 5.09 ERA in starts after only three days' rest, but was 10-4 with a 3.02 ERA when he had four or more days' rest between assignments.

For Palmer, moving to Atlanta represented not only a change of scenery from Montreal, but a change in team culture as well. "In Montreal, we were family," he recalled. "All the players and the wives and the families came to Montreal for one reason, for the Expos. Going to Atlanta, a lot of players lived in the area. … It wasn't the same. It was a little more laid back. It was a lot different atmosphere than Montreal."[16]

The lowlight of Palmer's season came on July 11 against the eventual world champion New York Mets. After former teammate Gary Carter smacked a three-run homer off Palmer in the first inning, he plunked the next Mets batter, Darryl Strawberry, in the hip. Strawberry rushed the mound, and Palmer knew immediately he was in a jam.

"I didn't know what to do when Strawberry came out," said Palmer. "I threw the glove instinctively. I knew he wasn't coming out to shake hands."[17]

Order was restored without much difficulty, and the umpires didn't throw anyone out of the game. Palmer probably wished he had been thrown out, as he ended up allowing seven earned runs in 1⅔ innings—Carter drove in all seven runs as he hit a grand slam off Palmer in the second—as the Mets won 11-0.

That little brouhaha was a blip in an otherwise fine season, and Palmer re-signed with the Braves for 1987, in what was probably the easiest arbitration case in history, as both Palmer and the Braves submitted the same figure, $725,000, to the arbitrator. The Braves even sweetened the pot by promising that Palmer would have a hotel room to himself on road trips.

The privacy didn't prevent Palmer from visiting the disabled list again, after he strained ligaments backing up a play at third base on June 18. Until then he was having a topsy-turvy year, losing his first four decisions, winning his next four, then losing the four after that. He returned with a bang on July 25, going 6⅓ scoreless innings for the victory as the Braves beat Philadelphia 2-1. He went 4-3 after his return from the DL, for an overall record of 8-11 with a 4.90 ERA.

The Braves wanted to ink Palmer to a contract again for 1988 but they offered him less money, so he signed instead with the Philadelphia Phillies for $675,000. It was another inconsistent season for Palmer; he lost his first five decisions, but rebounded to finish 7-9, with a 4.47 ERA. The highlight of his season was a complete-game one-hitter against St. Louis on August 2. He also won his next start, going six innings in a 7-4 Phillies win against the Cubs. He didn't know it at the time, but it was his last victory in the big leagues. He didn't pitch at all in September and went under the knife again on September 21 when he had surgery in Los Angeles for a torn rotator cuff.

The Phillies cut Palmer after the season and he signed with the Detroit Tigers for 1989, but after he went 0-3, the Tigers released him on July 13. The Cleveland Indians signed him on July 27 and sent him to their Triple-A team in Colorado Springs of the Pacific Coast League. He went 2-2 with the Sky Sox with a 4.23 ERA. The Indians cut him after that season. He signed with the Reno Silver Sox, an unaffiliated team in the Class-A California League in 1990, and, after going 1-0 in three starts, called it a career.

After his baseball career ended, he and his family moved to Atlanta where his wife at the time –they later divorced—had relatives. He became the pitching coach at Parkview High School in Lilburn, Georgia. In the eight years he coached there, Parkview won five Georgia High School Association championships and finished second the other three

times. The team was voted national Team of the Year by *Baseball America* in 2012, his last year with the club.

As of 2015, Palmer coached the baseball team at his old high school, and divided his time between Glens Falls and Atlanta, where he worked as a real-estate title examiner. He has two daughters Liza and Leah, in addition to his son.

Despite the injuries that hampered his career, Palmer looked back fondly on his time as a pitcher. "I had signed 10 one-year nonguaranteed contracts, so whether my arm hurt or not, I felt like I had to go out there and pitch," he said. "I was pitching for my job every year. "I have no regrets about that. It was what it was and I wouldn't change any of it."[18]

He also takes great pride in having played for an organization which, at the time, was one of the best in baseball. "In my mind, Montreal was one of the top two or three organizations in baseball," Palmer said. "I am so glad and so proud that I got to be a Montreal Expo during that period of time."[19]

SOURCES

In addition to the sources listed in the notes, the author consulted:

Chicago Tribune.

Galveston Daily News.

The Gazette (Montreal).

Gwinnett (Georgia) *Daily Post*.

Le Devoir (Montreal)

Ottawa Journal.

Troy Record.

Wustl.edu

NOTES

1. David Palmer, telephone interview, October 25, 2015.
2. Palmer interview.
3. Tim Wilkin, "A conversation with … former major leaguer Dave Lapoint," *Times Union* (Albany, New York), July 18, 2010.
4. Alain Usereau, *The Expos in Their Prime* (Jefferson, North Carolina: McFarland & Company, 2013), 61.
5. Palmer interview. Williams became the Expos' manager in 1977.
6. Palmer interview.
7. Gullickson was drafted in the first round of the 1977 draft and Sanderson was drafted in the third round that same year.
8. Usereau, 62.
9. Palmer interview.
10. Charlie Lea broke Palmer's team record of seven straight wins as a starter in 1983.
11. He did pitch 11 innings for the Class-A West Palm Beach Expos in 1981 and had one start at Memphis where he gave up one earned run without getting anybody out.
12. "Expos hurler says arm pain gone," *Galveston Daily News*, March 10, 1982.
13. Palmer interview.
14. "N.L. West," *The Sporting News*, February 24, 1986, 38.
15. Mike Dyer, "Palmer, Glad to Be Free of Expos, Looking Impressive With Braves," *Schenectady Gazette*, March 21, 1986.
16. Palmer interview.
17. "Strawberry Not "Hip" With Palmer," *Kerrville* (Texas) *Times*, July 13, 1986.
18. Palmer interview.
19. Palmer interview.

A FIVE-INNING PERFECTO FOR PALMER

APRIL 21, 1984: MONTREAL EXPOS 4, ST. LOUIS CARDINALS 0, AT BUSCH STADIUM (SECOND GAME OF A DOUBLEHEADER)

By Norm King

IF SIR EDWARD BULWER-Lytton were a sportswriter covering the game in which the Montreal Expos' David Palmer pitched five perfect innings for a 4-0 rain-shortened win, he could have started his story off with the line that he wrote and which Snoopy has made famous: "It was a dark and stormy night."[1]

Those immortal words accurately described the weather conditions in St. Louis on April 21, 1984, when the Expos and the Cardinals squared off in an early-season twi-night doubleheader at Busch Stadium. The two teams were still getting into the rhythm of the season and were squaring off for the first time that campaign, as Expos ace Steve Rogers took the mound in Game One against John Stuper. Both pitchers were making their first starts of the season, and each had something to prove. Rogers was back after a stint on the disabled list with shoulder soreness, while Stuper had just been called up from the Louisville Redbirds of the Triple-A American Association. Stuper probably wished he had stayed in the land of bourbon as the Expos pounded him for six runs, five earned, in 1⅓ innings. Rogers lasted 6⅔ innings, giving up three earned runs as the Expos won, 6-3.

They managed to finally complete Game One after a 94-minute rain delay in the eighth inning, but then the rains came again, making it questionable whether the second game would even start.

"It was a long, long, long, long night," recalled Palmer. "I was going to go to warm up, but the umpires said to wait and see what the weather does. Even the second game was delayed."[2]

This game was important to Palmer's career because it was his second start of the season after his return from Tommy John surgery. His previous start, on April 7 in Atlanta, marked the first time he had pitched since August 13, 1982. He went five innings in that initial outing, giving up one earned run and getting the win in a 7-2 Expos victory. He even hit the first home run of his major-league career.

Bob Forsch was Palmer's mound opponent on the 21st. This was Forsch's fourth start of 1984, and he came into the game with an 0-1 record. Forsch had pitched a no-hitter in his previous start against Montreal, on September 26, 1983, so the Expos wanted some revenge. That was going to be a tall order, as Expos manager Bill Virdon rested regulars Pete Rose, Gary Carter, Andre Dawson, and Argenis Salazar, who had all played in the first game.

Nonetheless, Forsch didn't fare much better than Stuper did, as Montreal's backup-laden lineup scored three runs in the first inning. Bryan Little got on with a one-out bunt single, and moved to third when George Hendrick made a two-base error on Tim Raines' fly ball to right. Tim Wallach walked to load the bases, then Terry Francona singled to score Little and Raines. Forsch loaded the bases again when he walked Jim Wohlford, which moved Wallach to third; Wallach scored on a sacrifice fly by Bobby Ramos.

Palmer and his cut fastball took the mound and worked to … well … perfection, right from the beginning, as he induced Lonnie Smith to ground to short, struck out Andy Van Slyke, then got Dane Iorg to ground to short as well. Forsch settled down in the second, retiring the side in order, but gave up a home run to Wallach in the third. Palmer, meanwhile, kept mowing Cardinal batters down, getting groundball after groundball—he got 11 groundouts, along with two strikeouts and two fly balls.

"[Palmer] was hitting the target, down and away (pitching to the lower outside corner of the strike zone), and that's the key," said Expos catcher Bobby Ramos.³

The Expos came to bat in the top of the sixth with the clock approaching midnight. Francona and Wohlford both singled, and then the rains came down again, in torrents. Palmer went to the training room to kept his arm warm and loose, and in keeping with the superstition of ignoring a pitcher while he's pitching a no-hitter, none of his teammates talked to him about the situation. The umpires eventually called the game after a 77-minute rain delay, at 1:05 A.M. on April 22.

After the game was called, Palmer told reporters he was pleased with how the season was unfolding to that point. "The good Lord is looking after me," he said. I hit a home run in my first start … and now a rain-shortened perfect game. I'll take it."⁴

Palmer's performance was the first perfect victory of fewer than nine innings since Dean Chance of the Twins threw five perfect innings against the Boston Red Sox in 1967. Before that, two pitchers performed the feat in 1907: Harry Vickers threw five perfect innings for the Philadelphia Athletics against the Washington Senators and Edwin Karger of the Cardinals pitched seven innings without allowing a baserunner against the Boston Doves (Braves).

Major League Baseball listed Palmer's performance as a perfect game until 1991, when it clarified the definition of a no-hitter to stipulate that the pitcher had to go nine or more innings to receive credit for a gem.

Palmer's five-inning win was the high point of an up-and-down season for him. He lost his next three decisions, then won his next four to finish with a 7-3 mark and a 3.84 ERA. Forsch had a dreadful 1984 campaign, missing three months due to injury and finishing with a 2-5 record and a 6.02 ERA.

SOURCES

In addition to the sources listed below, the author also used:

phrases.org

The Sporting News

mlb.com

NOTES

1 That sentence was the first one in Bulwer-Lytton's 1830 novel, *Paul Clifford*.
2 Telephone interview with David Palmer, October 26, 2015.
3 Brian Kappler, "Palmer Takes Shortcut to Record Book," *Montreal Gazette*, April 23, 1984.
4 Ibid.

MIKE WITT

By Paul Hensler

AFTER THE LANDMARK Messersmith-McNally decision was handed down by arbitrator Peter Seitz in December 1975, the California Angels quickly engaged in what some pundits referred to as "checkbook baseball," a process in which financially well-off teams like the Angels and the New York Yankees sought to bolster their rosters by bidding for the best free agents on the market rather than develop talent in their own farm system. In the case of the Angels, owner Gene Autry was generous — some thought foolishly so — in lavishing contracts on players whose mission was to provide a quick fix to a roster badly in need of fortification, with his ultimate goal of reaching the World Series now hopefully in sight.

Early beneficiaries of the Messersmith verdict included Bobby Grich, Don Baylor, and Joe Rudi, who contributed to California's success in winning the 1979 American League West Division title. However, several veteran pitchers signed during this time — among them Bruce Kison, John D'Acquisto, and Bill Travers — either did not meet expectations or became unfortunate examples of how money could be ill-spent on free agents.

But to label the California farm system as incapable of producing robust talent would be a mistake. Top prospects who emerged as major leaguers and went on to solid careers included Frank Tanana, Jerry Remy, Carney Lansford, Ken Landreaux, and Willie Mays Aikens, while Dickie Thon, another with "can't-miss" potential, had his ability severely hampered only when he suffered a beaning just as he was establishing himself as an All-Star. The only problem for the Angels was that in the case of most of these latter players, they achieved the better part of their notoriety wearing the uniforms of other teams, as they had been traded away in the late 1970s and early 1980s for talent that, in some instances, gave questionable value in return.

It was into this milieu that a high-school pitcher who was raised in the shadow of Anaheim Stadium was delivered to the California Angels. The team was wise to cultivate the talent of Mike Witt and let him develop into the mainstay of their pitching rotation, most notably during one of the franchise's most successful — and ultimately agonizing — seasons.

Michael Atwater Witt was born on July 20, 1960, in Fullerton, California, and spent his early years in nearby Buena Park. His physical development filled out to a height of 6-feet-7, leading many to assume that he would select basketball as his sport of choice. However, Witt maintained that baseball was always his first love and although playing on the court was enjoyable, he found that "basketball was so much more physical and intense, that the contrast to baseball provided a great way to compete in a different way, ultimately making the baseball player in me much better."[1]

Helped greatly by the influence of his father and oldest brother in his athletic ventures, Witt also benefited from the sacrifices that his mother made for the entire family, which also included Mike's other five siblings. Upon entering Anaheim's Servite High School, an all-boys Roman Catholic prep school, Witt excelled in baseball and basketball. Under the tutelage of coach Larry Toner, Witt's stellar pitching — he won all 14 of his decisions during his senior year — led the Friars to the 1978 CIF Southern Section 4-A baseball championship, and he captured honors as the conference's Player of the Year. There was no small amount of irony inherent in that title game: The contest was held at Anaheim Stadium, and Witt allowed only three hits in Servite's 6-1 victory. The pitching rubber toed by Witt that day was the same one trod upon by Angel standouts Frank

Tanana and Nolan Ryan, whom the youngster would see from the upper deck of The Big A before moving down to the field level later in the game "and watch three innings of Nolan Ryan up close."[2]

Witt's deeds on the mound not surprisingly attracted the attention of baseball scouts, and just weeks before his 18th birthday he was chosen by California in the fourth round of the 1978 amateur draft. There followed a difficult choice: Would Witt enroll at Santa Clara University, a Jesuit institution, on a full baseball-basketball scholarship, or embark on a career on the diamond at the lowest stretches of the minor leagues? In spite of his mother's doubts about passing up an outstanding collegiate offer, Witt opted for taking a chance on working his way onto the roster of the baseball team he loved.

Without breaking stride, Witt continued the torrid pace he set while finishing his time at Servite, going 7-1 with a 3.56 ERA for the Angels' Pioneer League Rookie team in Idaho Falls. Witt's first full year in professional baseball proved to be more challenging, however. The Angels fielded only one Class-A team in 1979, so Witt moved to Salinas — as did fellow 1978 draftee and future major-league slugger Tom Brunansky — but he was hit hard en route to an 8-10 record and an unimpressive 5.11 ERA. With Salinas again for part of 1980, Witt found his footing, winning seven of 10 decisions and posting a fine 2.10 ERA, but when he was promoted to Double-A El Paso, his mediocre record of 5-5 was accompanied by an inflated ERA of 5.79. The Angels noted his "difficulty in the pitching-rich Texas League" but also pointed out one particular flash of brilliance that came in a 13-strikeout performance, which included one streak of fanning seven consecutive batters.[3] Enamored by the emerging potential that prompted them to draft Witt in the first place, the Angels invited him to spring training in 1981 even though he had logged but a dozen appearances in Double-A.

Once in camp and displaying maturity beyond his years, Witt quickly began to establish himself among the starting pitchers thanks to a record of 3-0 and an ERA of 1.44 over 25 innings of work, and he forced manager Jim Fregosi's hand to add him to the Angels' Opening Day roster. General manager Buzzie Bavasi dismissed any notion that Witt was being moved too soon to the major-league level. "I rushed Sandy Koufax. I rushed Don Drysdale. I rushed Carl Erskine. If [Witt] can get them out, he can pitch with us," said the former Brooklyn and Los Angeles Dodgers executive.[4] Also in agreement over Witt's status was California's player personnel director, Gene Mauch, who concurred with the decision to promote the budding star.

Witt had every right to assume that his address for the 1981 season would be California's Triple-A affiliate in Salt Lake City, and he was stunned by his jump from Double-A to the major-league club. Reminiscing years later about his arrival in Anaheim, the pitcher said, "I won't forget looking at the halo around the 'A' and the logo of the state of California with a star by Anaheim, thinking, 'I'm actually wearing this [uniform].'"[5] Maintaining his composure even though he had realized another dream, Witt acknowledged that his rise to the big leagues had been facilitated by pitching coach Tom Morgan. Morgan had been a pitcher for several major-league teams, including the expansion Los Angeles Angels in 1961. In his duties as the Angel pitching mentor, Morgan had been instrumental in developing Nolan Ryan into a formidable hurler, and his influence over Witt was similar. "[Morgan] helped me with my motion and all of a sudden, everything fell into place," Witt said shortly after his rookie season.[6]

As to be expected of a player trying to find his way as a new major-leaguer, Witt did show inconsistency. Yet, he was one of only a handful of rookie pitchers in the American League who landed a spot in their team's rotation at the beginning of the 1981 season, along with Steve Crawford (Boston), Jerry Don Gleaton (Seattle), Gene Nelson (New York), and Howard Bailey (Detroit).[7] Entering the major leagues that year also had a labor-related peril when players went on strike and forced the cancellation of about one-third of scheduled games, mostly in June and July. Witt feared that his shaky performance through late May would spell a demotion to Salt Lake City as the likelihood of a work stoppage intensified. But he was spared the fate of time in Triple-A and instead became an unemployed pitcher during the strike. However, the interruption allowed him to regroup, and Witt completed his first season as an Angel with three impressive complete-game wins in which he allowed only four earned runs in 27 innings.

A portent of Witt's future performances was growing evident. His most notorious pitch, the curveball, was drawing praise from inside and outside the organization. Witt's manager, Gene Mauch, who had taken over from the fired Fregosi at the end of May, declared, "Once that kid realizes how valuable that thing he has in his right sleeve is, he's going to be some kind of pitcher," and Boston skipper Ralph Houk echoed the sentiment by stating, "He could be a big, big winner."[8] The final accounting showed Witt's record of 8-9 not being enough to merit AL Rookie of the Year laurels, but he was named the Angels' top rookie. Witt led all Angels pitchers with 75 strikeouts—as well as 11 hit batters—and his ERA of 3.28 was second to veteran Ken Forsch among the team's starters.

Entering the 1982 season, the Angels girded themselves for another run at the AL West pennant by executing a series of transactions that imported a host of veterans. Catcher Bob Boone, shortstop Tim Foli, and third baseman Doug DeCinces were acquired via trade or free-agent signing in order to address manifold weaknesses in the regular lineup. Owner Gene Autry also rolled the dice when he signed one of the biggest names on the free agent market, Reggie Jackson, the former Yankee finishing his contract in New York and looking to rebound from a mediocre performance in 1981. One of the Angels' best prospects, Daryl Sconiers, expressed trepidation that he would follow in the footsteps of other young talent groomed by California only to be sent to another team in a trade. For his own part, Witt did his best to ignore such talk. "I never concerned myself with what the front office was thinking," Witt said after his playing days were over. "I knew that everyone needed pitching, and that as long as I did my job, I would be okay."[9]

Witt opened the new campaign in less than spectacular fashion—he was chased in the third inning of his first start—but recovered to win three straight games. This Jekyll-and-Hyde pattern seemed to define Witt's season, and for most of May he was banished to the bullpen

to straighten out his difficulties. Witt posted three wins in August to keep the Angels in contention, but remained winless after his eighth victory on August 23. The final tally for his second season showed an 8-6 record, an ERA of 3.51, with 85 strikeouts in 179⅔ innings. Having his first taste of champagne when the Angels clinched the AL West, Witt also made one appearance in the American League Championship Series, a three-inning relief effort in Game Three at Milwaukee against the Brewers. He ended a Brewer threat by striking out Charlie Moore to close out the fourth inning but served up a two-run homer to Paul Molitor in the seventh, which became the margin of victory in Milwaukee's 5-3 win.

Nevertheless, critics were still in Witt's corner, including sportswriter Peter Gammons, who wrote, "No young pitcher in this league has a better curveball than California's Mike Witt." But Gammons' comment also included this ominous foreboding: "But in his August 18 start against Boston, he threw [the curve] 11 of his first 13 pitches."[10] The best weapon in Witt's repertoire was en route to becoming his worst enemy, as an early overreliance on his best pitch began to sow the seeds of future physical problems from which he would not recover. Also included in later commentary by Gammons was an observation that dealt with a problem Witt *would* address. "There have been knocks against his ability to concentrate, but we're talking about a kid who won't be 23 until July [1983]."[11] If anything was working to Witt's advantage besides his potential, his youthfulness served as a welcome counterweight to the age of Angels starters Geoff Zahn (37), Ken Forsch (36), Tommy John (40), Dave Goltz (34), and Bruce Kison (33).

In 1983 Witt stumbled badly leaving the gate when the season opened. He dropped his first three decisions in convincing fashion, allowing 14 earned runs in just 15 innings for an 8.40 ERA. Sent again to the bullpen because "suddenly, his breaking ball has a mind of its own," Witt exuded confidence that he would be able to correct his problems, especially in light of his demotion coming so early in the campaign.[12] Pitching coach Tom Morgan was called upon to shepherd Witt through mechanical adjustments in his windup and delivery, both of which were determined to be askew. Angels manager John McNamara, in his first year at California's helm, began to use Witt in short relief, thereby causing a tempest in the team's bullpen when Doug Corbett took exception to being displaced as the closer.

But Witt delivered when called upon, and a shift in his role seemed to be in the making. In his first seven relief appearances, he pitched 12⅔ scoreless innings and picked up three saves through May 10. Given several spot starts over the following months, Witt returned to the rotation on July 21 but posted only a 3-8 record through the end of the season. Although Witt set a career high for games pitched (43) and had early success in the role of closer, the year was a step backward for him. Ending with a 7-14 record and an uninspiring ERA of 4.91, the 23-year-old was clearly at a crossroads as he looked ahead to his fourth major-league season.

Two critical factors entered into Mike Witt's life, one in November 1983, and another shortly thereafter. The first was the culmination of a courtship with a young woman he had met in his first year with the Angels. Lisa Fenn worked as a secretary for the club and moved to the group-ticket sales department, and by late 1982 she and Mike began dating because "every time we turned around we ran into each other. … We got engaged right away and were married 11 months later."[13] The nuptials brought a large degree of stability to Mike's life, and he furthered his cause with the superb effort he displayed playing winter ball in Venezuela soon after his wedding. This experience in winter ball (in which Witt posted an 8-0 record) served as a springboard to help him at last reach the potential that was envisioned by so many observers inside and outside the Angels' organization. "With my home life set, something just clicked for me in winter ball before that 1984 season," Witt said years later, and recognizing that another dismal season-long performance might seriously damage his career, he added, "I found the [necessary] consistency and mental focus, knowing my job was on the line."[14]

In the offseason Angels manager McNamara took on a new pitching coach to replace the retiring Tom Morgan. Witt's development as a pitcher had been reported as being "arrested by his inability to get along with Morgan," but Marcel Lachemann, Morgan's replacement, brought a "rosy disposition" with him that was expected to smooth over any previous personality clashes.[15]

Despite having great success in the recently completed winter league, Witt lost any momentum from that experience when the American League season commenced. After a no-decision in his opening assignment—Witt pitched 7⅓ innings of scoreless ball at home against the Red Sox—he suffered through two starts in which he yielded six runs in each game, losing the first but escaping with a win in the second. After little better luck in his fourth start, in which Witt gave up five more runs in 7⅓ innings, he took the advice of first baseman Rod Carew and enlisted the services of Dr. Harvey Misel. Misel was a hypnotist who in 1975 helped future Hall of Famer

Carew ignore pain from a pulled leg muscle. Witt employed Dr. Misel's services to improve his concentration, and the results were dramatic: three complete games for three wins, with only two earned runs given up. But the bad vibes returned as Witt went winless in his last four starts in May. There ensued another turnaround in late June in which Witt reeled off a six-game winning streak and dropped his ERA to a season-low 3.36.

To be sure, more rough spots dotted the rest of his season, but Witt persevered and finally came into his own as the ace of the Angels staff. He led all pitchers in every major category: 15 wins (against 11 losses), 246⅔ innings in 34 starts, 196 strikeouts, and 9 complete games, which tied Geoff Zahn's mark. He put down 16 Seattle Mariners on strikes on July 23, prompting Mariners manager Del Crandall to muse, "We can't understand why he isn't 18-0" instead of 11-7 at that point in the season.[16] The lessons about concentrating were evidently gaining traction, although Witt was more concerned about reaching a level of consistent performance than focusing on accumulating strikeouts. He also credited his wife with providing a "settling influence" in his life, although Lisa offered a different perspective of the ups and downs of their marriage.[17] Admitting that she was a bundle of nerves whenever her husband was scheduled to pitch in an important game, Lisa also noted the difference between an everyday player—who has a chance to redeem himself the next game after a poor performance—and a starting pitcher. "There are four or five days between games. That's great if he's pitched a good game, but if he doesn't feel good about the last game, that's four or five days of brooding."[18]

Witt's performance against the Mariners matched Dwight Gooden for the best single-game strikeout total in the majors in 1984 (Gooden had two 16-K games in September), and his 15th victory was most special, coming on the final day of the season against the Texas Rangers at Arlington Stadium. Playing only for pride and the chance to finish the year at .500, the Angels sent Witt to the mound and received the ultimate performance from their new workhorse. Retiring all 18 Texas batters through six innings, Witt finally was staked to the only run he would need—Reggie Jackson plated Doug DeCinces on a fielder's choice in the top of the seventh—and then vanquished the final nine batters he faced to complete the 11th perfect game in major-league history.[19] Witt's only other similar feat came in his days playing Little League baseball in Fullerton, when he pitched a no-hitter, and his gem against the Rangers proved to be a farewell gift of sorts for his manager, as John McNamara was relieved of his duties and would be replaced by Gene Mauch for the 1985 season. The notoriety Witt received from his breakthrough season culminated in a cameo appearance on *The Jeffersons* television show.

After improving their record from 70-92 in 1983 to 81-81 a year later, the Angels looked forward to continuing their rise and breaking the bonds of another second-place finish. The team's media guide featured a caption exclaiming "We're So Exc!ted" *[sic]*, but

such glee did not translate to a promising beginning to Witt's 1985 season. Putting himself in a hole thanks in part to home-run balls he threw in each of his first three starts, Witt was 0-3 before finally pitching the type of game expected of him, a three-hit whitewashing of the Mariners in Seattle on April 25. Had he been given a bit more offensive support, his record for the first half of the year would have been better than 6-6, but most encouraging was his stretch from June 12 through September 12, when he was victorious in 10 of 11 decisions. Solidifying his place in the rotation, Witt lasted deep into many games, allowing Mauch to give the bullpen a rest, especially during the summer months. This expenditure of innings, however, spelled fatigue late in the season. In September Witt failed to last beyond the seventh inning on four occasions, but he caught a second wind on October 1 to beat Kansas City and put the Angels a game ahead of the Royals as the two teams dueled coming down the stretch. Five days later Witt also was the winner in the season's finale—once more against the Rangers in Texas—that put California in a disappointing second-place finish, one game behind eventual World Series champion Kansas City.

There was no doubt that Witt's stock was still on the rise. Repeating his 15-win season of 1984 and again leading Angels pitchers in starts (35), innings (250, which also enabled him to collect a $150,000 bonus), ERA (3.56, among starters), and strikeouts (180), Witt validated the faith expressed by the club in its three-year, $2.75 million contract that ran through 1987. With a rotation bolstered by another promising young starter who had gained a major-league toehold, the 1986 season shaped up to be possibly the best in the Angels' history. Kirk McCaskill, a Canadian who had been a standout hockey player at the University of Vermont, joined Witt and veterans Don Sutton and John Candelaria to give Mauch a formidable quartet on the mound, with closer Donnie Moore anchoring the bullpen. Among regular players was a fine blend of speed, power, and run production that positioned California to unseat the Royals as AL West champions.

Commencing the 1986 campaign better than others, Witt furnished quality innings for much of the first half of the season, and his 9-7 record with 3.08 ERA earned him a selection to the American League All-Star team. It was in August, however, when he lorded over opponents to such an extent that he garnered AL Pitcher of the Month honors. Winning all five of his starts, including three complete games and one shutout, Witt permitted only a single earned run in 43 innings for a 0.21 ERA, and as an improvement over the previous year, he averaged eight innings in his six starts during September.

After moving into first place in the AL West on July 7, the Angels never looked back, building a 10-game lead on September 26 to clinch the division title. Witt's statistics spoke for themselves as he walked away with club MVP honors in voting by his teammates: a record of 18 wins, 10 losses, an ERA of 2.84 in 269 innings, in which he gave up only 218 hits and fanned a career-high 208 batters with just 73 bases on balls. Reporting in *The Sporting News*, Moss Klein observed that Witt "may be second only to Roger Clemens as the league's most feared starter," and pointed out that four of his early-season losses could be attributed to lack of run support.[20] Praise from Witt's manager—"He's no longer 'young Mike Witt'"—indicated that Gene Mauch appreciated the hurler having blossomed into a mature and outstanding pitcher, and journalist Stan Isle told readers of his column that the Elias Sports Bureau found Witt to be among a select group of players in either league that it classed as "underrated."[21]

Now the center of attention, Witt was nonetheless blasé regarding the tributes. "I know how my teammates feel about me even without putting it into words," he said on the eve of the American League Championship Series against Boston. "I don't get caught up in being compared to other people."[22] At season's end, Witt finished third in voting for the AL Cy Young Award and placed 12th in balloting for the league's Most Valuable Player.

Encomiums aside, Witt's regular season had closed on a sour note as he attempted to become the Angels' first 20-game winner since Nolan Ryan turned the trick in 1974. Those hopes were dashed when he lost to the Rangers in his final home start on September 28 after giving up a grand slam to Pete Incaviglia. Witt was inspired to do his best on the field, but as Tom Singer of the *Los Angeles Herald Examiner* noted, the pitcher also was motivated by an undercurrent of revenge, namely "getting back at reporters for what he considered unfair treatment in his formative seasons."[23] According to Singer, throughout the 1986 season Witt "spent time dodging reporters, or giving them curt answers when cornered," tactics that led to Witt being unflatteringly dubbed "the Earl of Surl."[24]

Witt's loss to Texas—and with it the chance for a 19th victory—meant that it would be impossible for him to win 20 with only one more scheduled start remaining. After the defeat, Witt unloaded his suppressed feelings to the gathered scribes: "Maybe I've been waiting five years for this year, so you guys could come to me and get nothing [to write about]. I hope you're frustrated."[25] Harboring his bile about criticism in the press directed his way as he struggled in the early 1980s to establish himself in the Angels rotation, Witt admitted that his recent evasiveness was deliberate. He disdained the way the press treated him compared with veterans like Rod Carew, Reggie Jackson, and Doug DeCinces, who in Witt's view were given much more latitude when their performances were subpar. Kirk McCaskill confessed that Witt was "very bitter" about the predicament, and Witt considered taking teammate George Hendrick's lead by not speaking at all to the media.[26] Coming at a time when Witt was also thoughtfully involved with charity work for the Pediatric Cancer Research Center at Children's Hospital of Orange County, the unfortunate episode tainted what otherwise should have been one of the high-water marks of Witt's career.

And there still remained the issue of the next hurdle to the World Series, the ALCS, which opened in Boston's Fenway Park. To no one's surprise, Mauch chose Witt as the Game One starter, and the demons haunting the former Phillies manager since 1964—to say nothing of the 1982 debacle in which his Angels blew a two-games-to-none lead over the Brewers—were seemingly in the process of being exorcised after Witt dispatched the Red Sox and their ace Roger Clemens 8-1 in a complete-game effort. Allowing just five hits and two walks, Witt benefited from an early four-run outburst and subsequent three-run cushion in the eighth inning. Although McCaskill suffered a loss in Game Two, the Angels were satisfied at splitting the first two contests on the road as the series moved to Anaheim.

In Game Three John Candelaria outdueled Oil Can Boyd, 5-3, and when the Angels staged a frantic rally with three runs in the bottom of the ninth and pushed a run across in the bottom of the 11th to take Game Four, 4-3, California was one victory away from reaching the World Series for the first time. Game Five meant that it would be Mike Witt's turn to take the mound, and if he could pitch anywhere near as well as he had in the series opener, the Angels were well-poised to claim the American League pennant.

On the warm, hazy afternoon of October 12, over 64,000 fans packed Anaheim Stadium in heightened anticipation. "Boston at Witt's End," read one bedsheet poster hanging from the upper deck, and the momentum from the previous night's victory was palpable. Witt and Bruce Hurst, who took the mound for Boston in the hope of holding the Angels at bay, pitched a scoreless first inning, but the Red Sox struck in the second when Jim Rice singled and Rich Gedman followed two batters later with a stinging line-drive home run to right field. Bob Boone cut the lead in half with a solo shot leading off the third, while Witt had his way with the Boston lineup, easily retiring Red Sox batters—with the notable exception of Gedman, who belted a double his second trip to the plate in the fifth. Hurst was giving no quarter and held the Angels in check until two were out in the sixth with the score at 2-1. Doug DeCinces smacked a double to right-center field, and Bobby Grich followed with a drive to deep center field. Dave Henderson, substituting for the injured Tony Armas, drew a bead on the fly ball and leaped to make what would have been a phenomenal catch at the wall, but in doing so, Henderson tipped the ball over the fence for a most improbable home run, giving the Angels a 3-2 lead.

Buoyed by the change in score, Witt set down three of the next four hitters in the seventh, Gedman again playing the bête noir by singling to right. In the home half of the inning, the Angels padded their margin with runs courtesy of Rob Wilfong's pinch-hit double and a sacrifice fly by Brian Downing. In the top of the eighth, California led 5-2, and Witt retired the side on nine pitches, but he flagged in the ninth, the most infamous inning in Angels history. Witt surrendered a base hit to Bill Buckner, who then gave way to pinch-runner Dave Stapleton. Rice was caught looking at a third strike, but Don Baylor—Witt's erstwhile teammate—drove a home run to left to cut the Boston deficit to one run. Dwight Evans was then retired on a popup to DeCinces at third, and the only thing now standing between the Angels and the World Series was Rich Gedman.

In light of Gedman's performance this day against Witt—made all the more ironic given that Gedman was a dreary 2-for-24 lifetime against Witt entering Game Five—it made sense that Gene Mauch would go to his bullpen, particularly left-hander Gary Lucas. The previous evening, Lucas had struck out the Boston catcher swinging on a 2-and-2 pitch, so the change in pitchers seemed a natural fit for the circumstances. Witt retired to the dugout as the crowd cheered and throbbed with anticipation of the final out. The ace had done all that could be expected of him by putting forth a yeoman effort to bring the Angels within one out of the AL title. But for California, ignominy followed: Lucas plunked Gedman with the only pitch he threw, and when Mauch brought in closer Donnie Moore to snuff out the threat, he served up a homer to Dave Henderson on a 2-and-2 pitch, giving Boston a 6-5 lead. Although the Angels tied the score in the bottom of the ninth, they eventually lost in the 11th inning, the series moving back to Boston, where California lost Games Six and Seven, a pair of routs that left everyone associated with the Angels—players, management, and fans—stunned at the improbable outcome after being one strike away from playing in the World Series.

In a revealing interview a few months after the ALCS meltdown, Witt displayed an extraordinary amount of candor in answering questions about the Game Five collapse and how the aftermath would affect himself and the team as they tried to recover. His wife, Lisa, saved various game accounts from the newspapers, which Mike read on occasion over the winter and made him understand further how close he had come to clinching the pennant for the Angels. Reliving the final inning, Witt said that the base hit by Buckner to lead off was on a pitch that he had retired the Red Sox first baseman with his other trips to the plate, and the strikeout of Rice on three straight pitches came on a delivery that he could not recall. But when Baylor touched him for the two-run homer, Witt "couldn't believe it at the time. ... The last thing on my mind was that it was a home run. ... He just went out and got it [by using] the fat part of the bat."[27] Bearing down on Evans, Witt coaxed the popout on an 0-and-2 offering, a situation in which DeCinces told Witt that he had handled the Boston right fielder "perfectly."[28] Naturally the outcome of the game—to say nothing of the rest of the series—"was a huge letdown. To see 20,000 people lined up around the rail ready to jump down [to celebrate] ... *we had it!*"[29] Lastly, the entire club was shell-shocked in the knowledge of having to return to Boston: "The mood of the team during those last two games. ... I don't even remember playing there."[30]

Recognizing a possible repeat of the psychological damage that lingered after the 1982 ALCS loss to the Brewers, Witt looked forward to 1987 because the nucleus of the pitching staff was ostensibly intact, and the record shows that new faces from the farm system, such as Jack Howell, Mark McLemore, and Devon White, would be on hand to augment a lineup solidified by 1986 wunderkind Wally Joyner and Dick Schofield, a very capable shortstop. Witt anticipated that coming so close to a league title in 1986 and playing before huge crowds would have the benefit of motivating the Angels to execute with the same intensity. "It made us *real* hungry," he said, and now it was up to players and manager to perform.³¹ When asked about his personal role as a team leader, Witt preferred to let his work on the mound do the speaking rather than serve as a cheerleader in the clubhouse, an attitude showing a large degree of maturity on his part by recognizing the possibility that he could be overstepping his bounds by becoming too vocal.

But the record also shows that in spite of the Angels' best efforts to put the ALCS demons to rest, the team ruined a hopeful start to the 1987 season by going into a tailspin in the latter part of May, losing 12 of their last 15 games in the month, including nine in a row. Although they recovered to reach second place by early August, the bottom fell out for good in September due to a 7-19 record, and the Angels landed in the basement of the AL West, tied with Texas for sixth place. Witt did lead by example, as evidenced by his naming as Player of the Week for the first week of June, and his 11 wins with a 3.31 ERA at the halfway point of the season earned him a spot on the American League All-Star team for the second time.

However, Witt's 5-9 record after the break contributed to an ERA that swelled to 4.01 by the end of the campaign. The final log showed 16 wins, 14 losses, and a team-high 192 strikeouts, and Witt suffered from a lack of run support, as he was backed by two runs or less in eight of his losses. Among his 36 starts — the most by an Angel pitcher since Nolan Ryan's 37 a decade earlier — were 10 complete games. Not known at this time was the fact that Witt had ascended as high as he would rise as a major-league pitcher, and a new and disturbing trend began to emerge in his performances.

Although Witt was the mainstay of the rotation, "there were evident cracks in his dominance," and as questions regarding his right shoulder persisted as the season played out, Witt, "[who] was abrasive with the press in the best of times … was defensive about the condition of the shoulder."³² As his fastball, once in the low 90s, waned to the mid-80s, the issue of a salary drive with free agency pending certainly had to be in his mind, too: Witt was in the final year of his three-year deal, and he wanted to pitch at least 240 innings in order to collect a $250,000 bonus. In the previous two seasons, he reaped a total of $350,000 for innings pitched and sought a repeat reward. In 1987 he crossed the threshold by lasting until at least the eighth inning in 16 of his 36 starts, but doing so turned out to be a Pyrrhic victory.

Once on the market, Witt attracted the attention of the New York Yankees — who were always willing to spend, and likely bid up the signing price for him — and he later confessed, "I was signed, sealed, and delivered to New York. … But [George] Steinbrenner gave me a week before he wanted to announce it, and during that week, I changed my mind."³³ The change of heart — because of both his and his wife's family ties to the area — returned him to Anaheim for $2.8 million over the next two years. If any doubts nagged California management, it was not obvious in the sentiments expressed by Gene Mauch or general manager Mike Port. Mauch expected that with offseason rest and recuperation, "that good Mike Witt fastball [will] come back," and Port defended the new contract by offering Witt's ability to reach 247 innings as proof of his well-being.³⁴ "If we had any suspicions, we wouldn't have spent two months pursuing him."³⁵

In an attempt to regain the form he displayed in the course of helping the Angels win the AL West, Witt employed modern technology by "enlist[ing] biomechanics experts to dissect his delivery with the use of computer graphics."³⁶ Pitching coach Marcel Lachemann helped him with small adjustments that seemed to make a huge improvement, and Witt blazed through 1988 spring training undefeated in four decisions. In 21 innings, Witt yielded only three walks while fanning 22 batters. The Angels could only hope for a continuation of his renaissance during the regular season, but such was not the case. Under new skipper Cookie Rojas, Witt was selected for another Opening Day start, yet inconsistency remained the lanky right-hander's bugbear, as he finished April with losses in two of his three decisions and an alarming 5.29 ERA. The month of May was no kinder, as Witt lost four straight before salvaging a

win with a shutout of the Orioles. "There's nothing physically wrong with him, I'm sure of that," pled Rojas in defense of his faltering ace, yet Lachemann remained concerned because "something's out of whack."[37] The eight bases on balls Witt issued in a May 18 start—along with sloppiness shown by others on the field—were more than GM Port could bear, and he threatened to make some trades in order to shake the Angels from their lethargy.

Rojas urged Witt to forgo his strategy of "nibbling at the plate with breaking pitches" and challenge hitters with more fastballs, a tactic that paid off when he reeled off four straight wins in June.[38] From this point until the end of the season, Witt's ERA hovered just above 4.00,

but to his credit, his competitive fire propelled him to boost his record from a dismal 1-6 in mid-May to 13-12 by early September. His victory on September 8 was his 100th in an Angels uniform—and also was a game in which he failed to fan a single batter—but a skein of four defeats to end that month produced a final accounting that hinted at a worrisome downturn: 13-16 record, 4.15 ERA—a career high—with 263 hits allowed in 249⅔ innings, and only 133 strikeouts, his lowest total since 1983. The sway that he had held over American League hitters had embarked on a decidedly downward trend, and the team in general reflected the decline by finishing 75-79 under Rojas (who was fired in late September) and going winless in eight games with interim manager Moose Stubing in charge. The Angels' fourth-place finish made the near-AL pennant of 1986 seem like ancient history.

Former Texas skipper Doug Rader was brought in to revive the Angels' fortunes for 1989. Not only was a new field leader in the dugout, but Mike Port was busy importing new talent—including some reclamation projects—that he hoped would ignite the Angels on several fronts. Lance Parrish, Claudell Washington, Bob McClure, and Bert Blyleven were added to the roster and fueled a resurgence that kept California in a position to overtake the reigning AL champion Oakland Athletics. In spring training Moss Klein told readers of his *Sporting News* column, "California has an intriguing starting rotation. The names are impressive: Mike Witt, Bert Blyleven, Kirk McCaskill, and Dan Petry, along with Chuck Finley."[39]

Petry became a nonfactor, but picking up the slack in decisive fashion was a rookie southpaw from the University of Michigan who captivated crowds and inspired athletes of all abilities. Jim Abbott had been born without a right hand, but he did not let this handicap block his path to a superb collegiate career. The native of Flint, Michigan, was named to the US Olympic team, was the winning pitcher in the Gold Medal game, and subsequently was signed as the Angels' top pick in the 1988 draft. Jumping right into the rotation without spending a day in the minor leagues, the 21-year-old Abbott finished with 12 wins and as many loses, but impressed teammates, coaches, opponents, and fans alike with his grit and athleticism.

As stunning as Abbott was, so too were Blyleven and Finley, the former posting a 17-5 record after appearing to be at the end of his career following a 17-loss season in 1988 that was marked by a 5.43 ERA, the latter enjoying a breakthrough season of his own—as had Witt years earlier—with 16 wins and a nifty 2.57 ERA. And having recovered from several arm ailments over the past two years, McCaskill provided a pleasant surprise with 15 wins along with a 2.93 ERA. But the odd man out was Mike Witt, whose value continued to fall.

Digging himself a hole once again to commence the season, the erratic Witt quickly bottomed out on April 25 when he served up home runs to three

Baltimore hitters who collectively were batting less than .200. "You'd think he could locate the ball more effectively and consistently," grumbled Rader after the Orioles' slugfest, but Witt persevered and his manager continued to send him to the mound every fifth day.[40] Still exhibiting his workhorse ethic, Witt pitched into the seventh inning during 21 of his 33 starts, and in 11 of his losses the offense backed him with only two runs or less. Neither did the bullpen do Witt any favors by relinquishing leads that he had turned over to them. But there were only five complete games among his starts, not a single one of them a shutout, and the team's media guide later noted that Witt "has posted losing records both at home and on road in each of last two seasons."[41] In a *Sporting News* feature article lauding the vaunted starting rotation, Witt was referred to as "the titular ace of the staff," and was "losing speed, stuff and games at an alarming rate since 1986 [and] was only a stopper on the payroll" with his $1.4 million salary.[42] Lachemann, his pitching coach, held out hope for Witt to get on track, but "he no longer blows people away, and has been a frustrating holdout from [catcher Lance] Parrish's game of pitching inside."[43]

Witt was victimized by home runs at a disturbing rate in the first half of season—18 times—and at least was able to keep the ball in the park at a more acceptable rate in the second half, with only eight surrendered. Yet at just 28 years of age, Witt had evolved into an enigma for which there appeared no easy answer. He pitched his final game of 1989 at the end of September, his 15th loss against nine wins, and in 220 innings compiled an ERA of 4.54 with only 123 strikeouts to show for his efforts. That finale versus the Texas Rangers was a stark contrast to his season-ending perfect game—also against Texas –five years earlier. This time he failed to survive the seventh inning and was charged with four runs, all earned.

In the postseason, Witt was not eligible for free agency but could submit to salary arbitration if he was unable to agree with the Angels on a new contract. Astonishingly, Angels owner Gene Autry showed his generous side once more and brought the flagging ace back at a very modest salary cut of only $100,000, with Witt's one-year deal calling for $1.3 million. But by the time Witt signed in mid-January of 1990 for the coming season, he had little chance of holding a spot in California's rotation because Autry had already lavished a $16 million contract on one of the prime free agents available, former Seattle Mariners ace Mark Langston, who also was a three-time strikeout leader of the American League and a Gold Glove winner.

With Witt having fallen to fifth best of five Angels starters, it was obvious that he would cede his place in the rotation to Langston, and he faced the reality of time in the Angels bullpen or perhaps being traded in the very near future. As spring-training camps got under way, Witt was resigned to his fate, saying, "As long as I'm in the big leagues, that's all that matters."[44] The cover of the team's 1990 media guide spoke volumes about the players it expected to be the key personnel that year: pitchers Langston, Finley, and Blyleven, along with veteran slugger Brian Downing, Wally Joyner, and Chili Davis. One of the franchise's best pitchers had been relegated to the role of an afterthought.

As Opening Day drew near, Mike Port sought help for the outfield, and it was believed that the Yankees' Dave Winfield—a resident of nearby Beverly Hills—might be lured to Anaheim via a trade if the 10-and-5 clause of the outfielder's contract could be amicably brokered.[45] As rumors swirled that Witt would be sent to New York in exchange for Winfield, Witt had been relegated to the Angels bullpen, but the demotion allowed him to participate in one of the game's more unusual mound feats. In California's third game of the season, Langston was slated to make his home debut in an Angels uniform, which he did in spectacular fashion by throwing seven innings of no-hit ball against his former club, the Mariners. But a labor dispute between the Major League Baseball Players Association and the owners resulted in a lockout that shortened the timeframe of spring training, and with all pitchers not having the full benefit of a normal preseason preparation period, Langston was pulled by manager Doug Rader in order to prevent the southpaw, whose pitch count was at 99, from pitching too much too early.[46]

Called from the pen to complete the game was Witt, who entered to a mixture of cheers from fans wishing him well and boos from those who preferred to see Langston remain in the contest in hopes of finishing it on his own. But Witt did not disappoint, retiring all six batters he faced—four on groundballs to second along with a pair of strikeouts—to preserve the no-hitter.

Credited with a save, Witt claimed, "The fact that it was a no-hitter wasn't really foremost in my mind. It was in my mind, but it was a 1-0 game, and the foremost thought in my mind was keeping guys off base, because it would have brought the winning run to the plate."[47] When questioned about the significance of the game vis-a-vis his new role in the bullpen and the persistent trade rumors, Witt frankly admitted that he would rather be in his accustomed place in the starting rotation. "I have three 'druthers,'" he declared. "My first would be to start here [with the Angels], my second would be to start somewhere else, and my third would be to pitch here from the bullpen."[48]

Stoically trying to ignore the trade talk, Witt had some difficulty adjusting to his job as a reliever. He blew two save opportunities that resulted in losses and lost a third game while pitching into extra innings. But by May 10 Witt had pared his ERA to a tidy 1.77 in 20⅓ innings while allowing only one home run; then three days later the *New York Times* reported that Witt had been put in a situation that was not among his three "druthers." "Witt Appears Headed For Yanks and Bullpen," read the headline, meaning that relief duty for a team other than the Angels was now on Witt's immediate horizon. "It's not something I look at as being permanent," he told the *Times*. "I have no aspirations of being the next Dennis Eckersley."[49] Pointing to the fact that he was 29 years old, Witt was prepared to return to a starting role to build on the numbers—especially wins—he had accumulated serving in a rotation.

When completion of the trade for Winfield seemed imminent despite the continuing legal wrangling over his 10-and-5 status, the Angels revealed how anxious they were to move their erstwhile ace. The club said that the Yankees could keep Witt regardless of whether an arbitrator ruled in favor of Winfield and allowed the outfielder to remain in New York. Now officially displaced as an Angel, Witt forged ahead by joining the Yankees, who were on the road in Seattle.

Once donning pinstripes, Witt took a place in the New York rotation and pitched into at least the sixth inning in his first four starts, resulting in three no-decisions and one loss. However, in his fifth start, on June 8, he heard a dreaded "pop" in his arm during the second inning. Promptly removed from the game, he was placed on the disabled list for the first time in his career. Laid up for two months and refusing to serve a rehabilitation assignment in the minor leagues, Witt returned and remained in the Yankees rotation despite several inglorious outings. Besides his professional pride and work ethic, there was another motivating factor for Witt to perform well: major league owners were awaiting the outcome of a collusion judgment, and if they found themselves on the losing side of the arbitrator's ruling, several players—including Witt—stood to gain free agency. Witt's two-month salary drive enabled him to finish his service in the Bronx with a record of 5-6 and an ERA of 4.47 in 96⅔ innings. The fact that he remained in the rotation and came back after his injury to pitch at times like the old Mike Witt—including one shutout and another complete game as well as five other appearances in which he lasted into the seventh inning—furnished enough proof to the Yankees that he was worth keeping, even though Witt informed close friends that he might seek a new address on the West Coast should free agency become a reality.

In early December Witt indeed was allowed to test the open market but New York also offered salary arbitration to him. He attracted the attention of the Toronto Blue Jays, but George Steinbrenner's checkbook was the biggest factor in persuading Witt to remain a Yankee. He re-signed with the Yankees for three years at a total of $8 million, a staggering sum considering the injury he had recently suffered. And during spring training of 1991, the dark clouds above Witt began to take on a more ominous form; though he was expected to be the Yankees' starter on Opening Day, a strain in his right elbow grew increasingly worrisome. New York pitching coach Mark Connor was content to let Witt skip two starts in the Grapefruit League and remarked, "We're not ready to panic. Mike feels that he can throw right now. We want to proceed with caution."[50]

A mechanical adjustment was believed to be the cure, yet Witt himself was mystified by the existence of any discomfort. Again landing on the disabled list, he was in danger of becoming another overpaid free agent unable to perform due to injury. Along with several other notable starting pitchers, Witt landed on Moss Klein's "season-opening A.L. All-Disabled List staff" and did not make his first appearance until June 7.[51] His start that day was a five-inning, no-decision, but the following week he bowed out after just 17 pitches to four Minnesota batters and was done for the year. With an 0-1 record and a 10.13 ERA in a mere 5⅓ innings, Witt now faced the grim reality of Tommy John surgery to have any hope of a return. In late July he returned to Southern California and on July 25, he underwent an operation on his right elbow to replace the ulnar collateral ligament and faced a full year of rehabilitation. His only credited work in 1992 came in three starts with the Yankees' Gulf Coast team, but Witt seemed to be on the right track. He posted a 1-0 record, allowed no earned runs in 12 innings, and fanned 13 batters.

Witt soldiered on, and after nearly two years away from the game, during which time he "lived with an asterisk beside his name that denoted his constant presence on the disabled list," he at last returned on April 25, 1993.[52] After 96 pitches, Witt was lifted by manager Buck Showalter, who was inclined to not read too deeply into the pitcher's statistically unimpressive line of five hits in four innings, five runs — all earned, including four courtesy of a grand slam — two walks, and one hit batter. The skipper was "very satisfied" by the "good stuff" he saw Witt delivering, and in his next start Witt spun seven innings of three-hit ball — including a solo homer — saying afterward that his elbow "felt fine, never better."[53] Witt also attributed his successful rejuvenation to his brother Steve, a former prospect in the Philadelphia Phillies' system who served as his catcher during workout sessions at Witt's home.

One good outing begat another, and Witt compiled a modest string of starts in which he held the opposition in check and ostensibly secured his place in the Yankee rotation. But he slumped during a four-game stretch in which his ERA approached 12.00, and on June 1 his right elbow was bruised when it was struck by a line drive off the bat of Cleveland's Paul Sorrento, and Witt took two weeks off before returning against the Twins. That game proved to be Witt's finale, a no-decision in which he lasted until the sixth inning. Placed on the disabled list the following day — and five weeks short of his 33rd birthday — he would never again appear in a major-league game. Granted free agency once more at the end of the season, Witt was done as a major-league pitcher, and he would retire to his home in Southern California to spend time with Lisa and their children, daughter Kellen Marie and sons Justin and Kevin. He would take much pleasure in serving as a pitching coach at Dana Hills High School in the late 1990s and as a varsity assistant and pitching coach at Santa Margarita High School beginning in 2000, as his sons followed their father's footsteps onto the diamond.

At the height of his fame, Mike Witt divulged some tips for youngsters regarding his work ethic and his philosophy on pitching. While instructing the proper technique for gripping a curveball, he presciently warned underage pitchers on the hazards of throwing that pitch. "Wait until you are at least 15 years old. If you throw too many when you are young, you are bound to hurt your elbow," he cautioned.[54] Generally speaking, Witt distilled his guidance to one basic suggestion, namely practice. This was advice perhaps offered in an easier-said-than-done tone, because Witt himself fell victim to the siren song of the curveball, which he used to devastating effect, but it was also a pitch that came with the associated cost of harm to his own well-being.

Witt's achievements over 10 seasons in Anaheim—109 wins against 107 losses, 3.76 ERA, and 1,283 strikeouts as well as selection to two American League All-Star teams—earned him induction into the team's Hall of Fame on August 22, 2015. When the curveball worked for Witt, it was one of the best in baseball during the mid-1980s. That signature pitch enabled him to etch his name in the record books for a perfect game and, a bit more unusually, a shared no-hitter, but his bringing the California Angels to within one out their first American League pennant may provide the best defining moment of Witt's career. The story of a local kid with star potential playing for his hometown team appeared to reach its peak in Game Five of the 1986 ALCS, the climax of a steady ascent to the precipice of a championship, only to have the game's ending spoiled by fate. So too was the trajectory of Witt's years in baseball such that his rise seemed destined to place him in company with Cy Young Award winners, only to have the latter stages of his big-league journey hampered by injuries. In both that single game and in his career, for Mike Witt it was so close yet so far.

SOURCES

In addition to the sources cited in the notes, the author also consulted:

articles.latimes.com.

baseball-reference.com.

1993 Sporting News Baseball Yearbook.

Orange County Register.

Angels VIEW Magazine, 1982 Vol. 1 Book III.

1991 New York Yankees Yearbook.

Carew, Rod, and Ira Berkow. *Carew* (New York: Simon and Schuster, 1979).

Siegel, Barry, ed. *1991 Official Baseball Register* (St. Louis: The Sporting News, 1991).

Siwoff, Seymour, Steve Hirdt, and Peter Hirdt. *1987 Elias Baseball Analyst* (New York: Collier Books, 1987).

NOTES

1 Mike Witt, email correspondence with author, October 15, 2015.

2 Marcia C. Smith, "Mike Witt '78 Inducted into Angels Baseball Hall of Fame," *Orange County Register*, August 23, 2015.

3 *1981 California Angels Media Digest*, 139.

4 John Strege, "Young Angels Get Big Surprise," *The Sporting News*, May 2, 1981: 18.

5 Maria C. Smith.

6 *1982 California Angels Media Digest*, 57.

7 Peter Gammons, "AL Beat," *The Sporting News*, April 25, 1981: 7. Two other rookies, Dave Righetti of the Yankees and Boston's Bob Ojeda, also joined the crop of notable young AL talent.

8 Mauch and Houk quoted in *1982 California Angels Media Digest*, 57.

9 Witt email correspondence.

10 Peter Gammons, "AL Beat," *The Sporting News*, August 30, 1982: 25.

11 Peter Gammons, "AL Beat," *The Sporting News*, December 27 1982: 46.

12 John Strege, "Witt Looks for His Bender in Bullpen," *The Sporting News*, May 2, 1983: 16.

13 "Lisa Witt's Magic Kingdom," *Halo Magazine*, 1986: 55.

14 Marcia C. Smith.

15 Tom Singer, "Lachemann Eager to Rebuild Staff," *The Sporting News*, February 13, 1984: 38. Years later, Witt nonetheless credited Morgan for success he attained with the Angels.

16 Tom Singer, "K's King Witt 'Concentrates,'" *The Sporting News*, August 6, 1984: 18.

17 Ibid.

18 "Lisa Witt's Magic Kingdom."

19 At the time, Witt's was considered the 13th perfect game, but a decree requiring a full nine innings to be considered a perfect game reduced the number to 11.

20 Moss Klein, "AL Beat," *The Sporting News*, July 28, 1986: 26.

21 Tom Singer, "Mature Witt Gives Halos Durability," *The Sporting News*, August 11, 1986: 20; Stan Isle, *The Sporting News*, September 15, 1986: 10.

22 Witt quoted in Tom Singer, "Nobody Does It Better," *Halo Magazine*, 1986 ALCS Issue, October 1968: 9.

23 Tom Singer, "For a Bitter Witt, Mum's the Word," *The Sporting News*, October 13, 1986: 31.

24 Ibid.

25 Ibid.

26 Ibid.

27 "Q&A with Mike Witt," *Halo Magazine*, 1987, 9.

28 Ibid.

29 Ibid. Emphasis added.

30 Ibid.

31 Ibid. Emphasis in original.

32 Tom Singer, "Witt Runs Hot and Cold," *The Sporting News*, July 20, 1987: 24.

33 Tom Power, "Witt Decided There's No Place Like Home," *Halo Magazine*, 1989, 61.

34 Angels notes column, *The Sporting News*, January 11, 1988: 49.

35 Ibid. The Oakland Athletics were also interested in signing Witt.

36 Tom Singer, Angels notes column, *The Sporting News*, April 4, 1988: 41.

37 Tom Singer, Angels notes column, *The Sporting News*, May 16, 1988: 23.

38 Tom Singer, Angels notes column, *The Sporting News*, June 13, 1988: 20.

39 Moss Klein, "AL Beat," *The Sporting News*, March 20, 1989: 40.

40 Tom Singer, Angels notes column, *The Sporting News*, May 8, 1989: 23.

41 *1990 California Angels Media Digest*, 92.

42 Tom Singer, "Heavenly Arms: Angels Pulling Off a Joke on Logic," *The Sporting News*, June 12, 1989: 10.

43 "Heavenly Arms": 11.

44 Dave Cunningham, Angels notes column, *The Sporting News*, March 19, 1990: 31.

45 As a veteran with at least 10 years of service time, the last five of which were with the same club, Winfield had the right to refuse a trade to any team that was not among a group of clubs to which he had given prior consent. However, there was a dispute as to whether Winfield's long-term contract with the Yankees, which he signed in 1980, included a provision in which he had waived his 10-and-5 rights.

46 Dave Cunningham, "Langston and Witt: An Odd Couple for a No-Hitter," *The Sporting News*, April 29, 1990: 8.

47 "Q&A with Mike Witt."

48 Ibid.

49 Michael Martinez, "Witt Appears Headed For Yanks and Bullpen," *New York Times*, May 13, 1990: S2.

50 Jack Curry, "Witt Misses First Start With Elbow Soreness," *New York Times*, March 20, 1991: D26.

51 Moss Klein, "AL Beat," *The Sporting News*, April 15, 1991: 18.

52 Jack Curry, "Subs Steal the Show After Early Witt Exit," *New York Times*, April 26, 1993: C7.

53 Ibid.; Filip Bondy, "Witt Ices Mariners And Then His Elbow," *New York Times*, May 2, 1993: S1.

54 "Witt's Advice Is Simple: Practice," *Halo Magazine*, 1986: 45.

MIKE WITT'S PERFECT GAME
SEPTEMBER 30, 1984: CALIFORNIA ANGELS 1, TEXAS RANGERS 0, AT ARLINGTON STADIUM, ARLINGTON, TEXAS

By Paul Hensler

SEASON-ENDING GAMES rarely hold much fascination for many fans or players, and such was the case when the Texas Rangers hosted the California Angels in the finale of 1984. For Mike Witt, the circumstances of the visiting pitcher in his last start also served as the conclusion of a salary drive, and the lanky right-hander capped his season—the first in which the 24-year-old worked exclusively as a starter—in a most resounding way.

With the season nearly over, California's star-studded roster had failed to deliver a divisional pennant, and some in the media claimed the Angels were too old to be competitive. California nonetheless held the top spot in the AL West for a seven-week stretch through early July, but the team slumped, notably in the second half of September, and failed to overtake Kansas City. As the Angels' prospects dimmed, manager John McNamara's team could only look back on a few bright spots in a season gone sour. Witt had already secured his place as the best pitcher on the staff and sought his 15th victory on the campaign's last day.

On the afternoon of September 30 in Arlington, Texas, 8,375 fans settled down to watch the matchup of Rangers knuckleballer Charlie Hough and the Angels' up-and-coming Witt. Hough retired the visiting Angels in the top of the first inning when Rob Wilfong tried unsuccessfully to bunt his way on, Daryl Sconiers struck out, and Fred Lynn grounded out to second. In the home half of the first, Witt fanned Mickey Rivers, induced Wayne Tolleson to fly out to left field, and coaxed a grounder to second from Gary Ward. Hough and Witt again matched zeros in the second inning. Doug DeCinces opened for the Angels with a single but was erased on a double play, and Reggie Jackson flied out. Witt countered with a groundout by Larry Parrish, a flyout by Pete O'Brien, and a strikeout of George Wright.

The Angels had a chance to score first when Mike Brown led off the third with a triple, but Bob Boone (groundout), Dick Schofield (popup), and Wilfong (groundout) failed to take advantage. Witt answered with strikeouts of Tommy Dunbar and Donnie Scott, then closed out his first pass through the Texas lineup by getting Curtis Wilkerson to ground out to shortstop Schofield. California had a runner in scoring position in the fourth—Lynn singled and moved to second on a wild pitch—but he would go no further. Witt retired Texas again in order in the bottom of the fourth on groundouts by Rivers and Tolleson, then a fly ball by Ward.

Brown worked Hough for a one-out walk in the fifth but was left stranded, then Witt breezed past Parrish and O'Brien on grounders before fanning Wright to end the fifth. In the sixth inning, a two-out walk to Lynn was all for naught when the center fielder was cut down stealing. Witt deftly handled the bottom of the Rangers order on a pair of groundouts to second sandwiched around a Scott strikeout.

In the seventh the Angels plated what would be the only run of the game. DeCinces led off with a single and advanced on a passed ball of a Hough knuckler. After Brian Downing moved DeCinces to third by grounding to second, Jackson reached on a fielder's choice as DeCinces scored. Brown's second hit of the day, a double, put Jackson on third, but Boone grounded to third baseman Larry Parrish, who cut down Jackson trying to score. Schofield walked to load the bases, but Wilfong grounded back to Hough to end the threat.

After the seventh-inning stretch, Witt struck out Rivers but then threw three straight balls to Tolleson, who then "squared around twice to fake [a] bunt," recalled Witt, who noted, "That is generally frowned upon by baseball's unwritten rules."[1] The Rangers second baseman ended his at-bat by grounding out to Wilfong, as did Ward to end the inning. The Angels went quietly in the eighth, Lynn's single going by the boards when DeCinces hit into a double play. In the Texas eighth, Parrish led off by nearly ruining Witt's effort. The right-handed slugger got hold of a Witt offering and sent it deep the opposite way. The drive was hauled in by Brown at the base of the wall in right field and proved to be the hardest-struck ball of the day. "When Parrish hit it, I thought it had home run possibilities," admitted Witt after the game, but upon seeing that the ball would not leave the park, the pitcher was relieved to find his right fielder camped under it.[2] Surviving Parrish's scare, Witt bore down and got O'Brien and Wright on strikeouts, making it 24 consecutive batters retired.

In the top of the ninth, another Angels stir yielded no runs. With two outs, Brown singled and was replaced by pinch-runner Gary Pettis, who was cut down stealing. Only three outs now separated Witt from becoming the 11th major-league pitcher to pitch a perfect game, and McNamara made several adjustments in the field to minimize any weaknesses on defense.[3] Bobby Grich had replaced Sconiers at first base in the eighth inning. In the ninth, future Gold Glove winner Pettis remained in the game in center field, Lynn moved from center to right, and Derrel Thomas entered to give the Angels more speed in left by replacing Downing. It was up to Witt to serve as his own closer.

Dunbar led off the home half of the ninth by striking out for the second time, and Bob Jones pinch-hit for Scott, grounding out to second base. Marv Foley came to bat in place of Wilkerson and replicated Jones's feat by grounding to second to give Witt the first perfect game in the majors since Len Barker's gem in May 1981. This was also the seventh no-hit game in Angel history, Bo Belinsky, Clyde Wright, and the great Nolan Ryan — on four occasions — authoring the others. Hough's outing was exemplary, too — a complete game, only one run (which was unearned, at that), three walks, and three strikeouts — but the day belonged to Witt. "My control with all pitches was the key to the perfect game," he observed years later. "Both fastball and curveball were exceptional that day."[4] Keeping his concentration on the task at hand in perspective, Witt also claimed that visions of a perfect game "never occurred until I had two outs in the ninth," although he confessed, "I was aware of the *no-hitter* in the fourth."[5]

Alluding to the pace of the contest, which lasted a brisk hour and 49 minutes, as well as the trust he placed in his stellar backstop, Witt noted, "There was not a lot of conversation going on during the game. When a pitcher is on, there is not a lot to talk about. My mindset with Bob [Boone] catching was to basically follow his lead."[6] Witt threw 94 pitches in total, 70 for strikes, and 23 of those were first-pitch strikes. Afterward there was some griping on the part of the Rangers, such as O'Brien's claim that home-plate umpire Greg Kosc "widened the strike zone at the end," and Rivers hinted that since this game was the season's finale, some players were hurrying to be done with it: "I don't want to take anything away from [Witt], but everyone had their bags packed and were in a rush to get out."[7]

On hand to see her husband's feat was Lisa Witt, who "just happened to be on that road trip and had a front row seat ... right next to our dugout."[8] Mike's spouse was aware that he was pitching a no-hitter but she later revealed, "I didn't even know there was such a thing as a perfect game."[9] Returning to Anaheim after the contest, the Witts were besieged by the press, including a request for a 3:00 A.M. wakeup call to appear on ABC's *Good Morning America*. Witt garnered *Sports Illustrated* "Player of the Week" honors as a tribute to his feat. The perfect game served as a supreme milestone in Witt's young career, as he parlayed his overall 1984 performance — 15 wins, 11 losses, 34 starts, 3.47 ERA, and 196 strikeouts in 246⅔ innings—into a three-year, $2.75 million contract.

Lauded as one of the best young pitchers in baseball, Witt was later twice named to the AL All-Star team before arm problems began to take their toll. Working out of the California bullpen in April 1990, Witt combined on a no-hitter with Mark Langston during one of his last appearances in an Angel uniform.

NOTES

1. Mike Witt email correspondence with author, October 15, 2015.
2. Tom Singer, "Hitless Rangers Are Left at Witt's End," *The Sporting News*, October 8, 1984: 19.
3. At the time of Witt's feat, he was listed as the 13th perfect game pitcher rather than the 11th. The earlier achievements by Ernie Shore and Don Larsen were later removed from the list of sanctioned perfect games.
4. Mike Witt email.
5. Mike Witt email; Singer, "Hitless Rangers." Emphasis added.
6. Mike Witt email.
7. Singer, "Hitless Rangers."
8. Mike Witt email.
9. "Lisa Witt's Magic Kingdom," *Halo Magazine*, 1986, Vol.1, Book II, 55.

MIKE SCOTT

By Rory Costello

THE SPLIT-FINGER FASTBALL became a popular weapon for pitchers in the 1980s. Few if any used it better than righty Mike Scott. With the splitter, he went from mediocrity to ace. Though many believed he was doing something else to make the ball move so much — namely, scuffing it — that was never proven conclusively. Scott tapped into what made Gaylord Perry so effective on the mound: mind games. The mere idea of a defaced ball was a stealthy agent against batters. In 1986, when he won the Cy Young Award with the Houston Astros, Scott said, "I think the hitters lose some of their concentration when they worry about other things besides hitting."[1]

Scott's prime lasted for five seasons: 1985 through 1989. During that period, he won 86 games and lost 49, with a 2.93 ERA. He struck out 1,038 batters in 1,192⅓ innings, and his WHIP (walks plus hits per inning pitched) was an outstanding 1.06. He won a career-high 20 games in 1989 and was runner-up for another NL Cy Young Award. That year, though, he hurt his shoulder and began to struggle. Scott pitched his last game in the majors in April 1991, aged just 35.

Michael Warren Scott was born on April 26, 1955, in Santa Monica, California. His father, Warren Scott, worked in human resources for Chevron, the oil company. His mother, Kathy, worked for North American Rockwell.[2] There were two other children in the family: a brother named Jerry and a sister named Susie.[3]

Scott grew up in Hawthorne, a town about 15 miles southeast of Santa Monica. In 2002, in an interview with the *Astros Daily* website, he said, "I played basketball as well as baseball. I liked basketball better, but thought I had a better chance to go further in baseball."[4] According to another Hawthorne resident, Dean Morris, "Mike was simply a natural who could do anything, including surfing and golf."

Morris said Scott's father was an excellent Little League coach who "hit infield drills harder than I ever experienced in high school or at Stanford. … Warren never dished out more than he believed we could handle and he helped to create lots of great competitors."[5] In 1990, Mr. and Mrs. Scott received the George and Barbara Bush Little League Parents of the Year Award.[6]

Scott went to Hawthorne High School, where he was team captain and made all-league in both basketball and baseball. As a senior, the pitcher was 9-1 with a 0.67 ERA; he also hit four homers.[7] Even so, he wasn't drafted out of high school, and he didn't have any scholarship offers either. He was about to attend junior college, but then he got a call from Wayne Wright, the head baseball coach at Pepperdine University in Malibu, just a little farther up the Pacific coast from Santa Monica. Scott retained very fond memories of his school and its team. Looking back in 2014, he said, "I couldn't have been happier. If I could go back and select any college in the country to go to, it would absolutely be Pepperdine. I got what you should get out of college. What a university is supposed to do is have you ready for your next step in life, and I was ready."[8]

With the Waves, Scott earned all-conference honors in the West Coast Athletic Conference for three straight years. During his career there, he was 26-14 with a 2.10 ERA, setting school records for wins, strikeouts, and innings pitched. (All have since been surpassed.) He threw a perfect game against Cal-Lutheran on February 17, 1976.[9]

Scott also took part in international baseball competition. He was a member of the United States College All-Star team, led by Paul Molitor, that defeated the Japanese College All-Stars in 1975. In Game Two of the best-of-seven series, Scott pitched the final seven innings in relief of Floyd Bannister, allowing just one run. He got the win when Ken

Phelps hit a solo homer in the 13th.[10] That October, Scott also pitched for the United States in the Pan American Games. In Mexico City, Team USA's squad was also loaded with future big leaguers. They went 6-2 and took the silver medal behind Cuba.

The New York Mets drafted Scott in the second round of the 1976 amateur draft, after his junior year. "I was surprised when the Mets drafted me," he said, "because I hadn't heard much from them. I had heard from and talked to a few teams, but the Mets weren't one of them."[11]

The 21-year-old was first assigned to Double-A. He pitched well for the Jackson (Mississippi) Mets of the Texas League in 1976 and 1977. His 14 wins and 14 complete games led the league in '77, earning him promotion to Triple-A near the end of the season.

Scott went into the 1977 season as a married man. His wife, Vicki, also grew up in Hawthorne and went to high school with Mike. They had two daughters, Kimberlee and Kelsey. They celebrated their 38th anniversary on February 26, 2015.

Scott had a merely fair year in 1978 (10-10, 3.94 ERA) with the Mets' top affiliate, Tidewater. "I threw a fastball, a curveball and a slider," he said. "The higher the level I went, the more I realized I needed an off-speed pitch."[12]

Nonetheless, Scott made the big club's roster in spring training 1979. General manager Joe McDonald was not able to add a veteran reliever, so Scott became the last man kept on the 10-member pitching staff. He got the good word from manager Joe Torre, who called out, "Don't forget you need a jacket for traveling."[13] Later that summer, New York sportswriter Jack Lang wrote that the franchise's stinginess then was also a factor. "McDonald and the people at the Mets who count pennies shoved Neil Allen, Mike Scott, and Jesse Orosco down Torre's throat. … They just weren't ready this year."[14]

Indeed, Scott was sent back down to Tidewater in mid-June. After performing well there (8-4, 3.18), he was recalled in September. "I went to Puerto Rico to play winter ball in 1979," Scott remembered, "but I was only there a couple of weeks. I came home when my daughter was born."[15] Scott also spent the bulk of the 1980 season at Tidewater, cementing his status as a good prospect (13-7, 2.96). Again he was called up when the rosters expanded in September, and he never pitched again in the minors.

During his time with the Mets, from 1979 through 1982, Scott posted a record of 14-27 with a 4.64 ERA. The team was dreadful in those years, yet according to the general manager, Frank Cashen (who was hired in February 1980), Scott "was a nice young man and he always had a good arm, but he was just trying to be mediocre."[16]

Scott himself noted, "I really didn't have any mentors with the Mets."[17] That statement is surprising because in 1982, the team had two excellent pitching instructors in manager George Bamberger and coach Bill Monbouquette. Jesse Orosco, for one, benefited greatly from their tutelage.

On December 10, 1982, Scott was traded to Houston for outfielder Danny Heep. Heep was a useful reserve in New York for four seasons, and he too remained in the majors as late as 1991. In retrospect, however, Scott's development via the splitter skewed the deal heavily in the Astros' favor. Yet at the time, Jack Lang's acerbic comment was, "One by one, the New York Mets are ridding themselves of their disappointments."[18]

In Scott's own view, "I probably needed a change, I wasn't going anywhere with the Mets. The change of scenery was a good thing."[19]

With Houston in 1983, Scott pitched fairly well (10-6, 3.72), although he missed the first month of the season with shoulder tendinitis. In 1984, however, he had a poor year (5-11, 4.68). "I didn't know if my career was over," he told author Pat Jordan in a *People* magazine interview in 1987, "but I did know it wasn't moving very fast." Jordan wrote, "He still had a good 95-mph fastball that was as straight as a draftsman's ruler, and control that was adequate, but his curveball and slider appeared only in his dreams. 'Batters,' he says, 'just sat back on my fastball and ripped it.'"[20]

After the 1984 season, Scott went to the Astros' annual postseason golf holiday, which owner John McMullen hosted. At dinner one night, teammate Enos Cabell, who had been with the Detroit Tigers in 1983, told Scott about what Tigers pitching coach Roger Craig had done for that staff, notably with the splitter. Craig was in temporary retirement after Detroit won the 1984 World Series. McMullen overheard the conversation and took it up with Houston's general manager, Al Rosen. The team's manager, Bob Lillis, was an old teammate and good friend of Craig's. This enabled an approach.[21]

As Scott recalled, "Al Rosen arranged the meeting, I spent a week in San Diego with Roger Craig for about an hour a day. The first time I threw the pitch [competitively] was in spring training and I was amazed at how successful the pitch could be."[22]

According to Pat Jordan (a former pro pitcher himself, as described in his classic memoir, *A False Spring*), "Scott has been able to elevate the pitch to an art form for several reasons: His oversize hands allow him to get a comfortable grip on the ball for better control, and he can throw it with consistently high speed (usually in the mid-80s). More important, perhaps, was the realization that he had to surrender his career to the pitch or be out of baseball for good. 'I was just looking for a decent second pitch,' says Scott. 'I never thought it would become the pitch it has.'"[23]

In 1985, Scott—who turned 30 years old early that season—emerged as a star. He was 18-8 with a 3.29 ERA. "He was throwing the split-finger at least 35 percent of the time, sometimes more. He discovered that the more he threw it, the better it got. And if for some reason it wasn't working quite as well as it had been, he simply readjusted his grip and got it back."[24]

Already, however, the scuffing accusations swirled. After a game at Wrigley Field on May 26, Cubs manager Jim Frey had umpire John Kibler check Scott on the mound. The players saw something drop from Scott's glove. After the inning was over, Frey said that his first baseman, Leon Durham, found a small piece of sandpaper. Frey later sent an advisory letter with the alleged evidence to Chub Feeney, president of the National League.[25]

Houston won the National League West in 1986. The Astros were a deep and well-balanced team, but pitching was a great strength of the club. The staff was led by Scott, who added a cut fastball to his repertoire. His won-lost record in the regular season was not spectacular (18-10), but he led the league in ERA (2.22), strikeouts (306), and shutouts (five). He became an All-Star for the first time that summer. In mid-August, Scott Ostler of the *Los Angeles Times* stated, "Mike Scott is the best pitcher in baseball right now. … This season, he is a monster."[26]

On September 25 Scott threw a no-hitter against San Francisco to clinch the division title. The Giants manager was none other than Roger Craig, who said afterward, "I told one of my coaches in the fourth or fifth inning, 'We're not going to get a hit off of him.' It was unbelievable."[27]

In his next and final outing of the regular season—again versus the Giants—Scott made a bid to match Johnny Vander Meer's unique feat: back-to-back no-hitters. The first San Francisco hit did not come until Will Clark led off the seventh with a double. Clark scored, and Scott left trailing 1-0, but the Astros tied it in the ninth and won it in the 10th.

In the National League Championship Series against the New York Mets, Scott had authoritative complete-game victories in Game One and Game Four. After Game Four, he said, "I don't know if I've ever thrown better than in the last four or five games."²⁸ He became the second of just three Most Valuable Players from the losing team in an LCS.²⁹

Scott had extraordinary command of his splitter in that series. "I've never seen anything like it in my life," said Mets outfielder Len Dykstra. "It's like a Wiffle ball moving in the wind." First baseman Keith Hernandez said, "He painted us with it."³⁰

Yet the Mets also complained long and loudly about Scott. They harped on the belief that scuffing was helping his splitter to "drop off the table." Their manager, Davey Johnson, showed a group of reporters eight balls that were abraded in exactly the same spot—a mark about the size of a 50-cent piece. Johnson said, "It [sandpaper] is in his palm. He doesn't rotate the ball, he just makes a grinding motion. It's blatant to me." However, Chub Feeney called Scott "innocent until proven guilty"—though he added, "We will be watching closely the next time he pitches."³¹

Doug Harvey, the crew chief of the umpires for the 1986 NLCS, emphasized, "I have never found any evidence that Scott has been doing anything wrong."³² A quarter-century later, Scott himself remained cagey. "They can believe whatever they want to believe. Every ball that hits the ground has something on it. ... I've thrown balls that were scuffed but I haven't scuffed every ball that I've thrown."³³

The lingering threat of Scott in Game Seven was in the Mets' heads. Ron Darling, who would have been the opposing starter, said in 2006, "I felt I couldn't give up any runs because Mike Scott wasn't going to."³⁴ Second baseman Wally Backman said, "If we had lost [Game Six, an excruciating 16-inning battle] and had to face Scott tomorrow, I wouldn't have slept at all."³⁵

The Astros did not win a pennant until 2005. With regard to the 1986 NLCS, Scott said, "The loss was extremely tough for the team, and nothing good came out of it."³⁶ Yet if there had been a Game Seven, he was not one to issue a Joe Namath-style boast. "I've been asked that a hundred times," he later said, "and who knows? I could've been knocked out in the first inning. You never know what's going to happen. There's no guarantee."³⁷

In 1987 Scott was an NL All-Star once more. His marquee numbers weren't as impressive (16-13, 3.23) for a sub-.500 team, but he still struck out nearly a batter an inning. He finished seventh in the Cy Young voting that year.

Another noteworthy outing against San Francisco came on September 7, 1987. The Giants reached Scott for two runs in the first inning, but he then retired the last 26 men he faced. Craig and opposing pitcher Mike LaCoss were both ejected after arguing that Scott was defacing the ball. "He was caught red-handed," Craig said. "He put something down his shirt. Two of the umps saw it but said they didn't have the right to search him."

Scott's response: "I'm used to it by now. I'm sure they did find a scrape on the ball [one such ball was confiscated in the eighth inning, and Scott received a warning]. I threw it in the dirt a couple of times and [Harry] Spilman fouled one off and hit a groundball."³⁸ Looking back, he noted, "Craig's players were complaining, so he did what a manager should do when his players are complaining—he had the umpire check."³⁹

Scott received no Cy Young consideration in 1988 (14-8, 2.92), nor was he an All-Star. Nonetheless, Atlanta Braves manager Russ Nixon said, "He's one of the premier pitchers in baseball." That remark came on June 12, after Scott came within an out of his second no-hitter. Ken Oberkfell broke it up with a line single to right field. Catcher Alan Ashby, who also handled Scott in the no-hitter against San Francisco, said, "If you're comparing him to two years ago, he was great today. Two years ago he was superhuman." Scott concurred, saying, "I don't think I had the stuff I had against the Giants."⁴⁰

Scott had two other one-hitters in the majors. The first was on April 15, 1987, versus the Los Angeles Dodgers. The spoiler was Mariano Duncan, with a third-inning single. The other came against the Pittsburgh Pirates on May 19, 1989. That time Glenn Wilson singled to lead off the eighth.

When Scott won 20 games in 1989, he lost just 10 and posted a 3.10 ERA. He made his third All-Star team (though he did not appear in the game). He received four of the 24 first-place votes for the Cy Young Award. Mark Davis, who had a career year out of the bullpen for the San Diego Padres, got 19; the other went to Orel Hershiser.

By that time, though, Scott had developed a tear in his rotator cuff. In 2003 he said, "The second half of 1989, I was done. I had a real good start in 1989. I won a lot of games before the All-Star game and barely hung on. I had a real good chance to win a lot more than 20 that year, but I just barely got there. I remember the 20th game was against LA and my arm was just done."[41]

In 1990 Scott got off to a poor start—after his first nine outings, he was 1-5 with a 6.33 ERA. However, he corrected a flaw in his stride and despite his injury, he still logged more than 200 innings, finishing with a record of 9-13, 3.81. He was the subject of trade rumors during the season—the Astros parted with several veteran pitchers that year. In December, he had arthroscopy on his labrum and was asked not to throw until spring training began in February 1991.[42]

When Opening Day 1991 came around, Scott was on the mound for the Astros. He was hit hard in that start, though, as well as his next five days later. He went on the disabled list the next day. He started to throw lightly in late April, but suffered a setback when he tried to work the shoulder harder. The Houston front office decided to rest him completely for another month. "It's back to square one," Scott said.[43]

In late June, Scott reported from his home in California, "Things are about the same. I haven't been able to do much of anything." He ruled out open surgery in view of the recovery time—indeed, that was why he had chosen the less invasive arthroscopic procedure before. Astros general manager Bill Wood said, "We've all faced the possibility that we've seen the last of him in a uniform." Team physician Bill Bryan observed, "It probably falls into the category of when the car is ready to break down, it breaks down."[44]

Shortly thereafter, Bryan described the problem more clearly. "If you don't have the ball held tightly in the socket of the shoulder joint, you cannot pitch with velocity, you cannot pitch with control and it hurts." Scott did open up the slim possibility of a major operation, but said that it was very doubtful—even though his shoulder was so painful that he could not swim or lift weights.[45]

In retrospect, Scott did not associate his injury with heavy use of the splitter. When asked in 2003 if he thought it shortened his career, he responded, "I think it extended my career. … Eventually I had a rotator cuff tear that just happens to pitchers. … I don't buy into that it's a pitch that will hurt your arm."[46]

On September 25, 1991—the fifth anniversary of his no-hitter—the Astros honored Scott with a special day at the Astrodome. He said then that his pitching days were over, and in November, he made his retirement official.[47]

The Astros paid tribute to Scott once again on October 3, 1992, by retiring his uniform number, 33. "It was a great honor," he said, "and nice to share that honor with José Cruz, who I have always had a lot of respect for."[48]

In retirement, Scott played a lot of golf—he finally had his shoulder fixed for this reason in 2002—and played the stock market. He said, "I tell people I'm a broker with one client—myself." He also kept his hand in with baseball to a small extent, helping out with the team at Aliso Niguel High School.[49]

Travel was also a frequent activity for the Scotts—"England, Scotland, Ireland, Wales, Spain, Morocco, New Zealand, Australia and a family trip to Hawaii every year." They had two granddaughters as of 2015: Drew (8) and Sawyer (3).[50]

Pat Murphy, a college teammate of Scott's, summed him up as a player and man in 2014. "He had a quiet confidence about him. He didn't say a lot but had a great arm. He went out there and just did it, didn't make a big deal of himself. He was a leader that way. And he's the exact same guy 40 years later as he was as a freshman. He's humble, a great family man and a great person."[51]

With thanks to Mike Scott for his help.

NOTES

1. Charley Feeney, "Umps: Scott Doesn't Scuff," *Pittsburgh Post-Gazette*, October 14, 1986, 32.

2. David A. Goss, "Michael Warren Scott," *Biographical Dictionary of American Sports* (David L. Porter, editor) (Westport, Connecticut: Greenwood Publishing, 2000), 1376.

3. Warren L. Scott obituary, greenhillsmortuary.com, November 2, 2013.

4. Ray Kerby, "An Interview with Mike Scott," astrosdaily,com, February 4, 2002.

5. Cougartown.com (website devoted to happenings in and around Hawthorne and Hawthorne High School), Feedback page 1145.

6. First given in 1981, this award is presented annually to the parents of a major-league baseball player who were actively involved in their sons' Little League experience. Lance and Robin Van Auken, *Play Ball! The Story of Little League Baseball* (University Park, Pennsylvania: Pennsylvania State University Press, 2001), 228.

7. Goss, "Michael Warren Scott."

8. "Mike Scott Inducted into WCC Hall of Honor," pepperdinesports.com, March 8, 2014. See also Pepperdine Baseball Records Book, 2015 (pepperdinesports.com).

9. "Mike Scott Inducted into WCC Hall of Honor."

10. "U.S. Stars Rip Japan Twice," *Desert Sun* (Palm Springs, California), June 23, 1975: B4.

11. Kerby, "An Interview with Mike Scott."

12. Kerby, "An Interview with Mike Scott."

13. Jack Lang, "Three Kid Hurlers Surprised by Mets," *The Sporting News*, April 21, 1979: 5.

14. Jack Lang, "Mets Get Two Vets to Replace Kid Hurlers," *The Sporting News*, June 30, 1979: 27.

15. Letter from Mike Scott to Rory Costello, received December 12, 2015 (hereafter "Scott letter").

16. Ron Fimrite, "No Wonder He's Hot," *Sports Illustrated*, January 12, 1987.

17. Kerby, "An Interview with Mike Scott."

18. Jack Lang, "Mets Trying Hard to Unload Zachry," *The Sporting News*, January 3, 1983: 32.

19. Kerby, "An Interview with Mike Scott."

20. Pat Jordan, "Mike Scott Got a Grip on the Split-Fingered Fastball and Threw His Career a Nice Curve." *People*, July 6, 1987.

21. Fimrite, "No Wonder He's Hot."

22. Kerby, "An Interview with Mike Scott."

23. Jordan, "Mike Scott Got a Grip on the Split-Fingered Fastball and Threw His Career a Nice Curve."

24. Fimrite, "No Wonder He's Hot."

25. Joe Mooshil, "Scott 'Roughed Up' by Frey," Associated Press, June 5, 1985.

26. Scott Ostler, "Great Scott, He Throws a 'Splitter'," *Los Angeles Times*, August 14, 1986.

27. "Scott's No-Hitter Clinches for Astros." Associated Press, September 26, 1986.

28. Joseph Durso, "Scott Stymies Mets; Series Tied, 2-2," *New York Times*, October 13, 1986.

29. The other League Championship Series MVPs from losing teams, as of 2015, were Fred Lynn (1982, California Angels) and Jeffrey Leonard (1987, San Francisco Giants).

30. Durso, "Scott Stymies Mets; Series Tied, 2-2."

31. "Mets accuse Houston's Mike Scott of Scuffing Baseball" and "Feeney Clears Scott—for Now," Associated Press, October 15, 1986.

32. Charley Feeney, "Umps: Scott Doesn't Scuff," *Pittsburgh Post-Gazette*, October 14, 1986: 32.

33. "Network Recalls 1986 Postseason," Major League Baseball press release, November 4, 2011 (m.mlb.com/news/article/25882718/). Quote from in an interview Scott gave for Major League Baseball's documentary *A Postseason to Remember: 1986*.

34. Richard Sandomir, "Mets' Announcers Slide Into New Roles," *New York Times*, October 14, 2006.

35. Wire service reports, October 17, 1986.

36. Kerby, "An Interview with Mike Scott."

37. Phillip Lee, "Classic Catches Up with Mike Scott," *ESPN Classic*, November 19, 2003.

38. "Scott Accused of Scuffing Again," United Press International, September 8, 1987.

39. Kerby, "An Interview with Mike Scott."

40. Michael A. Lutz, "Mike Scott Misses No-Hitter by 1 Out," Associated Press, June 13, 1988.

41. Lee, "Classic Catches Up with Mike Scott."

42. "Astros' Scott Hesitant About Upcoming Year," Associated Press, February 11, 1991.

43. "Astros Halt Comeback of Scott," *Victoria* (Texas) *Advocate*, May 10, 1991: B1.

44. "Scott May Be Through with Injured Shoulder," Associated Press, June 28, 1991.

45. Mike Forman, "Scott May Call It Quits," *Victoria Advocate*, July 7, 1991: B1.

46. Lee, "Classic Catches Up with Mike Scott."

47. "Astros' Mike Scott Will Retire," Associated Press, November 21, 1991.

48. Kerby, "An Interview with Mike Scott."

49. Lee, "Classic Catches Up with Mike Scott."

50. Scott letter.

51. "Mike Scott Inducted into WCC Hall of Honor."

MIKE SCOTT NO-HITS THE GIANTS
SEPTEMBER 25, 1986: HOUSTON ASTROS 2, SAN FRANCISCO GIANTS 0, AT THE ASTRODOME

By Frederick C. Bush

MOST PRESEASON PROGnosticators had predicted that Houston would finish in third place or lower in 1986, but as the Astros prepared to face the San Francisco Giants on September 25, they knew that a victory would clinch their first National League West title since 1980. The Astros featured a powerhouse pitching staff whose 3.15 team ERA that season was second in the NL only to the 3.11 posted by the New York Mets. The fact that staff ace Mike Scott was the starter on this day gave the Astros favorable odds to clinch the division before 32,808 hometown fans in the Astrodome.

The prowess of the Astros' pitching staff already had been on prominent display the previous two nights. On September 23 Jim Deshaies tied a major-league record by striking out the first eight Los Angeles Dodgers batters he faced on his way to a two-hit shutout in which he totaled 10 strikeouts. The next night, Nolan Ryan held the Giants hitless into the seventh inning, registered 12 strikeouts in eight innings, and combined with Charlie Kerfeld on a two-hit shutout. On this day, Scott's performance would make his fellow moundsmen almost appear to be slackers.

The game began on an inauspicious note as Scott hit Giants leadoff batter Dan Gladden with his first pitch. He later confessed, "I was out of control. The crowd was into it, and I was pumped up."[1] Gladden stole second base and, after Robby Thompson flied out, advanced to third on Will Clark's groundout. Scott retired the next hitter, Candy Maldonado, to end what would be the Giants' only scoring threat that day.

In the bottom of the first inning, Giants starter Juan Berenguer retaliated against the Astros by hitting their leadoff man, Billy Hatcher, with his first pitch. Hatcher turned the tables by stealing second base, just as Gladden had done for the Giants, but he was erased from the basepaths when Giants catcher Phil Ouellette gunned him down as he tried to steal third. Berenguer allowed back-to-back singles to Denny Walling and Glenn Davis but pitched out of trouble to keep the game scoreless.

In the top of the second inning, Scott walked Chili Davis, who also proceeded to steal second base. But at this point Scott settled down. He struck out Bob Brenly and Ouellette and retired Jose Uribe on a pop fly to second baseman Bill Doran to begin a string of innings in which he retired 19 consecutive batters. By the end of the game, he had thrown 69 of his 102 pitches for strikes and had struck out 13 Giants.

Scott held the Giants spellbound throughout the game with his split-fingered fastball. Giants manager Roger Craig had to be struck by the irony that he was the man who had taught Scott the pitch after the 1984 season. Scott had finished that campaign 5-11 with a 4.68 ERA and had sought help from Craig, who at the time was out of baseball. Craig recalled, "The first three times I worked with him he didn't pick it up, then he just got it. Right then I knew the guy was going to have a good one, but I didn't know he'd be that good."[2] Scott threw the split-finger so well now that many opponents, including Craig, had accused of him of scuffing the ball. No such accusations were forthcoming on this day, though, and Craig claimed to be so impressed by Scott that sometime in the fourth or fifth inning he told one of his coaches that the Giants would not get a hit off him.[3]

Though Berenguer's performance did not match Scott's, he did keep the Astros off the scoreboard for four innings. In the top of the fifth, however, Walling gave Scott all the run support he would need in this game when he hit a one-out solo home run over the wall in right-center field to give the Astros a 1-0 lead.

Scott was well aware of the game situation, saying, "About the fifth inning, I knew they didn't have a hit, but I didn't think about going for (the no-hitter) until the seventh. At that point, I decided to go for it."4 Scott had struck out the side in the bottom of the sixth inning and, after he decided "to go for it," he struck out the first two batters in the seventh inning as well. In the bottom of the seventh, Walling scored his second run of the game on Jose Cruz's two-out single to give the Astros their final margin of 2-0.

Scott allowed one final baserunner in the eighth inning on a one-out walk to Ouellette. The next batter, Harry Spilman, who was pinch-hitting for Uribe, almost broke up the no-hitter with a sharp grounder, but Doran scooped up the ball on the run and fired it to shortstop Craig Reynolds to get the force out on Ouellette at second base. The only other time the Astrodome crowd gasped at the thought that Scott might lose his shot at a no-hitter occurred in the very next at-bat. Mike Aldrete, who had spoiled Nolan Ryan's no-hit bid in the previous game, hit a long fly ball that Hatcher caught "in full stride 10 feet from the fence" in center field.5 Ryan, who had pitched five no-hitters but had never seen a teammate pitch one, said, "I was nervous. ... Any little thing can end it. Now I know what I've put everybody else through."6

From that point on, the spotlight was solely on Scott, who would get to bask in its full glow. He struck out Gladden and Thompson to start the ninth inning and then got Clark to hit a weak grounder to the first baseman, Davis, who retired Clark himself and started the victory celebration. Scott had made a slow trot to cover first base and admitted, "I told (Davis) to take it himself because I didn't want to bobble it."7

When it was over, Scott had accomplished the dual feat of pitching a no-hitter and clinching a division title, which was a first in major-league history. The New York Yankees' Allie Reynolds had come closest to the achievement when he had clinched a tie for the American League pennant with a no-hitter against the Boston Red Sox on September 28, 1951. As for Scott's team, the Astros, they won the right to face the New York Mets, their 1962 NL expansion brethren, in what was now being called the "Silver Anniversary Series."8

Scott's no-hitter was the most dominant performance of the Astros' three consecutive shutouts, prompting Deshaies to quip, "It sure is hard to sustain any kind of fame around this place."9 The Astrodome crowd was so excited that they did not want to leave the stadium. So many fans stayed to celebrate that Scott was carried back onto the field to a new round of cheers a full 30 minutes after the last pitch. Kerfeld, the Astros' popular reliever, was elated for both his team and its fans and declared, "Shakespeare couldn't have written this any better. We wanted to get this one for the city of Houston and we got it."10

After the celebration was over, the Astros made it clear that there was one additional accolade they believed Scott had earned. Catcher Alan Ashby said, "I personally felt he had the Cy Young Award wrapped up already, but if this doesn't win it for him, then something is really fouled up in the system."11 In spite of the superlative season that Scott already had been enjoying, the Dodgers' Fernando Valenzuela was mentioned most often as the likely recipient of that award and, as coincidence would have it, Valenzuela had won his 20th game of the season with a two-hit victory over the Astros just three days earlier. Scott finished the season with an 18-10 record and led the league with 306 strikeouts, a 2.22 ERA, and 275⅓ innings pitched, but it was most likely his no-hitter that vaulted him past Valenzuela and garnered him the 1986 NL Cy Young Award.

NOTES

1 Neil Hohlfeld, "Great Scott! Astros clinch, Pitcher saves best for last," *Houston Chronicle*, September 26, 1986.

2 Roy S. Johnson, "Astros Clinch With Pizzazz On No-Hitter By Scott," *New York Times*, September 26, 1986.

3 Neil Hohlfeld, "'Great Scott' Clincher," *The Sporting News*, October 6, 1986: 12.

4 Hohlfeld, "Great Scott! Astros clinch, Pitcher saves best for last."

NO-HITTERS

5 Johnson, "Astros Clinch With Pizzazz."

6 Hohlfeld, "'Great Scott' Clincher."

7 Johnson, "Astros Clinch With Pizzazz."

8 Ivy McLemore, "Great Scott! Astros clinch NL West with no-hitter," *Houston Post*, September 26, 1986, astrosdaily.com/history/19860925/, accessed June 10, 2015.

9 Hohlfeld, "'Great Scott' Clincher."

10 McLemore, "Great Scott! Astros clinch NL West with no-hitter."

11 Eddie Sefko, "Astros agree: Cy Young Award should go to Scott," *Houston Chronicle*, September 26, 1986.

TOM BROWNING

By Joe Cox

DURING A SEVEN-YEAR period from 1985 to 1991, Tom Browning was the most durable starting pitcher in major-league baseball. In a career that spanned 12 major-league seasons and just shy of 2,000 innings pitched, Browning was most notable for working the majority of his career as a sturdy, dependable starter who would take the ball every time his turn in the rotation came around. Browning was quite successful in his prime, winning 15 or more games four times, pitching a perfect game in 1988, and contributing to the Reds' World Series title in 1990.

Thomas Leo Browning was born on April 28, 1960, in Casper, Wyoming, one of five children. Browning's parents divorced in his childhood, and his mother later married an electrical worker who was transferred to New York. The Browning family moved to upstate New York, where Tom played locally against future pros like Jim Deshaies and Andy Van Slyke.[1]

Browning played college baseball at LeMoyne College in nearby Syracuse, New York, and subsequently transferred to Tennessee Wesleyan. Browning was always a gifted player, but never a superior prospect. As he himself wrote in 2006, "I couldn't rely on natural talent—because I didn't have much of it. I wasn't the hardest thrower, the fastest runner, or the most gifted athlete. But I had a solid and durable arm, and I worked hard."[2] That hard work paid off, as the Cincinnati Reds made Browning their ninth-round draft choice in the 1982 amateur draft.

Browning pitched 88 innings of rookie-league ball in Billings, Montana, in 1982, going 4-8 with a 3.89 ERA. Significant improvement could be seen the following season, when he was 8-1 with a 1.49 ERA and 101 strikeouts in 78⅔ innings at A-level Tampa. It was at Tampa that Browning learned the screwball from minor-league pitching instructor Harry Dorish.[3] For a pitcher who never had dominant stuff, the lesson was a pivotal one for Browning's future. He later wrote that it "revolutionized my ability to get hitters out; and it was a big reason for my eventual success."[4] Browning finished 1983 with Double-A Waterbury, where he pitched better than his 4-10 record and 3.53 ERA might indicate.

In 1984 Browning spent almost the entire season at Triple-A Wichita, posting a 12-10 mark and a 3.95 ERA in 189⅓ innings. As a September call-up to Cincinnati, Browning won his first start on September 9, working into the ninth inning and allowing only one run to the Dodgers. He pitched three times, finishing 1-0 with a 1.54 ERA in 23⅓ innings.

The Reds had finished fifth in the division in 1984, after last-place finishes in 1982 and 1983. While the Cincinnati brass, including player-manager Pete Rose, hoped for big things from Browning, there was little reason to expect what lay ahead in 1985. Indeed, early in the season, one national columnist authoritatively noted, "No rookie pitcher will come close to Dwight Gooden's 17-9 record and 276 strikeouts of '84."[5] This ended up being only half true.

Rose plugged Browning into the rotation as the Reds' fourth starter, and in the first half of the season, Browning delivered solid results. He reached the All-Star break with a 7-7 record and a 3.73 ERA. The Reds were a solid 44-41. Browning continued to be up and down, and on August 9 he lost a tough 3-1 decision to the Dodgers, dropping him to 9-9 with a 3.77 ERA.

The next eight weeks, however, were something altogether unexpected. In his next 12 starts, Browning amassed 11 wins and no losses, going from a .500 pitcher to a 20-game winner. Twice he pitched shutouts, but he also gritted out ugly 8-5 and 10-6 wins. Still, on September 28, when he beat the Astros, Browning reached a 20-9 mark, making him the first rookie to win 20 games since Bob Grim of the 1954

Yankees.⁶ Browning's 3.55 ERA and 155 strikeouts both indicated his ability to roll with the punches and gut his way through wins rather than dominate his opponents. One particularly memorable win came on September 11, when Browning and the Reds beat the Padres as Pete Rose broke Ty Cobb's career hits record in the first inning. Milestone accomplishments aside, Cincinnati finished second in the NL West, and Browning ended up sixth in the NL Cy Young Award voting and second in the Rookie of the Year race, losing out to Vince Coleman and his 110 stolen bases. *The Sporting News's* NL Rookie Pitcher of the Year award served as a consolation prize.

It was probably inevitable that Browning would struggle to repeat his incredible rookie campaign—and that he would have an occasionally difficult relationship with the Reds' penny-pinching owner, Marge Schott. First, Browning angered Schott by filming ads for an auto dealership that competed with Schott's own.⁷ Then he held out through most of spring training for a new contract, eventually becoming the last Cincinnati player to sign,⁸ inking a one-year deal that would soon become annual tradition between Browning and the Reds.

Browning began 1986 badly, losing his first four decisions and finishing April with a 6.08 ERA. He gradually improved, and the Reds again finished second in their division, although they were a distant follower of the Houston Astros. Browning started 39 games (leading the NL), and worked 243⅓ innings, finishing the season at 14-13 with a 3.81 ERA.

Still, if 1986 had been a disappointment, 1987 was much worse. Browning again signed a one-year deal during spring training, and then struggled with a sore arm, pitching as if the entire season was spring training. Writing after his career, Browning attributed the injury to a martial-arts workout with pitcher John Denny.⁹ Manager Rose, who was usually sympathetic to Browning, jumped on his case, questioning Browning's toughness.¹⁰ In mid-June Browning, with a 7.76 ERA, was sent down to Double-A Nashville for five starts. He was scarcely better in the minors, accruing a 6.07 ERA. Browning did improve on his return to Cincinnati, eventually winning his last three

starts of the season, raising his record to 10-13 and lowering his ERA to 5.02. Again, the Reds ended up in second place, six games behind the Giants.

The 1985 season was Browning's best and 1990 was probably his most fulfilling year from a team standpoint, but 1988 had to be the oddest season of Browning's career. Once again a one-year contract was extended, and Browning signed it. His arm had healed, and his pitching had more or less returned to normal. Few other things had. Early in the season, Rose bumped NL umpire Dave Pallone in an altercation and was suspended for 30 days, one of the most severe punishments for an on-field offense in modern baseball history.

On June 6, 1988, Browning flirted with a no-hitter, reaching one out in the ninth inning before allowing a solitary single to future Hall of Famer Tony Gwynn. Browning won his last six decisions before the All-Star break and reached midseason with an 8-3 record and a 3.38 ERA. In the second half of the season, he continued strong. After opening the season at 2-3, for the remainder of the year, Browning was 16-2, finishing with a 3.41 ERA to accompany his 18-5 mark. On September 16, 1988, Browning pitched a perfect game at home against the LA Dodgers, the first perfect game in the National League in 23 years. The Dodgers went on to win the World Series, as Cincinnati again finished second in the NL West.

Browning was almost as sharp in 1989, although the positive moments of the season have been historically forgotten because the Pete Rose gambling scandal was a black cloud over Cincinnati's season. The Reds finished in fifth place, and late in the year Rose accepted a lifetime ban from baseball in settlement of his case. Against that backdrop, for the third time in four seasons, Browning led the NL in games started. His 249⅔ innings pitched were second in the league, and his 15-12 record was an incomplete picture of Browning's season. His 3.39 ERA was the best mark of his career, and his 3.6 WAR was his second best to date. On July 4 Browning flirted with a second perfect game, setting down 24 straight Phillies before Dickie Thon doubled to lead off the ninth inning. Another highlight was the entire month of August, just when the Rose settlement was finalized. Browning won all six of his starts and posted a 1.70 ERA, thus earning NL Pitcher of the Month honors.

On paper, there was little reason to suspect that 1990 would be a memorable season for the Reds. Cincinnati had an outstanding bullpen and a new manager, Lou Piniella, but few would have expected a championship season with wire-to-wire leadership in the standings. But the Reds won their first nine games and started the year 30-12, en route to the first World Series title in Cincinnati since 1976. Tagged as the Opening Day starter for the second time in his career, Browning was a solid contributor to the team, finishing 15-9 with a 3.80 ERA. He led the team in starts, innings pitched, and wins, and finished second to Jose Rijo in WAR, with a career-best 4.1 mark. In the NLCS, Browning beat Pittsburgh in a crucial series-evening second game, 2-1. He lost Game Five, but after the Reds finished off the Pirates in Game Six, Browning was in for an eventful World Series.

Browning was slated to start Game Three, and was watching Game Two from the dugout at Riverfront Stadium when his wife, Debbie, went into labor. Browning hurried to the hospital, but as Game Two dragged into extra innings, in the pre-cellphone era, the Reds' broadcasting team put out a radio bulletin for Browning to call the clubhouse, because he might be needed back at the ballpark.[11] Fortunately for the Reds, Joe Oliver singled home the winning run in the bottom of the 10th inning, and Browning had the rest of the night off. Two days later he pitched six solid innings, winning Game Three at Oakland, 8-3. The following night, the Reds closed out a shocking Series sweep and Browning was a world champion.

Two months into the 1991 season, Browning looked like a Cy Young Award candidate. With a win on June 14, he was 9-4 with a 3.43 ERA. Browning was rewarded with his only career All-Star Game selection. Cincinnati was in second place at the break, but slid to fifth, and Browning stumbled in the second half, finishing 14-14 with a 4.18 ERA. Browning placed much of the blame for his poor second half on a hip injury sustained in a Houston bar fight.[12]

Browning's poor finish to 1991 was the beginning of the end of his days of effective pitching. A knee injury sustained in a home-plate collision with Houston catcher Scott Servais ended Browning's 1992 season on July 1,[13] but even when he was healthy, he had just a 6-5 record and a 5.07 ERA to show for his trouble. The 1993 season included a citation for marijuana possession[14] and a finger injury[15] as well as a 7-7 record and a 4.74 ERA. If the season was notable at all, it was for an incident on July 7, when Browning sneaked out of the ballpark and caught part of the Cubs-Reds game on a rooftop adjoining Wrigley Field—while still in uniform.[16]

Browning was pitching better in 1994, with a 3-1 record and a 4.20 ERA in seven starts, but he sustained a horrific injury, breaking his arm while throwing a pitch on May 9 against San Diego. Browning later admitted that he instantly feared that he had been shot, writing, "I thought my arm was blown clear off my body. I couldn't feel it."[17]

Browning's career with Cincinnati was over. In 1995 he pitched for Kansas City, throwing some good games in the minor leagues, but losing his only two major-league starts as a Royal. He retired in spring training the following year.

Browning's life after baseball has been a varied one. In 2006 he wrote a book, *Tom Browning's Tales From the Reds Dugout*, with team employee Dann Stupp. In that same year, he was inducted into the Cincinnati Reds Hall of Fame. Browning has also worked as a broadcaster and a pitching coach, most recently for the A-level Dayton Dragons in 2015.

Tom Browning's career totals include a record of 123-90, a 3.94 ERA, and exactly 1,000 career strikeouts in 1,921 innings pitched. He was once an All-Star and once a world champion. As of the beginning of the 2016 season, Browning was ranked 12th in Reds history in wins, innings pitched, and strikeouts. He flirted with no-hitters on several occasions, but is perhaps best remembered for his 1988 perfect game.

NOTES

1 Michael Coffey, *27 Men Out: Baseball's Perfect Games* (New York: Atria Books, 2004), 176-77.
2 Tom Browning and Dann Stupp, *Tom Browning's Tales From the Reds Dugout* (Champaign, Illinois: Sports Publishing, 2006), 1.
3 Coffey, 178.
4 Browning and Stupp, 23.
5 Bill Conlin, "After '84, Rookie Pickings Seem Slim," *The Sporting News*, April 15, 1985.
6 Hal McCoy, "Taste of Victory Surprises Browning," *The Sporting News*, October 14, 1985.
7 Browning and Stupp, 55.
8 Information reported in Cincinnati Reds news within *The Sporting News*, March 24, 1986.
9 Browning and Stupp, 62.
10 Coffey, 183.
11 Browning and Stupp, 130-131.
12 Browning and Stupp, 144-145.
13 Associated Press, "Browning Sidelined for Rest of Season," *Los Angeles Times*, July 3, 1992.
14 Associated Press, "Browning Faces Drug Charge," *New York Times*, July 31, 1993.
15 Browning and Stupp, 171.
16 Browning and Stupp, 167-168.
17 Browning and Stupp, 175.

As an aside, baseball-reference.com is eternally invaluable for factual background.

TOM BROWNING'S PERFECT GAME
SEPTEMBER 16, 1988: CINCINNATI REDS 1, LOS ANGELES DODGERS 0, AT RIVERFRONT STADIUM

By Joe Cox

ON THE EVENING OF September 16, 1988, in Cincinnati, a relatively sparse crowd endured a rainy night, moving the evening's game between the Dodgers and the Reds well into the night hours. The scheduled 7:35 P.M. start was washed out, and for the fans in the stands and the players in the clubhouse, a lengthy evening of waiting began, as the umpires pondered whether the game could be played. But in retrospect, what was a few hours of waiting, anyway? Cincinnati had waited over a decade for a no-hitter, since Tom Seaver's 1978 masterpiece. In fact, the Reds and their fans had endured a 119-year wait (since the franchise's inception) for a perfect game. As several thousand of the announced crowd of 16,591 drifted out of the ballpark, they didn't realize that they had failed to wait out a historic game.

One person who didn't recognize the nature of the occasion was Tom Browning, the burly Reds left-hander who was scheduled to pitch the game. Browning later recalled that at around 9:30 P.M., he began to undress and put his street clothes back on before the groundskeeper indicated that the weather report showed a dry spell, during which the game might be played after all. It was late September, and the schedule was crowded. Browning admitted, "If it was earlier in the season and we had a chance to make it up sometime later, the game probably would have been called."[1]

Instead, at 10:02 P.M., after a nearly 2½-hour delay, the third-place Reds faced off against the Dodgers, who were safely in the driver's seat for the NL West title, en route to a shocking World Series triumph over Oakland. Browning would face rookie Dodgers righty Tim Belcher, who was 10-4 coming in, and would end up third in the 1988 NL Rookie of the Year race. Unlike his opponent, Browning was a veteran, completing his fourth full major-league season. Despite a rough 1987 campaign, Browning had won 60 games in his young career in the major leagues. He was having a solid 1988 season, and in fact, on June 6, he had nearly completed a no-hitter, getting down to the last two outs before allowing a base hit to Tony Gwynn. This time around, Browning would not be denied.

Once the game finally started, both Browning and Belcher were putting on a pitching clinic. Into the middle of the sixth inning, neither team managed a base hit, and the game's only runner came in the home half of the second, when Belcher walked Eric Davis. For his part, Browning had been even more meticulous. He had not even reached a three-ball count on any Dodger in the game's first six innings. The delayed start of the game seemed to enhance the strike zone of home-plate umpire Jim Quick. Dodgers star Kirk Gibson, who would win the 1988 NL MVP Award, later remarked, "It was a huge strike zone, ridiculous. Not to take anything away from either pitcher ... but when the plate gets too big, it's just hard to handle."[2]

If an enhanced strike zone wasn't enough for Browning, Mickey Hatcher of the Dodgers asserted that he was also lucky. "Everything that we hit was right at somebody," recalled Hatcher.[3] That said, a viewing of the game indicates that few balls were even hit hard. Dodgers catcher Rick Dempsey, remembered by Reds catcher Jeff Reed as "the only guy who gave us trouble all night,"[4] grounded sharply to Cincinnati third baseman Chris Sabo to lead off the third inning. Sabo made another tough play on a chopper from LA first baseman Mike Marshall to lead off the fifth inning. Otherwise, Browning was essentially cruising along.

As was Belcher. Browning acknowledged that by the game's middle innings, he had a touch of anxiety that he might be headed for a Harvey Haddix-like night. He noted, "Retiring 27 straight wouldn't make a lick of difference if we didn't have at least one run on the board."[5] With two outs in the home sixth inning, Belcher finally cracked. Cincinnati All-Star shortstop Barry Larkin doubled to right field and the next batter, Chris Sabo, grounded to third base and Dodgers third baseman Jeff Hamilton bounced an errant throw across the diamond, allowing Larkin to hustle home with the only run of the game. (Sabo's groundball was scored as an infield single.)

Staked to a lead, Browning was now free to focus on perfection. Alfredo Griffin led off the top of the seventh inning by grounding to second baseman Ron Oester. Mickey Hatcher then popped up to first baseman Nick Esasky. The dangerous Kirk Gibson battled to a 2-and-2 count before looking at a called third strike and promptly erupting in protest at Jim Quick, who ejected him from the game. After the dust settled, Browning had just six outs to go.

After the game Browning said it was in the eighth inning that he believed that he could actually complete the perfect game.[6] The Dodgers were rapidly becoming believers as well. Mike Marshall led off the inning by lifting a fly ball into the right-center-field alley, which Paul O'Neill tracked down easily. John Shelby then struck out for the third time in the game, marking Browning's sixth's strikeout of the night. With two out, Jeff Hamilton hit a soft grounder up the middle that Larkin handled easily, leaving Browning just three outs from perfection.

When Browning batted in the bottom of the eighth, he drew an intense ovation, even after striking out. As he returned to the mound to face down history in the ninth inning, Browning later recalled, "Inside, I was a wreck. I was as nervous as nervous could be. I was just trying to keep my composure."[7]

Browning's first foe in the ninth was Rick Dempsey. After a strike and a ball, Browning's third pitch was a changeup that caught a fair bit of the plate, and Dempsey slashed a high drive to right field, but it hung up on the warning track and Paul O'Neill flagged it down. Two outs to go. Second baseman Steve Sax was up next, and he elected to go after the first pitch. He grounded the ball up the middle, a challenging but not especially difficult play for Barry Larkin, who fielded it and threw Sax out at first by a step and a half. One out to go.

Second-year third baseman Tracy Woodson pinch-hit for Belcher, who had allowed just three hits and a solitary unearned run in eight innings pitched. For the 1988 season, Woodson pinch-hit 10 times, getting three hits in nine at-bats. Overall, he hit .249 for the season. And he now stood between Browning and perfection.

Woodson fouled off the first pitch into the first-base stands for strike one. The second pitch dipped inside for a ball. The next pitch missed the plate away, and Woodson held an advantage in the count. The next pitch was grounded foul up the third base line, and now Browning was one pitch away from history.

The next pitch was to be a fastball—high and inside. "[I]t went really high," wrote Browning years later. "And for reasons I'll never understand, [Woodson] felt obligated to swing."[8] And he missed. The perfect game was complete, and Browning was a 1-0 winner.

A few minutes before midnight, the Cincinnati Reds mobbed Browning, piling on top of him in jubilant celebration, and splitting his lip somewhere in the process.[9] Rookie third baseman Sabo yelled, "We're going to Cooperstown!"[10]

Congratulations poured in for Browning, and owner Marge Schott even gave his wife, Debbie, a mink coat.[11] Years later Browning indicated that he was honored to be remembered for the achievement—still the only perfect game in Reds history—but was amused that he was still sometimes called "Mr. Perfect." "I was only perfect for an hour and 52 minutes," he wrote. "Most of the other time, I was imperfect—and stubborn, immature, and even a bit of a wiseass."[12] Maybe so, but on one memorable, rainy night, Tom Browning owned a portion of baseball history—a perfect portion. All around, it was a moment worth the wait.

SOURCES

In addition to the sources cited in the Notes, the Reds' closed-circuit video of the game was commercially available on iTunes as of 2016. Despite the fact that the pitches were shot far above home plate, it was very helpful in reviewing the game.

NOTES

1. Tom Browning and Dann Stupp, *Tom Browning's Tales From the Reds Dugout* (Champaign, Illinois: Sports Publishing, 2006), 80-81.
2. James Buckley Jr., *Perfect: The Inside Story of Baseball's Twenty Perfect Games* (Chicago: Triumph Books, 2012), 154.
3. Buckley, 151.
4. Michael Coffey, *27 Men Out: Baseball's Perfect Games* (New York: Atria Books, 2004), 191.
5. Browning and Stupp, 82.
6. Sam McManis, "For Browning, It's Perfectly Easy," *Los Angeles Times*, September 17, 1988.
7. Browning and Stupp, 85.
8. Browning and Stupp, 86.
9. Browning and Stupp, 88.
10. Coffey, 194.
11. Browning and Stupp, 93-95.
12. Browning and Stupp, 98.

ANDY HAWKINS

By Stew Thornley

ANDY HAWKINS IS FAMIL-iar with tough luck. He is best remembered for pitching a 1990 no-hitter — that he lost. He followed that five days later with 11 shutout innings before losing in the 12th. He also got no decision in his final start of the 1988 season despite 10 scoreless innings. The opposing pitcher who matched goose eggs with him was Orel Hershisher, who, by getting the chance to pitch an extra inning (made possible by Hawkins's performance), passed Don Drysdale's record of 58 consecutive scoreless innings.

Melton Andrew "Andy" Hawkins was born to Mel and Linda Hawkins in Waco, Texas, on January 21, 1960. Another son, Mike, rounded out the family five years later. In addition to being a banker and a rancher, Mel was involved in coaching from the time his older son started pitching in Little League when he was 8 until he made the high-school team six years later.[1]

"Andy Hawkins needed to be pushed," wrote Tom Friend in the *Los Angeles Times* in 1985. "Mel Hawkins learned that early, because Andy grew early. He was bigger than most kids, and so he tended to relax at the sports he played."[2]

The label of "Timid Texan" stuck with the 6-foot-3 right-hander even after he established himself in the major leagues. Dick Williams, his manager with the San Diego Padres, once said he "pitched like a pussycat." The challenge angered Hawkins, but over time it appeared to be effective in the response it got.[3]

Growing up, Hawkins also played basketball and football. In the latter sport, he was a punter, kicker, cornerback, and tight end at Midway High School in Waco. His strongest skill was punting, and he received a scholarship from Baylor University in Waco. Hawkins also knew he was likely to be a high draft pick in baseball.

In June of 1978 Hawkins was the second pitcher taken (one spot behind Mike Morgan) and the fifth player drafted overall, and he gave up his Baylor scholarship to sign with the San Diego Padres. Assigned to Walla Walla in the Northwest League, Hawkins pitched well, compiling an 8-3 won-lost record with a 2.12 earned-run average in 102 innings.

Promoted the next year to Reno in the California League, Hawkins didn't do as well. "I have never struggled anything like that in my life," he said. "I was seriously down, and I was considering going back to Waco to play football and giving up baseball." Hawkins credited his manager, Eddie Watt, with helping him. "He talked me through it and kept me going. I made some changes. I give Eddie Watt a lot of credit. Eddie Watt is a good man."[4]

Watt was his manager again in 1981, with Amarillo in the Texas League, as Hawkins continued his progression to the big leagues. He moved up to Hawaii in the Pacific Coast League in 1982. At midseason he had an ERA of 2.17 in 132⅔ innings with the Islanders. Soon after pitching three straight shutouts and 30 consecutive scoreless innings,[5] Hawkins was called up by the Padres and displaced Juan Eichelberger in the starting rotation.

That fall, at the direction of the Padres, Hawkins pitched for Bayamon in the Puerto Rican League and hurled a no-hitter his first time out. Williams and San Diego general manager Jack McKeon came to the island to watch Hawkins — who upped his record to 3-0 while they were there — and other young players, including Tony Gwynn. "I loved it," Hawkins said of pitching in Puerto Rico for manager Art Howe and with pitching coach Mike Cuellar.[6]

A team on the rise, the Padres had an abundance of starting pitching, including Dave Dravecky, Ed Whitson, Eric Show, Tim Lollar, and Mark Thurmond. Hawkins started the 1983 season back in the Pacific Coast League, with Las Vegas, was

sharp in his first two games, and was called up when Whitson hurt his knee. He continued his strong pitching, posting a 1.93 ERA in his first six games and getting his first shutout with a win over Steve Carlton in Philadelphia.

Hawkins ended up back in the minors during the season, but by 1984, he was up to stay although he battled to keep his spot among the starting pitchers. Hawkins said it was a "mix and match"[7] between him and the left-handed Dravecky for the fifth spot. The Padres won the National League West Division and went with four starters in the postseason, putting both Dravecky and Hawkins in the bullpen.

The relievers stood out in the National League best-of-five playoffs in helping the Padres come back from a two-game deficit. In the deciding game, the Chicago Cubs had a 3-0 lead over San Diego after five innings. Hawkins relieved Show in the second, and he, Dravecky, Craig Lefferts, and Rich "Goose" Gossage held the Cubs scoreless the rest of the way. San Diego came back to win the game, 6-3, and advance to the World Series against the Detroit Tigers.

The Tigers won the first game and quickly took a 3-0 lead in the next one. With two out in the top of the first, Hawkins relieved Whitson. Hawkins had pitched 2⅔ innings of one-hit relief in Game One and was ready to go again the next night. "I said [to pitching coach Harry Dunlop] I could go in Game 2," Hawkins said. "I had nothing to rest up for."[8]

Hawkins pitched through the sixth and allowed only a bloop single to Kirk Gibson. While he was in the game, San Diego came back with runs in the first and fourth and then took the lead in the fifth on a three-run homer by Kurt Bevacqua. Craig Lefferts shut down the Tigers over the final three innings, and Hawkins was awarded the win.

At this point, through the final two games of the playoffs and the first two of the World Series, the bullpen had produced a string of more than 20 consecutive scoreless innings. "I never saw middle relief carry a team like this in postseason play," said Dick Williams.[9]

Detroit won the next three games to win the World Series. Hawkins pitched four innings in the final game, but the lone run he gave up put the Tigers ahead to stay, and he was charged with the loss. Nevertheless, he had an outstanding postseason, giving up only that run in more than 15 innings, and as of 2015 Hawkins remained the only pitcher to win a World Series game for the San Diego Padres.

Hawkins looked back on the "pussycat" comment from his manager earlier in the season. "The rap against me in the past, I guess, was that I was afraid to challenge hitters, that I wasn't aggressive enough, that I'd pitch for the corners," he said. "Well, I want to say that I wasn't afraid to throw strikes earlier this year. It was just that I was so erratic I couldn't throw strikes. Now, hopefully, that's all behind me."[10]

Williams believed his challenge had the right effect on Hawkins. "Hawks is coming after the hitters now," Williams said. "He's a very nice person, a gentleman, but on the mound you've got to be a little mean now and then."[11]

Hawkins was back in the rotation in 1985, and he credited new pitching coach Galen Cisco for helping him develop a cut fastball. "It was a good pitch for me," he said.[12] With the cutter in his arsenal of pitches, Hawkins won his first 10 starts of the season and his first 11 decisions before losing on June 19. He finished the year with an 18-8 won-lost record and career-best ERA of 3.15 (in seasons in which he pitched at least 162 innings, the number needed to qualify for a percentage title).

Hawkins dealt with injuries during his big season and beyond. He missed a start with a circulatory problem in the index finger of his right hand in July 1985. Two years later he spent time on the disabled list with tendinitis in his pitching shoulder. In 1988 he said in mid-August that his arm had been "dead for a month," adding that there was "nothing medical about it" and that "it happens every year about this time."[13]

Hawkins's final start of the 1988 season, which turned out to be his last with the Padres, came at home against the Dodgers on September 28. His mound counterpart was Orel Hershiser, who came into the game with 49 straight scoreless innings pitched, nine short of the major-league record held by Don Drysdale. With this also being Hershiser's final start of the regular season, it appeared that even if he could keep the shutout streak going, he could only tie Drysdale by the end of the season.

However, Hawkins was equally as impressive that night, and a scoreless game through nine meant Hershiser was able to take the mound again, keep the Padres off the board for another inning, and pass Drysdale for the record. "He was just fantastic," Hawkins said of Hershiser. "Everything he did he was right that year. We got to see it up close that night. He was dominant."[14] Both starters were long gone when the Padres finally won the game, 2-1, in 16 innings.

Hawkins was a free agent after the 1988 season and, with San Diego pursuing Bruce Hurst, he didn't think the Padres were interested in keeping him. He went with the best offer he received, a three-year deal from the New York Yankees worth a reported $3.6 million. (Hawkins's salary with the Padres in 1988 had been $453,000).[15] Gossage, a former teammate on the Padres as well as a former Yankees pitcher, said he thought Hawkins could handle the atmosphere and pressure of New York. Hawkins also liked that the Yankees seemed on the verge of another winning season and needed pitching, so the thought of donning pinstripes was "appealing to me. … I thought, 'I'll go to New York, and I'll get into three pennant races.' It never happened."[16]

The Yankees dropped below .500 and finished in fifth place in 1989. Hawkins had 11 wins by mid-July after two straight shutouts, but he dropped seven of his last 11 decisions and finished with a record of 15-15. The next year he was on the verge of being released in June but kept his spot on the team only because right-hander Mike Witt got hurt.

On July 1, 1990, Hawkins took the mound against Greg Hibbard at Comiskey Park in Chicago. The pair matched hitless innings through five. Although the Yankees got a few hits after that, they could not break through on the scoreboard, and the game was scoreless into the last of the eighth. Hawkins retired the first two batters before Sammy Sosa hit a grounder that Mike Blowers couldn't field cleanly at third. Immediately an "H" for hit appeared on the scoreboard. Hawkins thought his no-hitter was done. However, the scoreboard operator was premature, flashing the hit before official scorer Bob Rosenberg was able to make his decision, which was an error. Hawkins said, "So I went from, 'Oh, it's over' to 'I gotta get it back going again.'"[17]

Hawkins walked two batters but appeared to be out of the inning when Robin Ventura lifted a fly to left. The swirling winds caused Jim Leyritz to circle the ball and then put out his glove, only to have the ball clank off it. Three runs scored as Ventura pulled into second on the error. Ivan Calderon then sent a fly to right. Jesse Barfield fought the sun and lost, the ball bouncing out of his glove for another error and another run. Hawkins finally got Dan Pasqua to pop out to end the inning.

When the Yankees were retired in the top of the ninth, ending the game, Hawkins had a no-hitter, but he lost the game, 4-0. "I've never seen anything so incredible," said his manager, Stump Merrill. "You're not going to see a better performance. We gave them six outs in the eighth inning. As far as I'm concerned, Andy pitched a nine-inning no-hitter."[18]

Hawkins followed that strange outing with another great performance, holding the Minnesota Twins scoreless through 11 innings, only to lose the game on a pair of two-out, run-scoring singles in the 12th. As of 2015 he is the last starting pitcher ever to pitch into the 12th inning in the majors.

Hawkins's hopes for postseason runs with New York didn't come through, and the Yankees' expectations of Hawkins, who had received the richest contract for a starting pitcher in the team's history,[19] also fell short. By the end of the 1990 season Hawkins and Dave LaPoint, another free-agent signing after 1988, were dropped from the rotation and replaced by a couple of September call-ups.

The Yankees released Hawkins early in the 1991 season. The Oakland Athletics picked him up in mid-May but released him three months later. In 1992 Hawkins pitched in the Seattle Mariners organization for Calgary in the Pacific Coast League. It marked the end of his playing career.

Hawkins returned to Texas and, in his words, did "odds and ends" over the next few years, including working as a construction foreman and ranch manager. When he decided to explore jobs in baseball, he started with the Texas Rangers, who were only about 100 miles from his ranch outside Waco.[20] He began as a pitching coach in the Rangers organization starting in 2001, working at various levels of the team's farm system. He was with the Kansas City Royals organization in 2005 before returning to the Rangers and serving as pitching coach for their Oklahoma RedHawks team in the Pacific Coast League. In August 2008 Hawkins joined the Rangers as the interim pitching coach. The next year he became the bullpen coach for the Rangers and continued in that role as of 2015.

Hawkins and his first wife, Jackie (Taylor) had four children, Katy, Libby, Curtis, and Maggie. As of 2015 he lived with his wife, Jodi (McCabe), outside Phoenix in Surprise, Arizona, which is also where the Rangers have their spring training.

NOTES

1. Author interview with Andy Hawkins, August 12, 2015.
2. *Los Angeles Times,* May 30, 1985, articles.latimes.com/1985-05-30/sports/sp-5168_1_minor-leagues.
3. Steve Walker, "A Trip to the San Diego Bullpen Turns 'Pussycat' Padre Pitcher Andy Hawkins into a Tiger" *People,* July 8, 1985: 48.
4. Author interview with Andy Hawkins, August 12, 2015.
5. *The Sporting News,* July 26, 1982: 41.
6. *The Sporting News,* November 29, 1982: 67; Author interview with Andy Hawkins, August 12, 2015.
7. Author interview with Andy Hawkins, August 12, 2015.
8. "Dirty Kurt, Handy Andy Tame Tigers," *The Sporting News,* October 22, 1984: 13.
9. Ibid.
10. Ibid.
11. Ibid.
12. Author interview with Andy Hawkins, August 12, 2015.
13. *The Sporting News,* August 29, 1988: 21.
14. Author interview with Andy Hawkins, August 12, 2015.
15. *The Sporting News,* December 19, 1988: 56.
16. Author interview with Andy Hawkins, August 12, 2015.
17. Author interview with Andy Hawkins, August 12, 2015.
18. "3 No-Hitters, Two Celebrations," *The Sporting News,* July 9, 1990: 15.
19. *The Sporting News,* January 2, 1989: 50.
20. Author interview with Andy Hawkins, August 12, 2015.

JULY 1, 1990: CHICAGO WHITE SOX 4, NEW YORK YANKEES 0, AT COMISKEY PARK I

By Stew Thornley

IN 1906 THE CHICAGO WHITE Sox won the World Series with a team called the Hitless Wonders. On July 1, 1990, the White Sox truly were hitless but still victorious.

The 80th anniversary of Comiskey Park that day was also its last. Across the street to the north, a new Comiskey Park was rising and visible above the roof of the existing ballpark.

It was also Bat Day, an event that caused a delay in getting fans into the park. The gates were not opened until barely an hour before game time because the souvenir bats were late in arriving; the bats handed out to the kids were not the only ones slow in showing up.[1]

Andy Hawkins of the New York Yankees and Greg Hibbard of the White Sox combined to retire the first 29 batters in the game. Hibbard took a perfect game into the sixth before allowing a pair of one-out infield hits; he made it through seven innings without allowing a run but ended up as the forgotten man in the game.

Hawkins was making the most of a reprieve from a month before. With a won-lost record of 1-4 in early June, he was given the choice of a demotion to the minors or a release; he chose the latter. However, Mike Witt injured his elbow the next night, and Hawkins stayed with the Yankees. By the end of June, he was still winless over nearly the last two months although he had been pitching better, just without good fortune. His luck didn't improve with the coming of a new month.[2]

As Hibbard cruised through the opening innings, Hawkins put down the first 14 hitters he faced before walking a pair in the fifth. Sammy Sosa then crushed a ball to left that surely meant the end of the no-hitter and shutout—except that a stiff wind from the north kept the ball in and moved it toward the left-field line, and Jim Leyritz corralled it on the warning track to end the inning. The *USA Today* box score listed the game-time weather as 70 degrees with the wind at 16 miles per hour.[3] What this information didn't convey was how the wind swirled inside the ballpark, a challenge for fielders that would become a factor a few innings later.

The game was still scoreless, and the White Sox still hitless, with two out in the eighth when Sosa hit a grounder to third. Mike Blowers tried to backhand the ball, knocked it down, and then threw too late to get a sliding Sosa at first. A novice scoreboard operator jumped the gun and immediately flashed a hit on the board.[4] But official scorer Bob Rosenberg hadn't even had the chance to rule on the play; when he did, it was an error.

Many thought he had first called a hit and then changed it to an error, but Rosenberg said, "I called it [an error] right away. The Yankees in the dugout were giving me the finger," he said of what happened before the correct decision made it onto the scoreboard.[5]

Hawkins didn't remember any obscene gestures directed toward Rosenberg, but he did see waving and "commotion over there in the dugout." He thought his no-hitter was gone, but "the next thing I know I hear this cheer go up [an indication of the error finally being flashed on the scoreboard], so I went from, 'Oh, it's over' to 'I gotta get it back going again.'"[6]

The scoring decision finally set straight, the game continued. Sosa stole second, and Hawkins walked the next two hitters, causing stirring in the New York bullpen and a mound visit from manager Stump Merrill.

Hawkins got Robin Ventura to lift a fly to left. Leyritz followed the ball through the wind, found the range, and then had the ball hit off his glove and roll into the corner. Three runs scored as Ventura pulled into second. Suddenly Hawkins went from needing three outs for a no-hitter to just one out, since the error meant the White Sox would probably not be batting in the ninth.

It looked as if he had his out as Ivan Calderon hit an easy fly to right. But Jesse Barfield, battling the sun, had the ball pop in and out of his glove for another error as Ventura scored. After Hawkins retired Dan Pasqua on a pop fly to short, he walked off the mound with a no-hitter — albeit down by four runs — as the fans gave him an ovation. The game ended a few minutes later as the Yankees went down in the ninth.

Ironically, the two outfield butchers who cost Hawkins the game were also the two who made his no-hitter possible with fine catches to start the game. Leyritz charged and slid to make a shoestring catch of Lance Johnson's blooper leading off the bottom of the first. Barfield then ran and leaped to catch a shot hit by the next batter, Ventura.

The Sunday no-hitter by Hawkins was the third of the weekend in the majors. Two nights before, Dave Stewart of the Athletics and Fernando Valenzuela of the Dodgers had hitless outings, with different outcomes than Hawkins. "This is not even close to the way I envisioned a no-hitter would be," Hawkins told Michael Martinez of the *New York Times* after the game. "You dream of one, but you never think it's going to be a loss. You think of Stewart and Fernando, coming off the field in jubilation. Not this."[7]

Pitching a no-hitter and losing is a rare event. Ken Johnson had this happen to him in 1964. Of Hawkins, Johnson said, "I'm sorry to hear he joined me. I was very happy being the only man to lose a no-hitter."[8]

However, Johnson had not been alone in this distinction. Baltimore pitchers Steve Barber and Stu Miller combined on a losing no-hitter for Baltimore on April 30, 1967, and there was one other game that resembled the one pitched by Hawkins. In the Players League in 1890 Charles "Silver" King of Chicago no-hit Brooklyn but lost 1-0, a result that meant that King, like Hawkins, pitched only eight innings because Brooklyn did not have to bat in the bottom of the ninth. (Since Hawkins, there have been two other of these eight-inning-type no-hitters.)

"If Comiskey II, currently under construction across 35th Street, lasts another 80 years, it will not house a stranger game," wrote Bill Jauss in the *Chicago Tribune*.[9]

Hawkins's struggles continued beyond the bizzaro in Comiskey I. He didn't win again until late July. Not only that, in the meantime, he was the losing pitcher in another no-hitter with the White Sox, this one by Chicago's Melido Perez although the game was called by rain in the top of the seventh on July 12.

Rain-shortened no-hitters such as these usually weren't considered as "real" no-hitters by sentiments of the time. But no-hitters in games played to their natural conclusion were treated with the lofty status of others, even if the pitcher went only eight innings.

However, the next year Hawkins's game was dropped from the list of "official" no-hitters by a committee fiat because he had pitched fewer than nine innings.

Regardless of the ruling of a committee, his great pitching and bad luck created far more of a buzz than just about any official no-hitter. The game story made the top of the front page (not just the front sports page) in *USA Today* with the headline "Yankee's no-hitter is no winner" and a jump to the sports section for more on this "Unbelievable game."[10] The game led sportscasts and also had prominence on regular news programs.

On the 25th anniversary of the game, Grant Brisbee in *SBNation* chronicled the event in words and video, making clear that this was a no-hitter like no other.[11]

NOTES

1 Memory of the author, who attended this game.
2 Michael Martinez, "Hawkins lucky to be around for this one," *New York Times*, July 2, 1990: 3E.
3 *USA Today*, July 2, 1990.

4   Bob Logan, "Scoreboard operator makes biggest error in White Sox' win," *Arlington* (Illinois) *Daily Herald*, July 2, 1990: section 4, page 8.

5   Telephone interview with Bob Rosenberg, August 1, 2015.

6   Author interview with Andy Hawkins, August 12, 2015. Until this interview, Hawkins was not aware that the errant decision on the scoreboard was the result of an incompetent operator and not the result of the official scorer first ruling a hit and then changing it to an error.

7   Michael Martinez, "Hawkins hurls no-hit gem, but Yanks blow it." *New York Times*, July 2, 1990: 1E.

8   "An asterisk for the books," *Minneapolis Star Tribune*, July 2, 1990: 1C.

9   Bill Jauss, "Sox's hitless victory a real wonder," *Chicago Tribune*, July 2, 1990: section 3, page 1.

10 Mel Antonen, "Yankee's no-hitter is no winner," *USA Today*, Monday, July 2, 1990: 1A.

11 Grant Brisbee, sbnation.com/2015/7/1/8841355/andy-hawkins-no-hitter-yankees-white-sox. Brisbee gets a few facts wrong (such as the claim of Hawkins striking out 17 in the game—it was 3—and on the number of pitches it took for Hawkins to retire the first two batters in the bottom of the eighth), but his tone is appropriate for conveying the significance of this no-hitter. For the record, the author's scorebook shows that Hawkins retired the first two batters in the eighth on 10 pitches (not 14, as claimed by Brisbee), and the scorebook showing of 131 pitches in the game for Hawkins (including 37 in the eighth inning) is consistent with the total listed by *USA Today* in its box score the next day.

DAVE STIEB

By Joe Cox

HE WON THE SECOND-most games of any pitcher in the 1980s, was a seven-time All-Star, and helped transform the Toronto Blue Jays from expansion basement-dwellers to world champions. But Dave Stieb may be best known for his terrible luck in attempting to close out no-hitters. Four times in five years, Stieb reached the ninth inning with no-hitters. Three times in 12 months, he actually reached the last out of a no-hitter. Each time he missed out on finishing the bid. Just when it looked as if Stieb would never join the no-hit club, on September 2, 1990, he successfully completed the game that, a quarter-century later, remained the only no-hitter in Blue Jays history.

David Andrew Stieb was born on July 22, 1957, in Santa Ana, California. Stieb's father was a contractor. His older brother, Steve, was a catcher in the Atlanta Braves system for three seasons, batting .217 as a professional and never reaching above Double-A ball. Dave initially made a splash in baseball as an outfielder, rather than as a pitcher. He described himself as having "decent power and an exceptional arm," but noted that he "had never tossed a competitive pitch until I played for Southern Illinois University—and then only in emergencies."[1] In fact, Stieb hit .394 with 12 home runs and 48 RBIs in 1978 as a junior, and was named to *The Sporting News*'s All-American squad.[2] Stieb noted in his autobiography that he pitched a grand total of 17 innings that season.[3]

But when Toronto drafted Stieb in the fifth round of the 1978 major-league draft, they saw him as a pitcher. Stieb later recalled that Toronto asked him if he would mind pitching, and while he was initially reluctant, his attitude changed when Toronto officials told him, "The quickest way to make it would be pitching."[4] Stieb pitched a grand total of 128 innings in the minor leagues in 1978 and 1979 before Toronto called him to the big-league club, where he proceeded to grow up as a pitcher on baseball's biggest stage.

Stieb described his stuff in 1986 as featuring a tailing fastball, a regular fastball, a slow, straight overhand curve, a near side-arm hard curve, a batting-practice fastball, which Stieb called a "dead fish," and a slider, which quickly became Stieb's out pitch.[5]

In the early years of the Blue Jays, Stieb could be brilliant, but often still lose games. As a rookie in 1979, Stieb compiled an 8-8 record with a 4.31 ERA. The rest of the Blue Jays' staff went 45-101, and Stieb's eight victories were only one shy of the team lead. The Blue Jays finished in last place in 1980 and 1981, as well, and the struggles behind him gave Stieb a reputation for hard-fought competitiveness—and for not always accepting the mediocrity that surrounded him in those early seasons in Toronto. Withering glares might be shot at opponents, umpires, or even Blue Jays who made errors behind Stieb. In time he would learn to control such outbursts, but his reputation as a fierce competitor was made. Speaking of such behavior, Blue Jays catcher Ernie Whitt said of Stieb, "That's just his makeup, the way he competes. He's like that on the golf course, playing cards, whatever."[6]

In 1980 Stieb made his first All-Star Game appearance. While he finished the season 12-15 with a 3.71 ERA, Stieb pitched 14 complete games and finished among the top seven or eight AL pitchers in pitching WAR. In a strike-shortened 1981 campaign, Stieb again was an All-Star, and his 11-10 mark (with a 3.19 ERA) marked the first time a Blue Jays pitcher had worked 150 innings and completed the season with a winning record.[7] Stieb was unhappy playing for such a poor team, and Toronto engaged in serious trade discussions in the offseason involving him, including one contemplated deal that would have moved him to Philadelphia for six players including Ryne Sandberg.[8]

Stieb was eventually considered too valuable to trade. The following season, 1982, saw Toronto approach respectability with the best season in the franchise's young history. The Jays won 78 games, led by Stieb, who tallied 17 victories, and 19 complete games, pitching 288⅓ innings and finishing fourth in AL Cy Young Award balloting. Stieb won the AL Pitcher of the Year award from *The Sporting News*.

Stieb's hard feelings about Toronto were largely smoothed over when he inked a six-year, $5 million contract before the 1983 season. At the end of May Stieb was 8-3 with a 1.66 ERA. He started and won the All-Star Game, and his 17 victories and 3.04 ERA helped Toronto to its first winning season.

Stieb won 16 more games in 1984 as Toronto finished second in its division to the World Series winner, the Detroit Tigers. For the third consecutive season, Stieb led the American League in WAR for pitchers. He again started the All-Star Game.

In 1985 Stieb led Toronto to its first postseason appearance. He was just 14-13, but led the league with a 2.48 ERA, and was again an All-Star. On August 24, 1985, Stieb completed eight hitless innings against the White Sox before Rudy Law led off the ninth inning with a home run to spoil the no-hit bid. Still, Stieb helped Toronto win the division. The LCS had changed formats to best four of seven, and when Stieb shut out Kansas City for eight innings to win Game One, Toronto was in good shape. In Game Four Stieb worked six innings of one-run baseball. When Toronto rallied to win in the ninth inning, the Jays held a 3-games-to-1 lead in the series. However, Toronto lost the last three games, and thus the series, with Stieb taking the loss in Game Seven. Still, Toronto extended his contract through 1995.

After winning at least 11 games for six seasons and posting an ERA of no higher than 3.71, Stieb had a miserable 1986 campaign. At the All-Star break, instead of starting the midsummer classic, he was stuck at home with a 2-9 record and a 5.80 ERA. One contemporary account blamed Stieb's poor performance on some lingering elbow issues, which had caused him to move away from his trademark slider.[9] Whatever the problem, Stieb did improve in

the second half of the year, but finished just 7-12, with a 4.74 ERA. The Jays also struggled, finishing fourth in the AL East.

The 1987 season represented something of a return to form for Stieb. He started cold, but finished the year at 13-9, with a 4.09 ERA in 185 innings. The season ended in disaster for the Blue Jays, though, as they held a 3½-game lead for the AL East title with just seven games to play. Toronto lost all seven, and Detroit won the division outright with a 1-0 win over the Jays on the last day of the season. During that horrific stretch run, Stieb contributed a disappointing loss in which he was knocked out in the fifth inning. Manager Jimy Williams had bounced Stieb in and out of the starting rotation during the last month of the season.

During the offseason Toronto shopped Stieb extensively, but decided to keep him.[10] One columnist called Stieb "erratic" and opined that he "will likely never be as good as he was a few years ago."[11] In fact, after two straight difficult seasons, Stieb strung together three more excellent seasons from 1988 to 1990, nearly equaling his work from 1982 to 1984 as the peak performances of his career.

Stieb reached the 1988 All-Star break with a 10-5 record and a 2.93 ERA, which earned him his sixth All-Star Game selection of the 1980s. Stieb faltered a bit in midseason, but finished 1988 with a series of games that demonstrated both how good and how unlucky he could be.

Stieb gave up one run in seven innings to Detroit on September 13 to claim his 13th win of the season. On September 18 he shut out Cleveland on four hits for his 14th win. On September 24 Stieb faced the Indians again, this time in Cleveland, and nearly made baseball history. He completed 8⅔ hitless innings against Cleveland and had a 2-and-2 count on Julio Franco. Franco grounded the next pitch to second base, where the ball hit a divot left at the Stadium from a Cleveland Browns game and ricocheted over the head of second baseman Manuel Lee for a single, spoiling the no-hitter.[12] A disappointed Stieb then got the last out and completed his second straight shutout. After the game he told reporters, "I needed one ounce of luck right there and what did I get? Bad luck. Oh well."[13]

Unbelievably, in his next start, the last of the year, on September 30, Stieb again flirted with a no-hitter, retiring 26 Baltimore Orioles without yielding a base hit. Again, he was disappointed, as pinch-hitter Jim Traber blooped a 2-and-2 pitch into right field for a single. Stieb retired the next hitter to end the game. "It's a heartbreaker," he admitted after the game. "I'm just wrecked. You get through it all, the ball hits the bat, and you wait. Then it doesn't happen."[14]

Stieb's final line for 1988 featured a 16-8 mark and a 3.04 ERA, as well as a 31⅓-inning scoreless streak to end the year. In his last three starts of the 1988 season, he pitched three shutouts, allowing just six hits over the 27 innings and twice falling one pitch shy of no-hitters. Even Stieb's harshest critics had to admit that he had shown the ability to again dominate opposing hitters.

After he finished 1988 so well, Stieb and the Blue Jays both had a poor beginning to 1989. Manager Jimy Williams was fired on May 14, at which point Toronto was 12-24 and Stieb had a 4.84 ERA. Longtime Jays coach Cito Gaston succeeded Williams, and the team rallied to a 77-49 mark for the rest of the season, winning the AL East. The memorable season was also highlighted by the unveiling of the Skydome, Toronto's state-of-the-art new stadium.

The year was memorable for other reasons for Stieb, who finished the season at 17-8 with a 3.35 ERA. He again suffered no-hit heartbreak when on August 4 he set down the first 26 Yankees he faced before Roberto Kelly broke up the perfect game with a double. Stieb struck out 11 batters, and held on to win the game, 2-1, but had yet again lost a no-hitter on the last batter. Stieb also lost both of his starts in the ALCS, as the Jays lost to Oakland in five games.

The 1990 season proved to be an odd one, both for Stieb and for the Blue Jays. Stieb was 11-3 at the All-Star break, and was chosen for his seventh (and final) All-Star squad. On September 2 he no-hit the Indians in Municipal Stadium, the Blue Jays first (and as of a quarter-century later, only) no-hitter.

In his next start, on September 8, Stieb won his 18th game of the year. He made five more starts, but did not win another game. The Blue Jays, who spent most of the season in second place, had a late-season surge, and led the AL East race by 1½ games with eight games to play. They lost six of the last eight, and on the last day of the season needed to beat Baltimore and have Boston lose to Chicago to force a tie for the division crown. Stieb pitched well, working into the eighth inning, but the bullpen lost the lead around the same time that Boston edged out Chicago, and Toronto was knocked out of the playoffs.

Still, Stieb had begun the 1990s with an 18-6 season and a 2.93 ERA, good for fifth in the Cy Young Award voting. But the rest of his career included just 10 more major-league victories. Stieb was effective early in the 1991 season, going 4-3 with a 3.17 ERA, but shoulder tendinitis and a herniated disc in his back limited him to just nine starts, the last of which came on May 22.

In 1992 Toronto had finally formed the nucleus to win a championship. Unfortunately or Stieb, he was reduced to a bit player. He was 4-6 with a 5.04 ERA in 96⅓ innings for Toronto, and his last appearance of the year came on August 8. Accordingly, when the Blue Jays beat the Atlanta Braves in the World Series, Stieb savored the moment, but as an injured spectator instead of as a starting pitcher. "It was very bittersweet," Stieb admitted. He recalled that when the Series ended he "celebrated like I won the last game … but I don't look at it like somebody that played in it and won it."[15]

The Blue Jays did not renew Stieb's contract after the season, and he signed a free-agent deal with the Chicago White Sox for 1993. Stieb made only four starts with Chicago, going 1-3 with a 6.04 ERA, before he was released. Stieb signed a minor-league deal with the Kansas City Royals, but six weeks later was released again, and decided to retire from baseball.

This held until 1998, when Stieb was in spring training as a coach for Toronto. He had thrown on numerous occasions, and did not notice the old elbow soreness. Eventually he was talked into asking manager Tim Johnson for a shot to pitch.[16] Stieb went to the minors and worked his way back to the Blue Jays for one last hurrah. Stieb pitched 19 times, including just three starts, and went 1-2 with a 4.83 ERA. After the season, Toronto approached Stieb about continuing his career as a reliever, but he elected instead to again retire, this time for good.

Stieb continued to serve the Blue Jays as a coach for a few years, but gradually drifted back home to Nevada, where he was part of a construction company and spent much of his time with his family. As of 2016 Stieb remained Toronto's leader in many pitching categories, including wins (175), innings pitched (2,873), and strikeouts (1,658). Stieb threw five one-hit games in his career, but treasures the memories of the September 1990 day when he finally nailed down his no-hit masterpiece.

NOTES

1. Dave Stieb with Kevin Boland, *Tomorrow I'll Be Perfect* (Garden City, New York: Doubleday & Company, Inc., 1986), 14.
2. Lou Pavlovich, "Horner and Gibson Stand Out in Selections," *The Sporting News*, July 8, 1978.
3. Stieb with Boland, 31.
4. Murray Chass, "Switch Helps Stieb's Career," *New York Times*, June 3, 1982.
5. Stieb with Boland, 80-81.
6. "Stieb Cools Temper, Gets Hot," *St. Louis Post-Dispatch*, July 31, 1985.
7. Neil MacCarl, "Losing Took Toll on Jays' Mattick," *The Sporting News*, October 24, 1981.
8. Peter Gammons, "'82 Will Be Brighter for These 10 Players," *The Sporting News*, January 2, 1982.
9. Moss Klein, "Beneath 30-Year Malaise, Pulse Felt in Tribe," *The Sporting News*, May 12, 1986.
10. Neil MacCarl, "Blue Jays," *The Sporting News*, January 4, 1988.
11. Moss Klein, "Blue Jays at Critical Point; Next Is Critical List," *The Sporting News*, May 2, 1988.
12. "Perez: One-Legged No-Hitter," *The Sporting News*, October 3, 1988.
13. Associated Press, "Stieb Loses No-Hitter With Two Outs in 9th," *Chicago Tribune*, September 25, 1988.
14. Dan Hafner, "Baseball Roundup: Out Away, It's Oh, No for Stieb No-Hitter Again," *Los Angeles Times*, October 1, 1988.
15. Dave Stieb, telephone interview with author, January 23, 2016.
16. Stieb interview.

SEPTEMBER 2, 1990: TORONTO BLUE JAYS 3, CLEVELAND INDIANS 0, AT CLEVELAND STADIUM

By Adrian Fung

IF THERE WAS EVER A PITCHer who was the face of bad luck, it had to be Dave Stieb. Three times, the ace right-hander of the Toronto Blue Jays was one out away from pitching the franchise's first no-hitter. All three times, he came up empty. On September 24, 1988, at Cleveland Stadium, Julio Franco hit a routine grounder to the right side of the infield but the ball took an unexpected high hop over the head of startled second baseman Manny Lee for a single, ending Stieb's no-hit bid.

Six days later, in Toronto in his next and final start of the season, Baltimore pinch-hitter Jim Traber flared a drop-shot single down the right-field line with one out to go, breaking up Stieb's second consecutive gem.

Finally, on August 4, 1989, pitching in Toronto's newly-opened futuristic SkyDome, Stieb struck out 11 and retired the first 26 Yankees in order but Roberto Kelly lined a 2-0 slider for a double into left field that spoiled a third no-hit bid—a perfect game attempt—for Stieb that again, came down to the last out.

On this late summer afternoon in Cleveland, the Blue Jays handed the ball to their star-crossed ace, looking to get back in the hunt for the American League East Division title. In just two weeks, Toronto had dropped out of a first-place tie, falling 6½ games behind the Red Sox. Stieb, at least, was on his way to finishing 1990 with an 18-6 record and a 2.93 ERA. In what would be his last good season, his 18 wins established a new team pitching record for single-season wins and his ERA ranked fifth in the league. Meanwhile, the Indians were completing another mediocre season, but were gathering promising young prospects such as Carlos Baerga, Albert Belle, Charles Nagy, and catcher Sandy Alomar Jr. who would win the 1990 American League Rookie of the Year Award. Even so, the Blue Jays had won the first two of the holiday weekend three-game series and were 7-2 on the season against the Tribe.

As Stieb warmed up in the visitors' bullpen, he didn't feel totally sharp. "His stuff was okay, he was growling a bit about it but he's a perfectionist,"[1] said pitching coach Galen Cisco, hours later.

The game began under cloudy skies when Stieb walked speedy Cleveland leadoff man Alex Cole. After Stieb threw over to first base four straight times, Cole took off for second but battery-mate Pat Borders helped out Stieb by throwing out Cole. Borders did it again in the second, throwing out Baerga, attempting to steal, to end the inning.

In the third, Stieb struck out the side. He was then staked to a lead in the top of the fourth when first baseman Fred McGriff launched a solo home run the opposite way to left-center field. The Blue Jays doubled their lead the next inning when Kenny Williams and Manny Lee hit back-to-back doubles off Cleveland starter Bud Black.

Meanwhile, Stieb found his groove. He retired Cleveland in order in the fourth and fifth innings then struck out the side for a second time in the sixth. Remarkably, since Cleveland first baseman Brook Jacoby flew out to left for the second out of the second inning, Stieb had not allowed an Indian to hit the ball out of the infield, setting down 12 straight batters on eight strikeouts, three groundouts and an infield popup.

Still, Stieb reflected after the game that he wasn't as sharp as he would have liked. "I didn't have great control. I couldn't find my release point in the early innings. I hung pitches but got away with them. They helped me out a few times by swinging at bad pitches. They hit balls right at people," he said.²

"We were doing what we could to break Stieb's concentration. We were yelling at him from the bench, trying to do anything to get him out of his rhythm," said Tom Brookens, Cleveland's third baseman. "The thing that makes him so tough is that he has a hard slider that doesn't break a whole lot, another slider that breaks a foot or more and a curve," Brookens added.³

As the pregame clouds melted away, batters now had to deal with pitches coming from the bright mound area into the darkness at home plate and with Stieb regaining command of his arsenal of pitches, he coaxed the first two batters to ground out to the middle infielders to begin the seventh. Cleveland finally hit the ball into the outfield, when Dion James' drive to right-center was caught by a hustling Williams to make it 15 straight retired in order.

Veteran Ken Phelps led off the bottom of the eighth and lined an inside slider hard down the right field line…but the ball landed *just* foul. No-hit king Nolan Ryan once said about a ball drilled right at a teammate during one of his no-hitters, "A foot or two either way, it was a base hit, maybe a double to the wall. It shows how much luck goes into throwing a no-hitter."⁴ On this afternoon, Stieb strangely, was the beneficiary of *good* luck.

Would this finally be his lucky day?

Stieb pitched carefully to Phelps, staying outside and walked him. Down by only two runs, the next three Indians batters swung early hoping to get a hit, but Stieb efficiently used just four pitches to stifle any chance of a Cleveland rally by inducing three straight fly balls to end the inning.

In the top of the ninth, Stieb got some breathing room. McGriff led off with his second home run of the day, capping an excellent weekend that included a 5-for-5 game the night before.⁵ Toronto now led 3-0 and observing the tradition of not speaking to a pitcher working on a no-hitter, the entire team gave Stieb exaggerated space on the bench.

"I think I was more nervous sitting on the bench than he (Stieb) was out there pitching," confessed left fielder George Bell. "My hands were all sweaty, but I had a lot of confidence in Dave today."⁶

Pinch-hitter Chris James began the bottom of the ninth by lofting an easy fly ball to left field. Candy Maldonado was next, also coming off the bench. The veteran slugger was on his way to a career-high 22 home runs in 1990 but was also a strikeout-prone free-swinger. After showing Maldonado mostly sliders, Stieb threw a neck-high fastball on 2-2 and got him to swing through it.

The sizable pro-Toronto sections of the crowd that had traveled across the border to support the Blue Jays during Labor Day weekend exploded in cheers of relief and anticipation.

Here was Dave Stieb at the intersection of history and disappointment for a fourth time. Standing in his way was Cole who battled to three-ball counts in each of his first three plate appearances. Stieb approached Cole cautiously and walked him on four pitches. Borders came halfway to the mound, making a cursory attempt to break the tension, offered brief words of encouragement to Stieb who quickly took the ball and ascended the hill.

With a three-run lead, McGriff played at normal depth, off the first-base bag and Cole took second on defensive indifference. The only thing that mattered now was the batter.

Stieb's 123rd pitch of the day was a breaking ball and Jerry Browne—ironically acquired by Cleveland in exchange for nemesis Julio Franco—lined the ball to right field. It looked like a straightforward play but as the ball descended out of the bright sky towards right fielder Junior Felix, could the sun be the bearer of bad luck at the last instant? Veteran broadcaster Don Chevrier described the moment: "Into right field…He has…GOT IT! No-hitter for Dave Stieb! The long frustration is finally over! The first in Toronto Blue Jay history, recorded here in Cleveland this afternoon."⁷

Stieb jogged off the mound and clasped his right hand to his cap as if disbelieving he had finally achieved what had eluded him so many times in the past. Borders was first to congratulate him and soon the entire team hoisted Stieb onto their shoulders.

A relieved smile spread across his face as he shook hands with his teammates. It had taken him two hours and 27 minutes to make personal and team history.

"We all knew Dave had lost the no-hitter three times before, but me, I think positive," Felix said.[8] "I had it all the way, no problem," he continued, referring to his difficult game-ending shadows-to-sunlight catch. "It makes me part of the glory."[9]

While Felix would go down in the record books as the man who recorded the last out, it was Stieb who finally was able to bask in the glory of joining the no-hit club. For the man whose 1986 autobiography was prophetically titled *Tomorrow I'll be Perfect*, Stieb was modest in his assessment of what he accomplished.[10]

"I can hardly believe what I did today. I wasn't nervous and, no doubt, being there so many times before helped but like I've said before, I'd given up caring about no-hitters," Stieb started, thinking back on the trail of disappointment that preceded his achievement. He echoed Ryan's sentiments on chance and no-hitters: "I've come to realize that there's just so much luck involved in a no-hitter. That's what today was—all luck."[11]

NOTES

1. Larry Millson, "Outside pitches tough on Indians," *The Globe and Mail*, September 4, 1990: C9.
2. Allan Ryan, "FINALLY! Stieb gets no-hitter after five near-misses and a scary final out," *Toronto Star*, September 3, 1990: D1.
3. Allan Ryan.
4. Nolan Ryan and Harvey Frommer, *Throwing Heat* (New York: Doubleday, 1988), 93.
5. Larry Millson, "McGriff in charge," *The Globe and Mail*, September 4, 1990: C9.
6. "Jays sweat it out on the bench as Sir David mows down Tribe," *Toronto Star*, September 3, 1990: D1.
7. "Toronto Blue Jays at Cleveland Indians," *Labatt's Blue Jays Baseball*, CTV Television Network (Toronto: CFTO, September 2, 1990).
8. "Jays sweat it out..."
9. Allan Ryan.
10. Dave Stieb and Kevin Boland, *Tomorrow I'll Be Perfect* (New York: Doubleday, 1986).
11. Allan Ryan, "Stieb pitches Jays' 1st no-hitter," *Toronto Star*, September 3, 1990: A1.

DENNIS MARTINEZ

By Rory Costello

IN 1976, DENNIS MARTÍNEZ became the first Nicaraguan to play in the big leagues—and he remains by far the most successful. Indeed, his 245 major-league wins are the most by any Latino pitcher, two ahead of Juan Marichal. Martínez got more than half of those wins after overcoming an alcohol problem that nearly derailed his career. His single most outstanding performance came on July 28, 1991, when he became the 13th pitcher to throw a perfect game.

El Presidente—as Martínez is often known in the U.S.—was a nickname he first received in 1979 from Orioles teammate Ken Singleton.[1] In later years, Martínez's name was bandied about as a candidate for president of Nicaragua, but only by a fringe party. The U.S. press ran with the idea, and it went mainstream in the States. His countrymen refer to Martínez as *El Chirizo*, which refers to his shock of mestizo hair. Without dispute, though, he has long been an enormous hero at home. In 1998, Nicaragua renamed its national stadium in his honor.

Denis José Martínez Ortiz was born on May 14, 1955—or maybe 1954. Journalist Tito Rondón, who grew up in Nicaragua and is an authority on baseball there, noted that the daily *La Prensa*'s listing of the Nicaraguan team competing in the 1972 Amateur World Series showed 1954. Various other local press sources also show the earlier date of birth, but pending official confirmation, this biography will use 1955, in accord with Martínez's own belief.

Rondón added, "When he signed with the Orioles, he chose the name José Dennis Martínez. As mother's maiden name he wrote 'Emilia,' his mom's first name—Emilia Ortiz de Martínez was her complete name. The Major League name became official when Dennis became an American citizen [in 1993]. When the stadium in Managua was named after him and they put up his name in lights, he insisted (and it was done) that they add the second 'n'."[2]

Martínez comes from Granada, a small city on the western shore of Lake Nicaragua and not far from the Pacific Ocean. Doña Emilia was in her forties when she gave birth to Dennis, her seventh child. He followed three brothers (Enrique, Guillermo, and Carlos) and three sisters (Lilliam, Aminta, and Adilia).[3] He came ten years after his previous sibling, and this meant that he grew up a lonely child, as he told Bruce Newman of *Sports Illustrated* in 1991.[4]

What's more, Dennis's father, Edmundo Martínez, became estranged from Emilia while she was expecting Dennis. He too had a drinking problem. Edmundo had inherited land from his father, and Emilia ran a stall in which she sold the products that came from the farm.[5] "My dad was...the quietest, most lovely drunk I ever saw," Martínez told Newman. "He was very gentle...But when he was drinking, he would sell our pigs to get money for liquor."[6]

"Emilia was a wonderful, honest, hard-working woman," said Tito Rondón. "When Dennis reached the majors, he asked her to retire, and he kept asking her, but she never did. She always went to the market to put up her stall and sell fruit, cheeses, beef and other staples."

In 2012, Martínez also recalled his childhood in a chat with *La Prensa*. "I was a rascal when I was a kid [the word he used was *pícaro*, the root of picaresque]. I grew up in the streets. They called me a bum, but I was a baseball bum." He recalled using balls made of socks and that he was 13 years old when he held a real baseball for the first time.[7] In sandlot ball, however, he was a third baseman.[8]

According to Tito Rondón, "Dennis started to play in an organized way as an infielder in a youth league in the area between Granada, Masaya, and Jinotepe in 1971." He also did some pitching and first attracted national attention that year when he led his team, Prego Junior, to the juvenile championship of

Nicaragua. He threw a 1-0 shutout, allowing just a single infield hit and driving in the game's only run with a homer.

Nicaragua's first winter professional baseball league had folded in 1967, but an amateur summer league was established there in 1970. Founder Carlos García called it the First Division, and indeed it featured the nation's best players. In 1972, Martínez stepped up to that level. The skinny 17-year-old pitched for his hometown team, the Granada Tiburones (Sharks). Tito Rondón recalled, "Before the season he tried out for San Fernando from Masaya. Their old catcher 'Guaracha' Castellón would say tongue in cheek, years later, 'My claim to fame is that I fired Dennis Martínez from San Fernando.'

"Dennis then decided to try out for the Tiburones, and manager Heberto Portobanco also told him that he could not make the team. But he liked his strong arm, so he asked his brother, coach Joaquín 'Chapuliche' Portobanco, to take the youngster to the bullpen and teach him how to throw so they could evaluate him as a pitcher. He made the Granada team and the national squad."

Most of the other Nicaraguan big-leaguers (12 altogether as of early 2013) also started in this league. Number two was pitcher Tony Chévez of León, whom the Orioles signed along with Martínez. Chévez was the bigger star at home, and expectations were higher for him.[9] Yet after a fine early minor-league career, he pitched just four games with the 1977 Orioles. He hurt his shoulder in the fourth outing and was never the same.

That year, the Nicaraguan playoffs featured star performances from Martínez and Chévez. It was a four-team round robin that came down to a best-of-three tiebreaker between León and Granada. After Martínez won Game One on June 21, the series finished with a doubleheader on June 22 at the National Stadium in the capital city, Managua. In the opener, Chévez won 5-0—but in the nightcap, Granada beat León with five innings from Martínez in relief.[10] "You just took the ball," said Chévez in 2009. "Everybody was watching."[11]

In August 1972, the Torneo de la Amistad (Friendship Tournament) was held in Santo Domingo, Dominican Republic. Rookie Martínez got a surprise start against Cuba in a game that Nicaragua won, 5-4—its first victory over the regional powerhouse in 20 years.[12] Later that year, the 20th Amateur World Series was held in Managua from November 15 through December 3. The hosts, Nicaragua, won the bronze medal with a 13-2 record. Martínez pitched in five games, starting two; he was 1-1, 1.86.

Less than three weeks later, on December 23, 1972, Managua suffered its devastating earthquake. That New Year's Eve, as Roberto Clemente left for Nicaragua on his mercy mission, his plane went down off Puerto Rico, killing all on board. Martínez had come to know Clemente because Roberto had managed the Puerto Rican team in the Amateur World Series. More than 40 years later, Martínez said, "I had two idols—one as a pitcher, Juan Marichal, and the other, Clemente, as a human being. I took him as an example. He got me to think more about helping your neighbor, helping children, which was his goal and now mine too."[13]

In 1973, there was a split in Nicaragua's top amateur ranks that would last through 1977. Two leagues evolved under rival federations: the Roberto Clemente League and the Hope and Reconstruction League, or ESPERE. Martínez played for the Granada entry in ESPERE in 1973.

When he was nearly 18, on April 29, 1973, Martínez married Luz Marina García, a fellow student from Granada. "She was 15," said Tito Rondón. "Dennis signed several months later, and left Nicaragua in March 1974. Friends told her to leave him, that in the U.S. he would forget her. But he had told her to wait for him, and she had faith in him. And in 1977, when he returned to the U.S., to the Orioles, she was with him." They had four children: Dennis Jr., Erica, Gilberto, and Ricardo. Martínez has often credited the support of his wife in helping his life get back on track and remain there.

Owing to a conflict between international baseball organizations FIBA and FEMBA, two Amateur World Series were held in parallel in 1973. The FEMBA event took place (without Cuba) in Managua from November 22 through December 5. Following the quake, the National Stadium was in ruins and the Nicaraguan economy was still suffering. Yet the hosts still spent a precious $500,000 to stage the tourney.[14]

Nicaragua faced the U.S. in the gold medal game, held in León; 9,000 fans thronged the 6,000-seat stadium. The Nicaraguans had to settle for silver, though, as Martínez lost a 1-0, 10-inning duel to Rich Wortham, who pitched in four seasons in the majors (1978-80; 1983). "I heard Dennis plead with his teammates, 'Please get me just one run, one is all I need,'" recalled Tito Rondón, who got to sit in the dugout for the first six innings. "But Wortham was much superior to the Nica hitters. Dennis had tougher foes and he tired in the 10th."

Manager Tony Castaño told Chévez—and Martínez too, one may infer –"You gotta go north. There's nothing for you here."[15] He tipped off his fellow Cuban, Julio Blanco Herrera, a bird dog for Baltimore.[16] Regional scouting supervisor Ray Poitevint then entered the picture. He later said, "Dennis looked like a pencil. But he had natural talent, as much as anyone. And he was hungry. He wanted to be something."[17] When he was signed, Martínez weighed a mere 135 pounds.[18] As a scout, though, Poitevint projected how his prospect would look when mature. Martínez filled out to 160 pounds by the time he reached Baltimore, eventually weighing 185 as a veteran. He stood 6-feet-1.

Tito Rondón and a colleague named Hans Bendixen were actually in Poitevint's hotel room, having an engrossing conversation about scouting with Ray and Julio Blanco Herrera, when Doña Emilia arrived with Dennis. "The signing was cloak and dagger stuff," said Rondón. "Ray and Julio asked us a favor; not to publish or talk about it." Accounts vary as to the bonus Baltimore paid, but whether it was $10,000 or as little as $3,000, Poitevint later called it "the best money I ever spent."[19]

According to Tito Rondón, keeping the signing quiet enabled Martínez to play for Granada at the beginning of the 1974 Nicaraguan season. At that time, he was also an engineering student at La Universidad Nacional Autónoma—he had a good mind for mathematics. He went there for just the first year, though, before going to the United States—Doña Emilia was not best pleased that he quit school.[20]

In March 1974, Dennis and Tony started their pro careers with Miami in the Florida State League (Class A). They had traveled the world before with the national team and had pitched in big stadiums, so they were not overwhelmed. Martínez ascended rapidly through the Baltimore system. In his first year with Miami, he was 15-6 with a 2.06 ERA. He struck out 162 men and allowed just four homers in 179 innings. He started the 1975 season with Miami again, but after going 12-4, 2.61, he was promoted to Double-A Asheville. He finished the season with two games at Triple-A Rochester.

Martínez pitched strongly again at Rochester in 1976 (14-8, 2.50). There were warning signs—"Unnamed teammates stated that the pitcher had developed 'bad night-time habits,' and enjoyed the party life." Even so, he was the International

League's Pitcher of the Year, winning the Triple Crown of pitching. It was only the second time it had been done in the league's history.[21]

Thus, in September the big club rewarded him with his first call to the majors. Rochester manager Joe Altobelli thought that Martínez would be a better big-league pitcher than Mark Fidrych, who was then enjoying his marvelous rookie year for the Detroit Tigers. Baltimore superscout Jim Russo agreed, saying, "We haven't rushed Dennis, and our patience should pay off." (Of course, the Orioles had that luxury back then, since their pitching was so deep.) Russo added, "Martínez and Fidrych have similar styles. They keep the ball down and have exceptional sinking stuff."[22]

Martínez later described his repertoire to Orioles historian John Eisenberg. "My stuff was decent. I had a good curveball. My fastball was decent. My curveball made my fastball better. Everyone was aware of my curveball, so my fastball went right by them. But mostly, I had a big heart...It isn't the stuff you have, it's how you execute it. With desire, determination, that's how I did it."[23] Looking back in 2011, he added, "As soon as I got a changeup, I blossomed."[24]

Martínez's debut came in long relief against the Tigers at Memorial Stadium on September 14, Ross Grimsley and Dave Pagan gave up seven runs between them in the first four innings. The rookie entered and struck out the first three batters he faced. He didn't allow a run the rest of the way either, and he got the win because the Orioles scored four in the bottom of the seventh. After that he started three times, losing two of them, including a 1-0 decision to Boston at Fenway Park in the second-last game of the season.

As part of his development, that winter Martínez went to play in Puerto Rico with the Caguas Criollos. Thomas Van Hyning, who has chronicled Puerto Rico's winter league in two books, wrote, "Martínez was part of the Baltimore-Caguas axis between 1976-77 and 1980-81. During this period he helped Caguas win three titles." Van Hyning added, "Puerto Rico was a second home to Martínez...the quality of play appealed to [him], and he gave it his all, including the 1978-79 championship game when he bested Mayagüez's Jack Morris."[25]

Wayne Garland, who won 20 games for Baltimore in 1976, signed as a free agent with the Cleveland Indians. Martínez therefore had a good chance to crack the starting rotation in 1977. Instead, he wound up as a swingman, starting 13 games in 42 appearances. He was 14-7, though his ERA was 4.10. In those days, four-man rotations were still the norm; Jim Palmer, Rudy May, Grimsley, and Mike Flanagan—who won the #4 starter job—started 143 games among them that year, completing 59. Manager Earl Weaver "was inclined to go with Martínez and Scott McGregor when he had to make a call on the bullpen...mainly because both rookies have displayed an ability to get the ball over the plate."[26]

Martínez entered Baltimore's rotation in 1978, along with McGregor. In December 1977, May had been traded to the Montreal Expos, and later the same month, Grimsley signed with the same club as a free agent. Martínez was 16-11, 3.52 in 40 games (38 starts). He had a poor first half, but at the All-Star break, pitching coach Ray Miller asked Dennis's wife what Martínez was doing differently that he hadn't done in the minors. Luz Marina replied that he was dipping his shoulder.[27] He also addressed how he was tipping his pitches with facial expressions by sticking a big chaw of tobacco and bubblegum in his cheek—it became his visual trademark.[28] In the second half, Martínez was 9-4, 2.30. He threw complete games in 11 of his last 14 starts, and in two of the other three games, he went 11 and 8 innings.

When Baltimore won the AL pennant in 1979, Martínez led the league in starts (39), complete games (18), and innings pitched (292 1/3). His results were so-so, though—15-16, 3.66. After losing two of his first three starts, Martínez reeled off 10 straight wins in 14 outings from April 22 through June 20. He didn't pitch that badly the rest of the way, but had little to show for it—he didn't really pitch well enough to win much of the time either.

Some Orioles insiders, according to New York sportswriter Dick Young, cited Martínez's insistence that Dave Skaggs catch him rather than Rick

Dempsey.²⁹ Skaggs joked, "When I die, they're going to bury me 60 feet, six inches away from Dennis Martínez."³⁰ Martínez told John Eisenberg, "I had a lot of disagreements with Dempsey. Whatever I was doing, it wasn't good enough or I wasn't doing things the right way."³¹ Dempsey too acknowledged the battle and the two-way frustrations, but he said, "Earl made sure I knew what he wanted us to do with each hitter. I know Dennis didn't like it, but we won that way."³²

At least at some level, worries about his family back in Nicaragua may have been a factor too. The Sandinista revolution was in full swing, and amid the civil war, Martínez could not reach Doña Emilia by telephone. Dictator Anastasio Somoza Debayle resigned on July 17. It was soon thereafter that Ken Singleton said, "You're going to be *El Presidente*," and the name stuck.

In the postseason, Martínez started Game Three of the AL Championship Series versus the California Angels. At Anaheim Stadium, he took a 3-2 lead into the ninth inning, but after Rod Carew's one-out double, Weaver called for Don Stanhouse, who couldn't hold the lead.

Martínez appeared twice in the World Series against the Pittsburgh Pirates. He started Game Four at Three Rivers Stadium, got knocked out of the box in the second inning—but the Orioles' six-run rally in the eighth inning got him off the hook. In Game Seven, he was the fifth pitcher that Weaver used in the ninth inning, when the Pirates scored two crucial insurance runs. Dennis came on with the bases loaded and hit Bill Robinson with a pitch, but then got Willie Stargell to hit into a double play.

The 1980 season was a setback for Martínez. A sore shoulder kept him out of action for most of two months from mid-May through mid-July. He was able to pitch only 99 2/3 innings, with 12 starts in 25 appearances. Bullpen coach Elrod Hendricks made an interesting observation—Martínez had not played winter ball in the 1979-80 season. "A lot of Latin pitchers cannot go without pitching in the winter," Ellie said. "They simply develop their arms a different way."³³

Trade rumors circulated around Martínez after that off year, but his market value was low, and it turned out to be better for them that he stayed. *El Presidente* bounced back nicely in the strike season of 1981—his 14 wins led the AL, and he lost just five while posting a 3.32 ERA. He came in fifth in the voting for the Cy Young Award. General Manager Hank Peters said that June, "We didn't want to break up our pitching staff and we've always felt Dennis had the arm and the ability. It was just a matter of him putting it all together."³⁴

Martínez signed a five-year contract with Baltimore after the '81 season. He was a workhorse again in 1982, starting 39 games and going 16-12. However, his ERA was on the high side at 4.21. That September, he had to return to Nicaragua for the funeral of his father.³⁵ "He was walking and a truck hit him and killed him in Granada," Martínez recalled in 1985, suspecting that alcohol was likely a factor.³⁶ Despite Edmundo's grave alcoholism, Dennis still loved his father greatly—though he later

regretted drinking together with him when he went back home.[37]

The year 1983 was when Martínez's personal problems came to a head. It was reflected in his performance on the mound—7-16, with a career-high ERA of 5.53. The Orioles did not use him in either the AL Championship Series against the Chicago White Sox or the World Series against the Philadelphia Phillies. Nonetheless, Martínez is still proud of his championship ring from '83, even though he thought the '79 squad was more talented. "This was the year I got help for my alcohol problem," he said in 2002. "It was a bad year, but I got a new start."[38]

After Martínez was arrested for drunk driving in December 1983, the Orioles staged an intervention. He entered rehab in Baltimore's Sheppard Pratt Hospital. He told UPI sportswriter Milton Richman that he was still in denial at first, but then his counselor encouraged Martínez to find strength in prayer. "That," he told Richman, "was the turning point of my life."[39] He stayed in control with the ongoing help of Alcoholics Anonymous meetings.[40]

It took more than three years for Martínez to re-emerge as an effective pitcher, though. He was 6-9, 5.02 in 1984. "I was happy to see the improvement in my mental problem," he told Richman. "That was my prime concern. Baseball was second."[41]

As part of his effort to rebound on the field, Dennis returned to Puerto Rico near the end of the 1984-85 winter season, joining the Santurce Cangrejeros.[42] Martínez got another chance to be a rotation regular for Baltimore in 1985 after Mike Flanagan ruptured an Achilles tendon. He did post a 13-11 record, but his ERA remained lofty at 5.15. "Physically, he is back," said Ray Miller that June. "Mentally, he is in the upward direction."[43]

Martínez's stock fell in 1986. He pitched just four games for Baltimore in April and then—bothered again by a sore shoulder—suffered a demotion to Rochester. In mid-June, the Orioles traded him to Montreal with a player to be named later, receiving a player to be named later in return. During the second half of the season, he started 15 games and relieved in four for the Expos, with no particular success (3-6, 4.59). He considered quitting.

After the '86 season, Montreal refused to offer more than $250,000 to Martínez, who had been making $500,000 in the last year of his Baltimore pact.[44] He became a free agent, but there were no takers, and he was barred from re-signing with the Expos until May 1, 1987. He went back to the minors again to get in shape, pitching for the independent Miami Marlins (Class A). He then re-signed with Montreal for the minimum salary. He was just 3-2, 4.46 for the Expos' Triple-A club in Indianapolis, but when Montreal farmed out Jay Tibbs in June, Martínez got another chance.

From then on, it all came together. During six and a half seasons with the Expos, Martínez was consistently among the best pitchers in the National League. His winning percentage was good (97-66, .595), but that wasn't all. His ERA was 2.96, including a major-league-best 2.39 in 1991. He was an NL All-Star in 1990, becoming the oldest player to make his All-Star debut, and repeated that honor in '91 and '92. He again received Cy Young consideration in 1991.

Along with attaining inner peace, Martínez had become a master craftsman on the mound. In 1988, he told Montreal sportswriter Ian MacDonald, "Before, when I was drinking, I used to think I was good. I didn't think about pitching. . .I used to just try to throw the ball past the hitter. Now I think. I don't say it makes it easy, but it makes it easier." He moved the ball around, changed speeds, focused on the weaknesses of the hitters, and made constant adjustments, setting up batters based on their reactions from pitch to pitch.[45] He also hid the ball well with his motion and threw from varied arm angles.

Many insights also come from James Buckley's book *Perfect: The Inside Story of Baseball's Twenty Perfect Games*. Ron Hassey, the catcher for Martínez's flawless gem, said, "He had to hit his spots; he had to have his command to get guys out. But Dennis had outstanding control, and he knew how to pitch." Center fielder Marquis Grissom said, "It was like an artist making a painting." Opposing catcher Mike Scioscia also noted how fine Martínez's command was, saying, "We might have played 20 innings against him and never gotten a hit." Tito Rondón, then with *La Prensa*, said, "Dennis Martínez was already the most popular man in [Nicaragua] before he pitched a perfect game. Now he's just more popular."[46]

In December 1993, the 38-year-old veteran signed as a free agent with the Cleveland Indians. General manager John Hart viewed his club as a contender, and owner Richard Jacobs was willing to open up his wallet. Montreal had been paying Martínez around $3 million a year from 1991 on, but Cleveland gave him a two-year contract for $9 million. This was vast wealth by the standards of Nicaragua, where his needy countrymen already counted heavily on him.

Martínez continued to pitch well for the Indians—32-17 (.653) with a 3.58 ERA in his three seasons there. He was particularly effective in 1995, when he made the AL All-Star team and helped Cleveland to win the pennant. In his first return to the postseason since 1979, he started once against Boston in the Division Series, getting a no-decision. He was 1-1 in the ALCS against Seattle, including seven scoreless innings in the decisive Game Six against fearsome Randy Johnson, even though his whole body hurt.[47] He was 0-1 in two starts against Atlanta in the World Series.

Martínez pitched only once in 1996 after the end of July, though—elbow problems disabled him. He became a free agent again that November, and it took him until late the following February before he landed with a new team, because his elbow was perceived as too risky. The Seattle Mariners finally took a chance, and as he approached his 42nd birthday, Martínez won a spot on the roster.

He was a good influence in the clubhouse and showed initial signs that he was not done yet, but Martínez made only nine ineffective starts for the Mariners. Although his elbow held up, a surprising 29 walks in 49 innings led to a 1-5 record and 7.71 ERA. Seattle released him in May 1997. The following month, he decided to retire, citing the lack of an opportunity to keep pitching.[48] He established the Dennis Martínez Foundation in 1997, with the goal of helping children, primarily in Nicaragua but also elsewhere in Latin America.

In the winter of 1997-98, however, Martínez decided to go back to Puerto Rico once more to play winter ball. As he had the previous year, he was again hoping to catch on with the Florida Marlins, since he had made his home in Miami for many years and the Nicaraguan population in south Florida was sizable. Various teams watched Martínez in his playoff showcase with the Mayagüez Indios, but Atlanta was the only one to show serious interest.[49]

During his 23rd and final season in the majors, Martínez was mainly a reliever, making five starts in 53 appearances. He was 4-6, 4.45 in 91 innings pitched. On June 2, he finally tied his old idol Juan Marichal for most wins in the majors by a Latino pitcher. It came with a complete-game 12-hit shutout at Milwaukee. He went ahead with a victory in relief over the Giants in San Francisco on August 9. His last win, #245, came in middle relief at Atlanta's Turner Field on September 25. He retired all four New York Mets he faced.

Martínez got into four NLCS games for Atlanta in 1998, getting one of the Braves' two wins against the San Diego Padres. In February 1999, he announced his final retirement, saying, "There is nothing more to do."[50]

A couple of months later, the Nicaraguan Baseball Federation named Martínez coordinator of the national team for the Pan American Games, to be held in Winnipeg that July. He said that he might even join the team if it needed pitching.[51] When July rolled around, he was still planning to work an inning or two in exhibition games, with an eye toward appearing against Cuba or the U.S. if Nicaragua made it as far as the semifinals. He was motivated because the Pan Am Games were an Olympic qualifying event.[52] It only got as far as an exhibition appearance in Panama, though.[53] A bad knee was one reason, but Mexico knocked out Nicaragua in the quarterfinals.

After retiring, Martínez worked for the Nicaraguan Visitors and Travel Bureau. He also helped coach at Westminster Christian High School in Miami. His youngest son, Ricky, was a player there.

In the spring of 2005, with all his children out of school except for Ricky, he returned to the Orioles organization as a pitching instructor in camp. Old teammate Mike Flanagan, who was in the Baltimore front office, had kept in touch with him over the years about a possible return.[54]

Martínez spent six years (2007-12) as a minor-league pitching coach in the St. Louis Cardinals organization. He enjoyed helping many young prospects develop; among them was his son Ricky, who signed with the Cardinals as a non-drafted free agent in 2010. However, Dennis was hoping to get a shot at the big-league level.[55] In November 2012, he got that chance when the Houston Astros named him as their bullpen coach.

Martínez also remained involved with the Nicaraguan baseball scene. He managed the national team in the 2011 Baseball World Cup, as well as the 2013 World Baseball Classic qualifying tournaments, held in September and November 2012. Son Ricky was part of the squad for the WBC qualifiers.

In 2004, Martínez became eligible for the Baseball Hall of Fame in Cooperstown. He received 16 votes from the Baseball Writers Association of America. That level of support meant he was "one and done"—off the ballot in 2005. Five years later, baseball author Joe Posnanski wrote, "When you add it all up he has a very similar case to Jack Morris, who is gaining Hall of Fame momentum."[56] It remains to be seen if the Veterans Committee may eventually consider Martínez. In 2011, however, he became a member of the Latino Baseball Hall of Fame in La Romana, Dominican Republic.

One may conjecture that without the lost years in the middle of his career, Dennis Martínez might be an even stronger candidate for Cooperstown. But the flip side of that argument is that his career only became what it did because of the resurrection. "I never did," he said when asked in 2002 if he thought he would pitch for 23 years. "I think after recovery I had more of an effort to live life. And the competitor in me wanted to keep going. I did everything that God allowed me to do.

"I think the key to my longevity was staying in shape and changing my life after my addiction. Before that, I did not take good care of myself…But I had my family and I had a lot to play for."[57]

NOTES

1 "Former Oriole Dennis Martinez ponders political pitch," *Baltimore Sun*, January 7, 1994.

2 E-mail from Tito Rondón to Rory Costello, March 6, 2013 (based on Rondón's personal knowledge of the situation).

3 "Pésame a Denis Martínez por la pérdida de su madre," *La Prensa* (Managua, Nicaragua), May 4, 2001.

4 Bruce Newman, "Return of the Native," *Sports Illustrated*, December 30, 1991.

5 Bob Finnigan, "13 Years Of Sobriety, Dennis Martinez Has Been A Responsible Family Man, A National Hero In His Native Nicaragua And One Of Baseball's Best Pitchers," *Seattle Times*, April 25, 1997.

6 Newman, "Return of the Native"

7 Amalia del Cid, "Denis Martínez," *La Prensa*, October 14, 2012.

8 Newman, "Return of the Native"; Finnigan, "13 Years Of Sobriety"

9 Hernández, Gerald. "Everth Cabrera es el décimo nicaragüense en Grandes Ligas, quiere triunfar en San Diego". Puro Béisbol website (http://purobeisbol.com.mx/content/view/1255/1/). See also George Vecsey, "Nicaragua's Best Pitcher," *New York Times*, September 27, 1981: S3.

10 Ruiz Borge, Martín. "Asoma el tercer duelo," *El Nuevo Dia* (Managua, Nicaragua), March 16, 2003.

11 Rory Costello, "Tony Chévez," SABR BioProject (http://sabr.org/bioproj/person/94643812)

12 Edgard Tijerino, "Denis, prepárate," *El Nuevo Diario*, September 18, 2011.

13 Antolín Maldonado Ríos, "Dennis Martínez fue influenciado por Clemente," *El Nuevo Día*, January 4, 2013.

14 Jordan, Pat. "Dubious Triumph In Florida," *Sports Illustrated*, December 9, 1974.

15 "Tony Chévez"

16 Edgard Tijerino, "¡Qué difícil fue!" *La Prensa*, January 13, 2003.

17 John Eisenberg, *From 33rd Street to Camden Yards* (New York, New York: Contemporary Books, 2001), 282.

18 Steve Henson, "The Frontiersman: Poitevint Blazes Trail for Angels as Global Scout," *Los Angeles Times*, September 17, 1993.

19 Finnigan, "13 Years Of Sobriety." The Orioles made Julio Blanco Herrera a full scout as a result of the Martínez/Chévez signing.

20 Vecsey, "Nicaragua's Best Pitcher"

NO-HITTERS

21 Brian Bennett, On *a Silver Diamond: The Story of Rochester Community Baseball from 1956-1996* (Scottsville, New York: Triphammer Publishing, 1997), chapter 4.

22 "A Better Bird," *The Sporting News*, September 18, 1976, 32.

23 Eisenberg, *From 33rd Street to Camden Yards*, 283.

24 Derrick Goold, "Dennis Martinez makes his mark as pitching instructor," *St. Louis Post-Dispatch*, August 14, 2011.

25 Thomas Van Hyning, *Puerto Rico's Winter League* (Jefferson, North Carolina: McFarland & Co., 1995), 160.

26 Jim Henneman, "Orioles Toss Burning Problem to Fireman Drago," *The Sporting News*, July 2, 1977, 18.

27 Peter May, "If Birds Ever Need a Pitching Coach…," United Press International, September 13, 1978.

28 Newman, "Return of the Native"

29 Dick Young, Young Ideas," *The Sporting News*, October 20, 1979, 20.

30 Phil Pepe, "Phil Pepe's Patter," *The Sporting News*, November 3, 1979, 16.

31 Eisenberg, *From 33rd Street to Camden Yards*, 305.

32 Newman, "Return of the Native"

33 Peter Gammons, "Don't Expect Many of Those Deadline Deals," *The Sporting News*, June 21, 1980.

34 Ken Nigro, "Dennis Martinez Is O's New Ace," *The Sporting News*, June 27, 1981, 15.

35 Tom Flaherty, "Orioles Serve Weaver One Last Hot Roll," *The Sporting News*, October 4, 1982, 12.

36 Milton Richman, "Orioles' Dennis Martinez Has a New Goal: Staying Sober," United Press International, March 10, 1985.

37 Edgard Tijerino, "Era mi padre, lo quería," *El Nuevo Diario*, August 28, 2011. Finnigan, "13 Years Of Sobriety"

38 Gary Washburn, "Where have you gone, Dennis Martinez?" MLB.com, September 12, 2002 (http://baltimore.orioles.mlb.com/news/article.jsp?ymd=20020912&content_id=126757&vkey=news_bal&fext=.jsp&c_id=bal)

39 Richman, "Orioles' Dennis Martinez Has a New Goal: Staying Sober"

40 By most accounts, he stayed consistently sober, but according to one story, he had a few relapses. Ian MacDonald, "The only Montreal Expo to ever pitch a perfect game is now teaching a new generation," Canwest News Service, March 15, 2008.

41 Richman, "Orioles' Dennis Martinez Has a New Goal: Staying Sober"

42 Van Hyning, *Puerto Rico's Winter League*, 160.

43 Jim Henneman, "Martinez's Pitching Quiets Trade Talks," *The Sporting News*, June 17, 1985, 20.

44 *The Sporting News*, December 22, 1986, 48.

45 Ian MacDonald, "Heeding Expos' Call for Arms," *The Sporting News*, September 12, 1988, 15.

46 James Buckley Jr., *Perfect: The Inside Story of Baseball's Twenty Perfect Games* (Chicago, Illinois: Triumph Books LLC, 2012), 166, 167, 169.

47 Terry Pluto, *Our Tribe* (New York, NY: Simon & Schuster, 1999), 237.

48 "Dennis Martinez Retires From Baseball," *Seattle Times*, June 18, 1997.

49 Mike Berardino, "Martinez Making A Brave Comeback Try," *Palm Beach Sun-Sentinel*, March 8, 1998.

50 "Dennis Martinez retires," Associated Press, February 7, 1999.

51 "Still pitching?" *Seattle Times*, April 19, 1999.

52 Stephen Canella and Jeff Pearlman, "Dennis Martinez's Plans — One More Time: Pan Am Games," *Sports Illustrated*, July 19, 1999. This article also confirmed that Martínez showed his year of birth as 1954 in documentation he presented for the event.

53 Dick Heller, "Coach Martinez makes pitch for himself in Pan Am Games," *Washington Times*, July 12, 1999.

54 Gary Washburn, "'El Presidente' happy in new job," MLB.com, February 20, 2005 (http://mlb.mlb.com/news/article.jsp?ymd=20050220&content_id=946722)

55 Goold, "Dennis Martinez makes his mark as pitching instructor"

56 Joe Posnanski, "Taking a look at the Hall of Fame ballot's one-and-done club," SI.com, December 2, 2009 (http://sportsillustrated.cnn.com/2009/writers/joe_posnanski/12/01/hall.of.fame/index.html)

57 Washburn, "Where have you gone, Dennis Martinez?"

DENNIS MARTÍNEZ'S PERFECT GAME
JULY 28, 1991: MONTREAL EXPOS 2 — LOS ANGELES DODGERS 0, AT DODGER STADIUM, LOS ANGELES

By Rory Costello

"EL PRESIDENTE! EL Perfecto!"

That was broadcaster Dave Van Horne's call on July 28, 1991, at Dodger Stadium, after Dennis Martínez completed the only perfect game in Montreal Expos history.

Other Montreal pitchers had thrown no-hitters—Bill Stoneman in 1969 and 1972, and Charlie Lea in 1981. Also, just two days before Martínez's gem, Mark Gardner went nine no-hit innings against Los Angeles—but Montreal could not score. Gardner then lost his no-no and the game in the 10th inning.[1] But Martínez became just the 13th man to throw a perfect game in major-league history.

Martinez's masterpiece symbolized his personal redemption. The pitcher, whose father was an alcoholic, became one too. It nearly derailed his career. As early as 1976, in Triple A, there were warning signs.[2] In 1983 his alcohol problem came to a head, and he got help. "It was a bad year," he later said, "but I got a new start."[3]

Though it took more than three years for Martínez to re-emerge fully, he became a master craftsman on the mound. The Expos acquired him from Baltimore in June 1986, and from June 1987 through 1993, Martinez was consistently among the best pitchers in the National League.

In 1988 he had said, "Before, when I was drinking, I used to think I was good. I didn't think about pitching. ... I used to just try to throw the ball past the hitter. Now I think. I don't say it makes it easy, but it makes it easier."[4]

That thinking process made him a very crafty pitcher. He moved the ball around, changed speeds, focused on the weaknesses of the hitters, and made constant adjustments, setting up batters based on their reactions from pitch to pitch. He also hid the ball well with his motion and threw from varied arm angles. In some respects, Martinez had his finest season in 1991. He led the NL in ERA at 2.39—never rising above 2.42—and finished fifth in the Cy Young Award voting.

"He's been this way all year," catcher Ron Hassey remarked after the perfect game. "There's been only one or two games when he hasn't had the kind of stuff he had today."[5]

However, as *El Presidente* took the hill at Dodger Stadium on July 28, he hadn't won since a complete-game 4-3 victory at Pittsburgh on July 5. In three starts after that, he had two no-decisions, sandwiched around one of his few shaky outings in '91, a loss to San Diego at home.

It was a typical summer Sunday afternoon in Los Angeles: 95 degrees and hazy. A big crowd of 45,560 was at the game. Martinez had attended Mass that morning, as he did each Sunday. "To me, that was the key point to the day," he later said.[6]

Never overpowering, Martinez fooled the Dodgers "with curveballs and sinkers and guts."[7] As Expos historian Jonah Keri wrote, "Though there weren't advanced pitch-tracking systems back then ... you'd swear he threw 50 of his trademark knee-buckling curveballs."[8] Ken Singleton, the color commentator who teamed with Dave Van Horne on the TSN (Canada's only sports network at the time) telecast, said, "It's not your run-of-the-mill curveball that's coming up there today."[9]

Two of those benders came at critical junctures. As Bill Plaschke of the *Los Angeles Times* put it, "Hassey and Martinez combined on two big, bold pitches that may have saved the perfect game. With two out in the seventh inning and a full count on Eddie Murray, Martinez dared to throw a curveball. Murray jumped at it, grounding it to second base. With one out in the eighth inning and a full count on Kal Daniels, Martinez threw another curveball. Daniels swung through it for a strikeout."[10]

The Dodgers came close to a hit several times. With one out in the fourth, Montreal third baseman Tim Wallach handled Juan Samuel's smash on the lip of the infield grass. With one out in the fifth, Daniels grounded to second base. Delino DeShields backed onto the outfield grass, waiting for a big hop. Daniels — once a fast runner, but slowed by several knee operations — got out of the box slowly but was still out by just half a step.

El Presidente also helped himself with one out in the seventh. The speedy Samuel pushed a bunt up the first-base line, but Martinez raced over, barehanded the ball, and threw out Samuel while falling forward. In the fourth inning, he had fought off a sore hip, caused by landing in a hole on the slippery mound dug by opposing pitcher Mike Morgan.

There was a play that almost led to an error. With one out in the sixth, DeShields fielded Alfredo Griffin's grounder, but his low throw to first nearly pulled Larry Walker off the bag.

Morgan also had a perfect game through five innings until Hassey led off the sixth with a single. The Expos' two runs — both unearned — came in the top of the seventh inning. Griffin, the Dodgers' shortstop, committed an error, and after a sacrifice bunt and a groundout, Walker got Montreal's big hit, a triple. Walker scored when Griffin made his second error of the inning on a Hassey groundball. Morgan went on to throw a complete game himself, allowing just four hits while walking one.

The last man between Martinez and perfection was pinch-hitter Chris Gwynn, younger brother of Tony. The lefty swinger almost ended the dream when he slapped a 1-and-1 pitch barely foul down the third-base line. Expos center fielder Marquis Grissom said, "I don't think anybody wanted the ball hit to them. I was so overexcited out there. I was just thinking, 'Please, no line drives, nothing hard.' I don't want to be the one to ruin history."[11]

Martinez left the 1-and-2 pitch up, and Gwynn lifted it to right-center. "I hit it well," said Gwynn, "but I knew it wasn't enough to get out."[12] Grissom said, "It was a routine fly ball. But I had to get over there and get it. I had to forget what was at stake."[13]

After Grissom gloved the ball, celebration ensued, led by Wallach. When the swarm abated, Martinez then enjoyed an interlude alone in the dugout. "There was nothing in my mind," he said. "I had no words to say, I could only cry. I didn't know how to express myself. I didn't know how to respond to this kind of game."[14]

Martinez's command was exceptional. He needed just 96 pitches, 66 of which were strikes. He went to a two-ball count on only eight hitters, and of these, only three went to a three-ball count. There were 17 groundouts, five strikeouts, two foul outs, and just three fair balls hit out of the infield.[15]

Hassey, who also caught Len Barker's perfect game of May 15, 1981, became the first major-league catcher to handle two of them. "This was a lot different than Lenny's," Hassey said. "Lenny was … a wild pitcher. Dennis is a pitcher's pitcher."[16]

The catcher added, "We had a game plan, and we went out and did it. You give the credit to Dennis. He's the guy who had to throw the pitches. I'm just the guy who's catching them and helping him."[17] Other Expos said, however, that Hassey was being too modest.[18]

Jonah Keri wrote, "In the clubhouse afterwards, Walker showered Martinez with beer, and the conquering hero carefully wiped it off his face. Later that night, teammates and friends toasted him with champagne; Martinez raised his glass, then set it down without taking a sip."[19] After the game, the sober man offered hope to others with drinking problems, saying, "It's never too late to do something about it."[20]

Martinez, the first player from Nicaragua to reach the majors, was already a hero in his homeland. He got the nickname *El Presidente* in 1979 from Ken Singleton, then a teammate with the Orioles. Tito Rondón, who in 1991 was sports editor of the Nicaraguan newspaper *La Prensa*, said, "Dennis Martínez was already the most popular man in the country before he pitched a perfect game. Now he's just more popular."[21]

"I thank God for this game that He gave me late in my career," said Martinez.[22] As it turned out, the veteran remained active through the 1998 season, when he turned 44. He threw eight more shutouts, including two of his six career two-hitters (he also had a one-hitter in 1985). He amassed 245 regular-season victories in the majors, still the record for Latin American hurlers as of 2015—but win number 174 was his finest hour.

SOURCES

In addition to the sources cited in the notes, another important article consulted by the author was:

"Perfect Sunday," *Washington* (Pennsylvania) *Observer-Reporter*, July 29, 1991.

NOTES

1. Also worthy of mention are two rain-shortened performances. On April 21, 1984, David Palmer retired the first 15 St. Louis Cardinals he faced, but the game was called. On September 24, 1988, Pascual Pérez pitched five hitless innings against the Philadelphia Phillies, but that game was called in the top of the sixth. In September 1991 the Committee for Statistical Accuracy issued a retroactive ruling that these, among 50 games that had been listed as no-hitters, no longer qualified as such. The irony is that the committee made this decision after being asked to rule whether Mark Gardner's achievement deserved to be called a no-hitter.
2. Brian Bennett, *On a Silver Diamond: The Story of Rochester Community Baseball From 1956-1996* (Scottsville, New York: Triphammer Publishing, 1997), Chapter 4.
3. Gary Washburn, "Where Have You Gone, Dennis Martinez?" MLB.com, September 12, 2002.
4. Ian MacDonald, "Heeding Expos' Call for Arms," *The Sporting News*, September 12, 1988.
5. Wendy Lane, "Dennis Martinez: Simply Perfect," *Lexington* (North Carolina) *Dispatch*, July 29, 1991.
6. James Buckley Jr., *Perfect: The Inside Story of Baseball's Twenty Perfect Games* (Chicago: Triumph Books, 2012), 160.
7. Bill Plaschke, "Martinez Perfect Against L.A.," *Los Angeles Times*, July 29, 1991.
8. Jonah Keri, *Up, Up and Away* (Toronto: Random House Canada, 2014), 267.
9. TSN broadcast of the perfect game, accessed via YouTube.com.
10. Plaschke, "Notebook: Perfect Game Not New to Hassey," *Los Angeles Times*, July 29, 1991.
11. Plaschke, "Perfection Brings Expos' Martinez to Tears." (This is an alternate version of "Martinez Perfect Against L.A.")
12. Lane.
13. Plaschke, "Perfection Brings Expos' Martinez to Tears."
14. Plaschke, "Martinez Perfect Against L.A."
15. Ibid.
16. Plaschke, "Notebook: Perfect Game Not New to Hassey."
17. Lane.
18. Plaschke, "Notebook: Perfect Game Not New to Hassey."
19. Keri, 268.
20. Lane.
21. Buckley, *Perfect*, 169.
22. Lane.

WILSON ÁLVAREZ

By Leonte Landino

WILSON WAS MEANT TO be. The no-hitter he pitched for the White Sox on August 11, 1991, changed not only his life, but also the way a country's new generation embraced baseball.

Asked about the game over the years, he would repeat, "It was a gift from God."[1] Indeed, it seems it was.

Wilson Álvarez became the fourth youngest pitcher in history to accomplish the feat.[2] He was the 13th Chicago White Sox pitcher to throw a no-hitter, and his was the 14th hitless game in franchise history. It was the first for a Venezuelan pitcher. And this was just his second major-league start.

The world of major-league baseball first heard the name of left-hander Wilson Álvarez in July 1989, when the Texas Rangers called him up for a spot start on July 24. In his native Venezuela, Álvarez was already a well-known name, mostly in Maracaibo, his hometown, where he had been in the news since he was a boy starring in the little leagues.

Wilson Álvarez was born in Maracaibo on March 24, 1970, the son of William Álvarez, an upholsterer, and Ada Álvarez, a homemaker. Maracaibo is one of the most baseball-crazy corners of the world, the place where Luis Aparicio became an idol and where every kid dreams about being a major-leaguer. Wilson and his three brothers, William, Walter, and Willy, were no different. (There was also a daughter, Wendy.)

It was Ada who took the time to take her sons to the Santa Lucía Little League field every weekend for games and during the week for practice.

Maracaibo is the epicenter of the Little League system in Venezuela, home to the Coquivacoa Little League, the first Venezuelan league affiliated with the Williamsport, Pennsylvania-based organization. In 1955 Frank Poteraj, an American oil worker, committed to bring organized baseball for boys to the area and founded the league, encouraging the subsequent affiliation of other leagues. As of 2017, 23 of the 37 affiliated leagues in the country actively operate in the state of Zulia, and of the five Latin American teams that have won the Little League World Series title, two have been from Maracaibo.

It was in these challenging and competitive surroundings that Wilson Álvarez grew up, learned baseball, and began to shine. While in Little League between the ages of 11 and 16, he pitched 12 no-hit games, gaining notoriety as a top prospect.

In August 1984 Venezuela celebrated the induction of Luis Aparicio to the National Baseball Hall of Fame. The National Sports Institute issued a commemorative magazine.[3] Aparicio's picture was on the cover and most of the issue was dedicated to his legacy. The last page, however, showed a picture of 14-year-old lefty Wilson Álvarez, who had recently thrown a 21-strikeout no-hitter in a national youth baseball tournament.

Aparicio's induction in Cooperstown was celebrated on August 11, 1984. Exactly seven years later, and around the same time in the afternoon that Aparicio made his acceptance speech, the kid from the back cover was pitching a no-hitter, and for one of Aparicio's old teams, the White Sox.

After the hype surrounding his amateur career, the 16-year-old Álvarez was signed on September 23, 1986, by the Texas Rangers as an international free agent and was assigned to Águilas del Zulia of the Venezuelan Winter League. In his first season, he started one game, had nine appearances as a reliever, and allowed 12 runs in 9⅓ innings pitched, finishing his first professional season with a record of 0-1 and an 11.57 ERA.

A couple months after the winter season Álvarez traveled to his first spring training in the United States and was assigned for 1987 to the White Sox' team in the Gulf Coast League. He posted a record

of 2-5, 5.24 in his first 10 starts. He was promoted to the Class-A South Atlantic League, going 1-5 with a 6.47 ERA in six starts for the Gastonia Rangers. He finished his first year with a combined 3-10 won-lost record and a disastrous rate of 5.2 walks per nine innings.

"Those days were tough," he recalled. "It was tough to adapt to a new culture, new friends, language, food and all. The expectations were high back home and I felt things were not going on the right direction, although I trusted that I could pitch and do my job."

Álvarez grew to become 6-feet-1 and 175 pounds.

Álvarez was always a very shy person, very quiet. Some people confused his lethargy with laziness. During his first two years in the minors, the results were disappointing, but only in terms of stats—something not overly significant for a minor leaguer; the "stuff" was there. His fastball was lively; he was working on his command, curveball, and slider.

The level of play in the Venezuelan League was higher than rookie ball and Single-A. During those years, a mix of major leaguers and top-ranked prospects made this winter circuit one of the most competitive. It is not a secret that the aim of Caribbean baseball is winning, not on player development as in the minor leagues.

Between 1987 and 1990 Álvarez's game was getting shaped by the competitiveness of winter baseball. He became a fan favorite with Zulia, a team managed by Manny Trillo in '87, Pete Mackanin in '88 and '89, and Rubén Amaro Sr. in 1990.

In 1989 Mackanin took the team and his star young arm to another level, winning the league title and the 1989 Caribbean Series in Mazatlán, México. Led by catcher Joe Girardi and first baseman Carlos Quintana, the team also featured top-caliber major-league prospects including Phil Stephenson, Cris Colón, Pete Castellano, Eddie Zambrano, and major-league journeyman infielder Angel Salazar.

Playing with bright major-league prospects and for coaches like Trillo, Amaro, and Mackanin helped shape Álvarez's character. "Zulia was a very competitive team," he recalled. "Those guys played with hard-core passion for the game and for the franchise. Most of them were hometown locals just like me and it was a matter of pride to win. It was a completely different scenario than what we were seeing in those years in the minors. The Venezuelan League was about passion. It was tough baseball. Many, many good players were there … major leaguers, foreign players, people wanted us to win and there was a lot of pressure and fun and they had confidence in me, which I always appreciated."

The Rangers sent Álvarez to Triple-A Oklahoma City for a brief stint in 1988, but he spent most of the season with Class-A Gastonia, where he was 4-11 but recorded a 2.98 ERA. He started 1989 in the Florida State League for the Port Charlotte Rangers, where, going 7-4 with a 2.11 ERA in the first half of the season, he showed at age 19 that his three years of professional experience were really paying off. His strikeout-to-walk ratio improved and his curveball and changeup command was effective after coming back from the Winter League. He was promoted to Double A, joining the Tulsa Drillers of the Texas League the first week of July.

The big-league club was challenging Oakland in the divisional race and after several years the White Sox had a shot at the postseason. They knew their farm system was loaded with great talent from Latin America thanks to the labors of assistant GM Sandy Johnson.

Rangers general manager Tom Grieve decided to start showing off his talent pool by calling up players who could either help or become fodder for trades. In June the White Sox called up 20-year-old Dominican outfielder Sammy Sosa. And on July 24, after just three weeks in Tulsa, Álvarez was called up to start against the Toronto Blue Jays in place of the injured Hough. The 19-year-old became the first player born in the 1970s to play in the major leagues.

Álvarez's first pitch, to Junior Félix, was a strike. On his fifth pitch, Félix hit a single to center field. Tony Fernández was up next and he hit a home run to left. On a 2-and-2 count, Kelly Gruber went back-to-back deep to center field. George Bell walked. Fred McGriff got four balls in a row. Manager Bobby Valentine took Álvarez out of the game, bringing in Dominican veteran Cecilio Guante in relief.

The rookie departed after facing five batters and surrendering three hits and two walks for three runs. Having recorded no outs, he carried an earned-run average of infinity.

"Most people thought (calling up Álvarez) was because (White Sox GM Larry Himes) was at the game," Grieve told the *Chicago Tribune*. "The purpose of that callup was to win that game and he was the best one we had for that job."[4]

"They called me up to show me so they could trade me," Álvarez declared. "I was devastated. I thought it was going to be almost impossible to get back to the majors. The next day they sent me down back to Tulsa and the day after they told me I was traded to the Chicago White Sox."

Álvarez took the news badly. His confidence was hurt. The Rangers needed to add a veteran bat for the rest of the season and the White Sox were an aging team with a poor farm system. Chicago sent veteran All-Star Harold Baines and Venezuelan infielder Fred Manrique to Texas for Álvarez, skinny outfielder Sammy Sosa, and infielder Scott Fletcher.

A few days later Álvarez was pitching for the Birmingham Barons of the Double-A Southern League. He pitched just six more games the rest of the season and then returned to Zulia, where his confidence returned with the comfort of playing at home.

The 1990 season offered a fresh start for the lefty and after his solid performance in Venezuela he was sent to Triple-A Vancouver. That year he married Daihanna, who was pregnant; he started the season with a record of 7-7 and an ERA of 6.00. He was demoted to Double-A Birmingham by midseason.

On the personal side, his wife gave birth prematurely to their first child, a boy. After complications from a pulmonary infection, the baby died on August 11, just five days old.

"That was hard. We were so excited for the birth of the baby. I couldn't concentrate on baseball. Losing a child was something we couldn't understand and we were both so young and hopeful that all was going to be fine with my career, our family. But it wasn't."

Álvarez finished the season with seven more starts in Double A, going 5-1 and improving his ERA to 4.27. Birmingham pitching coach Rick Peterson helped him face his emotional struggles.

By spring training of 1991 Álvarez was coming off his best season in winter ball, having gone 3-3 in nine starts for Zulia with an ERA of 1.38, establishing himself as one of the top hurlers of the circuit at the age of 20. He looked like a veteran on the mound and was ready to prove to the White Sox that he belonged in the majors. His fastball was in the mid-90s, and he had better command of his slider and curveball. The White Sox assigned him again to Birmingham and after 23 starts, he was 10-6 with a 1.83 ERA and 165 strikeouts in 152⅓ innings. The stuff was there and the moment to return to the majors was getting close. The White Sox were reshaping their team, and Álvarez was in their plans.

To ensure that Álvarez was fit for the job, the White Sox called him up on August 11. He would face the Baltimore Orioles that Sunday afternoon at Memorial Stadium. It was his second major-league start.

"I couldn't believe I was getting back and pitching on the same day when we lost our baby," he said. "I had a million things on my mind, I was nervous because I was afraid that I was not going to be able to make an out like in 1989. I didn't know what to think or do because of the chance to pitch back on this level. When we arrived on the bus to the ballpark I realized I had left my bag with all my clothes and equipment at the lobby of the hotel. The team sent a person to get my stuff where my wife was waiting. When the bag arrived I got dressed and ran to the bullpen with the belt on my hand to prepare for the game and only was able to warm up for a half-hour."

That afternoon the baseball gods were behind Álvarez. Facing a tough Orioles lineup with hitters like Cal Ripken, Randy Milligan, Chris Hoiles, and Dwight Evans, he managed to make outs step-by-step, with his solid fastball, circle change, slider, and splitter. Everything worked just fine. The White Sox scored twice in the top of the first and Álvarez struck out the side, all three swinging, in the bottom of the inning. The White Sox scored two more runs in the second, and after walking Dwight Evans in the second, Álvarez resumed mowing Baltimore batters down. The next baserunner reached on a walk in the sixth. Álvarez walked five batters in all, and his catcher, Ron Karkovice, made an error in the seventh, but Álvarez didn't give up a hit. The White Sox defense did its part with a memorable sliding catch in the seventh inning by center fielder Lance Johnson that helped preserve the gem. Álvarez had himself a no-hitter.

"He didn't realize he was there," recalled teammate and countryman Ozzie Guillén. "I'd heard about his performance in the little leagues in Venezuela and in Chicago we knew him as the kid we got in the Harold Baines trade. I never got to actually know him until that day when we needed a pitcher and he came over for a start. I always think that he didn't believe he was pitching that day and he just let go all his talent from the mound."[5] It was a historic achievement for a Venezuelan pitcher. The whole country watched the game on television and the no-hitter became a national storyline of pride and greatness—a mark for a whole generation.

For the next seven days, every major newspaper in Venezuela sold out their advertising pages to one company or another, each congratulating Álvarez for his game. Even a month after the game, the congratulatory messages were around—billboards in streets with his picture and graffiti on walls with thank-you messages. Everybody was part of the celebration.

Álvarez was the second major-league pitcher to hurl a no-hitter in his second major-league start. He stayed with the White Sox for the rest of the season and established himself in the pitching rotation. He ended his major-league season with a record of 3-2 in nine starts, with a 3.51 ERA.

After his no-hitter, Venezuelan fans followed every game that Álvarez pitched over the next 12 years, hoping to see another no-hitter. It became part of the fan psyche.

After the season Álvarez went back to Venezuela to pitch for Zulia and was received as a hero in his hometown. For Zulia he became the first winner of the pitching Triple Crown, leading the league in wins (8-0), ERA (1.47), and strikeouts (64). He was named the Pitcher of the Year and led the Águilas to the league championship and a spot in the 1992 Caribbean Series.

After his 8-0 record and extraordinary year of 1991, Álvarez became better known as El Intocable (The Untouchable).

Álvarez started the 1992 season as a reliever for the White Sox but he struggled, in large part due to a walk rate of almost six per nine innings. He joined the rotation in mid-June and ended the season with an ERA of 5.20, starting only 9 games out of 34 appearances. That winter he returned to Venezuela; he pitched six games with a 4.08 ERA.

By this time, Major League Baseball had become more and more aware of the workload of Latin players and began limiting performances in winter ball for key players. The White Sox saw Álvarez as an important part of their plans, and fans in Venezuela had to adjust to seeing fewer major-league stars.

"I wanted to pitch every year and all season in Venezuela," said Álvarez. "The (White Sox) considered that pitching in Venezuela was a risk, but also necessary to keep in shape during the off months. For me it was a continual growing but also a matter of pride, to be able to pitch in front of my family and friends and for the team who gave me so much. Even with limitations, I tried by all means to pitch back home."

Álvarez was excited to pitch in "El Juego de la Chinita," a celebratory game honoring the Virgin of Chiquinquirá, the patron of Maracaibo. This game has been played on November 18 since 1933; Luis Aparicio made his debut in professional baseball in El Juego in 1953, playing for Gavilanes.

"It was special to pitch that day. It's a spiritual thing. It's the energy of the fans. The ballpark is packed with over 25,000 people all excited and being part of the celebration that embraced the city. Those games were special and it was an honor for me and for my family to be in the center of the mound representing what we are," Álvarez said.

In 1993 Álvarez was a full-time starter for the White Sox alongside Jack McDowell (Cy Young Award winner in 1993), Cuban-American prospect Alex Fernandez, and Jason Bere. This quartet won 67 out of the White Sox' 92 victories as they clinched the AL West. Álvarez (15-8) led the starters with a 2.95 ERA.

The White Sox advanced to the ALCS, against Álvarez's nemesis, the Toronto Blue Jays, who won the first two games of the series. Álvarez took the mound for Game Three.

"It was a huge game for me, for all people behind me, and I always remembered when I could not record an out in 1989. It was the time to be the face of my team and step up," he said.

Álvarez threw a real gem, a complete-game 6-1 win at SkyDome, allowing only seven hits and two walks. The win lifted morale and Chicago won the next game, but couldn't contain the Blue Jays' offense in the final two games. The Blue Jays won the ALCS and followed with a World Series victory over the Philadelphia Phillies.

In 1994 Álvarez was named to the American League squad for the All-Star Game. He pitched the bottom of the eighth inning, retiring the side in order. For the season he was 12-8, 3.45.

Álvarez spent 1995 and 1996 as a solid member of the White Sox rotation, starting 64 games. He improved his strikeout-to-walk rate and won 23 games (8-11 and 15-10, with ERAs of 4.32 and 4.22).

At the July trading deadline in 1997, Álvarez was 9-8 with a 3.03 ERA. The White Sox looked revamp the team with a younger roster. It was Álvarez's final year before free agency. Rather than lose Álvarez the White Sox traded him to the San Francisco Giants along with pitchers Danny Darwin and Roberto Hernández in a nine-player deal.

"I was not comfortable with the Giants," Álvarez said. It was a difficult change switching leagues. I struggled. I never felt comfortable in the dugout.

Roberto and I got into a place where we never felt totally welcome. Barry Bonds was not the nicest person in the world and he was the leader of that clubhouse. Overall it was not a good experience."

During his time with the White Sox, Álvarez was 67-50 but lost 30 games in which the team scored two or fewer runs. After his stint with the Giants he became one of the most sought-after lefties in baseball. The New York Yankees were a top contender for his services, but he chose to sign with the expansion Tampa Bay Devil Rays for five years and $35 million.

Álvarez said, "Signing with Tampa Bay was a decision my family and I took. We stayed living in the Sarasota area after signing with the White Sox and being close to home was the most important factor in place. My daughters were going to school and I was just several miles from the new ballpark. They also offered me the chance of being the number-one starter in the rotation. It was a new challenge and I took it."

Álvarez became the first starter in the Devil Rays' history and threw the first official pitch at Tropicana Field. But his season didn't go as planned. He ended up with a 6-14 record and an ERA of 4.73. Again run support was lacking, perhaps understandably on an expansion team. Álvarez felt some pressure from fans who were expecting a solid performance from the new team and their highly-prized free agent.

Tampa Bay was an inconsistent team. The Devil Rays had signed big names such as Álvarez, Roberto Hernández, sluggers Fred McGriff and José Canseco, and future Hall of Famer Wade Boggs. The rotation was not deep and the bullpen was inconsistent, and the team finished with a 63-99 record. The Devil Rays improved to 69-93 in their second season. Álvarez was 9-9 (4.22).

Álvarez came back to Venezuela and played winter ball in 1999, winning some key games for Zulia, including five games in the postseason that helped the team reach the finals. Zulia won the title, Álvarez's fourth title with the team. He pitched the opening game for the 2000 Caribbean Series, but lost the game on unearned runs.

When the 2000 season arrived, expectations were high for the Devil Rays but injuries plagued their roster. Five days before the start of the season, Álvarez was placed on the disabled list with shoulder tendinitis.[6] He had to undergo arthroscopic surgery. The 18-month rehab process cost him two seasons; he pretty much had to learn again how to throw a baseball. Returning to the field in 2002, he was able to pitch in only three games before June.

"It was the most frustrating time of my life" Álvarez said. "I didn't think it was too bad at the beginning but then the recovery was not progressing and the surgery was the option. It was hard for me because I wanted to show fans in Tampa that I could bring something for the team, but my condition was not there. I had to relearn how to pitch, how to gain velocity, how to move my arm. The process is long and painful and sometimes you feel like quitting, but my family supported me at all times to go back and compete. I gave everything I could to Tampa Bay, but the injury came in a very wrong time for me and for the team. I understand the frustration of fans and the organization."

In 2002 Álvarez was able to pitch only 75 innings in 23 games; it was more of a process to regain confidence in his pitches and to work on a change of approach. He was no longer the power lefty and was about to become a specialist. He had to rely more on location.

By the end of the season Álvarez had reinvented himself as a pitcher, with a fresh shoulder, but the Devil Rays released him. He signed with the Los Angeles Dodgers who planned to use him as a reliever. He turned in a solid performance, posting a record of 6-2 with a 2.37 ERA in 21 games, assuring himself a spot in the bullpen as a lefty specialist and occasional starter. In 2004 he pitched in 40 games, 15 of them as a starter.

After signing a new free-agent contract with the Dodgers after the 2004 season, Álvarez was set back again with shoulder injuries in 2005 and on August 1 he opted for retirement instead of another surgery.

On December 30, 2005, Álvarez pitched one last time for Zulia, taking the mound before a handful of fans in Maracaibo with the team eliminated from contention. He wore his number-47 jersey for the last time and retired the side in one inning of work. It was a sentimental afternoon in honor of a local boy who had reached the highest levels of the game.

After Álvarez's no-hitter, five more Venezuelan-born pitchers (as of 2017) pitched no-hit games: Anibal Sánchez in 2006 for the Marlins, Carlos Zambrano in 2008 for the Cubs, Johan Santana in 2012 for the Mets, Félix Hernández, a perfect game in 2012 for the Mariners, and Henderson Álvarez in 2013 for the Marlins. (The list should be six: Armando Galarraga lost his perfect game for the Tigers in 2010 when umpire Jim Joyce incorrectly called a batter safe at first base.[7]) For each one of these pitchers, Wilson Álvarez was an inspiration due both to his successful 14-year major-league career and the impact the no-hitter had in a baseball crazed-country.

Wilson Álvarez was the first Venezuelan pitcher with over 100 wins in the major leagues, compiling a record of 102-92 with a 3.96 ERA in 355 games. He made the All-Star team in 1994. In Venezuela he pitched for 12 seasons with a record of 29-18 and a career ERA of 2.49. He was elected to the Venezuelan Baseball Hall of Fame in 2011 and the Caribbean Series Hall of Fame in 2010.

After retiring Álvarez became the pitching coach for the Gulf Coast League Orioles (Rookie) near his residence in Sarasota, Florida. He and his wife, Daihanna, had three daughters, Vivianna, Vanessa, and Valentina. He has returned to the Venezuelan League as a pitching coach for Caribes de Anzoátegui and Águilas del Zulia, where he remained a fan favorite and an icon of the team, being part of four of the five titles in the history of this franchise.

Álvarez reflected, "When you retire it is like all that attention that you had, is gone, from one day to another and it never comes back. So another stage of your life begins and you discover it while still being young."[8]

In the 2016-17 season, Álvarez as pitching coach helped guide a young staff to a solid season. Zulia went to the finals for the first time since 2000 and won the title in six games over Cardenales de Lara. In the Caribbean Series the team lost to the Criollos de Caguas of Puerto Rico in the semifinals.

Álvarez's number-47 jersey remained one of the top sellers among fans, and on December 14, 2016, the team officially retired his number.

"This is the most important moment of my life because I'm here with my family, my teammates, my friends and my beloved team," Álvarez responded.[9] His parents and siblings were at the ceremony, after which he threw out the ceremonial first pitch.

Álvarez established a music label, "47Music," run by his wife, to support new artists in the Latin Pop genre.

Despite the passage of time, new generations of fans in Venezuela still hear the echoes from August 11, 1991, when a country shouted together: "Wilson threw a no-hitter!"

From Álvarez: "It was a gift from God."

SOURCES

This article draws on personal interviews and both on- and off-record conversations with Wilson Alvarez between 1995 and 2017.

The author also consulted ¡A La Carga!, the official magazine of Águilas del Zulia (Maracaibo, Venezuela: Tripleplay Sports Productions, 1997-2002), *Baseball Zone* (Maracaibo: Tripleplay Sports Productions, March 2001), *Diario Panorama* (Maracaibo) and the *Dallas Morning News*.

NOTES

1. All quotations by Wilson Álvarez are from interviews with the author unless otherwise attributed.
2. The younger ones were Amos Rusie (7,367 days), John Ward (7,411 days), and Vida Blue (7,725 days.) Alvarez was 7,810 days old.
3. *Revista IND.* (Caracas, August 1984).
4. Alan Solomon, "Alvarez: The Making of the Sox' No-Hit Kid," *Chicago Tribune*, August 13, 1991: B1.
5. Conversation with Ozzie Guillén about Álvarez's no-hitter, March 24, 2017.
6. articles.latimes.com/2000/apr/01/sports/sp-14936.
7. See Andres Galarraga and Jim Joyce, with Daniel Paisner, *Nobody's Perfect* (New York: Atlantic Monthly Press, 2011).
8. eljuegoperfecto.blogspot.com/2010_01_01_archive.html.
9. noticiaaldia.com/2016/12/wilson-alvarez-este-es-el-momento-mas-importante.

WILSON ÁLVAREZ NO-HITTER

AUGUST 11, 1991: CHICAGO WHITE SOX 7, BALTIMORE ORIOLES 0, AT MEMORIAL STADIUM, BALTIMORE

By Leonte Landino

THE WILSON ÁLVAREZ NO-hitter journey began in the Maracaibo Little Leagues. The boy from Parroquia Santa Lucía became known for constantly achieving seamless performances.

As a kid, Álvarez threw 11 no-hitters.[1] His 12th provided the foundation for a career in the major leagues.

The Texas Rangers called the 19-year-old Álvarez up in 1989 for an emergency start against the Toronto Blue Jays. Expectations were huge for the lefty, but after facing only five batters and allowing three hits and three runs, including two home runs, he was returned to the minors after the game and was eventually traded to the Chicago White Sox.

The White Sox provided a fresh start. Álvarez spent 1990 and half of 1991 in the minors. He married his wife, Daihanna, in 1990 and on August 11, their first child died five days after he was born of a pulmonary infection.

On August 11, 1991, the White Sox gave Álvarez a second chance.

"I couldn't believe I was getting back and pitching on the same day when we lost our baby, Álvarez said. "I had a million things on my mind, I was nervous because I was afraid that I was not going to be able to make an out like in 1989. I didn't know what to think or do because of the chance to pitch back on this level. When we arrived on the bus to the ballpark I realized I had left my bag with all my clothes and equipment at the lobby of the hotel. The team sent a person to get my stuff where my wife was waiting. When the bag arrived I got dressed and ran to the bullpen with the belt in my hand to prepare for the game and only was able to warm up for half an hour."[2]

The White Sox players were getting dressed in the clubhouse. Ozzie Guillén, a fellow Venezuelan, remembers that veteran pitcher Charlie Hough said: "Something special is going to happen at this ballpark today."[3]

A crowd of more than 40,000 filled Baltimore's Memorial Stadium that Sunday. The Orioles were in sixth place but they had a collection of power hitters in their lineup, led by Cal Ripken.

Back home in Venezuela, Venevisión, the country's largest national television network, planned to broadcast the game on its traditional *Game of the Week* so the whole country could follow White Sox shortstop Guillén, a national idol. But the night before, Álvarez's sudden callup spread across the country by word of mouth. By 1:00 P.M., Venezuela had stopped to watch Álvarez.

White Sox bats began the game doing their part. Robin Ventura singled and Frank Thomas hit a home run off Orioles starter Dave Johnson. Álvarez came to the mound with a 2-0 lead.

The first pitch to Orioles center fielder Mike Deveraux was a strike. Five pitches later, Álvarez had his first major-league out, a strikeout. Second baseman Juan Bell struck out on five pitches. And it took five more to strike out Cal Ripken. Three up, three down.

Álvarez finally had the chance to breathe at the major-league level. "After that first inning I got trust in myself. I knew I belonged at that level. I said to myself that this was the level where I wanted to be and there was no turning back."

The second inning started with a walk to Dwight Evans but Álvarez quickly got out of trouble when Randy Milligan grounded into a double play. David Seguí grounded out to end the second. In the third

Chris Hoiles and Leo Gomez were retired by consecutive fly balls and Bob Melvin struck out swinging. The fourth and fifth innings saw six straight outs by popups and lineouts.

In the Chicago second, Ozzie Guillén led off with a double and the White Sox scored two more runs for a 4-0 lead. They scored three more in the top of the sixth.

In the bottom of the sixth with one out, Álvarez walked Leo Gomez but retired Melvin and Deveraux on a pop fly and strikeout.

In the dugout, nobody was talking to Álvarez. He thought it was because he was the new guy in the clubhouse. He was lonely in the dugout. His mind was not on the game, but on the loss of his child. He was not savoring the moment but only pitching as if he were a robot in spikes. He was in a mechanical mode, amazed about where he was, after all he had to go through, after all the years learning the game and working his way from Maracaibo, which seemed to be a far and distant land.

In Venezuela everybody remembers that afternoon. People called one another to confirm that everyone was watching the game, in case anybody was missing it or had stepped out. The whisper was universal … "Wilson is pitching a no-hitter."

In the seventh inning with one out, Cal Ripken hit a slow grounder that sank almost in front of the plate. Catcher Ron Karkovice picked up the ball, but threw wild to first; Ripken took second on the error. Evans was out on a pop fly, but Milligan walked. With two runners on base David Seguí popped to right field for the third out.

In the eighth inning Hoiles, leading off, hit a ball between right field and center that looked unreachable, but center fielder Lance Johnson appeared out of nowhere and made a magnificent sliding catch that saved the gem. When Johnson lifted his glove, Wilson saw the scoreboard for the first time during the afternoon.

"I saw the board and I said to myself, 'Wow … they don't have any hits.' I didn't realize I was pitching this good or this far in the game. That's when my heart started pumping and I got nervous."[4]

He was able to get two more outs in the eighth inning. Johnson caught the third out and pointed out the scoreboard with zero hits after the play.

The Orioles were losing, 7-0, but when Álvarez came out in the ninth the 40,000 fans at Memorial Stadium were cheering for the rookie. It was a surreal afternoon. The vibe was felt back in Venezuela. Álvarez was doing what no Venezuelan had ever done.

Deveraux flied out for the first out and Juan Bell fanned. With two outs, Cal Ripken was up, the most feared hitter on the team. Karkovice called semi-intentional walks for him and veteran Dwight Evans, so Álvarez could face Randy Milligan. Álvarez was visibly nervous at this point. To those watching, Álvarez looked different than he had the first six innings. He was sweating, kind of lost, looking at the sky at all times. Ozzie Guillén approached the mound and said, "Kid, don't think about anything that is happening here, just keep pitching the way you have been pitching and don't worry about anything."[5]

Pitching to Milligan, Álvarez threw a strike. Then Milligan fouled one off, then fouled off another, then took a ball. The count was 1-and-2. Álvarez threw a curveball in the dirt and Milligan swung and missed. It was done.

"No-Hit-No-Run!" screamed Gonzalo López Silvero, the Venevisión announcer. He kept screaming it, again and again.

Álvarez was astonished, always looking at the sky. "You took my son and gave me this instead," he said.[6] Meanwhile Karkovice was hugging him and the White Sox were jumping around him as if they had just won the World Series.

Two years earlier, Álvarez was unable to get anybody out. This day he got everybody. In the meantime, he lost a child and became one of the idols of his country. This achievement took him to another level. He was the first one. The best in Venezuelan baseball history.

Álvarez followed Bobo Holloman as the second in history to get a no-hitter in his first or second major-league start.[7] From then, in every one of his starts he had that feeling that he could do it again. He became better known as "El Intocable" (The Untouchable).

Wilson Álvarez's no-hitter opened the doors of big-league baseball for him. He played six more years with the White Sox, becoming an ace of the rotation, helping the White Sox in the 1993 postseason and winning Game Three of the ALCS against his nemesis, the Blue Jays. In 1997 was traded to the San Francisco Giants and in 1998 signed as a free agent with the Tampa Bay Devil Rays, becoming the first starter for the new franchise. He finished his career with the Los Angeles Dodgers in 2005, becoming the first Venezuelan pitcher with over 100 wins in the majors.[8]

NOTES

1. *Revista IND.* (Caracas, Venezuela), August 1984.
2. All quotations by Wilson Álvarez are from interviews with the author unless otherwise attributed.
3. Personal conversation with Ozzie Guillén about Álvarez's no-hitter, March 2017.
4. Baseball Zone—Tripleplay Sports Productions. Maracaibo, Venezuela, March 2001.
5. Conversation with Ozzie Guillén.
6. *A La Carga!*—Oficial Magazine of Aguilas del Zulia (Maracaibo: Tripleplay Sports Productions), 1997-2002.
7. "Rookie No-Hitters," MLB.com, mlb.mlb.com/mlb/history/rare_feats/index.jsp?feature=rookie_no_hitter.
8. "Wilson Álvarez," baseball-reference.com/players/a/alvarwi01.shtml.

MATT YOUNG

By Alan Raylesberg

MATT YOUNG'S PLACE IN baseball history is secure. On April 12, 1992, then 33-year-old Matt Young became only the third pitcher to throw a complete-game no-hitter and lose the game. Pitching in the first game of a doubleheader for the visiting Boston Red Sox against the Indians in Cleveland, Young lost 2-1. Since his complete game was only eight innings long, Young's gem is not recognized as an official no-hitter. Official or not, Young, Andy Hawkins, and Ken Johnson (who had an "official" nine-inning complete game) remain, as of the end of 2016, the only major-league pitchers to lose a complete game in which they did not allow a hit.

Matthew John Young was born on August 9, 1958, in Pasadena, California, one of eight children of William and Mary Ellen Young. William Young was a building contractor and disabled veteran who died in 2005.[1] As a youngster, Matt played baseball in the Arcadia/Sierra Madre Little Leagues, the same leagues that produced major-league pitchers Tim and Todd Worrell.[2] He attended St. Francis High School in La Canada Flintridge, a city in Los Angeles County. There Matt starred as a left-handed pitcher. St. Francis is a Catholic college-preparatory school for boys, and more than 99 of its graduates go on to higher education.[3] Young is one of a number of notable alumni of St. Francis, including Jason Hirsh (Colorado Rockies), Mark Loretta (Los Angeles Dodgers), and Gregg Zaun (Baltimore Orioles).[4] After graduating from St. Francis in 1976, Young attended Pasadena City College, Jackie Robinson's alma mater, in 1977 and 1978. Besides Robinson, other alumni who made it to professional baseball include Irv Noren (Yankees), Alan Wiggins (Padres), and Brandon Kintzler (Brewers).[5] Young was an All-Metropolitan Conference First Team selection as a pitcher and was inducted into the college's Hall of Fame in 2015.[6]

While attending Pasadena City College, Young was selected in the second round of the January 1978 amateur draft by the Boston Red Sox. Instead of signing with the Red Sox, Young accepted a scholarship to the University of California, Los Angeles and pitched for the Bruins in 1979 and 1980.[7] UCLA has a long tradition of sending players to the major leagues, including Jackie Robinson.[8] Young's roommate at UCLA was Tim Leary, another Southern California native who would go on to pitch 13 years in the major leagues.[9] As of the end of 2016, UCLA had sent approximately 90 players to the majors.[10] Writing for CBSSports.com in 2013, Danny Knobler chose Young as one of the top 10 major-league players from UCLA, noting that he was then "the only UCLA pitcher ever to make an All-Star team."[11]

In the June 1980 amateur draft, Young was selected again, by the Seattle Mariners in the second round. A predraft scouting report on Young rated him a 50 (on the 20-80 scale) in "overall future potential," noting that he had a "plus fast ball," "fields his position well," and "looks good on mound as far as delivery, etc."[12] Young's weaknesses, according to the scouting report, was that his "curve has not improved in 2 years at UCLA, tends to lose close games—question his courage."[13] Young spent three years in the Seattle farm system, advancing each year from Class A to Double A to Triple A before debuting with the Mariners at the age of 24 on April 6, 1983.

Young pitched 10 years in the majors, for the Mariners, Dodgers, Athletics, Red Sox, and Indians. He was a strapping figure on the mound, at 6-feet-3, 205 pounds, and a hard thrower. He pitched in 333 games, including 163 starts, with a record of 55-95 and a 4.40 ERA. He had 20 complete games in his career, 5 shutouts, and 25 saves.

In his debut season of 1983, Young pitched 203 innings for the Mariners, going 11-15 with a 3.27 ERA, which ranked him in the top 10 for ERA in the American League. He made the All-Star team and pitched a scoreless eighth inning in the midsummer classic, with future Hall of Famer Johnny Bench being one of the three batters he retired. On June 3 Young pitched a two-hit shutout against the Yankees.[14]

An arthritic condition surfaced in 1984, affecting Young's lower back and knees[15] and limiting him to 22 appearances, all starts, for the Mariners, with a record of 6-8 and a 5.72 ERA. Young was healthy in 1985 and started 35 games for the Mariners (12-19, 4.91). Scouting Young as a possible acquisition for the Minnesota Twins, a Twins scout praised Young's abilities: "[h]e has good movement and good velocity on his fastball … throws a good slider and a soft curve … throws strikes and challenges a hitter."[16] Young was converted to a reliever in 1986, appearing in 65 games for Seattle while starting five. He had 13 saves to go with an 8-6 record and a 3.82 ERA.

After the 1986 season Young was traded to the Los Angeles Dodgers. He was "a hot commodity" at the Winter Meetings and the Dodgers got him "cheaply," according to the *Los Angeles Times*, for "unproven" starter Dennis Powell and second-base prospect Mike Watters.[17] Ross Newhan, writing in the *Los Angeles Times* in December 1986, mentioned Young in the same breath as Sandy Koufax. Newhan noted that Koufax had to retire because of arthritic pain in his left elbow and that the recently acquired Young required medication to control arthritis that became evident in 1984.[18] Young, whose father had rheumatoid arthritis, said at the time that "[t]oo much was made about [the arthritis] in the first place. … I haven't had a problem for 2½ years."[19]

The Dodgers did their homework before acquiring Young. Advance scout Phil Regan, who was Young's pitching coach in Seattle, recommended him for relief work, noting that "[i]n the last two years, Matt never refused the ball as either a starter or reliever."[20] Another Dodgers scout, Mel Didier, called Young "one of the hardest throwers in the American League [who] can pitch three days in a row with outstanding stuff."[21] Manager Tom Lasorda expected Young to fill the Dodgers' need for a left-handed reliever in the bullpen, commenting: "I'm impressed. I like the way he throws."[22]

Young signed a one-year contract with the Dodgers for $350,000, avoiding salary arbitration.[23] In what turned out to be his only season with the Dodgers, he pitched in 47 games, all in relief, finishing 31 of them, while going 5-8 with a 4.47 ERA. After the season Young was traded to the Oakland A's as part of a three-team trade that sent Dodgers pitcher Bob Welch to Oakland and brought the Dodgers Alfredo Griffin and Jay Howell from Oakland and Jesse Orosco from the Mets.[24]

After being traded, Young had to undergo Tommy John surgery and missed the entire 1988 season. Returning for the 1989 season after a short stint in the minors, Young pitched in 26 games (four starts) as a member of the 1989 World Series-winner A's. He made one relief appearance in the American League Championship Series but did not pitch in the World Series, in which the A's swept the San Francisco Giants.

In 1990 Young returned to the Mariners as a free agent, signing a one-year contract for $587,000, "cheap" even at the prices of that era.[25] Young signed with Seattle in part because of the opportunity to once again be a starting pitcher. And, indeed he got that chance in Seattle and took maximum advantage of it. Young posted a 3.51 ERA while going 8-18 with 33 starts and a team-best seven complete games. Mariners pitching coach Mike Paul said, "[t]he improvement in Matt Young from April until now has been phenomenal in our eyes. He's just gotten better as the season's gone along."[26] His 8-18 record was not indicative of how well Young, then 32 years old, pitched for a Mariners team that did not score many runs for him.

The 1990 season was a "bounceback" season for Young. Mike Paul said, "When he started the year, there was always the question of, 'Do I still have it? Can I get people out? Well, he's held up very well with the run support he's been given this year."[27] Young said, "I may not be a better pitcher than I was [back in 1983 when he debuted with the Mariners] but I think I'm a smarter pitcher. I realize my limitations, my capabilities. I know now that I can't strike anybody out until I get two strikes on them."[28] Young threw harder after his surgery than he did before. "My velocity has picked up by two or three mph on an average on my fastball," he said. "[b]efore my surgery, I threw anywhere from 87 to 89. Now [in 1990] I'm throwing 89 to 92."[29] In 1990 Young made the baseball record books when he struck out four batters in an inning (including future Hall of Famer Wade Boggs) on September 9 against the Red Sox. As of the end of 2016, he was one of only 78 pitchers to accomplish the feat and one of 20 left-handers.

Hitting free agency once again after the 1990 season, Young signed with the Red Sox for three years and $6.4 million. His annual salary of $2,266,667 far exceeded his previous high salary of $587,000 the year before.[30] *The Sporting News* reported that the signing was part of the "Red Sox spending binge" as the defending AL East Champions (having lost to Oakland in the 1989 ALCS) signed four free agents (Jack Clark, Danny Darwin, Tom Brunansky, and Young) for a total of $31.45 million.[31] *The Sporting News* also highlighted Young's salary in an article that compared free-agent salaries to those of MLB umpires, commenting on the large sum paid to Young, who had only an 8-18 record the year before.[32]

In his first season for the Red Sox, 1991, Young started 16 games, relieved in three, and went 3-7 with a 5.18 ERA. He spent time on the disabled list with a slightly torn rotator cuff.[33] His disappointing season earned him the nicknames "Sigh Young" and "Door Matt."[34] As the 1991 season came to a close, rumors abounded that the Red Sox would "dump" Young.[35] *The Sporting News* commented that the signing of Young and Darwin was a "big blunder,"[36] referring to them (along with Clark) as the "Fenway Flops."[37] While free-agent salaries in 1991 were significantly lower than those in later years, "escalating salaries" and the "huge" amounts paid to free agents were still an issue.[38] Young's contract was mentioned in articles noting that free-agent salaries had reached "obscene levels,"[39] were "spiraling out of control,"[40] and were a sign of "insanity."[41]

The Red Sox decided to keep Young in 1992. The decision looked great when Young, in his first start of the year, pitched his no-hitter on April 12, 1992. Facing the Cleveland Indians in the first game of a doubleheader, he gave up single runs in the first and third innings as he struggled with his control. Those two runs were the difference in a 2-1 defeat as Young walked seven and struck out six.[42] The game put Young in the record book not only for the no hitter but also because the doubleheader set a record that still stood as of 2016, for the fewest hits allowed by one team in a doubleheader—two—thanks to Roger Clemens pitching a two-hit shutout in the second game.

The no-hitter was the highlight of Young's 1992 season. He started eight times, relieved 20 times and was 0-4 with a 4.58 ERA. He had a short stint on the disabled list in July.[43] In that season Young, under the tutelage of new Red Sox manager Butch Hobson, worked on and improved his longtime difficulty in throwing to the bases.[44] Like Steve Sax and Chuck Knoblauch in the 1980s and '90s and Jon Lester and

Dellin Betances later on, Young had the "yips" when it came to making throws.[45] Young's "mental block" was so bad that during the entire 1991 season he did not attempt a single pickoff throw to first base.[46] Young recognized the problem with self-effacing humor, stating, "I'm a mental case" and attributing his throwing problems to self-doubt that began when he made a critical throwing error during a 1984 game, in his second year in the majors. Michael Madden, writing in the Boston Globe in 1992, remarked that 'just a simple toss to first base would have been a victory [for Young] but that when Young (having worked hard on his fielding) picked off a runner in his second start of the season, it "truly was a marvel."[47]

Despite the improvement in his throwing, Young's disappointing 1992 season led to his being released by the Red Sox before the start of the 1993 season. After signing with Boston for three years for $6.35 million, Young left after only two seasons and a total of only three wins.[48] After his release, Young signed with the Cleveland Indians, where he ended his major-league career in 1993 with a 1-6 won-lost record in 22 appearances (eight starts). His last big-league appearance was on August 6, 1993, and he was released by the Indians on August 9.[49] Toronto signed him three days later, assigning him to Triple-A Syracuse before releasing him in September.

In 1993 The Sporting News disclosed that Young "had a Cy Young of his very own." The newspaper was not referring to the award but to the fact that Matt Young had a pet Dalmatian named Cy. He and his pet, along with other major leaguers and their pets, were featured in a 20-card set of baseball cards from Milk-Bone, the dog-biscuit company.[50]

Off the field, Young had a role in a piece of baseball labor history. After player strikes in 1981 and 1985, the collective-bargaining agreement expired in 1989. In 1990 Young was named to an 18-player negotiating committee to work with Players Association executive director Donald Fehr in negotiations with Major League Baseball.[51] That year the owners locked out the players during spring training before the owners and the union reached a new agreement in March. After serving on the negotiating committee, Young became the player representative for the Red Sox during the 1992 season.[52]

After his release by the Blue Jays, Young returned home to Pasadena. He coached Connie Mack youth baseball[53] and pursued business interests, including real-estate investments with a friend, former Mariners minor-league pitcher Tracy Harris.[54] Young's two children had athletic careers of their own. His son, Clayton (born in 1985), played two years of varsity baseball at the same high school his father attended, where he was selected as the team's most improved player.[55] A tall (6-feet-5) left-handed pitcher like his father, Clayton then played baseball at Glendale Community College and San Diego State. He was drafted in the 37th round in 2003 by the Kansas City Royals, and again in 2005 by the New York Yankees in the 38th round. Young's daughter, Brynne (born in 1982), played volleyball for four years at the University of San Diego.[56] Matt's younger brother, Bill, was also an athlete, having pitched for St. Francis High School before becoming a major-league scout.[57]

While he never achieved the success of his namesake, Cy Young, Matt Young pitched in 333 games over 10 years in the major leagues. His performance in one of those games—on April 12, 1992—ensures that he will be long remembered by baseball fans everywhere.

SOURCES

The author gratefully acknowledges the assistance of Frank Harris, the reference services librarian at the County of Los Angeles Public Library, for providing background information regarding Matt Young and his family.

NOTES

1. Obituary of William J. Young, *Pasadena Star-News*, November 16, 2005; Sierra Madre Area City Directory (1959) and (1968) listings for William J. Young; Mike Downey, "Dodgers Call Gets This Lefty Off the Hook," *Los Angeles Times*, December 14, 1986.

2. "Dodger Thoughts: Spring Training Opening Chat and Earliest Dodger Stadium Memory," Comment No. 53, March 11, 2005, dodgerthoughts.baseball.toaster.com/archives/156845.html.

3. St. Francis High School website, sfhs.com

4. The Baseball Cube, thebaseballcube.com/hs/profile.asp?HS=2123.

NO-HITTERS

5 Baseball-Reference.com, baseball-reference.com/schools/index.cgi?key_school=f372b08a.

6 "PCC 2015-16 Sports Hall of Fame Selections Announced," pasadena.edu/news-and-events/news/2015-2016-sports-hall-of-fame-selections.php.

7 Ibid.

8 University of California, Los Angeles Baseball Players Who Made It to the Major Leagues, Baseball Almanac, baseball-almanac.com/college/university_of_california_la_baseball_players.shtml.

9 "AL Report," *The Sporting News*, June 20, 1983.

10 Baseball Reference.com, baseball-reference.com/schools/index.cgi?key_school=47d2ae18.

11 Danny Knobler, "On the List of UCLA's Best, Jackie Robinson Stands Out," *CBSSports.com*, June 26, 2013, cbssports.com/mlb/writer/danny-knobler/22537300/on-the-list-of-uclas-best-jackie-robinson-stands-out. Young is also the answer to a great trivia question: Who are the only two major leaguers to play at both Pasadena City College and UCLA? Answer: Jackie Robinson and Matt Young. In 2015 Gerrit Cole became the second UCLA pitcher to make an All-Star team.

12 Scouting Report by Joe Stephenson available at Diamond Mines, scouts.baseballhall.org/report?reportid=01601&playerid=youngma01

13 Ibid.

14 *The Sporting News*, June 20, 1983.

15 Ross Newhan, "New Dodger Matt Young Says His Arthritic Condition Is Under Control," *Los Angeles Times*, December 14, 1986.

16 Scouting Report by Lee Irwin available at Diamond Mines, scouts.baseballhall.org/report?reportid=06538&playerid=youngma01.

17 Newhan.

18 Ibid.

19 Ibid.

20 Ibid.

21 Ibid.

22 "N.L. West," *The Sporting News*, April 1, 1987.

23 "Sports People: Comings and Goings," *New York Times*, February 7, 1987.

24 The trade also included pitcher Jack Savage going from the Dodgers to the Mets and the A's sending pitchers Kevin Tapani and Wally Whitehurst to the Mets. See Baseball-Reference.com.

25 Jim Cour, "Mariners Hail Matt Young Despite Record," *Los Angeles Times*, September 13, 1990.

26 Ibid.

27 Ibid.

28 Ibid.

29 Ibid.

30 Murray Chass, "Record Opening Day Salaries: Not Peanuts or Cracker Jack," *New York Times*, April 10, 1991.

31 "A.L. East," *The Sporting News*, February 18, 1991; "Game Report," *The Sporting News*, July 22, 1991.

32 "Sports Voices: Shame on Baseball: Umpires Deserve Better," *The Sporting News*, April 15, 1991.

33 "A.L. East," *The Sporting News*, August 5, 1991.

34 Dan Shaughnessy, "Leave It to Red Sox, and Young, to Lose a No-Hitter," *Boston Globe*, April 13, 1992.

35 "A.L. East," *The Sporting News*, September 30, 1991.

36 "A.L. Report," *The Sporting News*, May 6, 1991.

37 "A.L. Report," *The Sporting News*, July 8, 1991.

38 "Sports Voices: TSN Poll Line," *The Sporting News*, December 9, 1991.

39 "A.L. Report," *The Sporting News*, October 14, 1991.

40 "Sports Voices: TSN Poll Line," *The Sporting News*, December 9, 1991.

41 Bob Verdi, "Sports Voices: In This Age of Skyrocketing Salaries, Survival Is Players' Ultimate Mission," *The Sporting News*, March 23, 1992.

42 See Alan Raylesberg, "April 12, 1992: Cleveland Indians 2, Boston Red Sox 1 at Fenway Park, First Game of a Doubleheader," SABR GamesProject.

43 "Transactions," *New York Times*, July 1, 1992.

44 Michael Madden, "Young Is Still Being Thrown Off," *Boston Globe*, March 19, 1992; Dan Shaughnessy, "Rolling Out the Unwelcome Matt. After Two Star-crossed Seasons, Red Sox Finally Release Young," *Boston Globe*, March 31, 1993.

45 Nick Cafardo, "Yapping About Lester's Yips Overblown," *Boston Globe*, April 12, 2015 (stating that Matt Young had to roll balls to first base).

46 Madden.

47 Ibid.

48 Shaughnessy, "Rolling Out the Unwelcome Matt" (discussing Young's disappointing Red Sox career and stating that "[t]he signing of Matt Young probably was the worst free agent signing in baseball history").

49 "Transactions," *New York Times*, August 8, 1993.

50 "Openers: Pet Names," *The Sporting News*, May 31, 1993.

51 "A.L. Report," *The Sporting News*, January 1, 1990.

52 "A.L. East," *The Sporting News*, March 22, 1993.

53 "St. Francis Wins Third Straight," *Glendale* (California) *News-Press*, June 8, 2001.

NO-HITTERS

54 Dan Raley, "Where Are They Now? Pitcher Tracy Harris, Former M's Farm Hand," Seattlepi.com, May 9, 2006, seattlepi.com/sports/baseball/article/Where-Are-They-Now-Pitcher-Tracy-Harris.

55 San Diego State Official Athletic Site, Biography of Clayton Young, goaztecs.com/sports/m-basebl/mtt/young_clayton00.html.

56 Ibid.; University of San Diego Women's Volleyball, Biography of Brynne Young, usdtoreros.com/sports/w-volley/mtt/young_brynne00.html.

57 "High School Baseball/Southern Section Previews: San Fernando League," *Los Angeles Times*, March 7, 1992.

APRIL 12, 1992: CLEVELAND INDIANS 2, BOSTON RED SOX 1 AT MUNICIPAL STADIUM

By Alan Raylesberg

SUNDAY, APRIL 12, 1992, WAS a windy, 41-degree day in Cleveland as the Boston Red Sox faced the Indians in a doubleheader at the old Cleveland (Municipal) Stadium, often referred to as "The Mistake by the Lake." The more than 20,000 in attendance that day were about to witness something that had occurred only twice before—a complete-game no-hitter in a losing effort. Matt Young, who the following season would be pitching for the Indians, was the losing pitcher for Boston that day. Young did not allow a hit and struck out six in his eight innings. He was wild, however, walking seven batters, two of whom scored to give Cleveland a 2-1 triumph.

Twenty-eight years earlier, on April 23, 1964, Ken Johnson of the Houston Colt .45s pitched a nine-inning complete-game no-hitter at home against Cincinnati but lost 1-0. On July 1, 1990, Andy Hawkins of the visiting New York Yankees held the Chicago White Sox hitless over eight innings but lost 4-0 when four unearned runs scored on two outfield errors. Before the 1992 season, apparently motivated by the Hawkins feat, the major leagues' committee for statistical accuracy, chaired by then-Commissioner Fay Vincent, changed the rules to, among other things, not recognize complete games of less than nine innings as no-hitters. Fifty no-hitters were demoted to "notable achievements" in the official record book. Young's game, coming after the committee's ruling, never achieved no-hit status.

The April 12 doubleheader was significant for another reason. Young's gem was the first game. In the second game, Roger Clemens pitched a two-hit shutout as Boston won 3-0. The combined total of two hits allowed by Red Sox pitchers set a record that still stood as of 2016 for the fewest hits allowed by a team in a doubleheader.

The 1992 Boston Red Sox were hoping to win the World Series for the first time since 1918. In 1990, under manager Joe Morgan, they had won the AL East, only to lose in the ALCS. In 1991 the Red Sox paid over $31 million to sign four free agents, including Young. Young had a disappointing 1991 campaign as the Red Sox finished second. As the 1992 season began, the Red Sox had a new manager, Butch Hobson, and, as Young made his first start of the season on April 12, optimism was in the air.

Boston came into the game 1-2, having lost two to the Yankees in their season-opening series before beating Cleveland, 7-5, on Saturday, in a 19-inning marathon. Young was a big, hard-throwing left-hander (6-foot-3, 205 pounds) who often struggled with his control. Lack of control got him into trouble in the bottom of the first, when he walked the Indians' speedy leadoff hitter, Kenny Lofton. Lofton stole second and third and then scored on Carlos Baerga's one out grounder to give Cleveland a 1-0 lead.

Young's lack of control got him into trouble again in the third, as he walked the first two batters. After a force out and a steal of second, another groundball by Baerga made it 2-0. Boston got one run back in the fourth on a pop-fly single by Luis Rivera off the Indians starter, Charles Nagy. That was the last run scored in the game.

While Young held the Indians hitless the rest of the way, it was not without difficulty. In the fifth Lofton walked for the third time and again stole second and third before Young got the final out. Cleveland's Mark Whiten drew yet another walk in the sixth but was caught stealing (1-3-6-3). In the seventh the Indians almost got a hit when third baseman Wade Boggs robbed Brook Jacoby with a diving stop of a sharp grounder. The next two batters walked before Young got out of the inning.

The Red Sox had their chances but could not tie it, loading the bases in the sixth and having the first two batters reach base in the ninth before Indians reliever Derek Lilliquist snuffed out the rally. Young had held the Indians hitless but the Red Sox had lost. Boston left 11 men on base and that, along with the two runners who walked and scored for Cleveland, was the story of the game.

Boston's rookie catcher John Flaherty was playing his first major-league game and got a hit in his first at-bat. Flaherty went on to play in the major leagues for 14 seasons. After Young's game Flaherty displayed the sense of humor that would serve him well as a Yankees broadcaster after his playing career, remarking "[J]ust another day, caught a no-hitter, got my first major-league hit."[1]

As the *Boston Globe* reported, Young "had the Indians fooled with a tricky change up" but was done in by the walks and steals.[2] The rap on Young over the years was that "he'll usually beat himself."[3] The *Globe's* Dan Shaughnessy wrote, "[o]nce again, Young pitched well enough to lose."[4] Said Young, "I look at seven walks and I don't feel I pitched that well."[5]

Young's game, even though it was considered not to be a no-hitter according to the recently revised baseball rules, was the first time a Red Sox pitcher had held an opponent hitless since September 16, 1965, when Dave Morehead pitched a 2-0 no-hitter against the Indians at Fenway Park. Commenting on having pitched a no-hitter that wasn't, Young said, "Sure … they didn't get any hits. The game's over. People can make rules all they want. It doesn't matter to me."[6] Young told the *Globe* that "pitching a no-hitter that is not recognized is like being in purgatory."[7] And when asked what he would say "if he called home," Young—who clearly had a good sense of humor about the whole thing—replied, "I'd say I've got some good news and some bad news."[8] Young did not bother to keep the game ball. "I don't think it's really hit me yet," he said after the game.

"I'm kind of upset about losing the game. A loss is a loss."[9]

Roger Clemens was surprised to hear that it was not a no-hitter.[10] "I didn't know that (until later). I congratulated him and everything," Clemens said.[11] Young's sense of humor was intact here as well. After Clemens' 3-0 win in the second game, he commented, "Some guys get all the runs."[12]

Writing in the *New York Times*, Murray Chass noted that Young was philosophical about his no-hitter not being recognized as such.[13] Chass wrote, "Young shrugged off the bureaucratic trashing of his feat by saying a no-hitter is supposed to be when the pitcher strikes out the last batter, the catcher runs to the mound and everyone jumps around."[14] None of that happened, of course, on April 12, 1992.

Chass noted, "Until 1990, no pitcher had ever experienced the kind of game Young pitched," that is until Andy Hawkins did it in July of that year.[15] "Now two pitchers have been snubbed by the Committee for Statistical Accuracy, which sounds like something left over from the old Soviet Union."[16] Chass's advice to Young: "Matt Young shouldn't let anyone tell him that he didn't pitch a no-hitter. …"[17]

The day after the no-hitter that wasn't was Opening Day at Fenway Park. Young was warmly received by the crowd.[18] Fay Vincent was in attendance and heard shouts of "It's a no-hitter, Fay!"[19] Vincent defended the rule change, stating, "Look, it wasn't just I. It was a committee that looked at it very carefully. I think we're correct. A no-hitter has to be, in effect, a victory. It's got to go nine innings. … It's not that Matt Young and Andy Hawkins didn't do something significant. … Eight innings is not a complete game if you're pitching a no-hitter, because you're losing."[20]

Young said he didn't have a chance to talk to Vincent about the no-hitter rule, but still felt he pitched one.[21] Vincent was unmoved. "Matt Young said it very well. In a no-hitter, the catcher runs out, jumps in your arms to celebrate a victory. Matt and I agree. … It's the asterisk no-hitter—a distinguished achievement in a game in which there was no hit."[22]

The *Globe's* Shaughnessy remarked that "years from now it will probably be forgotten that Roger Clemens rescued the Sox with a two-hit shutout in Game 2."[23] In fact, as of the end of 2016 — nearly 25 years after that doubleheader — both games are remembered for the records (or non-records) that were set. As Shaughnessy wrote: "And so April 12, 1992, goes down in Red Sox history. It was the day Matt Young threw a no-hitter. Not."[24]

SOURCES

Retrosheet.org and Baseball Reference.com were the source of play-by-play information.

NOTES

1. Mike Shalin, "First Day, Big Day, Sox' Flaherty Makes Historic Debut," *Boston Herald,* April 13, 1992.
2. Dan Shaughnessy, "Leave It to Red Sox, And Young, to Lose a No-Hitter," *Boston Globe*, April 13, 1992.
3. Ibid.
4. Ibid.
5. Ibid.
6. Ibid.
7. Ibid. See also "Rules Deprive Matt Young of a No-Hitter: Baseball: Red Sox Pitcher Doesn't Go the Required Nine Innings in 2-1 Loss to Indians. In Second Game, Cleveland Gets Two Hits and Loses," *Los Angeles Times*, April 13, 1992.
8. Shaughnessy.
9. Ibid.
10. Mike Shalin, "Roger's Few Runs Look Big to Young," *Boston Herald,* April 13, 1992.
11. Ibid.
12. Ibid.
13. Murray Chass, "What Is a No-Hitter? Matt Young Knows," *New York Times*, April 17, 1992.
14. Ibid.
15. Ibid.
16. Ibid.
17. Ibid.
18. Nick Cafardo," Red Sox Notebook: Fenway Opener/Red Sox-Orioles," *Boston Globe*, April 14, 1992. Young received the longest ovation during introductions.
19. Ibid.
20. Ibid.
21. Ibid.
22. Ibid.
23. Shaughnessy.
24. Ibid.

KENNY ROGERS

By Thomas E. Schott

IT WAS STRAWBERRY FIELDS forever where Kenny Rogers grew up, on a 15-acre strawberry farm in Dover, Florida, in the heart of Hillsborough County, just a bit west of Plant City, home of the annual state Strawberry Festival. Plant City was also where the Cincinnati Reds held spring training for many years, so Rogers grew up in baseball country, too, where kids play baseball year-round and where half a dozen or so major-league teams train in the spring in and around the Tampa area.

Kenneth Scott Rogers was born on November 10, 1964, in Savannah, Georgia, to Edgar "Earl" Rogers, a career US Air Force member, and his wife, Carol. When Earl retired to his Florida strawberry patch, he fully expected his son to follow in his footsteps as a farmer, and that certainly appeared the youngster's path. Until his senior year at Plant City High School, Kenny had only dabbled in some Little League baseball, but that year he played right field for the school team, and that was when he caught the attention of cigar-chomping Texas Rangers scout Joe Marchese. At about 5-feet-9 and 140 pounds, the skinny 17-year-old kid would have been barely noticeable but for his arm. Marchese watched him throw two balls over third and two over the catcher's head from right field, and when he approached him later, he told Rogers, "You're going to be a pitcher. That's what you're going to be." Rogers was skeptical, but receptive to the idea.[1]

So on Marchese's advice, the Rangers drafted the young lefty in the 39th round in 1982, and Rogers began his tortuous seven-year trek to the big leagues. By his own admission, "[I]t was hard"—and discouraging. "[T]wice I told them to release me so I could go and get a real life."[2]

Indeed, Rogers claimed the only reason Sarasota manager Tom Grieve in the Gulf States Rookie League didn't release him during his first two years was because "I brought the coaches strawberries from my father's farm."[3] Early on, "the book on him everywhere was 'dumb and durable,'" said Tom House, who along with Dave Egan, another former southpaw pitcher, helped tutor Rogers to respectability. On his good days, the youngster could be optimistic. In 1985 he told his girlfriend, Rebecca Lynn Lewis, whom he married four years later, that he expected to play three seasons in the majors. But his record in the minors hardly indicated a big-league pitcher in the making.[4]

The minors for Rogers could fairly be characterized as odd, at the very least. His time in the Texas Rangers' minor-league system extended from 1982 to 1988, during which time he lost more than twice as many games as he won (19-39), amassed a not-too-sterling 4.20 ERA—actually a bit lower than his major-league 4.27—and a similarly lackluster 1.397 WHIP. He spent twice as much time with Class-A teams, all or parts of six seasons with relatively much better numbers, as he did with Double-A teams. And strangest of all, he spent not a day in Triple-A baseball until 2006, when he pitched 3⅔ innings on a rehab assignment to Toledo in the International League.

Still only 24 years old, Rogers made the big team coming out of spring training in 1989, and began his major-league career inauspiciously, walking the first hitter he faced on four pitches in the Rangers' third game of the season, on April 6. He picked up his first major-league victory three days later, when Toronto's Tom Henke blew a save and the Rangers jumped on him for two runs in the bottom of the ninth. Rogers went on to appear in 73 games that season, becoming a fixture in middle relief from the Texas bullpen. And oddly, in a career filled with oddities, the 2.93 ERA he achieved in his first season was the lowest he ever earned either as a starter or reliever in his 20-year career. As one writer so aptly observed, Rogers' first 10 days in the majors "stands almost as a microcosm of what was to follow: indifferent, lightly worn failure, followed by modest effectiveness, mixed with carelessness saved by stunning skill and redeemed, as often as not, by luck."[5]

The Rangers used Rogers primarily as a setup man out of the bullpen through 1992. In his sophomore year, he spelled Jeff Russell as the team's closer when the latter was injured, achieving 15 saves but blowing six. He also started a dozen games during that four-year stretch. But he started none in 1992—ironically, for that was the year Rogers, still smarting from his second straight defeat in salary arbitration with the club, started lobbying for a starting role during spring training. He then proceeded to lead the AL in game appearances (81) that season with a nice 3.10 ERA strictly as a reliever.[6]

With his durability established and the Texas rotation in sore need, Rogers got his wish in the 1993 season and became a starter. He almost lost his job a few times, especially during a shaky May when he went 1-3 and gave up 24 earned runs in 19⅓ innings, including a stretch of three starts in which he couldn't get past three innings and gave up 16 runs on 18 hits and 8 walks. But he managed to finish the year with a creditable record of 16-10, with a 4.10 ERA for a Texas team that won 86 games and finished second in their division. With a little leverage this time for salary negotiations this time—up till now, he'd never gotten what he thought he deserved—Rogers agreed to a $2.3 million contract for the 1994 season.[7]

That season was cut short by the players strike, but not before Rogers achieved the pinnacle of pitching prowess: He threw a perfect game against the California Angels. It was the first ever by a left-hander in the American League. Using only 98 pitches on the evening of July 28 in the Rangers' brand-new Ballpark at Arlington, he shut down the Angels 4-0. Rookie Rusty Greer preserved the gem with a spectacular diving catch in center field in the ninth on a leadoff slicing liner off the bat of Rex Hubbard. Only one other hitter, Chili Davis in the eighth, even hit the ball hard off Rogers. But Kenny didn't have time to luxuriate in his accomplishment. (A Player of the Week Award and an appearance on Letterman quickly faded.) Two weeks after his

gem, the strike began, and that news dominated the airwaves for weeks.[8]

In 1995 Rogers' free-agency year, the Rangers had given him a nice bump to $3.75 million for his services, and the lefty delivered. He was named to the All-Star team (the first of four selections to the midsummer classic) and went 17-7 with a 3.38 ERA for the year. A workhorse, he pitched 208 innings with a 1.288 WHIP and 5.8 WAR (wins above replacement), to lead the team. Naturally, he expected to be handsomely rewarded for his efforts, and the Rangers made what one of their executives called "the absolute best offer we could"—a four-year deal for $17.5 million. But this didn't satisfy Rogers. He claimed he thought negotiations "had just begun" with the Rangers when George Steinbrenner's perennially flush New York Yankees signed him to a four-year pact at $20 million. Going to New York turned out to be one of the worst decisions Rogers ever made in a career in which he made several.[9]

Rogers' time with the Bronx Bombers was, to put it mildly, a disaster. Trouble began in spring training, 1996. Rogers claimed he wasn't able "to get comfortable on the mound." Yankees pitching coach Mel Stottlemyre and manager Joe Torre thought he might be pressing because of his big contract.[10] Whatever the reason, the lefty didn't improve, and the ubiquitous New York media, after first wondering why the Yankees hadn't put their expensive acquisition into the starting rotation when the season opened, soon found out why.[11] By September, with the Yankees holding a comfortable nine-game lead over Boston in the AL East, the season had so unraveled for Rogers that observers were wondering whether he was "too far gone" to be of much use. At that point, Rogers was 10-8 with a 5.00 ERA, and a friend described him as "very depressed" and perhaps hurt as well. This happened to be true on both counts: Rogers had been struck on the left shoulder by a line drive in spring training, and "he didn't help himself by keeping the injury secret and incurring Torre's seldom seen wrath."[12]

The Yankees cruised easily into the postseason and eventually to a world championship. Rogers, with a chance for redemption, failed miserably. Starting three games, one each in the Division Series, League Championship Series, and World Series, he achieved a 14.14 ERA in only seven total innings pitched, gave up 15 hits, 11 earned runs, and two homers, while walking six and striking out four. Even after a personal exhortation from The Boss—Steinbrenner himself—his Series start in Game Four against the Atlanta Braves was a horror: two innings, 13 batters, five hits, five runs, a homer, and two walks. Amazingly, because of Yankee resilience, the lefty didn't absorb a loss for any of these awful postseason outings. In fact, the Bombers won them all.[13]

The 1997 season brought more of the same. In early May, the *New York Post* declared "Kenny Starting To Crack" in a massive headline. Manager Torre thought his pitcher's problems more mental than physical: Rogers strayed from his game plan, too impatient. "He over-complicates it." Basically Rogers suffered a crisis of confidence. "Rogers' approach to pitching any given game," columnist Tom Keegan observed, "is a case study in a man's inability to weather failure. He throws one bad pitch and wants to reinvent himself as a pitcher." Unsurprisingly, the Yankees were shopping Rogers on the trading market as early as June. Torre made no secret of what he thought, in his 1998 book *Chasing the Dream*: Rogers was "one of the most difficult players I ever managed."[14]

Although a July trade that would have sent Rogers to the San Diego Padres fell through, New York succeeded in November in offloading their problem pitcher (plus half his $10 million salary for two years) to the Oakland A's in exchange for utility infielder Scott Brosius. Once on the opposite coast, Rogers seemed to experience a rebirth. In 1998 he won 16 games losing 8 with a 3.17 ERA to go with it. He pitched 238⅔ innings, more than any other season in his career. He also achieved his career fourth-best strikeout/walk ratio (2.06), and his career-best WHIP (1.182), and by far his best WAR (7.58, second in the AL for pitchers).[15]

All the more strange, then, that the 34-year-old southpaw's performance fell off so notably in 1999. He was 5-3 with a 4.30 ERA and was giving up more than 10 hits per nine innings when the A's traded him on July 23 to the New York Mets for a couple of prospects. More than one writer found it "curious" that the A's would do this, especially since they were contending for a wild-card playoff spot. But the real reason did not surprise anybody who knew Kenny. "Rogers did not endear himself to the organization. … He was disgruntled, and wanted out." He had become a persona non grata and a clubhouse problem with the A's since he announced in spring training that he would not be re-signing with the team at the end of his contract. The A's general manager, Billy Beane, declared the trade with the Mets essential: "You had 24 guys pulling one direction, and one guy pulling in the other."[16]

Rogers didn't seem likely to endear himself to the Mets either. Beat writer Selena Roberts said there was "something unnerving" about the man, "a disturbing unknown" with an "aloof personality" that kept teammates and coaches at a distance. Moreover, "he is incapable of telling a story that doesn't twist and bend." Rogers had arrived at the Mets with a hamstring injury and two different explanations about how it happened. "You know Kenny," said his new manager, Bobby Valentine, who knew him well from Texas. "He always says he's fine." Problem was, the writer continued, "how do you trust Rogers? How do you know when he's healthy and when he's not?"[17]

Rogers put up some serviceable numbers in the 76 innings he pitched for the Mets in 1999 (5-1, 4.07 ERA). Presumably he had helped the Mets reach the playoffs as the wild-card team, but he provided no help at all in the ensuing postseason. The Atlanta Braves eliminated the Mets in the NLCS, in the bottom of the 11th inning of the sixth game—when Rogers, in relief, walked in the winning walk-off run on five pitches. Which crowned an egregious playoff performance: 3 games lost, 12 innings pitched, 16 hits (including two home runs), 9 walks, 8 strikeouts, and an ERA of 7.09.

As a free agent at season's end, Rogers decided to take another drink at the original well and signed a three-year deal with the Texas Rangers for $22.5 million. Kenny claimed it had been "no secret" that he wanted to return, and he wanted to repeat his previous success in Texas and hoped to stay more than the three years. He wouldn't, at least not consecutive years, because he again opted for free agency at the end of this contract. The years Rogers pitched on this stay with the Rangers could not be described as particularly distinguished. He went 31-28 for the period with an ERA of 4.64; he continued to amass innings pitched (558⅔) and posted a lousy 1.461 WHIP. A couple of events stood out for him: he won the first pair of his five career Gold Glove Awards in 2000 and 2002 (the others came in 2004-06).[18] And the 2001 season marked the first time Rogers had ever gone onto the disabled list in his 14-year career. In July he had to undergo season-ending surgery to correct a circulation problem in his left shoulder.[19]

One thing remaining constant, though, was Rogers' disdain for Rangers salary proposals after service with the team.[20] At the conclusion of the 2002 season, Texas offered the 37-year-old a two-year deal for $10.5 million. Rogers spurned the offer and then had to swallow his pride and squeeze his pocketbook to accept a one-year $2 million offer from the Minnesota Twins that didn't come until mid-March. "My pride and ego got in the way," he admitted.[21] But having served his time with the Twins (13-8, 4.57 ERA), the greener pastures in Arlington, Texas, beckoned once again. And why not? As desperate for pitching as Rogers was for a job, the Rangers were willing to sign a 38-year-old pitcher for two years, albeit at the relatively cheap price of $6 million. "I never wanted to leave," Rogers claimed, a bit disingenuously. "It's an extremely happy day to come back here and probably finish my career here."[22]

No one could have suspected that at age 39, Rogers was about to embark on the most solid three-season span of his career, a time that made Kenny Rogers a household name in the baseball world, not only for several sterling pitching achievements, but arguably even more for less laudatory on-field occurrences. He spent the first two years, 2004-05, with Texas. And then, as was his custom, rejected their contract offer and accepted a two-year contract from the Detroit Tigers at $8 million a year.

It was a remarkable three years. Rogers made the All-Star team and won Gold Glove Awards in all three seasons; he went 49-25 with a 4.04 ERA and averaged 3.9 WAR per season for the period. He starred in the postseason for Detroit in 2006. But he could not avoid further clouding his image and reputation in the process.

Kenny Rogers had never been easy-going. One observer characterized him at the end of his career as "arrogant and pompous," to which "touchy" and "hot-headed" could easily be added.[23] The list of particulars bearing this out is a long one. Rogers could be a volatile teammate. He and another shave-tail Rangers pitcher, Kevin Brown, both barely into the big leagues, had angered veteran Texas players in camp in March 1991 by staging a one-day walkout to protest the team's negotiating tactics on pay. He and multiyear All-Star catcher Ivan "Pudge" Rodriguez got into a dugout squabble during the 1994 season. He shoved local sportswriter Simon Gonzalez out of the clubhouse that same year, and after a loss at home to the A's, he destroyed an exercise bike in the visitors clubhouse that cost him over $2,700 in docked pay. Rogers fought on a plane trip and continued it in a hotel elevator over a card game with A's teammate Jason McDonald in 1999. And Rogers raised the ire of manager Joe Torre and all his Yankees teammates when in the midst of a shellacking by the Seattle Mariners during 1997, he plunked utterly inoffensive Ken Griffey Jr. in the buttocks with a pitch. Rogers claimed it got away from him, but other Yankees, including Torre, didn't believe him. They attributed it to frustration.[24]

On June 17, 2005, a couple of weeks before the outburst that made him *SportsCenter* fodder for a week, Rogers had broken a bone in his nonpitching hand punching a water cooler in the dugout after being removed from a game. Up until then, the lefty had been having a marvelous season (9-2 with a league-leading 2.46 ERA).[25] But he wasn't happy. After winning 18 games in 2004, he approached Rangers owner Tom Hicks and requested a contract extension. Hicks refused. "Word got out that Rogers threatened to retire immediately if the contract wasn't extended." Though the lefty denied the story, the local media criticized him roundly, and Kenny blamed the Rangers "for spreading the news. And the media for circulating it." Rogers promptly ceased having anything to do with the media.[26]

With all this lurking in the background—not to mention tension with Texas manager Buck Showalter over a number of issues, a couple of untoward incidents with a reporter and cameraman, and some miscellaneous property destruction—on June 29, Rogers flipped his lid. Walking onto the field for warmup stretching that day, Rogers shoved two cameramen. When one of them, Larry Rodriguez of Dallas's Fox affiliate KDFW, resumed filming, Rogers shoved him again, knocked the camera to the ground, and kicked it. Rodriguez was hospitalized with pain in shoulder, arm, and neck, and he subsequently filed an assault complaint against the lefty. Official baseball reacted swiftly. Commissioner Bud Selig fined Rogers $50,000 and suspended him for 20 games (later reduced by an arbitrator to 13). On July 18 Rogers was booked on a charge of misdemeanor assault and released on bond. In the following weeks and months, the pitcher checked all the appropriate boxes: issuing public and private apologies, completing an anger-management course, and settling a lawsuit with Rodriguez for an undisclosed sum. But to the chagrin of many, he chose to participate in the All-Star Game (where he didn't fare well, giving up two earned runs on three hits in his one inning). And further besmirching of his reputation did not go away.[27]

Rogers delivered another good season in 2006, his first with the Detroit Tigers on a two-year deal. Remaining healthy, he started 34 games, pitched over 200 innings, and went 17-8. The Tigers won 95 games and went into the postseason as the AL's wild-card team. And in this, his fourth postseason with a fourth different team, Kenny finally found his stride. He helped pitch his team into the World Series. In one of the most emotional wins of his entire career, on October 6 at Comerica Park, he secured a win against future Hall of Famer Randy Johnson and the Yankees in the third game of the ALDS. Rogers threw 7⅔ innings of five-hit ball, surrendering no runs and striking out eight. Detroit went on to blow right past the Oakland A's in the ALCS, with Rogers winning the third game after another 7⅓ scoreless innings (two hits, six strikeouts).

But then fortune turned on the Tigers, who managed but a single win in the World Series against the St. Louis Cardinals. And that was the second game, the one Kenny Rogers started. Once again Rogers appeared peerless on the mound: He pitched eight scoreless innings on two hits, winning his third game of the playoffs. But controversy eclipsed his magnificent performance that night, and indeed spilled over into questions about his first two playoff victories as well. During the first inning, TV commentator Tim McCarver noticed and mentioned a dark smudge, a brown substance, on Rogers' pitching hand, below the thumb. It had disappeared when Rogers came out to pitch the second, but suspicions abounded. Was it pine tar? Had Rogers been cheating? Cardinals manager Tony LaRussa lodged no official complaint, and Rogers explained it had been a mixture of rosin and mud. Opinion ran the spectrum. Hall of Famers Bob Feller and Gaylord Perry, a master practitioner of doctoring baseballs, didn't doubt for an instant that Rogers cheated. Nor did many writers and fans. But nothing could be proven one way or another, since no one on the St. Louis side ever requested that the umpires examine Rogers' hand. So Kenny Rogers' 23 consecutive scoreless playoff innings pitched remains to this day the record for a left-hander, albeit under an inevitable cloud.[28]

Reality and his 42 years of age finally caught up with Rogers in 2007. Because of surgery to remove a blood clot in his left shoulder in late March, Rogers didn't start a game until June 22. And he was sidelined by injury again for the entire month of August. He finished out the year 3-4 with a 4.43 ERA, having pitched only 64 innings.[29] Offered a one-year contract with the Tigers for 2008 for $8 million, Rogers seized it eagerly. Amazingly, by then the oldest active major leaguer at 43 stayed healthy for the entire season. But he was clearly done: He won only three of 13 starts in the second half of the season, finishing the year 9-13 with a 5.70 ERA and 1.630 WHIP.[30]

As a durable pitcher for almost 20 seasons, Rogers' longevity assured that his name would appear on several all-time record lists. For example, with "one of the greatest pickoff moves in baseball history, he is second [to Steve Carlton] in all-time pickoffs with 93." He is also only one of eight pitchers with over 200 wins (219) never to have won 20 games in a season. He appears on numerous Rangers leader lists: first in appearances (528), second in wins (133), innings (1,909), and career WAR, third in starts (252) and K's (1,201).[31]

Rogers never formally retired from baseball. He just stopped playing. He served as a special pitching instructor for Detroit during spring training in 2010, and Texas, for whom he played 12 years, inducted him as the 14th member of the Rangers Hall of Fame on August 6, 2011. As of 2016 he, his wife, Becky, and their two children, Jessica and Trevor, resided in Westlake, Texas, a suburb of Dallas.[32]

SOURCES

Statistical information is from baseball-reference.com. Unless otherwise noted, all newspaper (except *The Sporting News*) and web sources cited in the notes are from clippings in Kenny Rogers file, Giamatti Research Center, Baseball Hall of Fame, Cooperstown, New York.

NOTES

1. Bob Nightengale, "Scout Saw Rogers' Talent," *USA Today*, October 10, 2006; Mark Cannizzaro, "Luck & Rogers a Perfect Match," *New York Post*, April 26, 1995.

2. Cannizzaro, "Luck & Rogers"; Bob Nightengale, "At 41, Rogers Finds a Good Fit," *USA Today*, October 10, 2006.

3. Jay Jaffe, "JAWS and the 2014 Hall of Fame Ballot: Kenny Rogers," *Sports Illustrated*, December 26, 2013.

4. Tim Kurkjian, "As Good as It Gets," *Sports Illustrated*, August 8, 1994.

5. Michael Coffey, *27 Men Out: Baseball's Perfect Games* (New York: Atria Books, 2004), 221.

6. Tony DeMarco, "Rogers Brings Suspense to Role as Team's Closer," *Fort Worth Star-Telegram*, July 15, 1990; T.R. Sullivan, "For Starters, Rogers Wants Spot in the Rotation," *Fort Worth Star-Telegram*, February 20, 1993.

7. *The Sporting News*, May 31, 1993: 30, August 23, 1993: 31; *New York Times*, February 3, 1994.

8. "Rangers' Rogers Perfect in 4-0 Win," *USA Today*, July 29, 1994; "Baseball: Rogers Throws Perfect Game for Rangers," *New York Times*, July 29, 1994; Kurkjian, "As Good as It Gets."

9. T.R. Sullivan, "Rogers Out," *The Sporting News*, January 8, 15, 1996.

10. Jim Salisbury, "Tape Reveals Rogers' Flaws," *New York Post*, March 21, 1996: 72.

11. Murray Chass, "A Healthy 17-Game Winner Winds Up in Yankee Limbo," *New York Times*, April 16, 1996. The Yankees were treating Rogers "like Cinderella," Chass wrote.

12. "Rogers's Shoulders Now Must Bear the Weight of a Race," *New York Times*, September 18, 1996. The unnamed friend was teammate hurler Andy Pettitte.

13. Jim Salisbury, "Boss to Kenny: I'm Waiting," *New York Post*, October 24, 1996.

14. Tom Keegan, "Kenny Starting to Crack," *New York Post*, May 6, 1997; "Vaughn Returned to Sender," *Oneonta* [New York] *Star*, July 7, 1997; Torre quoted in Jack Curry, "Torre and Rogers, Act II," *New York Times*, October 6, 2006.

15. Joel Sherman, "Kenny Rogers to Go," *New York Post*, November 8, 1997; Bill Madden, "Besides 'Stink,' No Rogers Regret," *New York Daily News*, February 2, 1998.

16 "Mets Take Gamble on Rogers," *Oneonta Star*, July 24, 1999; Gary Petersen, "Rogers Just Too Self-Conscious," *Contra Costa (California) Times*, July 11, 2005.

17 Selena Roberts, "Mets' Rogers Is a Pitcher of Mystery," *New York Times*, August 26, 1998.

18 Rogers, the former shortstop and outfielder, was always a good fielder, leading the league several times in assists and range factor for a pitcher. He also had a renowned pickoff move.

19 "Texas Signs lefty Rogers," *Oneonta Star*, December 30, 1999; "Rogers' Season Ends," *Albany (New York) Times Union*, July 21, 2001.

20 Randy Galloway, "Rogers' Past Tells Us a Lot About His Present," *Fort Worth Star-Telegram*, June 2, 2005. This article makes an excellent case that suppressed anger about the money Texas paid him always lurked in Rogers while he was with the Rangers.

21 *New York Times*, September 25, 2003.

22 *New York Post*, January 14, 2004. Rogers' stint with Minnesota involved his third trip to the postseason, where he pitched an inning and a third against the Yankees, gave up a hit, and struck out three.

23 "All-Time Bad Guys Team," For Baseball Junkies. baseballjunkies.blogspot.com/2012/05/all-time-bad-guys-team.html.

24 *The Sporting News*, March 18, 1991, April 18, 1994; *USA Today Baseball Weekly*, May 12-18, 1999: 3; Jim Reeves, "Lack of Control Was Displayed 11 years ago," *Fort Worth Star-Telegram*, July 2, 2005; Jack Curry, "Yanks Irked That Rogers Plunked Griffey," *New York Times*, August 24, 1997. Tino Martinez paid for Rogers' sin two innings later by getting hit on the leg with a pitch from the M's Jeff Fassaro.

25 Ben Shpigel, "Broken Right Hand Shelved Rogers," *Dallas Morning News*, July 28, 2005. See also "Rogers Pitching a Blue Streak," *Dallas Morning News*, May 21, 2005.

26 Galloway, "Rogers' Past Tells About His Present."

27 Jose De Jesus Ortiz, "Rogers Can't Handle Pressure," *Houston Chronicle*, July 3, 2005; ESPN, "Ranger Pitcher Confronts and Threatens Cameraman," espn.go.com/mlb/news/story?id=2097491; "Rogers to Sit 20 games," *New York Post*, July 2, 2005; Evan Grant, "Rogers: 'I Failed Miserably,'" Ernesto Londono, "Rangers' Rogers Charged With Assault," Evan Grant, "Ruling Ends Rogers' Penalty," Matt Mosley, "Cameraman Files Lawsuit Sgainst Rogers," Evan Grant, "Ex-Ranger Rogers May Have Changed His Persona," all in *The Dallas Morning News*, July 7, 18, August 10, October 6, 2005, April 7, 2006; Tim Dahlberg (Associated Press), "Rogers Should Walk Away From All-Star game," *Oneonta Star*, July 6, 2005.

28 Gene Wojciechowski, "Rogers Was Masterful, but Did He Cheat?" ESPN.com, October 23, 2006; Paul White, "Real Dirt on Rogers Unclear," *USA Today*, October 24, 2006; Bob Nightengale, "Hall of Famer Feller Blasts Rogers, Says, 'Of Course He Was Cheating,'" Jon Saraceno, "Spitball Master Watches Rogers With Admiration," Dan Vergano, "Did He or Didn't He? It's a Sticky Question," *USA Today*, October 25, 2006; Murray Chass, "Reassessing Hand That Rocked the Series," *New York Times*, November 5, 2006.

29 "Rogers Out After Surgery for a Blood Clot," *New York Times*, March 31, 2007..

30 *New York Daily News*, December 1, 2007.

31 Louis Horvath, "Rogers Inducted in Ranger Hall of Fame," accessed March 16, 2016, mlb.mlb.com/news/20110806/22851920.html; "Kenny Rogers," accessed March 12, 2016, tigersdetroit.wikia.com/wiki/Kenny_Rogers.

32 Email, Reference Librarian, Local History and Genealogy, Library of Congress, to Tom Schott, March 18, 2016.

KENNY ROGERS' PERFECT GAME
JULY 28, 1994: TEXAS RANGERS 4, LOS ANGELES ANGELS 0, AT THE BALLPARK AT ARLINGTON, TEXAS

By Thomas E. Schott

EVEN HAD KENNY ROGERS not tossed a perfect game on July 28, 1994, baseball fans would have remembered the date. Earlier that day, the executive committee of the Players Association had voted to go out on strike on August 12. The culmination of a long, bitter struggle between owners and players, the strike occurred over issues most fans didn't grasp or care about: salary caps and a revamped revenue-sharing plan. No one knew it at the time, but this, the eighth work stoppage in major-league history, would also be the longest — 232 days. It would cancel the rest of the 1994 season and the entire postseason including the World Series, and shorten the 1995 season to 114 games.[1]

Perhaps the sense of impending doom for the season explains the near-capacity crowd of 46,581 who jammed the Texas Rangers' brand new park, the Ballpark at Arlington, that evening. They, too, had come to watch a division leader, for the Rangers were atop the new four-team Western Division of the American League by 1½ games. Impressive, until you learn that the team wasn't even playing .500 ball and their opponents that night, the California Angels, stood last in the same division, but were only 6½ games back.[2]

Which is not to say that Texas didn't have some good players. The nucleus of a team that would dominate the AL West in the late '90s was already there: Iván "Pudge" Rodriguez, rookie Rusty Greer, Juan "Gonzo" Gonzalez. And other pretty good players who wouldn't be around then: Will Clark and José Canseco. By contrast, the visiting Angels had few to stir much excitement, beyond two-sport wunderkind Bo Jackson in his final season and 1993 Rookie of the Year outfielder Tim Salmon. And maybe aging lefty pitcher Mark Langston and rookie Jim Edmonds, but that's pushing it.

Nor were the starting pitchers anything special either. California's starter was a tall, skinny 21-year-old left-hander named Andrew Lorraine, a rookie pitching in his third major-league game. In his 7⅔ innings pitched so far, he had yielded 17 hits (three homers), 6 walks, and 11 earned runs. Hardly an auspicious start, but he fit on a team that suffered from a lot more than just pitching woes. "The team's last-place standing just before the All-Star break," observed a *Los Angeles Times* staffer earlier, "doesn't even begin to tell how bad this team really is."[3]

Lorraine's mound opponent Kenny Rogers, another left-hander, had been with Texas since 1989. Before that he had knocked around in the Rangers' farm system for seven years out of high school. He had been converted from outfielder to pitcher on the strength of his arm, so raw at the start that he didn't know what the stretch position was. He pitched primarily from the bullpen until 1993, when he became a full-time starter and did okay: 16-10 with a 4.10 ERA. He would make a lot of money from baseball throughout his career, but he never thought Texas paid him enough. For 13 straight years Rogers and the Rangers had lived together on one-year contracts. Rogers was even further irked that the Rangers had bested him in arbitration in 1992 and '93 and not given him what he wanted for this year. Plus, he was having only a fair season, at this point 10-6, 4.32 ERA, and opponents were hitting him hard; they had a .766 OPS against him and were hitting .295 with the ball in play.[4]

But Rogers would be virtually untouchable this typically hot evening in the Dallas area: clear and 88 degrees at game time. The Angels were riding a six-game losing streak. The Rangers were playing the first of four with California, their fourth game in a 10-day homestand, and they were in good spirits. One Fort Worth reporter described them "as loosey-goosey as I'd seen them all season."[5]

Rogers didn't show anything special in the first inning. It took him 15 pitches to retire the top of the Angels order one-two-three, including a couple of strikeouts, both called with the count 3-and-2. Rogers' second strikeout victim, of an eventual eight, was Edmonds, a left-handed hitter who would not have even been in the game had not Salmon been injured. Even more curious, the home-plate umpire who rang Edmonds up was a minor-league substitute named Ed Bean, called up as a fill-in for vacationing 17-year veteran Ken Kaiser. This night was only his seventh time calling balls and strikes in the big leagues.[6]

Another oddity stepped in for the Rangers: Right fielder Wallace McArthur "Butch" Davis, who, hitting .297, had been called up that very day from Oklahoma City. Davis grounded out to short, Pudge Rodriguez flied out. With two out, Rogers' teammates now gifted him with two runs. The number-three Rangers hitter, steroid-sculpted DH José Canseco, deposited a home run about one row deep in the left-field stands, and third baseman Dean Palmer singled home Will Clark, who had walked and advanced to second on a hit by Gonzalez. Greer flied out to end the inning. Texas added two more runs in the third, on solo home runs by Rodriguez and Canseco (his second).[7]

So the score stood 4-0 as the game entered its middle innings. Rogers was cruising, the only tough play thus far being Palmer's nice scoop and throw on a hot shot in the hole by LA shortstop Gary Disarcina to end the Angels third. Kenny had found his groove. It took him only 29 pitches to record the next nine outs, including the second swinging strikeout of Bo Jackson.[8]

By the top of the seventh the crowd, if not aware of it before, realized that no Angels had reached first base through six innings. (The TV audience had been informed, of course.) At this point Rogers decided to put a lump in everybody's throat by going to a 3-and-2 count on all three hitters (Chad Curtis, Spike Owen, Edmonds) in the seventh. He had almost "made it an ordinary night" in the fifth, going to a 3-and-0 count on J.T. Snow before retiring him on a fly to center. It had taken 19 pitches this inning for Kenny to get his three outs and he walked back to the dugout to a rising crescendo of cheers.[9]

The top half of the eighth brought up the heart of the California order again: Chili Davis, Bo, and Snow. With the crowd roaring on every pitch, Rogers got Davis on a sinking liner to Gonzalez in left, the hardest-hit ball by the Angels all night. Kenny had baffled Bo Jackson all night and did again, getting him to miss a third-strike fastball. Then he caught Snow looking at a third-strike "tumbling waterfall of a curveball," and the crowd erupted. Between innings, while Will Clark went up to hit, Canseco took over his position next to Rogers on the bench, just to be certain some chatty fool didn't approach and break one of baseball's most sacrosanct taboos.[10]

And then the ninth. Three outs to go. With the glare of myriad spotlights on him, Rogers looked "stricken, forlorn, scared." And had he foreseen the low sinking liner to right-center that the seven-hole Angels hitter, second baseman Rex Hudler, stroked on a 0-and-2 count, it might have given him heart palpitations. Instead it just caused momentary paralysis as he watched Rusty Greer come charging in from center, make a desperate dive, backhand the ball about a foot from being a base hit, and then slide 15 feet. Practically every perfect game has a golden defensive play, and this was Rogers'. The final two Angels hitters were anticlimax: a routine grounder to short by catcher Chris Turner and then a routine fly ball to center by Disarcina.

Rogers entered the record books as the 12th pitcher of the century to pitch a perfect game, and the first left-hander in the AL ever. It had taken 98 pitches. He had gone to three balls on only six hitters. The closest the Angels had come to a hit was Hudler's flare in the ninth. Otherwise, with the stuff he had that night, a curve breaking 3½ feet for strikes, a wicked change, and a hopping fastball, Rogers could've probably beaten anybody.[11]

SOURCES

In addition to the sources cited in the Notes, the author relied on baseball-reference.com.

NOTES

1 The strike gave rise to a host of what-might-have-beens. Up until the disastrous strike, baseball had been enjoying a golden season. In the NL, San Diego outfielder Tony Gwynn, hitting .394, flirted with the magic .400 average; Giant Matt Williams had 43 homers and was on a pace to tie, if not beat Roger Maris's season mark of 61. The Montreal Expos sported the best record in the franchise's history, 74-40, and led their division by six games, and the Yankees after years of drought had a comfortable lead in the AL East and appeared on track for the postseason. Had it not been for the strike, 1994 might have been seen as the first year of their dominance of the rest of the twentieth century.

2 James Buckley Jr., *Perfect: The Inside Story of Baseball's Twenty Perfect Games* (Chicago: Triumph Books, 2002), 176. By the time the season came to its inglorious close on August 12, the Rangers, who still led the division (by one game) at 52-62, had the fourth-worst record in the league. But the three teams with still worse records were all in the Western Division.

3 Gebe Martinez, "Plot in Angels Movie Hits Close to Home: Baseball : Celluloid Team Bears the Same Logo—and Losing Ways—as the Real Thing," *Los Angeles Times*, July 11, 1994; accessed April 13, 2016, articles.latimes.com/1994-07-11/local/me-14387_1_california-angels-baseball.. The Angels finished the 1994 season with the worst record in the AL: 47-68.

4 Buckley, *Perfect*, 175; Michael Coffey, *27 Men Out: Baseball's Perfect Games* (New York: Atria Books, 2004), 227.

5 Jim Reeves, "On a Hot Summer Night," *The Sporting News*, August 8, 1994: 16.

6 Coffey, *27 Men Out*, 231. Bean worked only three dozen major-league games, all in 1994.

7 A veteran minor leaguer, the 36-year-old Butch Davis had been up and down with several clubs since 1983. He played the four-game Angel series, and that ended his major-league career. Davis wasn't unknown to Ranger fans. In 1993 he functioned as a regular bench guy and appeared in 62 games. But this game was the first time he appeared in the major leagues in 1994.

8 Coffey, *27 Men Out*, 234; Reeves, "Hot Summer Night." Intent on facing the meat of the California order in the fifth inning, Rogers did not notice the small fire on the concrete floor of the Texas dugout—Canseco's old red baseball shoes burning, doused with alcohol set alight by outfielder and trickster Chris James, not because José was "hot" (a speculation by the TV broadcasters), but because they stank. Loosey goosey indeed, but also an indication of the mood of the team behind a pitcher with a perfect game in progress.

9 Coffey, *27 Men Out*, 235.

10 Material in this paragraph and the one that follows is from Coffey, 238. A video of Greer's great catch is at m.mlb.com/cutfour/2015/07/28/139026162/rusty-greers-catch-saves-kenny-rogers-perfect-game.

11 Oddly enough, three of the next four perfect games in the AL were thrown by lefties—David Wells, Mark Buehrle, and Dallas Braden.

HIDEO NOMO

By Bill Staples Jr.

LIKE BABE RUTH, HE WAS A savior for the major leagues when the game was at risk of losing fans. Like Jackie Robinson, he was a courageous pioneer who blazed a trail and opened new doors of opportunity for others to follow. Like Fernando Valenzuela, he was the pride of a specific ethnic community, yet adored by people of all races and creeds. Like Bob Gibson, he was a fierce competitor on the mound, and a friend to all who knew him off the field. Like Luis Tiant, his twisted and contorted windup fooled hitters on every team, and delighted fans in every ballpark. Like Nolan Ryan, his dedication to conditioning and training was legendary, and unmatched by his peers. Like Sandy Koufax, he was a fireball who appeared suddenly and blinded the competition, then faded away. Like Ted Williams, Ernie Banks, Tony Gwynn, and countless other greats, he was blessed by the baseball gods with the passion and skills to play the game at a higher level, but was denied the glory of ever winning a World Series. And finally, like Buck O'Neil, his career statistics on the field will (most likely) prevent him from being enshrined in Cooperstown, despite the fact that he is arguably one of the game's most important ambassadors. When you stop and realize that all of these qualities are embodied in a single ballplayer, you begin to fully appreciate his career, his legacy, and the undeniable truth that there is no one else in the history of game quite like Hideo Nomo.

Nomo was born on August 31, 1968, into a working-class family in the industrial section of Osaka, Japan. His father, Shizuo, and mother, Kayoko, had great hopes for their son, naming him Hideo (pronounced He-day-oh), which translates literally to "excelling man," but is commonly understood to mean "superman" or "hero" in Japanese.[1]

He started playing baseball with his father at age 5 and by the time he was 12 his dream was to become a professional ballplayer. In the fifth grade he invented his corkscrew "tornado" windup to impress his father, and to fool batters. "By twisting my body and by using this force, I was able to throw harder. And at the same time, with that motion, it would be difficult for batters to pick up the ball," he explained.[2]

When Hideo reached middle-school ball he dominated batters with his speed, and frightened them with his lack of control. At times he would walk the bases loaded only to strike out the side. The head coach of Kindai High School, the top school-baseball program in Osaka, told Nomo, "Young man, with that tornado windup, you'll never make it."[3] Nomo used the criticism as inspiration when he enrolled in the lesser-known Seiyo Industrial High School. There he dominated the local competition, and even pitched a perfect game.

Despite his 6-foot-2, 200-pound frame, when he graduated from high school in 1987 Nomo failed to catch the attention of college and pro scouts. Instead, he joined the Shin-Nitetsu Sakai, a company-sponsored club in the semipro industrial leagues, where he perfected both his corkscrew motion and his forkball. He was so dedicated to mastering the forkball grip that at night before going to sleep he taped a tennis ball between his index and middle fingers.[4]

Nomo earned a spot on Team Japan, which won a silver medal in the 1988 Olympics in Seoul, South Korea. The next year he received offers from a record eight teams in the 1989 Nippon Professional Baseball draft. Nomo signed with the Osaka-based Kintetsu Buffaloes and received a bonus of 100 million yen (roughly $1 million US) and a guarantee that the team would not try to change his pitching form.[5]

Buffaloes manger Akira Ogi was an easygoing character who endeared himself to Nomo. As a result, Nomo gave Ogi-san everything he had on the mound. Armed with a blazing fastball and a wicked forkball, Nomo tied for the league lead in wins (18-8)

and led with a 2.91 ERA and 287 strikeouts in 235 innings. He won the Rookie of the Year award, the Most Valuable Player award, and the Sawamura Award, given to the best pitcher in NPB. For the next three seasons he led the Pacific League in wins and strikeouts. And because of his unorthodox windup, he also earned the nickname "Tatsu-maki"—Japanese for "The Tornado."[6]

The young Nomo also bonded with teammate Masato Yoshii, a veteran pitcher three years his senior. Masato took Hideo under his wing when he first turned pro, and in addition to teaching Nomo the ins and outs of professional baseball, he also shared with him his dream of one day playing in the US major leagues. "Masato was a diehard major-league baseball fan for a long time," said translator Kota Ishijima, who worked with both Nomo and Yoshii with the Mets. "Their relationship was quite strong. With regard to regard to Hideo's interest in playing in the major leagues, Yoshii strongly influenced him."[7]

After the 1990 season, the Japanese all-stars battled the visiting major-league all-stars, winning four games in the best-of-seven series. Nomo's performance caught the eye of several Americans, including Ken Griffey Jr. and Randy Johnson. The Big Unit approached Nomo at a private dinner in Japan and told him, "You belong in MLB."[8] With Johnson's praise, and the strong influence of Kintetsu teammate Masato Yoshii, Nomo could not shake the thought of going to America to compete in the majors.

In 1994 manager Ogi was replaced by Keishi Suzuki, a Japanese Hall of Fame pitcher with an impressive résumé: 317-238 record, fourth all-time in wins; 3,061 strikeouts, and 340 games pitched without a walk, an NPB record. Suzuki followed a militaristic training regimen and believed that the remedy for a sore arm was to throw more. "Throw until you die," he said.[9] By the time Nomo left the NPB, he had thrown more than 140 pitches in a single game 61 times. The excessive pitch counts took their toll on the righty. He was injured most of the 1994 season and finished with an 8-7 record, appearing in only 114 innings, down 53 percent from 243⅓ the previous season.[10]

After the 1994 season Nomo met baseball agent Don Nomura, who had translated the Japanese Uniform Players Contract searching for loopholes to recruit players to the United States. With the help of California-based agent Arn Tellem, they found one—the voluntary-retirement clause. It stated that if a player retired and returned to NPB, he was bound to his former team. However, there was no provision for players who retired and went to another country to play. This was Nomo's out. After the '94 season, he declared his retirement from NPB at age 26.

After interviewing with several major-league teams, including the Los Angeles Dodgers, San Francisco Giants, and Seattle Mariners, Nomo found a personal connection with Dodgers owner Peter O'Malley and signed with the team in February 1995.

That spring the relationship between the major leagues and its fans was at an all-time low. The previous season was killed by the players strike, a conflict that many perceived as an unrelatable argument over money between billionaires (the owners) and millionaires (the players). The 1994 World Series was canceled. Fans were disgusted and some vowed never to step foot in a major-league ballpark again. Many fans had a change of heart after Nomo arrived in America.

Nomo signed a minor-league contract with the Dodgers' Double-A team, the San Antonio Missions, who had just hired new pitching coach Luis Tiant, a fellow tornado-style pitcher. Nomo reported to spring camp in Vero Beach, Florida at the end of February and immediately impressed Tiant. "He's a smart pitcher. … (If) you're good, you're good, no matter where you pitch," Tiant said in his endearing Cuban accent.[11]

By the end of April the Dodgers were convinced Nomo was ready for the big leagues, but wanted the rookie to get a tune-up start with one of their minor-league clubs.[12] In his American professional baseball debut, Nomo pitched 5⅓ innings for the Bakersfield Blaze of the California League against the Rancho Cucamonga Quakes. With little run support, the Blaze lost 2-1, but the Dodgers were pleased with Nomo's performance and called him up. They announced that he would make his first start on May 2 against the San Francisco Giants in Candlestick Park.[13]

With his start against the Giants, Nomo became the first Japanese-born player to join a major-league team after officially retiring from the NPB. When he joined the Dodgers, only one other Japanese native, Masanori Murakami, had played in the major leagues. Murakami returned to Japan after playing with the Giants in 1964-65.[14]

His predecessor offered Nomo congratulatory a message in the press: "I wish him all the best and hope he has great success as a Japanese major-leaguer. I would like to see him do well against everybody — except for the San Francisco Giants."[15]

Murakami's jest helped fuel Nomo when he pitched against San Francisco. By the end of his career, he had compiled a 13-7 record against the Giants, 4-5 when pitching in Los Angeles and 9-2 in San Francisco, an .818 winning percentage in the Bay City. Throughout his career Nomo was "a Giant killer" in their own ballparks, Candlestick/3Com Park and PacBell/AT&T Park. (Nomo's personal best in any opposing city was .833 Tropicana Field in St. Petersburg.)

In his major-league debut, Nomo pitched five scoreless innings, allowing one hit. He left the 0-0 game after the fifth inning and did not get a decision. (The Dodgers lost to the Giants 4-3 in 15 innings.) Among the 200 members of the media present, most were from Japan. Only 16,099 fans paid to see the game at Candlestick Park (just 28 percent of the 58,000 capacity). However, millions in Japan watched the game live on television, where the first pitch was thrown at 5:33 A.M.

After six starts, Nomo ended May with five no-decisions and one loss. June would be a different story. He recorded his first major-league win against the New York Mets on June 2, a 2-1 victory. In eight innings he allowed just two hits, a home run and single, both to Bobby Bonilla. Nomo went undefeated for the entire month of June, going into the midseason break with a 6-1 record, a 1.99 ERA, and 119 strikeouts in 90⅓ innings pitched.

Nomo had one of the greatest Junes in Dodgers history. In each his six starts, he pitched at least eight innings. He gave up just five earned runs in 50⅓ innings, allowing 25 hits and 16 walks while striking out 60. In winning six straight games, he capped the month with back-to-back complete-game, 13-strikeout shutouts. No other Dodgers pitcher had ever thrown back-to-back shutouts with 13 or more strikeouts.[16]

Shortly before the 1995 All-Star Game, Atlanta Braves pitcher Greg Maddux suffered a groin injury running to first base.[17] Maddux's injury made Nomo the potential starter for the National League. The Braves ace said, "I think more people want to watch him pitch than me, to be honest." Nomo got the official nod to start from NL manager Felipe Alou.

The game was played on July 11 in Texas at The Ballpark in Arlington in front of 50,920 fans. Fittingly, Nomo's boyhood idol, Nolan Ryan, threw out the ceremonial first pitch. Nomo pitched two innings and faced six batters. He struck out three (Kenny Lofton, Edgar Martinez, and Albert Belle), allowed one hit (a single by Carlos Baerga, who was caught stealing) and no walks. The NL won the game, 3-2, on a home run by Jeff Conine in the eighth.[18] Nomo had a great outing, but would never pitch in another All-Star Game.

Nomo's spotlight in the All-Star Game also helped heal a nation and improve relations between the United States and Japan. His brilliance in the 1995 season was a source of great pride and a much-needed morale boost for the Japanese.[19] The country had recently experienced acts of terrorism, a massive earthquake, economic recession, and rising unemployment. Nomo's performance was welcome relief for his country.[20]

In the late 1980s to early 1990s US-Japan relations were poor due to American perceptions of unfair trade practices in Japan. Some American politicians engaged in "Japan bashing" through policy and public-relations stunts like destroying Japanese-made products with sledgehammers on the evening news.[21] Critics observed that there was a lot of "unwarranted, irrational, racially tinged hostility toward the Japanese."[22] Attitudes in the United States toward Japan started to change when Nomo arrived.

"Nomo's impact will be so great as to recast the image of the Japanese people in the American imagination," wrote the *Mainichi News*.[23] Historians compared Nomo to Babe Ruth, who visited Japan in 1934. The US ambassador said then that Ruth was so popular in Japan that "one Babe is better than a hundred ambassadors." For the same reason, one Japanese scholar observed, in 1995, "Nomo is better than 100 Japanese ambassadors to Washington."[24]

At the end of the season Nomo was named NL Rookie of Year after notching a 13-6 record and a 2.54 ERA, and leading the league with 236 strikeouts in 191⅓ innings. "I think I had a great year with the Dodgers, and I'm satisfied," he said.[25] "My next goal is to pitch for the Dodgers in the World Series."[26]

Nomo's Rookie of the Year Award was a disappointment for Braves rookie Chipper Jones, who had his sights set on winning the award when he was drafted years earlier. A key contributor to the Braves' 1995 postseason success, Jones said, "He's got something I don't have, but I've got something he doesn't have — a World Series ring."[27]

In 1996 Nomo went 16-11, pitched his major-league career high of 228⅓ innings, and reduced his to a career-low 3.4 per nine innings pitched. His performance helped the Dodgers finish with a 90-72 record, one game behind the Western Division-leading San Diego Padres. Los Angeles secured the wild-card spot in the postseason, but was swept by the Braves in the Division Series. (Nomo started the third and final game of the series and gave up five runs in 3⅔ innings.)

While a World Series championship eluded Nomo in 1996, the Japanese righty found himself once again making history on the mound. On April 13 he struck out a career-high 17 batters in a 3-1 victory over the Florida Marlins.[28] On September 17 he pitched a no-hitter against the Colorado Rockies at hitter-friendly Coors Field.

Nomo was 3-0 against Colorado in his career, but the mile-high altitude had never been kind to him. He had never won a game in the Rockies' home ballpark.[29] Furthermore, Colorado was an offensive powerhouse in 1996. By the end of the season the Rockies led the NL in home runs (221) and stolen bases (201). Their lineup included three 40-home-run hitters, Andres Galarraga (47), Ellis Burks (40), and Vinny Castilla (40). Dante Bichette and Eric Young were also among the top offensive performers in the National League.

Nomo dominated the Rockies hitters in the game and won 9-0. In the improbable no-hitter, he struck out eight and walked four. Dodgers manager Bill Russell was stunned by Nomo's achievement. He said, "That was huge, especially to do it in Colorado. With the hitters they have over there and for Nomo to throw a no-hitter … is a tremendous effort."[30]

"(Nomo) probably doesn't realize how unbelievable that accomplishment is," said teammate Eric Karros. "People in Japan probably don't know Coors Field, but I'm betting it won't be done again."[31]

Karros was correct in his prediction. As of the 2016 season, no other pitcher had thrown a no-hitter in Coors Field. More than 20 years later, some argue that Nomo's feat, particularly against one of the best-hitting teams of all time — was "the greatest regular-season pitching performance in baseball history."[32]

In 1997 Nomo set a major-league record for starting pitchers by reaching 500 strikeouts in 444⅔ innings. That was one-third of an inning less than Dwight Gooden's record of 445 innings set in 1985.[33] Nomo's record was later broken by Kerry Wood (404⅔), Yu Darvish (401⅔), and the late Jose Fernandez of the Marlins, who surpassed them all in 2016 by reaching the milestone in 400 innings.[34]

On paper Nomo's 1997 season looked somewhat average, and even uneventful. Unbeknownst to him and those around him though, his career began its downward spiral that season. The critical moment occurred on July 26 when the Phillies' Scott Rolen knocked Nomo out of a game with a line drive off his pitching arm. Rolen's shot was the only hit Nomo allowed in 3⅔ innings. The Dodgers won the game, 4-1, but the smash changed everything for Nomo.

He quickly returned to pitching, but by the end of the season his elbow required surgery to remove bone chips and calcium deposits. In hindsight, the career-altering impact of Rolen's line drive off suggests parallels to the beanball that leveled Boston Red Sox slugger Tony Conigliario in 1967. Both athletes eventually returned to the field and displayed flashes of their former brilliance, but neither was ever truly the same player again.

Rolen was the batter Nomo hit most often during his career. Nomo hit the Phillies shortstop three times, all after the line-drive incident. According to Nomo each hit-by-pitch was an honest mistake. "Absolutely not intentional," he declared. "He's a great hitter. I was just trying to jam him inside. I will not give him any more sweet pitches."[35]

The 1998 season marked the beginning of the end of "Nomomania" in Los Angeles. With a 2-7 record and 5.05 ERA, the 29-year-old right-hander was removed from the Dodgers' 40-man roster after complaining when he learned that his name had been included in trade talks with Seattle for Randy Johnson.[36] Both the Yankees and Mets expressed an interest in Nomo, but the Mets appealed to him most because of familiar faces in the clubhouse. Among them were rookie pitcher Masato Yoshii, one of Nomo's best friends from Japan; his former Dodgers catcher, Mike Piazza; and Dave Wallace, his former Dodgers pitching coach, now a senior adviser for New York.[37] On June 4 the Dodgers traded Nomo with Brad Clontz to the Mets for Greg McMichael and Dave Mlicki.

Getting Nomo's career back on track was the Mets' top priority. Even his new teammates tried to help. Mets outfielder Butch Huskey thought he had the solution. He said the right-hander was tipping his pitches. "You could figure out what pitch he was throwing," Huskey said: When Nomo was throwing a fastball, his left pinkie was visible at the height of his windup. When he threw a splitter, his pinkie was in his glove. Huskey said that ex-Mets Tim Bogar and Bill Spiers discovered the flaw during Nomo's rookie season. Mets pitching coach Bob Apodaca alerted Nomo. "He's a professional. I don't want him to be overly concerned," Apodaca said. "It might just be a matter of putting his hand up higher in his glove. Or getting a bigger glove."[38]

The change of scenery or glove size didn't help Nomo in New York. He pitched only slightly better for the Mets the second half of 1998. After spring training in 1999, the Mets released him, choosing to give the aging Orel Hershiser a try instead.[39]

Nomo signed a minor-league contract with the Chicago Cubs, who gave him an extended spring training and required him to start three games with the Triple-A Iowa Cubs. After assessing his performance, the Cubs would either put him on the major-league roster or release him. Rick Kranitz, the Cubs' roving pitching instructor, declared, "I don't see why he can't pitch in the big leagues. The ball's jumping out of his hand."[40] But Nomo was released after his final start.

Nomo next signed with the Milwaukee Brewers. He pitched one solid outing for the Double-A Huntsville Stars and the Brewers brought him up. In Milwaukee, Nomo returned to his lucky jersey Number 11 that he once wore with the Kintetsu Buffaloes in Japan. Nomo had a good season, going 12-8. Nomo got his groove back, thanks in part to a close relationship with manager Phil Garner.[41]

"He seems to do well for people he likes," Garner observed.[42]

On September 8, 1999, Nomo became the third-fastest starting pitcher to reach 1,000 strikeouts, trailing only Roger Clemens and Dwight Gooden.

Unable to come to an agreement on a long-term contract with Milwaukee, Nomo entered the 2000 season as a free agent. He signed a one-year contract with the Detroit Tigers for $1.25 million and the chance to earn an addition $3.25 million in performance bonuses. In Detroit he reunited with Phil Garner, now the Tigers manager.

With the Tigers Nomo had to abandon his lucky jersey number 11, which had been worn by former manager Sparky Anderson and would be retired when Anderson was elected to the Hall of Fame. So Nomo settled for 23, previously worn by Kirk Gibson. When asked what he knew of Gibson, Nomo said, "He played well for the Dodgers and the Tigers." Nomo hoped to do the same.

In the season opener in Oakland, Nomo pitched a three-hitter and struck out eight in seven innings. The Tigers won, 7-4, and the season started on a promising note for Nomo and his new team. By the end of the season Nomo led the Tigers pitching staff with 181 strikeouts in 190 innings pitched, but also held the dubious distinction of leading the team in home runs allowed. He gave up a career-high 31 homers, six of them to the Boston Red Sox. His season was also marred by nagging injuries. In August he experienced discomfort in his throwing hand, radiating pain that originated in the first knuckle of his middle finger and shot down both sides of the finger. The Tigers training staff suspected that the injury was the result of Nomo's spreading his fingers to throw his forkball.

Despite the injuries, home runs allowed, and losses (he was 8-12), Nomo enjoyed his time as a Tiger. One night in Milwaukee after pitching six innings, he wore an eight-foot-tall costume of an Italian sausage and secretly participated in—and won—County Stadium's nightly Sausage Race.[43]

Nomo's enjoyable season came to a sour end when the Tigers released him. The Red Sox came calling and signed him to a one-year, $3.25 million contract with a signing bonus of $1.25 million.[44] Unlike the Tigers, the Red Sox were impressed that Nomo was sixth among AL starters with 181 strikeouts and third in strikeouts per nine innings (8.57). Nomo also had 17 quality starts (six innings or more and three earned runs or less allowed). They believed there was still some gas in Nomo's tank and that his arm could help the team. "I'm happy to be part of the Red Sox team," Nomo said. "I'm going with the Red Sox because they have a strong chance to go to the World Series." As he did in Milwaukee, Nomo donned his lucky jersey number 11 in Boston.

In his first start with the Red Sox, on April 4, 2001, Nomo pitched the second no-hitter of his career, defeating the Baltimore Orioles, 3-0, in Camden Yards. He joined Cy Young, Jim Bunning, and Nolan Ryan as the only major-league pitchers to throw a no-hitter in both the American and National Leagues. (Randy Johnson joined the group with his perfect game in 2004.)

Nomo struck out 11 and walked three. The no-hitter was the first thrown at Camden Yards. It also was the first of four no-hitters caught by Boston's Jason Varitek in his career. And it was the earliest calendar date on which a no-hitter had been pitched. (Bob Feller threw a no-hitter on Opening Day in 1940, but that occurred on April 16.)[45] The old Nomo was back, and it wasn't just for one game. He went on to finish the 2001 season with a 13-10 record and lead the American League in strikeouts with 220.

The major-league game with the largest viewing audience in Japan had been Nomo's debut game. On May 2 Nomo pitched in the game with the second largest audience. The Red Sox played the Seattle Mariners in Seattle and Ichiro Suzuki was in his first season with the Mariners.[46] The game started at noon in Japan and was an instant classic.[47] The Mariners won, 5-1. Nomo held Suzuki hitless but drilled him in the middle of the back with a fastball. The blow left the Mariners' leadoff hitter gasping for breath. "It was a fastball that I wanted to throw inside," Nomo said. "The cutter stuck on my fingers longer than I wanted, so the ball was more inside than I wanted." Ichiro joked about the incident later, saying, "I never imagined that my first hit-by-pitch would be done by a Japanese pitcher in Major League Baseball."[48]

After rejuvenating his career in Boston, Nomo turned down Red Sox offer of $19 million for three years and re-signed with the Dodgers. He earned close to $22 million over the next three seasons in Los Angeles. But by turning down the Red Sox offer he missed an opportunity to achieve the one goal that eluded him during his major-league career. Had he stayed in Boston, he might have been a member of the historic 2004 Red Sox team that "Reversed the Curse" and won the organization's first World Series in 86 years.[49]

When Nomo returned to Los Angeles in 2002 he quickly learned that this was not the same Dodgers organization he once knew. The O'Malley family had sold the team to Rupert Murdoch, the owner of News Corporation, the giant media conglomerate.

In Nomo's first season back, the Dodgers finished 92-70. They held first place for 30 games throughout the season, but finished in third place in a strong NL West behind the wild-card San Francisco Giants, who advanced to the World Series against the Anaheim Angels. Nomo finished the season with 193 strikeouts in 220⅓ innings and a 16-6 record, the best winning percentage (.727) of his major-league career. He was 9-5 at the All-Star break and got on a hot streak, winning 11 of 12 games in the second half.

In 2003 the Dodgers improved to second place despite a worse record (85-77) than the season before. Nomo started a team-high 33 games and compiled a 16-13 record with 177 strikeouts in 218⅓ innings. He pitched two shutouts and two two-hitters. His 3.09 ERA was the sixth best in the NL and the second best of his career. The Dodgers pitching staff had three players from Japan: Nomo, Masao Kida, and Kaz Ishii.

Nomo missed two weeks in September with shoulder inflammation and had surgery in the off-season to "clean up" the rotator cuff. Afterward, the velocity on his fastball dropped dramatically, from the 90-mph range down to the low to mid-80s. "I can't get strength behind my pitches," Nomo complained. The Dodgers noticed the decline in velocity at the beginning of spring training but hoped he would come around.

Manager Jim Tracey proclaimed Nomo the staff ace after the departure of Kevin Brown.[50] But the ace never appeared. In July the Dodgers placed Nomo on the 15-day disabled list with rotator-cuff inflammation.[51]

After achieving the best winning percentage of his career the previous season, Nomo struggled in 2004. He finished with a 4-11 record (a .267 winning percentage, a career low) and an 8.25 ERA, the highest ERA ever for a pitcher with at least 15 decisions. The Dodgers sent Nomo to Triple-A Las Vegas for a brief stint and eventually released him at the end of the season.

Nomo signed a minor-league contract with Tampa Bay for 2005. With the Devil Rays he returned to his lucky uniform number. One reporter commented that Nomo wore number 11 "any season when he feels he has something to prove."[52] At the start of the season, Nomo had 196 career wins between Japan and the major leagues, and desperately wanted win number 200. "In Japan, 200 wins is a big deal," a Japanese sportswriter said. "It will ensure Nomo's spot in the Japanese Baseball Hall of Fame, if he hasn't earned one already."[53]

After the rotator-cuff injury and the attempt to repair it, Nomo was clearly no longer the pitcher he used to be. "It's his guts, his competitiveness that makes him an effective pitcher," said Tampa Bay general manager Chuck LaMar.[54] On June 15 Nomo allowed two runs in seven innings as the Devil Rays defeated the Milwaukee Brewers, 5-3. It was career win 200, qualifying him for the Japanese Golden Players Club, known in Japan as the Meikyukai.[55] Membership in the Meikyukai is automatic for position players with 2,000 hits and pitchers with 200 victories. Nomo's win made him the 45th member of the Golden Players Club and the 16th pitcher.[56]

"He's had a great career and this is a special win," said Tampa Bay manager Lou Piniella. "We didn't have champagne, but we had the beer, so he got doused with beer and everybody gave him a standing ovation, which was really respectful of a heck of a competitor and a great pitcher."⁵⁷ But by midseason Nomo was sitting on an unimpressive 5-8 record and a 7.24 ERA, and with a stockpile of young arms in the Tampa Bay farm system, the team released him.

The 36-year-old veteran was immediately picked up by the New York Yankees but pitched only at Triple-A Columbus. After the season his contract with the Yankees was not renewed.

In March 2006 Nomo signed with the Chicago White Sox, the defending World Series champions. He started one game for Triple-A Charlotte and afterward was put on the disabled list with a sore elbow. He was released in June. Nomo resurfaced 16 months later and about 20 pounds heavier, signing with the Leones del Caracas in the Venezuelan League. The 39-year-old pitcher arrived in Venezuela in October 2007 because of his friendship with Leones manager Carlos Hernandez, Nomo's batterymate during his first two seasons in the major leagues. When asked if this was a first step to returning to the majors, Nomo answered, "I'm taking things slow, this is a first step, if all goes well, I'll think about looking for the opportunity to return."

In January 2008 Nomo agreed to a minor-league contract with the Kansas City Royals. Despite his history of shoulder problems, the Royals were intrigued with Nomo as a middle reliever and as a mentor for rookie pitcher Yasuhiko Yabuta. "Hideo has a lot of experience and can help guide him along and serve as a role model," said Royals GM Dayton Moore.

Nomo pitched three games in relief in April as a member of the Royals. Against the heart of the Yankees lineup, he surrendered home runs to Alex Rodriguez and Jorge Posada in the ninth inning. Undeterred, the veteran struck out fellow countryman Hideki Matsui to end the inning. Against the Mariners, Nomo faced Ichiro Suzuki, who struck out swinging on a 2-and-2 pitch.

In his third and final appearance for the Royals, on April 18, Nomo relieved Yabuta in the bottom of the eighth inning against Oakland. He faced four Oakland hitters and allowed a single, double, and a home run—a triple shy of the cycle, and a heartbreaker for anyone rooting for a Nomo career comeback. Travis Buck went down swinging to end the inning. It was the final strikeout of Nomo's 12-year major-league career. The Royals released him a week later.

In July 2008 Nomo announced his retirement from professional baseball at age 39.⁵⁸ Slugger Hideki Matsui said, "He was a pioneer for all of us. He helped all of us come to the major leagues. All of the players who have come from Japan owe him a debt of gratitude."⁵⁹

"Before Hideo came over here everyone had an image of major-league baseball and people looked at players over here as monsters because they were so big," said Ichiro Suzuki. "We were able to watch more MLB games and were able to get an image of, 'Maybe I can play in the big leagues.'"⁶⁰

After retirement Nomo joined the Orix Buffaloes, the current incarnation of his former Japanese team. He traveled occasionally with the team during the 2009 season and worked with the pitchers.⁶¹ In 2010 he became a part-time adviser for the Hiroshima Carp, and also invested in a team in Japan's Industrial League.⁶²

Nomo had participated in instructional camps in the past, but in retirement he found a new passion in coaching and helping to develop young players. He founded the Nomo Project, an initiative designed to help introduce young Japanese players to the experience of playing baseball in America.⁶³

In 2011 Nomo partnered with Segetoshi Hasagawa to create the USA-Japan Youth Baseball Games, a tournament for players 15 and younger. Nomo's Junior All-Japan team joined with Hasegawa's Southern California-based ROX Baseball Club, the Japan-based International Baseball Exchange Committee team and the Urban Youth Academy team to make up the participants in the tournament.⁶⁴

In 2014, his first year of eligibility for election to the Hall of Fame, Nomo received only six votes (1.1 percent) and was thus removed from the Cooperstown ballot. The voting on the other side of the Pacific was a different story. For the Japanese Baseball Hall of Fame, he received 82.4 percent of the 324 votes, well above the 75 percent needed for induction.[65]

Nomo joined the elite group with Victor Starfin (1960) and Sadaharu Oh (1994) as the only people elected to Japan's Baseball Hall of Fame in their first year of eligibility. He also became the youngest person ever to be inducted, at the age of 45 years and 4 months. When Nomo learned that he had been elected to the Japanese Baseball Hall of Fame, he was doing what he loved most: He was on the field helping to develop future All-Star players with his own boys baseball tournament.

Nomo's son, Takahiro, joined the family business of baseball after graduating from Menlo College in California in 2015. He was named the team translator for the Nippon Ham Fighters, winners of the 2016 Japan Series (Japan's equivalent of the World Series).[66] In 2016 Nomo and former Dodgers executive Acey Kohrogi joined the San Diego Padres to help increase the team's presence in the Pacific Rim.

In reflecting on Nomo's legacy, Dave Wallace, former Dodgers pitching coach, said, "He was the first one. He had everything to lose and nothing to gain. He set the table for a lot of other guys, who are now reaping the benefits. Japanese players will always owe him for that."[67]

Since Nomo's arrival in 1995, a total of 58 other Japanese-born players have pursued their major-league dreams in America.

"For him to come over and leave a successful career behind in Japan the way he did … he had to have some guts to do that," said former Dodgers teammate Eric Karros. "And then to succeed the way he did with the media watching him 24 hours a day? There may be better players from Japan who come to MLB, but Nomo will always be the man," he said. "There's Nomo up here, then there's the rest."[68]

NOTES

1 Jrank.org, "Net. Hideo Nomo—Super Tornado," sports.jrank.org/pages/3447/Nomo-Hideo-Super-Tornado.html#ixzz4UAhMsTQV, accessed November 20, 2016.

2 Robert Whiting, *The Samurai Way of Baseball: The Impact of Ichiro and the New Wave from Japan* (New York: Little, Brown and Company, 2005), 98.

3 Alan M. Klein, *Growing the Game: The Globalization of Major League Baseball* (New Haven: Yale University Press, 2006), 71.

4 Whiting, *The Samurai Way of Baseball*, 99.

5 Ibid.

6 Jrank.org, "Net. Hideo Nomo—Super Tornado."

7 Kota Ishijima, Nomo's former translator, email interview, January 13, 2017.

8 Whiting, *The Samurai Way of Baseball*, 97.

9 Whiting, 101.

10 Ken Daley, "Dodgers Forgo MRI Exam for Pitcher Nomo," *Los Angeles Daily News*, February 14, 1995.

11 Ken Daley, "Spark(y) Is Lacking in Game—Anderson, Lasorda Differ on Dispute," *Los Angeles Daily News*, March 4, 1995.

12 Cindy Martinez Rhodes, "Spirit Not Snubbed by Nomo's Start for Blaze," *Riverside* (California) *Press-Enterprise*, April 26, 1995.

13 Eric Noland, "Dodgers Notes—Nomo Not Nervous About Making Debut at Candlestick," *Los Angeles Daily News*, May 1, 1995.

14 Ibid.

15 Ken Daley, "Japanese Import Delivers—Dodgers' Nomo Fulfills Dream in Pitching Debut," *Los Angeles Daily News*, May 3, 1995.

16 Craig Minami, "Dodger Rookie Hideo Nomo Starts 1995 All-Star Game," *True Blue LA*, July 12, 2013.

17 "Injured Maddux Decides to Skip All-Star Appearance—Braves Ace Strained his Groin Thursday Night Against Dodgers," *Kansas City Star*, July 8, 1995.

18 Craig Minami, "Dodger Rookie Hideo Nomo Starts 1995 All-Star Game."

19 Cameron W. Barr, "A Welcome Ray of Sunlight for Gloomy Japan," *Christian Science Monitor*, July 5, 1995.

20 Ibid.

21 Martin Tolchin, "The Nation: Japan-Bashing, Becomes a Trade Bill Issue," *New York Times*, February 28, 1988.

22 Ibid.

23 Cameron W. Barr.

24 Ibid.

25 Chuck Johnson, "Top Rookie Nomo 'Really Appreciates' New Teammates," *USA Today*, November 10, 1995.

26 Dave Allen, "L.A.'s Nomo Is Rookie of the Year," *Deseret News* (Salt Lake City), November 10, 1995.

27 Chuck Johnson.

28 Gordon Edes, "Nomo Baffles Marlins, Strikes Out 17," *South Florida Sun Sentinel* (Fort Lauderdale), April 14, 1996.

29 Video: MLB Classics, "9/17/96: Nomo's No-No," youtube.com/watch?v=Bv2_wo2l72A,, accessed November 27, 2016.

NO-HITTERS

30 "Dodgers' Nomo Pulled No-Hitter Right Out of Thin Air at Coors Field," Spokesman.com, September 19, 1996.

31 Ibid.

32 Ibid.

33 "Nomo Returns to the Dodgers," *Deseret News,* (Salt Lake City), December 21, 2001.

34 Zachary D. Rymer, "Fastest Starter to 500, How Far Can Jose Fernandez Climb MLB's All-Time K List?" Bleacher-Report.com, July 18, 2016.

35 Don Bostrom, "Swollen Elbow Causes Rolen to Miss First Game," *Allentown* (Pennsylvania) *Morning Call,* August 26, 1997.

36 Jack Curry, "Nomo Released by Dodgers, May Land With Mets," *Fort Worth Star-Telegram,* June 2, 1998.

37 Ibid.

38 Thomas Hill, "Mets Finger Pinkie as Nomo's Weak Spot," *New York Daily News,* June 8, 1998.

39 T.J. Quinn, "Official Sayonara for Nomo—Yoshii May Be History Soon," *The Record* (Hackensack, New Jersey), March 27, 1999.

40 Dave Van Dycke, "Nomo Still Presenting A Puzzle - Theories Abound, But Cubs Taking A Look," *Chicago Sun-Times,* April 18, 1999.

41 Tom Haudricourt, "They Go Hand in Glove—Nomo's Comfort Zone With Garner Leads Him to Detroit," *Milwaukee Journal Sentinel,* February 28, 2000.

42 Ibid.

43 "Names in the Game," Associated Press Archive, July 9, 2000.

44 Sean McAdam, "Red Sox Acquire Hideo Nomo," *Providence Journal,* December 15, 2000.

45 Murray Chass, "Baseball: Nomo Hurls a No-Hitter in His Red Sox Debut," *New York Times,* April 5, 2001.

46 Jeff Horrigan, "Baseball—Sox Slip Up in Seattle—Ichiro, Mariners Sail to 5-1 Victory," *Boston Herald*, May 3, 2001.

47 Ibid.

48 Ibid.

49 MLB.com, "Red Sox Break the Curse," m.mlb.com/video/v19983103/ws2004-gm4-red-sox-complete-a-fourgame-series-sweep, accessed October 29, 2016.

50 Bill Plunkett, "Dodgers' Winning Streak Ends at Six," *Orange County Register* (Santa Ana, California), May 13, 2004.

51 Rich Hammond, "Dodgers Notebook: Injured or Not, Nomo on DL," *Los Angeles Daily News,* July 2, 2004.

52 Roger Mooney, "Japan's Wonder: Rays' Nomo Left Everything to Play Ball in America," *Bradenton* (Florida) *Herald*, April 15, 2005.

53 Ibid.

54 Ibid.

55 Carter Gaddis, "Rays' Nomo Finally Nails Down Victory No. 200," *Tampa Tribune,* June 16, 2005.

56 Ibid.

57 Ibid.

58 "Around the Bases," *Miami Herald,* July 18, 2008.

59 Roger Mooney.

60 Ibid.

61 NPBtracker.com, "Nomo Travels with Orix," npbtracker.com/2009/04/nomo-travels-with-orix/, April 15, 2009.

62 Robert Whiting, "Nomo's Legacy Should Land Him in Hall of Fame," *Japan Times,* October 24, 2010.

63 Ben Platt, "Japanese Youth Get Taste of American Baseball," MLB.com, August 24, 2011.

64 Ibid.

65 Kaz Nagatsuka, "Nomo Inducted Into Japanese Baseball Hall of Fame," *Japan Times,* January 17, 2014.

66 Kei Nakamura, "Sports Graphic Number Web (Japanese)," January 30, 2015, number.bunshun.jp/articles/-/822582, accessed December 30, 2016.

67 Robert Whiting, "Nomo's Legacy Should Land Him in Hall of Fame."

68 Ibid.

NOMO NO-HITS THE ROCKIES AT HITTER-FRIENDLY COORS FIELD

SEPTEMBER 17, 1996: LOS ANGELES DODGERS 9, COLORADO ROCKIES 0, AT COORS FIELD, DENVER

By Bill Staples Jr.

ON A TYPICAL WORKDAY IN Tokyo, rush-hour traffic is notorious for being among the busiest on the planet.[1] One can only imagine what it was like on Wednesday, September 18, 1996, at 4:30 P.M. (Tokyo time) when word began to spread about the possibility of a *no hitto no ran* (the Japanese words for "no-hitter").[2]

Approximately 5,795 miles (9,326 km) east of Tokyo in Denver, Colorado, Japan's favorite son and Dodgers pitching sensation Hideo Nomo was about to take a 9-0 lead and a no-hitter into the ninth inning against the Rockies. At 5 P.M. large monitors in busy intersections aired the game, causing commuters to stop in their tracks and tune in to watch Nomo make history.[3]

Prior to this date there were 241 major-league no-hitters, but number 242 was the first one thrown by a Japanese-born pitcher.[4] So it was only fitting that Nomo's historic performance was broadcast on NHK television to millions of fans in Japan by Masanori Murakami, the first Japanese-born player in major-league history.[5] At the time, however, viewers did not know that Nomo's no-hitter occurred in a game that almost didn't happen.

Shortly before the projected 7:05 P.M. start time in Denver, Coors Field was hit with heavy rain and thunderstorms. After a two-hour rain delay, sprinkles continued to fall but umpire crew chief Bill Hohn and his crew decided that conditions were good enough to play.[6]

The official attendance was 50,066, but only about 30,000 fans endured the rain delay and 46-degree temperature to see the 9:05 P.M. start. The damp weather not only affected actual attendance, it influenced on-field performance as well. Because the light rain made the mound slippery, Nomo had to abandon his full windup and pitch from the stretch, even with no runners on base.[7]

As for the hitters, the humidity in the air deadened hard-hit balls that might have normally sailed over the outfield fences at Coors Field. After the game, Dodgers catcher Mike Piazza observed, "It was a little muggy and the ball didn't carry as well as it usually does here."[8]

Entering the game, the 28-year-old Nomo had a 15-10 record and a 3.29 ERA, and had pitched 207⅔ innings in 30 games. The Dodgers held a half-game lead over the San Diego Padres for first place in the National League West.

Nomo was 3-0 against Colorado in his career, but the mile-high altitude had never been kind to him. Vin Scully observed, "With Nomo it is a case of *where* he is pitching. ... See what he does at Dodger Stadium and then at Coors Field."[9] (See Table 1 below.)

Table 1: Rocked in Colorado - Nomo vs. Rockies at Coors Field vs. Dodger Stadium, 1995-96

Date	Location	Score	Result for Nomo
May 7, 1995	Coors Field	10-12	No decision
June 29, 1995	Dodger Stadium	3-0	Win
April 30, 1996	Dodger Stadium	7-4	Win
June 30, 1996	Coors Field	15-16	No decision
July 5, 1996	Dodger Stadium	8-1	Win
Sept. 17, 1996	Coors Field	9-0	Win (no-hitter)

Nomo wasn't the only pitcher to struggle in Denver. In fact, great pitching was a rarity in the Mile High City. Prior to Nomo's no-hitter, only three major-league pitchers had thrown a complete-game shutout at Coors Field: Pat Rapp (Florida Marlins, 1995, one-hitter), Tom Glavine (Atlanta Braves, 1995, six-hitter), and Mark Thompson (Colorado Rockies, 1996, seven-hitter vs. Florida).

Nomo's past performance against Colorado at Coors Field wasn't the only Dodgers cause for concern. The Rockies were an offensive powerhouse in 1996. By the end of the season they would lead the NL in home runs (221) and stolen bases (201). Their lineup included three 40-home-run hitters: Andres Galarraga (47), Ellis Burks (40), and Vinny Castilla (40). Dante Bichette and Eric Young were also among the top offensive performers in the NL.

Burks led the league in runs scored (142), slugging percentage (.639), and total bases (392), and finished third in the National League MVP vote. Before the Dodgers series, he was coming off a stellar Player-of-the-Week performance, hitting .643. He was hot, and given that Rockies had previously scored 28 runs in two games Nomo started at Coors Field, no doubt Burks and the other Rockies hitters were eager to face the Japanese righty again.

The matchup on the mound featured two pitchers who won silver medals in the Olympics for their respective countries, Bill Swift with Team USA in 1984, and Nomo with Team Japan in 1988.[10] Swift started strong for the Rockies, retiring the first three Dodgers hitters on two groundouts and a strikeout. Nomo, on the other hand, got off to a rough start.

Rockies leadoff hitter Young hit a fly ball to deep center field for the first out. Nomo walked Quinton McCracken, who stole second and advanced to third on a fly to deep right field by Burks. In the dugout, Dodgers manager Bill Russell and pitching coach Dave Wallace had reason for concern; Nomo had thrown 10 wild pitches already this season as a result of his nasty forkball. With two outs and the Rockies' possible first run just 90 feet away, Nomo buckled down and struck out Bichette with a 2-and-2 forkball to end the threat. The first inning seem to set the tone for Nomo's pitching for the rest of the evening. Mixing fastballs and sinking split-fingers for strikes, and strategically placing balls out of the zone, he kept hitters off balance, eventually walking four over nine innings.

In fact, only three times did the Rockies threaten to end Nomo's no-hit bid with sharply-hit balls. In the fourth inning Galarraga came close when he hit a fielder's-choice grounder to shortstop Greg Gagne. In the seventh Galarraga hit a hard line drive to Raul Mondesi, and Castilla hit a high fly to Wayne Kirby in center field. On any other night those fly balls might have left the ballpark in Denver.

In the top of the ninth the world tuned in to watch Nomo make history. Murakami called the play-by-play for NHK Television in Japan. Vin Scully narrated the moment for fans in America via ESPN. All the while, none of his Dodgers teammates would talk to Nomo in the dugout. He sat quietly, alone on the bench as his teammates batted. With his right hand kept warm wrapped in a towel, he silently high-fived teammate Chad Curtis after Curtis scored in the top of the ninth, and fist-bumped Tim Wallach to celebrate a two-run home run that put the Dodgers up 9-0.

The Dodgers batters were merciless on Rockies pitching in the ninth, which forced Nomo to bat. The Rockies fans gave him a standing ovation as he removed his jacket and stepped into the batter's box. With two outs and two runners on, and the prospect of securing a no-hitter just moments away, Nomo struck out swinging.

For Nomo, his final inning mirrored the efficiency with which Swift started the game. Leadoff hitter Young grounded out to Delino DeShields at second base. McCracken did the same. With Nomo one out away from making history, Burks, the Rockies' hottest hitter, stepped into the box. With a 2-and-2 count, Nomo's signature forkball fooled the slugger, who swung and missed.

It seemed that the magnitude of what Nomo achieved was appreciated by everyone. Except Nomo. "You may not believe me, but I'm glad we picked up the win at this time rather than I accomplished a no-hitter," he said through his translator. "We're battling for the division title, so this is a big win."[11]

Both managers were impressed with Nomo's achievement. Dodgers manager Russell said, "That was huge, especially to do it in Colorado. With the hitters they have over there and for Nomo to throw a no-hitter … is a tremendous effort." Rockies manager Don Baylor agreed: "In this ballpark, that was an incredible feat."[12]

"(Nomo) probably doesn't realize how unbelievable that accomplishment is," said teammate Eric Karros. "People in Japan probably don't know Coors Field, but I'm betting it won't be done again."[13] Karros was correct in his prediction. As of the 2016 season, no other pitcher had thrown a no-hitter in Coors Field.

In fact, prior to Rapp's one-hitter in 1995, the last time a pitcher came close to a no-hitter in Denver was in 1957, when Ryne Duren pitched seven innings of no-hit ball for the Denver Bears, the Triple-A affiliate of the New York Yankees. Duren finished the game with a one-hitter.[14]

Almost 20 years later, Jack Moore of Vice Sports suggested that Nomo's no-no—as the first and only ever no-hitter at Coors Field, and against one of the best hitting teams of all time—is arguably "the greatest regular-season pitching performance in baseball history."[15]

SOURCES

In addition to the sources cited in the Notes, the author relied on Baseball-Reference.com.

NOTES

1. Japan-guide.com, "2016 Survey: How Many Times Have You Visited Japan?" japan-guide.com/e/e2020.html, accessed November 27, 2016.

2. Dexter Thomas, translator, provided Japanese words for "perfect game" and "no-hitter," via email exchange, December 26, 2016. See also Samuel E. Martin, *Reference Grammar of Japanese* (Honolulu: University of Hawai'i Press, 2003), 380.

3. Video: MLB Classics, "9/17/96: Nomo's No-No," youtube.com/watch?v=Bv2_w02l72A, accessed November 27, 2016.

4. No-hitters.com, "No-Hitter List | Baseball No-Hitters at NoNoHitters.Com," nonohitters.com/no-hitters, accessed November 27, 2016.

5. Video: MLB Classics, "9/17/96: Nomo's No-No."

6. Ibid.

7. Jack Moore, "Throwback Thursday: Hideo Nomo Defies the Odds for a Coors Field No-No," VICE Sports, September 17, 2015.

8. Associated Press, "Dodgers' Nomo Pulled No-Hitter Right Out of Thin Air at Coors Field," Spokesman.com, September 19, 1996.

9. Video: MLB Classics, "9/17/96: Nomo's No-No."

10. In both the 1984 and 1988 Summer Olympic Games, baseball was a demonstration sport. Medals were awarded, but the medals were not "official" and did not count in the respective nations' medal totals.

11. "Dodgers' Nomo Pulled No-Hitter Right Out of Thin Air at Coors Field."

12. Ibid.

13. Ibid.

14. Bob Kravitz, "Nomo's No-Hitter in Coors Field Is Nothing Short of Incredible," *St Louis Post-Dispatch,* September 19, 1996.

15. Jack Moore, "Vice Sports - Throwback Thursday: Hideo Nomo Defies The Odds For A Coors Field No-No," September 17, 2015, https://sports.vice.com/en_us/article/throwback-thursday-hideo-nomo-defies-the-odds-for-a-coors-field-no-no, accessed December 30, 2016.

NOMO JOINS ELITE COMPANY WITH NO-HITTERS IN BOTH LEAGUES

APRIL 4, 2001: BOSTON RED SOX 3, BALTIMORE ORIOLES 0, AT ORIOLES PARK AT CAMDEN YARDS, BALTIMORE

By Bill Staples Jr.

IN HIS FIRST START WITH THE Boston Red Sox, Hideo Nomo pitched a no-hitter, defeating the Baltimore Orioles, 3-0, at Camden Yards. In doing so, he joined Cy Young, Jim Bunning, and Nolan Ryan as the only pitchers in major-league history to throw no-hitters in both the American and National Leagues.[1] (Randy Johnson joined the group with his perfect game in 2004.[2]) Of the five members in this elite club, Nomo is the only one not enshrined in Cooperstown. (See Table 1.)

After pitching six full seasons in the major leagues, Nomo signed a one-year, $4.5 million contract with Boston in December 2001.[3] "I'm going with the Red Sox because they have a strong chance to go to the World Series," Nomo said.[4] Individual awards and accomplishments are nice, but his ultimate goal had always been to win the World Series.[5]

In his first two seasons with the Los Angeles Dodgers, Nomo recorded a 29-17 record (.630 winning percentage). However, in his final three seasons he was 16-19 (.457). His struggles were due primarily to a lack of command caused by injuries. The Dodgers traded Nomo in midseason 1998 to the New York Mets. Afterward, he had one-year stints with Milwaukee and Detroit, where he finished with a combined 20-20 record.[6]

The Boston pitching staff included past and future All-Stars Pedro Martinez, Tim Wakefield, David Cone, Bret Saberhagen, and Derek Lowe.[7] The signing of the 32-year-old righty not only gave the Red Sox another weapon in their arsenal, it also gave them the distinction of becoming the first major-league team with two Japanese-born pitchers on their roster.

For Japanese teammate Tomo Ohka, it was a dream come true. He was 14 years old when Nomo earned MVP honors as a rookie in the Japanese Pacific League in 1990. Nomo was Ohka's childhood hero. He admired Nomo for his accomplishments on the mound and for his role as a pioneer for other Japanese players entering the major leagues.

Despite a rocky 2001 spring training, where he had an 0-3 record and a double-digit ERA, injuries to Cone and Saberhagen allowed Nomo to secure the number-two spot in the rotation behind Martinez.[8]

The Red Sox opened the season with three games against the Orioles in Baltimore. Boston manager Jimy Williams told the press, "You never know when you're going to see a special game. You really don't. That's why I like baseball."[9] The Orioles won walk-off 2-1 victories in the first and third games of the series. But the middle game of the season-opening series belonged to Boston, courtesy of Nomo.

Nomo's first no-hitter, in Denver in 1996, was in a game whose start was delayed by rain. His start in Baltimore was also delayed, for 45 minutes, because of a power outage that hit in the bottom of the first inning.[10] Entering the game the Baltimore lineup was 8-for-51 (.157) against Nomo. David Segui, 5-for-13 (.387) with two home runs, was the only Orioles hitter with any success against him.

Also working in Nomo's favor that night was the presence of home-plate umpire Eric Cooper. During the offseason the major leagues had decided to expand the strike zone vertically, and at times Cooper appeared to be struggling with his interpretation of the new rules. A few questionable called third strikes might have created doubt in the heads of Orioles hitters, perhaps forcing them to chase pitches normally outside their comfort zone.[11]

In traditional Nomo fashion, he started off slow on the mound and gained strength as the game progressed. In the first inning, three of four Orioles hitters made solid contact. The number-three hitter, Nomo's old Dodgers teammate Delino DeShields, reached base on a walk.

In the second inning, Melvin Mora blasted a fly ball to the center-field warning track that found Carl Everett's glove. Cal Ripken reached first on an error by third baseman Shea Hillenbrand and advanced to second on a Nomo splitter that was too hot for catcher Jason Varitek to handle. (It was ruled a wild pitch.) Baltimore's rally ended when Brook Fordyce became the first of Nomo's 11 strikeout victims.

Nomo's no-hit bid was threatened again by Brady Anderson's warning-track fly to right field in the third inning, a hot fielder's-choice grounder to second by Segui in the fourth, and a laser hit by Ripken to right field for an out in the fifth.

In the sixth inning Nomo started to dominate. The righty had great command of his fastball, forkball, and splitter, and gave the Orioles nothing to hit down the middle of the plate. By peppering the corners and changing speeds, Nomo struck out eight batters from the sixth through the eighth. Baltimore outfielder Jerry Hairston was fooled all night, striking out three times. All but two Orioles (Ripken and Chris Richard) struck out at least once.

In the bottom of the ninth inning, the only thing standing between Nomo and his second no-hitter were Anderson, Mike Bordick, and DeShields. "As I was going into the ninth inning, I was not nervous," Nomo said after the game.[12] Perhaps that was because he knew the stats were in his favor. Up to this point the last three Orioles batters were a combined 2-for-31 (.065) against Nomo.

Anderson (0-11 vs. Nomo) grounded back to Nomo. Knowing that Bordick (1-8) was a notorious fastball hitter, Nomo pitched away from the right-handed hitter. On a 2-and-1 count, Bordick slapped an outside pitch toward no-man's land behind second base in shallow center field. Second baseman Mike Lansing, a late-inning defensive replacement, chased the ball down and snagged it out of the air. The play saved the no-hitter and generated a semi-emotional glove slap from the stoic Nomo. For the final out, DeShields (1-12) hit a shallow fly to left field, where Troy O'Leary tucked it away easily.

While this was Nomo's second no-hitter, the achievement represented many firsts. The crowd of 35,602 applauded Nomo for giving them the first no-hitter at Camden Yards (and, as of 2016, the only one).

His feat also marked the earliest calendar date (April 4) on which a no-hitter had been pitched. Bob Feller threw a no-hitter on Opening Day in 1940, but that occurred on April 16.

For Varitek, Nomo's no-hitter was the first of four he would catch during his career. It was the 15th by a Red Sox pitcher.

After the game, Nomo said, "Today was my first time throwing for the Boston Red Sox, and I am obviously very happy with my performance."[13]

Nomo finished the season with a 13-10 record, leading the American League in strikeouts (220) and strikeouts per nine innings pitched (10.00). He also led the league in walks (96, one more than Cleveland's C.C. Sabathia).

Nomo pitched two one-hit games for Boston in 2001. He carried a no-hitter into the seventh inning against the Minnesota Twins, eventually winning 2-0 and allowing one hit and five walks, while striking out eight. Nomo vowed to pitching coach Joe Kerrigan that he would walk fewer hitters, and made good on his promise with a one-hit shutout against the Toronto Blue Jays in which he struck out 14 and walked none.[14]

NO-HITTERS

Table 1: Pitchers With No-Hitters in Both the American and National Leagues

Pitcher	First League No-Hitter	Second League No-Hitter	No-Hitters Career Total	HOF Induction Year
Cy Young	Cleveland Spiders (NL) Saturday, September 18, 1897 Cleveland Spiders 6, Cincinnati Reds 0; League Park (Cleveland)	Boston Americans (AL) Thursday, May 5, 1904 Boston Americans 3, Philadelphia Athletics 0; Huntington Avenue Grounds (Boston)	3	1937
Jim Bunning	Detroit Tigers (AL) Sunday, July 20, 1958 Detroit Tigers 3, Boston Red Sox 0; Fenway Park	Philadelphia Phillies (NL) Sunday, June 21, 1964 Philadelphia Phillies 6, New York Mets 0; Shea Stadium	2	1996
Nolan Ryan	California Angels (AL) Tuesday, May 15, 1973 California Angels 3, Kansas City Royals 0; Royals Stadium	Houston Astros (NL) Saturday, Sept. 26, 1981 Houston Astros 5, Los Angeles Dodgers 0; Astrodome	7	1999
Hideo Nomo	Los Angeles Dodgers (NL) Tuesday, Sept. 17, 1996 Los Angeles Dodgers 9, Colorado Rockies 0; Coors Field	Boston Red Sox (AL) Wednesday, April 4, 2001 Boston Red Sox 3, Baltimore Orioles 0; Orioles Park at Camden Yards	2	2014*
Randy Johnson	Seattle Mariners (AL) Saturday, June 2, 1990 Seattle Mariners 2, Detroit Tigers 0; Kingdome	Arizona Diamondbacks (NL) Tuesday, May 18, 2004 Arizona Diamondbacks 2, Atlanta Braves 0; Turner Field	2	2015

Inducted into the Japanese Baseball Hall of Fame in 2014.

NO-HITTERS

SOURCES

In addition to the sources cited in the Notes, the author relied on Baseball-Reference.com, baseball-almanac.com, and video of the game, at MLB Classics, "9/4/01: Nomo's Second No-No," youtube.com/watch?v=qfwNcsSPzCY, accessed November 27, 2016.* See also BaseballPilgrimages.com, "No-Hitters Thrown in Current Major League Ballparks," baseballpilgrimages.com/ballparks/no-hitters.html, accessed November 28, 2016.

*YouTube has listed the wrong date for the game, but the link still works as of February 2017.

NOTES

1 Murray Chass, "Baseball; Nomo Hurls a No-Hitter in His Red Sox Debut," *New York Times,* April 5, 2001.

2 FoxSports.com, "12 Years Ago, Randy Johnson Made MLB History with This Perfect Game," foxsports.com/mlb/story/arizona-diamondbacks-atlanta-braves-randy-johnson-perfect-game-12-years-ago-051816, accessed November 28, 2016.

3 David Heuschkel, "Nomo Ready to Leave Sox," *Hartford Courant,* December 6, 2001.

4 Sean McAdam, "Red Sox Acquire Hideo Nomo," *Providence Journal,* December 15, 2000.

5 Lawrence Rocca, "Nomomania Revisted — Baseball: The International Popularity of the Dodgers' Right-Hander Is Already on the Rise," *Orange County Register* (Santa Ana, California), February 19, 1996.

6 Baseball-Reference.com, "Hideo Nomo," baseball-reference.com/players/n/nomohi01.shtml, accessed November 28, 2016.

7 Baseball-Reference.com, "2001 Boston Red Sox Roster," baseball-reference.com/teams/BOS/2001.shtml, accessed November 28, 2016.

8 Video: MLB Classics. "9/4/01: Nomo's Second No-No," youtube.com/watch?v=qfwNcsSPzCY, accessed November 28, 2016.

9 Phil O'Neill, "Japanese Blitz Will Sack Nomo / No-Hitter Will Attract Extra Media," *Worcester* (Massachusetts) *Telegram & Gazette,* April 6, 2001.

10 Ibid.

11 Joe Capozzi, "Discomfort Zone," *Palm Beach Post,* March 1, 2001.

12 "Second No-No for Nomo, This One Against O's," *New York Daily News,* April 5, 2001.

13 Ibid.

14 David Kamerman, "Hideo Nomo Spins 1-Hit Gem for Red Sox," *Boston Globe,* May 26, 2001.

DAVID "BOOMER" WELLS

by Norm King

YOU HAVE TO LOVE A GUY who takes the mound in the House That Ruth Built wearing a Cap That Ruth Wore.

David Wells did just that at Yankee Stadium on June 28, 1997, when he took the hill to pitch against Cleveland sporting his Yankee pinstripes and his Yankee cap. The problem was that it wasn't the standard-issue model his teammates were wearing; it was a cap Ruth wore in 1934 that Wells had purchased for $35,000. Yankees manager Joe Torre found out about it after the first inning and ordered Wells to remove it.

Such was the career of David Lee "Boomer" Wells, whose reverence for New York Yankees traditions contrasted with his iconoclastic attitude toward just about everything else during his 21-year major-league career with nine different teams. He retired with a career 239-157 career won-lost record (.604 winning percentage), a 10-5 record in the playoffs, two World Series rings, and a perfect game.

Wells was born on May 20, 1963, in Torrance, California. His childhood was, to say the least, unconventional. His mother, Eugenia Ann Wells, was a biker chick with the handle Attitude Annie. Annie wasn't exactly your typical suburban soccer mom as she had five children from four different men. Wells didn't meet his father, David Pritt, until he was 22 years old.

Growing up, Wells was the only kid in the neighborhood, and possibly in the country, who could bring the Hell's Angels to his Little League games. Annie's boyfriend was Crazy Charlie Mendez, a longtime member of the San Diego chapter, and he would bring his confreres to Wells's games when he pitched. Not only that, the bikers would each give him a dollar (or 25 cents) for every batter he struck out, and $5 (or $1) every time he won.[1] And no matter how much the gang members owed him, he never worried about them welching.

"I could pull in $100 a game, and nobody dared screw around with me," said Wells. "Try, and I'd say, 'I'll get my mom's boyfriend on you.'"[2]

Charlie didn't generally abuse Wells, but he wasn't afraid to smack him if it meant teaching an important life lesson. Once, when he was 12, Wells walked into the kitchen with his fists up; Charlie greeted him with a left hook. "I said, 'What did you do that for,'" recalled Wells. "He said, 'Anytime you put your hands up, you'd better use 'em.' Other than that, he treated me like a king."[3]

Wells pitched for a very good Point Loma High School team that competed for the city championship in 1981 and 1982. If some of the stories about his high-school career are true, his coach may very well have ended up with ulcers. He once told teammates during a game that he was going to deliberately walk the bases loaded, then strike out the side on nine pitches, and proceeded to do just that. On another occasion, Wells was going for a second perfect game when the first baseman told Wells he needed one out for the gem. Coach Steve Saracino heard the player and told him he was off the team if the batter got a hit. Well, the batter did get a hit, and Saracino followed through on his threat. The following Monday, Wells convinced his teammates to boycott practice unless the first baseman was reinstated. Saracino relented.

Wells was the starter for two championship games, losing in 1981 to Darren Balsley and Mt. Carmel High School, then coming back to beat Mt. Carmel the following year. Balsley was Wells's pitching coach during both of his stints with the San Diego Padres.

That ability to pitch in critical ballgames and being chosen for the American Baseball Coaches Association second All-American team may have encouraged the Toronto Blue Jays to pick Wells in the second round of the 1982 amateur draft. Being drafted by a team that had one of our feathered friends as a nickname didn't impress Boomer.

"I said, 'Man, if I ever sign, I'm never playing for those guys, ever,'" Wells said. "A Blue Jay? I mean, a bird? And I signed with the Blue Jays out of high school. I'm like, how cliché is that?"[4]

Wells's first stop up the minor-league ladder didn't make him very happy, either. The Jays sent him to the Medicine Hat (Alberta) Blue Jays of the rookie-level Pioneer League, where as a 19-year-old he had a moderately successful season, going 4-3 but with a 5.18 ERA. He walked 32 and struck out 53 in 64⅓ innings pitched.

Wells continued his climb through the minor-league ranks south of the 49th Parallel over the next few years as he developed his skills as a pitcher. In 1984 his ERA improved to 3.73, to go along with a 6-5 pitching record with Kinston of the Class-A Carolina League He had only 15 appearances in 1984, seven with Kinston and eight with Knoxville of the Double-A Southern League before becoming just the third pitcher in history to undergo Tommy John surgery. (The first two were Brent Strom of San Diego in 1977 and, of course, Tommy John.) The operation caused Wells to miss all of the 1985 season.

When Wells returned in 1986, he had to start again from the beginning, and advanced from Single A to Double A before landing with the Jays' Triple-A International League affiliate in Syracuse, where he spent parts of the next three seasons. He got called up to the Jays in the middle of the 1987 season and made a less than memorable major-league debut on June 30, 1987, against the New York Yankees. He gave up four earned runs in four innings of work and took the loss in a 4-0 Yankees win. Then he decided to celebrate July 4 in Kansas City by getting lit up for five earned runs in only 1⅓ innings for his second loss as the Jays got Royally routed 9-1. Wells found a plane ticket back to Syracuse in his locker after that game.

He returned as a September call-up as the Jays battled the Detroit Tigers for the East Division crown. The team used him as a reliever, and that's how

he got his first major-league victory. On September 2 he came in against the California Angels with two out in the top of the eighth inning with the score tied 5-5 in Toronto's Exhibition Stadium. George Bell's two-run home run in the bottom of the inning put Toronto ahead, and Wells got the victory despite giving up an earned run in the ninth.

The Jays weren't afraid to use Wells in critical situations as the season wound down. Holding a one-game lead over Detroit going into the last weekend of the season, Toronto visited Tiger Stadium for the three-game series that would decide the division champion. In the first game, on October 2, Wells took over for Jim Clancy, who had given up four runs in two-plus innings of work. He held the Tigers scoreless the rest of the way, but the Jays still lost 4-3. Detroit ended up winning the crown.

Despite being the subject of offseason trade rumors—the Associated Press said he may have been part of a trade to the Yankees—Wells started the 1988 season in the Jays bullpen.[5] He still had his rookie status, and in a July 10 article, Associated Press sportswriter Jim Donaghy chose Wells as the mid-season top rookie in the American League with a 3-5 record and four saves.[6] Any chance Donaghy ever had of being offered a job as a scout quickly went out the window as the Jays announced the next day that they had sent Wells down to Syracuse the next day. They recalled him in late August, and he pitched in four games from August 26 until the end of the season without any decisions or saves.

Wells began the 1990 season in the bullpen, but a slump by teammate John Cerutti changed the direction of Wells's career. Cerutti lost five of his first six decisions, so Jays manager Cito Gaston decided that some time in the bullpen would help him out of his funk; Gaston promoted Wells into the starting rotation on May 24 as a temporary measure. Even Wells expected to return to the bullpen. "Several times throughout June, he told reporters it was only a matter of time until he returned to the bullpen," wrote Mike DiGiovanna in the *Los Angeles Times*.[7]

Wells's assignment to the rotation turned out to be as temporary a measure as income tax. He was a starter for the rest of the season, finishing the year with an 11-6 record—his first win was in relief—with a 3.14 ERA and 189 innings pitched.

The 1991 Blue Jays began a string of three straight American League East Division titles, but for Wells the season had mixed results. On August 9 he and Gaston got into an argument on the mound after Wells had given up five runs on nine hits against the Boston Red Sox, with Wells throwing the ball away as he stormed off the mound. The two later fought under the stands.

The spat and scuffle happened during a period when Wells lost six of eight decisions between July 29 and September 8, during which his ERA rose from 2.73 to 3.75, more than one run per nine innings. Not surprisingly, Wells was relegated to the bullpen for the rest of the season.

After winning the American League East in 1985, 1989, and 1991 only to lose in the ALCS, the Blue Jays finally went all the way in 1992. They not only reached the World Series for the first time, but defeated the Atlanta Braves in six games to win it all.

For Wells, a season that culminated a championship ring got off to a lucrative start when the Jays more than doubled his salary from $800,000 to $2,063,000. That was a pretty good raise for a swingman.[8] In fact, he did so much swinging between the bullpen and the rotation that he could easily have had motion sickness. He started in his first two appearances, defeating Baltimore 3-1, and losing 1-0 to the Red Sox, which earned a ticket to the relief corps.[9] He returned to the rotation on June 24, and was inconsistent, going 5-6 between then and August 25. A 6-3 loss to the White Sox in which he gave up all six runs (three earned) convinced Gaston that Wells could better serve the team as a reliever, where he remained the rest of the season. He finished with a 7-9 record and a 5.40 ERA. He didn't play in the ALCS, which the Jays won in six games over Oakland, but he was excellent in the fall classic, appearing in four games and giving up only one hit and no runs in 4⅓ innings of relief.

After the season Wells felt that he had earned the right to be a starter. "I think I proved something not pitching for 21 days and getting into the World Series and showing I can pitch," he said.[10] Instead, the Jays gave him his unconditional release on March 30, 1993. In a 2000 *Sports Illustrated* article on Wells, former Blue Jays general manager Gord Ash explained that the team had grown tired of his inconsistency, his temper, his weight and his fondness for drinking beer—lots and lots of beer. "We did everything we could to control him," said Ash.[11]

Whatever bothered the Blue Jays didn't seem to be of concern to other teams, as Wells garnered interest from 16 other clubs within three days of his release. He signed a one-year deal with the Detroit Tigers on April 3 that included a $900,000 salary, plus $550,000 in bonus incentives. He also became a starter on a team that had the worst team ERA (4.60) in the American League in 1992.

Sparky Anderson was Detroit's manager, and besides having a penchant for removing pitchers from games early—he was nicknamed Captain Hook—he also let players be themselves, and Wells thrived without being pressured to conform. He went 11-9, although his ERA was still high at 4.19, and struck out 139 batters in 187 innings.

Those numbers proved lucrative to Wells; before the 1994 season he signed a three-year contract with Detroit worth $7.5 million. But as is so often the case, fate intervened to make management gnash its teeth over the deal. Wells went on the disabled list on April 19 to recover from having bone chips removed from his elbow. He may as well have stayed there because when he returned to the mound in June, he proceeded to lose his next three starts, and finished the strike-shortened season with a 5-7 record and a 3.96 ERA.

The 1995 season almost changed baseball history. The Tigers were going nowhere and the Yankees, in the middle of a playoff hunt, wanted Wells for their rotation, and were willing to trade a minor-league starter for him. That minor leaguer, according to Jerry Green of the *Detroit News*, was somebody named Mariano Rivera. Yankees general manager Gene Michael eventually nixed the deal after Rivera's fastball began showing improvement. Instead, the Tigers traded Wells to the eventual National League Central Division champion Cincinnati Reds on July 31 for pitchers C.J. Nitkowski and Dave Tuttle. Wells had been the only bright light on a miserable Tigers pitching staff; he had a 10-3 record with a 3.04 ERA when he left Detroit, and had even pitched a third of an inning in the All-Star Game.

After he stopped pinching himself at being traded to a contender, Wells joined the Reds' rotation for the stretch run having won his last eight decisions in a row. Before his first start, against the New York Mets on August 2, Wells met with his new boss, the infamous team owner Marge Schott, who gave him some unusual encouragement.

"Reds owner Marge Schott, with her dog in tow, sought out Wells in the dugout a few minutes before the game and had an animated conversation," the newspapers reported the next day. "Schott, who is picking up the remainder of Wells' $2 million salary, patted the pitcher's belly, squeezed his elbow and waved goodbye."[12] The pep talk worked because he pitched 7⅓ innings in a 6-2 Reds victory for his ninth consecutive win.

Wells was 6-5 with Cincinnati, giving him a 16-8 record for the season, with a 3.24 ERA as Cincinnati won the NL Central division title. In his first-ever postseason start, he helped the Reds clinch the Division Series with a 10-1 win to sweep the Dodgers. In Game Three of the NLCS against the Atlanta Braves, he gave up three earned runs in six innings of a 5-2 loss. Atlanta swept Cincinnati in four straight and went on to defeat Cleveland in the World Series.

While she may have enjoyed rubbing Wells's belly, the notoriously parsimonious Schott did not want to pay the $3 million he was due for 1996 and so the Reds traded him to Baltimore for center fielder Curtis Goodwin and minor leaguer Trovin Valdez. The trade reunited Wells with Pat Gillick, his general manager in Toronto, who now held the same position with the Orioles.

Health issues hounded Wells in the spring and early in the season. He was hospitalized with a rapid heartbeat during spring training, but was released after an overnight stay. He also missed time in May with gout, returning on May 20, his birthday. His teammates welcomed him back and acknowledged his birthday by scoring 13 runs to give him his first win in five starts since April 16.

"It's a nice gift, all those runs, but you still have to go out there and do the job," Wells said. "Still, it's a great advantage when you get that type of run support."[13]

The win was a high point in an otherwise mediocre season for Wells, as he went 11-14 with a 5.14 ERA. Nonetheless, the Orioles' 88-74 record was good enough to get them the wild-card playoff spot. Wells made a huge postseason contribution. He won Game One of the ALDS against the powerhouse Cleveland Indians and went seven frames in the clincher as Baltimore won in 12 innings to pull off the upset. He also earned the only Orioles victory in the ALCS as they lost to the Yankees in five games.

Just as Victor Kiam liked Remington Razors so much that he bought the company, the Yankees went out and signed Wells, the only pitcher to beat them in the ALCS, to a three-year, $13.5 million contract on December 24, 1996. The Yankees may have regretted their decision just three weeks later when he broke his pitching hand in a fight on January 14, 1997, while he was in San Diego attending his mother's funeral. Wells ruffled the Yankees corporate feathers again when he said that he would like to wear Babe Ruth's number 3, which the Yankees had retired in 1948.

"I asked for 03 and they wouldn't do that," said the longtime admirer of the Sultan of Swat. I'm hoping Mr. (Charlie) Hayes will give up No. 33.[14] That way, I can be Babe Ruth twice over."[15]

The number issue was less serious than Wells's injury problems when spring training began. While he was still recovering from his broken hand, he had a recurrence of the gout that had bothered him the previous season. But for all the issues and headlines, Wells did produce. He went 16-10 with a 4.21 ERA and helped the Yankees win the American League wild-card playoff spot with a 96-66 record. The Yankees lost to Cleveland in the ALDS, but Wells pitched a 6-1 five-hitter at Jacobs Field to win Game Three, his only start.

Wells arrived at spring training for the 1998 season just three months shy of his 35th birthday. He strained a rib muscle early on and didn't get his first spring-training start until March 14. He proceeded to have a season for the ages, going 18-4 with a 3.49 ERA, followed by a 4-0 run in the playoffs—he was chosen MVP in the ALCS—as the Yankees won the World Series. Wells also started the All-Star Game, and just for fun, he gave himself an early birthday present by pitching a perfect game at Yankee Stadium against the Minnesota Twins on May 17. It was the first perfect game in Yankee Stadium since fellow Point Loma alumnus Don Larsen performed the feat against the Brooklyn Dodgers in Game Five of the 1956 World Series.

The circumstances surrounding his perfecto would be difficult to believe if it involved anybody but Wells. Manager Joe Torre had pulled him from a May 6 start against Texas after he gave up seven earned runs in 2⅔ innings. Torre complained that Wells was out of shape and the two, along with pitching coach Mel Stottlemyre, had a long discussion about the situation. Judging by what he wrote in his autobiography, Wells was hardly in game shape when he showed up to face Minnesota.

"In his 2003 autobiography *Perfect, I'm Not*, Wells conceded that he pitched his gem 'half-drunk, with bloodshot eyes, monster breath, and a raging, skull-rattling hangover,' having gone to bed at 5 a.m. and gotten just an hour of sleep," wrote Jay Jaffe in *Sports Illustrated*.[16]

In the Broadway musical *Damn Yankees*, the character Lola sings a song with the line, "Whatever Lola wants, Lola gets." George Steinbrenner, owner of the damn Yankees, was like Lola because he also got whatever he wanted, and after the 1998 season, he wanted Blue Jays pitcher Roger Clemens for his team, and to get him, the Yankees traded Wells back to Toronto, along with pitcher Graeme Lloyd and second baseman Homer Bush. Wells was not pleased at going back to Toronto, but Jays general manager Ash assured him that he would be treated differently this time around.

"We did everything we could to control Boomer," Ash said, referring to Wells's first stint with Toronto. "We learned the hard way: The worst way to control him is to try and control him."[17]

Hard way or not, the lesson was well learned. Boomer was allowed to be Boomer, heavy-metal music blaring in the locker room and all, and the result was the first of two marvelous seasons. Maybe he was partying like it was 1999, since it was, because he got off to a slow start and by the end of May was 5-5 with a stratospheric 6.30 ERA. Nonetheless, the Jays inked Wells to a one-year, $11.5 million contract extension on June 20, which spurred him on to a 17-10 record with an improved 4.82 ERA; he also led the league with seven complete games.

Cue the *Twilight Zone* music at this point, because it was in the year 2000 that Wells decided to have the only 20-win season of his career when he went 20-8, with a 4.11 ERA and a league-leading nine complete games. He also started the All-Star Game—his former manager Joe Torre selected him for the honor—as the Jays were in the pennant race for the whole season before finishing with an 83-79 record, 4½ games behind the eventual world champion Yankees.

Although the Blue Jays were willing to allow Wells to be himself, they felt enough was enough in early January, 2001, when Wells accused the Blue Jays organization of not doing enough to win and said that Toronto fans were "terrible."[18] They traded him to the Chicago White Sox for four players who ended up playing a total of 65 games for Toronto. From the standpoint of number of games played, it actually turned out to be an even trade. Wells went 5-7 with a 4.47 ERA, and didn't pitch after June 28 because of back spasms. He ended up having season-ending surgery.

Just as with a great Broadway play, Wells had a New York revival when he signed for a second stint with the Yankees in 2002, because Steinbrenner wanted the now-39-year-old back in the fold. "David Wells is a winner and he belongs in pinstripes," said Steinbrenner in a statement. "People say we're going out on a limb, but we'll see. We're betting on The Boomer."[19]

It turned out to be a good bet because Steinbrenner, a breeder, knew good horseflesh. Wells not only recovered from his back injury, he won six of his first seven decisions, and went on to have a 19-7 record, leading the rotation in both victories and winning percentage (.731) as the Yankees won the American League East with a 103-58 record. The usually clutch Wells couldn't carry that regular season success into the playoffs as he got pounded in his lone start against the eventual World Series champion Anaheim Angels, who touched him for eight earned runs in 4⅔ innings in Game Four of the ALDS.

Wells was hot again in 2003, perhaps because of the hot water he found himself in prior to the season when his autobiography came out. Besides his description of his condition the day of his perfect game, he also said that a number of players were taking steroids. The resulting controversy was a pain in the Yankee brass and they fined him $100,000.

That little fracas aside, Wells was doing it again on the mound at age 40, going 15-7 with a 4.14 ERA as the Yankees went back to the World Series after a one-year drought. He defeated the Twins, 8-1, in the ALDS and Boston, 4-2, in the ALCS, but the World Series against the Florida Marlins was another matter. Wells lost Game One, 3-2, and had to leave Game Five due to tightness in his back after pitching a perfect first inning in a game the Yankees lost, 6-4.

Wells's run in the Bronx ended after New York lost the World Series, so he decided to go home, and signed as a free agent with the Padres. At first it looked as though he couldn't go home again, as he lost his first two starts, went on the disabled list due to a cut on his wrist, and by June 18 was 2-5. But damned if the old coot didn't go 10-3 the rest of the way to finish 12-8, with a not-too-shabby 3.73 ERA.

The 2004 Red Sox called themselves "idiots" for their distinctive and often offbeat personalities, so perhaps it was no surprise that they signed Wells for the 2005 season. After all, he only had to replace three-time Cy Young Award winner Pedro Martinez, who won 16 games in 2004. Wells had the wags shaking their heads again as he went 15-7 in his summer of being 42, with a 4.45 ERA that was actually below the team ERA of 4.74. The Red Sox made the playoffs again as the wild card, but even Wells couldn't prevent them from being swept by the eventual world champion Chicago White Sox. He gave up five runs, but only two earned, in 6⅔ innings of Game Two, which the White Sox won 5-4.

Age started creeping up on Wells in 2006, as he went a combined 3-5 with the Red Sox and Padres. He had one last shot in the playoffs with San Diego, and didn't pitch badly in his only start in the ALDS, giving up two runs in five innings in Game Two to the St. Louis Cardinals, but that was all the Redbirds needed for a 2-0 win as they went on to win it all. Wells had a last hurrah, of sorts, in 2007; he had a 5-8 record with a 5.54 ERA when the Padres released him on August 13. But the Los Angeles Dodgers picked him up 11 days later, and he went 4-1 with them, albeit with a 5.12 ERA. He called it a career at age 44 after the season.

Wells was able to retire financially secure after earning more than $58 million playing baseball. He returned to San Diego to live with his wife, Nina, a former runway model whom he married in 2000, and their two sons, Brandon Miles and Lars Van. He got very active in community and charitable causes, raising money for diabetes research (he was diagnosed with the disease in 2007) and helped push through a school bond to pay for major upgrades to his high school's baseball field, which now bears his name. As of 2015, he was the coach of the school's team.

"If you can give back," he said in a 2014 interview, "it's a home run."[20]

SOURCES

In addition to the sources cited in the notes, the author used the following:

Abca.org.

Bluebirdbanter.com.

Hardballtimes.com.

Herald-Zeitung (New Braunfels, Texas).

Indiana (Pennsylvania) *Gazette*.

Kokomo (Indiana) *Tribune*.

Mlbreports.com.

New York Times.

Philly.com.

Plhsalumni.org.

Razon, Max. *Born Under a Bad Sign* (Bloomington, Indiana: Xlibris, 2009).

Salina (Kansas) *Journal*.

USA Today.

Special thanks to Tom Larwin and the members of the Ted Williams SABR chapter for their assistance.

NOTES

1 Accounts differ on the amounts. The higher numbers appear in a 1997 *Sports Illustrated* article, but Wells gave the lower numbers during a 2014 interview on the YES Network.

2 Franz Lidz, "The Unvarnished Ruth Free-Spirited Lefthander David Wells May Get Tattooed By Hitters Every Now And Then, But He's Fulfilling His Dream — Pitching For The Yankees, The Team Of His Idol, The Babe," *Sports Illustrated*, September 8, 1997.

3 Ibid.

4 YESnetwork.com interview.

5 "Cardinals talking with Horner," *Index-Journal* (Greenwood, South Carolina), January 8, 1988.

6 Donaghy's article appeared in the July 10, 1988, edition of the *Altoona Mirror*.

7 Mike DiGiovanna, "He Started a Reliever but Is Winning as a Starter," *Los Angeles Times*, July 13, 1990.

8 In baseball, a swingman is a pitcher who works as both a starter and reliever.

9 Wells went only four innings in the loss to Boston because of a 58-minute rain delay. Pat Hentgen replaced him in the fifth.

10 Steve Milton, "Toronto Blue Jays," *The Sporting News*, November 9, 1992: 46.

11 Jeff Pearlman, "Heavy Duty They said he wouldn't last, but Toronto's large-livin' lefthander, David Wells, has become baseball's most reliable pitcher — and a clubhouse wise man to boot," *Sports Illustrated*, July 10, 2000.

12 "Los Angeles Tops Colorado," *News Record* (North Hills, Pennsylvania), August 3, 1995.

13 "Orioles celebrate Wells' birthday, 13-1," *Gettysburg Times*, May 21, 1996.

14 Hayes, a Yankees teammate, gave Wells the number, and wore number 13 for the 1997 season.

15 "Wells has Ruthian request," *The Capital* (Annapolis, Maryland), February 11, 1997.

16 Jay Jaffe, "15 years ago today: David Wells' perfect game," *Sports Illustrated*, May 17, 2013. Wells later said he was misquoted.

17 Jaffe.

18 Rick Gano, "Blue Jays trade Wells to White Sox," *Daily Journal* (Ukiah, California), January 15, 2001.

19 "Slimmer Wells returns to Yankee Stadium," *Santa Cruz* (California) *Sentinel* January 11, 2002.

20 Andrea Naversen, "At Home With David & Nina Wells," *Ranch & Coast*, May 12, 2014.

PERFECTLY WELLS, THANK YOU.
MAY 17, 1998: NEW YORK YANKEES 4 – MINNESOTA TWINS 0, AT YANKEE STADIUM

By Norm King

DAVID WELLS POSITIVELY reeks of New York Yankees history. During one game he wore a game-used Babe Ruth cap he had purchased for $35,000. He wore number 33 when he played in the Bronx as a tribute to the Babe's iconic number 3, which was retired, and because they wouldn't let him wear the number 03. Hell, he even attended Point Loma High School in San Diego, which was the alma mater of Don Larsen, who pitched a perfect game for New York against the Brooklyn Dodgers in the 1956 World Series.

Who more appropriate, then, to pitch the first perfect game in Yankee Stadium since Larsen's own perfecto? Well, a lot of people, actually, based on Wells's performances since the season began. Yankees manager Joe Torre had expressed his hopes to Wells in a handwritten note: "You are one of the guys who can provide the leadership we need to get back to October," wrote Torre. "Being a great pitcher or player is all about responsibility."[1]

At game time the responsibility needed to be a great pitcher was still missing. In an April 30 start, Wells gave up four earned runs in 6⅓ innings during a 9-8 Yankees home win against the Seattle Mariners. He was worse the following start, on May 6 against Texas, when he almost blew a 9-0 lead he held after two innings, by giving up seven earned runs in the third. New York would win that one, 15-13. Wells was showing signs of finding his groove his next start on May 12, going eight innings in a 3-2 win over Kansas City, in which he retired the last 10 batters he faced. He had a 4-1 record going into the game with the Minnesota Twins, but a less than impressive 5.23 ERA.

His warm-up session prior to the game didn't inspire Wells with great confidence. "I went out into the bullpen and I was fighting myself a little bit," he said. "I launched a couple of balls into the stands out of frustration."[2]

Maybe he was being too hard on himself, because pitching coach Mel Stottlemyre liked what he was seeing, and felt Wells was going to have a good outing. "I felt like he was going to have a very special game," said Stottlemyre. "I always think of a shutout as being a particularly special game."[3]

Wells was dominant right from the beginning, as he barely broke a sweat while setting the Twins down on nine pitches in the first. The top of the second was almost as easy, except that it took 13 pitches to get through the heart of the Twins order: Marty Cordova (groundout), Ron Coomer (strikeout), and Alex Ochoa (foul popup to the catcher).

Wells got the only run he would need in the bottom of the second. Bernie Williams doubled to left, moved to third on a passed ball, and scored on a wild pitch by Twins starter LaTroy Hawkins.

Critical to any pitcher's success is how well he communicates with his catcher—Steve Carlton, for example, kept Tim McCarver on a major-league roster by employing him as his personal catcher when he was with the Phillies. On this day, the connection between Wells and his catcher, Jorge Posada, was almost other-worldly.

"Every (signal) I put down, he threw. It seemed like I was thinking everything along with him. It was freaky," Posada said. "I was putting down everything he wanted to throw. I'd tell him to throw it in the dirt and he threw it in the dirt. He was unbelievable that day."[4]

That "freaky" connection was particularly strong in the third inning, when Wells struck out the side. That was also the inning when the no-hitter came closest to ending, as Javier Valentin smacked a long fly ball down the left-field line that was foul by 20 feet. Valentin worked Wells to a full count before whiffing. It was the first of only four times that day that Wells went to a three-ball count on a hitter.

Whether a pitcher is pitching a perfect game or not, a 1-0 score is still pretty tight. Bernie Williams provided Wells a bit of breathing room when he smacked the first pitch he saw from Hawkins in the fourth deep to right to make the score 2-0. Wells probably didn't need the cushion, as he continued mowin''em down, striking out the first two batters in each of the fifth and the sixth. Then came the seventh.

If there was any inning in which Wells faced the prospect of losing his perfect game, it was the seventh. After Matt Lawton flied out to center, he went to 3-and-2 counts on the next two hitters, but Brent Gates grounded to first and Paul Molitor struck out swinging. That's when Wells's teammates began exhibiting the behavior that only happens when one of their teammates is pitching a no-hitter.

Anyone who watches the video of Wells's gem will notice that Torre sat in the dugout with his hands in his pockets the entire game doing his best imitation of a Buddha statue. That type of Zen calmness is needed by around the seventh during a no-hitter, because the players know what's happening and allow the traditional superstitions of baseball to take over, which generally means avoiding the pitcher like the plague.

"Nervousness gnawed at David Wells in the seventh inning yesterday, when he began realizing he might pitch a perfect game," wrote Buster Olney in the *New York Times*. He … desperately needed his superstitious Yankee teammates to speak and ease the mounting tension.

"But nobody would oblige him, save for (Yankee teammate) David Cone, who removed his good-luck sunglasses and approached Wells. 'I think it's time,' Cone said, his delivery perfectly dry, 'to break out the knuckleball.'"[5]

The Yankees also handled their nervousness in a productive manner in their half of the seventh, by smacking baseballs around Yankee Stadium. With one out, Williams doubled to left for his third hit of the game. Darryl Strawberry followed with a run-scoring triple. Chad Curtis brought Strawberry home with a single to make the score 4-0, leaving the rest up to Wells.

The eighth inning was marked by a relatively tough play when Ron Coomer hit a ball up the middle that Wells thought would go for a base hit, but second baseman Chuck Knoblauch knocked it down and threw it to first in time for the second out of the inning.[6] After Ochoa popped out to first to end the frame, Wells's teammates had a chance to worry about having to play the ninth.

"[With a] no-hitter, I mean, you can still make an error and the guy will still get the no-hitter and you're off the hook," said Derek Jeter. "But with a perfect game there's no room for any flaws, no errors, nothing."[7]

The team was flawless in the ninth, as Jon Shave flied out to right fielder Paul O'Neill, Valentin struck out—Wells's 11th strikeout of the game—and Pat Meares flied out to O'Neill to complete the 13th perfect game since 1900 and launch the pandemonium. Wells's teammates mobbed him, then carried him off on their shoulders, which wasn't easy to do considering he weighed 250 pounds.

In his 2003 autobiography, *Perfect I'm Not*, Wells claimed he had been out partying with the cast of *Saturday Night Live* until 5:00 A.M. the morning of the game and was hung over when he took the mound. Whether that's true or not doesn't really matter, because not only did Wells show how pitching could be an art form that day, he went on to have an 18-4 season with a league-leading five shutouts. He also won a World Series ring, which was—there's no other word for it—perfect.

SOURCES

In addition to the sources listed in the notes, the author also consulted:

Sports Illustrated.

Youtube.com.

NO-HITTERS

NOTES

1. Tyler Kepner, "Baseball: Wells's Book has Teammates Amused and Torre Concerned," *New York Times*, March 1, 2003.
2. David Wells, video interview, mlb.com.
3. Mel Stottlemyre, video interview, mlb.com.
4. Peter Botte, "Jorge Posada's favorite moment: Catching David Wells' perfect game," *New York Daily News*, September 19, 2008.
5. Buster Olney, "Baseball: Rarest Gem for Yankees' Wells: A Perfect Game," *New York Times*, May 18, 1998.
6. This game took place the season before Knoblauch suddenly developed an inability to throw the ball to first base. He had 13 errors in 1998, then 26 in 1999, followed by 15 in only 82 games in 2000. The Yankees moved him to left field for the 2001 season.
7. Derek Jeter, video interview, mlb.com.

DAVID CONE

By Tara Krieger

I like to think of the world's greatest athlete coming up to bat against me—Tiger Woods, Wayne Gretzky, I don't care who it is—and I'm looking at him thinking, you have no chance.[1]

THERE WAS A MOMENT IN the third game of the 1996 World Series that felt eerily familiar for David Cone. Bases loaded, no gas in the tank. He had been burned in that situation a year before.

Game Five, American League Division Series, Seattle, 1995: On his 147th pitch, Cone had walked pinch-hitter Doug Strange in the eighth inning to allow the tying run in the Yankees' eventual 11th-inning postseason exit.

No doubt he had replayed that moment all season. But 1996 had brought its own trials—a life-threatening aneurysm that had sidelined him for four months, so that now his stamina was the equivalent of coming out of spring training.[2] The defending champion Atlanta Braves had embarrassed the Yankees at home in the first two World Series games, and now 24 million pairs of eyes were on Cone in Atlanta.[3]

On the winning side of a 2-0 duel against future Hall of Famer Tom Glavine, a tiring Cone had loaded the bases with one out in the sixth and cleanup hitter Fred McGriff at bat. Yankees manager Joe Torre jogged to the mound.

"David," said Torre, his face inches away from his star right-hander's. "This is really important; I need to know the truth. Are you okay?"

"I'm fine," Cone said, "I can get McGriff."

Torre asked if he was sure.

"I'm losing my splitter a bit, but it's more mechanical than anything."

"I wanted to hear him say it," Torre said afterward. "If he had hesitated, I would have taken him out. But he didn't."[4]

"I lied," Cone said. "But I had to make him believe my lie."[5]

McGriff popped up to short, and Cone eventually escaped with a one-run lead. The Yankees ultimately took Game Three, and the next three games, for their first championship in 18 years.

Typical Cone to believe the improbable—he was often at his best when the odds were stacked against him. Despite developing a reputation as a free spirit in his early years with the Mets, and then in midcareer as a hired gun after jumping multiple teams in time for their playoff push, Cone's candor facing the New York media had turned him into a sort of elder spokesman. He was a player representative when team owners threatened to shut the MLB Players Association down. When his fastball began to slow as he hit his 30s, he became, as he often said, "a finesse pitcher without the finesse," adopting new arm angles and sometimes inventing pitches on the spot to compensate for any flaws in his abilities.[6]

In some ways, David Cone's place among the pitching elite seems improbable—he doesn't look like a prototypical athlete. His baseball cards claim he is 6-feet-1 and 180 pounds,[7] but standing next to teammates he often resembled the runt younger brother, what with his slight hunch and a face that sportswriters ad nauseam likened to a "choirboy."[8] And his high school didn't have a baseball team.

In fact, ask a teenage Cone where he saw himself as an adult, and he figured he'd follow his fictional hero, Oscar Madison of *The Odd Couple*, into journalism, complete with the greasy, wrinkled sweatshirt and half-eaten bologna sandwich behind the couch. That was as good a dream as any for a kid growing up in the blue-collar Northeast district of Kansas City.

And yet, in other ways, the youngest of four children—a girl followed by three boys—born to Joan Sylvia Curran, a secretary and travel agent, and Edwin Mack Cone seemed intended to be an athlete from his birth on January 2, 1963. He was almost named Theodore Samuel Cone; Theodore after Ted Williams, Samuel after New York Giants linebacker Sam Huff.[9] Instead, he was David Brian Cone.

Ed Cone once had professional dreams as a sidearmer, or perhaps going into business like his father and namesake, who managed a hotel chain and knew the local political bosses. Instead, Ed Cone worked as a mechanic, first at a steel plant, then at a meatpacking factory. He rose long before the sun to repair large hunks of metal for over 60 hours a week, often in rooms kept at freezing temperatures.

"There was never a suggestion that my success in sports, if it came along, would be some kind of avenue to financial success for him," David Cone said. "He wasn't proving anything through me. With him, sports was an avenue for his kids to get a better education. We were sports-crazy in my family, but the real obsession was always school. You might say it didn't work out that way with me."[10]

Fierce Wiffle-Ball games would take place in the Cones' backyard under the floodlights Ed and Joan Cone had installed for evening baseball. The family affectionately called it Conedlestick Park or Coneway Park. Pitching came naturally as soon as David realized the Wiffle Ball could bend and dive depending on his grip.[11] Ed Cone helped him fine-tune his mechanics.

Frequently playing alongside boys his older brothers' ages, David got used to fighting for what was his. He was cut from his first little league team at age 7, because he was too small. He made it the next year, with Ed Cone as the new coach. David was also the star shooting guard on Ed Cone's junior-high basketball team.[12] Friends recalled the legendary squabbles between father and son — at least one particular temper tantrum ended with David being sent home.[13]

"He commanded respect, but there was a fear factor, too," David said of his father's coaching style.[14]

Cone described his parents as "tough, hard-nosed, blue-collar people. They went by the sort of kick-the-bird-out-of-the-nest type of theory. You had to fly or fall to the ground. In some ways, I really appreciate that. In other ways, maybe we both regret that we

haven't fostered that close, affectionate relationship that some families have. Part of my resiliency and so-called toughness, emotionally, is due to that background. Part of the problems I have emotionally, too, are due to that background."[15]

However, the tight-knit Cone clan knew family first. When David's older brother Danny got into a fistfight with a neighbor on their front porch, Joan Cone wrestled her son away from the larger man's blows. The neighbor's ire escalated into weapon-wielding[16] death threats, so Ed Cone grabbed a .22 and shot him. (The wound was superficial.) David, 14, learned that day not to "be bullied by anybody. The worst thing you could be called in this world is someone who didn't stand up for his family."[17]

Such attitude translated to sports. He played basketball with such intensity that he once struck an opponent who had caused him to foul out with a metal protector he had been wearing over an injured finger.[18] Another opponent who violently slammed a ball at his chest received it back in the face.[19]

This isn't to paint Cone as the belligerent sort — he just hated getting beat. At Rockhurst High School,[20] the all-boys Jesuit prep he attended as an alternative to the subpar Kansas City public-education system, he was generally an above-average student, charming and well-liked. His senior year, he led the football team, as its starting quarterback, and the basketball team, as a guard, to the district finals.

Rockhurst had no baseball team. His junior year, Cone, also a sportswriter for the school newspaper, had gathered over 700 signatures on a petition, as well as a potential field and coaching staff, but it was a no-go.[21] Instead, Cone played summer ball in the Ban Johnson League, a gangly adolescent mowing down college-age men interested in going pro.

At 16, he was called to an invitation-only tryout with his hometown Royals, where the scouts gave him a second look from among a couple of hundred talents.[22] He also pitched in an open tryout with the Cardinals. At 17, he hit 88 mph on the radar gun[23] and was telling his parents — much to his mother's concern — that he wanted to forgo college for the major leagues.[24]

Cone was considering a partial scholarship at the University of Missouri (in baseball, with a chance to walk on to the football team). But on June 8, 1981, a Western Union wire announced that the Kansas City Royals selected him in the third round of the free-agent draft.[25] It helped that his father and Royals scout Carl Blando had known each other since childhood.

Having grown up idolizing the likes of Dennis Leonard and George Brett, Cone was all too eager to sign on the dotted line for $17,500. Similar draftees were receiving $30,000, but Cone had never seen so much money in his life. He wouldn't be so cavalier about his worth in future negotiations.

Cone immediately reported to Sarasota for rookie ball, where he had a 2.55 ERA in 67 innings pitched, second most on the team. The next year, 1982, Cone split between Class-A Charleston and Fort Myers, going 16-3 with a 2.08 ERA, including seven complete games.

Then, in an exhibition game against the Pirates in March 1983, he tore the ACL in his left knee in a collision at home plate. If the hip-length cast from surgery didn't say it emphatically enough, Cone's season was done. Between the countless hours he spent on an exercise bike rebuilding his strength, he took a minimum-wage job at a conveyor belt company. For four months, he cut and bonded strips of rubber, frequently slicing his hands as an occupational casualty — not the smartest idea for a pitcher. The uncertainty of a comeback plagued him with visions of a future in manual labor, just like his father.[26]

Cone struggled with his control in 1984 at Double-A Memphis (110 strikeouts, 114 walks), and in 1985 at Triple-A Omaha (115 strikeouts, 93 walks). Such prolonged mediocrity may have prevented a September call-up with the big-league club, which won its first World Series title that fall.

Nor could he manage his money, as notices from the Internal Revenue Service went ignored. His first paycheck in 1985 was for $83; Uncle Sam had taken around 90 percent.[27]

Moved to the Omaha bullpen to start 1986, Cone rediscovered the strike zone, fanning 63 and walking 25 in 71 innings. The Royals were noticing. On June 8 — five years to the day after his draft — Cone replaced a concussion-suffering Mark Gubicza on the big-league roster. He relieved Bret Saberhagen in the top of the ninth against Minnesota and allowed three singles and a run. Three days later, he was summoned for mop-up work against Seattle (4⅔ innings, five earned runs, four strikeouts). After two more brief, scoreless relief appearances, he was returned to Triple A.

Rejoining the parent club as a September call-up, Cone appeared seven times from the bullpen, including four shutout innings with five strikeouts on September 20. His final line in his first major-league season: no decisions, a 5.56 ERA, 21 strikeouts, and 13 walks in 22⅔ innings.

"David had a fastball and a slider back then," said Jamie Quirk, an Omaha teammate. "He was almost there but he kept trying to strike everybody out. I wanted to persuade him to be in the strike zone more and set the batters up — let them hit the ball now and then but where you wanted them to hit it. He got the idea some days."[28]

Were there any doubts Cone was ready for "The Show," he spent the offseason helping the Ponce Leones capture the Puerto Rican Winter League pennant and the Caribbean World Series championship. He was named the league's Player of the Year.

Cone headed to Royals spring training in 1987 energized with two pitches that would become signatures: a side-arm slider (the "Laredo"), which he learned from Gaylord Perry, and a split-finger fastball. A day after being told he made the team—March 27—he was traded to the Mets.

Apparently the Royals needed a catcher, and they eyed Ed Hearn. Throw in pitching never-really-weres Rick Anderson and Mauro Gozzo, and Cone was headed to New York with outfield prospect Chris Jelic. Hearn would play a total of 13 more games in his major-league career. It may be the worst trade in Royals history.[29]

For Cone, the news that he was being ripped from his hometown and sent to some unfamiliar city hit him like a sucker punch to the gut. He had a spot in the Royals rotation, and now he was concerned about starting the season in Triple A if the Mets, the reigning world champions, could not fit him on their roster.

Cone needed not worry about his place in New York. During his first session at the Mets' spring training facility, his pitches moved so much that catcher Barry Lyons could barely hold onto them—Cone said pitching coach Mel Stottlemyre's jaw was "literally dropping."[30] Cone would start the season at Shea Stadium.

And players—a roster oozing with as much zany debauchery as raw talent—took swiftly to his congenial, slightly goofy nature. Lyons was lockered next to Cone when he first arrived. "We hit it off," Lyons said.[31] And first baseman Keith Hernandez, according to Cone, "made me feel more welcome in one day than the Royals had in six years."[32]

"[T]he Mets were a perfect fit for me," Cone said. "I'd do anything in the world to fit in with that wild group of guys."[33]

Injuries (and Dwight Gooden checking into rehab) forced Cone into the rotation. His first start in blue-and-orange, on April 27, was mortification—10 runs (7 earned) in five innings. Undeterred, two starts later, on May 12, he went the distance for his first big-league win.

Just as Cone's place in the rotation seemed secure, a fastball by the Giants' Atlee Hammaker fractured his pinky as he squared for a bunt on May 27.[34] Surgery followed, and Cone would not return until the middle of August, the pinky permanently, grossly misshapen.

Cone finished 5-6 with a 3.71 ERA in 99⅓ innings, as the injury-ravaged Mets, despite the second-best record in the National League, missed the playoffs.

Injuries worked to his advantage—Cone exploded into the rotation permanently in 1988 after Rick Aguilera's elbow went bad. His first start, on May 3, was a complete-game shutout against Atlanta. Two weeks later, he struck out 12 in seven innings of a 1-0 win at San Diego. In fact, Cone won every one of his starts in May, as well as his final eight starts of the season. He recorded double-digit strikeouts seven times that season, averaging almost 7⅔ innings per start, including eight complete games (four shutouts), and another two he went 10 innings. Former President Nixon was waiting in the Shea Stadium dugout to shake Cone's hand upon his 20th win.

Cone's line included a league-best .870 winning percentage (20-3), a 2.22 ERA, 213 strikeouts (both second-best in the NL), a NL All-Star team selection, and third place, behind winner Orel Hershiser and runner-up Danny Jackson, in the NL Cy Young Award voting.

It wasn't hard to be a David Cone fan in the late 1980s.[35] A friend of his, Andrew Levy, with a bunch of college pals, started the "Coneheads" (after the *Saturday Night Live* sketch),[36] who wore pointy rubber head coverings and occupied "Cone's Co'ner" in the left-field upper deck. For every strikeout, they'd string orange construction cones from the rafters.

"I can tell you that the Coneheads were a motivating factor whenever I took the mound," Cone said in hindsight. "I didn't want to let them down."[37]

Candid, articulate, and slightly idiosyncratic, Cone embraced the New York media. He chatted with the writers regularly, sometimes showed up at their pickup basketball games,[38] and was one of the few starters who didn't mind being interviewed the day of his turn in the rotation. Reporters lapped up his clubhouse antics, such as when leaving tickets for Vanna White (a "Total ruse. Just for fun," he said[39]) became an ongoing spoof. When the Dodgers' Pedro Guerrero hurled his bat at Cone and charged the mound after Cone's slow curve hit him near his head, Cone was readily available after the game to claim the offending pitch was unintentional.

"If I'm going to hit somebody," Cone said, "it'll be a 90 mile-per-hour fastball."[40]

Another time, after Phillies broadcaster Chris Wheeler lightly criticized his batting average, Cone appeared in the booth in full uniform. "It's a hard .143," he defended himself on air.[41]

The 1988 Mets won the division by 15 games and were the overwhelming favorite against the Los Angeles Dodgers in the NLCS. Enter Bob Klapisch, writer for the *Daily News*. Under the guise of Cone realizing his other childhood dream of becoming a sportswriter, Klapisch agreed to turn daily clubhouse interviews into a ghostwritten column.

After the Mets had won the opener with a ninth-inning rally off reliever Jay Howell, Klapisch-as-Cone wrote that Dodgers starter Hershiser "was lucky for eight innings," and that the Mets knew they'd win when he came out: "Seeing Howell and his curveball reminded us of a high school pitcher."

"Bob Klapisch just kind of asked me some questions in the clubhouse, and things got a little crazy in the aftermath of a big win in Game One of the playoffs," Cone said, "and I never got a chance to read it before it went out, and I got credit for the byline. To this day, I still can't believe I allowed that to happen, that I wouldn't at least see the final copy before I put my name on it."[42]

The Dodgers passed out copies and pinned it to their bulletin board. And lit up Cone for five runs in two innings that night. He'd only allowed five earned runs once, and he'd never been knocked out of a start before the fourth inning all season.

"It definitely affected how I pitched," Cone said. "It was the first time I felt physically inhibited by nerves. My legs felt heavy from being so nervous."[43]

Cone apologized to Howell the next day and dropped the column soon afterward. In its final iteration—which Cone wrote himself—the contrite righty admitted he'd said every word, a "feeble attempt at humor" which he was "naïve" to think wouldn't make print.[44]

"I had a choice to make, either stand up and be honest, or run away and hide," Cone said, "so that was an early hard lesson to learn."[45] Klapisch later praised Cone for owning his mistake, when he just as easily could have said he'd been misquoted.[46]

Cone recovered with a perfect ninth inning in relief in the Mets' Game Three win, and a complete-game victory in Game Six to stave off elimination. But the Mets lost in seven games, and some baseball insiders still believe that Cone's column cost the Mets the pennant.[47]

Cone wasn't as overpowering in 1989, but still tallied formidable numbers, with 190 strikeouts (fourth in the NL) and a 3.52 ERA. A third-year player ineligible for arbitration, he was a bargain at $332,500. But after that year he commanded $1.3 million in front of the arbitrator—and won.

Cone immediately flew to Kansas City and told his father, whose long hours at the plant had hastened arthritis, to quit his job.

"Nothing I've done in my life has meant more than that moment," Cone said.[48] A year later, when his salary nearly doubled to $2.35 million, he bought a condominium for his parents in Florida. Another arbitration win in 1992 yielded a $4.25 million salary.

Armed with the splitter, which teammate Ron Darling helped him perfect,[49] and the Laredo, which came from the side and broke six inches off the plate,[50] in addition to his usual four-seam fastball and curve, Cone topped the NL in strikeouts in both 1990 (233) and 1991 (241). He averaged more than a strikeout per inning both years, and had mastered pitch control, with a league-high 3.585 strikeout-to-walk ratio in 1990, and a second-best 3.301 in 1991. If sabermetrics were general parlance in 1991, Cone would have been ninth in WAR for pitchers (4.4), and would have led the league in Fielding Independent Pitching (2.52).

"My agent, Steve Fehr, was very progressive with numbers, the early sabermetrics movement," Cone said. "We used some of those numbers in arbitration cases against the Mets in the early '90s, and we actually won those cases. ... A lot of it was based on numbers, trying to look inside the numbers, past won-loss record, and trying to get a better look at what the pitcher really did. So I was an early believer, really."[51]

Perhaps the Mets' sinking fortunes were partially to blame for Cone's underwhelming 14-8, 14-10, and 14-14 records between 1989 and 1991. Frustrated by a 20-22 start in 1990, general manager Frank Cashen replaced manager Davey Johnson with third-base coach Bud Harrelson. The Mets battled back to first place in early September, but couldn't stay ahead of the division-winning Pirates. In 1991 the team finished fifth, and Harrelson was dismissed. By late 1992, the Mets, with one of the game's highest payrolls, were hovering dangerously close to last place. The wild egos that had previously held the team together had given way to infighting, and age and injury had slowly sapped the team of its talent. Daily appearances on Page Six were not as easily ignored.

Cone still loved New York, but was slowly falling from favor with the Mets organization. There were on-field embarrassments, such as on April 30, 1990, when he allowed two Atlanta runs to score while he argued with the umpire over whether he had stepped on first base for the force out. Or on June 4, 1991, when Cone shook off a pitchout from bench coach Doc Edwards, and he and Harrelson erupted in a shouting and poking match in the dugout. The altercation overshadowed a 13-strikeout win in which Cone did not allow an earned run.

Even after these humiliations, Cone was at his locker, answering questions. Fittingly, in 1991 Cone switched his number from 44 to 17, to honor Keith Hernandez, the Mets' previous press point-man.

Still, his off-the-field behavior was a delicate dance. Cone never had the addiction problems of some of his teammates, but he often ran with them — carousing, staying out late, and frequently not going to bed alone.

In September 1991, three women sued Cone and the Mets for $8.1 million, claiming he had made death threats. According to Cone, at least one had been harassing Sid Fernandez's wife in the stands, and although he'd "dropped 90,000 F-bombs," he never threatened their life. "It was a farce of a lawsuit, to get publicity," he said.[52]

Three weeks later, the phone rang early in the morning in Cone's hotel room in Philadelphia, where he was scheduled to pitch that day. It was the final day of the season, and Cone had staggered in at 6:30 A.M. after another all-nighter with his Mets teammates.

Cashen broke the news: A woman who had been with Cone the night before was accusing him of rape, and police were investigating. He could skip his start if he wanted. Cone refused, despite near-hallucinations of a cop interrupting play at Veterans Stadium to arrest him.[53]

"If anything, it made me stronger," he says. "It gave me a cause. Either fold or get mentally strong, that's how I was thinking. I chose to get strong."[54]

Cone was at his best — three hits, one walk, no runs, 19 strikeouts (18 of which were swinging). The last tied an NL record, with Tom Seaver and Steve Carlton.[55] Within three days, police had concluded the allegations were "unfounded."[56]

In February 1992, another woman alleged she was Cone's girlfriend and she had been gang-raped by teammates Dwight Gooden, Daryl Boston, and Vince Coleman. Cone admitted he had been with the woman a few times, but wasn't currently seeing her. The police would drop the investigation.[57]

Not a month went by when perhaps the juiciest scandal hit the tabloids: WEIRD SEX ACT IN THE BULLPEN, famously howled the *New York Post* back page on March 26, 1992. The three women from the previous fall had amended their lawsuit to add other lurid claims, including that Cone had masturbated in front of them in the Shea Stadium bullpen in 1989. There was nothing to it — the suit never reached trial[58] — but the baseless gossip has become part of Cone lore. Angry fans would taunt, "Masturbation!" or make rude gestures from the stands during the season.

"Even though both cases were cleared up, my name was completely cleared, the damage had been done," Cone reflected years afterward. "I've had to live with that. There was part of me that said, at some point, 'Be more careful, cover your ass a little better, but you can still live, you can still have fun.' I thought there was a lot of reckless journalism, but I sort of came full circle and said, 'Now, wait a minute — you did put yourself in a position to be taken advantage of a couple of times.'"[59]

A few days later, Cone, fed up with the nosy tabloids, initiated a petition to ban all reporters from the clubhouse; his teammates were happy to oblige.[60] The Mets' media boycott lasted until they headed north on April 3.[61]

"I look back at that, I think we as players probably overreacted during that time," Cone said. "We should've handled that situation better. But we did feel like for the first time we were under attack, and we thought a lot of the stuff that was coming our way was not truthful, it was kind of reckless at times. We all collectively did it, realized we couldn't go on once we got into it, and looking back, probably would've played it differently back then."[62]

Eventually, Cone had to take it. He fielded lewd questions from Don Imus and Howard Stern on air. He invited cartoonists who'd depicted his "weird act" to send him autographed copies.

However, as the Mets spiraled, even Cone's personality couldn't save him. On August 27, 1992, the Mets, mindful Cone was facing free agency that fall, traded him to Toronto for Jeff Kent and Ryan Thompson. At the time Cone was 13-7 with a 2.88 ERA, and leading the NL in shutouts (5) and strikeouts (214). Had he not been traded to the AL, the Mets' only All-Star Game representative that year would've won his third straight NL strikeout title, as the Braves' John Smoltz only passed him by one (215) in his final start. Cone's season strikeout total was 261.

"The trade was a wake-up call for me," Cone said. "It was time to take a hard look at myself – what am I doing wrong here? Or at least, what are the perceptions of what I'm doing wrong? You're getting a reputation as a kid with great stuff, some of the best stuff in the big leagues as far as pitching goes, and also one of the biggest flakes. I kind of looked at that and said, 'Is this how I want to be remembered?' Not that I had any great revelations or made any great changes in my life, but I certainly looked at it and tried to address it."[63]

"Excited" was what he told the press. The Blue Jays were hurtling toward a division title. Cone's four wins sealed the deal,[64] and Toronto beat the Braves in the World Series to bring a championship to Canada for the first time.

"It was like I was hitchhiking on the side of the road and got a ride to the World Series –unbelievable," Cone told cheering fans at the victory parade.[65]

It was Cone's first ring, but he felt "rented, like I was hired long enough to ensure the win."[66]

Toronto wasn't home — rather than find an apartment, Cone stayed in the Skydome Hotel. This impermanence was further emphasized when mere days after the parade, Cone was back in New York, hosting a charity auction and appearing on the David Letterman TV show.

Cone could have returned to New York the next year — he made clear he was interested in signing with the Yankees,[67] and he'd maintained his New York apartment. But Cone became disillusioned with the Yankees' disorganized negotiating tactics — which he later learned were because their first choice had been Greg Maddux. When the Royals stepped in with an "unbelievable" three-year, $18 million offer, including a $9 million bonus, the choice was clear. Cone was going home to Kansas City as baseball's highest-paid pitcher.[68]

According to Cone, Ewing Kauffman, the Royals owner, who was dying of bone cancer, "made the offer with the caveat of, not 'take it or leave it,' but 'you need to decide pretty soon,' especially considering the uneven structure of the contract, the way he presented it. It was, 'Take a little bit of time, but not too much. Make your decision.' He was a good salesman."[69]

In 1993 Cone finished in the top 10 in the AL in ERA (3.33), strikeouts (191), innings pitched (254), complete games (6), and hits allowed per nine innings (7.264). What stands out is that he went 11-14—the Royals' weak offense[70] barely supported Cone, with 2.93 runs per start.[71]

The next year, Kansas City gave him the support (5.11 runs per start), and Cone went 16-5 with a 2.94 ERA—including three consecutive shutouts in May—and a selection to the AL All-Star team. The Baseball Writers Association of America bestowed upon him the AL Cy Young Award that fall.

Outside events overshadowed those accolades. The MLB Players Association went on strike August 12, the World Series canceled for the first time since 1904. Cone, encouraged by Steve Fehr, union executive director Donald Fehr's brother, was involved as a player representative with the Mets, but his role grew that fall when players chose him as the AL representative. Cone attributed his leadership role in union negotiations to "timing."

"Sometimes, it's by default," he said. "I was one of the more established pitchers at that time. Some of the players, they get involved, they're worried about angering the owners, or losing their job, or getting labeled. Most of the guys back then, especially, that served on the Players Association boards, they had to be prominent guys or had to be the type of players that felt secure to be able to represent their teams without feeling like they were going to lose their jobs or feeling like there would be repercussions for their involvement."[72]

Part of Cone's role was to boost morale of those concerned players, so that they would not feel pressure to cross picket lines. At his most grandstanding during a rally, he bent over with his rear end to the crowd to remind players that "the owners are trying to stick it up your ass without Vaseline. That's what this strike is about. This is about your rights, not your money."[73]

Baseball's antiquated antitrust exemption had opened the door for owner collusion to suppress player salaries in recent collective-bargaining agreements. At the height of the strike, the owners unilaterally imposed a salary cap and made plans to bring in replacement players to start the 1995 season if the MLBPA didn't concede. It threatened the union's existence. Cone spent the winter in Washington, tirelessly lobbying senators and representatives to repeal the antitrust exemption.[74]

His efforts ultimately resulted in the Curt Flood Act of 1998, a partial repeal, so that players could bring antitrust lawsuits "involving conduct that directly relates to or affects" their employment.[75] Cone believes the partial repeal is "one of the reasons why we've had labor peace for so long" since the strike.[76]

Cone also was among those urging the National Labor Relations Board to seek an injunction against the owners beginning the season with replacement players. On March 30, 1995, Federal Judge Sonia Sotomayor granted the injunction, and the players returned to work. Cone returned the favor in 2009 when he testified in favor of now-Justice Sotomayor's nomination to the US Supreme Court.[77]

Cone took at least one day off from his strike activities, November 12, 1994, to marry Lynn DiGioia, an interior designer from Connecticut. They met in Puerto Rico in 1987 and had dated on and off since.

The strike had been over but a week when the Royals traded Cone back to the Blue Jays for rookie Chris Stynes and minor leaguers Tony Medrano and Dave Sinnes.

"I don't blame my union activities for them trading me, but I know it didn't help," Cone said, noting that the $5 million price tag in the last year of his contract probably had something to do with it.[78]

Cone's second turn in Toronto didn't last much longer than the first. The last-place Blue Jays sent him to the Yankees near the trade deadline, July 28, for prospects Marty Janzen, Jason Jarvis, and Mike Gordon. The Yankees were languishing in mediocrity, but general manager Gene Michael ardently believed Cone was the missing piece to send them to the postseason for the first time since 1981.[79] Which he did, going 9-2 as the Yankees captured the AL wild card. It was the textbook definition of a "hired gun."

Cone had now mastered the art of appearing both straightforward and rehearsed with the press. During his first homestand in pinstripes, he reviewed his new team's media guide in full view of reporters, knowing the story would play better than if he had done it privately.[80] He also gently alerted a grateful in-game broadcasting team that the clubhouse could hear their between-inning banter, and that they should exercise some discretion before they embarrass themselves.[81]

Wearing number 36 in honor of Robin Roberts,[82] a still-durable Cone led the league with 229 ⅓ innings pitched. He threw 135 pitches in the ALDS opener victory against Seattle. But he blew a 4-2 lead in the eighth inning of Game Five, the tying blow coming on the aforementioned walk to Doug Strange on pitch 147. He still patiently answered reporters' questions afterward, albeit teary-eyed.

A free agent again, Cone almost didn't re-sign after the Yankees retracted their initial offer. He and Fehr had all but reached a deal with Baltimore[83] when Yankees owner George Steinbrenner allegedly jumped in from a pay phone and reinstated the bid—a three-year, $18 million deal with an additional $1.5 million in options.[84] Cone signed.

Now a seasoned New Yorker, Cone embraced his role as a leader by welcoming newer players. When Joe Girardi's early struggles led to frequent taunting on sports talk radio, Cone advised the first-year Yankees catcher that his critics would "lay off" if Girardi interacted with them rather than hiding from the press.[85] Girardi rebounded.

Cone pitched seven shutout innings in the Yankees' Opening Day victory in Cleveland, but coldness, numbness, and blueness persisted in his pitching hand for weeks after he'd left the 38-degree weather. An angiogram showed blood clots, and Cone was prescribed blood thinners. But a second angiogram on May 7 revealed a potentially life-threatening diagnosis: an aneurysm—the weakening and ballooning of an artery—in his right shoulder.

"I didn't even know what it was or what it meant," Cone said. "It was very scary. I just wanted to know if my career was over at that point."[86]

Vein-graft surgery was scheduled three days later, as doctors replaced the offending section of artery with a piece from Cone's left thigh. How long he would be out was anyone's guess.

The procedure had not left structural damage to his shoulder, and once the graft healed, Cone could throw again. After two rehab starts at Double-A Norwich, Cone boarded a plane to rejoin the Yankees in Oakland on Labor Day.

He walked two batters in the first. Then, no hits for seven innings. But he was being held to a strict pitch count, so manager Joe Torre replaced him with Mariano Rivera after pitch number 85.[87]

"If they had left the decision up to David, they would have needed a tractor to get him out of there," said Ed Cone, who had watched the game from behind the first-base dugout at the Oakland Coliseum.[88]

Cone would pick up two more wins and a loss, finishing 7-2 with a 2.88 ERA in 11 starts. He was shelled for six runs against Texas in the ALDS, and he was wild (five walks, six innings, 133 pitches) against the Orioles in the ALCS. But his gritty performance in the third game of the World Series jump-started the Yankees' march to their first championship since 1978.

He was no longer a hired gun.

The first half 1997, Cone showed the devastating promise the Yankees had hoped for when they re-signed him. Named to the AL All-Star team, he had 12 wins and a 2.68 ERA by early August. He'd hit double digits in strikeouts in six games, including June 23, when he fanned 16 Tigers, and averaged over 10 strikeouts per nine innings. Then he spent most of September on the disabled list for right-shoulder tendonitis and inflammation. He was chased from his one postseason start in the fourth inning, allowing six Cleveland runs in the ALDS.

The problem was a bone spur that required off-season arthroscopic shoulder surgery. It wasn't even clear that Cone would be ready to join the Opening Day roster in 1998, but again he flouted expectation. Despite a rocky first two starts, Cone quietly built up his record.

Now 35, Cone was learning to adjust to his own vulnerabilities—in terms of when he could throw (warmer weather suited him), how much he could throw, and the types of pitches he could throw.

"A lot of wear and tear just took its toll and I lost some velocity," Cone said of his later years, when he relied more on finesse, "so I had to adjust, get more creative, probably throw more breaking stuff, less fastballs, change angles a bit more."[89]

He skipped a start in early June when his mother's Jack Russell terrier, Veronica, nipped at his index finger. It paved the way for Orlando "El Duque" Hernandez, a Cuban defector with a peculiar high leg kick, to make his major-league debut. Cone, who joked about being "Wally Pipped,"[90] wasn't slowed in the slightest, striking out 14 Marlins five days later.

A pair of Adidas commercials airing around that time showcased Cone's self-deprecating humor. In one, the advice that he "rest that arm" led a fan entourage to embarrassingly baby him.[91] The other, depicting fans at a club doing "The El Duque," ended with Cone awkwardly grinding in the men's room in response to Luis Sojo's suggestion, "Hey, Coney, why don't you have a dance?"

Cone was also the only player bold enough to sidle up to teammate and drinking buddy David Wells as he was in the middle of throwing a perfect game on May 17. "I think it's time to break out the knuckleball," he said.[92] Wells laughed. Tension released.

Despite arm fatigue toward September, Cone won his 20th game in his final start—the decade gap between 20-win seasons still a major-league record. He chugged through the postseason, winning the rubber games of both the ALDS and the ALCS, and starting Game Three of the World Series in San Diego (a cortisone shot to the shoulder helped), as the Yankees capped their incredible 114-48 season with Cone's third ring.

On July 18, 1999, against the Montreal Expos, Cone accomplished what only 15 other pitchers had done in major-league history—he threw a perfect game.[93] Cone had come close before—aside from the aneurysm comeback game, he'd also taken a no-hitter into the eighth in 1991—but this was his first no-hitter. The timing almost seemed contrived: The Yankees honored Yogi Berra prior to the game,[94] and Don Larsen, the only man with a World Series perfecto, had thrown out the first pitch and watched the feat unfold at Yankee Stadium.

"It makes you stop and think about the Yankee magic and the mystique of this ballpark," Cone said afterward.[95]

An All-Star again in 1999, Cone was 10-4 with a 2.65 ERA, averaging 6⅔ innings per start the day he was perfect. Afterward, he was anything but—2-5 with a 4.82 ERA, averaging 5.46 innings.[96] Although he insisted he felt better physically in 1999 than he did the previous season,[97] his velocity was down—his fastball topping off in the mid-80s. Nonetheless, Cone's big-game mentality kicked in with two October victories—he struck out nine Red Sox in the ALCS and allowed one Braves hit in seven innings in Game Two of the World Series—as the Yankees won their third championship in four years.

Before 1999, Cone had leveraged his option into a one-year, $8 million salary. Now, the Yankees, concerned about Cone's age, 37, and his tired second half, refused to accommodate his request for a two-year contract before 2000. Instead, the parties agreed to a one-year, $12 million deal.

Then Cone, in his words, "fell on my face,"[98] going 4-14 with a 6.91 ERA—or, as fans derided him, $3 million per win. In a Twilight Zonesque twist, the entire debacle was chronicled in Roger Angell's book, *A Pitcher's Story*, on which Cone had agreed to cooperate before his season went south.

By early August Cone was 1-10.[99] After extended mechanical work at the Yankees' training facility, he won three of five starts. But on September 5, in front of family and friends in Kansas City, he dislocated his left shoulder fielding a bunt. As the injury wasn't to his pitching arm, Cone returned to the rotation after missing one turn, with disastrous results (23 earned runs, 14⅔ innings) in his final four starts.

Perhaps as a nod to Cone's team history, Torre put Cone on the postseason roster. With the Yankees clinging to a 3-2 lead in Game Four of the Subway Series against the Mets, Cone was summoned to face Mike Piazza with two outs in the fifth.[100] He popped up the future Hall of Famer on five pitches, and the

Yankees won their fourth title in five years the following night.

The Yankees couldn't guarantee Cone a spot in the 2001 rotation, so they parted ways—Cone likened the split to a "divorce."

"I want to go where I'm needed, and there isn't a great need for me here with the Yankees," Cone said then.[101]

Cone discovered where he was needed when Red Sox pitching coach Joe Kerrigan visited him that offseason and diagnosed flaws in Cone's motion.[102] Cone signed with Boston for $1 million, with another million in deferred payments.

New York newspapers called him a traitor—the Yankees' $12 million liability had taken the money and run to their bitter rivals.

Cone shrugged it off. "It's better to be booed than forgotten," he said.[103]

A sore shoulder delayed Cone's Boston debut until May, but the season was somewhat redemptive—9-7, 4.31 ERA, in spite of him being kept to low pitch counts and often given an extra day of rest. On September 2 the old Cone resurfaced, as he dueled Mike Mussina, his replacement in the Yankees rotation, over eight scoreless innings. He lost on an unearned run in the ninth—as Mussina came within one strike of a perfect game.[104]

The Red Sox didn't re-sign him, and Cone spent 2002 as a spectator. He led the Yankee Stadium Bleacher Creatures in their first-inning roll call of the starting lineup on Opening Day ("I've always wanted to watch a game from out here."[105]) and was pulled into the broadcast booth of the upstart YES Network for a few games.

He claimed he didn't really throw that year,[106] though news outlets kept hinting at a comeback. Before the 2003 season, John Franco and Al Leiter talked him into going to spring training. Cone made the Mets as the fourth starter, at age 40.

And for one "magical" night (his word),[107] the Coneheads returned to Shea. Wearing Dwight Gooden's old number 16, Cone pitched five shutout innings for his 194th career win. Then reality set in.

Cone said he "gave it a good shot, but just physically couldn't do it anymore. And it wasn't really my arm at that point, it was more my hip. My hip just gave me a bunch of problems that year. All those years of landing on my left hip, as a right-handed pitcher, kind of took its toll."[108]

He announced his retirement on May 30, six wins shy of 200. His 2,668 strikeouts ranked 18th all-time, then.[109] When he became eligible for the Hall of Fame in 2009, only 3.9 percent of the BBWAA voted for him—a player needs 5 percent to remain on the ballot.[110]

"I think one of the problems for me was the way I finished my career," Cone said. "I didn't finish off my career and get my numbers up there from a quantitative career perspective, just kind of fell a little short." The Hall of Fame Braves trio of Greg Maddux, Tom Glavine, and John Smoltz, for instance, "got started a little younger, and they lasted a little longer," and "they stayed healthy the whole time."[111]

After spending his entire adult life gripping a baseball, Cone's transition game wasn't seamless. He has always had his charities. His own David Cone Foundation has supported several not-for-profit organizations, including the Ban Johnson League that made him, Joe Torre's Safe at Home Foundation (domestic violence), and various medical causes, in particular the ALS Association and cancer research. He guest-bartended at Foley's New York Pub to raise funds for Hurricane Sandy victims.[112] He took a pie to the face to promote gastroparesis awareness.[113]

But finding his career niche took time. Coaching was always in the back of his mind, but "the window closes for opportunities for pitching coaches. To go back on the road full-time would be a big commitment; you have to be ready for that."[114]

Cone has two sons now. Brian was born in 2006, though David and Lynn divorced in 2011. Cone and his fiancée, Taja Abitbol, a restaurateur and real estate agent from Queens, have a son, Sammy, born in December 2011. As of 2017 they lived in Manhattan's Greenwich Village.

Would Cone encourage his boys to follow in his footsteps? "Absolutely—I wouldn't discourage it,"

Cone said. "Certainly if they showed the interest and the promise and that's what they wanted to try to pursue, I would try to help them in any way I could." But, he cautioned, "It was something I was always worried about as a father. I didn't want to push them or have them feel like they had to compete with their father or feel like they had to be as good as their father. I was always more protective in that regard."[115]

For a would-be sportswriter-turned-athlete, Cone's second career should have seemed obvious—media. In 2008 he became a part-time color commentator for the YES Network, among a rotating team of announcers providing in-game and studio analysis. His remarks have not always been the most filtered—asides have included recitations of song lyrics ("Rapper's Delight," "Call Me Maybe"), unintentional innuendos (a pitcher asked to warm up but not called upon got "jerked off" in the bullpen), or poking fun at his broadcast colleagues. ("It is high, it is far, it is off my forehead!" he said in John Sterling's voice when a pop foul got too close for comfort in the adjacent radio booth.). Yet Cone has won praise as a perceptive student of sabermetrics, with observations ranging from complicated statistics to technical analysis of how the ball spins across the plate—attention to detail not often found in an ex-ballplayer behind the microphone.

"Every year it's become a little easier, knowing what the job entails, when to use sabremetrics and when not to," said Cone. "I try to be an easy listen. I try to tell you something you don't know."[116]

The easy way out would've been to rest on his laurels and regale in tall tales about his days in uniform, as so many ex-players have done. But Cone has always been at his best when challenged to defy conventional expectation.

SOURCES

Statistics, unless otherwise noted, are from Baseball-Reference.com or Retrosheet.org. Special thanks to Andrew Levy for putting me in touch with David Cone.

NOTES

1 Roger Angell, *A Pitcher's Story* (New York: Warner Books, 2001), 29.

2 Announcer Tim McCarver made such an observation in the World Series Game Three broadcast on Fox, October 22, 1996.

3 The attendance at Fulton County Stadium that night was 51,843; another 23.99 million viewers watched the game on television, according to Nielsen ratings. Cone had lost Game One of the ALDS against Texas; he pitched better in Game Two of the ALCS against the Orioles, which the Yankees also eventually lost.

4 John Harper & Bob Klapisch, *Champions! The Saga of the 1996 New York Yankees* (New York: Villard Books, 1996), 197-98.

5 Angell, 45. Cone has suggested more recently that he was only joking at the time about having "lied" about his ability to finish the inning, but admits that he was "exhausted" and drained from the "pressure of the moment," and that it never really occurred to him that he might not be able to pitch out of the inning. Podcast, "30 With Murti: David Cone and the 1996 Yankees," May 5, 2016, newyork.cbslocal.com/2016/05/05/remembering-the-1996-yankees-david-cone-30-with-murti/.

6 Torre once dubbed Cone "Thomas Edison every day." Craig Wolff, "Uptown Local: David Cone is the toast of New York, but he's still a backyard K.C. boy in a pinch," *ESPN the Magazine*, October 5, 1998, espn.com/espn/magazine/archives/news/story?page=magazine-19981005-article25.

7 Cone is probably closer to 5-feet-11; he himself has admitted being under 6 feet tall. See, e.g., Bob Klapisch, "Klapisch: Q-and-A with David Cone," *North Jersey.com*, February 25, 2017, northjersey.com/story/sports/columnists/bob-klapisch/2017/02/25/klapisch-a-q-and-a-with-david-cone/98423578/.

8 See, e.g., Ian O'Connor, "A Pair of Aces Jack, Cone hold Yank Cards," *New York Daily News*, August 3, 1995, nydailynews.com/archives/sports/pair-aces-jack-cone-hold-yank-cards-article-1.696298; Jennifer Frey, "A Grown-Up David Cone Takes to Life as a Leader," *Washington Post*, March 24, 1996, washingtonpost.com/archive/sports/1996/03/24/a-grown-up-david-cone-takes-to-life-as-a-leader/20719712-5429-4492-bbbc-dc6f5cdb0a7b/?utm_term=.d476711dd8ff; Chris Smith, "Wild Pitcher," *New York Magazine*, October 18, 1999, nymag.com/nymetro/news/sports/features/2138/; Angell, 14.

9 Angell, 76.

10 Angell, 80.

11 "I was 12 years old, in 1975, when Luis Tiant was in the World Series with the Red Sox," Cone said. "I just kind of fell in love with him, started copying him in the backyard. He had that kind of style." Interview with author, February 24, 2017.

12 Angell, 79.

13 John Ed Bradley, "The Headliner," *Sports Illustrated*, April 5, 1993, si.com/vault/1993/04/05/128316/the-headliner-strikeout-king-david-cone-hopes-the-news-he-makes-as-a-kansas-city-royal-will-be-about-baseball-not-off-the-field-shenanigans.

14 Angell, 78.

15 Chris Smith, "Wild Pitcher."

16 The Cones saw the neighbor brandishing something shiny, which could have been a gun. It turned out to be a knife.

17 John Ed Bradley.

18 Angell, 79.

19 John Ed Bradley.

20 Until 2016, Cone might have been Rockhurst's most famous graduate—if not for a suddenly prominent politician from Virginia named Tim Kaine.

21 Angell, 116. Rockhurst restored its baseball program in 1989, and a few years later Cone made a large donation toward the school's athletic programs.

22 Angell, 118-19.

23 John Ed Bradley.

24 Angell, 119.

25 Interestingly, four members of the Mets' 1990 rotation were chosen during that draft: Cone's future roommate Sid Fernandez (73rd overall pick) was chosen immediately ahead of Cone (74th) by the Dodgers; Ron Darling (9th) was selected by the Rangers in the first round; and Frank Viola (37th) was chosen by the Twins in the second round. Longtime Mets closer John Franco was also part of the 1981 draft, selected by the Dodgers in the fifth round.

26 See Angell, 124.

27 John Ed Bradley.

28 Angell, 147.

29 See, e.g., Peter Botte, "Ed Hearn, known for Mets trade that got David Cone, flopped with Royals but finds success in life," *New York Daily News*, October 27, 2015, nydailynews.com/sports/baseball/mets/ed-hearn-finds-success-royals-flop-mets-cone-article-1.2412564.

30 Angell, 153.

31 Robert David Jaffee, "Former NY Mets Catcher Barry Lyons Roars Back From Depression," *Huffington Post*, January 28, 2014, huffingtonpost.com/robert-david-jaffee/former-ny-mets-catcher-ba_b_4681263.html. Years later, after Hurricane Katrina had destroyed Lyons' home, Cone and friend Andrew Levy helped bring Lyons out of a spiral of depression and addiction.

32 Angell, 154.

33 Angell, 149.

34 Cone, a left-handed batter, described the pitch hitting "the bottom hand around the [k]nob of the bat. Like cracking a walnut." Twitter, June 25, 2013, twitter.com/Baldassano/status/349594799944380416.

35 Dashing initial hopes of many New Yorkers, Cone is not Jewish. His last name originates from the Irish "McCone," not "Cohen."

36 Cone hasn't appeared on *SNL* in a Conehead, but he did show up twice on the late-night sketch comedy. The first time was among a group of players upstaging host Ben Stiller after the Yankees won the World Series in 1998. The second was in drag with pal David Wells and host Derek Jeter in 2001—he played a "skank" in a leopard-print halter top and metallic black miniskirt who pulled underwear from his bra.

37 Vincent M. Mallozzi, "Live From New York, It's a Conehead," *New York Times*, October 29, 2006, nytimes.com/2006/10/29/sports/baseball/29cheer.html.

38 John Feinstein, *Play Ball: The Life and Troubled Times of Major League Baseball* (New York: Villard, 1993). Excerpt available at Google Books.

39 Correspondence with author, March 3, 2017.

40 Sam McManis, "HIT, THROW AND RUN: Guerrero Throws Bat at Pitcher; Dodgers Lose, 5-2," *Los Angeles Times*, May 23, 1988, articles.latimes.com/1988-05-23/sports/sp-2199_1_dodgers-lose.

41 Paul Hagen, "Now There's No Way Phils Can Lose 100," *Philadelphia Daily News*, September 28, 1988. Cone batted .234 in 1989, the highest average for any pitcher with more than 35 at-bats.

42 Interview with author, February 24, 2017.

43 Ibid.

44 Sam McManis, "BASEBALL PLAYOFFS: Cone Winds Up Eating His Words: Met Pitcher Apologizes; Career as a Columnist Is Over," *Los Angeles Times*, October 8, 1988, articles.latimes.com/1988-10-08/sports/sp-3095_1_david-cone; Robbie Andreu, "Cone Writes His Wrong. He Quits," *Sun-Sentinel*, October 8, 1988, articles.sun-sentinel.com/1988-10-08/sports/8802280502_1_bob-klapisch-column-gag-order (excerpts from column quoted).

45 Interview with author, February 24, 2017.

46 Gerard Cosloy, "Klapisch Recalls Controversial Cone Column," *Can't Stop the Bleeding*, September 11, 2006, cantstopthebleeding.com/klapisch-recalls-controversial-cone-column (excerpted from the *Bergen Record*).

47 See, e.g., Murray Chass, "ON BASEBALL: Yankees Must Beware Fate of the 1988 Mets," *New York Times*, June 25, 1996, nytimes.com/1996/06/25/sports/on-baseball-yankees-must-beware-fate-of-the-1988-mets.html (Joe McIlvaine claimed the column "absolutely" contributed to the Mets' NLCS loss.); Buster Olney, *The Last Night of the Yankee Dynasty* (New York: HarperCollins, 2004), 166. (Mets manager Davey Johnson "would say his greatest regret of that season was 'David Cone's literary career.'")

48 Angell, 90.

49 David Laurila, "Q&A: David Cone, Stat-head All-Star," *FanGraphs*, November 20, 2012, fangraphs.com/blogs/qa-david-cone-stat-head-all-star.

50 Joe Sexton, "BASEBALL: Dawson Slaps Laredo Slider and Mets Go South," *New York Times*, August 10, 1991, nytimes.com/1991/08/10/sports/baseball-dawson-slaps-laredo-slider-and-mets-go-south.html.

51 Interview with author, February 24, 2017.

52 John Ed Bradley.

53 Angell, 175; John Ed Bradley, si.com/vault/1993/04/05/128316/the-headliner-strikeout-king-david-cone-hopes-the-news-he-makes-as-a-kansas-city-royal-will-be-about-baseball-not-off-the-field-shenanigans.

54 John Ed Bradley.

55 Kerry Wood (1998) and Max Scherzer (2016) have since surpassed that record, with 20 K's.

56 Allen Barra, "The New Whitey Ford," *The Village Voice*, October 12, 1999, villagevoice.com/news/the-new-whitey-ford-6420696.

57 Ibid.; Michael Marriott, "BASEBALL; State Attorney Says 3 Mets Will Not Face Criminal Charges," *New York Times*, April 10, 1992, nytimes.com/1992/04/10/sports/baseball-state-attorney-says-3-mets-will-not-face-criminal-charges.html.

58 Two of the women dropped out of the suit, and the third woman settled privately over words that were exchanged—the worst thing Cone had apparently done was call her a "groupie." See Angell, 176-77.

59 Chris Smith, "Wild Pitcher."

60 Eric Pooley, "Why Are These Guys Laughing?" *New York Magazine*, April 13, 1992, 58, 60.

61 Bruce Kauffman, "Battered Mets Banish the Messenger," *AJR*, May 1992, ajrarchive.org/Article.asp?id=2061.

62 Interview with author, February 24, 2017.

63 Chris Smith, "Wild Pitcher."

64 The Blue Jays won the AL East over Milwaukee by four games.

65 Archived news footage from 1992 Blue Jays victory parade, available at youtube.com/watch?v=F5jxknTz7tI&t=682s (last visited March 11, 2017).

66 Allen Barra, "The New Whitey Ford."

67 Joe Sexton, "BASEBALL; Royals Make Cone Game's Highest-Paid Pitcher," *New York Times*, December 9, 1992, nytimes.com/1992/12/09/sports/baseball-royals-make-cone-game-s-highest-paid-pitcher.html.

68 Cone clarified that the "highest-paid" label was only "the highest average annual value"—the contract was actually "back-loaded," in that after the bonus, he was to make $2 million the first two years, and $5 million the third year. At least Greg Maddux, when he signed with the Braves a day after Cone did, was making more from a salary standpoint. Interview with author, February 24, 2017.

69 Interview with author, February 24, 2017.

70 Kansas City's offense was last in the AL in runs scored (675) and team on-base percentage (.320).

71 By comparison, the White Sox' Jack McDowell, who won the AL Cy Young Award, had similar numbers to Cone—except that he went 22-10.

72 Interview with author, February 24, 2017.

73 Angell, 247. Former MLBPA head Marvin Miller praised Cone as "one of the most articulate spokesmen for players' rights I've ever seen." Allen Barra, "The New Whitey Ford."

74 Before the Senate Judiciary Subcommittee, Cone forcefully testified that the negotiation process with the owners was "such a joke." See "Kansas City Royals Pitcher David Cone on baseball strike—1995 Senate Judiciary Subcmte Hearing," *C-SPAN*.org, February 15, 1995, c-span.org/video/?c4510189/kansas-city-royals-pitcher-david-cone-baseball-strike. Cone has often been asked whether he would consider going into politics. He generally demurs –"too many skeletons."

75 S.53—Curt Flood Act of 1998, 105th Cong., congress.gov/bill/105th-congress/senate-bill/53.

76 Interview with author, February 24, 2017.

77 See "Sotomayor Confirmation Hearing, Day 4, Legal Issues Panel," *C-SPAN*.org, c-span.org/video/?c1446191/clip-sotomayor-confirmation-hearing-day-4-legal-issues-panel.

78 Interview with author, February 24, 2017.

79 Andrew Mearns, "This Day in Yankees History: David Cone, Hired Gun—July 28, 1995," *Pinstripe Alley*, July 28, 2012, pinstripealley.com/2012/7/28/3198562/this-day-in-yankees-history-david-cone-hired-gun-july-28-1995.

80 See Ian O'Connor, "A Pair of Aces Jack, Cone Hold Yank, Cards," *New York Daily News*, August 3, 1995, nydailynews.com/archives/sports/pair-aces-jack-cone-hold-yank-cards-article-1.696298.

81 George Vecsey, "Sports of the Times; Cone Faces Unfinished Business," *New York Times*, December 22, 1995, nytimes.com/1995/12/22/sports/sports-of-the-times-cone-faces-unfinished-business.html.

82 Roberts, a Hall of Fame pitcher, had also been active in the early days of the MLBPA, helping persuade the players to hire Marvin Miller as union head.

83 The Orioles attracted Cone, in part, because he'd worked with new general manager Pat Gillick (with the Blue Jays) and new manager Davey Johnson (Mets) before, and he respected owner Peter Angelos for not hiring replacement players during the strike. Harper & Klapisch, 14-15.

84 The Mets also made a last-minute offer, but the money wasn't there.

85 Podcast, "30 With Murti: David Cone and the 1996 Yankees."

86 Ibid.

NO-HITTERS

87 Only a controversial ninth-inning single stood between Rivera completing a combined no-hitter.

88 Jack Curry, "Sensational Comeback for Cone: Seven Innings, No Runs, No Hits," *New York Times*, September 3, 1996, nytimes.com/1996/09/03/sports/sensational-comeback-for-cone-seven-innings-no-runs-no-hits.html.

89 Interview with author, February 24, 2017.

90 Pipp was the Yankees first baseman whose injury contributed to the rise of his replacement, Lou Gehrig.

91 tvspots.tv/video/5213/adidas—rest-that-arm.

92 Buster Olney, "BASEBALL; Rarest Gem for Yankees' Wells: A Perfect Game," *New York Times*, May 18, 1998, nytimes.com/1998/05/18/sports/baseball-rarest-gem-for-yankees-wells-a-perfect-game.html.

93 As of March 2017, 23 pitchers had thrown perfect games—seven since Cone.

94 Berra's number 8 was emblazoned behind home plate throughout the game, and Cone threw 88 pitches.

95 Murray Chass, "BASEBALL; On Day Made for Legends, Cone Pitches Perfect Game," *New York Times*, July 19, 1999, nytimes.com/1999/07/19/sports/baseball-on-day-made-for-legends-cone-pitches-perfect-game.html?ref=davidcone.

96 Cone still finished with the second-lowest ERA in the AL, at 3.44.

97 Jack Curry, "Baseball: Cone's Velocity Returns, Showing His Arm Is Sound," *New York Times*, August 17, 1999, nytimes.com/1999/08/17/sports/baseball-cone-s-velocity-returns-showing-his-arm-is-sound.html.

98 Joe DiLessio, "David Cone on Advanced Stats, the End of His Playing Career, and Riding on David Wells's Motorcycle," *New York Magazine*, May 26, 2011, nymag.com/daily/sports/2011/05/david_cone_on_advanced_stats_t.html. As perceptive triviaheads have indicated, "David Cone" anagrams to "Odd Cave-In."

99 Cone lasted once beyond the seventh inning all season, in a no-decision on May 9.

100 Cone had pitched a perfect inning of relief against Seattle in the ALCS, and Torre considered starting him in Game Four instead of the struggling Denny Neagle. Cone encouraged Torre to start Neagle over him, because, Cone claimed, he had gotten comfortable coming from the bullpen.

101 Angell, 283.

102 The Mets, Rangers, and Royals (as a closer) also expressed mild interest in Cone that offseason.

103 Joel Sherman, "Cone-Tamination; Is Complete," *New York Post*, February 19, 2001, nypost.com/2001/02/19/cone-tamination-is-complete/.

104 Cone is also the answer to the trivia question of who threw the final pitch to Cal Ripken, Jr. The Orioles Iron Man went 0-for-3 as Cone hurled another eight innings without allowing an earned run on October 6.

105 Jack Curry, "ON BASEBALL; That Face In a Crowd Is Cone's," *New York Times*, April 6, 2002, nytimes.com/2002/04/06/sports/on-baseball-that-face-in-a-crowd-is-cone-s.html.

106 News outlets in 2002 claimed that Cone was still throwing regularly. When the author asked Cone if he had been throwing throughout 2002, he replied, "No, not really. I just kind of took the year off." Interview with author, February 24, 2017.

107 "David Cone Announces Retirement," UPI Wire, May 30, 2003, upi.com/David-Cone-announces-retirement/76971054333945/.

108 Interview with author, February 24, 2017.

109 As of 2017, Cone had slipped to 23rd all-time, surpassed by Pedro Martinez, Curt Schilling, John Smoltz, Mike Mussina, and CC Sabathia.

110 Cone's career pitching Wins Above Replacement, at 61.7, ranks right between Hall of Famers Juan Marichal and Don Drysdale—51st all-time.

111 Interview with author, February 24, 2017.

112 David G. Palacio, "After Sandy: Baseball's David Cone Serves Beer To Help Victims," *The Midtown Gazette*, November 17, 2012, themidtowngazette.com/2012/11/after-sandy-local-ball-player-serves-beer-to-help-hurricane-victims/.

113 The video was posted to social media: https://www.facebook.com/gastroparesispiefacechallenge/videos/466237433765594/

114 Interview with author, February 24, 2017.

115 Ibid.

116 Bob Klapisch, "Klapisch: Q-and-A with David Cone," *North Jersey.com*, February 25, 2017, northjersey.com/story/sports/columnists/bob-klapisch/2017/02/25/klapisch-a-q-and-a-with-david-cone/98423578/.

DAVID CONE PITCHES A PERFECT GAME

JULY 18, 1999: NEW YORK YANKEES 6, MONTREAL EXPOS 0, AT YANKEE STADIUM

By Tara Krieger

PRESSURE WAS DAVID Cone's lifeblood. In 1996, with the Yankees, the right-hander threw seven no-hit innings on his return from a career-threatening aneurysm that had sidelined him most of the season. Only a strict pitch count prevented him from going all nine against a power-hitting Oakland club that Labor Day.

"I'll never wonder if this could have been my last opportunity to throw one," said Cone of not completing the no-hitter. "I wouldn't think that way."[1]

Perhaps the stakes weren't high enough. Or improbable enough.

Cone was 36 on July 18, 1999. At the time, only Cy Young himself had thrown a perfect game at an older age.[2] But Cone (9-4, 2.86 ERA) had pitched for the American League All-Star team days before. The previous season, he won 20 games. He had contributed to two World Series championships in the past three years (1996 and 1998) and the Yankees would win a third in four years that fall. Sportswriters were casually floating the words "aura and mystique" and speaking of "ghosts" at old Yankee Stadium to connect the team's near-invincibility to the dynasties of old.

The strongest link to those dynasties was at the Stadium that afternoon—Hall of Fame catcher Yogi Berra, owner of a record 10 championship rings, whom the Yankees chose to honor for rekindling his connection to the team. Berra and owner George Steinbrenner had recently repaired a 14-year rift, in which Berra refused to set foot in Yankee Stadium after Big George had fired him as manager. With Joe DiMaggio's passing that spring, Berra was the greatest living Yankee.

Don Larsen, whose perfecto Berra had caught during the 1956 World Series, threw the ceremonial first pitch to Berra behind the plate.

Cone, keenly aware of the battery's historical significance, casually asked Larsen if he would "run and jump in Yogi's arms" to re-create the moment.

"You got it wrong, kid," Larsen snapped back. "He jumped into my arms."[3]

Fans settled for a handshake. "Perfect, it's absolutely perfect, and it has been a perfect day today," Yankees television announcer Bobby Murcer remarked prophetically as Berra and Larsen retreated to the dugout.

Cone began his warm-ups with catcher Joe Girardi. Interleague play being only in its third season, he had never faced the Montreal Expos in any recent incarnation.[4]

The Expos, at 33-54, had the fewest wins in baseball and were on a five-game losing streak that straddled the All-Star break. And they were tired, their bus having arrived in New York at 3:30 A.M.[5] for this rare Sunday opener of a three-game set. Their starter was Javier Vazquez, nearly 23 and newly recalled from Triple-A Ottawa, where he spent a month after going 2-4 with a 6.63 ERA with Montreal. The rest of the lineup was also young; the starting nine were, on average, under 26 years old. The Yankees' batting order, in contrast, included just two players under 30, all but one of whom had been or would be an All-Star during their careers.

Tickets didn't exactly sell out, as 41,930 fans showed up to fight the 95-degree heat. But Cone preferred pitching in hotter weather, particularly since his aneurysm surgery two years earlier.

Cone struck out leadoff hitter Wilton Guerrero looking on three pitches. Then the Yankees' defense saved him when Terry Jones and Rondell White both swung deep into the outfield. Right fielder Paul O'Neill one-handedly speared Jones's ball—Cone was sure it was a triple[6] — diving into a somersault in the right-center gap, and left fielder Ricky Ledee ran down White's fly near the track in left-center. Inning over.

In the top of the second, Cone fanned cleanup hitter Vladimir Guerrero and induced two weak grounders to the infield. He struck out the side in the third.

Vazquez, conversely, gave up the game in the bottom of the second. It started with a one-out walk to Chili Davis. The next batter, Ledee, homered into the empty blue seats in the right-field upper deck.

Vazquez then hit Scott Brosius's backside, allowing Girardi to drive him in on a double to center. Girardi was tagged out rounding second, but Vazquez walked Chuck Knoblauch. Derek Jeter's two-run homer in front of the numbers by Monument Park completed the Yankees' five-run inning.

Then, a sudden downpour, and the grounds crew applied the tarp with one out in the Yankees' half of the third. Cone played catch with batboy Luigi "Squeegee" Castillo to stay loose during the 33-minute delay. After play resumed, Cone continued rolling, with a seven-pitch fourth, weak fly ball after weak fly ball. The whispers started in the broadcast booth in the fifth.

"Now that would be the coincidences of coincidences. He pitched a perfect game on Yogi Berra Day? Come on," marveled broadcaster Tim McCarver after the 14th out. "It can't happen, so we just won't look for it."[7]

But it *was* progressively the all-consuming discussion among the Yankees' radio and television announcers for the game's remainder — the idea that mentioning it would hex the pitcher meant little in the booth by the late 1990s. On the bench, however, Cone's teammates, still believing they could spread bad mojo, kept their distance. The Yankees clubhouse, where Cone routinely retreated between innings to change his undershirt, was uncharacteristically deserted. An odd feeling for Cone, who a year earlier had been the one breaking the tension when former teammate David Wells was on his way to his own perfecto.

Only Davis dared cross that line. When Girardi was late to his post one inning, the Yankees designated hitter jumped in and squatted.

"You know, I used to catch in the minor leagues," Davis said to Cone. "I could catch your stuff."

Cone laughed. "That's all I needed," Cone recalled a decade later, "Chili was my guy."[8]

In the Expos' seventh, Wilton Guerrero hit a chopper toward the middle of the diamond that Brosius[9] stabbed and threw to first for the 19th out. Back-to-back strikeouts followed, heading into the seventh-inning stretch.

"It was a sports psychiatrist's kind of a Class 101 — it was negative thoughts and positive thoughts going both ways," Cone later remembered. "It was, 'You can do this,' and the other part was, 'Don't blow it.' So it was a constant battle of, 'Don't get too far ahead of yourself—you still have to win the game, you still have a few more innings to go,' but with each out and each inning, that anxiety kinda grew."[10]

Jose Vidro provided the most anxiety with one out in the eighth. He lined a hard grounder up the middle that Knoblauch grabbed on the outfield grass. The Yankees second baseman, who had become notoriously unable to hit his targets recently, spun, planted, and fired on the money to first baseman Tino Martinez. Cone then caught Brad Fullmer looking. Three outs left.

Unfortunately for Cone, a seemingly interminable bottom of the eighth grew longer when back-to-back hits from O'Neill and Bernie Williams plated another run and chased Vazquez. Reliever Bobby Ayala induced Davis to ground into a double play, effectively extinguishing the Yankees' rally.

"I've never been happier to see a double play hit by one of our guys," Cone said.[11]

Then it was the ninth, and Cone's every pitch was met with a standing ovation, followed by silence, save for isolated whistles. He fanned Chris Widger on three straight sliders. He induced pinch-hitter Ryan McGuire to fly out in shallow left to Ledee, who nearly lost the ball in the sun.[12]

And on a 1-and-1 count, Orlando Cabrera popped up along the third-base line about 30 feet in front of the bag. Cone pointed to the sky, and his hands fell on his head as if to say "that's it." He sank to his knees as the ball hit Brosius's glove for Out 27.

There was no jumping into Cone's arms for Girardi—he had scarcely charged in and wrapped Cone in a "bear hug" before teammates buried them, then carried Cone off the field.[13]

Cone had thrown 88 pitches—with Berra's retired number 8 etched behind home plate all day.[14] Not once did Cone reach a three-ball count on any hitter. In the pressroom, Cone embraced Larsen "as if he was my father."[15]

"You probably have a better chance of winning the lottery than this happening,"[16] Cone said—"the stars aligned" for him to pitch a perfect game on Yogi Berra Day.[17] Thus, his swift decline in the aftermath of being untouchable seemed both incredible and inevitable; some say the no-hitter was Cone's deal with the devil.[18] Following the perfecto, Cone went 2-5 (4.82 ERA) to finish 1999, and then was 4-14 (6.91) in 2000.[19]

Vazquez pitched back-to-back complete games following his losing decision, going 7-3 with a 3.77 ERA to end the season.[20]

"It was probably as much fun as I've had losing a game in my career," Vazquez said. "Watching David Cone control the game, remembering the atmosphere, Don Larsen and Yogi Berra were there, it was unbelievable."[21]

NOTES

1. Jack Curry, "Sensational Comeback for Cone: Seven Innings, No Runs, No Hits," *New York Times*, September 3, 1996. nytimes.com/1996/09/03/sports/sensational-comeback-for-cone-seven-innings-no-runs-no-hits.html.

2. In 2004 Randy Johnson completed a perfecto at the spry age of 40.

3. Steve Serby, "'My Head Was on Fire': David Cone Relives Perfect Game, 15 Years Later," *New York Post*, July 17, 2014. nypost.com/2014/07/17/my-head-was-on-fire-15-years-later-david-cone-relives-perfect-game/.

4. Cone's career record against Montreal—stemming mostly from his years with the Mets—was 10-8 with a 2.84 ERA.

5. The Expos had boarded the bus after a night game in Baltimore.

6. Serby. Cone's memory of the game in 2014 erroneously attributed the at-bat to Wilton Guerrero.

7. Fox network television broadcast of the David Cone's perfect game. See youtube.com/watch?v=wwod7qO4y40 (last visited March 16, 2017).

8. Tyler Kepner, "Cone's Magic Moment, 10 Years Later," *New York Times*, July 18, 2009. bats.blogs.nytimes.com/2009/07/18/cones-magic-moment-10-years-later/?_r=0.

9. Brosius won a Gold Glove in 1999.

10. Serby.

11. Murray Chass, "Baseball: On Day Made for Legends, Cone Pitches Perfect Game," *New York Times*, July 19, 1999. nytimes.com/1999/07/19/sports/baseball-on-day-made-for-legends-cone-pitches-perfect-game.html.

12. From the dugout, Yankees manager Joe Torre, celebrating his 59th birthday, was uncertain the ball was caught. Bench coach Don Zimmer assured him it was. "I'm glad he was right," Torre said after the game. Ralph Vacchiano, "David Cone Throws a Perfect Game for Yankees on Yogi Berra Day at the Stadium in 1999," *New York Daily News*, July 18, 2015. nydailynews.com/sports/baseball/yankees/yankees-david-cone-throws-perfect-game-yogi-day-1999-article-1.2294698 (reprint of original article from July 19, 1999).

13. Ibid.

14. "IT'S DEJA VU ALL OVER AGAIN..." flashed the Yankees jumbotron immediately after the game.

15. "I Was There When: David Cone's Perfect Game," December 23, 2013, m.mlb.com/nyy/video/topic/70621568/v31277587/i-was-there-when-david-cones-perfect-game.

16. Murray Chass, "BASEBALL; On Day Made for Legends, Cone Pitches Perfect Game," *New York Times*, July 19, 1999, nytimes.com/1999/07/19/sports/baseball-on-day-made-for-legends-cone-pitches-perfect-game.html.

17. Nick Diunte, "Yogi Berra Still Fresh on the Mind of David Cone at Cancer Fundraiser," *Examiner*, September 27, 2015, examiner.com/article/yogi-berra-still-fresh-on-the-mind-of-david-cone-at-cancer-fundraiser [broken link]; *see* web.archive.org/web/20160129113409/http://www.examiner.com/article/yogi-berra-still-fresh-on-the-mind-of-david-cone-at-cancer-fundraiser.

18. Murray Chass, "Sports of the Times; Cone Sold His Soul to the Devil," *New York Times*, July 25, 2000. nytimes.com/2000/07/25/

19 Cone remembered, "I kind of fell on my face in the year 2000."— Joe DiLessio, "David Cone on Advanced Stats, the End of His Playing Career, and Riding on David Wells's Motorcycle," *New York Magazine*, May 26, 2011. nymag.com/daily/sports/2011/05/david_cone_on_advanced_stats_t.html.

20 Four years later, he was traded to the Yankees, only to be sent to Arizona after one All-Star season in the infamous deal that put Randy Johnson in pinstripes. He returned to the Yankees in 2010, the year before he retired.

21 Mark Feinsand, "Vazquez 'thrilled' to be a Yankee," MLB.com, December 18, 2003, originally published at yankees.mlb.com/NASApp/mlb/nyy/news/nyy_news.jsp?ymd=20031218&content_id=620683&vkey=news_nyy&fext=.jsp&c_id=nya [broken link]; *for full text, see* forums.nyyfans.com/showthread.php/54600-mlb.com-Vazquez-thrilled-to-be-a-Yankee.

DEREK LOWE

By Bill Nowlin

IN 2004, AS THE BOSTON RED Sox won their first world championship in 86 years, right-handed sinkerball pitcher Derek Lowe earned the rare distinction of winning the clinching game in the Division Series, the League Championship Series, and the World Series itself.

He won 176 regular-season games pitching for seven different major-league teams, but his most notable tenure was with Boston, where he also threw a no-hitter in 2002, was a two-time All-Star, and was 70-55 with a 3.72 earned-run average.

He began his career with the Seattle Mariners, but came to Boston midway through his first season in one of the most lopsided trades in baseball history.

Lowe was born and raised in the Detroit suburb of Dearborn, Michigan, on June 1, 1973, the son of Don and Dianne Lowe. Dianne worked as a nurse and Don as a repairman. Derek grew up in an athletic family and told writer Herb Crehan, "Everyone in the family was involved in sports: uncles, aunts, cousins, everyone. I wouldn't change a thing about the way I grew up. I played whatever sport was in season: golf, soccer, basketball, and baseball. Playing and adapting to the different sports made me a better athlete."[1]

He graduated from Dearborn's Edsel Ford High School, where he lettered in four sports: basketball, golf, and soccer, as well as baseball. And he was an All-League honoree in four sports. He was expected to attend Eastern Michigan University on a basketball scholarship (Lowe was 6-feet-6 and is listed in baseball-reference at 230 pounds.) His all-league selection in baseball had been as a shortstop, though, not a pitcher, but he was drafted as a pitcher—despite winning only a pair of games in high school. "I was pitching my sophomore year against the number one team in the state in the playoffs, and the other team had kids that were getting looked at for the draft, so pro scouts were at the game. I lost the game but Seattle Mariners scout Ken Medeja noticed and started following my high school career. Seattle was drafting tall pitchers at that time hoping they would fill out in time and I fit that build. Long story short, I was drafted in the eighth round even though only winning two high school games."[2]

Unsurprisingly, Lowe was a Tigers fan growing up. "Chet Lemon. He was my man," he said in 2003. "But then I started playing shortstop, and I wanted to be Alan Trammell."[3]

"He was a typical high school kid," said Pat Wyka, athletic director at Edsel Ford for 25 years. "He wasn't 100 percent focused. ... He did not have a good senior pitching season." But he was good enough to catch the eye of the Mariners' scouts.[4]

In the June 1991 player draft, it was the Seattle Mariners who drafted Lowe, in the eighth round, the 214th pick overall. Starting out with 213 prospects having been rated higher in the draft, Lowe wasted no time in signing, on June 7. Medeja is credited with the signing. The 18-year-old Lowe was sent to rookie league in Arizona, started 12 games, and built a 5-3 record with a 2.41 ERA, striking out 60 and walking 21.

He was advanced slowly through the system, working for Bellingham, Washington, in 1992, where he was 7-3 with a 2.42 ERA, nearly identical to that from rookie league. Lowe struggled at higher levels of play and was 21-25 over the next three seasons while giving up more than five runs per nine innings. He split 1996 between the Port City Roosters in Double A (in North Carolina) and the Mariners' Triple-A Tacoma Rainiers of the Pacific Coast League.

Lowe began the 1997 season with Tacoma but a very early-season injury sent Seattle left-hander Tim Davis to the 15-day disabled list and resulted in Lowe's being called up to join the major-league Mariners on April 24. His debut came two days later in Toronto. The score was tied, 3-3, when he was brought on in relief to pitch the bottom of the sixth. He got through his first three innings and got the first out in the bottom of the ninth. Otis Nixon reached on a single to third base and then stole second. Another infield single, to shortstop, put two men on; Nixon had to hold at second base. Manager Lou Piniella called on Norm Charlton to relieve. Charlton got a fly out but then yielded a single, which resulted in the loss of the game being charged to Lowe.

After another relief stint, Lowe was optioned back to Tacoma, but then recalled again and got his first start on May 27 against the Twins. He worked five innings and gave up four runs, but had a no-decision. Lowe's first win came—in Detroit—on June 6, thanks to a pair of two-run homers by Jose Cruz Jr. Lowe appeared in six June games and three in July. He held a 2-4 record with a 6.96 ERA in 53 innings, when he was optioned back to Tacoma in July

That's when the Mariners dealt Lowe to Boston in a July 31 trading-deadline deal. The Mariners really need to bolster their bullpen and acquired Heathcliff Slocumb from the Red Sox for Lowe and minor-league catcher Jason Varitek. Years later, Varitek said that he and Lowe were pretty raw: "He was a one-pitch pitcher, and I couldn't catch, hit, or throw."[5]

With Boston's Triple-A Pawtucket Red Sox, Lowe was 4-0 in 1997 with a 2.37 ERA (the last time he worked in the minor leagues) and in September he was called up to the big-league club, where he was 0-2 in 16 innings but with a solid 3.38 ERA.

Lowe's first two games in 1998 were starts, and losses. He relieved in 13 games, then got a few starts again, losing all five decisions in his next eight starts. He was 0-7 by the end of June, with an ERA of 4.23. He finished the year 3-9, with the three wins all coming in relief. His 4.02 earned-run average was, however, slightly better than the team's 4.18. The Red Sox made it to the postseason, losing the Division Series to Cleveland, three games to one. Lowe worked 4⅓ innings in the ALDS, giving up one run on three hits, the eighth run of nine in a 9-5 Game Two loss.

The Red Sox noted that Lowe had pitched much better in relief than when starting, and in 1999 they had him work exclusively out of the bullpen, pitching in 74 games, closing 32 of them and earning 15 saves (he was 6-3). His ERA for the year was 2.63. Come the postseason, one earned run in four innings cost him a loss in Game One of the Division Series, again against the Indians. Lowe won Game Three thanks to a big six-run bottom of the seventh at Fenway Park. The Red Sox advanced to the ALCS, facing the Yankees.

Lowe had a superb 2000 season, closing 64 games (most in the league) and earning a league-leading 42 saves (tied with Todd Jones of the Tigers). His ERA was an enviable 2.56 and he was honored in midseason by being named to the American League All-Star team. Won-lost records tend not to mean much for relievers; he was 4-4.

One could see 2001 as a transition year. By July 29 Lowe was 4-8, with 21 saves and a 4.15 earned-run average. There was a mixed bag of closers—by year's end, Lowe had closed 50 games, but Rod Beck had closed 28, Ugueth Urbina (acquired from the Expos on July 31) had 13, and Rolando Arrojo 11. The team also changed managers in midseason, with pitching coach Joe Kerrigan replacing Jimy Williams as manager. Lowe finished 5-10 with a 3.53 ERA; the team's ERA was 4.15.

Grady Little became Red Sox skipper for 2002; the team itself was under new ownership. Tony Cloninger became the pitching coach. Lowe returned to starting games and in his fifth start (April 27) he threw a no-hitter against the Tampa Bay Devil Rays, with only one third-inning base on balls. Lowe had an interesting take on the battle of wits between batter and pitcher when it comes to a no-hitter: "You need some luck, or good fortune, and you need to remember the pressure is on the batter because you are pitching well and they aren't having any success."[6]

It was the first time a pitcher had both had a 40-save season and thrown a no-hitter. Lowe won a career-high 21 games in 2002, against only eight losses, with a season ERA of 2.58 and a WHIP of 0.974. He was again named to the All-Star team. After the season, Lowe placed third in the Cy Young Award voting.

In 2003, when the Red Sox came to within a few innings of making it to the World Series, Lowe worked to a 17-7 record, though with an ERA of almost two runs per game higher—4.47. The number of walks he'd allowed had jumped from 48 in 2002 to 72 in 2003. Walks haunted him in the 2003 postseason, too. In Game One of the ALDS, he came into a 4-4 tie game in Oakland to pitch the bottom of the 11th, and then again the 12th. In the bottom of the 12th, he walked two batters, sandwiched around a couple of groundouts, and then issued an intentional walk to load the bases—before giving up the one hit he'd allowed, an unexpected bunt single by catcher Ramon Hernandez.

In ALDS Game Three, Lowe started and gave the Red Sox seven innings of one-run ball. They won the game on Trot Nixon's two-run homer in the bottom of the 11th. In the deciding Game Five, back in Oakland, Boston was ahead 4-3 heading into the bottom of the ninth. Scott Williamson walked the first two batters he faced. Grady Little called on Lowe, who retired the side with two strikeouts after a sacrifice. In the ALCS, Lowe lost both Game Two (6-2) and Game Five (4-2), ending up with an 0-3 record for the 2003 postseason. After the Sox lost to the Yankees in extra innings in Game Seven, Lowe said, "That was the quietest clubhouse I have ever been in. Nobody said a word. Of course there wasn't anything to say."[7]

That was reversed in 2004, as noted above. Lowe had a mediocre regular season, again slipping a full run in ERA from 4.47 to 5.42. His record was 14-12. In the postseason, new manager Terry Francona, well aware of how Lowe had slipped, said he was asking him to work out of the bullpen. Lowe thought about going home, but Francona asked him to sleep on it. He accepted the assignment. And he won the clinching game in all three rounds of the postseason—getting the win in relief in the deciding Division Series game, winning Game Seven of the ALCS (allowing just one run in six innings) and winning Game Four of the World Series with seven shutout innings. He had also started Game Four of the ALCS, allowing three runs in 5⅓ innings. Afterward, he admitted Francona had been right: "I probably would have left me off the roster I had pitched so poorly. But it was tough to go back to the bullpen."[8] All's well that ends well; he had a world championship ring.

Lowe was a free agent and in January 2005 signed a four-year deal with the Los Angeles Dodgers. There were rumors that the Red Sox had concerns about his drinking, and did not put on a push to re-sign him. Lowe started 35 games for the Dodgers in 2005, tied for the lead in the National League. He cut down his walks, struck out more batters, and brought his ERA down nearly two runs (a one-hitter—a single by the first batter in the game—on August 31 helped) to 3.61, but his record was just 12-15 (the Dodgers were 71-91). He won 16 games in 2006, enough to tie for the league lead with five others. Lowe's four years with Los Angeles were remarkably consistent, year to year, and he never missed a turn in the rotation, leading the league once more in starts in 2008 (and once more tied with several others). In that year's postseason he won the first game of the Division Series, but lost the first game of the NLCS, 3-2.

And then it was on to Atlanta for three seasons, Lowe again cashing in as a free agent and again twice leading the league in games started (in 2009 and in 2011, tied with five others in 2009 and two others in 2011). But he also led the National League in losses in 2011 (9-17, after winning 31 games in the two prior years). His ERA had crept back up over 5 (to 5.05). He'd started 2009 well enough, but the second half of the season was subpar by his standards. And 2010 was, as well, even a little more so; but suddenly in September Lowe got a second wind and reeled off five consecutive wins, becoming Pitcher of the Month and helping the Braves secure the wild card as he himself finished with an even 4.00 ERA on the season. He pitched very well in the Division Series against the San Francisco Giants, but ended up with an 0-2 record, saddled with losses of 1-0 and 3-2.

Like most pitchers, Lowe didn't hit that well (.149, with a .201 on-base percentage, in 534 plate appearances). His one home run was one of the bright spots of his 2011 season. On August 31 he homered at Turner Field, leading off the third inning against Washington Nationals pitcher John Lannan. Lowe worked a 3-and-2 count, with a couple of fouls mixed in, homering to deep left field on the eighth pitch to give Atlanta a 2-0 lead in a game Lowe won, 3-1.

Lowe was pretty good fielding his position, with a career .975 percentage, five times tied for being best among pitchers.

After the 2011 season, the Braves didn't see enough of a future in Lowe, given those 17 losses and his declining effectiveness, so they settled for some degree of salary relief and swapped him on the last day of October to the Cleveland Indians for 23-year-old lefty minor leaguer Chris Jones, with the Braves paying a reported two-thirds of Lowe's hefty salary for the final year of their four-year deal.

The Indians saw him as a fourth or fifth starter, but as a veteran with experience who might provide some help. Indeed, hoping for a comeback season, Lowe got off to an excellent start with the 2012 Indians and was 6-1 by May 15, but seemed to run out of steam and was 2-7 over June and July, while watching his ERA climb from 2.15 on May 20 to 5.52. The team released him on August 10.

The Red Sox and Orioles both showed some interest, and Lowe himself said he just needed a "tune-up." But three days later the team he had caught on with was the New York Yankees. He was asked to work back in the bullpen. On the 13th, he had what was only his second relief appearance (excluding the postseason) since 2001. He threw four innings of two-hit scoreless relief in his first game and was credited with a save. Over the remainder of the season, Lowe won one and lost one, with a 3.04 earned-run average in 17 relief appearances, and pitched in the postseason for the last time, throwing two innings of relief in three games, giving up three runs in three Yankees losses though never involved in any of the decisions.

Lowe ended his career with a win. A free agent again, he wanted to continue as a starting pitcher but the versatility he offered had appeal and he signed a minor-league deal with the Texas Rangers in the spring of 2013. Expected to make the big-league team, he did just that. The Rangers used him in relief nine times. When starter Nick Tepesch was struck by a line drive in the top of the second inning of the April 20 home game against visiting Seattle, Lowe was brought in for long relief and worked four full innings of no-hit relief, credited in the ultimate 5-0 win. But after he was tagged for eight runs over his final three appearances, in 2⅓ innings, the Rangers designated him for assignment on May 20. There was no interest from other teams and in mid-July Lowe announced his retirement.

Lowe said he'd go back to rooting for the Tigers. "I'm not going to go to the Hall of Fame, so I don't feel like I need to have a retirement speech," he said. "But I was able to play 17 years on some pretty cool teams and win a World Series. So, everyone's got to stop playing at some point, and this is my time."[9]

Lowe has been married twice. He had two children with his first wife, Trinka, and adopted the son she had from a prior relationship. Lowe later became involved with Fox Sports Net broadcaster Carolyn Hughes during the first of his Dodgers years while she was covering the team. His first wife, Trinka, had apparently had an affair with married German soccer star Stefan Effenberg.[10] Following divorces from their respective spouses, Lowe and Hughes married in December 2008.

In his years since baseball, Derek Lowe has been able to enjoy being retired from the game. In June 2016 he said, "I am just splitting time between Florida and my home state of Michigan, spending a lot of time with family, and golfing quite a bit."[11]

Lowe is a survivor of squamous cell carcinoma and has donated time to a number of causes that fight cancer, including the Melanoma Foundation of New England and the National Council on Skin Cancer Prevention.

SOURCES

In addition to the sources noted in this biography, the author also accessed Lowe's player file from the National Baseball Hall of Fame, the *Encyclopedia of Minor League Baseball*, Retrosheet.org, Baseball-Reference.com, Rod Nelson of SABR's Scouts Committee, and the SABR Minor Leagues Database, accessed online at Baseball-Reference.com.

NOTES

1 Herb Crehan, "Derek Lowe Remembers the 2004 World Championship," BostonBaseballHistory.com, June 30, 2014.

2 Email to author, June 15, 2016.

3 Associated Press, "Baseball the Right Choice for Lowe," ESPN.go, March 11, 2003, at sports.espn.go.com/mlb/news/story?id=1392434.

4 Ibid.

5 Tony Massarotti, "'Tek Support," *Boston Herald*, April 28, 2002: B24.

6 Crehan.

7 Ibid.

8 Ibid.

9 Tom Pelissero, "Derek Lowe 'Officially' Threw His Last MLB Pitch," *USA Today*, July 17, 2013.

10 "Inside Track," *Boston Herald*, September 8, 2008.

11 Email to author, June 15, 2016.

APRIL 27, 2002: BOSTON RED SOX 10, TAMPA BAY DEVIL RAYS 0, AT FENWAY PARK

By Bill Nowlin

TO THROW A NO-HITTER typically takes a pitcher and catcher working in sync, among any number of other things going right. Red Sox right-hander Derek Lowe had Jason Varitek behind the plate; both pitcher and catcher had come to the Red Sox together in the same trade.

This was the second major-league no-hitter caught by Varitek; he had previously caught Hideo Nomo's on April 4, 2001. Tek later caught no-hitters by Clay Buchholz (September 1, 2007) and Jon Lester (May 19, 2008). No other catcher has caught four regular-season no-hitters, but if one includes the postseason (and why not?) Carlos Ruiz matched the accomplishment in 2015.[1]

After Jon Lester's 2008 no-hitter, Varitek said, "I'm very fortunate. It's so exciting to be part of one as a catcher. Each one's so different."[2]

Of course, it was Lowe who threw the no-hitter. He had worked primarily as a reliever through the 2001 season. In 2000, he'd led the American League in closes (64) and saves (42). He'd appeared in 67 games in 2001 but had a bit of an offyear. "I was booed off the field," he remembered.[3] In fact, he was so reviled, he said, that when he had to use the bathroom in the bullpen, "I kind of slithered along the wall so they wouldn't see me."[4] He added, "It's tough when you don't do well—especially in this town. When you don't win, you get it from everyone. It's not like in other cities, where you can just drift away."[5]

Lowe was given the opportunity to become a starter in 2002. It paid off; he had a 21-8 season with a 2.58 earned-run average.

In his first 2002 start, Lowe allowed the Orioles just one hit in seven innings of work, a base hit in the bottom of the eighth. On April 15 against the Yankees, he'd allowed just two hits, again in seven innings. He was 3-1 (2.73) when Tampa Bay came to Fenway on April 27. It was Kids' Opening Day.

Lowe was a sinkerball/groundball kind of pitcher, and he worked well with Varitek. He struck out six batters and got 13 groundball outs. Only five balls were hit out of the infield. But all it takes is one to drop in, or hit off the wall, and there's no no-hitter. He walked one batter in the third, and he faced only that one batter over the minimum. Even with all the scoring the Red Sox did, the game lasted only 2:28.

In the first inning Lowe struck out the first batter, then saw a flyball to deep center get reeled in by Rickey Henderson, then induced a grounder to short. Had the wind been blowing out, Randy Winn's deep fly to Henderson might have hit the wall or gone out. It was the closest thing to a hit the Rays rendered all Saturday afternoon. Boston took a 1-0 lead on a Henderson leadoff homer (the 80th leadoff shot of his long career).

There were three groundouts in the second. After a leadoff walk to Brent Abernathy in the third, there were three more groundouts. The Red Sox scored six more times in the bottom of the third, giving Lowe a comfortable cushion. While all that scoring was going on, Boston pitching coach Tony Cloninger said of Lowe, "He came up [to the clubhouse] and he was kind of dissatisfied with his mechanics. I just followed him up here and he was by the mirror working on mechanics a little bit. I said, 'Hey, don't worry about things. Just keep pitching the way you are. You're pitching a good game.'"[6]

In the fourth, there was a K, another fly ball (tracked down by Trot Nixon in right field, the only other ball struck that came close), and another groundout. In the fifth, it was two more groundouts bracketing a fly ball. And in the sixth inning, Lowe struck out the side. It's a safe bet that almost everyone in Fenway Park knew of the possibility at that point.

Nine pitches in the seventh inning set down three Rays in order—a strikeout, an unassisted groundout to first baseman Jose Offerman, and another fly ball to Nixon. The first and fourth innings had also been nine-pitch innings, as was the ninth.

The Red Sox added one more run in the fourth, and—after Lowe got the Rays on a fly ball to Manny Ramirez in left, a foul out to first base, and a 6-3 groundout, they added two more in the bottom of the eighth, the final run coming in when Shea Hillenbrand was hit by a pitch with the bases loaded.

There was a potential downside to adding on those couple of extra runs. Sitting on the bench was Lowe, waiting, well aware that he needed to get only three more outs before giving up a hit. "It was hard," he said. "Obviously, in a perfect world, you go 1-2-3 and run back out there. But the hitters don't care what's going on. They want to go out there and get RBIs, get hits."[7]

Varitek and Nixon both struck out and then it was time for Lowe to take the mound again and work the ninth. That's the time it can really get to you. "I saw Nomo do it. I thought, 'What would it be like to actually do it?' The second it comes into your mind, you've got to get back to the real world."[8]

"You've got a ground ball pitcher in Derek, so anytime a ball could just go right through the infield," said Varitek.[9] The Rays hitters were impatient; Lowe threw only 28 pitches over the final three innings.

In the ninth, nothing went through the infield. Russ Johnson popped to Rey Sanchez at second base. Felix Escalona flied out to Henderson in center field; Henderson got a very good jump on the ball and caught it without drama. "I just told it to stay in the glove," he said.[10] And the final batter, Jason Tyner, grounded out on a 2-and-2 pitch, Sanchez to Offerman at first base. Both fielded the ball cleanly. Lowe had his no-hitter. "I got him on a changeup with that last pitch," he said. "I didn't know how to react. I never stepped in this path before. …You know, it's funny, but it was after the game that I got nervous and jittery. I felt as though I still had to do something."[11] A day later, he said he'd been "overtaken by 'a weird feeling' that he was somehow out of place, apparently unaccustomed to glory after last year's trials. 'I just was embarrassed,' he said. 'I wanted to have everybody get off the field and get back to the clubhouse.'"[12]

It was the first no-hitter at Fenway Park since Dave Morehead's in 1965.[13] Because he'd saved so many games in 2000, he became the third pitcher (joining Dennis Eckersley and Dave Righetti) to have had both a 40-save season and a no-hitter.

"Jason called a great game," Lowe said, "I didn't shake him off once."[14] Tek said he had done so, once, in the sixth or seventh inning. It took all of 97 pitches. He threw first-pitch strikes to 20 of the 28 batters.

Varitek thought back to the years he'd spent as Lowe's teammate since coming to Boston in 1995: "I was pretty bad, and he was a one-pitch pitcher on one side of the plate. And that's where we've come from. I couldn't hit, catch, or throw, and he couldn't throw except for one pitch over one side of the plate, so we've come a long way. … I understand Derek, and that's half the battle—understanding your pitchers."[15] It's almost hard to believe," wrote Bob Hohler, that "Varitek once wanted almost nothing to do with Lowe because he had such a hard time catching his sinking fastball."[16]

Red Sox owner John Henry was seated next to the Red Sox dugout. "I think I was the only person in the ballpark not standing," he said. "I don't like to stand up with two strikes and two outs."[17]

Lowe had the last word: "It's almost surreal. You almost don't think it's you. I still don't feel I did what I did, as amazing as it sounds. You still think it's happened to somebody else."[18]

NOTES

1 The no-hitters caught by Ruiz are: a combined no-hitter with Cole Hamels, Jake Diekman, Ken Giles, and Jonathan Papelbon on September 1, 2014, against the Braves; two in 2010 by Roy Halladay (May 29 against the Marlins and October 6 in the NLDS against the Reds), and then a complete game by Cole Hamels (July 25, 2015, against the Cubs).

NO-HITTERS

2 Gordon Edes, "Varitek Gets His Mitts on History, Too," *Boston Globe*, May 20, 2008: D3. Edes also quoted pitching coach John Farrell: "That's a team effort, and Jason had a huge impact. Jon threw every pitch, but Jason's guidance got him to that point."

3 Ken McGuire, Associated Press, "Lowe Fires No-Hitter," April 28, 2002.

4 Bob Hohler, "High Time for Lowe; Fenway Sees First No-Hitter in 37 Years," *Boston Globe*, April 20, 2002: A1.

5 Jackie MacMullan, "Lowe's Theater Show-Stopper Status Was Tough to Picture," *Boston Globe*, April 28, 2002: D1.

6 David Heuschkel, "Hey, Lowe! Once Reviled Closer Nearly Perfect in First Fenway No-Hitter Since '65," *Hartford Courant*, April 28, 2002: E1.

7 Ibid.

8 Murray Chass, "Lowe No-Hits the Devil Rays, And Tames the Green Monster," *New York Times*, April 28, 2002: G1.

9 David Heuschkel.

10 Bob Hohler, "'Lucky Charm' Keyed the Sox' Hit Parade," *Boston Globe*, April 28, 2002: D13.

11 Jackie MacMullan.

12 Bob Hohler, "A Stunning Feat; No-No Afterglow Overwhelms Lowe," *Boston Globe*, April 29, 2002: D1.

13 The author of this game account was at the September 16, 1965 Morehead no-hitter, too.

14 Murray Chass, G5.

15 Michael Smith, "The Day Came To Stand Still; Wary Teammates Held Their Ground," *Boston Globe*, April 29, 2002: D12.

16 Hohler, "A Stunning Feat."

17 Mike Shalin, "Henry Seated as a Witness," *Boston Herald*, April 28, 2002: B23.

18 Tony Massarotti, "Lowe Soars to New High, No-Hits Rays," *Boston Herald*, April 28, 2002: B22. And David Heuschkel, *Hartford Courant*. After the game, first baseman Jose Offerman presented Lowe the game-winning ball on a platter, and the Hall of Fame asked him to donate something from the game. "Now you go there and see your hat and grubby old pair of shoes. And you can say, 'I've done something to be in here.'" Tony Massarotti, "'Tek Support," *Boston Herald*, April 28, 2002: B24.

RANDY JOHNSON

By Joseph Wancho

HEADING INTO THE 2004 season, it seemed as if he had accomplished all he could in his 16-year career. At 40 years old he showed no signs of letting up. He had won five Cy Young awards, and was one of only five pitchers to win the award in both the American and National Leagues. He was named World Series co-MVP in 2001, and was tabbed as the starting pitcher for four All-Star Games. He led both leagues in strikeouts and ERA in multiple seasons and led the National League in wins in 2002 with 24. He twirled the first no-hitter in Seattle Mariners history on June 2, 1990. His collection of hardware rivaled the tool department of the local Home Depot.

Yet Randy Johnson added one more feat to his baseball immortality. The Arizona left-hander was sporting a 3-4 record heading into a May 18 matchup with the Atlanta Braves at Turner Field. In three of his losses, the Diamondbacks offense had done its own version of molting. But instead of shedding skin, it was runs, as they pushed only three across the dish while Johnson was on the hill in those defeats. The latest was a 1-0 loss to the New York Mets on May 12.

But on this evening, Johnson carried the team on his back, striking out 13 Braves on the way to pitching a perfect game. The Diamondbacks' offense was by no means explosive, but its two runs proved to be more than enough. "It was like a surreal experience," said Atlanta's Chipper Jones. "When you wake up, you think, no, he couldn't have thrown a perfect game against us. You think it had to be a dream."[1]

"A game like this was pretty special," said Johnson, who reached a three-ball count on only one batter. "It doesn't come along very often. It didn't faze me. Everything was locked in. Winning the game was the biggest, most important thing."[2] In the bottom of the ninth inning, Arizona second baseman Matt Kata threw out the first batter. Johnson struck out the next two batters. At the end, pinch-hitter Eddie Perez was overmatched when the last of Johnson's 117 pitches was clocked at 98 MPH. "This is one of those nights where a superior athlete was on the top of his game," said Arizona manager Bob Brenly. "There was a tremendous rhythm out there. His focus, his concentration, his stuff, everything was as good as it possibly could be. Everything he's done to this point pales in comparison."[3]

Brenly knew what he was talking about. As of 2014, Johnson was the oldest pitcher by over three years to reach perfection. It was the 17th perfect game in major-league history, and the first since David Cone in 1999.

Randall David Johnson was born on September 10, 1963, in Walnut Creek, California. He was one of six children (three boys and three girls) born to Rollen and Karen Johnson. Rollen Johnson, commonly known as Bud, worked as a police officer and security guard. As a youngster, Randy honed his craft by pitching against the garage door. He tried to emulate another left-handed pitcher, Oakland's Vida Blue, one of Johnson's boyhood idols. Even as a youngster, Johnson threw hard, often loosening the nails in the wood siding with one of his pitches. His father would hand him a hammer, "Pound them back in, son," Bud would instruct him.[4]

Randy was a two-sport star at Livermore High School, excelling in basketball and baseball. He was drafted by the Atlanta Braves in the fourth round of the 1982 free-agent draft. However, Johnson put the major leagues on hold and accepted a scholarship to play basketball and baseball at the University of Southern California. After two years he left the hardwood behind to concentrate on baseball. Johnson was a teammate of Mark McGwire at USC, and learned under the tutelage of the legendary coach Rod Dedeaux. His first appearance in a PAC-10 game, when he was a freshman, came in relief against

Stanford, and resulted in an embarrassing moment. "A player on Stanford had just hit a grand slam when Coach Rod Dedeaux called me into the game. He said to me, 'Do you know what you're going to do?' I said 'Yeah, I'm pitching from the stretch.' He said to me, 'Why are you going to pitch from the stretch?' And I said 'Because there's a man over there at first.' I was looking at Stanford's first base coach. Dedeaux just looked at me and walked back to the dugout."[5]

After three seasons for the Trojans, Johnson was again selected in the 1985 amateur draft. Montreal picked the 6-foot-0 left-hander in the second round and Johnson signed with the Expos. He ascended through the minor-league chain, making various stops from Jamestown (Rookie League) in 1985 to Triple-A Indianapolis. He had tremendous upside, as he threw a blistering fastball to go with his intimidating stature on the pitcher's mound. However, he did have control issues (128 walks at Double-A Jacksonville in 1987) and was temperamental (he missed two months of the?? What season? season with a hairline fracture in his right hand after punching a concrete wall). Johnson credited coaches Joe Kerrigan and Rick Williams for his development. "Kerrigan was my pitching coach at the Double-A and Triple-A levels of the Montreal Expos' system and Williams was the roving pitching instructor in the minors. Both of these coaches helped me greatly because they made me grow up and become a better person. They helped me develop into a big-league pitcher. I owe a great deal to them."[6]

Johnson made his major-league debut on September 15, 1988, with a win in a start against the Pittsburgh Pirates at Stade Olympique in Montreal. But the Expos were expecting big things in 1989, and traded their prized hurler to the Seattle Mariners for a proven left-handed pitcher, Mark Langston, on July 31, 1989, in a five-player swap. Before leaving the Expos Johnson acquired his famous nickname. During batting practice in 1988, Johnson collided head-on with outfielder Tim Raines. The 5-foot-8 Raines looked up at Johnson and exclaimed, "You're a big unit." The nickname stuck.

Johnson made 22 starts for Seattle in 1989, posting a 7-9 record. The next season he served notice of his arrival, when on June 2, 1990, he tossed the Mariners' first no-hit game. Johnson blanked Detroit at the Kingdome, 2-0. He fanned eight Tigers, but also walked six batters. "I'll never forget this moment," said Johnson. "When I struck out Mike Heath for the last out, I didn't know how to react. I just stood there."[7] Johnson had the Tigers off balance for much of the game. "He was throwing completely backwards," said Detroit second baseman Tony Phillips. "He was throwing fastballs when he should have been throwing breaking balls."[8]

But Johnson's control was still an issue. He led the American League in walks for three straight years (1990-1992). He looked to a highly-placed source for some sound advice. Future Hall of Famer Nolan Ryan, then pitching for the Texas Rangers, told Johnson he needed to cut down on his walks as well as develop a secondary pitch to go with his blazing fastball. "I told Randy he could be the most dominating pitcher in baseball if he just worked on his game," recalled Ryan. "He was a lot like me when I was younger. He was just pitching and not doing a lot of thinking."[9]

Johnson also found resolve and courage from another source. Bud Johnson had been suffering with an ailing heart, and he died on Christmas Day of 1992. Randy, who was en route to see his father, missed the opportunity to say goodbye. "From that day on I got a lot more strength and determination to be the best player I could be," said Johnson, "and not to get sidetracked and not to look at things (in games) as pressure, but challenges. What my dad went through was pressure. That was life and death. This is a game."[10]

From 1992 through 1995 the switch was flipped and the Big Unit led the American League in strikeouts four straight years. He joined an elite club in accomplishing that feat during four (or more) consecutive seasons.[11] In 1993 he struck out 308 batters, and it was the first of five seasons in his career that he would top 300 strikeouts in a season. He won his first Cy Young Award in 1995 with a record of 18-2, a league-leading 2.48 ERA, and 294 strikeouts. "I got an individual award, but this is a team award," said Johnson. "Without the success of my teammates, this wouldn't have happened."[12]

The 1995 American League West Division ended in a tie between Seattle and the California Angels. A one-game playoff was played on October 2 at the Kingdome. With Johnson on the hill, the M's cruised to an easy 9-1 victory and faced the New York Yankees in the Divisional Series. After dropping the first two games in New York, the Mariners evened the series at two wins apiece. Johnson, who had won Game Three, came back to pitch three innings of relief as the Mariners won Game Five, 6-5 in 11 innings. Seattle's magical season ended in the American League Championship Series, as they lost to the Cleveland Indians in six games. In the clincher, Johnson lost to Dennis Martinez, 4-0.

Johnson had major back surgery in 1996 and started only eight games. He made a full comeback in 1997, posting a 20-4 record and a 2.28 ERA with 291 strikeouts. Twice he struck out 19 batters in a game, against the Oakland Athletics on June 24, a 4-1 defeat, against the Chicago White Sox on August 8, a 5-0 victory. In that game he struck out Frank Thomas and Albert Belle three times each. "Basically, with him I just look for one pitch—his fastball," said Chicago second baseman Ray Durham. "If he's getting his slider over, I'm out anyway."[13]

Johnson started the All-Star Game in Cleveland on July 8, 1997. In the second inning he uncorked a throw over the head of the Colorado Rockies' Larry Walker. Walker, a left-handed batter and a former teammate of Johnson's in Montreal, turned his batting helmet around and hit right-handed to the amusement of all. On the next pitch he returned to the left side of the plate. Walker's Colorado teammate Dante Bichette said of Johnson, "He's the most dominating pitcher right now. When he came up, he had that fastball and the strikeouts. But he didn't have that look in his eye. Now he's got that possessed look in his eye. If you just look at him you could get intimidated."[14] The Rockies faced Johnson on June 13, 1997, and could manage only two hits and one run against him in eight innings.

The Mariners won the American League West Division by six games over the Anaheim Angels in 1997. Their postseason was short-lived; they were eliminated in four games by Baltimore in the ALDS. Johnson lost both of his starts to Mike Mussina in the series.

Johnson entered the last year of his Mariners contract in 1998. Seattle had committed to long-term deals with Alex Rodriguez and Junior Griffey, so Johnson expected a big payday too. But Seattle management had its doubts about his durability. The 34-year-old ace was a power pitcher who had pitched more than 200 innings in six of the last eight season and had had back surgery. The Mariners looked to trade Johnson even though an estimated 9,000 more fans pushed their way through the turnstiles at the Kingdome every time Johnson toed the rubber.[15]

Johnson did not take to the constant trade talk well, and his record on the mound (9-10, 4.33 ERA) may have reflected his feelings. At the trading deadline on July 31, Johnson was dealt to Houston for pitchers Freddy Garcia and John Halama and infielder Carlos Guillen. The Astros were atop the National League Central Division by 3½ games over the Chicago Cubs at the time. Adding Johnson instantly made Houston the favorite to take the NL flag. Chipper Jones of Atlanta summed up the feeling of the senior circuit: "I think those were gulps you heard around midnight Friday from Atlanta, San Diego and Chicago. Picking up Johnson has to make Houston the favorite. In a (seven-game) series, you are going to have to face Randy at least twice, which means you may have to win four games against pitchers like (Mike) Hampton and (Shane) Reynolds. Those guys could be Number 1 starters on a lot of other teams."[16]

When the news hit of the trade broke, the Astros were in Pittsburgh. First baseman Jeff Bagwell was in a bar across from Three Rivers Stadium with some teammates and club officials. When the word came of the trade, Bagwell bought drinks for everyone in the house. In Johnson's first start, two days later, he struck out 12 Pirates to get the win. It was the most strikeouts by an Astros left-hander in 29 years. Johnson was as solid as advertised. He went 10-1 with a 1.28 ERA. The Astros won their division by a comfortable 12½ games.

But the euphoria was tempered quickly when San Diego toppled Houston in four games in the Division Series. Johnson lost Game One, a tight 2-1 contest in which Padres starter Kevin Brown rang up 16 strikeouts. Johnson also lost Game Four, surrendering just one earned run in six innings of a 6-1 loss.

The Arizona Diamondbacks, after their inaugural season, wanted to make a splash in the free-agent market. They signed Johnson to a four year, $52 million pact. The return on their investment was substantial. Johnson won the Cy Young Award each season from 1999 through 2002. He joined Pedro Martinez and Gaylord Perry as the only pitchers to win the award in both leagues (Roy Halladay and Roger Clemens followed), and he tied Greg Maddux for the most consecutive years winning the award. On September 10, 2000, Johnson struck out Mike Lowell of the Florida Marlins for his 3,000th strikeout. On May 8, 2001, he struck out 20 Cincinnati batters. In each of the four years Johnson won the Cy Young Award, he struck out more than 300, topping out at 372 in 2001. He won at least 20 games twice, and won the ERA crown three times. In 2002 Johnson won the "Triple Crown" for pitchers, leading the league in wins (24), ERA (2.32), and strikeouts (334). He was the second pitcher in National League history to do so (Dwight Gooden of the Mets was the first, in 1985).

But for all of his accomplishments, Johnson always maintained that individual awards meant nothing if the team didn't win. "The outcome of the game takes precedence over anyone's accomplishments," he said in commenting on a loss in 2000. "You can get all the strikeouts you want, but I made a mistake (on a throwing error in the game in which he notched his 3,000 strikeout, a 4-3 loss)."[17]

Johnson was joined in Arizona by veteran right-hander Curt Schilling via trade during the 2000 season. They were polar opposites: Johnson was a surly, introverted type, Schilling had an extroverted, funny personality. Where Johnson was all business on the mound, Schilling was a bit more relaxed, easygoing. Johnson was quiet, Schilling talked nonstop. They fed off each other to form a fearsome one-two punch in the Diamondbacks rotation. Randy welcomed Curt's arrival. "What helped most with Curt was that he's one of the few pitchers who knows the expectations put upon that ace in a rotation of five pitchers," said Johnson. "So I can share experiences and feelings with him that I couldn't share with anybody."[18] Said Arizona first baseman Mark Grace, "Randy is a pussycat, a very, very nice man. He just doesn't enjoy the spotlight as much as Schilling."[19]

Arizona catcher Damian Miller also shared a different viewpoint of Johnson. "Randy puts a lot of faith in me," said Miller. "He wants me to do whatever I can to get him through seven or eight innings. If I have to yell at him, I yell at him. One thing about Randy: He's got the three Cy Youngs, but if I've got something to say, he looks me right in the eye and listens to it. He doesn't feel like he's above his catcher. He wants his catcher to get in his face."²⁰

But the Big Unit saved his best for the baseball's biggest stage, the World Series, in 2001. The Diamondbacks rode Johnson and Schilling (both 20-game winners) to a division crown and a berth in the World Series against the New York Yankees. With the Diamondbacks trailing three games to two, Johnson won his second game, hurling seven strong innings during a 15-2 pasting of the Yankees. Game Seven was much closer, as the Yankees took a 2-1 lead in the eighth inning. Johnson, as he did in 1995, came on in relief and retired all four batters he faced. He was the pitcher of record when the Diamondbacks scored two runs off Mariano Rivera in the bottom of the ninth inning to capture their first world championship. Johnson and Schilling were named co-MVPs of the Series. When Arizona manager Bob Brenly asked Johnson how he felt after Game Six, and whether he would be able to come out of the bullpen for Game Seven, Johnson answered, "This is the World Series, I'll be ready."

Johnson signed a new two-year deal with Arizona in 2003, reported at $33 million. The deal made Johnson the highest-paid pitcher in major-league history. But arthroscopic surgery on his right knee curtailed his season (6-8, 4.26 ERA in 2003). He rebounded in 2004 to lead the league in starts (35) and strikeouts (290) while winning 16 games.

Johnson authored a book with Jim Rosenthal titled *Randy Johnson's Power Pitching: The Big Unit's Secret to Dominaton, Intimidation and Winning* (Three Rivers Press, 2003). The book was written to guide youngsters on how to be complete pitchers. Pitching coaches Tom House and Mark Connor contributed to the manuscript.

After the 2004 season the Diamondbacks sought to cut some salary and knew that it might be a problem keeping Johnson. Johnson was sold to the New York Yankees on January 11, 2005, for pitchers Javier Vazquez and Brad Halsey, catching prospect Dioner Navarro, and $9 million. Johnson won 17 games in 2005 and 2006 for the Yankees, although his ERA ballooned to 5.00 in 2006. Both years the Yankees won the American League East Division. However, they were bounced from the division playoff round both years, with Johnson failing to register a win. "When Randy came here, he didn't have the same stuff he used to have," said Yankee closer Mariano Rivera. "Randy only pitched here as a visitor and maybe he wasn't comfortable. He's the only one who really knows. But he worked, worked hard. We didn't win as much as we wanted to, but I know every time out there, he pitched as hard as he could."²¹

After the 2006 season, Johnson had lower-back surgery, and was sold back to the Diamondbacks for four players on January 9, 2007. But more back surgery limited Johnson to 10 starts in 2007.

After an 11-10 season in 2008, Johnson signed a one-year deal with the San Francisco Giants. He got his 300th win as a Giant, against the Washington Nationals on June 4, 2009. It was a game that was unlike others earlier in his career; he pitched six innings and struck out only two. His 13-year-old son,

Tanner, served as batboy. "I'm just happy that my family and friends were able to come," said Johnson. "My son being batboy—those are kind of moments that I relish the most. My family's been with me the whole time. They've seen what I've done."[22] Johnson, who was now 45 years old, quipped that all he needed was 211 more victories to catch Cy Young.

Johnson retired after the 2009 season. In 22 major-league seasons, his record was 303-166 with a 3.29 ERA. He struck out 4,875, second to Nolan Ryan (5,714). He threw 37 shutouts and pitched 100 complete games. He was nominated to the All-Star Game 10 times.

In retirement Johnson surrendered his time to his other two passions: his family, wife Lisa and their four children (Johnson also had a daughter from a previous relationship), and photojournalism. He enjoyed doing the things he missed while playing, and enjoyed seeing his children grow up from their teen years. It may seem odd to some that for someone who shunned the camera lens as a player, Johnson embraced it so much as a hobby. But he took classes at USC and applied his skills at various concerts and NASCAR events. He made numerous trips to visit the troops in Afghanistan. Johnson aided many charities, mostly cystic fibrosis where his fundraising efforts have raised more than a million dollars. Occasionally he scheduled appearances at sports memorabilia/card shows.

In 2006 Johnson perhaps took a departure from his rather withdrawn demeanor and appeared in an episode of *The Simpsons*. The cartoon show debuted on March 19, 2006, in the 17th season of the series. Johnson played himself in the role.

SOURCES

Ancestry.com

baseball-reference.com/

retrosheet.org/

Johnson's file at the Baseball Hall of Fame

NOTES

1. *Sports Illustrated*, May 31, 2004.
2. *USA Today*, May 19, 2004.
3. Ibid.
4. *Sports Illustrated*, December 17, 2001.
5. *Baseball Digest*, November 1996, 33.
6. Randy Johnson player file at the National Baseball Hall of Fame.
7. *USA Today*, June 4, 1990.
8. Ibid.
9. *New York Post*, June 21, 1997.
10. *USA Today Baseball Weekly*, July 2-9, 1997, 36.
11. The others are Rube Waddell, Dizzy Dean, Lefty Grove, Bob Feller, and Nolan Ryan in the American League, and Grover Cleveland Alexander, Dazzy Vance, and Dizzy Dean in the National League.
12. *USA Today*, November 11, 1995.
13. *USA Today*, August 11, 1997. Despite his professed inability to hit Johnson, Durham had a career .297 batting average (although 10 strikeouts in 37 at-bats) against Johnson.
14. *New York Post*, June 21, 1997.
15. *USA Today Baseball Weekly*, March 4-10 1998, 8.
16. *Sports Illustrated*, August 10, 1998, 34-38.
17. *Arizona Republic* (Phoenix), September 11, 2000.
18. *Sports Illustrated*, December 17, 2001.
19. *New York Times*, September 29, 2002.
20. *The Sporting News*, November 5, 2001.
21. *New York Post*, January 12, 2007.
22. Mlb.com, June 4, 2009.

RANDY JOHNSON'S PERFECT GAME
MAY 18, 2004: ARIZONA DIAMONDBACKS 2, ATLANTA BRAVES 0, AT TURNER FIELD, ATLANTA

By Joseph Wancho

IF THERE WAS A TEAM THAT needed the proverbial "shot in the arm," it was the Arizona Diamondbacks. They were in the midst of a five-game losing streak when they visited Turner Field to start a three-game series with Atlanta on May 18, 2004. The Diamondbacks were in last place in the National League's West Division, trailing the Los Angeles Dodgers by 8½ games. The offense was struggling, having scored just eight runs over the last five losses. Arizona had just been swept by its cellar-dweller brethren in the East Division, the Montreal Expos. The Diamondbacks managed to cross the plate four times in the three-game series.

But if you need a stopper, someone to stop the bleeding, who better than Randy Johnson? The five-time Cy Young Award winner may have been 40 years old, but he could still bring the heat. Unfortunately, the Big Unit was not immune to the putrid offensive support by his mates. In his last two outings, Johnson had hurled admirably but loss nonetheless. On May 7 he gave up two earned runs, struck out 10, and lost to the Phillies, 4-1. In his next start, against the Mets on May 12, he surrendered one earned run and whiffed seven batters, but took the loss, 1-0, dropping his record to 3-4.

The Atlanta Braves' fortunes in the early part of 2004 were a bit better than those of their guests. Although their record was 17-19, they were in a virtual tie for third place with New York in the NL East Division. They trailed the front-running Florida Marlins by only 3½ games.

Atlanta's starting pitcher was Mike Hampton, a left-handed pitcher who was having his own problems. He sported a 0-4 record and a 7.41 ERA thus far in the young season. Johnson and Hampton were not unfamiliar with each other, as they were teammates in 1993 with Seattle and in 1998 in Houston.

After a scoreless first inning, Arizona struck first. With two outs in the top of the second, Danny Bautista singled to right field. Alex Cintron followed with a double to center, Bautista scored, and the visitors led 1-0. In the Braves half of the second inning, Johnson struck out Johnny Estrada and J.D. Drew. Six up and six down for the Big Unit, and he also had four K's.

In an era where baseball games tended to approach or exceed three hours in length, this game was clipping right along. Hampton was giving a good account of himself, having given up only the single run. In the home half of the fifth inning, the Braves went down in order, all on balls hit to the outfield. Drew hit a liner to the corner in right field that was hauled in by Bautista with a basket catch. It was the only inning in which Johnson did not record at least one strikeout in the game. In the sixth inning, Hampton tapped a slow roller that shortstop Cintron scooped up and fired to first base, nipping the Braves pitcher by a half-step.

In the top of the seventh, Cintron was involved in the scoring again. After a one-out double down the left-field line, Cintron scored on a single by Chad Tracy. The Diamondbacks' lead was pushed out to 2-0. As for the Braves, their parade to the plate came in threes. Three batters came to bat, three batters sent back to the dugout.

In the eighth inning, Andruw Jones flied out, but not before losing his bat trying to catch up to a Johnson fastball. And that was the diet Randy fed the Braves, a fastball that was moving and a superb slider. As Johnson came up to bat in the ninth inning, a good portion of the 23,381 fans at the Braves ballpark cheered him. He grounded out, short to first.

As Johnson trudged out to the mound for the bottom of the ninth inning, the cheers increased. The first batter, Mark DeRosa, grounded out to second baseman Matt Kata. Johnson struck out Nick Green and then pinch-hitter Eddie Perez. His last pitch to Perez was a 98-mph fastball. The Big Unit could still hum it in there, as he recorded his 13th strikeout. His teammates mobbed him; Johnson had thrown the first no-hitter in Diamondbacks history.

"He could smell it at the end," said the Braves' catcher, Johnny Estrada. "This was a legitimate perfect game any way you slice it."[1] Added Chipper Jones, who struck out all three times he came to bat, "It was a situation where a dominant pitcher caught a struggling team."[2]

Although Johnson did not seem to be affected by the pressure of the situation, his manager, Bob Brenly, started fidgeting around the sixth inning. Johnson at times looked bored sitting in the dugout. "It didn't faze me," he said."Winning the game was the biggest, most important thing."[3] But he also acknowledged that the feat was a big deal. He became only the fifth pitcher in major-league history to hurl a no-hitter in each league. (Cy Young, Jim Bunning, Nolan Ryan, and Hideo Nomo preceded him.) Johnson threw his first on June 2, 1990, against the Detroit Tigers while a member of the Seattle Mariners. "A game like this was pretty special. It doesn't come along very often. Not bad for being 40 years old. Everything was locked in."[4]

"This is one of those nights where a superior athlete was on top of his game," said Brenly. "There was a tremendous rhythm out there. His focus, his concentration, his stuff, everything was as good as it could be. Everything he's done up to this point pales in comparison."[5]

Although the perfect game was obviously the highlight of Arizona's season, the Diamondbacks could not overcome a disappointing season. They completed the year with a 51-111 record, 42 games out of first place. Johnson posted a 16-14 record and led the league with 290 strikeouts. No other pitcher on the Diamondbacks staff had more than seven wins.

The Braves wound up in their customary position atop the NL East Division. It was their 10th consecutive division title. They lost in the NLDS to Houston in five games. Mike Hampton, who went the distance against Johnson on May 18 and pitched his best game of the season, used the game as a catapult to a strong season. He went 13-4 the rest of the season, with a 4.28 ERA.

NOTES

1 "Johnson K's 13 in perfect effort," ESPN.com, May 19, 2004.
2 Ibid.
3 "Johnson Simply Perfect at 40," *USA Today*, May 19, 2004.
4 Ibid.
5 Ibid.

DALLAS BRADEN

By Dirk Lammers

FANS MIGHT THINK IT'S A no-brainer to pick Dallas Braden's most cherished moment of his injury-shortened pro career, but the southpaw actually ranks his May 9, 2010, perfect game for the Oakland A's "a distant second."[1]

The memory that truly brings out the goose bumps is Braden's May 11, 2005, start for his hometown Stockton Ports, the Athletics' California-based A-ball affiliate. Braden had struck out 10 by the ninth inning, and only the "beer batter" (a cherished minor-league tradition) stood in the way of a five-hit, complete-game victory. Banner Island Ballpark maintained beer sales up through the ninth inning, and Braden rewarded the 1,800 or so fans who endured with an 11th and final strikeout that cut the price of their final pours.[2]

"To do that in my hometown wearing the name of my hometown across my chest, with friends and family in the stands, and waiting for that last strike hearing them chant, 'Let's go Dallas, clap, clap, clap-clap-clap,' I'm getting goose bumps right now thinking about it," he said.

Braden was promoted to Double-A three days later, but he never lost his appreciation for his gritty hometown and blue-collar upbringing.

Dallas Lee Braden was born on August 13, 1983, in Phoenix, Arizona. His mother, Jodie Atwood, wondered why her son wasn't eating for the first two days of his life when doctors discovered he was born without a uvula, a small piece of tissue in the back of the throat. Atwood took her infant son west to Stockton, her mother's city of residence, so the boy could undergo emergency mouth surgery.

Atwood put down roots in Stockton, and the single mother and son sometimes resided with Braden's grandmother, Peggy Lindsey, who managed a motel, and sometimes lived in their own apartments.

"It's been us three, my entire life," Braden said. "It had to be us three, because we didn't have the money."

Baseball hooked Braden by age 4 when he first slipped on a glove given to him by a neighbor. As Braden's arm showed promise and velocity beyond his years, Atwood moved to a different Stockton neighborhood so her son could join the Hoover Tyler Little League. "And sacrifices like that began very early on," he said.

Atwood by this time had started her own home-cleaning business, and she'd often hold her son out of school so he could help her clean an extra house or two. She'd always explain her reasoning for such decisions.

"Every step of the way, it was with my future in mind," Braden said. "And being able to look back and reflect on that, it honestly feels like she didn't take a breath without thinking that I might be able to catch some of the air that she let out."

As Braden reached working age, his mother agreed that he could forgo taking on a job if he continued working hard on the diamond.

Braden excelled as a baseball player at Stockton's Amos Alonzo Stagg High School, although his poor grades and truancy twice got him booted off the team.[3] He was a senior en route to a 9-1 record when his mother awoke one morning complaining of a headache. He attended class and baseball practice that day, but she wasn't there to pick him up. A friend's mother took him to the hospital, where devastating news awaited.

"They must have missed something in the blood work and the cancer has gone to her brain and this is now terminal, inoperable tumors," he learned. "Like, 'We didn't see this. We're sorry.'"

Atwood underwent chemotherapy treatments, but they did little good. She died on May 20, 2001, just a few months after her diagnosis, with peace that her son was about to fulfill her dream by completing high school. The loss of the woman Braden called his best friend was devastating.

"You talk about the rock or a guiding light in every sense of the word, in every possible embodiment, that was her," Braden said.

Two weeks after his mother's death, the Atlanta Braves selected Braden in the 46th round of the 2001 amateur draft. But at 5-feet-9 and 140 pounds "soaking wet in a cotton uniform," he didn't think he was ready for the pros.

"I needed to grow up physically," he said. "I needed to grow up mentally."

Braden turned to Grandma Peggy, who was always there to provide support and guidance. The pair drove north to American River College in Sacramento to ask if the school was holding tryouts. When head coach Kevin Higgins told them the roster was pretty much set, Lindsey piped in that her grandson had been drafted by the Atlanta Braves *and* was a left-handed pitcher. "That's when he perks up," Braden recalled.

Braden spent two seasons with the Beavers, winning 12 games and earning an honorable mention for all-conference pitcher in 2003.[4] He transferred to Texas Tech, where he grew as a ballplayer and a man under head coach Larry Hays, a "tremendous leader, tremendous father figure."

Moving from the streets of Stockton to the Bible Belt was quite a culture shock for Braden, who had always played with a "me against the world" chip on his shoulder. He said that in Stockton he learned to avoid looking at others, and he now had to find a way to accept people for who they were.

"I learned to be able to sort of turn that into a character if I had to or out of necessity," he said. "Meaning, I can tap into this, but I don't have to live this rigid anymore."

The Oakland Athletics selected Braden—now 6-foot-1, 185 pounds—in the 24th round of the 2004 amateur draft. He signed and reported to Vancouver, posting a 2-0 record in a relief role for the Canadians before heading east to start for the Kane County Cougars. The lefty was throwing an

88-92 mph fastball at the time with a straight change and a screwball.

"The screwball was the moneymaker for me," he said. "I was able to get some swings and misses on that pitch."

Braden began the 2005 season in Stockton, compiling a 6-0 record for his hometown Ports and occasionally fanning the "beer batter" before his promotion to Double-A Midland. He posted a 9-5 record for the RockHounds, but lingering arm troubles forced him to undergo shoulder surgery during the 2005-2006 offseason. Braden began the 2006 season on a rehab assignment before returning to Stockton for three starts (2-0) and Midland for one. The 2007 season was poised to be Braden's breakout season after he posted a sub-1.00 ERA during winter ball.

"I go through spring training, and they're telling me, 'You're going to be our guy in Triple-A and when the phone rings you're the first one on the plane,'" Braden said.

But the plan went awry just days before the Athletics broke camp. The Washington Nationals released Braden's friend Colby Lewis, and the A's signed the right-hander and gave him Braden's promised spot in Triple A. A dejected Braden headed back to Midland, but two starts later he got the bump to Sacramento. When Oakland's Rich Harden landed on the 15-day disabled list with a strained left hamstring, the A's called up Braden to start an April 24, 2007, road game at Camden Yards in Baltimore.

The 23-year-old rookie "couldn't feel anything" but tossed six innings of three-hit ball to lead the A's to a 4-2 win over the Baltimore Orioles. It was Braden's only win of the season, as he finished with a 1-8 record and a 6.72 ERA.

Braden spent the first half of the 2008 season bouncing between Oakland and Sacramento, serving in a relief role while with the parent club. He worked his way into the rotation for the second half of the 2008 season and pitched well enough to keep the job into 2009. By this time he was strictly fastball-straight change, although he occasionally mixed in a modified screwball that found its movement through finger pressure rather than arm stress.

"At no point was I going to overpower you with anything, but I will stare you down with the meanest 85 you ever felt," Braden said. "And I had to pitch that way."

Braden was throwing some of his best stuff at the start of the 2010 season when a walk-by incident landed him in the New York tabloids.

The A's were hosting the Yankees on April 22, 2010, when Robinson Cano popped a flare up the third-base line that was ruled foul. Baserunner Alex Rodriguez, who had rounded second and was nearing third, strolled across the pitcher's mound as he headed back to first. The unprecedented trespass prompted Braden to howl, "Get off my $@*&#% mound!" and A-Rod's shrug like it was no big deal further infuriated Braden.

"Right over the rubber," Braden said. "That is like me coming to get a ball from the umpire after a foul ball and then digging in to your batter's box."

Braden continued jawing at Rodriguez after squeezing his glove to complete Cano's 3-6-1 inning-ending double play. The fired-up pitcher chucked the ball into the dugout, kicked a stack of Gatorade cups, and slammed down his glove.

Seventeen days later, Braden landed on front pages for a more admirable accomplishment—he threw the 19th perfect game in major-league history. It was Mother's Day, a somber yet significant holiday for a man who lost his mom to melanoma when he was 17. Grandma Peggy was in the crowd at Oakland that afternoon, and after she and Braden shared a touching on-field moment celebrating the perfecto, she quipped, "Stick it, A-Rod," in earshot of reporters.[5]

The quote landed on the cover of the *New York Daily News*, and Braden was invited to deliver David Letterman's Top 10 list of "thoughts that went through Dallas Braden's mind while he threw his perfect game."

"No. 3: Even *I've* never heard of me," the pitcher deadpanned.[6]

Braden was warming up in the bullpen for his final start of the 2010 season when he felt his shoulder pop. He made it into the fifth frame before catcher Kurt Suzuki walked to the mound and asked, "What the hell is wrong with you? What do you got?"

"And I said, 'Nothing, that's the problem,'" Braden said. "And he goes, 'Well, let's throw the changeup.'"

Braden spotted enough well-placed changeups to finish out the inning and secure a win, but the shoulder problems persisted into the spring of 2011. Neither stretching nor anti-inflammatories provided much relief, and Braden made just three starts that season. When he walked off the Oakland mound in the fifth inning of his start on April 16, 2011, against Detroit, he knew he had thrown his last career pitch.

It was hard for Braden to sit in the training room and "look these guys in the eye, cash a paycheck and actually put this uniform like I deserve to," he said. "I didn't know how to fake it."

Braden endured two additional surgeries before declaring his arm "a shredded mess" and retiring in January 2014.[7] He joined ESPN as a *Baseball Tonight* studio analyst for the 2014 season and married actress

Megan Barrick that November. They took up residence in the Los Angeles area.

In 2015 Braden added in-game analyst to his ESPN résumé as the network signed him to a multiyear extension.

Phil Orlins, ESPN's MLB senior coordinating producer, said Braden "oozes passion and enthusiasm," bringing "energy, knowledge, and a blue-collar personality that connects with our viewers."[8]

That authenticity continued to endear him to the community of Stockton, where the Ports retired his number 50 jersey in 2015. Braden said he was ecstatic that his short career continued to let him make a living hanging around ballparks.

"I'm still afforded an opportunity to be around some of the best athletes in the world, to be around some of the most beautiful cathedrals man will ever make, to see the big green fields that are baseball diamonds," Braden said. "I'm so thankful the game has given me the opportunity to still be around it."

NOTES

1. Author interview with Dallas Braden, January 5, 2016. All quotations in this biography are taken from this interview unless otherwise noted.
2. Jagdip Dhillon, "Braden enthralls hometown crowd with shutout," Recordnet.com, recordnet.com/article/20050512/A_SPORTS/305129920, accessed January 26, 2016.
3. Susan Slusser, "Braden throws 19th perfect game," SF Gate, sfgate.com/sports/article/Braden-throws-19th-perfect-game-3264978.php, accessed January 26, 2016.
4. Thanks to Doug Jumelet, Head Baseball Coach at American River College.
5. Carl Steward, "Steward: 'Grandma Peggy' gets the final word on A's pitcher Dallas Braden, and on A-Rod," Inside Bay Area, insidebayarea.com/ci_15052220, accessed January 25, 2016.
6. CBS, "Dallas Braden's Top 10 on Letterman," Youtube.com, youtu.be/Hx1sxa2dwws, accessed January 26, 2016.
7. Susan Slusser, "Ex-A's pitcher Dallas Braden says he is hanging it up," SF Gate, blog.sfgate.com/athletics/2014/01/14/ex-as-pitcher-dallas-braden-says-he-is-hanging-it-up/.
8. Ben Cafardo, "ESPN reaches multi-year extension with MLB analyst Dallas Braden," ESPN Front Row, espnfrontrow.com/2015/03/espn-reaches-multi-year-extension-mlb-analyst-dallas-braden/, accessed January 26, 2016.

MAY 9, 2010: ATHLETICS 4, RAYS 0, AT OAKLAND–ALAMEDA COUNTY COLISEUM

By Dirk Lammers

BALLPLAYERS ARE TRAINED to always know the count, but perhaps it was Dallas Braden's blissful ignorance of the balls and strikes on May 9, 2010, that helped him finalize a coveted spot on the perfect-game list alongside Hall of Famers Cy Young, Sandy Koufax, and Randy Johnson.

The Oakland Athletics southpaw retired the first 26 Tampa Bay Rays he faced at Oakland-Alameda County Coliseum that Sunday afternoon, and only the pesky veteran Gabe Kapler stood between Braden and baseball's 19th perfect game.

With a 2-and-1 count, Braden threw a down-and-away fastball he described as "painted," but umpire Jim Wolf disagreed. The count was 3-and-1, but in Braden's head it was 2-and-2. Catcher Landon Powell, knowing the correct count, called for a changeup. Braden, stubbornly thinking 2-and-2, shook off Powell.

Kapler was likely looking changeup, and Braden's fastball jammed him into grounding to shortstop Cliff Pennington, who threw over to first baseman Daric Barton to complete the perfecto.

Powell often ribs Braden for sharing his Larsen-Berraesque moment with the wrong ballplayer.

"Barty was right there so I just jumped into his arms," Braden said. "Landon came up and he's yelling at me, 'You're supposed to come to me! You're supposed to come to me!'"[1]

Braden's perfect afternoon began with a less-than-perfect morning.

It was Mother's Day, a holiday Braden despises because of the pain it carries. His mother, Jodie Atwood, was his rock and guiding light, but melanoma took her from him during his senior year in high school. Atwood was Braden's best friend, and she repeatedly made sacrifices so he could play the sport he loved.

Braden had stayed out late with friends the night before his Mother's Day start, and he was a little slow getting up for a game that carried an earlier-than-usual start time. Peggy Lindsey, Braden's beloved grandmother, who raised him after his mother's death, dropped by the house to feed the pond fish and greet the dog, but Braden slept right through it. Lindsey called him on her way to the stadium to make sure he would be on the mound.

Braden's pregame routine at the ballpark typically took three hours. But on this day he arrived an hour before game time, which means he didn't get his pregame massage or stretch time, didn't drink his Red Bull, and didn't get to go over the hitters, watch video, or look over the pregame scouting report. His spikes were dirty, his glove was unoiled, and his hat was unstarched.

"Everything about the day was about as backward and as wrong as it's ever been for me making a start," he said.

But Braden buttoned up his white "Athletics" jersey, which on this day featured a small pink ribbon stitched over the script's "c," and stepped onto the hill.

Rays leadoff hitter Jason Bartlett quickly woke the fielders by lining an 0-and-1 fastball down the third-base line, but Kevin Kouzmanoff leaped over the bag to glove the game's first out. Five more Rays outs followed before the Athletics got on the board.

Kouzmanoff and Eric Chavez led off the bottom of the second inning with singles, and Kouzmanoff scored on Powell's single to left. The A's added another run in the third inning by stringing together consecutive singles by Barton, Ryan Sweeney, and Kouzmanoff.

Meanwhile, Kouzmanoff continued aiding Braden in the field. In the third inning, he snagged a slow dribbler off the bat of Bartlett and fired to first to steal what looked like a sure infield hit. He also chased down three foul popups — one near the steps of the Oakland dugout — to keep the perfecto intact.

"He was literally everywhere that day," Braden said.

As the game reached the midway point, Braden sat alone in the dugout and looked up at the scoreboard during a Rays mound visit. There was a zero in the "R" column, a zero in the "H" column, and he couldn't recall issuing a single walk.

"Oh my God, really?" he thought. "I just said to myself, 'Don't baby it. Don't baby it.'"

Braden thought he hadn't been afraid up until this point, so why start now?

"Hell, you haven't even been conscious," Braden told himself. "Don't screw this up by trying to be a part of it now. Just do what you've been doing."

Braden's fastball hovered just above the mid-80s, but he used 68-mph changeups — often on two-strike counts — to induce six Rays strikeouts. And the few hard-hit balls always found teammates' gloves.

"The guy had the pitches when he needed them," Rays third baseman Evan Longoria told the *San Francisco Chronicle*. "I didn't see two pitches in the same spot the whole game."[2]

With one out in the ninth, Dioner Navarro drove a sharp liner right at left fielder Eric Patterson, who took a step in before backtracking a stride and wrapping his mitt around out number 26. Kapler's groundout followed, sending the A's and their 12,000 or so fans into pandemonium.

After celebrating with teammates and coaches, Braden looked to the crowd for Lindsey, a regular at A's home games that featured Braden on the mound.

"Where's Gram?" Braden yelled. "Where's Gram?"

Braden looked toward Grandma Peggy's seat, but moments earlier she had climbed up onto the top of the dugout — much to the chagrin of the security guards — to watch the 27th out. Lindsey made her way down to the field, and the two locked in an emotion-filled embrace, remembering the mother/daughter they'd lost to cancer.

Braden pulled out the Celtic cross he wears around his neck to honor his mother and grandfather.

"I kissed it, and she kissed it, and that was all we needed," he said.

Powell, Braden's batterymate, teared up while witnessing the poignant scene.

"It was hard to fight 'em back," Powell told the *Oakland Tribune*. "He's had a lot of things happen to him in his life, and even the last few years has had some unlucky things happen to him in the game of baseball. So that was special to see."[3]

Braden's victory gave him a 4-2 record in the young season. But whatever was to come in his career, the Stockton native would forever occupy a spot on a list that numerous Hall of Fame pitchers couldn't reach. Will that feeling ever sink in?

"It doesn't," he said. "It shouldn't."

NOTES

1 Author interview with Dallas Braden, January 5, 2016. All quotations are from this interview unless otherwise indicated.

2 Susan Slusser, "Braden throws 19th perfect game," SF Gate, sfgate.com/sports/article/Braden-throws-19th-perfect-game-3264978.php, accessed January 26, 2016.

3 Carl Steward, "Steward: 'Grandma Peggy' gets the final word on A's pitcher Dallas Braden, and on A-Rod," Inside Bay Area, insidebayarea.com/ci_15052220, accessed January 25, 2016.

ROY HALLADAY

By Alan Cohen

"Toronto will forever hold a special place in my heart. The memories will last a lifetime and so will my gratitude."

– Roy Halladay's closing statement in his farewell letter to the Toronto fans in December 2009

"My father took me to meet him and we set up lessons. He never took any money. It used to frustrate us. When newspapermen used to phone him and ask about kids he'd say, 'I'll answer any questions as long as you don't put my name in the story.' He said he received enough watching the kids pitch. He didn't need anything else."

– Roy Halladay talking about his mentor, Bus Campbell, in 1997[1]

"Load your gun (put your hands up over your head). Show your billfold to the catcher (pivot). Pick up a piece of dirt (with your leg)."

—Bus Campbell's mantra

To most baseball fans, Bus Campbell's name is unknown. Born in 1921, he was a baseball lifer, starting by helping little leaguers in 1947 on the playgrounds near Denver. After working in construction, he went back to college, got his degree in physical education, and became a high school teacher and pitching coach in 1959. He spent most of his career in Littleton, Colorado, except for a short stint as a pitching coach at the University of Iowa. From Iowa he returned to the Denver area, where he remained a fixture on the playgrounds for decades, offering his wisdom to anyone who would listen.

Although he never played professionally, Campbell guided more than 100 pitchers to the major leagues, never seeking the spotlight for himself. He also worked as a regional scout for several major-league teams. In 1990 Robert Bruce "Bus" Campbell, three years after being inducted into the Colorado Sports Hall of Fame, entered the life of 13-year-old Roy Halladay. The youngster's father asked for help in guiding Roy, who was showing promise as a pitcher. Campbell, then 69 and scouting for the Toronto Blue Jays, helped mold the youngster into an accomplished pitcher. Halladay's appreciation for Campbell was such that he set aside a portion of his signing bonus and awarded his mentor, who was like a grandfather to him, with a grandfather clock as a Christmas present in 1995.[2]

And Bus Campbell would not be the last great influence on Halladay.

One of three children, and the only boy, Harry LeRoy Halladay III was born on May 14, 1977, in Denver. His parents, Roy and Linda, raised their family, which included Roy and his sisters Heather and Miranda, in Arvada, Colorado. The move to Arvada was predicated on finding a basement big enough to accommodate the 60 foot 6 inch distance from home plate to the mound, allowing young Roy, during the winter months, to throw balls against mattresses hung from the walls.[3] Roy II was a commercial pilot and flying became a passion for the younger Halladay as well. Older sister Miranda blazed a sports path of her own, earning a basketball scholarship to Idaho State University.

As a child, when not showing his passion for building and operating model airplanes, Roy played Little League, Babe Ruth, and American Legion baseball. He was initially mentored by his father before receiving guidance from Bus Campbell. In high school, Halladay played for coach Jim Capra and pitched a no-hitter against Pomona in his first start. As his senior year dawned in 1994, the big leaguers were on strike, but young Roy was not fazed. He had been 7-1 as a sophomore. As a junior, he was 9-0 with two saves and 68 strikeouts in 53⅔ innings. In the playoffs he won two games. In the semifinals, he pitched a seven-inning complete-game win and in the finals he pitched 4⅔ innings in relief. He viewed his success philosophically. "It's a little fun and kind of scary at the same time. But I think (senior year) will be more fun than anything. When you get a (pitching) gun back there, it's, I don't know if it is natural or what, but you always try to get the best reading you can. It's something I'm going to work on this year and just go out there and stay in control."[4] On the eve of his best season yet, Roy added, "(The opportunity to excel at the next level is) something that I'm striving for. I've been getting ready since last summer and this winter. It's crucial that I have a good year. I'm always looking to get to the next level. The higher I get, the better. I think it depends on what's available."[5]

Halladay graduated from Arvada West High School in 1995. He played baseball and basketball and ran cross-country in the fall (a Bus Campbell suggestion). He was a first team All-Conference and All-State selection for three years and named League and State MVP twice. In basketball, he was also a member of the second All-State team. He was named the top player in Colorado by *USA Today*, and was selected first team All-America by the National High School Baseball Coaches Association. After his junior year, he participated in the Junior Olympics, leading his West squad to the Bronze Medal with a 12-3 win. The Toronto Blue Jays selected Halladay in the first round of the 1995 amateur draft, with the 17th overall pick. Over the course of his three-year high-school career, he was 26-2 with two no-hitters. In his senior year, the 6-foot-6 Halladay was 10-1 with a 0.55 ERA and 105 strikeouts in 63 innings.[6] In the state tournament, he showed off his bat, going 2-for-3 in a semifinal win. He was the inaugural winner of Colorado's Bauldie Moschetti Trophy, named in honor of the legendary Colorado high-school baseball coach and mentor.[7]

On the day he was drafted by the Blue Jays (the phone call came from his old mentor Campbell), Halladay said, "I'm just kind of speechless. They've been talking to me more than anybody else lately, and they said they would pick me if they got the chance. They've been calling all morning, getting Social Security number and things, so it sounded pretty positive."[8] With his father acting as his agent, Roy anticipated signing with the Blue Jays quickly. "I'd be very, very surprised—completely shocked—if I didn't sign. Right now, my thinking is it would be awfully hard to pass up the Blue Jays. They've been a great organization, and they figure to be successful for a long time to come."[9] The Blue Jays had won back-to-back World Series in 1992 and 1993, but then hit a postseason dry spell that would extend until 2015.

Halladay passed up a scholarship to the University of Arizona and signed with Toronto on June 30, 1995, for a bonus estimated at a club-record $895,000.

Before signing, he hired an agent, Greg Landry, who would remain with him through his entire career. He made his professional debut in October with Toronto's team in the Rookie Gulf Coast League, where he struck out 48 batters in 50⅓ innings. Though his won-lost record was only 3-5, he showed enough to be selected the fifth-best prospect in the league.[10] In 1996 with Dunedin in the Class-A Florida State League, Halladay went 15-7, well above the norm on a team that went 67-70. It was a season when the 19-year-old Halladay, who had the most wins that season of any pitcher in the Toronto minor-league organization, matured into a team leader. In his first start, he opened eyes with a three-hit, eight-strikeout performance, but was not involved in the decision. "When I first came here, I didn't know what to expect," he said. "But I kept throwing a lot (in spring training) and doing well. The first time I started (in the team's second game of the season), I think I was able to prove I belong here. That game was a big confidence-builder to me."[11] He also mastered the changeup in 1996. He was named his team's most valuable player, and was chosen for the league all-star team.

In 1997 Halladay spent time in training with the Blue Jays and made his first spring appearance in a Toronto uniform on March 3, pitching two shutout innings, striking out four, against the Chicago White Sox. A week later, he was assigned to Knoxville of the Double-A Southern League, but before he departed for the minor-league camp, Blue Jays manager Cito Gaston gave his assessment of the 19-year-old: "He's a kid who won't be in the minors long. Whether it's confidence or believing in himself, he has it all. He's calm and cool out there." In his final spring performance with Toronto, Halladay retired the last eight batters he faced.[12] Halladay split 1997 between Knoxville and Triple-A Syracuse. In seven games in Knoxville he was 2-3 with a 5.40 ERA and 30 strikeouts in 36⅔ innings. His first appearance with Syracuse came on his 20th birthday (he was the youngest player in the league) and the opposition did not treat him well. He was tagged with the loss as Columbus defeated Syracuse, 5-3. He got off to a rocky start (0-5) with the SkyChiefs and wound up with a 7-10 record and a 4.58 ERA.

Halladay returned to Syracuse in 1998 and went 9-5 with a 3.79 ERA, despite missing more than a month with a strained right shoulder. He was called up to Toronto at the end of the season. He made his major-league debut with a start at Tampa Bay on September 20. After five innings he left the game with a 5-3 lead, but the bullpen faltered and he was denied his first win. In his second start, against Detroit a week later in Toronto, he carried a no-hitter and a 2-0 lead into the ninth inning. With two outs, Tigers pinch-hitter Bobby Higginson hit a home run that broke up the no-hitter and ended the shutout. After Higginson's homer, Halladay got the final out for his first major-league win. "I took some things out of it," he said. "I gained some confidence, so I think that it was a good thing that it happened. Depending on how I take that this year, that'll show whether it was good or not."[13] It would take a while, but Halladay would have career moments that would put that brush with history in the rearview mirror, once and for all—it was definitely a good thing.

Halladay made the Blue Jays roster in 1999. He split his time between the starting rotation and the bullpen, starting half his 36 games. He pitched 149 innings, going 8-7 with a 3.92 ERA. In his first appearance of the season, he appeared in relief on April 7, pitching three innings against the Twins to earn the only save of his career. He pitched his first career shutout against Detroit on May 20, winning 7-0.

The following season was a disappointment. In his first eight appearances with the Blue Jays through May 15, Halladay was 2-4 with an 11.97 ERA. He spent the next month with Triple-A Syracuse, and returned to the Jays on June 24, going seven innings against the Boston Red Sox for the win. He was largely ineffective in his eight appearances after being recalled and at the end of July, sporting a 10.63 ERA, he was again sent to Syracuse. He was recalled again in September and finished the 2000 season with a 4-7 record and a 10.64 ERA. During the offseason, Roy, his wife, Brandy, and their infant son, Braden, relocated to Florida to escape the demands there were in Colorado because of Halladay's celebrity status.

During spring training in 2001, Halladay was "very distracted by the big picture. I'd be thinking about pitching seven innings and giving up three runs instead of about the pitch I was about to throw."[14] But two men — Harvey Dorfman and Mel Queen — entered his life, and his career was turned around.

As Halladay faced his demons during the spring of 2001, Brandy made an impulse purchase, buying *The Mental ABC's of Pitching* by Harvey Dorfman. The book and Dorfman's *The Mental Game of Baseball* became bibles to him as he climbed his way to achievement. In 2002 Halladay met Dorfman and all the pieces fell into place.[15]

The Blue Jays realized that a drastic change of scenery was needed to get Halladay back on his game and sent him to Class A: Dunedin of the Florida State League. General manager Gordon Ash and manager Buck Martinez, knowing that the news would be devastating, had Tim Hewes, the team's counselor, inform Halladay of the decision.[16] It was a trying time for Halladay, who even placed a call to his mentor Campbell, then 82 years old. Campbell said, "Your problem isn't physical, it's mental. You've got to get help."[17]

But as much as the still-young 230-pound right-hander needed help grasping the mental aspects of the game, his pitching fundamentals also needed work. His high-velocity fastball, delivered from an over-the-top motion, was coming in flat and was an easy target for batters, regardless of speed.

Halladay worked his way back up through the minors to the majors in 2001. At Dunedin he was 0-1 in 13 games with a 3.97 ERA, but did earn two saves. He made some steps forward at Dunedin, and his next step would bring greater rewards. That step took him to a Double-A ballpark in Kodak, Tennessee, near Knoxville, home of the Tennessee Smokies of the Southern League.

The Blue Jays brought former pitching coach and farm director Mel Queen out of retirement to work with the 24-year-old Halladay. Roy's move from Class A to Double A was not so much as a promotion but as a place where he would work under Queen's tutelage, and regain the form that had made him one of the best pitching prospects in baseball. Queen was essential in the turnaround for Halladay, rebuilding his delivery, teaching him new grips on his pitches, and helping him develop a stronger mental approach. "You're wasting talent, Doc," was the first thing Queen told Halladay. "I verbally abused him pretty hard that first week," Queen said. "A lot of guys wouldn't have taken it. A lot of guys would have walked away. A lot of guys would've punched me. I basically told him he wasn't a very intelligent young man. In fact, as far as baseball-wise, I told him he was pretty naïve and stupid. And that's got to change."[18]

Queen's methods worked. In five games with Tennessee, Halladay had a 2-1 record and a 2.12 ERA. His next and final minor-league stop was at Syracuse, where he pitched in two games. He made it back to Toronto at the beginning of July and pitched in 17 games, going 5-3 with a 3.16 ERA.

After showing sporadic signs of brilliance in prior seasons, Halladay emerged as a dominant pitcher in 2002. He went 19-7 with a 2.93 ERA in a league-leading 239⅓ innings. On June 7 at Toronto he had one of his best performances, yielding only two hits while shutting out the Rockies, 8-0, but the team was only 24-34 at the time, and only 20,032 saw his effort. No other Blue Jays pitcher had more than 10 wins and the team finished at 78-84, in third place in the AL East. Halladay was named to his first All-Star team, but was ineffective, yielding three runs in one inning, including a two-run homer by Barry Bonds. He completed only two games in 2002. That changed the next season.

There still were times when Halladay doubted himself. One of his closest friends in baseball was Chris Carpenter. The two were first teammates at Syracuse in 1997, and were with Toronto until August 2002. In midseason Harvey Dorfman happened to be in town, and the two approached him. "A few questions" turned into a career-saving collaboration between Dorfman and Halladay. Dorfman instilled in Halladay the concept that he should hold himself accountable and responsible. "Being responsible means that when things go wrong, I can right them."[19]

That season Blue Jays radio play-by-play man Tom Cheek began calling Halladay "Doc," after a famous figure of the nineteenth-century Wild West, John Henry "Doc" Holliday. In 2003, he took dead aim on greatness. That was a season that saw this assessment from Jon Siegel of the *Washington Times*: "Roy Halladay is a 6-foot-6 mountain man who looks even more menacing with his red beard and no moustache. And that's before the Denver native unleashes his overpowering right arm."[20] This venture into hyperbole was on the eve of Halladay's trying to tie one of the American League's most cherished records. On August 1 he went for his 16th win in a row, a record shared by seven pitchers. After going 0-for-April (0-2), Halladay had spent the next three months winning 15 straight games. He lost to the Anaheim Angels that evening and had a bumpy (2-4) August. But he came back to go have five complete-game wins, including two shutouts in September, to finish at 22-7. In his first Cy Young Award season, he led the American League in wins, innings pitched (266), complete games (9), and shutouts (2), with a league-leading strikeout-to-walk ratio of 6.38. Pitching coach Gil Patterson said, "There's no panic, no overthrowing, no stress—just conviction and strength. Umpires, errors, runs, who the hitter is doesn't affect him."[21]

In 2004 Halladay had right-shoulder problems and made two trips to the disabled list. His season was first interrupted on May 28, after he defeated the Angels the night before. He felt soreness and was on the DL from May 28 through June 11. After returning he was largely ineffective, and was back on the DL from July 17 through September 20 with shoulder fatigue. He returned for three late-season appearances and there was encouragement when on the last weekend of the season he held the New York Yankees to one run in eight innings to even his record at 8-8. For the season he pitched 133 innings and his ERA rose to 4.20.

Halladay was back in form in 2005. Through July 3, he was 12-4 with five complete games and two shutouts. His ERA stood at 2.33 as he took the mound against the Texas Rangers on July 8. In the third inning disaster struck. Kevin Mench lined a ball off Halladay's left shin. Roy fielded the ball and throw out Mench from a seated position. But he had to leave the game. X-rays revealed that he had suffered a nondisplaced fracture in his lower leg.[22] His season was over. He was leading the American League in innings pitched and had been named to the All-Star team. Despite pitching in only 19 games, he led the league in complete games.

Halladay came back in 2006 to go 16-5 with a 3.19 ERA and lead the league in won-loss percentage (.762). He was named to his fourth All-Star team and pitched two innings, allowing one run on a wild pitch. In his best performance of the season, on May 13 at Tampa Bay, he allowed only three hits as the Blue Jays won 8-1. However, the team again missed the playoffs, finishing second in the AL East with an 87-75 record. It was his first season since 2003 with more than 30 starts (32) and more than 200 innings pitched (220).

Halladay's success continued into 2007. He was 4-0 with a 2.28 ERA in April, and didn't slow down. Again he had a 16-win season, this time with seven losses and a 3.71 ERA. His best effort of the season was an 8-0, three-hit shutout of Seattle on July 22. He had a league-leading seven complete games, and it was the first of five consecutive seasons in which he led his league in complete games. He was not selected for the All-Star Game, but finished in the Cy Young Award voting.

Halladay's ERA came down to 2.78 in 2008 and he was again a 20-game winner. He struck out a career-high 206 (a number he exceeded in each of the next four seasons). He returned to All-Star competition and pitched a scoreless fourth inning, retiring the three batters he faced. His record for the season was 20-11 and he led the league in complete games (9), shutouts (2), and innings pitched (246). In his best game of the season, he blanked the Yankees 5-0 on two hits on July 11. When the Cy Young ballots were tabulated, he finished second to Cleveland's Cliff Lee.

The 2009 season presented challenges that had little to do with Halladay's pitching. Before the 2006 season he had signed a contract extension through 2010, and the Blue Jays were faced with a decision. They had not been to the postseason since their back-to-back championships in 1992-1993. Attendance was down and although Halladay was happy in Toronto, he would become a free agent after the 2010 season. Halladay, acknowledged by many as the best pitcher in baseball, had yet to show his mastery in postseason competition. When the Blue Jays were in fourth place as the season entered July, rumors started to surface that he was on the trading block. On July 6, with Halladay's concurrence, general manager J.P. Ricciardi let it be known that he was seeking offers. As Doc had a no-trade clause in his contract, Ricciardi entered negotiations with contending teams authorized by Halladay.[23] The Philadelphia Phillies were at the top of Halladay's list.

Roy and Brandy's two sons, Braden and Ryan, were born while he was with the Blue Jays. Ryan was named for Doc's childhood hero, Nolan Ryan. When he was 13, Halladay had purchased *Nolan Ryan's Pitcher's Bible* and followed Ryan's conditioning protocol.

Together, Roy and Brandy worked with Toronto's Hospital for Sick Children. Starting in 2005, he and Brandy hosted "Doc's Box" at Skydome (in conjunction with the Jays Care Foundation), where they invited children and their families from the hospital to a luxury suite. In 2008 Halladay was presented the annual George Gross/Toronto Sun Sportsperson of the Year Award. Halladay donated the $1,000 he received to a fund set up for Isaac McFadden. Isaac had been diagnosed in 2005, when he was 18 months old, with a rare disease, and Halladay and Isaac had grown close over the years. Halladay matched the award with a gift of his own.[24]

Halladay was not traded in 2009, as general manager Ruben Amaro Jr. of the Phillies, was not willing to pay the asking price. Doc had taken a 10-2 record into July and during the trade talk had been named to his sixth All-Star team. He started the All-Star Game for the first time and allowed three runs (two earned) in two innings. For the season, he was 17-10, with an ERA of 2.79. In 239 innings, he struck out 208 batters. Again he led the league in complete games (9). His most impressive performance of the season came on September 4, a 6-0 shutout of the Yankees. Ramiro Pena's double in the sixth inning was the Yankees' only hit. The win was only the Blue Jays' 60th against 74 losses. They finished in fourth place in the AL East, and on the final weekend of the season, Ricciardi was fired as general manager. Once again, Halladay watched the postseason on television.

On the eve of the trading deadline when it looked as though he would be traded, Halladay had said, "I really feel like I've fulfilled a lot of obligations, and at some point, you have to be a little bit selfish on what you want (a postseason appearance). I've gotten to the point where I can make a decision on what's best. It's purely based on having a chance to win. I really do hope it's here (Toronto). But I think for me, I hate to look back and regret that I had that three- or four-year window and I didn't take the chance to give myself the best opportunity, and that's really all I'm trying to do, whether it's here or someplace else."[25] New GM Alex Anthopoulos, at the 2009 winter meetings, resumed discussions with Amaro of the Phillies and completed a deal that had Halladay move to Philadelphia in exchange for pitcher Kyle Drabek, outfielder Michael Taylor, and catcher Travis d'Arnaud.

Doc left Toronto a fan favorite; as a token of his appreciation, he bought a full-page newspaper ad thanking the fans for their support, passion, and devotion since he first signed in 1995. The Phillies gave him a contract that extended through 2013 and his 2010 season would, by itself, justify the big investment.

As the Phillies surged to an early league lead, Halladay was a major key to their success. On May 29 the Phillies led the NL East by 1½ games and Halladay sported a 6-3 record with four complete games and two shutouts. His ERA was 2.22 and he had struck out 59 batters in 77 innings. The Phillies were in Miami to play the Marlins at Sun Life Stadium, which was best suited for football. That night, before 25,086 spectators, he faced 27 batters and retired each one for a perfect game. He struck out a season-high 11 batters. In the All-Star Game, he pitched two-thirds of an inning, giving up two hits but getting a double-play ball and facing only three batters.

During the second half of the season, the Phillies battled the Atlanta Braves and New York Mets for East Division supremacy. On July 21 they trailed the division-leading Braves by seven games. Then they caught fire. From July 22 through the end of the season, they were 49-19 and won the division by six games. Halladay during this stretch went 11-2, capping his 21-10 season with an 8-0 shutout at Washington on September 27 that clinched the division title for the Phillies. Doc finished the season with a 2.44 ERA. In winning his second career Cy Young Award (he was a unanimous selection), he led the league in complete games (9) and shutouts (4). His 7.30 ratio of strikeouts (219) to walks (30) was the league's best. For the first time in his career, Halladay appeared in the postseason.

On October 6, in the first game of the Division Series against Cincinnati, the Phillies' ace, Roy Halladay, took the mound. At his home park, in front of 46,411 spectators and in view of a national television audience, Halladay pitched a gem. The Phillies jumped off to a 4-0 lead with three second-inning runs. And Doc did the rest. He retired the first 14 batters he saw, five by strikeout, before yielding a fifth-inning walk to Jay Bruce. Bruce was the only Reds baserunner. Halladay's no-hitter, the second in postseason history, secured his place in baseball history.

The Phillies swept the Reds in three games and faced the San Francisco Giants in the League Championship Series. In the opener, Halladay was matched with the Giants' Tim Lincecum. Roy extended his string of postseason hitless innings to 11⅓ before yielding a solo home run to Cody Ross in the third inning. The Phillies trailed 4-3 when Halladay was removed for a pinch-hitter in the bottom of the seventh inning and the Giants held on to take a 1-0 lead in the series. Through four games, the Giants had a 3-1 lead and Halladay and Lincecum dueled once again in Game Five. Halladay came out on top in the rematch to keep the Phillies alive. He was removed for a pinch-hitter after hurling six innings in Philadelphia's 4-2 win. The Giants clinched the LCS in the next game.

Halladay was back in dominating form for the Phillies in the following season, but it was time tinged with sadness as two of his mentors, Harvey Dorfman and Mel Queen, died within three months of each other in early 2011. Through June, Doc had a 10-3 record with a 2.40 ERA. On July 2 the Phillies visited Toronto and he was welcomed by 44,078 fans. He picked the occasion to hurl his sixth complete game of the season as the Phillies won 5-3 to extend their record to 53-31. Their first-place lead was four games. National League manager Bruce Bochy selected Halladay to start the All-Star Game on July 12, and Halladay turned in the best of his seven All-Star Game performances. In his two innings, he retired six consecutive batters as the National League won, 5-1. He continued to excel after the All-Star break and posted a 19-6 mark for the season. He led the National League with eight complete games and a 6.29 strikeout-to-walk ratio. His 2.35 ERA was his best since his abbreviated 1998 season and his 220 strikeouts were a career high. He finished second in the Cy Young Award balloting, the seventh time he had finished in the top five in the voting.

The Phillies faced the St. Louis Cardinals in the Division Series and Halladay started Game One. He yielded three first-inning runs on a Lance Berkman three-run homer, but the Phillies came back with a vengeance, scoring 11 unanswered runs while Halladay was retiring the last 21 batters he faced. The bullpen yielded three ninth-inning runs, and Philadelphia won 11-6.

In the decisive Game Five, Halladay faced longtime friend and former Blue Jays teammate Chris Carpenter in a duel that, after the first two batters, met all expectations. The two had been teammates in Toronto from 1997 through 2002. Those first two batters, Rafael Furcal and Skip Schumaker, of the Cardinals, tripled and doubled, and St. Louis had all the offense it would need. Carpenter shut down Philadelphia on three hits for the 1-0 win. Halladay came out for a pinch-hitter after hurling eight innings and allowing four hits after the first inning. The Phillies were eliminated three games to two, and Halladay had appeared in his last postseason game.

Halladay turned 35 on the date of his team's 36th game—May 14, 2012. He was 3-3 at the time, and uncharacteristically had yet to complete a game. He had soreness in his right shoulder, and lasted only two innings in a start on May 27. Diagnosed with a strained right latissimus dorsi (a large muscle in the back), he was placed on the disabled list on May 29. The condition did not require surgery,[26] and he returned to action on July 17. Over the balance of the season Halladay went 7-3 with an unsightly ERA of 4.93. The Phillies were unsuccessful in defending their division title, slipping to third place with an 81-81 record. Halladay's 11-9 record brought him to within one win of 200 career victories. His 4.49 ERA for the season was his worst since his disastrous 2000 season.

As 2013 dawned, there were question marks and nobody realized that more than Halladay. "I think any player would honestly tell you, 'You never know.' Every year you come into spring training, and you come in hoping that you're going to feel good and you'll be able to pick up where you left off. But there's no guarantees. I know that. And I've known that my whole career."[27] After faring poorly in his first two starts, failing to get past the fourth inning either time, Halladay took the mound in Miami. The Marlins were in their new ballpark, Marlins Park, and a Sunday-afternoon crowd of 21,412 was on hand. Halladay was his old self, allowing only one run on five hits, but his mates were able to get only one run in the first eight innings. In the ninth inning, Laynce Nix batted for Halladay and put the Phillies ahead 2-1 with a home run. Jonathan Papelbon came on to seal the deal, saving Halladay's 200th win.

Halladay followed that effort with an 8-2 win over the Cardinals five days later, but his season was one of frustration. After getting hammered by the Marlins on May 5, he complained of shoulder discomfort and had arthroscopic surgery shortly afterward to fix a bone spur, a frayed labrum, and a partially torn rotator cuff. He was out of action until August 25, when he returned and pitched six innings as the Phillies defeated the Arizona Diamondbacks, 9-5. By then it was clear that there would be no more seasons for Roy Halladay. He finished the 2013 season with a 4-5 record. In his final start, against the Marlins on September 23, he faced only three batters, walking two. He left the game with "arm fatigue." One of the runners scored and he absorbed the loss. His final season showed him with a 4-5 record and a 6.82 ERA.

That arm fatigue came after 41,091 pitches at the major-league level. In a 16-season career, he was 203-105 with an ERA of 3.38. In an era when complete games were rare, he had 67, leading his league seven times. Of those complete games, 20 were shutouts.

"There was always somebody with a Toronto jersey on. Always. There were fans saying, 'Brandy, remember me?' Every year I saw somebody that knew my name, because it was always so personal. Toronto, as big as it is, still felt so small to us. It still felt like home."[28]

—Brandy Halladay at Roy Halladay's retirement in Toronto

After the 2013 season, with his Philadelphia contract at an end, Halladay signed a one-day contract to go back to the Blue Jays and announced his retirement at a press conference. He was inducted into the Canadian Baseball Hall of Fame in 2017.

Having displayed a work ethic second to none, a compassion for teammates and community that was the envy of his peers, and a pitching style and achievement reminiscent of a bygone era, Roy Halladay left the sport, and the sport was much the better having had him for 16 seasons.

A place in Cooperstown could be occupied by Halladay as early as 2019. Until then, the words of Cole Hamels bring Roy Halladay into focus:

"That's how we labeled him: This guy is the Immortal, we're all just humans, and we're lucky enough to play baseball with him."[29]

SOURCES

In addition to the sources shown in the Notes, the author used Baseball-Reference.com and the Roy Halladay player file at the Baseball Hall of Fame Library. The author is particularly grateful for the help extended by Cassidy Lent and Matt Rothenberg at the library. The following sources were also used:

Monnig, Alex. *Roy Halladay: Superstar Pitcher* (Minneapolis: Abdo Publishing, 2012)

Schwarz, Alan. "Simply Unhittable," *New York Times*, April 5, 2009: SP1.

NOTES

1. Jack Etkin, "Bus-Man's Holiday—Long Time Pitching Coach Never Stops Teaching Colorado's Top Prospects," *Rocky Mountain News* (Denver), June 1, 1997: 14C.
2. Ibid.
3. Jim Salisbury and Todd Zolecki, *The Rotation: A Season with the Phillies and One of the Greatest Pitching Staffs Ever Assembled* (Philadelphia: Running Press, 2012), 43.
4. Jeff Hamrick, "Arvada West's Halladay Takes Turn in Spotlight," *Rocky Mountain News*, March 16, 1995: 12B.
5. Neil H. Devlin, "Halladay: Ready, Willing, and Able," *Denver Post*, March 21, 1995: B-10.
6. Norm Clarke, *Rocky Mountain News*, October 24, 1995: 2B.
7. Neil H. Devlin, *Denver Post*, June 18, 1995: B-10.
8. Devlin, "Blue Jays Declare Halladay Arvada West Pitcher is No. 1 in Toronto," *Denver Post*, June 2, 1995: D-1.
9. Randy Holtz, "Toronto Gets Halladay with 17th Selection," *Rocky Mountain News*, June 2, 1995: 9B.
10. Etkin and Tracy Ringolsby, *Rocky Mountain News*, October 9, 1995: 21B.
11. Bob Putnam, "Don't Let Age Fool You, He's a Vet," *St. Petersburg Times*, July 28, 1996: 9C.
12. Anwar S. Richardson, *Tampa Tribune*, March 9, 1997.
13. Matt Michael, "High Standards: Near No-Hitter Puts Pressure on Roy Halladay," *Syracuse Herald-American*, March 28, 1999.
14. Phil Sheridan, "Halladay Pays Homage to a Treasured Mentor," *Philadelphia Inquirer*, March 2, 2001: D1, D3.
15. Etkin, "Toronto Blue Jays Roy Halladay 2003 Pitcher of the Year," *Baseball Digest*, January 2004: 22.
16. Salisbury and Zolecki, 43.
17. Geoff Baker, "To Hell and Back: How Doc Halladay's 95 Days of Purgatory Turned Him into a Dominant Pitcher," *Toronto Star*, September 27, 2003.
18. Ibid.
19. Etkin, *Baseball Digest*, January 2004.
20. Jon Siegel, "Halladay Guns for Sweet 16 in Streak," *Washington Times*, August 1, 2003.
21. Ibid.
22. Stephen Hawkins (Associated Press), "Halladay to Miss at Least a Month, All-Star Start," July 9, 2005.
23. Tyler Kepner, "Toronto's Towering Ace Lingers at the Exit: Suitors are Circling as the Blue Jays Ponder Trading Away Halladay," *New York Times*, July 26, 2009: SP1.
24. Bob Elliott, "Little Man Has Doc's Heart," *Toronto Sun*, June 27, 2010.
25. Kepner.
26. Jayson Stark, "Roy Halladay Out 6-8 Weeks," ESPN.com, May 29, 2012.
27. Stark, "A Defining Year Awaits Roy Halladay," ESPN.com, February 13, 2013.
28. David Cooper, "Blue Jays: Toronto Will Always be 'Home' for the Halladays," *Toronto Star*, December 11, 2013.
29. "Even in the Twilight of His career, the Phillies Roy Halladay Remains a Legend Among Peers," Yahoo Sports, March 1, 2013.

27 UP AND 27 DOWN
MAY 29, 2010: PHILADELPHIA PHILLIES 1, FLORIDA MARLINS 0, AT SUN LIFE STADIUM, MIAMI

By Alan Cohen

"Steps back up onto the mound, tucks the ball in his right hand. Now into the glove. Holds it in front of the letters. Nods yes. The wind; the one-two pitch. Swing, and a groundball to the left side. Castro's got it. Spins, throws. He got him! A perfect game for Roy Halladay! 27 up and 27 down! Halladay is mobbed at the mound as the Phillies celebrate perfection tonight in Miami!" — Phillies radio play-by-play broadcaster Scott Franzke[1]

Early in my bullpen (pregame warmup), I was hitting spots more than I have been. I felt I just carried that out there."[2]

– Roy "Doc" Halladay after pitching the 20th major-league perfect game

BEFORE A SATURDAY NIGHT crowd of 25,086 in Miami (many of whom were Phillies fans, and others lured by a postgame concert and fireworks show), Roy Halladay, in his first season with the Phillies, was going for his seventh win of the season. The Phillies had not been scoring of late. The Mets had shut them out in three consecutive games and Philadelphia came into the game having lost five of their previous six games, four by shutout. Their National League lead had shrunk to 1½ games. And Halladay was coming off his worst start of the season. On Sunday, May 23, he had lasted only 5⅔ innings against the Boston Red Sox, yielding seven runs (six earned) in an 8-3 loss. When he was removed from the game, Doc approached manager Charlie Manuel in the dugout and told him, "I'm better than that."[3]

The Marlins' pitcher, Josh Johnson (5-1), was up to the task. The 26-year-old was coming off a 15-5 season in which he had been selected to the All-Star team for the first time. He had won his prior two starts and had not been scored on in 18 innings coming into the game, seeing his ERA shrink from 3.35 to 2.43. The two pitchers matched up well not only in ability, but in size. Halladay was big at 6-feet-6 and 230 pounds; Johnson was even bigger at 6-feet-7 and 250 pounds.

In filling out his lineup card for the game Phillies manager Manuel had some decisions to make regarding the left side of his infield. Shortstop Jimmy Rollins and third baseman Placido Polanco were injured. The replacements he chose, Wilson Valdez and Juan Castro, became major factors in preserving the perfect game.

Over the first two innings, Johnson pitched out of jams as Halladay retired the first six batters, with four strikeouts and two groundballs. It wasn't that easy: Two of the batters in the first inning thought they had worked out walks only to have home-plate umpire Mike DiMuro bring them back to the batter's box. The leadoff batter, Chris Coghlan, looked at a 3-and-2 pitch, and the third batter in the inning, Hanley Ramirez, looked at a 3-and-1 pitch for strike two before grounding out.

In the third inning the Marlins' defense allowed the only run Halladay would need. With one out, Valdez, who had doubled in the first inning, singled to center field. Chase Utley then lined a ball to deep center field that was misplayed by the Marlins' Cameron Maybin. Maybin misjudged the ball and started charging in. He reversed direction, but was unable to complete the play. The ball went off

Maybin's glove for a three-base error and the score was 1-0.[4] Afterward, Maybin said, "J.J. (Johnson) did a great job of competing. Unfortunately, one play—that was the ballgame."[5]

Halladay continued to have 3-and-1 and 3-and-2 counts against batters (seven during the course of the game) and still retired each man he faced. In the sixth inning, with one out, Maybin hit a roller to the right of shortstop Valdez. Going into the hole, Valdez grabbed the ball and threw to first just in time to get the out. Two innings later, Florida's Jorge Cantu banged a low liner toward third base. Castro went to his knees, short-hopped the ball, and threw to first.

Johnson came out of the game after pitching seven innings and throwing 121 pitches. He stuck out six batters and walked only one while allowing six hits. Relievers Clay Hensley and Juan Carlos Oviedo each pitched perfect innings, setting the stage for Halladay to emerge from the visitors' dugout for the bottom of the ninth.

> *"Once you think it's possible is probably two outs in the ninth. Up to that point you obviously are aware of it, but it's never something you think is possible. Really, once I got to two outs it felt like I had a chance. It's not something you expect"*— Roy Halladay [6]

The Marlins' last swings were taken by three pinch-hitters. Mike Lamb's long fly ball to center field dropped into the glove of Shane Victorino at the edge of the warning track; Wes Helms struck out looking; and on a 1-and-2 count Ronny Paulino grounded to Castro. Ranging to his left, Castro grabbed the ball, spun around and threw a perfect strike to the waiting glove of Ryan Howard for the final out. The game was over in 2:13, with Halladay having thrown 115 pitches, 72 of which were strikes, to complete his masterpiece.

In the Marlins clubhouse after the game, there was some griping about the umpire's calls but Halladay's mastery was acknowledged by Marlins manager Fredi Gonzalez. "You've got to take your hat off to Doc," Gonzalez said. "That's why he is who he is. That's what (the Phillies) got him for."[7]

Johnson was the hard-luck loser. He would go on to post an 11-6 record in 2010 with a league-leading 2.30 ERA. He was named to his second All-Star team, but would be unable, due to injury, to replicate his success in future seasons. His last big-league season was 2013.

After the game, Halladay hastened to share the credit with his catcher, Carlos Ruiz. "We felt like we got in a groove early and about the fifth or sixth, I was just following Chooch. I can't say enough about the job he did today. Mixed pitches. For me, it was really a no-brainer."[8] Ruiz said, "His tempo was real good, so I was feeling great because whatever I put down, he was going to throw it. He would hit the spot. He was painting everything. He hit the corners."[9]

Marlins owner Jeffrey Luria went so far as to offer to give Halladay the pitching rubber as a memento. There was one minor issue. The field had been darkened for the fireworks show. That did not stop the Marlins grounds crew. With the fireworks exploding and the music playing, workers dug out the rubber in the darkness and made the presentation to Halladay.[10]

The perfect game was the second thrown in the major leagues in 2010. Twenty days earlier, in Oakland, Dallas Braden of the A's had hurled a perfect game against the Tampa Bay Rays.

It was not the first time Halladay had flirted with a no-hitter. In his second career start, in 1998, he had taken a no-hitter into the ninth inning against the Tigers only to see it foiled by Bobby Higginson's pinch-hit homer with two outs in the final inning. He had also hurled a one-hitter against the Yankees in 2009. The next time Halladay pursued a no-hitter would be in his first postseason appearance, four months down the road. When he no-hit Cincinnati in the first game of the National League Divisional Series, he joined Don Larsen, as the only two pitchers to hurl no-hitters in postseason play.

Catcher Carlos Ruiz went on to catch three more no-hitters during his time with the Phillies. The four no-hitters tied him with Jason Varitek for the major-league record.

Halladay would pitch to a 21-10 record in 2010 and win the National League Cy Young Award. He had previously been accorded the same honor, in 2003, in the American League while pitching for Toronto. He had one more season of success in 2011, when he would join the small group of pitchers who started All-Star Games in each league. He retired at the end of the 2013 season with 203 career wins.

SOURCES

In addition to the sources cited in the Notes, the author used Baseball-Reference.com and:

Kepner, Tyler. "20 Days Later, It's Halladay's Turn at Perfection," *New York Times*, May 30, 2010: SP3.

NOTES

1 Matt Geib, "Tales of Roy Halliday's Perfect Game," *Philadelphia Inquirer*, May 31, 2010.
2 Tim Reynolds, "Phillies' Halladay Throws Perfect Game," *Associated Press*, May 29, 2010.
3 Matt Geib.
4 Joe Capozzi, "A Perfect Halladay," *Palm Beach Post*, May 30, 2010: 1C.
5 Tim Reynolds.
6 Juan C. Rodriguez, "Halladay Perfect," *Orlando Sentinel*, May 30, 2010: C8.
7 Tim Reynolds.
8 Ibid.
9 Matt Geib.
10 Clark Spencer, "Phillies 1, Marlins 0: Phillies Roy Halladay Throws Perfect Game Against Florida Marlins," *Miami Herald*, May 30, 2010.

OCTOBER 6, 2010
PHILADELPHIA PHILLIES 4, CINCINNATI REDS 0, AT CITIZENS BANK PARK
GAME ONE OF THE NATIONAL LEAGUE DIVISION SERIES

By Alan Cohen

"It's surreal, it really is. I just wanted to pitch here (Philadelphia), pitch in the post-season. To go out and have a game like that, it's a dream come true." [1] — Roy Halladay, October 6, 2010.

"When it gets that loud, it's hard to ignore. I thought especially the last three innings, it got louder every inning. It' probably—obviously—one of the most electric atmospheres I've ever been in. It was pretty neat." [2] — Roy Halladay, October 6, 2010.

AS THE DINNER HOUR approached in Philadelphia, 46,411 fans, virtually all rooting for the Phillies, congregated at the ballpark in Philadelphia and were greeted by the type of cold and rainy weather that is not unusual in the fall months. Millions of people nationwide gathered, in more comfortable surroundings, around television sets for the first game of the National League Division Series. The Phillies had won the NL East and were facing the Cincinnati Reds, the NL Central winner. The Reds were appearing in the postseason for the first time since 1995.

Philadelphia's Roy Halladay was making his first postseason appearance after 12 frustrating years in Toronto. He wanted to be traded to Philadelphia as early as midway in the 2009 season, and after the season, he got his wish. In his first season with the Phillies, he had gone 21-10 and was acknowledged as the best pitcher in the game. Would he be able to confirm that status in the postseason?

Cincinnati countered with Edinson Volquez. He had started 12 games since re-joining the club in mid-July. He had begun the season at Class-A and made three minor-league stops, appearing in eight games, before being recalled by the Reds and joining their rotation. He had a 4-3 record with an ERA of 4.31, but down the stretch, he gave the Reds a strong boost when, on September 21, he allowed one run and scattered three hits in eight innings, as the Reds won, 4-3, to extend their NL Central lead to eight games.

After Halladay retired the side in order, using only 10 pitches (per Baseball-Reference.com) in the top of the first inning, the Phillies broke on top with a run in their first at-bat.[3] Shane Victorino doubled with one out, stole third base, and came around to score on a fly ball by Chase Utley, barely beating the throw with a head-first slide. Volquez was having trouble with the elements. "I had problems in the first inning, the feeling with the ball. It was kind of cold and raining, a little wet with the grip. I couldn't control some of them (pitches) with the rain."[4]

In the next inning, Halladay continued his mastery with another three quick outs. The Phillies, with two out in their half of the inning, broke things open. Carlos Ruiz walked as Volquez seemed to be pitching around him.[5] Wilson Valdez, playing third base for the Phillies in place of Placido Polanco, then hit a ball up the middle that was fielded by shortstop Orlando Cabrera. Cabrera tried to force Ruiz at second but the throw was wide.[6] The official scorer credited Valdez with a single. Halladay aided his own cause, driving in Ruiz with a line-drive single to left field that fell in front of Jonny Gomes, as Gomes tried to make a sliding catch on the play. Halladay, who had rarely had the opportunity to bat in his days in the American League (3-for-38 in interleague play) had taken his hitting seriously since joining the Phillies, going 13-for-92 with five RBIs during the 2010 season. From July 23 through August 14, he hit in five consecutive games, each one a Phillies victory. As he stood on first after his RBI single, Halladay saw the Phillies' fans, as a group, standing and waving their "Fightin' Phils" rally towels.[7]

A walk to Jimmy Rollins loaded the bases and Victorino, with his second hit of the game, a single, delivered two runs and forced a pitching change. The Reds brought in Travis Wood, in his first relief appearance of the year, to get the final out of the inning but the damage was done and the Phillies had more than ample run support. Halladay kept rolling along and was backed up by good fortune and good defensive work. Reds pitcher Wood, with two out in the third inning, hit a sinking liner to right field that was hauled in by Jayson Werth, who had been perfectly positioned on the play. An inning later, it was Rollins' turn to shine, going into the hole between shortstop and third to gather in a ground ball off the bat of Joey Votto.

The Reds finally got a base runner in the fifth inning when Jay Bruce walked on a 3-2 cutter with two out. He would be the only Cincinnati base runner of the game. And the Phillies continued to back up Halladay with their gloves. In the top of the sixth inning, after Wood had pitched 3 1/3 scoreless innings in relief, he was removed as Reds manager Dusty Baker inserted Juan Francisco as a pinch-hitter. Francisco had been added to the roster at the last second as a replacement for the injured Jim Edmonds. He hit a hard smash up the middle, but Rollins ranged over to make the play and throw on to first for the second out of the inning.

Pitchers were in complete command for each side in the seventh and eighth innings as there was not a single hit. The score, as the game went to the ninth inning remained 4-0. Halladay took the mound and the noise was deafening. As John Gonzalez wrote in the *Philadelphia Inquirer*, it was a "choreographed mass that couldn't possibly believe its good fortune and needed to express its happiness in unison."[8]

"I was panicking as I reached for the ball. My hand was shaking, it's still shaking. When the ball came off the bat, I had to reach back a little bit to pick it up and throw it, and that's why I went to my knee." [9] — Philadelphia catcher Carlos Ruiz.

Ramon Hernandez and Miguel Cairo each hit harmless pop-ups and there were two quick ninth-inning outs. Brandon Phillips came up to bat for the fifth time as the Reds' final chance to extend the game. With the count at 0-2, he was protecting the plate when Halladay's pitch caromed off the bat of and fell about 10 feet in front of home plate in fair territory. Ruiz threw off his mask and chased after the ball, almost tripping over it. His motion took him past the ball. He reached back to grab the ball, went to one knee, and threw to Ryan Howard at first base to secure Halladay's second no-hitter of 2010. The game was over in 2:34. Doc had thrown a perfect game against the Marlins on May 29. But this effort was on center stage, and much more economical. In May, Halladay had thrown 115 pitches (72 for strikes). This time around, only 25 of his 104 pitchers were balls. He stuck out eight Reds batters.

The following day was a day off for both teams, but Halladay, as always, was among the first at the ballpark to begin his workout regimen. When the series resumed, the Phillies won the next two games and advanced to the League Championship serious where they lost to the eventual World Series winning San Francisco Giants, missing out of a third consecutive trip to the World Series.

Halladay would never play in a World Series.

Opposing manager Baker said, "The thing about it is, you know, I don't think he threw anything down the heart of the plate. Everything was on the corners and moving. I don't know what his percentage was, but it looked like he threw 90% for first-pitch strikes (it was 25-of-28 for 89%). Any time you do that with the stuff he has, then he can go to work on you after that."[10]

And Philadelphia pitching coast Rich Dupree observed, properly so: "The marathon is over. The

11 years of grinding and working are over. Now it's time to really enjoy it and cherish it, and I think he understands that. If you work so long to get hereto get into the postseason, you might as well be yourself and enjoy it and run with it. Tonight, he did."[11]

SOURCES

In addition to those sources cited in the notes, the author used Baseball-Reference.com.

NOTES

1 Associated Press, "Phillies' Halladay No-Hits Reds," *Daily Star* (Oneonta, New York), October 7, 2010:13.

2 John Erardi, "Phillies Good to the Last Out: For All of Halladay's Dominance, It Took Smooth Play on a Tricky Hope to Seal Gem," *Cincinnati Enquirer*, October 7, 2010: D4

3 Sal Donnellon's game account says Halladay threw 11 pitches in the first inning. See Sal Donnellon, "The Pitcher: Philly Has His Number Now," *Philadelphia Daily News*, October 7, 2010: 76.

4 Tom Groeschen, "Overshadowed, Underwhelming: Early Struggles Relegate Volquez to Bit Player in Historic Game," *Cincinnati Enquirer*, October 7, 2010: D4

5 Bob Brookover, "On Day After, Doc Sticks to Routine," *Philadelphia Inquirer*, October 8, 2010: D5.

6 John Fay, "Three Keys," *Cincinnati Enquirer*, October 7, 2010: D5.

7 Erardi, "Shades of 1981, . . . and 1990," *Cincinnati Enquirer*, October 7, 2010: D7

8 John Gonzalez, "Finally Sports Paupers No More," *Philadelphia Inquirer*, October 7, 2010: E2.

9 Erardi: D4

10 Sal Donnellon.

11 David Hale, "Halladay Finally Gets to Celebrate: Playoff Debut One for History Books," *Cincinnati Enquirer*, October 7, 2010: D4.

STEVE BARBER

By Warren Corbett

STEVE BARBER WAS A WILD left-handed pitcher with a cannonball sinker, a chip on his shoulder, and a pain in his elbow.

Barber was anointed as the majors' fastest pitcher before he appeared in a regular-season game. He was the first 20-game winner in the modern history of the Baltimore Orioles, but his arm went bad before the team grew into the powerhouse of the American League. After leaving Baltimore, he latched on with eight other teams, proving that a left-hander with a live fastball and a pulse can always find work. A charter member of the doomed Seattle Pilots, he was depicted in Ball Four as a man who wouldn't lead, follow, or get out of the way.

Stephen David Barber was born on February 22, 1938, in Takoma Park, Maryland, just outside Washington, and grew up nearby in Silver Spring. His father, Stanley, a post-office clerk at the time of the 1940 census, was killed in a tractor accident when Steve was 15.[1] His mother, the former Helen Johnson, worked as a secretary and moved in with her parents to raise Steve and his younger brother, Richard.

The girls at Montgomery Blair High School thought Steve looked like the actor Paul Newman, with his wavy hair and blue eyes.[2] Big-league scouts thought he looked like a prospect when he went 8-0 and pitched a no-hitter as a senior. But Steve followed his mother's wishes and went to the University of Maryland.

That didn't work; he quit midway through his freshman year. "I dropped out of Maryland before I flunked out," he said.[3] The Orioles' area scout, Walter Youse, heard that Barber was on the loose and gave him a train ticket to the club's minor-league spring camp at Thomasville, Georgia, in March 1957.

The camp was a cattle call for hundreds of hopefuls trying out for nine farm clubs. Barber, wearing uniform number 285, stood out from the herd well enough to win a contract. He signed for $500, plus $50 for bus fare home to visit his family before he reported to Class D ball in Paris, Texas.

Barber was stuck in Class D and C, the basement of the minors, for three years. He found his way from Paris to Dublin, Georgia, to Aberdeen, South Dakota, to Pensacola, Florida, but he couldn't find home plate. He walked 446 in 477 innings. He also struck out almost one batter per inning, explaining why the Orioles didn't give up on him.

"By '59 I'd been screwed around for three years," Barber said. "No one would work with me or teach me anything that would give me any control." He became so frustrated that he stormed out of spring training in 1958 and went home briefly. His Pensacola manager, Lou Fitzgerald, once told him, "I don't care if you walk five hundred guys, you're pitching nine innings tonight." When Barber walked the bases loaded in the first, Fitzgerald came to the mound to say, "Well, you've got four hundred ninety-seven to go."

Barber was wild after hours as well. He and Pensacola teammates Bo Belinsky and Steve Dalkowski made up a trio of hard-throwing, hard-partying lefties. Somebody labeled them "The Lost Boys." They all drank, but nobody could keep up with Dalkowski, who was even faster and much wilder than Barber on and off the field.

Harry Dalton, an assistant in the Orioles' front office, told Barber, "I hear you have an attitude problem." Barber replied, "It seems to me that if I make it, it's all well and good for you, but if I don't it's no big deal because you don't have any money invested in me."[4]

Near the end of the 1959 season, another Orioles executive, Eddie Robinson, watched Barber pitch and brought him to Baltimore to work out in September. Manager Paul Richards liked what he saw and asked, "How come I never heard of you?" The cheeky busher

answered, "Probably because I'm not one of your fucking bonus babies."⁵ Barber took his case to general manager Lee MacPhail and demanded to be sent to the fall instructional league in Florida, where the Orioles polished their top prospects. Barber told the boss, "Mr. MacPhail, if you send me down there to play for [Orioles coaches] Luman Harris and Harry Brecheen this winter, there won't be any more minor-league ball for me."⁶

Barber got his way. In Florida Brecheen worked with him to tweak his delivery and perfect his slider. On a cold, windy afternoon Richards sat in his car with the heater running and watched Barber buzz through a lineup of the Milwaukee Braves' best prospects. "The ball was just singing," teammate Boog Powell remembered. "He's breaking bat after bat."⁷ Richards said, "I think we found our left-hander for next year."⁸ The lost boy from Class D had been discovered.

Barber continued to break bats in spring training in 1960, even when he was pitching batting practice. Orioles outfielder Jackie Brandt said, "Barber threw a shot put," a heavy sinking fastball that tailed away from right-handed hitters.⁹ He featured a slider and an occasional changeup, but never developed much of a curve. In an exhibition game he shut out the mighty Yankees for four innings, striking out Yogi Berra twice and Mickey Mantle once.

A photographer for *This Week*, a Sunday newspaper supplement, came to Florida on an assignment to find the fastest fastball. Mantle and Bill Skowron of the Yankees urged him to check out the Orioles' kid lefty. Radar guns did not yet exist, so the photographer used a high-speed movie camera to time six fireballers. Barber registered 95.55 mph, outpacing the big-name pitchers: Don Drysdale, who also topped 95, Sandy Koufax, Ryne Duren, Herb Score, and Bob Turley.¹⁰

The Orioles had never had a winning record in their first six seasons after the St. Louis Browns moved to Baltimore, but they had been building a strong farm system. In 1960 Richards and MacPhail decided to place their bets on the kids. Three rookies—first baseman Jim Gentile, second baseman Marv Breeding, and shortstop Ron Hansen—joined the 23-year-old "veteran" Brooks Robinson in the infield. A fling of young pitchers called the Kiddie Korps included Barber and right-handers Milt Pappas, Chuck Estrada, Jack Fisher, and Jerry Walker. Estrada was the oldest at 22, a week older than Barber.

In his first major-league game, on April 21, Barber gave up three runs to the Washington Senators before he was relieved in the fifth, but two of the runs were unearned. Richards said he was a victim of bloop hits. Three days later at Yankee Stadium, New York pounded out a 12-0 lead in the first two innings. Richards called on Barber to mop up. He held the Yankees scoreless for four innings, allowing only a single to Berra. In his next start he beat the Boston Red Sox with a complete-game six-hitter. He was a sensation, the unknown who rocketed from Class D to the majors. Baltimore fans embraced the Maryland boy as a hometown hero.

Barber showed typical rookie inconsistency, going more than a month without a victory before he faced the Kansas City Athletics on July 28. He walked five in the first five innings. Hank Bauer delivered Kansas City's first hit in the sixth. Barber allowed no more baserunners and finished a one-hitter with 10 strikeouts. On September 11 he held the Athletics scoreless through eight innings, but loaded the bases with two away in the ninth. Richards summoned a reliever to get the final out. Barber, denied his shutout, pitched a tantrum, throwing equipment around the clubhouse. That fire was just what the manager liked to see. "I was proud of that boy," Richards said. "I told him he could knock down all the lockers he wants to as long as he battles them on the mound, too."[11]

The young Orioles shoved their way into the pennant race. On September 16 they trailed the Yankees by just .001 in the standings when Barber opened a series in New York against Whitey Ford. The Baby Bird walked seven and gave up two home runs while Ford shut out the Orioles until the ninth. The Yankees swept the four-game series, killing Baltimore's pennant hopes. The Orioles finished second, the best showing in their short history. It was a turning point for the franchise.

Barber ended his first year with a 10-7 record and 3.22 ERA, though he led the league in walks and wild pitches. He made *The Sporting News* all-rookie team along with Estrada, Gentile, Breeding, and Hansen, who was voted Rookie of the Year.

Newly married in the spring of 1961, Barber shut out the Minnesota Twins in his first start, then added two more shutouts by the end of May. He continued to pile up victories and scoreless innings, but his control still deserted him occasionally. On August 13 he slogged through 11 innings against Boston, walking 11 and striking out the same number, before an error by the Red Sox pitcher let in the winning run. Barber's wife, Ann, keeping score in the stands, counted 193 pitches. Boston's Pete Runnels, the reigning batting champ, said Barber had the best stuff in the league: "He knocks the bat right out of your hand."[12]

After a slow start, the Orioles got hot in July and stayed that way. They won 95 games, but couldn't catch the Yankees and Tigers. Barber turned in a sparkling sophomore season, finishing 18-12, 3.33. He tied for the AL lead with eight shutouts, two of them over the Yankees, and opponents batted just .217 against him. But he and Estrada walked the most batters in the league.

Real life intruded on Barber's blossoming baseball career. After the Berlin Wall was erected in August 1961, President Kennedy called 148,000 military reservists to active duty. Like many ballplayers, Barber had secured a spot in the reserves to avoid being drafted for two years' service. He reported to Fort Bragg, North Carolina, as soon as the baseball season ended, and just before American and Soviet tanks faced off on opposite sides of the wall in one of the most perilous moments of the Cold War.

Barber's first child, Steve Jr., was born while he was serving his country driving an Army trash truck. The reservists' orders said they could be held on active duty for up to a year, so the Orioles made plans to use Barber as a weekend pitcher in 1962, whenever he could get a pass. He squeezed in three weeks of spring training while on leave, then began flying each weekend from Fort Bragg to where the Orioles were playing.

An extra day or two of rest seemed to agree with Private First Class Barber. He won his first three starts and was 4-2 at the end of May. But he faltered during a 25-day furlough in June (was the baby keeping him awake?) and stood at 6-6 when the Army released him on July 9. He won his ninth game on the 28th; a week later he was in a hospital with mononucleosis. That effectively ended his season.

The Orioles failed to build on their success of 1960 and '61. Richards had left to join the expansion Houston Colt .45s, and the amiable Billy Hitchcock replaced him. The young players reacted as if they had been let out of jail with the departure of the stern Richards. Outfielder Barry Shetrone said there was no discipline and much drinking. Barber and Estrada argued with Hitchcock when he came to the mound to relieve them. The club dropped from 95 wins to 85 losses and finished seventh. After the season GM MacPhail got rid of several of the playboys and traded for the veteran Luis Aparicio to play shortstop and bat leadoff. But he kept the manager.

Baltimore started strong in 1963, and so did Barber. His record was 12-5 by the end of June and he made his first All-Star team, but passed up the game because of a calf injury. Ann fed him a steak, french fries, and salad before every start. One day she substituted green beans, and he lost.

As the Orioles fell back to finish fourth, Barber kept winning without the beans. He beat the Angels on September 18 for his 20th victory, the first 20th-century Oriole to reach that milestone. His walks declined and his strikeout rate rose. His 2.75 ERA was eighth best in the league. The club rewarded Barber with an $8,000 raise to a reported $26,000.

Baltimore got a new manager in 1964: Hank Bauer, a mainstay of the Yankees dynasty whose biography always includes the words "tough" and "ex-marine." Barber landed in Bauer's doghouse early when he sat out three weeks with a sore back. After he recovered, his control was poor and he was serving up home runs because his sinker wasn't sinking.

The Orioles spent most of the season in first place, but Barber blamed himself for losing the pennant. He lost five of his last six decisions. The truth was that the Yankees got hot in September to nose one game ahead of the White Sox and two up on the Orioles. Barber was pitching in bad luck down the stretch; he lost three games while giving up a total of five earned runs. Still, his 9-13, 3.84 record looked like failure.

By this time Steve and Ann Barber had divorced. Steve married his second wife, Patricia, in January 1965. He regained his control and his sinker to go 15-10 with a 2.69 ERA, the lowest of his career to date. But he was still frustrated by Bauer's quick hooks; he completed only seven of 32 starts.

The Orioles won the 1966 pennant on December 9, 1965, the day they acquired Frank Robinson from Cincinnati. Robinson won the AL Triple Crown, giving the club the slugger it needed. More important, he became the indispensable leader. With Robinson setting the tone, Barber said, "It was the closest knit group I've ever been around."[13]

By the All-Star break the Orioles were turning the pennant race into a runaway. Barber was the ace of the pitching staff, leading the league with a 10-3 record and a 1.96 ERA. Then his arm gave out. He pitched only 14 innings after the break. The diagnosis was elbow tendinitis, and the pain dogged him for the rest of his career.

On the last day of the season Barber and 21-year-old right-hander Wally Bunker started a doubleheader to audition for a World Series start. Barber walked the bases loaded in the second and was relieved. Left off the Series roster, he watched from the stands as the Orioles swept the heavily favored Los Angeles Dodgers. "The biggest thrill of my career was being part of that team," he said later. "Also the biggest disappointment, not getting to pitch in the World Series."[14]

Barber dug himself deeper into management's doghouse during spring training in 1967. As the club's player representative, he announced that the Orioles wanted to be paid for all radio and TV interviews. The players backed down, but Bauer showed little patience with his sore-armed pitcher. Barber was sent to the minor-league camp for a week. When he returned, he pitched like a man trying to save his job. In his first start he held the Angels hitless until Jim Fregosi doubled with one out in the ninth, then finished a one-hit shutout.

Two weeks later Barber again took a no-hitter into the ninth, against Detroit. The closest call was Jim Northrup's liner back to the mound in the second. It hit Barber in the backside and he threw Northrup out. The Orioles eked out a 1-0 lead, but Barber was staggering all the way, walking seven in the first eight innings. He walked the first two batters in the ninth, then retired the next two. On the verge of achieving a pitcher's dream, he threw a wild pitch that allowed the tying run to score. Rattled, he walked the batter. No-hitter or not, Bauer brought in Stu Miller to get the final out.

With runners at first and third, Miller got Don Wert to slap a grounder up the middle that Luis Aparicio speared and flipped to second baseman Mark Belanger for the force out to end the inning. But Belanger dropped the ball as the winning run scored.

Barber became the second pitcher to lose a no-hit game. He walked 10, hit two, unleashed the wild pitch, and made a throwing error. He said, "I was pitching so bad that day that I should have gotten beat 10-1."[15]

He got worse. By July 4 Barber stood at 4-9 with a 4.10 ERA and no control. He had allowed seven bases on balls per nine innings. The Orioles dumped him to the Yankees for three minor leaguers. (Barber had earned a reputation as a Yankee-killer with a 15-10 record against them.)

"I'm not coming to the Yankees as a broken-down pitcher with nothing left," the 29-year-old said.[16] But his results didn't improve: 6-9, 4.05 with New York. One of the victories was the 100th of his career, a shutout of the Minnesota Twins. The 1967 Yankees were a broken-down team. They finished ninth.

The next spring Barber couldn't straighten his left arm and was sent down to Triple-A Syracuse. Rejoining the big club in June, he went 6-5 in 19 starts with a 3.23 ERA, no better than average in the Year of the Pitcher. The Yankees left him unprotected in the expansion draft after the 1968 season, but neither the new Kansas City Royals nor Seattle Pilots jumped at the chance to acquire a sore-armed 30-year-old pitcher. Seattle made Barber the 37th player chosen in the draft.

Pilots teammate Jim Bouton made Barber a villain in his celebrated 1969 diary, *Ball Four*. Bouton described watching Barber spend day after day taking heat treatment and cortisone shots for his arm, insisting all the while that it didn't hurt. Barber came out of a game in May after facing only three batters and didn't pitch again for three weeks. When he refused a rehab assignment in the minors, Bouton wrote, "'You son of a bitch,' I said to myself. 'You're the guy who won't go down in order to help out the club. Instead you hang around here, can't pitch, and now other guys are sent down because of you.'"[17] Barber spent more than a month on the disabled list and finished with a 4-7 record and 4.80 ERA. He was the losing pitcher in the final game in the Pilots' history.

Barber went to spring training in 1970 declaring himself pain-free and optimistic: "This could be my biggest year in baseball."[18] The Pilots released him a month later, just before the bankrupt franchise was transferred to Milwaukee.

Barber milked another five years out of his dying arm as a vagabond relief pitcher. Chicago Cubs: released. Atlanta Braves: released. California Angels: traded. Milwaukee Brewers: released. When the San Francisco Giants became the fifth team to release him, in August 1974, the handwriting on the wall looked like a mural. Barber hooked on with the Cardinals' Tulsa farm club and pitched the last six games of his career in Triple A. At 37, he still wasn't ready to give up. The next spring he wangled a tryout with the Cleveland Indians, managed by his former teammate Frank Robinson, but nothing came of it.

Barber owned a car-stereo business in Arizona, then moved to Las Vegas and opened a car-care shop. Jim Bouton sneered, "He has a bunch of cars lined up getting cortisone shots, whirlpool massage, and diathermy treatments."[19] (Barber never forgave Bouton for *Ball Four*.) He later worked as a manager in a car dealership and a hearing-aid salesman. Nearing retirement age, Barber drove a school bus for children with disabilities for several years.

In 1988 Barber was inducted into the Orioles Hall of Fame. "I'm not sure I have the kind of accomplishments that are worthy of this kind of honor," he said. "But I'll take it."[20] His final record shows 121 victories, 106 losses, and a 3.36 ERA.

Steve Barber died in Henderson, Nevada, on February 4, 2007, just short of his 69th birthday, of complications from pneumonia. His wife, Pat, their daughters Tracy and Danielle, and his son, Steve Jr., and daughter, Kelly, from his first marriage survived.

NOTES

1. Stanley and Helen Barber were living in the home of her parents, Sarah and Emil Johnson (a carpenter) at the time of the 1940 census.

2. Blair High alumni include bestselling author Nora Roberts, actress Goldie Hawn, Olympic gymnast Dominique Dawes, Watergate reporter Carl Bernstein, TV anchor Connie Chung, Internet provocateur Matt Drudge, and major leaguers Johnny Klippstein and Sonny Jackson.

3. George Minot, "Steve Barber Has Control So Now He's Big Leaguer," *Washington Post*, May 9, 1960: A20.

4. John Eisenberg, *From 33rd Street to Camden Yards: An Oral History of the Baltimore Orioles* (New York: Contemporary Books, 2001), 92.

5. Eisenberg, 93.

6. William Tanton, "Steve Barber Steps In," *Baltimore Sun* Sunday magazine, June 26, 1960: 184.

7. Eisenberg, 98.

8. Susan Reimer, "Barber Comes Home, Enters Through Hall," *Baltimore Sun*, August 6, 1988: 1B.

9. Eisenberg, 98.

10. Leslie Lieber, "Who's the Fastest Pitcher?" *This Week*, June 19, 1960: 11.

11. Doug Brown, "Greybeard Philley Filling Big Bill for Flag-Hungry Birds," *The Sporting News*, September 21, 1960: 7.

12. Lou Hatter, "Birds' Barber Draws Praise," *Baltimore Sun*, September 17, 1961: 1D.

13. Eisenberg, 167.

14. Eisenberg, 176.

15. Reimer, "Barber Comes Home." The first pitcher to lose a no-hitter was Ken Johnson of Houston, who lost to Cincinnati, 1-0, on April 23, 1964. Pete Rose reached on Johnson's ninth-inning error and scored on an error by Nellie Fox.

16. Jim Ogle, "Barber Delighted." *The Sporting News*, July 22, 1967: 15.

17. Jim Bouton, *Ball Four* (repr. New York: Collier Books, 1990), 180-181.

18. Hy Zimmerman, "Pilots' Painless Barber Impressive," *Seattle Times*, February 26, 1970: 66.

19. Bouton, 405.

20. Reimer, "Barber Comes Home."

STU MILLER

By Warren Corbett

THE ASTROPHYSICIST NEIL deGrasse Tyson estimates that the slowest pitch that could reach home plate on the fly would travel around 30 miles per hour.[1] Stu Miller didn't defy the laws of physics, but he challenged the equation that says Velocity = Success.

"He's got three speeds of pitches — slow, slower and reverse," the sportswriter Jim Murray said.[2] Murray described Miller's signature changeup as a moth flitting across the plate; others called it a butterfly.

Throwing fog instead of smoke, Miller was the relief ace for two pennant winners during a 16-year major-league career. The right-hander changed speeds on his fastball and curve, and delivered side-arm as well as overhand. He said his secret was throwing softly with the same arm speed as his fastball. Others thought the secret was his head fake. He jerked his head to the left an instant before releasing the ball. He called it a shrug, and insisted he didn't do it on purpose: "I can't help it. My head snaps involuntarily."[3] The unique motion discombobulated the batter's timing. Frank Robinson, who played with and against Miller, said, "(H)itters knew what was coming and they still couldn't hit it."[4]

Another sportswriter, Tex Maule, jeered, "It's doubtful that Miller could throw a baseball through a wet paper sack."[5] Miller quietly resented such put-downs. He hated being called a junkman. "I don't throw underhand or drop-kick the ball to the plate," he protested. "I don't throw a knuckle ball or forkball. I throw only three pitches — fast ball, curve and slider."[6] He said he had to have a decent fastball to set up his slow stuff. "Effective pitching relies simply on throwing the batter's timing off. Combine that with variety and control, you've got the advantage."[7]

To clear up some misconceptions: Encyclopedias say Miller was 5-feet-11-inches tall. Anyone who stood next to him knew better; several said 5-8 was more like it. His weight increased, by his own reckoning, from 150 pounds to 175 as he got older. He was routinely called "little Stu Miller," but no, he was not blown off the mound by a gust of wind during an All-Star Game.

Stuart Leonard Miller was born in Northampton, Massachusetts, on the day after Christmas in 1927, the second son of George and Edna Miller. The Miller family owned a furniture-manufacturing business, but the company went broke in the Depression. "It was a hardscrabble way of life," Stu said. "Dad didn't do much of anything because there wasn't any work. Somehow we got by, same as everybody else."[8] Stu contributed to the family treasury by digging potatoes for 10 cents an hour and delivering groceries.

He learned baseball from his father. His older brother, Gordon, was a left-handed pitcher, so Stu, like most little brothers, got the dirty job: catcher. They played sandlot ball; Stu didn't even try out for his high-school team. After graduation in 1945 he served two years in the US Navy as an aerologist (then the Navy term for a meteorologist), with sea duty aboard the light aircraft carrier Saipan. He also picked up pitching experience on service teams.

Miller's entry into professional baseball was as unlikely as his success in the game. He was hanging around home, driving a cab and preparing to start college in 1949 when the St. Louis Cardinals held a tryout camp in Northampton. "I had no idea about playing major-league baseball at all," he recalled. "Me at a hundred and forty-nine pounds."[9] He went to the tryout because he had nothing better to do and wasn't enthusiastic about college. He didn't have much of a fastball even as a 21-year-old, but St. Louis signed him for a $100 bonus and $150 a month. Miller thought the Cardinals needed warm bodies to fill the rosters of nearly two dozen farm clubs.

After giving up more than six runs per game in his first season, Miller had to repeat Class-D ball in 1950. His manager in Hamilton, Ontario, Vedie Himsl, taught him the changeup. "I didn't know what a changeup was," Miller said, "but he explained that it's a pitch that you throw with the same arm motion and it makes the hitter think it's a fastball, but it's not."[10] Miller caught on quickly and advanced to Triple A two years later.

He was enjoying his best season at Columbus in 1952—11-5, 2.34, four shutouts—while the parent club was trying out pitchers by the carload. The Cardinals had some old pitchers, some young pitchers, but few good pitchers. Asked for a report on Miller, Columbus manager Johnny Keane told the front office, "He will not impress you physically, but don't let that fool you. I guarantee he will win in the majors."[11]

Called up in August, Miller shut out the Cubs in his debut and allowed only one earned run in his first three starts, all complete games. National League hitters had never seen anything like him. He posted a 6-3 record and 2.05 ERA, giving up just 63 hits in 88 innings. Still, manager Eddie Stanky wasn't sold; the slight, quiet Miller reminded him of a stenographer. Stanky also resented the rookie's passion for bridge. (Miller qualified as a Junior Master in duplicate bridge while playing ball.) "Eddie Stanky couldn't stand me, and the feeling was mutual," Miller said.[12]

Stanky got it right; the league quickly caught up with Miller. He was bombed in his first start of 1953, and struggled to prove himself for the next four years. His problem is easy to spot: 19 home runs allowed in 137⅔ innings in 1953, 19 in 114 innings in '56. When he couldn't keep the ball down, he paid for it. He was demoted to the minors for the second half of 1954 and all of '55. "I just wasn't pitching well and I certainly didn't belong on a major-league roster," he said decades later.[13] On May 11, 1956, the Cardinals traded him to the Philadelphia Phillies in a swap of pitchers: Miller, Harvey Haddix, and Ben Flowers for Murry Dickson and Herm Wehmeier.

Miller showed no improvement in Philadelphia, and the Phils passed him on to the New York Giants. He opened the 1957 season in Triple A, but was called up in May and began to blossom when manager Bill Rigney used him primarily as a reliever. Miller's 3.63 ERA was by far the best since his abbreviated rookie year.

In the Giants' new home in San Francisco in 1958, Miller turned into a different pitcher at age 30. A really good one. He kept the ball in the park, his control improved, and his strikeout rate jumped to 5.9 per nine innings, fifth highest in the league. Opening the season in the bullpen, he didn't allow a run in five of his first six appearances. Rigney, short of pitching, put him into the rotation. His first start was a three-hit shutout. At season's end, Miller's 2.47 ERA led the league. In 20 starts and 21 relief appearances, his record was only 6-9, but the Giants scored no more than two runs in six of his losses.

Miller had always been more effective as a reliever than as a starter. He seldom completed a game and often weakened in his third and fourth times through the opposing lineup. In 1958 the difference was dramatic: 0.81 ERA in relief, 3.01 when starting. But baseball's conventional wisdom still held that the bullpen was for second-rate pitchers, so managers kept running Miller out as a starter.

That changed in 1959. The Giants acquired right-handers Sam Jones and Jack Sanford to fill out their rotation with lefties Johnny Antonelli and Mike McCormick. Rigney installed Miller as his bullpen stopper. Rigney used him in the usual fashion for the time, bringing him in whenever a starter faltered, whether it was the fourth inning or the ninth. Miller's calm temperament fit the relief role. Giants pitcher Billy O'Dell said, "The ballgame would be getting tense, and I'd look down at the end of the bench and Stu was working crossword puzzles."[14]

The Giants, with a powerful lineup including Willie Mays, Orlando Cepeda, and midseason call-up Willie McCovey, spent most of the '59 season atop the standings in a three-way race with the defending champion Milwaukee Braves and the surprising Los Angeles Dodgers. But their pitching was thin behind the first four starters and Miller, who started nine times with 50 games in relief. Rigney worked his reliable five into the ground in August and September, probably costing San Francisco the pennant.

The Giants were two games up on Los Angeles and Milwaukee when they faced the Dodgers in a three-game series beginning September 19. LA won both ends of a Saturday doubleheader to climb into a tie for the lead. Miller appeared in both games, throwing 55 pitches. In Sunday's finale, Rigney called on him in the ninth, but he had nothing left. He surrendered four runs (two inherited) as the Dodgers nailed down a sweep and stood alone in first place.

The Giants went on to lose five straight, but they still had a chance to tie for the pennant on the season's final day. McCormick held the Cardinals scoreless for seven innings, protecting a 1-0 lead. In the eighth two singles and an error loaded the bases, and McCormick issued his only walk of the game to force in the tying run. Miller relieved, making his 12th appearance in 25 days. Gino Cimoli's RBI single won the game for St. Louis and lost the pennant for San Francisco.

Miller could console himself with the knowledge that he had won his second consecutive ERA title; the newspaper stats showed him just ahead of his teammate Sam Jones. But when the official figures were posted, Jones came in at 2.826 to Miller's 2.844. Miller believed he had been robbed. He thought the league didn't like it when he won the title the year before with a losing record. Besides, he said, "I guess they just didn't want a junkball pitcher like me to win."[15] If there had been a conspiracy, it more probably would have gone Miller's way, because no black pitcher had led either league in ERA before Jones.

In 1960 an awful first half saw Miller's ERA rise above 7.00. He rebounded to finish at 3.90. The next year a new manager, Alvin Dark, used him exclusively in relief for the first time, and almost exclusively in the late innings. Miller prospered in the role, going 14-5 with a 2.66 ERA and a league-leading 17 saves. The save was not yet an official statistic, but *The Sporting News* had begun counting them. The baseball bible named Miller the NL's fireman of the year, based on a primitive formula of wins in relief plus saves, without accounting for blown saves. Miller blew eight opportunities, meaning he was less effective than the average pitcher in close games.

Miller made his only All-Star team in 1961 and stumbled into a legend. The first of two All-Star Games was played at San Francisco's Candlestick Park on an uncommonly hot July day—several fans collapsed—until the notorious wind kicked up in the eighth inning. Miller relieved in the ninth with the National League leading, 3–2, one out, and two runners on. As he came set to face his first batter, a blast of wind staggered him—he thought it was 65 mph, but probably not. "My whole body waved, and Stan Landes, the National League umpire behind the plate, called a balk on me. I went up to him and said, 'Stan, the wind pushed me.' He said, 'I know that, Stu, but rules are rules.'"[16]

The moment is calcified in history: The gale "blew little Stu Miller right off the mound."[17] He spent the rest of his life denying it. "I wasn't blown off that mound. I just waved a little. But I'll always be the guy who was blown away, no matter what I say. There were 44,000 people in the park that day, but over the years I bet I've had at least 100,000 people tell me they saw me flying in the air. You'd think I'd been blown out into the Bay."[18]

Almost forgotten in the hubbub, Miller was the game's winning pitcher. In 1961's second All-Star Game, with 16 family members watching in Boston, he worked three scoreless innings and struck out Mickey Mantle, Elston Howard, and Roy Sievers in succession just before the game was called because of rain with the score tied.

The 1962 Giants started strong and held first place for most of May, then spent the next four months chasing the Dodgers. Willie Mays anchored the league's most dangerous lineup with 49 home runs and a .999 OPS (on-base plus slugging percentage). Jack Sanford won 16 straight decisions. Miller had an up-and-down year, sharing late-inning duties with the veteran Don Larsen and young side-armer Bobby Bolin, but he came through when it counted most.

The Giants trailed Los Angeles by two games going into their final series of the season against Houston. Miller pitched in both ends of a doubleheader, working six scoreless innings, as the teams split the first two games. The next day the Giants had to win or go home. Miller relieved in the eighth with the score tied. He set down the last six batters in a row and Mays delivered a game-winning homer to lift San Francisco into a first-place tie with Los Angeles. Both teams had won 101 games.

The Giants won the first game of the best-of-three playoff and took a 5–0 lead into the sixth inning of Game Two. When Sanford walked the leadoff batter, Miller took over and pitched to four men, retiring only one. Two runs came in; Billy O'Dell and Don Larsen conspired to cough up five more before the inning was over. The Dodgers went on to win, 8–7, but the Giants took the third game to give San Francisco its first World Series.

Alvin Dark had evidently lost confidence in Miller after the playoff debacle. In the World Series Dark used him only to mop up in two games that were already lost as the Yankees beat the Giants in seven. Although Miller saved 19 regular-season games in 23 opportunities, his ERA jumped to 4.12, reflecting his inconsistent performance. In December the Giants shipped him to Baltimore in a six-player deal. The key man for the Orioles was a power-hitting young catcher, John Orsino, while the Giants wanted left-hander Billy Hoeft to balance their bullpen.

Miller wasn't surprised by the trade, but it upended his family life. He had married Jayne Munro, a hometown girl, after his rookie season, and they settled in the Bay area. They raised four sons and two daughters. Miller had opened an insurance agency, Miller & Merritt. Traded from coast to coast, he brought his family along during the season. He swapped houses with one of the men he was traded for, pitcher Jack Fisher. Miller rented Fisher's Baltimore home and Fisher took the Millers' house in San Mateo. Miller continued renting his home to Giants players for the rest of his career, even though the place seemed to be jinxed; his first three tenants were soon traded.

Miller joined a young Orioles team that had fallen to seventh place in 1962. Manager Billy Hitchcock used him to finish games, although the term *closer* did not yet exist and his role was far different from the modern closer's. He usually entered in the seventh inning or later and was a true fireman, often called in with runners on base. At 35, Miller had his busiest season with an American League-record 71 appearances.

AL hitters, seeing Miller's array of junk and quirky motion for the first time, were flummoxed. He struck out more than one batter per inning in 1963, a rare feat in that era, as opponents batted just .232 against him. He was credited with 26 saves, an unofficial major-league record (later recalculated to be 27), and blew only three save chances. He was the first to win *The Sporting News* fireman award for a second time. Although Steve Barber won 20 games, local broadcasters and writers voted Miller the team's most valuable player.

Under new manager Hank Bauer, Miller recorded 22 saves in 1964, and turned in his best all-around season in 1965. He did not allow a run in 17 straight appearances covering 31 innings. His ERA shrank to 1.89 with a 14-7 record, 24 saves and only one blown save. He was again named the club's MVP.

Except for the 1962 season, the Orioles had been pennant contenders since 1960, but always fell short. In 1966 two new stars put them over the top. Frank Robinson came from Cincinnati in a trade and emerged as the team leader. Robinson won the Triple

Crown as the Orioles battered opposing pitchers. They led the league in runs scored, batting average, on-base percentage, and slugging.

Twenty-year-old Jim Palmer, in his first year as a starter, won 15 games to lead a young rotation. Lefty Steve Barber, 28, was the ace, joined by Dave McNally, 23; Wally Bunker, 21; and John Miller, 25. But the youngsters were inconsistent, and Bauer was impatient. General manager Harry Dalton built a veteran bullpen behind them: Miller, 6-foot-6 sidearmer Dick Hall, swingman Eddie Watt, and Moe Drabowsky, an undistinguished 30-year-old prankster who turned into an outstanding middle reliever. When Miller and Hall suffered arm problems early in the season, Dalton acquired knuckleballer Eddie Fisher, who had won *The Sporting News* fireman award with the White Sox the year before, giving the club a five-deep bullpen.

Baltimore needed all bullpen hands on deck, because the starters completed only 23 games, the second fewest in the league. After Barber went down with a sore elbow in July, the relievers shouldered an even bigger load. Fisher shared the late-inning responsibilities with Miller; they combined for 14 victories and 32 saves.

The bats and the bullpen carried the Orioles to the pennant, but Bauer needed only one relief pitcher in the World Series against the Los Angeles Dodgers. Drabowsky relieved McNally and picked up the win in Game One, then Palmer, Bunker, and McNally pitched consecutive complete-game shutouts to sweep the favored Dodgers.

Miller finished 406 games in his career, but he got his most famous final out on April 30, 1967. Steve Barber started against Detroit and had a terrible day. He walked 10 batters, plunked two, threw a wild pitch, and committed an error — but he didn't allow a hit through 8⅔ innings. The Orioles led 1-0 in the ninth when Barber walked the first two hitters and bounced a wild pitch in front of the plate to let in the tying run. After another walk, Hank Bauer removed his no-hit pitcher and brought in Miller with two away. Miller induced a grounder through the middle that was flagged down by shortstop Luis Aparicio, who flipped to Mark Belanger at second for the out that would end the inning. But Belanger dropped the ball as the winning run crossed the plate. Miller recorded the third out, one batter too late. The Orioles were only the second team to lose a no-hitter.

The 39-year-old Miller's age caught up with him in 1967. He needed more rest and appeared in only 42 games, his lightest workload since he began relieving full time. He posted an excellent 2.55 ERA, but failed too often with the game on the line. He gave up the winning run in seven tie games and blew four saves in 12 opportunities. With a 3-10 record, Miller recognized that his time was up in Baltimore. He told a writer, "I'll be pitching somewhere next year."[19]

The Orioles sold Miller to the Atlanta Braves in April 1968, but his new club released him three weeks later. The Cardinals gave him an unsuccessful trial with their Triple-A Tulsa farm club. He hoped to hang on for the expansion draft that was scheduled in the fall to stock two new big-league teams, but he confessed years later that he had lost the desire to play. By midseason Miller had signed on as pitching coach for the Giants farm team in Fresno, California.

When he retired, Miller ranked third in career saves with 153, behind Hoyt Wilhelm and Roy Face. The save did not become an official statistic until 1969, and managers had no thought of holding back their top relievers for save situations, much less reserving them for the ninth inning. Miller pitched more than one inning in 107 of his saves.

Miller returned to his insurance business in the San Francisco Bay area, and later owned a liquor store for many years. He died at 87 on January 4, 2015, at his home in Cameron Park, California. Jayne Munro Miller, his wife of 62 years, died a month after her husband.

NOTES

1   Mike Fast, "How Slow Could You Throw?" *The Hardball Times*, June 4, 2010. hardballtimes.com/tht-live/how-slow-could-you-throw/, accessed January 28, 2016. See the comments for Tyson's estimate. A 30-mph pitch would have to be an "eephus," leaving the pitcher's hand on an upward trajectory of about 45 degrees.

NO-HITTERS

2 Jim Murray, "The Junk Dealer," *Los Angeles Times*, August 4, 1961. In Miller's file at the National Baseball Hall of Fame library, Cooperstown, New York.

3 Walter Judge, "Li'l Stu Fools 'Em With Head Motion," *San Francisco Examiner*, January 26, 1959, in HOF file.

4 John Eisenberg, *From 33rd Street to Camden Yards: An Oral History of the Baltimore Orioles* (New York: Contemporary Books, 2001), 171.

5 Tex Maule, "The Young Pitchers Take Command," *Sports Illustrated*, June 26, 1961. si.com/vault/1961/06/26/581768/the-young-pitchers-take-command, accessed January 26, 2016.

6 "Stu Miller Explains How," Associated Press-*Baltimore Sun*, April 4, 1966: C4.

7 Lou Hatter, "Miller Edgy as Speaker," *Baltimore Sun*, September 8, 1965: 19.

8 Stu Miller, telephone interviews by Ed Evans, 2013.

9 Mike Mandel, *The S.F. Giants, an Oral History* (self-published, 1979), 59.

10 Miller interview by Ed Evans.

11 Robert L. Burnes, "Stu Miller fooled everybody," *St. Louis Globe-Democrat*, July 16, 1980: D2.

12 Miller interview by Ed Evans.

13 Mandel, 60.

14 Danny Peary, ed., *We Played the Game* (New York: Black Dog & Leventhal, 1994), 508.

15 Mandel, 60.

16 Ron Fimrite, "Gone With the Wind?" *Sports Illustrated*, September 1, 1986. si.com/vault/1986/09/01/113879/gone-with-the-wind-the-giants-want-out-of-blustery-candlestick-park-and-one-of-these-days-they-just-might-get-their-wish, accessed January 26, 2016. The balk rule, 6.02(a)(1), states that a balk should be called when "The pitcher, while touching his plate, makes any motion naturally associated with his pitch and fails to make such delivery. ..." Official Baseball Rules, 2015 edition.

17 Bob Stevens, "Giants Label Lefty Pierce Prize Catch," *The Sporting News*, January 3, 1962: 17.

18 Fimrite, "Gone With the Wind?"

19 Doug Brown, "Stu Pushes 40, Set for Relief Pull Again," *The Sporting News*, December 9, 1967: 41.

APRIL 30, 1967: DETROIT TIGERS 2, BALTIMORE ORIOLES 1, AT MEMORIAL STADIUM, BALTIMORE

STEVE BARBER AND STU MILLER COMBINE FOR NO-HITTER IN A LOSS

By Jimmy Keenan

IN LATE APRIL OF 1967, THE Detroit Tigers traveled to Baltimore to play four games against the defending world champion Orioles at Memorial Stadium. The Orioles' Dave McNally bested the Tigers' Denny McLain in the first contest, 5-3. Detroit's Mickey Lolich evened the score the following day by defeating Wally Bunker, 4-2. On April 30, 1967, the two teams wrapped up the series with a Sunday afternoon doubleheader. Orioles manager Hank Bauer gave the starting assignment to southpaw Steve Barber in the opener, while Tigers skipper Mayo Smith went with right-hander Earl Wilson.

Barber, making his third start of the season, had been battling tendonitis in his pitching elbow since late in the 1966 season. The Birds lefty retired the side in the first inning without giving up a hit, allowing only a walk to Tigers center fielder Mickey Stanley. This would be a common theme for Barber throughout the game.

Wilson, who entered the game with a 12-5 lifetime record against Baltimore, allowed just two singles, one to Andy Etchebarren and the other to Frank Robinson, in the first seven innings. On the Orioles' side, Barber was even better, holding the Tigers hitless through eight frames. The downside was Detroit had a man on base every inning except the fifth via a walk, error or hit batsman.

The Birds finally got to Wilson in the bottom of the eighth. Curt Blefary started off with a base on balls. A sacrifice bunt from Woody Held moved Blefary over to second. Wilson then intentionally walked Charlie Lau, who pinch-hit for Etchebarren to get to Barber. The Orioles pitcher worked Wilson for a free pass to load the bases. Luis Aparicio followed with a sacrifice fly to Tigers right fielder Al Kaline, Blefary scoring on the play. Kaline's throw from the outfield got by catcher Bill Freehan allowing Lau and Barber to advance a base. With runners on second and third, Baltimore's Russ Snyder flew out to first baseman Norm Cash to end the inning.

Barber, with his no-hitter still intact, was continuing to have difficulty throwing strikes, walking Cash and Ray Oyler to start off the ninth. Dick Tracewski was sent in to run for Cash while Jake Wood replaced Oyler on the bases. The next batter, Wilson, helped his own cause by executing a sacrifice bunt that advanced both runners.

Willie Horton, pinch-hitting for Dick McAuliffe, popped up to catcher Larry Haney, who had replaced Etchebarren, for the first out. With the count 1-2 on Mickey Stanley, Barber threw a changeup that bounced in the dirt past Haney. Tracewski came home from third on the errant toss with Wood moving over to third. Barber eventually walked Stanley, his 10th free pass of the afternoon, which drew manager Hank Bauer out of the Oriole dugout. When Bauer got to the mound he told Barber, "I tried to get it for you," referring to the no-hitter. A frustrated Barber replied, "If you can't get the ball over the plate you don't deserve to win."[1] Barber received a rousing ovation from the 26,884 fans at Memorial Stadium as he walked off the field.

With the score tied at one apiece, Bauer brought in Stu Miller from the Orioles bullpen. The first batter he faced, Don Wert, smacked a ground ball up the middle that shortstop Luis Aparicio ranged far to his left and caught on the run. Aparicio then gave a backhanded toss to second baseman Mark Belanger, who had just entered the game as a defensive replacement, for the force out. The normally sure-handed Belanger's bare hand got in the way of the throw causing the ball to drop out of his glove. The error allowed Wood to score the Tigers' second run of the game. The next hitter, Al Kaline, hit a sharp grounder that caromed off third baseman's Brooks Robinson's glove. The ball took a fortuitous bounce into the waiting hands of Aparicio, who threw to Belanger covering second for final out of the inning.

Fred Gladding came in to pitch the ninth for Detroit. He retired Frank Robinson and Brooks Robinson on fly balls before striking out Mike Epstein to preserve the 2-1 Tigers win.

There seems to be at least one outstanding defensive gem in every no-hitter and in this game it was Barber who made the play. The Birds pitcher pounced off the mound and threw out Jim Northrup at first base after taking a hard shot off his leg from the Detroit left fielder in the second inning.

Detroit's Norm Cash spoke to the press about Barber after the game, "All his pitches were really moving. He was hard to hit. None of his pitches were down the middle."[2]

Speaking to reporters about coming out of the game without giving up a hit Barber remarked,"If I hadn't been pitching a no-hitter I would have been out long before that. I was out of gas in the fifth inning. I'm not upset about losing the no-hitter. I'm more concerned about losing the game. No-hitters are not worth anything in the books unless you win."[3]

Orioles right fielder Frank Robinson joked with Barber who was icing his sore elbow in the training room, "Next time give up a hit in the first inning, will you Steve? You make me feel like an old 31 standing out there through that."[4]

Barber came close to pitching a no-hitter earlier in the season. In his first start of the year on April 16 he held the California Angels hitless for eight innings, allowing only three walks, until Jim Fregosi doubled with one out in the ninth. Summing up his pitching performance against the Tigers, Barber told Doug Brown of *The Sporting News*, "I was aiming at the middle all day, but I couldn't hit it. I had no idea where I was throwing. I haven't been so wild since I was a rookie in 1960. I can't understand it. But I'm going to find out. I don't think Hank [Orioles manager Hank Bauer] could stand this all season."[5]

AUTHOR'S NOTE

Barber and Stu Miller's collaborative no-hit effort was the second time in baseball history that multiple pitchers had combined to lose a no-hitter. On May 26, 1956, the Reds' Johnny Klippstein, Hershell Freeman, and Johnny Black combined to hold the Milwaukee Braves hitless for nine innings. Black gave up a double with two outs in the 10th before serving up the game-winner in the 11th inning, losing 2-1. Prior to 1967, the other major-league pitcher to lose a no-hitter in a nine-inning game was the Astros Ken Johnson who lost to the Cincinnati Reds 1-0 on April 23, 1964.

NOTES

1 Murray Chass, "Ninth Inning Walks Give Tigers 2-1 Triumph," *The Day*, May 1 1967, 27.

2 Ibid.

3 Ibid.

4 Doug Brown, "Steve Drops 2-1 Verdict to Bengals," *The Sporting News* May 13, 1967, 7.

5 Ibid.

VIDA BLUE

By Richard J. Puerzer

VIDA BLUE BURST ONTO the scene in major-league baseball as a fireballing left-hander for the Oakland A's and served as one of the primary characters in the A's streak of five division championships and three World Series championships. His career, which spanned from 1969 to 1986, would see high points, including the multiple World Series championships and outstanding pitching performances, as well as dark days, such as his suspension from the game for drug use and his involvement in one of the most publicized contract holdouts in the history of the game. In many ways, the ups and downs of Blue's baseball career, both on and off of the field, reflected the times during which he played perhaps more than any other of his contemporaries.

Vida Rochelle Blue, Jr. was born on July 28, 1949, in Mansfield, Louisiana, a small town in the northern part of the state. He was the eldest of six children born to Vida Blue, Sr. and Sallie Blue. His father was a laborer, and Blue remembered having everything he needed, although not everything that he wanted, as he grew up.[1] He recalled Mansfield as a town that was still segregated, with a white high school and a black high school, DeSoto High, which Blue attended. As a youngster Blue played baseball and football with his peers. He was a good athlete, and could throw a baseball very hard when he was still quite young.

When he entered high school, the school did not have a baseball team. However, the principal recognized Blue's talent and formed a school baseball team around him.[2] Blue's pitching prowess got the attention of scouts, including Kansas City A's scout Ray Swallow. Despite Blue's wildness—he once pitched a no-hitter and struck out 21 in a seven-inning game, but lost the game due to ten walks—his skill was evident. Blue was equally renowned as a high-school football player, starring as a quarterback. He was recruited by major colleges, including Notre Dame, Purdue, and Houston. Houston was recruiting Blue to play quarterback at a time when there were no African-Americans playing quarterback for major colleges. But Blue's father died during his senior year in high school, and he decided that he needed to support his family. Baseball would provide that support sooner than football might. He was selected by the Kansas City Athletics in the second round of the 1967 draft and was offered a two-year contract a $12,500 per year. Although he later said he had a stronger desire to play football than baseball, Blue signed with the A's.

Blue's professional baseball career began in the Arizona winter instructional league in 1967. He pitched in nine games, striking out 26 batters while walking 22 in 34 innings. At age 18, he reported to spring training with the A's for the 1968 season, then was assigned to the Burlington Bees of the Class A Midwest League. Blue started the season opener against the Quad City Angels and struck out 17 while giving up only three hits in eight innings. On June 19, in the first game of a doubleheader, Blue pitched a no-hitter in the seven-inning game. Throughout the season, Blue developed his curveball to go along with his dominant fastball, and improved his control. He finished with a record of 8-11 in 24 games, pitching 152 innings and striking out 231 while walking 80.[3]

For the 1969 season, Blue was assigned to Double-A Birmingham. He pitched in 15 Southern League games, going 10-3, with 112 strikeouts and 52 walks in 104 innings. Oakland A's owner Charlie Finley was anxious to bring Blue up to the majors, seeing him as his next pitching star. Blue was called up in July, and made his major-league debut on July 20, starting against the California Angels. He lost the game, pitching into the sixth inning and giving up home runs to Aurelio Rodriguez and Jim Spencer. He started three more games, including a win on July 29 over the New York Yankees, before being sent

to the bullpen for the rest of the season. In his first major league season, he finished with a record of 1-1, pitched 42 innings, struck out 24 while walking 18, and finished with an earned-run average of 6.64. Joe DiMaggio, then a coach with the A's, said of Blue, "It was a shame to bring up a kid like that when he hasn't pitched two pro years. He throws as hard as anybody, but he hasn't learned to pitch yet."[4]

Blue was sent to the Triple-A Iowa Oaks (American Association) to start the 1970 season. There he crossed paths with fellow pitcher Juan Pizarro. Blue learned a great deal from the veteran Pizarro, and later said that "[Pizarro] helped me more than any single person in my career."[5] With Pizarro's help, Blue made adjustments in his delivery that helped him to achieve greatness. He was rested for a few weeks in the middle of the season because of an injury, but came back to finish the season. In 17 games, Blue put together a record of 12-3 while striking out 165 in 133 innings.

He was called up to the A's in September, and started the first game of a Labor Day doubleheader against the White Sox in Chicago's Comiskey Park. Although he helped himself by hitting a three-run home run, he was knocked out of the game after giving up four runs in less than five innings. However, in his next outing he pitched a complete-game one-hitter against the Kansas City Royals, giving up a single to Pat Kelly with two outs in the eighth inning. After a lackluster start against the Milwaukee Brewers, Blue faced the division-leading Minnesota Twins on September 21. He was matched against Jim Perry, who would win 23 games and the Cy Young Award that season. Blue was the star that night, however, throwing a no-hitter and walking only one batter. Finley telephoned the locker room after the game to congratulate his new star pitcher and tell him he would receive a $2,000 bonus for the performance. Blue made two more starts that season and finished the season as one of the young star pitchers in baseball. Along with Catfish Hunter, Blue Moon Odom, and Rollie Fingers, the A's pitching staff was one of the primary reasons the A's would have high expectations for the next few seasons.

Although Blue made a spectacular splash in 1970, his 1971 season ranked among the great pitching seasons of all time. The A's made the franchise's first postseason appearance since 1931. It may have been their best season of the 1970s despite the fact that they won the World Series in the following three seasons, 1972-1974.

Blue pitched the 1971 season opener for the A's in Washington against the Senators, and took the loss, pitching only into the second inning. He then won ten straight games, including nine complete games, and over the course of the season received the attention of the nation. He appeared on the cover of *Sports Illustrated* and *Time*. As a hard-throwing left-hander, the press compared Blue favorably to Sandy Koufax. However, this comparison was clearly difficult for Blue as Koufax was one of the greatest pitchers ever, and his prowess was nearly impossible to match. Veteran player Tommy Davis was one of Blue's best friends and a roommate that season. Davis helped him to navigate through the heavy load of press requests, as well other demands for his time.

Anything Blue did drew the attention of the press. For example, it became known that he carried two dimes in his pocket when he pitched. Although it was likely a charm Blue used in his pursuit of winning 20 games, he would not verify that to the press, which drew even more attention.

Blue's start on July 9 against the California Angels was perhaps his best performance of the season. Although he did not get a decision in the game (he was going for his 18th win), he went 11 innings, gave up seven hits, no walks, and no runs while striking out 17 batters. The A's eventually won the game 1-0 in 20 innings. In his next appearance, Blue started the All-Star Game for the American League. Although he gave up home runs to Henry Aaron and Johnny Bench, he was the winning pitcher, the youngest in All-Star Game history. Blue's performance declined slightly in the second half of the season. He won his 20th game on August 7, and won his next two starts, raising the question of whether he could win 30 games for the season. But after number 22, he won only two and lost four of his last nine starts of the season. Surely he tired as the season wore on. The previous season, between the minors and majors, Blue pitched only 171 innings. In 1971, he pitched 312 innings. He finished the season with a record of 24-8 and a league-leading ERA of 1.82, and allowed the fewest runners per inning in the American League.

In the American League Championship Series, Blue faced off against the defending champion Baltimore Orioles and pitcher Dave McNally in Game One in Baltimore. The Orioles matched the A's in wins, with 101, and the opening game would be a test of Blue. He had a 3-0 lead going into the bottom of the fourth inning, but gave up a run in that inning, and four more in the eighth to lose the game. The A's were swept in three games, bringing an anticlimactic close to Blue's magical season.

Despite his dominant regular-season performance, Blue had competition for the American League Cy Young Award. Detroit's Mickey Lolich had surpassed Blue in wins with 25 to Blue's 24, and in strikeouts, 308 to 301 (although Lolich pitched a staggering 376 innings). However, Blue edged out Lolich to win the Cy Young Award. Blue actually had an easier time winning the American League Most Valuable Player Award, finishing well ahead of teammate Sal Bando in the voting.

In 1971 Blue became involved in his first controversy with owner Charlie Finley. Finley offered Blue $2,000 to change his middle name legally to "True." The always creative Finley saw the nickname as another way to market his pitching superstar. Blue declined the offer. He liked his name, thought it unique as it was, and had no desire to change it. Finley however would not let the idea rest. When Blue pitched, his name appeared on the scoreboard as "True Blue." Finley instructed the A's radio and television announcers to refer to Blue by the nickname. Blue asked them to stop, and also asked the team's public-relations people not to refer to him as True Blue in press releases or to use the name on the scoreboard. This situation began the friction between Blue and Finley that blew up after the end of the season.

After his spectacular 1971 season, Blue demanded a pay raise. In 1971 he had made $14,750 in salary and $6,365.58 as his share of the postseason money, and also got a Cadillac as a bonus from Finley. Finley offered a raise, but not nearly what Blue wanted. Bob Gerst, an attorney representing Blue, presented an opening offer to Finley of $115,000. Later he told Finley that Blue would accept $85,000, which was a little less than the average salary paid to the top ten highest paid pitchers in baseball. Finley said he would pay Blue no more than $50,000. Finley held firm, making the negotiations public and declaring that Blue would not be seeking so much if he had not hired a lawyer to represent him. Both sides made their case to the press and the public, and the acrimonious situation became referred to as "The Holdout." The situation also served to elevate scrutiny of the reserve clause, which was under new attack by the players. Marvin Miller, director of the Players Association, was critical of Finley and the reserve system. The holdout extended into spring training. On March 16 Blue and Gerst held a televised press conference to announce that Blue was withdrawing from baseball to take a position with the Dura Steel Products Company. While Blue actually did work for the company for a time, this was obviously an effort to combat Finley as it was clearly Blue's desire to play baseball.

When the season started, Blue was placed on the restricted list, meaning he could not play for the first 30 days of the season. The major-league season was delayed ten days by a players strike in spring training, and opened on April 15 without Vida Blue. In late April Commissioner Bowie Kuhn organized a meeting between Finley, Blue, and Gerst. They reached an agreement on a $63,000 deal. However, Finley and Blue couldn't agree on the wording of the announcement of the agreement. Finley did not want to appear as conceding anything, and insisted that he was paying Blue $50,000, an additional $5,000 signing bonus, plus $8,000 for Blue's college fund. Blue wanted the deal to state what it was: payment of $63,000. Finally, on May 2, Blue signed for the package.[6]

Although Blue had missed only 18 playing days, he had not been conditioning and practicing as he would have during spring training and was not ready to pitch. He did not make his first appearance, which was only one inning long, until May 24. The 1972 season was tough for Blue. Although he did post a relatively good ERA of 2.80 and allowed only 165 baserunners in 151 innings, he finished with a disappointing record of 6-10. His team, of course, won the American League West and faced the Detroit Tigers in the League Championship Series. Blue pitched exclusively out of the buillpen, pitching middle relief in Games One, Three, and Four. In each appearance, the games were in the balance, and Blue acquitted himself well. In the fifth and decisive game, Blue relieved Blue Moon Odom in the sixth inning of a 2-1 game, and pitched the final four innings for the save. In the World Series against the Cincinnati Reds, Blue pitched in relief in Game One, picking up the save, as well as in Games Three and Four. With the A's leading three games to two, he started Game Six. He was not as sharp as a starter as he had been in relief, and allowed three runs, including a Johnny Bench home run, in 5⅔ innings, and took the loss. The A's won Game Seven,

In 1973 Blue returned to form as an All-Star-caliber pitcher. He went 20-9, with an ERA of 3.28. While he was not the power pitcher that he was in 1971, striking out 158 in 263⅔ innings, he was described by many as a smarter pitcher. A *Sports Illustrated* article quoted teammate Sal Bando as saying, "In the first part of 1971 Vida was overpowering everybody, now he is overmatching them."[7] The article described Blue's pitching style: "He jogs out to his position and works with quick efficiency, throwing his left-handed darts out of a fluid, high-kicking motion." Blue's pitching repertoire included his highly regarded fastball as well as a good curveball and changeup.

For the first four months of the 1973 season, Blue pitched well, but was often inconsistent. He hit his stride in August, winning six straight starts, including four complete games. He put together another streak of five consecutive wins in September, helping to lead the A's to a division win over the Kansas City Royals. In the American League Championship Series, Blue started Game One against the Baltimore Orioles' ace, Jim Palmer. Blue did not make it out of the first inning, giving up three hits and two walks before being relieved by Horacio Piña. Baltimore got four runs in the inning, and won, 6-0. Blue again faced Palmer in Game Four and pitched much better. Through six innings he shut out the Orioles, giving up only two hits as the A's held a 4-0 lead. However, after getting one out in the seventh, Blue gave up a walk to Earl Williams, a single to Don Baylor, an RBI single to Brooks Robinson, and a three-run home run to Andy Etchebarren, tying the game, 4-4. He was relieved by Rollie Fingers, who went on to lose the game, 5-4. In the World Series against the New York Mets, Blue's postseason troubles continued. He started Games Two and Five, both against Jerry Koosman. In Game Two, a high-scoring affair, Blue gave up solo home runs to Cleon Jones and Wayne Garrett. He was relieved in the sixth inning after allowing two baserunners who would later score. The Mets went on to win the game 10-7 in 12 innings.

In Game Five, Blue gave up two runs in 5⅔ innings and lost to Koosman who, with reliever Tug McGraw, shut out the A's, 2-0. The A's won the Series, softening the effects of Blue's lackluster pitching.

In 1974, although his won-lost record was not as impressive as in 1973, Blue pitched equally well. He finished with a record of 17-15 and an ERA of 3.25. He was durable, making 40 starts, and struck out 174 batters in 282⅓ innings. The A's faced off again against the Orioles in the AL Championship Series. With the series tied one game apiece, Blue started Game Three, matched up again against Jim Palmer. Unlike 1973, Blue pitched brilliantly. He pitched two-hit, no-walk shutout, striking out seven in the 1-0 win. In the World Series against the Los Angeles Dodgers, Blue started Games Two and Five, matched up against Don Sutton in both games. In Game Two he was bested by the Dodgers, giving up a run in the second and a two-run homer to Joe Ferguson in the sixth, taking the 3-2 loss. In Game Five Blue pitched five shutout innings before giving up two tying runs in the sixth. After allowing a walk in the seventh, Blue was relieved by Blue Moon Odom, who went on to win the game for the A's.

The 1975 season was Vida Blue's best since his masterful 1971 season. He started the All-Star Game and finished the season with a record of 22-11 and an ERA of 3.01. With the departure of Catfish Hunter to the Yankees, Blue and Ken Holtzman starred on the A's pitching staff and helped to lead the A's to their best record since 1971. Among his pitching highlights that season, Blue was the starter and one of four A's pitchers to pitch a combined no-hitter against the California Angels on September 28, in the last game of the season. However, after three straight World Series championships, the A's were swept in the AL Championship Series by the Boston Red Sox. Blue started Game Two against Reggie Cleveland. He gave up a two-run home run in the fourth inning to Carl Yastrzemski and two more hits before being relieved. Although he had ten more seasons in the major leagues, this was Blue's last postseason appearance. Over his career, his postseason numbers were unexceptional, with a record of 1-5 and an ERA of 4.31 in 17 appearances.

The 1976 season was another controversial year in Blue's career, although the controversy was not of his doing. Starting with the departure of Catfish Hunter to the Yankees before the 1975 season and the trade of Reggie Jackson and Ken Holtzman to the Orioles before the 1976 season, the dynastic A's were being dismantled. Through mid-June, the A's were in fifth place in the West Division, 11 games behind the Royals. Blue had a record of 6-6 in 15 starts, with an ERA of 3.09. Then, just a few hours before the June 15 trade deadline, Charlie Finley announced that he was selling Blue to the New York Yankees for $1.5 million, and Joe Rudi and Rollie Fingers to the Red Sox for $2 million. However, the transactions were held up by Commissioner Bowie Kuhn. Kuhn and Finley had battled over a number of issues over the years, but this event brought their rancorous relationship to a breaking point. In retrospect, the attempted sale of these players was yet another step in the process of transitioning from the rule of the reserve system and moving toward free agency for players. It foreshadowed transactions in the years to come. Kuhn justified his concern with the transactions, stating: "The issue is whether the assignment of the contracts is appropriate or not under the circumstances. That's the issue I have to wrestle with. I have to consider these transactions in the best interest of baseball."[8]

On the 18th Kuhn announced that the sale of the three players would not be in the best interests of baseball, and disallowed them. Blue thus remained with the A's. However, with all of the legal threats made by Finley after Kuhn's ruling, Blue did not pitch again until July 2. Both he and the A's improved over the remainder of the season. Blue finished 1976 with a record of 18-13 and an ERA of 2.35, and the A's finished in second place, 2½ games behind the Royals.

In 1977 the team was truly dismantled, not by Finley's actions, but by his inaction in signing his players who were now eligible for free agency. Joe Rudi, Rollie Fingers, and Sal Bando, who had all been with the team throughout the championship years, left the A's via free agency. However, Blue had signed a three-year contract before the "trade" to the Yankees, and was ineligible for free agency. The 1977 season was a forgettable one for Blue. He led the league in losses with a record of 14-19, and had an ERA of 3.83. The A's finished last in the American League West, behind even the expansion Seattle Mariners.

During 1978 spring training, Blue was traded to the San Francisco Giants, giving him a new opportunity. For Blue the A's got seven players and $300,000. The new environment with the Giants and distance from Charlie Finley helped to restore his career as he became the ace of the Giants' pitching staff. The Giants were a solid squad, and were in first place as late as August 15 before fading and finishing in third for the 1978 season. Blue started the All-Star Game for the National League, making him the first pitcher to start the game for both leagues. He had a very good year overall, going 18-10 with a 2.79 ERA. He finished third in the balloting for the NL Cy Young Award and was named *The Sporting News* National League Pitcher of the Year. Although he was only 28 years old and his career would extend on for several years, 1978 was Blue's last great year. In 1979 he and the Giants saw a significant decline. Blue finished the season with a record of 14-14 and an ERA of 5.01 while the Giants finished 19½ games under .500 and in fourth place. In 1980 Blue rebounded a bit, with a record of 14-10 and an ERA of 2.97. In the strike-shortened 1981 season, he went 8-6 with a 2.45 ERA. It was the first full season in Blue's career in which he did not win 14 or more games. He did pitch and get the win in the All-Star Game, becoming the only pitcher to win the game for each league.

On March 30, 1982, at the end of spring training, Blue was traded with another player to the Kansas City Royals for four players. He pitched pretty well for the Royals, with a record of 13-12 an ERA of 3.78, and led the pitching staff in strikeouts. He did fade at the end of the season. After throwing a one-hitter against the Mariners on September 13, Blue started four more games, losing his last three decisions while his ERA grew from 3.36 to 3.78. In 1983 Blue struggled mightily. After seven starts and a record of 0-3 he was relegated to the bullpen. He stayed in the pen and made spot starts, but did not pitch well in either role. With a record of 0-5 and an ERA of 6.01, he was released by the Royals on August 5.

At the time, Blue's problems on the field paled in comparison with his problems off the field. Blue and Royals teammates Willie Wilson, Jerry Martin, and Willie Mays Aikens were implicated in buying cocaine. Blue pleaded guilty to cocaine possession and served 81 days in prison. On December 15, 1983, he was suspended for a year by Commissioner Kuhn. He was out for the 1984 season, then after being reinstated he signed with the Giants in the spring of 1985. Considering that he had missed a full season, Blue pitched respectably as both a starter and reliever, going 8-8 with a 4.47 ERA in 1985. In 1986, he returned to the Giants, pitching exclusively as a starter, and went 10-10 with an ERA of 3.27. Blue was a free agent after the season and signed with the A's for 1987, but abruptly retired during spring training. It was rumored that he had tested positive for drugs and retired rather than face another possible drug suspension. In announcing his retirement, Blue suggested that he still struggled with drug addiction, stating, "I reached the point where I had to choose between baseball and life."[9] In an autobiography published in 2011, he indicated that he had struggled with substance abuse for much of his career: "Along with all the glory that I'd achieved, there was a growing darkness reaching for me. And the light began to dim as early as 1972."[10] It makes one wonder what his career might have been but for his struggle with drugs.

In 1992 Blue became eligible for election to the Baseball Hall of Fame. He received a modicum of support in the four years he was considered, with his highest vote total, 8.7 percent, occurring in 1993. He was automatically removed from the ballot in 1995 because of his low vote totals. Some have wondered why Blue did not receive more serious consideration for the Hall of Fame, considering that his career numbers are quite similar to those of his former teammate, Hall of Famer Catfish Hunter. Perhaps the negative impressions created by his drug problems led to his lack of consideration. Regardless of his worthiness for the Hall of Fame, Vida Blue was one of the top pitchers of his time. In his 2001 *Historical Baseball Abstract*, Bill James ranked Blue as the 86th best pitcher in the history of baseball. Blue finished his career with 209 wins and 161 losses, 2,175 strikeouts, three 20-win seasons, a Cy Young Award, and a Most Valuable Player Award in his 17-year major-league career.

After retirement Blue retained a close association with baseball. He played in the Senior Professional Baseball Association in 1989 and 1990. He became active in philanthropic work, and spoke to a number of audiences about his struggle with substance addiction. Most recently, Blue served as a television analyst for the San Francisco Giants.

SOURCES

Blue, Vida, as told to Marty Friedman, *Vida Blue: A Life* (Nashville, Indiana: Unlimited Publishing LLC, 2011).

Clark, Tom, *Champagne and Baloney: The Rise and Fall of Finley's A's* (New York: Harper and Row, 1976).

Clark, Tom, *Baseball: The Figures* (Berkeley, California: Serendipity Books, 1976).

Clark, Tom, *Blue* (Los Angeles: Black Sparrow Press, 1974).

Clark, Tom, *Fan Poems* (Plainfield, Vermont: North Atlantic Books, 1976).

James, Bill, *The New Bill James Historical Baseball Abstract* (New York: The Free Press, 2001).

James, Bill, and Rob Neyer, *The Neyer/James Guide To Pitchers* (New York: Fireside, 2004).

Kuhn, Bowie, *Hardball: The Education of a Baseball Commissioner* (New York: Times Books, 1987).

Libby, Bill, and Vida Blue. *Vida: His Own Story* (Englewood Cliffs, New Jersey: Prentice-Hall, Inc., 1972).

Markusen, Bruce, *A Baseball Dynasty: Charlie Finley's Swingin' A's* (Haworth, New Jersey: St. Johann Press, 2002).

Neyer, Rob, and Eddie Epstein, *Baseball Dynasties* (New York: W.W. Norton and Company, 2000).

baseball-reference.com

NOTES

1 Bill Libby and Vida Blue, *Vida: His Own Story*, 16.
2 Libby, 20.
3 Libby, 43-45.
4 Libby, 49.
5 Libby, 51.
6 Libby, 231-248.
7 Ron Fimrite, "Vida's Down With the Growing-Up Blues," *Sports Illustrated*. September 10, 1973.
8 Ron Fimrite, "Bowie Stops Charlie's Checks," *Sports Illustrated*, June 28, 1976.
9 Ron Fimrite, "Oakland A's Pitcher Vida Blue," *Sports Illustrated*, May 19, 1997.
10 Vida Blue, as told to Marty Friedman, *Vida Blue: A Life*, 55.

GLENN ABBOTT

By Clifford Corn

WILLIAM GLENN ABBOTT is filled with stories and memories and good feelings about his days in the major leagues.

The former American League pitcher is forthright, open, and honest as he conjures up a past filled with recollections of warm summer days in big-league cities around the country. And although he played his last big-league game in August 1984 — when the Detroit Tigers cut him after a terrible stretch following the All-Star break — he continues to make his presence felt in the game he loves by coaching up-and-coming young arms in the Pacific Coast League.

Abbott's tale is a long and interesting one: a leap from being a member of the World Series-winning Oakland A's of the 1970s to the expansion Seattle Mariners to the impressive Tigers teams of 1983 and '84.

William Glenn Abbott was born on February 16, 1951, in Little Rock, Arkansas.

"When I was a kid, everybody played baseball," he told an interviewer in 2008. "I always loved it. When I was 14 or15, we'd ride bicycles over to the baseball fields and would play a little workup or something and then help prepare the field. It's just what kids did then.

"The Cardinals were big in Little Rock. I can remember when Dick Allen came to Little Rock; he was the first black to play there. I remember Ferguson Jenkins and guys like that who played there. ... I've always loved it and played the game. This is not a job to me. I really enjoy what I do. It's my 39th season, and I love it. I like working with the young kids."

In his early days with the sport, Abbott played the infield and caught as well as pitched.

That changed when he entered high school. "I realized that I had the chance to go on beyond high-school ball," he said "I realized that I had some ability and didn't want to take a chance of breaking a finger or something like that."

Abbott played baseball and basketball in high school and had planned to continue with both sports in college. But he was drafted out of high school in the eighth round by the Oakland A's in June 1969, and signed immediately. He was 18 years old. For a couple of years during the offseason, he attended State College of Arkansas, now called the University of Central Arkansas. He made the big leagues when he was 22 years old.

Starting in the Rookie-classification Northwestern League, Abbott quickly worked his way through minor-league ball and made his debut with Oakland on July 29, 1973, when he started against the Texas Rangers. He was taken out in the fourth inning with Oakland leading, 4-2, and Texas runners on second and third (the A's eventually won, 7-4).

Though Abbott's major-league pitching record was just 62-83, he had his moments.

September 28, 1975, the last game of the season, was a good example. Abbott was the second of four pitchers who combined to throw a no-hitter against the California Angels. Abbott pitched one inning and retired the side in order.

Abbott said the A's were preparing for the playoff series against the Boston Red Sox, and the manager, Alvin Dark, already had decided that Vida Blue would start but pitch no more than five innings. Abbott was slated to pitch the sixth, Paul Lindblad would throw the seventh inning, and Rollie Fingers would wrap things up in the eighth and ninth, regardless of the score.

"When I went out to take the mound in the sixth inning, the home crowd was booing — people were booing," Abbott said. "But they weren't booing me. They were booing because Vida Blue came out of the game and he was pitching a no-hitter. I said to myself, 'Lord, please don't let me give up a hit.'" And he didn't.

Abbott pitched for Oakland for four seasons and compiled a 13-16 record.

His years with the A's brought a lot of smiles. "I was on a team where you hear all the stuff about how wild they were, with all the fights and stuff. But the players were all-for-one when they were at the ballpark and on the field. They expected to win. In my first year we won the league championship." Oakland went on to win the World Series as well.

His next stop in an 11-year major league career was with the Seattle Mariners, when he became the 24th pick in the 1976 expansion draft.

Abbott viewed the change from winning a title in Oakland to moving to an expansion team in Seattle as a positive experience as well.

"I went from a team that expected to win to a team that didn't have a lot of confidence," he said. "They thought they could win but weren't sure. It was a big adjustment. In expansion, you always have a bunch of Triple-A players who never had a chance to play in the majors. It's a big step to make. If you can play Double-A ball, you can pretty much play Triple-A ball. But they don't understand the jump to the majors. It's like daylight and dark. A lot of guys can't comprehend that."

Abbott's promise was realized in the 1977 campaign, the first of the Mariners' existence. He compiled a 12-13 record with a 4.45 ERA, fanning 100 batters. He was the longest-serving of the original Mariners players—his last game for Seattle was on August 21, 1983. In all, his record with the Mariners was 44-62 with an ERA that ranged from 3.94 to 5.27.

Abbott missed the 1982 season because of floating bone chips in his elbow. His arm problems were compounded by a serious bout of viral meningitis. He lost 30 pounds, as well as some vision and hearing, and still had repercussions from the illness into June 1983. He was finally able to pitch again in midsummer of 1983.

Abbott was purchased by the Tigers on August 23, 1983, for $100,000, and stayed with Detroit for parts of two seasons.

"Detroit is a good baseball town, and I wanted an opportunity to go to a winning ball club," he said during an interview at PGE Park in Portland, Oregon, his baseball home in 2008, where he was the pitching coach for the Portland Beavers, the San Diego Padres' Triple-A affiliate. "You really appreciate a chance like that. It's huge to get that opportunity."

He was released by the Detroit organization on August 14, 1984, during the height of the championship run to the World Series. Abbott immediately started a coaching career that topped his pitching career for longevity.

Standing 6-foot-6, Abbott had a playing weight of around 200 pounds, and added a few pounds after his coaching career started. To an interviewer, his native Arkansas showed up in his easy drawl: the word "four" became a two-syllable word when it left Abbott's mouth.

In talking about the differences between the two leagues, Abbott made a definitive observation about his playing days: "National League umps were far more consistent back then," he said, though he wouldn't comment on the current umpiring situation in the major leagues.

"I wish I could have played in National League as a pitcher," he said. "I like the game a lot better. There's more things going on, more decisions to be made, pitcher having to hit, et cetera. It's also a better league to pitch in. The designated hitter means that teams like Boston and New York have no weaknesses in the lineup."

The right-hander's feelings about his time with the Tigers?

"I knew I had a chance to go to a contending ball club, and you don't realize how important that is until later. I was very fortunate," he said.

He made his Tigers debut on August 27, pitching seven innings against Toronto and leaving with the scored tied, 2-2. His best game for the Tigers that season was a 5-0 shutout of the Cleveland Indians on September 14. His mark with the Tigers in '83 was 2-1 with a 1.93 ERA in seven starts.

"The Tigers made a run in '83 and came up a game or two short [actually six games behind Baltimore]. I pitched well for them then, with Sparky [Anderson, the manager] and [pitching coach] Roger Craig as the pitching coach. And in '84, that team started 35-5 and set a record. We set the [American League] record in Anaheim for the most consecutive games won on the road and got a standing ovation.

"But I was in the bullpen and wasn't getting a chance to pitch much because the starters were so good. It made it really difficult; it's difficult to perform at a high level if you don't get the chance to play. But Jack Morris and Dan Petry and those guys were just dealing."

Abbott took the second loss of the '84 season when the Tigers were 16-1 but recalled few details of the 19-inning game in his interview, despite the fact that he committed two errors that contributed to the loss.

"Two errors? That's bad. Maybe that's why I can't remember," he said.

During Detroit's wire-to-wire American League East championship run in 1984, Abbott pitched in 13 games, eight of them starts, with a 3-4 record and a 5.93 ERA before he was cut. His best game that season was a complete-game victory over the Chicago White Sox on July 16, in which he gave up only five hits and one walk.]

Abbott had fond recollections of his teammates from that charmed 1984 season, even though it was a truncated one for him.

Of Sparky Anderson, he said: "He didn't talk to you much. He would say hi, but that's the way managers were then. I had no problems with Sparky at all. He was a pretty positive guy. He had some good players on the team. It was amazing; those guys came to play. They never even complained about playing charity games against Cincinnati on an off day."

Roger Craig, the Tigers' pitching coach during Abbott's tenure in Detroit, "was one of the most positive people I've ever been around. He was always telling you how good you were. You have to be positive with the guys, and Roger was always that way."

Jack Morris, the Tigers' acknowledged ace throughout the 1980s, according to Abbott, "had tremendous confidence. He was probably the best pitcher of that decade — or one of the best, I'll say that. He was just getting better and better at the time. Jack was a winning-type pitcher. He threw a no-hitter in April in one of the first televised games [of the season] in Chicago. I remember a fan was yelling after every inning, 'Hey Morris, you got a no-hitter going' — trying to get him off stride. And about the eighth inning, Jack said back to him, 'Damn right. Stay right there 'cause you're gonna see one.' He was a quality pitcher."

Dan Petry, considered the number two man in Detroit's rotation for most of the 1980s, "didn't say a lot," Abbott said, "but he was very consistent. You knew what you were going to get every time you went out there."

Abbott also had good words for two relievers who not only saved his bacon on more than one occasion in 1984, but that of other Tigers hurlers during the championship season. Guillermo Hernandez, the 1984 AL Cy Young Award winner and Most Valuable Player, "couldn't do anything wrong," he recalled. Aurelio "Senor Smoke" Lopez, who notched a 10-1 record and 14 saves in the midst of Hernandez' spectacular season, "also was very consistent." Abbott said.

Alan Trammell, Detroit's shortstop and the World Series MVP in 1984, "was just as solid as they come. He was a ballplayer. He could handle the bat so well. He was underrated at that time. Howard Johnson was coming along at that time, too, playing third base. They were all very professional, and they expected to win. There was a lot of confidence — a good atmosphere to be in.

"Darrell Evans did a good job. It was the end of his career, but he was very consistent and made a tremendous impact on the club. Whittaker and Trammell and Lance Parrish and Kirk Gibson and Dave Rozema — it makes a difference when your players come up together. You've got to have talent, but you need chemistry, too, and it all fell together with the Tigers."

Abbott said he got a ring and a share of the World Series money that year, even though he left the ballclub in August.

"It might have been a three-quarter share; I can't remember. It just makes you feel good that your teammates appreciate you," he said.

His time in the majors flew by, but the memories lingered.

"I had never seen a no-hitter in professional games, and in the first three years I was in the league, I saw one every year, including being involved in the one against the Angels when I was with Oakland. (It was actually four.) The Angels at that time were a bad ballclub, but Vida Blue was on that day. It was just five innings, but he walked through them.

"I had a chance to play with guys like Catfish Hunter. They made a big impression on me. They were very professional about the way they approached the game."

One of his greatest thrills was pitching in Yankee Stadium for the first time. "It was really an experience to go see those monuments for the first time. If you love baseball, that is really something. That's why I hate to see Yankee Stadium moving. It's one thing that bothers me. There's so much history. If you think of the people who played there, Yankee Stadium is like hallowed ground. You hate to see that happen, but I understand it when teams have to go to larger parks.

"The dugouts in Tiger Stadium were so small that everybody couldn't sit down when you came off the field. It was like a bunker in the bullpen."

As for Detroit's fans: "The Tigers have great fans. Everywhere you go you'd hear people talking about the Tigers. Every night they had big crowds. It was really a unique experience. It was really a cool deal there. I really enjoyed that — very much."

Abbott came to the Binghamton (New York) Mets, the New York Mets' AA-level entry in the Eastern League, as pitching coach after serving the Savannah Sand Gnats in the same capacity in 2011. Abbott's Sand Gnats staff led the South Atlantic League in 2011 with a 3.26 ERA. They also combined for the most saves (50) and lowest WHIP (1.223).

Prior to his time with the Mets, Abbott was a pitching coach for five years in the San Diego Padres' system, spent four seasons in the Texas Rangers organization, and logged 13 years at various levels with the Oakland Athletics. The Arkansas native began his coaching career with the Little Falls Mets in 1985, the year after the Tigers cut him loose, working with his old friend Mel Stottlemyre; this began a five-year tenure with the Mets' organization before heading to Oakland.

After getting drafted by the Athletics in the eighth round in 1969, Abbott spent 11 seasons in the major leagues as a starting pitcher for the A's (1973-76), Seattle Mariners (1977-83), and Detroit Tigers (1983-84). In 248 career games, the right-hander made 206 starts, went 62-83, amassed a 4.39 ERA, struck out 484 batters, and hurled five shutouts.

As a member of the Athletics in 1975, Abbott was part of the first four-pitcher no-hitter in MLB history. On Sept. 28, he combined with Vida Blue, Paul Linblad and Rollie Fingers to baffle the Angels on the final day of the regular season.

Abbott was married in 1973. He and his wife, Patti, live in Arkansas in the offseason, and wherever he is working during the season. The eldest of their three children. Todd, pitched in the Oakland minor-league system from 1995 through 1998 and became a high-school teacher and baseball coach in Bentonville, Arkansas. Their second son, Jeff, also became a teacher, in Bolivar, Missouri. Daughter Amy, the youngest child, is married with two children and lives in North Little Rock.

Even though Glenn Abbott hasn't thrown a pitch in the major leagues since 1984, he has never stopped being a positive influence on the game he loves.

After being let go by Detroit, Abbott coached with the New York Mets for five years, working with old friend Mel Stottlemyre, and then joined the Oakland organization for 13 more years. He was with the Texas Rangers for three years before joining the San Diego Padres' organization. He took on a new assignment for the Padres in 2010, becoming pitching coach for their Double-A affiliate, the San Antonio Missions.

SOURCES

http://www.baseball-reference.com

http://www.wikipedia.org

Corn, Clifford. Interview with Glenn Abbott, April 21, 2008.

PAUL LINDBLAD

By Paul Hofmann

PAUL LINDBLAD WASN'T one of the Oakland A's most celebrated stars or eccentric personalities, but he was a valuable part of a formidable bullpen that contributed to the team's string of five consecutive division championships and three consecutive World Series titles. Though somewhat overlooked in the annals of Athletics history, Lindblad was without question an integral part of the Swingin' A's dynasty of the early 1970s.

Paul Aaron Linblad was born on August 9, 1941, to George and Helen (Walters) Lindblad in Chanute, Kansas.[1] He was the oldest of five boys. Chanute, a mill town in the southeast corner of the state, had 11,000 residents at the time. The Lindblads settled in Chanute after George was discharged from the Navy and went to work for the Santa Fe Railroad. The job required George to spend a great deal of time away from the family, commuting to and from Kansas City. George Lindblad was a strict and highly critical father.[2] Although he always wanted Paul to play professional baseball, he rarely encouraged him or was satisfied with his son's performance on the field. Over time, this contributed to a strained relationship between the two. Paul's mother was a homemaker.

Paul Lindblad's journey to the major leagues is a story of love, persistence, and faith. His baseball career began on the baseball diamond in Katy Park. He began playing Little League baseball, progressed to American Legion baseball, and was introduced to the world of semipro baseball on the Kansas prairies. It was there that he fell in love with the game of baseball and also the woman he would marry.

Paul, known as Junior, was a standout athlete.[3] He attended Chanute High School, where by all accounts he was a good student. He did well in math and drafting, subjects that would serve him well when he entered the construction business after baseball. Paul was a three-year letterman on the basketball team and the 1959 state high school champion in the javelin.[4] The school did not have a baseball team.

American Legion baseball dominated the landscape of rural Midwest America and Lindblad led the Chanute Legion team to a regional title and a berth in the state tournament, where the team lost by one run in the first round.

After high school, Lindblad attended Chanute Junior College, which was conveniently located in the same building as the high school. He played semipro baseball, threw the javelin (he finished second at the National Junior College Championships in 1961), and continued his relationship with his high-school sweetheart, Kathy, who was still attending high school.

After earning an associate's degree in business from Chanute Junior College, Lindblad was awarded an athletic scholarship to play baseball at the University of Kansas. He arrived in Lawrence, Kansas, in the fall of 1961 and found it difficult to be away from Kathy. He frequently made the 100-mile trip back home to Chanute to see her on weekends, and they decided to marry. The Lindblads were married on November 4, 1961. Soon after, Lindblad withdrew from school, moved to Kansas City, and took a job with the Sante Fe Railroad. He worked for the railroad for almost a year before signing a contract with the Kansas City Athletics prior to the 1963 season. His $2,000 signing bonus helped the young couple who by this time were the proud parents of a daughter they named Cindy.

The Athletics sent Lindblad to the Burlington Bees of the Class-A Midwestern League, where the 21-year-old established himself as a bona-fide major-league prospect, winning 10 games with a 1.58 earned-run average before a sore elbow forced the Bees to shut him down. The elbow pain was severe enough for the A's to send Lindblad to the Mayo Clinic to have it checked. The pain was so severe, his wife said, that he questioned his future in baseball.[5]

But there was no structural damage to his arm and a winter of rest was all that was required.

In 1964 Lindblad was assigned to the Birmingham Barons of the Double-A Southern League. The Barons were the first integrated professional sports team in Alabama, and Lindblad observed firsthand the segregation that continued to dominate the South. His teammates included future Athletics Bert Campaneris, Tommie Reynolds, and John "Blue Moon" Odom. (The team's story and the 1964 Southern League pennant race are chronicled in Larry Colton's *Southern League: A True Story of Baseball, Civil Rights, and the Deep South's Most Compelling Pennant Race*.)

Lindblad had an up-and-down season for Birmingham, winning his first five starts, then falling into a slump in June and dropping four straight. It was the first time the lefthander had to deal with the ebbs and flows of pitching professionally. Despite struggling in June, Lindblad earned a $1,000 promotion bonus after sticking with Birmingham for more than 90 days. The bonus again came in handy as the Lindblads were expecting their second daughter, whom they named Paula. He finished 1964 with a respectable 11-8 season, 3.32 ERA, and 139 strikeouts, the highest strikeout total of his career. Lindblad was never an overpowering pitcher. His fastball topped out at around 90 mph and his best pitch was his slider. His greatest asset on the mound was his pinpoint control, the ability to put any pitch wherever he wanted it. Lynn Ranabargar, a longtime Chanute resident, said, "If he wanted a curveball low and outside, that is exactly where it was. If he wanted a fastball high and tight, all he had to know was how far off the chin they want it and that's where it went."[6]

Understanding that he was not an overpowering pitcher and that his future in baseball depended on his ability to stay healthy and be a fundamentally sound player, Lindblad jogged daily basis and ran extra wind sprints to keep himself in the best shape possible. He also took great pride in making sure he made the routine plays.

The 1965 season brought with it a promotion to Kansas City's Triple-A affiliate, the Vancouver Mounties of the Pacific Coast League. In 28 starts Lindblad posted a 12-11 record and a 3.67 ERA, which earned him a late-season call-up to the A's, a team on its way to and finishing last in the American League. On September 15, 1965, he made his major-league debut against the soon-to-be crowned American League champion Minnesota Twins. He tossed a perfect seventh inning, striking out Bob Allison and Jimmie Hall. He pitched in three more games for the Athletics that fall. On September 22 he suffered his first major-league loss after yielding a fifth inning, two-run homer to Washington Senators shortstop Eddie Brinkman. Despite an unimpressive 11.05 ERA in 7⅓ innings, he was in the major leagues to stay.

During his early years in professional baseball, Lindblad played winter ball in Venezuela and the Caribbean. During this time he became interested in collecting coins. When he wasn't playing ball, Lindblad explored his surroundings and often purchased old coins from the local people. Later he took his numismatic interests to the extreme of buying a metal detector, which he carried with him on road trips. Bruce Markusen wrote regarding Lindblad's penchant for searching for hidden treasures in *Baseball's Last Dynasty: Charlie Finley's Oakland A's:*

> Don Mincher, who played with Lindblad in Washington, Oakland, and Texas remembered the left-handed reliever as a man of boundless energy, who always needed to keep busy. Mincher recalled Lindblad's trademark habit of searching for money with a metal detector. "He'd go to the ballparks and look for pennies and nickels all day long." By Lindblad's own estimation he collected an average of $11 per city on road trips and gave the money to his children, who like Lindblad himself enjoyed collecting coins. When the metal detector beeped, Lindblad used a small screwdriver to dig into the turf and warning track. Yet, Lindblad had to be careful not to dig too deep, for fear of striking a water hose or electrical line. Trips to Cleveland's Municipal Stadium posed a special problem, since groundskeepers Harold and Marshall Bossard took special pride in maintaining the grass field. "If I dig too deep into the Indians' field," Lindblad said, "those two guys would tan my hide."7

The A's broke camp in Bradenton, Florida, in 1966 with the 23-year-old Lindblad on the pitching staff. As a minor leaguer he had been used almost exclusively as a starter. However, his role with the A's was less defined and the next two seasons would go a long way toward shaping his role as a long and middle reliever. In 1966 and 1967 he started 24 games and worked in 60 as a reliever. On August 12, 1966, against the Minnesota Twins, Lindblad threw wild on a pickoff attempt at second base, allowing the Twins' Cesar Tovar to advance to third. Tovar then stole home off a rattled Lindblad. But the throwing error was noteworthy in that Lindblad would not commit another error until May 6, 1974, a record 385 errorless games streak that covered nearly eight years. He finished 1967 with a 5-8 record, with six saves and a 3.58 ERA.

On July 16, 1967, Lindblad tossed a three-hit shutout against the Chicago White Sox at Comiskey Park. It was the only complete game of his career. He made only 12 more starts the rest of his career. The Athletics struggled on the field and at the gate in 1967, winning only 10 of their final 40 games and drawing just 726,639 fans all season. Fearing a collapse of the franchise, baseball owners allowed owner Charles Finley to relocate the team to Oakland. The Lindblads were excited and nervous about moving their young family so far away from Kansas.8

Lindblad's first season in Oakland saw him settle into a role that would define the remainder of his major-league career. He appeared in 48 games, 47 in relief, and compiled a 4-3 record with two saves and a 2.40 ERA. He followed with two more solid seasons in 1969 and 1970. In 1969 he pitched in 60 games, winning nine and losing =six with a 4.14 ERA. Soon after the end of the 1969 season, Paul and Kathy welcomed their third child, a son they named Troy. In 1970 Lindblad made 62 appearances on his way to recording an 8-2 mark with three saves and a 2.70 ERA. Just as the 28-year-old Lindblad was establishing himself as a major leaguer, so too were the A's establishing themselves as contenders. The perpetual doormats of the American League finished 1970 in second place, nine games behind the Twins in the American League's West Division.

Early in the 1971 season Lindblad's career took an unexpected turn. On May 8 he was dealt with Frank Fernandez and Don Mincher to the Washington Senators for first baseman Mike Epstein and left-handed reliever Darold Knowles. Both players were key acquisitions that allowed the A's to get over the hump. After being an integral part of the Athletics rebuilding process, Lindblad now found himself playing for a Senators club that was battling the Cleveland Indians for last place in the American League East. A year later the team relocated to Arlington, Texas, and became the Texas Rangers. Lindblad spent two productive seasons with the Senators/Rangers franchise.

In 1971 he appeared in 43 games for the Senators, finishing with a 6-4 record with eight saves and a 2.58 ERA. With Texas in 1972, he led all American League hurlers with 66 appearances and finished the season with a 5-8 mark, nine saves, and a 2.62 ERA. During these two years Lindblad solidified himself as one of the most reliable left-handed relievers in the American League. Meanwhile, his former teammates in Oakland were celebrating their 1972 World Series title.

In November 1972 Finley reacquired Lindblad in exchange for A's farmhand Bill McNulty and outfielder Brant Alyea. Finley's revolving-door style of managing player personnel often resulted in his reacquiring players he had previously traded, and when Finley dealt Lindblad to the Senators, he told Paul that he would try to reacquire him. Despite the many well-documented disputes Finley had with many of the players he employed, Kathy Lindblad said Paul's relationship with Finley was always friendly and respectful. The relationship extended beyond his playing days. Finley occasionally called Paul just to "catch up on things."[9] Lindblad's first season back with the A's was not one of his better ones. He pitched in only 36 games, making three spot starts. He finished the year 1-5 as his ERA rose more than a run per game, to 3.69. Heading into the postseason, Darold Knowles was the first left-handed option out of the bullpen and Lindblad did not appear in the A's five-game ALCS victory over the Baltimore Orioles.

Lindblad did pitch in three games during the 1973 World Series against the New York Mets. In Game Two he relieved in the 12th inning after the Mets had taken a 7-6 lead off Rollie Fingers. Lindblad induced back-to-back groundballs to second baseman Mike Andrews, both of which Andrews fumbled, leading to three more runs that put the game away.

In Game Three, also an extra-inning affair, Lindblad came on in the ninth inning, worked two innings, and earned the victory, one of the greatest moments of his life, according to his wife.[10] In addition to earning the victory, Lindblad became a footnote in baseball trivia when he became the last pitcher to face Willie Mays. In the bottom half of the 10th the Mets' aging slugger pinch-hit, and Lindblad got him to ground into a fielder's choice. The A's scored the winning run in the top of the 11th. The victory was Lindblad's only postseason win. He pitched once more in the Series, throwing a scoreless inning in Game Four.

Among the three World Series rings won by Lindblad, the 1973 ring was the one he was most proud of and routinely wore, despite the fact that it originally contained no diamonds.[11] He felt he had contributed more to this team's success than the other two teams that won World Series titles. The ring was lost when Lindblad placed it in a briefcase that was later stolen. Kathy Lindblad still has her husband's rings from the 1974 and 1978 World Series.[12]

The Athletics and Lindblad followed up their 1973 World Series title with another championship season in 1974. Lindblad pitched more than 100 innings for the first time since 1967 and had a 4-4 record with a career-low 2.06 ERA as he filled the void created by the struggles of fellow lefty Darold Knowles. However, his contributions ended at the conclusion of the regular season. The A's received such solid starting pitching performances throughout the American League Championship Series and the World Series that Lindblad didn't make a single postseason appearance.

The 1975 season was perhaps Lindblad's finest. With Knowles having been traded to Chicago, his workload increased significantly. He came out of the bullpen 68 times and pitched 122⅓ innings, both career highs, on his way to posting a 9-1 record with seven saves and a 2.72 ERA. The effort earned the attention of sportswriters across the country as Lindblad garnered a handful of votes and finished 18th in the American League MVP voting, during a season when the A's won their fifth consecutive American League West championship.

On September 28, 1975, the final day of the 1975 season, Lindblad combined with Vida Blue, Glen Abbott, and Rollie Fingers to toss a no-hitter against the California Angels. Lindblad pitched a 1-2-3 seventh inning, retiring Leroy Stanton on a groundout to third, striking out John Balaz, and getting Bruce

Bochte to ground out to second. It was the first time in the major leagues that four pitchers combined for a no-hitter.

The A's were swept by the Boston Red Sox in the 1975 ALCS. Lindblad, who pitched in two of the three games, was one of the few A's pitchers who were remotely effective. In 4⅓ innings he allowed one run to a heavy hitting Red Sox lineup that included Carl Yastrzemski, Fred Lynn, and a host of other big bats.

The 1976 season was Lindblad's last in Oakland. The 34-year-old again proved to be a reliable member of the bullpen as he went 6-5 with a 3.06 ERA. The A's championship run ended as the team finished with an 87-74 record, 2½ games behind the Kansas City Royals. With many of the key pieces of the A's dynasty already departed, the franchise's glory days were clearly in the rear-view mirror. In an effort to cut costs, Finley sold off as many of the A's assets as possible. Lindblad still had value and before the start of the 1977 season he was sold to the Texas Rangers for $400,000.

Lindblad spent a little more than a season and a half with the Rangers before being purchased by the New York Yankees on August 1, 1978. The Yankees needed to bolster their bullpen in an effort to chase down the front-running Red Sox. The Yankees caught the Red Sox and went on to win a one-game playoff to advance to the American League Championship Series and eventually the World Series. Lindblad made his final appearance in the majors in Game One of the 1978 World Series. Coming on in relief in the fifth inning he pitched 2⅓ innings and gave up three earned runs as the Dodgers battered four Yankees pitchers for 11 runs in the opening game blowout.

The Yankees' acquisition of Lindblad reunited him with his good friend and longtime A's roommate, Catfish Hunter. In addition to collecting coins, Lindblad loved the outdoors, particularly hunting and fishing, activities he and Hunter relished together.

After the season the Yankees sold Lindblad to the Seattle Mariners, who released the 37-year-old lefthander at the end of spring training. After 14 seasons in the majors, Lindblad's career had ended, and he retired to his home in Arlington, Texas. Lindblad finished his career with a 68-63 record and 64 saves in 385 games, with a 3.29 ERA and the admiration of many who remembered him as the perfect teammate.

Lindblad became a custom homebuilder in Arlington. He returned to baseball as a minor-league pitching coach in the Milwaukee Brewers organization in 1987 and worked in that capacity until 1993, when he was diagnosed with early-onset familial Alzheimer's disease (FAD), the same disease that afflicted his mother and later three of his brothers. Early-onset Alzheimer's is a rare form of the disease that is known to be entirely inherited.[13]

The disease progressed rapidly and had a dramatic impact on Lindblad's behavior and his physical appearance. He began to get progressively more upset at little things and was unable to control his anger, often lashing out at Kathy.[14] According to Kathy, he didn't recognize her or his children and wasn't the same gentle, caring man she had married.[15]

In 1997 Lindblad was moved to a facility that specialized in assisted-living care for those suffering from Alzheimer's. Lindblad spent the final nine years of his life in Peach Tree Place in Arlingtons.[16] He died from complications of the disease on January 1, 2006. He was 64 years old.

After Lindblad's death, the field at Katy Stadium in Katy Park in Chanute was renamed Paul Lindblad Field. On October 5, 2008, Lindblad was inducted into the Kansas Sports Hall of Fame.

SOURCES

Colton, Larry, *Southern League: A True Story of Baseball, Civil Rights, and the Deep South's Most Compelling Pennant Race* (New York: Grand Central Publishing, 2013).

Markusen, Bruce. *Baseball's Last Dynasty: Charlie Finley's Oakland A's* (Indianapolis: Masters Press, 1998).

McDowell, Brian, "Legion tournament honors Lindblad's legacy," *Chanute Tribune*, July 5, 2013. Retrieved from chanute.com/sports/article_593e439e-e5c1-11e2-9e26-0014bcf6878.html

Wolters, Levi. "Hall of Fame Induction Ceremony Sunday," *Wichita Business Journal*, October 2, 2008.

Chanute Area Chamber of Commerce and Office of Tourism (2012). Retrieved from chanutechamber.com

Chanute Historical Society. Retrieved from chanutehistory.org/

Chanute, Kansas. Retrieved from en.wikipedia.org/wiki/Chanute,_Kansas

Kansas City Athletics: Historical Moments. Retrieved from sportsencyclopedia.com/al/kcityas/kca_s.html

Markusen, Bruce, "Thinking of Paul Lindblad." Retrieved from bruce.mlblogs.com/2006/01/17/thinking-of-paul-lindblad/

Paul Aaron Lindblad 1941-2006. Retrieved from thedeadballera.com/Obits/Obits_L/Lindblad.Paul.Obit.html

Paul Lindblad. Retrieved from baseballlibrary.com/ballplayers/player.php?name=Paul_Lindblad_1941&page=chronology

Types of Alzheimer's: Early-Onset, Late-Onset and Familial (2013). Retrieved from webmd.com/alzheimers/guide/alzheimers-types

Wade Funeral Home, Arlington, Texas, Paul Aaron Lindblad August 9, 1941-January 1, 2006. [Funeral Program, 2006].

W.E. Alford, personal communications, December 10 and December 12, 2013

Lindblad, Kathy, personal communications, December 11, 16, and 17, 2013

NOTES

1 Wade Funeral Home, "Paul Aaron Lindblad 1941-2006."

2 Personal correspondence with Kathy Lindblad, December 17, 2013.

3 Personal correspondence with W.E. Alford, December 10, 2013.

4 Larry Colton, *Southern League: A True Story of Baseball, Civil Rights, and the Deep South's Most Compelling Pennant Race* (New York: Grand Central Publishing, 2013).

5 Personal correspondence with Kathy Lindblad, December 16, 2013.

6 Brian McDowell, "Legion tournament honors Lindblad's legacy," *Chanute Tribune*, July 5, 2013.

7 Bruce Markusen, *Baseball's Last Dynasty: Charlie Finley's Oakland A's* (Indianapolis: Masters Press, 1998), 177-178.

8 Personal correspondence with Kathy Lindblad, December 16, 2013.

9 Personal correspondence with Kathy Lindblad, December 11, 2013.

10 Personal correspondence with Kathy Lindblad, December 17, 2013.

11 Personal correspondence with Kathy Lindblad, December 11, 2013.

12 Personal correspondence with Kathy Lindblad, December 11, 2013.

13 Types of Alzheimer's: Early-Onset, Late-Onset and Familial (2013).

14 Colton.

15 Personal Correspondence with Kathy Lindblad, December 17, 2013.

16 Colton.

ROLLIE FINGERS

By Dale Voiss

ROLLIE FINGERS WAS clearly excited as he caught a leaping Ted Simmons, his catcher, after Fingers struck out Detroit's Lou Whitaker to nail down the victory and the second-half American League East title for his Milwaukee Brewers in 1981. (The unprecedented split season was devised after the players' two-month strike was settled.) The Brewers were in the postseason for the first time in their 13-year history. They lost in the first round to the first-half champion New York Yankees, three games to two, but Fingers, whose 28 saves that season preserved 45 percent of the Brewers' 62 victories, won not just the Cy Young Award but the American League Most Valuable Player award as well. Only five pitchers (Don Newcombe, Sandy Koufax, Bob Gibson, Denny McLain, and Vida Blue) did that before Fingers, and only four (Willie Hernandez, Roger Clemens, Dennis Eckersley, Justin Verlander) had done it after him, as of 2014.

Roland Glen Fingers developed his mustache, perhaps the most colorful in major-league baseball, on his own. But he credited his father with teaching him how to pitch. Roland was born on August 25, 1946, in Steubenville, Ohio, to George and Pearl (Stafford) Fingers. His father, a steelworker, had pitched in the St. Louis Cardinals farm system for four years and had been a roommate of Stan Musial.

One day, after returning home from a tough day in the steel mill, George Fingers said, "That's it, we're moving to California," Roland Fingers recalled in a TV appearance with Tim McCarver in August 2010. He sold his house for $1,500, bought a car, and moved the family to Rancho Cucamonga, California, where he went to work in yet another steel mill. On the drive west, the family couldn't afford to stay in hotels, and they were forced to sleep in sleeping bags by the side of the road.

At Upland High School (Upland and adjoining Rancho Cucamonga are east of Los Angeles), Fingers played left field and pitched on the baseball team. He also played American Legion baseball for the Upland Post. In August 1964, after graduating from high school, Fingers pitched his Legion team to the national American Legion title and was named the tournament's player of the year. After winning local and regional tournaments, Upland went to the national tournament in Little Rock, Arkansas. Playing the outfield, Fingers belted three hits and made two running catches in Upland's victory over a Detroit team in the opener of the round robin. He pitched a three-hitter against a team from Charlotte, North Carolina, to wrap up the title. For the Legion season he finished with an 11-2 record, a 0.67 earned-run average, and 102 strikeouts in 81 innings. In the regional and national tournaments, he batted .450 (18-for-40).

After the tournament Fingers returned home to California to discuss his baseball future with his parents. The free-agent draft hadn't been instituted yet, and Fingers had already received offers from more than a dozen major-league organizations. He was prepared to turn them all down to attend Chaffey Junior College at Alta Loma, California.

The Los Angeles Dodgers offered Fingers a $20,000 bonus to sign a contract. But because they already had a solid pitching staff, led by Fingers' boyhood heroes Sandy Koufax and Don Drysdale, he felt it would take him years to make the majors with the Dodgers. Instad, he accepted a $13,000 offer from the Kansas City Athletics, signing the contract on Christmas Eve of 1964.

The Athletics originally wanted Fingers as an outfielder but decided in his first spring training to have him pitch. At Leesburg, in the Class A Florida State League in 1985, he won 8 games and lost 15, with a 2.98 ERA. In late August he went to Cooperstown, where in a ceremony at the Baseball Hall of Fame he received the American Legion player of the year award from the previous summer.

Fingers spent the 1966 season with the Modesto Reds of the Class A California League. Still a starter, he went 11-6 in 22 games with a 2.77 ERA. Among his teammates that season were future Hall of Famers Reggie Jackson and Tony La Russa.

In the spring of 1967, Fingers married his high-school sweetheart, Jill Cutler, who had been the statistician for the Upland High School baseball team. He moved up the A's ladder again, to Birmingham of the Double-A Southern League. Pitching on Opening Day, he suffered a fractured cheekbone and jawbone, and lost some teeth when he was hit by a line drive off the bat of Fred Kovner of Evansville. Fingers' jaw was wired shut for five weeks. He returned to the mound in two months and finished the season with a 6-5 record and a 2.21 ERA. After Birmingham's season ended, to get in some more work, Fingers pitched for the Athletics' entry in the Arizona Fall Instructional League.

The Athletics moved from Kansas City to Oakland after the 1967 season, but Fingers stayed in Birmingham in 1968 for a second straight year. He started the season with eight straight victories, including a two-hit, 5-0 shutout of Evansville, and ended the season with a 10-4 record and a 3.00 ERA. This performance earned him a call-up to Oakland in September, and Fingers would never again pitch in a minor-league game. He pitched just once for the A's after his call-up, allowing four runs on four hits in relief in a 13-0 loss to the World Series-bound Detroit Tigers on September 15. The four hits included a home run by Tigers catcher Bill Freehan.

In the winter of 1968-69, Fingers pitched for the La Guaira club of the Venezuelan Winter League, and worked on developing a slider to supplement his "out" pitch, the fastball.

In 1969 the Athletics' new manager, Hank Bauer, installed a four-man starting rotation — Blue Moon Odom, Chuck Dobson, Catfish Hunter, and Jim Nash — and said that to keep the starters on four days' rest, Fingers would start when the A's played more than four straight days. Fingers made his first start of the season on April 22 in Minnesota. He shut out the Twins on five hits, 7-0, facing just 32 batters. He made his next start five days later in Seattle, going 8⅓ innings and allowing five runs on six hits in a 13-5 win over the Pilots. Seven days later he started against Seattle again, this time at Oakland, and lost, 6-4, giving up 11 hits in six-plus innings. He didn't start again until May 30, when he was shelled by the Cleveland Indians, lasting just one-third of an inning in a 9-2 loss. For the next 3½ months, Fingers worked out of the bullpen; he did not start again until September 15, when he lost to the Twins. In the remaining two weeks of the season he made three more appearances as a starter. In 60 games, including eight starts, Fingers was 6-7 with 12 saves.

Hank Bauer was fired in September and replaced by third-base coach John McNamara, who had been Fingers' manager at Birmingham in 1967. Under

McNamara in 1970, Fingers got 19 starts and made 26 relief appearances, posting a 7-9 record.

Dick Williams replaced McNamara for 1971. Fingers began the season in the rotation and started eight games, winning one and losing three. His last start of the season came on May 15, after which Williams made Fingers the closer. Except for two starts early in the 1973 season, Fingers was a closer for the next 15 years. In that 1971 season he earned 17 saves in 20 opportunities, the fourth highest saves total in the American League.

The A's won 101 games that year to win the American League's West Division by 16 games over the Kansas City Royals, but were swept by the Baltimore Orioles in the American League Championship Series. Fingers pitched in two games in the series, allowing two runs in 2⅓ innings.

The division championship in 1971 was the first of five straight for the A's. Their rise to the top was fueled by the talent they got out of their minor-league system in the 1960s, players like Fingers, Reggie Jackson, Bert Campaneris, Joe Rudi, Sal Bando, Catfish Hunter, Blue Moon Odom, and Vida Blue. As these players came together, they jelled as a team and brought success to Oakland. The A's appearance in the 1971 ALCS was the first postseason play for the franchise and its predecessors since the Philadelphia Athletics lost the 1931 World Series to the St. Louis Cardinals.

In 1972-74 the A's won three straight World Series. Over that span, in a time when the semiautomatic ninth-inning closer was not as much of a fixture as it became two decades later, Fingers had 61 saves and a 27-22 won-lost record with an ERA of 2.34. In each of those seasons he pitched between 111 and 126 innings—numbers unheard of among closers of the 21st century. He made the American League All-Star team in 1973 and 1974. (He was also an All-Star in 1975, 1976, 1978, 1981, and 1982.)

Reggie Jackson, Oakland's star outfielder, showed up for spring training in 1972 with a mustache. His teammates did not like the idea of Jackson with a mustache so they all started growing facial hair to protest. Team owner Charles Finley, instead of making everyone shave, as the players hoped he would, offered a cash prize to the player who could grow the best facial hair by Opening Day. Finley felt the look would help sell tickets. Fingers grew a handlebar mustache that curled at the tips. It won the contest, and the mustache became his trademark look.

After the 1972 season Finley sent Fingers a contract calling for a $1,000 raise for 1973. Fingers phoned Finley to argue about the contract. Finley would not budge, so Fingers slammed down the receiver and vowed never to talk to Finley again. He hired agent Jerry Kapstein to represent him in negotiations with Finley and kept his word never to speak to Finley again.

In each of the three seasons from 1974 to 1976, Fingers pitched in at least 70 games, leading the league in appearances in 1974 and 1975. During that span, he saved 62 games for Oakland and had a better than 3-to-1 strikeout-to-walk ratio.

In June 1976, anticipating that he might lose them to free agency after the season, Finley sold Fingers and Joe Rudi to the Boston Red Sox, and Vida Blue to the New York Yankees for a total of $3.5 million ($1 million each for Fingers and Rudi and $1.5 million for Blue). Baseball Commissioner Bowie Kuhn rescinded the deals, saying they were not in the best interests of baseball. Finley's argument had been that if the three became free agents at the end of the season, he would not get anything in return if they signed elsewhere. Kuhn, on the other hand, said that if he allowed the sale to go through, "the door would be opened wide to the buying of success by the more affluent clubs." Finley sued Kuhn for restraint of trade but lost the suit.

After the 1976 season, with Fingers and several teammates eligible for free agency, Finley chose not to sign them and they all went their separate ways. In an attempt to prevent teams from making offers to Fingers, Finley stated that he was washed up, but the San Diego Padres signed Fingers anyway, for a salary of slightly over $250,000, almost triple his highest salary as an Athletic. (The Dodgers, Cardinals, Giants, and Pirates had also wooed Fingers.) Among the players leaving Oakland that winter were Don Baylor, Joe Rudi, Sal Bando, Bert Campaneris, and Gene Tenace, who also signed with the Padres. In signing, Fingers said he was glad to move to the National League because he was a low-ball pitcher and NL umpires were more likely to call the low-ball strike. Fingers' signing with the Padres came shortly after his wedding to the former Danielle Lamar on November 14. (His first marriage had ended in divorce in 1974, and this one would, too.) A former A's teammate, pitcher Ken Holtzman, was Fingers' best man at the ceremony in the Oakland suburb of Lafayette.

On the Padres, Fingers was reunited with former Athletics manager John McNamara. But McNamara, who took over the Padres in 1974, was fired 48 games into the 1977 season and was replaced by Alvin Dark. At the time Fingers signed, many believed that McNamara would move him into the rotation. This would leave the closer role to Butch Metzger, who had saved 16 games for the Padres in 1976 and earned the NL Rookie of the Year Award. McNamara surprised many by giving the closer job to Fingers and using Metzger in middle relief.

In San Diego, Fingers joined a staff anchored by 1976 Cy Young Award winner Randy Jones. Jones had won 22 games for the Padres in 1976, but an arm injury in September threatened his 1977 season. Jones recovered enough to start the season but went a disappointing 6-12 in 27 games. Meanwhile, Fingers saved 35 games, more than half of the Padres' 69 wins.

Fingers spent four years in San Diego as the Padres' closer, going 34-40 while earning 108 saves in 265 outings. The Padres had just one winning season in the four years and never finished higher than fourth in the six-team National League Western Division. Fingers could hardly be blamed; during his stay in San Diego he won the unofficial National League Fireman of the Year Award three times, in 1977, 1978, and 1980. In his final year in San Diego, Fingers surpassed Hoyt Wilhelm's career record for saves. (As an indication of how the use of closers has changed over the years, Fingers' career total of 341 put him, as of the beginning of the 2014 season, only 11th among closers; the leader as of that year was Mariano Rivera, with 652.)

After the 1980 season Fingers returned to the American League. The Padres traded him, Tenace, and pitcher Bob Shirley to the St Louis Cardinals for seven players; then the Cardinals sent Fingers, catcher Ted Simmons, and pitcher Pete Vuckovich to the Milwaukee Brewers for outfielders Sixto Lezcano and David Green and pitchers Lary Sorensen and Dave LaPoint. When Fingers arrived in Milwaukee, the Brewers were coming off three straight winning seasons. They were led by an explosive offense that included future Hall of Famers Robin Yount and Paul Molitor. But they struggled to find a consistent closer. Fingers was seen by many as the final piece of the puzzle that could send the team to their first postseason appearance. Fingers did not disappoint. In what was regarded as one of the greatest seasons a relief pitcher had up to then, he saved 28 of the team's 62 victories as the Brewers sailed to the second-half American League East title in the strike-shortened 1981 season. Fingers' dominating performance, which included a minuscule 1.04 earned-run average, landed him not only the Cy Young Award but the MVP award as well. Fingers had one victory and one save as the Brewers fell to the Yankees three games to two in the divisional playoffs.

In 1982 Fingers saved 29 games through late August as the Brewers led the American League East for most of the season. The team had really taken off when hitting coach Harvey Kuenn replaced Buck Rodgers as manager in early June. Rodgers' removal had been precipitated by the team's poor play (the Brewers were 23-24 when he was fired) along with criticism of Rodgers by several players, including Fingers.

On August 30 the Brewers obtained right-handed pitcher Don Sutton from the Houston Astros in exchange for three prospects. Sutton, a future Cooperstown inductee, joined the team the next day and started the second game of a doubleheader September 2 against the Cleveland Indians. The Brewers lost the game, 4-2. The loss, however, was not the worst news the team received that night. In the first game of the doubleheader Fingers tore a muscle in his right forearm. The injury kept him out of action for the remainder of the season. Rookie Pete Ladd replaced him as the closer, and the Brewers, without Fingers, advanced to the World Series, which they lost to the Cardinals in seven games.

This tendinitis injury left Fingers sidelined for the entire 1983 season. He returned to form for the Brewers in 1984, saving 23 games for a team that disappointed nearly everyone by finishing 67-94, last in the American League East, under manager Rene Lachemann.

In 1985 Fingers, now 38 years old, returned to the Milwaukee bullpen but clearly wasn't his old self. He saved 17 games but had eight blown saves and finished with a 1-6 record and a 5.04 ERA. The Brewers released him after the season. He received overtures from the Cincinnati Reds, but a team rule against facial hair would have forced him to shave his trademark handlebar mustache, so he declined the Reds' offer and retired.

Fingers went to work for a communications company in the San Diego area, where he worked for about a dozen years. He followed that with a short stint at a printing company, also in the San Diego area.

In January 1992, on just his second appearance on the ballot, Fingers was elected to the Baseball Hall of Fame, along with pitcher Tom Seaver. Before his induction the Brewers retired his uniform number, 34. The following year the Athletics followed suit by also retiring number 34.

Golf became a major passion for Fingers in retirement. He carried a handicap of 2 to 3 for most of his adult life. Fingers played over a decade, with several other pro athletes, on the Celebrity Golf Tour, where he was known to finish as high as third.

In 1999 Fingers moved from his home in California to Las Vegas, where he took a job with Billy Walters, who owned several golf courses in the area. After less than a year he left Walters Golf and later got involved with a golf company that developed a product which helps clean up lakes.

In January 2007 the state of Wisconsin listed Fingers as number eight on its list of tax delinquents. The state Department of Revenue alleged that he owed nearly $1.5 million in income tax from his days as a pitcher for the Brewers. In July the state filed documents saying that two of the three cases it had filed against Fingers had been satisfied, with the third case, for more than $58,000, still pending. The next month Fingers said that his name had been cleared and he had never been delinquent.

As of 2014 Fingers still resided in Las Vegas. Of his five children, a son, Jason, was drafted by the Kansas City Royals in the tenth round of the June 2000 amateur draft. He pitched for Spokane of the Class A Northwest League in 2000 and Burlington in the Class A Midwest League in 2001 before ending his baseball career. During the summer of 1970 Fingers' younger brother, Gordon, pitched in eight games for Coos Bay-North Bend, Oakland's entry in the Northwest League.

SOURCES

Wisconsin State Journal (Madison, Wisconsin), November 4, 1981.

The Sporting News, September 12, 1964, August 7, 1965, April 27, 1967, November 25, 1967, November 16, 1968, January 11, 1969, February 8, 1969, April 19, 1969, July 3, 1976, December 11, 1976, March 12, 1977.

Armour, Mark. "Charles Finley." SABR BioProject.

Fingers' Hall of Fame induction speech, 1992

Online interview with Fingers by Jimmy Scott, at jimmyscottshighandtight.com/node/824

"Fingers still takes pioneer route," at lasvegasgolf.com/departments/features/rollie-fingers-golf-326.htm

OAKLAND USES FOUR PITCHERS TO NO-HIT ANGELS ON FINAL DAY OF THE SEASON

SEPTEMBER 28, 1975: OAKLAND ATHLETICS 5, CALIFORNIA ANGELS 0, AT OAKLAND–ALAMEDA COUNTY STADIUM

By Michael Huber

ON THE VERY LAST DAY OF the 1975 season, the Oakland Athletics employed four pitchers to no-hit the California Angels. Before a home crowd of 22,131, Oakland's manager Alvin Dark had a plan to have Vida Blue, his ace starter, go only five innings and then rest him for the playoffs. Relievers Glenn Abbott, Paul Lindblad, and Rollie Fingers knew beforehand when they were expected to enter the game; they combined for four perfect innings. Oakland had already clinched the Western Division title, and the League Championship Series was almost a week away. California finished the season in last place, 22½ games behind the A's. Reggie Jackson slugged his 35th and 36th home runs, pacing the A's to a 5-0 victory over the Angels.

The Oakland pitching staff overmatched the Angels batters. No California hitter had better than a .288 average entering the game. Further, this was the first major-league start of the season for the Angels' starter, Gary Ross.[1]

Blue walked Dave Chalk with one out in the top of the first inning, but Chalk was erased when Leroy Stanton grounded into a double play. In the bottom of the first, Claudell Washington singled off Ross with one out and moved to second on a walk to Gene Tenace. Reggie Jackson moved both runners up a base with a fly ball to deep center field. Sal Bando followed with a single, driving in the two runners, and Oakland had a 2-0 lead.

Blue retired the Angels in order in the second and third innings. After Tenace flied out to start the A's half of the third, Jackson homered to make it 3-0. After Blue retired the first two batters in the top of the fourth, Stanton reached on an error by shortstop Bert Campaneris and stole second base, but John Balaz popped out to first. Blue walked designated hitter Paul Dade in the fifth, but again California could not muster a hit or run. Blue left the game after the fifth having allowed just the two walks. After the game he said, "I knew I was coming out. It didn't matter to me at all. All I care about is my earned-run average. I'll take my record of 22-11 and run."[2] He added, "I knew I was only going five and then somebody else was coming in—Mean Joe Greene, the Count of Monte Cristo, or somebody."[3]

Abbott entered the game to start the sixth inning for Oakland and retired Ike Hampton, Jerry Remy, and Chalk in order. Abbott said, "I thought maybe with a no-hitter going they'd let Vida stay in for one more inning. I never gave much thought to a no-hitter at that stage of the game, but I didn't want to give up a hit and be a goat."[4]

In the top of the seventh, Athletics manager Dark moved Tenace to first base and sent Ray Fosse behind the plate. Ted Martinez took over at second base and Dal Maxvill at short, and Lindblad came in to pitch. Lindblad struck out Balaz in between groundouts by Stanton and Bruce Bochte. Three up and three down. Veteran southpaw Lindblad commented, "I was in the right spot at the right time. Funny thing is, I really didn't realize we had a no-hitter going. All I knew is we had three runs and if they scored four off me I'd get the loss."[5] He also told reporters, "I was just concerned about pitching my inning and getting out of there. In 1966, I pitched seven innings of no-hit ball against Houston in spring training and John Wyatt didn't give up any hits in the last two."[6]

A's slugger Jackson smashed a second round-tripper in the Oakland seventh with Washington aboard, raising the lead to 5-0, and that was all the scoring in the game. Oakland rookie pitcher Mike Norris had been told by Dark to be ready to pitch in the eighth inning. The plan was for him to get one out, because Fingers needed 1⅔ innings of scoreless ball to lower his earned run average below 3.00. However, with the no-hitter looming, Dark instead brought in Fingers to start the eighth. California skipper Dick Williams sent up four left-handed pinch-hitters against Fingers, who retired them all. Then he got Mickey Rivers to ground out to shortstop Maxvill with two outs in the ninth, and the no-hitter was preserved. This was the 36-year-old infielder's last major-league game; he was released in the offseason.

Fingers, Oakland's famously moustachioed closer, said after the game, "I was a little nervous although the pressure was less than it is in a playoff or World Series game. The guys in the dugout were razzing me so much that I knew if I gave up a hit I'd hear about it all winter long."[7] But home-plate umpire Bill Kunkel, interviewed after the game, said, "The way Rollie was pitching, he must have thought it was the World Series."[8] It was Kunkel's first major-league no-hit game as an umpire, and it came without any controversial calls.

Oakland had five runs on nine hits and three walks. Bando and Jackson were each 2-for-4, and the pair knocked in all five runs. Each also struck out once.

This was the first major-league no-hitter in which more than two hurlers, and the third combined no-hitter ever.[9] Through the end of the 2015 season, there have been 11 combined no-hit games. Three times a team has used four pitchers and twice a team has used six pitchers.[10] Both of the six-man combinations were interleague contests.[11]

Vida Blue had been named to the American League All-Star squad that July and finished sixth in the voting for the 1975 Cy Young Award. In his previous outing, on September 24, Blue pitched six innings and gave up 10 hits in earning a 13-2 victory over the Chicago White Sox. He finished the month of September with a 5-1 record and two complete games, allowing 15 earned runs in 49⅓ innings (2.74 ERA).

This was the second no-hitter for Blue. He defeated the Minnesota Twins, 6-0, on September 21, 1970, yielding only one walk to prevent a perfect game.[12] It was only his second season in the big leagues. That was the last no-hitter for the Athletics until this combined effort, which was the third no-hit game of the 1975 season. California's Nolan Ryan pitched his fourth career no-hitter (1-0) against the Baltimore Orioles on June 1, and San Francisco's Ed Halicki no-hit the New York Mets, 6-0, on August 24.[13]

The Athletics beat the Milwaukee Brewers on June 4 and moved into first place in the AL West, then spent the rest of the season atop the division. Dark's decision to rest his ace in the final game was second-guessed. Blue started Game Two of the American League Championship Series against the Boston Red Sox. He pitched three innings and allowed three earned runs but did not figure in the decision (Oakland lost to Boston, 6-3).

SOURCES

In addition to the sources mentioned in the notes, the author consulted baseball-reference.com, mlb.com, and retrosheet.org.

NOTES

1. Ross had been traded to the Angels by the San Diego Padres on September 17 for Bobby Valentine and a player to be named later (Rudy Meoli). He spent the bulk of the season pitching for the Hawaii Islanders of the Pacific Coast League.
2. "4 A's Combine for Historic No-Hitter," *Chicago Tribune*, September 29, 1975.
3. *The Sporting News*, October 11, 1975: 34.
4. *Chicago Tribune*.
5. Ibid.

NO-HITTERS

6 Ron Bergman, "A's Add Bizarre Note to Finale: Four Pitchers Share a No-Hitter," *The Sporting News*, October 11, 1975.

7 *Chicago Tribune*.

8 Bergman.

9 The first combined no-hitter was played on June 23, 1917. Boston's Babe Ruth was ejected for arguing with the umpire after walking Washington's leadoff batter. Ernie Shore entered, the leadoff man was caught stealing, and Shore retired the next 26 hitters in a row.

10 The six-pitcher combos occurred on June 11, 2003 (Houston Astros beating the New York Yankees), and June 8, 2012 (Seattle Mariners beating the Los Angeles Dodgers).

11 For further details, see sportingcharts.com/articles/mlb/history-of-combined-no-hitters.aspx.

12 In the 1970 no-hitter, before an Oakland crowd of just 4,284, Blue outdueled Jim Perry, who won the American League Cy Young Award that season. Perry allowed two earned runs, and his 1970 record dropped to 23-12 with the loss.

13 "4 A's Pitchers Combine for No-Hitter," *New York Times*, September 29, 1975.

ASTROS NO-NO-NO-NO-NO-NO-HIT YANKEES

JUNE 11, 2003: HOUSTON ASTROS 8, NEW YORK YANKEES 0, AT YANKEE STADIUM

by Michael Huber

On June 11, 2003, six Houston Astros combined to pitch a record-setting no-hitter against the New York Yankees in an interleague affair. Roy Oswalt, Peter Munro, Kirk Saarloos, Brad Lidge, Octovio Dotel, and Billy Wagner "shut down the Bronx Bombers in the House That Ruth Built …"[1]

The Yankees' starter was Jeff Weaver, who was making his first start in 12 days. He allowed a first-inning leadoff double to Craig Biggio. Biggio moved to third on a fly ball and scored on a wild pitch by Weaver with two outs. The Astros added a run in the second on a triple by Orlando Merced and a sacrifice fly by Omar Vizcaino.

Roy Oswalt, the Astros' ace, started off strong, retiring the Yankees in order in the bottom of the first, striking out Derek Jeter and Jason Giambi. But Oswalt had to leave the game with a groin pull after only two pitches in the bottom of the second inning. The Yankees and their fans might have been optimistic that this would be a high-scoring game with Oswalt gone. Instead, "what seemed like a potential blowout became the first no-hitter against the Yankees in the Bronx since 1952."[2] Jimy Williams, the Astros manager, sent reliever after reliever into this unexpected situation, and each man kept putting zeroes on the scorecard. Peter Munro came in to pitch for Oswalt. He walked Jorge Posada on a full count, then retired Robin Ventura, Hideki Matsui, and Todd Zeile in order.

Houston kept the pressure on Weaver. Geoff Blum singled to begin the third inning, and with two outs Lance Berkman launched a home run, giving the Astros a 4-0 lead. With two outs in the bottom of the fourth inning, Munro walked Zeile. Williams pulled Munro in favor of Kirk Saarloos, who got Raul Mondesi to fly to left field for the third out.

The closest the New Yorkers came to getting a hit was in the bottom of the fifth inning. Alfonso Soriano lined a 1-and-1 pitch from Saarloos into left field. Left fielder Berkman "ran in, stuck out his glove and made a tumbling catch."[3] Berkman played the line drive down, stating, "It wasn't that close. It probably looked more spectacular than it really was."[4] According to the *New York Times*, "Berkman dived forward like a punt returner protecting a football on the 10-yard line and made a nifty catch."[5]

Brad Lidge became the fourth Houston pitcher in the top of the sixth, and in two innings he faced six batters, getting six outs, including strikeouts of Zeile and Mondesi to end the seventh. In the Astros' seventh inning, two singles and an error by Jeter led to the fifth Astros tally and chased Weaver. Chris Hammond came out of the Yankees bullpen and retired Jeff Kent and Berkman to end the inning. Jason Anderson became the third Yankees hurler in the eighth and allowed a run on a double to Richard Hidalgo, who motored to third on a wild pitch and scored on a single by Brad Ausmus.

In the home half of the eighth inning, Williams called on Octavio Dotel, the hard-throwing set-up man in the Astros bullpen. He threw three pitches past Juan Rivera for out number one. Soriano fouled off three straight pitches before swinging and missing at a wild pitch in the dirt. The ball got past Ausmus, and Soriano raced to first base, safe. Derek Jeter took Dotel to a full count, then struck out swinging. Giambi fouled off a few pitches and then whiffed on a 2-and-2 count. Four strikeouts in an inning, all swinging. Dotel became the 45th major-league pitcher to strike out four batters in one inning. Later he said, "I knew that we had a no-hitter but I didn't feel any pressure because I said if they get a base hit, who cares? There were five of us. It's not like one person was throwing a no-hitter. It's kind of different, but it's good too."[6] By this time, fans were exiting the Stadium, "obviously not wanting to see the Yankees on the dubious end of history."[7]

The Astros added two more runs in the top of the ninth. Alberto Reyes yielded Hidalgo's two-out double, which plated Jeff Bagwell and Berkman. The score was now 8–0.

Even with the big lead, the bottom of the ninth meant it was time for Billy Wagner, the Astros' closer. He struck out Posada and pinch-hitter Bubba Trammell. That meant that Astros pitchers had struck out eight Yankees batters in a row, the seventh and eighth Yankees in a row to fan. The previous five pitchers had all gone to the clubhouse after being replaced. They "were afraid to jinx the no-hitter by leaving the clubhouse and joining their teammates on the bench," so they watched Wagner pitch a 1-2-3 finale on the monitor instead of watching it live. When Matsui grounded Wagner's first pitch to first baseman Bagwell, who flipped the ball to Wagner covering first base for the final out, they stormed the field, some in shorts and T-shirts. Five of the pitchers (all but Oswalt) posed in front of the dugout for a photo.

Wagner was awestruck about the whole experience. "Your first appearance in Yankee Stadium, and it's a no-hitter, and you're part of it. It doesn't get any better than that. That's a storybook ending for our bullpen to go out and battle. To be able to achieve something like that, it's really special."[8] After the on-field celebration, the Astros filed back to the clubhouse. To their amazement, the Yankees had placed bottles of champagne in front of the six pitchers' lockers. Wagner appreciated that, saying, "That's how the Yankees are, they're pretty classy."[9]

The Yankees managed six baserunners: three walks, a hit batsman, a batter who reached on an error, and Soriano's dropped third strike. All three walks were given up by Munro. "I was a little erratic," he said after the game. "I was walking some guys, and that was probably why. It's a good thing I didn't do too much damage."[10]

Astros manager Williams also admitted to the press, "I'll be very honest with you. I didn't know they didn't have any hits until the seventh. We had already used four pitchers, and we got a lead and were trying to win this game. I knew they had a lot of baserunners, so when you have baserunners you think, 'Well somebody must have gotten on with a hit.' Then I looked up there and there was a zero there. I started trying to remember when they got a hit."[11]

This was the first time that more than four pitchers had combined for a no-hitter.[12] The Orioles' Hoyt Wilhelm had no-hit the Yankees in Baltimore in 1958, and this game marked the first in 7,048 games in which the New York team had been no-hit, and it was the last as of 2015. It was played on the 65th anniversary of the first of Johnny Vander Meer's two consecutive no-hitters. It was the second no-hitter of the 2003 season, and the third in interleague play (including the Yankees' Don Larsen's perfect game in the 1956 World Series against the Brooklyn Dodgers).[13]

After the game, Yankees skipper Joe Torre told reporters, "There's no question that (the New York Yankees) weren't very good tonight, but you don't want to diminish how well they (the Houston Astros) pitched."[14] He added, "This is one of the worst games I've ever been involved in."[15] The loss caused New York to relinquish first place in the American League East, falling a half-game behind Boston. Astros pitchers struck out 13 Yankees batters, including Jeter three times and Giambi, Ziele, and Mondesi twice each. On the other side, every starting player for Houston got at least one hit. Ausmus led the way with a 3-for-4 effort.

Saarloos, who pitched the fifth inning, did not earn the win. Since the starter, Oswalt, departed early and did not pitch five innings, the official scorer decided who would get the victory, and he gave the W to Lidge, who pitched the sixth and seventh innings, striking out a pair and not allowing any Yankee to reach base. Ten years after the game, Saarloos said in an interview, "Every once in a while I joke around about how I threw a no-hitter at Yankee Stadium and that I'm in the Hall of Fame. I leave some of the details out."[16]

SOURCES

In addition to the sources mentioned in the notes, the author consulted baseball-reference.com, mlb.com, and retrosheet.org.

NOTES

1 "Houston Astros vs. New York Yankees No Hitter Box Score June 11, 2003, baseball-almanac.com/boxscore/06112003.shtml. (Hereafter box score).

2 Benjamin Hoffman, "A No-Hitter So Rare It Took 6 Pitchers," nytimes.com/2013/05/02/sports/baseball/6-pitchers-0-hits-when-the-astros-made-history-in-the-bronx.html?_r=0.

3 "Yanks no-hit for first time in 45 years by record six Astros," cbssports.com/mlb/gametracker/recap/MLB_20030611_HOU@NYY.

4 Ibid.

5 Jack Curry, "Team Effort: 6 Astros Pitchers, 0 Yankee Hits," *New York Times*, June 12, 2003.

6 Box score.

7 Curry.

8 Box score.

9 "Yanks no-hit."

10 Hoffman.

11 Jose de Jesus Ortiz, "Houston's performance one for the books," *Houston Chronicle*, June 12, 2003.

12 On June 8, 2012, almost exactly nine years later, Seattle's Kevin Millwood, Charlie Furbush, Stephen Pryor, Lucas Luetge, Brandon League, and Tom Wilhelmsen combined to no-hit the Los Angeles Dodgers, 1-0, in an interleague contest.

13 The first no-hitter of the 2003 campaign was by Philadelphia's Kevin Millwood against San Francisco on April 27. Millwood was also involved in the 2012 six-pitcher no-hitter. (See Note 12.)

14 Box score.

15 "Yanks no-hit."

16 Hoffman.

AHEAD OF THEIR TIME: NEGRO LEAGUES NO-HITTERS

By Dirk Lammers

Just take the ball and throw it where you want to. Throw strikes.

Home plate don't move.

—Satchel Paige

THREE DECADES BEFORE Don Larsen threw his perfect game in the '56 World Series, a 22-year-old Negro League pitcher "down the Shore" beat his big-city counterpart to the postseason punch.

Claude "Red" Grier joined the Atlantic City Bacharach Giants midway through the 1925 season after spending a year and a half with the Washington (and later Wilmington) Potomacs. Grier boasted "a wide assortment of pitches and good control," James Overmyer wrote in *Black Ball and the Boardwalk*, and the southpaw helped lead the 1926 Bacharach Giants to an Eastern Colored League championship.[1]

Atlantic City was set to face the Negro National League champion Chicago American Giants in the third-ever Colored World Series, with three of the games staged at neutral sites.

Game One ended in a tie, and Grier took the loss in Game Two.

On October 3, 1926, Grier got the start for Game Three at Maryland Baseball Park in Baltimore and dominated the American Giants lineup for a 10-0 no-hit victory in front of just 2,857 fans.

Grier's gem is one of the dozens of no-nos thrown in the Negro Leagues before the majors integrated in 1947, though incomplete game accounts and the gray lines between professional, semipro, minor league, and barnstorming teams make it tough to come up with an exact number.

There's no doubt that many Negro League pitchers could have etched their spots into the major-league record books if baseball had welcomed them earlier, but their numerous accomplishments received far less media attention.

"Cannonball" Dick Redding, who played for a variety of teams from 1911 through 1928, has been cited as throwing as many as 30 career no-hitters—seven in 1912 alone—but it's difficult to uncover enough box scores to prove or disprove those estimates.

Redding's August 28, 1912, no-no for the Lincoln Giants against the Cuban Stars in Atlantic City is considered the first documented no-hitter between two high-level African American teams.

"Redding's speed was terrific, and the Cubans were helpless before his delivery," noted a *New York Press* game account uncovered by researcher Gary Ashwill. "This was the second hitless game Redding has pitched this season."[2]

The other 1912 no-no, according to the *Press*, was an August 5 perfect game against the Cherokee Indians during that club's East Coast barnstorming tour. If there are others (and there most certainly are), they're difficult to dig up.

Another Negro League pitcher of note is the Kansas City Monarchs' Hilton Smith, who threw the Negro American League's first no-hitter on May 16, 1937. Smith led the Monarchs to a 4-0 win over the Chicago American Giants.

Fans across the nation gushed over Bob Feller in 1940 when the Iowa farm sensation pitched the majors' first Opening Day no-hitter, but detailed game accounts are scarce on Leon Day's 1946 Opening Day no-no for the Newark Eagles of the Negro National League.

Like Feller prior to his second no-no, the quiet, soft-spoken Day had just returned from serving his country in World War II, having stormed Utah Beach during the Allied Forces' invasion of France. In James A. Riley's book *Of Monarchs and Black Barons:*

Essays on Baseball's Negro Leagues, Day said he had few opportunities to pitch while stationed overseas.

"I was discharged in February at Fort Dix, and went home to Newark until spring training," Day recalled. "We trained in Tampa that year, but my arm wasn't too good."[3]

Day, as usual, was way too modest. The right-hander took the mound at Newark's Ruppert Stadium on May 5, 1946, and used his illusory no-wind-up delivery to no-hit the Philadelphia Stars for a 2-0 win. He allowed just three runners to reach first via a pair of walks and an error, but he struck out just six batters. For Day, any game with a "K" count below 10 was a sign that he "didn't have good stuff."[4]

In stark contrast to Leon Day's modesty was the larger-than-life Satchel Paige, who estimated he threw 55 no-hitters over his long, storied career that included stints with numerous teams. When Paige wasn't pitching in league games, he was barnstorming across the country competing against anyone who would take the ball field against his All-Stars. Just two Paige no-hitters are documented. On July 15, 1932, he threw the first no-no at the newly built Greenlee Field in Pittsburgh's Hill District, the nation's first black-built and black-owned major-league ballpark. His Pittsburgh Crawfords topped the New York Black Yankees 6-0.

"The elongated speed ball artist from the far South was at his best and literally had the Yanks eating out of his hand," said a *Pittsburgh Courier* account.[5]

Paige's second no-no for the Crawfords came against the Homestead Grays. On July 4, 1934, Paige struck out a Negro National League–record 17 batters.

It would be 14 years before he finally got the opportunity to face big-league batters in the regular season. In 1948, at the age of 42, he made his major-league debut with the Cleveland Indians.

The list of Negro Leagues no-hitters, as best as anyone has been able to verify, includes other such greats thrown by Bill Gatewood, "Smokey" Joe Williams, and Jesse "Nip" Winters.

Negro Leagues No-Hitters List

The following is a list of 34 Negro Leagues no-hitters, but ongoing research may turn up more. Former Negro League pitchers such as "Toothpick" Sam Jones who threw their no-nos in the majors appear on the official Major League Baseball list.

John Goodgame
West Baden Sprudels
Friday, April 21, 1911 / West Baden Sprudels 3, French Lick Plutos 0

"Cannonball" Dick Redding
Lincoln Giants
Wednesday, August 28, 1912 / Lincoln Giants 1, Cuban Stars 0

Louis Decatur "Dicta" Johnson
Chicago American Giants
Sunday, June 8, 1913 / Chicago American Giants 9, Paterson Smart Set 0

Charles Dougherty
Chicago American Giants
Monday, June 9, 1913 / Chicago American Giants 8, Paterson Smart Set 0

Frank Wickware
Chicago American Giants
Wednesday, August 26, 1914 / Chicago American Giants 1, Indianapolis ABCs 0

Dizzy Dismukes
Indianapolis ABCs
Sunday, May 9, 1915 / Indianapolis ABCs 5, Chicago Giants 0

Dick Whitworth
Chicago American Giants
Sunday, September 19, 1915 (first game of doubleheader) / Chicago American Giants 4, Chicago Giants 0

Bill Gatewood
St. Louis Giants
Saturday, May 13, 1916 / St. Louis Giants 4, Cuban Stars 1

NO-HITTERS

Gatewood's first of two no-hitters on this list.

Bernardo Baró
Cuban Stars
Sunday, July 21, 1918 (first game of doubleheader) / Cuban Stars 11, Indianapolis ABCs 0

"Smokey" Joe Williams
Lincoln Giants
Sunday, May 4, 1919 (first game of doubleheader) / Lincoln Giants 1, Brooklyn Royal Giants 0

Tom Johnson
Chicago American Giants
Tuesday, June 17, 1919 / Chicago American Giants 7, Detroit Stars 3

Bill Gatewood
Detroit Stars
Monday, June 6, 1921 / Detroit Stars 4, Cincinnati Cubans 0
First Negro National League no-hitter; Gatewood's second of two no-hitters on this list.

Phil Cockrell
Hilldale (Darby, Pennsylvania)
Monday, September 5, 1921 (second game of doubleheader) / Hilldale 3, Detroit Stars 0
Cockrell's first of two no-hitters on this list.

Bill Force
Detroit Stars
Tuesday, June 27, 1922 / Detroit Stars 3, St. Louis Giants 0

Jesse "Nip" Winters
Atlantic City Bacharach Giants
Wednesday, July 26, 1922 / Atlantic City Bacharach Giants 7, Indianapolis ABCs 1
Winters's first of two no-hitters on this list.

Phil Cockrell
Hilldale (Darby, Pennsylvania)
Saturday, August 19, 1922/ Hilldale 5, Chicago American Giants 0
Cockrell's second of two no-hitters on this list.

José Méndez (5 innings), **Bullet Rogan** (4 innings)
Kansas City Monarchs
Sunday, August 5, 1923 (second game of doubleheader) / Kansas City Monarchs 7, Milwaukee Bears 0
Méndez pitched 5 perfect innings; Rogan allowed one base runner.

Jesse "Nip" Winters
Hilldale (Darby, Pennsylvania)
Wednesday, September 3, 1924 (first game of doubleheader) / Hilldale 2, Harrisburg Giants 0
First Eastern Colored League no-hitter; Winters's second of two no-hitters on this list.

Andy Cooper
Detroit Stars
Sunday, June 28, 1925 (second game of doubleheader) / Detroit Stars 1, Indianapolis ABCs 0

Rube Currie
Chicago American Giants
Tuesday, July 13, 1926 / Chicago American Giants 16, Dayton Marcos 0

Claude "Red" Grier
Atlantic City Bacharach Giants
Sunday, October 3, 1926 / Atlantic City Bacharach Giants 10, Chicago American Giants 0
Game Three of 1926 Colored World Series.

Laymon Yokely
Baltimore Black Sox
Sunday, May 15, 1927 (second game of doubleheader) / Baltimore Black Sox 8, Cuban Stars 0

Joe Strong
Baltimore Black Sox
Thursday, August 4, 1927 / Baltimore Black Sox 2, Hilldale 1 (11 inn.)

Willie Powell
Chicago American Giants
Sunday, August 14, 1927 / Chicago American Giants 5, Memphis Red Sox 0

"Army" Cooper (7 1/3 innings), **Chet Brewer** (1 2/3 innings)
Kansas City Monarchs

Saturday, June 29, 1929 / Kansas City Monarchs 4, Chicago American Giants 0
Cooper was relieved with one out in the eighth after walking bases loaded.

Paul Carter
Hilldale (Darby, Pennsylvania)
Monday, September 7, 1931 (second game of doubleheader) / Hilldale 6, Baltimore Black Sox 0

Satchel Paige
Pittsburgh Crawfords
Friday, July 8, 1932 (second game of doubleheader) / Pittsburgh Crawfords 6, New York Black Yankees 0
Paige's first of two no-hitters on this list.

Bill Foster
Chicago American Giants
Sunday, September 24, 1933 (first game of doubleheader) / Chicago American Giants 6, New Orleans Crescent Stars 0

Satchel Paige
Pittsburgh Crawfords
Wednesday, July 4, 1934 / Pittsburgh Crawfords 4, Homestead Grays 0
Paige struck out 17 batters; his second of two no-hitters on this list.

Hilton Smith
Kansas City Monarchs
Sunday, May 16, 1937 (first game of doubleheader)/ Kansas City Monarchs 4, Chicago American Giants 0

First Negro American League no-hitter.

"Schoolboy" Johnny Taylor
Negro All-Star Team
Sunday, September 19, 1937 / Negro All-Star Team 2, Paige's Dominican All-Stars 0

Benefit All-Star Game played at the Polo Grounds.

Gene Smith
St. Louis Stars
Friday, June 27, 1941 / St. Louis Stars 6, New York Black Yankees 1

Leon Day
Newark Eagles
Sunday, May 5, 1946 / Newark Eagles 2, Philadelphia Stars 0
An Opening Day no-hitter.

Eugene Marvin Collins
Kansas City Monarchs
Sunday, May 22, 1949 / Kansas City Monarchs 14, Houston Eagles 0

SOURCES

SABR Negro League Committee and Noir Tech Research using the *Chicago Defender, Chicago Tribune, Baltimore Afro American, Kansas City Call, Kansas City Star-Times, Pittsburgh Courier,* and *St. Louis Argus.*

This article was initially published in Dirk Lammers' book *Baseball's No-Hit Wonders* (Lakewood, Colorado: Unbridled Books, 2016), and appears in this volume courtesy of publisher Fred Ramey, Unbridled Books.

NOTES

1   James E. Overmyer, *Black Ball and the Boardwalk: The Bacharach Giants of Atlantic City, 1916–1929* (Jefferson, North Carolina: McFarland, 2014), 133.

2   "Redding Pitches Hitless Game," *New York Press,* August 29, 1912: 7.

3   James A. Riley, *Of Monarchs and Black Barons: Essays on Baseball's Negro Leagues* (Jefferson, North Carolina: McFarland, 2012), 153.

4   Ibid., 155.

5   "New York Yanks Win Series from Crawfords," *Pittsburgh Courier,* July 16, 1932: 15.

PITCHERS WHO THREW COMPLETE-GAME NO-HITTERS IN BOTH THE MINOR AND MAJOR LEAGUES

By Chuck McGill

IN THE MAJOR LEAGUES, there have been just under 300 officially recognized no-hitters, as well as 48 no-hitters that were indeed complete games but which were stricken from the official list by a rule definition announced in 1991.

In the minor leagues, from 1877 through 2016, there have been 4,275 known no-hitters thrown by about 3,700 different pitchers or groups of pitchers (when two or more pitchers combined to throw a no-hitter).

We have defined a "minor-league game" as one thrown for a team listed as in the minor leagues in *The Encyclopedia of Minor League Baseball* or listed as a minor-league team (for the year in question) on Baseball-Reference.com. Any game of any legal length—that is, five innings or more, is eligible for the list. This also includes extra-inning games in which a pitcher held the opponent hitless for at least the first nine innings.

The list below includes all 43 pitchers who have thrown a no-hitter in both the minor leagues and the major leagues. The schedule includes all games of legal length, including tie games.

Pitcher	Date	League	Team	Opponent	Score	Innings
Ed Cushman	9/28/1884	Union Association	Milwaukee Brewers	Washington Nationals	5-0	
	6/18/1889	International Association	Toledo White Stockings	Rochester Jingoes	8-0	9
Sam Kimber	9/26/1883	Inter-State Association	Brooklyn Greys	Reading Actives	13-0	7
	10/4/1884	American Association	Brooklyn Atlantics	Toledo Blue Stockings	0-0	
Matt Kiloy	10/6/1886	American Association	Baltimore Orioles	Pittsburgh Alleghenys	6-0	
	5/2/1894	Pennsylvania State League	Allentown Kelly's Killers	Easton	9-0	9
Ted Breitenstein	10/4/1891	National League	St. Louis Browns	Louisville Colonels	8-0	
	4/22/1898	National League	Cincinnati Reds	Pittsburgh Pirates	11-0	
	8/15/1909	Southern League	New Orleans Pelicans	Montgomery Climbers	2-0	9
Bumpus Jones	10/15/1892	National League	Cincinnati Reds	Pittsburgh Pirates	7-1	

NO-HITTERS

	6/5/1898	Western League	Columbus Senators	Kansas City Blues	3-2	9
Cy Young	7/25/1890	Tri-State League	Canton Nadjys	McKeesport	4-1	9	18 strikeouts
	9/18/1897	**National League**	**Cleveland Spiders**	**Cincinnati Reds**	**6-0**		
	5/4/1904	**American League**	**Boston Pilgrims**	**Philadelphia Athletics**	**3-0**		Perfect Game
	6/30/1908	**American League**	**Boston Red Sox**	**New York Highlanders**	**8-0**		
Christy Mathewson	6/12/1900	Virginia League	Norfolk Phenoms	Hampton Crabs	1-0	9
	7/15/1901	**National League**	**New York Giants**	**St. Louis Cardinals**	**5-0**	
	6/13/1905	**National League**	**New York Giants**	**Chicago Cubs**	**1-0**	
Jesse Tannehill	9/7/1895	Virginia State League	Richmond Blue Birds	Roanoke Magicians	10-0	9
	8/17/1904	**American League**	**Boston Pilgrims**	**Chicago White Sox**	**6-0**	
Weldon Henley	6/7/1902	Southern League	Atlanta Crackers	Little Rock Travelers	12-0	9
	7/22/1905	**American League**	**Philadelphia Athletics**	**St. Louis Browns**	**6-0**	
Johnny Lush	5/1/1906	**National League**	**Philadelphia Phillies**	**Brooklyn Superbas**	**6-0**	
	9/20/1914	Pacific Coast League	Portland Beavers	Venice Tigers	0-1	9
Jeff Pfeffer	5/8/1907	**National League**	**Boston Doves**	**Cincinnati Reds**	**6-0**	
	5/5/1910	Central League	Fort Wayne Billikens	Zanesville Potters	0-1	9
Nick Maddox	8/22/1907	Central League	Wheeling Stogies	Terre Haute Hottentots	3-0	?
	9/20/1907	**National League**	**Pittsburgh Pirates**	**Brooklyn Superbas**	**2-1**	
Nap Rucker	6/24/1905	South Atlantic	Augusta Tourists	Columbia Gamecocks	3-0	9
	9/5/1908	**National League**	**Brooklyn Superbas**	**Boston Doves**	**6-0**	
Chief Bender	5/12/1910	**American League**	**Philadelphia Athletics**	**Cleveland Naps**	**4-0**	
	8/19/1920	Eastern League	New Haven Weissmen	Bridgeport Americans	3-0	9
Joe Wood	5/21/1908	American Association	Kansas City Blues	Milwaukee Brewers	1-0	9
	7/29/1911	**American League**	**Boston Red Sox**	**St. Louis Browns**	**5-0**	
Earl Hamilton	8/14/1909	Virginia League	Portsmouth Truckers	Danville Red Sox	4-0	9

NO-HITTERS

Pitcher	Date	League	Team	Opponent	Score	IP
	8/30/1912	American League	St. Louis Browns	Detroit Tigers	5-1	
Ed Lafitte	7/12/1909	Eastern League	Providence Clamdiggers	Jersey City Skeeters	0-2	9
	9/19/1914	Federal League	Brooklyn Tip-Tops	Kansas City Packers	6-2	
Rube Marquard	9/3/1908	American Association	Indianapolis Indians	Columbus Senators	7-0	9
	4/15/1915	National League	New York Giants	Brooklyn Robins	2-0	
Frank Allen	9/1/1909	Southern League	Mobile Sea Gulls	Montgomery Climbers	1-0	7
	4/24/1915	Federal League	Pittsburgh Rebels	St. Louis Terriers	2-0	
Jimmy Lavender	7/5/1913	Ohio State League	Huntington Blue Sox	Hamilton Maroons	2-0	?
	8/31/1915	National League	Chicago Cubs	New York Giants	2-0	
Eddie Cicotte	8/16/1906	Western League	Des Moines Champions	Omaha Rourkes	3-1	?
	4/14/1917	American League	Chicago White Sox	St. Louis Browns	11-0	
Fred Toney	5/10/1909	Blue Grass League	Winchester Hustlers	Lexington Colts	1-0	17
	5/2/1917	National League	Cincinnati Reds	Chicago Cubs	1-0	
Ernie Koob	5/5/1917	American League	St. Louis Browns	Chicago White Sox	1-0	
	5/11/1920	American Association	Louisville Colonels	Kansas City Blues	4-0	
Bob Groom	6/16/1907	Pacific Coast League	Portland Beavers	Los Angeles Angels	1-0	9
	5/6/1917	American League	St. Louis Browns	Chicago White Sox	3-0	
Jesse Haines	6/24/1915	Southern Michigan League	Saginaw Ducks	Flint Vehicles	3-2	?
	7/17/1924	National League	St. Louis Cardinals	Boston Braves	5-0	
Dazzy Vance	5/30/1915	Western League	St. Joseph Drummers	Wichita Wolves	2-1	9
	9/13/1925	National League	Brooklyn Robins	Philadelphia Phillies	10-1	
Paul Dean	8/30/1932	American Association	Columbus Red Birds	Kansas City Blues	3-0	9
	9/21/1934	National League	St. Louis Cardinals	Brooklyn Dodgers	3-0	
Johnny Vander Meer	6/11/1938	National League	Cincinnati Reds	Boston Bees	3-0	

NO-HITTERS

	6/15/1938	**National League**	**Cincinnati Reds**	**Brooklyn Dodgers**	**6-0**		
	7/15/1952	Texas League	Tulsa Oilers	Beaumont Roughnecks	12-0	?	
Tex Carleton	9/14/1929	International League	Rochester Red Wings	Toronto Maple Leafs	3-1	9	
	4/30/1940	**National League**	**Brooklyn Dodgers**	**Cincinnati Reds**	**3-0**		
Lon Warneke	8/15/1930	International League	Reading Keys	Buffalo Bisons	1-0	7	
	8/30/1941	**National League**	**St. Louis Cardinals**	**Cincinnati Reds**	**2-0**		
Don Black	7/22/1941	Virginia League	Petersburg Rebels	Staunton Presidents	1-0	?	
	8/4/1942	Virginia League	Petersburg Rebels	Pulaski Counts	4-0	?	
	7/10/1947	**American League**	**Cleveland Indians**	**Philadelphia Athletics**	**3-0**		
Allie Reynolds	9/2/1942	Eastern League	Wilkes-Barre Barons	Elmira Pioneers	0-1	11	No hits through 10 innings
	7/12/1951	**American League**	**New York Yankees**	**Cleveland Indians**	**1-0**		
	9/28/1951	**American League**	**New York Yankees**	**Boston Red Sox**	**8-0**		
Virgil Trucks	5/18/1938	Alabama-Florida League	Andalusia Bulldogs	Evergreen Greenies	1-0	9	19 strikeouts
	6/4/1938	Alabama-Florida League	Andalusia Bulldogs	Dothan Browns	6-0	?	
	5/26/1940	Texas League	Beaumont Exporters	Tulsa Oilers	1-0	7	
	5/31/1941	International League	Buffalo Bisons	Montreal Royals	0-1	10	
	5/15/1952	**American League**	**Detroit Tigers**	**Washington Senators**	**1-0**		
	8/25/1952	**American League**	**Detroit Tigers**	**New York Yankees**	**1-0**		
Jim Wilson	8/17/1949	International League	Buffalo Bisons	Jersey City Skeeters	5-0	7	
	6/12/1954	**National League**	**Milwaukee Braves**	**Philadelphia Phillies**	**2-0**		
Bo Belinsky	**5/5/1962**	**American League**	**Los Angeles Angels**	**Baltimore Orioles**	**2-0**		
	8/18/1968	Pacific Coast League	Hawaii Islanders	Tacoma Cubs	1-0	?	
Jack Kralick	6/17/1955	Kitty League	Madisonville Miners	Union City Dodgers	1-0	?	
	8/8/1956	Northern League	Duluth-Superior White Sox	Fargo-Moorhead Twins	5-0	7	
	8/26/1962	**American League**	**Minnesota Twins**	**Kansas City Athletics**	**1-0**		

NO-HITTERS

Player	Date	League	Team	Opponent	Score	
Tom Phoebus	8/15/1966	International League	Rochester Red Wings	Buffalo Bisons	1-0	7
	4/27/1968	**American League**	**Baltimore Orioles**	**Boston Red Sox**	**6-0**	
Jim Palmer	6/19/1964	Northern League	Aberdeen Pheasants	Duluth-Superior Dukes	8-0	9
	8/13/1969	**American League**	**Baltimore Orioles**	**Oakland Athletics**	**8-0**	
Bill Singer	4/23/1964	Pacific Coast League	Spokane Indians	Dallas Rangers	3-0	7
	7/20/1970	**National League**	**Los Angeles Dodgers**	**Phildaelphia Phillies**	**5-0**	
Vida Blue	6/19/1968	Midwest League	Burlington Bees	Appleton Foxes	4-0	7
	9/21/1970	**American League**	**Oakland Athletics**	**Minnesota Twins**	**6-0**	
Bob Forsch	5/13/1972	Texas League	Arkansas Travelers	Memphis Blues	4-0	7
	5/25/1973	American Association	Tulsa Oilers	Denver Bears	5-0	
	4/16/1978	**National League**	**St. Louis Cardinals**	**Philadelphia Phillies**	**5-0**	
	9/26/1983	**National League**	**St. Louis Cardinals**	**Montreal Expos**	**3-0**	
Tom Browning	7/31/1984	American Association	Wichita Aeros	Iowa Cubs	2-0	7
	9/16/1988	**National League**	**Cincinnati Reds**	**Los Angeles Dodgers**	**1-0**	Perfect Game
Jose Jimenez	8/27/1998	Texas League	Arkansas Travelers	Shreveport Captains	6-0	
	6/25/1999	**National League**	**St. Louis Cardinals**	**Arizona Diamondbacks**	**1-0**	
Bud Smith	5/6/2000	Texas League	Arkansas Travelers	Midland RockHounds	5-0	
	6/11/2000	Texas League	Arkansas Travelers	San Antonio Missions	1-0	
	9/3/2001	**National League**	**St. Louis Cardinals**	**San Diego Padres**	**4-0**	

NO-NOS KNOCKED OFF THE BOOKS

By Dirk Lammers

BASEBALL'S OFFICIAL NO-hitter list used to chronicle an additional 50 outstanding pitching performances before the Committee for Statistical Accuracy chaired by then MLB Commissioner Fay Vincent established the first official definition of a no-hitter in September 1991

The definition, which simply declared a no-hitter to be a game of nine innings or more that ends with no hits, had the effect of:

- Eliminating 36 no-hitters that were shortened by rain, darkness or other reasons. (Devern Hansack threw the only post-ruling rain-shortened no-hitter in 2006.)
- Erasing two no-hitters that resulted in losing efforts by the away team in which the home team didn't bat in the bottom of the ninth. (Two such no-nos have been thrown since 1991 that would have qualified under the old rules.)
- Wiping out 12 no-hitters by pitchers who threw nine innings of no-hit ball only to yield a hit in extra innings. (Pedro Martínez was since kept out of the no-no club, even though he retired the first 27 batters of a game in 1995).

The accomplishments listed here aren't considered official no-hitters, but they are recognized in other sections of the Elias Sports Bureau record books in their own categories.

No-hitters through nine innings broken up in extra innings

Earl Moore
Cleveland Blues (AL)
Thursday, May 9, 1901
Chicago White Sox 4, Cleveland Blues 2 (10 innings)
League Park (Cleveland)
Game went 10 innings. Moore gave up leadoff single in 10th and allowed one more hit in a losing effort.

Bob Wicker
Chicago Cubs (NL)
Saturday, June 11, 1904
Chicago Cubs 1, New York Giants 0 (12 innings)
Polo Grounds (New York)
Game went 12 innings. Wicker gave up just one single with one out in the 10th and got the victory.

Harry McIntire
Brooklyn Superbas (NL)
Wednesday, August 1, 1906
Pittsburgh Pirates 1, Brooklyn Superbas 0 (13 innings)
Washington Park (Brooklyn)
Game went 13 innings. McIntire gave up a single with two out in the 11th and allowed three more hits in a losing effort.

Red Ames
New York Giants (NL)
Thursday, April 15, 1909
Brooklyn Superbas 3, New York Giants 0 (13 innings)
Polo Grounds (New York)
Game went 13 innings. Ames gave up single with one out in 10th and allowed seven more hits in a losing effort.

Tom Hughes
New York Highlanders (AL)
Tuesday, August 30, 1910 (Second game of doubleheader)
Cleveland Naps 5, New York Highlanders 0 (11 innings)
Hilltop Park (New York)
Game went 11 innings. Hughes gave up single with one out in 10th and allowed six more hits and five 11th-inning runs in a losing effort.

NO-HITTERS

Jim Scott
Chicago White Sox (AL)
Thursday, May 14, 1914
Washington Senators 1, Chicago White Sox 0 (10 innings)
National Park (Washington)
Game went 10 innings. Scott gave up a leadoff single in 10th and allowed one more hit in a losing effort.

Hippo Vaughn
Chicago Cubs (NL)
Wednesday, May 2, 1917
Cincinnati Reds 1, Chicago Cubs 0 (10 innings)
Weeghman Park (Chicago)
This remains the only time in Major League history that both pitchers had no-hitters through nine innings. Vaughn gave up a single with one out in 10th and allowed one more hit in a losing effort. The Reds' Fred Toney is credited with a no-hitter, completing the accomplishment in 10 innings.

Louis "Buck" ("Bobo") Newsom
St. Louis Browns (AL)
Tuesday, September 18, 1934
Boston Red Sox 2, St. Louis Browns 1 (10 innings)
Sportsman's Park (St. Louis)
Game went 10 innings. Newsom gave up a single with two out in the 10th (the only hit against him) but lost the game.

Johnny Klippstein (7 inn.), Hersch Freeman (1 inn.), Joe Black (3 inn.)
Cincinnati Reds (NL)
Saturday, May 26, 1956
Milwaukee Braves 2, Cincinnati Reds 1 (11 innings)
Milwaukee County Stadium (Milwaukee)
Game went 11 innings Black gave up a double with two out in 10th and allowed two more hits for the loss.

Harvey Haddix
Pittsburgh Pirates (NL)
Tuesday, May 26, 1959
Milwaukee Braves 1, Pittsburgh Pirates 0 (13 innings)
Milwaukee County Stadium (Milwaukee)
Haddix threw a perfect game through 12, retiring the first 36 batters he faced. He lost the perfect game in the top of the 13th when Pirates third baseman Don Hoak committed an error, letting Felix Mantilla reach first. After a sacrifice bunt by Eddie Mathews and an intentional walk to Hank Aaron, Haddix lost the no-hitter (and the game) on a Joe Adcock walk-off homer. The homer was ruled a double because Aaron walked off the field before rounding the bases, and the final score was ruled 1-0.

Jim Maloney
Cincinnati Reds (NL)
Monday, June 14, 1965
New York Mets 1, Cincinnati Reds 0 (11 innings)
Crosley Field (Cincinnati)
Game went 11 innings. Maloney gave up leadoff home run in the 11th and allowed one more hit in the losing effort.

Mark Gardner (9 inn.), Jeff Fassero (0 inn.)
Montreal Expos (NL)
Friday, July 26, 1991
Los Angeles Dodgers 1, Montreal Expos 0 (10 innings)
Dodger Stadium (Los Angeles)
Game went 10 innings. Gardner gave up a leadoff single in 10th and allowed one more hit before Fassero came in. Fassero gave up a game-winning hit but Gardner had responsibility for the baserunner and was charged with the loss.

Pedro Martínez (9 inn.), Mel Rojas (1 inn.)
Montreal Expos (NL)
Saturday, June 3, 1995
Montreal Expos 1, San Diego Padres 0 (10 innings)
Jack Murphy Stadium (San Diego)
Game went 10 innings. Martínez had a perfect game through nine. After he gave up a leadoff double in the 10th, Rojas came in and retired the next three batters.

No-hitters lost by the away team in which the game ended after 8 1/2 innings:
Silver King
Chicago Pirates (PL)
Saturday, June 21, 1890
Brooklyn Ward's Wonders 1, Chicago Pirates 0
South Side Park (Chicago)

NO-HITTERS

Home team led after 8 1/2 innings so didn't have to bat in ninth. No-hit pitcher threw just eight innings.

Andy Hawkins
New York Yankees (AL)
Sunday, July 1, 1990
Chicago White Sox 4, New York Yankees 0
Comiskey Park (Chicago)
Home team led after 8 1/2 innings so didn't have to bat in ninth. No-hit pitcher threw just eight innings.

Matt Young
Boston Red Sox (AL)
Sunday, April 12, 1992 (First game of doubleheader)
Cleveland Indians 2, Boston Red Sox 1
Cleveland Stadium (Cleveland)
Home team led after 8 1/2 innings so didn't have to bat in ninth. No-hit pitcher threw just eight innings.

Jered Weaver (6 inn.), Jose Arrendondo (2 inn.)
Los Angeles Angels (IL)
Saturday, June 28, 2008
Los Angeles Dodgers 1, Los Angeles Angels 0
Dodger Stadium (Los Angeles)
Home team led after 8 1/2 innings so didn't have to bat in ninth. No-hit pitchers threw just eight innings.

No-hitters that fell shy of nine innings due to weather, darkness or other reason

Larry McKeon
Indianapolis Hoosiers (AA)
Tuesday, May 6, 1884
Indianapolis Hoosiers 0, Cincinnati Red Stockings 0 (6 innings)
League Park (Cincinnati)
Game called due to rain.

Charlie Geggus
Washington Nationals (UA)
Thursday, August 21, 1884
Washington Nationals 12, Wilmington Quicksteps 1 (8 innings)
Capitol Grounds (Washington)
Game called by consent.

Charlie "Pretzels" Getzien
Detroit Wolverines (NL)
Wednesday, October 1, 1884
Detroit Wolverines 1, Philadelphia Phillies 0 (6 innings)
Recreation Park (Detroit)
Game called due to rain.

Charlie Sweeney (2 inn.), Henry Boyle (3 inn.)
St. Louis Maroons (UA)
Sunday, October 5, 1884
St. Paul Whitecaps 1, St. Louis Maroons 0 (5 innings)
Union Grounds (St. Louis)
Game called due to rain.

Fred "Dupee" Shaw
Providence Grays (NL)
Wednesday, October 7, 1885 (First game of doubleheader)
Providence Grays 4, Buffalo Bisons 0 (5 innings)
Olympic Park (Buffalo)
Planned five-inning doubleheader.

George Van Haltren
Chicago White Stockings (NL)
Thursday, June 21, 1888
Chicago White Stockings 1, Pittsburgh Alleghenys 0 (6 innings)
West Side Park (Chicago)
Game called due to rain.

Ed Crane
New York Giants (NL)
Thursday, September 27, 1888
New York Giants 3, Washington Nationals 0 (7 innings)
Polo Grounds (New York)
Game called due to darkness.

Matt Kilroy
Baltimore Orioles (AA)
Saturday, July 29, 1889 (Second game of doubleheader)
Baltimore Orioles 0, St. Louis Browns 0 (7 innings)
Oriole Park (Baltimore)
Game called due to darkness.

George Nicol
St. Louis Browns (AA)
Tuesday, September 23, 1890

NO-HITTERS

St. Louis Browns 21, Philadelphia Athletics 2 (7 innings)
Sportsman's Park (St. Louis)
Game called due to darkness.

Hank Gastright
Columbus Solons (AA)
Sunday, October 12, 1890
Columbus Solons 6, Toledo Maumees 0 (8 innings)
Recreation Park (Columbus)
Game called due to darkness.

Jack Stivetts
Boston Braves (NL)
Saturday, October 15, 1892 (Second game of doubleheader)
Boston Braves 4, Washington Senators 0 (5 innings)
Boundary Field (Washington, D.C.)
Game called by mutual consent.

Elton "Ice Box" Chamberlain
Cincinnati Reds (NL)
Saturday, September 23, 1893 (Second game of doubleheader)
Cincinnati Reds 6, Boston Beaneaters 0 (7 innings)
League Park (Cincinnati)
Game called due to darkness.

Ed Stein
Brooklyn Grooms (NL)
Saturday, June 2, 1894
Brooklyn Grooms 1, Chicago White Stockings 0 (6 innings)
Eastern Park (Brooklyn)
Game called due to rain.

Red Ames
New York Giants (NL)
Monday, September 14, 1903 (Second game of doubleheader)
New York Giants 5, St. Louis Cardinals 0 (5 innings)
Robison Field (St. Louis)
Game called due to darkness.

Rube Waddell
Philadelphia Athletics (AL)
Tuesday, August 15, 1905
Philadelphia Athletics 2, St. Louis Browns 0 (5 innings)
Columbia Park (Philadelphia)
Game called due to rain.

Jake Weimer
Cincinnati Reds (NL)
Friday, August 24, 1906 (Second game of doubleheader)
Cincinnati Reds 1, Brooklyn Superbas 0 (7 innings)
Palace of the Fans (Cincinnati)
Nightcap planned as seven-inning game.

Jim Dygert (3 inn.), Rube Waddell (2 inn.)
Philadelphia Athletics (AL)
Wednesday, August 29, 1906
Philadelphia Athletics 4, Chicago White Sox 3 (5 innings)
Columbia Park (Philadelphia)
Game called due to rain.

Grant "Stoney" McGlynn
St. Louis Cardinals (NL)
Monday, September 24, 1906 (Second game of doubleheader)
St. Louis Cardinals 1, Brooklyn Superbas 1 (7 innings)
Washington Park (Brooklyn)
Game called due to darkness.

Al "Lefty" Leifield
Pittsburgh Pirates (NL)
Wednesday, September 26, 1906 (Second game of doubleheader)
Pittsburgh Pirates 8, Philadelphia Phillies 0 (6 innings)
National League Park (Philadelphia)
Game called due to darkness.

Ed Walsh
Chicago White Sox (AL)
Sunday, May 26, 1907
Chicago White Sox 8, New York Highlanders 1 (5 innings)
South Side Park (Chicago)
Game called due to rain.

Ed Karger

NO-HITTERS

St. Louis Cardinals (NL)
Sunday, August 11, 1907 (Second game of doubleheader)
St. Louis Cardinals 4, Boston Doves 0 (7 innings)
Robison Field (St. Louis)
Perfect game; nightcap planned as seven-inning game.

Howie Camnitz
Pittsburgh Pirates (NL)
Friday, August 23, 1907 (Second game of doubleheader)
Pittsburgh Pirates 1, New York Giants 0 (5 innings)
Polo Grounds (New York)
Game called due to darkness.

Harry "Rube" Vickers
Philadelphia Athletics (AL)
Saturday, October 5, 1907 (Second game of doubleheader)
Philadelphia Athletics 4, Washington Senators 0 (5 innings)
National Park (Washington, D.C.)
Perfect game, called because of darkness.

Johnny Lush
St. Louis Cardinals (NL)
Thursday, August 6, 1908
St. Louis Cardinals 2, Brooklyn Superbas 0 (6 innings)
Washington Park (Brooklyn)
(Game called due to rain.)

Len "King" Cole
Chicago Cubs (NL)
Sunday, July 31, 1910 (Second game of doubleheader)
Chicago Cubs 4, St. Louis Cardinals 0 (7 innings)
Robison Field (St. Louis)
Teams agreed to call the game at 5 p.m. Central so teams could catch their trains.

Jay Carl Cashion
Washington Senators (AL)
Tuesday, August 20, 1912 (Second game of doubleheader)
Washington Senators 2, Cleveland Naps 0 (6 innings)
Griffith Stadium (Washington, D.C.)
Game called at end of sixth to allow Cleveland to catch a train.

Walter Johnson
Washington Senators (AL)
Monday, August 25, 1924 (First game of doubleheader)
Washington Senators 2, St. Louis Browns 0 (7 innings)
Griffith Stadium (Washington, D.C.)
Game called due to rain; second game of doubleheader canceled.

Fred Frankhouse
Brooklyn Dodgers (NL)
Friday, August 27, 1937 (First game of doubleheader)
Brooklyn Dodgers 5, Cincinnati Reds 0 (8 innings)
Ebbets Field (Brooklyn)
Opener called due to rain after 7 2/3 (second game of doubleheader canceled)

Johnny Whitehead
St. Louis Browns (AL)
Monday, August 5, 1940 (Second game of doubleheader)
St. Louis Browns 4, Detroit Tigers 0 (6 innings)
Sportsman's Park (St. Louis)
Game called due to rain.

Jim Tobin
Boston Braves (NL)
Thursday, June 22, 1944 (Second game of doubleheader)
Boston Braves 7, Philadelphia Phillies 0 (5 innings)
Braves Field (Boston)
Game called due to darkness.

Mike McCormick
San Francisco Giants (NL)
Friday, June 12, 1959
San Francisco Giants 3, Philadelphia Phillies 0 (5 innings)
Connie Mack Stadium (Philadelphia)
Game called due to rain. McCormick allowed a single and then walked the bases loaded in the sixth inning, but because that inning was never completed statistically the hit never happened.

NO-HITTERS

"Toothpick" Sam Jones
San Francisco Giants (NL)
Friday, September 26, 1959
San Francisco Giants 4, St. Louis Cardinals 0 (7 innings)
Busch Stadium I (St. Louis)
Game called due to rain.

Dean Chance
Minnesota Twins (AL)
Thursday, August 6, 1967
Minnesota Twins 2, Boston Red Sox 0 (5 innings)
Metropolitan Stadium (Minneapolis)
Perfect game, called because of rain.

David Palmer
Montreal Expos (NL)
Saturday, April 21, 1984 (Second game of doubleheader)
Montreal Expos 4, St. Louis Cardinals 0 (5 innings)
Busch Stadium (St. Louis)
Perfect game, called because of rain.

Pascual Pérez
Montreal Expos (NL)
Saturday, September 24, 1988
Montreal Expos 1, Philadelphia Phillies 0 (5 innings)
Veterans Stadium (Philadelphia)
Game called due to rain.

Mélido Pérez
Chicago White Sox (AL)
Thursday, July 12, 1990
Chicago White Sox 8, New York Yankees 0 (6 innings)
Yankee Stadium (New York)
Game called due to rain.

Devern Hansack
Boston Red Sox (AL)
Sunday, October 1, 2006
Boston Red Sox 9, Baltimore Orioles 0 (5 innings)
Fenway Park (Boston)
Game called due to rain.

Thanks to Dirk Lammers and his website NoNoHitters.com.

WHEN IS A NO-HITTER NOT A NO-HITTER

OCTOBER 1, 2006: BOSTON RED SOX 9, BALTIMORE ORIOLES 0, AT FENWAY PARK

By Bill Nowlin

WHEN DOES A PITCHER throw a complete-game shutout without giving up even one base hit, leaving the game with a win, but somehow that's not a no-hitter? It sort of defies logic. You pitched. You were the only pitcher for your team. You won the game. It's in the record books as a complete-game win. And you never gave up a hit.

The answer is fairly well known, however unsatisfying it may be. According to an edict from major-league baseball, if you pitch fewer than nine innings, a game such as that is not a no-hitter. Even though there were no hits. And it is counted as a complete game.

Pitching in only his second game in the majors, Nicaraguan righty Devern Hansack of the Boston Red Sox faced the Baltimore Orioles at Fenway Park. It was Sunday, October 1 — the very last game of the 2006 regular season.

The Orioles were solidly in fourth place with a record of 70-91. The Red Sox were in third place but just one game behind the Toronto Blue Jays (Boston was 85-76 and Toronto was 86-75). If Toronto lost its game against the New York Yankees and Boston won its game, the two teams would be tied at 86-76. Neither had a shot at a wild-card berth, however.

Hansack hadn't even been in Organized Baseball at the beginning of 2005. He was on the Nicaraguan team, playing at an international tournament in The Netherlands, when a tip to Red Sox international scouting chief Craig Shipley resulted in a $3,000 offer for Hansack to sign a contract with the Red Sox. He enjoyed a very good year at Double-A Portland, helping the team to the postseason and being named the team's MVP. He had been brought up to the majors in the waning days of the year. At Fenway Park, he was working out of a temporary locker in the Red Sox clubhouse.

Hansack lost his first start, 5-3, in Toronto on September 23. Now, with little on the line, he was asked to pitch the last game and close out the season. Pitching for the O's was right-hander Hayden Penn.

The game was delayed for quite a long time by bad weather, a mere 3-hour and 23-minute rain delay. Both teams wanted to get the game in. It didn't get underway until 5:28 P.M. The game time temperature was 56 degrees, with a 12 mph wind coming in from center field. There was a continuous drizzle, and the field condition was wet. But home-plate umpire Rob Drake set himself behind Boston catcher Jason Varitek and gave Hansack the signal to start the game.

The attendance was purportedly 35,826. In reality, most of those who had purchased tickets never showed up. A groundout, a strikeout, and a fly ball to center, and the O's were set down in order on 11 pitches.

Even though David Ortiz popped up foul to the catcher, the two batters before him had gotten on base and Mike Lowell hit a three-run homer. Red Sox, 3-0.

With one out in the top of the second, Hansack walked Fernando Tatis, but two pitches later retired the side on a double play. Tatis was the only Orioles batter to reach base in the game. Hansack retired the side in order in the third.

In the bottom of the third, Penn imploded. He got two men out, but two walks sandwiched around a single loaded the bases. Then he walked Carlos Pena, forcing in the fourth Red Sox run. And on the first pitch he saw, center fielder Gabe Kapler hit a bases-clearing double to left. It was now 7-0 in favor of the Red Sox, and Baltimore manager Sam Perlozzo called in Julio Manon to take over for Penn. Manon did his job and secured the third out.

In the fourth Hansack had another 1-2-3 inning. Manon gave up a solo home run, hit over the Green Monster, to Mark Loretta. With an 8-0 lead, and the weather still very unpleasant, the Red Sox replaced David Ortiz, Loretta, and Trot Nixon. For Nixon, it was his last game for the Red Sox, and manager Terry Francona had sent him out to right field, only to call him back in so that the fans could give him a final round of applause.

Two strikeouts and a fly ball to center field, and Hansack retired the Orioles in the top of the fifth. Given that the Red Sox held the lead, it was now an official game. Hansack had walked the one batter, and struck out six, but not given up a hit. In fact, none of the balls the Orioles hit was even close to a base hit.

But the umpires hadn't given up on the game, so the Red Sox batted again in the bottom of the fifth as Hansack tried to keep as warm and dry as he could sitting on the bench in the Boston dugout. Eric Hinske hit a solo home run for Boston, off new Baltimore pitcher Russ Ortiz, and the score stood 9-0. Pena reached first on a base on balls, but this time Kapler hit into a double play and Alex Cora grounded out to end the Red Sox fifth.

At this point, play was halted due to a worsening of the weather, and the tarp pulled over the infield in the vain hope that the game could be resumed.

Had he been aware that he was pitching a no-hitter, as it was in progress? "Well, in the beginning, I didn't take notice until I came out after the fourth inning."[1]

It proved impossible to continue and after another 41-minute rain delay, the game was called. Those present had seen a no-hitter. But not according to major-league baseball. Back in 1991, the powers that were—the committee for statistical accuracy—had decided to issue a definition of a "no-hitter." It wasn't a game in which one team failed to get a hit. According to the committee's edict, "A no-hitter is a game in which a pitcher or pitchers complete a game of nine innings or more without allowing a hit."[2]

Perhaps the game that prompted someone feeling the need to define "no-hitter" was the six-inning, rain-shortened no-hitter at Yankee Stadium on July 12, 1990, when Melido Perez no-hit the Yankees, 8-0. It was a no-hitter the day he threw the game. A year later it was not. Perez was deprived of his no-hitter because of a committee ruling.

It wasn't just Perez who lost his no-hitter. So, too, did 35 other pitchers, some of whom had gone to their graves believing they'd pitched a no-hitter (something everyone else had believed, too). A half-dozen or so of the pitchers who in effect had to turn in their honors were still among the living. For years, some of them had "no-hitter" on their résumé, maybe a ball signed by the umpire or by their catcher or teammates—only to wake up one day and been told they had no longer earned that distinction.[3]

Not only did all those pitchers lose their distinction, but so did their catchers.

Jason Varitek of the Boston Red Sox didn't lose the honor, because he never had it. The definition of a no-hitter had been changed (in 1991), years before Varitek caught Hansack's game. But the consequence of the edict deprived him of what would have been a unique accomplishment—the only catcher in major-league history to have caught five no-hitters.

Varitek had previously caught "official" no-hitters by Hideo Nomo (in 2001) and Derek Lowe (2002), and later caught ones by Clay Buchholz (2007) and Jon Lester (2008). Working in sync with your pitcher and calling a no-hitter is in very large part an accomplishment by the catcher as well, and Varitek holds the record with four. As Buchholz told Dirk Lammers, "Pitchers put a lot of trust in their catchers, whether it'd be knowing you can bounce a curveball with a runner on third and know if they're going to block it and pitch calling. That was really early in my career, so I didn't really have any idea who I was throwing to, what they hit well, what they didn't hit well."[4]

Carlos Ruiz has subsequently caught four "official" no-hitters as well—two by Roy Halladay in 2010 (the first one a perfect game), one in 2014 (a combined effort involving four pitchers), and one in 2015. So Ruiz has now tied Varitek, but had Hansack's no-hitter not been ruled a "notable achievement," Varitek would have five.

Hansack's complete-game shutout was the first one a Red Sox pitcher had thrown since Pedro Martinez had done it on August 12, 2004.

"I wasn't disappointed because nobody can stop the rain," Hansack said after the game. "That was fun, wasn't it, seeing him change speeds with the rain dripping off his cap," manager Francona said. "The way he was able to throw strikes, he was really something special."[5]

NOTES

1   Author interview with Devern Hansack, September 23, 2016.

2   The committee was prompted by Commissioner Fay Vincent. Another determination made by the committee was to reaffirm prior practice (since 1968) that no asterisk needed to be placed next to the names of players like Roger Maris, who had hit 61 homers in a 162-game season, surpassing Babe Ruth's 60 struck when the seasons were 154 games long. The decision was that "Rain-shortened games or others ... of fewer than nine innings will be considered 'notable achievements,' not no-hitters, and will be listed separately." Murray Chass, "Maris's Feat Finally Recognized 30 Years After Hitting 61 Homers," *New York Times*, September 5, 1991.

3   Dirk Lammers, in his enjoyable and comprehensive book *Baseball's No-Hit Wonders* lists the 36 pitchers and provides dates and details of their games. In sequential and not alphabetical order, they were nineteenth-century pitchers Larry McKeon, Charlie Geggus, Charlie "Pretzels" Getzien, Charlie Sweeny, Henry Boyle, Fred "Dupee" Shaw, George Van Haltren, Ed Crane, Matt Kilroy, George Nicol, Hank Gastright, Jack Stivetts, Elton "Ice Box" Chamberlain, and Ed Stein. (Sweeny and Boyle had pitched a combined no-hitter.) Those twentieth-century pitchers who had their honors scrubbed from the books were Red Ames, Rube Waddell, Jake Weimer, Jim Dygert (who joined Waddell in a combined no-hitter—making Rube a two-time "loser"), Stoney McGlynn, Lefty Leifield, Ed Walsh, Ed Karger, Howie Camnitz, Harry "Rube" Vickers, Johnny Lush, Len "King" Cole, Jay Carl Cashion, Walter Johnson, Fred Frankhouse, Johnny Whitehead, Jim Tobin, Mike McCormick, "Toothpick" Sam Jones, Dean Chance, David Palmer, Pascual Perez, and Melido Perez. See Dirk Lammers, *Baseball's No-Hit Wonders* (Lakewood, Colorado: Unbridled Books, 2016), 381-387.

4   Dirk Lammers interview with Clay Buchholz, May 20, 2015. Ibid., 261.

5   Howard Ulman, Associated Press, October 1, 2006. A blogger noted that with the win, Hansack became the "sixth-winningest Nicaraguan pitcher in MLB history" (see smoaky.com/forum/index.php?showtopic=59716):

   1. Dennis Martinez, 245.

   2. Vicente Padilla, 66.

   3. Albert (DeSouza) Williams, 35.

   4. Porfi Altamirano, 7.

   5. Oswaldo Mairena, 2.

   6. Devern Hansack, 1.

DEVERN HANSACK

By Bill Nowlin

DEVERN HANSACK'S BRIEF career in major-league baseball contains a number of ingredients that offer some fascination. He was the son of a baker and a lobster fisherman from Pearl Lagoon, Nicaragua, who made it all the way to the big leagues as a right-handed pitcher with the Boston Red Sox. On the very last day of the 2006 season, in just his second start in the majors, he threw what some would argue was a no-hitter (more on that later). And he was — albeit with a minor contribution — a member of the 2007 world champion Red Sox.

Devern Brandon Hansack was born on February 5, 1978, in Pearl Lagoon, a town on the Miskito Coast of Nicaragua. Those who have not traveled in the region may have never heard of the Miskito Coast, sometimes spelled Mosquito Coast and named after the Miskito Indians in the area. It's an area on the Caribbean coast of Central America, embracing parts of Honduras and Nicaragua. English is the primary language, dating back to days when the region had been colonized by England. Livingston, Guatemala, reflects that historical influence as well, as does the country of Belize (which was named British Honduras until it became Belize in 1973).[1]

Pearl Lagoon itself is a municipality of under 9,000 people, and lacks roads. Access is by boat, though in 2007 it became possible to arrive by road. It is located about 25 miles north of the larger (around 50,000 people) city of Bluefields, and is the largest coastal lagoon in Nicaragua. In a Spanish-speaking country like Nicaragua, it may seem surprising that there are communities with English-language names like Bluefields and Pearl Lagoon, but that reflects the Moskito Coast culture.

The Lonely Planet website paints an idyllic picture of Pearl Lagoon (which would be Laguna de Perlas if one were to translate it into Spanish): "At last, you've arrived in the real Caribbean. Here are dirt roads and palm trees, reggae music, and an English-speaking Creole community that fishes the local waters for shrimp, fish and lobster, and still refers to Spanish-speaking Nicaraguans as 'the Spaniards.' You can feel the stress roll off your shoulders as soon as you get off the boat from Bluefields. And the best part is that despite its obvious charms, this town still sees very few tourists — which means you may well be the only foreigner buzzing through the mangroves and jungle that surround Pearl Lagoon (the bay). The bay is a timeless expanse of black water and home to more than a dozen ethnic fishing villages."[2]

The NicaTour.net site explains: "You notice the wooden fishing boats. Fishing is the principal activity of the inhabitants and an important natural resource. The people that live in the villages near the lagoon are busy all day. There is constant activity around the boats and fishing gear since fishing is the primary source of income for these families." It goes on to point out that Pearl Lagoon "was considered the second capital of the Mosquitia kingdom when the last Mosco king took up residence in the city. He arrived here after Henry Clarence deposed him in Bluefields in 1894."[3]

And yet Pearl Lagoon has long had an active interest in baseball, with several local teams. This fairly small community has produced yet another major leaguer, also a right-handed pitcher, Albert Williams. Though originally drafted by the Pirates, Williams (born in 1954) was later released and signed as a free agent by the Minnesota Twins. The 6-foot-4, 190-pound righty played his full big-league career for the Twins, working in 120 games (97 of them as a starter) from 1980 through his final season in 1984. Over the course of those five seasons, Williams was 35-38, with a 4.24 ERA. Between his time in the Pirates' minor-league system and his signing with the Twins, he played a 1979 season split between Caracas and Panama in the Inter-American League.

Williams was well-known in Pearl Lagoon, of course, but after he made the big leagues, he didn't return back to Nicaragua and so, while Hansack knew about Williams, he never met him.

Devern has been playing baseball from his earliest childhood. His first baseball was handmade for him by his father.[4] "As soon as we grew up, that's what we would want in our hand—we would make a bat out of any tree, something to have swinging. He made both. You had to have your own little bat and your own little ball. Then you could get in a game." A glove came later—"not much of a glove, you know, a little cardboard."[5]

Was he a pretty good hitter? "I was a pretty good hitter. I was a center fielder at those times."[6]

Devern had nine siblings. His mother is Melissa McCoy, a baker by trade, specializing in coconut bread and meat patties. His father, George Hansack, was a lobster fisherman and also farmed coconut trees.[7]

Hansack was initially signed by scouts Andres Reiner and Calixto Vargas for the Houston Astros in 1999, for a reported $10,000. They had both visited Bluefields and seen him play for the Pearl Lagoon team. The Astros had him play baseball in Venezuela for the seasons of 2000 and 2001. He'd first been spotted by an Astros scout while playing in an Atlantic Coast tournament. It was reportedly in Venezuela, and not in Nicaragua, where he learned Spanish.[8] In 2002 he pitched in 12 games (10 starts) for the New York-Penn League's Tri-City ValleyCats. He was 3-4, with a 3.60 ERA. The 2003 season, he worked out of Lexington, Kentucky, for the Single-A South Atlantic League's Lexington Legends. There Hansack was 10-6, with a 4.52 ERA.

At the end of spring training in 2004, the Astros released Hansack. He left professional baseball at the time. In 2005, the Red Sox vice president for international scouting, Craig Shipley, got a tip from the third-base coach of the Nicaraguan national team, Hubert Silva, and subsequently watched Hansack pitch in a World Cup international baseball tournament in The Netherlands.[9]

Murray Chass of the *New York Times* said that Shipley liked what he saw. "He was pretty easy to like," Shipley said. "He was throwing 93, 94 and had a good slider, an above-average slider."[10] Shipley wanted to sign him, but for strategic reasons he let Hansack return to Nicaragua without a conversation.

Chass continued, "After Hansack returned home, Shipley sent Jon Dipuglia, the Latin American scouting cross-checker, to Nicaragua to sign him. 'We didn't make contact with him in Holland,' Shipley said, explaining his strategy. 'When you make contact, the player starts talking to others on the club and they say, "I know this guy with that team and that guy with that team," and you could lose the chance to sign him. I also didn't want scouts who were there to see me talking to him.'"[11] A deal was struck and Hansack became property of the Red Sox organization.

ESPN's Amy K. Nelson wrote that Shipley had signed Hansack for a $3,000 bonus, adding, "Hansack went on to become the Red Sox's Double-A pitcher of the year while living in a Dominican fan's basement apartment in Portland, Maine."[12]

In 2006 he pitched for the Portland (Maine) Sea Dogs, the Double-A Eastern League affiliate of the Boston Red Sox. And he made it to the major leagues. With Portland, Hansack was 8-7 with an ERA of 3.26. He was an older player for a Double-A team, 28 at the time, but Nick Cafardo of the *Boston Globe* wrote in late July that Hansack "has been effective as a starter for Portland since taking a regular turn in the rotation June 17. He's allowed three runs or fewer in all eight of his starts, with no earned runs allowed in four of those starts."[13]

The fourth time was the charm. On September 17 Portland won its first Eastern League championship, three games to two, over the Akron Aeros. Hansack pitched eight innings, allowing three runs, striking out eight and walking no one. He got the win, and was named the team's MVP. Nelson said that Boston's Theo Epstein had been at the celebration and took Hansack aside, saying, "Have fun, but not too much, I need to talk with you."[14]

Two days later Hansack was called up to Boston. "To me, it was a big surprise," he said. "To win a championship and get called up, it was amazing."[15]

The 2006 Red Sox were in second place on September 19, but they weren't in contention. They were 11 games out of first place with 11 games to play.

Hansack was given a start—his major-league debut—on September 23 in Toronto. "A Pearl Lagoon boy is here," he said. "I can't believe I'm here. … Boston signed me and gave me a second chance. I can tell any young guy who wants to do something, there's a second chance. Just put your mind to it."[16]

Hansack lost the game at Rogers Centre, 5-3, pitching five-plus innings. After pretty much cruising through the first three innings, he gave up back-to-back solo home runs in the fourth inning to Lyle Overbay and Troy Glaus. The Red Sox tied the game, 2-2, in the top of the sixth, but Hansack gave up a double and a single to the first two batters in the bottom of the sixth and Red Sox manager Terry Francona made a move, bringing in lefty Javier Lopez. One of the inherited runners scored. After the game, Francona said of Hansack, "He threw strikes, he threw his breaking ball over the plate. I thought he showed some poise. He left two fastballs back to back, right over the middle of the plate. I thought he represented himself pretty well. Right from the first pitch of the game, he looked like he belonged. Pounded the zone, which was good to see right off the bat. He did OK."[17]

Eight days later, there was the "no-hitter." On October 1 at Fenway Park, the last game on the schedule for both the Red Sox and the Orioles, Hansack waited out a 3-hour, 23-minute rain delay and finally took the mound. He set down the Orioles in order in the first inning, working throughout the game in a continuous drizzle. There was a window that had opened in the weather. "I started warming up quick," he recalled. Rain was coming off his cap. "It was dripping. It was making it hard for me to throw."[18] Likewise, the O's pitchers, of course—and they gave up nine runs in five innings.

Hansack faced the minimum 15, walking Fernando Tatis in the second but moments later inducing a one-out double play that took Tatis off the basepaths and closed that inning. No other Baltimore batter reached first base. The game was called after five innings, a 9-0 shutout. It's in the books as a complete game, a shutout, and there were no hits by the Baltimore batters.

"For the fans there, it was a no-hitter. I was very excited, surprised, because I was out of baseball so long," Hansack said.[19]

"What an end of the season for him," Francona added. "It was fun, wasn't it? One day he's pumping his chest down in Portland, a couple of weeks later, he's winning a game and giving up no hits in a game in Boston. Good for him, and good for us."[20]

Sportswriter Gordon Edes dubbed Hansack "perhaps the most improbable of the 14 pitchers who have started for the Sox this season."[21]

"I don't know why it doesn't come up as a no-hitter," Hansack said 10 years later. Neither do many fans. Had the exact game been pitched in 1990, it would have been declared a no-hitter at the time. There was, however, a "rules change" in 1991 a new definition was promulgated: To be deemed a "no-hitter," a game had to go at least nine innings. It was, nonetheless, quite a way to end a season.

Working with Jason Varitek as his catcher that day was "the best. As rookies coming up, we aren't going to shake off Varitek, right? Whatever he called, I tried to throw."[22]

In January 2007, Amy K. Nelson actually traveled to Pearl Lagoon to see what the place was like. Hansack showed her the house in which he had been born and still lived, just behind the center-field scoreboard.

Come the 2007 season, with the idea of trying Jonathan Papelbon as a starter instead of reliever, the Red Sox looked over quite a number of pitchers during spring training for the open slot in the bullpen. Amalie Benjamin wrote that Hansack's "stuff still intrigues the Red Sox."[23] It didn't take long in spring training, however, to come to the decision to keep Papelbon in the pen. Hansack was placed with Pawtucket to start the season.

He had a terrific start with the PawSox, striking out 20 batters in his first 10⅔ innings, and winning his first two games, allowing only one earned run. On May 3 Boston's Mike Timlin was diagnosed with right shoulder tendinitis, placed on the 15-day disabled list, and Hansack was called up.

On May 8, at Rogers Centre, Josh Beckett pitched seven innings of one-run ball. Francona asked Hansack to work the bottom of the eighth. He did, but he struggled. He walked the first two batters, then induced a grounder to get a force out at second base. A single drove in one run (the Red Sox still led, 9-2), with a strikeout and another walk—loading the bases—following. J.C. Romero came on and struck out the last batter. Hansack was optioned back to Pawtucket, the Red Sox preferring to see him starting there.

On May 17 Josh Beckett tore some skin on a finger, and Hansack was recalled. The next evening, in the second game of a day/night doubleheader against visiting Atlanta, Hansack was given a start. A solo homer by Chipper Jones marred his first inning. In the second inning, a Matt Diaz double drove in a second run. And in the fourth, Diaz homered. An error followed by another double made it 4-0, Braves. Hansack completed the fourth, but had taken a ball hit off his finger and was replaced by Joel Pineiro come the fifth. X-rays were negative. The final score was 14-0, Braves, and Hansack was the losing pitcher. After the game he was sent back to Pawtucket with Kason Gabbard brought in to take his place.

For Pawtucket in 2007, Hansack started in 23 (of 25) games and was 10-7, 3.61.

On September 1, 2007, rookie Clay Buchholz threw a no-hitter in his second major-league start. There had been close ones—notably Billy Rohr, in 1967—but no Red Sox rookie had ever thrown a no-hitter before—since Hansack's five-inning no-hitter was deemed not to qualify.

On September 4, after rosters expanded, Hansack rejoined the Red Sox. He pitched three full innings in Baltimore on September 8. The Sox were already down, 11-4, at the midpoint of the game. Hansack pitched the fifth, sixth, and seventh, allowing two hits and no runs. It was his last appearance of the season. The Red Sox had a 5½-game lead over the pack, in first place in the American League East, but it was a fragile lead that dipped to as little as a game and a half on September 19 and again on the 23rd. They held on and won the division, and ultimately the World Series.

For his part, Hansack had a 0-1 record (4.70) to go with the world-championship ring the Red Sox presented to all who had been on the team at any point in the season.

There had been one curious incident during a Sunday night game at Fenway Park on September 16. The Yankees were in town. While Mariano Rivera was warming up in the bullpen, a ball flew out of the adjacent Red Sox bullpen and struck him on the hand. "It came in hot," Yankees reliever Ron Villone told the New York Post. "He couldn't feel his arm; it was numb. We were in the bullpen saying, 'Oh no.'" Blame was pinned on Boston's Eric Gagne, but he said it hadn't come from him, that it had come from Hansack, who was warming up beside him at the time. Rivera got into the game, and earned a save.[24]

Hansack played in the Dominican Winter League, and put in some work in Boston over the winter as well. In mid-March he was assigned to Pawtucket, and started 25 games there in 2008. He was 6-10 with a 4.08 ERA, though after a slow start, at one point in June he threw 25 consecutive scoreless innings and into July and August had made 10 quality starts in a row. After Pawtucket was eliminated from the International League playoffs (Hansack had pitched six hitless innings in Game Two), and with the Boston Red Sox very much still in contention, Hansack was brought up to Boston on September 7.

The Sox were in second place, but only two games back, when Hansack pitched in his first major-league game of the 2008 season, throwing the final three innings (without giving up a hit) on September 13 against the Blue Jays. It was a game the Red Sox lost, 8-1. His next game was on September 17, at Tampa Bay. Starter Tim Wakefield was struggling and had given up five runs before Hansack took over in the third. He got two outs, but was charged with two unearned runs before he, too, was replaced. The loss dropped Boston back to two games behind. Hansack pitched in two more games. On September 26 he was the last pitcher in a 19-8 loss to the Yankees. He was charged with three earned runs in 2⅓ innings. As he had in 2006, he pitched in the last regular-season game of 2008. It was Red Sox against Yankees, at Fenway Park, and the score was tied, 3-3, after nine innings. Hansack pitched the top of the 10th and got the Yankees 1-2-3, with two groundouts bracketing a strikeout. And Boston scored in the bottom of the 10th, so Hansack got the win. He was 1-0 (4.05) in 2008.

Though he'd pitched in three seasons for the Red Sox, had a no-hitter ("unofficial" though it was), and contributed to two teams that went to the playoffs (the Red Sox did in 2008, though they lost in the ALCS), he was not a familiar face to most Sox fans. Keith O'Brien wrote that he "would likely not be recognized if he wore his uniform on the Red Line."[25]

That fall Hansack went to the Florida Instructional League for more work. He remained on the 40-man roster. On March 28 he was optioned to Pawtucket. On April 22, to clear room for Jeff Bailey, the Red Sox put Hansack on unconditional-release waivers. He wasn't claimed so the Red Sox signed him to a minor-league deal, as he worked rehabbing in extended spring training. He did pitch for Pawtucket, but only for one inning—the last of his professional career.

Hansack had to undergo rotator cuff and a difficult labrum surgery, both at the same time. He was unable to return to pitching professionally. He has normal use of his shoulder, and eight years later could still pitch, but not with the same force as previously.

In subsequent years, Hansack spent some time coaching at home in Pearl Lagoon, and was briefly appointed as an assistant baseball coach at the University of Maine at Farmington beginning in September 2013. A year later, on September 5, 2014, he was invited to throw out the ceremonial first pitch before a Portland Sea Dogs playoff game.

A number of his brothers and sisters work on cruise ships, some docking out of Miami and others out of Europe. Others work in Managua at call centers for businesses like Target. His sister Val works for the mayor of Pearl Lagoon.

At the time this biography was written in September 2016, Devern and his wife, Christine Forsley (a Mainer—they met while Devern was in Portland), lived in Carrabassett Valley, Maine, with their two young children, Ruby and Brandon, near the Sugarloaf Ski resort. Devern returns home to Pearl Lagoon for visits and to get in some fishing, shrimping, and lobstering, particularly during the cold wintertime in Maine. In the early autumn of 2016, he was knitting his own throw net to take to Nicaragua with him, the better to shrimp and fish with.[26]

SOURCES

In addition to the sources noted in this biography, the author also accessed Retrosheet.org, Baseball-Reference.com, Rod Nelson of SABR's Scouts Committee, and the SABR Minor Leagues Database, accessed online at Baseball-Reference.com. Thanks to Chris Bessey, to Christine Forsley, and to Devern Hansack.

NOTES

1. "Belize was a British crown colony from 1862 until 1964, when it became self-governing. Belize became fully independent from the United Kingdom in 1981. Belize was the last continental possession of the United Kingdom in the Americas." See sunofbelize.com/en/british_honduras.php.
2. lonelyplanet.com/nicaragua/caribbean-coast/laguna-de-perlas/introduction#ixzz4JfIAFubF.
3. nicatour.net/en/nicaragua/pearls-lagoon.cfm.
4. Email from Christine Forsley on September 22, 2016.
5. Author interview with Devern Hansack on September 23, 2016.
6. Ibid.
7. Email from Christine Forsley on September 22, 2016.
8. Amy K. Nelson, "From Pearl Lagoon to the Back Bay," February 13, 2007, ESPN.com at espn.com/mlb/news/story?id=2762971.
9. Silva had already played a role in the Red Sox signing pitcher Mario Pena from Managua. In later years, Silva appeared in the news packaging a couple of players (Corby McCoy and Luis Garcia) in 2012-13 for the New York Yankees. baseballamerica.com/online/prospects/international-affairs/2013/2614690.html.
10. Murray Chass, "Lobsterman From Nicaragua Could Join Red Sox Cast," *New York Times*, January 14, 2007.
11. Ibid. Hansack himself said that Shipley spoke with him personally, and was not aware of the intrigue that Chass detailed.
12. Amy K. Nelson.
13. Nick Cafardo, "Masterson Is a Cape Crusader," *Boston Globe*, July 28, 2006: C6.
14. Amy K. Nelson.
15. Nick Cafardo, "A Sparring Session," *Boston Globe*, September 20, 2006: F5.
16. Amy K. Nelson.
17. Gordon Edes, "Lowell Unmoved by Offseason Possibilities," *Boston Globe*, September 24, 2006: C11.
18. Author interview with Devern Hansack on September 23, 2016.
19. Mike Shalin, "Red Sox Bracket 2006 Season with Wins," MLB.com, October 1, 2006. m.mlb.com/news/article/1693280//.
20. Ibid.
21. Ibid.
22. Author interview with Devern Hansack on September 23, 2016.
23. Amalie Benjamin, "Pitcher Aiming for Spot; Delcarmen Bids for Place on Sox," *Boston Globe*, March 20, 2007: E1.
24. Gordon Edes, "Ramirez Will Make the Call; Slugger's Return Now Up to Him," *Boston Globe*, September 18, 2007: D5.
25. Keith O'Brien, "Latino Sox Fans Lost in Lineup Shuffle," *Boston Globe*, September 23, 2008: A1.
26. Email from Christine Forsley on September 22, 2016.

THE CURSE OF KING KORN

By John T. Saccoman

YOU HAVE HEARD OF THE Curse of the Bambino and the Curse of the Billy Goat, but what about the "Curse of King Korn?" In 1962 the Bohack supermarket chain announced incentives for various Mets "firsts" in the form of King Korn trading stamps.[1] These could be turned in for merchandise at redemption centers. For example, the first Mets grand slam netted Rod Kanehl 50,000 of the stamps.[2] Smaller achievements merited a smaller number; however, the bounty for a no-hitter was 500,000 of the King Korn trading stamps.[3] It would be 50 years before someone could theoretically collect on that offer. More on that later.

If we define "no-hitter" to be a complete-game effort by a single pitcher in a major-league baseball game, then there have been some inexplicably lengthy periods in which a team did not have a no-hitter.

The longest streak of no-hitter futility was authored by the Philadelphia Phillies. On May 1, 1906, southpaw Johnny Lush no-hit the Brooklyn Superbas, winning 6-0. Phillies would not pitch another no-hitter for 8,945 games.[4] In the 8,946th game, on Father's Day, June 21, 1964, Jim Bunning pitched a perfecto at Shea Stadium against the hapless Mets, prevailing by the same 6-0 tally.

The only major-league franchise to have never had a no-hitter thrown by one of its pitchers is the San Diego Padres. This streak, as of the 2017 season, is 7,652 games. Perhaps their best chance came on July 21, 1970, in the team's second year of existence. Clay Kirby, pitching against the Mets (there they are again), had a no-hitter through eight innings in San Diego. The Mets had scored a run in the first inning via two walks, three stolen bases, and a fielder's choice, giving them a 1-0 lead entering the bottom of the eighth. Padres manager Preston Gomez, with two outs, nobody on, and his hurler authoring a no-hitter, elected to pinch-hit for Kirby. It didn't work. The Mets won, 3-0, with three hits in the ninth inning off reliever Jack Baldschun. Gomez pulled an identical stunt on September 4, 1974, while managing the Houston Astros. It didn't work then, either.

When we think of the 1970s Baltimore Orioles, we think of the dominant starting rotation. Jim Palmer. Mike Cuellar. Dave McNally. Pat Dobson. Steve Stone. Mike Flanagan. The list goes on. However, this franchise is mired in the second longest current no-hitter drought. On August 13, 1969, Jim Palmer tossed a no-no at the Oakland Athletics, defeating them by an 8-0 score. They haven't seen another one since, a streak that has spanned 7,514 games, as of 2017.[5]

Now, about that curse of King Korn:

This particular curse did not last as long as the better-known curses (respectively, 86 years and 71 years), and, in fact, it is not the longest in major-league history. However, a curse might be the only way to explain the Mets' drought, which topped 8,000 games.

From the inception of the ballclub in 1962 through May 31, 2012, the New York Mets participated in 8,019 regular-season games, or roughly 7.64 peercent of all major-league games played in that time. From the 1962 season through May 31, 2012, there were 124 one-pitcher no-hitters thrown in major-league baseball. If we assume that no-hitters are random events, then the Mets should have participated in more than nine one-pitcher no-hitters. When one conjures up an image of the Mets, rarely is a high-powered offense the first thing that comes to mind. It is pitching, and specifically, power pitching, that is the historical calling card of the franchise, particularly when it has been successful.

Through the 2011 season, they had been the victim of a one-pitcher no-hitter six times. Since the team might have been expected to participate in nine no-hitters, it would not be unreasonable to assume that Mets pitchers no-hit the opposition three times. Couple that with the fact that Tom Seaver, Dwight Gooden, David Cone, Nolan Ryan, Mike Scott, Warren Spahn, Bret Saberhagen, and Dean Chance all pitched for the Mets, won Cy Young Awards and pitched no-no's, we might conclude that Mets hurlers authored even more than three no-hitters. Except that they didn't. The first five pitched their no-hitters after they left the Mets, while the last three did it before they joined the team. Another pitcher who meets these three criteria, Hideo Nomo, pitched one no-hitter before and one after his Mets stint.

In fact, 23 of the 125 one-pitcher no-hitters thrown in the "Mets Era" were thrown by pitchers who at one time wore the uniform (either in the majors or the minors), but not at the time of their masterpiece.

Then, in the 8,020th regular-season game of their existence, it happened. Johann Santana, a former Cy Young Award winner, pitched a no-hitter while wearing a Mets uniform, beating the St. Louis Cardinals, 8-0, on Friday, June 1, 2012, at Citi Field.

And what about King Korn?

Well, Bohack's stopped issuing King Korn Stamps as of June 23, 1969.[6] That means that Tom Seaver likely would not have received any had his one-hitter the next month been a no-no. (He had retired the first 25 Chicago Cubs he faced, and later referred to it as his "imperfect game.")

Thus, while Johan Santana never received any King Korn trading stamps, he did receive a $5.5 million buyout from the Mets after the 2013 season.

NOTES

1. Janet Paskin, *Tales from the 1962 New York Mets Dugout: A Collection of the Greatest Stories from the Mets Inaugural Season* (New York: Sports Publishing, 2012), 75.

2. Steve Rushin, "Bad Beyond Belief," *Sports Illustrated*, May 25, 1992. si.com/vault/1992/05/25/126550/bad-beyond-belief-thirty-years-ago-the-newborn-new-york-mets-made-baseball-history-of-the-most-dubious-kind. Rushin, in his article, quotes Kanehl: "King Korn had a store in Chicago, and I traded the stamps in there," says Kanehl, who now manages a Garcia's Mexican Restaurant in Rancho Mirage, California. "I got a living-room suite, a Deepfreeze, an end table—a lot of junk." Kanehl died in 2004.

3. Phil Mushnick, nypost.com/2012/06/04/mistakes-second-nature-for-espn/.

4. nonohitters.com/philadelphia-phillies-no-hitters.

5. Four pitchers combined for a no-hitter on Saturday, July 13, 1991, at Oakland-Alameda County Coliseum for the Baltimore Orioles. The Mets have never enjoyed a combined no-hitter.

6. *Wall Street Journal*, June 9, 1969 (accessed via ProQuest).

THE "MOST-HITTERS"

By Bill Nowlin

A WEEK BEFORE THE *No-Hitters* manuscript was to be delivered to our book designer, I was prompted to wonder: OK, in a no-hitter, we have a game in which one pitcher gave up no hits. Zero. But what was the opposite? What was the game in which the *most* hits were surrendered by one pitcher? What were the "most-hitters"? Naturally, I turned to SABR's Lyle Spatz and asked him.

His answer: 36 hits. Louisville's Jack Wadsworth had a game in 1894 during which he gave up 36 hits.

If you want to count only the years since 1900, there are four games tied for the "honor" with 26 hits apiece. Lyle listed them:

26 Al Orth Phillies 1900
26 Doc Parker Reds 1901
26 Al Travers Tigers 1912 (Ty Cobb strike game)
26 Hod Lisenbee A's 1936

I had also asked Lyle which extra-inning game saw a pitcher give up the most base hits. He directed me to Eddie Rommel who in 1932 had given up 29 hits while pitching the last 17 innings of an 18-inning game. That alone seemed to offer the likelihood of a good story.

Short of writing up Games Project accounts of all six games—which I recommend to a willing author—an editor with a little more than a week to wrap up all the editorial jobs of producing a book provides some brief accounts of the games in question.

August 17, 1894: Jack Wadsworth (36 hits)

Wadsworth played professional baseball from 1890 through 1990, most of it in the minor leagues, but he pitched four seasons in the National League, for Cleveland in 1890 (2-16), Baltimore in 1893 (0-3), and the Louisville Colonels in 1894 and 1895. He was 4-18 with Louisville in 1894 and 0-1 in 1895. Simple addition shows a career major-league record of 6-38; he had a 6.85 earned-run average. One of his losses—not surprisingly, given the 36 base hits he allowed—was the August 17 game in Philadelphia. The Colonels were in 11th place at the time; they finished the season in 12th (last) place. The Phillies finished fourth.

The home team did not always bat last at the time, so the Phillies batted in all nine innings; the only one in which they did not score was the second. While Kid Carsey of the Phillies held the Colonels to four runs on eight hits (Wadsworth had one of them), the Phillies scored 29 runs on 36 hits, totaling 49 bases. Wadsworth apparently had no trouble getting the ball over the plate; he walked only three. But that was perhaps his problem—the ball being straight and over the plate. Despite all the runners circling the bases (there were 12 left on base), the entire game was played in 2 hours and 5 minutes. At game's end, wrote the *Philadelphia Inquirer*, "Wadsworth's arm hung limp and the Louisville fielders' tongues were hanging out, the result of their running after long hits."[1]

Right fielder Sam Thompson had the best day at the plate, 6-for-7 with 12 total bases, including a home run. Mike Grady, Joe Sullivan, and Billy Hamilton each had five hits. "Poor old Wadsworth!" lamented the *Oregonian* in Portland.[2] Both teams brought on a catcher in relief during the game, but both starting pitchers went the distance.[3] The *Evening Star* of Washington, DC, suggested one of the reasons for the success of the Philadelphia batters: "It is claimed that [Phillies manager Arthur] Irwin discovered Wadsworth's signs."[4]

April 19, 1900: Al Orth (26 hits)

Highlighting the magnitude of Wadsworth's accomplishment is the fact that the closest anyone has come to matching it still fell 10 base hits short. Al Orth was 14-14 (3.78) for the 1900 Phillies, but he almost blew his first start, on Opening Day (and

Patriots Day) at the Boston Beaneaters' South End Grounds in front of large crowd of around 10,000 fans. Staked to a healthy 17-8 lead heading into the bottom of the ninth, and with several thousand dispirited Boston fans having beat an early exit, Orth let things fell apart. He'd given up 17 hits through eight, though the hits were, in the kind view of the *Boston Globe*, "well distributed."[5] Buck Freeman pinch-hit and homered to kick things off for Boston, then Shad Barry bunted for a base hit. There followed, in all, nine hits accounting for nine runs—and Boston had tied it up, 17-17. Had Fred Tenney singled, it would have been all over, but he grounded out to Delahanty at first base and the game went to the 10th inning. Tenney was the only Beaneater who never made a hit.

The Phillies scored two runs in the top of the 10th, thanks to an error by Bobby Lowe. Bill Bernhard took over for Orth, and retired the Bostons 1-2-3. Orth thus gave up 26 hits but his team won the game.

June 21, 1901: Doc Parker (26 hits)

Cincinnati's Harley Parker had pitched two innings for the Cubs in 1893. He was 4-2 for the Cubs in 1895 and 1-5 in 1896. He was a doctor, and had been pitching in weekend semipro games around Chicago but reappeared in the majors in 1901, joining the Cincinnati Reds on June 19—and wound up pitching in only one game. The game was at Brooklyn's Washington Park. The *Brooklyn Eagle* wrote, "It was a case of 'biff and run' from the sound of the bell."[6]

The Brooklyn Superbas won, 21-3. They scored in every one of the first seven innings; every player on the team banked at least one base hit. Wee Willie Keeler was 5-for-5 and scored five times, too, before checking out of the game to give Cozy Dolan a chance to get some playing time in right field. Had they even tried in the bottom of the eighth? Maybe not. The *Eagle* averred, "[T]hey grew tired of circling the bases. They just lobbed at the ball in the eighth and allowed themselves to be retired without attempting to run out the hits, which were fielded slowly and painfully by the tired and weary Cincinnatis."[7]

The Superbas didn't even have to bat in the bottom of the ninth; they'd already won. So Parker had been hit for 26 base hits, with 34 total bases, in eight innings of work.

The *Cincinnati Post* wrote of its Reds, "They played like amateurs against Brooklyn. Parker won't linger long if he showed the best he had in stock."[8] The loss was the 10th in 11 games, the only game not a loss being a 6-6, 12-inning tie. The Reds finished in last place.

May 18, 1912: Al Travers (26 hits):

As with Harley Parker in 1901, Travers pitched in just one game in the year in question—in fact, it was the only major-league game in which he ever appeared. He was 20 years old at the time he was asked to take the mound pitching for the Detroit Tigers at Philadelphia's Shibe Park, "a student at nearby St. Joseph's College. A few years later, he would become Father Aloysius S. Travers, S.J., and to this day he is the only Catholic priest ever to play in a major league game."[9]

Three days earlier, Ty Cobb had climbed into the stands at New York's Hilltop Park and savagely beaten a disabled spectator who had just one hand and only two fingers on the other hand. AL President Ban Johnson saw the incident first-hand and he handed Cobb an indefinite suspension from baseball. As many as 13 Tigers went on strike in support of Cobb. The *Washington Post* editorialized in support of Cobb, blaming the police for not having removed the "blackguard" who had been verbally abusing him.[10]

It's not that Travers had been a standout college pitcher; "he later confessed that he had never pitched a game in his life."[11] The replacement third baseman had never before played baseball. It was a farce (in the words of the *Philadelphia Inquirer*, "the greatest farce in the baseball line that has ever been unloaded upon the public since the inception of the game."[12] The Tigers fielded a "joke team of schoolboys … and the world's champions 'fattened' on the 'strikebreakers.'"[13]

Travers was actually somewhat effective in the early going; the score was only 6-2 after four innings. Perhaps the Athletics were keyed up to face major-league pitching and simply didn't know how to handle his slow curves. But then they scored eight times in the fifth and added another 10 runs. The final was 24-2, Travers having given up 26 hits and walking seven. He struck out one.

September 11, 1936: Hod Lisenbee (26 hits):

Hod Lisenbee was something of a veteran. In his rookie year with the 1927 Washington Senators, he was 18-9. Though he never had another year that good, he pitched in some 682 minor- and major-league games. Arm problems dogged him throughout, problems apparently never satisfactorily diagnosed, but they didn't keep him for trying. When he took the mound on September 11, 1936, for the Philadelphia Athletics in Chicago. He'd appeared in 15 games for the A's with an earned-run average of 4.91 and a record of 1-5.

The White Sox jumped on him for four hits and four runs in the first inning, only one run of which was earned. He gave up two singles over the next three innings; the score was 4-1 at midpoint. In the bottom of the fifth, however, he gave up four more runs on six hits. In the sixth it was three more runs on four more hits. With the score now 11-1, the game was out of hand but manager Connie Mack still wouldn't pull Lisenbee. After six hits (four runs) in the seventh and four more hits (two more runs) in the eighth, the score was 17-1. Philadelphia scored once in the top of the ninth, but fell 15 runs of short of forcing Lisenbee to take the mound in the bottom of the innings. Lisenbee's ERA jumped in one game, from 4.91 up to 6.03.

The most hits in extra innings / July 10, 1932: Ed Rommel (29 hits):

Eddie Rommel pitched 13 seasons for the Philadelphia Athletics (he was 171-119), and 1932 was the last of those 13 seasons. Twice — in 1922 and 1925 — he had been a 20-game winner. From 1928 on, he'd worked more as a reliever. In 1932 he pitched exclusively in relief. He was without a decision through July 9, and had just worked two innings on July 8 and three more on July 9.

On July 10 he pitched again in relief, in Cleveland. Lew Krausse started the game and gave up three runs on four hits in the first inning. Rommel was brought in. He never left, working 17 innings. In the end, he faced off in a duel of relievers as Wes Ferrell threw 11⅓ innings as Cleveland's third pitcher in the game. Four times, the lead switched. When the A's scored seven times in the top of the seventh, they took a 13-8 lead — the fifth time the lead had changed, only to see the Indians score six times in the bottom of the seventh (and effect another lead change).

After nine innings, the score was tied, 15-15. Then followed six scoreless innings. The Athletics scored twice in the top of the 16th when Jimmie Foxx slammed his third home run of the game. (He drove in eight runs.) It looked as though Rommel might get a win. But four more hits — a double, followed by three singles –tied the score again. There was no scoring in the 17th. With two outs in the top of the 18th, Foxx singled (his sixth hit of the game) and scored on Eric McNair's double. Rommel had already given up 29 hits, but in the bottom of the 18th he wrapped two strikeouts around a groundout and left the field with a "W."

The two teams combined for 58 hits, 25 by the A's and 33 by the Indians. Rommel gave up 29 hits, 20 of them from the second inning through the ninth, and then only nine hits over the next nine innings.

He'd endured, he'd improved, and in the end, Rommel had given up 29 hits and he had won the game.

Cleveland's Johnny Burnett had nine hits all by himself, eight of them off Rommel.

It was Rommel's last season. Starting in 1938, he became an American League umpire and served for 22 years, working 3,369 big-league ballgames.

NOTES

1   "Phillies Make New Records," *Philadelphia Inquirer*, August 18, 1894: 3.

2   "The National League," *Oregonian* (Portland), August 18, 1894: 2.

3   "It Rained Hits for Phillies," *Boston Journal*, August 18, 1894: 3.

4   "Other League Games," *Evening Star* (Washington, DC), August 18, 1894: 7. The pitcher, rather than his catcher, was the one indicating which pitch he planned to throw.

5. T.H. Murnane, "Runs Galore," *Boston Globe*, April 20, 1900: 1.
6. "Base Hits Galore for the Champions," *Brooklyn Eagle*, June 22, 1901: 8.
7. Ibid.
8. Ren Mulford Jr., "Simply Awful," *Cincinnati Post*, June 22, 1901: 2.
9. Greg Livacari, "Al Travers," SABR BioProject, sabr.org/bioproj/person/8b444434.
10. "Baseball Rowdies," *Washington Post*, May 19, 1912: ES4.
11. Ibid.
12. "Tigers Quit Field; Cobb Is Suspended," *Philadelphia Inquirer*, May 19, 1912: 17.
13. "Famous Detroit Ball Team Strikes," *St. Louis Post-Dispatch*, May 19, 1912: A1.

CONTRIBUTORS

MARC Z AARON is a Certified Public Accountant and Certified Valuation Analyst practicing in Randolph, Vermont and living in Grantham, New Hampshire. He is an avid baseball fan from his childhood growing up in The Bronx, and remains to this day a born and bred Yankee fan. Marc has four sons and coached little league for six years. He is a contributor to SABR's BioProject and his first book was published in March 2016— *Who's On First: Replacement Players in World War II* with co-editor Bill Nowlin.

Marc loves tennis as much as baseball and is a tournament tennis player on the local, regional and national levels. He has been a ranked player in New England for his age grouping.

A fantasy baseball player in a countless number of leagues, Marc is also an adjunct professor of economics at Vermont Technical College, the University of New York in Prague, and the Anglo-American University in Prague.

Biggest thrill has been speaking with Sandy Koufax by phone!

BOB BAILEY has been contributing to SABR Publications since 1988. He has writing extensively on the Nineteenth Century Louisville Colonels and the Junior World Series of the twentieth century. In 2013 he was one of the Associate Editors of SABR's *Inventing Baseball*. He has published two books on baseball topics. "*History of the Junior World Series* was a finalist for the 2004 Casey Award and *Baseball Burial Sites* cataloged over 8,000 burial locations for players and others associated with baseball. For the past 10 years he has edited "Nineteenth Century Notes," the newsletter of SABR's Nineteenth Century Committee.

PARKER BENA is a lobbyist by trade. He lives in Jefferson City, Missouri with his wife Karen and his three sons Jordan, Jeremy, and Brendan, three cats, and a Chocolate Lab named Shimmy. He is a devoted fan of the St. Louis Cardinals, following their doings on Fox Sports Midwest, and is especially fascinated with nineteenth century baseball. He contributed a biography of Daryl Patterson to *Sock It To 'Em Tigers* and also a game account to *Inventing Baseball: The Greatest Games if the Nineteenth Century*.

RAY BIRCH is a retired public school teacher from North Kingstown, Rhode Island, and a holder of three degrees from his alma mater, Rhode Island College. He has written biographies for the SABR Bio Project publications about the 1918, 1967 and 1975 Boston Red Sox, as well as ones for their publications about Cuban players and the Red Sox players from the 1950s. Ray enjoys using the research tools that SABR provides as well as those that are available on the Internet. Ray enjoys reading and spending time with his five children and eight grandchildren.

WARREN CORBETT is the author of *The Wizard of Waxahachie: Paul Richards and the End of Baseball as We Knew It*, and a contributor to SABR's BioProject.

CLIFF CORN has lived in Oregon since 1956, when he arrived there immediately after graduating from high school in Kansas. Cliff taught high school mathematics for 31 years, retiring in 1991. An avid baseball fan since 1951, Cliff saw several A's game when the franchise was in Kansas City and initially wrote the biography of Glenn Abbott for the book *Mustaches and Mayhem: Charlie O's Three-Time Champions. The Oakland Athletics: 1972-74*, edited by Chip Greene and published by SABR in 2015.

RORY COSTELLO has fond memories of a paperback he owned as a kid: *No-Hitter* by New York sportswriter Phil Pepe. He still hopes to see one in person at the ballpark someday. Rory lives in Brooklyn, New York with his wife Noriko and son Kai.

JOE COX is the author of *Almost Perfect: The Heartbreaking Pursuit of Pitching's Holy Grail*, published by Lyons Press. He is working on another baseball book for Lyons, to come in early 2018. Joe has co-written or assisted in writing several other sports books, including a biography of broadcaster Claude Sullivan, who was the voice of the Cincinnati Reds for a few years in the 1960s. Otherwise, Joe practices law and lives with his wife and children near Bowling Green, Kentucky.

JOHN DIFONZO grew up in Somerville, Massachusetts where he was the Sports Editor for his high school newspaper. He is a lifelong Red Sox fan and season-ticket holder since 2004 currently living in Beacon Hill with his wife Gabriella. John is a graduate of Tufts University and holds a Master of Science in Global Financial Analysis from Bentley University and is a CFA chartholder.

CHARLES F. FABER was a native of Iowa who lived in Lexington, Kentucky, until his passing in August 2016. He held degrees from Coe College, Columbia University, and the University of Chicago. A retired public school and university teacher and administrator, he contributed to numerous SABR projects, including editing *The 1934 St. Louis Cardinals*. Among his publications are dozens of professional journal articles, encyclopedia entries, and research reports in fields such as school administration, education law, and country music. In addition to textbooks, he wrote 10 books (mostly on baseball) published by McFarland. His last book, co-authored with his grandson Zachariah Webb, was *The Hunt for a Reds October*, published by McFarland in 2015.

ADRIAN FUNG lives and works in Toronto. At age 7, he attended his first MLB game in the summer of 1986 at the now-demolished Canadian National Exhibition Stadium. Cal Ripken Jr., in game 706 of the streak, hit a three-run home run that day. Adrian also attended Tom Seaver's last game and Andrew McCutchen's first game. After monitoring SABR activities from afar for over a decade, Adrian finally joined SABR (Hanlan's Point Chapter - Toronto) in 2014 and has contributed several stories to SABR Games Project, mostly about memorable games in Blue Jays history. He also writes for the maverick hockey website, thePensblog.com under the *nom de guerre* "PenguinsMarch."

BEN GIRARD is a writer and historian from St. Louis, Missouri currently researching perceptions of race and drugs in pre-World War II America. He inherited a life-long passion for Cardinals baseball from his mother, Diane, who inherited it from her father, Al, and her aunt, Jo. Ben has Ken Burns' *Baseball* to thank for his love of history. He uses any excuse to recount his first-hand experiences of Mark McGwire's 62nd home run of 1998 and Game Six of the 2011 World Series. The Bob Forsch biography, and the game reports of Forsch's no-hitters, are Ben's first contributions to SABR.

A SABR member since 2006, **CHIP GREENE** is a frequent contributor to SABR's BioProject book series, for whom he edited *Mustaches and Mayhem*, the story of the three-time champion Oakland A's. Chip and his wife, Elaine, live in Waynesboro, Pennsylvania.

PAUL HENSLER received his Master's degree in History from Trinity College in Hartford, Connecticut, and is a member of SABR as well as the Phi Alpha Theta National History Honor Society. A contributor to several SABR publications and *NINE: A Journal of Baseball History and Culture*, Paul will have his second book, *The New Boys of Summer: Baseball's Radical Transformation of the Late Sixties*, published by Rowman & Littlefield in late 2017. For more information, please visit www.paulhensler.com.

PAUL HOFMANN is the Associate Vice President for International Programs at Sacramento State University. He is a native of Detroit, Michigan and lifelong Detroit sports fan. His research interests include 19th century and pre-World War II Japanese baseball. He is also an avid baseball card collector. Paul currently resides in Folsom, California.

NO-HITTERS

SABR member **MICHAEL HUBER** is Professor of Mathematics at Muhlenberg College in Allentown, Pennsylvania, where he teaches an undergraduate course titled "Reasoning With Sabermetrics." He has published his sabermetrics research in several books and journals, including *The Baseball Research Journal*, *Chance*, and *Base Ball*, and he genuinely enjoys contributing to SABR's Baseball Games Project. He has been rooting for the Baltimore Orioles for close to 50 years, and he was present when the Orioles pitched a combined no-hitter against Oakland on July 13, 1991.

JOHN RICHMOND HUSMAN has been a SABR member since 1982 and is a former chair of the 19th Century Committee. He is a great grandson of 19th century pitcher J. Lee Richmond and is historian for the Toledo Mud Hens.

JIMMY KEENAN has been a SABR member since 2001. His grandfather, Jimmy Lyston, and four other family members were all professional baseball players. A frequent contributor to SABR publications, Keenan is the author of the following books; *The Lystons: A Story of One Baltimore Family* and *Our National Pastime and The Life, Times and Tragic Death of Pitcher Win Mercer*. He is a 2010 inductee into the Oldtimers Baseball Association of Maryland's Hall of Fame and a 2012 inductee into the Baltimore's Boys of Summer Hall of Fame.

A SABR member since 2010, **NORM KING** lives in Ottawa Ontario. His baseball research focuses on his dear departed Montreal Expos. He has written biographies of numerous Expos players and personnel, including Bob Bailey, Warren Cromartie, Steve Rogers, and Hall of Fame broadcaster Dave Van Horne. Norm thought he was crazy about missing his team until he met people from Brooklyn who are still unhappy that the Dodgers moved to Los Angeles. He was senior editor and main writer of the SABR book: *Au jeu/Play Ball: The 50 Greatest Games in the History of the Montreal Expos*, the top-selling SABR book of 2016.

TARA KRIEGER has been an active member of SABR since 2005. Although her current day job is as an attorney with the City of New York, she has previously been on staff as a sports writer at *Newsday* and as an editorial producer for MLB Advanced Media. With SABR, she is an editor and contributor to BioProject and has participated in the publication of several SABR books, including *Van Lingle Mungo*, *The Miracle Has Landed*, *Bridging Two Dynasties*, *Go-Go to Glory*, and *Minnesotans in Baseball*. She also presented original research, "Andy Coakley vs. the Cubs: Baseball's Forgotten Labor Struggle," at the 2015 SABR national convention in Chicago.

DIRK LAMMERS is an award-winning Associated Press journalist and baseball blogger. He is an oft-quoted authority on no-hitters and the creator of NoNoHitters.com, the acclaimed gathering point for all things related to pitching's greatest feat. His book *Baseball's No-Hit Wonders* was published by Unbridled Books in 2016.

LEONTE LANDINO is a Venezuelan baseball journalist, writer and producer for baseball properties at ESPN International, covering since 1995 stories around Latin baseball and the daily beat of Major League Baseball, the Winter Leagues, the Caribbean Series, and the World Baseball Classic. Has contributed with SABR with extensive research on Luis Castro and various bio-projects as well as serving as chair of the Luis Castro/Latin American Chapter. Landino is an active baseball speaker on international issues, sabermetrics and new technologies in baseball and media. Lives in Terryville, Connecticut with his wife Mariana and daughter Anabella.

JIM LEEKE is a writer and creative director in Columbus, Ohio, where he also cofounded the nonprofit Anglo-American Baseball Project. He has written several biographies for SABR's BioProject, all of players who served in the U.S. armed forces during World War One. His latest book is *From the Dugouts to the Trenches: Baseball during the Great War*.

BOB LEMOINE barely had a handful of hits in his Little League career and seems to think he's an expert on no-hitters. From Maine originally, he works as a high school librarian in New Hampshire. He has contributed to several SABR projects, including co-editing *Boston's First Nine: the 1871-75 Boston Red Stockings* with Bill Nowlin in 2016. An upcoming book will focus on the Boston Beaneaters of the 1890s.

LEN LEVIN is a retired newspaper editor who now edits the decisions of the Rhode Island Supreme Court. He also spends a lot of time going to baseball games (he has seen three no-hitters) and editing for SABR.

Born in Rhode Island, **CHUCK MCGILL**'s biggest regret about baseball was passing up the opportunity to go to what became the longest professional baseball game on record, the Pawtucket Red Sox against the Rochester Red Wings on April 18, 1981. He has lived in Vermont for most of the past 30 years, and is a lifelong Boston Red Sox and Fred Lynn fan. He specializes in minor-league no-hitter research.

DAVID NEMEC is a novelist and baseball historian. He has written *The Great Encyclopedia of Nineteenth Century Major League Baseball*; *The Beer and Whisky League*, a history of the American Association's 10-year sojourn as a rebel major league; *Major League Baseball Profiles: 1871-1900*; and many other baseball history and memorabilia books. His most recent novel, *The Picture Maker*, was translated into Czech and published in April 2016 in the Czech Republic under the title *Zajatec Predstav*. Nemec's contributions to the 1871-75 Boston Red Stockings' book are expanded and updated versions of biographies that originally appeared in *Major League Baseball Profiles: 1871-1900*.

Red Sox fan **BILL NOWLIN** has never seen the Red Sox held hitless but has been fortunate to see Red Sox pitchers throw four no-hitters — Dave Morehead, Derek Lowe, Jon Lester, and Devern Hansack.* He has written or edited more than 60 books, mostly about baseball, and has served on SABR's Board of Directors since 2004. He's also in the International Bluegrass Music Hall of Fame. (*See his article on Hansack in this book.)

LEN PASCULLI, a life-long New Jersey resident, joined SABR in 2001. Len is a lawyer, an adjunct professor, and a father of three. He married Jan, his college sweetheart (Penn State), in 1977. Besides playing at Mets' Dream Camp in 2001, at the Doubleday Farms Baseball Dream Camp (in Carlisle, PA) annually, writing for SABR's BioProject, and pulling out his remaining curly hair while managing his Rotisserie League baseball team, Len's interests include basketball, travel, and theater (watching, not performing).

JACOB POMRENKE is the Director of Editorial Content for the Society for American Baseball Research. He is also the editor of *Scandal on the South Side: The 1919 Chicago White Sox*, published in 2015, and chairman of SABR's Black Sox Scandal Research Committee. He lives in Scottsdale, Arizona, with his wife, Tracy Greer, and their cats, Nixey Callahan and Bones Ely.

RICHARD J. PUERZER is an associate professor and chairperson of the Department of Engineering at Hofstra University. He has contributed to a number of SABR Books, including *Mustaches and Mayhem: The Oakland Athletics: 1972-1974 (2015)* and *The 1986 New York Mets: There Was More Than Game Six (2016)*. His writings on baseball have also appeared in: *Nine: A Journal of Baseball History and Culture*, *Black Ball*, *The National Pastime*, *The Cooperstown Symposium on Baseball and American Culture* proceedings, and *Spitball*.

ALAN RAYLESBERG is an attorney in New York City. He is a lifelong baseball fan who enjoys baseball history and roots for the Yankees and the Mets. Alan also has a strong interest in baseball analytics and is a devotee of baseball simulation games, participating both in draft leagues and historical replays.

STEPHEN V. RICE, Ph.D., hails from Detroit, Michigan, and lives in Collierville, Tennessee. During his childhood he pored over statistics in the baseball encyclopedia and wondered about the players. The numbers don't say much about the players; they don't tell us who they were or what they were like. Now he writes biographies for the SABR BioProject, to help tell their stories. In his day job, he is a software architect in the Computational Biology department at St. Jude Children's Research Hospital in Memphis.

CARL RIECHERS retired from United Parcel Service in 2012 after 35 years of service. With more free time, he became a SABR member that same year. Born and raised in the suburbs of St. Louis, he became a big fan of the Cardinals. He and his wife Janet have three children and is the proud grandpa of two.

PAUL ROGERS is co-author of several baseball books including *The Whiz Kids and the 1950 Pennant* (Temple University Press, 1996) with boyhood hero Robin Roberts, and *Lucky Me: My 65 Years in Baseball* (SMU Press 2011) with Eddie Robinson. Paul is president of the Ernie Banks - Bobby Bragan DFW Chapter of SABR and a frequent contributor to the SABR BioProject, but his real job is as a law professor at Southern Methodist University, where he served as dean of the law school for nine years. He has also served as SMU's faculty athletic representative for 30 years.

JOHN T. SACCOMAN is a Professor of Mathematics and Computer Science at Seton Hall University in New Jersey. An avid fan of the New York Mets, he team-teaches one of the earliest known Sabermetrics courses there with its founder, Rev. Gabe Costa. They, along with Mike Huber, have co-authored three books published by McFarland— *Understanding Sabermetrics*, *Practicing Sabermetrics* and *Reasoning with Sabermetrics*. John resides in northern New Jersey with his Bosox-loving wife Mary and tries to get to Citi Field whenever possible with his Boston-area son, Ryan.

STEVEN SCHMITT is author of *A History of Badger Baseball—The Rise and Fall of America's Pastime at the University of Wisconsin*. He has also authored SABR biographies on John DeMerit and Hawk Taylor in *Thar's Joy in Braveland—The 1957 Milwaukee Braves* and individual biographies on Ty Cline, Steve Ridzik, Ken Johnson, Johnny Gerlach and Stony McGlynn (in progress). Schmitt has bachelor's and master's degrees from the University of Wisconsin—Madison School of Journalism and Mass Communication and resides in Madison, Wisconsin.

THOMAS E. SCHOTT, Tom, is a professional historian, holder of a Ph.D. in American history from LSU, retired historian for the DoD, free-lance editor, Texas Ranger fan, nephew of SABR co-founder the late Arthur O. Schott, writer/editor of numerous books and articles on the American Civil War, baseball, and American biography. Erstwhile poet. All of these and more. Lives in Norman, Oklahoma, with wife of 49 years, Susan. Daughter, two sons in Florida, two grandchildren.

JOE SCHUSTER is the author of the novel *The Might Have Been* (Ballantine Books), which was a finalist for the CASEY Award for the best baseball book of 2012, as well as the short nonfiction book, *One Season in the Sun* (Gemma Open Door), which focuses on ballplayers whose major league careers lasted a few weeks or less. A member of the faculty of Webster University in St. Louis, he writes frequently for the Cardinals *Gameday* magazine. He is married and the father of five rabid Redbird fans.

From an early age **DAVID E. SKELTON** developed a lifelong love of baseball when the lights from Philadelphia's Connie Mack Stadium shone through his bedroom window. Long removed from Philly, he resides with his family in central Texas where he is employed in the oil & gas industry. An avid collector, he joined SABR in 2012.

LYLE SPATZ is the chairman emeritus of SABR's Baseball Records Committee. He is the author of three books of baseball history, co-author of another, and has contributed chapters to several more, including *The Dictionary of Literary Biography* and *The Biographical Dictionary of American Sports*. His articles have appeared in *The Washington Post*, *The New York Times*, other newspapers, and numerous baseball magazines. He has taught baseball history to Elderhostel groups and also presented papers at the Babe Ruth Conference at Hofstra University and at the Jackie Robinson Conference at Long Island University.

BILL STAPLES, JR. has a passion for researching and telling the untold stories of the "international pastime." His areas of expertise include Japanese American and Negro Leagues baseball history as a context for exploring the themes of civil rights, cross-cultural relations, and globalization. He is a board member of the Nisei Baseball Research Project, member of the Japanese American Citizens League, and chairman of the SABR Asian Baseball Committee. He is the author of *Kenichi Zenimura, Japanese American Baseball Pioneer* (McFarland, 2011), winner of the 2012 SABR Baseball Research Award. Bill lives in Chandler, Arizona, with his wife and two children and is an active community volunteer and youth coach.

STEW THORNLEY is an official scorer for Major League Baseball and has written about the role of official scorers and no-hitters. He also keeps a list of no-hitters that have been broken up in the ninth inning on his website, milkeespress.com. He has been a member of the Society for American Baseball Research since 1979.

CASEY TIBBITTS is an information technology manager living in San Diego, California. He is the author of the historical novel *Place of Honor* and a lifelong student of Major League Baseball's history and traditions.

ADAM J. ULREY used to be the featured writer for *Inside Ducks Sports*, and spent 10 years on the radio doing a sportstalk show in the beautiful Willamette Valley. He enjoys building his own Bamboo Fly rods and has a small catering business. He spends most of his free time in the outdoors doing everything from hiking to fishing in his own stream. But his favorite past time is spending time with his wife Jhody and son Camran. He also has two beautiful dogs named Montana and Behr.

JOE WANCHO resides in Westlake, Ohio and is a lifelong Cleveland Indians fan. He has been a SABR member since 2005 and is the chair of the Minor League Research Committee.

A lifelong Pirates fan, **GREGORY H. WOLF** was born in Pittsburgh, but now resides in the Chicagoland area with his wife, Margaret, and daughter, Gabriela. A Professor of German Studies and holder of the Dennis and Jean Bauman Endowed Chair in the Humanities at North Central College in Naperville, Illinois, he edited more than half a dozen books for SABR books while hard at work on several more.

NO-HITTERS

NO-HITTERS
SABR BioProject Team Books

In 2002, the Society for American Baseball Research launched an effort to write and publish biographies of every player, manager, and individual who has made a contribution to baseball. Over the past decade, the BioProject Committee has produced over 6,000 biographical articles. Many have been part of efforts to create theme- or team-oriented books, spearheaded by chapters or other committees of SABR.

THE 1986 BOSTON RED SOX:
THERE WAS MORE THAN GAME SIX
One of a two-book series on the rivals that met in the 1986 World Series, the Boston Red Sox and the New York Mets, including biographies of every player, coach, broadcaster, and other important figures in the top organizations in baseball that year. .
Edited by Leslie Heaphy and Bill Nowlin
$19.95 paperback (ISBN 978-1-943816-19-4)
$9.99 ebook (ISBN 978-1-943816-18-7)
8.5"X11", 420 pages, over 200 photos

THE 1986 NEW YORK METS:
THERE WAS MORE THAN GAME SIX
The other book in the "rivalry" set from the 1986 World Series. This book re-tells the story of that year's classic World Series and this is the story of each of the players, coaches, managers, and broadcasters, their lives in baseball and the way the 1986 season fit into their lives.
Edited by Leslie Heaphy and Bill Nowlin
$19.95 paperback (ISBN 978-1-943816-13-2)
$9.99 ebook (ISBN 978-1-943816-12-5)
8.5"X11", 392 pages, over 100 photos

SCANDAL ON THE SOUTH SIDE:
THE 1919 CHICAGO WHITE SOX
The Black Sox Scandal isn't the only story worth telling about the 1919 Chicago White Sox. The team roster included three future Hall of Famers, a 20-year-old spitballer who would win 300 games in the minors, and even a batboy who later became a celebrity with the "Murderers' Row" New York Yankees. All of their stories are included in Scandal on the South Side with a timeline of the 1919 season.
Edited by Jacob Pomrenke
$19.95 paperback (ISBN 978-1-933599-95-3)
$9.99 ebook (ISBN 978-1-933599-94-6)
8.5"x11", 324 pages, 55 historic photos

WINNING ON THE NORTH SIDE
THE 1929 CHICAGO CUBS
Celebrate the 1929 Chicago Cubs, one of the most exciting teams in baseball history. Future Hall of Famers Hack Wilson, '29 NL MVP Rogers Hornsby, and Kiki Cuyler, along with Riggs Stephenson formed one of the most potent quartets in baseball history. The magical season came to an ignominious end in the World Series and helped craft the future "lovable loser" image of the team.
Edited by Gregory H. Wolf
$19.95 paperback (ISBN 978-1-933599-89-2)
$9.99 ebook (ISBN 978-1-933599-88-5)
8.5"x11", 314 pages, 59 photos

DETROIT THE UNCONQUERABLE:
THE 1935 WORLD CHAMPION TIGERS
Biographies of every player, coach, and broadcaster involved with the 1935 World Champion Detroit Tigers baseball team, written by members of the Society for American Baseball Research. Also includes a season in review and other articles about the 1935 team. Hank Greenberg, Mickey Cochrane, Charlie Gehringer, Schoolboy Rowe, and more.
Edited by Scott Ferkovich
$19.95 paperback (ISBN 9978-1-933599-78-6)
$9.99 ebook (ISBN 978-1-933599-79-3)
8.5"X11", 230 pages, 52 photos

THE TEAM THAT TIME WON'T FORGET:
THE 1951 NEW YORK GIANTS
Because of Bobby Thomson's dramatic "Shot Heard 'Round the World" in the bottom of the ninth of the decisive playoff game against the Brooklyn Dodgers, the team will forever be in baseball public's consciousness. Includes a foreword by Giants outfielder Monte Irvin.
Edited by Bill Nowlin and C. Paul Rogers III
$19.95 paperback (ISBN 978-1-933599-99-1)
$9.99 ebook (ISBN 978-1-933599-98-4)
8.5"X11", 282 pages, 47 photos

A PENNANT FOR THE TWIN CITIES:
THE 1965 MINNESOTA TWINS
This volume celebrates the 1965 Minnesota Twins, who captured the American League pennant in just their fifth season in the Twin Cities. Led by an All-Star cast, from Harmon Killebrew, Tony Oliva, Zoilo Versalles, and Mudcat Grant to Bob Allison, Jim Kaat, Earl Battey, and Jim Perry, the Twins won 102 games, but bowed to the Los Angeles Dodgers and Sandy Koufax in Game Seven
Edited by Gregory H. Wolf
$19.95 paperback (ISBN 978-1-943816-09-5)
$9.99 ebook (ISBN 978-1-943816-08-8)
8.5"X11", 405 pages, over 80 photos

MUSTACHES AND MAYHEM: CHARLIE O'S THREE TIME CHAMPIONS:
THE OAKLAND ATHLETICS: 1972-74
The Oakland Athletics captured major league baseball's crown each year from 1972 through 1974. Led by future Hall of Famers Reggie Jackson, Catfish Hunter and Rollie Fingers, the Athletics were a largely homegrown group who came of age together. Biographies of every player, coach, manager, and broadcaster (and mascot) from 1972 through 1974 are included, along with season recaps.
Edited by Chip Greene
$29.95 paperback (ISBN 978-1-943816-07-1)
$9.99 ebook (ISBN 978-1-943816-06-4)
8.5"X11", 600 pages, almost 100 photos

SABR Members can purchase each book at a significant discount (often 50% off) and receive the ebook edtions free as a member benefit. Each book is available in a trade paperback edition as well as ebooks suitable for reading on a home computer or Nook, Kindle, or iPad/tablet.
To learn more about becoming a member of SABR, visit the website: sabr.org/join

NO-HITTERS
The SABR Digital Library

The Society for American Baseball Research, the top baseball research organization in the world, disseminates some of the best in baseball history, analysis, and biography through our publishing programs. The SABR Digital Library contains a mix of books old and new, and focuses on a tandem program of paperback and ebook publication, making these materials widely available for both on digital devices and as traditional printed books.

GREATEST GAMES BOOKS

TIGERS BY THE TALE:
GREAT GAMES AT MICHIGAN AND TRUMBULL
For over 100 years, Michigan and Trumbull was the scene of some of the most exciting baseball ever. This book portrays 50 classic games at the corner, spanning the earliest days of Bennett Park until Tiger Stadium's final closing act. From Ty Cobb to Mickey Cochrane, Hank Greenberg to Al Kaline, and Willie Horton to Alan Trammell.
Edited by Scott Ferkovich
$12.95 paperback (ISBN 978-1-943816-21-7)
$6.99 ebook (ISBN 978-1-943816-20-0)
8.5"x11", 160 pages, 22 photos

FROM THE BRAVES TO THE BREWERS: GREAT GAMES AND HISTORY AT MILWAUKEE'S COUNTY STADIUM
The National Pastime provides in-depth articles focused on the geographic region where the national SABR convention is taking place annually. The SABR 45 convention took place in Chicago, and here are 45 articles on baseball in and around the bat-and-ball crazed Windy City: 25 that appeared in the souvenir book of the convention plus another 20 articles available in ebook only.
Edited by Gregory H. Wolf
$19.95 paperback (ISBN 978-1-943816-23-1)
$9.99 ebook (ISBN 978-1-943816-22-4)
8.5"X11", 290 pages, 58 photos

BRAVES FIELD:
MEMORABLE MOMENTS AT BOSTON'S LOST DIAMOND
From its opening on August 18, 1915, to the sudden departure of the Boston Braves to Milwaukee before the 1953 baseball season, Braves Field was home to Boston's National League baseball club and also hosted many other events: from NFL football to championship boxing. The most memorable moments to occur in Braves Field history are portrayed here.
Edited by Bill Nowlin and Bob Brady
$19.95 paperback (ISBN 978-1-933599-93-9)
$9.99 ebook (ISBN 978-1-933599-92-2)
8.5"X11", 282 pages, 182 photos

AU JEU/PLAY BALL: THE 50 GREATEST GAMES IN THE HISTORY OF THE MONTREAL EXPOS
The 50 greatest games in Montreal Expos history. The games described here recount the exploits of the many great players who wore Expos uniforms over the years—Bill Stoneman, Gary Carter, Andre Dawson, Steve Rogers, Pedro Martinez, from the earliest days of the franchise, to the glory years of 1979-1981, the what-might-have-been years of the early 1990s, and the sad, final days.and others.
Edited by Norm King
$12.95 paperback (ISBN 978-1-943816-15-6)
$5.99 ebook (ISBN978-1-943816-14-9)
8.5"x11", 162 pages, 50 photos

ORIGINAL SABR RESEARCH

CALLING THE GAME:
BASEBALL BROADCASTING FROM 1920 TO THE PRESENT
An exhaustive, meticulously researched history of bringing the national pastime out of the ballparks and into living rooms via the airwaves. Every play-by-play announcer, color commentator, and ex-ballplayer, every broadcast deal, radio station, and TV network. Plus a foreword by "Voice of the Chicago Cubs" Pat Hughes, and an afterword by Jacques Doucet, the "Voice of the Montreal Expos" 1972-2004.
by Stuart Shea
$24.95 paperback (ISBN 978-1-933599-40-3)
$9.99 ebook (ISBN 978-1-933599-41-0)
7"X10", 712 pages, 40 photos

BIOPROJECT BOOKS

WHO'S ON FIRST:
REPLACEMENT PLAYERS IN WORLD WAR II
During World War II, 533 players made the major league debuts. More than 60% of the players in the 1941 Opening Day lineups departed for the service and were replaced by first-timers and oldsters. Hod Lisenbee was 46. POW Bert Shepard had an artificial leg, and Pete Gray had only one arm. The 1944 St. Louis Browns had 13 players classified 4-F. These are their stories.
Edited by Marc Z Aaron and Bill Nowlin
$19.95 paperback (ISBN 978-1-933599-91-5)
$9.99 ebook (ISBN 978-1-933599-90-8)
8.5"X11", 422 pages, 67 photos

VAN LINGLE MUNGO:
THE MAN, THE SONG, THE PLAYERS
40 baseball players with intriguing names have been named in renditions of Dave Frishberg's classic 1969 song, Van Lingle Mungo. This book presents biographies of all 40 players and additional information about one of the greatest baseball novelty songs of all time.
Edited by Bill Nowlin
$19.95 paperback (ISBN 978-1-933599-76-2)
$9.99 ebook (ISBN 978-1-933599-77-9)
8.5"X11", 278 pages, 46 photos

NUCLEAR POWERED BASEBALL
Nuclear Powered Baseball tells the stories of each player—past and present—featured in the classic Simpsons episode "Homer at the Bat." Wade Boggs, Ken Griffey Jr., Ozzie Smith, Nap Lajoie, Don Mattingly, and many more. We've also included a few very entertaining takes on the now-famous episode from prominent baseball writers Jonah Keri, Joe Posnanski, Erik Malinowski, and Bradley Woodrum
Edited by Emily Hawks and Bill Nowlin
$19.95 paperback (ISBN 978-1-943816-11-8)
$9.99 ebook (ISBN 978-1-943816-10-1)
8.5"X11", 250 pages

SABR Members can purchase each book at a significant discount (often 50% off) and receive the ebook edtions free as a member benefit. Each book is available in a trade paperback edition as well as ebooks suitable for reading on a home computer or Nook, Kindle, or iPad/tablet.
To learn more about becoming a member of SABR, visit the website: sabr.org/join

NO-HITTERS

SABR BioProject Books

In 2002, the Society for American Baseball Research launched an effort to write and publish biographies of every player, manager, and individual who has made a contribution to baseball. Over the past decade, the BioProject Committee has produced over 2,200 biographical articles. Many have been part of efforts to create theme- or team-oriented books, spearheaded by chapters or other committees of SABR.

THE YEAR OF THE BLUE SNOW:
THE 1964 PHILADELPHIA PHILLIES
Catcher Gus Triandos dubbed the Philadelphia Phillies' 1964 season "the year of the blue snow," a rare thing that happens once in a great while. This book sheds light on lingering questions about the 1964 season—but any book about a team is really about the players. This work offers life stories of all the players and others (managers, coaches, owners, and broadcasters) associated with this star-crossed team, as well as essays of analysis and history.
Edited by Mel Marmer and Bill Nowlin
$19.95 paperback (ISBN 978-1-933599-51-9)
$9.99 ebook (ISBN 978-1-933599-52-6)
8.5"X11", 356 PAGES, over 70 photos

THE MIRACLE BRAVES OF 1914
BOSTON'S ORIGINAL WORST-TO-FIRST CHAMPIONS
Long before the Red Sox "Impossible Dream" season, Boston's now nearly forgotten "other" team, the 1914 Boston Braves, performed a baseball "miracle" that resounds to this very day. The "Miracle Braves" were Boston's first "worst-to-first" winners of the World Series. Refusing to throw in the towel at the midseason mark, George Stallings engineered a remarkable second-half climb in the standings all the way to first place.
Edited by Bill Nowlin
$19.95 paperback (ISBN 978-1-933599-69-4)
$9.99 ebook (ISBN 978-1-933599-70-0)
8.5"X11", 392 PAGES, over 100 photos

DETROIT TIGERS 1984:
WHAT A START! WHAT A FINISH!
The 1984 Detroit tigers roared out of the gate, winning their first nine games of the season and compiling an eye-popping 35-5 record after the campaign's first 40 games—still the best start ever for any team in major league history. This book brings together biographical profiles of every Tiger from that magical season, plus those of field management, top executives, the broadcasters—even venerable Tiger Stadium and the city itself.
Edited by Mark Pattison and David Raglin
$19.95 paperback (ISBN 978-1-933599-44-1)
$9.99 ebook (ISBN 978-1-933599-45-8)
8.5"x11", 250 pages (Over 230,000 words!)

THAR'S JOY IN BRAVELAND!
THE 1957 MILWAUKEE BRAVES
Few teams in baseball history have captured the hearts of their fans like the Milwaukee Braves of the 1950s. During the Braves' 13-year tenure in Milwaukee (1953-1965), they had a winning record every season, won two consecutive NL pennants (1957 and 1958), lost two more in the final week of the season (1956 and 1959), and set big-league attendance records along the way.
Edited by Gregory H. Wolf
$19.95 paperback (ISBN 978-1-933599-71-7)
$9.99 ebook (ISBN 978-1-933599-72-4)
8.5"x11", 330 pages, over 60 photos

SWEET '60: THE 1960 PITTSBURGH PIRATES
A portrait of the 1960 team which pulled off one of the biggest upsets of the last 60 years. When Bill Mazeroski's home run left the park to win in Game Seven of the World Series, beating the New York Yankees, David had toppled Goliath. It was a blow that awakened a generation, one that millions of people saw on television, one of TV's first iconic World Series moments.
Edited by Clifton Blue Parker and Bill Nowlin
$19.95 paperback (ISBN 978-1-933599-48-9)
$9.99 ebook (ISBN 978-1-933599-49-6)
8.5"X11", 340 pages, 75 photos

NEW CENTURY, NEW TEAM:
THE 1901 BOSTON AMERICANS
The team now known as the Boston Red Sox played its first season in 1901. Boston had a well-established National League team, but the American League went head-to-head with the N.L. in Chicago, Philadelphia, and Boston. Chicago won the American League pennant and Boston finished second, only four games behind.
Edited by Bill Nowlin
$19.95 paperback (ISBN 978-1-933599-58-8)
$9.99 ebook (ISBN 978-1-933599-59-5)
8.5"X11", 268 pages, over 125 photos

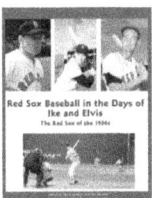

RED SOX BASEBALL IN THE DAYS OF IKE AND ELVIS: *THE RED SOX OF THE 1950S*
Although the Red Sox spent most of the 1950s far out of contention, the team was filled with fascinating players who captured the heart of their fans. In *Red Sox Baseball*, members of SABR present 46 biographies on players such as Ted Williams and Pumpsie Green as well as season-by-season recaps.
Edited by Mark Armour and Bill Nowlin
$19.95 paperback (ISBN 978-1-933599-24-3)
$9.99 ebook (ISBN 978-1-933599-34-2)
8.5"X11", 372 PAGES, over 100 photos

CAN HE PLAY?
A LOOK AT BASEBALL SCOUTS AND THEIR PROFESSION
They dig through tons of coal to find a single diamond. Here in the world of scouts, we meet the "King of Weeds," a Ph.D. we call "Baseball's Renaissance Man," a husband-and-wife team, pioneering Latin scouts, and a Japanese-American interned during World War II who became a successful scout—and many, many more.
Edited by Jim Sandoval and Bill Nowlin
$19.95 paperback (ISBN 978-1-933599-23-6)
$9.99 ebook (ISBN 978-1-933599-25-0)
8.5"X11", 200 PAGES, over 100 photos

SABR Members can purchase each book at a significant discount (often 50% off) and receive the ebook editions free as a member benefit. Each book is available in a trade paperback edition as well as ebooks suitable for reading on a home computer or Nook, Kindle, or iPad/tablet.
To learn more about becoming a member of SABR, visit the website: sabr.org/join

NO-HITTERS

THE SABR DIGITAL LIBRARY

The Society for American Baseball Research, the top baseball research organization in the world, disseminates some of the best in baseball history, analysis, and biography through our publishing programs. The SABR Digital Library contains a mix of books old and new, and focuses on a tandem program of paperback and ebook publication, making these materials widely available for both on digital devices and as traditional printed books.

CLASSIC REPRINTS

BASE-BALL: HOW TO BECOME A PLAYER
by John Montgomery Ward
John Montgomery Ward (1860-1925) tossed the second perfect game in major league history and later became the game's best shortstop and a great, inventive manager. His classic handbook on baseball skills and strategy was published in 1888. Illustrated with woodcuts, the book is divided into chapters for each position on the field as well as chapters on the origin of the game, theory and strategy, training, base-running, and batting.
$4.99 ebook (ISBN 978-1-933599-47-2)
$9.95 paperback (ISBN 978-0910137539)
156 PAGES, 4.5"X7" replica edition

BATTING by F. C. Lane
First published in 1925, Batting collects the wisdom and insights of over 250 hitters and baseball figures. Lane interviewed extensively and compiled tips and advice on everything from batting stances to beanballs. Legendary baseball figures such as Ty Cobb, Casey Stengel, Cy Young, Walter Johnson, Rogers Hornsby, and Babe Ruth reveal the secrets of such integral and interesting parts of the game as how to choose a bat, the ways to beat a slump, and how to outguess the pitcher.
$14.95 paperback (ISBN 978-0-910137-86-7)
$7.99 ebook (ISBN 978-1-933599-46-5)
240 PAGES, 5"X7"

RUN, RABBIT, RUN
by Walter "Rabbit" Maranville
"Rabbit" Maranville was the Joe Garagiola of Grandpa's day, the baseball comedian of the times. In a twenty-four-year career that began in 1912, Rabbit found a lot of funny situations to laugh at, and no wonder: he caused most of them! The book also includes an introduction by the late Harold Seymour and a historical account of Maranville's life and Hall-of-Fame career by Bob Carroll.
$9.95 paperback (ISBN 978-1-933599-26-7)
$5.99 ebook (ISBN 978-1-933599-27-4)
100 PAGES, 5.5"X8.5", 15 rare photos

MEMORIES OF A BALLPLAYER
by Bill Werber and C. Paul Rogers III
Bill Werber's claim to fame is unique: he was the last living person to have a direct connection to the 1927 Yankees, "Murderers' Row," a team hailed by many as the best of all time. Rich in anecdotes and humor, Memories of a Ballplayer is a clear-eyed memoir of the world of big-league baseball in the 1930s. Werber played with or against some of the most productive hitters of all time, including Babe Ruth, Ted Williams, Lou Gehrig, and Joe DiMaggio.
$14.95 paperback (ISNB 978-0-910137-84-3)
$6.99 ebook (ISBN 978-1-933599-47-2)
250 PAGES, 6"X9"

ORIGINAL SABR RESEARCH

INVENTING BASEBALL: THE 100 GREATEST GAMES OF THE NINETEENTH CENTURY
SABR's Nineteenth Century Committee brings to life the greatest games from the game's early years. From the "prisoner of war" game that took place among captive Union soldiers during the Civil War (immortalized in a famous lithograph), to the first intercollegiate game (Amherst versus Williams), to the first professional no-hitter, the games in this volume span 1833–1900 and detail the athletic exploits of such players as Cap Anson, Moses "Fleetwood" Walker, Charlie Comiskey, and Mike "King" Kelly.
Edited by Bill Felber
$19.95 paperback (ISBN 978-1-933599-42-7)
$9.99 ebook (ISBN 978-1-933599-43-4)
302 PAGES, 8"x10", 200 photos

NINETEENTH CENTURY STARS: 2012 EDITION
First published in 1989, Nineteenth Century Stars was SABR's initial attempt to capture the stories of baseball players from before 1900. With a collection of 136 fascinating biographies, SABR has re-released Nineteenth Century Stars for 2012 with revised statistics and new form. The 2012 version also includes a preface by **John Thorn**.
Edited by Robert L. Tiemann and Mark Rucker
$19.95 paperback (ISBN 978-1-933599-28-1)
$9.99 ebook (ISBN 978-1-933599-29-8)
300 PAGES, 6"X9"

GREAT HITTING PITCHERS
Published in 1979, Great Hitting Pitchers was one of SABR's early publications. Edited by SABR founder Bob Davids, the book compiles stories and records about pitchers excelling in the batter's box. Newly updated in 2012 by Mike Cook, Great Hitting Pitchers contain tables including data from 1979-2011, corrections to reflect recent records, and a new chapter on recent new members in the club of "great hitting pitchers" like Tom Glavine and Mike Hampton.
Edited by L. Robert Davids
$9.95 paperback (ISBN 978-1-933599-30-4)
$5.99 ebook (ISBN 978-1-933599-31-1)
102 PAGES, 5.5"x8.5"

THE FENWAY PROJECT
Sixty-four SABR members—avid fans, historians, statisticians, and game enthusiasts—recorded their experiences of a single game. Some wrote from inside the Green Monster's manual scoreboard, the Braves clubhouse, or the broadcast booth, while others took in the essence of Fenway from the grandstand or bleachers. The result is a fascinating look at the charms and challenges of Fenway Park, and the allure of being a baseball fan.
Edited by Bill Nowlin and Cecilia Tan
$9.99 ebook (ISBN 978-1-933599-50-2)
175 pages, 100 photos

SABR Members can purchase each book at a significant discount (often 50% off) and receive the ebook editions free as a member benefit. Each book is available in a trade paperback edition as well as ebooks suitable for reading on a home computer or Nook, Kindle, or iPad/tablet.
To learn more about becoming a member of SABR, visit the website: sabr.org/join

Society for American Baseball Research

Cronkite School at ASU
555 N. Central Ave. #416, Phoenix, AZ 85004
602.496.1460 (phone)
SABR.org

Become a SABR member today!

If you're interested in baseball — writing about it, reading about it, talking about it — there's a place for you in the Society for American Baseball Research. Our members include everyone from academics to professional sportswriters to amateur historians and statisticians to students and casual fans who enjoy reading about baseball and occasionally gathering with other members to talk baseball. What unites all SABR members is an interest in the game and joy in learning more about it.

SABR membership is open to any baseball fan; we offer 1-year and 3-year memberships. Here's a list of some of the key benefits you'll receive as a SABR member:

- Receive two editions (spring and fall) of the *Baseball Research Journal*, our flagship publication
- Receive expanded e-book edition of *The National Pastime*, our annual convention journal
- 8-10 new e-books published by the SABR Digital Library, all FREE to members
- "This Week in SABR" e-newsletter, sent to members every Friday
- Join dozens of research committees, from Statistical Analysis to Women in Baseball.
- Join one of 70 regional chapters in the U.S., Canada, Latin America, and abroad
- Participate in online discussion groups
- Ask and answer baseball research questions on the SABR-L e-mail listserv
- Complete archives of *The Sporting News* dating back to 1886 and other research resources
- Promote your research in "This Week in SABR"
- Diamond Dollars Case Competition
- Yoseloff Scholarships
- Discounts on SABR national conferences, including the SABR National Convention, the SABR Analytics Conference, Jerry Malloy Negro League Conference, Frederick Ivor-Campbell 19th Century Conference
- Publish your research in peer-reviewed SABR journals
- Collaborate with SABR researchers and experts
- Contribute to Baseball Biography Project or the SABR Games Project
- List your new book in the SABR Bookshelf
- Lead a SABR research committee or chapter
- Networking opportunities at SABR Analytics Conference
- Meet baseball authors and historians at SABR events and chapter meetings
- 50% discounts on paperback versions of SABR e-books
- 20% discount on MLB.TV and MiLB.TV subscriptions
- Discounts with other partners in the baseball community
- SABR research awards

We hope you'll join the most passionate international community of baseball fans at SABR! Check us out online at SABR.org/join.

SABR MEMBERSHIP FORM

	Annual	3-year	Senior	3-yr Sr.	Under 30
U.S.:	❑ $65	❑ $175	❑ $45	❑ $129	❑ $45
Canada/Mexico:	❑ $75	❑ $205	❑ $55	❑ $159	❑ $55
Overseas:	❑ $84	❑ $232	❑ $64	❑ $186	❑ $55

Add a Family Member: $15 each family member at same address (list names on back)
Senior: 65 or older before 12/31 of the current year
All dues amounts in U.S. dollars or equivalent

Participate in Our Donor Program!
Support the preservation of baseball research. Designate your gift toward:
❑ General Fund   ❑ Endowment Fund   ❑ Research Resources   ❑ _____
❑ I want to maximize the impact of my gift; do not send any donor premiums
❑ I would like this gift to remain anonymous.

Note: Any donation not designated will be placed in the General Fund.
SABR is a 501 (c) (3) not-for-profit organization & donations are tax-deductible to the extent allowed by law.

Name _____

E-mail* _____

Address _____

City _____ ST _____ ZIP _____

Phone _____ Birthday _____

* Your e-mail address on file ensures you will receive the most recent SABR news.

Dues $_____
Donation $_____
Amount Enclosed $_____

Do you work for a matching grant corporation? Call (602) 496-1460 for details.

If you wish to pay by credit card, please contact the SABR office at (602) 496-1460 or visit the SABR Store online at SABR.org/join. We accept Visa, Mastercard & Discover.

Do you wish to receive the *Baseball Research Journal* electronically?: ❑ Yes   ❑ No
Our e-books are available in PDF, Kindle, or EPUB (iBooks, iPad, Nook) formats.

Mail to: SABR, Cronkite School at ASU, 555 N. Central Ave. #416, Phoenix, AZ 85004